Casualty Insurance Claims

Coverage/Investigation/Law

by Pat Magarick, J.D., LL.M.

Third Edition

Clark Boardman Company, Ltd.
New York, New York   1988

To my wife, Trudy, with love,
who earned this dedication with her love, devotion, forbearance,
and proofreading
during the several years that this book was being written

Copyright 1988 by Clark Boardman Company, Ltd.

Library of Congress Cataloging-in-Publication Data
Magarick, Pat.
　Casualty insurance claims: coverage, investigation, law/by Pat Magarick.
　　p.　cm.
　Includes bibliographies and index.
　ISBN 0-87632-559-2
　1. Insurance, Casualty—Law and legislation—United States.
2. Insurance, Casualty—United States—Adjustment of Claims.
I. Title.
KF1215.M29 1987
346.73'0865—dc19
[347.306865]　　　　　　　　　　　　　　　　　　　　　87-16624
　　　　　　　　　　　　　　　　　　　　　　　　　　　　CIP

Acknowledgments

The bibliographies incorporated at the end of most of the chapters in this book are not complete or by any means comprehensive. The books and articles mentioned are those that have provided me with much useful material. Three publications deserve special thanks for their consistently fine articles: the Insurance Counsel Journal (ICJ), the Federation of Insurance Counsel Quarterly (FIC), and Ashley's Bad Faith Law Reports.

While I have been diligent in attempting to track down important articles, I am sure that some work was overlooked and to the authors, whoever they are, I tender my apologies.

I have not always mentioned the standard law texts which are known to all lawyers and most experienced claim people, but Professors Larson, Keeton, and O'Connell whose work is prodigious and to whom I owe a special debt, must be mentioned.

I would also like to acknowledge a debt to the following:

Automobile Liability Insurance Cases, originally written by Norman K. Risjord and June M. Austin and now published by John C. Risjord, Kansas City, Mo.

The American Insurance Association Tort Case Bulletins, which are excellent digests of case law, important to claim people and lawyers involved in negligence practice. They are published by the American Insurance Association (AIA), 85 John Street, New York, N.Y. 10038.

The Defense Research Institute (DRI), publishers of "For The Defense" and many other very helpful publications in many of the areas covered in this book. They are located at 1100 West Wells Street, Milwaukee, Wi. 53233.

Fidelity, Casualty & Surety Bulletins (FC&S), edited by Eugene F. Wolters, has also been very helpful in allowing me to keep up with the latest changes and developments in casualty insurance policies and their interpretation. They are published by The National Underwriter Co., 420 Fourth Street, Cincinnati, Oh. 45202.

My thanks also to *The Insurance Services Office (ISO)* whose people have always been courteous and helpful, and who have permitted me to reproduce parts of their policies. They are located in New York City.

Finally, thanks are also due to the *American Educational Institute,* Basking Ridge, N.J., for their publication, "Claims Law," edited by James H. Donaldson.

Special Appreciation

I would like to give special thanks to James N. Rodbard, of the firm of Conklin, Loesch & Caravas, Troy, Michigan, for his excellent help in the writing and editing of several important chapters of this book and to Dr. Leonard A. Stine of Highland Park, Illinois, for his very valuable help with the medical section of this book.

Preface to Third Edition

The publication of the third edition of this book makes some marked and radical changes that I think are noteworthy. The thrust of the text is no longer confined to, and directed at, the new claim representative, but has been enlarged and given much greater depth in some important areas that will be helpful to the experienced claim representative, house counsel, and attorneys who want to familiarize themselves with this branch of insurance practice.

Some fields of law have been touched upon very lightly because they are basic principles of law where many texts and other reference material is readily available. As new areas of casualty liability develop, they will be discussed and added in subsequent updates. Notable changes have been made in Products Liability, with the usual broadening of basic principles of law and concomitant changes in policy wording that required extensive comment. "Plain English" policies are proliferating and have entered the commercial market as well as policies written for the individual, and particular and extensive coverage has been given to the new 1986 Commercial General Liability policy.

Professional liability concepts have been enlarged to include many new professions and even some trades. In the area of medical malpractice, the last few years have seen what almost amounts to a revolution in the attitude and willingness of doctors to testify against each other. As verdicts increased astronomically, legislators were forced to take action to curtail the epidemic which was threatening the very nature and practice of the medical sciences. In the meantime, great advances have been made in the medical professions that have had a decided effect on the insurance industry. Enormous progress has been made in the areas of diagnosis, recovery, and rehabilitation, but along with such progress has come even more enormous increases in medical costs and liability exposure to those that practice in the medical fields.

Professional responsibility for the malpractice of lawyers, accountants, architects and engineers, teachers and athletic directors, some trades people, and even claim representatives have increased greatly as the courts have expanded the areas of liability and minimized defenses.

Accountability by insurance companies for their settlement practices in both first and third party cases has dramatically enlarged the field of extra-contractual liability.

In addition, where structured settlements play such an important role today, and where advance payments are often made without taking a release, old thinking and habits of doing business have also had to change.

The desirability of taking signed and recorded statements, the effect of releases, and many other practices that were heretofore considered as sacrosanct, have undergone radical reconsideration.

All of these factors, and others not mentioned, dictated the need for this new edition of the first book of its kind in the insurance industry. I have been most gratified by the acceptance which the previous editions have received by insurance companies, independent adjusters, and lawyers. One reason for this I ascribe to my attempt to "tell it like it is," from many years of actual practice and experience, together with constant study of the law and related fields. I most fervently hope that it will continue to be a practical book and, because of its enlarged scope, I have greatly increased the number of case citations.

Finally, it is impossible to confine subjects such as Statutes of Limitations, Strict Liability, Comparative Negligence, Emotional Distress, Punitive Damages, and many others to one section in and of themselves. These and other subjects impinge on one another so that each are mentioned many times as they touch on each other. Accordingly, and inevitably, there will be some overlapping and a little repetition, although an attempt was made to keep this at a minimum.

Specialized areas such as Fidelity, Accident and Health, and Crime Insurance have been omitted from this edition since these are subjects rarely included within the bounds of Casualty insurance.

Preface to First Edition

This book will help you, whether you are an experienced claim representative or a novice, to do a better job in investigating and reporting casualty claims. The increasing specialized knowledge required of the casualty claim representative is rapidly giving the occupation professional status. This status necessitates the development of additional educational facilities.

Casualty claim work encompasses broad fields of learning. Some, like law and medicine, are closely allied. Others are only occasionally touched upon. It is not an exact science in the sense that definite answers can always be given to arising problems. Policies and laws governing their interpretation do not remain static. It is therefore essential that the intelligent claim representative keep abreast with the changes as they take place.

Most of the larger companies have some educational program for new claims personnel. Some of these programs are formal, well-planned courses that attempt to do a thorough job. Others are less adequate in varying degrees. There are too few texts or claim manuals to which the new claim representative can turn. Here is a book to fill that gap.

It was with the intent to diminish the feeling of helplessness common to most new claim personnel in a new undertaking that this book was written. We believe that it will help fill a definite need in the industry, not only for the new employee, but also for those hardworking and sincere individuals who, while striving to improve their work, nonetheless continue to make errors because they have no readily available source of guidance. The book will also prove useful to the more experienced employee as a refresher.

Various insurance societies throughout the country have some specialized education for the new claim person, but it is usually open only to those already employed in the industry. Some universities and law schools also give courses in casualty claim handling; but, for the most part, the need for additional educational facilities for claim personnel is still felt in the insurance industry.

Chapter Contents

Chapter 1   The Occupation of Claim Representative and Claim Handling Procedures
Chapter 2   Casualty Insurance
Chapter 3   General Principles of Investigation
Chapter 4   Signed and Recorded Statements
Chapter 5   Securing the Physical Facts
Chapter 6   Obtaining Medical Information
Chapter 7   Medicine—Fundamentals
Chapter 8   Injury and Disease
Chapter 9   General Principles of Law–Part I
Chapter 10 General Principles of Law–Part II
Chapter 11 Intrafamily Tort Relationships and Immunities
Chapter 12 Governmental and Charitable Immunities
Chapter 13 Suits—Practice and Procedure
Chapter 14 Practical Considerations of Suits and Casualty Litigation
Chapter 15 Fraud
Chapter 16 Claims—Reserves, Reserving, and Statistics
Chapter 17 Settlements and Settlement Negotiations
Chapter 18 Releases
Chapter 19 Coverage Problems
Chapter 20 Some Important Casualty Policy Provisions
Chapter 21 Liability for Bad Faith and Punitive Damages
Chapter 22 Automobile Policies and Coverages
Chapter 23 Some Laws Applicable to the Use of Automobiles
Chapter 24 Protection Against the Irresponsible Motorist
Chapter 25 Automobile Liability Investigation and Checklists
Chapter 26 Public or General Liability Policies and Coverages
Chapter 27 "Occurrence"
Chapter 28 Investigation of Public or General Liability Claims
Chapter 29 Products Liability
Chapter 30 Products Liability—Duty to Warn and Recall
Chapter 31 Products Liability—Some Defenses and Related Problems
Chapter 32 Products Liability—Punitive Damages
Chapter 33 Investigation of Products Liability Claims

Chapter 34 Environmental Pollution
Chapter 35 Professional Liability—Physicians
Chapter 36 Professional Liability—Dentists, Nurses, Hospitals, and Druggists—and the Investigation of Medical Malpractice Claims
Chapter 37 Professional Liability—Lawyers
Chapter 38 Other Areas of Professional Liability
Chapter 39 Handling Workers' Compensation Cases
Chapter 40 Workers' Compensation-Employers' Liability Policy and Investigation
Chapter 41 Federal Employer-Employee and Other Federal Legislation
Chapter 42 Wrongful Termination of Employment
Chapter 43 Subrogation—Salvage—Contribution
Chapter 44 Reporting and Reports

Table of Contents

CHAPTER 1
The Occupation of Claim Representative and Claim Handling Procedures

§ 1.01	The Good Claims Representative	1-1
	[1] Qualifications	1-2
	[2] Training and Education	1-4
§ 1.02	Claim Handling Procedures	1-5
	[1] Proper Preparation	1-6
	[2] Prompt and Thorough Investigation	1-11
	[3] Decision and Action	1-12
	[4] Adequate Reporting	1-13
	[5] Self-Discipline	1-14

CHAPTER 2
Casualty Insurance

§ 2.01	Kinds of Insurance	2-1
§ 2.02	State Regulation and Control	2-4
§ 2.03	Major Subdivisions of an Insurance Company	2-4
§ 2.04	Five Kinds of Carriers	2-6
§ 2.05	The Agent and His Authority	2-7
§ 2.06	The Policy Contract	2-8
§ 2.07	The Four Parts of a Standard Casualty Policy	2-9
§ 2.08	Indemnity Contracts	2-10
§ 2.09	Endorsements	2-10
§ 2.10	Binders	2-11

CHAPTER 3
General Principles of Investigation

§ 3.01	Making the Investigation Thorough and Precise	3-1
§ 3.02	The Value of Contacts	3-3
§ 3.03	Timing the Investigation	3-4
§ 3.04	The Interview	3-4
	[1] Interviewing the Insured	3-5
	[2] Interviewing the Claimant	3-6

CASUALTY INSURANCE CLAIMS

	[3]	Interviewing the Claimant's Attorney	3-7
§ 3.05		Discovering the Witnesses	3-8
	[1]	Locating the Missing Witness	3-10
	[2]	Interviewing the Witnesses	3-11
§ 3.06		Investigating the Special Damages	3-13
§ 3.07		General Investigation of Fatal Claims	3-15
§ 3.08		Confidential Report to the Underwriters	3-15

CHAPTER 4
Signed and Recorded Statements

§ 4.01		Preparing and Planning the Statement	4-3
§ 4.02		Approach to Interview with Witness	4-3
§ 4.03		Rules for Better Signed Statements	4-4
§ 4.04		Construction of a Signed Statement	4-8
§ 4.05		Example of a Narrative Statement	4-12
§ 4.06		Translator's Affidavit	4-17
§ 4.07		Illiterate Witnesses	4-17
§ 4.08		Negative Signed Statements	4-18
§ 4.09		Statements Obtained by Mail	4-19
§ 4.10		Statements Taken from Children	4-19
§ 4.11		Question and Answer Statements	4-20
§ 4.12		Statements Taken by a Court Reporter	4-22
	[1]	Objections to Use of a Court Reporter	4-22
	[2]	Reasons for Obtaining Statement by a Court Reporter	4-23
	[3]	Limitations	4-23
§ 4.13		Statements Taken by Recording Devices	4-24
	[1]	Advantages in Using Recording Devices	4-26
	[2]	Disadvantages in Using Recording Devices	4-27
	[3]	Admissibility	4-28
	[4]	Obtaining the Facts	4-28
	[5]	Telephone Recording Devices	4-30

CHAPTER 5
Securing the Physical Facts

§ 5.01	Diagrams	5-2
§ 5.02	Photographs	5-7
§ 5.03	Movies	5-11
§ 5.04	Surveys and Plats	5-11
§ 5.05	Advertising Catalogs and Instructional Material	5-12
§ 5.06	Laboratory Testing	5-12

TABLE OF CONTENTS

§ 5.07	Preliminary Hearings		5-13
§ 5.08	Records		5-14
	[1]	Weather Reports	5-14
	[2]	Police Reports	5-14
	[3]	Motor Vehicle Records	5-15
		[a] Driving Records	5-16
	[4]	Birth, Death, and Marriage Certificates	5-16
	[5]	Coroner's Report	5-16
	[6]	Autopsy Report	5-17
	[7]	School Records and Information	5-17
	[8]	Income Tax Reports	5-17
	[9]	Military Records	5-18
	[10]	Civil Aeronautics Board Reports	5-18
	[11]	Newspaper Reports	5-18
§ 5.09	Company Engineering Department		5-18
§ 5.10	Choosing an Expert		5-19
§ 5.11	Bibliography		5-19

CHAPTER 6
Obtaining Medical Information

§ 6.01	Information to be Obtained from the Claimant	6-3
§ 6.02	Medical Liens	6-5
§ 6.03	Information to be Obtained from the Attending Physician	6-6
§ 6.04	Medical Report Form	6-6
§ 6.05	Dental Records	6-8
§ 6.06	Hospital Records	6-8
§ 6.07	Medical Examinations	6-9
	[1] Choosing the Examining Doctor	6-12
	[2] Expensive Diagnostic Procedures	6-14
§ 6.08	Autopsy and Coroner's Reports	6-15
§ 6.09	Military Records	6-15

CHAPTER 7
Medicine—Fundamentals

§ 7.01	Trauma	7-2
§ 7.02	Medical Terminology	7-2
§ 7.03	Wounds	7-8
§ 7.04	Some Branches of Medicine	7-9
§ 7.05	Structure of the Human Body	7-10
§ 7.06	Bones and Bone Structure	7-11
§ 7.07	Fractures	7-11

xv

[1]	Kinds and Combinations of Fractures	7-12
[2]	Fractures Designated by Location and Shape	7-13
[3]	Reduction and Resulting Effects of Fractures	7-13
[4]	Checklist for Claims Involving Fractures	7-14

CHAPTER 8
Injury and Disease

§ 8.01		Examples of Common Diseases and Injuries	8-2
	[1]	Ankylosis	8-2
	[2]	Arthritis	8-2
	[3]	Backaches and Herniated Discs	8-2
	[4]	Burns	8-5
	[5]	Bursitis	8-6
	[6]	Diabetes	8-6
	[7]	Eye Injuries	8-7
	[8]	Head Injuries	8-8
	[9]	Heart Disease	8-12
	[10]	Hernia	8-13
	[11]	Miscellaneous Injuries, Diseases, and Neurosis	8-14
	[12]	Multiple Sclerosis	8-16
	[13]	Occupational Diseases	8-17
	[14]	Osteomyelitis	8-19
	[15]	Osteoporosis	8-20
	[16]	Trichinosis	8-20
	[17]	Tuberculosis	8-20
	[18]	Tumors and their Relationship to Trauma	8-21
§ 8.02		Drug and Alcohol Abuse	8-22
§ 8.03		Some of the Newer Diagnostic Tools and Procedures	8-22
	[1]	Angiography	8-22
	[2]	Digital Subtraction Angiography (DSA)	8-22
	[3]	Balloon Angioplasty of the Arteries	8-22
	[4]	Tomography	8-23
	[5]	Computerized Tomography (C-T SCAN)	8-23
	[6]	Magnetic Resonance Imaging (MRI)	8-23
	[7]	Ultrasound	8-23
§ 8.04		Rehabilitation	8-24
§ 8.05		Bibliography	8-24

TABLE OF CONTENTS

CHAPTER 9
General Principles of Law–Part I

§ 9.01	Introduction	9-2
§ 9.02	Widespread General Knowledge Required	9-2
§ 9.03	Law Degree Not Essential	9-2
§ 9.04	Common and Statutory Law	9-3
§ 9.05	Law of Negligence as it Applies to Casualty Claims	9-4
	[1] Definition of Torts	9-4
	[2] Negligence	9-5
	[a] Degrees of Negligence	9-5
§ 9.06	Defenses	9-6
	[1] Contributory Negligence	9-7
	[2] Comparative Negligence	9-8
	[a] "Pure" Form of Comparative Negligence	9-8
	[b] "Modified" Form of Comparative Negligence	9-9
	[c] "Slight" Form of Comparative Negligence	9-10
§ 9.07	Unforeseeability	9-10
§ 9.08	Proximate Cause	9-11
§ 9.09	Intervening Cause	9-11
§ 9.10	Act of God	9-12
§ 9.11	Legislative Sanction	9-12
§ 9.12	Willful and Wanton Misconduct	9-12
§ 9.13	Last Clear Chance Doctrine	9-13
§ 9.14	Assumption of Risk Doctrine	9-14
§ 9.15	Multiple Defendants	9-16
	[1] Joint and Several Liability	9-17
	[2] Contribution Among Joint Tortfeasors	9-17
	[3] Counterclaim or Set-off	9-19
	[4] Declaratory Judgment Actions	9-19
	[5] Settlement in Multiple Claims Under Comparative Negligence	9-19
	[6] Mary Carter Agreements	9-21
	[7] Release and Covenant Not to Sue	9-21
§ 9.16	Nuisance	9-22
	[1] Attractive Nuisance Doctrine	9-23
	[2] Strict Liability	9-23
	[a] Dangerous Instrumentalities	9-24
	[b] Dangerous Activities	9-25
	[c] Inherent Defects	9-25

CASUALTY INSURANCE CLAIMS

	[d]	Blasting Operations	9-26
	[e]	Animals	9-26
	[f]	Aircraft	9-27
	[g]	Food and Drugs and Other Product Liability Cases	9-27
§ 9.17	Statutes of Limitations		9-27
§ 9.18	Bibliography		9-29

CHAPTER 10
General Principles of Law–Part II

§ 10.01	Conflict of Laws		10-2
	[1]	Lex Loci Delicti Rule	10-2
	[2]	Best Interests Rule	10-3
§ 10.02	Contracts		10-3
	[1]	In General	10-3
	[2]	General Principles of Contract Law	10-5
	[3]	Hold Harmless Agreements	10-6
	[4]	Exculpatory Contracts	10-6
§ 10.03	Damages		10-6
	[1]	In General	10-6
	[2]	Special Damages	10-7
	[3]	Property Damage	10-8
	[4]	Bodily Injury Damages	10-8
	[5]	Compensatory Damages	10-8
	[6]	Consequential Damages	10-9
	[7]	Exemplary or Punitive Damages	10-9
	[8]	Collateral Source Rule	10-10
	[9]	Loss of Consortium	10-11
	[10]	Actions for Wrongful Death and Survival Rights	10-11
	[11]	Joint Tortfeasors Liability for Damages	10-12
	[12]	Recovery Over	10-12
	[13]	Damages for Fright or Emotional Distress	10-13
§ 10.04	Evidence		10-14
	[1]	Classifications of Evidence	10-14
		[a] Hearsay Evidence	10-15
		[b] Res Gestae	10-15
		[c] Judicial Notice	10-16
	[2]	Burden of Proof	10-16
	[3]	Best Evidence Rule	10-16
	[4]	Opinion versus Fact	10-17
	[5]	Res Ipsa Loquitur	10-17
	[6]	Competency of Non-Expert Witnesses	10-18

TABLE OF CONTENTS

	[7]	Privileged Communications	10-19
	[8]	Expert Testimony	10-20
§ 10.05	Agency		10-21
	[1]	Imputed Negligence (Respondeat Superior)	10-21
	[2]	Determination of Agent's Negligence	10-22
		[a] Sub-Agency	10-22
		[b] Temporary or Special Employee	10-23
		[c] Deviation	10-23
		[d] Joint Venture Agency Liability	10-24
	[3]	Implied Agency Created by Statute	10-25
	[4]	Family Purpose Doctrine	10-26
	[5]	Independent Contractor	10-26
§ 10.06	Bailments		10-27
	[1]	Kinds of Bailments	10-28
		[a] Custody versus Bailment	10-28
		[b] Rental versus Bailment	10-29
		[c] Theft versus Bailment	10-29
	[2]	Acts of Employees	10-30
	[3]	Contributory or Comparative Negligence as a Defense	10-30
	[4]	Particular Bailments	10-30

CHAPTER 11
Intrafamily Tort Relationships and Immunities

§ 11.01	Minor Children		11-2
§ 11.02	Parental Liability for the Torts of Children		11-2
§ 11.03	The Doctrines of Parental and Spousal Immunities		11-5
	[1]	History and Background	11-5
	[2]	Parental Immunity Doctrine Still Effective	11-6
		[a] Fraud, Collusion, and Insurance as Factors	11-6
		[b] Effect of Insurance	11-7
	[3]	Abolition and Curtailment of the Parental Immunity Doctrine	11-9
	[4]	Emancipation	11-10
	[5]	Effect of the Death of Either Party	11-11
	[6]	Intentional, Willful and Wanton Torts	11-11
	[7]	Gross Negligence and Drunken Driving	11-12
	[8]	Change in Intrafamily Immunity Doctrines	11-13
§ 11.04	Husband/Wife Immunity Doctrine		11-13
	[1]	Historical Background	11-13
	[2]	Married Women Acts	11-14

	[3]	Present Trends Abrogating Husband/Wife Immunity	11-14
	[4]	Husband/Wife Immunity Still Holds	11-16
	[5]	Torts Committed Before Marriage	11-17
	[6]	The Insurance Factor in Husband/Wife Immunity	11-17
§ 11.05	Prenatal Injury		11-18
	[1]	Introduction	11-18
	[2]	Early Decisions	11-19
		[a] The Restriction of Viability	11-20
		[b] When Fetus is "Quick"	11-21
		[c] "At Time of Conception"	11-22
	[3]	Right to Recover for Death of Stillborn Child	11-22
		[a] Recovery Limited to Pecuniary Loss	11-23
		[b] Right of Action for Child Born Alive May Be Time Limited	11-23
	[4]	Requirement of Viability in Death Caused by Prenatal Injury	11-24
§ 11.06	Child's Right of Action for Wrongful Life		11-24
§ 11.07	Bibliography		11-26

CHAPTER 12

Governmental and Charitable Immunities

§ 12.01	Governmental Immunity		12-1
	[1]	History and Introduction	12-1
	[2]	Federal Immunities	12-2
		[a] Absolute Immunity—Judicial and Legislative	12-5
	[3]	State and Municipal Immunities	12-6
	[4]	"Governmental" or "Planning" Acts and Quasi-Immunities	12-8
	[5]	Riots and Civil Disturbances	12-9
	[6]	Ministerial or Proprietary Acts versus Governmental Acts	12-10
	[7]	Defense of Discretionary Acts	12-11
§ 12.02	Effect of Insurance Coverage on Immunity		12-12
§ 12.03	Punitive Damages in Governmental Immunity Cases		12-13
§ 12.04	The Doctrine of Charitable Immunity		12-15
	[1]	Charitable Immunity Practically Abolished	12-17
	[2]	Effect of Insurance Coverage on the Charitable Immunity Doctrine	12-18

TABLE OF CONTENTS

§ 12.05 Bibliography 12-19

CHAPTER 13
Suits—Practice and Procedure

§ 13.01	The Courts and Their Jurisdictions........................	13-1
§ 13.02	Service of Process...	13-4
	[1] Waiver of Proper Service.............................	13-6
	[2] Long Arm Statutes	13-6
§ 13.03	Change of Venue	13-10
§ 13.04	Pleadings...	13-12
§ 13.05	Insurance Policy as Evidence	13-17
§ 13.06	Trial..	13-18
§ 13.07	Appeal	13-18
§ 13.08	Liens	13-18
§ 13.09	Costs—Determination of Award	13-19
§ 13.10	Claim Department and Defense Counsel Action	13-21
§ 13.11	Excess Ad Damnum...	13-22

CHAPTER 14
Practical Considerations of Suits and Casualty Litigation

§ 14.01	Legal Expenses...	14-2
§ 14.02	Dealing With Defense Counsel..............................	14-3
	[1] Checklist in Defense Counsel Relationships	14-3
	[2] Settlement Reevaluation	14-4
	[a] Defense Counsel's Review....................	14-5
	[b] Claim Manager's or Supervisor's Review..	14-6
	[3] Reservation of Rights or Nonwaiver Agreements..	14-7
	[4] Availability of Witnesses...............................	14-7
	[5] Trial Preparation...	14-7
	[6] Trial and Disposition.....................................	14-9
	[7] Appeal...	14-10
	[8] Checklist for Suit Preparation......................	14-11
§ 14.03	Law Reporting Systems	14-13
	[1] Available Computer Systems........................	14-18
§ 14.04	Bibliography	14-19

CHAPTER 15
Fraud

§ 15.01	Fraud by the Claimant Concerning the Facts of an Accident	15-2

xxi

§ 15.02	Fraud Regarding Allegations of Injury	15-3
§ 15.03	Fraud Practiced by Repairmen or Doctors Without Collusion by the Claimant	15-4
§ 15.04	Fraudulent Acts of an Insured	15-4
§ 15.05	Beware of Danger Signals	15-5
§ 15.06	Investigation of Claims Involving Fraud	15-7
	[1] Undercover Investigations	15-8
	[2] Index Bureau	15-9
§ 15.07	Medical Fraud and Psychosomatic Illness	15-10
§ 15.08	Medical Fraud—Overtreatment and Incompetence	15-11
	[1] Misused Medical Terminology	15-12
	[2] Iatrogeny	15-13
§ 15.09	Bibliography	15-13

CHAPTER 16
Claims—Reserves, Reserving, and Statistics

§ 16.01	What Are Reserves?	16-1
§ 16.02	Various Types of Claims Reserves	16-4
	[1] Unearned Premium Reserves	16-4
	[2] Incurred But Not Reported Reserves (IBNR)	16-4
	[3] Actual Claim Reserves	16-5
	[4] Expense Reserves	16-6
	[5] One-Shot Cases	16-6
	[6] Delayed Reserving System	16-7
§ 16.03	Importance of Prompt Reporting	16-7
	[1] Automobile and General Liability Claim Reserving	16-7
	[2] Liability Suit Reserving	16-10
	[3] Fatal Cases Reserving	16-12
	[4] Property Damage Claims Reserving	16-12
	[5] Workers' Compensation Cases Reserving	16-13
§ 16.04	Reserve Revisions	16-14
§ 16.05	Claim Inventory or Reserve Reconciliation	16-15
§ 16.06	Reducing Outstanding Reserves	16-15
§ 16.07	Additional Factors to Consider in Reserving Policy	16-16
§ 16.08	Admissibility of Reserves in Evidence	16-16
§ 16.09	Claim Statistics	16-17
§ 16.10	Claim Department Responsibility	16-18
	[1] Claims	16-18
	[2] Suits	16-19

TABLE OF CONTENTS

	[3]	Average Reserves	16-21
	[4]	Claim Expenses	16-21
	[5]	Settlement Figures	16-22
	[6]	Statistical Forms	16-22
§ 16.11		The Age of the Computer	16-22
§ 16.12		Bibliography	16-25

CHAPTER 17
Settlements and Settlement Negotiations

§ 17.01	Introduction	17-2
§ 17.02	First-call Settlements	17-3
§ 17.03	General Rules Concerning Settlements	17-3
	[1] Demands Made After Settlement	17-4
	[2] Protecting Medical Bills	17-4
	[3] Dealing With the Claimant's Attorney	17-5
§ 17.04	Evaluating Bodily Injury Claims	17-5
§ 17.05	Decisions Concerning Evaluation	17-8
§ 17.06	Control	17-9
	[1] Maintaining Control of Death Cases	17-10
§ 17.07	The Proper Approach to Settlement Negotiations	17-10
§ 17.08	Offer Versus Demand	17-12
§ 17.09	Obtaining the Release	17-13
§ 17.10	Negotiating With Attorneys	17-14
§ 17.11	Disposition of Injury Claims Involving Minors	17-18
	[1] Medical Information	17-18
	[2] Indemnification Release	17-18
	[3] Investigation	17-19
	[4] Emancipated Child	17-20
	[5] Settlement With Court Approval	17-20
	[6] Closing Records	17-21
§ 17.12	Advance Payments	17-21
	[1] Advantages	17-22
	[2] Choosing the Cases	17-23
	[3] Some Reasonable Limitations	17-23
	[4] Method of Payment	17-24
	[5] Admission of Liability	17-25
	[6] Written Permission to Settle	17-26
	[7] Statute of Limitations	17-26
	[8] Follow-up	17-27
	[9] Closing the Case	17-27
§ 17.13	Structured Settlements	17-28
	[1] Introduction	17-28

	[2]	Tax Considerations	17-29
	[3]	Legal Aspects	17-32
	[4]	Model Structured Settlement Act	17-32
	[5]	Workers' Compensation Cases	17-33
§ 17.14	Bibliography		17-34

CHAPTER 18
Releases

§ 18.01	New Developments	18-1
§ 18.02	Contractual Aspects	18-2
§ 18.03	Release Forms	18-4
	[1] Execution of Release Forms	18-8
§ 18.04	Fraud	18-11
§ 18.05	Indecent Haste	18-11
§ 18.06	"Fairly and Knowingly Made"	18-12
§ 18.07	"In Full Satisfaction of All Claims Against Others"	18-12
§ 18.08	Mistake Concerning Injuries or Facts	18-13
§ 18.09	Respondeat Superior	18-14
§ 18.10	Joint Tortfeasors	18-14
	[1] Statutory Enactment—Uniform Contribution Acts	18-15
§ 18.11	Releases in Death Claims	18-16
§ 18.12	Alleged Subsequent Malpractice by Doctors	18-17
§ 18.13	Bad Faith Allegations to Induce Settlement	18-18
	[1] Assignment of Insured's Claim for Bad Faith	18-18
§ 18.14	Mary Carter Agreements	18-19
§ 18.15	Laches	18-20
§ 18.16	Bibliography	18-20

CHAPTER 19
Coverage Problems

§ 19.01	Typical Coverage Problems	19-2
§ 19.02	Importance of Immediate Investigation	19-3
§ 19.03	Disclaimer of Coverage	19-4
§ 19.04	Reservation of Rights	19-5
	[1] Wording of the Letter of Reservation	19-7
§ 19.05	Nonwaiver Agreements	19-7
§ 19.06	Declaratory Judgment Actions	19-8
§ 19.07	Plain Language Policies	19-9
§ 19.08	The Doctrine of Reasonable Expectations	19-10

TABLE OF CONTENTS

	[1]	Ambiguity in the Policy Provisions	19-11
	[2]	Existing Means for Balancing the Equities	19-12
	[3]	Commercial Policies	19-13
§ 19.09	Bibliography		19-15

CHAPTER 20
Some Important Casualty Policy Provisions

§ 20.01	Accident and Occurrence		20-3
	[1]	Self-Defense	20-4
§ 20.02	Duties of the Insurer		20-5
	[1]	Duty to Defend	20-5
	[2]	Determination of Insurer's Duty	20-7
	[3]	Duty to Appeal	20-10
	[4]	Family Automobile Policy	20-10
§ 20.03	Notice of Accident or Occurrence		20-11
	[1]	Prejudice	20-12
	[2]	Notice by Others On Behalf of the Insured	20-14
	[3]	"As Soon As Practicable"	20-14
	[4]	Written Notice	20-14
	[5]	Disclaimer Letter	20-15
	[6]	Investigation of Delayed Notice Cases	20-15
§ 20.04	Assistance and Cooperation		20-16
	[1]	Prejudice	20-17
	[2]	Nonappearance at Trial	20-18
	[3]	Statutory Protection for Injured Claimants	20-18
§ 20.05	"Other Insurance" Clause		20-19
§ 20.06	Policy Cancellation		20-21
	[1]	Written Notice of Cancellation	20-23
	[2]	Cancellation Because of Nonpayment of Premium	20-24
	[3]	Renewal of Coverage	20-25

CHAPTER 21
Liability for Bad Faith and Punitive Damages

§ 21.01	In General			21-1
	[1]	Original Concept		21-2
	[2]	Fraud or Bad Faith Doctrine		21-2
	[3]	Negligence		21-3
		[a]	Determining the Insurer's Negligence	21-4
		[b]	Absolute Liability for Excess Verdict	21-4
		[c]	Suggestions for Defensive Action	21-4

§ 21.02	Conditional Time Limitation Offers.............................		21-6
§ 21.03	Guiding Principles for Primary and Excess Insurers...		21-8
§ 21.04	Unfair Claim Settlement Practices Statutes.............		21-11
§ 21.05	Checklist for the Investigation of Excess Liability Claims...		21-15
§ 21.06	Insurance Coverage for Punitive Damages............		21-17
	[1]	Public Policy...	21-17
	[2]	Insurance Coverage.....................................	21-18
	[3]	Vicarious Liability—Employer-Employee Relationships...	21-19
§ 21.07	Bibliography...		21-20

CHAPTER 22
Automobile Policies and Coverages

§ 22.01	Introduction...		22-2
§ 22.02	History of the Automobile Liability Policy............		22-2
	[1]	Indemnity versus Liability.........................	22-2
	[2]	The Omnibus Clause—Permissive User of the Automobile...	22-3
	[3]	Some More Recent Decisions Regarding the Omnibus Clause.................................	22-5
	[4]	Other Early Differences..............................	22-6
	[5]	Standardization..	22-6
	[6]	Legislation..	22-7
§ 22.03	A Review and Comparison of the Family and Personal Auto Policies...................................		22-8
	[1]	Exclusions..	22-10
	[2]	Limits of Liability.......................................	22-10
	[3]	Out of State Coverage and Financial Responsibility..	22-11
	[4]	Other Insurance...	22-11
	[5]	Reduction in Coverage in Personal Auto Form..	22-12
§ 22.04	Medical Payments Coverage.....................................		22-12
	[1]	Exclusions..	22-13
	[2]	Limit of Liability...	22-15
	[3]	Other Insurance..	22-15
§ 22.05	Physical Damage—Motor Vehicle Claims...............		22-16
	[1]	Coverage...	22-16
	[2]	Salvage..	22-18
	[3]	Insurable Interest..	22-19
	[4]	Subrogation..	22-19

TABLE OF CONTENTS

	[5]	Decisions Concerning Policy Interpretation	22-20
	[6]	Checklists	22-20
		[a] Total Loss Claims	22-20
		[b] Theft Losses Investigation	22-21
		[c] Fire Losses Investigation	22-21
§ 22.06	Uninsured Motorist Coverage	22-22
	[1] Exclusions	22-23
	[2] Differences in Coverage	22-24
§ 22.07	Underinsured Motorist Coverage	22-24
	[1] Multiple Claimants	22-25
§ 22.08	Conditions for All Parts of the Personal Auto Policy	22-25
	[1] Duties After an Accident	22-25
	[2] Other Conditions	22-26
§ 22.09	Business Auto Policy	22-28
§ 22.10	Garage Policy	22-31
	[1] Care, Custody or Control Exclusion	22-33

CHAPTER 23
Some Laws Applicable to the Use of Automobiles

§ 23.01	Guest Statutes	23-2
	[1] Purpose of the Guest Statutes	23-3
	[2] Who Is a Guest?	23-3
	[3] Joint Venture	23-4
	[4] Share the Ride Arrangements	23-4
	[5] What Does Payment or Compensation Comprise?	23-4
	[6] Owner Occupant	23-5
	[7] Contributory or Comparative Negligence of Guests	23-5
	[8] Infants as Guests	23-6
	[9] Entering, Leaving, or Outside the Vehicle	23-6
	[10] Gross Negligence or Willful and Wanton Misconduct	23-7
	[11] Examples of Gross Negligence or Willful and Wanton Misconduct	23-7
§ 23.02	Checklist for Investigation of Guest Statute Cases	23-8
§ 23.03	Liquor Law Liability	23-9
	[1] Dram Shop and Liquor Control Statutes	23-10
	[2] Exclusivity of Dram Shop Legislation	23-11
	[3] Recent Trends	23-12

	[4]	Social Hosts and Company Parties	23-13
	[5]	Uninvited Guest	23-14
	[6]	Employer Hosts	23-14
	[7]	Minors or Incompetent Guests	23-15
	[8]	Common Law Defenses	23-16
	[9]	Noninnocent Participant	23-16
	[10]	Intoxication Defined	23-16
	[11]	Extraterritoriality in Dram Shop Jurisdiction	23-17
	[12]	Suit by the Intoxicated Person	23-17
	[13]	Insurance Coverage for Liquor Law Liability	23-18
§ 23.04	Seat Belt Defense		23-19
	[1]	Statutory Enactments	23-20
§ 23.05	Bibliography		23-21

CHAPTER 24
Protection Against the Irresponsible Motorist

§ 24.01	Financial Responsibility Laws		24-2
	[1]	Policy Wording	24-3
	[2]	Motor Carrier Act of 1980	24-5
§ 24.02	Assigned Risk Plans		24-6
§ 24.03	Unsatisfied Judgment Laws		24-7
§ 24.04	Compulsory Insurance		24-8
§ 24.05	Uninsured and Underinsured Motorist Coverage		24-8
	[1]	Stacking of Recoveries	24-9
	[2]	Hit-and-Run Cases	24-10
	[3]	Statute of Limitations	24-12
	[4]	Investigation of Uninsured Motorist Claims	24-12
§ 24.06	No-Fault Automobile Plans and Legislation—Personal Injury Protection (P.I.P.) Coverage		24-14
	[1]	Introduction	24-14
	[2]	History	24-14
	[3]	The Keeton–O'Connell Plan	24-16
	[4]	Complete Personal Protection Automobile Insurance Plan	24-16
	[5]	Present Trends—Personal Injury Protection (P.I.P.) Coverage	24-17
		[a] Policy Coverage	24-18
		[b] Multiple Coverages	24-20
		[c] Subrogation	24-20

TABLE OF CONTENTS

CHAPTER 25
Automobile Liability Investigation and Checklists

§ 25.01	Coverage Information	25-1
§ 25.02	Checklist on Policy Declarations	25-3
§ 25.03	Identification of the Insured's Vehicle	25-3
§ 25.04	Information to be Obtained from the Insured's Driver	25-4
§ 25.05	Information to be Obtained from the Claimant	25-9
§ 25.06	Witnesses	25-11
§ 25.07	Physical Facts or Objective Findings	25-11
§ 25.08	Further Details	25-13
§ 25.09	Evaluating Automobile Property Damage Claims	25-14
§ 25.10	Good Investigations Are Still Necessary	25-14
§ 25.11	Guide for Property Damage Settlement Decision	25-15
	[1] Loss of Use	25-18

CHAPTER 26
Public or General Liability Policies and Coverages

§ 26.01	Introduction	26-1
§ 26.02	Commercial General Liability Policy	26-3
	[1] The "Occurrence" Policy	26-5
	[2] The "Claims-Made" Policy	26-5
	[3] Extended Reporting Period	26-6
	[4] Section I—Coverages	26-9
	[a] Coverage A—Bodily Injury and Property Damage Liability	26-9
	[b] Duty to Defend	26-10
	[c] Exclusions in the Master Forms	26-11
	[5] Section II—Who Is an Insured	26-16
	[6] Section III—Limits of Insurance	26-16
	[7] Section IV—Commercial General Liability Conditions	26-16
	[a] Notice of Accident	26-16
	[8] Section V—Extended Reporting Periods	26-18
§ 26.03	Personal and Advertising Injury Liability	26-18
	[1] Definitions	26-20
	[2] Privileged Communications	26-22
	[3] Investigation of Personal Injury Cases	26-23
	[a] Defamation	26-23
	[b] False Arrest or Imprisonment	26-23
	[4] Damages	26-24

CASUALTY INSURANCE CLAIMS

§ 26.04	Advertising Injury	26-24
§ 26.05	Medical Payments	26-25
§ 26.06	Contractual Liability	26-26
§ 26.07	Products—Completed Operations	26-26
	[1] Covered Territory	26-29
	[2] Completed Operations	26-30
§ 26.08	Liquor Liability Coverage Form	26-30
§ 26.09	Pollution Liability Coverage	26-31
§ 26.10	Endorsements	26-33

CHAPTER 27
"Occurrence"

§ 27.01	Introduction	27-1
§ 27.02	"Occurrence" Is an "Accident"	27-2
§ 27.03	Manifestation Theory	27-3
§ 27.04	Exposure Theory	27-4
§ 27.05	Triple-Trigger Theory	27-5
§ 27.06	Injury In Fact	27-6
§ 27.07	"Cause of Injury" Determines Number of Occurrences	27-6
§ 27.08	Statute of Limitations	27-9
§ 27.09	Stacking and Proration	27-10
§ 27.10	Doctrine of Reasonable Expectations	27-12
§ 27.11	Neither Expected Nor Intended from the Standpoint of the Insured	27-13
§ 27.12	Self-Defense	27-15

CHAPTER 28
Investigation of Public or General Liability Claims

§ 28.01	In General	28-1
§ 28.02	General Checklist for the Investigation of Public or General Liability Claims	28-2
§ 28.03	Checklists for Special Investigations	28-11
	[1] Claims Involving Tenancy	28-11
	[2] Sidewalk Claims	28-12
	[3] Waxed Floors	28-14
	[4] Stairways	28-14
	[5] Falling Objects	28-15
	[6] Elevators	28-16
	[7] Escalators	28-18
	[8] Construction Cases	28-18

TABLE OF CONTENTS

    [9]   Sports Events, Fairgrounds, and
           Amusement Parks 28-20
    [10] Golfing Accidents 28-22
    [11] Animals 28-22
    [12] Blasting Operations 28-23

CHAPTER 29
Products Liability

§ 29.01	Coverage	29-2
§ 29.02	Products Hazard	29-2
§ 29.03	Containers	29-2
§ 29.04	Exclusions	29-3
§ 29.05	Limits of Liability	29-5
§ 29.06	Territorial Extension	29-5
§ 29.07	Persons Insured	29-6
§ 29.08	Vendor's Endorsement	29-6
§ 29.09	Legal Aspects of Products Liability	29-8
	[1] Intervening Acts	29-9
§ 29.10	Sales—Breach of Warranty	29-10
	[1] Express Warranty (U.C.C. § 2-313)	29-11
	[2] Merchantability and Fitness for Use	29-11
	[3] Implied Warranty—Merchantability Code (U.C.C. § 3-316)	29-12
	[4] Implied Warranty—Fitness for Particular Purpose	29-12
	[5] Multiple Grounds for the Same Action	29-13
	[6] Statute of Limitations in Warranty Actions	29-14
§ 29.11	Strict Liability	29-14
	[1] Vendor's Liability	29-16
	[2] Statutory Enactments	29-17
	[3] Insurance Protection	29-18
§ 29.12	Design Defects	29-18
	[1] Unreasonably Dangerous	29-19
	[2] Crashworthiness and Second Injury Liability	29-22
	[3] Seat Belts	29-24
	[4] Strict Liability in Design Defect Cases	29-24
	[5] Open and Obvious Danger	29-25
	[6] State-of-the-Art Defense	29-26

CHAPTER 30
Products Liability—Duty to Warn and Recall

§ 30.01		Duty to Warn..	30-1
	[1]	Negligence and Strict Liability in Duty to Warn..	30-3
	[2]	Foreseeability...	30-4
	[3]	Open and Obvious Condition..........................	30-5
	[4]	Design Defects...	30-6
	[5]	Dangers That Are Common Knowledge......	30-6
	[6]	Adequacy of Warning.....................................	30-7
	[7]	Proximate Cause..	30-9
	[8]	To Whom the Duty is Owed...........................	30-9
	[9]	Alterations...	30-10
	[10]	Component Part..	30-10
	[11]	Continuing Duty to Warn...............................	30-10
	[12]	Continuing Duty to Warn in Drug Cases....	30-11
	[13]	Method of Warning in Drug Cases...............	30-11
	[14]	Post-Accident Warnings................................	30-12
	[15]	Pre-Accident Governmental Standards Compliance...	30-13
	[16]	Model Act—Duty to Warn.............................	30-14
§ 30.02		Recall..	30-14
	[1]	Coverage from Loss Resulting from Recall	30-15
	[2]	"Sistership" Exclusion.....................................	30-15
	[3]	Recall Letter..	30-16
	[4]	Recall as a Defense...	30-17
	[5]	Assumption of Risk in Recall Cases..............	30-17
	[6]	Admissibility in Evidence of Recall Letter..	30-18

CHAPTER 31
Products Liability—Some Defenses and Related Problems

§ 31.01		Some Products Liability Defenses..........................	31-1
	[1]	Assumption of Risk in Products Liability Cases...	31-1
	[2]	Contributory Negligence................................	31-3
	[3]	Comparative Negligence as a Defense to Strict Liability..	31-4
	[4]	Comparative Causation...................................	31-6
§ 31.02		Used, Rebuilt, Reconditioned, or Altered Products...	31-6
	[1]	Liability of Manufacturer for Reconditioned Products.................................	31-6

TABLE OF CONTENTS

	[2]	Dealer Preparation	31-7
	[3]	Drugs and Related Products	31-8
	[4]	Duty to Warn in Prescription Drug Cases	31-10
	[5]	Hypersensitivity to Certain Drugs	31-10
	[6]	Pre-Marketing Testing	31-11
	[7]	Drug Addiction	31-11
	[8]	Statutes of Limitation in Drug Related Cases	31-12
	[9]	Handguns	31-12
	[10]	Subsequent Modification or Repair	31-14
§ 31.03		Federal Rules of Evidence	31-14
§ 31.04		Post-Settlement Problems	31-15
§ 31.05		Changes in Standards	31-15
§ 31.06		"Market Share" Liability and Similar Theories	31-16
§ 31.07		Successor Corporations	31-19
	[1]	Punitive Damages Against Successor Corporations	31-21
§ 31.08		Statutes of Limitations or Repose	31-21
	[1]	Statutes of Repose	31-22
	[2]	Implantations or Insertions	31-22
§ 31.09		Service versus Product	31-24

CHAPTER 32
Products Liability—Punitive Damages

§ 32.01		Punitive Damages	ˋ 32-1
	[1]	Multiple Exposure	32-1
	[2]	First Come, First Served	32-3
	[3]	Justification for Punitive Damages	32-3
	[4]	Phraseology Used in Justifying Punitive Damage Awards	32-5
	[5]	Settlement of Underlying Suit	32-7
	[6]	Collateral Estoppel	32-7
	[7]	Wrongful Death Statutes	32-8
	[8]	Strict Liability	32-9
	[9]	Negligence as a Basis for Awarding Punitive Damages	32-11
	[10]	Breach of Warranty	32-11
	[11]	Insurance for Punitive Damages	32-12
	[12]	Amounts Awarded—Model Uniform Products Liability Act	32-12

CHAPTER 33
Investigation of Products Liability Claims

§ 33.01	In General	33-1
§ 33.02	Strict Liability—Areas for Investigation	33-3
§ 33.03	Products Liability Investigation—General Checklist	33-4
§ 33.04	Products Liability—Some Specific Investigations Checklists	33-6
	[1] Automobiles	33-6
	[2] Bottling Claims	33-8
	[3] Crop Dusting	33-9
	[4] Drugs and Cosmetics	33-10
	[5] Food Consumption on Premises of Vendor	33-11
	[6] Design Defect Cases	33-12
	[7] Warning Defects Cases	33-12
	[8] Altered Products—Liability of Original Manufacturer	33-13
	[9] Product Recall	33-13
	[10] Market Share Liability for Fungible Products	33-14
§ 33.05	Bibliography	33-14

CHAPTER 34
Environmental Pollution

§ 34.01	Introduction	34-1
§ 34.02	Class Actions	34-2
§ 34.03	Mass Tort Litigation	34-2
§ 34.04	State Rules	34-5
§ 34.05	Federal Acts and Statutes Concerning Pollution	34-5
§ 34.06	Grounds for Bringing Environmental Pollution Actions	34-6
§ 34.07	Insurance Coverage	34-9
	[1] Occurrence and Accident Defined	34-10
	[2] Sudden and Accidental Discharges	34-11
	[3] Completed Operations Hazard Exclusion	34-11
	[4] Policies Intended to Cover Pollution Damage	34-12
	[5] First-Party Cases	34-12
	[6] Emotional Distress	34-13
	[7] Clean-up Costs	34-14
§ 34.08	Statutes of Limitation	34-14
§ 34.09	Investigation of Environmental Pollution Claims Checklist	34-15

TABLE OF CONTENTS

§ 34.10   Bibliography 34-16

CHAPTER 35
Professional Liability—Physicians

§ 35.01	Introduction..	35-2
§ 35.02	Physicians, Surgeons and Dentists Professional Liability Policies	35-4
	[1] Insuring Agreements..	35-5
	[2] Persons Insured	35-5
	[3] Limits of Liability	35-5
	[4] Medical Incident	35-6
	[5] Exclusions	35-6
	[6] Consent of Insured to Settle	35-7
	[7] Each Claim..	35-7
	[8] Protracted Treatment	35-8
	[9] Coverage for Insured's Employees......................	35-8
	[10] Notice of Accident...	35-8
	[11] Claims-Made Policies..	35-9
	[12] Sexual Wrongdoing..	35-9
§ 35.03	Some General Principles of Medical Malpractice Liability Law	35-11
	[1] Standard of Care..	35-11
	[2] *Res Ipsa Loquitur*...	35-13
	[3] Honest Error in Judgment	35-14
	[4] Informed Consent...	35-14
	[a] Exceptions to the "Informed Consent" Doctrine	35-17
	[b] Forms and Videotapes..........................	35-18
	[5] Defenses to Actions for Medical Malpractice..	35-18
	[6] Referral to Specialist	35-19
	[7] Abandonment	35-20
	[8] Psychiatrist and Psychotherapist Responsibility for Wrongful Release of Mentally Ill Patients	35-20
	[9] Second Injury...	35-22
	[10] Respondeat Superior or Captain-of-the-Ship Doctrine.........................	35-22
	[11] Contracts to Cure	35-23
	[12] Multiple Defendants..	35-24
	[13] Good Samaritan Doctrine	35-25
	[14] Malpractice Actions for Wrongful Birth and Wrongful Life..	35-26

	[a]	Wrongful Birth	35-26
	[b]	Wrongful Life	35-28
	[c]	Wrongful Pregnancy or Wrongful Conception	35-29
	[d]	"Benefits of Parenthood" Doctrine	35-30
	[e]	Damages Recoverable for Wrongful Birth Cases	35-31
	[15]	Actions Based on Contract	35-33
	[16]	Statutes of Limitations	35-33
	[a]	Discovery Rule—Foreign Substance Left in Body	35-34
	[b]	Continuing Negligence Rule	35-36
	[c]	Fraudulent Concealment	35-36
§ 35.04	Arbitration of Medical Malpractice Cases		35-37
§ 35.05	Recent Medical Malpractice Legislation		35-38
§ 35.06	Action for Wrongful Suit by Physicians		35-39
	[1]	Malicious Prosecution	35-40

CHAPTER 36
Professional Liability—Dentists, Nurses, Hospitals, and Druggists—and the Investigation of Medical Malpractice Claims

§ 36.01	Dentists		36-2
	[1]	Duty of Care	36-2
	[2]	Expert Testimony	36-3
	[3]	Contributory and Comparative Negligence	36-3
	[4]	Releases	36-3
	[5]	Statutes of Limitations	36-3
§ 36.02	Nurses		36-4
	[1]	Duty of Care	36-5
	[2]	Locality Rule	36-6
	[3]	Some Areas of Responsibilities	36-6
	[4]	Charitable Immunity	36-7
§ 36.03	Hospitals		36-7
	[1]	Coverage	36-7
	[2]	Who is Covered	36-8
	[3]	Hospital Liability	36-8
	[4]	Corporate Liability	36-9
	[5]	Standard of Care—Locality Rule	36-9
	[6]	Vicarious Liability of a Hospital	36-10
	[7]	Ostensible Agency Doctrine	36-12
	[8]	Product/Service Distinction	36-13
	[9]	Negligent Release of Mental Patient	36-14

TABLE OF CONTENTS

	[10]	Blood Transfusions	36-14
	[11]	Charitable Immunity	36-15
	[12]	Pleadings	36-15
§ 36.04	Druggists		36-16
§ 36.05	Investigation of Medical Malpractice Claims		36-16
	[1]	In General	36-16
	[2]	Checklists	36-19
		[a] Qualifications of the Insured	36-19
		[b] Factual Details	36-20
		[c] Information to be Obtained from or Concerning the Injured	36-20
		[d] Hospital Records	36-21
		[e] Druggist's Malpractice Claims	36-23
§ 36.06	Bibliography		36-24

CHAPTER 37
Professional Liability—Lawyers

§ 37.01	In General		37-1
§ 37.02	Policy Coverages		37-2
	[1]	Occurrence Policies	37-3
	[2]	Claims-Made Policies	37-3
	[3]	Exclusions	37-4
	[4]	Other ISO Policy Provisions	37-5
	[5]	Nonstandard Policy Forms	37-6
	[6]	Professional Services	37-6
§ 37.03	Grounds Upon Which Actions May Be Brought		37-7
	[1]	Privity of Contract	37-7
	[2]	Actions in Negligence—Standard of Care	37-8
	[3]	"Errors-in-Judgment" Rule	37-9
	[4]	Duty to Research the Law	37-11
	[5]	The Age of the Computer	37-11
	[6]	The Doctrine of "Informed Consent"	37-12
	[7]	The "But For" Rule	37-13
	[8]	Conflict of Interests	37-13
	[9]	Statute of Limitations	37-15
§ 37.04	Some Suggestions for the Investigation of Lawyer's Malpractice Cases		37-16
§ 37.05	Checklist for Avoiding Legal Malpractice		37-16
§ 37.06	Bibliography		37-18

CHAPTER 38
Other Areas of Professional Liability

§ 38.01	Accountants		38-2
	[1]	Definition of the Practice of Accounting	38-2
	[2]	Liability to Client—Standard of Reasonable Care	38-3
	[3]	Restatement (Second) of Torts	38-3
	[4]	Liability to Third Parties—Privity of Contract	38-4
	[5]	Statutory Liability—Federal Security Act	38-5
	[6]	Accountants' Professional Liability Policy	38-5
§ 38.02	Claim Adjusters		38-6
	[1]	Agency Obligations	38-7
§ 38.03	Architects and Engineers		38-8
	[1]	General Areas of Possible Liability	38-8
	[2]	Hold Harmless Agreements	38-9
	[3]	Statute of Limitations	38-10
	[4]	Legislation Concerning Statutes of Limitations	38-11
	[5]	Checklist for Investigation of Cases Involving Architects and Engineers	38-11
§ 38.04	Directors and Officers		38-12
	[1]	Indemnification	38-13
	[2]	Insurance	38-13
	[3]	The Insurance Policy	38-14
§ 38.05	Educators		38-15
	[1]	In General	38-15
	[2]	Students Participation in Sports or Other Athletics	38-16
§ 38.06	Insurance Agents		38-17
	[1]	Standard of Care	38-18
	[2]	Insurance Agent's Authority	38-18
	[3]	Ratification	38-19
	[4]	Professional Liability Coverage for Insurance Agents	38-19
	[5]	Binders	38-20
	[6]	Actions By Company Against Agent	38-20
	[7]	Actions By Insured Against Agent	38-21
	[8]	Actions By Third Parties Against Agent	38-22
	[9]	Some Defenses for Malpractice Actions	38-23
	[10]	Checklist for Insurance Agents to Prevent Some Actions for Malpractice	38-24
§ 38.07	Bibliography		38-25

TABLE OF CONTENTS

CHAPTER 39
Handling Workers' Compensation Cases

§ 39.01	General Principles		39-3
	[1]	Types of Compensation Acts	39-3
	[2]	State Provisions for Obtaining Coverage	39-4
§ 39.02	Administration		39-4
§ 39.03	Benefits		39-6
	[1]	In General	39-6
	[2]	Medical Benefits	39-6
	[3]	Indemnity Benefits	39-7
	[4]	Benefits to Dependents in Fatal Cases	39-8
	[5]	Waiting Period	39-8
	[6]	Second Injury or Special Disability Funds	39-8
§ 39.04	Those Entitled to Coverage		39-9
	[1]	Exempted Groups	39-9
	[2]	Injured Must Be an Employee	39-10
	[3]	Determining Who is an Employee and Who is an Employer	39-10
		[a] General Contractors	39-11
		[b] Subcontractor	39-11
		[c] Independent Contractor	39-11
		[d] Checklist for Determining Claimant's Status	39-12
		[e] Partners and Corporate Officers	39-13
		[f] Dual Employment	39-13
		[g] Loaned Employees	39-13
		[h] Volunteers	39-14
		[i] Casual Employees	39-14
		[j] Statutory Employers	39-14
		[k] Checklist for Determining Type of Employee	39-15
§ 39.05	Personal Injury By Accident Arising Out of and In the Course of the Employment		39-15
	[1]	Personal Injury	39-16
	[2]	Accident	39-16
	[3]	"Arising Out of the Employment"	39-16
	[4]	"In the Course Of"	39-18
§ 39.06	Exclusive Remedy in Workers' Compensation		39-19
	[1]	Remedy Exclusive Even Where No Compensation Award is Made	39-21
	[2]	Derivative Suits	39-22

CASUALTY INSURANCE CLAIMS

	[3]	Action for Loss of Consortium	39-23
	[4]	Recent Trends in California	39-24
	[5]	Dual Capacity Doctrine	39-25
	[6]	Insurance Coverage Dilemma	39-28
	[7]	Intentional Injury	39-28
	[8]	Sexual Harassment	39-29
	[9]	Exclusivity in Occupational Disease Cases	39-29
	[10]	Election to Sue Employer	39-30
§ 39.07	Third Party Action		39-30
§ 39.08	Punitive Damages Arising Out of Compensation Cases		39-31
§ 39.09	Jurisdiction and Extraterritoriality		39-31
	[1]	Jurisdiction	39-32
§ 39.10	Notice of Accident or Disease		39-33
§ 39.11	Liability of Successive Insurers		39-34
§ 39.12	Illegal Employment of Minors		39-35
§ 39.13	Malpractice as Related to Workers' Compensation		39-36
§ 39.14	Final Determination		39-36
§ 39.15	Rehabilitation		39-36
§ 39.16	Structured Settlements in Workers' Compensation Cases		39-37

CHAPTER 40
Workers' Compensation-Employers' Liability Policy and Investigation

§ 40.01	In General			40-1
	[1]	Coverage A—Workers' Compensation		40-2
	[2]	Coverage B—Employers' Liability		40-4
	[3]	Occupational Disease		40-5
	[4]	Voluntary Compensation Endorsement		40-7
	[5]	Extra-Legal Medical Benefits Endorsement		40-7
§ 40.02	Workers' Compensation Investigation			40-7
	[1]	Unfair Claim Practices Acts		40-9
	[2]	Index Bureau Reports		40-9
	[3]	Checklists		40-10
		[a]	Coverage	40-10
		[b]	Factual Information	40-12
		[c]	Information to be Obtained from Insured	40-14
		[d]	Information to be Obtained from Claimant	40-16
		[e]	Medical Investigation	40-18

TABLE OF CONTENTS

	[4] Physical Facts	40-19
	[5] Subrogation	40-20
§ 40.03	Occupational Disease Investigation	40-20
	[1] Checklist	40-21
§ 40.04	Non-Occupational Disability Laws	40-22
§ 40.05	Bibliography	40-22

CHAPTER 41
Federal Employer-Employee and Other Federal Legislation

§ 41.01	Federal Employees' Compensation Act (FECA)	41-2
§ 41.02	Federal Employers' Liability Act	41-2
§ 41.03	Longshore and Harbor Workers' Compensation Act	41-3
§ 41.04	Defense Base Act	41-6
§ 41.05	War Hazards Compensation Act	41-6
§ 41.06	Economic Opportunity Act	41-7
§ 41.07	The Jones Act (Merchant Marine Act, Revised 7th ed. 1976)	41-7
§ 41.08	Seaworthiness	41-8
§ 41.09	Federal Tort Claims Act	41-9
§ 41.10	Occupational Safety and Health Act (OSHA)	41-10
§ 41.11	Death on the High Seas Act (1976) (DOHSA)	41-11
§ 41.12	Racketeer Influenced and Corrupt Organizations Act (RICO)	41-12
§ 41.13	Bibliography	41-14

CHAPTER 42
Wrongful Termination of Employment

§ 42.01	Introduction	42-1
§ 42.02	Actions Brought in Contract	42-2
§ 42.03	Implied Contracts—Personnel Manuals	42-3
§ 42.04	Public Policy Exceptions to the "At-Will" Doctrine	42-4
§ 42.05	Implied Covenant of Good Faith and Fair Dealing	42-6
§ 42.06	Tort of Wrongful Discharge	42-7
	[1] Fraud	42-7
	[2] Intentional Infliction of Emotional Distress	42-8
	[3] Employment Discrimination	42-8
	[4] Other Grounds for Tort Actions	42-9
§ 42.07	Some Insurance Problems in Termination of Employment Cases	42-9

CASUALTY INSURANCE CLAIMS

	[1]	Umbrella Policies	42-9
	[2]	Errors and Omissions and Directors and Officers Liability Policies	42-10
	[3]	Comprehensive and Commercial General Liability Policies	42-11
	[4]	Occurrence—Pattern and Practice	42-12
	[5]	"Civil Suit"	42-13
	[6]	Public Policy in Insurance Coverage	42-13
	[7]	Workers' Compensation Policy	42-14
§ 42.08		Checklist for Handling Termination Cases	42-15
§ 42.09		Bibliography	42-16

CHAPTER 43
Subrogation—Salvage—Contribution

§ 43.01		Subrogation	43-1
	[1]	Policy Wording	43-2
	[2]	Applicable Insurance Lines	43-3
	[3]	Third Party Recovery	43-3
	[4]	Third Party Settlement by Insured	43-4
	[5]	Sample Form Lien Letters	43-5
	[6]	Other Subrogation Rights	43-5
	[7]	Right of Action	43-6
	[8]	Defenses to Subrogation Actions	43-6
	[9]	Voluntary Payment	43-6
	[10]	Waiver of Subrogation Rights	43-7
	[11]	Loan Receipts	43-7
	[12]	Practical Application of Subrogation Rights	43-9
	[13]	Some Factors to Consider	43-9
	[14]	Subrogation Receipt	43-10
	[15]	Knock-For-Knock Agreements	43-11
	[16]	Subrogation Agreement	43-11
	[17]	Arbitration	43-12
	[18]	Deductible Feature of Collision Policy	43-12
	[19]	Subrogation Apportionment—Excess Carrier	43-13
	[20]	Recovery Expenses	43-13
	[21]	A Few Recent Cases Involving Subrogation	43-13
	[22]	Subrogation Under the Workers' Compensation Acts	43-14
§ 43.02		Salvage	43-15
	[1]	In General	43-15
	[2]	Checklist for Claims Involving Salvage	43-16

TABLE OF CONTENTS

§ 43.03	Contribution	43-16
§ 43.04	Bibliography	43-17

CHAPTER 44
Reporting and Reports

§ 44.01	Introduction		44-1
§ 44.02	Reporting		44-2
	[1]	Necessity for Reporting	44-2
	[2]	Necessity for Prompt Reporting	44-3
	[3]	Manner and Form of Reporting	44-4
	[4]	The Art of Dictating a Report	44-5
	[5]	Objectionable Material	44-6
§ 44.03	Reports		44-7
	[1]	Casualty Claim Investigation Report Outline (Other than Compensation)	44-7
		[a] Suits	44-12
	[2]	Compensation Claim Investigation Report Outline	44-12
	[3]	Special Report Outlines	44-17
	[4]	Interim Reports	44-17
	[5]	Final Reports	44-18

Index Ind.-1

Checklists

Chapter 3	**General Principles of Investigation**	
	Locating the Missing Witness.........................	3-10
	Investigating the Special Damages................	3-13
	General Investigation of Fatal Claims	3-15
	Confidential Report to the Underwriters.....	3-15
Chapter 5	**Securing the Physical Facts**	
	Diagrams..	5-2
Chapter 6	**Obtaining Medical Information**	
	Information to be Obtained from the Claimant...	6-3
Chapter 7	**Medicine—Fundamentals**	
	Claims Involving Fractures............................	7-14
Chapter 8	**Injury and Disease**	
	Arthritis...	8-2
	Backaches and Herniated Discs....................	8-2
	Head Injuries	8-8
	Miscellaneous Injuries, Diseases, and Neurosis...	8-14
Chapter 14	**Practical Considerations of Suits and Casualty Litigation**	
	Defense Counsel Relationships	14-3
	Suit Preparation	14-11
Chapter 15	**Fraud**	
	Investigation of Claims Involving Fraud......	15-7
Chapter 21	**Liability for Bad Faith and Punitive Damages**	
	Investigation of Excess Liability Claims.......	21-15
Chapter 22	**Automobile Policies and Coverages**	
	Total Loss Claims...	22-20
	Theft Losses Investigation.............................	22-21
	Fire Losses Investigation	22-21
Chapter 23	**Some Laws Applicable to the Use of Automobiles**	
	Investigation of Guest Statute Cases............	23-8
Chapter 24	**Protection Against the Irresponsible Motorist**	
	Investigation of Uninsured Motorist Claims	24-12

xlv

CASUALTY INSURANCE CLAIMS

Chapter 25 Automobile Liability Investigation and Checklists
    Coverage Information 25-1
    Policy Declarations 25-3
    Identification of the Insured's Vehicle 25-3
    Information to be Obtained from the
        Insured's Driver 25-4
    Information to be Obtained from the
        Claimant 25-9
    Physical Facts or Objective Findings 25-11
    Guide for Property Damage Settlement
        Decision 25-15

Chapter 26 Public or General Liability Policies and Coverages
    Investigation of Personal Injury Cases 26-23

Chapter 28 Investigation of Public or General Liability Claims
    General Checklist 28-2
    Special Investigations
        Claims Involving Tenancy 28-11
        Sidewalk Claims 28-12
        Waxed Floors 28-14
        Stairways 28-14
        Falling Objects 28-15
        Elevators 28-16
        Escalators 28-18
        Construction Cases 28-18
        Sports Events, Fairgrounds, and
            Amusement Parks 28-20
        Golfing Accidents 28-22
        Animals 28-22
        Blasting Operations 28-23

Chapter 33 Investigation of Products Liability Claims
    General Checklist 33-4
    Some Specific Investigations
        Automobiles 33-6
        Bottling Claims 33-8
        Crop Dusting 33-9
        Drugs and Cosmetics 33-10
        Food Consumption on Premises of
            Vendor 33-11
        Design Defect Cases 33-12
        Warning Defects Cases 33-12
        Altered Products—Liability of Original
            Manufacturer 33-13

CHECKLISTS

	Product Recall	33-13
	Market Share Liability for Fungible Products	33-14
Chapter 34	**Environmental Pollution**	
	Investigation of Environmental Pollution Claims	34-15
Chapter 36	**Professional Liability—Dentists, Nurses, Hospitals, and Druggists—and the Investigation of Medical Malpractice Claims**	
	Qualifications of the Insured	36-19
	Factual Details	36-20
	Information to be Obtained from or Concerning the Injured	36-20
	Hospital Records	36-21
	Druggist's Malpractice Claims	36-23
Chapter 37	**Professional Liability—Lawyers**	
	Investigation of Lawyer's Malpractice Cases	37-16
	Avoiding Legal Malpractice	37-16
Chapter 38	**Others Areas of Professional Liability**	
	Investigation of Cases Involving Architects and Engineers	38-11
	Checklist for Insurance Agents to Prevent Some Actions for Malpractice	38-24
Chapter 39	**Handling Workers' Compensation Cases**	
	Determining Claimant's Status	39-12
	Determining Type of Employee	39-15
Chapter 40	**Workers' Compensation-Employers' Liability Policy and Investigation**	
	Coverage	40-10
	Factual Information	40-12
	Information to be Obtained from Insured	40-14
	Information to be Obtained from Claimant	40-16
	Medical Investigation	40-18
	Occupational Disease Investigation	40-20
Chapter 42	**Wrongful Termination of Employment**	
	Handling Termination Cases	42-15
Chapter 43	**Subrogation—Salvage—Contribution**	
	Claims Involving Salvage	43-16

CHAPTER 1

The Occupation of Claim Representative and Claim Handling Procedures

§ 1.01   The Good Claims Representative
         [1]   Qualifications
         [2]   Training and Education
§ 1.02   Claim Handling Procedures
         [1]   Proper Preparation
         [2]   Prompt and Thorough Investigation
         [3]   Decision and Action
         [4]   Adequate Reporting
         [5]   Self-Discipline

§ 1.01   The Good Claims Representative

Prompt, fair, sound, and equitable claim handling is the measure of an insurance company. Proper claim handling is the most important product that a company has to sell. The company is judged by the manner in which each person in the Claim Department performs his or her obligations. The day is past when all that a claim representative had to know was how to drive a hard bargain.

What is proper claim handling? It is synonymous with fair and ethical dealing. It calls for sympathy, tact, and understanding. But it is also the realization that the obligations of an insurance carrier run to the insureds, stockholders, and the general public, as well as to the individual claimant.

The claim representative, therefore, must work within the limits set by the insurance contract and resist an improper claim to the same extent that the company meets its just obligations in paying a claim.

To put it another way, although he or she must always be more than willing to settle a fair and proper claim, it is also his or her duty to decline payment on claims which have no merit or which are not covered under the policy provisions.

It is well recognized today that the Claim Department is the most important factor in creating goodwill among actual and prospective clients. Careless, thoughtless, or inefficient claim handling can easily destroy the reputation of a company, and can also do great harm to the industry as a whole.

[1] Qualifications

Everyone has certain aptitudes and qualifications which to some extent determine the means by which that individual will earn his livelihood. An individual's desire to enter a certain profession may be based, at least in part, on illusions, both about his or her own qualifications and about the occupation itself.

If personnel selection, with all its aptitude tests, were an exact science, a good deal of unhappiness created by placing a square peg in a round hole could be avoided. There are, however, certain universal attributes and characteristics which a claim representative must have to be a success in the casualty claim field:

1. **Integrity** is foremost. The temptations that beset the casualty claims person are many and varied. The pressures come not only directly from the occasional few with whom a claim is being settled, but also indirectly from those with whom he or she has constant business associations. These include appraisers, repair shops, replacement outlets, doctors, defense attorneys, and many others upon whom the claim representative must constantly call for paid services.

Lest this assertion be misconstrued, the instances of outright bribery are comparatively few. However, it is sometimes the practice of some people who are dependent upon claim people for business assignments to tender gifts or services of various kinds in appreciation. In some instances these are friendly gestures without wrongful intent or implication, but such practice undeniably builds actual or fancied obligations. For this reason, it is best that claim personnel refuse *all* gratuities.

As for "kick-backs," it cannot be stated too emphatically that this is outright dishonesty whether accepted as an alleged gratuity from a garage or claimant after a case is settled, or received as outright bribery.

2. **Courtesy.** A good claim representative is naturally courteous and should act accordingly. Courtesy and consideration must be shown to all people with whom the representative comes in contact.

Patience, tact, and diplomacy are as important as technical knowledge.

3. **Intelligence** is another important qualification. Intelligence is not to be confused with education, which is what this book is all about, nor is it something that can be accurately measured by the grades acquired in school or college. These may be some indication, but all too often have more to do with memory than they do with intelligence.

The new claim representative must have intelligence enough to grasp quickly, many problems about which he may know little or nothing. He must, for example, learn enough about automobile mechanics to determine whether repair bills are in order. He will shortly be drawn into problems involving fields new to him, such as construction, engineering, and chemistry, and must be able to analyze and investigate claims in these and many other specialized fields.

A good claim representative must try to satisfy the insured, the agent, the claimant or his attorney, and his superiors. He constantly comes in contact with people who, because of physical injury or financial loss, feel wronged and emotionally upset. Claimants who have suffered financial loss are primarily concerned with reimbursement, and, human nature being what it is, avarice plays a part in many of their demands. A claim representative has everyday dealings with those who, by training, are shrewd negotiators.

It is therefore obvious that the competent claim representative must be alert to all of these factors and must have the intelligence to deal with them promptly and properly in accordance with changing situations. He must be quick-thinking and adaptable.

4. **Personality.** The prospective claim representative must have a good personality. He should be well poised, able to meet all types of people on an equal basis and make them feel that he is neither inferior nor condescending. It is of the utmost importance that he is liked by those with whom he comes in contact.

5. **Education** is of course an important factor. There can be no doubt that a legal education is a definite advantage. In my opinion, however, the lack of a law degree should not be a major deterrent for the new prospect. There are too many examples of top-notch claim people whose formal education did not go beyond high school to permit too much weight to be given to this item.

Unfortunately, a high school education today may not mean very much. A prospective claim representative must at least have a basic understanding of the English language. If he expects to make progress he will have to do a lot of technical reading on insurance, law, and medicine, as well as peripheral reading involving the investigation and handling of specific products or other claims. He must have the ability to write and talk clearly and understandably. If he has not mastered these basics he will be wasting his time and creating an impression for his company that can be very harmful.

However, education can be a matter of self-training. It need not necessarily be considered only from the standpoint of classroom study.

6. **Tolerance** is another characteristic essential to the good claim representative. It is a broad term, often misused. It should include an attempt to understand differences in points of view, politics, way of life, as well as race, religion, and foreign background.

A claim representative meets all kinds of people who have all shades of opinion, background, economic status, race, and creed. If he is to be effective in his work he must not reveal his prejudices. It is, of course, Utopian to expect anyone to be without prejudices of any sort. We all have them in varying degrees. These prejudices, however, must not be of major proportions and must be kept under control. By constant self-examination and education, we may even be able to eliminate many of them.

7. **Intangibles.** A good claim representative should have further qualities that, for lack of a better term, may be called intangibles. These include common sense, imagination, initiative, persistence, and similar qualities which are essential. Here, again, it is not a mere matter of terminology. Common sense for instance is a quality that can be differentiated from both education and intelligence. It is a term difficult to define, but includes doing the right thing at the right time. The other requirements mentioned above are obvious and speak for themselves.

[2] **Training and Education**

Many theses have been written about the effectiveness of book learning compared to that of supervised work instruction in training programs. In claim work, each is important and each has its proper place.

There is no limit to the amount of knowledge a person can acquire in the casualty claim field. Constant study is **absolutely essential** to the development of a good claim representative, and a planned course of study is much more effective than haphazard reading.

Essential source material should encompass:

(a) A review of representative files covering all lines of business written in the company which the new employee may be required to handle.
(b) Familiarization with the principal types of policies issued.
(c) Familiarization with company manuals, bulletins, and general written instructions.
(d) Books and articles.
(e) Introduction to insurance and law magazines and journals.
(f) Introduction to the applicable Workers' Compensation Acts, where pertinent, FC&S Bulletins, and pertinent statutes and material that will be helpful in the long run.

Proficiency, however, often requires more than book knowledge. Actual performance is essential to the development of proper methods. Experience with agents, with contacts and procedures required to obtain reports, with important insureds and all persons who can help, is vitally necessary.

§ 1.02 Claim Handling Procedures

Since the present legal code of ethics permits advertising by lawyers, old-time ambulance chasing has become past history. The names of firms that specialize in negligence work can be obtained on every street corner and from just about every television and radio program. The big guns in the plaintiff's legal fraternity do not have to advertise since the inexperienced lawyers are only too willing to share their fees with those attorneys who have an established reputation in the accident field.

Accordingly, it will be rare that a bodily injury claimant will not be represented by an attorney. It is best to make this determination as soon as possible and, if the claimant is so represented, all further contact with the plaintiff concerning the claim must be made through the claimant's attorney.

That is not to say that *all* claimants will be so represented, and that is why it is so urgently important to assure the claimant who is not so represented, as soon as possible, that he or she will be dealt with fairly. Judgment is obviously necessary to avoid making any specific settlement promises unless the claim representative has enough information to warrant settlement. Otherwise, most of what is included in this chapter applies whether or not an attorney is representing the claimant. The subject of negotiating with lawyers will be dealt with in much more detail in subsequent chapters that apply to specifically related topics.

The average outside investigator and claim representative, these days, probably has more work than he or she can handle comfortably. It is also the policy of some companies to handle some liability injury cases, at least initially, by telephone. There is no objection to getting some advance information by telephone when making an appointment for a personal interview, as long as the questions asked do not drive the individual being questioned into the arms of the nearest attorney.

Nevertheless, while some corners will inevitably be cut, under some circumstances, it is the purpose of this book to tell how it should be done and hope that the reader has the opportunity to follow the suggestions made.

There is no better way of calling attention to the abilities of a claim representative than by doing exceptional work, which it is hoped this book may help him or her to do.

There are five general phases to good claim handling procedures:

1. Proper preparation;
2. Prompt and thorough investigation;
3. Decision and action;
4. Adequate reporting; and
5. Self-discipline.

Each of these elements will be discussed in detail, but by way of general introduction to the field of casualty claims handling and investigation, the comments in this chapter should set a proper perspective.

[1] **Proper Preparation**

Proper preparation enables the claim representative to plan an orderly investigation without loss of time or effort. Such preparation avoids the necessity for call-backs to the insured, claimant, or witnesses. Call-backs are not only a waste of time, but are bad public relations as well. An additional interview gives the impression that the company is uncertain, or is looking for an "out."

A thoroughly planned initial interview makes it more likely that the claim representative will obtain correct and complete information. Claimants and witnesses become suspicious when a call-back is made to get additional information which should have been obtained in the initial contact. Not only does the claim representative run the risk of losing control of the case, but greatly lessens the chances of getting the entire truth in the form of a signed statement.

It is obvious that proper preparation should begin at the very inception of a case—that is, at the receipt of the first report. It requires prompt and thorough analysis of the problems involved. Such an analysis must be based upon the facts at hand, the coverage information, and the applicable law. *It cannot be based upon guess and surmise.*

The investigation, once started, becomes a constantly shifting picture with new leads and new avenues of inquiry opening up as it develops. As we progress into the various specific areas of investigation that will involve the special coverages, we will discuss in much more detail the investigation needed in each specific instance. The discussion here will be limited to general principles. Suggested steps for the proper preparation in the handling of casualty claims are as follows:

1. **Review the Report.** Review the initial report carefully and make notes on the information contained therein. These notes should be made in the form of a worksheet which the investigator should have for every claim that he handles. Some companies have preprinted worksheets which outline the investigation to be made and leave space for the insertion of important information such as the file number, names of the insured, claimant, and witnesses, coverage information, facts, etc. If such preprinted sheets are not available, it is easy enough to make them up.

If the original report of accident is incomplete, a telephone call to the insured will usually provide sufficient details to enable the claim representative to arrange an orderly plan of action. Such a call may serve the double purpose of arranging for an appointment with the insured, since it will be necessary to obtain a detailed signed statement from him or her on any serious claim. Quite often, drawing a rough diagram from the facts at hand will help to clarify the picture.

It is, of course, obvious that not all claims will demand the same kind of investigation. The insured's first report may indicate that the matter is of minor importance and may contain sufficient information to avoid the necessity of further contact with him. Again, the matter may be important enough to warrant a phone call for additional information without personal contact. Each company has its own policy concerning the degree of investigation necessary, depending upon the importance of the case involved, and the supervisor will soon inform the claim representative concerning the company's attitude in this respect.

2. **Examine the Coverage.** Over the years, a mystique has been developed concerning coverage problems. In many companies the new claim representative is not required to do any policy reading and is, as a matter of fact, occasionally discouraged from doing so. I personally believe that instruction in coverage problems is of prime importance and should begin as soon as possible. It will certainly be of prime importance as long as the claim representative is involved in claim work. Certainly, if an insured is expected to know what is in his policy, the claim representative should at least be just as familiar with it. It cannot be expected that a new claim representative will be able to interpret a policy which is complicated or needs legal interpretation, but he should at least become familiar with the major problem areas as soon as possible.

Accordingly, the claim representative should examine the coverage carefully in the light of the facts at hand on all important cases involving anything other than the ordinary uncomplicated accident report. The application, or daily, and all endorsements should be "pulled" and examined. If the claim representative recognizes a coverage problem he should immediately consult with his supervisor concerning it and make a careful outline of the investigation needed for a proper determination of the problem involved. All of the facts connected with the problem should be obtained. Specific coverage questions will be discussed in detail subsequently.

In cases involving coverage questions, it is most important that as little as possible be left to guess work. A wrong decision can do untold harm in a relationship with the insured, his agent, and with the public at large.

3. **Outline the Projected Investigation.** After the facts and the coverage information have been reviewed, a complete outline of the projected investigation should be made. Here again is where a worksheet becomes invaluable. Enough space should be allocated so that the investigator can list everything that has to be done in the order

of its importance. He may get the impression that he does not have the time to do this, but in the long run the time spent in outlining the projected investigation will be more than made up by the time saved in wandering around aimlessly.

Where necessary, he should use all available technical aids such as textbooks, articles on related subjects, and the policy itself if needed to become familiar with it.

4. **Outline the Interview.** Some sort of an outline should be made of the points that are to be covered in each interview. While the interview is progressing, it is impossible to remember everything about a complicated claim. The use of proper notes reduces the possibility of overlooking an important point and avoids the necessity for call-backs.

5. **Consultations.** If there is any doubt or confusion about the direction of the investigation or the facts to be obtained, a claim representative should discuss the matter with his manager or supervisor to get additional ideas or clarification of the objectives.

To consult with someone else on an intricate problem is not an admission of weakness. The very act of talking over the situation will help clarify the objectives. The old adage that "two minds are better than one" has been proven time and again in claims work.

6. **Make an Itinerary.** If a claim representative were handling only one claim at a time it would be relatively easy to make an itinerary that would be efficient and most productive. Unfortunately, the economics of the situation are such that this is impossible since every claim representative is required to handle a sizable workload. Accordingly, it is essential that he consider the following factors in planning his itinerary for the day.

(a) The order of importance of the claim itself. He may have an important case that is going into suit where it is absolutely essential for him to obtain some information as soon as possible.

(b) The location of the stops that he is to make. It is important for him to try to arrange his itinerary so that he does not have to backtrack any more often than is absolutely necessary. If backtracking is required it might be more efficient for him to arrange to make several stops in different areas on different days.

(c) Where possible, and where advisable, he should make advance appointments which will have to be fitted into his itinerary. I am not advocating making appointments in all cases because there will be many instances where it will be advisable to try to surprise a witness or a claimant and not give him any advance notice that the claim representative wants to interview him. However, where the element of surprise is not involved, appointments will save a lot of time.

(d) Finally, in making an itinerary, the investigator will have to consider the likelihood that the individual he is seeking will be at home or at his place of business at the time when he will be there. Except on weekends it is obviously silly to call a business person at home during working hours or vice versa. Give consideration to this factor before making up the itinerary.

It will hardly ever be possible to make up a perfect itinerary in view of the above factors. However, if some of these factors are taken into consideration in making up the itinerary it will certainly be much more advantageous than to start making calls blindly without any advance planning.

To repeat, for the sake of emphasis: In a situation where a specific case is of prime importance, such a case should obviously receive preference. On an individual important case there can be no set formula. For instance, if sufficient facts have been obtained from the insured in his first report, or in a telephone conversation, it may be better to see the claimant personally on the first call. On the other hand, if at the time the claim representative is ready to start his investigation, he does not have sufficient facts to form a fairly clear picture of what happened, he may consider it advisable to see the insured first.

Where "ambulance chasing" is prevalent, it is usually more practical to make an attempt to see the claimant immediately. To see the insured first is usually wiser when coverage questions are involved, since a determination of the coverage problem may make it inadvisable to contact the claimant at all. Possibly the scene of the accident is on the route to the insured or to the claimant. In that case the claim representative might wish to examine the scene before he interviews the principals.

[2] Prompt and Thorough Investigation

A prompt investigation very often affords the opportunity to make first call settlements where the facts and injury so warrant. First call settlements have a definite advantage even where the payments appear at the time to be a little higher than the claim representative's opinion of the actual value of a claim.

By completing a justifiable first call settlement, the claim representative saves the time that would ordinarily be spent in additional investigation, reporting, and return calls to the claimant. This time can be used to better advantage on other cases. An early settlement saves the time of the typist and clerk on reports and office routine handling. It saves mailing costs on reports and conserves material. Such disposition leaves one less case for the home office examiner to review, and avoids the necessity for maintaining an open reserve. Finally, it eliminates the possibility of malingering and padding of special damages at some later date. When a claim representative pays top value to dispose of a case, he obviously does so to avoid trouble later. The longer a settlement is delayed, the more likelihood there is of difficulty in disposition.

Even if the first call settlement is impossible or inadvisable because of the extent of the injury or the attitude of the claimant, prompt contact with the claimant is advantageous. When approached promptly, the claimant is apprised of the company's interest and desire to act fairly. The claim representative is given time to establish firm relations with the claimant and maintain control before well-meaning friends or relatives give ill-advised counsel.

Prompt neighborhood investigation at the scene of an accident is very likely to disclose witnesses who have not come forward voluntarily. Promptness affords the opportunity to obtain signed statements from all of the witnesses while the facts are still fresh in their minds, and before they can be influenced by others. Timely investigation permits a claim representative to get the physical facts before conditions have changed. Photographs, for instance, should be obtained during the time of the year when the accident occurred and not after seasonal changes have denuded the trees of their leaves or streets and pavements of ice and snow. Although the danger of tampering with physical conditions is comparatively slight in most parts of the country, wear and tear alone may in time change the physical aspects of the location of an accident, and ordinary repairs may be made which alter the original condition.

Immediate investigation makes it more likely for a claim representative to obtain medical information or authorization to get such medical information.

A prompt interview with an insured, agent, or broker is much more likely to reveal the truth concerning a question of coverage or delayed notice.

Investigation soon after the accident will enable the claim representative to obtain more readily, a true and well-rounded picture. He will be less prone to confusion and uncertainty, and will be better prepared to meet the plaintiff's allegations, and may then make a determination concerning settlement or defense at the earliest opportunity. Finally, prompt investigation enables the claim representative to render his insureds and agents the kind of service that can make his company's product superior to others.

[3] **Decision and Action**

It is most important that a decision be made as promptly as possible on whether or not a case is one for settlement or declination. To do so is not only good business practice, but good for the reputation and public relations of our industry as well. A claimant has the right to know the attitude of the insurance carrier and its decision, so that his future actions may be guided accordingly. If the investigation is complete and the case is one to decline, the claim representative should do so courteously and promptly, and give proper explanation for the decision. The claimant then knows where he stands and the company will know all the sooner whether he intends to press the matter further.

Declination of a claim should never be made lightly, especially if injury is involved or might likely be alleged. This topic will also be discussed in much more detail in subsequent chapters, but is emphasized here because of the dangers of allegations concerning bad faith claim handling and actions for punitive damages.

Unless there is no policy, or if the accident happened before the inception or after the termination of a policy, supervisory advice should be obtained before declining a claim for coverage reasons. Even in situations like these, it is wise to discuss the matter with higher authority before making a definite declination. A binder may have been issued or for some other reason the matter may require additional investigation with the policyholder and his broker or agent.

Nevertheless, a decision must be made as promptly as possible in order to avoid waiver or estoppel, which will also be discussed in more detail in Chapter 14, *infra.*

Prompt decision is especially important in compensation cases where the claimant is disabled and depends upon indemnity payments to keep him going. Such payments are scrutinized very closely by most states and the time element involved in making them is of the utmost importance. If the claim is compensable and properly covered, the insurer's clerical department should be sure that the payments are made on time.

In today's atmosphere, where advance payments are not at all unusual, it becomes essential to determine as soon as possible what the ultimate decision is going to be on any particular case. Here, however, there is a diversity of opinion. Some companies feel that where the injury warrants control, and where this factor is of utmost importance, they may decide to make advance payments even though the liability picture is not altogether clear. This is a matter for individual company decision and again something which will be discussed in much more detail in Chapter 17, *infra.*

[4] Adequate Reporting

The matter of reporting is also a subject that will be treated at length in Chapter 44, *infra.* The job of a field claim representative in the handling of a casualty claim is by no means complete when he has progressed through the investigation or even the disposition of a claim.

The information he has obtained and the work he has done must be shown in the file so that his decision will stand scrutiny by anyone. Since he has nothing to conceal, he should welcome the most critical investigation of his files. His letters and other file material should be well worded and show exactly what he means. Careless wording can inadvertently create a false or distorted picture.

Claim files are no longer confidential after they have gone into suit and are also subject to insurance department examination. Accordingly, a claim representative should take no action or record any matter that could or should not be brought before any court, insurance department examiner, or other official representative without fear of embarrassment or criticism.

Pertinent material of a confidential nature definitely belongs in the file, but unnecessary or *derogatory* (as distinguished from descriptive) reference to race, religion, national origin, or even appearance, has no place in the files.

Every file must speak for itself. There should be no unanswered questions, or at least as few as possible. Why settlement was made, what amount was paid, or why the claim was denied, should be shown and fully explained in the report.

Finally, the field claim representative should try to anticipate the needs of the home office. His reports should be accurate and thorough enough to avoid, as much as possible, correspondence from the home office correcting errors or calling for clarification. He should use good English, write legibly, send readable copies, and try to be clear and logical in his thinking and reporting.

Again, this is a generalization. The company that the claim representative is working for may have practices that require as little as possible in the claim and suit files for reasons already mentioned. If that is the case the claim representative has no alternative but to follow his or her instructions.

[5] Self-Discipline

Some readers may find it surprising, in a text of this nature, that the subject of self-discipline in dealing with the investigation of a casualty claim needs discussion.

One of the most desirable features of claim handling is the fact that it is probably one of the fields that is freest of rigid outside discipline. Most companies, particularly in widespread areas, do not require the claim representative to report in to the office every day and as long as he gets his work done, he is left pretty much on his own. On a cold snowy winter day, he has nobody to answer to if he gets up an hour or two late or even if he does not work that particular morning, assuming that he has no important appointments.

If he does his job properly and makes the night calls, and the Saturday and Sunday calls that he invariably will have to make on occasion, he deserves a certain amount of time off at other times. However, in order to be fair to the company, he is required to exercise the greatest degree of self-discipline simply because it is not imposed upon him from the outside. Such self-discipline requires him to:

1. Get up in the morning at a regular hour and in time to put in a full day's work.

2. Give attention to old cases that are not a matter of utmost urgency, but which should not be neglected. See to it that the investigation that has to be done is completed and not to procrastinate at least beyond a reasonable time.
3. Make reports promptly and adequately.
4. Spend time in the office to the greatest advantage by planning itineraries and by making advance appointments where possible.

CHAPTER 2

Casualty Insurance

§ 2.01　Kinds of Insurance
§ 2.02　State Regulation and Control
§ 2.03　Major Subdivisions of an Insurance Company
§ 2.04　Five Kinds of Carriers
§ 2.05　The Agent and His Authority
§ 2.06　The Policy Contract
§ 2.07　The Four Parts of a Standard Casualty Policy
§ 2.08　Indemnity Contracts
§ 2.09　Endorsements
§ 2.10　Binders

Most of the textbooks on insurance go into lengthy and comprehensive discussions as to the definition of a loss or claim. From the point of view of a claim representative, a loss is damage to or disappearance of property which is ostensibly covered by a policy of insurance. The term "loss" is ordinarily applied to property owned or legally controlled by the insured and is used mostly in the fire and allied lines. Claims, on the other hand, usually refer to losses which are ostensibly covered under a casualty policy. These, for the most part, involve bodily injury but also include many types of property damage. With some exceptions mentioned hereafter, casualty insurance protects an insured from claims made against him or her as a result of his or her wrongdoing.

§ 2.01　Kinds of Insurance

Insurance coverages can generally be divided into two categories:

1. **First party coverages,** is insurance such as accident and health, inland marine, fire and allied lines, fidelity, burglary and robbery, and automobile collision and comprehensive policies. *First party* means the insured, who usually pays the premium, is also the claimant who receives the benefits from the policy when something goes wrong which is covered by

the insurance policy and which may or may not result from wrongdoing by others.

2. **Third party insurance** is liability insurance which protects the insured from claims resulting from his wrongdoing or alleged wrongdoing toward others, for which money damages may be recoverable against him. An example of this kind of coverage may be automobile liability, general liability, products liability, employers liability, professional liability, and personal injury liability.

Insurance policies are also classified by type of coverage provided, such as:

Life insurance, which cannot properly be fitted into either first party or third party categories, since the insured may not be paying the premiums, although this is an exception, and the insured does not directly benefit financially when a loss arises. It is for this reason referred to as a beneficiary contract.

Fire and allied lines pretty much speaks for itself. These are a branch of first party claims, although *fire legal liability* coverage, an offshoot, protects the insured from claims made against him when fire damage occurs to others resulting from the insureds alleged negligence.

Workers' compensation insurance, which is statutory in nature (arises by Acts of state legislators), is paid for by an employer to provide benefits to his employees as a result of injuries or disease suffered by them as a result of such employment. Such a policy is usually accompanied by *employers liability coverage* which protects the employer from claims made by employees in situations not covered by the workers' compensation act of that state.

Marine insurance has to do with liability arising out of, and damage to, ships and cargo and other matters dealing with shipping on waterways. This coverage, and that of surety bonds are areas and worlds unto themselves. They require highly specialized knowledge, and claims arising from such coverages are usually left in the hands of lawyers, or claim adjusters directly supervised by lawyers who specialize in admiralty or surety bond law.

Casualty insurance, the area with which this book is mostly concerned, is a catch-all designation, never clearly defined, but is generally agreed to encompass aviation and automobile liability and first party coverages, general liability, products liability, professional liability, otherwise known as malpractice insurance and personal injury insurance. Workers' compensation, inland marine, accident and health and fidelity, burglary and robbery coverages are also today often written by casualty insurance companies.

Of the coverages mentioned heretofore, *aviation and automobile coverages* are self-explanatory. *General liability* refers to liabilities incurred on private or business property, although not confined to a specific property in all cases. *Products liablity* is usually written as a part of the general liability policy. It is separately purchased and, generally speaking, protects manufacturers, wholesalers, and retailers from claims resulting from real or alleged defects in a particular product.

Professional liability policies, otherwise known as malpractice or errors and omissions insurance, is third party liability coverage purchased by professional people such as doctors, surgeons, nurses, druggists, dentists, lawyers, architects, engineers, teachers, accountants, and some business people, such as hairdressers and even company officers and directors whose services might subject them to liability claims. It may also be purchased by corporations such as hospitals and clinics.

Personal injury coverage, as distinguished from bodily injury which refers to actual physical injury to the body, is a term used to designate coverage for torts (wrongs committed for which the law provides monetary damages), such as false arrest, false imprisonment, wrongful entry or eviction, wrongful detention, malicious prosecution and libel, slander, or invasion of the right of privacy. This coverage is not ordinarily written on primary policies such as automobile or general liability, or as a policy in and of itself. It is usually reserved for personal excess liability policies, commonly referred to as umbrella or excess liability coverage, but has recently been added as a part of the new Commercial General Liability policy.

Excess and umbrella policies give additional and higher limit coverage over those stated in the primary policies which are required before an excess policy will be written. The primary policy is known as the underlying coverage.

In addition to the above policies, in many states part of the automobile policy includes medical payments, "no-fault" (P.I.P.), and "uninsured motorist" coverage which are hybrids of fairly recent development and will be discussed in some detail in Chapters 22-24, *infra.*

Finally, so that the reader will have some idea of what is meant by *inland marine coverage*, let it be said that this policy has very little to do with ordinary marine coverage. Loosely defined, it deals with transportation property risks on land, resulting from shipment of property by truck, rail, or air.

§ 2.02 State Regulation and Control

Since insurance comes under the jurisdiction of the various states, it is also regulated by them in various ways. Authority must be obtained to write various lines and rates must be submitted for approval. In addition, examinations of insurance companies are regularly made by the states. Among other items checked, are the claim files, with particular attention to the adequacy or redundancy of reserves.

In addition, areas of casualty insurance are governed by statutes enacted by the various states, including Financial Responsibility Statutes, Workers' Compensation Laws, "No Fault" insurance laws and other insurance laws which require casualty insurance to be carried on certain specific risks and which subject the insurance policies to the statutory requirements. "Unfair Claim Practices" acts also require insurers to conform to certain codes of ethical conduct.

§ 2.03 Major Subdivisions of an Insurance Company

So that the new claim representative will be able to get a proper perspective on the relative position which he will hold in the insurance company for which he is working, he must understand the need for close cooperation within the company, and should have some elementary knowledge of the major departments in the average company. These are:

1. **Agency or Production Department.** This is listed first because it is through this department that the policies (the insurance product) are sold. Some companies sell their policies through agencies or general agencies and others sell directly to the policyholder, but, in either event, production is channelled through this department. In the average company, the marketing, advertising, and public relations functions are performed by subdivisions of the agency or production department. If the company is large enough some of these functions are made into separate departments.

2. **Underwriting Department.** This department is responsible for the selection of the risks which the company is willing to accept. It sets the conditions involved in the acceptance of general classes of business and helps to establish the rates charged. It writes the tailor-made policies required on many large risks, and ordinarily supervises the submission of policy forms to the various state insurance departments for acceptance and rating.

In addition, usually, one of the subdivisions of the underwriting department, is the engineering division. The duties of this division are to inspect a property under consideration and report upon its physical characteristics so that the underwriting department will be able to decide whether or not they wish to accept the risk, and if so, at what rate. The engineering division also makes recommendations concerning physical corrections or additions which might make a previously undesirable risk acceptable.

3. **Claim Department.** This department, of course, involves the principal subject of this book. Within the claim department, or as an adjunct thereto, may be a legal and medical division, depending on the size of the company.

While the claim department has no control over the business that has been written, it has a great deal to do with the ultimate loss ratio. A good claim department can make the difference between profit and loss on a marginal risk.

4. **Accounting, Statistical, and Actuarial Department or Departments.** This department, concerned with figures, pretty well describes itself. The size of the company will determine whether these three functions are combined into one department or whether they are separate departments. In larger companies, the claim department may have a statistical unit of its own. In recent years, computers have revolutionized the gathering of statistics.

5. **Personnel Department.** Here again, if the operation is large enough, the claim department may do its own personnel recruiting. In any event, most companies will have a separate personnel department to attend to the myriad of problems that arise in employer-employee relationships.

6. **Training Department.** Depending on the size of the company and the attitude of management, some companies may have a separate training department for all other departments; some may have a training subdivision within the claim department, and others may have no training program at all.

7. Others. Finally, most companies will have separate departments or individuals to handle finances and investments, purchasing and supplies, building services, and other divisions which only touch the claim representative tangentially and needs no further discussion here.

§ 2.04 Five Kinds of Carriers

There are five methods of obtaining necessary insurance:

1. **Self-Insurance**—In many instances the state laws permit an insured to carry his own insurance with certain limitations and provisions. These usually require the filing of proof of financial responsibility by way of bonds, cash or other collateral. In ever increasing numbers, this is accomplished by the creation of "captive" insurance companies.

2. **Stock Companies**—Stock companies are controlled by directors elected by the stockholders and owned by the holders of the stock shares. Their principal distinguishing characteristic is that they are nonparticipating carriers (insureds do not share in either their profits or losses) and that they conduct their business through appointed agents and brokers.

3. **Mutual Companies**—Theoretically, a mutual company is an association of insureds who have banded together for the purpose of carrying on an insurance business for their own benefit.

Actually, an insured obtains a policy from a mutual company already in existence and merely becomes a participating member of the corporation as a result of his transaction. At one time a policyholder in a mutual company was entitled to share in its profits and, in some instances, obligated to bear a portion of its losses, according to the percentage of his interest determined by amount of premium paid.

About all of the mutual companies are now nonassessable, which means that insureds cannot be charged for a proportionate share of incurred losses. Today, in actuality, there is little if any difference in the ordinary insurance policy purchased from a stock or a mutual company or in the general manner in which they operate.

4. **Reciprocal Exchanges**—These are groups of individuals, firms, or corporations who band together under a common name in order to exchange contracts of insurance through a central office. They op-

erate through an attorney who is authorized by his subscribers to exchange insurance for them.

Contracts of insurance are issued only to members and the contracts are the several or individual obligations of the members of the exchange. A well-known example is Lloyds of London.

5. **State Funds**—The state fund is an insurance company operated by the state of its origin. So far, these have been limited to the field of workers' compensation insurance and recently (in Puerto Rico) automobile liability.

There are two types of state funds: (1) monopolistic, where no private company may write workers' compensation in that state, and (2) competitive, where the state fund competes with private carriers.

§ 2.05 The Agent and His Authority

Stock companies and some mutual companies distribute their product through representatives known as agents. In addition, some large companies have sales representatives who are direct employees of the insurance company, and are not independent agents in that they do not represent any other company. Brokers are purchasing agents for the buyer of insurance.

It is important to distinguish between a broker and an agent in those states recognizing such a difference. In most jurisdictions there must be some contract between the insurance company and the persons and organizations selling for the insurance company, giving some definite authority to the seller, before an agency can be created. The distinction between agents and brokers in recent years has fast been disappearing.

Some states, however, have a statute modifying this holding to the effect that any person who sells insurance for a company that accepts his business is considered an agent of that company.

Agents who have the authority to countersign and issue policies are usually held to have the power to bind by oral contract. Should the agent represent himself to the insured as having specifically bound a certain risk, and fail to do so either because of negligence or lack of authority, he may become personally liable to the insured.

In the creation of an insurance agency, the law will imply that the agent has received authorization to do certain acts and carry on such business as is necessary or proper for the execution of the agency. The law will also imply that the agent has received authority similar to that which is customarily given to agents in that particular industry.

A company is bound by the apparent authority which the agent has, and that apparent authority is measured by what a reasonably prudent man would be led to believe in view of the general conditions in the industry.

The company may, by its silence, after notice of certain acts of the agent, waive its right to object not only to the act in question but to any future acts of a similar nature. Such silent acquiescence is interpreted as implied authority. Acquiescence of the agent's past act—for instance, accepting premiums for the issuance of a previously unauthorized policy—amounts to a ratification and will bind the company.

The fraudulent acts of an agent will not bind his principal if the insured is aware of the fraud, and even more so if he is a party to it.

The reader should refer to § 38.06, *infra,* dealing with agents and brokers malpractice insurance.

§ 2.06 The Policy Contract

An insurance policy is a contract between the insured and the insurance carrier in which the carrier agrees to reimburse or hold the insured harmless against certain losses, in consideration for a premium paid.

The law of contracts, therefore, applies generally to insurance policies, with certain modifications which have developed in insurance law.

As in the case of other contracts, insurance policies may be subject to reformation if they contain terms not intended or agreed upon by both parties. Any ambiguity in the policy provisions are strictly construed against the insurer.

In order to be valid, an insurance policy must contain the following legal requirements:

1. There must have been an offer and an acceptance. A request by an insured, sometimes called an application (whether written or oral), comprises the offer. The issuance of a binder or the policy constitutes the acceptance.
2. Both the insured and the insurer must be parties capable of making a legal contract. If the policy is issued by a company

not licensed to write in that particular state or, under some circumstances, if the insured is a minor or an incompetent person, the contract of insurance may be void or, at least, voidable.

3. There must be a meeting of the minds. This implies mutual understanding and agreement as to the general nature of the instrument. It is by no means an implication that a policy can be voided simply because the insured did not understand all the terms of the policy agreement but merely implies in a broad sense that fraud or trickery can void a contract of insurance as well as any other contract.

4. There must be adequate consideration. This speaks for itself and concerns, on the one hand, the premium paid by the insured, and on the other, the promise to defend the insured and make good certain legal obligations in addition to settling claims and suits.

5. The policy must be issued for a lawful purpose. The courts have declared it against public policy to enforce an insurance contract issued for an illegal purpose.

6. There must be an insurable interest. This is the principle that takes an insurance contract out of the realm of gambling. In order to create a valid insurance contract, the insured must have an insurable interest in the subject of the policy.

§ 2.07 The Four Parts of a Standard Casualty Policy

1. **The Declarations.** These contain essential information given by the insured, such as his name and address, location of the risk, and other warranties or representations made by him, as well as a general description of the type of insurance coverage afforded, the contract period, limits of insurance, premium, and similar items.

In addition, the declarations of the standard automobile policy, for instance, may include the place of principal garaging of the automobile, a statement to the effect that the automobile is to be used principally for pleasure or business, unless otherwise indicated, and the ages of the principal drivers.

Some liability policies include the statement that during the past year no insurer has cancelled any similar insurance issued to the named insured, except as stated in the policy. Some states define what may or may not be asked in the application.

2. **Insuring Agreements.** The insuring agreements outline the coverage provided under the policy, the services to be rendered to the insured, and include definitions and limitations.

3. **Exclusions.** The exclusions limit the scope of the policy coverage and specifically outline the circumstances under which coverage is not provided. If an investigation discloses facts that fall specifically within any of the exclusions, there is no coverage unless the courts have abrogated the exclusion.

4. **Conditions.** The conditions set forth some of the rights and obligations of both parties to the insurance contract. They indicate the limits of liability, set forth the duties of the insured, and otherwise define the scope of the policy.

Various kinds of automobile policies such as the personal automobile policy, and tailor-made policies of many varieties, have a format quite different from the basic pattern herein outlined.

A detailed discussion of the various provisions of the automobile and general liability policies will be found in the chapters that are devoted to the interpretation of specific policies. New easy-to-read policies in so-called "plain language" have also been introduced and will be discussed separately.

§ 2.08 Indemnity Contracts

In general, it can no longer be stated that insurance contracts are contracts of indemnity. Indemnification of the insured implies reimbursement to him after he has suffered a direct and actual loss.

Liability policies, for instance, promise to pay "on behalf of the insured" and do not indemnify the insured directly.

The policy provisions, including the one concerning bankruptcy, have made this term almost meaningless today. The expression "to indemnify" has therefore practically been eliminated from third party liability policies.

§ 2.09 Endorsements

Standardization of many casualty policies has not done away with the need for specific endorsements covering particular needs. The complexities of casualty insurance requirements are such that no regular policy can cover all possible contingencies. Very often, therefore, it is necessary for a supplemental agreement to be attached to the main body of the policy, limiting, enlarging, or further delineating certain provisions, or extending or limiting coverage. These supplemental agreements are known as endorsements. Their legal effect is to supersede any conflicting provisions contained in the body of the policy.

By the same token, written or typed corrections or additions will usually supersede contradictory printed provisions. Just as there are standard forms of casualty policies, there are, today, many standard forms of endorsements.

A discussion of the important individual standard endorsements will be found in the chapters that deal with policy provisions.

§ 2.10 Binders

If insurance coverage is desired immediately and before a regular policy can be written up, the company will, upon proper application, issue a binder covering the risk temporarily in the form of a written memorandum. It is in all respects the equivalent of the policy subsequently to be issued and is effective during the time it will take to issue such policy or for a definitely stated period. If no definite period is stated, and no policy issued, it usually expires at 12 o'clock noon on the 15th day following the day upon which the binder takes effect.

Unless there was a definite understanding to the contrary, a binder cannot enlarge or diminish the scope of the regular policy intended to replace it.

As in any other contract, a binder must contain enough information to indicate a meeting of the minds between the carrier and the policyholder. Information such as the name of the policyholder, location, coverage dates, and other information sufficient to accurately identify the contract of insurance is essential.

A binder need not be in writing, but may be oral as well, however difficult it may be to prove its existence at some later date.

CHAPTER 3

General Principles of Investigation

§ 3.01   Making the Investigation Thorough and Precise
§ 3.02   The Value of Contacts
§ 3.03   Timing the Investigation
§ 3.04   The Interview
     [1]   Interviewing the Insured
     [2]   Interviewing the Claimant
     [3]   Interviewing the Claimant's Attorney
§ 3.05   Discovering the Witnesses
     [1]   Locating the Missing Witness
     [2]   Interviewing the Witnesses
§ 3.06   Investigating the Special Damages
§ 3.07   General Investigation of Fatal Claims
§ 3.08   Confidential Report to the Underwriters

    The investigation of a casualty claim bears little resemblance to the dramatic goings-on of our lurid fictional characters and cartoons. The claim representative will need some imagination and inquisitiveness, a little initiative and a lot of determination and persistence, not a "Dick Tracy" complex.

    An unknown witness cannot be located unless a neighborhood investigation is made; a proper neighborhood investigation can be made only by ringing doorbell after doorbell. The claim representative may not get a signed statement from the police officer who investigated the accident, but the chances are certainly in his favor that the police officer will discuss the accident with him and give him some pertinent information. He certainly would not get this if he decided it was useless to attempt to see the officer in the first place. His approach should be confident but never "hard-sell."

§ 3.01   Making the Investigation Thorough and Precise

    There are only three purposes involved in every investigation of a casualty claim: (1) to determine the facts, (2) to determine liability, and (3) to obtain and preserve the evidence. A claims person cannot be content with guesswork. Innuendo must, if possible, be tracked down. All allegations should be thoroughly checked for accuracy and must either be corroborated or denied by evidence that can be presented in court. An attitude of alert skepticism is decidedly healthy.

An investigation is made to determine the truth as nearly as possible. No useful purpose is served by philosophizing on the nebulous quality of the word "truth." The new claim representative will learn within the period of the first few months that four people can see an accident and give four different versions of how it happened. Moreover, each witness will be convinced that he is telling the truth. The problem, therefore, is to try to piece together enough versions and physical facts so that some pattern can be found to indicate most accurately how the accident actually occurred. Do not start an investigation with any preconceived notions or prejudices. Let the facts speak for themselves.

The constant objective of a good investigator should be to strive to obtain the facts. If he finds, as his investigation progresses, that liability rests with the insured, the quicker he realizes it, the sooner he will be able to work out settlement negotiations for the disposition of the case.

It does no one any good for a party to the accident, or a witness, to shave the truth under an ill-advised impression that he is favoring one side or the other. To be led into a belief that there is little or no liability, and then be confronted with proof to the contrary at trial, is disastrous.

Because of excessive demands, lack of liability, or for a number of other reasons, settlement of a claim may not be consummated and the case may have to be tried. It then becomes most important to translate the truth into some tangible form that can be presented as evidence in court.

This is accomplished by means of signed statements, affidavits, court reporters statements, photographs, diagrams, specialist's testimony, and, where possible, by actually producing the object which may be involved in the accident or allegation. It may, for instance, be alleged that a defective faucet broke in the claimant's hands, causing the claimant to be severely lacerated or burned by hot water. An examination of the handle might reveal that it was struck a sharp blow by a hard object, such as a hammer, and for this reason it might be advisable to introduce the handle itself, as well as expert testimony concerning it, in the trial. The object is naturally the best possible kind of evidence.

It is accordingly obvious that such a handle, or some similar evidence, should be put in a place of safekeeping and properly identified so that someone will be able to testify at the trial that it was preserved intact and in exactly the same condition from the time immediately after the accident until the moment it is presented in court.

To repeat what has already been stated: An effective investigation must be planned in advance and properly timed. There must be order in its execution. There can be no set pattern in the investigation of a casualty claim because of the varied circumstances in each case that call for individual handling.

§ 3.02 The Value of Contacts

A claim representative need not be a politican or a press agent to be a successful investigator, but it helps to have some elements of both. By establishing friendly contacts with the various police agencies, hospital and motor vehicle clerks, and various officials on both a high and low level, he will not only obtain a great deal more information, but will get it a lot more quickly.

Once he has established a good contact, a telephone call may save hours of travel and waiting time. The claim representative should never antagonize those upon whom he may subsequently have to call for information, no matter how great the provocation. He should take the time to establish friendly relations with police sergeants, hospital officials or clerks, record clerks, and others in similar positions upon whom he will be calling for the first few times. It will be time well spent.

If certain rules or regulations require the investigator to obtain forms or go through red tape routines which he feels are cumbersome, he should follow the procedure in good grace and not request short-cuts that will embarrass the clerks who have to abide by those rules.

Friendly contacts are invaluable for picking up gossip or hearsay which may often lead to pertinent information, if tracked down.

§ 3.03 Timing the Investigation

The scope of an investigation is determined as it develops. If the case is one to settle and if the demands are within reason, all efforts should be bent upon disposing of the case and eliminating or avoiding any investigation which will serve no ultimate purpose. Over-investigation can be just as costly in the long run as under-investigation. This is particularly applicable in property damage claims of the average kind where the liability has been determined and the damages established.

If the claim representative has decided that to see the claimant first is most advantageous in cases that warrant it, he will usually find it advisable to contact the insured by telephone and obtain his oral version of the accident before getting around to taking his signed statement.

If he cannot talk to the insured right away, he should see that the insured is notified to give no signed statement to anyone but his own company representative and to be cautious about any verbal information he may be forced to give in making a claim of his own against the other party.

As the investigation develops, new leads will be forthcoming. These should be followed through promptly. The investigator should keep a running account in the form of a checklist on his worksheet, of work accomplished and investigating still to be done.

§ 3.04 The Interview

Unless a claim representative is handling property damage, medical payments, or other run-of-the-mill claims, his investigation will be made by personal interviews. He will have to meet, question, and take statements from insureds, claimants, and witnesses. These people come from all economic groups and have various religious, cultural, economic, and national backgrounds. The claim representative must be tolerant, in the accepted usage of this term. It is a broad term and has often been misused, but, in my connotation, tolerance includes differences in point of view, politics, dress, mode of life, and other such matters as well as race, religion, and foreign background. A claim representative must not show his prejudices, if he has them.

The interview should always have a positive rather than a negative approach. If an investigator approaches a witness or a claimant with the attitude that he is not going to get a signed statement, he will be pretty certain not to get it. This does not mean that he should be cocky, but he will better his chances of success if his attitude is not defeatist.

A claim representative should try to be natural at all times. He does not need to be subservient, in the misguided belief that this will make the person he is interviewing more kindly disposed toward him. Usually, the result will be a loss of respect. Nor, on the other hand, is there any excuse for arrogance or an attitude of superiority. He must always remember that there, but for the grace of God, go I.

[1] Interviewing the Insured

The easiest interview a claim representative will have is with his insured. Usually the insured is looking forward to the visit so that he can unburden himself and let the claim representative carry the load for him. He feels he is entitled to this because of the premium he has paid. Sometimes an insured will take the arrogant position that since he paid for protection, all else required of him is superfluous, unnecessary annoyance. The claims person may have to deal firmly with him, and explain the facts of life concerning cooperation as outlined in the policy provisions. It may be necessary to call in the broker or agent for help, but by and large, when a claim representative sees the insured he will be dealing with a friendly witness.

The claim representative is usually the insured's first contact with an employee of the company with which he is insured. Because of this the claim representative's job is to make every effort to see that the interview is pleasant, affiable, and as smooth-running as possible. He should take all the time needed to get the information necessary to protect the insured's interests, but should not drag out the interview to the point of a social visit, especially if he has interrupted the insured or is engaging time which the insured could spend profitably in some other manner.

In this interview it is best to give the insured a briefing on what may be expected of him in the event that settlement negotiations fail and the case has to be tried. If the matter is brought up by the insured it is also well to acquaint him with the things the insurer cannot do for him. Some insureds, for example, expect company claim representatives to press their claim against the third party. It must be tactfully explained that it would be both unlawful and improper

§ 3.04[2]   CASUALTY INSURANCE CLAIMS

to do so unless, of course, there are subrogation rights involved. This will be discussed in Chapter 43, *infra*.

The problem of representation before a criminal court or traffic hearing will also often come up. The same explanation must be given in this respect. If the adjuster is a company representative he should remember that, although he may be the local attorney of record for his company, he is not in the general practice of law, and it would be both improper and unwise for him to represent an insured in either a criminal matter, traffic hearing, or an action against third parties not involving subrogation rights. The claim representative may always attend such hearings as an observer, but to take responsibility for the outcome is inadvisable.

[2] **Interviewing the Claimant**

As a novice in the field of claim adjusting, a claims person may, within the first few years, acquire a certain degree of cynicism. Shortly thereafter, he should finally reach a normal balanced perspective and understanding that most claimants, although subject to human foibles and stresses, are relatively honest.

He should not misrepresent himself. Aside from the ethics involved, any misrepresentation will usually boomerang and do him and his company more harm than good. His approach should at all times be one of helpful cooperation. If he feels a sincere sympathy, it will manifest itself. If he tries to feign a sympathy that does not exist, he will breed only antagonism. He is after all, seeking the truth, so he should tell the claimant just that.

Unless a claim representative has reached a point where it can be determined that a first-call settlement is possible, it is not advisable to make any definite commitment the first time he sees the claimant. Nor should he decline the claim until he has completed his investigation.

A claim representative should not miss the opportunity to obtain from the claimant written permission to get doctor and hospital records, whether he intends to use these immediately, or some time in the future. He will have no better opportunity to get this permission than on his initial visit.

If the claimant informs the claim representative that he is represented by an attorney and gives him the attorney's name and address, he should fold up his tent and go home. Any attempt to get a signed statement or further information after the claimant has disclosed the fact that he is being represented by counsel is unethical and deceitful. Any other conduct can lead to trouble.

An investigator must remember that the control he maintains will depend upon the impression he makes upon the claimant. If he indicates by attitude and gesture, as well as by words, that he intends to act fairly and ethically within the limits set by the policy, his batting average on settlements will be better than average.

Although the subject will be discussed in more detail in Chapter 17, a few words should be said here about advance payments to deserving claimants before settlement is consummated.

Each company has its own policy with reference to such payments. They are becoming more prevalent and have, in my opinion, helped to keep some serious cases under reasonable control.

The claim representative will learn the attitude of his company concerning such payments and act accordingly.

[3] Interviewing the Claimant's Attorney

Details concerning the information which should be obtained from the attorney will be covered in discussing the specific investigations of various types of claims. The discussion here will be confined to generalities.

As everyone knows, there is nothing more irritating than to be ignored. Therefore, if an attorney has informed the company by mail that he represents a claimant, he should be given the courtesy of acknowledging his letter at once. The claim representative should make an appointment to see him and keep that appointment.

Attorneys, like other human beings, are entirely individual in their make-up and reactions. A claim representative's approach to those who are honest, fair, and intelligent should, of course, be friendly, sincere, and frank. The attorneys who are uninformed in the field of negligence law, or those who are not above sharp practice, are much more difficult to deal with. With them, the claim representative must sometimes be guided by his instincts for self-preservation.

The dishonest attorney must be approached with an attitude of extreme skepticism. An attempt should be made to obtain as much information as possible by independent investigation and every allegation of the attorney should be checked carefully. In dealing with this type of person it is especially important to obtain negative as well as positive signed statements from all possible witnesses. Special damages and other allegations of injury, as well as facts, must be checked and rechecked.

Then, there is the arrogant type, who will try to browbeat and intimidate the new claim representative. Experience will soon give the claim representative the confidence needed to meet such a person on an equal plain. He should not try to outshout him. On the other hand, he should not be bluffed or intimidated either.

Finally, we have the shrewd attorney who plays his cards close to the chest. With him it is important that the claim representative does not reveal his defenses. He should give him just as much information of a general nature as is necessary to prove his point, but no more than the attorney gives him.

Each attorney must be treated as an individual and according to the manner in which it is expected that he will react. The longer a claim representative works in a certain area, the better acquainted he will become with the practicing attorneys. The more experience he has with them individually, the better he will be able to deal with them in the future. Experience and hearsay will be his best teachers.

§ 3.05 Discovering the Witnesses

The one question the investigator will probably ask more often than any other in the investigation of casualty claims is "Do you know or have you heard of anyone who saw the accident?" He will of course also try to learn this from the insured, the claimant, police officers, and many others, as well as outside witnesses. He will scan the Police and Motor Vehicle Bureau reports to determine the names of any possible witnesses. He will attend traffic hearings and criminal proceedings, and read the transcripts. He will interview coroners and read transcripts of the coroners inquests, all to determine the names of possible witnesses to an accident.

Most important, in serious cases where the effort is warranted, he will make neighborhood investigations, and if he wants the best results he will make them at the same hour of the day when the accident occurred, and as soon after the accident as possible.

Making a neighborhood investigation requires common sense and a great deal of persistence and determination. First of all it means calling on every store in the immediate vicinity that was open at the time of the accident and finding out not only whether the proprietor or the sales people saw the accident, but also whether there were

PRINCIPLES OF INVESTIGATION § 3.05

any customers in the store at the time. It also means checking with these people to determine whether they heard if anyone else had seen the accident.

Then comes the doorbell ringing! In addition to covering the first floor of the houses in the immediate vicinity, it also means ringing the bell of every apartment that has a window facing onto the scene of the accident.

Time after time, investigators have located witnesses who were looking out of a third or fifth story window down onto the scene of an accident. The investigator must ask all of these people whether they know of anyone else who might have seen the accident. Sometimes this involves interviewing four or five people before he tracks down the person referred to. This individual may be merely described generally since no one may know his name or address.

Most people's lives are set in a pretty well-defined pattern. If buses were present at the time of the accident, it will not be unusual to find some people in them at the same time and place on a subsequent day. Bus drivers can usually be interviewed through the company for whom they work. Very often the claim departments in these companies will do the preliminary interviewing for the investigator.

A claim representative may possibly learn that telephone linemen or other outside workers were present at the scene of the accident, and he will have to track them down. If it is warranted, delivery people, including those who deliver mail, parcels, newspapers, etc., who may have been working at the time of the accident should be checked out.

After a case has gone into suit, information may be obtained that may lead to the discovery of other witness, by means of interrogatories and depositions. If such information is obtained it should be followed up immediately.

Occasionally, in important cases a catchy advertisement in a local paper will bring forth a witness. All of this of course presupposes the fact that the extensive nature of the accident deserves this kind of attention.

Lest the adjuster whose territory includes an inner-city slum area laugh out loud at some of these suggestions, it should be remembered that what is written in this text assumes situations where the suggested investigation can be made without fear of bodily injury. Obviously, where conditions are dangerous, common sense and self preservation must prevail.

[1] Locating the Missing Witness

If the investigator contacts the witnesses promptly he should be sure to obtain from them the identifying information and the names and addresses of relatives or friends who have a permanent address, and follow this up with regular periodic check-ups concerning their availability so that he will have no worry about being able to locate the witnesses when he needs them. There will be occasions, however, since no one is infallible, when he will find it necessary to locate a witness that he has lost track of because the witness no longer lives at the last address that the investigator has for him.

There are various "skip-trace" organizations who specialize in locating missing persons for a reasonable fee. All claim representatives occasionally have use for such organizations.

There will, however, be many instances when, because of the time element, or because other methods have been unsuccessful, a claim representative may have to make every effort himself to locate a witness who has apparently disappeared. If so, he should know that there is no magic formula for locating a missing witness. Should he use some ingenuity, imagination, and a good deal of tenacity, he will probably accomplish his objective. It is very difficult for an individual in this country to disappear without leaving any trace whatsoever.

As a stimulant to the investigator's imagination, the following checklist is offered as leads for locating the missing witness:

- ☐ Registered letter, return receipt with address requested, sent to the last known address of the witness.
- ☐ Telephone directories.
- ☐ City directories.
- ☐ Interview janitor or landlord at last known address for any possible leads, including:
  - ○ Names and addresses of relatives or friends.
  - ○ Names of company or collector on an industrial life insurance policy.
  - ○ Name of credit or collection agencies or individuals.
  - ○ Name of any federal, veterans', or other organizations that the witness may have belonged to.
- ☐ Canvass the neighborhood or buildings for any possible leads from friends, relatives, or acquaintances. It is essential that such investigations be repeated several times because the investigator will never find everyone home the first time the canvass is made. There is also always the possibility that someone he saw before has since seen or heard from a missing witness.
- ☐ Business establishments, stores, and banks in the immediate vicinity.

PRINCIPLES OF INVESTIGATION § 3.05[2]

- [ ] Churches and church organizations.
- [ ] Local doctors and dentists who may have treated the witness at one time.
- [ ] Local parochial or public schools.
- [ ] Name of a moving firm whose vehicles may have been observed by the janitor or any of the neighbors.
- [ ] Any former employer of the witness or any member of his family. From this source, the investigator may obtain:
  - Union affiliations.
  - Names of references on employment records.
  - Type of work and employment.
  - Information from fellow workmen.
- [ ] Automobile or motor vehicle bureaus may have information concerning the witness's address if an automobile has been registered in his name, or if a driver's or chauffeur's license has been issued to him.
- [ ] Local election records.
- [ ] Utility and telephone companies.
- [ ] Military service or veteran's administration records.
- [ ] Credit accounts at department stores.
- [ ] Welfare agencies.
- [ ] Police records.
- [ ] Tax records.
- [ ] Marriage, birth, or death records of the witness or his immediate family.
- [ ] Judgment records.
- [ ] Golf, tennis, or other athletic clubs that the witness may have belonged to, including leads to any hobbies that the witness may have had.
- [ ] Credit card organizations.

[2] Interviewing the Witnesses

When we speak of witnesses, we cover an extremely wide area. An insured, or a claimant, is usually a witness to the accident, interested though he may be in the outcome. One who knows neither party and is not interested in the outcome, except as a matter of justice, is a disinterested witness. Witnesses are often designated as friendly or hostile, adverse or favorable. These terms are self-explanatory.

In interviewing witnesses, again a claim representative's approach must be one of genuine sincerity. He may have to explain to the witness why it is important to the insurance company to pay just and proper claims and to avoid time-consuming additional investigation and litigation expenses. However, if he can convince the average person that he is sincerely interested in seeing that justice is done, whether or not it affects his company adversely, he will usually get the witness's cooperation and, in most cases, his signed statement, without too much difficulty.

Occasionally, a witness will give an initial impression of hostility that is merely a defense mechanism on his part. He may believe that a version unfavorable to the claim representative will be received with antagonism. It is up to the claim representative to avoid jumping to conclusions and break this false barrier down.

To repeat, he should not misrepresent himself. He should gain the witness's confidence by his obvious honesty and fairness.

Unless the circumstances are extraordinary, it is advisable to have seen both the insured and the claimant and to have visited the scene of the accident before interviewing the witnesses. This presumes, of course, that the claimant is not represented by counsel. It does not imply that there should be undue delay in interviewing the witnesses. They should be seen as soon as possible. Time can only dim their memory.

The claim representative may wish to take a key witness on an important claim back to the scene of the accident so that he can refresh his memory and familiarize himself with distances and landmarks. While it is perfectly proper and often necessary to refresh the memory of the witness, a claim representative should not try to lead him in any definite direction.

If the witness is important to the case the claim representative should obtain not only his name and present address, but the name and address of someone such as his mother or another close relative who has a permanent residence and through whom the witness can always be located.

It is important that witnesses be interviewed under circumstances that are comfortable to them. The claim representative should not try to interview a witness at his place of business if such an interview might make him ill at ease. He should be seen at home if possible. He should take the time necessary to obtain a proper interview but he should not impose upon the witness. If there is no choice but to interview a witness at his place of employment, an attempt should be made to enlist the aid of his employer, but care must be used—it could boomerang.

A good claim representative will try to find some common bond with a witness on which to establish a basis of friendship and amity.

If the witness is busy or has only a very short time to give the claim representative he should take whatever information he can, but prepare the way for an additional interview later when the witness is not so rushed. On a follow-up, the average witness will usually go overboard to give whatever information he can, since he feels responsible for the extra call.

Although the matter of reporting will be discussed subsequently, it should be noted here that whenever a witness is interviewed the claim representative should obtain complete details and record them along with his impressions of that witness. Did he appear to be honest and sincere? Was he reluctant? Did he seem to be holding back any information? Did he give the impression that he was favoring either side? Was his manner of presentation such as to make him a good witness on the stand? Was his appearance favorable? Did he speak with an accent? Was he hesitant, or straightforward and direct in presentation? Did he appear intelligent and well educated, or slow, stupid or ignorant? Was he opinionated, timid or hesitant? Was he uncertain or positive in his statements? Was he friendly or belligerent? Did he have any speech impediment? What was the over-all impression of his credibility? What is his reputation? Does he have any physical deformities? Does he appear vindictive?

Whatever his reason, if a witness persists in refusing to give information about an accident which the claim representative has reason to believe he has seen or knows something about, it is important to obtain his negative signed statement so that he may be impeached if he tries subsequently to testify for the claimant at a trial.

Finally, before leaving the witness, a claim representative should try to determine whether the witness gave a signed statement to someone else.

§ 3.06 Investigating the Special Damages

Special damages is a term used in the investigation of casualty claims to denote losses that can be measured in definite sums of money. Allegations of special damages should not be taken at face value. If the nature of the case or the amount involved warrants it, the items should be checked for authenticity.

If special damages have been exaggerated, it is a good indication that other features of the claim may need careful scrutiny. It is also a lot easier to dispose of a claim for a fair value after the claimant has been confronted with proven exaggerations in his special damage allegations.

§ 3.06 CASUALTY INSURANCE CLAIMS

Special damages which are ordinarily encountered in casualty claim work, may be listed as follows:

- **Lost time and earnings.** It must be borne in mind that the claimant is entitled to his take-home pay only, and that he suffers no loss as a result of tax or other deductions, unless he is called upon to make up some items, such as insurance or hospitalization.
  - Where the employee is salaried:
    - Check the employer's payroll records. Do not be satisfied with a verbal corroboration made by some clerk. In some instances, even a written letter cannot be taken at face value.
    - Check the exact lost time.
    - Check the exact lost earnings. The employer may have paid all or part of the employee's salary.
    - Determine the amount of the regular salary.
    - Determine the amount of commissions and overtime, and obtain average salary for that particular time of the year.
    - Estimate tips and other gratuities, such as board and lodging.
    - Determine whether the injury has necessitated a change of job or employment.
    - Determine whether the injury has necessitated claimant's going on part-time work.
  - Where the claimant is self-employed:
    - Check income tax records, including federal, state and city, if any and where possible.
    - Social security tax, if possible.
    - Unemployment tax.
    - Examine private books and accounts.
- **Property Damage.** The following items will be discussed in great detail when we consider automobile property damage losses subsequently:
  - Estimate of repairs.
  - Appraisals and surveys.
  - Difference in value before and after the accident.
  - Exact amount of loss of use.
- **Medical Expenses.**
  - Doctors', specialists', and dentists' bills.
  - Travel expenses to and from doctors'.
  - Registered nurses' fees.
  - Practical nurses' fees.
  - Hospital or clinic bills.
  - Cost of ambulance.
  - X-rays.
  - Laboratory fees.
  - Prosthetic appliance or surgical apparatus.
  - Medicines, drugs, etc.
- **Funeral Expenses.**

PRINCIPLES OF INVESTIGATION § 3.08

§ 3.07 General Investigation of Fatal Claims

In the investigation of fatal claims, the following points should be checked:

- [ ] Duration of the time the decedent lived after the accident, to determine the amount of possible pain and suffering.
- [ ] Age of the decedent.
- [ ] General health of the decedent. Determined by:
  - Neighborhood canvass.
  - Life insurance examinations.
  - Army or school examinations.
- [ ] Medical history investigation, if warranted.
- [ ] General habits and morals, if warranted.
- [ ] Life expectancy.
- [ ] Earnings.
- [ ] Potential earning capacity and increases expected.
- [ ] Names and addresses of close relatives.
- [ ] Age, sex, and number of dependents and possible heirs.
- [ ] General economic condition and social status.
- [ ] Marital status with certificates or other documentary proof or written corroboration.
- [ ] Complete medical bills.
- [ ] Complete funeral expenses.
- [ ] Causal relationship between death and accident, derived from:
  - Coroner's report and transcript of hearing.
  - Death certificate.
  - Autopsy report.
  - Medical report.
  - Medical history.

§ 3.08 Confidential Report to the Underwriters

You will often hear it said that the claim department is the eyes and ears of an insurance company. As has already been seen, its activities extend far beyond the old concept of routine claims handling.

One of the important functions and duties of the claim representative is to report to the underwriting department any information that may affect the desirability of a risk or the adequacy of the premium rate.

Ordinarily, it is not the province of the claim department to recommend the cancellation of a risk. There are many reasons why the underwriter may decide to retain a risk, despite some undesirable features. It *is* the duty of the claim department to bring to the attention of the underwriting department any information that may aid them in arriving at a proper decision concerning cancellation, or which may necessitate corrective action. In the course of the investigation of an accident, much information will come to the attention of the claim representative that might affect the desirability of a risk. Final decision concerning cancellation, however, should rest strictly with the underwriting department.

Most companies have some form for this purpose which is variously termed "Questionable Risk Report," "Confidential Risk Report," or some similar designation used for the same purpose.

The types and kinds of deficiencies that should be noted and brought to the underwriters attention can be grouped roughly into five categories. These, and some examples of each, are:

☐ **Physical defects:**
   O Poor condition of automobile or buildings.
   O Defect of equipment, such as brakes, broken headlights, defective horn or steering mechanism on an automobile; defective machinery on compensation risks, and so forth.
   O Improper equipment.
   O Machinery safeguards not being used, or no safeguards provided.
   O Dangerous machinery.
   O Unoccupied premises.

☐ **Moral hazards:**
   O Bad reputation of insured or driver with reference to speeding, reckless driving, or criminal background.
   O Police record.
   O Philandering.
   O Intoxication.
   O Apparent collusion.
   O Fraudulent acts or false statements.
   O Illegal operation of vehicle, elevators, machinery, or equipment.

☐ **Physical infirmities:**
   O Glasses required and not used, poor eyesight, or blind in one eye.
   O Loss or impaired use of fingers, arm, or leg.
   O Insured or driver afflicted with epilepsy, heart condition, or other infirmity or disease which could momentarily disable driver.
   O Insured or driver aged or infirm.

☐ **Matters affecting premium:**
   O Age of driver.
   O Usual traveling distance on truck bearing local truckman's endorsement.
   O Principal garaging of automobiles.
   O Operations or employment not covered under compensation policy.
   O Improper classification of automobile or job.

§ 3.08 PRINCIPLES OF INVESTIGATION

☐ **Other hazards:**
- ○ Accident frequency or excessive traffic violations.
- ○ Poor class of drivers or employees.
- ○ Truck used to transport employees.
- ○ Gross negligence or wanton disregard involved in accident under investigation.
- ○ Improper registration or no driver's license.
- ○ Catastrophe hazard, such as transportation of butane gas, asphalt, or dynamite; fire trap, and so on.
- ○ Noncooperation.
- ○ Employment of minors.
- ○ Occupational disease exposure.
- ○ Unsafe practices.

Although it is not ordinarily the province of the claim department to recommend cancellation of a risk, as we have previously stated, a claim representative should always notify the underwriting department when such cancellation might adversely affect an open claim or suit.

In some instances involving serious accidents, it is essential that the goodwill and complete cooperation of the insured be maintained, especially where he has some influence over others, such as witnesses and perhaps even a claimant. In such instances, the claim department may wish to take a calculated risk and remain on the policy, since cancellation might antagonize and lose the friendship and cooperation of the insured. In this type of case it is the duty of the field claim representative to let the underwriter know the circumstances, and request that no cancellation be made until further notice by him, or upon disposition of the claim or suit.

CHAPTER 4

Signed and Recorded Statements

§ 4.01 Preparing and Planning the Statement
§ 4.02 Approach to Interview with Witness
§ 4.03 Rules for Better Signed Statements
§ 4.04 Construction of a Signed Statement
§ 4.05 Example of a Narrative Statement
§ 4.06 Translator's Affidavit
§ 4.07 Illiterate Witnesses
§ 4.08 Negative Signed Statements
§ 4.09 Statements Obtained by Mail
§ 4.10 Statements Taken from Children
§ 4.11 Question and Answer Statements
§ 4.12 Statements Taken by a Court Reporter
    [1] Objections to Use of a Court Reporter
    [2] Reasons for Obtaining Statement by a Court Reporter
    [3] Limitations
§ 4.13 Statements Taken by Recording Devices
    [1] Advantages in Using Recording Devices
    [2] Disadvantages in Using Recording Devices
    [3] Admissibility
    [4] Obtaining the Facts
    [5] Telephone Recording Devices

The ability to take a good written statement from a party to an accident or a witness thereto, is fast becoming a lost art. In this era of speed, where time must be carefully allocated, the expense factor usually makes shortcuts almost a necessity, even where those shortcuts are not as effective in the long run.

Progress is inevitable and the telephone and recording devices have, to a great extent, replaced the handwritten statement which in today's educational climate is, more often than not, illegible in any event.

Nevertheless, to be able to take a good statement is as fundamental to claim education as the ability to handle numbers is to a mathematician, despite the invention of calculators. Because it is an educational tool, this subject is given detailed prominence in this edition of this text.

Only a small percentage of the signed statements taken by an investigator may ever be used. However, all statements have potential importance, and the investigator must learn early in his training how to take a correct, proper, and complete statement.

Many bugaboos have been built around this subject. A claim representative therefore, may have some preconceived ideas about the manner in which a signed statement should be taken, and about the average person's reluctance to sign it. Experience will be the best teacher, but how to avoid a few of the pitfalls can be learned from the experience of others. Above all, relax and be natural. Over-anxiety is a sign of uncertainty and will be as obvious as timidity.

The proper time to get a signed statement is *NOW*. The longer it is delayed, the less likely it will be obtained.

If the purpose and reasons for obtaining signed statements are understood, the claim representative will be that much more qualified and prepared to answer questions asked by the witnesses.

Why is a signed statement so important in claims work?

1. It provides an opportunity to obtain details in a permanent record form while they are fresh in the minds of the witnesses. Unless an investigator can take shorthand, no notes will be as comprehensive as a complete statement taken from a witness.
2. It can be used as a subsequent refresher, if memory dims the details. This may become most important if the case goes into suit and, eventually, trial.[1]
3. Signed statements can sometimes be used as a substitute for the witness's personal testimony if the witness is not available to give his own version. Unless statements are taken by a court reporter, are depositions, or are notarized, it might be difficult to get them admitted into evidence. Signed statements are subject to the same rules of evidence as are other testimony.[2]
4. A witness's statement can be used to discredit him either before or during trial if he should attempt to change his story.[3]

---

[1] Astrowski v. Mockridge, 242 Minn. 265, 65 N.W.2d 185 (1954).
[2] Carradine v. New York, 209 N.Y.S.2d 143 (1960).
[3] Asaro v. Parisi, 297 F.2d 859 (1st Cir. 1962).

SIGNED AND RECORDED STATEMENTS § 4.02

5. Once the witness has signed a statement he is less likely to change his story, for he realizes that his statement can be used against him.
6. A signed statement is a reliable and usually accurate factual record of the information obtained for the file and for transmission to the home office.
7. It can be used as a means of convincing opposing counsel of the falsity of certain allegations and make him more amenable to a fair settlement figure.

§ 4.01 Preparing and Planning the Statement

To obtain a signed statement that is logical, concise, and chronological in form, the investigator must plan his work in advance. The average statement involving an automobile accident (or the usual stairway case, for instance) should not require the seasoned investigator to spend much preliminary time jotting down points of information he does not wish to forget in questioning the witness. For the new person in the field, I suggest such preliminary planning on every case until the taking of certain types of signed statements become second nature.

The less time that is available to take a statement, the more preliminary planning is necessary, so that the most information can be obtained in the least amount of time. Ordinarily, it is not only common courtesy, but intelligent handling, to see a witness when he has the time to spare. This is not always possible, and to arrange for another appointment without making any attempt to get a signed statement during the first interview can be disastrous. Any delay provides too many opportunities for the witness to change his mind or to be persuaded to change it.

§ 4.02 Approach to Interview with Witness

Everything that has been said about the interview with the witness applies equally to the obtaining of a signed statement. Obviously, anything that is done to antagonize the witness defeats the purpose for which he is being interviewed. The manner in which the witness's cooperation is gained is something personal to the investigator, and cannot be learned by reading a book.

To repeat, people are different. It is therefore necessary to approach them differently. Above all, the investigator should gain their interest on some common basis of appreciation or endeavor. Their confidence should be gained by sincerity and evident fairmindedness. Certainly do not simply introduce yourself, and then sit down and immediately pull out a writing pad. Rather, talk to the witness first, and put him at ease. The witness will shortly begin to talk about the accident quite naturally. You should let the witness talk, if both you and the witness have the time. You can then start taking notes of salient points that you wish to include in the statement. This will be the outline and preparation before writing the actual statement.

The investigator must watch for reactions from a witness and must be able to change his approach the moment he senses antagonism. The sight of a statement pad will often cause an immediate negative reaction. Accordingly, put the witness at ease by explaining your mission, and convince the witness of your desire to get the true facts. If the witness refuses to sign the statement, take the refusal in good grace. When the interview is concluded, the witness should be thanked for the time he has graciously given. This is good manners and creates goodwill as well.

§ 4.03 Rules for Better Signed Statements

For the most part, taking signed statements is a matter of common sense. The new claim representative, however, may find a few guidelines helpful in establishing a procedure. There are a number of elementary principles with which he should be familiar.

1. **Coverage problems.** Whenever a coverage problem is involved, two separate signed statements should be obtained from the insured; one covering the facts of the accident, and the other covering the information to be obtained on the coverage problem. The statement concerning coverage problems will usually contain references to the agent or broker as well as to the insured's carrier, which should not be in the statement concerning the facts of the accident. While it is more a fiction rather than a reality, most states still forbid the injection of insurance in the trial of an action for negligence.

2. **First person.** The statement should be written in the first person, in order to show that the witness is doing the talking.

3. **Separate statements.** No two people will ever see an accident exactly alike. It is therefore a better practice to obtain a separate

signed statement from each witness. The investigator should refrain from having one witness add either his signature to the statement of another, or even a paragraph to the effect that his version of the accident corresponds with a version as stated by the other witness. There are of course unusual circumstances that could make such a practice acceptable where the alternative would be no statement at all from the second witness, but this should be the exception rather than the rule.

4. **Legible writing.** The handwriting on the statement must be legible. If the handwriting of the investigator is difficult to decipher, he should get a portable typewriter or have the witness write the statement himself. Requests to have the witness write a statement may not always be granted, but the request will usually make the witness much more amenable to signing the one written or typed by the investigator.

Handwritten statements should be written in ink or ballpoint pen. Where the witness is willing to write his own signed statement, the investigator will have to help him with it and this of course is dangerous where the statement may have to be admitted into evidence. Where the witness writes his own statement without any direction whatsoever it will usually be inadequate, so the choice is one between the frying pan and the fire. In any event, the investigator should never request the witness who is self-conscious about his education or spelling to write his own statement.

5. **Narrative form.** Unless a court reporter's statement is being taken, the straight narrative form is the best form for the ordinary signed statement. The question and answer type of statement looks too legalistic for the average layman. It may breed suspicion whereas the ordinary narrative statement might not. Narrative, however, does not mean to imply that the investigator is to write a novel. He should be specific, brief, and to the point without overlooking important material. The question and answer form usually requires a great deal of extraneous writing. It may, for instance, require a whole series of questions to obtain personal and comparatively unimportant details about the witness before the claims person can get to the meat of the statement. In addition, if the answers are not written exactly as given it could lead to misinterpretation that might cause the entire statement to be discredited.

6. **Arrangement.** Although every effort should be made to arrange the statement chronologically for easy reading, the writer should not

be afraid to add paragraphs at the end, either upon request by the witness or to cover information that he forgot to include previously in the body of the statement. In other words, he should be orderly but need not make a fixation of it.

It has been said that the signed statement should be taken without paragraphing, under the belief that in breaking up the statements into paragraphs, there is some opportunity for the one who holds the statement, to add a few words after it has been signed. My own view is that although a certain amount of suspicion is healthy, it should not be overdone. Paragraphing makes for easier reading. That is more important than the suspicion that might be aroused by leaving part of the line unfilled.

7. **Solitary interview.** If the investigator can possibly avoid it, he should not try to take a signed statement from a witness when the witness is surrounded by family and friends. It is best to tactfully suggest that the noise and disturbance will be too great for concentration. Then, if possible, he should attempt to interview the witness alone where he will have his undivided attention. There are of course exceptions if the witness is an infant, in a hospital or other institution, or is illiterate or unfamiliar with the English language. Again, it is recognized that there may be times when gatherings are unavoidable and when the investigator must either take a signed statement under adverse conditions or not get one at all.

8. **Style.** Whenever it is appropriate, simple language and short sentences should be used. The written statement should record as closely as possible the witness's manner of speech, but bad grammar or objectionable verbiage should not be purposely used. Occasionally, the investigator will take down a direct quotation. When this is done he must, of course, use the exact language of the witness. However, uncalled-for bad grammar is an obvious condescension that leaves as bad an impression as the use of words that are far beyond the obvious knowledge of the witness. The investigator should refrain from using unfamiliar legal, medical, or technical language.

9. **Preprinted forms.** The claim representative should avoid the use of preprinted forms in taking signed statements. They serve no useful purpose and, again, will only create suspicion and be less effective if needed to be presented as evidence.

10. **Factual material.** Wherever possible, try to give factual information and avoid opinions or conclusions. While this is not *always*

possible or even advisable, some effort should be made to keep opinion and conclusion at a minimum, unless it is pertinent.

If any statements overheard by a witness immediately after an accident are included they should be quoted as close to verbatim as possible. If opinion based upon obvious circumstantial evidence is included it should be kept to a minimum, and wherever possible such words as "probably" and "perhaps" should be minimized.

Also, where possible, recognized designations of speed, distance, and direction should be used. To indicate speed, approximate miles per hour should be used instead of such words as "fast," "slow," or "moderate." The points of a compass rather than "right" or "left" should be given, and distance should be measured from such landmarks as large trees, mailboxes, buildings, etc. While it is advisable to be as definite as possible, it is not advisable to be dogmatically so. A statement that a car was traveling at thirty-seven miles-per-hour could be torn to pieces on cross-examination.

11. **Insurance.** All mention concerning the name of the company that is involved in the investigation, or the phrase "insurance company" should be avoided. It may be necessary to use this statement in a trial of a case.

12. **Conditions affecting statement.** A signed statement should not be taken from anyone who is under the influence of alcohol or narcotics, or who is in a state of shock following an accident. If a witness is obviously thick of tongue, drowsy, or unusually slow in his answers to ordinary questions, the investigator should be doubly cautious and make thorough inquiries concerning the witness's condition before obtaining a statement from him. This is one of the few exceptions to the rule of promptness.

To obtain an effective statement and to keep his ethics above reproach, the investigator must observe local laws, ordinances, or codes that regulate the time or place for the taking of statements. If, for instance, he must take a statement in a hospital under circumstances that permit it, he should try to have a nurse or attendant present as a witness. The attendant will also be able to attest to the fact that the patient was free from apparent unusual pain and from the influence of narcotics and that the witness appeared to be in a rational frame of mind.

13. **Objectionable phraseology.** The use of objectionable words or phrases should be avoided unless the investigator is directly quoting the remarks of the witness. Otherwise, any reference to race, reli-

gion, foreign background, or any evidence of bigotry or obscenity should be scrupulously avoided. A completely innocent remark concerning race, intended merely as a descriptive appellation, could easily be misinterpreted by a juror.

14. **Preserving the statement.** The investigator should refrain from physically mutilating a statement in any way. It is a valuable piece of evidence, and should not be soiled, torn or shopworn. In addition, it should not be date-stamped by an office clerk or by any other marking that might make it unacceptable as evidence.

§ 4.04 Construction of a Signed Statement

There will be times when, because of pressure, peculiarities of an individual, the facts of an accident, or for other reasons, the statement will not follow an orderly pattern.

By and large, however, the general construction of a signed statement obtained from a witness, be he insured, claimant, or disinterested outside witness, should follow an orderly, chronological form. This not only makes for easy reading, but indelibly impresses its pattern on the claim representative so that he will automatically obtain the necessary information because it fits into his regular routine.

An outline of a good construction pattern for a statement should include the following subjects, generally in the order given:

1. **Date, Time, and Address.** At the top, upper righthand corner of the statement always place the date and time when the statement was taken, and the address of the place where it was taken. By including the time, the investigator pins down the surrounding circumstances more definitely, and makes it more difficult for a witness to subsequently deny that he gave the statement.

2. **Identification of the Subject.** The first paragraph of the signed statement should be concerned with the identification of the subject who is giving the statement. It should include his name, age, and address. It is of primary concern that the authenticity of a statement be provable. Therefore, the more personal details, within reason (not readily available to anyone) that can be obtained and placed in a signed statement, the less likely it is that the witness will ever be able to deny that he gave it. It is suggested that such additional information as the witness's place of employment, social security number, or other pertinent data be added to the statement where warranted. The degree of identification of the subject should depend on the na-

ture of the accident and the type of witness with whom the investigator is dealing.

3. **Location and Reason for Witness's Presence.** This paragraph should be devoted to a description of the location of the accident and should include the reasons for the witness being there at the time. The direction in which the witness may have been walking or riding should be given, as well as the exact spot from which he viewed the accident. Naturally, in subsequent investigations the investigator should make it a point to check on the story given by a witness to determine whether he actually could have viewed the accident from the position where he said he was.

This paragraph should also include the introduction to the factual matter by indicating what attracted the witness's attention to the accident.

4. **Factual Details.** This paragraph should include the factual information concerning the details of the accident. It should, as far as possible, be confined to facts. Hearsay information should be avoided unless it involves spontaneous remarks made directly before or after the accident, or unless the remarks contain information which will attack the credibility of a witness.

If, from the investigator's own knowledge, he realizes that the information being given is obviously wrong because of an honest mistake on the part of the witness, he should try to clarify the situation before putting it down on paper. On the other hand, if there is any question of dishonesty, or if the witness stubbornly maintains his position on the situation, it should be taken down as is. By doing so, he may at least destroy his value as a witness for the opposition.

5. **Physical Description.** The physical description of the scene of the accident should be as complete as possible. It should include weather and lighting conditions, road surfaces, road and other measurements, and any other pertinent details.

Wherever possible, some effort should be made to get the witness to draw some form of crude diagram, illustrating the factual situation. Drawing the diagram will help clarify the facts and impress them with that much more certainty on the witness. Have the diagram signed as well as the statement. It is best to keep the names of other witnesses out of the signed statement. They may turn out to be unreliable and the statement if read in court might create an erroneous impression.

6. **Injuries and Damage.** The next section of the signed statement can include details concerning the nature of the property damage and the injuries received. This should include not only as complete a description of the damage as possible, but an estimate of the cost of repairs, if one has been obtained. Description of the injuries should be as complete and detailed as possible. It ought to be in the language used by the narrator. The names of all attending doctors and their addresses, should also be included. This will be discussed in greater detail when the problem of the medical investigation is considered.

7. **Special Damages.** In statements obtained from claimants, complete lists of all special damages should be obtained and itemized. The items that make up special damages have previously been covered.

8. **Police Action.** An indication of any possible arrests or other police action should be included toward the end of the statement.

9. **Corrections.** Having finished the body of the statement, it is now the duty and responsibility of the investigator to make sure that the statement contains the exact information given by the witness and that it does not deviate in any way from the information which he gave. Now, then, is the time to give him the statement, ask him to read it, and to point out any errors, any parts of the statement which are not clear, or any sections which the witness for any reason whatsoever wishes to have changed.

Wherever possible, all changes or corrections should be made by the witness in his own handwriting. If the witness shows any reluctance, or objects to making the corrections in his own handwriting, the investigator should make sure that each correction made is initialed by him. Under no circumstances should any portion of the statement be erased.

Rarely is a statement written first-draft without needing some minor corrections. The investigator should not look upon this as something objectionable. The fact that a witness has made corrections in the body of a statement in his own handwriting, or has initialed such corrections, is an admission that he has not only read, but studied the statement. It would be difficult indeed for him to try to testify subsequently that he had not read the statement or was not aware of what it contained after having corrected it.

10. **Acknowledgment.** Having placed the pen in the hands of the witness for the purpose of making corrections, it then becomes a mere matter of routine procedure, after he has completed his correc-

tions, to ask him to acknowledge the fact that he has read the statement and affirm the truth by adding in his own handwriting the words "I have read the above and preceding number of pages, and state that the information contained therein is true and correct," or words of a similar nature. This sentence should be written on the line following the end of the statement, allowing for no empty space in between.

11. **Signature.** If the investigator has obtained the acknowledgment that the witness has read the statement and affirms the information to be true, in his own handwriting, he should not have any difficulty with the signature. Most witnesses will append it automatically. It is preferable that he does not use the word "sign" in asking the witness to put his name down on the next line after the acknowledgment. "Sign" and "signature" have become dirty words in situations of this nature. Psychologically, they have connotations which should not be called up.

The person who continually bemoans the fact that he cannot obtain signed statements is one who is making excuses for certain deficiencies within himself. A positive attitude (and this does not mean an aggressive attitude), a matter-of-fact handling of the situation, and, above all, the absence of any hint of defeatism or timidity, will ordinarily accomplish the necessary results. No signature will ever be obtained without some effort or attempt to get it. Nor will it be obtained with an attitude or words that signify, "You don't want to sign this, do you?"

Each page of the statement should be initialed by the witness or, preferably, signed with his full name.

When a witness hesitates to put his signature on the statement, the investigator may point out that he is merely being asked to verify the truth of the statements he has made. It sometimes helps to ask the witness what phase of a statement he seems uncertain about, and to make sure to include whatever he wants, even if it happens to be irrelevant matter.

If the witness adamantly refuses to sign the statement, in some instances a third party who was present during the time the statement was taken might be induced to add his signature to a paragraph attesting to the fact that the statement was read by or to the witness, and that he affirmed it to be true and correct.

In some instances a witness may refuse to add his signature to a statement, but will not object to placing the letters "O.K." at the end.

Sometimes, he might be willing to answer the following questions as written out by the person who has obtained the statement: "Have you read the above and preceding pages?" "Is the information contained therein true and correct?" Affirmative answers to each of these questions in his own handwriting has the same effect as though he had signed the statement.

Occasionally, the very sight of a statement pad will affect a witness as a red flag affects a bull. He will vehemently and violently tell you that there is no use in your writing out a statement since he will absolutely refuse to sign it. The investigator should put his pad away, inform the witness that he is merely attempting to arrive at the truth, and ask the witness to give the facts.

12. **Witness to the Statement.** Whenever practical, signed statements should be witnessed by one or two disinterested parties who should place their full names and addresses on the statement. The investigator taking the statement should not ordinarily witness it.

§ 4.05 Example of a Narrative Statement

Obviously all statements taken will not have to be as complete and detailed as the example given here. The following will, however, illustrate the areas that should be covered in obtaining information from a person who has witnessed an accident that resulted in serious injuries or death to one or more of the parties involved.

> 987 Pearl Street, Apt. 16B
> New York, New York 10005
>
> January 10, 1987

I, John Paul Jones, live at the above address, where this statement is being made, and have so lived for the past three years. I am 28 years old, married to Minerva Sue Jones, and have two children, John Jr., 6 years old and Anne Marie, 2 years old. I am employed as a draftsman by the Community Shipping

Lines located at 23 Liberty Street, New York, New York. My social security number is 30-246-987.

On Monday night, January 5, 1987, at about ~~8:30~~ 8:00 P.M., I went out to mail an important letter that I wanted to get on its way as soon as possible. The mailbox is located about three blocks from my home—at the corner of John Street and Broadway. I turned west on Liberty Street as I left the building and was walking on the ~~north~~ south side of the street. I had crossed Nassau Street, heading toward Broadway and reached a point about 50 feet east of Broadway. Liberty Street is a one way street with traffic going west. There was very little traffic on this rather narrow, two car width street. ~~No cars were~~ I didn't see any cars parked on either side, so my vision was clear. Broadway is a rather wide street—wide enough for four cars to ride abreast.

As I recall it, there were some cars parked on the east side of Broadway facing north. There is a traffic light at the intersection which was working at the time. It was a clear cold night, probably around freezing, and the street had some icy spots. There isn't much lighting on Liberty Street but Broadway was very well lighted.

Just as I was about to cross over to the north side of Liberty Street, I looked to my right (east) and saw a car with one headlight racing west in the middle of the street. This car was about 200 yards from me when I first noticed it. I am a driver and have been driving for about 12 years—ever since I was 16, and judge that this auto was going at about 40 and 45 miles an hour. Despite the fact that I had one foot off the curb and into the street, the driver of this oncoming car did not sound his horn.

Suddenly, this car swung slightly to the south and was obviously skidding forward (west) in this position. I followed it with my eyes and saw it go through the red light at the intersection at Broadway and crash into the rear end of a car that was going south on the east side of Broadway, a one way street going south. I had not noticed the southbound car until just before the crash. The impact pushed the southbound car about ten feet west at which point both cars stopped. I was only about 50 feet from the collision and reached it in a few seconds. A woman in the southbound car was shrieking hysterically. She was in the left rear seat and appeared to be strapped in because she did not move right away. I did not actually see that she was strapped in but did notice that the driver, a young man of about 30 years of age and a woman who was sitting in the front seat along side of him, also about the same age, were strapped in with seat belts. Although the woman in the back seat was screaming, there was no evidence of injury and the other two people in that car did not seem to be seriously injured although they did seem to be stunned.

I did not examine the area closeby and cannot tell whether there were any visible skid marks. There were some icy spots on Liberty Street in the area, but I cannot describe them in size or area.

There was a whole group of people in the westbound car that seemed to laying all over each other after the accident. They looked like the "hippie type", with long hair and odd looking clothes in the "mod" style. There was practically no shouting or noise from the six or seven people in that car. Frankly, I could not tell how many were boys and how many were girls—they all more or less looked alike. Most of them appeared in a daze but I cannot tell whether this was as a result of the accident or not.

Within a few minutes there was a whole group of people around the accident and because of the crowds that were gathering, I really did not get a good look at the damage done to the cars except to notice that the front end of the westbound car was ~~stove~~ caved in. It was an old car and looked something like a 1970 Chevrolet although I am not sure. The other car had the left side caved in. It was a modern car—I think a Thunderbird.

I recognized one of the people in the crowd who was a woman that sells newspapers on the corner of Broadway and Liberty Street. There were several other people whose faces I recognized as being people from the neighborhood but I don't know where they live or what their names are. One is an elderly woman that usually goes walking with her little poodle in the area. She is short (about 5'2"), appears to be about 60 years of age, wears a fur coat but no hat.

The other one or two whose faces I recognized, I simply

do not know ~~cannot remember~~ whether they either live or work in the neighborhood.

The police arrived in about ten minutes and about ten minutes after that, an ambulance arrived. The hysterical woman in the southbound car had quieted down and she was able to walk out of the car and into the ambulance.

I did not notice any injuries on any of the people in the westbound car and none of them ∧ were taken to the hospital.
_{as far as I know}

There were two policemen at the scene who had come in a patrol car but I don't know what precinct they were from and I don't remember them well enough to describe them.

Shortly thereafter, a police tow truck came and moved the cars over to the side of the road and the crowd dispersed. I went home.

I have read the above and preceeding x pages and state that the information contained therein is true and correct.
Witnessed by:
Sarah M. Jones
1234 West End Ave., N.Y., N.Y., Apt. 12 C

Samuel K. Larkin
1945 N. 9 Ave., N.Y., N.Y., Apt. 3 D

SIGNED AND RECORDED STATEMENTS § 4.07

§ 4.06 Translator's Affidavit

Occasionally, a claim representative will encounter a witness who does not have sufficient understanding of the English language to be able to read the statement. In that event it is necessary to obtain a translator's affidavit or short statement appended to the bottom of the statement obtained from the witness.

The affidavit or appended statement should indicate that the translator read the statement to the witness in his own language, that the witness understood it, and affirmed the facts contained therein to be true and correct. Such a clause can read as follows:

> I, John Doe, residing at [Street], [City and State], state that I can fluently read and write Spanish as well as English. I further state that I have read the above and preceding statement of Maria Jiminez and that I have accurately translated it into the Spanish language which she understands. Maria Jiminez affirmed the fact that this is her statement, that she thoroughly understands it, and that the information contained therein is true and correct.

This paragraph should, of course, be signed by the translator and either witnessed or notarized.

Before obtaining the signature of the translator, the signature of the witness should be obtained at the bottom of the statement, even though written in a foreign language.

§ 4.07 Illiterate Witnesses

Because of the fact that the percentage of illiteracy in this country is surprisingly high, the investigator will encounter illiterate witnesses more often than he would think likely.

Sometimes an illiterate person will attempt to cover up his ignorance by what may appear to be an obstinate refusal to confirm the statement by reading it, or to sign it. With a moderate degree of perspicacity, the investigator should be able to recognize this subterfuge. In any event, obtaining a statement from an illiterate person requires the utmost tact and diplomacy. The investigator should avoid, as much as possible, embarrassment to the witness. He should read the statement to the witness, make whatever corrections are necessary, and, if possible, call in the services of a friend or some other reliable person in whom the witness has confidence and who the investigator believes to be reliable.

He should have that third person reread the corrected statement to the witness and obtain the witness's assurance that the statement is true and correct. Then, in place of his signature, he should have his mark placed at the bottom of the statement and append a paragraph on the same page to the effect that the statement has been read to the witness and that he has affirmed that the information contained therein is true and correct. Such an appended statement, to be signed by the third person who has read it to the witness, can read as follows:

> I, John Joe, residing at [Street], [City and State], read the above and preceding X pages to _____. She stated that she understood the statement, affirmed that it was hers, and that it is true and correct.

This paragraph should be signed by the person who read the statement to the witness and the corrections should all be initialed by him.

If a notary has been called in to assist either as translator or to read the statement to an illiterate person, the notary should add his own form of affidavit.

§ 4.08 Negative Signed Statements

In investigating serious or important claims the claim representative will obtain leads that will direct him to people who will deny any knowledge of the accident. In those instances where the denial is persistent, and where he believes there is a possibility that they are either covering up or may subsequently appear as witnesses for the opposition, he should make every effort to obtain a short, signed statement from such persons. It should state that they did not see the accident and from their own observation know nothing about it. Such a negative, signed statement will at least prevent that person from later appearing as a surprise witness for the opposition. If he does appear it will enable the defense attorney to discredit him on the stand.

SIGNED AND RECORDED STATEMENTS § 4.10

§ 4.09 Statements Obtained by Mail

If a case which the claim representative is investigating is of any consequence, it warrants a personal interview with every witness.

Occasionally, the obstacles to personal interview may be extreme, involving distance, weather conditions, or the time element. The investigator may, therefore, after due consideration, and at a calculated risk, determine that the most advisable course of action is to attempt to get information from a witness through the mail.

Having learned by now that the writing of a statement is an involved matter—proficiency in it requires practice—the investigator should not expect that the ordinary witness will always be able to write a satisfactory narrative account of an incident without his help. It is therefore preferable to outline a complete list of questions to which the witness should add his answers. He should make sure that the witness has plenty of space in which to do so.

Again, judgment must be used to avoid asking so many questions that the witness is discouraged. At the same time he should be comprehensive enough to get the information he needs. He should use great care and spend enough time to prepare the questions so that they will be pertinent and intelligible.

As much care should be used in framing the accompanying letter to the witness as in the preparation of the questions themselves. He must remember that he is imposing on the time of the witness and that the witness is doing him a favor in complying with his request.

§ 4.10 Statements Taken from Children

It has often been said that children make unreliable witnesses. Frankly, my own experience and that of many with whom I have discussed this subject, is to the contrary. Some children do have vivid imaginations and sometimes cross the borderline between truth and fantasy. This, however, is usually not hard to determine. For the most part a child who has sufficient mental development can be impressed with the importance of his remarks to the extent that he will make a reliably factual statement.

The average child who is able to read and write will, for the most part, give a more straightforward and honest account than the average adult.

Whether the statement should be written in the handwriting of the child, or whether the investigator should write it himself, is a matter of judgment involving elements of time and the child's age, personality, general intelligence, and education.

If the child has acquired reasonable skill in writing it is advisable to have him write the statement himself. In this case particularly, it is essential that all useless verbiage be eliminated in order not to tire the child or cause him to lose interest. Such a statement should always be obtained in the presence of a parent, adult relative, or friend. It is particularly important that the words used should not be incomprehensible to the child. His vocabulary, of course, will vary with his age and development.

There is, of course, an age and intelligence limit under which there is no point in attempting to take a signed statement from a child.

§ 4.11 Question and Answer Statements

It is obvious that a statement taken in question and answer form, covering an involved and complicated accident, could go on and on, almost interminably. There is, accordingly, little point in giving an example of a complete statement of this type. However, in an effort to illustrate some of the observations made in this chapter, the following example is given of some questions and possible replies that might be elicited during the early part of such an interrogation.

Some introductory remarks should be given by the interrogator, such as: "Just for the record, let me state that we are in the office of the Penny Steamship Lines on Dock number 36 in New York City, N.Y. It is 10 a.m. and today is June 2, 1986. We are alone in the small office of the supervisor."

Q. *What is your full name?*
A. John Michael McGregor.
Q. *Is McGregor spelled MC or MAC?*
A. MC.
Q. *Where do you live?*
A. 134 West 70th Street.
Q. *What city?*
A. New York.
Q. *Manhattan?*
A. Yes.
Q. *Is it an apartment house?*
A. Yes, I live in apartment 4-A.

SIGNED AND RECORDED STATEMENTS § 4.11

Q. How long have you lived there?
A. About 5, 6 years.
Q. In case you move, I'd like to have the name and address of a relative who could always reach you.
A. My mother always knows where I am. She lives in Queens.
Q. What is her full name?
A. Anne-Marie O'Rourke.
Q. O'Rourke?
A. Yes, my father died and she remarried.
Q. What is her exact address?
A. 116-44 Jamaica Avenue.
Q. Jamaica, Queens?
A. Yes.
Q. How long has your mother been living there?
A. Oh, about 15 years.
Q. How old are you?
A. 36 years.
Q. Are you married?
A. Yes.
Q. What is your wife's name?
A. Mary.
Q. Mary what?
A. Mary Agnes McGregor
Q. Do you have any children?
A. Yes, Joseph Jr. and Sue-Anne.
Q. How old are your children?
A. Joe is 14 and Sue-Anne is 10.
Q. Where do you work?
A. Oh, at the docks.
Q. What docks?
A. Penny Steamship Lines, dock 36.
Q. What do you do?
A. Stevedoring.

I have now asked twenty-two questions and have obtained only some background information on the witness, all of which could have been covered (as you have already seen) in one fair-sized paragraph taken in narrative form. It is obvious that in order to find out where the witness was at the time he observed the accident, where he was going, what first called his attention to the accident, and then to go on to develop the facts and other details would require literally dozens more questions and a lot more time. As indicated initially, this must be kept in mind when making a decision whether or not to take this kind of statement.

§ 4.12 Statements Taken by a Court Reporter

A court reporter is an experienced stenographer who takes notes on a stenographic machine, of the courtroom proceedings during the trial of a case. When court is not in session the court reporter's services are usually available for other stenographic purposes.

Some attorneys have said that any statement worth taking, should be taken by a court reporter. It is obvious that those who hold this view have no great number of cases that need investigation, or do not have to pay the bill for taking such statements. A statement properly taken, according to the rules outlined in these pages, can be every bit as effective, and sometimes more so, than a statement taken by a court reporter.

The skill required to take an effective court reporter's statement differs greatly from that required to secure a narrative statement. Once a question is asked, and an answer given, it is definitely on the record and cannot be erased.

[1] Objections to Use of a Court Reporter

An interrogator can draw out more details and obtain clarification, but if incorrect or objectionable remarks have been made, there is no way to cross them out. Unless great skill is exercised in questioning a witness, he can, and often will make objectionable references to insurance, give unfounded or biased opinions, and make derogatory or otherwise improper remarks that will become a part of the record before he can be stopped. Unless the interrogator is highly experienced, a witness will often reply to questions concerning an accident with vague terms to indicate directions and measurements which without further elucidation can make his statement all but valueless.

Any attempt to delete extraneous or inadmissible remarks from the record may destroy the effectiveness of the entire statement if this is later revealed. If a situation calls for the taking of a statement by a court reporter it may also call for the services of an attorney who is experienced in this type of interrogation.

Another important objection to the use of a court reporter's statement is the fact that the transcribed statement cannot be used and

SIGNED AND RECORDED STATEMENTS § 4.12[3]

introduced into court as physical evidence. If the case comes to trial it is necessary to produce the reporter to testify and if he is not readily available, is sick, or has died, the interrogator and his client are in real trouble.

In addition, a witness and a jury may be inclined to look upon a court reporter's statement with more suspicion and skepticism than they do when dealing with an ordinary narrative statement because of its legalistic aspect and because of the obvious expense involved in its procurement.

[2] Reasons for Obtaining Statement by a Court Reporter

When then, do we use this form of statement-taking at all? There are some situations where a statement should be taken by a court reporter for reasons herein indicated.

Occasionally, difficulties with a witness who is known to be antagonistic may be anticipated and the information to be obtained from him is of such importance as to call for a court reporter's statement because it will be recorded verbatim in the witness's own vocabulary and vernacular. It is also occasionally warranted because of the health or age of a witness or for other reasons which subsequently prevent a witness from personally appearing in court. Sometimes it is advisable where a witness is illiterate or in the rare event that a witness is blind, and may have heard pertinent remarks or outcries.

[3] Limitations

A reporter may be an excellent stenographer, but he is also a human being and accordingly there are limits to his abilities. If either participant to the interrogation talks too fast, or if they both talk at once, or inaudibly, the reporter is bound to have difficulty. If the questions of the interrogator are disjointed, confused and half thought out, the statement will be transcribed just as it was related and will come out no better than given.

While it is true that an experienced reporter can sometimes do a better job of interrogating than some attorneys, I do not hold with the thinking that he should be used as an assistant or backstop in the questioning. A reporter has a full-time job for which he has been educated and trained and should confine himself to his job of recording. Any injection into the realm of interrogating would also have to be recorded and could only result in giving the ultimate impression that the interrogator did not know his business.

With rare exceptions, court reporter's statements are no longer taken by an adjuster who is not an attorney. This is due to the fact that depositions, taken by an attorney for either side after a claim has gone into suit, have become a matter of common usage in almost every case involving serious injuries or death and even in some other suits.

For this reason, it is suggested that any thought of taking a court reporter's statement be discussed with company supervisors or the legal department before any attempt is made to do so.

§ 4.13 Statements Taken by Recording Devices

Cost effectiveness is the order of the day and there is no doubt that taking statements by machine is much quicker than taking them by hand. In addition, there has been such progress in recording devices within the past decade, and so much greater use of them by claim departments, that a reevaluation of their use must be made.

A recorder need no longer be carried in an attache case, nor does it weigh ten or more pounds. Good recorders that weigh in the neighborhood of one pound and are small enough to be carried in a jacket pocket can be purchased for a fraction of the cost of one a decade ago. They are now much easier to operate and can even be used clandestinely. Therein lies one of their chief dangers and temptations and is the cause of so much legal controversy. The adjuster must absolutely resist any temptation to use recorders clandestinely. Not only is it unethical, but such action will destroy its usefulness in a trial.

It should be noted that the original tape must be presented in evidence. Transcriptions are subject to too many conditions that might affect accuracy and are ordinarily not admissible unless accompanied by the original tape. In addition, deterioration can result if not properly stored. Accordingly, great care and a regular routine must be set up in order to preserve the originals in such a fashion that no tampering or deterioration or destruction by "wipe-out" will take place.

Transcription can, in rare instances, be helpful to make an unclear or softly spoken passage understandable if the trial judge permits it.

When taking recorded statements, it is advisable to use an outline so that essential information will not be overlooked. At the same

SIGNED AND RECORDED STATEMENTS § 4.13

time, it is also important to use such notes unobtrusively so that the person being interviewed is not unduly alarmed.

If the person being interviewed is soft-spoken, the recorder should be placed near enough to get a good recording. To avoid distraction, it should, if possible, be placed below eye-level and away from distracting noises so as to avoid interference. If an open window is permitting street noises to intrude, the person being interviewed should be asked permission to close it. In the all-too-often case of a blaring radio or television, a polite request should be made to turn it off, with an explanation that will not create ruffled feelings. Any other people that may be unavoidably in the room should be requested to hold any comments and questions until after the interview. However, if there is an interruption, the person making any comments should be identified. In interviewing a claimant, it is important to explain that only the facts are being recorded and any discussion or questions will be answered thereafter.

It is ordinarily best to keep all comments concerning insurance out of the record for reasons previously discussed.

It is most important that the interviewer speak clearly and loud enough, but not so loud as to upset the subject. The interviewer should try at all costs not to lead the witness, should ask simple and direct questions, and never try to be "cute" or "tricky."

In the event that a diagram is involved, the interviewer should explain for the record what is taking place and have the diagram signed or initialed by the person being interviewed.

In order to avoid any suspicion of tampering with the tape, the recorder should be kept on continuously during the interview. Any long silences should be explained, especially if the person being interviewed leaves the room for any reason.

When faced with an unresponsive answer to a question, the interviewer should repeat the question in a simpler way, or explain it more fully. If it becomes obvious that the person being interviewed is deliberately obfuscating the facts or issues, the interviewer should go on to the next matter.

The interviewer should avoid multiple questions and make sure that one question is answered before another is asked.

In any event, the interviewer must become thoroughly familiar with the recording device and be able to describe its operation with obvious knowledge, should such a description be required in a subsequent suit. Any fumbling with the equipment at the time a statement

§ 4.13[1]   CASUALTY INSURANCE CLAIMS

is being taken should, if possible, be avoided. It is, accordingly, imperative that the interviewer make sure that the batteries in the recorder do not need replacement at the time of the interview.

If the recording is not routinely transcribed, and a summary is made for the file, the claim representative or investigator must take every precaution to assure that the summary is accurate.

[1] Advantages in Using Recording Devices

There are many advantages in the use of recording devices over the taking of handwritten or typewritten statements:

1. The statement which is recorded is done in the witness's own words and in his own particular accent. It gives the trial attorney a chance to determine to some degree what impression the witness will make at trial.
2. The recording will indicate a witness's emphasis and inflections and will give an idea as to whether he is forceful and positive or weak and vacillating.
3. Recording can be an invaluable help in taking statements from illiterate witnesses.
4. Studies have been made that indicate that the use of recording devices shortens the time of the interview and saves the time of both the witness and the investigator. A word of caution here, however, is the fact that this type of statement must be taken at least partially in question and answer form, and we have already seen that the question and answer type of statement is much longer than the narrative form.
5. Since only a small percentage of the statements that an investigator takes are ever used at trial, it is only necessary to transcribe some of the statements which are taken.
6. In most cases, it is not necessary to have a witness sworn when taking his statement by means of a recording device.
7. Occasionally an antagonistic witness becomes interested in the "gadget" aspect of a recording device and gets so interested in listening to a playback of his voice that he loses his antagonism and becomes cooperative.
8. Negative statements are easier and quicker to obtain.
9. Taking statements by a recording device avoids the problem of illegible handwriting.

[2] Disadvantages in Using Recording Devices

Some of the disadvantages of taking a statement by means of a recording device are:

1. In taking this kind of a statement it is necessary for at least a good part of the statement to be in question and answer form. To be effective at this type of statement taking requires special training and experience. For those who have by many years of experience been used to taking narrative statements, it requires a change of habit that may be difficult.
2. Because a good part of this type of statement must be in question and answer form, transcription is often long and involved.
3. It is essential that the recording be clear and audible. This is sometimes difficult either because a witness speaks in a low voice, or away from the microphone, or slurs his words. Occasionally interference from outside sources such as television, radio, children playing and shouting, noises from workers, etc., can prevent proper recording.
   Carelessness, or a lack of familiarity with the device in some instances (particularly with tape or wire), can cause an entire section of the recording to be wiped out.
4. While most states admit evidence taken by recording devices when properly authenticated, the interrogator must know the laws, rules and regulations for admission. If he is not thoroughly familiar with them, he can destroy the value of the recording as evidence.
5. Occasionally, a witness will freeze when he is told that he is speaking into a recording device. This is another form of "mike fright" familiar to radio and television operators. This objection, however, is becoming less important as more people are becoming familiar with recording devices.
6. Where the local rules of procedure require that copies of a witness's statement be given to him, the claims persons will be required to make transcriptions for this purpose.
7. In reviewing a file, it is much easier to get at the "meat" of the material by reviewing a written or typed statement rather than listening to sections of a recording.
8. The recording device is another piece of equipment which the claims person must carry.

9. The cost factor in purchasing these devices for a large staff deserves some consideration.

[3] Admissibility

Ordinarily, statements taken by a recording device are subject to the same rules of evidence as written statements, and where properly authenticated and where a proper foundation has been laid, the majority view is that they are admissible as evidence.[4]

The personal injury case of *Steve M. Solomon Inc. v. Edgar*[5] set up requirements for laying a proper foundation for admissibility as follows:

1. It must be shown that the mechanical transcription device was capable of taking testimony.
2. It must be shown that the operator of the device was competent to operate it.
3. The authenticity and correctness of the recording must be established.
4. It must be shown that changes, additions, or deletions have not been made.
5. The manner of preservation of the record must be shown.
6. Speakers must be identified, and
7. It must be shown that the testimony elicited was freely and voluntarily made, without any kind of duress.

[4] Obtaining the Facts

In attempting to obtain a statement with a recording device, it is obvious that the interrogator explain the reason for using the device. It is suggested that the machine is being used for the purpose of accuracy in obtaining the facts in the words of the person being interviewed, and for the further purpose of saving the time of that person.

It is further suggested that the investigator explain the operation of the recorder as he sets it up, show how it works, and, on a sample disc, allow the witness or other subject to become familiar with it.

---

[4] 58 A.L.R.2d 1024 (1958).

[5] 88 S.W.2d 167 (Ga. App. 1955). *See also* Hinkle, "Recorded Statements Revisited," Insurance Adjuster Magazine, July 1977.

SIGNED AND RECORDED STATEMENTS § 4.13[4]

Once the machine is set-up to record the interview, the investigator must record his name and position (as investigator or attorney for one of the parties) and the place, date, and time of the interview. A few remarks of identification concerning the decorations in the room, the furniture, pictures, or any other distinguishing features can also be recorded. This will make it much more difficult for the person being interviewed to subsequently deny that it was his statement and that it was taken in his home. He must further record his own statement to the effect that this is a recording concerning an investigation of an accident which occurred at a certain time and place, that the witness understands that his remarks are being recorded, and that the statement is given voluntarily.

A statement taken by means of a recording device should preferably be a combination of question and answer, and narrative form. The introductory information should be obtained by question and answer, as previously illustrated, in order to identify the witness and obtain background information concerning him. When the interrogator has reached the point where he wishes to obtain a description of the accident, it is preferable at least to permit the witness to start his explanation in a running narrative account. Should the witness ramble however, and should it be necessary to get him back in line, the interrogator should have no hesitancy about cutting in at the end of a sentence and asking a few direct questions in order to get the witness back on the right track. Unless the witness starts to make statements which could seriously impair the value of the entire recording, it is best to wait until he has finished a sentence before the interrogator interjects. Otherwise, there may be an overlapping of two voices that could be difficult to understand.

Ordinarily, background movements like the entrance or exit of children, or a witness's wife going from one room to another, need not be mentioned, but where there is an interruption that causes a discontinuance of the conversation, the investigator should not stop the machine but should merely make an explanation into the microphone concerning the reason for the interruption and to the effect that the conversation will continue as soon as the witness has returned.

Before the recording begins, a witness should be cautioned against nodding or pointing or making other soundless answers. Where this is done in spite of such precautions, the interrogator must inject a direct question based upon the silent answer. For instance, the interrogator could say: "You have just nodded in answer to my question and I presume this is intended to mean yes."

The format of the statement can follow the same pattern as outlined previously in the taking of a written statement.

At the conclusion of the interview, the investigator should always ask the witness if there is information which he wishes to add to the statement or any corrections or additional explanations he would like to make. When he has replied, the final question asked by the claims person should be, "Is the information which you have given in this interview true and correct to the best of your knowledge?"

In the event that more than one tape is needed, proper explanation should be made both at the end of the first tape and at the beginning of the new one.

[5] **Telephone Recording Devices**

There is a Federal Communications Commission ruling that requires all telephone recording equipment to have an automatic beeper to warn the parties that the conversation is being recorded. It is accordingly important for the caller to explain the reason for the beeper and to inform the person being called that the conversation is being recorded.

The admissibility of conversations in evidence that are taken over the telephone by mechanical devices is a matter of federal or state decision, ruling or statute. Ordinarily, if the conversation is held openly and is properly founded, it will be admitted on the same basis as other statements.[6]

In the case of *Jackson v. Montgomery*,[7] the court enumerated four requirements for admissibility which I have paraphrased:

1. The witness must acknowledge the conversation took place.
2. The witness must have known that the conversation was being recorded and made no objection thereto.
3. The witness was made aware of the identity of the person calling, and who he was representing.

---

[6] Gale Oppenheimer v. Cohen, 140 N.Y.S.2d 546 (1955).
[7] 320 N.E.2d 770 (1974).

4. The interviewer must be able to give the exact time and place of the conversation and be able to testify as to its accuracy.[8]

It must always be kept in mind that a telephone interview is at best only a substitute for a personal interview and should be used as a last resort where a personal interview is not warranted because of the expense, distance, weather conditions, or other good reasons.

---

[8] *See also* 58 A.L.R. 1024 (1958), 11 A.L.R.3d 1296, (1967), 24 A.L.R.3d 1261 (1969), 49 A.L.R.3d 955 (1973), and 57 A.L.R.3d 172 (1974).

CHAPTER 5

Securing the Physical Facts

§ 5.01 Diagrams
§ 5.02 Photographs
§ 5.03 Movies
§ 5.04 Surveys and Plats
§ 5.05 Advertising Catalogs and Instructional Material
§ 5.06 Laboratory Testing
§ 5.07 Preliminary Hearings
§ 5.08 Records
    [1] Weather Reports
    [2] Police Reports
    [3] Motor Vehicle Records
        [a] Driving Records
    [4] Birth, Death, and Marriage Certificates
    [5] Coroner's Report
    [6] Autopsy Report
    [7] School Records and Information
    [8] Income Tax Reports
    [9] Military Records
    [10] Civil Aeronautics Board Reports
    [11] Newspaper Reports
§ 5.09 Company Engineering Department
§ 5.10 Choosing an Expert
§ 5.11 Bibliography

In casualty claim reporting, the term physical facts is an elastic catchall phrase. It is particularly concerned with the physical conditions at the scene of the accident, including any vehicles, machinery, or objects involved in the accident.

In general, these are the facts that speak for themselves. A thorough examination of the physical facts can help to determine whether the accident could have actually occurred as alleged by an insured, claimant, or witness.

In the investigation of a serious claim, the scene of the accident and any other objects involved in it should be scrutinized as soon as possible. Skid marks, debris, and other such markings do not remain visible for very long after an accident occurs. In stairway accidents, the steps should be seen before anyone has an opportunity to tamper with nosings or coverings. Furthermore, conditions change, snow and ice melt and disappear, foliage grows or diminishes with the seasons, buildings are erected and demolished, and other changes occur if enough time is allowed to elapse before checking the scene of the accident.

Although it is, of course, important to view the physical facts in an effort to determine the truth of the various allegations, it is just as important that evidence be obtained by means of photographs, surveys, and diagrams. It is equally important that certain objects involved in the accident be preserved for presentation in court in those cases which may have to be tried.

In order to secure these all-important physical facts immediately, an investigator should always carry a ruler and tape measure, and a camera, so that he can make measurements, draw diagrams, and take snapshots for the benefit of anyone reviewing the file.

Observation is a matter of training, and a good claim representative will soon be able to see many things at the scene of an accident that an untrained observer would ordinarily overlook. He should train himself to observe fully and to make a complete description of the scene of an accident, including all details that are or may become pertinent to the investigation and trial of a case.

Checklists of items to be observed, reported on, and shown on a diagram are given subsequently, since each type of accident and investigation is discussed separately.

Since this category of "physical facts" is used as a catchall, various reports and other items that do not readily fit into any other category have been included here.

§ 5.01 Diagrams

A diagram made by an investigator need not be a work of art, nor need it have the precision of a draftsman's blueprint. However, since its main purpose is to dispel confusion, not compound it, enough care and effort should go into its composition to make it understandable.

Diagrams drawn by the investigator have many advantages:

1. A visual drawing of the scene of an accident is mentally absorbed much quicker than a word description.
2. It is very often much easier to draw a diagram illustrating what occurred than it is to describe the occurrence in words.

3. A diagram will help the reviewer of the file, whether he be the local manager or the home office examiner, to understand the factual situation much better and to arrive at a determination of liability more quickly.
4. The drawing of a diagram will force the investigator to make a closer observation than he ordinarily would and help impress the physical facts that much more firmly in his mind.
5. Studying a complete diagram will often suggest leads to additional investigation that might uncover as-yet-unknown witnesses.

The method of drawing diagrams varies with the individual. Some investigators can make a complete and finished diagram at the scene of the accident without having to re-do it later. Others are so meticulous that they are not satisfied with a diagram drawn under adverse conditions on the spot; they re-do it subsequently at home or in the office.

Several aids can be purchased that are helpful in making diagrams. They run the gamut from cut-outs designed into rulers or celluloid squares, to elaborate diagram kits which include rubber stamps to represent all types of transportation equipment, traffic signals, and even human beings in various positions. Properly used, these aids can be very helpful. On the other hand, effective diagrams can be made without any of them. A diagram need not be elaborate to be effective. Although it should be complete and clearly understandable, a diagram drawn by an investigator is not made to be presented in court as evidence.

The quality of an investigator's work can usually be judged by the diagram he draws, and by whether he draws one at all.

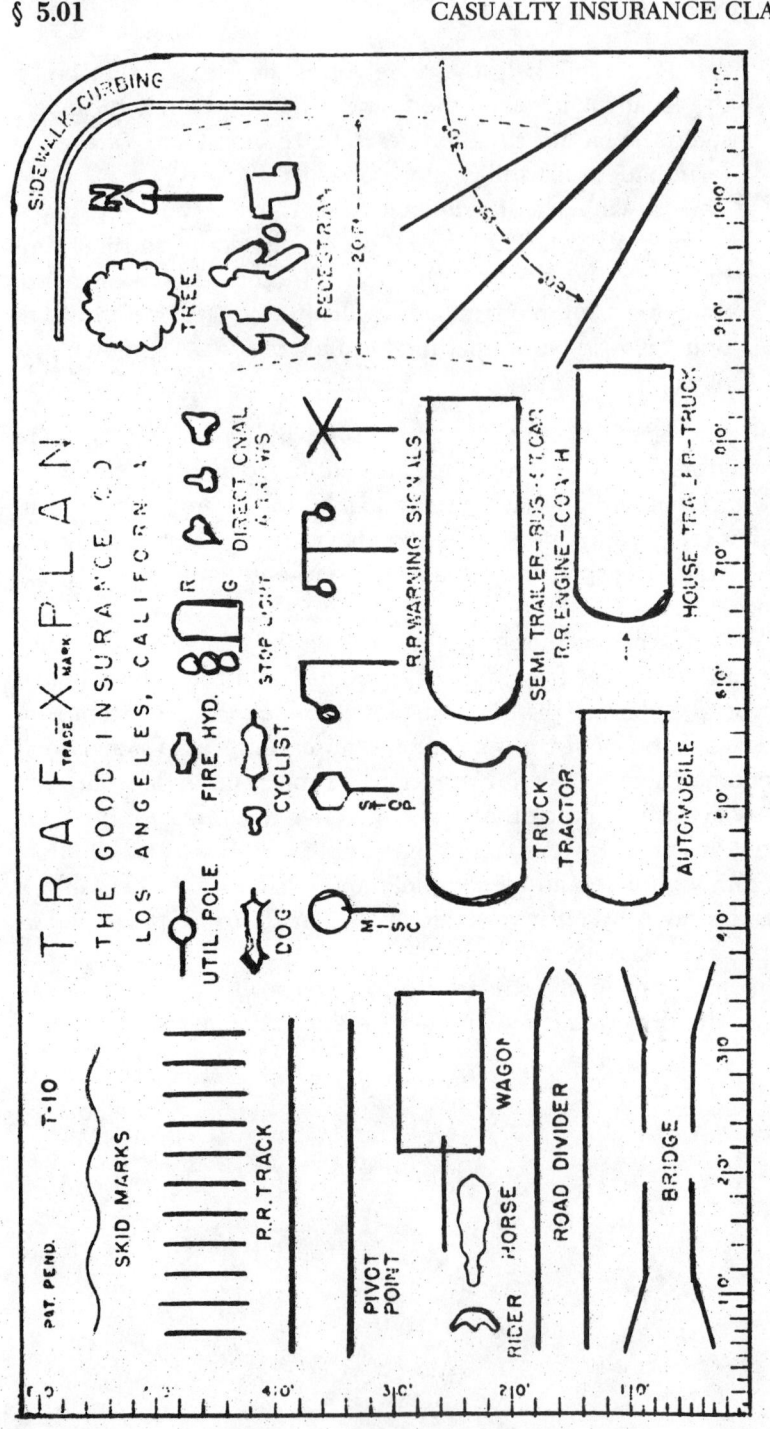

(a) Transparent Template For Making Diagrams

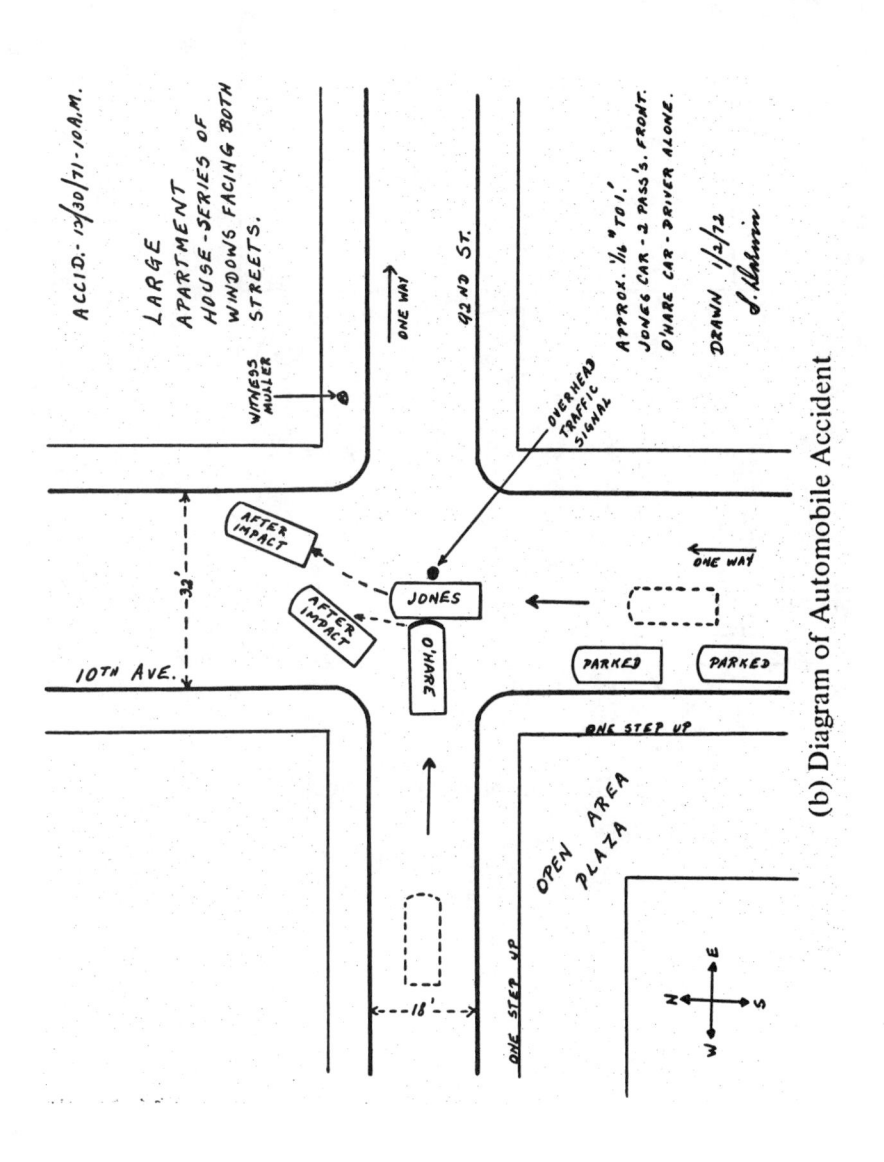

SECURING THE PHYSICAL FACTS § 5.01

(b) Diagram of Automobile Accident

§ 5.01 CASUALTY INSURANCE CLAIMS

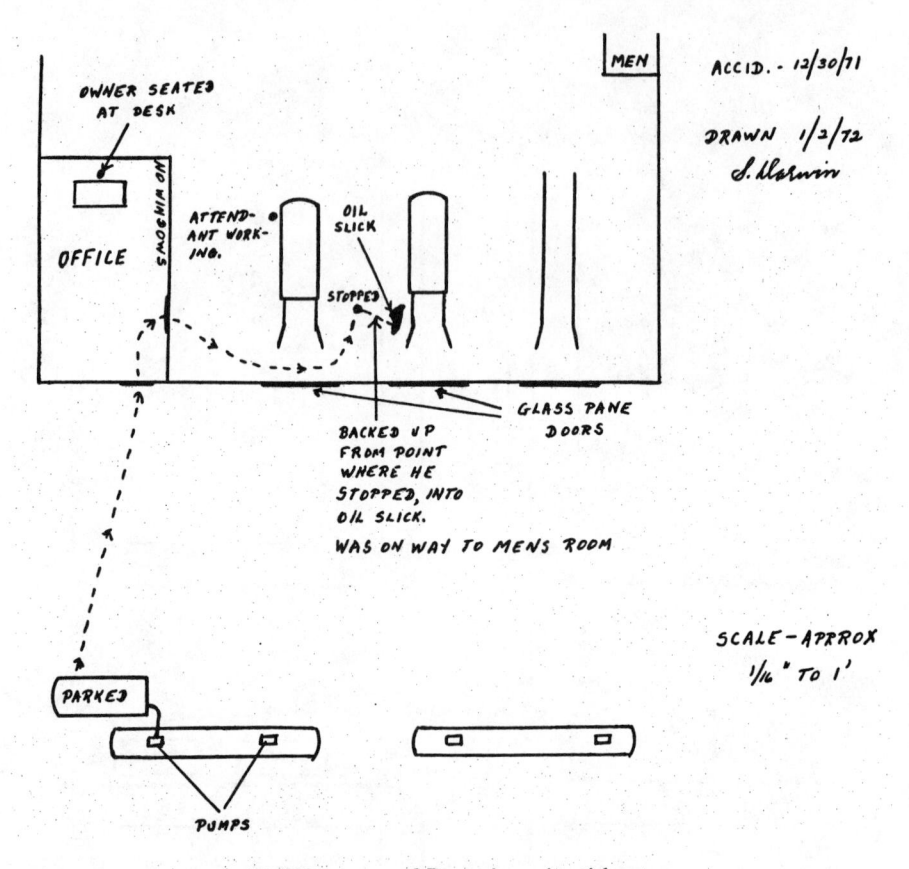

(c) Diagram of Premises Accident

The essential information which should be included in all diagrams is:

- [ ] All of the details of the physical facts, including the surrounding area, the makeup and general condition and composition of the streets or roads, lighting, defects, obstructions, points of vantage from which witnesses could have viewed the scene, traffic controls, and all other details which will be further itemized in discussions of investigations of automobile and other types of accident claims.
- [ ] Position of the vehicles involved in an automobile accident before, during, and after the accident.
- [ ] All measurements that have a direct bearing on the investigation, including distances from lighting, skidmarks, and street or object measurements.
- [ ] A compass indication at the top of the diagram, showing north to be the top of the page.
- [ ] If the diagram is done to scale, key to the scale in the lower right hand corner.
- [ ] A legend at the bottom of the diagram giving a label to all objects or vehicles involved and include the date and time the diagram was drawn, as well as the date and time of the accident.
- [ ] The signature of the diagram's maker.

§ 5.02 Photographs

Since the main purpose of taking photographs is to have a permanent record of conditions as they existed at the time of the accident, they should of course be taken as soon as possible, before any change has occurred in the scene or object being photographed.

For our purposes, photographs can be divided into a number of general classifications.

1. *Snapshots.* For the most part, these are chiefly to be used merely for the transmitting of information from the investigator to the file. They are not ordinarily used in the trial of a case because in many jurisdictions photographs are not admissible unless taken by a qualified expert. The average investigator does not have the experience to qualify as an expert; furthermore, it is not usually advisable to have the investigator for an insurance company testify at a trial, if this can be avoided. Snapshots should be taken in those cases in which the scene or object is difficult to describe or to draw in detail. Snapshots taken for this purpose require only the use of a simple camera that can be operated with a minimum of fuss and technical ability.

2. *Commercial photographs.* Commercial photographs are taken primarily to be used as evidence at a trial. It is therefore important that the photographer not only be well-qualified, but also have the necessary characteristics for a good and convincing witness. Accordingly, it is important that all photographs be properly identified on the reverse side or by an attached tab. In view of the large number of cases that require the use of a commercial photographer, cost, in the average case, should be a definite consideration. Not only must the investigator have a definite understanding about the price before engaging the services of a commercial photographer, but must specify the number of photographs desired. This should not be left to the discretion of the photographer.

The case that warrants commercial photographs also warrants the presence of the investigator at the scene of the accident while the photographs are being taken. Too often, where instructions are given to a photographer by telephone or letter, the shots taken are not the most desirable. In some instances, misunderstanding is so great that it makes the photographs absolutely worthless for the purposes for which they were intended. The investigator who has "lived" with a case, who knows exactly what is important to show, should be at the scene to direct the photographer.

The commercial photographer whose services are engaged should definitely understand that any photographs taken belong to the company that ordered them, and that no prints are to be made available to anyone else.

Commercial photographs can be important in the defense of a case not only by showing the entire scene of an accident, but by illustrating the point of contact through pictures of both vehicles that show the damage to them.

The investigator must remember that he is trying to show the condition as it existed at the time of the accident. He should see that the photographs are taken not only at the same time of year, but even at the same time of day or night, so that the shadow formations and lighting conditions will be similar. It is of course just as important that the weather conditions be the same.

Everyone has seen examples of trick photography, and photographic distortions made either intentionally or by accident. The angle of a shot, the type or combination of filters, the direction of the lighting, and the like, can so distort a picture that it bears little resemblance to the actual object represented. Such distortions should be guarded against not only in taking photographs but in examining those taken by others who are trying to present a different point of view.

3. *Superimposed photographs.* Some commercial photographers are also qualified to testify concerning surveys and measurements. They usually specialize in what are commonly termed "superimposed photographs." These consist of a thin sheet of transparent paper, placed over the photograph, with measurements drawn on the paper sheet.

In some instances, photographers specialize in marking a scene of an accident with rulers, chalk or other objects to indicate measurements shown up on the actual photograph itself. Care must be used so that the effectiveness of the photograph is not lost because of the markings and changes made by the photographer.

Superimposed photographs can sometimes serve a very useful purpose. Where the importance of a case warrants their use, the investigator should make sure that the person who does the work is well-qualified and has a previous history as an expert witness.

4. *Aerial photographs.* An investigator will not often have use for aerial photographs. For the most part, he will be interested in a detailed study of a small area, not an aerial shot of a vast area. In the exceptional case, it may sometimes be advisable to take an aerial photograph to show the general contour of a road or area over a considerable distance. Even though this should be kept in mind as a possibility, its use should be kept at a minimum.

5. *Panorama shots and enlargements.* The expense involved in panorama shots and enlargements should of necessity limit their use to important cases that are definitely pointed for defense. They are very effective in the courtroom and are not used often enough in those cases in which a detailed study of the scene is important to the defense of a case.

Commercial photographers who know their business can make overlapping photographs that will represent a considerable area. Though there is a certain amount of unavoidable distortion in such photographs, it may be unimportant if the extent of the area to be covered is of prime importance.

6. *Stereoscopic views.* Stereoscopic photography is valuable when it is important to present a three-dimensional picture. While the photography itself should not present any great problems for the commercial photographer, the finished prints must be viewed in a special

viewer or through special glasses. Consideration should be given to the taking of stereoscopic views when dealing with the defense of claims involving steps, curves, and inclines that would, in the ordinary photograph, blend into the background. These photographs can also be important when it is desirable to highlight a dent in a car that might be almost invisible in the ordinary flat-plane photograph.

7. *Color photographs.* There is no substitute for a good color photograph to show personal injury. It is, however, one thing to show an actual injury honestly, and quite another to highlight gore for the sake of inciting the jury's sympathy. Many of our courts have become more conservative in the admission of color photographs because of abuses by some attorneys who have taken progressive photographs during the course of an operation, or who have photographed undressed wounds. The tendency today is to permit only the part of the body that is essential to a proof of injury to be shown.

Color photography has an important place when color is a vital factor in an accident. For instance, a full-color photograph of a stop sign is far more effective than the same photograph in black and white. If it is desirable to show that damage on a vehicle was long-standing and that rust was encrusted in the damaged areas long before the accident occurred, color photography can be extremely valuable.

8. *Slides and projections.* Occasionally, detail of an object or an area is so important that it is advisable to project a picture of it onto a screen. Either black and white or color projection can create a dramatic and impressive effect.

However, the investigator must realize that it may be difficult to have a slide admitted in evidence and to obtain the judge's permission to project it onto a screen. When problems of admissibility arise, it may be necessary to use a highly-qualified expert who can, among other things, testify that a projected image can show gradations in tone and color that are impossible to reproduce in a print on paper.

9. *Police photographs.* Very often the police or detectives who make the investigation of an accident will take their own photographs. These shots are important because they have been taken by an impartial agency, usually very shortly after an accident. Many jurisdictions will release copies of such photographs on payment of a fee. The investigator should always determine whether such photographs have been taken and whether copies are available to him.

10. *Newspaper photographs.* Occasionally, a news photograph of a scene of an accident or vehicles involved in it is advantageous to the defense of a case. Ordinarily, copies of such a photograph are made available upon payment of a small fee. In many instances, photographs may have been taken by a free-lance photographer from whom not only the prints but sometimes the negatives can be bought.

§ 5.03 Movies

The taking of motion pictures is a specialized art, requiring professional competence if the movies are to be effective. Again, the investigator must remember that the pictures themselves have no value as evidence unless the person who took them can qualify as an expert.

Those who have had experience in this field have the equipment such as trailers, telephoto lenses, and the necessary know-how to take pictures of claimants without revealing the fact that the subject is being photographed.

The use of motion pictures in claim work is usually confined to checking on the activities of a claimant in order to refute his allegation of disability. This is a controversial matter involving advisability and jury reaction factors that require discussion with higher authority before taking action.

Ordinarily, it is not necessary to incur the expense of motion pictures unless some element of fraud is involved.

§ 5.04 Surveys and Plats

The purpose of the engineer's survey or a plat (a model reproduction) made to scale is to help the jury visualize the physical condition at the scene of the accident. Because of the expense involved, a survey should be ordered with discretion and only after the most careful consideration.

Both a survey or a plat can be helpful in the defense of an important case, but they can also be calamitous when improperly used at trial. Neither should be ordered without advice of competent counsel, and in the exceptional case only.

§ 5.05 Advertising Catalogs and Instructional Material

Ordinarily, if the investigation of a claim involves some product or piece of machinery, the investigator may find upon inquiry that there is a good deal of advertising or instructional material that will not only help explain the structure of the product or machine, but will give detailed diagrams of its operation. These are often extremely helpful in the defense of a case. The insured should always be requested to furnish whatever material of this nature he has concerning the object in question.

§ 5.06 Laboratory Testing

In addition to such basic factors as testing the adequacy of brakes or steering on an automobile that has been involved in an accident, products and professional liability coverages have proven the need for many kinds of laboratory tests that might be helpful in trying to determine liability.

Testing can determine the reason for the failure of structural material including metal, wood, and rope; the reason and breaking point of glass objects; the reason for malfunctioning of appliances and other mechanical and electrical equipment; the contamination of foods and drugs; and the allergenic qualities of contact materials such as chemical fabrics, detergents, cosmetics, etc.

A difficult problem is the determination of whether a foreign substance was actually present in a product or container when purchased or whether such article or product was tampered with, accidentally or purposely, after it was purchased.

The investigator must always be conscious of the fact that it is not enough for him to know that a certain product complained of was not contaminated, or that an object broke because it was struck by a hammer and not as alleged by the claimant. He must be able to prove this in court, and must therefore become familiar with the many different types of laboratory services which are available.

The federal government, most states, and many municipalities maintain health and other departments that conduct various kinds of laboratory tests, especially in order to check the cleanliness of establishments that serve or process food. Colleges and universities maintain bacteriological, chemical, mechanical, electrical, and other laboratories, and the professors who run them are ordinarily very cooperative if approached with tact.

SECURING THE PHYSICAL FACTS § 5.07

There are also private laboratories which can and will make all kinds of tests that might be required in determining liability on a case under investigation.

Technological knowledge has in recent years grown so perceptibly that areas of testing until recently impossible, are now commonplace. With the use of all sorts of new equipment and instruments, tests can be made to reveal the following:

1. Radiography—to reveal internal flaws in metals and welds by x-ray analysis.
2. Corrosion studies—to determine why a metal part may have failed.
3. Emission spectrograph—to determine whether there are any metallic impurities and the nature thereof.
4. Testing machines for a determination of the strength of materials, including their load capacity.
5. Air pollution surveys which today can determine the amount of foreign material in the air and the nature thereof.
6. Acoustics determination for noise levels.
7. Appliance testing for determination of electrical and mechanical safety and for defects of any kind.
8. Drug analysis to determine factors of irritation, allergy, contamination, toxicity, etc.
9. Food analysis to determine purity, toxicity, allergic qualities, etc.
10. Chemical testing of solvents and reagents to determine their inhalation toxicity, irritation potential, and harmful effects to eyes or membranes.
11. Testing of medical supplies and equipment to determine sterility, toxicity, and allergic propensities.
12. Tests to determine the strength of bottles containing beverages and to determine whether the bottle sustained outside force before breaking.
13. Tests to determine the contents of extraneous material in a bottled beverage or other processed drink, and many others.

§ 5.07 Preliminary Hearings

Although the defense attorney may not be able to use transcripts of a criminal or traffic hearing in the trial of a civil action, the information to be obtained from such transcripts is very often quite valuable in giving leads for the investigation of a claim.

Indiscriminate ordering of transcripts is an expensive luxury. Attendance at the trial or hearing by the investigator should enable him to determine whether a transcript will be helpful or necessary. It will also provide an opportunity to see some of the principals or witnesses as they are testifying and get an impression of their effectiveness as witnesses.

Transcripts which may be useful are (1) traffic hearings or motor vehicle department hearings; (2) criminal trials; or (3) coroner's hearings.

In any such hearing or trial, the claims man can only act as an observer. He must never act as the representative for the insured.

§ 5.08 Records

[1] Weather Reports

If the physical facts have changed, or if there is a possibility that the weather had a bearing on a claimant's allegations, it is exceedingly important that the investigator obtain a weather report. The successful defense of the case he is investigating may depend upon it.

The United States Weather Bureau, through its many local stations, publishes weather reports for particular localities. Weather may vary even within a small locality. It is therefore important that the investigator make sure his report covers the particular area involved in the accident.

The information contained in these reports ordinarily includes cloudiness or sunshine; precipitation (whether it be rain or snow), including the amount of precipitation at various hours throughout the day, as well as the average for the day; wind velocity; temperatures at various hours throughout the day, as well as the average temperature; and other exceedingly valuable information.

[2] Police Reports

Police reports made by various departments of the state and municipal governments can be exceedingly helpful in the investigation of an accident case. Most of these reports are a matter of public record and are available for a small fee. Others may not be available when criminal prosecution is involved, and still others are confidential reports that can only be obtained through confidential sources or by discovery processes.

A police report is usually made when an accident of a serious nature occurs. Depending on the jurisdiction, it may be made by state troopers, local municipal police, or the sheriff's office.

These reports are becoming more and more inclusive and contain much of the following information:

1. Date, time, and place of the accident.
2. Traffic details, usually including a small diagram.
3. Names of all parties and witnesses involved in the accident, including the owners and drivers of vehicles, or the owners of premises involved in an accident.
4. A description of the driver, including age and license number.
5. The names and addresses of all injured parties, and a digest of their injuries, including the place where they received medical attention.
6. Description of the accident, ranging from brief to detailed.
7. Names of witnesses to the accident.
8. Weather, lighting, and road conditions.
9. Description of motor vehicles involved in the accident.
10. Property damage sustained.

Occasionally, police reports will furnish even more detailed information in the form of questions requiring check-mark answers. These reports are ordinarily available in photostatic form or can be copied. In some cases, a small fee is charged.

Police officers often have more information in their notes than appears on the actual report. Sometimes this information is hearsay that can lead to profitable avenues of additional investigation. Therefore, it is always advisable for the investigator to see the police officers personally if the magnitude of the case warrants it.

[3] **Motor Vehicle Records**

Most states have a Motor Vehicle Department that is separate and distinct from the Police Department. This department usually requires each party to an accident that involves a certain minimum of property damage, ranging from $50.00 up, or that involves any bodily injury, to submit a report promptly. The forms are available, usually in photostatic reproduction, for a nominal fee.

Although these motor vehicle accident reports cover much the same ground as the police and state troopers' report, their importance is greater because they are usually made out by the drivers involved in the accident and often include admissions against interest. These reports may not be available in some areas.

[a] Driving Records

Within the Motor Vehicle Department, some states will provide a certified abstract of a driver's operating record for a nominal fee. This record usually contains the type of license the operator holds (private passenger, junior license, or truck), the number and type of accidents in which the driver was previously involved, a record of any traffic convictions, and a record of any suspensions, revocations, or restorations of a driver's license.

[4] Birth, Death, and Marriage Certificates

While it is common knowledge that certified copies of birth, death, and marriage certificates are available for small fees in all areas of the country, investigators may overlook these sources of information. In cases where dependency is a factor in the determination of damages, these records can obviously be important.

Information such as places of birth and marriage, name of the attending physician on a death certificate, and names of witnesses who were present for, or clergy who performed, a marriage ceremony, can all be helpful if it is necessary to trace a witness or to obtain some background information on a party to the litigation.

[5] Coroner's Report

A coroner's report may be available in cases involving the possibility of criminal prosecution as a result of a death. Most of the larger municipalities automatically conduct a coroner's inquest in a case where death has resulted from an accident.

Sometimes, for a small fee, a certified copy of an abstract of the coroner's report can be obtained and usually contains at least the following information:

1. Date, time, and place of the examination.
2. Name, age, occupation, and personal description of the deceased.

3. A detailed description of the injuries.
4. A history of the incident or the accident taken from police information.
5. Probable cause of death.

[6] Autopsy Report

Some of our larger municipalities have subdivisions in their medical departments that automatically perform autopsies in certain types of accident cases. These autopsy reports are sometimes available upon payment of a small fee, and are well worth obtaining.

No death case can be treated lightly. The leads that may be obtained from autopsy reports have proven invaluable in uncovering information that would not otherwise have been revealed.

[7] School Records and Information

School records, if obtainable, can be an important source of information, whether they be obtained from a primary or high school, or college.

Pertinent information that would have a direct bearing on the value of a claim may be developed from the following:

1. Attendance record before the accident (basis of comparison).
2. Time lost as a result of the accident and attendance record for some time subsequent to it.
3. Grades before and after the accident.
4. Physical, dental, or psychiatric examinations.
5. Aptitude, intelligence, or psychological examinations and tests.
6. Curriculum before and after accident.
7. Complaints to teachers, athletic directors, or principal.
8. Athletic activities before and after the accident.

[8] Income Tax Reports

Federal and state income tax reports can be a potent weapon in corroborating damages or in disproving special damage allegations. Although such records are ordinarily not a matter of public record, there may be legitimate ways to obtain this information. All too often an investigator knowing the federal and state income tax reports are confidential, gives no thought to the possibility of obtaining this in-

§ 5.08[9]   CASUALTY INSURANCE CLAIMS

formation even when a case goes into suit. He should consult local counsel to see if an attempt to get the records is feasible and warranted.

[9] Military Records

While it is not required by state law or ordinance, many veterans who are discharged from the army voluntarily record their discharge papers at the local county courthouse, making these documents a matter of available record. From them, the investigator can obtain such information as an individual's date and place of birth, education, service periods and places, and the date of discharge.

[10] Civil Aeronautics Board Reports

Every airplane accident is investigated by the Civil Aeronautics Board, and these reports should be reviewed by the investigator. They are detailed and contain a great deal of valuable information concerning the pilot, the airplane, and the passengers. These reports are available to interested parties, but are not necessarily admissible in court.

[11] Newspaper Reports

Occasionally, an important bit of information can be obtained from newspaper accounts of an accident. The investigator, however, should read all newspaper reports with an extremely jaundiced eye. After comparing newspaper accounts with the results of his own investigation, he sometimes begins to wonder whether or not it is the same accident. There are, however, occasions when such articles do reveal names of witnesses or other information not previously obtained.

§ 5.09 Company Engineering Department

Casualty insurance companies that do a considerable volume of business usually have their own engineering department whose prime function is to assist the underwriting department in risk selection, and to help in accident prevention work. All too often the cooperation between the engineering and claim departments in a casualty company is not what it should be. Company engineers can be of

SECURING THE PHYSICAL FACTS § 5.11

valuable assistance to the claim department, not only in the help which they themselves can give in the investigation of a claim, but in giving advice concerning the hiring of proper experts needed for the defense of a case, such as contractors, architects, chemists, or electricians.

§ 5.10 Choosing an Expert

In choosing the expert for defense testimony, consideration should be given to the following:

1. Background, education, or experience that make him acceptable as an expert to the particular court and give weight to his testimony.
2. Personal qualifications that make a good witness, such as acceptable appearance, poise, assurance, and so on.
3. Recognition as an expert in the place where the case is being tried. The better known he is, the more weight his testimony is likely to bear.
4. Reputation for honesty and fair dealing.

In the event that expert testimony is needed, the investigator should always take the precaution of having a definite advance understanding concerning fees.

§ 5.11 Bibliography

Physical Facts—General

Cox, "Preservation of Evidence." Address to Atlanta Claim Assoc. School, Atlanta, Ga., January 1963.
Hagenbaugh, "Proper Physical Evidence is a Vital Aid in Winning Lawsuits," Insurance Adjuster, April 1963.

Diagrams

Tucker & Staiger, "Models, Diagrams and Surveys." Address to Kansas City Claim Adjusters Assoc., March 9, 1951.

Documents, Records and Reports

Clapp, "Claims Investigation—Some Lightly Traveled Areas," Insurance Law Journal, March 1960.

Hoffman, "Checking Various Reports." Lecture, Univ. of Kansas City, Jan.-May term 1953.
Miller, "Government Records and Reports in Civil Legislation," Insurance Counsel Journal, July 1961.

Expert Witnesses

Davies, *Finding an Expert Witness in the Sciences,* 13 Clev.-Marq. L. Rev. 2, May 1964.
Dombroff, "Prepare and Present Your Expert Witness," F.T.D., August 1984.
Lawton, "Reconstruction: A Basic Tool in Determining Accident Causation," Insurance Counsel Journal, January 1969.
Peterson, "The Scientific Expert," Insurance Law Journal, January 1953.
"Using Experts to Best Advantage," Crawford News Letter, vol. IV, #4, April 1984.
Younger, "Expert Witnesses," Insurance Counsel Journal, April 1981.

Laboratory Tests

Carroll, "Why Did These Parts Fail?", Materials in Design Engineering. New York: Reinhold Pub. Co., July 1961.
Gregor, "Testing the Product," Industrial Design, November 1960.

Photographs, Movies, Videotape

Aldrich, "Traffic Accident Reconstruction: An Overview," Insurance Adjuster, December 1984.
Dombroff, "Videotape: An Innovative Evidentiary Use of an Engineering Technology," F.I.C. Quart., Winter 1983.
Hoffmaster, "Document With Photographs," The Independent Adjuster, Spring 1981.
Mackall, "I Now Offer this Photograph in Evidence," Insurance Counsel Journal, April 1953.
Scott, "Photographs." Address, Kansas City Claim Conference, February 23, 1951.
Witman, "Investigative Photography," L.A. Bar Bull., August 1951.

CHAPTER 6

Obtaining Medical Information

§ 6.01 Information to be Obtained from the Claimant
§ 6.02 Medical Liens
§ 6.03 Information to be Obtained from the Attending Physician
§ 6.04 Medical Report Form
§ 6.05 Dental Records
§ 6.06 Hospital Records
§ 6.07 Medical Examinations
    [1] Choosing the Examining Doctor
    [2] Expensive Diagnostic Procedures
§ 6.08 Autopsy and Coroner's Reports
§ 6.09 Military Records

The first time a trainee copies a hospital report, he may come out of the experience quite bewildered and not a little awed. Five years later, he may be inclined to criticize the diagnosis and sneer at the treatment.

The truth of the matter is that the average layman can, with some diligent study, acquire a good working knowledge of medical terminology and enough of an understanding of the field in which he is interested to discuss injuries, and even treatment, quite intelligently. To be realistic, however, the physician who has spent years studying and practicing medicine knows more than the claim representative about medical problems. Therefore while he should learn as much as he can, the claim representative should never try to replace the physician.

The scope of this book does not permit more than a mere basic discussion of the scientific aspects of medicine as it affects the claim practice. This vast field has been covered excellently in several massive texts written by competent physicians. Medico-legal textbooks should be available to the claim representative, and he should be able to discuss medical problems with a resident or examining physician, or with his home office.

Even if the office out of which he is working maintains a resident physician on its staff, there is still need for the claims person to have a certain familiarity with injuries or diseases which may result from, or may become aggravated by, accidental injury. He must, in any event, be able to:

1. **Evaluate the injury.** This can be done only if he is able to understand the medical reports and appraise their significance. If he cannot evaluate the injury, he obviously cannot evaluate the claim and must, therefore, depend entirely upon his supervisor to set a figure on its value.

2. **Help detect fraud or malingering.** Unless he has at least some fundamental knowledge of symptoms, causes, and effects, he will be completely at sea in determining the honesty or justice of a particular claim.

3. **Help determine whether proper treatment is being given,** especially in compensation claims. Claim adjusters, despite the common misconception, are human. They do become emotionally involved in their claims. It is natural, therefore, both from the humanitarian and business point of view, for the claim representative to be anxious for the claimant to receive the best possible treatment, so that he can make the quickest possible recovery.

Let me repeat these words of caution: he should not attempt to make any diagnosis of his own. He should not stand in judgment upon someone who knows this field a lot better than he does. Obviously, some doctors are not as competent as others, and some are even incompetent. The layman with specialized training in certain fields should at least be able to determine the advisability of calling in another physician for consultation or examination.

4. **Learn when to order a medical examination** and by whom it should be made. Ordering an examination shortly after a claimant has received a fracture and is still in a cast is not only useless, but a complete waste of money if there is no question about the genuineness of the injury or the honesty of the claim.

On the other hand, if there is or may be an element of fraud or malingering the claims representative may find it advisable to assign a medical examination as soon as possible, or at least after enough time has passed so that any subjective complaints should have materialized.

§ 6.01 Information to be Obtained from the Claimant

"Things ain't what they used to be in my day." We live today in a much more claim-wise and sophisticated era. In years past, it was the norm for an adjuster to see even a seriously injured claimant who was not represented by an attorney. Then it got to be a chase as to who got to the hospital first. Today, an adjuster is usually forbidden from getting anywhere near the claimant if he is in a hospital. So when the adjuster does meet up with the claimant who says "Talk to my lawyer," get the lawyer's name and telephone number and do just that.

Nevertheless, not all injured claimants will be represented by a lawyer when first seen by the adjuster. A request for an authorization to see medical and hospital records may drive the claimant into the arms of the nearest lawyer. So what does the adjuster do? He uses all the diplomacy of which he is capable and explains the fact that he wishes to be fair in his evaluation of the claimant's medical condition which he cannot properly do without the medical information.

What is hereafter written assumes a classic case of cooperation. This is what the adjuster should try to get, all things being equal, and if they are not equal he should get as much as he can. If he cannot get authorization, he should get as much verbal information as possible. So let's get on with what the adjuster should at least strive for.

The time to obtain written authorization to procure medical information is the first time the claim representative interviews the claimant. Authorization should be phrased in simple language, and the use of legal terminology should be avoided. The authorization need only state that the bearer is authorized to receive a medical report on the accident from the doctor or hospital involved. The authorization should, of course, be signed by the claimant. Enough copies should be given so that medical information can be obtained from each attending physician, hospital, clinic, or any other person or organization that rendered medical services.

Medical information obtained from the claimant should preferably be incorporated in a signed statement obtained from him, but, whether obtained orally or in writing, the information should include:

- ☐ Detailed description of all objective (noticeable) evidence of injury.
- ☐ Detailed account of any unconsciousness, giving exact duration.
- ☐ Complete list of subjective complaints (not accompanied by noticeable evidence of injury), when they first developed, and their duration.

§ 6.01   CASUALTY INSURANCE CLAIMS

- [ ] Assistance rendered at the scene of the accident.
- [ ] First aid rendered and by whom.
- [ ] Name of hospital or doctor to whom the claimant was taken immediately after the accident.
- [ ] Name and address of family physician who subsequently treated the claimant.
- [ ] Name and address of any specialists who were called in for consultation and treatment.
- [ ] Dates of all visits to physicians, specialists, hospitals, or clinics.
- [ ] Dates of visits made by doctors or specialists to the home of claimant.
- [ ] Dates of admission to and discharge from a hospital.
- [ ] Information concerning x-rays—by whom taken, when, and what part of the body they covered.
- [ ] Details of operations or casts.
- [ ] Details of the nature of the treatment rendered.
- [ ] Exact duration of confinement to bed.
- [ ] Exact duration of confinement to the home.
- [ ] Exact length of disability from work.
- [ ] Exact nature of present complaints, if any.
- [ ] Description of any scars or disfigurements (include snapshots or photographs, if obtainable).
- [ ] Complete details of previous medical history:
    - Family history, including inherited tendencies or weaknesses, and the history of family deaths that might have a connection with the present or future disability of the claimant.
    - Names and addresses of all doctors and hospitals that were involved in previous serious ailments that might have a connection with the present disability or which might have been aggravated by the accident.
    - Complete list of previous operations, with full details, including x-rays previously taken.
    - Details concerning any previous protracted treatments.
    - General observations regarding obesity, undue nervousness, unusual despair or other indications of a similar nature that may have a direct bearing on the injury, disability, or recovery. (Not to be included in any statement.)
    - History of previous diseases, such as cancer or heart condition, which may have been aggravated as a result of the accident.
    - History of previous ailments or diseases which might have left after-effects, such as scarlet fever, measles, and so on.
    - History of any previous diseases which might affect healing in any manner, such as tuberculosis, syphilis, gonorrhea, diabetes, and so on. (Tact is required.)
    - Special emphasis on previous injury to eyes, ears, or members of the body that may have impaired complete function or contributed to the cause of the accident.

- Previous dental history, if applicable.
- History of all extensive previous physical examinations, such as for life insurance, armed forces, or induction to the armed forces, employment, or school examinations.

In reporting the medical information, some comment should be made concerning the competency, qualifications, and reputation of the claimant's attending physician or physicians. If these are unknown to the claim representative, the qualifications of the attending physicians should be checked in the local medical directory or the *Directory of Medical Specialists*.

§ 6.02 Medical Liens

A number of states, and the Congress, in regard to veteran's hospitals, have by statute given hospitals and doctors a means of legally protecting their bills for services rendered in connection with casualty claims, by filing a lien. Such a lien requires the party on whom it is served to pay the medical bills out of any money paid in settlement of a third-party claim.

These statutes are known as Lien Laws. Where applicable, they require Notice of Lien to be given by hospitals or doctors to third parties alleged to be liable for the injuries received by the claimant. In some instances, notice is required to be given to the third party insurance carrier, if known. Sometimes the liens must be filed in the county clerk's office in order to become effective.

Failure to comply with the provisions of the Lien Law after notice obligates the third party or his insurance carrier to reimburse the hospital or doctor for the bills covered in the lien, regardless of any settlement which may have been made with the claimant.

Accordingly, it is obviously important to note the existence of any lien and take whatever steps may be necessary to insure payment of the bill before settlement is consummated. This may be done by issuing a separate draft to the claimant and the doctor or hospital for the amount of the bill at the time of settlement, if it is still unpaid.

In many jurisdictions, recognition of the lien will permit the investigator to obtain medical information from a hospital. Usually, there are certain prescribed forms which must be completed before the information will be released. The filing of a lien can sometimes be used to an advantage when all other avenues for obtaining medical information have previously failed.

§ 6.03 Information to be Obtained from the Attending Physician

This may become known as the age of the doctor and the lawyer. Any attempt to get direct information from the claimant's doctor without previous authorization from the injured or his lawyer will usually be futile, unless the case under investigation is a workers' compensation case. Nevertheless, with the permission of the injured or his attorney, if he has one, some attempt should be made to get some information directly from the doctor, or to at least get the doctor's report.

In the event that a claimant is not represented by a lawyer, the doctor should always be informed that he will be paid his regular fee for whatever time he expends giving information or in giving any reports.

Any information that may be obtained from the attending doctor is, of course, of prime importance. In some instances, a mailed request with a self-addressed return envelope, enclosing a medical form, has produced surprising results.

Prompt medical information obtained from the claimant's attending doctor will help to determine the need for a physical examination, and give the claim representative an opportunity to prepare the case properly for defense, if necessary.

If the attending doctor's qualifications or integrity are unquestionable, settlement can often be effected based on his information without the delay and expense of a physical examination. It is equally important to obtain the attending doctor's report where a physical examination is needed, so that the examining physician may have the benefit of the medical allegations before making his examination.

§ 6.04 Medical Report Form

Most casualty claim departments have some printed or mimeographed medical report forms to be completed by attending doctors. In many instances they are so detailed that they discourage a busy doctor. He may either ignore them completely or fill them in sketchily. In other instances, forms have been so whittled down that they lose much of their potential value.

To be most effective, the form should contain at least the following information:

1. **Personal and descriptive data.** This should include notation of the date, time, and place where the initial examination was made. It should also include at least the name, address, marital status, age, weight, height, and occupation of the claimant.
2. **History of the accident.** Whether or not detailed questions concerning the time, place, location and other factual details of the accident itself should be printed on the form is a matter of judgment. Suffice it to say that some provision must be made for the history or factual details concerning the accident.
3. **Previous medical history.** Here again the details included in the form may vary. For a checklist of the information that can be obtained under this category, see the list provided in § 6.01, *supra*, "Information to be Obtained from the Claimant."
4. **Details concerning the initial examination,** including any x-ray or laboratory test reports, and consultant's reports.
5. **Treatments rendered,** including the type and the dates of all office and home visits.
6. **Diagnosis.** This should include a detailed account of the doctor's findings concerning ailments and disability with special emphasis on trauma.
7. **Prognosis.** This concerns the estimated disability and possibility or probability of partial or ultimate recovery with emphasis on any possible partial or permanent disability.
8. **Conclusion and recommendations.** Here the doctor should comment on recommendations concerning future treatments, operations, or further hospitalization, as well as any other details that affect the medical picture.
9. **Diagrams.** Diagrams of various parts of the body are usually imprinted on the opposite side of the medical form to enable the doctor to show scars or indicate the location of fractures, burns, or other injuries.
10. **Doctor's bill.** Provision should always be made for the doctor to show the amount of his bill up to the time the report is made, with provision for estimated future medical expense, and the charge for the report.

§ 6.05 Dental Records

In all cases involving injury to teeth, the investigator should take special pains to obtain as complete a dental history as possible, including the general condition of the subject's teeth immediately before the accident, an account of any diseases of the mouth, details concerning bridgework or plates, pivots or caps, or other information that might have a bearing on the injury allegedly sustained as a result of the accident under investigation. For instance, it is not unusual to find that teeth which may have been knocked out as a result of an accident were in advanced stages of decay.

§ 6.06 Hospital Records

In investigating serious accidents a claim investigator should, if possible, make a transcript of the complete hospital record. He should not be content with an abstract of the hospital records merely because the abstract will save him the bother of copying the record. This copying is admittedly a time-consuming and tedious chore, but it pays off often enough to make it worthwhile. An extract is ordinarily only a very brief digest of the information contained in the record.

If a case is important enough to warrant such an examination, every paper in the hospital records should be carefully scrutinized. The records will usually contain:

1. **Admission information.** Besides the ordinary information about the date of admission and the history of the accident as given by the patient, there may be welfare board reports concerning the financial background of the claimant, policy reports, an itemized list of the clothes and possessions of the claimant at the time of admission, condition of the clothes, and other extremely valuable information.
   The history of the accident as given by a claimant to a hospital attendant immediately after an accident can be of extreme importance if the claimant seems inclined to change his story later.
2. **Examination reports** by attending physicians and interns, x-ray reports, notes and instructions by interns and doctors, details concerning treatment, pathologists' and laboratory reports.

3. **Nurses' notes.** Such notes, made for the benefit of the attending doctors and interns, contain comments that are often pertinent concerning a patient's attitude and morale, and will also indicate what drugs have been administered.
4. **Diagnoses and prognoses** of the various attending physicians and specialists and, of course, the date and circumstances under which the patient left the hospital.

Personal interviews with the intern or attendants who accompanied the claimant to the hospital, and the attending nurses, have often been sources of valuable information, both as to the details of the accident and to the claimant's medical condition. Leads may often be obtained through these people that may well be worth the time spent in locating them.

A nurse, whether in attendance in a hospital, nursing home or private home, spends much more time with a patient than a doctor, and sees the patient under conditions that tend to let down the bars which are present in the ordinary doctor-patient relationship. Not only does the nurse see the patient in unguarded moments, but gets to know much more about the character and make-up of the injured. The nurse is the one who hears all of the patient's subjective complaints, can observe the patient's attitude, and is the best judge as to whether or not the patient is exaggerating his injuries, consciously or otherwise. Accordingly, an alert investigator should not miss the opportunity to obtain some very valuable information from this source.[1]

§ 6.07 Medical Examinations

A proper medical examination can be a most important source of information. It is also a valuable defense weapon, but it should not be ordered indiscriminately. Consideration should be given to the ultimate objectives which are:

1. To help determine if the allegations of disability are true and to corroborate the injuries sustained.
2. To help determine if the alleged injuries or disability resulted from the accident.
3. To help determine the true extent of any disability.

---

[1] *See also* Hospital Records under Malpractice Section in § 36.05[2][d], *infra*.

4. To help determine if the claimant is receiving proper, sufficient, or too much treatment.
5. Obtain the history of the accident as given to the examining physician or corroborate any conflict with the previous information he gave to the hospital or other doctors.

If the object of the examination is merely to corroborate information, assuming maximum healing has taken place, the hospital records or the reputation of the claimant's attending physician and the information he gives, may be sufficient for the purpose. However, in order to avoid unpleasant surprise as a result of afterthoughts, where there is no allegation of further injury or disability an attempt should be made to tie this down in the form of a signed statement or a report from the doctor.

Medical examinations should never be assigned routinely as a matter of course. It is a costly measure at best.

When deciding on the advisability of a physical examination, the claim representative should obtain as much medical information as he can from the attending physician, hospital records or other sources. Otherwise, the examining doctor may be concentrating on the effect of a fracture and completely miss a subsequent allegation of neurosis. The claim representative must never forget that a medical examination can be a two-edged sword; made by the wrong doctor at the wrong time, or without sufficient preparation, it can do more harm than good.

Obviously, the doctor will be able to make a much more thorough examination and of greater value, if he is familiar at the outset with all the allegations and complaints.

All x-rays do not always show an exact picture. Not all parts of the body can be shown with clarity. Sometimes radiopaque material must be injected or inserted in the area to be x-rayed. Fractures of some parts of the skull are very difficult to determine and over- or under-exposure, faulty development, or the angle at which an x-ray is taken may often affect the value or readability of an x-ray.

Local custom and statutes vary with reference to the obtaining of physical examinations. When a case goes into suit, at least one physical examination is ordinarily permitted by law. However, in view of the fact that both the claimant and any attorney who he may have engaged are ordinarily anxious to obtain a settlement, they will in most instances cooperate to the extent of permitting at least one examination even when the case is not in suit. Since this may be the

OBTAINING MEDICAL INFORMATION § 6.07

only examination that is permitted, the claim representative must be intelligent about its use. He must make the best use of the examination that is permitted. Except in the unusual or long disability case, he would be hard put to justify more than one examination.

Reluctance on the part of either the claimant or his attorney to permit a medical examination is usually an indication that some attempt at exaggerating the injuries or the disability may be made.

As has been said before, judgment must be used in determining when a physical examination should be made. If there is no question of fraud or malingering, or the propriety of the necessity for further treatment, an examination should be delayed until the maximum healing has taken place. Otherwise, a physical examination should be obtained as soon as enough time has elapsed to develop any subjective complaints that might be alleged in the future.

Like any other expert that may be engaged, the physician making the examination should be properly qualified, impartial, and honest, and should make a good impression as a witness. If the allegations require the services of a specialist, a specialist should be engaged to make an examination. Barring unusual circumstances, a jury will not give as much credence to a general practitioner as it will to a specialist. This can cause disaster if the specialist is testifying for the opposition. The claim representative should not use doctors who may be even unconsciously biased in his favor. He is fooling only himself, and not the jury. He should make arrangements with a physician who is thorough and competent, but not too busy to make a proper examination and give a proper report.

He must also remember, the examining physician may have to testify at trial, and some specialists rate their services quite highly and should accordingly have an understanding with the doctor concerning his fees before engaging him. When the claim representative has decided who should make the examination, he should be given all the information available before the examination takes place.

Under no circumstances should an examining physician advise the claimant about treatment, or suggest a course of treatment. Occasionally, under rare circumstances, the attending physician may wish to consult with the doctor who makes an examination for the company, but even here the situation must be handled with the greatest tact and diplomacy to avoid putting the company in a position where it may be accused of practicing medicine. The repercussions are obvious. If there is any question about the treatment, the claim representative should let the examining physician discuss it with the plaintiff's attending doctor and report in detail to him.

Finally, the claim representative should make sure that the examining doctor's report is intelligible and that he thoroughly understands it. If not, he had better discuss it with the doctor until all questionable points are cleared up.

[1] Choosing the Examining Doctor

The claim representative, in making an assignment to a physician for a medical examination, or in evaluating the claimant's physician, should know how to interpret information obtained from the *American Medical Directory,* or from other medical directories published in this country. Such directories give information concerning the school or university from which a doctor graduated; the year of graduation; any specialties which he practices; any fellowships or special degrees or honors; any medical societies to which he belongs; his staff and hospital associations and other such valuable information that can help to determine a doctor's experience, education, and competence.

However, it is important to remember that such background information, while exceedingly important, is not the complete picture. There are many general practitioners who have, because of their varied experience, initiative and intelligence, become extremely competent medical practitioners despite their lack of a specialty or higher degree, and despite the fact that they may not have graduated from a name university or medical college. Such a general practitioner often has a reputation in a local area that would have great weight with a jury picked from the same area. It must also be recognized that a local physician will usually be favored by a jury from the same area.

The development of medicine is marked by an ever-growing list of specialties to which practicing physicians more and more confine themselves. In fact, general practice is itself becoming a specialty.

In rural areas, a country doctor must be a good practitioner who has some familiarity with all types of medicine, including surgery. In highly-populated cities, more and more medical people continue their studies along very specialized lines. With the growth of large clinics and medical centers, specialization is now commonplace.

In order to be able to determine the particular specialist to whom the claim representative may wish to assign a physical examination,

OBTAINING MEDICAL INFORMATION § 6.07[1]

he should have at least some familiarity with the more common specialties which are being practiced today. These are as follows:

1. *Allergy.* Deals with the unusual susceptibility of a person to a substance or substances usually harmless in similar amounts for the average person.
2. *Anesthesiology.* The study of anesthesia and anesthetics.
3. *Bacteriology.* The science that treats bacteria and other microscopic organisms. Examining physicians usually refer their specimens to bacteriologists for bacteriological tests.
4. *Cardiology.* The study of the heart and its functions.
5. *Clinical Pathology.* A branch of medicine pertaining to or founded on actual treatment or observation of patients.
6. *Dermatology.* The study of the skin and skin diseases.
7. *Gastroenterology.* The study of the stomach and intestines and their diseases.
8. *Gynecology.* Deals with women's diseases, especially those of the genital, urinary, and rectal areas.
9. *Internal medicine.* Deals with the diagnosis of ailments within the body and covers an area encompassed by many of the more specialized fields.
10. *Laryngology.* Specializes in ailments of the throat, larynx, and associated organs.
11. *Neurology.* Deals with the nervous system and its disorders.
12. *Obstetrics.* Deals with childbirth and the management of pregnancy and labor.
13. *Ophthalmology.* Concerns the eye and its diseases and disorders.
14. *Otology.* Deals with the ear and its diseases and disorders.
15. *Pathology.* Studies the essential nature of disease and concerns itself especially with the structural and functional changes which cause or are caused by disease.
16. *Pediatrics.* Concerns the treatment of a child and its development, and childrens' diseases and their treatment.
17. *Proctology.* Deals with ailments of the rectum.
18. *Psychiatry.* Specializes in the mind and its disorders.
19. *Radiology.* Concerns the use of x-ray in the diagnosis and treatment of disease.
20. *Rhinology.* Studies the nose and its diseases.
21. *Roentgenology.* Deals with the use of x-ray, both in diagnosis and treatment.

22. *Urology.* Specializes in disorders of the urinary tract and male reproduction organs.
23. *Surgery.* Specializes in operative procedures. It has been left for the last because it has subdivisions which should be familiar to the claim representative. Three fields of surgery with which he will most often come in contact are:
    a. *Neurological surgery.* Confined to the nervous system, especially the spinal cord, and the brain itself.
    b. *Orthopedic surgery.* Concerns itself with the preservation and restoration of the skeletal and muscular systems and is the branch with which we most often come in contact with in dealing with fractures.
    c. *Plastic surgery.* Deals with the restoration and the building up of tissues as they affect the general appearance of an individual. The claims representative will most often come in contact with this branch of medicine in dealing with permanent and disfiguring scars as a result of injury.

[2] **Expensive Diagnostic Procedures**

The examining physician must be made to understand that the use of expensive diagnostic procedures such as magnetic resonance imaging, C-T scans and similar procedures are not to be undertaken without specific approval by the claim department for several very important reasons.

1. Procedures involving an invasion of the body can create additional liabilities for which the insurance company may become liable.

2. The use of some of these procedures draws a fine line between the needs for examination purposes, and medical diagnostic treatment. Under no circumstances should an examiner chosen by the company to make a medical examination of an injured claimant be permitted to act in a manner that could be interpreted as treating that person. The obvious consequences of such treatment could far outweigh any possible benefits to be derived.

3. The expense involved in the use of these relatively new procedures would be considerable and are only warranted in the exceptional case after consultation with the house or consultant doctor, and after further consultation between claim supervisors and the examining doctor.

Obviously, if such procedures have already been used by the claimant's physician, every legitimate effort should be made to obtain copies or to take the doctor's deposition, if the case is in suit.

§ 6.08 Autopsy and Coroner's Reports

In Chapter 5, *supra*, we discussed important information that can be obtained from autopsy and coroner's reports. Such matters as personal information concerning the claimant, his background and employment, details concerning the accident, medical history, and information concerning possible drinking might all be found in these reports.

§ 6.09 Military Records

While some selective service records are privileged, that part of the record concerning physical disability and injury can usually be obtained. This information usually contains a complete medical history and a record of any injuries, ailments, or treatments while in the service, particularly where there may have been any disability resulting in a pension. These records are most important where there is any allegation of neurological or psychiatric complications and can, if necessary, be subpoenaed in an action in the federal courts. In state courts, the power of subpoena with reference to such records is discretionary with the judge.

Veteran records concerning disability are ordinarily very comprehensive and include among other items: (1) name, age, and other personal data; (2) military record; (3) a complete chronological medical history, including examination on admission, treatments, and examination on discharge; (4) a history of all accidents or injuries; (5) medical history; (6) nurses' notes, doctor's progress notes, and doctor's orders; (7) laboratory tests, x-rays, electrocardiograms, etc; (8) clinical notes and out-patient records; (9) consultation records; (10) report of the Board of Medical Service.

CHAPTER 7

Medicine—Fundamentals

§ 7.01　Trauma
§ 7.02　Medical Terminology
§ 7.03　Wounds
§ 7.04　Some Branches of Medicine
§ 7.05　Structure of the Human Body
§ 7.06　Bones and Bone Structure
§ 7.07　Fractures
　　　　[1]　Kinds and Combinations of Fractures
　　　　[2]　Fractures Designated by Location and Shape
　　　　[3]　Reduction and Resulting Effects of Fractures
　　　　[4]　Checklist for Claims Involving Fractures

Despite the many important advances made in the science of medicine, doctors are the first to admit that it is yet in its infancy. We are just beginning to scratch the surface of psychosomatic medicine. Today the terms "organic" and "functional" are widely used to designate the difference between that which visibly alters the structure of tissue, and disease which changes the body activity without changing the structure.

Organic change is visible to the eye, the microscope or the x-ray. It can be determined by laboratory tests, as with fractures, tumors and other structural changes.

Functional disease may result from emotional distress such as violent anger which could affect the stomach or the blood pressure. Fright, deep embarrassment, extreme worry, or other emotional disturbances can and do affect the function of otherwise healthy organs of the body.

Functional disturbances often lead to organic failures such as ulcers, vascular and heart conditions, and other actual organic changes. The influence of the mind on the body is just beginning to be understood.

I mention this by way of introduction to this chapter on medicine because it is often so difficult for the new claim representative to understand why there are so many qualifications to the medical reports and records that he will see. It may be simple enough for a doctor to determine that a claimant received a fracture as a result of an accident, but it is very difficult indeed to determine the extent of disability which may result from severe fright to a claimant who already has a heart or vascular disability or who suffers from some neurosis or psychosis.

Claim representatives are primarily concerned with injuries or disabilities resulting from accident or, lately, near-accident to the claimant or someone near and dear to him. What the claim representative reads in this chapter will not qualify him to make a diagnosis, but it is the hope of the author that it may enable him to have a better understanding of injury and disability that could help him in his work.

§ 7.01 Trauma

The dictionary definition for trauma is a wound or injury. When we speak of traumatic injury, we mean those injuries and disabilities which arise as a result of some outside or accidental force. Such injuries are distinguished from congenital conditions which are malformations or illnesses that predated the birth of the claimant or from diseases or illnesses acquired by infection.

There are of course many instances where infectious disease sets in as a result of a weakened condition caused by trauma and there are also situations where traumatic injury aggravated a congenital condition, so that our interest is not solely confined to trauma but merely to trauma as the original factor.

§ 7.02 Medical Terminology

About three-fourths of the medical language (medicine does have a language all of its own) is derived from the Greek and the Latin. In most instances, the prefixes, roots, and suffixes of a single word are derived from one language. There are, however, many hybrid words which are combinations of both or which include even a third language.

An understanding of some of the principal prefixes, roots, and suffixes, will go a long way toward an understanding of medical terminology.

It is important to remember that many of the prefixes may also be used as roots and in some cases, even as suffixes.

The listing herein made is not generically correct. The author is not primarily interested in word derivation but in listing such words or parts of words as will most readily help the layman to understand some basic medical terminology. A review of the various medical dictionaries and texts reveals quite a bit of disagreement on terminology and its derivation.

In order to keep the list from becoming too cumbersome, I have avoided such obvious prefixes such as anti, post, inter and the like, and have also taken the liberty of combining under the heading of prefixes, a number of terms which are also roots.

Prefixes and Roots

a-	from, without
ab-	away, from, lack of
ad-	to, toward, near
aden-	gland
ankyl-	crooked, looped
arthr-	joint
aur-	ear
bi-	life
brachi-	arm
brachy-	short
brady-	slow
bronch-	windpipe
calc-	bone, heel
cardi-	heart
cec-	blind
cephal-	head
cervic-	neck
cheil-	lip
cheir-	hand
chondr-	cartilage
cili-	eyelid
cost-	rib
crani-	skull
creat-	meat, flesh
crur-	shin, leg
cry-	cold
cyst-	bladder
cyt-	cell
dacry-	tear

dactyl-	finger, toe
dent-	tooth
derm-	skin
desm-	ligament, band
digit-	finger, toe
dys-	bad, improper
ect-	outside
ede-	swell
em-	in, on
en-	in, on
end-	within, inside
enter-	intestine
epi-	upon, in addition, after
eso-	inside
eu-	well, good, normal
exo-	outside
febri-	fever
fract-	break
front-	forehead, front
gangli-	swelling
gastro-	stomach
gloss-	tongue
glyc-	sweet
gyn-	woman
helc-	sore, ulcer
hem-	blood
hemat-	blood
hepat-	liver
hist-	tissue, web
hom-	same, common
horm-	impulse
hyde-	water, fluid
hyper-	greater, above, more
hypn-	sleep
hypo-	under, less, below
hyster-	womb
in-	fiber, in, on, negative
infra-	below, beneath
insul-	island
is-	equal
ischi-	hip
labi-	lip
lapar-	blank

MEDICINE—FUNDAMENTALS § 7.02

laryng-	windpipe
leuko-	white
lien-	spleen
lig-	tie, bind
lip-	fat
lith-	stone
lumb-	loin
lymph-	fluid, water
macr-	large, great, long
mal-	bad
mamm-	breast
man-	hand
mega-	large, great, big
mening-	membrane
ment-	mind
mes-	middle, fold
meta-	accompanying, after
micr-	small
morph-	form, shape
my-	muscular
mycl-	marrow
myx-	mucus
ne-	new, young
necr-	dead, corpse
nephr-	kidney
neur-	nerve
nos-	disease
ocul-	eye
odont-	tooth
olig-	small, little
omphal-	navel
oo-	ovary, egg
opthal-	eye
or-	mouth
orchi-	testicle
orth-	straight, right
oss-	bone
ost-	bone
ot-	ear
ov-	egg
oxy-	sharp
para-	beside, near
path-	disease, illness

7-5

ped-	child
pell-	skin
pend-	hand
pept-	digest
pharyng-	throat
phleb-	vein
phleg-	burn
phob-	fear
phrag-	fence, enclose
phys-	blow, inflate
pil-	hair
platy-	broad, flat
pleur-	rib, side
pneum-	breath, air
pneumo-	lung
pod-	foot
por-	callus
proct-	anus, rectum
pseud-	false
psyc-	mind
pub-	adult
pulmo-	lung
pur-	puss
py-	puss
pyel-	pelvis, basin
pyl-	door
rachi-	spine
salping-	tube
sarc-	flesh
scler-	hard
sep-	decay
ser-	fluid
somat-	body
spas-	pull
sten-	closing, narrow
strep-	twist
syn-	together, joining
tel-	end
ten-	tight
thec-	case
thel-	nipple
therap-	treatment
thorac-	chest

thromb-	lump, clot
tox-	poison
trache-	windpipe
traumat-	wound
trich-	hair
vesic-	bladder
vit-	life
zo-	animal, life

Suffixes

-algia	pain
-blast	germ, bud, child
-cele	tumor, hernia
-centesis	puncture
-cide	cut, kill
-clasis	breaking
-crescent	grow
-ectomy	cutting out
-emia	blood
-esis	splitting
-form	shape
-genic	producing
-ial	relating to
-ic	kind
-ismus	spasm
-itis	inflammation
-lysis	melting, dissolving
-myces	fungus
-ode	road, path
-odynia	pain
-oid	like, form
-ology	science
-oma	tumor
-oscopy	peering
-osis	affected with
-ostomy	opening
-otomy	opening
-ous	similar, like
-pathy	disease, illness
-phobia	fear
-phyl	leaf
-plasty	molding, remaking or revision
-plegia	striking, paralysis
-poiesis	making

-*pthesis*	wasting away
-*ptosis*	dropping, falling
-*rhagia*	bleeding, bursting
-*rhaphy*	suture, repair
-*rhea*	discharge
-*rhexis*	rupture, bursting
-*somatic*	body
-*trophy*	nourish
-*ye*	substance

§ 7.03 Wounds

A wound has been described as any rupture in the continuity of an internal or external surface. Ordinarily, we think of wounds as injuries which have caused some break in the skin, but this need not necessarily be so.

Generally speaking, there are seven types of common wounds.

1. *Abrasion.* This type of wound consists of a rubbing or scraping off of the skin or mucous membrane.
2. *Contusion.* This type of wound is ordinarily known as a bruise. There is no breaking of the skin in this type of wound. However, the force applied in a contusion may be sufficient to cause a break in the skin as a result of the bruising or crushing.
3. *Ecchymosis.* An ecchymosis is the result of a contusion wound and is simply the term used for the ordinary "black and blue" marks. It is caused by hemorrhage of blood vessels immediately under the skin where the blow was applied and the bursting of the blood vessels, causing the blood to flow into the area resulting in the discoloration.
4. *Hematoma.* This is a lump usually caused as a result of a contusion wound or blow of some sort. It may also be caused by a rupture of blood vessels beneath the skin which instead of diffusing over a larger surface, gather in one spot and push the skin out much in the manner of air let into a balloon.
5. *Incised.* If you think of the word incision, you will never have any difficulty in recognizing an incised wound. It is simply a sharp cut, with smooth edges.
6. *Laceration.* This is a wound made as a result of a tear. In this type of wound the breaking of the skin is usually rough and uneven but may on occasion be clean as in an incised wound.

7. *Puncture.* This type of wound is made by a pointed instrument and is usually deep and exceedingly narrow.

In the investigation of injuries involving wounds, it is important to learn the exact location, the size and extent, nature of the bleeding, number and kind of sutures, possible scarring or disfigurement, possible involvement of a joint, and the cause and extent of any possible infection.

§ 7.04 Some Branches of Medicine

The claim representative should have some familiarity with certain terms designating branches of medicine with which he may come in contact.

Allopathy originally referred to the curing of disease by inducing some other action in the body in an attempt to offset it. This meaning of the term, however, has been lost down through the ages and today the term is commonly used to designate our accepted and most prevalent method of medical practice.

Homeopathy is a system of medicine in which diseases were treated by drugs almost exclusively. Doctors practicing this branch of medicine subsequently were commonly referred to as "pill doctors." Today, however, there is practically no difference in the practice of this branch of medicine, since the schools that teach it also have a curriculum similar to those in any other recognized medical school, plus a few minor specialty courses.

Osteopathy was originally based on the theory that the body is capable of creating its own remedies against disease when it is in normal structural relationship. Today, it is a branch of medicine which utilizes accepted physical, medical, and surgical methods of diagnosis and therapy and, for the most part, schools teaching osteopathic medicine require the same general courses as required in other recognized medical colleges. While there are some parts of the country where osteopathy is still thought of as bone manipulation, the tendency is to make osteopathy just another branch of medicine with a few specialties of its own.

Chiropody or podiatry is a minor branch of medicine dealing with the treatment of minor ailments of the foot. The requirements for the practice of chiropody are not as stringent as those concerned with the practice of medicine generally. Chiropody or podiatry must not be confused with medical specialties previously listed. In all of the medical specialties, a medical degree is required, plus additional study. A medical degree is not necessary in the practice of chiropody or podiatry, but specialized education, training, and licensing are essential.

Chiropractic is a system of therapeutics based upon the allegation that disease is caused by an abnormal function of the nervous system. Treatment is attempted by manipulation, particularly of the spinal column. This is not recognized by all jurisdictions as a branch of medicine in all states. While chiropractors are permitted to testify as to certain conditions in some states, greater weight will normally be given to medical practitioners and specialists.

Acupuncture is the insertion of needles into living tissues for remedial purposes—so says Websters International Dictionary. It is a form of medicine practiced in China and Japan for centuries, and, until recently, treated with disdain by occidental medical practitioners. Presently, it is being taken seriously in many parts of the world, even by Western physicians, and particularly in France where it is practiced in conjunction with occidental medicine by some doctors. It is beginning to get some acceptance in this country.

Naturopaths. Outside the realm of recognized medical science, faith and nature healers go under various designations. Their theories do not require study for our purposes except for the Christian Science religion which is accepted as medical treatment for a determination of damages or expenses in some parts of the country.

§ 7.05 Structure of the Human Body

The human body and its functions can be divided into seven general areas:

1. The skeletal system or bone structure is the framework upon which the rest of the body is built. There are about 200 bones of various shapes and sizes in the human body.
2. The muscles are the padding and connecting tissue which move and support the framework.
3. The heart, blood, and blood vessels supply the nourishment and help clear away some waste matter from the system.
4. The digestive system is closely allied to the blood system since it supplies the fuel eventually carried by the bloodstream and disposes of the digestive wastes.

5. The lungs and respiratory system supply the oxygen without which the body could not live.
6. The brain and nervous system is the motivating force which controls the movements and reactions of the body.

Trauma may of course affect any of these systems or organs, but the one with which we most often come in contact in claims work, and the one with which we are most often concerned, is the bone structure.

§ 7.06 Bones and Bone Structure

Bones, like every part of the body, are composed of living cells, and, as with many other parts, have their own blood supply and the power to regenerate and repair when damaged or broken. As a bone heals the so-called soft scar tissue calcifies and becomes hardened, thereby forming new bone tissue, known as callus formation.

There are three basic properties that comprise the structure or makeup of bone. The thin outer coating or layer surrounding the bone is known as the periosteum. This coating adheres to the surface of the bones and contains the fine nerves which register pain when a bone is struck.

The hard outer structure which is encased by the periosteum has properties similar to the softer inner structure of the bone wall, but is less porous. The center of the bone contains the marrow, comprised for the most part of fat cells and some blood cells. (Marrow is found only in the long bones.)

Granulation is the medical term used to designate the healing process of bone, as with other living tissue. In bone, the granulation is subsequently absorbed by the callus matter which replaces it and finally becomes part of the bone.

Crepitus is the grating sound caused by a rubbing together of the two ends of a broken bone and is one of the diagnostic measures sometimes used to determine the type of fracture involved.

§ 7.07 Fractures

A fracture is a break in a bone. Any attempt at further definition would prove to be incorrect insofar as one form of fracture or another might be concerned. For instance, it has been said that a fracture

§ 7.07[1]   CASUALTY INSURANCE CLAIMS

is a breaking of bone "by sudden or accidental force." Such a definition would exclude pathological fractures, which are defined hereafter.

One medical dictionary by actual count, names and defines 115 different varieties of fractures. Many of them would be unfamiliar to the average physician let alone a claim representative. Quite a few may be used in combinations such as "compound-comminuted." Approximately 25 varieties however, are terms which are in common usage and with which the claim representative should be familiar. These are arbitrarily listed in two groups.

[1] Kinds and Combinations of Fractures

Comminuted fracture is one where a bone is broken into a number of fragments, indicating two or more breaks.

Complete fracture is one in which there is a break through the entire bone, usually with some separation.

Compound fracture is one in which one or both pieces of broken bone extend through the flesh to the outside or close to it, or where there is a connection by way of a wound from the outside internally toward the broken bone. A compound fracture may also be a break through tissue into and opening on the inside of the body.

Compression fracture is one where the bone fragments are driven together.

Depressed fracture is one where the fragments are pushed below the surface, usually as a result of a crushing blow to the skull.

Fissure fracture is a crack in the bone extending into but not completely through it, and is sometimes referred to as a *hairline* fracture.

Greenstick fracture is one where the bone has been bent but where the ends have not separated into two distinct pieces. Its name is almost self-explanatory.

Impacted fracture is one where the end of one fragment has been driven into the end of another.

Incomplete fracture is one where the break has not completely severed the bone. A fissure or greenstick fracture, for instance, are also incomplete fractures.

Pathological fracture is one caused by disease or weakness in a bone and may not be traumatic in origin. A pathological fracture may occur without any unusual or accidental force being applied.

Simple fracture is one where there is a clean break without any unusual complications. While it may involve a complete break of the bone, there would be no protrusion into or through the flesh or tissues. It is the opposite of a compound fracture.

Sprain fracture is one in which part of the bone has been torn off as a result of adhesion to a tendon or ligament to which it has been fastened.

[2] Fractures Designated by Location and Shape

Colles fracture involves the lower end of the radius in the wrist.

Linear fracture is one which extends lengthwise and runs parallel to the long axis of the bone.

Longitudinal fracture is one where the break in the bone extends in a longitudinal direction, paralleling the length of the bone.

Oblique fracture is one in which the break extends in an oblique direction.

Potts fracture is one involving the lower end of the fibula in the ankle.

Spiral fracture is one in which the fracture runs in a spiral direction, as its name indicates.

Starred fracture can best be described as one in which the fracture lines radiate from a center point similar to the design of a star.

Transverse fracture is one where the break is more or less at right angles to the bone.

[3] Reduction and Resulting Effects of Fractures

The method by which the fractured ends of a bone are placed in a position for healing is known as reduction.

Closed reduction involves manipulation from the outside, to place the fragments of the bone in alignment followed by immobilization, usually in a plaster cast.

Open reduction involves operative procedure in order to expose the fragments of the bone and may require immobilization by mechanically binding the ends of the bone together either by screws, wires or plates, which may or may not subsequently be removed after healing has taken place.

If there is perfect alignment of the ends of the bone, complete immobility, and good blood supply with no complications, the fracture will usually heal without deformity. There are, however, so many possible complications that complete fracture often leads to some degree of permanent deformity. The healing process may result in a good bony union but it is also possible that the union may become fibrous in nature. Disease or poor blood supply may result in delayed or even complete non-union of the fragments.

The jagged ends of a fractured bone might tear a large artery to the extent that the normal flow of blood is stopped, resulting in gangrene or necrosis, both terms which signify a deadening or rotting of tissue or bone which may result in emergency operation or even amputation.

In all compound fractures, infection is of course one of the prime dangers. The severing of a large vein might result in a blood clot. Injuries to nerves are quite common in severe fracture cases and the more severe the fracture, the greater the possibility of damage to nerves. Impairment of growth in children with an eventual shortening of a limb is not an uncommon result of serious fracture cases nor is stiffness of the joint resulting in partial disability.

Beside the clinical factors which may affect the healing of the fracture, age, sex and general body condition all may have some bearing on healing and subsequent disability. Diseases such as syphilis, tuberculosis, diabetes and others can sometimes retard healing.

Fractures are so often encountered in casualty claim work that time spent in studying the many available medical dictionaries and texts will be extremely profitable to the claim representative or lawyer.

[4] Checklist for Claims Involving Fractures

In the investigation of claims involving fractures, certain basic information is essential for a proper evaluation of the claim as well as to prevent the ever present possibility of exaggeration and build-up.

Here is the information which should be obtained as soon as possible:

- ☐ Exact location of the fracture.
- ☐ Exact bones involved.
- ☐ Type or kind of fractures.
- ☐ Whether or not a joint is involved.
- ☐ Whether or not there is deformity or over-riding.
- ☐ Whether there is fibrous, delayed or non-union.
- ☐ Whether there is any stiffening of the joint (ankylosis).
- ☐ Whether open reduction was performed and, if so, the procedure used and determination as to whether another operation will be necessary to remove pins or plates.

MEDICINE—FUNDAMENTALS § 7.07[4]

- ☐ Whether there was any impairment of motion.
- ☐ Whether the claimant had syphilis, tuberculosis, diabetes, or other diseases which might affect the healing period.
- ☐ Whether the claimant had any congenital condition or previous history of arthritis or other medical condition that might affect healing.
- ☐ Whether there was any history of infection.

CHAPTER 8

Injury and Disease

§ 8.01   Examples of Common Diseases and Injuries
       [1]   Ankylosis
       [2]   Arthritis
       [3]   Backaches and Herniated Discs
       [4]   Burns
       [5]   Bursitis
       [6]   Diabetes
       [7]   Eye Injuries
       [8]   Head Injuries
       [9]   Heart Disease
       [10] Hernia
       [11] Miscellaneous Injuries, Diseases, and Neurosis
       [12] Multiple Sclerosis
       [13] Occupational Diseases
       [14] Osteomyelitis
       [15] Osteoporosis
       [16] Trichinosis
       [17] Tuberculosis
       [18] Tumors and their Relationship to Trauma
§ 8.02   Drug and Alcohol Abuse
§ 8.03   Some of the Newer Diagnostic Tools and Procedures
       [1]   Angiography
       [2]   Digital Subtraction Angiography (DSA)
       [3]   Balloon Angioplasty of the Arteries
       [4]   Tomography
       [5]   Computerized Tomography (C-T SCAN)
       [6]   Magnetic Resonance Imaging (MRI)
       [7]   Ultrasound
§ 8.04   Rehabilitation
§ 8.05   Bibliography

So that a few of the more commonly encountered injuries and ailments of the human body will be at least somewhat familiar to the new claim representative, I have attempted in the next few pages to give in plain, simplified language, definitions and related data in a manner which I hope will be easily understood to the layman newly approaching this field.

§ 8.01 Examples of Common Diseases and Injuries

[1] Ankylosis

This term is used to designate a stiffening of a joint resulting in a total loss of motion. The condition may be caused by infection or as a result of a fracture into the joint.

[2] Arthritis

Arthritis is an inflammation, irritation, or degeneration, resulting in pain in a joint. It is usually manifested by a thickening or swelling of the joint.

There are many varieties and causes of arthritis—authorities have listed over 100 different kinds. They range from minor, unimportant and momentary pain to a deforming and exceedingly painful variety. The term arthritis has today become somewhat of a catch-all phrase, including various forms of rheumatism and inflamed muscles, tendons and bursae.

It is important to remember that trauma may not only cause arthritis, but may reactivate or aggravate many types of arthritis, so as to make the causal relationship between accident and injury almost impossible to disprove.

Where there is a serious allegation of traumatic arthritis or where there is an allegation of a reactivation or aggravation of one of the other varieties, it is well to:

- ☐ Obtain a complete medical history including earlier x-rays if available.
- ☐ Obtain current x-rays which might show joint changes that could not have developed except over a long period of time or which may indicate merely hysteria or malingering.
- ☐ Obtain accident description concerning trauma.
- ☐ Obtain history of previous accidents.

[3] Backaches and Herniated Discs

Allegations of back injury have been one of the most troublesome problems with which the claim representative has had to deal. In recent years, the problem has become aggravated, rather than diminished, because of the tendency to diagnose many back complaints as being caused by herniated discs.

Due to the fact that certain back injuries may be diagnosed purely on subjective complaints, it is a condition which lends itself to exag-

INJURY AND DISEASE § 8.01[3]

geration or even simulation in cases of outright fraud. It is at the same time one of the most common causes of legitimate complaint and can come from, or be aggravated by, a great variety of causes.

Back pain may be a residual effect of such diseases as tuberculosis, bronchitis, pneumonia, syphilis, influenza, and a number of others. It may arise as a result of infection of the teeth, sinuses, tonsils, or other parts of the body. Ailments of the kidney, prostate, rectum, or malignant diseases may cause this symptom. Sprains, strains, or arthritis may cause backaches as well as nerve conditions such as sciatica. Age and general degeneration play a factor and the condition may even be neurotic in origin.

Backaches may result from injury or disease of the bones, joints, ligaments, muscles, or nerves, and, of course, may be traumatic in origin or trauma may aggravate a preexisting condition and awaken symptoms which may not previously have been present.

Where a definite fracture that shows up in x-ray is involved, the problem becomes comparatively simple. It is in those vast areas of subjective complaint without objective findings, that we run into difficulties.

The condition that has gained much prominence in recent years is most commonly referred to as herniation of the intervertebral disc. This is variously referred to as a protruded disc, extruded disc, ruptured disc, herniation of the nucleus pulposus, etc.

The weight of medical opinion is frank to admit that it is extremely difficult to make a positive diagnosis on subjective allegations of a few of the symptoms. It is therefore important for the claim representative to be at least somewhat familiar with the basic anatomy of the spine, the effect of a protruded disc, and to generally know enough to be able to discuss it intelligently. In compensation cases, if there is no reason to suspect fraud it is important for the claim representative to recognize the early symptoms of this condition so as to make sure that the injured claimant receives competent medical attention at the earliest possible date.

Normally, the spine contains seven cervical vertebrae that form the neck, twelve dorsal or thoracic vertebrae located behind the chest, five lumbar vertebrae in the small of the back, five which are fused together to form the sacrum in the posterior wall of the pelvis, and four, also fused together, which are known as the coccyx and which form the remnant of a tail at the extreme lower end of the column.

Much of the spinal length is composed of discs of cartilage and fibrous tissue between the bodies of the vertebrae. These discs act as elastic cushions of great resilience which absorb the shock and jarring from above and below, occasioned by almost any movement of the body.

The spinal cord is contained within the bony rings formed by each vertebrae. The cord does not run the full length of the column, but terminates at the lower border of the first lumbar vertebrae. From that point down, a bundle of great nerves continue giving off branches that pass on either side.

The body of a vertebrae or the front portion is made up of comparatively soft, porous material. The rear part is composed of three spur-like protuberances. It is much stronger and harder than the front portion and accordingly much less subject to damage.

Between the bones, and adhesive to them, is the intervertebral disc. This disc is composed of an upper and lower plate of cartilage, a fibrous coating and a gelatinous central mass which is known as the nucleus pulposus.

When a disc becomes ruptured, the nucleus pulposus pushes its way either through or against the fibrous coating of the disc on the only open edge which is between the bones and when this bulging pushes against the spinal column, or nerve roots, pain and other symptoms develop.

It is important to note that from the age of thirty to thirty-five, the discs undergo degenerative changes which cause a weakening in the strength of the cartilage and fibrous wall. It must also be remembered that the normal spine in an adult, particularly in an elderly person, has some anomalies or pecularities due to the many factors heretofore mentioned.

While x-rays may be of material assistance in determining herniation of a disc, it is by no means infallible since the protrusion itself does not show up on the x-ray plate.

The *myelogram* procedure, which involves the injection of radio-opaque material into the spinal canal is by no means always revealing and the danger of possible side-effects if the opaque material is not completely removed after the procedure is a decided negative factor. New medical inventions such as the C-T Scanner and MRI now make diagnosis much more accurate.

The tendency today is toward conservative treatment and away from operative procedure. The reason for this is that in many case

INJURY AND DISEASE § 8.01[4]

studies where operative procedure was performed, it was found that there actually was no herniation. Even where the condition was present, operation was not always effective. Fusion of the bones, a fairly common procedure heretofore, is now being performed much less often.

The controversial nature of this subject is so broad as to be almost contradictory in many respects. We can accordingly only suggest that when an injury to the back is alleged, careful investigation be made along the following lines:

- ☐ Obtain the complete details concerning the accident including the exact time and place of the incident, and the exact manner in which it occurred.
- ☐ Check all witnesses to corroborate or deny the allegations made by the claimant.
- ☐ Describe the exact nature of the claimant's occupation and the type of work performed, with emphasis on any lifting, bending, or stretching operations.
- ☐ Obtain from the claimant a complete list of symptoms and complaints, and previous medical history.
- ☐ Obtain the complete medical history as well as the detailed medical report and the accident history from the claimant's physician.
- ☐ Obtain complete hospital report with all of the factual and medical information, as well as histories.
- ☐ Determine the reputation and competency of the attending physician.
- ☐ Check the claimant's complaints and the basis for the doctor's diagnosis to determine whether they were all subjective.
- ☐ Determine the proposed method of treatment.
- ☐ Check on any previous accidents in which the claimant might have been involved.
- ☐ Check on any doctors who previously attended the claimant, if they are known or can be learned.
- ☐ If necessary, obtain physical examination by a competent doctor but the claims representative should arm him with all of the medical data before he makes his examination.
- ☐ In compensation cases, or in liability cases that are drawnout, the claim representative should make periodic checkups on the claimant's activities.

[4] Burns

Burns are injuries to tissue, usually caused by heat or chemicals. They are ordinarily classed in three categories:

1. **First Degree** burns are the least severe and involve only the epidermis. Evidence of a first degree burn is merely the reddening of the skin in the area of the burn.
2. **Second Degree** burns are more severe and usually involve the area down to the dermis. These burns are ordinarily manifested by a blistering of the skin.
3. **Third Degree** burns are more severe and involve destruction of the skin with extensive damage to the tissues beneath. Third degree burns usually leave ugly scars or cause skin constrictions which frequently require grafting operations.

[5] Bursitis

Bursitis is an inflammation of the small fluid containing sac (bursa) which is found between some of the movable parts of the body to prevent friction. Although a bursa may be found in the area of the kneecap, the large toe joint or the elbow, the one that seems to cause the most trouble is the shoulder.

Bursitis may or may not be caused by trauma, but it can in any event be aggravated by trauma, whatever its original cause.

[6] Diabetes

Diabetes is a term used to designate two specific diseases. The one with which we are principally concerned is the variety known as "diabetes mellitus." It is characterized by profuse urination, sugar in the urine and loss of weight, among other symptoms, when uncontrolled.

The claim representative's interest in this disease is due to the many complications which cause it to retard healing or to develop other ailments, especially infections and vascular kidney disease and loss of vision. Advance cases of diabetes can also have a psychological effect that may hamper normal functioning of parts of the body that could make a claimant accident prone.

According to a well-known authority on this subject, from which the following information was taken,[1] this syndrome can be completely asymptomatic, or it can appear as an isolated disorder of any organic system. Often it is manifested by one of the long-term complications such as foot ulcer, blurring of the vision, and kidney dis-

---

[1] Dr. George F. Cahill, Jr.'s excellent article, "Diabetes Mellitus," in *Cecil Textbook of Medicine*, 16th ed. (Philadelphia: W.B. Saunders Co.) p. 1053 et seq.

INJURY AND DISEASE § 8.01[7]

ease. Other pathologic states noted to be more frequent in diabetics could involve heart damage in young males, recurrent skin infections and many other phenomena which ordinarily appear unrelated.

Insulin therapy has for years been used to control the disabling effects of diabetus mellitus with a great deal of success, but also with some possible complications resulting from improper dosage or diet.

Modern treatment techniques include the use of an infusion pump worn either over the shoulder or attached to a belt, but this is cumbersome at best and more recent developments involve insulin distributing implants.

Without going into the matter any further, it is sufficient to note that where the claimant is a diabetic, special care should be taken with the physical examination and the examining physician should always be notified of this condition before the examination is made.

[7] Eye Injuries

Eye injuries are always serious matters. There are many types of eye disabilities which can be caused or aggravated by trauma. It is most important to get prompt and skilled medical attention for anyone suffering from an eye injury. Foreign bodies imbedded in the cornea, for instance, may cause infections or result in a scarring of the surface of the eye which may affect vision.

The retina is that section of the eye that has to do with the recording of the visual image, and a loosening or detaching of the retina will seriously affect vision. A detached retina may be caused by trauma or aggravated by trauma, but investigation will usually reveal a preexisting disease which has weakened the eye so as to make it more subject to this condition.

In the investigation of any serious accident involving the eyes, it is important to obtain a complete and detailed medical history. Certain diseases of the brain, kidney, blood, and others such as glaucoma, may affect vision and have a bearing on the disability or causation. Other conditions may also be caused or aggravated by trauma and may even involve the clouding of the eye, known as cataracts. Onset of the cataract, however, usually preexists the trauma.

Sympathetic opthalmia is a condition whereby an inflammation develops as a result of injury or disease in one eye which may affect the sight of the healthy or uninjured eye. Where such a condition is suspected of developing, it is sometimes necessary to remove the injured or diseased eye before the condition develops in the good one. Removal of the eye is known as *enucleation,* but even this drastic measure does not always prevent a condition of sympathetic opthalmia.

Eye diseases which are not uncommonly related to claims work and with which the claim representative should have at least a nodding acquaintance, are:

1. **Conjunctivitis.** Inflammation of the conjunctiva. It does not cause loss of sight. This condition can be caused by traumas as well as infection.
2. **Glaucoma.** Increased pressure in the eyeball. It is not caused by trauma but may be aggravated or activated by it.
3. **Iritis.** Inflammation of the iris.
4. **Trachoma.** A highly contagious disease of the eyeball and eyelid. It causes scar tissues which might be alleged as traumatic but is not due to trauma.

The result of tests for vision is expressed by fractions. The common 20/20 vision indicates that at 20 feet, if you read the chart, it is indicative of normal vision. The numerator represents the distance between the subject and the test chart and the denominator is the distance at which the normal eye could read the letters read by the patient; 20/50 indicates about 25 percent loss of vision; 20/100 indicates about 50 percent loss of vision; 20/180 indicates 75 percent loss of vision.

So many effective excellent instruments have been developed to examine the eyes as to make malingering in this area rather difficult.

[8] **Head Injuries**

Next to back injuries, head injuries are the most troublesome to handle from a claim viewpoint, and usually present the most dangerous potential even where the initial trauma might appear to be of a minor nature. Here again, where many of the complaints are subjective in nature, the field is wide open for possible exaggeration and malingering.

The danger of a fractured skull is not in the fracture itself but in the possible damage which the impact may have caused to the brain. It is therefore most important to remember that a fracture may exist without causing brain damage and brain damage may be sustained without a fracture.

INJURY AND DISEASE § 8.01[8]

In all head injuries of any severity, prompt medical treatment is of the utmost importance. This is especially so if the claimant has suffered unconsciousness immediately following the injury. While it is not impossible or even uncommon for brain damage to have occurred without unconsciousness, it is generally accepted that the severity of the damage can roughly be measured by the extent of the unconsciousness following the injury. A term most commonly used and misused to indicate head injury, is concussion. This is a loose term used to designate either a direct blow to the head, or a jarring of the head as a result of an indirect blow. Its effect may be momentary and only minor in nature, or severe and prolonged, so that actually the term "concussion" on a medical report, in and of itself, means little. It can be ambiguous or indefinite.

The extra-ordinary danger arising from injury to the brain results from the fact that brain tissue does not regenerate itself once it has been destroyed.

Post concussion syndrome is another medical term which is very general in its nature and rather overworked in medical reports and testimony involving head injuries. Syndrome simply means a sign or a set of symptoms. The phrase is self-explanatory, and consists of a set of symptoms following a concussion, and usually associated with it. Ordinarily, the symptoms will consist of headaches, dizziness, nervous depression, etc.

As has already been stated, a fracture of the skull in and of itself is not always serious. There are, however, many types of head fractures, many of which usually result in some brain injury. For our purposes, skull fractures can be divided into the following classifications:

1. **Simple or fissure fracture** is usually a crack on the top (vault) of the skull and may extend in one or more lines from the point of impact. Ordinarily, this type of fracture does not penetrate to the lining of the brain and ordinarily does not involve brain injury. In any event the healing period without complications, should not exceed three months, usually with no residual aftereffects. Such a fracture can, however, become serious if bony growth forms on the inside of the fracture resulting in pressure on the brain. Ordinarily, x-ray may not show a fissure fracture.
2. A **basal fracture** (lower part of the skull) is usually more serious than a fracture on top of the head but need not necessarily be fatal. A basal fracture is usually indicated by nose and/or

§ 8.01[8]   CASUALTY INSURANCE CLAIMS

ear bleeding and/or black eyes and unconsciousness immediately following the accident. Older people sometimes develop neurotic tendencies following a basal skull fracture.
3. A **depressed fracture** can involve any part of the skull. It is a severe penetrating injury in which the bone fragments at the point of impact are driven down toward the brain. Splinters of bone may be driven into the meninges which is the brain covering and therein lies the danger of this type of fracture. It usually results in permanent disability in some degree and if it is not fatal, may result in loss of hearing, vision, smell, or epilepsy. It often requires emergency surgery.
4. A **compound fracture** of the skull usually involves depression as well as penetrating fragments of the bone in either direction. It is of course an exceedingly serious injury and if not fatal, usually results in permanent injury, the extent of which is measured by the extent of damage to the brain.
5. **Fracture to the facial bones or jaw.** The principal danger in this type of fracture is the possible resultant disfigurement especially where a claimant is female. This type of fracture may also affect vision, hearing, the bite, or cause partial paralysis because of nerve or muscle involvement.

Brain herniation is an expression used to designate a protrusion of part of the brain through an opening in the skull. Surprisingly, it is not always fatal.

There are often various symptoms usually associated with skull fractures that enable the doctor to make his diagnosis. These may include bleeding from the nose, ears, or mouth, dripping of spinal fluid from the nose or ear, unconsciousness, discoloration under the eye or behind the ear, vomiting, dizziness, loss of the sense of perception, etc. Fracture of the skull, where brain injury is involved, may also cause temporary or prolonged amnesia and personality change, as well as paralysis of a part of the body. Since the right half of the brain controls the nervous system of the left half of the body, brain damage to that side might cause paralysis to the left side of the body, but will not affect the side of the body upon which the trauma was received.

A symptom of brain damage resulting in scar tissue after laceration of the brain, is a form of epileptic seizure known as *Jacksonian Epilepsy.* This is a form of traumatic epilepsy and usually develops within one year of the injury, although in isolated cases it may develop much later. Wherever there is an allegation of epilepsy resulting from head injury, the claim representative must go into every angle of the claimant's previous medical history. He may find the epileptic seizures to be congenital rather than traumatic in origin and it may be that they long preexisted the alleged injury. It is also important to go into the medical history of the entire family since traumatic or *Jacksonian Epilepsy* will obviously not show up in the medical history of anyone beside the person who has allegedly received the injury. It is important to learn when the symptoms first manifested themselves and how long the attack lasted.

One method of determining deep seated brain injury is the use of the electroencephalogram. This machine records graphically the electrical waves which emanate from the normal brain in a certain pattern. Brain injury is manifested by the alteration in this pattern which is graphically transcribed. The electroencephalogram has definite limitations. Any number of elements such as anxiety, tension, loose connections on the instrument or in its application, and length of time since the accident, may disturb the wave pattern and cause an erroneous reading. It must also be remembered that approximately 10 percent of those who have epilepsy record normal brain waves on the electroencephalogram and approximately 10 percent of the normal population will record waves that could be diagnosed as an epileptic pattern.

Beside the usual factual and medical background information applicable to all medical investigations, the following checklist applies to head injuries:

- ☐ Determine if the claimant sustained any cuts, bruises, discolorations, or swellings.
- ☐ Determine if there was any unconsciousness. If so, how long?
- ☐ Determine when medical aid was first received.
- ☐ Find out if there was any bleeding from the nose, ears, or mouth.
- ☐ Learn if there was any dripping of spinal fluid from the nose, ears, or mouth.
- ☐ Determine if there was any nausea or vomiting.
- ☐ Find out how soon any of these symptoms developed.
- ☐ Learn if any x-rays, C-T scan and MRI were taken. If so, what was the result?
- ☐ In the medical history, determine if there were any other causes found for sudden unconsciousness, hypertension, or epilepsy.

[9] Heart Disease

Heart disease can come from any one of a number of causes and it is legally recognized that undue strain over a long period of time can produce heart disease.

The question as to whether a heart attack can be brought about by a single direct trauma is one which the doctors have argued for quite some time. Most authorities hold that in order for trauma to produce a direct heart attack there must have been a preexisting condition or disease closely allied to, and causing a weakening, which produced the heart attack.

In any event, where a heart attack does result from direct trauma or strain, it should be manifested within hours after the accident. Our main concern in heart disease is with allegations of aggravation, about which possibility, there can be no doubt.

In the investigation of injuries involving heart conditions, certain terms will be encountered quite frequently and it is important that the claims person acquire some familiarity with them:

1. **Arteriosclerosis** is a thickening or hardening of an artery wall which affects its elasticity.
2. **Blood pressure** is the pressure at which blood is maintained in the arteries. It is expressed by a fraction. The upper number of the fraction is the systolic pressure which is that reached at the end of the contraction of the heart. The lower figure is the diastolic pressure which is the measurement made when the chambers of the heart are relaxed. Normal blood pressure, when a person is in good health, is 120/80 to 140/90, depending on age. Blood pressure is variable and can be affected by weight and many other factors besides age. It is commonly believed that the normal systolic pressure should be 100 plus the age of the subject but authorities have stated that this is a very loose and inaccurate measure of normalcy.
3. **Coronary occlusion** is a term which the claims person may often hear synonymously used with coronary thrombosis. Both are often referred to as a "heart attack."
4. **Embolism** is a blood clot or a small body such as fat or air which is carried into the blood stream as a result of phlebitis, an operation, or a fracture. If the embolism is carried to the brain or the lungs it may be fatal.

INJURY AND DISEASE § 8.01[10]

5. **An infarct** is an area of damage in a tissue brought about by an obstruction of circulation to that particular area.
6. **Phlebitis** is an inflammation of a vein which may be caused by trauma and is frequently encountered in the leg or pelvis, especially after injury.
7. **Pulse.** The normal pulse of a person is 60 to 90.
8. **Thrombosis** is the development or presence of an obstruction in a cavity of the heart or in a blood vessel.
9. **Varicose veins** are excessively dilated veins, most commonly found in the legs. It is subject to many complications which may result from even minor trauma and often results in extensive disability.

In the investigation of an accident involving death, where there is any indication of preexisting heart disease it is always important to obtain an autopsy report.

[10] Hernia

A hernia or rupture is a protrusion of an organ or tissue from its normal position or enclosure. When we speak of a hernia we commonly think of a protrusion of the intestines through the abdominal wall, but this is only one form of hernia.

Ordinarily, a hernia occurs as a result of a congenital structural weakness. The weakness is increased as a result of continued strain until suddenly the least force, even a sneeze, may bring about the ultimate break.

A hernia may be caused as a result of a direct blow from the outside which causes a break in the abdominal wall or some other part of the body. Having said that, let us hasten to add that this seldom occurs unless there has been a weakening of the structure over a protracted period of time.

Correction of a hernia usually requires surgery, although many people go through life wearing trusses or surgical belts that keep their organs in place.

Recognizing the congenital nature of an incipient hernia, compensation boards were at one time quite strict in determining the compensability of this condition. This attitude has gradually changed, however, until today the pendulum has swung almost completely the other way.

There was a time when every claim representative who investigated compensation hernia cases had to know by heart the symptoms of sudden hernia brought about by a single strain, such as shock, pain, nausea, catching of the breath, etc. Today, in most states, it matters little what the symptoms were as long as there is a substantiated allegation that the hernia was first discovered as a result of some act arising out of and in the course of employment. There are, however, some states that still insist upon some measure of traumatic proof.

The principal kinds of hernia with which a claim representative should be familiar are:

1. **Femoral,** which is a hernia more commonly found in women and occurs in the pelvic area below the area of the inguinal hernia.
2. **Hydocele,** which is commonly designated as a hernia, is actually an abnormal collection of fluid around a testicle.
3. **Inguinal,** which is an intestinal hernia in the area of the groin and involves a breaking into the inguinal canal leading to the scrotum.
4. **Umbilical** hernia is a rupture at the navel (where the umbilical cord has been cut).
5. **Ventral** is the term used to designate any hernia through the forward abdominal wall.

The chief danger of hernias is the ever present possibility of strangulation. This occurs when a loop of the intestine is pushed through the narrow opening in the abdominal wall and squeezed in place, resulting in the curtailment of proper circulation and the obstruction of the bowel. If allowed to remain for any period of time, gangrene may develop with extremely serious consequences.

When "incarceration" takes place, the intestine is so wedged as to require surgery.

[11] Miscellaneous Injuries, Diseases, and Neurosis

Direct injuries to the nerves, while troublesome from a medical point of view, are not too bothersome to the claim representative.

Injuries to the spinal cord, for instance, result in immediate symptoms such as retention of urine, paralysis of the legs, loss of sensory function or reflex changes.

Injuries to the nerves as they spread out from the spinal cord very often occur together with fractures of the longer bones, such as the

INJURY AND DISEASE § 8.01[11]

femur, humerus, etc. In this event, because of immobilization of the fractured bone, the nerve injury may not be discovered immediately.

Traumatic neurosis, however, is something else again. We are not now discussing fraud or malingering. Neurosis, while purely subjective in nature with its origin in the nervous system of the claimant, is a very real and a very disabling condition. The difficulty lies in distinguishing actual neurosis from malingering or simulation.

Authorities have said that the person most subject to neurosis following trauma is usually a highly emotional individual, probably a chronic worrier. The female is more inclined to be predisposed in that direction than the male. Actual neurosis should be treated therefore, as an aggravation of a preexisting condition which may have been more or less dormant until reawakened by the accident.

Traumatic neurosis or hysteria may show up in many ways. Sometimes the claimant will show the same symptoms as appear in diseases such as epilepsy, arthritis, heart ailments, or other definite organic disturbances. Neurosis following head injuries usually show up in the form of dizzy spells, headaches, fatigue, exaggerated reflexes, and extreme irritability.

In the investigation of a claim involving neurosis, besides the ordinary medical investigation, the following points should be stressed:

- [ ] Obtain a history of the movements of the claimant immediately after the accident in an effort to determine whether he could move around on his own or had to be carried.
- [ ] If taken to a hospital determine how long he remained there. Was there any unconsciousness?
- [ ] Find out the exact nature of the medical treatment.
- [ ] Determine the time lag between the accident and the time when the symptoms were manifested.
- [ ] Determine the occupation of the claimant.
- [ ] Learn the previous medical history, not only of the individual claimant but of his family, since neurotic tendencies sometimes run through a family.
- [ ] Find out the history and interview the doctors who previously attended to the claimant for even apparently trivial ailments.
- [ ] Find out the previous employment history of the claimant. Determine if the claimant was a job-hopper.
- [ ] Determine the history of the claimant's marital background.
- [ ] Learn the claimant's personal habits and reputation in his neighborhood. Did he have any peculiar traits?

☐ Find out if the claimant received psychiatric treatment before or after the injury.

[12] Multiple Sclerosis

This is an insidious nervous disease believed to be of "slow" viral origin. It is chronic in nature and affects the central nervous system. It grows intermittently worse as the disease continues along its course.

Recovery from this dread disease is almost unknown. It may, however, run its course from one to twenty years, the average being about seven to nine years.

It is manifested by a gradual difficulty in walking which becomes progressively worse to the point of stumbling and ataxic gait. There is, of course, a lack of coordination. During the progression of the disease the patient will undergo remissions, during which, for varying lengths of time, the symptoms may diminish or disappear entirely. He will then have flare-ups with the remission periods being variable as the disease progresses. It has been said that no two cases are identical in the pattern of this disease. The patient develops tremors with increased violence, with marked disturbances of speech, and disturbance of the eyeballs, called nystagmus.

It is more common in the adult female from the age of about twenty to forty years. Its danger to a claim representative is that the cause of this disease is not known, and because of its sudden flare-ups it is often impossible to tell whether the reawakening of the disease caused the accident or whether the accident caused a flare-up of the disease. It is as yet unknown whether or not trauma will reawaken the disease and two specialists will testify on opposite sides of the fence, both being convinced of the truth of their assertions.

As a result of the questionable cause of the disease and the question as to whether trauma will affect it, compensation boards in the various states have taken different views with reference to the compensability of this disease.

There is little that can be said about the investigation of a case involving this disease, except to make every possible effort to determine whether there was any stumbling or awkwardness immediately preceding the accident which caused it, and to dig into the medical backgrounds for a complete history of the progress of the disease, showing as closely as possible the periods of remission and flare-ups.

INJURY AND DISEASE § 8.01[13]

[13] **Occupational Diseases**

Our main concern with this group of ailments, is in the field of workers' compensation. In the subsequent discussions on workers' compensation we will go into more detail concerning coverage under the policies and under the various workers' compensation acts.

Many occupational diseases will cause industrial skin conditions which usually are not too serious in nature, but which are not easy to cure. Workers who constantly use ammonia, chrome, hydrogen sulphide, manganese, phosphorus, or wood alcohol, for instance, are subject to chronic conditions in both the skin and internal organs that are more or less disabling, dependent upon the period of time and the amount or quantity of the product that has been absorbed.

A few of the more common occupational diseases and those with which a claims person should have some familiarity are:

1. **Anthrax** is a disease contracted by close contact with animals or animal products, such as hides, wool, and meat. It is an infection caused by the anthrax bacillus which may remain alive on the surface of animals such as sheep, goats, cattle or pigs, and other domestic animals for some time. It is a virulant disease and very often fatal. The individuals most subject to this disease are tanners and leather workers, butchers, wool workers, sheepherders, veterinarians, and others whose occupations are involved with the animals that carry the anthrax bacillus.

2. **Arsenic poisoning** is a chronic ailment resulting usually from the ingestion of minute particles of metallic arsenic. The condition, unless large quantities of the product are involved, is usually not too serious and clears up quickly when exposure is removed. Arsenic is used in tanning and leathermaking, dye manufacturing, glassmaking, and is sometimes present in agricultural products, such as insecticides and soil conditioners.

3. **Asbestosis** is one of the occupational lung diseases resulting from the inhalation of asbestos fibers used in certain insulating materials. Chronic exposure may result in respiratory distress caused by fibrosis or scarring of lung tissue. This disease greatly increases the incidence of lung cancer and malignant pleural disease.

4. **Benzene poisoning.** Benzene is a coal derivative like coal tar and not to be confused with the petroleum derivative, benzine. It is highly soluble and inhalation of its vapors are the chief cause of chronic poisoning. This product is rarely used in its pure form and is usually one element in a product containing other elements under the same trade name. It is another product that causes skin rashes, possible kidney damage, and may eventually be fatal. This product is used in the oil, dye, paint, and drug industries and is also used as a solvent of fats, resins, sulphur, etc.

5. **Carbon monoxide poisoning.** Carbon monoxide is a colorless, odorless, and very poisonous gas. It is contained in coal gas, illuminating gas, and automobile exhaust gases. The odor usually associated with illuminating gas is often mistaken for carbon monoxide, which is merely one element of illuminating gas (sometimes a purposeful additive) and is in itself practically odorless. Large doses of this gas are fatal. It has residual aftereffects resulting in headaches and sometimes epilepsy. Automobile mechanics and other people who work in enclosed garages are subject to carbon monoxide poisoning.

6. **Lead poisoning** is a disease caused by ingesting lead fumes or dust in tiny particles. It may cause vomiting, cramps and diarrhea, and in prolonged chronic form may lead to hardening of the arteries, delirium, or convulsions, and is also a carcinogenic agent. Lead is used in the manufacture of paints, storage batteries, agricultural insecticides and other agricultural products, as well as many other things. Care should be used in order to avoid ingesting or inhaling lead fumes or dust.

7. **Mercury poisoning** is caused by exposure to metal mercury in its various forms. Mercury is the only metal which is liquid at normal temperature. If taken internally, it is a deadly poison and it may also cause chronic ailments by contact with its fumes or skin contact with the metal. Chronic mercury poisoning is characterized by discoloration about the mouth, insomnia, and anemia. The individuals who are subject to mercury poisoning are mercury miners, manufacturers of thermometers and barometers, mirror manufacturers, light bulb manufacturers, furriers, and felt hat workers.

8. **Radium poisoning.** Exposure to radium rays may result in severe and deep-seated burns which may eventually develop into ulcers. When radium is taken internally, even in minute quantities over any length of time, it causes bone degeneration and eventual death. There is no known antidote for radium poisoning. This product is used by clock and watch makers, as well as manufacturers of various medicines. Since receiving wide publicity as a result of radium poisoning in the watch industry in the early days of the use of radium, many precautions have been taken and the disease is today, relatively rare.

9. **Silicosis.** Some gases and dust will cause an inflammation of the lungs when inhaled. When this inflammation heals it creates scar tissue (lesions), which makes the lung membrane nonpermeable so that oxygen cannot be defused into the blood stream. Silica is such a slow reacting dust. Inflammation will usually not set in until after approximately five years of exposure, and this is important in the investigation of any cases involving an allegation of silicosis. X-rays alone are not a positive method of diagnosis. Shadows shown on x-ray might be one of several other diseases such as tuberculosis, etc. Occupations with the greatest silicosis hazards are sandblasters, quarry workers, stone masons, slate workers, and those who do much drilling with pneumatic drills.

[14] Osteomyelitis

Osteomyelitis is a serious infection of the bone, which may or may not be traumatic in origin. It may also have previously become arrested and be reawakened as the result of trauma. It is a difficult disease to cure and usually requires surgical intervention, as a result of which the diseased tissue is usually removed.

It may affect the growing portion of a bone in a child, arresting further growth and resulting in permanent shortening of a limb. It may also affect a joint and result in permanent stiffening.

Osteomyelitis is extremely dangerous in that the infection may spread if carried into the blood stream to bones in other parts of the body. While it may remain dormant for many years, it may also be reawakened at any time and with little apparent cause.

In recent years the new antibiotic drugs have been very valuable in minimizing traumatic osteomyelitis and in the treatment of acute osteomyelitis which is not traumatic in origin.

[15] Osteoporosis

Osteoporosis is a term used to describe a loss of bone density and calcium, which occurs principally in post-menopausal women. It is a common precursor of life-threatening fractures. This disease may be detected by x-ray or bone density studies, and although its progressive seriousness is irreversible, this may be arrested by the oral administration of calcium or estrogenic hormones, plus exercise.

[16] Trichinosis

Trichinosis is a disease caused as a result of eating raw or rare pork which contains the live larvae of the trichinella spirallis, a small worm. Occasionally, beef may also be so infected. When the live larvae enter the intestinal track, they bore through the intestinal wall or are carried by the blood stream to the muscles into which they penetrate and form cysts. This is evidenced by severe muscle pain, swelling, and high fever.

The safest precaution is to refuse to eat pork that has not been thoroughly cooked, usually for a duration of approximately two hours. It is known that heat over this period of time will kill the larvae.

This disease is important to the claim representative because of the possibility of products liability claims. Many products are made either entirely or partially of pork and, while the conditions in raising hogs is constantly minimizing the prevalence of this disease, it is still alleged often enough to warrant mentioning.

[17] Tuberculosis

Tuberculosis an infectious disease caused by the tubercle bacillus which produce lesions called tubercles. The result is a process which causes degeneration, necrosis, and ulceration. This disease is important because it can spread to most parts of the body and is not confined to the lungs, as is commonly believed. If the disease settles in a joint it may cause permanent stiffening.

It is important to claim representatives because trauma or overwork may cause a lowering of resistance that makes the body more

INJURY AND DISEASE § 8.01[18]

susceptible to this disease. There is also no question that trauma and overwork can certainly aggravate or activate the disease. Chemotherapy treatment available today makes it almost always curable.

[18] Tumors and their Relationship to Trauma

A tumor is a new and multi-cellular growth of unknown origin and apparently serving no useful purpose.

Tumors may be of two varieties:

1. **Benign tumors** are harmless except for any congestion which they might cause and which, when mechanically removed, cause no aftereffects.
2. **Malignant tumors** may spread rapidly to any part of the body and may be treated successfully by operations, chemotherapy, x-ray or radium, but which may after treatment reoccur or develop in some other part of the body.

There have been many theories as to the causation of malignant tumors, some of them involving the theory of misplaced cells within other tissue during fetal development, the presence or absence of some substance which stimulates excessive growth, heredity, infection, and trauma.

It is believed that chronic irritation may be a factor in establishing or awakening a malignant tumor. It is important here to distinguish between one severe injury such as is usually involved in claim work, and a repeated irritation as a result of many minor factors, such as lung cancer from cigarette smoking, or lip cancer, believed to result from constant pipe smoking.

A definite diagnosis of cancer is seldom made without a biopsy, which is a microscopic examination of a minute particle of the allegedly affected tissue.

There seems to be a relationship that certain oils, tars, and chemicals with which certain workers come in contact, result in cancer. Deep and continued x-ray may not only be a healing factor in cancer, but deep and continued x-ray burns may develop a cancer which may not have been there previously.

A malignant tumor may affect any part of the body including the skin. While accidental injuries generally call attention to a suspected malignant tumor, there is so far no proof that a single trauma will cause cancer and there are even those who doubt that a single traumatic act will even reactivate a cancer.

§ 8.02 Drug and Alcohol Abuse

No review of medicine, as related to trauma, would be acceptable without at least a mention of alcohol and other drug-related abuses. Obviously, many drugs have their proper use in the healing arts. It is the abuse by unthinking and irresponsible people in all economic classes that has posed such a huge problem for the world in almost all activities and professions, but particularly in the field of insurance claim work. The use of drugs and alcohol is a primary cause of serious accidents and to discuss the problem adequately would take volumes. Nevertheless, it must be pointed out that where there is any suspicion or possibility of drug abuse as having been a cause or a contributing cause of an accident, every effort and every investigative and medical tool should be used to determine if drug use or abuse played any part in the accident under investigation.

§ 8.03 Some of the Newer Diagnostic Tools and Procedures

In the past decade, remarkable progress has been made in the discovery of new diagnostic tools and procedures. Following are some of the more important and accessible procedures.

[1] Angiography

Angiography is the study of an organ or arteries by x-rays, after the insertion of a catheter into the arteries, and the injection of a radio-opaque dye. This procedure has been used for such studies as the mapping of obstructive lesions in the coronary arteries of the heart or the carotid arteries to the brain, diagnosis of renal tumors, or localization of gastro-intestinal bleeding points.

[2] Digital Subtraction Angiography (DSA)

This procedure involves converting into a digital computerized form, the x-ray pictures taken before and after angiography, and subtracting the one from the other. The result is a much clearer and uncluttered picture of the blood vessels.

[3] Balloon Angioplasty of the Arteries

This procedure is known as PTCA or precutaneous transluminal coronary angioplasty. After localizing by angiography an area of nar-

INJURY AND DISEASE § 8.03[7]

rowing or incomplete obstruction in an artery, a balloon on the intra-arterial catheter may be expanded in that location to stretch out the obstructed area. This procedure may avoid the necessity of a more serious surgical procedure.

[4] Tomography

This procedure is another method of clarifying the usual x-ray picture by using an x-ray tube that rotates about the patient and results in a series of single-plane clear pictures by blurring out the structures on either side of that plane. Tomography helps to define and localize a suspicious shadow on a routine x-ray, for example, a lung tumor or mediastinal lesion.

[5] Computerized Tomography (C-T SCAN)

Otherwise popularly known as the CAT SCAN, computerized tomography is a newer application of the principles of tomography, utilizing highly sophisticated (and expensive) equipment that converts to a digital computer and permits the visual reconstruction of a three-dimensional concept of many organs and other parts of the body. This method has been particularly helpful in such diagnoses as brain tumors, brain hemorrhage, spinal stenosis, herniated spinal discs, tumors of the pancreas, and others previously elucidated only by risky invasive procedures.

[6] Magnetic Resonance Imaging (MRI)

This procedure was previously referred to as NMR or nuclear magnetic resonance. It is an even newer technique for visualizing certain parts of the body by utilizing a huge electro-magnet to line up the nuclei of atoms within the body, and a radio-frequency generator to stimulate a realignment of those nuclei, with a computer to evaluate the changes. This technique results in an image of certain soft tissues and organs, such as the brain, nervous system, etc., that is reputed in some instances to be even superior to the results of a C-T scan.

[7] Ultrasound

This procedure is also a noninvasive method of visualizing parts of the body by the use of sonar (sound wave) equipment. Its use is much less expensive than either C-T or MRI scanning. It is said to be particularly useful in the visualization of the gall bladder, liver, kidneys, ovaries, a fetus in utero, heart muscles and valves (echocardiography), carotid arteries, the prostate gland, and other organs and tissues. By utilizing *Doppler equipment,* the flow of blood in vessels can be measured.

§ 8.04 Rehabilitation

In recent years, clinics throughout the country have done remarkable work in rehabilitating seriously injured and crippled workers. This is a field which has come to prominence recently as a result of the work being done on paraplegics who have lost the use of their limbs as a result of a spinal injury or a stroke.

Where the injury is real, whether the claim be one of liability or workers' compensation, it is important to the claim representative as well as to the claimant that the injured receive prompt and competent medical attention so that disability will be kept to a minimum. It is very often cheaper and certainly more humane in the long run to make a greater initial expenditure for proper medical service.

Proper rehabilitation will help to reduce the convalescent periods as well as the actual period of hospitilization. It may also avoid permanent disability. Rehabilitation includes many factors such as morale, general attitude, and other intangible factors as well as treatment of the actual physical disability itself. Some companies that write a lot of workers' compensation coverage have established or support rehabilitation hospitals or clinics. It is a fast growing field of medical science.

§ 8.05 Bibliography

Dorland's Illustrated Medical Dictionary. Philadelphia: W.B. Saunders Co.
Gaines, "Cardiovascular Injuries," Insurance Law Journal, September 1971.
Gray and Gordy, *Attorneys Textbook of Medicine.* New York: Matthew Bender & Co.
Schmidt, *Attorneys Dictionary of Medicine and Word Finder.* New York: Matthew Bender & Co.
Stedman's Medical Dictionary. Baltimore: Williams & Wilkins Co.
Williamson, "Malingering Potential," Insurance Adjuster, January 1963.

CHAPTER 9

General Principles of Law–Part I

§ 9.01 Introduction
§ 9.02 Widespread General Knowledge Required
§ 9.03 Law Degree Not Essential
§ 9.04 Common and Statutory Law
§ 9.05 Law of Negligence as it Applies to Casualty Claims
    [1] Definition of Torts
    [2] Negligence
        [a] Degrees of Negligence
§ 9.06 Defenses
    [1] Contributory Negligence
    [2] Comparative Negligence
        [a] "Pure" Form of Comparative Negligence
        [b] "Modified" Form of Comparative Negligence
        [c] "Slight" Form of Comparative Negligence
§ 9.07 Unforeseeability
§ 9.08 Proximate Cause
§ 9.09 Intervening Cause
§ 9.10 Act of God
§ 9.11 Legislative Sanction
§ 9.12 Willful and Wanton Misconduct
§ 9.13 Last Clear Chance Doctrine
§ 9.14 Assumption of Risk Doctrine
§ 9.15 Multiple Defendants
    [1] Joint and Several Liability
    [2] Contribution Among Joint Tortfeasors
    [3] Counterclaim or Set-off
    [4] Declaratory Judgment Actions
    [5] Settlement in Multiple Claims Under Comparative Negligence
    [6] Mary Carter Agreements
    [7] Release and Covenant Not to Sue
§ 9.16 Nuisance
    [1] Attractive Nuisance Doctrine
    [2] Strict Liability
        [a] Dangerous Instrumentalities
        [b] Dangerous Activities
        [c] Inherent Defects
        [d] Blasting Operations
        [e] Animals

    [f] Aircraft
    [g] Food and Drugs and Other Product Liability Cases
§ 9.17 Statutes of Limitations
§ 9.18 Bibliography

§ 9.01 Introduction

By the time someone becomes a seasoned claim representative, he will have learned a good deal of law, whether he has had a previous legal education or not.

It is a common misconception of those not engaged in claim work to believe that the only field of law with which the claims person must become familiar is negligence law. Tort law, of which negligence is a branch, is the preoccupation of this book, but there are many other phases of law with which this book is directly concerned.

§ 9.02 Widespread General Knowledge Required

Every time a release is used, or a policy interpreted, the law of Contracts comes into play. Real Property law is often touched upon in the handling of owners, landlords, and tenants cases; Agency and Bailments play a large part in the handling of casualty claims. Whenever a draft is issued in payment of a claim, the law of Bills and Notes is involved. Almost every time a claim involves participants in different jurisdictions, the claim adjuster is directly concerned with Conflict of Laws. Bus and railroad claims deal with the law of Carriers. Domestic Relations and Decedents Estates law is involved to some extent whenever a husband and wife or child are claimants, or when death occurs as a result of an automobile accident. The seasoned claim representative must become familiar with Practice and Procedure, both in his local state courts and in the federal courts.

It is obvious, therefore, that without a basic knowledge of the law of a particular jurisdiction, one is inept in the handling of casualty claims.

§ 9.03 Law Degree Not Essential

The lack of familiarity in the broad field of law may appear quite disturbing to a new claim representative who has had no previous legal education. It would be foolish to deny that the person who has had some legal training has a definite advantage in learning claim work. The trainee without legal training, however, need not be dismayed. He will painlessly absorb a little law every time he investigates a claim, and with diligent application and outside study over a reasonable period of time, should be able to learn as much as is necessary to make him proficient in his work.

There is, of course, a certain basic knowledge that the new claim representative will have to gain in the shortest possible time. The intelligent trainee will learn these fundamentals in short order.

In one respect, the trainee without previous legal education has a definite advantage. Rather than charge headlong into a situation, he will usually hesitate and seek advice. All too often the trainee with a law school degree acts rashly under the assumption that he knows all the answers before he has become seasoned enough to realize that he still has much to learn.

Law is not an exact science. Seldom can it be said that a ruling has no exceptions, or is uniform in all jurisdictions. Law is never static. New decisions constantly limit or enlarge old concepts, or create new ones.

Throughout this text, the claim representative will find that the phrase most often repeated is "learn the law of your jurisdiction." Be familiar with it as it is today, not as it was yesterday, except as a matter of history.

Discussion of the law cannot be confined to one section of a text on claim handling. It permeates the entire book and is a vital part of all discussions of investigation and policy contracts.

The following pages of this chapter will be devoted to a brief outline of the principles of law essential to a proper understanding of casualty claims work. Let these principles help to achieve investigative proficiency. Do not, however, try to apply them too rigidly or dogmatically.

§ 9.04 Common and Statutory Law

The system of law which we practice in the United States is based upon the English Common Law, which developed from decisions written up and handed down as precedents in situations of a similar nature which arose subsequently.

Ordinarily, the courts gave great weight to previous decisions involving similar facts, but as social, environmental, and physical conditions began to change rapidly, the courts began to break the precedent patterns more and more, particularly where matters of public policy were involved. Today, there is nothing "holy" about previous decisions (stare decisis), and it is often difficult to predict when a court will disregard a decision previously establishing a rule of law heretofore accepted as precedent.

There is another segment of the law based upon legislative enactment by either the federal (Congress) or the state legislative bodies. This law is specifically embodied as statutes and can be referred to as the written or statutory law.

The two parts must, however, be considered together, in view of the fact that a suit based upon statutory law must be interpreted by the courts and the court decisions sometimes seem to go far afield from what appears to be the intent of the statutes. In some cases, therefore, statutes are subsequently amended to clarify the original intent as interpreted by the courts. "Round and round we go."

§ 9.05 Law of Negligence as it Applies to Casualty Claims

[1] Definition of Torts

Very few jurists agree upon an exact definition of a tort. As a matter of fact many believe that the term is impossible of exact definition. This, however, is of little help to anyone looking for an introduction to the field. For lack of a more exact definition let us use the following: a tort is a civil wrong resulting from a violation of a legal right not created by contract, for which monetary redress is provided. The violation referred to may be either an act of commission or omission.

Putting it more simply: if you do something that you are not supposed to do, or fail to do something that you should do, you may be responsible in money damages to someone who has been injured as a result of your action or failure to act.

The legal rights of which we speak may be based on judicial decisions or may have been created as a result of legislative enactments called statutes.

Probably the most commonly used term in casualty claim work is "liability." Legal liability is the phrase used in most of the casualty policies and can be defined synonymously with legal responsibility. Liability is not confined to negligence only, since there are other factors besides negligence that might create liability on the part of an insured.

The law of torts embraces a vast field, including assault and battery, false imprisonment, malicious prosecution, conversion, nuisance, and trespass, as well as negligence.

Since most of the casualty policies with which we will deal in this text predicate liability resulting from some accidental injury or damage, the greatest concern involves the law of negligence.

[2] Negligence

Negligence is failure to exercise reasonable care in some act or omission, the result of which is injury to the person or damage to the property of someone else. Reasonable care is that degree of care which the ordinary prudent person would use under similar circumstances.

In order to establish negligence, there must be the breach of a legal duty to use care. Where there is no legal duty, there can be no negligence. Injury or damage alone is not sufficient to warrant recovery.

Although the various elements will be discussed in more detail, those factors necessary to constitute a good cause of action based on negligence are:

1. A legal duty owed to the plaintiff.
2. Some violation of that duty by act or omission.
3. A violation not of the kind to be expected from the reasonably prudent person under similar circumstances.
4. Proximate cause between the negligence and the injury or damage.
5. Definite and tangible damage or injury to the plaintiff.

While negligence implies carelessness, it stops short of an intentional wrong.

[a] Degrees of Negligence

In an effort to determine the degree of care which an ordinarily prudent person would use under similar circumstances, some courts have divided care into three general categories: slight, ordinary, and great. A few have added a fourth, which, for lack of a better term, is called willful and wanton conduct.

Admittedly, these are broad terms and difficult to define with any degree of exactness. They are used, conversely, to help define the three degrees of negligence as follows:

1. **Slight negligence** may be imputed as a result of the failure to use a high degree of care. It implies a situation in which the reasonably prudent person would exercise a greater degree of care than he would under ordinary circumstances.
2. **Ordinary negligence,** by analogy, can be construed as requiring that degree of care which might be expected under average circumstances. It implies the care used by the ordinarily prudent person when no unusual conditions are involved.
3. **Gross negligence** implies a failure to exercise even slight care. The act or omission must be of an exaggerated or aggravated nature.

Willful and wanton conduct is almost indistinguishable from intentional harm in some jurisdictions. This implies such disregard for the safety of others as to be unreasonable, but which is still negligent conduct and just short of deliberate and intentional action.

Although negligence is a legal term to be defined by the judge, whether or not the facts demand a conclusion of negligence is in most instances up to a jury to determine, but is the province of the judge when there is a non-jury trial. The courts have occasionally held that some facts have spelled out a conclusion of negligence as a matter of law. This usually involves circumstances where the degree of care used was obviously inadequate under the circumstances. Violation of a statute (state law), for instance, creates a presumption of negligence as a matter of law, but the violation of an ordinance (city or municipal law) is usually regarded merely as evidence of possible negligence.

§ 9.06 Defenses

Up to now, for the most part, affirmative actions that may be brought by a plaintiff and the duties owed him in various situations have been discussed.

The following subsections will be devoted to the defenses available to a defendant in those tort actions which might fall within the province of casualty claim work.

[1] Contributory Negligence

The doctrine of contributory negligence originated in the English common law decision of *Butterfield v. Forrester*[1] where the court stated that "One person being at fault will not dispense with another's using ordinary care for himself."[2] The doctrine consists of the plaintiff's failure to use reasonable care under circumstances where such failure contributed to the accident and the resulting injury or damage to the plaintiff.

Contributory negligence was, until fairly recent years in most jurisdictions, a valid defense to the affirmative allegations of negligence on the part of the defendant. It was not a good defense where the defendant's actions were willful or wanton, going beyond mere negligence.

Contributory negligence implies conduct on the part of the plaintiff that contributes to his injury or damage as a result of his failure to use the degree of care necessary for his own protection. It must have been a contributing factor to the injury or harm that the plaintiff has suffered as a result of the chain of circumstances set in motion by the original negligence of the defendant.

The standard of conduct required is exactly the same as that required in any negligence action, namely, that degree of prudence or care required of the ordinarily reasonable and prudent person under similar circumstances.

Theoretically, the percentage of negligence with which the plaintiff can be charged is immaterial in defeating his right of action, in cases where this defense is proper. In other words, according to the law, even if his own contributory negligence was only 10 percent of all of the negligence in the accident, this would be sufficient to bar his recovery. In practice, however, the theory is rarely applied so stringently.

The general rule concerning infants or insane persons requires them to conform to a standard of care of which they are capable. There is no uniformity concerning infants with respect to contributory negligence. Most jurisdictions will, as a matter of law, hold an infant below a certain age as being incapable of being charged with contributory negligence. In some jurisdictions a child of a certain age could be charged with contributory negligence if it could be shown

---

[1] 11 East 60 (1809).
[2] *Prosser & Keeton on Torts*, (5th ed.) §65.

that the child had the mental capacity to recognize the danger and act with prudence to avoid it.

This doctrine was finally recognized as being too harsh and consequently encouraged exceptions (1) where the defendant was willful and wanton, as already noted, (2) where the defense was founded on the defendant's violation of a statute, or (3) in the origin of "last clear chance" and other rules of law.

Over the years, most states have abolished contributory negligence as a complete defense, until now only a few states still hold to this doctrine[3] and I would not be at all surprised if these states fall in line very shortly.

[2] Comparative Negligence

Comparative negligence, in various forms, was adopted in this country in the early 1900's. It was incorporated in the Federal Employers Liability Act in 1910, the Jones Act in 1920, and in other federal acts since then.

The first state to adopt the principle of comparative negligence, and in its pure form, at that, was Mississippi. For a short time most of the other states that adopted comparative negligence took the short step of accepting the limited or modified form, but this soon changed and the trend now seems to be in the direction of the pure form, permitting recovery or offset in proportion to the percentage of negligence.

[a] "Pure" Form of Comparative Negligence

In the "pure" form of comparative negligence, damages are apportioned in accordance with the degree of negligence of each of the parties involved in the accident or incident. No matter how great the degree of negligence, as long as it is not 100 percent, at least theoretically, recovery may be made by the plaintiff for an amount which discounts his own negligence.[4]

---

[3] **Ala.:** Golden v. McCurry, 392 So. 2d 815 (1980) (court stated that any change should come from the legislature).
Md.: Harrison v. Montgomery Cty. Bd. of Ed., 456 A.2d 894 (Md. App. 1983).
Tenn.: Gross v. Nashville Gas Co., 608 S.W.2d 860 (App. 1980).
[4] **Alas.:** Kaatz v. State, 540 P.2d 1037 (1975).
Cal.: Li v. Yellow Cab Co., 532 P.2d 1226 (1975).
Fla.: Hoffman v. Jones, 280 So. 2d 431 (1973).

[b] "Modified" Form of Comparative Negligence

The "modified" form of comparative negligence comes in two basic varieties: (1) where recovery can only be made if the negligence of the plaintiff is less than 50 percent, and (2) if his negligence is at least no more than that of the plaintiff (50 percent or less). The decisions are not always clearly defined.[5]

Quite a few other states have adopted some form of modified comparative negligence and the list is growing constantly, although the "pure" form is gaining.

Ill.: Alvis v. Ribar, 421 N.E.2d 886 (1981); Coney v. J.L.G. Indus., 454 N.E.2d 197 (1983).
Iowa: Goetzman v. Wichern, 327 N.W.2d 742 (1982).
Kan.: Kennedy v. City of Sawyer, 618 P.2d 788 (1980) (in products liability cases only).
Ky.: Hilen v. Hays, 673 S.W.2d 713 (1984) (because it is fairer, simple to administer and more just).
La.: By statute.
Mich.: Placek v. City of Sterling Heights, 275 N.W.2d 511 (1979).
Miss.: By statute.
Mo.: Gustafson v. Benda, 661 S.W.2d 11 (Mo. 1983).
Mont.: Trust Corp. of Mont. v. Piper Aircraft Corp., 506 F. Supp. 1093 (1981) (products liability case).
N.H.: Hanson v. N.H. Pre-Mix Concrete Co., 268 A.2d 841 (1970).
N.Y.: By statute.
N.D.: Day v. General Motors Corp., 345 N.W.2d 349 (1984) (in strict liability cases).
R.I.: By statute.
Tex.: Duncan v. Cessna Aircraft Co., 665 S.W.2d 414 (1984) (in strict liability cases).
Wash.: Lamborn v. Phillips Pac. Chem. Co., 575 P.2d 217 (1978).

[5] **Ark.:** Missouri-Pacific R.R. Co. v. Star City Gravel Co., 452 F. Supp. 480 (1978).
Ga.: Zayre of Ga. v. Ray, 160 S.E.2d 648 (1968).
Idaho: Sippi v. Betty, 579 P.2d 683 (1978); Odenwalt v. Zaring & Bannock Creek Stockmen's Ass'n, 624 P.2d 283 (1980).
Minn.: Marrier v. Memorial Rescue Service, 207 N.W.2d 706 (1973).
N.J.: Van Horn v. Blanchard Co., 414 A.2d 265 (N.J. Super. 1980).
S.C.: Langley v. Boyter, 325 S.E.2d 550 (S.C. App. 1984) (where court stated "We hold the doctrine of contributory negligence as it has previously been applied in S.C. abrogated and replaced with the modified form of comparative negligence which permits recovery by a person who has been negligent in causing an accident, so long as his negligence is not greater than . . . that of the plaintiff.").
Vt.: Stannard v. Harris, 380 A.2d 101 (1977).
W. Va.: Bradley v. Appalachian Power Co., 256 S.E.2d 879 (1979).
Wis.: Wisconsin Natural Gas Co. v. Ford, Bacon & Davis Constr. Co., 291 N.W.2d 825 (1980); Reiter v. Dyken, 290 N.W.2d 510 (1980).
Wyo.: Board of City Comm'rs of City of Campbell v. Ridenour, 623 P.2d 1174 (1981).

[c] "Slight" Form of Comparative Negligence

The third form of comparative negligence is known as "slight" negligence. In this type, the plaintiff can make some form of recovery if his contribution to the accident was only "slight," but his recovery is still reduced by his percentage of negligence. If the jury finds his negligence to be more than slight he makes no recovery at all. At the moment, I believe that there are only two states that follow this doctrine.[6]

A determination of "slight" or "great" is, I suppose, no more nebulous than is a determination of percentage of negligence. It seems to me, however, that it is merely sticking a cautious toe unto the cold waters of comparative negligence. Merely a first step.

§ 9.07 Unforeseeability

As has previously been stated, one basis for liability on the grounds of negligence is predicated upon the failure of the defendant to act as the ordinarily prudent person would. If such a hypothetical person was unable to see any danger, obviously, he could not be required to take any action. A defendant is not obligated to anticipate an unforeseeable emergency. His responsibility is limited to those situations which the ordinarily prudent person could foresee under similar circumstances.

Reasonable foresight must be distinguished from unforeseeable consequences. Should the defendant act in a negligent manner, setting in motion a chain of circumstances that result in some unforeseen consequence, the prevailing view of our courts should hold him liable for such consequence. Here, however, we are talking about reasonable foresight before any question of negligence arises.

There are many gradations and shadings of foreseeable results, unforeseeable results, and foreseeable and unforeseeable forces that in themselves have consumed a major portion of some texts on this subject.

It must, however, be realized that the interpretation of a jury to the instructions of a trial judge varies greatly and, in my opinion, unforeseeability often plays little part in its deliberations. A claim representative must always realize in making an evaluation of a case that

---

[6] **Neb.:** Malcolm v. Dox, 100 N.W.2d 538 (1960).
S.D.: Wilson v. Great Northern Ry., 157 N.W.2d 19 (1968).

PRINCIPLES OF LAW—PART I § 9.09

it is the jury who makes the determinations concerning the facts, and it is the jury who has to apply unforseeability to the facts as brought out in the trial.

§ 9.08 Proximate Cause

One of the elements necessary to entitle the plaintiff to make a recovery in an action based on negligence is that the negligence of a defendant must have been the proximate cause of the injury or damage to him.

Proximate cause is a term difficult to define with any exactitude because its application depends upon the reasoning of the courts and the interpretation given by the jury in different circumstances in each particular case. Generally speaking, the injury or damage must be the natural and probable consequence of the defendant's negligence in order to constitute proximate cause. This means that the injury or damage might have been reasonably anticipated and was the natural consequence of the defendant's negligence.

Many so-called rules have been promulgated as a yardstick for measuring proximate cause. Some of these have variously been termed the "but for" rule, the "last wrongdoer" rule, the "cause versus condition" rule, and many other designations. No one of these has been found completely satisfactory by the majority of our courts.

§ 9.09 Intervening Cause

Again, broadly speaking, an intervening cause is some new and independent force that breaks the chain of connection between the original negligence of the defendant and the ultimate injury or damage to the plaintiff. Such intervening cause may be sufficient to avoid liability on the part of the defendant for his original negligence.

It is a force that comes into operation to produce the end result after the original act of negligence by the defendant has been committed.

If the intervening cause could have reasonably been foreseen by the defendant it will not relieve him of liability. It must have been one that could not have been reasonably foreseen by the ordinarily prudent person.

§ 9.10 Act of God

An act of God, sometimes referred to as the "force of nature" may be the cause of, or an intervening cause of, an accident, and has been accepted in many jurisdictions as a proper defense to relieve a defendant from liability. In doing so however, the courts have, for the most part, held that in order for this rule to be applicable there must not have been an act or failure on the part of the defendant that contributed to the disastrous result. Such obvious forces could be tornados, floods, earthquakes, or similar upheavals beyond the control of man.

§ 9.11 Legislative Sanction

By legislative enactment, conduct otherwise sufficient to create liability, may be sanctioned. In order to be effective such sanction or authorization must be either expressly or clearly implied. It is not sufficient that the end result only, be authorized. For instance, permission to erect a factory and manufacture a certain product would not necessarily sanction the escape of toxic fumes, but permission to erect a boiler factory might imply permission to create a certain amount of unavoidable noise.

§ 9.12 Willful and Wanton Misconduct

During the time when contributory negligence was the prevelant doctrine, a major exception was made by most jurisdictions for acts which were considered to be willful and wanton. It was held that such acts went beyond the scope of mere negligence, and was defined as an act that produced injury or damage, committed knowingly, intentionally and in reckless disregard for the safety of others. The recklessness of the defendant negated any allegation of contributory negligence on the part of the plaintiff. The doctrine, as originally interpreted, posed a problem for those jurisdictions which also favored the doctrine of comparative negligence.

Accordingly, in the comparative negligence states, the courts began to interpret "willful and wanton" misconduct as an aggravated form of gross negligence in the calculation of percentages of negligence, rather than as a complete defense.

PRINCIPLES OF LAW—PART I § 9.13

Some courts chose to abrogate the willful and wanton doctrine altogether.[7]

Nevada held to the doctrine of willful and wanton misconduct as an all or nothing ruling that was made an exception to the comparative negligence doctrine, as did other states.[8]

§ 9.13 Last Clear Chance Doctrine

Even before the days of comparative negligence, the rule of "last clear chance" had not been adopted universally, and where it was adopted, it was not uniformly applied.

This is another doctrine that was imposed to avoid the harshness of contributory negligence and to create liability upon a defendant in a negligence action where contributory negligence might ordinarily have been a good defense.

There are those who argue that this ruling is merely an application of the "proximate cause" rule and not an avoidance of the defense of contributory negligence. I have my doubts.

In effect, it imposes a duty upon one who recognizes the imminent danger of another to do something to avoid injury to that other person regardless of the fact that the other person was placed in the position of peril by his own negligence.

To invoke the doctrine, four elements are usually necessary and, in some instances, a fifth has been added:

(1) The plaintiff must be in imminent danger;
(2) The defendant must have been aware of that danger, or, in some states, able to have become aware of it through the exercise of ordinary care;
(3) There must have been time for the defendant to avoid the danger;
(4) There must have been a failure to react reasonably by the defendant; and
(5) Some jurisdictions hold that the plaintiff's position of danger must be one from which he cannot extricate himself.

---

[7] **Ark.:** Billingsly v. Westrac Co., 365 F.2d 619 (8th Cir. 1966).
N.J.: Draney v. Bachman, 351 A.2d 409 (N.J. Super. 1976).
Wis.: Bielski v. Schultz, 114 N.W.2d 105 (1962).
[8] **Nev.:** Davies v. Butler, 602 P.2d 605 (1979).
Okla.: Amoco Pipeline Co. v. Montgomery, 487 F. Supp. 1268 (1980).

Because of the many interpretations based upon the rule of "last clear chance" the situation became somewhat chaotic. The result was a welter of rules within rules.

In Missouri, the "humanitarian doctrine," for instance, extends the rule and seems to take the imperiled plaintiff where it finds him. It is apparently immaterial that the plaintiff not only brought about, but, by his own actions, continues his position of peril.

Another similar doctrine, that of "discovered peril," is usually applied where the plaintiff's danger is known to the defendant. Other such doctrines are called "imminent peril" rule, "discovered negligence," "emergency" rule, "ultimate negligence," and on and on. This is a nearly perfect example of the ludicrous attempts made by some of our judiciary to gain a degree of immortality by creating yet another rule or doctrine, even if it means the mere change of a word here and there.

At any rate, "it has been recognized . . . that the last clear chance doctrine is, in the final analysis, merely a means of ameliorating the harshness of the contributory negligence rule."[9]

Accordingly, some states have simply abolished this doctrine as it could apply to their comparative negligence statutes.[10] Some states still refuse to abolish it,[11] but do modify this doctrine under certain circumstances.[12]

Actually, as Heft and Heft state:[13]

> No real reason exists under the philosophy of comparative negligence to continue the rule of "last clear chance," since the doctrine's component parts—the degree of negligence of the plaintiff, its remoteness in time, the degree of defendant's negligence, the efficiency of its causation, the defendant's awareness of the plaintiff's peril, the defendant's opportunity to avoid doing damage and his failure to do so—remain as factors to be considered by the jury in measuring and comparing the parties' relative fault.

§ 9.14 Assumption of Risk Doctrine

One who voluntarily places himself in a position of possible danger, with full knowledge of that danger, is assumed to have taken

---

[9] Kaatz v. State, 540 P.2d 1037 (Alas. 1975).
[10] **Wyo.:** Danculovich v. Brown, 593 P.2d 197 (1979).
[11] **N.H.:** Hanson v. N.H. Pre-Mix Concrete Co., 268 A.2d 841 (1970).
[12] **S.D.:** Wilson v. Great Northern Ry., 157 N.W.2d 19 (1968).
[13] *Comparative Negligence Manual* § 1.220.

the risk of possible injury and to have relieved the defendant of certain duties toward him.

Assumption of risk is most often applied in cases of sports activities in which the plaintiff is either a participant or spectator, and in hazardous occupations that do not fall within the Workers' Compensation Act, although it may be applied in many other circumstances.

Negligence need not be a factor in this defense, since in its strict application the defendant is relieved from any legal duty and the plaintiff may have acted in a reasonably prudent manner in assuming the risk.

The defense of assumption of risk is sometimes confused with the defense of contributory negligence because of a possible overlapping of the two defenses. The two essential elements in assumption of risk are:

1. Knowledge and understanding of the risk involved.
2. Voluntary assumption of it.

The defense of assumption of risk may arise as a result of express agreement or by implication from the conduct of the parties.

One who accepts a gratuitous pass to a place of amusement, or for a free ride on a railroad or vehicle, usually agrees by accepting a printed ticket stating that no responsibiliity will arise as a result of the owner's negligence. A similar situation may arise as a result of a lease of property.

The only time that the courts will void such agreements is when the plaintiff has been placed at a disadvantage so that the situation is inequitable, or against public policy. Accordingly, such agreements have not been held binding in situations involving gross negligence or willful and wanton misconduct.

In recent years, assumption of risk as a defense has also been related, by some courts, to the defense of contributory negligence. This has most often been a factor in products liability suits brought under strict liability. In such cases, some courts have held that in those jurisdictions that have abolished contributory negligence as a complete defense, the doctrine of assumption of risk is no longer available.[14]

Accordingly, adoption of comparative negligence has been, and

---

[14] Me.: Austin v. Raybestos-Manhattan Co., 471 A.2d 280 (1984).
Tex.: Duncan v. Cessna Aircraft Co., 665 S.W.2d 414 (1984).

§ 9.15　　　　　　　　　　CASUALTY INSURANCE CLAIMS

is being more often, interpreted as the demise of assumption of risk.[15]

§ 9.15 Multiple Defendants

In the effort to arrive at a fair distribution of liability and damages under the comparative negligence doctrine where there are multiple defendants, some major problems are involved concerning the degree of fault and the responsibility for injuries committed and damages done.

The degree of fault itself can be subdivided into three categories:

1. Where the percentage of fault, whether more or less than 50 percent, is measured against each of the parties who are defendants to the suit.[16]
2. Where the statutes specifically provide that plaintiff's negligence must be less than the combined percentage of negligence of all of the defendants.[17]
3. Where plaintiff's negligence must be as much as, or less than, the combined percentage of negligence of all tortfeasors, whether or not they are defendants in the suit.[18]

---

[15] **Tex.:** Farley v. M.M. Cattle Co., 529 S.W.2d 751 (1975).

Wyo.: Barnette v. Doyle, 622 P.2d 1349 (1981); Brittain v. Booth, 601 P.2d 534 (1979).

Contra: **Mont.:** Zahrte v. Sturm, Ruger & Co., 661 P.2d 17 (1983) (comparative negligence principles apply to assumption of risk).

[16] **Minn.:** Marier v. Memorial Rescue Services, 207 N.W.2d 706 (1973).

N.J.: Rawson v. Lohson, 366 A.2d 1022 (1976).

Wis.: Natural Gas Co. v. Ford, Bacon & Davis, 291 N.W.2d 825 (1980); Soczka v. Rechner, 242 N.W.2d 910 (1976); Bielski v. Schulze, 114 N.W.2d 105 (1962) (landmark case).

[17] **Ark.:** Riddell & McGraw v. Little, 488 S.W.2d 34 (1970); Walton v. Tull, 356 S.W.2d 20 (1962) (with a few exceptions as noted).

Kan.: Negley v. Massey Ferguson, Inc., 625 P.2d 472 (1981); Langhofer v. Reiss, 620 P.2d 1173 (1980).

Mass.: Graci v. Damon, 383 N.E.2d 842 (1978).

Okla.: Laubach v. Morgan, 588 P.2d 1071 (1978).

Pa.: *See* Elder v. Orluck, 483 A.2d 474 (Pa. Super. 1984).

See also appropriate articles in bibliography, and Donaldson, *Claims Law,* vol. I, Comparative Negligence Section, New Jersey: American Educational Inst., Inc., P.O. Box 356, Basking Ridge, N.J. 07920.

[18] **Cal.:** American Motorcycle Ass'n v. Superior Court of Los Angeles, 578 P.2d 899 (1978).

Idaho: Pocatello Industrial Park Co. v. Steel West, Inc., 621 P.2d 399 (1980).

Kan.: Brown v. Keill, 580 P.2d 867 (1978) (court stated that true apportionment

Classification is very difficult because many of the statutes are ambiguous. Some have been rewritten and others will be, in regard to the responsibilities of defendants and plaintiffs in cases involving multiple defendants where comparative negligence is being practiced. None is completely equitable in every case and in an effort to achieve justice in each case, exceptions and new formulas keep cropping up as new situations develop.

[1] Joint and Several Liability

The confusion is compounded when an attempt is made to allocate responsibility for payment of damages in those cases involving joint and several liability.

To use the commonly accepted meaning of "joint and several," all tortfeasors are held both severally (individually) and jointly liable for *all* damages caused by all of the defendants. Quite a few jurisdictions have, at one time or another, given lip-service to this legal precept in dealing with comparative negligence cases, while at the same time, making exceptions to it.

[2] Contribution Among Joint Tortfeasors

At common law, all joint tortfeasors were severally and jointly liable to the injured. The plaintiff could sue one or all, or any number, at his discretion and the defendant could not compel inclusion of the other tortfeasors. If a judgment was rendered the plaintiff could press for payment against any one or more of the defendants for the entire judgment, and there was no right of recovery by the tortfeasor who paid the verdict against the other tortfeasors. This view was held by the majority of our courts until quite recently.

As a result of this obvious inequity, several exceptions were made that had previously permitted some defendants to avoid responsibility at the whim of the plaintiff, or because of other reasons, including

---

cannot be achieved unless the apportionment includes all tortfeasors guilty of causing negligence, whether or not they are parties to the case.).
Minn.: Lines v. Ryan, 272 N.W.2d 896 (1978).
W. Va.: Bowman v. Barnes, 382 S.E.2d 613 (1981).
Wyo.: Global Van Lines, Inc. v. Nebeker, 541 F.2d 865 (10th Cir. 1976).

collusion.[19] Contribution before payment of the judgment, or in the form of "equitable indemnity" was finally recognized by some courts as being one way to correct this situation. In addition, most states have now passed legislation which, in varying degrees, permit recovery among joint tortfeasors. This is particularly true where one joint tortfeasor has paid a judgment for more than his share of the liability. There is no uniformity to the way that the courts and legislatures have attacked this problem.[20]

Several cases have held that if a jury apportions the damages, joint tortfeasors become severally liable only for the amount of the award rendered against each defendant for his percentage of negligence or damages.[21]

In a few decisions, it was held that all tortfeasors, whether a party to the underlying suit or not, must be included in an apportionment of a special verdict to determine the percentages of negligence, after which damages are prorated.[22]

The entire situation concerning the apportionment of damages in jurisdictions that have some form of comparative negligence is in a state of flux, as courts reverse previous decisions in an effort to accommodate new factual requirements. No sooner is one state placed in a certain category, then the next decision may change it.

---

[19] See Prosser & Keeton on Torts (5th ed.) pp. 337-38; Donaldson, Claims Law (4th ed.) § 117.

[20] Alas.: Arctic Structures v. Wedmore, 605 P.2d 426 (1979).
Cal.: American Motorcycle Ass'n v. Superior Court, 578 P.2d 899 (1978).
Conn.: Fox v. Fox, 362 A.2d 854 (1975).
Fla.: Licenberg v. Issen, 318 So. 2d 386 (1975); Kennedy & Cohen, Inc. v. Van Eyck, 347 So. 2d 1085 (App. 1979).
Ga.: Church's Fried Chicken v. Lewis, 256 S.E.2d 916 (1979).
Idaho: Tucker v. Union Oil Co., 603 P.2d 156 (1979).
Me.: Packard v. Whitten, 274 A.2d 169 (1971).
Mich.: Weeks v. Feltner, 297 N.W.2d 678 (Mich. App. 1980).
Minn.: Lange v. Schweitzer, 295 N.W.2d 387 (1980); Tolbert v. Gerber Indus., 255 N.W.2d 362 (1977).
Miss.: Saucier v. Walker, 203 So. 2d 299 (1967).
Neb.: Lindgren v. City of Gering, 292 N.W.2d 921 (1980).
Wash.: Seattle-First Nat'l Bank v. Shoreline Concrete Co., 588 P.2d 1308 (1978).
W. Va.: Bradley v. Appalachian Power Co., 256 S.E.2d 879 (1979).
Wis.: Bielski v. Schulze, 114 N.W.2d 105 (1962).
[21] Kan.: Brown v. Keill, 580 P.2d 874 (1974).
Ky.: D.D. Williamson & Co. v. Allied Chem. Corp., 569 S.W.2d 672 (1978).
Vt.: Howard v. Spafford, 321 A.2d 74 (1974).
[22] Kan.: Stueve v. American Honda Motors, 457 F. Supp. 740 (1978).
Wis.: Connor v. West Shore Equip. Co., 227 N.W.2d 660 (1974).

[3] Counterclaim or Set-off

While comparative negligence poses no great mathematical problems where the defendant has interposed a counterclaim or set-off, it has been argued that in some cases this can result in a "windfall" for insurers. Where there is a large variance in damages, the combined liabilities of both parties can be less than the total percentage of both parties if the one with the greater injury has the most responsibility for the accident.[23]

The jurisdictions that have been faced with this situation have so far favored full recovery by both claimants where insurance is involved, allowing no set-off.[24]

Once again, it must be noted that the statutes which mention this subject at all, vary widely as to set-off.

[4] Declaratory Judgment Actions

In most jurisdictions, declaratory judgment may be permitted to help solve some of the problems involving multiple defendants in comparative liability states.

Since a request for contribution often may not properly be made prior to judgment, declaratory relief has its advantages. A request for declaratory relief permits all claims to be tried in one action and avoids any necessity for a preexisting judgment. In such an action, the judge can make the necessary allocations to the parties involved in the incident.[25]

[5] Settlement in Multiple Claims Under Comparative Negligence

The desire to include all possible defendants is not confined to plaintiffs only. Manufacturers, wholesalers, retailers, doctors, hospitals, nurses, specialists, and on and on, are nowadays brought into suits as codefendants by both parties to a negligence action where

---

[23] Cal.: Jess v. Herrmann, 604 P.2d at 208 (1979).

[24] Fla.: Stuyvesant Ins. Co. v. Bournazian, 342 So. 2d at 471 (1977); Hoffman v. Jones, 280 So. 2d 431 (1973).

See Rogers & Shaw, "A Comparative Negligence Checklist to Avoid Unnecessary Litigation," 72 Ky. L.J. 25 (1983-84).

[25] Adler, "Allocation of Responsibility After American Motorcycle Association v. Superior Court," 6 Pepperdine L. Rev. 1 (1978-79).

§ 9.15[5]   CASUALTY INSURANCE CLAIMS

comparative negligence has been adopted, with the result that the situation can become very complicated.

The problem is compounded when settlement is attempted between some of the parties, with others taking a backseat or actually opposing settlement. Many solutions have been tried, with none of them being satisfactory under all of the various circumstances. In several states, a tortfeasor who settles with the plaintiff is insulated from any further liability to that plaintiff and against any claims for further contribution.[26]

In the *American Motorcycle* case,[27] the court stated:

> While we recognize that Section 877 (Cal. Code) by its terms, releases a settling tortfeasor from liability for contribution and not partial indemnity, we conclude that from a realistic perspective, the legislative policy underlying the provision dictates that a tortfeasor who has entered into a "good faith settlement" . . . with the plaintiff must also be discharged from any claim for partial or comparative indemnity that may be pressed by a concurrent tortfeasor.

In some jurisdictions, a judgment is reduced by the amount paid in settlement, rather than by an amount measured by the percentage of negligence.[28] In other jurisdictions, any judgment is reduced only by the settler's percentage of negligence as compared with all other tortfeasors involved in the accident.[29]

Since the Uniform Contribution Among Tortfeasors Act states that any settlement agreement cannot effect persons not party to it, any settlement agreements made in states that follow this Act must take this into consideration.

---

[26] **Cal.:** American Motorcycle Ass'n v. Superior Court, 146 Cal. Rptr. 182 (1978).

La.: Garrett v. Safeco Ins. Co., 433 So. 2d 209 (La. App. 1983) (the nonsettling tortfeasor's rights of contribution are replaced by his right to have plaintiff's recovery against him diminished in proportion to the settling tortfeasor's percentage of fault).

[27] American Motorcycle Ass'n v. Superior Court, 146 Cal. Rptr. 182 (1978).

[28] **Cal.:** Lemos v. Eichel, 147 Cal. Rptr. 603 (1978); American Motorcycle Ass'n v. Superior Court, 146 Cal. Rptr. 182 (1978).

[29] **Kan.:** Brown v. Keill, 580 P.2d 867 (1978); Nagunst v. Western Union Tel. Co., 76 F.R.D. 631 (1977).

For a more comprehensive discussion of this subject, *see* Adler, "Allocation of Responsibility After American Motorcycle Association v. Superior Court," 6 Pepperdine L. Rev. 1 (1978-79).

[6] Mary Carter Agreements

While *Mary Carter Agreements* have been used in an attempt to make as large a recovery as possible for a particular plaintiff, it is my belief that such agreements in comparative negligence cases only invite further litigation and are not a good avenue for final disposition. There are always exceptional situations that call for unusual methods to get at the wrongdoers, but for my own views on *Mary Carter Agreements* in general, see § 18.14, *infra*, devoted to this subject.

[7] Release and Covenant Not to Sue

Paul Berg, in his article, "Comparative Contribution and its Alternatives: The Equitable Distribution of Accident Losses,"[30] suggests that it is possible to draft a release (covenant not to sue) that will protect the settling tortfeasor in cases of multiple tortfeasors under the various comparative negligence statutes by having "the plaintiff simply covenant that he will not execute against any of the non-settling tortfeasors for more than such tortfeasor's proportion of the judgment."

Mr. Berg admits, however, that the effect of such a covenant is to require the plaintiff to bear the secondary loss of nonjoined tortfeasors. Obviously there will be many plaintiffs who will not be willing to sign such a covenant. It is certainly not the ideal solution, if such will ever be found.

Some comparative negligence statutes do not limit contribution to the payment of a judgment and permit its application where a fair and reasonable settlement has been made by one or more of the tortfeasors against the others, unless there is a legal bar to such inclusion, such as insanity, infancy, etc.

In a paper written by Richard A. Bowman,[31] he states that:

> Wisconsin, which pioneered the application of comparative negligence strict liability, has developed a device permitting plaintiff to settle with one co-defendant and proceed to trial against the non-settling parties. The so-called release, named after the case of *Pierringer v. Hoger* [124 N.W.2d 106 (Wis. 1963)] provides that when plaintiff reaches a settlement with co-defendant, he release only that proportion of the responsibility which is later found in a jury trial to be attributable

---

[30] Insurance Counsel Journal, October 1976.
[31] "Contribution in Products Liability Cases," Bowman & Brooke, 600 Midwest Plaza West, Minneapolis, Minn. 55402.

§ 9.16   CASUALTY INSURANCE CLAIMS

to (the one with whom he settled) and he does not release any of the responsibility which is ultimately placed on any parties other than (the one who settled). The *Pierringer Release* also provides that the plaintiff will indemnify (the settling defendant) in the event that he is called upon to make contribution to (the other parties).

Mr. Bowman states that there are pitfalls in the use of such a release if the plaintiff has settled for an inadequate amount, but that possible defect is always present in any settlement.

§ 9.16   Nuisance

In its broadest meaning, a nuisance is a wrongful maintenance or use of property that results in some damage or injury. The term implies unreasonable personal conduct or use of property. Reasonable care is not an element on which liability may be predicated, and in this respect nuisance differs from negligence. The fact therefore, that a person in control of the property upon which a nuisance was created may allege that due care was used in the property's maintenance, would have no bearing upon ultimate liability if the action was predicated on the theory of nuisance.

Ordinarily, one must have created a nuisance, caused it to be created, or adopted it after its creation by a predecessor, in order to be held liable for a nuisance.

A nuisance need not arise as a result of a violation of a statute or ordinance. The courts have held that keeping a quantity of dynamite in a dangerous place or manner is a nuisance. Obnoxious fumes, ringing of bells, and erecting dangerous structures have all been held to be nuisances under certain circumstances.

Just as a nuisance may arise as a result of legislative enactment, so may an otherwise objectionable act or situation be sanctioned by statute. For instance, the blowing of a loud whistle, which might ordinarily be considered objectionable, may be sanctioned by enactment because of its very useful purpose.

A property owner may be held responsible for a nuisance if he has created it and permits it to remain, even though he may subsequently lease the property and no longer occupy it, and despite a clause in the lease holding the lessee responsible. He may also be held liable if he takes over property upon which a nuisance has been erected, and knowingly maintains it in that condition. He may further be held responsible if a nuisance has been created as a result of failure to maintain property which he has bound himself to maintain by lease or agreement.

Ordinarily, the sale of property upon which the previous owner has created a nuisance will not release that owner from liability. However, the subsequent buyer does not ordinarily become liable unless he has actual or constructive notice and has permitted a reasonable time to elapse without abating the nuisance.

[1] Attractive Nuisance Doctrine

The attractive nuisance doctrine is predicated on the theory that young children who lack mature judgment should be protected from certain actions common to children of tender years.

Accordingly, the courts of some states hold the owner or person who occupies land upon which there is an object ordinarily attractive to children, liable for injuries to children playing in or upon such an object if the object has inherent dangers to children.

The courts are not uniform in the application of this doctrine. More logical reasoning seems to hold that the child must have been lured to the object by its attractive nature before liability can be incurred.

Although a minority of our courts do not recognize the attractive nuisance doctrine as such, a few of them arrive at the same result by different reasoning, though denying the theory itself.

[2] Strict Liability

The basis for responsibility for injury, death, or property damage to an innocent victim has undergone various changes in the history of the common law. Initially the law was more concerned with the damage to the victim than it was with the intent or carelessness of the person causing the damage.

As outlined in Prosser & Keeton,[32] the general feeling was that "the law doth not so much regard the intent of the actor, as the loss and damage of the party suffering," or, as is said colloquially—"if you break it, you pay for it."

For the last few centuries, the negligence of an individual or legal entity which depends on whether or not his or her actions were reasonable under the circumstances that led to the accident that caused

---

[32] *The Law of Torts* (5th ed. 1984).

the death, injury, or damage has become the very basis upon which most of our modern tort law is founded.

Within the last half century or so, the law seems to have turned back upon itself and in some instances, at least, has again accepted the old original principle that liability may be applied without any wrongdoing and that reasonable care is immaterial. We are now, in certain circumstances, adopting the principle that liability can be imposed without fault, which gives no consideration to negligence, good or bad faith, knowledge, or ignorance.[33]

Since the doctrine of strict liability still has many qualifications, defining it as absolute liability is not quite correct. The basic concept is that there are certain circumstances that call for a degree of responsibility beyond that required in ordinary situations involving negligence and began with the development in the following areas.

[a] Dangerous Instrumentalities

When an obviously dangerous instrumentality is being used, stored, or transported, the highest degree of care is called for. Thus, one who stores nitroglycerin, for instance, would have to use every possible precaution to avoid injury or damage to others arising out of anything that might happen to explode the nitroglycerin. Again, anyone who leaves a loaded gun in a situation where a child could get his hands on it, would be responsible for injuries resulting from the child's use of that gun. Contributory negligence, except in unusual circumstances, would be no defense in these instances. If the inherently dangerous quality of an object is not obvious, and *if no notice* has been given concerning its dangerous characteristics, as a general rule, the manufacturer of such article alone, or perhaps the retailer as well, may be responsible for damage or injury resulting from its use. In this respect, drug manufacturers and suppliers are often held responsible for injuries and side effects resulting from the use of those drugs where insufficient warning has been given concerning their use or consumption. Strict liability has become a very important factor in products liability suits. This subject will be treated in greater detail when we discuss the handling of products liability claims in Chapter 30, *infra*.

---

[33] Fresno Air Service v. Wood, 43 Cal. Rptr. 276 (1965); Anselm v. Travelers Ins. Co., 192 So. 2d 599 (La. App. 1966).

Another instance of a similar nature would be the storage of inflammable gas or explosives in populated areas where the danger of a mishap is obvious.

Crop dusting is still another example of a situation that is so obviously dangerous that the highest degree of care is called for to avoid doing damage to crops not involved in the dusting or causing injury to animals or human beings that might be affected by dusting or spraying of highly toxic chemicals.

Other examples of situations that call for the highest degree of care would be in the erection or maintenance of dams, the drilling of oil wells, particularly off-shore, some mining operations of a particularly dangerous nature, and other operations that have a very hazardous potential.

[b] Dangerous Activities

The Restatement (Second) of Torts § 520 provides;

In determining whether an activity is abnormally dangerous, the following factors are to be considered: (a) whether the activity involves a high degree of risk of some harm to the person, land or chattels of others; (b) whether the gravity of the harm which may result from it is likely to be great; (c) whether the risk cannot be eliminated by the exercise of reasonable care; (d) whether the activity is not a matter of common usage; (e) whether the activity is inappropriate to the place where it is carried on; and (f) the value of the activity to the community."[34]

[c] Inherent Defects

One who owns or controls the use of a defective automobile may become liable for damages or injuries resulting from its operation by someone else, if that defect was a direct cause of such injury. The driver, as well, may have a good cause of action if he was unaware of the defect.

If the defect was not open and obvious the owner must have had actual or constructive notice of it, and the defect must have been of an inherently dangerous character in order to make him liable.

If notice of the defect is given to the driver, a few jurisdictions absolve the owner of further responsibility. The majority view how-

---

[34] *See also* Vandall, "Design Defects in Products Liability: Rethinking Negligence and Strict Liability," 43 Ohio St. L. J. 61 (1982).

§ 9.16[2][d]   CASUALTY INSURANCE CLAIMS

ever, still holds him liable to all but those who had knowledge of the defect. (See Chapter 29, Products Liability, for a more comprehensive discussion of this subject.)

[d] **Blasting Operations**

Those who use dynamite or other high explosives in blasting operations, do so at their own peril. In most jurisdictions they are held absolutely responsible for damage or injury done as a result of flying debris.

While the trend is also in the direction of holding the user absolutely responsible when the damage is indirect, there are still some jurisdictions that require a showing of negligence in the blasting operation. Damage or injury resulting from concussion of the air or vibration of the ground after the explosion is beginning to be recognized as the absolute responsibility of the user where the blasting has been done in a dense population or in surroundings which obviously call for an extra degree of caution. Opinion is much more divided where such damage results from blasting incidents in areas that are unpopulated and not obviously likely to cause damage or injury.

[e] **Animals**

Another area where strict liability is being imposed, deals with the care and maintenance of wild animals. Where the dangerous propensities of an animal is known, or should have been known, there can be no question that most jurisdictions will hold the owner to a degree of strict liability.

Even in cases involving domestic animals, such as dogs, where vicious propensities have been shown that were either known or should have been known to the owner, the courts will often permit recovery regardless of negligence, although the proof of dangerous propensities actually may bring the problem within the bounds of foreseeability and consequently, negligence.[35]

Most of the states that hold strict accountability where animals are concerned, do so by means of statutory enactment.

---

[35] Nelson v. Hall, 211 Cal. Rptr. 668 (Cal. App. 1985).

[f] Aircraft

Again by statutory enactment, quite a few states hold the owner or lessee of aircraft absolutely responsible for any ground damage which occurs resulting from any accident involving the aircraft. So far, such statutes are in the minority and may remain so in view of the fact that the courts already require a greater degree of responsibility than the owner of an ordinary vehicle when it comes to ground damage.

[g] Food and Drugs and Other Product Liability Cases

Many of the states have enacted statutes holding the vendor or manufacturer of certain foods and drugs responsible for accidents arising from their use or distribution. Other statutes deal with the question of labelling, particularly where poisonous drugs or chemicals are involved.

In recent years, the doctrine of strict liability has spread to new areas. In California, a court held that a landlord could be held strictly liable when a tenant fell against an untempered glass shower door that shattered.[36] Strict liability has been applied to "ultrahazardous activities," where the risk is such that harm may result from the very nature of the activity itself, regardless of protective measures taken by the enterprise.[37] Another court applied strict liability when damage occurred because the defendant installed a defective water heater in violation of a plumbing code.[38]

This subject will be discussed further in Chapter 29, *infra*, dealing with products liability.

§ 9.17 Statutes of Limitations

Statutes of limitations are legislative enactments which limit the time within which actions at law may be brought upon certain claims. We are primarily concerned with those statutes limiting the

---

[36] Becker v. IRM Corp., 213 Cal. Rptr. 213 (1985).

[37] Herbert v. Gulf States Utility Co., 426 So. 2d Ill. (La. 1983). *See also* Robertson, "Ruminations on Comparative Fault, Duty Risk Analysis, Affirmative Defenses and Defensive Doctrines in Negligence Liability in Louisiana," 44 La. L. Rev. 1341 (May 1984).

[38] Citizens Gas & Coke Util. v. American Econ. Ins. Co., 447 N.E.2d 329 (Ind. App. 1985).

time within which a third party action may be brought against an insured covered by a liability policy of insurance.

The limitation periods can and usually do differ in any one jurisdiction for personal injury as a result of ordinary tort, property damage, contract, assault and battery, malpractice, and wrongful death. There is also no uniformity on these limitations between the states, but there are similarities in some types of actions.

A statute of limitation, in order to bar an action, must be affirmatively pleaded after the time of limitation has run.

In tort actions, limitations usually begin to run from the date on which the act causing the injury is committed (though not always, as will be noted). This may or may not be the date on which actual damage is sustained or injury manifested.

Generally speaking, statutes of limitations run for and against all persons unless specifically excepted by the act. The laws of the jurisdiction in which the action accured usually governs, although this is no longer an absolute. In recent years, this has begun to change.

By special provision, most statutes of limitations are generally suspended from running against insane persons, infants for various periods (except in a few jurisdictions), and imprisoned persons. In these instances, the statute usually commences to run from the date the disability is removed or from the date the infant reaches majority.

In addition, some states have enacted statutes which suspend the running of the statutes of limitations where:

1. The defendant is absent from the jurisdiction at the time the cause of action accrues, or departs from the jurisdiction thereafter.
2. The defendant conceals himself within the jurisdiction in order to avoid service of legal process.

In these instances the statute again commences to run upon the return of the defendant to the jurisdiction where the cause accrued, or at such time as the defendant discontinues his concealment.

Mere visits to the jurisdiction for pleasure or business are not usually sufficient to commence the running of the statute.

Usually where personal service on the defendant is unnecessary, the absence of the defendant from the jurisdiction has no effect on the running of the statute. Hence, where the vehicle and traffic laws of the jurisdiction where the cause of action arose permits valid service of process to be made on the Motor Vehicle Commissioner or some other designated official on behalf of the defendant, the nonresidency of the defendant or the fact that he cannot be found within the state does not suspend the running of the statute of limitations. The same is true if the defendant has designated an agent within the state to accept process on his behalf.

It can therefore be seen that unauthorized acceptance of improper service might possibly prejudice an insured's rights, creating a condition under which an insurance carrier might become directly responsible.

A defendant may by his agreement, representations, or conduct be estopped from asserting the statute of limitations as a defense to an action. By the same token, an insurance carrier may by the conduct or misrepresentations of its claim representative, create an estoppel. For instance, where a claim representative has by his conduct or assertions lulled the plaintiff into a false sense of security by false representations or fraudulent concealment, it has been held that the defendant may be estopped from setting up the statute of limitations as a defense to an action. Some courts have even gone further and held that a defendant may be estopped where he has either intentionally or negligently misled the plaintiff by his representations. It has been held that inducing the plaintiff to believe that an amicable adjustment of a claim will be made without suit is sufficient misrepresentation to create an estoppel.

§ 9.18 Bibliography

Adler, "Allocation of Responsibility After American Motorcycle Association v. Superior Court," 6 Pepperdine L. Rev. 1 (1978).

"Applying Comparative Fault to Strict Liability Actions," D.R.I. article in Insurance Adjuster Magazine, June 1985.

Berg, "Comparative Contribution and Its Alternatives: The Equitable Distribution of Accident Losses," Insurance Counsel Journal, October 1976.

Boone, "Multiple-Party Litigation and Comparative Negligence," Insurance Counsel Journal, July 1978.

Bowman, "Contribution in Products Liability Cases," paper written by Mr. Bowman of the firm of Bowman & Brooke, 600 Midwest Plaza West, Minneapolis, Minn., 55402.

Carestia, "The Interaction of Comparative Negligence and Strict Products Liability—Where Are We?", 47 Insurance Counsel Journal 53 (1980).

Colley & Thomas, "Comparative Negligence Principles and Strict Liability: Theoretical Confluence or Confusion?", 19 Trial 58 (November 1983).

Gordon & Crowley, "Indemnity Issues in Settlement of Multi-Party Actions in Comparative Negligence Jurisdictions," Insurance Counsel Journal, July 1981.

Greenlee & Rochelle, "Comparative Negligence and Strict Liability—A Marriage of Necessity," Land & Water L. Rev., vol. XVIII (1983).

Hasenfus, "The Role of Recklessness in American Systems of Comparative Fault," 43 Ohio State L. J. 399 (1982).

Kulig, "Comparative Negligence and Strict Products Liability: Where Do We Stand? Where Do We Go?", 29 Vill. L. R. 695 (1983-84).

Robertson, "Ruminations on Comparative Fault, Duty Risk Analysis, Affirmative Defenses and Defensive Doctrines in Negligence Liability in Louisiana," 44 La. L. Rev. (1984).

Schwartz, "Contributory and Comparative Negligence: A Reappraisal," 87 Yale L. J. (1978).

CHAPTER 10

General Principles of Law– Part II

§ 10.01 Conflict of Laws
    [1]   Lex Loci Delicti Rule
    [2]   Best Interests Rule
§ 10.02 Contracts
    [1]   In General
    [2]   General Principles of Contract Law
    [3]   Hold Harmless Agreements
    [4]   Exculpatory Contracts
§ 10.03 Damages
    [1]   In General
    [2]   Special Damages
    [3]   Property Damage
    [4]   Bodily Injury Damages
    [5]   Compensatory Damages
    [6]   Consequential Damages
    [7]   Exemplary or Punitive Damages
    [8]   Collateral Source Rule
    [9]   Loss of Consortium
    [10] Actions for Wrongful Death and Survival Rights
    [11] Joint Tortfeasors Liability for Damages
    [12] Recovery Over
    [13] Damages for Fright or Emotional Distress
§ 10.04 Evidence
    [1]   Classifications of Evidence
        [a] Hearsay Evidence
        [b] Res Gestae
        [c] Judicial Notice
    [2]   Burden of Proof
    [3]   Best Evidence Rule
    [4]   Opinion versus Fact
    [5]   Res Ipsa Loquitur
    [6]   Competency of Non-Expert Witnesses
    [7]   Privileged Communications
    [8]   Expert Testimony
§ 10.05 Agency
    [1]   Imputed Negligence (Respondeat Superior)
    [2]   Determination of Agent's Negligence

§ 10.01

           [a] Sub-Agency
           [b] Temporary or Special Employee
           [c] Deviation
           [d] Joint Venture Agency Liability
    [3] Implied Agency Created by Statute
    [4] Family Purpose Doctrine
    [5] Independent Contractor

§ 10.06 Bailments
    [1] Kinds of Bailments
           [a] Custody versus Bailment
           [b] Rental versus Bailment
           [c] Theft versus Bailment
    [2] Acts of Employees
    [3] Contributory or Comparative Negligence as a Defense
    [4] Particular Bailments

§ 10.01 Conflict of Laws

It should come as no great shock to learn that there is no uniformity in many of the laws of our states. It is also true in many instances that the laws of two states may be contradictory, and that conflicts between these laws will arise.

This chapter will attempt to outline a few rules that have been used as a guide to reconcile differences in the laws of various jurisdictions.

Most of the conflicts with which claim representatives will be concerned will arise out of automobile accidents that occurred outside of the home state of the owner-driver. The problems involved will be affected by the laws of the state that takes jurisdiction, and particularly by the "long arm" statutes and decisions that determine jurisdiction.

Ordinarily, procedure should conform to the jurisdiction where the suit is being tried. Procedural matters include rules of evidence, burden of proof, statutes of limitation, service of process, and other laws of like nature.

[1] Lex Loci Delicti Rule

The general rule in accidents based on tort used to be that the law of the state in which the accident took place governed a suit brought in another state. This legal rule is referred to as *lex loci delicti* or "territorial rule." Under this theory it was felt that the rights of the parties were vested at the moment of impact as defined by the law of the state in which the accident took place.

[2] Best Interests Rule

In recent years the territorial rule, as with so many other staid old precepts, has gone by the boards under the headings of *best interests* rule, *center of gravity* rule, and *interest weighing* theory. The old territorial rule has been abrogated and there is today almost no way to predict the law that will apply in a negligence suit involving a conflict of interests where the lex loci rule has been abrogated.

Pennsylvania decided that a wife could not sue her husband in Pennsylvania when the accident happened in Colorado, despite the fact that Colorado permitted such action.[1]

New York decided that the plaintiff was not bound by the death limitation statute of the state where the accident occurred.[2]

On the other hand, in *Cipolla v. Shaposka*,[3] the Pennsylvania courts decided that the out of state guest laws where the accident occurred applied in an action brought in Pennsylvania.

Wisconsin's courts attempted to set some guidelines in *Zelinger v. State Sand & Gravel Co.*,[4] but the guidelines set down, in my opinion, have not added any help to the confusing situation except to indicate that the court will apparently apply the "better rule of law." You can bet that in those states which follow this reasoning, the "better" rule of law will usually be that applicable in the state where the suit is brought.

§ 10.02 Contracts

[1] In General

At first glance, it might appear as though the law of contracts would have little to do with an understanding of casualty claim work. Nevertheless, it is essential for the claim representative to be familiar with many aspects of contract law for the following reasons.

1. **An insurance policy is a contract.** Despite the fact that in the vast majority of the cases the insurance policy is written by the insur-

---

[1] McSwain v. McSwain, 420 Pa. 86, 215 A.2d 677 (1966).
[2] Miller v. Miller, 22 N.Y.2d 12, 237 N.E.2d 877 (1968).
[3] 429 Pa. 563, 267 A.2d 854 (1970).
[4] 38 Wis. 2d 98, 156 N.W.2d 466 (1968).

ance company, and the only input required from the insured to activate the contract is to complete an application honestly, purchase the policy, and pay the premiums, it is nevertheless a valid contract unless some breach has been committed by either party.

However, it is because the insured usually has nothing to do with the writing of the policy (*contract of adhesion*) that the courts hold the insurance company to much more strict accounting than they do the insured. Any ambiguity in the policy contract is strictly construed against the insurance company that wrote the policy.

2. **Releases are contracts.** Not too long ago, no knowledgeable claim representative would dream of settling a claim, or making payment on it, without taking a signed and often notarized release from all possible claimants who might have a cause of action resulting from the covered incident.

Such a release is a contract and the subject of releases will be discussed in some detail in Chapter 18, at which time it will be noted that the attitude of insurance companies and the courts has changed considerably since the early days of insurance policies as we know them in this country.

3. **Arbitration agreements are contracts** which are becoming much more prevalent as our courts are becoming overcrowded and legal costs are skyrocketing.

Some types of insurance policies encourage arbitration in their provisions. These are usually under first party insurance policies and the arbitration provisions may or may not be enforceable, depending on the jurisdiction involved and the wording of the provisions.

4. **Legal retainers and contingent fee agreements,** which are usually required contracts by attorneys when a claimant engages the services of a lawyer, are also agreements with which the claims person must be familiar.

Contingent fee contracts, which predicate payment to the lawyer on a proportionate share of the recovery, are legal in the United States, but, to my knowledge, in very few if any other countries.

The argument that poor people could not otherwise afford counsel would be valid only if there were no measures that could be taken to correct this situation. The reverse side of this coin is that contingent fee contracts breed the kind of abuses with which the claim representative will become all too familiar in the course of his work, and which has made us by far the most claim-conscious society in the world.

5. **Leases and land purchasing agreements,** often involved in the handling of general liability claims, are also contracts and are often important to determine liability or coverage.

6. **Structured settlements,** which will also be discussed in subsequent chapters, usually involve the creation of complicated contracts.

[2] **General Principles of Contract Law**

While the breach of a contract is not a tort, and does not usually involve the law of negligence, the claim adjuster often comes in contact with the law of contracts, not only in the cited examples previously listed, but in many other areas such as liens, property rights, and others both express and implied. In addition, in recent years, the courts have also held that in some instances, such as bad faith refusal to settle a claim or suit, a breach of the policy contract may give rise to the creation of a tort. Here again, we will see, in later chapters, that this is becoming an aspect of the law which is of ever increasing importance to the claims person.

To get back to a very brief discussion of some general basic principles of law concerned with contracts:

1. Ordinarily, the law of the jurisdiction so specified in the contract would be applicable, all else being equal.

2. If there is no statement or understanding as to the applicable law, the law of the place of performance of the contract *may apply* if so stated in the body of the contract or elsewhere, specifically.

3. If the contract is silent as to the applicable law, the governing law is ordinarily that of the place where the contract was made.

In order to create a valid contract, there must be "a meeting of the minds," which simply means that the parties to the contract must be in agreement on its terms. Adequate consideration must be shown to and by both parties, which may or may not include monetary payment on the part of either, although it usually does include payment on the part of one of the parties to the contract.

Since a casualty policy is a contract, interpretations of policy provisions would ordinarily be subject to the law of the jurisdiction where the policy was purchased. This law may often be different from the law of jurisdiction where the accident itself occurred, which may have been in a different state. Accordingly, where policy interpretation is also involved in a claim or suit based on the alleged wrongdoing of the insured, jurisdiction can become a very sticky problem, especially since many exceptions have been made to the general principles involving insurance policies in recent years.

A contract, to be held enforceable, must not be made to induce acts of a criminal nature, and engaging in such a contract is a crime, in and of itself.

[3] Hold Harmless Agreements

Hold harmless agreements are drawn with the intent to exonerate one party to the agreement, usually from negligent acts of the other party, such as subcontractors and their employees who perform work for others, often on the property of others. Such agreements usually apply only to the negligence of the contractor or subcontractor or their employees.

[4] Exculpatory Contracts

In some instances, private contracts that do not affect the general public interest may contain exonerating clauses, otherwise known as *exculpatory contracts* concerning the liabilities of the contracting individuals or legal entities, which are enforceable. Such contracts must be clear and unambiguous and are often involved in the area of sports, recreation activities, amusement ride participation, or as audience to sporting events, amusement parks, or theaters.

Obviously, when such an event, arena, or theater is insured, the claim adjuster must have, or acquire, a good degree of familiarity with the law involved, and must at least know enough to look with great skepticism on exculpatory language, especially that printed on the back of tickets of admission, which are often ineffective, and to be aware of the fact that minors may have special dispensations in the eyes of the law.

§ 10.03 Damages

[1] In General

The sum recoverable by a plaintiff who has sustained injuries or loss because of wrongful acts of the defendant is known as damages. In order to be recoverable, the damages must be a natural and proximate consequence of the wrongful acts. Foreseeability is not necessary. However, failure to get proper treatment would be an intervening cause that might mitigate the damages.

Aggravation of a preexisting injury or ailment is recoverable damage in an action based on negligence. Usually, existing disease or prior injury resulting in a diminution of life expectancy will mitigate damages in an action for wrongful death.

The amount of damages demanded in the pleadings is known in legal phraseology as the "ad damnum." The sum awarded cannot, in some jurisdictions, exceed the amount demanded in the ad damnum. However, many courts have permitted the plaintiff's attorney to amend pleadings, increasing the amount demanded even after a sum had been awarded in excess of the original demand.

Determination of the amount of damages to be awarded is within the province of the jury. The judge of appellate courts have the right to review the amount awarded but are reluctant to reduce the verdict or set it aside unless it is palpably unreasonable, a result of obvious passion or prejudice, or against the weight of the evidence. Although a verdict may be set aside because it is either excessive or unreasonably low, it is much rarer that a verdict will be set aside because the amount is small.

[2] Special Damages

Compensatory damages are those allowed as a result of actual injury.

Consequential damages are those which, though not immediate, subsequently follow from the original injury.

Both of these terms used together are commonly known as "special damages" in ordinary claim parlance, and are discussed in greater detail in Chapter 3, *supra*. The items which usually fall within the category of special damages are:

1. Actual loss from time of injury or death.
    a. Lost earnings.
    b. Medical expense.
    c. Funeral expense in death cases.
    d. Any property damage loss.
2. Future expected loss (must be reasonably probable).
    a. Expected lost earnings and earning capacity including probable promotions.
    b. Future expected medical expense including nursing or general care.
3. Pain and suffering, and disfigurement.

4. Loss of services or support.
   a. Loss of service of a child or spouse.
   b. Loss of support by dependents.
   c. Loss of consortium (marital relations).
5. Emotional distress in some jurisdictions and under some circumstances.

[3] Property Damage

The ordinary measure of damages for property is the reasonable cost of repairs.

In cases involving damaged automobiles, most courts have permitted recovery for reasonable loss of use while the car is being repaired. Where the damage is so great as to make repairing impractical or more costly, the measure of damage becomes the difference between the value of the vehicle before and its value after the accident. In this event, damages for loss of use may or may not be allowed.

A more detailed discussion of this subject will be found in Chapters 22 to 25, *infra*, dealing with the various automobile policies and the investigation of automobile property damage and physical damage claims.

[4] Bodily Injury Damages

One who has been injured by the defendant owes the latter no duty in mitigating the extent of the injury except that he may not heedlessly aggravate it. It is sufficient for him to employ a doctor. He need not employ the best doctor nor need he usually employ a specialist. Should he aggravate his condition or retard his recovery innocently, the defendant will be held liable for such additional damage.

A problem is presented where the aggravation is due to improper treatment on the part of the claimant's physician. Here, too, the claimant may have a right of action against the original wrongdoer and a malpractice action against the physician, but he cannot recover for the full damage from both.

[5] Compensatory Damages

These are damages awarded in a suit verdict for any monetary losses sustained by the plaintiff as a result of an injury sustained. They are, in effect, included within the category of special damages.

[6] Consequential Damages

Consequential damages are those that do not directly and immediately result from the wrongful act or omission of the defendant, but which are losses resulting from the consequences of such a wrongful act.

[7] Exemplary or Punitive Damages

In any discussion of insurance coverage for punitive damages, I am frankly partisan. The fact that, historically, punitive damages were nothing more than damages for pain and suffering, has no bearing on the present discussion since the situation has changed completely over the years. Punitive or exemplary damages are now awarded in certain cases over and above regular compensatory damages.

Punitive means "punishment." They are not damages despite the designation, but are penalties for wrongdoing. Whether the rationale be deterrent or punitive, logic demands that the loss be suffered by the wrongdoer and by no one else. The sole purpose and full effect of imposing punitive damages awarded against an insured is lost if the insurer is required to pay them for the insured under a policy of insurance, which is so in many states.

The question as to whether or not such a penalty is effective or not is completely immaterial. If it is not effective it should be eliminated as it has been in a few states.

Punitive damages assessed against an insurance company for its alleged wrongdoing is not involved in this discussion and will be treated in Chapter 17 dealing with an insured's duties to settle claims.

Where an employer is held responsible for punitive damages awarded against an employee driver or other wrongdoer, the question becomes academic. The word "punitive" in such cases is obviously a misnomer and there is no logical argument against coverage for damages that must be paid by the party who was not the wrongdoer.

Those states which have disallowed or rejected the propriety of insurance coverage for punitive damages, have usually done so on the basis of public policy.

The decision in *Northwestern National Casualty Co. v. McNulty*[5] stated the position very aptly:

> Where a person is able to insure himself against punishment, he gains a freedom from misconduct inconsistent with the establishment of sanctions against such misconduct. It is not disputed that insurance against criminal fines or penalties would be void as a violation of public policy. The same public policy should invalidate any contract of insurance against the civil punishment that punitive damages represent.

The states which have held that punitive damages are covered and payable under the automobile or other liability policies, usually do so on the basis that punitive damages are liabilities imposed by law and that there is nothing specific in the policy to hold that such damages are not covered.

These decisions either disregard or brush aside the public policy arguments.[6]

[8] Collateral Source Rule

The collateral source rule was originally promulgated as such in this country in 1871, although the principle had been recognized even earlier.

The rule was outlined rather well, although not as grammatically as it could have been, in 1938 by the Iowa court which held:

> The weight of authority is conclusive to the effect that a defendant owes to the injured, compensation for injuries, the proximate cause of which was his own negligence, and that the payment by a third party could not relieve him of this obligation; that regardless of the motive impelling their payment, whether from affection, philanthropy or contract, that the injured is the beneficiary of the bounty, and not the defendant who caused the injury.[7]

The collateral source rule permits recovery by a plaintiff who may already have been compensated for his or her "out-of-pocket" expenses by a first party insurer for the same injury. The defendant may not offset such payments in a liability suit against him.

---

[5] 307 F.2d 432 (1962).
[6] For a detailed discussion of punitive damages, *see* Magarick, *Excess Liability*. New York: Clark Boardman Company, Ltd.
[7] Clark v. Berry Seed Co., 225 La. 262, 280 N.W. 505 (1938).

Insurers have attempted, usually successfully, to make "Medical Payments," and "P.I.P." (No-Fault) payments not subject to the collateral source rule.

The reasoning behind this rule, as stated by the courts, was the fear that the wrongdoer might escape the full burden for compensating the injured.[8]

[9] Loss of Consortium

When consortium reared its ugly head, the old common law was a definite believer in a double standard of values. Although it recognized the husband's right to damages for the loss of his wife's connubial services, it apparently did not think of sex as a commodity of monetary value to the wife.

Whether this was originally based on physiological ignorance, a common acceptance of our oldest profession, or for other reasons, is a matter of conjecture. A wife simply was not permitted to recover for loss of services as an item of damages.

In 1950, the federal court for the first time upset the old common law by granting a cause of action for loss of consortium to a wife.[9] Since then most states have followed suit.

The fact of the matter is that consortium actually embraces such material items as loss of support and loss of services in addition to such nebulous factors as sex, love, and companionship.

[10] Actions for Wrongful Death and Survival Rights

Generally speaking, at common law, no right of action was granted for the loss of human life, and death on either side terminated any action which might have been started for injury arising out of negligence.

Every state has now enacted some form of wrongful death or survival statute which permits recovery under certain circumstances in the event of death arising out of negligent acts. These statutes vary considerably.

Some of the acts are unlimited in scope, but most of them set some limitation on the rights of the various parties concerned. Many of them limit the parties entitled to recovery; some limit those who may

---

[8] Grayson v. Williams, 256 F.2d 61 (10th Cir. 1958).
[9] Hitaffer v. Argonne Co., 183 F.2d 811 (D.C. 1950).

bring the action; others limit the amount recoverable in one form or another. A few differentiate between death resulting before and after suit has been started.

Once again, the claim representative will have to familiarize himself with the statutes of his particular jurisdiction.

[11] Joint Tortfeasors Liability for Damages

Where two or more persons act together so as to cause injury or damage to the plaintiff, each will be held liable for the entire damage.

The courts have used the term "joint tortfeasors" very loosely to include almost any group of two or more persons whose negligence contributed to the injury or damage.

Actually, joint tortfeasors are those who by prearranged design participate in an act which becomes tortious and which causes the harm. Otherwise they are merely concurrent tortfeasors.

In most jurisdictions, if the plaintiff has suffered damage or injury at the hands of two or more concurrent tortfeasors, apportionment of the damages will be made, if this can be done on some reasonable basis. If it is impossible to determine the extent of the damage or injury done by each defendant (and it usually is), each may be held for the entire loss or injury.

[12] Recovery Over

As we have seen, the law sometimes applies a vicarious liability to someone who does not actually commit a negligent or tortious act. For instance, an owner is responsible for the negligent acts of his independent contractor if the acts were illegal.

The person who has become vicariously liable to a plaintiff as a result of the negligence of another, may in certain circumstances have a right of action to be indemnified by the primary wrongdoer. This right is called the right of "recovery over."

Joint tortfeasors ordinarily do not have a right of recovery over against each other. However, several states have enacted statutes permitting one tortfeasor to bring an action against a joint tortfeasor, seeking contribution from him. It therefore becomes important, in determining whether or not such a right exists, to find out whether the liability of the defendants was primary or secondary, or joint or concurrent.

The right of recovery between joint or concurrent tortfeasors is called contribution, and is a bird of a different feather.

Recovery over is not limited to an attempt to recover for a judgment entered. It may be enforced in some cases of voluntary payment or settlement. However, in that event there must be no question of ultimate liability and notice of the claim or suit must have been given the primary wrongdoer and demand made upon him to settle or take over the defense.

This is important to claims people because in any such action the insurer stands in the shoes of the insured. They must therefore know when to go after a primary carrier where the insured is only secondarily liable. Proper notice must also be given to the wrongdoer.

[13] Damages for Fright or Emotional Distress

The claim representative's interest in the problem of possible recovery for injury without physical contact is primarily confined to the field of negligence. It will merely be stated in passing that most jurisdictions recognize the right of recovery if fright or emotional disturbance results from willful acts.

If negligence only is involved, there are still some states that do not permit recovery and follow the "impact" ruling in the old case of *Mitchell v. Rochester Ry. Co.,*[10] although the trend is definitely in the opposite direction. The majority of the jurisdictions now hold that fright or mental distress without impact of any kind, is recoverable injury.[11] If, however, such fright arose out of jeopardy to someone else, most states still do not allow recovery. A few jurisdictions have indicated possible recovery where the peril was to someone very dear, such as a child or other close relative.[12]

While there can be no doubt that there are some instances where recovery for shock or fright is justified, claim people should view the average claim of this nature with skepticism. The field is entirely too open to possible exaggeration and fraud. By means of detailed investigation, every effort should be exerted to prove the authenticity of the allegations both of circumstances and injury.

---

[10] 151 N.Y. 107, 45 N.E. 354 (1896).
[11] Batalla v. State, 10 N.Y.2d 34, 176 N.E.2d 729 (1961).
[12] Dillon v. Legg, 69 Cal. Rptr. 72, 441 P.2d 912 (1968).

§ 10.04 Evidence

Fundamentally, evidence is simply verbal, documentary, or other tangible and probative matter that substantiates or impugns allegations made by either party to an action. The end result of the presentation of the evidence may or may not be its acceptance as proof. Evidence is submitted to and judged by the jury. They decide whether or not it amounts to proof.

The prime purpose of the claim representative's initial investigation is to find the facts in order to determine the truth. The facts obtained must be transformed into evidence so that when the claim goes into suit, the allegations made by the defense may be substantiated, and those made by the plaintiff refuted, if untrue.

This and subsequent chapters, discuss the form and content of various types of documentary evidence, the means used to turn facts into evidence acceptable in court, and what facts constitute evidence.

Unless the investigation produces tangible or other probative evidence, the insurer will have little if any defense if a claim goes into suit.

[1] Classifications of Evidence

Ordinarily, evidence is divided into two categories, direct and circumstantial.

Direct evidence will usually substantiate an allegation in and of itself, and needs no other proof. An example of direct evidence is sworn testimony of individuals who have actual knowledge of the facts. Direct evidence, however, need not call for the presence of an individual, but may involve medical or hospital reports or documents of various kinds. It may also involve the physical presence of an object which by its very appearance may corroborate certain allegations.

For our purpose, direct evidence can be divided into two classes:

1. Verbal or oral, which involves the direct testimony of witnesses, doctors, appraisers, or other specialists who will substantiate the information given to the investigator.
2. Documentary evidence, which includes hospital reports, and records, photographs, motion pictures, diagrams and surveys, property damage estimates, signed statements, and letters.

[a] Hearsay Evidence

It must be understood that the definitions which are given in this section of the book are attempted simplifications of legal definitions made to be understandable to the average layman. In some instances, as in the hearsay rule, attempts at complete definition have been made by some of our most famous jurists without entirely satisfying everyone.

In general, hearsay evidence is based not on the personal knowledge of the person giving the testimony, but on what someone told him.

Although it is a general principle of law that hearsay evidence is usually not admissible evidence, there are so many exceptions to the general rule that its complete study is a project in itself.

The reason behind the rule is a good one. It is not fair to permit someone to make certain assertions based on the purported knowledge of someone else when that other person is not in court to be questioned and cross-examined.

Without any attempt to delve into the matter very deeply, we can say that some of the exceptions to the hearsay rule involve matters of public or general interest, declarations made immediately preceding death, declarations of pain and suffering, declarations against interest, and some others which we need not mention. This is a matter for attorneys who specialize in trial work, and should not be too much the concern of the claim representative, be he attorney or layman.

[b] Res Gestae

This is another phrase with which one should have at least some familiarity, although, again, the relationship need not become too intimate.

A literal translation of the words, res gestae, would be meaningless to the layman. In effect, it is a rule which holds that, under certain circumstances, a person may testify as to what another has said when his declarations were spontaneously made immediately after, or concurrent with, an incident or act. Such statements, to be admissible, must tend to elucidate or explain the nature of the act or occurrence.

This doctrine is another exception to the hearsay rule, and is applied when it is impossible to produce the actual person who made the declarations or statements. An example is the spontaneous declaration by one who has been mortally wounded saying, "John Smith

§ 10.04[1][c]   CASUALTY INSURANCE CLAIMS

stabbed me." Another example is an outcry by a driver immediately after an accident stating, "God, my brakes didn't hold."

This doctrine is complex and again not uniformly applied in our various jurisdictions but important in the investigation of an accident.

[c] **Judicial Notice**

Sometimes a judge will accept a fact which is recognized to be within his own knowledge, and of such common knowledge as to make it unnecessary to establish proof. This is known as judicial notice.

Such a fact cannot be something which the judge has learned privately but must be a matter of common knowledge to others as well as himself. If, for instance, it were to be proven that a driver of an automobile had drunk a quart of gin shortly before an accident, a judge might take judicial knowledge of the fact that as a result the driver was intoxicated at the time of the accident.

Other matters of which the court may take judicial notice include geographical locations, certain physical conditions, physical handicaps, obvious reactions involved in driving an automobile, conditions attractive to small children, certain accepted scientific and medical conditions, and many more.

Judicial notice may also be taken of certain court decisions and legislative acts and ordinances, and federal and state rules and regulations. The areas of permissible judicial notice of laws and regulations are usually governed by the statutes of the particular jurisdiction in which the suit is being tried.

[2] **Burden of Proof**

The lawbooks say that the burden of proof to establish the defendant's negligence is upon the plaintiff. Please do not take this too literally. There are too many exceptions to the general rule to permit it to have much weight in the investigation of a claim or suit.

[3] **Best Evidence Rule**

The best evidence rule simply states that in matters involving writings, the original must be produced, unless some valid reason can be shown for not producing it, such as its destruction or loss.

Where it can be validly explained, the court may permit a photostat or copy to be admitted in place of the original. Such copy is known as "secondary evidence."

[4] Opinion versus Fact

In the taking of signed statements, the need for confining such statements to matters of fact is discussed in Chapter 4.

This restriction is based on the general rule that witnesses may not testify on their opinions or conclusions, but only on the facts, from which the jury may formulate its own opinion and draw its own conclusions.

One exception to the general rule is a case in which the facts are so obscure that they make any determination impossible without some expression of opinion. An ordinary witness may, under certain circumstances, express an opinion that did not require special study or skill for him to form.

For instance, some jurisdictions will permit a man to testify on his opinion of the intoxication of another, or as to the approximate weight or size of an object, or as to distance or speed, which is especially important in automobile accidents. These so-called opinions, however, are so closely related to fact as to make the two hardly distinguishable.

A professional opinion from a qualified expert may, as we shall see, be accepted as testimony. It is hard to imagine a situation in which such testimony would not involve an expression of opinion.

[5] Res Ipsa Loquitur

"The thing speaks for itself" is a literal translation of a very controversial legal phrase. In other words, an incident or a situation may be of such a nature that the courts will presume negligence on the part of a defendant where actual negligence might be very difficult or impossible to prove. The derailing of a railroad train, for instance, would be a case where the *res ipsa* doctrine might be applied.

In order to invoke the doctrine it must be shown that something under the control of the defendant has caused damage which ordinarily would not have occurred if care had been used to prevent it. Direct evidence of negligence must either be absent or difficult to obtain.

The doctrine will usually be applied where an inference of negligence can be drawn from the circumstances of the accident alone and where the actual act or omission which caused the injury or damage is not apparent.

As long as the facts of the accident are established and the instrumentality causing the damage was owned or controlled by the defendant, and there can be no causal connection other than by an inference or presumption of negligence by the defendant, the doctrine may be applied. Two elements are essential: (1) the object causing the damage or injury must have been controlled by the defendant, and (2) it is reasonable to infer or presume that the accident would not have occurred unless the defendant's negligence was involved.

As in other fields of law that have a direct bearing on casualty claim handling, there is little uniformity in the application of this doctrine. I must, therefore, repeat the theme that runs throughout this book: *become familiar with the law of your jurisdiction.*

[6] Competency of Non-Expert Witnesses

A witness may be any person who can help to determine the facts of an accident and who has the ability to present the information in a court of law. He or she may not speak English, may be deaf, unable to speak or have speech defects. As long as the information can be transmitted accurately as the witness saw it, he or she will be permitted to testify if proper help is available in the form of a translator or therapist who can transmit the information to the judge and jury.

The witness may appear to be partial to one of the litigants because of relationship, employment, social friendship, or for any one of a number of other reasons. As long as the association is not clandestine, the witness will be permitted to testify, and if the partiality becomes evident it will be up to the judge and jury to determine what weight, if any, to give to the testimony.

The same thing applies to antagonistic witnesses. Impartial witnesses who have no ax to grind and who are in court for the sole purpose of trying to help arrive at the truth, are obviously the ones who will make the best impression.

The witness need not be an adult. Witnesses who are young children will be examined by the judge to help him determine whether the witness is capable of understanding the facts and able to give an honest and accurate account. He will also have to determine whether he thinks the child understands the nature of his oath to tell the truth.

Past criminal record is also no disqualification to a witness in a civil tort suit, nor is adjudged incompetency. The judge and jury must determine what weight to give such testimony.

In handling a claim that will most likely go into suit, it is very important for the claim representative, in evaluating a claim or suit, to make some judgment as to the appearance, sincerity, and apparent honesty of a witness, all of which will have some bearing on the weight given to his testimony.

Lying under oath in a courtroom is a crime, and while prosecutions for perjury are made in criminal cases, I have yet to see one in a tort case. It is important for the claim representative to be aware of this fact of life.

[7] Privileged Communications

Privileged communications are those based on an intimate relationship between the parties and which the law recognizes as confidential and not permitted to be admitted in evidence in court. Information obtained as a result of such a relationship cannot be divulged in a court of law without the consent of the person for whom the privilege is granted.

Although there are other situations in some jurisdictions granting privilege, the claim representative should be aware of the four major categories:

1. Husband and wife.
2. Physician and patient.
3. Clergyman and parishioner.
4. Attorney and client.

The old common law rule that one spouse may not testify against the other spouse has been substantially modified by statute. Today such testimony is admitted in most jurisdictions unless the information is of a very confidential nature.

On the contrary, at common law, communications between physician and patient were not held to be privileged. In this case, a change has been made by statute and by judicial decision granting privilege to the patient under certain circumstances.

In the field of negligence law it is rare that any attempt would be made to exercise such a privilege at trial where the injured plaintiff is trying to establish verification of his allegations concerning injury and disability. The subject gets complicated when a question of previous medical attention could have a detrimental effect on present allegations, but this is a matter for legal determination with which the claim representative need not be too concerned.

In situations involving clergymen and parishioners, there is almost unanimous agreement that statements made in confidence by such parishioners to clergymen are privileged.

The lawyer-client privilege is much more involved and requires a knowledge of local laws and judicial attitudes best left to the representing attorneys.

[8] **Expert Testimony**

The law recognizes that only persons specially trained in their fields may formulate acceptable opinion on facts falling within those fields. They testify when some special technical or scientific knowledge is required. Such experts may be engineers, automobile damage appraisers and, especially, physicians and surgeons.

It is obvious that a doctor is more qualified to make a prognosis than a layman who has not been trained in medicine. For the same reason an orthopedist who has spent a good deal of time studying the specialty is more qualified to testify concerning a bone disease than an ordinary medical practitioner. Although the general practitioner would be permitted to testify concerning a bone disease, a jury would probably give more weight to the opinion of an orthopedist.

The qualification of a witness to testify as an expert is usually determined by the trial court. His testimony will not be reviewed unless an obvious error has been made or some discretionary power abused.

It is not essential that an expert obtain his knowledge by formal education. For instance, an automobile property damage appraiser may not have gotten through the fourth grade of grammar school, but he will qualify as an expert mechanic if he has spent a number of years doing automobile repair work.

Naturally, since the qualification of experts is within the province of the particular judge, there is wide variance in all jurisdictions. For example, it is recognized in many jurisdictions that photography is a highly specialized profession and that those competent in the field can by various artifices create many illusions which do not reflect actual conditions. It is also recognized that lack of photographic skill can accidentally produce distorted impressions.

Some courts, therefore, will permit in evidence only those photographs that have been taken by recognized reputable specialists in the field. Others will admit snapshots taken by novices, under certain circumstances.

If a claim is expected to go into suit it is important that the findings of the investigation be bolstered by experts who will be able to testify in the jurisdiction where the case is to be tried.

§ 10.05 Agency

[1] Imputed Negligence (Respondeat Superior)

Should someone who is trying to impress the reader with his knowledge of the law use the term *respondeat superior,* he should not let it throw him. His informant is simply talking about the responsibility of an employer for the acts of his employee, or a principal for the acts of his agent. In other words, a person is held responsible when someone else acts for him at his request or with his consent.

The legal phraseology for employer-employee relationship is known as master and servant. The distinction between the two lies in the fact that whereas in a master-servant relationship there is employment for wages, in a principal-agent relationship there need not be.

Our concern with agency is confined to responsibility for the tortious or negligent acts of an agent or servant.

A principal or master is liable for the negligent acts of his agent or servant if those acts were performed either in the course of his employment and within the scope of his authority for the master, or at the express or implied direction of the principal. In either event, the servant or agent must be subject to the control and direction of the master or principal. Responsibility may go beyond mere negligence, and in certain circumstances may also include willful or intentional acts.

Since the master or principal can be reached only through the acts of the servant or agent, if the agent is exonerated from any wrongdoing, then the principal must also be.

An agency may be created orally, in writing, expressly, or by implication or estoppel. An agent and his principal, or a master and servant may be sued individually or jointly. A principal or master, in the event a recovery is obtained against him, may have a right of action against the agent or servant for the recovery of any judgment rendered against him, provided he did not contribute to or concur in the wrongful acts.

This, however, does not apply to the ordinary claim arising out of an automobile accident where insurance is carried on the automobile in question, since the driver of the automobile would be an additional insured under the policy if he was driving with the permission of the owner. This will be discussed at greater length in Chapter 22 when we cover the "Omnibus Clause" of the Standard Automobile Liability and Personal Automobile policies.

[2] Determination of Agent's Negligence

Determination of an agent's or servant's negligence is measured by the same yardstick used in all other actions based on negligence. There must be some legal duty owed to the plaintiff which has been breached by some lack of reasonable care.

In most jurisdictions the contributory negligence of a parent is not imputed to his child, although there are a few exceptions. Ordinarily, the negligence of one spouse will not be imputed to the other simply because of the marital relationship, except where community property laws are involved.

Generally speaking (and forgetting for the moment statutory or implied agency), an owner of an automobile is not responsible for the negligent acts of another driver if the car is being used for the purely personal benefit of the driver, whether or not permission has been granted to use the automobile. However, if he was using the vehicle with the permission of the owner, he would be covered by the owner's insurance policy.

Some courts have made an exception where the principal entrusted the automobile to a known incompetent or habitually drunken driver, but responsibility here rests on negligence rather than agency.

[a] Sub-Agency

When is an agent permitted to transfer his agency duties in part or in whole, to another person? Ordinarily, discretionary duties requiring the use of judgment cannot be delegated. However, unless specifically forbidden to do so, an agent may in certain circumstances delegate his duties to another:

1. If he is specifically authorized to do so by his principal.

PRINCIPLES OF LAW—PART II § 10.05[2][c]

2. If the act is unlawful for him but not for another person.
3. If the act to be performed is purely mechanical.
4. If it is common custom or usage in the industry to do so.

[b] Temporary or Special Employee

In some instances, an individual who is a regular or general employee of an employer may be loaned, hired, or directed to do work for a different employer for a temporary period or to do a specific job. In such event, responsibility for the employee's negligence may rest with a temporary rather than a general employer.

Most courts hold that determination depends on control, as in all agency questions, and all of the facts concerning control would have to be developed. An important factor in determining control is in whose business the employee was engaged at the time of the incident, although this alone is usually not enough. Checklists that will help in making a determination as to control may be found in Chapter 39 dealing with the investigation of the independent contractor relationship.

[c] Deviation

Once again we are forced to talk in generalities, because there is not uniformity concerning the responsibility of a principal or master for the negligence of his agent or servant where there has been some material deviation from the authority granted. The problem will most frequently concern the investigator in the investigation of automobile liability claims.

In order to determine whether there has been any deviation from the scope of the authority granted, it is obviously necessary to learn the limits of that authority. As previously stated, such authority may be either expressed or implied. It may be restricted by instructions not to do certain things or it may be directive by orders to do certain things. For instance, a principal for some good reason might direct an agent to take a certain route; he may have given permission to use the automobile for a certain limited time; he may have directed that the car be driven no faster than a certain speed; or he may have expressly forbidden the agent to use the car for the agent's personal business or pleasure or to go to certain places.

In any consideration of whether or not permission to use the automobile was granted to the driver, we again run into the general problem of deviation. For instance, if an owner specifically prohibited the use of the car in a certain territory or beyond a certain area or time limit, an accident which occurred outside of that limit might not be the responsibility of the owner since the permission granted was restrictive and use beyond the restriction no longer could imply permission in some cases.

In any event, where there is some express limitation of authority, the principal is usually not held responsible if there has been a *material* deviation from that limitation if it can be proved.

Even where no express instructions were given concerning the route to be taken, there may be sufficient deviation on the part of the driver so that his negligence will not be imputed to the principal. Such deviation, however, must be more than "merely a longer route" and must be of sufficient nature to show that the driver was not in the course of his agency at the particular time of the accident.

In certain circumstances the deviation may be so great as to amount to an abandonment of the agency or employment, possibly involving embezzlement or theft of the automobile. In such instances the liability of the agent could not be imputed to the principal unless the principal was guilty of some negligence in entrusting the automobile to the agent.

Where unquestionable deviation has occurred, responsibility of the owner or principal is suspended until such time as the driver returns to the course from which he deviated. A few courts hold that he need only start back, even though he may not as yet have reached the original course, to reinstate the agency relationship.

An agency situation may be created by implication if no previous objection was made in similar circumstances.

[d] Joint Venture Agency Liability

A joint venture is akin to a limited partnership. Technically, it involves a business enterprise in which all of the participants have an equal voice and share in the profits or losses. Each is considered the agent of the other insofar as the joint venture is concerned.

A few of our courts have ruled that any use of one vehicle by two or more persons for any common purpose is a joint venture. They have declared each party to be the agent of the other in an action brought by a third party as a result of an automobile accident based on negligence.

The prevailing view requires a showing of mutual right to control the vehicle, whether physically present or not, before the principal of joint venture will be applied. Common purpose or sharing in the expenses is usually not enough.

Where the principle is applied, the negligence of the driver is imputed to the joint-adventure passenger to defeat the latter's claim for injuries against a third party, if contributory negligence is a good defense. It must be remembered that these doctrines are more theoretical than practical since the automobile statutes, heretofore mentioned, make theories such as these obsolete.

[3] Implied Agency Created by Statute

All states have adopted laws governing the use of motor vehicles. Some of these statutes are incorporated in the insurance laws as well as in the motor vehicle laws.

In legislation of this type, it is unnecessary to show actual agency in order to hold the owner or other responsible parties liable for the negligent acts of the driver as long as the facts fall within the provisions of the particular statute.

Such vicarious (or substituted) liability imposed by statute falls for the most part in five general categories:

1. Where permission by the owner of an automobile creates an implied agency and makes the owner responsible for the negligent acts of any driver.
2. Where permission by the owner creates only a presumption of agency which may be rebutted.
3. Where permission by an owner to a minor imputes his negligence to the owner.
4. Where permission to a minor by an owner who has custody of him creates an implied agency.
5. Where anyone who signs the application for a driver's license or a learner's permit of an infant (ages vary) becomes responsible for the negligent acts of that infant.

In this last instance, most statutes provide that request for cancellation of the license or permit by the endorser relieves him of responsibility after the time limitation has expired.

[4] Family Purpose Doctrine

Some states have, by judicial decision, accepted a rule to the effect that an owner of an automobile may be held liable for the negligence of the driver if that driver was a member of his immediate family and was driving with the permission of the owner. This is known as the *Family Purpose Doctrine*, but again we have a situation where the doctrine is not uniformly applied. Some courts require that the automobile be purchased and kept for family use in order to create liability on the part of the owner. Others insist that the purpose of the errand resulting in the accident must have been for the general benefit of family. Where the doctrine is applicable, it avoids the necessity for proving agency. As automobile insurance and statutes became more prevalent, some of these doctrines became obsolete.

[5] Independent Contractor

An owner of property, generally speaking, is not liable for the negligence of an independent contractor with whom he has arranged to perform some work.

Having made that rather positive statement, we may proceed to cloud the issue by saying that there is no easy way to make an absolute distinction between an agent or employee and an independent contractor. The fact that an individual may have called himself an independent contractor and may have thought of himself as such is immaterial if the circumstances do not fit the pattern required in the particular jurisdiction.

Generally speaking, determination as to status depends upon control of the operation. If the principal maintains some control over the method of work or means of operation, the situation is usually one of employer-employee relationship and not that of independent contractor.

Some general factors (but by no means all of them) usually necessary to determine the status of a party are the following:

1. How was he hired? Was a definite salary set by the hour, day or week, or was there a lump-sum price agreement?
2. Was there any limitation on hiring?
3. Who pays social security, unemployment, or other taxes?
4. Who owned the tools and supplied the materials?
5. Who directed the work?
6. Who hired and paid additional help? Who fired them?

The subject of employer-employee, independent contractor relationship in compensation claims is discussed in some detail in "Handling Workers' Compensation Cases," Chapter 39, and includes a comprehensive checklist for the investigation necessary to a determination of that relationship. How many of these factors would have to be considered depends upon the court making the determination.

There are some situations in which the property owner or the one who hires the independent contractor (assuming his status as such has been determined) can be held responsible for his acts:

1. If the work which the independent contractor is required to do is unlawful.
2. If the work constitutes a public nuisance.
3. If there is any interference on the part of the owner which results in injury to the third party.
4. If by statute the owner is required to make certain repairs.
5. If the property owner has obligated himself to make certain repairs.
6. If the work to be done is inherently dangerous.
7. If the owner has failed to use reasonable care in the selection of the contractor.

§ 10.06 Bailments

Release of custody of personal property to another for some definite reason or purpose, with the intent and understanding that the property be returned after the purpose has been served, is known as a *bailment*. In order to establish a bailment there must be a voluntary relinquishing of possession by the owner and a taking of possession by the one to whom it is given.

The person who relinquishes possession of the object he owns is known as the *bailor*. The person to whom he gives it is known as the *bailee*.

Claim representatives will also be interested in this branch of the law, particularly in the investigation and disposition of claims arising under the Garage Keepers Legal Liability policy and also under claims arising out of warehouse losses under the Owners, Landlords and Tenants policy in addition to claims handled under Inland Marine policies.

[1] Kinds of Bailments

Bailments are usually divided into three classes:

1. *Bailments for the sole benefit of the bailor.* These are known as gratuitous bailments on the part of the bailee. An example of this type of bailment would be a request by a housewife to a neighbor to keep some meat in the neighbor's freezing compartment. In a bailment of this type the only duty which the bailee owes to the bailor is one of slight care.
2. *Bailments for the sole benefit of the bailee.* An example of this type of bailment would be the borrowing of a lawnmower without recompense of any kind. Since the bailment was for the sole benefit of the bailee, in this type of case he must exercise the greatest degree of care to avoid liability for any damage to the property.
3. *Bailments for the mutual benefit of both parties.* This is the ordinary situation where an object of any kind is rented or hired for a fee. It is the type most often encountered in casualty claim work. The degree of care which the bailee must exercise in this instance in order to avoid liability, is ordinary care.

[a] Custody versus Bailment

The mere fact that possession was voluntarily released by one party and temporarily transferred to the possession of someone else does not in and of itself make the transaction a bailment. The additional fact that such a relinquishment of possession is for mutual benefit of both parties is still not enough. While the word "consideration" was not used in the definition of a bailment, it is about as close a definition as we can get to the third element that is necessary to complete a bailment. This in fact is the only element that distinguishes a bailment from mere granting of custody over the property to someone else.

An example of granting mere custody would be the providing of tools by an employer to an employee for a specific job. In such an instance the employee merely has custody of property owned by the employer and is not acting as a bailee of such property. The employee is merely serving the interests of the employer, and not his own, except incidentally for the salary he receives.

This kind of situation is pertinent in incidents involving the driving of an automobile owned by the employer and temporarily in the custody of the employee, but again keep in mind the insurance policy provisions regarding permissive user of the vehicle.

[b] Rental versus Bailment

In the handling and disposition of automobile garage, parking lot, and warehouse cases there is an additional determination which must be made before the question of liability can properly be resolved. This involves the distinction between an express or implied rental agreement in which the sole intent of the parties is simply to rent an area for the storing of an object, and a bailment where the control of the object is vested in the bailee, and in which his responsibility is greater.

How, therefore, are we to distinguish between a bailment and a rental? The answer again seems to lie with the word "control." In other words, if the object has been placed in the possession of another with the intent that that other person have complete control over it while it is in his possession, then it can be considered a bailment. An example is the leaving of an automobile and keys with another person so that the automobile can be moved at will, even though the understanding is that it be moved only within the restricted area.

Most of the courts have declared garage owners to be bailees, whereas, in some instances, a parking lot owner may be considered only a landlord.

In addition to liability arising under the implied bailment, a direct liability may be created by contract between the parties. Where only a landlord-tenant relationship exists, the landlord may ordinarily issue a printed ticket exempting himself from liability or limiting his liability, and where the surrounding facts point to a rental arrangement only, the courts will usually sustain such a contract.

Where it has been determined, however, that a bailment exists the courts have declared almost without exception that the bailee may neither exempt himself from liability nor even limit his liability.

[c] Theft versus Bailment

Here again the concern is with the effect of the terminology on a policy involving first party automobile coverage. It is sometimes very difficult to determine whether an automobile is actually stolen or whether it was placed voluntarily in the hands of someone else, who then either misappropriated it or alleged claims over it which may or may not have been justified.

While there may have been some legal question as to the rights between the parties, if the object was turned over voluntarily to the correct individual who then accepted possession, it is not a theft. True, all of the elements of a bailment may not be present but often enough factors are present to conclude that the transaction was a bailment rather than a theft.

The important thing to remember is whether or not possession was relinquished voluntarily and whether or not it was accepted by the person to whom it was intended to be given.

[2] Acts of Employees

We have already learned that where an employee acts within the scope of his employment, the employer is directly responsible for his acts.

Even when an employee of a bailee acts outside the scope of his authority most jurisdictions still hold the bailee liable, but some do not unless the bailee was negligent in hiring the employee or had knowledge of previous careless or larcenous propensities.

[3] Contributory or Comparative Negligence as a Defense

Contributory negligence in a bailor or his agent is usually a good defense in an action brought against the bailee for his primary negligence. For instance, should a bailor or his agent leave an automobile with the keys in it on the street outside of a garage without informing the bailee or obtaining his consent, such an act might be considered sufficient contributory negligence to avoid responsibility on the part of the bailee. Many jurisdictions have in fact enacted legislation to this effect.

[4] Particular Bailments

1. *Storekeepers.* The custodian of a clothing store is ordinarily responsible for the clothes which the customer puts down temporarily while trying on the new clothes. He would not be responsible for anything more than the particular clothes that the customer had to lay aside momentarily, including what happened to be within those clothes at the time.

2. *Restaurants.* While there is some difference of opinion, ordinarily in most jurisdictions the restaurant owner is not liable for the loss of an overcoat or a hat when hooks or clothesracks have been provided close to the seat of a customer, particularly where notice of no responsibility has been posted. Where a checkroom has been provided, however, there is responsibility in most jurisdictions, even where no fee has been paid.

CHAPTER 11

Intrafamily Tort Relationships and Immunities

§ 11.01 Minor Children
§ 11.02 Parental Liability for the Torts of Children
§ 11.03 The Doctrines of Parental and Spousal Immunities
    [1] History and Background
    [2] Parental Immunity Doctrine Still Effective
        [a] Fraud, Collusion, and Insurance as Factors
        [b] Effect of Insurance
    [3] Abolition and Curtailment of the Parental Immunity Doctrine
    [4] Emancipation
    [5] Effect of the Death of Either Party
    [6] Intentional, Willful and Wanton Torts
    [7] Gross Negligence and Drunken Driving
    [8] Change in Intrafamily Immunity Doctrines
§ 11.04 Husband/Wife Immunity Doctrine
    [1] Historical Background
    [2] Married Women Acts
    [3] Present Trends Abrogating Husband/Wife Immunity
    [4] Husband/Wife Immunity Still Holds
    [5] Torts Committed Before Marriage
    [6] The Insurance Factor in Husband/Wife Immunity
§ 11.05 Prenatal Injury
    [1] Introduction
    [2] Early Decisions
        [a] The Restriction of Viability
        [b] When Fetus is "Quick"
        [c] "At Time of Conception"
    [3] Right to Recover for Death of Stillborn Child
        [a] Recovery Limited to Pecuniary Loss
        [b] Right of Action for Child Born Alive May Be Time Limited
    [4] Requirement of Viability in Death Caused by Prenatal Injury
§ 11.06 Child's Right of Action for Wrongful Life
§ 11.07 Bibliography

§ 11.01 Minor Children

The courts have generally held that infants and insane persons cannot, in most instances, be held liable for their torts unless a specific state of mind, such as malice, can be shown in order to create liability.

Since negligence presumes a capacity for exercising due care, in those actions based on negligence, the standard of care required of an infant should be, and usually is, that which is ordinarily shown by the average infant of similar age and mentality, under similar circumstances.

In most jurisdictions there is a legal presumption that a child under seven years of age is incapable of recognizing an act as tortious, which would ordinarily be construed as negligence. Where a child is over the age of seven, the courts usually try to determine negligence according to the degree of responsibility which a child of like age and mentality should ordinarily exhibit. Obviously, a child who could not be charged with negligence, cannot be held responsible for contributory or comparative negligence.

The age of majority, after which a person is no longer legally considered a child, varies. For centuries, all jurisdictions held twenty-one to be the age of majority. In recent years some states have taken a second look at what the age of majority should be. Permission to allow young people to drink beer at the age of eighteen subsequently resulted in a negative reaction from legislators who were inundated with demands to curtail drunken driving.

§ 11.02 Parental Liability for the Torts of Children

Parental responsibility for tortious acts of their children is another recent development of legislative, rather than common law. At common law, a parent was not liable for torts committed by his or her children.[1]

It was accordingly a big step for legislators to begin enacting statutes and ordinances holding parents liable for the tortious acts of their children. While almost all states have enacted statutes, and many cities and towns have passed ordinances concerning tortious acts of children, there is very little uniformity in these enactments. Most of them limit liability to deliberate acts, referred to legally as

---

[1] 54 A.L.R.3d 964 (1973).

INTRAFAMILY TORTS AND IMMUNITIES § 11.02

willful and wanton acts. In addition, the amount for which the parent may become liable is usually as small as several hundred dollars, but as of this writing, does not usually exceed $5,000.[2] Attacks have been made on such statutes as being unfair and unlikely to curb juvenile delinquency.[3]

Generally speaking, the attacks on the constitutionality of such enactments has been upheld so long as they are limited in nature, especially concerning the amount that can be recovered from the parents.

In one case, the Georgia statute was declared unconstitutional;[4] the parent's liability in the Georgia statute was unlimited, and the legislature has since reenacted a revised version of the statute which, by implication, the courts have indicated will be held to be constitutional.

Some states have adopted automobile "consent" statutes in lieu of, or in addition to, parental responsibility statutes. Such Acts make the owner of a vehicle responsible for the negligence of any driver who drives the vehicle with the permission of the owner. In view of the universal coverage given to permissive drivers, such Acts are helpful only where the vehicle involved in an accident is uninsured. Here again is an exercise in futility since an uninsured owner is usually not financially responsible in any event. It would be far better for society if all states enacted legislation making at least minimum liability insurance coverage mandatory at the time title of a vehicle is acquired by a new owner.

At common law there are also various exceptions even to the courts that hold to no liability for parents where:

1. The child who committed the tort was acting under the specific direction of the parent.

2. The parent acquiesced to, encouraged, or ratified the tortious act of the child.

3. A parent knowingly entrusted a dangerous instrumentality to a child who did not have the mental capacity or maturity to realize the dangers involved in its use.

The automobile consent statutes come into play in those jurisdictions that have enacted them in this kind of a situation, but even

---

[2] 8 A.L.R.3d 615 (1966).
[3] Comment, "Parental Responsibility Ordinances," 19 Wayne L. Rev. 1551 (1973).
[4] Corley v Lewless, 182 S.E.2d 766 (1971).

without such statutes it is obvious that an automobile in the hands of an irresponsible child is a very dangerous instrument.

Certainly, a loaded gun would be a dangerous instrument, even if it were not directly entrusted to a child. Placing such a gun or other dangerous instrument where a child could get at it would be enough to justify placing liability on the parent who gave or carelessly left the dangerous instrument where the child could reach it. An air rifle in the hands of a young child is another obvious instance of a dangerous instrument.

On the other hand, an object that could be lethal if used for violent purposes not intended as its regular purpose, may not, in and of itself, be considered a dangerous instrumentality. Such objects could, for instance, be a hard baseball or a bat, a hammer or heavy wrench, or other such object.

4. The act of the child was illegal and the benefit thereof accepted or instigated by the parent. Obviously, if the child stole or robbed something of value from someone, and the parent accepted such property knowing how it was obtained, the parent would also be held responsible for the tortious act of the child.

5. The child previously exhibited vicious propensities which were known, or should have been known, to the parent, and the parent took no responsible precautions to avoid harm to others. The parent could be held responsible for the tortious acts of the child.

6. The child committed a tortious act while in the employ of, or while acting as servant or agent of, his or her parent. The rules of agency would apply and the parent could, with the usual agency exceptions, be held liable for the tortious acts of the child.

In these kinds of situations there is always the question of the age of reason or maturity of the child. Judicial guidelines often set the arbitrary age of seven as being the age at which the average child could be considered responsible. However, as everyone knows, all children do not mentally develop at the same pace and common sense is a rare attribute even in adults. Accordingly, it is obvious that not all children can be adjudged mature at any specific age, and each situation must be considered in the light of all of the facts involved.

§ 11.03 The Doctrines of Parental and Spousal Immunities

[1] History and Background

In the late 1800's, as a result of being wrongfully committed to an insane asylum, and held there against her will for eleven days, a young woman, separated from her husband but still a minor, sued her mother for false imprisonment in the state of Mississippi.[5] In that case, the court held that:

> The peace of society, and of the families composing society, and a sound public policy, designed to subserve the repose of families and the best interests of society, forbid to the minor child a right to appear in court in the assertion of a claim to civil redress for personal injuries suffered at the hands of the parent. The state, through its criminal laws, will give the minor child protection from parental violence and wrongdoing, and this is all the child can be heard to demand.

Thus the doctrine of parental immunity was born. How quaint the reasoning of the court sounds today. It conjures up visions of stern and humorless Victorian judges who pontificated homilies from somewhere above the arena of everyday life.

The *Hewlett* decision[6] was shortly followed by two other cases, also involving intentional and brutal torts.[7]

In *Roller v. Roller*[8] the court gave "preservation of the domestic peace and tranquility in the home" as a reason for granting parental immunity to a father who had brutally raped his minor daughter.

There was, and still is, some basis for granting leeway to a parent in the pursuit of parental duties, but subsequent rethinking, and changing attitudes created so many exceptions to the general rule that we have now come almost 180 degrees in the opposite direction and are well on our way to abolishing all intrafamilial immunities.

Nevertheless, for a period of more than sixty years this doctrine spread to all corners of our country, and it was not until the 1960's that a number of courts began to seriously question the propriety of the doctrine itself and to start reversing the trend.[9]

---

[5] Hewlett v. George, 9 S. 885 (1890).

[6] *Id.*

[7] **Tenn.:** McKelvey v. McKelvey, 77 S.W. 664 (1903).
Wash.: Roller v. Roller, 79 P. 788 (1905).

[8] Roller v. Roller, 79 P. 788 (1905).

[9] *See* Prosser, W.L., *Prosser on Torts* (4th ed. 1971); Poust, "Parent-Child Tort Immunity: Common Sense to Some—Nonsense to Others," 36 Insurance Counsel Journal 374 (July 1969).

§11.03[2]   CASUALTY INSURANCE CLAIMS

Generally speaking, the doctrine of immunity works both ways. In those jurisdictions where it applies, and in those that have modified or abolished it, the same position appears to hold whether the suit is by the child against the parent or by the parent against the child.[10]

[2] Parental Immunity Doctrine Still Effective

Even today, the parental immunity doctrine still plays an important part in situations involving actions by children against their parents and vice versa, despite the definite trend toward limiting or abolishing it.

Since the situation is in a period of rapid transition, it is often difficult to state with any degree of certainty that any particular jurisdiction still holds to the doctrine, or whether because of so many exceptions to it the jurisdiction should be more accurately placed in the abolition category. The record is changing on almost a daily basis.

The word "complete" cannot be used with reference to parental immunity or its abolition in most jurisdictions even at the time of this writing. Many states still basically hold to the doctrine of parental immunity where mere negligence is involved and where there are only one or two exceptions.

[a] Fraud, Collusion, and Insurance as Factors

While the argument that parental immunity fostered fraud and collusion in suits between parents and children predated the advent of widespread insurance coverage,[11] it is today so obviously and closely tied in with insurance coverage for accidents, and particularly for automobile accidents, that the two arguments must be considered in conjunction with each other.

The fact of insurance coverage has been used both to justify retention of the parental immunity doctrine, and to refute it.

A few states have abolished the doctrine of parental immunity by statute in cases involving automobiles, motor vehicles, or insurance,

---

[10] *See* 60 A.L.R.2d 1285 (1958).
[11] Hinkle, "Intrafamily Litigation—Parent and Child," Insurance Law Journal, March 1968.

INTRAFAMILY TORTS AND IMMUNITIES § 11.03[2][b]

which is at least the more honest approach.[12]

In some cases, the insurance exception has been narrowed to the extent of the policy limits only, so that if judgments rendered are over the policy limits, the immunity doctrine would apply and still be effective for any amount of the judgment over those limits.

[b] Effect of Insurance

I think it is completely naive and unrealistic not to recognize that there is at least a much greater chance of collusion in intrafamily suits, where insurance is involved, than in a case involving unrelated parties. It is, in my opinion, just as naive for a court to state that "Our court system, with its attorneys and juries is experienced and reasonably well fitted to ferret out the chicanery which might exist in such cases.[13]

Just as naive is a statement by several courts to the effect that the danger of collusion might even in fact be lessened because of the insured's duty to cooperate and because the insured is represented by counsel appointed by the insurer.[14] The "duty to cooperate" clause in the insurance policy has not deterred fraudulent conduct in the past and is certainly not going to deter it in suits where family members are pitted against each other.

As to the fact that counsel for the insured is appointed by the insurance company, the courts have made it very clear that such counsel is the representative of the insured and the attorney owes him his first and primary duty.

Of much more serious import are the decisions that hold that insurance coverage negates the argument concerning domestic tranquility. Obviously, if there is insurance, it is not likely that the domes-

---

[12] **Conn.:** Ooms v. Ooms, 316 A.2d 783 (1972).
N.C.: Triplett v. Triplett, 237 S.E.2d 546 (1977).
S.C.: Elam v. Elam, 268 S.E.2d 109 (1980) (Court held the statute totally abolishing parental immunity to be unconstitutional on the basis of equal protection).
See also Casey, "The Trend of Interspousal and Parental Immunity: Cakewalk Liability," Insurance Counsel Journal, July 1971.
[13] **N.H.:** Briere v. Briere, 224 A.2d 588 (1966).
[14] **Kan.:** Nocktonick v. Nocktonick, 611 P.2d 135 (1980).
Mass.: Sorensen v. Sorensen, 339 N.E.2d 907 (1975).

tic peace of the family would be affected by a suit between family members.[15]

Insurance would also negate any argument to the effect that a verdict in a family case would lower the family reserves. It probably would increase it considerably if a verdict was rendered. I don't hold either of these arguments to be very satisfactory. The fact of the matter is that the presence of insurance is an inducement to sue, all else being equal.

In my opinion, the only worthwhile reason given for the retention of the family immunity doctrines that deserves serious consideration, involves the problem of possible fraud and collusion resulting from the insurance factor.

Now that insurance is a fact of life, especially where an automobile is involved, it is a reasonable assumption that such coverage is at least an inducement to some degree of fraud and collusion.

Despite the conditioned reflex caused by many years on the defense side of insurance claims and suits, I have come to the conclusion that to eliminate the possibility of fraud and collusion by adhering to the family immunity doctrines merely because of the insurance factor, would be palpably unfair. However, it is obvious that in all suits involving children against parents and vice versa, where there is even the suspicion that an attempt is being made to "make the most" of an accident, all aspects of such a claim or suit should be scrutinized by both judge and jury with a great deal of skepticism.

The only answer that I have to this very puzzling dilemma is that special care must be exercised in the investigation and trial of suits involving family members ostensibly pitted against each other when it is obvious that it is to the benefit of both parties to the action to arrive at a verdict for the plaintiff.

Most liability policies agree to pay "on behalf of the insured, all sums which he shall become legally obligated to pay as damages," or wording to the same effect in the modern "simple language" policies.

For a short time, attempts were made to exclude family members and especially the named insured from coverage as a claimant, but objections from agents and state insurance departments were so vo-

---

[15] **Alas.:** Hebel v. Hebel, 435 P.2d 8 (1967).
Cal.: Gibson v. Gibson, 92 Cal. Rptr. 288 (1971).
N.Y.: Gelbman v. Gelbman, 297 N.Y.S.2d 529 (1969).
Wash.: Borst v. Borst, 251 P.2d 149 (1952).
Wis.: Goller v. White, 122 N.W.2d 193 (1963).

ciferous that such exclusions were, for the most part, withdrawn. It appears as though some judges do not know the facts of life when they assume that insurance carriers can, without insurance state department approval, put any exclusions in the policy that they believe warranted.

Public policy is also a consideration that is not static. It has been used both for and against immunity. In a 1982 case, for instance,[16] the Florida court stated that the presence of insurance is the basis for recognizing that changing conditions have made a change in the public policy as the basis first for and then against parental immunity.

[3] Abolition and Curtailment of the Parental Immunity Doctrine

Many jurisdictions have made very heavy inroads on the parental immunity doctrine with so many and varied exceptions, that it becomes rather obvious from the decisions themselves, and from the dicta, that the present trend is definitely in the direction of abolishing this doctrine altogether, or so weakening it that it will have only minor (no pun intended) application.[17]

---

[16] Ard v. Ard, 414 So. 2d 1066 (1982), *overruling* Florida Farm Bur. Ins. Co. v. Gov't Employees Ins. Co., 387 So.2d 932 (1980).

[17] **Alas.:** Hebel v. Hebel, 435 P.2d 8 (1967) (auto accident).
Ariz.: Streenz v. Streenz, 471 P.2d 282 (1970) (auto accident and insurance).
Cal.: Gibson v. Gibson, 92 Cal. Rptr. 288 (1971) (action by minor against parent).
Colo.: Trevarton v. Trevarton, 378 P.2d 640 (1963), *but see* Horton v. Reaves, 526 P.2d 304 (1974).
Del.: Williams v. Williams, 369 A.2d 669 (Super. 1976).
Fla.: Ard v. Ard, 395 So. 2d 586 (App. 1981) (crack in the dike).
Hi.: Peterson v. City & County of Honolulu, 462 P.2d 1007 (1970); Tamashire v. De Gama, 450 P.2d 998 (1969).
Ill.: Schenk v. Schenk, 241 N.E.2d 12 (1968). Illinois presents a mixed bag of cases as indicated in previous notations, but the large crack in the immunity doctrine is obvious.
Kan.: Noctonick v. Noctonick, 611 P.2d 135 (1980) (M.V. exception).
Ky.: Rigdon v. Rigdon, 465 S.W.2d 921 (1971).
La.: Rouley v. State Farm Mut. Auto. Ins. Co., 235 So. 2d 786 (1964); Deshotel v. Travelers Ind. Co., 243 So. 2d 259 (1971); *but see* Bondurant v. Bondurant, 386 So. 2d 705 (1980).
Mass.: Sorenson v. Sorenson, 339 N.E.2d 907 (1975).
Mich.: Paige v. Bing Constr. Co., 233 N.W.2d 46 (App. 1975).
Minn.: Cherry v. Cherry, 203 N.W.2d 352 (1972).
N.H.: Briere v. Briere, 224 A.2d 588 (1966).
N.J.: Gross v. Sears, Roebuck & Co., 386 A.2d 442 (App. 1978); Convery v. Macyka, 394 A.2d 1250 (1978). In this state, too, we see the former position changing radically.

Where, for all practical purposes, the parental immunity doctrine has been abolished, the measure of negligence is the ordinary one of reasonableness under the circumstances.

[4] Emancipation

A minor child may become emancipated:

1. By reaching the age of majority.
2. By legal and binding agreement with his or her parents under some circumstances.
3. By the parents forfeiture of his or her rights as a result of failure to fulfill parental duties and responsibilities.
4. By proper method set up by statute in that jurisdiction.

When emancipated, a minor child may bring an action against a parent in the same manner in which he or she would bring suit against any third party.[18]

If however, the child was not emancipated *at the time of the alleged wrongdoing*, it has been held that emancipation does not give the child any rights which it did not have at the time the tort was committed.[19]

Nev.: Rupert v. Stiene, 528 P.2d 1013 (1974).
N.Y.: Gelbman v. Gelbman, 297 N.Y.S.2d 529 (1969) (landmark case changing some previously held views).
N.D.: Nuelle v. Wells, 154 N.W.2d 364 (1967).
Pa.: Falco v. Pados, 282 A.2d 351 (1971).
Va.: Smith v. Kaufman, 183 S.E.2d 190 (1971).
Vt.: Wood v. Wood, 370 A.2d 191 (1971).
Wash.: Merrick v. Sutterlin, 610 P.2d 891 (1980).
W. Va.: Lee v. Comer, 224 S.E.2d 721 (1976) (doctrine of parental immunity must be the exception rather than the rule).
Wis.: Goller v. White, 122 N.W.2d 193 (another landmark case).

[18] **Ky.:** Carricato v. Carricato, 384 S.W.2d 85 (1964) (child, age 20 years and 10 months declared emancipated).
Mo.: Wurth v. Wurth, 313 S.W.2d 161 (1959) (child, age 19, employed and paying board was held to be emancipated).
Tenn.: Brickey v. Brickey, 31 CCH 1325 (1964) (child, 19, married but still living at home while attending college, was held to be emancipated. Suit by mother against child).

[19] **Mass.:** Luster v. Luster, 13 N.E.2d 438 (1938).
Okla.: Tucker v. Tucker, 395 P.2d 67 (1964).

[5] Effect of the Death of Either Party

A mixed bag of some early and some more recent cases have ruled that the death of either party in an action between a parent and child would have no effect on the parental immunity doctrine.[20]

It has, however, been reasoned that the death of one of the parties in an action between a parent and child would no longer disturb "the domestic tranquility of the home" and these cases have accordingly held that such an action would abrogate parental immunity.[21]

[6] Intentional, Willful and Wanton Torts

Even in those jurisdictions that basically hold to the doctrine of parental immunity, the exception most often made is where the tor-

---

[20] **Fla.:** Russell, Admin. v. Meehan, 141 So. 2d 332 (1962).
Me.: Downs v. Poulin, 216 A.2d 29 (1966).
N.Y.: In re Estate of Jennings, 236 N.Y.S.2d 531 (1963).
N.C.: Capps v. Smith, 139 S.E.2d 19 (1964).
Okla.: Hill v. Graham, 424 P.2d 35 (1967) (death statute does not change the previous rights of the living); *but see* Stewart v. Harris, 434 P.2d 902 (1967), which appears to be contradictory.
Ore.: Chaffin v. Chaffin, 397 P.2d 771 (1964) (unless more than mere negligence is involved).
R.I.: Castillucci v. Castillucci, 188 A.2d 467 (1963).
S.C.: Maxey v. Sauls, 130 S.E.2d 570 (1963).

[21] **Ala.:** Bonner v. Williams, 370 F.2d 301 (5th Cir. 1967).
Ga.: Union Bank v. First Nat'l Bank, 362 F.2d 311 (5th Cir. 1966), *but see* Harrell v. Gardner, 154 S.E.2d 265 (1967), despite death statute.
Ill.: Jordan v. Jordan, 182 N.E.2d 365 (1962).
Ky.: Harlen Nat'l Bank v. Gross, 346 S.W.2d 482 (1961) *overruling* Harralson v. Thomas, 269 S.W.2d 276 (1954).
Mass.: Oliveria v. Oliveria, 25 N.E.2d 766 (1940).
Minn.: Albrecht v. Pothoff, 257 N.W. 377 (1934).
Mo.: Brennecke v. Kilpatrick, 336 S.W.2d 68 (1960).
N.H.: Gaudreau v. Gaudreau, 215 A.2d 695 (1965); Dean v. Smith, 211 A.2d 410 (1965).
N.J.: Palcsey v. Tepper, 176 A.2d 818 (1962), *but see* Heyman v. Gordon, 190 A.2d 670 (1963).
Pa.: Vidmar v. Sigmund, 162 A.2d 15 (1960).
S.C.: Maxey v. Sauls, 130 S.E.2d 570 (1963).
Tenn.: Logan v. Reaves, 354 S.W.2d 789 (1962).
W. Va.: Morgan v. Leuck, 72 S.E.2d 825 (1952).
Wis.: Krause v. Home Mut. Ins. Co., 112 N.W.2d 134 (1961).

tious act was viciously intentional or willful and wanton, as the courts often phrase it.[22]

There undoubtedly may be some controversy as to whether certain acts under specific circumstances would be considered as cruel and vicious, but I doubt whether any court would today enforce the parental immunity doctrine if the tortious acts involved excessively cruel and vicious acts.

[7] Gross Negligence and Drunken Driving

Despite the allegation of drunken driving, an Ohio court, in the case of *Teramano v. Teramano*,[23] held that in a case of injury committed solely because of the parents intoxication "there would be no evidence of actual intent to injure and that there would be no evidence upon which a jury would be justified in presuming malicious intent or abandonment of the parental relationship."

As to evil intent, I can go along, but I think that very few courts would today agree that a parent who was driving an automobile while intoxicated was not guilty of abandoning his or her parental responsibilities toward a child who was riding in that car.

Many courts today equate drunken driving with wanton and willful conduct, or, at least, gross negligence sufficient to warrant an exception to the parental immunity doctrine under such circumstances.[24]

---

[22] **Ariz.:** Windhauer v. O'Connor, 477 P.2d 561 (App., 1970).
 Ark.: Brown v. Cole, 129 S.W.2d 245 (1939) (involved the murder of a step-son).
 Cal.: Rosenfield v. Rosenfield, 34 Cal. Rptr. 479 (1963); People v. Stewart, 10 Cal. Rptr. 219 (1961). California has since abolished the parental immunity doctrine.
 Ga.: Buttrum v. Buttrum, 105 S.E.2d 510 (1958).
 Ill.: Brandt v. Keller, 109 N.E.2d 729 (1963).
 Md.: Mahnke v. Moore, 77 A.2d 923 (1951).
 Mich.: Rodebaugh v. Grand Trunk Western R.R., 145 N.W.2d 401 (1966).
 Neb.: Pullen v. Novak, 99 N.W.2d 16 (1959).
 N.J.: Small v. Rockfeld, 330 A.2d 335 (1974) (exception to the doctrine made for intentional acts or gross negligence).
 N.Y.: Harbin v. Harbin, 227 N.Y.S.2d 1023 (1962).
 Pa.: Vidmar v. Sigmund, 162 A.2d 15 (1960) (illegitimate child sued alleged father).
 Utah: Ellington v. Forest, 618 P.2d 37 (1980).
 Wash.: Stevens v. Murphy, 421 P.2d 668 (1966).
[23] 216 N.E.2d 375 (1966).
[24] **Ga.:** Buttrum v. Buttrum, 105 S.E.2d 510 (1958).
 Ill.: Nudd v. Matsoukus, 131 N.E.2d 525 (1956).
 Ore.: Cowgill v. Boock, 218 P.2d 445 (1950).
 Wash.: Hoffman v. Tracy, 406 P.2d 323 (1965).

INTRAFAMILY TORTS AND IMMUNITIES § 11.04[1]

In most cases, gross negligence, in and of itself, has not been held sufficient to warrant the abrogation of the parental immunity doctrine.[25]

[8] Change in Intrafamily Immunity Doctrines

Some states have taken the prerogative of abolishing the intrafamily immunity doctrines. Others have made it clear that they feel that any such change must be made by the legislatures and not by the courts.[26] Some courts that hold to the immunity doctrine have argued that since the immunity doctrine was a creation of the courts, the courts, accordingly, also have the right to change or abrogate such doctrine.[27]

§ 11.04 Husband/Wife Immunity Doctrine

[1] Historical Background

At common law, in matters that did not involve criminal jurisdiction, marriage, for the most part, merged a wife's legal interests with those of her husband. She could not, for instance, sue or be sued without joining her husband on her side of any issue or controversy, and he was entitled to any judgment that was obtained.

In matters involving torts, the husband became liable for any torts committed by his wife and was a partner with her in any action she might wish to bring for torts committed against her.[28] The end result was to nullify any right to sue her husband which a wife might otherwise have had and vice versa.

---

[25] **S.C.:** Maxey v. Sauls, 130 S.E.2d 570 (1963); Gunn v. Rollings, 157 S.E.2d 590 (1967).

[26] **Del.:** Alfree v. Alfree, 410 A.2d 161 (1979) (interspousal).
   Ill.: Mroczynski v. McGrath, 216 N.E.2d 137 (1966); Woodman v. Litchfield Community School Dist., 242 N.E.2d 780 (1968).
   Me.: Downs v. Poulin, 216 A.2d 29 (1966).
   Md.: Latz v. Latz, 272 A.2d 435 (App. 1971).
   Mo.: Brawner v. Brawner, 327 S.W.2d 808 (1959) (interspousal).
   Ore.: Smith v. Smith, 297 P.2d 572 (1955).
   See also 92 A.L.R.3d 901 (1979).

[27] **Ind.:** Brooks v. Robinson, 284 N.E.2d 794 (1972).
   Nev.: Rupert v. Stienne, 528 P.2d 1013 (1974).
   Va.: Surratt v. Thompson, 183 S.E.2d 200 (1971).
   Wash.: Freehe v. Freehe, 500 P.2d 771 (1972).

[28] **Mass.:** Nolin v. Pearson, 77 N.E. 800 (1906).
   See also Prosser, *The Handbook of Torts* (3d & 4th eds.).

§ 11.04[2] CASUALTY INSURANCE CLAIMS

Some early cases even justified husband/wife immunity by using many of the same arguments propounded to justify parental immunity, such as disruption of the family tranquility and the probability of fraud and collusion in such suits, plus the old legal concept that the husband and wife were one legal unit.[29]

In recent years, however, many more courts are holding such views to be obsolete, and in at least one case, despite statutory wording to the contrary.[30]

[2] **Married Women Acts**

About the middle of the nineteenth century, the state legislatures began to enact various married women emancipation statutes that spread rapidly throughout the country, and which are today almost universal. The scope of the Acts vary, as does the language and interpretation given to them by the state supreme courts. Originally, many of these statutes were not generally specific as to a wife's right to sue her husband in tort, but with amendments and more liberal interpretations in recent years, married women were finally given the freedom by our courts to sue and be sued for torts in their own name and without the necessity of joining their husband in the suit.[31]

When it came to actions for injury resulting from torts committed by a husband or wife against each other however, since many of the statutes were not specific on this subject, many of the early decisions favored the doctrine of immunity between the spouses and refused to permit the husband or wife to sue each other for torts resulting in injury, for reasons that today appear to be specious at best.

[3] **Present Trends Abrogating Husband/Wife Immunity**

The change in the attitude of many of the courts, and even some of the legislatures, became evident as far back as the 1930's. Since

---

[29] **Del.:** Alfree v. Alfree, 40 A.2d 161 (1979).
Fla.: Corren v. Corren, 47 So. 2d 774 (1950): Raisen v. Raisen, 379 So. 2d 352 (1979).
Ga.: Robeson v. International Indem. Co., 282 S.E.2d 896 (1981).
Kan.: Guffy v. Guffy, 631 P.2d 646 (1981).
Ohio: Thomas v. Herron, 253 N.E.2d 772 (1969) (even though alleged tort occurred before marriage).
See also Williams, "Intraspousal Tort Immunity in New Jersey: Dismantling the Barrier to Personal Injury Litigation,"10 Rutgers (Camden) L. J. 661 (1979).
[30] Sorensen v. Sorensen, 339 N.E.2d 907 (Mass. 1975).
[31] *See* McCurdy, "Personal Injury Torts Between Spouses," 4 Vill. L. Rev. 303 (1959).

INTRAFAMILY TORTS AND IMMUNITIES § 11.04[3]

then, the trend has been unmistakably in the direction of drastically curbing, or even abolishing the intraspousal immunity doctrine altogether.[32]

---

[32] **Ala.:** Penton v. Penton, 135 S. 481 (1931) (statute construed as abrogating the immunity doctrine).
  Alas.: Cramer v. Cramer, 379 P.2d 95 (1963) (statute construed as abrogating immunity doctrine).
  Ariz.: Windauer v. O'Connor, 485 P.2d 1157 (1971) (involving divorce and intentional tort), *but see* Burns v. Burns, 526 P.2d 717 (1974).
  Ark.: Leach v. Leach, 300 S.W.2d 15 (1957) (immunity doctrine abrogated).
  Cal.: Klein v. Klein, 26 Cal. Rptr. 102 (1962); Self v. Self, 26 Cal Rptr. 97 (1962) (immunity doctrine abrogated).
  Colo.: Rains v. Rains, 46 P.2d 740 (1935) (statute construed as abrogating immunity doctrine).
  Conn.: Silverman v. Silverman, 145 A.2d 826 (1958). *See also* Imperati v. Imperati, No. 18 6844 (Conn. Super. Ct. 1983).
  Idaho: Rogers v. Yellowstone Park Co., 539 P.2d 566 (1974).
  Ind.: Brooks v. Robinson, 284 N.E.2d 794 (1972).
  Iowa: Shook v. Crabb, 281 N.W.2d 616 (1979).
  Ky.: Layne v. Layne, 433 S.W.2d 116 (1968).
  La.: United States v. Haynes, 445 F.2d 907 (5th Cir. 1971) (involving direct action statute).
  Me.: MacDonald v. MacDonald, 412 A.2d 71 (1980).
  Md.: Lusby v. Lusby, 390 A.2d 77 (1978) (involving intentional tort); Boblitz v. Boblitz, 462 A.2d 506 (Md. 1983) (court of appeals abrogated interspousal immunity).
  Mass.: Lewis v. Lewis, 351 N.E.2d 526 (1976) (classic case); Brown v. Brown, 409 N.E.2d 717 (1980).
  Mich.: Hosko v. Hosko, 187 N.W.2d 236 (1971) (statute construed as abrogating immunity doctrine).
  Minn.: Beaudette v. Frana, 173 N.W.2d 416 (1969).
  Neb.: Imig v. March, 279 N.W.2d 382 (1979).
  Nev.: Rupert v. Stienne, 528 P.2d 1013 (1974) (motor vehicle exception).
  N.H.: Taylor v. Bullock, 279 A.2d 585 (1971) (even after divorce).
  N.J.: Immer v. Risko, 267 A.2d 481 (1970) (despite ambiguous statutory wording); Darrow v. Hanover Township, 278 A.2d 200 (1971) (interpreted prospectively); Merenoff v. Merenoff, 388 A.2d 951 (1978).
  N.M.: Maestras v. Overton, 531 P.2d 947 (1975).
  N.Y.: Weicker v. Weicker, 283 N.Y.S.2d 385 (1967); Holodook v. Spencer, 364 N.Y.S.2d 859 (1974).
  N.C.: Cox v. Shaw, 139 S.E.2d 676 (1965).
  N.D.: Fitzmaurice v. Fitzmaurice, 242 N.W.2d 526 (1932).
  Ohio: Varholla v. Varholla, 383 N.E.2d 888 (1978); Damm v. Elyria Lodge Co., 107 N.E.2d 337, *but see* Lyons v. Lyons, 208 N.E.2d 533 (involving motor vehicle exception).
  Ore.: Apitz v. Dames, 287 P.2d 585 (1955) (exception for intentional tort committed during marriage).
  Pa.: Hack v. Hack, 433 A.2d 859 (1981) (immunity doctrine abrogated).
  R.I.: Digby v. Digby, 388 A.2d 1 (1978) (involved motor vehicle exception).
  S.C.: Fowler v. Fowler, 130 S.E.2d 568 (1963).
  S.D.: Scotvold v. Scotvold, 298 N.W.2d 266 (1941).

§ 11.04[4] CASUALTY INSURANCE CLAIMS

[4] **Husband/Wife Immunity Still Holds**

Old doctrines sometimes die hard and some jurisdictions still basically hold fast to the doctrine of intraspousal immunity where the tort, committed during marriage, was due to ordinary negligence, and where both parties remained married and were living together at the time the tort was committed.[33]

Tex.: Bounds v. Caudle, 540 S.W.2d 925 (1977) (involved intentional tort).
Utah: Stoker v. Stoker, 616 P.2d 590 (1980) (involved intentional tort).
Vt.: Richard v. Richard, 300 A.2d 68 (1973).
Va.: Surratt v. Thompson, 183 S.E.2d 200 (1971).
Wash.: Freehe v. Freehe, 500 P.2d 771 (1972).
W. Va.: Coffindatter v. Coffindatter, 244 S.E.2d 338 (1978).
Wis.: Bodenhagen v. Farmers Mut. Ins. Co., 95 N.W.2d 822 (1959).
See also 92 A.L.R.3d 901, 923 (1979) and Bibliography at end of Chapter.

[33] **Ariz.:** Schwartz v. Schwartz, 447 P.2d 254 (1968); Burns v. Burns, 526 P.2d 717 (1974), *but see* Windaver v. O'Connor, 485 P.2d 1157 (1971) (intentional tort).
Del.: Saunders v. Hill, 202 A.2d 807 (1964) (despite death of both parties); Alfree v. Alfree, 410 A.2d 161 (1977).
D.C.: Mountjoy v. Mountjoy, 206 A.2d 733 (1965).
Fla.: Mims v. Mims, 305 So. 2d 787 (1974); Raisen v. Raisen, 379 So. 2d 352 (1970).
Ga.: Robeson v. International Ind. Co., 282 S.E.2d 896 (1981).
Ill.: Heckendorn v. First Nat'l Bank, 166 N.E.2d 571 (1960) (despite death of one party); Calvert v. Morgan, 190 N.E.2d 1 (1963).
Ind.: Brooks v. Robinson, 284 N.E.2d 794 (1972).
Kan.: Guffy v. Guffy, 631 P.2d 646 (1981).
Md.: Ennis v. Donovan, 161 A.2d 698 (1960), *but see* Lusby v. Lusby, 390 A.2d 77 (1978).
Miss.: Scales v. Scales, 151 S. 551 (1934), *but see* Deposit & Guar. Bank v. Nelson, 54 So. 2d 476 (1951), involving the murder of a wife.
Mo.: Ebel v. Fergusen, 478 S.W.2d 334 (1972).
Nev.: Morrisett v. Morrisett, 397 P.2d 184 (1964), *but see* Rupert v. Stienne, 528 P.2d 1013 (1974).
Ohio: Lyons v. Lyons, 208 N.E.2d 533 (1965).
Okla.: Hale v. Hale, 462 P.2d 681 (1967) (death does not change the rights of the living. Mother sued father for the death of their son).
Ore.: Chaffin v. Chaffin, 397 P.2d 771 (1964); Smith v. Smith, 287 P.2d 580 (1955), *but see* Apitz v. Dames, 287 P.2d 585 (1955), dealing with an intentional tort.
R.I.: Castellucci v. Castellucci, 188 A.2d 467 (1963) (despite death of one party), *but see* Digby v. Digby, 388 A.2d 1 (1978).
Tenn.: Gordon v. Pollard, 336 S.W.2d 25 (1960) (marriage annulled).
Texas: Latiolais v. Latiolais, 361 S.W.2d 252 (1962), *but see* Bounds v. Caudle, 560 S.W.2d 925 (1977), dealing with an intentional tort.
Utah: Rubaclava v. Gisseman, 384 P.2d 389 (1963) (despite death of one party), *but see* Stoker v. Stoker, 616 P.2d 590 (1980), which dealth with an intentional tort.
Va.: Furey v. Furey, 71 S.E.2d 191 (1952), *but see* Surratt v. Thompson, 183 S.E.2d 200 (1971).

[5] Torts Committed Before Marriage

Some jurisdictions have held to the husband/wife immunity doctrine even where the torts were committed before the parties were married,[34] and even if the tort was the result of gross negligence, and in some cases, willful and wanton or deliberate and intentional.[35]

A few cases have granted spousal immunity even after the parties have been divorced or after their marriage has been annulled,[36] while other jurisdictions have abrogated the immunity doctrine where the suit was brought after the parties were divorced or had obtained an annullment.[37]

[6] The Insurance Factor in Husband/Wife Immunity

As with parental immunity, some states abrogate interspousal immunity for torts resulting from the use of a motor vehicle, or from an insured accident.[38]

The presence of insurance coverage has been used as an argument both for and against the immunity doctrines, as was pointed out in

---

[34] **Fla.:** Amendola v. Amendola, 121 So. 2d 805 (1960).
Ga.: Carmichael v. Carmichael, 187 S.E. 116 (1936).
Ind.: Brooks v. Robinson, 270 N.E.2d 338 (App. 1971).
Md.: Hudson v. Hudson, 174 A.2d 339 (1961).
N.J.: Orr v. Orr, 176 A.2d 241 (1961). A mixed up state.
Ohio: Thomas v. Herron, 253 N.E.2d 772 (1969).
Pa.: Meisel v. Little, 180 A.2d 772 (1963), *but see* Hack v. Hack, 433 A.2d 859 (1981).
R.I.: Benevides v. Kelly, 157 A.2d 821 (1960).
Texas: Latiolais v. Latiolais, 361 S.W.2d 252 (1962), *but see* Bounds v. Caudle, 560 S.W.2d 925 (1977).

[35] **Ga.:** Wright v. Wright, 70 S.E.2d 152 (1952) (willful).
Kan.: Fisher v. Toler, 401 P.2d 1012 (1965) (assault).
Ill.: Hindman v. Hindman, 124 N.E.2d 344 (1965) (willful). Another mixed up state.
Ore.: Chaffin v. Chaffin, 397 P.2d 771 (1964) (gross negligence).

[36] **Miss.:** Ensminger v. Campbell, 134 So. 2d 728 (1961) (divorced).
Mo.: Ebel v. Fergusen, 478 S.W.2d 334 (1972).
Tenn.: Gordon v. Pollard, 336 S.W.2d 25 (1960) (annulled).

[37] **Ariz.:** Windauer v. O'Connor, 485 P.2d 1157 (1971).
La.: Gemillion v. Caffey, 71 So. 2d 670 (1954) (divorce after assault).
Md.: Lusby v. Lusby, 390 A.2d 77 (1978).

[38] **Ariz.:** Fernandez v. Romo, 649 P.2d 878 (1982).
Conn.: Imperati v. Imperati, No. 18 6844 (Conn. Super. Ct. 1983).
Neb.: Rupert v. Stienne, 528 P.2d 1013 (1974).
N.J.: Merenoff v. Merenoff, 388 A.2d 951 (1978); Immer v. Risko, 267 A.2d 481 (1970).
R.I.: Digby v. Digby, 388 A.2d 1 (1978).
Vt.: Richard v. Richard, 300 A.2d 637 (1973).

the discussion of parental immunity. Here too, some courts reasoned that the presence of insurance is an invitation to fraud and collusion and accordingly held that insurance coverage would not affect the intraspousal immunity doctrine where it would otherwise apply.[39]

§ 11.05 Prenatal Injury

[1] Introduction

Traditionally, up to recent years, an infant had no right to recover for injuries sustained before birth. An unborn child was considered to be part of the mother.[40] The legal terminology for an unborn child, derived from the French, is "en ventre sa mere." In medical terminology, at least after a certain stage of development, an unborn child is known as a fetus. The indefinite time at which a fetus may be able to be born and continue to live, usually between six and seven months, is known as viability.

As with other formerly entrenched legal concepts, this one is also being breached. The case of *Bonbrest v. Kotz* [41] was the first case to hold that a viable child could recover for prenatal injury where there was no statutory law either way and many jurisdictions have now followed the new ruling.

The next step concerned prenatal injuries to nonviable children and in the case of *Kelly v. Gregory* [42] recovery was allowed to an unborn child that received injuries while it was a three month fetus. The few jurisdictions which have followed this lead have reasoned that a child has a separate existence from the moment of conception.[43]

Since most jurisdictions still require viability of the unborn child as a prerequisite for recovery to prenatal injuries, the problem requires a determination of just when a child becomes viable. Despite my rather loose definition of viability, medical testimony is at vari-

---

[39] **Ariz.:** Burns v. Burns, 526 P.2d 717 (1974), *but see* Fernandez v. Romo, 649 P.2d 878 (1982).
Ohio: Lyons v. Lyons, 208 N.E.2d 533 (1965); Varholla v. Varholla, 383 N.E.2d 888 (1978).
Ore.: Smith v. Smith, 287 P.2d 583 (1955).
Va.: Brumfield v. Brumfield, 74 S.E.2d 170 (1953).
[40] Deitrich v. Inhabitants of Northampton, 133 Mass. 14 (1884).
[41] 65 F. Supp. 138 (D.C. 1946).
[42] 125 N.Y.S.2d 696 (1953).
[43] Smith v. Brennan, 31 N.J. 353, 157 A.2d 497 (1960).

ance, resulting in a battle of medical experts when a trial of this nature takes place.

Some courts have declared a child viable when a mother feels life. Others have held that a child is viable when its fetal heartbeats are audible.

In a very erudite article on the subject of an infant's right to recover in an action at law, in his or her own name, for a tort inflicted before it was born,[44] Robert J. Del Tufo stated that "in ascertaining the medical and legal status of the fetus, investigation must range from biological fact to philosophical abstraction." Add to that the rather hysterical atmosphere concerning the "right to life" movement and you have a situation where decisions will, as often as not, be rendered on the basis of emotion rather than logic.

The problems involved in a determination of the rights of an unborn child before birth are many and complex. While distinctions have been attempted to be made, differentiating "viable" from "quick," and whether such distinctions should even be made is very questionable. The term "fetus" itself has been used rather loosely to designate almost any stage of development of the unborn child in the mother's womb. The medical dictionaries refer to the word "fetus" as "the later stages of development when the body structures are in the recognizable form of its kind." Most of the so-called "keywords" used by the courts in a discussion of prenatal rights are vague, indefinite, and inconclusive. In addition, attitudes have changed in recent years, as social and scientific developments have become much more rapid and the doctrine of stare decisis is withering on the vine.

[2] Early Decisions

Until 1946 no jurisdiction recognized a common law right of action by an infant or his or her representative to bring an action for injuries received before birth.[45] The case of *Bonbrest v. Kotz* [46] was

---

[44] Del Tufo, "Recovery for Prenatal Torts: Action for Wrongful Death, 15 Rutgers L. Rev. 61 (1960).

[45] **Ill.:** Allaire v. St. Lukes Hosp., 56 N.E. 638 (1900).

Mass.: Dietrich v. Northampton, 138 Mass. 14 (1884) (first U.S. opinion on this subject. Justice Holmes, interpreting the Massachusetts statute, held that the fetus is a part of the mother's body and not a "person" in and of itself).

N.Y.: Drobner v. Peters, 133 N.E. 567 (1921;.

[46] 65 F. Supp. 138 (D.C. 1946).

the first to recognize the separate right of one who was injured before birth, to bring an action in his or her own name against the tortfeasor who caused the injury. Other courts quickly followed this lead until Alabama finally made it unanimous in 1972.[47]

It was finally recognized that a cause of action by one who was injured before birth should not be denied merely because of the difficulty in proving the facts or causal relationship of the tort,[48] or because of the possibility of fraudulent claims.[49]

Finally, it was pointed out that since the law had long recognized the separate right of action of unborn children to protect property and inheritance rights, it was obviously an anachronism not to do so in suits involving injury incurred prenatally.[50]

[a] The Restriction of Viability

A few states still held onto the "viable" condition, to the effect that a tort must have been inflicted on the fetus after it had become "viable."[51]

Having decided that a child has a right of action for prenatal injuries, decisions such as these then proceeded to becloud the issue in typical juridical fashion by holding that the injured fetus must have reached a certain state of development in order to justify recovery.[52]

A general composite definition of viable holds that where the fetus has reached a state of development so as to create a likelihood that it could be born alive and able to continue life outside the mother's womb, it may be considered to be viable. About the most succinct definition of viable was enunciated in the very first case that decided

---

[47] **Ala.:** Huskey v. Smith, 265 So. 2d 596 (1972).
U.S.: Roe v. Wade, 410 U.S. 113 (1972).
[48] **Mo.:** Steggall v. Morris, 258 S.W.2d 577 (1963).
N.H.: Bennett v. Hymers, 147 A.2d 108 (1958).
N.Y.: Woods v. Lancet, 102 N.E.2d 691 (1951).
[49] **Md.:** Damaswiecz v. Gorsuch, 79 A.2d 550 (1957).
N.J.: Smith v. Brennan, 157 A.2d 497 (1960).
[50] **D.C.:** Bonbrest v. Kotz, 65 F. Supp. 138 (D.C. 1946).
U.S.: Roe v. Wade, 410 U.S. 113 (1972).
[51] **D.C.:** Bonbrest v. Kotz, 65 F. Supp. 138 (1946).
Mo.: Steggall v. Morris, 258 S.W.2d 577 (1953).
Ore.: Mallison v. Pomeroy, 291 P.2d 225 (1955).
S.C.: Hall v. Murphy, 113 S.E.2d 790 (1960); Sox v. United States, 187 F. Supp. 465 (1960).
[52] *See* other cases in 40 A.L.R.3d 1222 (1971).

INTRAFAMILY TORTS AND IMMUNITIES § 11.05[2][b]

in favor of an action by someone who received prenatal injuries.[53] This case defined viable as "when a fetus had developed to the point of maturity to survive apart from its mother." Despite this excellent definition, at the time the decision was made there was no scientific way to make such a determination with any degree of certainty. Modern medical scientific advances have made "viability" considerably shorter, especially since Justice Blackmun put a tail on the Bonbrest decision. In *Roe v. Wade*,[54] he defined viability as "the interim point at which the fetus becomes . . . potentially able to live outside the mother's womb, *albeit with artificial aid."* (Italics added.) I have no doubt that in the near future viability will be almost synonymous with conception. No decision that I have read so far has been able to explain to my satisfaction why injury must be restricted to a period after the fetus is viable in order to justify a right of action. As a matter of fact, it has been pointed out that up to the time of the *Brennan* decision in 1960,[55] no jurisdiction which has approved recovery for injury to a viable fetus has later denied recovery to a child who survived an injury inflicted before it was viable. In fact, many courts have specifically rejected the viability requirement,[56] and the trend is almost unanimously in this direction.[57]

[b] When Fetus is "Quick"

Some decisions have held that the right of a person to bring an action for prenatal injury depends upon whether or not the fetus has become "quick." In the case of *Damasiewicz v. Gorsuch*,[58] a Maryland court held that "quick" was as effective a determining point as "viable" and then went on to imply that neither was really necessary.

"Quick" has been defined as the time when a fetus has developed to the state where it moves within the mother's body.[59]

---

[53] Bonbrest v. Kotz, 65 F. Supp. 138 (D.C. 1946).
[54] 410 U.S. 113 (1972).
[55] Smith v. Brennan, 157 A.2d 497 (N.J. 1960).
[56] Ga.: Hornbuckle v. Plantation Pipe Line Co., 93 S.E.2d 727 (1956).
N.J.: Smith v. Brennan, 157 A.2d 504 (1960).
N.Y.: Kelly v. Gregory, 125 N.Y.S.2d 696 (1953).
[57] Simon, "Parental Liability for Prenatal Injury," 14 Colum. J.L. & Soc. Probs. 47-90 (1978).
[58] 79 A.2d 550 (1957).
[59] State v. Timm, 12 N.W.2d 670 (Wis. 1944).

[c] "At Time of Conception"

Black's Legal Dictionary defines conception as being "the beginning of pregnancy," and even though this can still not be determined with absolute certainty, there is really no need to do so. All of the nonsense about viability, quick, etc. should be eliminated from further consideration because to do otherwise is not logical and practically all new decisions recognize this fact.[60]

[3] Right to Recover for Death of Stillborn Child

While I believe that granting the right of action to a person who has suffered prenatal injuries is fair and logical, I cannot agree that there is either justice or logic in permitting such an action to heirs and representatives of a child stillborn. Such an action could not possibly benefit the child, and the mother has an action of her own for injury and pain and suffering caused to her. Nor is there any similarity between the rights granted in property actions and those involving the death of the child for torts inflicted before birth.

In any event, what guarantee is there that the cost of raising and educating a child these days will not far exceed any possible benefit that might be derived financially?

Nevertheless, many jurisdictions do permit recovery even in the case of a stillborn child.[61] On the other hand, there seem to be more

---

[60] **Ga.:** Hornbuckle v. Plantation Pipe Line Co., 93 S.E.2d 727 (1956); Tucker v. Carmichael, 65 S.E.2d 909 (1951) (court held that "when life begins" is synonymous with "conception" and should be as effective as "viable").

Ill.: Daley v. Meier, 178 N.E.2d 691 (1961).

N.J.: Smith v. Brennan, 157 A.2d 497 (1960).

N.Y.: Kelly v. Gregory, 125 N.Y.S.2d 696 (1953).

Wis.: Puhl v. Milwaukee Auto. Ins. Co., 99 N.W.2d 163 (1959) ("Biological separability" theory is conditioned on birth of a living child).

U.S.: Rowe v. Wade, 410 U.S. 113 (1972).

[61] **Conn.:** Hatala v. Markiewicz, 224 A.2d 406 (1967); Simon v. Mallin, 380 A.2d 1353 (1977).

Kan.: Hale v. Manion, 368 P.2d 1 (1962).

Ky.: Mitchell v. Couch, 285 S.W.2d 901 (1955).

Idaho: Volk v. Baldazo, 651 P.2d 11 (1982).

Ill.: Chrisofogeorges v. Brandenburg, 304 N.E.2d 88 (1973).

La.: Danos v. St. Pierre, 402 So. 2d 633 (1981).

Mass.: Mone v. Greyhound Lines, Inc., 331 N.E.2d 916 (1975).

Mo.: O'Grady v. Brown, 654 S.W.2d 904 (1983) (decision limited to viable fetus only); Acton v. Shields, 386 S.W.2d 363 (1965) (statute, however, also requires pecuniary loss).

N.M.: Salazar v. St. Vincent Hosp., 619 P.2d 826 (1980).

INTRAFAMILY TORTS AND IMMUNITIES § 11.05[3][b]

decisions holding that no right of action exists for the representatives, executors, or heirs of a child who is stillborn.[62]

[a] Recovery Limited to Pecuniary Loss

A few of the decisions, based on their respective statutes, hold that any recovery for the death of an unborn child must be limited to the pecuniary loss suffered by the parents.[63]

[b] Right of Action for Child Born Alive May Be Time Limited

In discussing the rights of unborn children, a number of cases

---

Vt.: Vaillancourt v. Medical Center Hosp., 425 A.2d 92 (1980).
Wash.: Seattle-First Nat'l Bank v. Rankin, 367 P.2d 835 (1962).
[62] **Cal.:** Justus v. Atchison, 139 Cal. Rptr. 97 (1977); Norman v. Murphy, 268 P.2d 178 (unborn child is not a "person" as required by statute).
Fla.: Stern v. Miller, 348 So. 2d 303 (1977).
Iowa: Weitl v. Moes, 311 N.W.2d 259 (1981), *but see* Dunn v. Rose, Way, Inc., 333 N.W.2d 830 (1983), where action was permitted only if brought by parents and not in the name of the stillborn child).
Mass.: Leccase v. McDonough, 279 N.E.2d 339 (1972); Keyes v. Construction Service Co., 165 N.E.2d 912 (1960).
Mo.: Acton v. Shields, 386 S.W.2d 363 (1965) (statute requires pecuniary loss so there was no need to determine "person").
Neb.: Drabbels v. Skelly Oil Co., 50 N.W.2d 229 (1951).
N.J.: Graf v. Taggert, 204 A.2d 140 (1964) (statute limited recovery to pecuniary loss which was too speculative to determine. No need to decide whether unborn child was a "person").
N.Y.: Endresz v. Friedberg, 301 N.Y.S.2d 65 (1969); In re Logan, 156 N.Y.S.2d 152 (1956), *aff'd,* 166 N.Y.S.2d 3 (1957).
Okla.: Howell v. Rushing, 261 P.2d 217 (1953).
Pa.: Carroll v. Skloff, 202 A.2d 9 (1964); Scott v. Kopp, 431 A.2d 959 (1981).
R.I.: Gorman v. Budlong, 49 A. 704 (1901).
Tenn.: Hogan v. McDaniel, 319 S.W.2d 221 (1958); Durrett v. Owens, 371 S.W.2d 433 (1963) (no right of action for stillborn).
Tex.: Magnolia Coca Cola Bottling Co. v. Jordan, 78 S.W.2d 944 (1935).
Wis.: Puhl v. Milwaukee Auto. Ins. Co., 99 N.W.2d 163 (1959) (right of action exists only if child is born alive).
[63] **Mass.:** Keyes Construction Service, Inc., 165 N.E.2d 912 (1960) (recovery granted).
Mo.: Acton v. Shields, 386 S.W.2d 363 (1965) (no recovery since there was no pecuniary loss).
S.C.: Hall v. Murphy, 113 S.E.2d 790 (1960) (recovery granted).
Tenn.: Shousha v. Matthews Drivurself Service, Inc., 358 S.W.2d 471 (1962) (recovery granted).

§ 11.05[4]

place time limits on when an action might be brought on the basis of the death of an injured child, who had been born alive but died shortly after its birth.[64]

[4] **Requirement of Viability in Death Caused by Prenatal Injury**

Finally we come back to a discussion of the need for an unborn child to be considered as viable before a right of action is given to the unborn infant. There are some jurisdictions that still hold this to be a requirement for recovery by the heirs even where the child dies shortly after birth in some circumstances.

In the case of *Amann v. Faidy* [65] the prenatally injured child was born alive and received its injury while it was viable and both seem to have been a requirement to recovery.

In *Verkennes v. Corniea* [66] the child was viable when injured and the court made a point of this factor.

§ 11.06 **Child's Right of Action for Wrongful Life**

Wrongful life claims involve the allegation that life itself is the injury, as distinguished from wrongful injuries committed upon the prenatal child.

An action for wrongful life by a child against the attending doctor or its parents, is a recent development arising out of some remarkable medical advances that can reveal defects in the fetus that would show up in the child subsequent to birth. It also involves knowledge recently developed concerning the effects of certain diseases of the pregnant mother on the child when born. Techniques known as amniosentesis and ultrasound can reveal genetic defects, and the aftereffects of certain diseases on pregnant mothers have also become common knowledge. It has, accordingly, become routine for obstetri-

---

[64] Ala.: Haskey v. Smith, 265 So. 2d 596 (1972).
Ill.: Amann v. Faidy, 114 N.E.2d 412 (1953).
Mass.: Keyes v. Construction Service, Inc., 165 N.E.2d 912 (1960).
S.C.: Hall v. Murphy, 113 S.E.2d 790 (1960) (viable child born alive).
Tenn.: Shousha v. Matthews Drivurself Service, 358 S.W.2d 471 (1962).
Wis.: Puhl v. Milwaukee Auto. Ins. Co., 99 N.W. 2d 163 (1959).
[65] 114 N.E.2d 412 (Ill. 1953).
[66] 38 N.W.2d 838 (Minn. 1949).

cians to make such tests if requested to do so after the doctor has informed the parents of their advisability.

So far, such actions by children against their parents who knew, or should have reasonably known, that such tests would have revealed serious defects in the unborn child have not met with much success, except in a few instances.[67]

Suits for wrongful life, where the action is brought by a child who suffered serious defects, or by its parents, must be distinguished from "dissatisfied life" claims where a healthy child brings a suit, usually for illegitimacy, against its parents.[68]

The case of *Geitman v. Cosgrove*[69] is an early case involving a child who brought an action against the attending physician for wrongful life. The child suffered from serious defects in sight, hearing, and speech as a result of rubella (German Measles) contracted by the mother during pregnancy. The attending doctors had informed the mother that her disease would have no effect on the child born of this pregnancy. The trial court dismissed the suit before it reached the jury and the supreme court affirmed the decision on the basis that any reasonable calculation of compensatory damages would be impossible, among other grounds. The value of defective life versus no life poses an unanswerable question and most courts thus far have refused to face it.[70]

The first case to hold that there was no reason in public policy to bar a child from stating a cause of action for wrongful life against her mother was *Curlender v. Bio-Science Laboratories*.[71] In a subsequent

---

[67] Cal.: Turpin v. Sartini, 182 Cal. Rptr. 337 (1982).
N.J.: Procanik v. Cillo, 478 A.2d 755 (1984).
Wash.: Harebeson v. Parke-Davis, 656 P.2d 483 (1983).
[68] Zapeda v. Zapeda, 190 N.E.2d 849 (Ill. App. 1963) (all such suits, including this one, have, to date, been rejected).
See also Kohnen & Zoellner, "Wrongful Life: Existence v. Nonexistence—Is Life Always Preferable?", FIC Quarterly, Spring 1986.
[69] 227 A.2d 689 (N.J. 1970).
[70] Fla.: Public Health Trust v. Brown, 388 So. 2d 1084 (App. 1980).
N.Y.: Howard v. Lecher, 397 N.Y.S.2d 363 (1977); Becker v. Schwartz, 413 N.Y.S.2d 895 (1978).
Pa.: Gildiner v. The Jefferson Univ. Hosp., 451 F. Supp. 692 (1978).
Tex.: Jacobs v. Theimer, 519 S.W.2d 846 (1975).
Wis.: Dumer v. St. Michaels Hosp., 233 N.W.2d 372 (1975).
[71] 165 Cal. Rptr. 477 (1980).

article on this subject,[72] the author states that "the hypothesized duty (to abort) is irreconcilable with a woman's constitutionally protected right of privacy." The decision in the *Curlender* case was subsequently overruled in the case of *Turpin v. Sartini*.[73]

While the right of privacy of a mother to terminate a pregnancy is not mentioned in the Constitution, the Supreme Court has, by interpretation of the ninth and fourteenth amendments, recognized a woman's right of privacy so far as her own body is concerned, and the right to make a decision concerning abortion. It has also been held that procreation is a basic personal right.[74]

The California legislature reacted to the *Curlender* decision by enacting a statute precluding *parental* liability for wrongful life.[75]

To cite as an example, some of the great works of art, literature, and music have been created by handicapped people, as an argument favoring defective birth, is to miss the point that such a decision is purely a personal one. Obviously, the individual who has decided to bring an action in all good faith, does not believe that such a life is a blessing.

While this problem poses an interesting philosophical question, that is no satisfaction to a person who rues the day he or she was born. A monetary award, in these days of reconstructive miracles, might at least give a person born with defects a fair chance to have them corrected.

§ 11.07 Bibliography

Brinker, "Interspousal Tort Immunity in Missouri," 47 Mo. L. Rev. 519 (1982).

Casey, "The Trend of Interspousal and Parental Immunity—Cakewalk Liability," Insurance Counsel Journal, July 1978.

Chernaik, "Recovery for Prenatal Injuries: The Right of a Child Against Its Mother," 10 Suffolk U.L. Rev. 582 (1976).

Comment, Levin, "Constitutionality of Legislative Imposition of Vicarious Parental Liability for Delinquent Acts of Juveniles," 12 U. Balt. L. Rev. 171 (1982).

---

[72] Waters, "Wrongful Life: The Implications of Suits in Wrongful Life Brought by Children Against Their Parents," 31 Drake L. Rev. 411 (Spring 1981).

[73] 182 Cal. Rptr. 337 (1982).

[74] Roe v. Wade, 410 U.S. 113 (1973).

[75] *See* California Civil Code § 43.6. *See also* Kohnen & Zoellner, *supra* note 68.

Comment, "Negligence and the Unborn Child: A Time for Change," 18 S.D.L. Rev. 204-20 (1975).
Comment, "Prenatal Injuries and Wrongful Death," 18 Vand. L. Rev. 847 (March 1965).
Comment, "The Reasonable Parent Standard: An Alternative to Parent-Child Tort Immunity," 47 U. Colo. L. Rev. 795 (1976).
Comment, "Torts—Interspousal Immunity—Unliquidated Tort Claims Between Spouses No Longer Barred—Pennsylvania Abrogates Doctrine of Interspousal Immunity as Unsupported by Law, Logic or Public Policy," 27 Vill. L. Rev. 432 (1981-82).
Comment, "Wrongful Life and a Fundamental Right to be Born Healthy," 27 Buffalo L. Rev. 537 (1978).
Del Tufo, "Recovery for Prenatal Torts: Actions for Wrongful Death," 15 Rutgers L. Rev. 61 (1960).
Dinsdale, "Child v. Parent: A Viable New Tort of Wrongful Life?", 24 Ariz. L. Rev. 391 (Spring 1982).
Hinkle, "Intrafamily Litigation—Parent and Child," Insurance Law Journal, March 1968.
Hollister, "Parent-Child Immunity: A Doctrine in Search of Justification," 50 Fordham L. Rev. 489 (March 1982).
Lederleitner, "Immunity for the Modern Day Parent," Insurance Law Journal, May 1971.
Marvin, "Discerning the Parent's Liability for the Harm Inflicted by a Nondiscerning Child," 44 La. L. Rev. 1213 (May 1984).
Miller, "No Recovery for Injury to a Viable Fetus Which Is Stillborn," Insurance Counsel Journal, January 1969.
Poust, "Parent-Child Tort Immunity: Common Sense to Some—Nonsense to Others, 36 Insurance Counsel Journal 374 (July 1969).
Prosser & Keeton (5th ed.) p. 913, ¶123.
Robertson, "Toward Rational Boundaries of Tort Liability for Injury to the Unborn," Duke L.J. 1401 (1978).
Simon, "Parental Liability for Prenatal Injury," 14 Colum. J.L. & Soc. Probs. 47-59 (1978).
Thompson, "Intrafamily Immunity: A Vanishing Myth?", F.I.C. Quarterly, Spring 1982.
Waters, "Wrongful Life: The Implications of Suits in Wrongful Life Brought by Children Against Their Parents," 31 Drake L. Rev. 411 (Spring 1982).

CHAPTER 12

Governmental and Charitable Immunities

§ 12.01 Governmental Immunity
    [1] History and Introduction
    [2] Federal Immunities
        [a] Absolute Immunity—Judicial and Legislative
    [3] State and Municipal Immunities
    [4] "Governmental" or "Planning" Acts and Quasi-Immunities
    [5] Riots and Civil Disturbances
    [6] Ministerial or Proprietary Acts versus Governmental Acts
    [7] Defense of Discretionary Acts
§ 12.02 Effect of Insurance Coverage on Immunity
§ 12.03 Punitive Damages in Governmental Immunity Cases
§ 12.04 The Doctrine of Charitable Immunity
    [1] Charitable Immunity Practically Abolished
    [2] Effect of Insurance Coverage on the Charitable Immunity Doctrine
§ 12.05 Bibliography

§ 12.01 Governmental Immunity

[1] History and Introduction

The theory of governmental immunity had its roots in the days when English Kings were held to be above the courts. In view of the fact the king appointed the judges, he was considered to have immunity from their jurisdiction. Accordingly, the rule of sovereign immunity was established.

The doctrine of governmental immunity was adopted in the United States in the case of *Cohen v. Virginia*,[1] and reaffirmed in the early 1900's in the case of *Kawananoka v. Polyblank*,[2] in which Justice Holmes stated that the doctrine of governmental immunity was applicable "on the logical and practical ground that there can be no

---

[1] 19 U.S. 264 (1821).
[2] 205 U.S. 349 (1907).

legal right against the authority that makes the law on which the right depends."

It is only in very recent years that the trend in our courts and legislative bodies has been in the opposite direction, and seems to be going that way at an ever-increasing rate.

The trend is generally to breach the immunity doctrine one way or another. Without further pretense, the courts have said "It is plainly unjust to refuse relief (on the basis of governmental immunity) to persons injured by the wrongful conduct of the state."[3]

A number of states have established administrative agencies to hear and make a determination of claims against the state.[4] Most states have special procedural, monetary and other requirements and limitations, especially where administrative agencies have been set up to handle claims against the state.

In the discussion of governmental immunities, we are dealing with three separate governmental entities: (1) federal, (2) state, and (3) municipal. Of necessity, this section will be confined to highlighting the major problems involved.

[2] Federal Immunities

Before the enactment of the Federal Tort Claims Act of 1946, the only way suit could be instituted against the United States government was when it consented to be sued under several narrow statutes which preceded the Act, or to have Congress pass a private bill to cover an individual situation. Such a process was so burdensome that Congress finally passed the Federal Tort Claims Act (FTCA) in order to alleviate the hardship.[5]

Jurisdiction over actions involving the federal government and its employees is vested exclusively in the federal courts and no such action can be maintained in the state courts.

While one section of the FTCA provides for liability on the part of the federal government to the same degree as that which would be imposed on a private individual, other parts of the Act seem to

---

[3] Willis v. Dep't of Conservation & Ecol., 264 A.2d 34 (N.J. 1970).

[4] *Prosser & Keaton on Torts* (5th ed. 1984) names Alabama, Arkansas, Georgia, Kentucky, North Carolina, Tennessee, West Virginia, and Wisconsin.

[5] *Prosser & Keeton on Torts* (5th ed. 1984), p. 1034.

exclude actions based on strict liability.[6] As Professor Van Alstyne put it, "To bury sovereign immunity beneath a respectable mound . . . is a notable achievement. To keep it decently interred however, is another problem."[7]

One great exception that has been made to the doctrine of governmental immunity for federal officers is where the tort involved violated a constitutional right of an individual.[8]

The Act contains other exceptions where immunity is retained. The case of *Ferris v. United States* [9] closed the door to certain specific categories of governmental employees. Members of the armed services, for instance, are denied the right to sue the government except where injury or death was due to an act that was not incidental to enlistment in the services.[10] The same applies to federal prisoners whose injuries were received while they were prisoners.[11]

Probably the most important exception where the employee's immunity still prevails involves governmental conduct when the act was done while the employee was performing discretionary functions or duties, which in federal court terminology have usually been referred to as "policy" or "planning judgment" acts.[12] The theme of exception for "discretionary" acts runs throughout many of the decisions not only at the federal level, but, as will be seen, at the state and municipal level as well.

The courts have distinguished "policy" or "planning" activities from "operational" acts which carry out the directives of the planners. Acts on the "operational" level have been held not to be immune from suit.[13] Unfortunately, there is no uniformity in the decisions as to what is or is not "operational," "planning," or "discretionary."

---

[6] *See Prosser & Keeton* (5th ed.) for cases listed in fn. 42, p. 1036.

[7] "Government Tort Liability: A Decade of Change," U. Ill. Law Forum (1966).

[8] Butz v. Economou, 438 U.S. 478 (1978); Harlow v. Fitzgerald, 457 U.S. 800 (1982).

[9] 340 U.S. 135 (1950).

[10] United States v. Brown, 348 U.S. 110 (1954); Brooks v. United States, 337 U.S. 49 (1949).

[11] United States v. Demko, 385 U.S. 149 (1966) (unless the prisoner is not covered by a compensation plan); United States v. Muniz, 374 U.S. 150 (1963). Other exceptions have been made as noted by *Prosser & Keeton on Torts* (5th ed. 1984).

[12] Dalehite v. United States, 346 U.S. 15 (1953); Stanley v. State, 197 N.W.2d 599 (Iowa 1972) (this case gives a good review of federal immunity).

[13] Indian Towing Co. v. United States, 350 U.S. 61 (1955).

§ 12.01[2]   CASUALTY INSURANCE CLAIMS

Even where the basic governmental immunity might apply, the immunity is removed in situations involving intentional torts.[14]

Early attacks on governmental immunity made distinctions between the immunity of the government itself and that of its employees, and whether or not such employees were engaged in "governmental" or mere "proprietary" duties. These questions are still being hotly debated to this day and the battle seems to be getting more intense. As we shall see, in some cases the courts declare the battle to be between "discretionary" and "ministerial" functions. Other decisions make distinctions between "operational" and "proprietary" duties; still others between "planning" and "operational" and more. There is absolutely no uniformity, even in terminology; all of which seems to add up to whether the employee had an executive job and was functioning in an executive capacity at the time, or was a clerical employee who carried out regular routine duties.

This, in itself, is by no means any kind of yardstick for granting or not granting immunity since some so-called lower level employees such as police officers and firemen are faced daily with decisionmaking problems upon which their actions must depend. The question as to where we can draw a line between employees whose actions may be immune from suit and those whose actions may not be immune, even assuming governmental duties are involved, is absolutely impossible to determine by any definite standard. Even two courts in the same jurisdiction differ on this point.

Another area of confusion revolves around the eleventh amendment which reads "The Judicial power of the United States shall not be construed to extend to any suit in law or equity, commenced or prosecuted against one of the United States or Citizens of another state. . . ." Thus, governmental immunity protects states from suits in their own courts while the eleventh amendment immunity protects states from suits in federal court. That's what was supposed to happen, but it didn't, by a long shot.

Under three congressional acts, the United States has waived some of its own immunities by permitting some suits or reviews of some

---

[14] Moffett v. United States, 430 F. Supp. 34 (Tenn. 1976). *See also* Schiff, "Torts—Government Immunity—The Intentional Torts Exception to the Federal Tort Claims Act Does Not Preclude an Action Against the Federal Government for Negligent Failure to Discharge or Supervise Federal Employee Who Subsequently Commits Intentionally Tortious Conduct," 29 Vill. L. Rev. 1017 (June 1984).

GOVERNMENTAL IMMUNITIES § 12.01[2][a]

decisions.[15] Practically all states have, by statute and/or court decision, made various exceptions to a greater or lesser degree on the idea of total governmental immunity.

[a] Absolute Immunity—Judicial and Legislative

The only person who is absolutely immune from liability, even in a situation that might involve a violation of Constitutional rights, is the President of the United States while in office.[16]

However, even in those states where governmental immunities have been all but abolished, the immunities holding legislators and judges immune from acts committed while they were in the course of their official duties, are still held valid.[17] The judges and legislators, however, must have acted within the scope of their judicial and legislative functions to be held immune from suit in most cases.[18]

In the case of *Stump v. Sparkman*[19] the court made some effort to define "judicial function" by stating that if the act is a function normally performed by a judge in his judicial capacity, such an act creates immunity for the judge, even where the act may be considered excessive.

Immunity is also granted to judicial officials who are acting in a quasi-judicial capacity at the time of the alleged wrongdoing,[20] but some courts have hedged on granting absolute immunity to such "quasi-judicial" functionaries unless they are acting under superior orders.[21]

The immunity granted to legislators is also absolute, so long as they

---

[15] *See Prosser & Keeton on Torts* (5th ed.) for more on this subject.

[16] Nixon v. Fitzgerald, 457 U.S. 731 (1982).

[17] Restatement (Second) of Torts, § 895 B, comment c. *See* Stump v. Sparkman, 435 U.S. 349 (1978); Huendling v. Jensen, 168 N.W.2d 745 (Iowa 1969) (even where a corrupt justice of the peace used his judicial power to collect civil debts for a commission); Allen v. Secor, 195 So. 2d 586 (Fla. 1967); Pierson v. Ray, 386 U.S. 547 (1967).

[18] Rankin v. Howard, 633 F.2d 844 (9th Cir. 1980) (judge); Harris v. Harvey, 605 F.2d 330 (7th Cir. 1979) (judge); Hutchinson v. Proxmire, 443 U.S. 111 (1979) (senator); Zarcone v. Perry, 572 F.2d 52 (2d Cir. 1978) (judge); Stump v. Sparkman, 435 U.S. 349 (1978) (judge); Pierson v. Ray, 386 U.S. 547 (1967) (judge); Tenney v. Brandhove, 341 U.S. 367 (1951).

[19] 435 U.S. 349 (1978).

[20] Imbler v. Pachtman, 424 U.S. 409 (1976).

[21] Tymiak v. Omodt, 676 F.2d 306 (8th Cir. 1982); Tarter v. Hury, 646 F.2d 1010 (5th Cir. 1981); Morrison v. Jones, 607 F.2d 1269 (9th Cir. 1979); Imbler v. Pachtman, 424 U.S. 409 (1976).

act within the scope of their legislative duties.[22]

Qualified immunity may also be given to certain legislative, as well as judicial employees, if their functions were legislative or judicial at the time of the alleged wrongdoing.[23]

Executive officials are usually granted qualified immunity if they were acting within the scope of their official duties.[24] The case of *Wood v. Strickland* [25] held that an executive official in the performance of his discretionary acts, will be held immune from civil suit unless:

1. He knew, or reasonably should have known that his actions violated the plaintiff's constitutional rights;
2. He took the action with malicious intent to cause a deprivation of constitutional rights.

The good faith of such official does not in and of itself, grant him immunity.[26] Good faith does however have a bearing in the case of officials who have the privilege of qualified immunity in some states. The question of who may be entitled to qualified immunity and as to what part discretion plays in the granting of immunity, involves so many types of "officials" and so many diverse situations that each case deserves detailed legal research in the particular jurisdiction involved. Executive officials, for instance, have been so diverse a group as to include a state governor, president of a state university, members of the state National Guard, members of various police organizations, and state hospital employees, among others, and, again, jurisdictions differ.

[3] **State and Municipal Immunities**

In a very general way, the Supreme Court noted that in a dual system of government, cities are not sovereign and do not receive all of the federal deference of the states that create them.[27] Accordingly, while governmental immunities are more leniently granted

---

[22] Gravel v. United States, 408 U.S. 606 (1972).
[23] Butz v. Economou, 438 U.S. 478 (1978); Blake v. Rupe, 651 P.2d 1096 (Wyo. 1982); Johnson v. Granholm, 662 F.2d 449 (6th Cir. 1981); Dineen v. Daughan, 381 A.2d 663 (Me. 1978) (libel action, attorney's pleadings held immune).
[24] Wood v. Strickland, 420 U.S. 308 (1975).
[25] *Id.*
[26] Owen v. City of Independence, 445 U.S. 622, 100 S. Ct. 1398 (1980).
[27] City of Lafayette v. Louisiana Power & Light Co., 435 U.S. 389 (1978).

GOVERNMENTAL IMMUNITIES § 12.01[3]

to states and their employees, the judicial attitude of a particular jurisdiction reflects pretty much the same basic principles of law for both. However, the confusion is just as great, or perhaps more so, since there are many more municipalities than there are states.

The immunity granted to states and municipalities and their employees is always conditional to a greater or lesser degree, either as a result of common law decision, legislative enactment, or judicial interpretation of legislative intent.

The previously held opinion that there must have been a violation of the Constitution by "a policy statement, ordinance, regulation or decision" before a tort action could be maintained against a municipality[28] was overturned in the case of *Monell v. Dep't of Social Services*[29] where the Supreme Court held that a municipality was a "person" subject to suit under section 1983 of title 42. As has, and will be seen, such positive statements cannot be taken at face value in dealing with governmental immunities. For instance, in the case of *Owens v. Haas*,[30] the Federal Court of Appeals stated that "if the failure to supervise or the lack of a proper training program was so severe as to reach the level of 'gross negligence' or 'deliberate indifference' to the deprivation of the plaintiff's constitutional rights," a municipality may be held liable. In this case, the brutal and premeditated beating of a prisoner by several guards was indication of "a deliberate indifference to the plaintiff's constitutional rights in failing to properly train the prison guards."

Ordinarily, a single instance, such as the use of excessive force, would not, of itself, be sufficient to create an indication of acquiescence or deliberate indifference by the municipality.[31] Nevertheless, in the *Monell* case,[32] the Supreme Court did not abolish the traditional common law municipal immunities, despite the previously mentioned action under section 1983 of title 42.[33] It was held that any other interpretation would require Congressional action.[34]

---

[28] Monroe v. Pape, 365 U.S. 167 (1961).
[29] Monell v. Dep't of Social Services, 436 U.S. 658 (1978).
[30] 601 F.2d 1242 (2d Cir.), *cert. denied*, 440 U.S. 980 (1979).
[31] Cattan v. City of New York, 523 F. Supp. 598 (N.Y. 1981); Turpin v. West Haven, 449 U.S. 1016 (1980).
[32] 436 U.S. 658 (1978).
[33] Procunier v. Navarette, 434 U.S. 555 (1978).
[34] Owens v. Haas, 601 F.2d 1242 (1979). *See also* the excellent article by Moskowitz, Rothstein & Flanagan, "The Defense of Municipalities: A Primer on Municipal Liability," Insurance Counsel Journal, April 1984.

[4] "Governmental" or "Planning" Acts and Quasi-Immunities

A governmental "official" acting within the scope of his or her official functions, is generally immune from suit as an individual. The major problems encountered in this area involve quasi-officials or those at a lower level who commit torts. The question of immunity then depends on whether or not the employee was acting in pursuit of his governmental duties at the time of the wrongdoing.

The distinction becomes more difficult when we get down to the lower level of municipalities. In one area, there is at least some general understanding that at the functioning street level, policemen and women are in a special category since the everyday work that they are required to do involves constant decisionmaking upon which lives can depend. In some states specific protection is given to police members (and firemen) on the basis of a "public duty" exception, so that to members of these groups, immunity is still granted in varying degrees.[35] With some basic exceptions, municipalities and the police members have been accorded immunity while acting within the course of their work, and if no great excesses are committed.[36]

Other jobs are more difficult to place in the governmental immunity category. A court in Wyoming held that the issuance of a certificate of title for an automobile was a governmental duty warranting immunity for the county clerk and the clerk who was following his boss' governmental planning as well.[37] In New Jersey, a building inspector who was allegedly negligent in granting a certificate of occupancy, was held immune since his act was held to be governmental in nature.[38] In Iowa, a Conservation Board and its members were held immune from suit arising out of an alleged nuisance committed in the maintenance of a city park.[39] A Kansas court also held a municipality immune from suit for the commission of an alleged nuisance,

---

[35] Mendez v. Blackburn, 226 So. 2d 340 (Fla. 1969); Magenheimer v. State ex rel. Dalton, 90 N.E.2d 813 (Ind. App. 1950); Jahnke v. City of Des Moines, 191 N.W.2d 780 (Iowa 1971); Wilson v. Nepstad, 282 N.W.2d 664 (Iowa 1979).

[36] Pa.: Smeltz v. Copeland, 269 A.2d 466 (1970).

[37] Denver Buick v. Pearson, 465 P.2d 512 (Wyo. 1970).

[38] Fiduccia v. Summit Hill Constr. Co., 262 A.2d 920 (1970).

[39] Iseminger v. Black Hawk City, 175 N.W.2d 374 (1970).

GOVERNMENTAL IMMUNITIES § 12.01[5]

and other states have done likewise.[40] City park care was held to be governmental in Alabama,[41] but in New Mexico the court deemed such activity to be proprietary in nature and not cloaked with immunity.[42]

As is obvious, some courts favor governmental immunity,[43] while others take a much more lenient attitude in favor of protecting the rights of the plaintiff by increasingly breaching that immunity.[44]

Often, judicial decisions are made with little or no regard or discussion of the question of governmental immunity, particularly where justice appears to call for redress.[45]

In the case of *Anderson v. City of Minneapolis,*[46] the court held that despite the doctrine of governmental immunity, the state can be held liable for damages resulting from obviously dangerous defects in plans and construction where the state had notice of the danger and while negligence was involved during the time that the state had control.

[5] Riots and Civil Disturbances

Injury or damage resulting from riots are ordinarily covered by special enactment both at the state and federal level. The statutes go both ways, some imposing strict liability on the part of the government or municipality, some retaining governmental immunity, and others making exceptions in cases where insurance covers the losses.

---

[40] Woods v. Kansas Turnpike Auth., 472 P.2d 219 (1970). *See also Prosser & Keeton on Torts* (5th ed.) pp. 1054-55.
[41] Jones v. City of Birmingham, 224 So. 2d 492 (1969).
[42] Murphy v. City of Carlsbad, 348 P.2d 492 (N.M. 1960).
[43] **Cal.:** Lipman v. Brisbane Elem. School Dist., 11 Cal. Rptr. 97 (1964).
Conn.: Donnelly v. Ives, 268 A.2d 406 (1970).
Mich.: Thomas v. State Highway Dep't, 247 N.W.2d 530 (1970).
Ore.: Smith v. Cooper, 475 P.2d 78 (1970).
[44] **Cal.:** Johnson v. State, 73 Cal. Rptr. 240 (1968) (California goes both ways).
Iowa: Lewis v. State, 256 N.W.2d 181 (1977) (Iowa goes both ways, but it is to be noted that there is more leniency in breaching immunity at the municipal level).
La.: Breaux v. State, 326 So. 2d 481 (1976).
Neb.: Daniels v. Anderson, 237 N.W.2d 397 (1975).
Wash.: King v. City of Seattle, 525 P.2d 228 (1974).
[45] **N.Y.:** Bartels v. City of Westchester, 429 N.Y.S.2d 906 (1980).
Neb.: Koepf v. City of York, 251 N.W.2d 866 (1977).
[46] 296 N.W.2d 383 (Minn. 1980).

[6] Ministerial or Proprietary Acts versus Governmental Acts

Those jurisdictions that have not done away with governmental immunity have, in many instances, breached this doctrine partially by making a distinction between "proprietary" and "governmental" acts which resulted in injury or damage.

While there is much legislation and many decisions on this subject, as already noted, neither term has been clearly defined. The determination of what may be a ministerial or a proprietary act is often quite arbitrary. Governmental functions are ordinarily more easy to determine.

It has generally been held that governmental duties encompass those areas that would pose threats to the quality and efficiency of the government if damages or even litigation were permitted to be brought against them.

Another generality holds that when an official or governmental policy is implemented and becomes a ministerial or proprietary act, an employee may no longer be granted governmental immunity.[47] To put it another way, some decisions have held that when a ministerial act in execution of a discretionary policy is performed negligently, the defense of governmental immunity is no longer available to the municipality or its employees.[48]

In the *Puffer* case[49] the court held that a clerk's decision to issue a marriage license is discretionary and entitled to a good faith defense, but the act of issuing the license is clerical (ministerial) and therefore not entitled to immunity.[50]

In the Oklahoma case of *Hershel v. University Hospital Foundation*,[51] the court held that as to proprietary functions of a state, immunity no longer applies. This was carried a step further in

---

[47] Owen v. City of Independence, 445 U.S. 622 (1980) (stated that "[w]hile the city retained its immunity for decisions as to whether the public interest required acting in one manner or another, once any particular decision was made, the city was fully liable for any injuries incurred in the execution of its judgment.").

[48] N.Y.: Libertella v. Maenza, 229 N.Y.S.2d 299 (1962); Puffer v. City of Binghamton, 301 N.Y.S.2d 274 (1969).

[49] 301 N.Y.S.2d 274 (1969).

[50] *See* "The Defense of Municipalities: A Primer on Municipal Liability," by Moskowitz, Rothstein & Flanagan, Insurance Counsel Journal, April 1984, p. 259, for a more detailed discussion of this subject.

[51] 610 P.2d 237 (1980).

GOVERNMENTAL IMMUNITIES § 12.01[7]

the same jurisdiction in the case of *Vanderpool v. Oklahoma*,[52] where the court stated that:

> A state or local governmental entity is liable for money damages for injury or loss of property . . . caused by the negligence or wrongful act or omission of any governmental entity or any employee or agent of the government entity while acting within the scope of the governmental entity's office . . . under circumstances where the entity, if a private person, would be liable to the claimant.

The court however, made specific exceptions for acts or omissions (1) in the exercise of legislative or judicial functions, and (2) administrative functions involving a determination of fundamental governmental policy.

In South Dakota, there is the same kind of confusion in trying to measure immunity by the standards of the type of position the tortfeasor held at the time. On the one hand, several cases held that state employees were not clothed with governmental immunity on an analysis of the employee's function.[53] On the other hand, Ms. Miner says in her article[54] that three other decisions held to the contrary that such employees were to be held immune.[55]

[7] **Defense of Discretionary Acts**

In most cases, the question of whether or not an act is discretionary in nature usually depends on whether it is one requiring decision-making. Going a step further, we have the defense of a discretionary act by someone whose job is only proprietary in nature; in other words, the clerks and service employees who carry out the guidelines set by the executives.

Even where the position of the employee is "planning" or "governmental" in nature, the question as to whether or not his or her wrongdoing required discretionary action is often vital.

---

[52] 672 P.2d 1153 (1983)

[53] National Bank of S. Dakota v. Leir, 325 N.W.2d 845 (1982); Kruger v. Wilson, 325 N.W.2d 851 (1982); Smith v. Greek, 328 N.W.2d 261 (1982). *See also* C. Miner, "An Analysis of S. Dakota's Sovereign Immunity Law: Governmental v. Official Immunity," S.D.L. Rev. (Spring 1983) which cites these cases.

[54] C. Miner, "An Analysis of S. Dakota's Sovereign Immunity Law: Governmental v. Official Immunity," S.D.L. Rev. (Spring 1983).

[55] Guillaume v. Staum, 328 N.W.2d 259 (1982); Arndt v. Hannum Trucking Co., 324 N.W.2d 680 (1982); Merrill v. Birhanzel, 310 N.W.2d 522 (1981).

§ 12.02   CASUALTY INSURANCE CLAIMS

This question of discretionary action is by far the most commonly cited defense for governmental employees seeking the cloak of governmental immunity.[56] A number of decisions have declared similar acts to be proprietary or ministerial in nature, and, accordingly, not protected by immunity.[57]

§ 12.02   Effect of Insurance Coverage on Immunity

About one-third of our states require municipalities and their entities to purchase insurance coverage for a required amount. Such insurance coverage may be specifically required by statute in blanket form or for special projects.

In some cases, insurance coverage may be authorized but not required. Often, in this kind of a situation, immunity is almost always waived to the extent of the coverage provided by the policy itself.

---

[56] **Ariz.:** Ryan v. State, 656 P.2d 616 (1982).
  Fla.: Raven v. Coates, 125 So. 2d 770 (1961), *but see* Commercial Carrier Corp. v. Indian River County, 371 So. 2d 1010 (1979) where the court held that this case represented an implicit exception to the immunity waiver passed by the Florida legislature in 1973. *See also* McDonald, "Sovereign Immunity, Revisited But Still Not Refined," 12 Fla. St. U. L. Rev. 401 (1984), which cites another case, Dep't of Transportation v. Webb, 438 So. 2d 780 (1980).
  La.: Stewart v. Schneider Enterprises, 386 So. 2d 1351 (1980).
  N.Y.: Riss v. City of N.Y., 293 N.Y.S.2d 897 (1968); Puffer v. City of Binghamton, 301 N.Y.S.2d 274 (1969).
  Va.: Lawhorne v. Harlan, 200 S.E.2d 569 (1973).
  Wash.: J. & B. Dev. Co. v. King City, 631 P.2d 1002 (1981).
  Wis.: Coffey v. City of Milwaukee, 247 N.W.2d 132 (1976).

[57] **Alas.:** State v. Stanley, 506 P.2d 1284 (1973).
  Ariz.: Jesik v. Maricopa Comm. College, 611 P.2d 547 (1980).
  Fla.: Ankers v. District School Bd. of Pasco City, 406 So. 2d 72 (App. 1981).
  La.: Sansonni v. Jefferson Parish School Bd., 344 So. 2d 42 (App. 1977).
  Mass.: Morash & Sons v. Commonwealth, 296 N.E.2d 461 (1973).
  N.J.: Weeks v. City of Newark, 162 A.2d 312 (1960) (where payment of a fee was held to be immaterial).
  N.M.: Murphy v. City of Carlsbad, 348 P.2d 492 (1960) (city park care held to be proprietary act, *but see* Jones v. City of Birmingham, 224 So. 2d 632 (Ala. 1969), where the same kind of act was held to be governmental).
  N.C.: Rice v. Lumberton, 69 S.E.2d 543 (1952).
  Ohio: Ranells v. City of Cleveland, 321 N.E.2d 885 (1975).
  Wyo.: Connett v. Fremont School Dist., 581 P.2d 1097 (1978); Town of Douglas v. York, 445 P.2d 760 (1968) (payment of a fee for service was construed as making the service proprietary and not subject to immunity. *See* Weeks v. City of Newark, 162 A.2d 312 (N.J. 1960), a similar hospital case where the court ruled otherwise).

GOVERNMENTAL IMMUNITIES § 12.03

A few states have retained the immunity doctrine and held it applicable even where there is insurance coverage. It is to be noted, however, that ordinarily where such insurance is obtained, the insurance policy contains an endorsement to the effect that any immunity that the entity may have will be waived to the extent of the insurance coverage provided.

Another type of endorsement requires the (usually) written consent of the insured in order to waive immunity. Such an endorsement implies that the right of the insured and the insurer to assert immunity is preserved unless otherwise agreed.

Where there is immunity, some early decisions have held that the immunity persists, even if insurance is obtained, so long as the policy has no endorsement to the contrary.[58]

In a South Dakota case,[59] it was held that the purchase of insurance coverage does not affect the sovereign immunity of state engineers. In Iowa, a section of the state code authorizes a municipality to purchase insurance but holds that such insurance constitutes a waiver of the governmental immunity defense only to the extent of the insurance coverage for that incident.

While some states do not completely waive immunity upon purchase of insurance, they may do so in certain specific instances.

In the case of *Holden v. Bundek*,[60] the court held that waiver of immunity is granted only when insurance coverage is purchased, and not merely because such insurance was authorized to be purchased. In some states that authorize the purchase of insurance coverage, such purchase may not waive governmental immunity unless the statutes of that state specifically so provide.[61]

§ 12.03 Punitive Damages in Governmental Immunity Cases

While the courts and the legislatures have been rapidly eroding vast areas of previously held governmental immunities, they have been very reluctant to open the door far enough to grant punitive

---

[58] McGrath Bldg. Co. v. City of Bettendorf, 85 N.W.2d 616 (Iowa 1957); Kesman v. Fallowfield Tp. School Dist., 29 A.2d 17 (Pa. 1942); Mann v. Cty. Bd. of Arlington, 98 S.E.2d 515 (Va. 1957).

[59] Arnt v. Hannum Trucking Co., 324 N.W.2d 680 (S.D. 1982).

[60] 317 A.2d 29 (Del. 1972).

[61] McGrath Bldg. Co. v. City of Bettendorf, 85 N.W.2d 616 (Iowa 1957). *See also* 68 A.L.R.2d 1429 (1959).

damages. Both have developed rules and legislation prohibiting the awarding of such damages.

By far, the majority of the decisions to date on this subject have ruled against the imposition of punitive damages in torts involving governmental wrongdoings.[62]

In *City of Newport v. Facts Concert*,[63] the Supreme Court held that punitive damages cannot be awarded in any case under title 43 of section 1983 of the U.S. Code, against a municipality for its alleged bad faith actions. The Court pointed out that there is nothing in the Act that indicates any intention of revoking common law immunity of a municipality as a matter of public policy.

In subsequent actions, lower federal courts have held that other entities of municipalities such as school boards and boards of supervisors are also to be held immune from punitive damage awards.[64]

In another decision brought under the Clayton Act,[65] however, the court, while acknowledging the *City of Newport* decision, held that Section 4 of the Clayton Act specifically mandates an award of treble damages, regardless of the defendant.

It is to be assumed that in all cases involving governmental immunity the wrongdoing must have been committed within the scope of the employee's official functions and duties even, as has

---

[62] **Alas.:** University of Alas. v. Hendrickson, 552 P.2d 148 (1975) (state university is an integral part of the state).
D.C.: Smith v. District of Columbia, 336 A.2d 831 (App. 1975).
Fla.: Fisher v. City of Miami, 172 So. 2d 455 (1965) (as previously noted, there is a good degree of confusion in Florida decisions).
Hi.: Lauer v. Y.M.C.A. of Honolulu, 557 P.2d 1334 (1976).
Ill.: George v. Chicago Transit Auth., 374 N.E.2d 679 (1978).
Kan.: McHugh v. City of Wichita, 563 P.2d 497 (App. 1977).
Me.: Foss v. Maine Turnpike Authority, 309 A.2d 339 (1973).
Md.: Herilla v. Mayor & City Counsel of Balt., 378 A.2d 162 (1977).
Minn.: Disforge v. City of W. St. Paul, 42 N.W.2d 533 (1950).
Miss.: Urban Renewal Agency of Aberdeen v. Tackett, 255 So. 2d 904 (1971).
Mo.: Chappel v. City of Springfield, 423 S.W.2d 810 (1968).
N.M.: Rascoe v. Town of Farmington, 304 P.2d 575 (1956).
Ohio: Ranells v. City of Cleveland, 321 N.E.2d 885 (1975).
Okla.: Nixon v. Oklahoma City, 555 P.2d 1283 (1976).
S.C.: Lineberger v. City of Greenville, 178 S.C. 47 (1935).
Tex.: Cole v. City of Houston, 442 S.W.2d 445 (App. 1969).
[63] 453 U.S. 246 (1981).
[64] *See* Tolbert v. City of Nelson, 527 F. Supp. 836 (Va. 1981); Tyler v. Board of Ed. of New Castle County, 519 F. Supp. 834 (Del. 1981).
[65] Grason Elec. Co. v. Sacramento Mun. Utility, 526 F. Supp. 276 (Cal. 1981).

been noted, where the defendant is a judge.[66]

The minority view, by far, implies that punitive damages might be assessed against a government agency (usually a municipality) as a result of torts committed by its employees, and in almost all such cases the wording is merely dicta interpretation that such an award could be made in situations involving severe wrongdoing.[67]

In a 1983 case,[68] the Court held that complete immunity from punitive damage awards does not extend to actions brought against municipal employees such as prison guards. Even here, however, the Court made some rigid guidelines by stating that such damages could be awarded only if (1) the guard was found guilty of gross negligence or (2) if he acted with reckless disregard to the plaintiff's rights. Malice was not required to be shown. The Court nevertheless acknowledged that some municipal employees were entitled to qualified immunity for discretionary acts while in the performance of their governmental functions.

§ 12.04 The Doctrine of Charitable Immunity

The doctrine of charitable immunity is a relatively young doctrine that has all but perished before it got a chance to mature. It thrived when charities were small, private institutions and, for the most part, were outside the realm of government and big business.[69] As they grew in size and wealth, and as insurance became available and accepted, the need for protection diminished and the doctrine of charitable immunity became less important.

---

[66] Zarcone v. Perry, 572 F.2d 52 (2d Cir. 1978) (in this case the judge had a coffee vendor brought before him in handcuffs for selling bad coffee. Such action was held to be outside the scope of the judge's official functions).

[67] **Iowa:** Young v. City of Des Moines, 262 N.W.2d 612 (1978) (A 1982 legislative amendment, however, changed this situation by specifically stating that punitive damages were not to be granted.)
Ky.: City of Covington v. Faulhaber, 197 S.W.2d 1065 (by implication only).
N.Y.: Lockhaas v. State, 407 N.Y.S.2d 298 (1978) (except for misconduct foreseeable by officials or where wanton or reckless conduct was involved in the employment of the wrongdoer).
Ore.: Gigler v. City of Klamath Falls, 537 P.2d 121 (1975) (implication that outrageous conduct might warrant awarding of punitive damages).

[68] Smith v. Wade, 461 U.S. 30 (1983).

[69] *See* Toth, "Church Liability for Negligence," Insurance Law Journal, February 1962.

Old arguments to the effect that donations to charities would be affected if the doctrine was abolished, that charities should not be responsible for the acts of their employees, and that beneficiaries should assume the risk of charitable negligence as a part of the beneficial package, have all been given well deserved short shrift in recent years.[70]

Charitable institutions have been variously defined legally, but frankly I am not satisfied with any definition that I have seen. My own definition, a composite, would hold that an organization is charitable when it has been created primarily to benefit mankind or a section thereof, by way of education, medical, health or spiritual assistance or research, without profit, or for a nominal fee. Charitable institutions include such organizations as hospitals, churches, schools and colleges, orphanages, scientific research institutions, or other foundations with similar beneficial motivations.

At common law, charitable organizations were immune from liability for their negligent acts. With the passing of time, great inroads have been made on the charitable immunity doctrine. Today there are very few jurisdictions that still hold to this doctrine and even they may soon disappear.

To the contrary, more and more states are adopting an attitude of no immunity whatsoever for charitable organizations, as a result of statutory enactment and judicial decision, and are holding them to the same degree of care and liability as noncharitable organizations.

The majority of states still hold to some middle position of partial immunity for charitable organizations in certain situations.

1. Some states grant immunity when actions are brought by nonpaying beneficiary patients or inmates who are recipients of its charity.[71]

2. Some of the decisions differentiate between negligent acts arising out of charitable functions, where they still hold to the immunity doctrine, and acts arising out of noncharitable fundraising duties such as benefits, bingo games, etc.[72]

3. Another category of exceptions to the immunity doctrine involves the selection of employees by the charitable organization.

---

[70] *See* Restatement (Second) of Torts § 895 E.
[71] **La.:** Grant v. Touro Infirmary, 223 So. 2d 148 (1969).
Nev.: Springer v. Federated Church, 283 P.2d 1071 (1955).
[72] **Ohio:** Blankenship v. Alter, 167 N.E.2d 922 (1960).

These decisions have ruled that immunity is waived in those situations where the organization has been negligent in its selection or retention of employees.[73]

4. The *trust fund* rationale in favor of charitable immunity was based on the illusory argument that the capital funds of a charitable organization are held in trust for the beneficial purpose of that charity and should not be depleted for the purpose of satisfying tort judgments.[74] This reasoning for the retention of the charitable immunity doctrine should not be confused with actual, legal trust funds set up so that such funds may not be reached for any but trust purposes.

5. Probably the strongest argument favoring the retention of the charitable immunity doctrine was on the basis of *public policy*. It was, and occasionally still is, argued that it is preferable for society that the rights of the individual injured be subservient to the interests of the general public.[75]

[1] **Charitable Immunity Practically Abolished**

Recent movement has clearly been in the direction of eventual abolition of the doctrine of charitable immunity. In 1985, for instance, Ohio abolished its immunity for charitable institutions in *Albritton v. Neighborhood Centers Association for Child Development*.[76] The court stated that:

> The "rule" [charitable immunity doctrine] has been devoured by exceptions: immunity for hospitals has been abolished; where the injured party is not a beneficiary of the charity or pays for the services rendered; or where the charity operates a business enterprise for profit. The very existence of these exceptions militates strongly against all of the policy arguments in favor of the doctrine. There is no compelling precedential reason for its retention.

Many other courts feel much the same way.[77]

---

[73] **Ga.:** Bailey v. YMCA, 130 S.E.2d 242 (Ga. App. 1963).
N.C.: Habuda v. Trustees of Rex Hosp., 164 S.E.2d 17 (1968).
[74] **Tex.:** Southern Methodist Univ. v. Clayton, 176 S.W.2d 749 (1943).
[75] Discussed in the case of Foster v. Roman Catholic Diocese, 70 A.2d 230 (1950).
[76] 466 N.E.2d 867 (1985).
[77] **D.C.:** Heimbuck v. President & Dir's of Georgetown College, 251 F. Supp. 614 (1966).
Ind.: Harris v. Y.W.C.A., 237 N.E.2d 242 (1968).

§ 12.04[2]

Quite a few jurisdictions continue to make exceptions to the charitable immunity doctrine, heading more gradually in the direction of complete abrogation of the doctrine.[78]

[2] Effect of Insurance Coverage on the Charitable Immunity Doctrine

The question as to whether or not the charitable immunity doctrine is waived if insurance coverage has been obtained is almost totally academic.

For all practical purposes, when casualty insurance is provided to a charitable institution, the policy contains an endorsement to the effect that as to the coverage provided, immunity is waived.

In the case of *Abernathy v. Sisters of St. Mary's*,[79] the Missouri Supreme Court stated that "Today, public liability insurance is available to charitable institutions to indemnify them against losses by way of damages for their negligence, and it is common knowledge that most charitable institutions carry such insurance and pay the premiums thereon as a part of their normal cost of operation."

Several other cases have expressed this obvious view as well.[80]

Md.: Sanner v. Trustees of Sheppard & Enoch Pratt Hosp., 398 F.2d 226 (1968); Howard v. Bishop Byrne Council Home, 238 A.2d 863 (1968).
Mass.: Colby v. Carney Hosp., 254 N.E.2d 407 (1969).
Mo.: Abernathy v. Sisters of St. Mary's, 446 S.W.2d 599 (1969).
Ore.: Hungerford v. Portland Sanitarium, 384 P.2d 1009 (1963).
S.C.: Hupman v. Erskine College, 281 S.C. 43 (1984).
Tex.: Howle v. Camp Amon Carter, 470 S.W.2d 629 (1971).
Wash.: Pierce v. Yakima Valley Mem. Hosp., 260 P.2d 765 (1943).
W. Va.: Adkins v. St. Francis Hosp., 143 S.E.2d 154 (1965).
Wyo.: Lutheran Hosp. v. Yepsen, 469 P.2d 409 (1970).
[78] La.: Grant v. Touro Infirmary, 223 So. 2d 148 (1969).
N.J.: Kirby v. Columbian Institute, 243 A.2d 853 (1968); Jacobson v. Atlantic City Hosp., 392 F.2d 149 (1968).
N.C.: Habuda v. Trustees of Rex Hosp., 164 S.E.2d 17 (1968).
R.I.: Brown v. Church of Holy Name of Jesus, 252 A.2d 176 (1969).
Va.: Egerton v. R.E. Lee Mem. Church, 395 F.2d 381 (1968).
[79] 446 S.W.2d 599 (1969).
[80] La.: Grant v. Touro Infirmary, 223 So. 2d 148 (1969).
N.C.: Hill v. James Walker Mem. Hosp., 407 F.2d 1036 (1969).

§ 12.05 Bibliography

Charitable Immunity

Freeman, "Circumventing Immunities: Charitable and Governmental," Case & Comment, July-August 1971.

Note, "Charitable Immunity in Massachusetts: Its Creation, Endurance, Demise and Extinction," 4 Suffolk U.L. Rev. 553 (1970).

Note, "Diminishing Doctrine of Charitable Immunity: An Analysis," 19 Drake L. Rev. 187 (1969).

"Tort Liability of Non-Profit Charitable Corporations," 1 Univ. of San Fernando Valley Law Rev. 190 (1968).

Toth, "Church Liability for Negligence," Insurance Law Journal, February 1962.

Governmental Immunities

Comment, Miner, "An Analysis of South Dakota's Sovereign Immunity Law: Governmental v. Official Immunity," 28 S.D.L. Rev. 317 (Spring 1983). (A good source of historical background.)

Comment, "Negligence of Municipal Employees: Re-Defining the Scope of Police Liability," 35 U. Fla. L. Rev. 720 (1984).

Greenhill, "Recent Developments in Governmental and Charitable Immunities," Speech at F.I.C. meeting, Florida, January 1970.

Hopkins, "Municipal Tort Liability in Iowa," 31 Drake L. Rev. 855 (1981-82).

McDonald, "Sovereign Immunity—Revisited But Still Not Refined," 12 Fla. St. U. L. Rev. 401 (1984). (Emphasis on Florida law.)

Moskowitz, Rothstein & Flanagan, "The Defense of Municipalities: A Primer on Municipal Liability,' Insurance Counsel Journal, April 1984.

Note, Robinson, "Municipal Immunity Statutory Limitations of Recovery is Constitutional," 11 Stetson L. Rev. 372 (1982). (Concentrates on Florida law.)

Van Alstyne, "Governmental Tort Liability: A Decade of Change," 1966 Univ. of Ill. Law Forum 919 (Spring 1966).

CHAPTER 13

Suits—Practice and Procedure

§ 13.01 The Courts and Their Jurisdictions
§ 13.02 Service of Process
    [1] Waiver of Proper Service
    [2] Long Arm Statutes
§ 13.03 Change of Venue
§ 13.04 Pleadings
§ 13.05 Insurance Policy as Evidence
§ 13.06 Trial
§ 13.07 Appeal
§ 13.08 Liens
§ 13.09 Costs—Determination of Award
§ 13.10 Claim Department and Defense Counsel Action
§ 13.11 Excess Ad Damnum

Although claim representatives are not primarily interested in technicalities of trial work, there are some matters with which the claim representative must be familiar when a claim goes into suit. Not only must he understand the technical terminology which he will have to use in discussing a claim with an attorney, but it will be of vital importance for him to be able to follow intelligently the pleadings of a case in order to be able to recognize danger signals and avoid pitfalls in his investigation.

The principles of practice with which claims people are chiefly concerned involve the (1) jurisdiction of the court; (2) service of process; (3) pleadings; (4) trial; and (5) appeal.

§ 13.01 The Courts and Their Jurisdictions

Courts are divided into many classifications. There are those, for instance, which deal strictly with criminal matters and those concerned only with civil actions. The latter are subdivided into courts which deal with wills and descedents' estates, domestic relations and other specialties. In some jurisdictions there is a distinction between courts of equity and courts of law. Courts of equity are more concerned with natural justice where legal technicalities may prevent complete remedy in a court of law. In addition, federal courts are different in some respects from all of the others.

Designations for various courts of original, appellate, and inferior jurisdiction vary from state to state but can be outlined in the following manner:

(a) *Justice of the Peace, Magistrates, or Small Claims Courts.* These inferior courts are usually limited in their jurisdiction. The courts may be limited by the dollar value of the claim to, for example, a maximum of $1,000 or $5,000. Parties appearing in small claims court are typically required to waive the right of appeal of the court's decision, and there is generally no right to a jury trial. Ordinarily, justice of the peace courts, and sometimes magistrates courts, are presided over by judges who have had no formal legal training. Practices and procedure, as well as the rules of evidence, are less formally adhered to than in the basic trial court.

(b) *Municipal Courts or District Courts.* Also inferior to the court of original jurisdiction, municipal or district courts are presided over by lawyers who have been elected or appointed to the bench. Jury trials may be had in these courts and there may be some limited equity jurisdiction. These courts are also limited by the amount of damages that may be sought, such as a $10,000 maximum. The rules of civil procedure and evidence are followed in these courts.

(c) *Circuit Courts, Superior Courts, or Common Pleas Courts.* These are the typical designations for the courts of original jurisdiction. They are called courts of original jurisdiction because most cases are first litigated in these courts. They are distinguished from appellate courts which review the record made in the trial courts.[1] These courts are, in some cases, unlimited in the subject matter of the claims that may be brought before them. Some of the courts require that the amount of damages claimed, or in controversy, exceed a certain amount before the court has jurisdiction to hear them. Equitable relief may generally also be the basis for jurisdiction.

(d) *Appellate and Supreme Courts.* These courts are also variously termed. In New York, there is an intermediate appellate court called the Appellate Division of the Supreme Court (which, in New York, is the court of original jurisdiction) and the highest appellate court is called the court of appeals. In Pennsylvania, the intermediate ap-

---

[1] Green, *Basic Civil Procedure* (2d ed. 1979), p. 4.

peals court is the superior court and the highest court in the state is the Pennsylvania Supreme Court. In Illinois, the intermediate appeals court is the Illinois Appellate Court and the intermediate appeals court in Michigan is called the court of appeals. The function of appellate courts is to review decisions of the trial courts for errors. The decisions of appellate courts may affirm or reverse the trial court, generally on both law and fact. Based on the nature of the matter that has been appealed, on reversal, the appellate courts may order the case remanded to the trial court for retrial of all or part of the case. The courts may also reverse and enter an appropriate order which effectively terminates the litigation, unless appealed to the court of highest authority of that state. Thereafter, it can only be appealed to the U.S. Supreme Court if a federal constitutional question is involved.

(e) *Federal Courts.* The federal judiciary, established by Article III of the United States Constitution and organized by the Congress under constitutional mandate, exists as a separate forum for deciding cases and controversies under certain circumstances. The basic jurisdiction of the federal courts is limited by the citizenship of the parties, the dollar amount in controversy, and the subject matter of the case. In the federal courts, any person or entity may sue another person or entity on questions arising under the federal constitution, statutes, or federal law. However, if one party is suing another over a question of state law or statute, there must be diversity of citizenship between the plaintiff and defendant and the amount in controversy, currently a $10,000 minimum, must be alleged. It should also be noted that the federal courts may also decide equitable matters and issue declaratory judgments under the Declaratory Judgment Act, discussed hereafter.

The basic organization of the federal judiciary is similar to that of its state court counterpart. The court of original jurisdiction is the United States District Court, spread out over more than 100 judicial districts, each of which may or may not be separated into subdivisions. For instance, there is a United States District Court for the Eastern District of Michigan which is divided into northern and southern subdivisions. Appeals from the district court are heard by one of thirteen federal courts of appeals. These courts were formerly known as circuit courts and are still geographically designated by circuit. For instance, the Court of Appeals for the Third Circuit hears appeals arising from the district courts in Pennsylvania, New Jersey, and Delaware, while the Ninth Circuit Court of Appeals hears appeals from the seven westernmost states in the continental United States, Alaska, and Hawaii. Finally, all appeals from the courts of appeals, as well as appeals from the highest state appellate courts, are heard by the United States Supreme Court. In addition, the Supreme Court has original jurisdiction over a few select matters.

§ 13.02 Service of Process

Service of process, or notification from the court that a lawsuit has been filed, is the method used to notify the defendant that an action is being brought against him. This is done by means of a summons to answer the complaint. There is always a time limitation for appearing and answering the summons, if properly served on the defendant. It is most important when an insured notifies his carrier that he has been served that the claim representative determine exactly when, upon whom, and how service was made. Failing to appear or answer a summons after the time required for appearance or answer has expired may result in a default judgment against an insured. While a plaintiff's counsel is sometimes willing to set aside a default, by stipulation, moving the court to do so can be costly, even if the default is set aside.

Service of a summons may ordinarily be made in three ways.

1. **Personal service.** This is the manner of service in which claim representatives are primarily concerned. It involves serving a summons directly on the individual who is being sued. There are prescribed rules concerning this procedure which are strictly or loosely construed according to the jurisdiction involved.

2. **Substituted service.** Until statutes were enacted permitting substituted service, the law required that actual service be made on the defendant or his legal representative in the state where the action was being brought. With the advent of the automobile and its wide use across state boundaries, came the realization that a hardship was being worked on innocent victims of accidents. Service could not be made on an out-of-state tortfeasor who usually returned to his home state before he could be served with the summons. This situation has now been corrected by statute or court rule. The rules vary in minor details but their general effect is the same. They permit service to be made by mail on some designated state official, such as the Secretary of State, Motor Vehicle Commissioner, or someone in a similar

position. Such official is deemed to be the agent (for the purpose of accepting service) of a nonresident automobile operator or owner who has been involved in an accident within that state. These acts are usually referred to as nonresident motorist acts.

Where substituted service is made, notice must be given to the defendant. Once again, it becomes important for the claim representative to know the local laws, since an attempt may be made to serve an insured improperly. This can happen in the following instances:

(1) The death of the insured may make the statute inoperative;
(2) The insured may not have received the notice of the suit;
(3) The insured may not actually be a nonresident;
(4) Service may not have been made in accordance with the statutory requirements.

3. Service by publication. Though in certain instances prescribed by statute or court rule, service by publication may be made, such service is usually not a matter with which the claim representative is concerned. It is sufficient here to note that in some instances in which it is impossible to reach the defendant by personal or substituted service, some statutes permit service by publication.

Another legal document with which the claim representative should be familiar is the subpoena. This is a document ordering a witness to personally appear or to produce documentary evidence before a court or at some place designated by one of the parties. Its authority stems from the court, but in most instances it may be filled out by the attorney and served by his representative. In some instances the subpoena must be issued directly by the judge.

A common policy condition requires the insured to forward immediately to the company, every summons or other process received by him or his representative. Upon receipt and acceptance of such summons, the company assumes the obligation of properly defending the insured.

Each state prescribes the manner by which a summons may properly be served. After the insurer has received notification that the insured has been served with a summons, the claim representative should immediately determine: (1) the time and place where service was made, (2) the person upon whom such service was made, and (3) the person upon whom such service was made if by a method other than personal service, such as through the Secretary of State or by mail directly to the insured. The company can then determine whether the service was proper.

[1] Waiver of Proper Service

In the event that service of summons was made improperly, the claim representative or defense attorney must not, by any act of commission or omission, waive proper service or admit to proper service without the written consent of the insured. By doing so without his consent, an insured is placed in a position of jeopardy and exposure. It is quite possible that by such action the insurance company would be considered to have waived any possible policy defenses, and, in some instances, might even be held for an excess verdict.

Therefore, if there is any doubt whatsoever about the propriety of service, but it appears to be to the best interests of the insured as well as the carrier to accept service as proper, a letter or a signed statement should be obtained from the insured along the following lines:

I, [insured], reside at _____. I am insured with the _____ Insurance Company, under policy _____. On [date], summons in the action of _____ vs. _____, brought in the _____ Court, County of _____, State of _____, came to my attention.

(describe manner)

I hereby request the _____ Insurance Company to accept service of this summons as proper and in accordance with all legal requirements, and to enter a defense of this suit in my behalf.

[2] Long Arm Statutes

While the rules of substituted service may ordinarily apply to nonresident motorists, there are similar statutes, commonly referred to as long arm statutes, which also permit residents of one state to obtain jurisdiction over residents of another state and proceed against the nonresident defendant in the plaintiff's chosen forum.

These statutes are varied. Some permit service by mail through the Secretary of State of the jurisdiction of the nonresident defendant, as previously noted. Others permit personal service of process in the foreign state on the nonresident defendant.

Many long arm statutes were enacted to enable residents of a state to reach manufacturers, wholesalers, or retailers in product liability suits where the defendant's only connection with the state in which the suit was filed was the sale of the product within that state. The reasoning in permitting a plaintiff to sue a defendant in a state foreign to the defendant is based upon the fact that the defendant, usually a corporation, either conducts business within the state, has an office or agent in the state, or "owns, uses or possesses" some real or personal property situated in the plaintiff's home state. Ordinarily, these statutes provide that torts committed within the plaintiff's state form a basis for long arm jurisdiction. The concept underlying long arm jurisdiction is that a state may exercise personal jurisdiction over a nonresident defendant if there is some connection between the defendant and the forum state. These connections have been noted above and have been characterized by the United States Supreme Court as "minimum contacts" which when made the basis for jurisdiction of the nonresident defendant should not offend traditional notions of fair play and substantial justice, and which do not offend the due process clause of the fourteenth amendment to the United States Constitution.[2]

In *International Shoe Co. v. State of Washington*,[3] the Supreme Court redefined the meaning of "present" within a jurisdiction for the purposes of the due process clause of the fourteenth amendment, and held that it was not necessary for the defendant to be physically present in the state in order to receive process. The court required

---

[2] The following cases deal with long arm statutes:

Ariz: Phillips v. Anchor Hocking Glass Corp, 413 P.2d 732 (1966).

Colo: Alliance Clothing, Ltd. v. District Court, 532 P.2d 351 (1975); Texair Flyers v. District Court, 506 P.2d 367 (1973); Safari Outfitters, Inc. v. Superior Court, 449 P.2d 367 (1973); Granite State Volkswagen v. District Court, 492 P.2d 624 (1972).

N.M.: Blount v. T.D. Publishing Corp, 423 P.2d 421 (1967).

N.Y.: Babcock v. Jackson, 191 N.E.2d 279 (1963).

N.C.: Bylam v. National Cibo House Corp., 143 S.E.2d 225 (1965).

Pa: McAndrew v. Burnett, 374 F. Supp. 460 (1974); Cipolla v. Shoposka, 267 A.2d 854 (1970).

Vt.: Miller v. Cousins Properties, Inc., 378 F. Supp. 711 (1974).

Wis.: State ex rel. Rush v. Circuit Court, 244 N.W. 766 (1932).

U.S.: Pennoyer v. Neff, 95 U.S. 714 (1877); International Shoe Co. v. State of Washington, 326 U.S. 310 (1945); McGee v. International Life Ins. Co., 355 U.S. 220 (1957); Hanson v. Denckla, 357 U.S. 235 (1958); L.D. Reeder Contractors v. Higgins Indus., 265 F.2d 768 (9th Cir. 1959); Rosenblatt v. American Cyanamid Co., 392 U.S. 110 (1965); Aftanese v. Economy Boiler Co., 343 F.2d 187 (8th Cir. 1965).

[3] 326 U.S. 310 (1945).

only that the defendant maintain "minimal contacts within the state" so that the institution of such a suit "would not offend the traditional notions of fair play and substantial justice."

In the case of *McGee v. International Life Insurance Co,*[4] the United States Supreme Court upheld the jurisdiction of the California courts by stating that there was no violation of due process in a suit based on an insurance contract which had been delivered in California, and for which premiums had been collected from California where the insured was a California resident.

While the necessity for the "presence" of a defendant was not abandoned, some cases considerably relaxed the requirement.[5]

In 1966, the New York Court of Appeals made what I consider to be a very unfair and illogical decision involving insurance legal practice in *Seider v Roth.*[6] Despite the fact that the New York Court of Appeals subsequently affirmed the holding in *Seider,* in the later case of *Simpson v. Loehmann,*[7] it might have been viewed as a local aberration had not a few states, unaware that the *Seider* doctrine is a double-edged sword which could affect their citizens adversely, adopted the decision either judicially or by statute.[8] Accordingly, this decision warrants review.

In *Seider,* the insured was a Canadian resident who bought his automobile insurance policy in Canada. He was involved in an automobile accident in Vermont. The other party involved in the accident (the plaintiffs) were New York residents. The only other contact with New York State was the fact that the insurance company that insured the Canadian resident also conducted business in the State of New York.

The court of appeals held that the duties of an insurer to defend and to indemnify the insured is a debt, attachable as a piece of property within the State of New York, or establishing *in rem* jurisdiction over the insurance company. The New York courts were able to obtain jurisdiction over the insurance company by means of the attachment statute.

---

[4] 355 U.S. 220 (1957).
[5] **Ill.:** Gray v. American Radiator & Sanitary Corp., 176 N.E.2d 761 (1961).
Minn.: Atkins v. Jones & Laughlin Steel Corp., 104 N.W.2d 888 (1960).
N.Y.: Johnson v. Equitable Life Assur. Soc., 254 N.Y.S.2d 258 (App. Div. 1964).
[6] 269 N.Y.S.2d 99, 216 N.E.2d 312 (1966).
[7] 287 N.Y.S.2d 633, 234 N.E.2d 669 (1967).
[8] **Minn.:** Minn. Stat. § 1 571.495 (1978).
N.H.: Forbes v. Boynton, 313 A.2d 129 (1973).

The fact that the duties referred to (defense payment of the claim) would not arise until after liability was established, or after suit was brought; that both duties were intangible and impossible to translate into specific sums in advance of certain definite requirements that make them contingent obligations and not transferrable, did not impress the court. The majority held that the obligation was present and that it was a debt which could be attached to the extent of the policy limits. This decision, in effect, permits direct action against an insurer, which heretofore could only be accomplished by legislative action.[9]

The dissent stated that "it is well established that an indebtedness is not attachable unless it is absolutely payable at present, or in the future and not dependable upon *any* contingency." Here, the existence of a policy is used as the basis for jurisdiction to start the very action necessary to activate the insurer's obligation under the policy. The promise to defend the insured is presumed to be the *res* (property) which is attachable and which provides the basis for jurisdiction for a civil suit which must be commenced before the duty to defend can possibly accrue.

In *Simpson v. Loehmann*,[10] the court of appeals, in a 4–3 decision, refused to consider further arguments that attachment offends due process, that it imposes an undue burden on the insurance industry and upon interstate commerce, and that it impairs the obligations of the insurance contract. In a separate opinion, Judge Breitel harshly criticized the *Seider* decision, but concurred in the court's holding "only because the institutional stability of a court is more important than any single tolerable error which I believe it committed."

I couldn't disagree more. Is injustice more tolerable than the "stability of a court"?

The *Seider* decision and others that have followed it were obviously decided in order to open more liberal and claim conscious forums to plaintiffs. The New Hampshire court all but said as much in adopting the *Seider* doctrine in a case against New York State defendants. In the case of *Forbes v. Boynton*,[11] the New Hampshire Supreme

---

[9] Judge Henry Friendly of the Second Circuit Court of Appeals arrived at the same conclusion and upheld the *Seider* decision in the case of Minichiello v. Rosenberg, 410 F.2d 106 (2d Cir. 1968).

[10] 287 N.Y.S.2d 633, 234 N.E.2d 669 (1967).

[11] 313 A.2d 129 (N.H. 1973).

§ 13.03 CASUALTY INSURANCE CLAIMS

Court brought the level of judicial decisionmaking down to that of a street brawl. The court held that

> we are not holding that the *Seider* rule is to be applied generally to all cases of foreign motorists insured by a company with an office in this state and licensed to do business in New Hampshire. We are merely holding that under the circumstances of this case in a suit by a resident of New Hampshire against a resident of New York, where the *Seider* rule prevails, . . .

This clearly implies that the New Hampshire Supreme Court was inspired by the desire to get back at the New York Court of Appeals for having made the *Seider* decision in the first place. This is not, in my opinion, a very good reason for perpetuating and compounding the error of the *Seider* rule.

However, the light of reason has once again prevailed and no less than the United States Supreme Court has held that a Minnesota garnishment statute based on the *Seider* decision could not be used as the basis for obtaining jurisdiction over a foreign defendant whose only contact with the state was that his insurance carrier had an office in the state in which the suit was filed.[12]

In *Rush v. Saychuk*,[13] the Supreme Court held that the state court's exercise of jurisdiction over defendant and his insurer's local office offended the traditional notions of fair play and substantial justice. It further held that the defendant's minimum contacts with the state could not be established by treating an attachment proceeding as the functional equivalent of a direct action against the insurer, considering the insured a nominal defendant, in order to obtain jurisdiction over the insurer. If the state court did not have jurisdiction over the insured, it could not then reach the insurer.

§ 13.03 Change of Venue

Once the court has jurisdiction over the parties, the question may still remain as to whether the venue, or situs of the forum, is proper or convenient. A court may have jurisdiction over the parties and the subject matter, but the county or federal judicial district in which the suit is filed may be improper because the parties or witnesses are not to be found in that county or judicial district. Most states have

---

[12] Rush v. Saychuk, 444 U.S. 320 (1980).
[13] *Id.*

§ 13.03

enacted venue statutes or rules of court which designate the proper forum in which a case is to be litigated.

For instance, a typical venue statute may provide that within a particular jurisdiction (state), the action is to be brought in the county in which the defendant resides, has a principal place of business, or conducts business. If the defendant does not meet any of these criteria (as in the case of a defendant from outside the state who has minimum contacts with the state for due process purposes) then the action is to be brought where the plaintiff resides, has its principal place of business, or conducts business. As an alternative, the case may be tried in the county where the cause of action arose.

If a plaintiff files suit in county A and defendant resides in the same state, but in county B, venue is said to be improper. The court is typically required, on motion or on its own initiative, to transfer the case to county B.

Venue may also be changed even if it is proper as to the parties or properly laid. This may be accomplished under the doctrine of *forum non conveniens* (for the convenience of the parties and witnesses). The granting or denial of such a motion for change of venue is usually discretionary with the court and will be reversed on appeal only if the court abuses its discretion.

Suppose there is an auto accident in county A, in the rural part of the state. The plaintiff is a resident of county B. The defendant is from county Z which is an urban center. County Z is notorious for runaway juries and multi-million dollar verdicts. All the witnesses to the accident are from counties A and B.

Even if venue is properly laid in county Z, there may be significant prejudice to the defendant if the case is tried in that county, and a change of venue could be advantageous to the defendant. These are considerations that claim representatives should be aware of once the preliminary facts of the law suit are established. Of importance is the fact that many statutes and court rules require that a motion for change of venue must be brought at the time or shortly after the defendant answers plaintiff's complaint or else objections to venue will be waived.

A related issue that may be faced by the claim representative is whether to remove a case filed in state court to federal court. Under

§ 13.04   CASUALTY INSURANCE CLAIMS

the Federal Judiciary Code,[14] an action brought in state court, over which the federal district court has original jurisdiction (diversity of citizenship and amount in controversy, or federal subject matter jurisdiction) may be removed to the federal court and tried in that forum. This option may be preferable if an out-of-state insured is sued in an urban court where large jury verdicts are feared or where federal procedural rules may be to the insured's advantage. Cases tried in federal court usually come up for trial sooner than in state courts.

§ 13.04 Pleadings

The pleadings in a lawsuit consist of all documents that are filed with the court or formally exchanged by the parties and make up, along with hearing transcripts, the record of the case. While many of the pleadings are of little or no concern to the claim representative, there are some basic documents with which the claim representative should be familiar and should make part of his claim file.

A few of the pleadings with which the claim representative should have some familiarity are:

1. **Petition, Complaint, or Declaration.** This is the initial statement or allegations of the plaintiff's lawsuit. It is usually prepared in numbered paragraphs alleging specific facts and conclusions of law. It contains statements which identify the parties, allegations that the court has jurisdiction over the parties, and the subject matter and a factual background for the claim. The substantive allegations of legal wrongs committed against the plaintiff follow, typically in a count by count manner, i.e., Count I—Negligence, Count II—Breach of Implied Warranty, Count III—Strict Liability and Tort, and so on.

Finally, the complaint or petition contains a prayer for relief which seeks a specific damage amount, or more typically whatever amount above the jurisdictional minimum the court, or the jury, sees fit to award the plaintiff. It is important that the claim representative handling the particular case reads the complaint or petition very carefully, and uses it as a guide for the direction his investigation should take. It can be very embarrassing to him if he has made a detailed investigation involving a defect at a certain location only to

---

[14] 28 U.S.C. § 1441.

learn that the petition or complaint alleges that the accident occurred in an entirely different area.

2. **Answer and Affirmative Defenses or Affidavit of Defense.** This is a paragraph-by-paragraph response to the allegations in the complaint or petition. The defendant may respond by admitting the allegations in a particular paragraph, such as the residence of the defendant. Defendant will deny that the plaintiff is entitled to any damages and will neither admit nor deny factual issues which plaintiff will have to prove to make his case. In many jurisdictions, a defendant is also required, with his answer, to raise any affirmative defenses he has to plaintiff's claims. An affirmative defense must be proven by the defendant. An affirmative defense which is not raised in the answer is, in many cases, deemed waived and may not be raised at a later time.

3. **Counter-Claims, Cross-Claims, and Third-Party Claims.** When the defendant is served with a complaint, the allegations may give the defendant a right to proceed in a cause of action against the plaintiff, a codefendant, if there is one, or a third party. Defendant may file a counter-claim against the plaintiff if defendant has a cause of action that arises out of the same transaction or occurrence from which plaintiff's claims arise. Defendant may allege, in the case of an automobile negligence action, that not only was he not negligent, but that defendant has been injured by the plaintiff's actions. A cross-claim may be filed between codefendants to an action brought by the plaintiff. The cross-claim (as well as third party complaint), particularly in a casualty claim, usually seeks indemnity and/or contribution from the cross-defendant for any liability imposed on the cross-plaintiff as a result of the claims of the plaintiff in the main case. A third-party complaint may be filed against a stranger to the lawsuit by one of the defendants, asserting a right against the third party which the plaintiff would have the right to assert if the third party had been sued as a defendant. The third party, in turn, may bring in a fourth party defendant, and so on, ad infinitum.

While a counter-claim may be handled by the same attorney who is the defense counsel chosen by the insurer, the defendant must be made to understand that he is "on his own" as to the counter-claim and that the insurer can assume no responsibility for the result of that action, nor assume any extra expense involved in such a counter-claim.

4. **Demurrer or Judgment on the Pleadings.** As a response to a plaintiff's complaint, the defendant may file a demurrer to the allegations, asserting that even if all the facts alleged in plaintiff's complaint are true, it nevertheless fails to state a claim on which relief may be granted. In other words, plaintiff's complaint does not state a legally recognized right to recover. Described another way, the plaintiff makes certain allegations to which the defendant replies "so what?" In many jurisdictions, the demurrer takes the form of a motion for judgment on the pleadings filed by the defendant, instead of the answer. The defendant, in essence, asks the court to rule that as a matter of law, plaintiff's complaint fails to state a claim, and asks the court to dismiss the complaint at the outset.

5. **Motions.** Motions are requests to the court by either side to take some action with reference to the case. For instance, a motion may request that the court allow a party to amend the complaint, or add an affirmative defense. It may ask the court to order the opposing party to comply with discovery requests, or it may ask the court to dismiss the complaint or enter judgment in favor of the plaintiff.

6. **Bill of Particulars.** In some jurisdictions, a defendant may request a more detailed statement from a plaintiff of his cause of action. A bill of particulars is the plaintiff's reply to such a demand. It is a more detailed accounting of his original claim and usually itemizes special damages as well as some of the allegations of fact. Its effect is to confine the action, limit the scope of proof, and give more definite information concerning the original allegations.

7. **Discovery Pleadings.** Discovery has become the basic means by which the parties uncover the factual basis for the claims and defenses in the lawsuit. The basic premise behind discovery is that all parties to a litigation should have access to all information about the respective claims and defenses that is relevant, and not privileged. In this way, a suit will proceed to trial with "all the cards face up on the table." Discovery facilitates full disclosure of the facts and prevents unfair surprise by one of the parties at the time of trial. Discovery also aids the parties in narrowing the facts and issues which will ultimately be tried. Without knowledge of the facts of the case, the claim representative is disadvantaged and is not able to realistically evaluate the case. Discovery is undertaken by a variety of methods. Parties and witnesses may be deposed and the parties may serve written questions on each other which must be answered in writing. Parties may have access to documentary and physical evidence and

may be permitted access on land to perform inspections. Requests for admissions may be served on a party asking him to admit, or specifically deny, certain facts. Failure to answer these requests within a certain time period is deemed an admission of those facts. Depositions on oral questioning is a sworn interrogation of the parties or witnesses by the attorneys for the parties. Interrogation is reduced to a typed transcript, which in some states must be filed with the court. The person being deposed is questioned by the attorneys as to his knowledge of the facts surrounding the claim. This interrogation, in the form of question and answer, is usually governed by the jurisdiction's rules of evidence.

Written *interrogatories* are a series of typed questions served on a party by the opposing party which requires full written response within a prescribed time period. Serving interrogatories on the opposing party is typically the first discovery taken once the lawsuit is filed. However, it should be noted that the Federal Rules and many state court rules permit some type of discovery prior to the time a matter is placed in suit for the purpose of perpetuating the deponent's testimony.[15]

Another early discovery device is the request for production of documents or evidence relevant to the lawsuit. In some cases, the parties will be entitled to perform inspections of the evidence. This is particularly important in product liability suits where expert testimony is often required, and that testimony is based on a thorough and detailed inspection of the product. As mentioned above, requests for admissions are useful means by which certain factual allegations may be disproved or conclusively established ahead of trial. Most of the modern discovery procedures in effect in the state courts are derived from the federal discovery rules found in the Federal Rules of Civil Procedure.[16]

Finally, the claim representative will be wise to keep abreast of the developments as discovery progresses. There may be an occasion when the opposing party will not be cooperating with counsel for the insured by tardiness or refusal to answer interrogatories, etc. In this case, most jurisdictions provide for sanctions for failure to comply with discovery request ranging from the award of costs to the offended party to dismissal with prejudice of plaintiff's complaint. Such action, however, is quite rare.

---

[15] *See* Federal Rules of Civil Procedure, Rule 27.
[16] Specifically, Rules 26-37.

8. **Dispositive Motions.** Perhaps the most important pretrial motion filed will be the dispositive motion, or motion, which if granted, will dispose of the litigation. The dispositive motion asks the court to rule that, as a matter of law, the plaintiff is either entitled to the relief claimed or is entitled to no relief at all. There are three basic dispositive motions, called by various names depending upon the jurisdiction:

1. Judgment on the Pleadings;
2. Accelerated Judgment; and
3. Summary Judgment or Disposition.

Judgment on the pleadings has been discussed at 4, above. Accelerated judgment motions allege that there is some deficiency in the proceedings which deprives the court of jurisdiction over the action, such as lack of jurisdiction over the parties, property or subject matter; process issued was insufficient; service of process insufficient; plaintiff lacks capacity to sue; another action has been instituted between the same parties involving the same claim; the claim is barred by release, payment, prior judgment, immunity granted by law, statute of limitations, statute of frauds, infancy or disability of the moving party, or assignment or other disposition of the claim before commencement of the action. The essential feature of the motion for accelerated judgment is that the moving party is alleging some defect in the proceedings which destroys plaintiff's cause of action, apart from the validity of the substantive claim.

A motion for summary judgment alleges that given all the facts, the parties have adduced or are capable of adducing, there is no issue or question or dispute as to the facts. When the facts are viewed in the light most favorable to the nonmoving party, the moving party is entitled to judgment as a matter of law. For instance, in a slip and fall case, the plaintiff may have alleged in his complaint that he slipped on a loose step while descending a wooden staircase. When he is deposed, he testifies that he does not know how he happened to fall; that one minute he was at the top of the stairs and the next minute he was flying down the steps head first. The defendant will argue, in his motion for summary judgment, that there was no issue as to any material fact that plaintiff does not know how he fell and that defendant is entitled to summary judgment dismissing the plaintiff's claim for failure to prove causation (one of the elements of negligence.) The court should grant the motion because, while the plaintiff may allege a valid claim in his complaint, the undisputed fact is that he cannot attribute his fall to the loose step. When the claim representative conducts his investigation, he should always have in mind the facts that the plaintiff will be required to establish in order to support the claim and the possibility of a summary judgment motion.

§ 13.05 Insurance Policy as Evidence

An insurance policy is admissible into evidence in any action involving the existence, construction, or effectiveness of the policy itself. Issues involving delayed notice, payment of premium, the application or similar matters would, of course, be pertinent to the production of the policy itself.

However, in negligence actions, it has long been determined that the existence of a policy of insurance could have an effect on the verdict and would not be pertinent to the issues of the suit. It has been the general rule for many years that where the sole issue involved is the determination of negligence, insurance is not a pertinent issue and should not be mentioned. The insurance policy should not be admissible in evidence.[17]

Some states have enacted statutes which strictly forbid the joinder of an insurance company as a codefendant in an original action brought by an injured person, or his personal representative in a case where death is involved, for the same reasons that insurance may not be mentioned in a personal injury case.

The basis for rules excluding the mention of insurance in a personal injury claim is to prevent the prejudice of the defendant. Theoretically, and practically, if a jury is apprised of the fact that the defendant is insured, it may be tempted to award the plaintiff a greater sum than the plaintiff might be due, simply because there is a "deep pocket" available. Judging from the escalation in jury awards, it may well be presupposed that juries in most tort cases assume that the defendant is insured. Nevertheless, the mention of insurance is still forbidden at the time of trial.

There are an increasing number of jurisdictions that hold "an insurance contract is no longer a secret, private, confidential arrangement between the insurance carrier and the individual, but is an

---

[17] Johanek v. Aberle, 27 F.R.D. 272 (D.C. Mont. 1961).

agreement that embraces those whose personal property may be injured by the negligent act of the insured."[18]

Discovery of the policy limits of a defendant is permitted, and, in some cases, a party may obtain discovery of the existence and contents of an insuring agreement if the carrier may not be liable to satisfy part or all of the judgment entered in an action or to indemnify or reimburse payments made in satisfaction of a judgment.[19] However, it should again be noted that disclosure does not make the agreement admissible at trial.

§ 13.06 Trial

In organizing a case for trial, the investigator's main concern is in preparing, gathering, and preserving the evidence to be presented. Further discussion of this subject is included in Chapter 14. Trial of a civil action may be had with or without a jury, but in most cases a party must specifically demand a jury trial.

§ 13.07 Appeal

The defeated party in the court of original jurisdiction has the right, for certain specified reasons and within a specified time, to appeal to have his case reviewed by a higher court. In most jurisdictions, judgment must be entered by the court by written order before the time starts running on the appeal. Under the Federal Rules of Civil Procedure, a party appealing a judgment or final order must file a notice of appeal to the court of appeals within thirty days of the entry of order. The time period in state courts vary.

§ 13.08 Liens

A number of states have, by statute, given hospitals and doctors the means for legally protecting their bills for services rendered in connection with casualty claims. The same right has been given compensation carriers with reference to their subrogation rights against third parties and their insurers.

These statutes are known as Lien Laws and, where applicable, require notice of lien to be given to third parties alleged to be liable

---

[18] Maddox v. Grauman, 205 Ky. 422, 265 S.W.2d 39 (1954).
[19] *See generally* Federal Rules of Civil Procedure 26(b)(2) and (3).

SUITS—PRACTICE AND PROCEDURE § 13.09

for the injuries received by the claimant. In some instances, notice is required to be given to the third party insurance carrier if known. The liens are usually required to be filed in the county clerk's office in order to become effective.

Failure to comply with the directions of a lien after a notice obligates the third party or his insurance carrier to reimburse the hospital or doctor for the bills covered in the lien, may require that those parties also be paid in addition to any settlement which may have been made with a claimant. The same rule applies to compensation liens.

It is important to consider the lienholder's interest before a settlement draft is issued. Protection may be obtained by issuing a separate draft to the lienholder, or by including the lienholder as an additional payee on the draft issued in settlement of the claim. The former is probably the more practical procedure.

It is important to remember that all attorneys who have been retained to handle a case for a claimant have a claim on any settlement proceeds for services rendered by them. Some states have given lien status to their letters of representation.

§ 13.09 Costs—Determination of Award

Costs are certain allowances authorized by statute to reimburse successful litigants in most situations, for a portion of their expenses incurred in prosecuting or defending an action or special proceeding.[20] They are generally considered as a penalty and are in the nature of incidental damages.[21]

Costs are a strictly statutory creation. Despite the fact that there is no common law right to costs, the awarding of such incidental damages has been declared constitutional.[22]

In the absence of specific wording to the contrary, costs may be awarded only against a party to the action, and only a party to the action is entitled to recover costs.[23] They belong to the party at interest and are not awarded to any attorney except in unusual circumstances, in the absence of an agreement to the contrary.[24]

---

[20] Caperna v. Williams Bauer Corp., 57 N.Y.S.2d 254 (1945).
[21] Tobias Tile Co. v. Topping Realty Co., 186 N.Y.S. 734 (1921).
[22] Hayman v. Morris, 37 N.Y.S.2d 884 (1942).
[23] H.D.S. Mercantile Corp. v. Monet Fashions, Inc., 234 N.Y.S.2d 547 (1962).
[24] Graham v. Fisher, 297 N.Y.S. 199 (1937).

§ 13.09 CASUALTY INSURANCE CLAIMS

While a successful litigant may, under certain circumstances, be denied costs, he is never required to pay them.[25]

The amount of costs that may be awarded are usually specified in the statutes involved. By any standard, these are very low. Ordinarily the court has some jurisdiction, but is usually limited by the statute as to the amount it can award. The sum usually includes, in addition to a small specific amount, filing fees, ordinary legal fees of witnesses and referees, reasonable fees by commissioners in taking of depositions, publication fees, copying and printing fees, and other such items.

Under ordinary circumstances, lawyer's fees are not assessed as costs,[26] but are taxed separately for various reasons.

In the event of fraud or bad faith, or for some very extraordinary circumstances, a court may be granted the authority to assess attorney's fees as costs.[27] Items such as investigative fees, travel and subsistence expenses for witnesses from distant places, extra expenses of trial such as movies, maps, laboratory tests, etc., are not included in the ordinary designation of costs.

The assessment of costs is practically never a deterrent for the bringing of a suit. A great number of suits which are brought in the courts, particularly in the negligence field, are unjustified either because the demand is beyond all reason or because the facts do not warrant an equitable recovery. To counter the filing of seemingly frivolous lawsuits, the Federal Rules of Civil Procedure and many state court rules and statutes expressly provide for the imposition of sanctions on an attorney or party who signs a pleading in violation of the requirement that:

> The signature of an attorney or party constitutes a certificate by him that he has read the pleading, motion, or other paper; that to the best of his knowledge, information, and belief formed after reasonable inquiry it is well grounded in fact and is warranted by existing law or good faith argument for the extension, modification, or reversal of existing law, and that it is not interposed for any improper purpose, such as to harass or to cause unnecessary delay or needless increase in the cost of litigation.[28]

---

[25] In re Leary's Estate, 14 N.Y.S.2d 960 (1939).
[26] Maryland Cas. Co. v. United States, 108 F.2d 784 (4th Cir. 1940).
[27] Gordan v. Woods, 202 F.2d 476 (1st Cir. 1953).
[28] Federal Rules of Civil Procedure, Rule 11.

SUITS—PRACTICE AND PROCEDURE   § 13.10

In some cases, particularly in federal court, parties found to violate this or similar rules have been taxed costs and actual attorney fees incurred by the opposing party. These amounts have occasionally reached hundreds of thousands of dollars. The claim representative should keep this in mind, particularly when dealing with the claimant's attorney prior to the time the case is put into suit. Impressing upon the claimant attorney that if the case is put into suit the insured will seek sanctions under Rule 11 or similar state rules, may help in effecting an early and reasonable settlement of the suit, especially if the courts in that jurisdiction have the reputation for taxing costs and actual attorney's fees for frivolous lawsuits.

§ 13.10 Claim Department and Defense Counsel Action

Assuming that a suit is one for proper defense by the insurance carrier, all pleadings received from an insured or his agent or attorney should be acknowledged promptly. Such acknowledgment gives the company the opportunity of affirming in writing the fact that the insured was properly served.

No suit can be properly investigated or adjusted unless the claim representative has thoroughly read and understood the complaint. This is, after all, the basis for the plaintiff's action, and is the framework upon which his attorney intends to build his case. The complaint contains the broad general allegations that usually tell whether the incident falls within the terms of the policy. It also contains much additional important information that may furnish leads for investigation.

Check the pleadings. Defense counsel's case will depend upon the ability to muster sufficient information that can be presented in court to refute the allegations made by the plaintiff's attorney. The complaint should therefore be checked carefully to determine the answers to the following questions:

1. Do the facts alleged indicate a cause of action?
2. Are the proper parties named as plaintiffs and defendants?
3. Are the defendants properly covered under the policy? Questions of corporate entity, copartnership, trust, agency, and so on, should be especially scrutinized.
4. Has suit been instituted in the proper jurisdiction?
5. Has the statute of limitations run?

§ 13.11 CASUALTY INSURANCE CLAIMS

6. Are the allegations of the complaint sufficiently covered in the investigation?
7. Does the complaint indicate a need for additional investigation to combat the allegations?

§ 13.11 Excess Ad Damnum

In many instances, an insurance company will receive pleadings wherein the amount of the judgment demanded exceeds the amount of coverage provided by the policy of insurance.

The company's monetary responsibility to an insured is limited by the amount of coverage he has purchased. Any judgment obtained against him over and above this amount is usually his own personal responsibility. Therefore, when the amount of money demanded in the pleadings exceeds the amount of the coverage, it is the duty of the insurance company to inform the insured promptly in writing of his possible exposure above the limits of the policy.

Such a letter is usually referred to as an *excess ad damnum* letter. It should inform the insured that although the company will see to it that he is defended, he may, if he desires, engage his own counsel at his own expense, to collaborate with counsel for the insurance company. Such a letter can read as follows, absent of any complications.

> Summons and Complaint personally served upon you in the action of _____ vs. _____ , brought in the _____ Court, County of _____, State of _____, has been received.
>
> The judgment demanded in this suit is in the amount of _____ dollars. Policy _____, which our company issued to you, provides coverage up to _____ dollars for injury sustained by any one person, and a total of _____ dollars for injury sustained by more than one person in any one accident.
>
> Since the amount demanded in judgment exceeds the amount of coverage provided by this policy of insurance, you may if you so desire, engage the services of personal counsel at your own expense, to collaborate with our attorneys [*Give their name and address.*]
>
> Please notify us immediately in the event of a change in your address, so that we may reach you promptly at any time, particularly since your full cooperation is a requirement of the policy.
>
> You may be assured that we will protect your interests to the best of our ability whether you associate your personal counsel with ours or not. We must, however, make it very clear that we will under no circumstances be responsible for the payment of any sum in excess of our policy limits.

CHAPTER 14

Practical Considerations of Suits and Casualty Litigation

§ 14.01 Legal Expenses
§ 14.02 Dealing With Defense Counsel
    [1]   Checklist in Defense Counsel Relationships
    [2]   Settlement Reevaluation
        [a]   Defense Counsel's Review
        [b]   Claim Manager's or Supervisor's Review
    [3]   Reservation of Rights or Nonwaiver Agreements
    [4]   Availability of Witnesses
    [5]   Trial Preparation
    [6]   Trial and Disposition
    [7]   Appeal
    [8]   Checklist for Suit Preparation
§ 14.03 Law Reporting Systems
    [1]   Available Computer Systems
§ 14.04 Bibliography

From a review of various decisions on the subject, the word suit can be defined generally as a proceeding in a court of justice for the enforcement of a right or for the redress of an injury. For our purposes, any civil action in a court of law may be considered as a suit.

Litigation is costly and time-consuming. The claim representative should make every effort to keep suits at a minimum, without sacrificing the principles of good claim handling. There are, of course, many instances where a decision to permit a claim to go into suit may be proper for the following reasons:

1. *Excessive demand.* If faced with the proposition of paying much more than the case appears to be worth, or defending a suit, there is little choice but to defend a suit.
2. *Some fraudulent aspect to the claim.* Where the fraud is more than mere "puffing," defending a suit often becomes a matter of principle even though the defense may sometimes be more costly than settlement.

§ 14.01   CASUALTY INSURANCE CLAIMS

   3. *Little or no liability.* If the demand is based on injury and disregards liability, the investigation may make defense advisable.

Other things being equal, however, consideration should be given to the expense factor when an attempt is made to dispose of a claim that will probably go into suit unless it is settled. At the same time, the company must not earn the reputation of being an "easy mark" for any attorneys who may care to institute suits. For this reason, if a fair offer has been made while a case is in claim, an increase in the offer is not justified simply because suit has been instituted.

§ 14.01 Legal Expenses

If there is a definite understanding with trial counsel concerning legal fees before engaging his services, argument and misunderstanding will be minimized when his bill is presented. Within reasonable limits an attorney has a right to charge what he believes his services are worth. As long as the company knows in advance approximately what the charges will be, it has little room for complaint if it chooses to engage him. On the other hand, trial counsel has a duty to submit an itemized bill for services rendered, so that the company knows exactly for what it is being charged.

Transcripts of testimony in criminal, traffic, or other hearings should be ordered with discretion, and only when it will be obviously advantageous to have complete copies. Such transcripts are expensive and serve no good purpose if they cannot be used to aid the defense of a suit.

Requests for examination before trial (deposition) should be made with discretion by counsel for the insurance carrier, and only after considering carefully the advantages to be gained. Depositions should never be undertaken indiscriminately simply because the law permits it. In some cases depositions should be taken only if essential witnesses will not be available for the trial and if their testimony is necessary for the defense of a case.

Some companies want their attorneys to press for recovery of costs in the event of a defendant's verdict because they feel that such action is a deterrent to those attorneys who bring obviously groundless actions in the hope that they may get a "nuisance settlement" or a freak verdict. Costs are a punitive measure of damages and should be used accordingly. In the U.S. the amount permitted to be recovered is so small that it is often meaningless and not even economically worth the effort to recover. The fact that an attorney is not personally affected by the assessment of costs does nothing to influence his attitude in instituting a suit. Where the choice of suit is made by the attorney, he should be personally responsible for the payment of meaningful costs, which could have a decided effect on unjustified suits.

A fairly effective deterrent to the institution of unjustified suits is the insistence by defense counsel that the plaintiff file a bond for costs whenever the law permits this to be done.

§ 14.02 Dealing With Defense Counsel

Defense counsel, by and large, resent instructions from claim representatives, especially when they are called upon to take only limited action in some suits. They often fail to recognize that in most such instances, the claim representatives expect that the case will be settled before trial, and consider the suit as merely a holding operation.

The attorney, on the other hand, believes that if settlement expectations do not materialize such a "holding operation" could decidedly prejudice his ability to properly defend the case, particularly if depositions are not obtained from witnesses or experts who subsequently become unavailable for one reason or another. Here, it is simply a matter of judgment. The claim representative or his supervisor must have experience enough to be able to properly evaluate settlement opportunities dispassionately and avoid unnecessary risks. Defense counsel must be forthright in pointing out the dangers of short-cutting, to the claims people. The great danger here is that by putting himself on record in writing, the defense counsel can prejudice the insurer in the event of a possible excess verdict.

Nevertheless, the buck must stop with the claim department. It is the claim representative, clothed with the proper authority, who must make the final decision, with full consideration of the views of defense counsel and with guidance from supervisors and home office if necessary. Defense counsel must recognize this fact in dealing with a well-run claim department.

[1] Checklist in Defense Counsel Relationships

☐ Have an understanding of counsel's fees before making any assignment.

§ 14.02[2]   CASUALTY INSURANCE CLAIMS

- ☐ Upon assignment, promptly send defense counsel a complete and legible copy of all pertinent documents in the claim file, assuming this is not a summons-first-notice case:
  - ○ All inter and intra memos and instructions.
  - ○ Coverage information including policy limits. If a coverage problem exists, be aware of the fact that a conflict of interests is inherent and that a separate attorney will probably have to be appointed to represent the insured or the insurance company.
  - ○ Check to determine if any other insured could possibly be involved that might cause an additional conflict of interests.
  - ○ If the file is not self-explanatory, give reasons why the case went into suit.
  - ○ Request appropriate reports and opinions but be aware that such opinions may be used against the insurer if not fully accepted.
  - ○ If the insurer desires the services of a particular member of a law firm, make your views known diplomatically or preferably have such an understanding in advance.
- ☐ Complete the investigation as soon as possible and forward investigation reports and material promptly to defense counsel.
- ☐ Discuss reserve information if this is company practice.
- ☐ Request suggestions for additional investigation.
- ☐ Suggest what reports are expected from counsel and in what format, and inform counsel promptly of any changes in home office requirements.
- ☐ Inform counsel promptly of any settlement negotiations. Counsel should be made to understand exactly what part he or she is to play in such negotiations. If counsel is to enter into such negotiations, request him to keep insurer advised immediately. Make sure that he has a definite understanding concerning his settlement authority and that of those in the company with whom he is dealing.
- ☐ Request copies of all legal papers that are pertinent and specify as to depositions or digests.
- ☐ Notify counsel immediately of any change in claim supervision.
- ☐ Answer all correspondence promptly with any requested information or indicate that you will try to get it, especially when authority to act is requested.
- ☐ Request counsel to make constant reevaluations and to keep company informed of them and all important developments.
- ☐ Promptly pay all justified bills from or forwarded by counsel.

[2] Settlement Reevaluation

Quite a few factors have developed in recent years that stack the odds against an insurer in making a determination as to whether or not a suit should be permitted to go to trial.

SUITS AND CASUALTY LITIGATION § 14.02[2][a]

The proliferation of bad faith or negligence actions for damages in excess of the policy limits, punitive damages, unfair claim practices acts used to grant individual rights of action, skyrocketing defense costs, the shocking increase in amounts awarded by juries, and other factors of a lesser nature are matters to be seriously considered, in addition to the common factors that must be weighed and which have previously been discussed.

Overemphasis on these considerations, however, can lead into a fear trap that beclouds good judgment. Unjust and overvalued demands should still be faced with decided resistance. There will be many occasions where a fair decision dictates the necessity for trial. In such instances, the claim representative's attendance at trial, with enough settlement authority is crucial. Even when there is a gut reaction against settlement, the claim representative should always keep his mind open enough to face realities. An entrenched, stubborn, and arbitrary position is usually the position of a claim representative who is more interested in justifying his previous judgment than he is in making a fair evaluation.

In making the following suggestions concerning reports requested from defense counsel and from field office to the home or regional office, it must always be kept in mind that in most jurisdictions, copies of such reports may have to be given to plaintiff's counsel. Each company must therefore adopt a policy concerning what material they want in the claim file. The following suggestions assume a desire to have a complete claim file, especially in jurisdictions where privileged communications are honored as such.

[a] Defense Counsel's Review

Trial counsel should be requested to furnish the company with a complete review of the file as soon as reasonably possible after he receives it. Such a review should contain the attorney's opinion on liability and settlement value at that particular time, his opinion as to whether the investigation already made is sufficiently complete, as well as his recommendations for further investigation and future action.

If the attorney has sufficient information, he should research the law and report on it, make reserve recommendations, and evaluate the claim, on the basis of his recommendation, in respect to settlement or trial.

§ 14.02[2][b] CASUALTY INSURANCE CLAIMS

Ordinarily, and particularly in important cases, when trial date has been set, the file should again be reviewed most thoroughly by the defense attorney.

Trial counsel's last pretrial review should be made early enough so that it will not be necessary for anyone in the home office to make a sudden snap decision without full information. Nothing is more irritating to a home office examiner than to receive a last minute telephone call requesting settlement authority just before a case is to be tried, particularly if the authority requested is considerably more than the attorney's previous evaluations.

Points to review. Depending on the importance of the case, such a review should include:

1. A complete review of the facts upon which the attorney's opinion of liability is predicated.
2. A review of the law.
3. Attorney's opinion on whether the case will reach the jury.
4. Medical review and opinion on its effect on the jury.
5. Review of the special damages and an indication of their credibility.
6. Attorney's opinion on the impression which the insured, claimant, and all other witnesses may make upon the jury.
7. Attorney's opinion about the ability, qualifications, peculiarities, and prejudices of the plaintiff's attorney, the trial judge, and local juries.
8. Opinion on the trend of recent verdicts.
9. Opinion on the likelihood of a verdict.
10. Attorney's settlement evaluation in actual dollars.
11. Report on previous negotiations giving the last demand and offer.
12. Last-minute instructions for additional investigation and work to be completed by the claim representative.

[b] **Claim Manager's or Supervisor's Review**

Most companies like to have the opinion of the claim manager or supervisor, in addition to that of trial counsel, particularly since the claim representative can add information concerning trial counsel, who may not be familiar to the home office. If necessary, such information should include:

1. Opinion of trial counsel's ability and standing in the community.
2. Opinion of the plaintiff's attorney's ability and standing.
3. Trend of recent verdicts in that locality.
4. Opinion on liability and additional investigation needed, as well as an estimate of settlement value.
5. Report on settlement negotiations.
6. Any additional recommendations, including report on the availability of all witnesses, the plaintiff, and the defendant.
7. Condition of all evidence and review of physical facts.
8. Review of the reserves and recommendations for any necessary change.

[3] **Reservation of Rights or Nonwaiver Agreements**

There are many instances in which it may be advisable to appear for an insured, his driver, or others, despite the fact that there may be an unresolved coverage question. Appearance is often made by the insurance company in order to control the defense and avoid the possibility of a default judgment.

In such instances, it is important that the investigation necessary to resolve the coverage questions be made immediately and that the factual information be submitted as soon as possible so that a proper determination can be made promptly.

[4] **Availability of Witnesses**

A regular periodic check-up on the availability of all witnesses should be made from the time a claim first goes into suit until final disposition of it has been made. It is always advisable in checking on a witness to obtain the name and address of a close relative through whom the witness may be contacted in the event that the witness moves about frequently.

The likelihood of losing track of a witness is greatly reduced if such a check-up is made on a semi-annual basis.

[5] **Trial Preparation**

Only a very small percentage of the claims handled should ever be tried. Trial should be the last resort of an insurance carrier, after every fair means of amicable settlement has failed.

It is therefore clear that by the time the claim representative has reached the pretrial stage in the handling of a claim, he will have mustered all his forces either to convince the plaintiff's attorney to make a reasonable settlement, or to be as well prepared as possible for actual trial.

Trial counsel's pretrial preparation is a field of study in itself, about which much has already been written. Our main concern is to determine what is needed from the insurer's point of view.

Actually, pretrial preparation begins at the inception of a claim and involves everything from the initial investigation on through the various steps that have been previously outlined. In this particular discussion, however, we are particularly concerned with the steps which must be taken after we have learned the trial date.

At this stage, it is absolutely essential that the claim representative and the defense attorney work in close cooperation, so that each can perform his own particular duties without interference or going at cross purposes.

As soon as trial date has been determined, complete and thorough review of the file should be made by both trial counsel and claim supervisor to determine whether the investigation is complete in all respects and to make sure that there are no loose ends.

Most companies place ultimate responsibility for the handling of a suit on the shoulders of the claim supervisor. They believe that he is the proper person to be at least a party to settlement negotiations, if not actually to conduct them. It is also his responsibility to see that the investigation is completed and to carry out any instructions for additional investigation that may be given him by the trial counsel.

Such instruction should not be construed as a reflection on the ability or thoroughness of the investigator. As every experienced adjuster knows, a good claim supervisor who reviews a file can come up with at least a few additional ideas, no matter who previously investigated or handled the claim. It is essential that any investigation suggested by the attorney be completed as promptly as possible, for obvious reasons.

The file should also be reviewed carefully by in-house counsel to see that all pleadings are in order, all motions properly filed, and all necessary depositions taken or arranged for. It is of considerable importance that arrangements for any depositions be made sufficiently in advance of trial so that any leads obtained can be investigated in good time.

Here again is another chance to try to dispose of the case by settlement, if this is warranted. A closed suit eliminates trial expense, danger of an excessive verdict, lowers the overhead, and permits the claim representative to devote his attention to other claims. Such a settlement attempt presumes, however, that the plaintiff's attorney will be reasonable in his demands.

It has often been argued that any approach to the plaintiff's attorney with a view to entering settlement negotiations is a sign of weakness and puts the company at a disadvantage. I have never been able to agree with this negative line of reasoning. My own experience has been that whenever enough facts have been gathered to make a determination of liability and a valuation of the injury, the proper time has come to enter into settlement negotiations, whether the matter be in claim or in suit. The problem of approach requires common sense.

The claim representative may indicate a desire to determine the demand before bending all his energies toward completion of the investigation, or he may base his approach upon year-end review and clean-up, or upon a request from the home office. It is high time that both sides recognized the desirability of an amicable settlement and that any initiative taken to reach such an accomplishment is no sign of weakness on the part of either one.

Trial counsel, on his part, must at least see the insured and the principal witnesses in advance of actual trial. He must get to know what they look like, and how they answer questions at first hand. The claim representative should help to see that this is arranged, and to reassure the insured and all witnesses concerning the actual trial. To most laymen a courtroom is a rather awesome environment, and if they are assured that we only want them to tell the truth in their own particular way, much of the apprehension will disappear and they will, as a result, make better witnesses.

In the event of any difficulty with an insured, it is occasionally necessary to remind him that one of the conditions of the policy requires that at the company's request, he must attend hearings and trial, and assist in effecting settlements, securing and giving evidence, obtaining the attendance of witnesses, and in the conduct of the suit.

[6] **Trial and Disposition**

If the case must be tried, it should be done with a determination to win. The probabilities are that if settlement has been impossible before now, the demand was too high because of either the injury or the liability. Some advantage is therefore with the insured, however slight it may appear.

Whenever possible, the claim manager or casualty supervisor should personally attend all important trials so that he may be able to evaluate the suit at any moment should settlement possibilities appear favorable. Attendance at the trial also permits the claim representative to assist trial counsel in obtaining any last minute information or investigation, or to secure the attendance of a reluctant witness, if necessary. It is most important however, that he remain in the background.

In the event that settlement is effected before trial is completed, documentary evidence must be obtained indicating that all court records have been cleared and that there has been a proper entry or filing of the dismissal order, stipulation, withdrawal or other closing paper, whatever it may be called in a particular jurisdiction. Should voluntary judgment be entered, it is necessary to see that judgment is satisfied in the same manner as though verdict has been rendered against the defendant.

[7] Appeal

The defeated party in a court of original jurisdiction has the right, for certain specified reasons and within a specified time, to appeal to have his case reviewed by a higher court.

In some jurisdictions some overt act is required of the victorious party in order to start the running of the time for appeal. In Michigan, for instance, "Proof of Service on Opposing Counsel" is required.

The claim representative must know his local rules and see that they are complied with. It is sometimes advisable to "backstop" outside counsel in matters of this kind.

When a verdict has been rendered in favor of a plaintiff, trial counsel should prepare an immediate review of the trial, giving all the pertinent facts and his opinion on whether or not the case should be appealed. Such an opinion should not be based on prejudice, pique, or resentment, but on an unbiased and clear analysis of all of the factors and probable expense involved. The review should be forwarded to the insurance company in sufficient time for proper consideration to be given to the problem without the pressure of having time run out too soon.

SUITS AND CASUALTY LITIGATION § 14.02[8]

Two factors must be given serious consideration in any decision concerning the advisability of appeal: (1) the expense factor, and (2) the possibility of creating bad law. At all times, the insured's best interests must be kept uppermost.

In some jurisdictions, an overt act is required of the victorious party in order to start the running of the time for appeal. If this is necessary in his jurisdiction, it should be made sure that it is followed through in accordance with the requirement.

In the event that the insurance carrier's trial counsel is victorious, the claim representative should be cautious about taking down the reserve on a case until he is sure that there will be no appeal.

[8] Checklist for Suit Preparation

A. Some Preliminary Guidelines for Defense Counsel:

- ☐ Review the case shortly after it has been received and outline carefully the investigation needed. Pretrial investigation begins on the day the attorney gets first notice of the suit.
- ☐ Do not evaluate the case until the basic investigation has been received and then do so carefully in the light of all pertinent information.
- ☐ Make periodic reviews of the file to make sure that the requested investigation is being completed.
- ☐ Arrange the file chronologically so that all information is available with the least confusion. Keep the file neat and in order.
- ☐ Outline and index the case.
- ☐ See that all pleadings have been reviewed and are in order, all motions have been properly filed, all interrogatories have been made and answered, and all necessary depositions have been taken.
- ☐ Determine if proper consideration has been given to the venue where the case is to be tried.
- ☐ Make sure that the necessary investigation, reports and records have been received and all loose ends have been followed up.
- ☐ Determine if all avenues for possible settlement have been explored without success.
- ☐ Make sure that final check has been made to determine the availability of all witnesses, including the defendant, any passengers, outside witnesses, doctors, appraisers and engineers, photographers and any other experts.
- ☐ See that arrangements have been made for service of subpoenas or court orders where required, in order to produce witnesses, police officers, hospital and salary records and any other needed records, or witnesses.
- ☐ See that arrangements have been made to see the defendant and other key witnesses in order to properly evaluate them and to determine that there has been no lapse of memory concerning important details.

§ 14.02[8] CASUALTY INSURANCE CLAIMS

☐ See the scene of the accident where this is warranted.

B. Final Review of Files by Claim Supervisor and Defense Counsel:

☐ **Coverage Information.** Review the policy and the facts to make sure that all questions concerning coverage have been resolved. If a question still exists, make sure that proper reservation of rights letter has been sent or nonwaiver agreement obtained.
  ○ Consider the advisability of declaratory judgment action. Make sure that a proper excess ad damnum letter has been sent where necessary. Make sure that all proper precautions have been taken to avoid possibility of an excess verdict.

☐ **Review the Facts.** Determine if the following statements and reports have been obtained.
  ○ Insured's or defendant's statement.
  ○ Plaintiff's version or statement.
  ○ All witnesses' statements including passengers and outside witnesses as well as negative witnesses.
  ○ Expert witnesses' reports. Make sure that these experts are properly qualified to testify.
  ○ Police, motor vehicle, hospital, coroners, P.U.C. and I.C.C. Reports and other reports and records that give a history of the accident.

☐ **Review the Physical Evidence.** Check to make sure that all evidence and exhibits are available and identifiable. Make sure that they are in proper condition for presentation as evidence.
  ○ Equipment of any kind including products, parts, broken bottles, descriptive, advertising or instructional material, labels, etc.
  ○ Certified copies of public records.
  ○ Determine whether all necessary photographs are on file such as snapshots, commercial photographs, enlargements, color photographs, overlays, aerial views, panorama shots, etc. Scrutinize the pictures in order to make sure that there is no danger of distortion. Height, angle, depth, filters, or developing can all alter proper view of the situation.
  ○ Review any movies that were taken and make sure that they were taken by an expert who can testify concerning the rate of speed at which the film was taken and that the result was a true version of what was photographed. Make sure that the movies can be qualified for admission by being able to prove that they were not tampered with or cut in any fashion.
  ○ Determine whether all other visual aids have been obtained and are ready for presentation, such as plats, diagrams, mats, cut-outs, scale models and other demonstrative evidence, including medical charts and models.
  ○ Determine whether all survey and appraisal reports are available including chemical and other laboratory analysis and tests.

SUITS AND CASUALTY LITIGATION § 14.03

- ○ Determine if all necessary reports have been obtained, such as index bureau reports, police, motor vehicle, P.U.S., I.C.C., hospital records, coroner's reports, school records, autopsy, and other public records as well as any other governmental, state or municipal records. Make sure that the proper subpoenas have been served so that the reports may be used at trial if necessary.
- ☐ **Medical Information:** Review and evaluate all medical reports such as:
  - ○ Plaintiff's or plaintiff's attorney's version of injuries and disability.
  - ○ Autopsy reports.
  - ○ Reports of attending doctors, dentists, and surgeons. Evaluate their potential as witnesses.
  - ○ Hospital records.
  - ○ Veteran's records.
  - ○ X-ray records and x-ray plates where necessary.
  - ○ Determine whether a physical examination has been made if needed and make sure of the availability of the examining doctor. Have a pre-trial interview with him in order to evaluate his testimony.
- ☐ **Special Damages.** Check to see if these have been obtained and determine whether they have been checked as authentic:
  - ○ Wage and salary records including income tax reports if available. Employer's records or plaintiff's account books.
  - ○ Medical bills, including doctors, dentists, nurses, ambulance, hospital and all other similar bills.
  - ○ Property damage of any kind including automobiles, clothes, jewelry, etc.

§ 14.03 Law Reporting Systems

The report of the cases is the primary means by which lawyers and judges are guided as to the state of the law in the jurisdiction. The guiding principle in legal decisionmaking is that like cases with like factual circumstances will be decided in the same way, and that future decisionmaking will follow past decisionmaking. This is the principle behind the rule of *stare decisis* which requires that courts regard the rule of law applied to past decisions with a similar fact situation as binding precedent on later cases. As previously indicated, this rule is still given lip service, while being all but abandoned as social and political conditions rapidly change.

The report of the case, or opinion, is the primary source of the common law. The common law came to the United States as part of our English legal heritage. The opinions of the English judges and their announcement of rules of law, whether based on custom or the edict of the king, is the foundation of American common law. It was not uncommon, as late as the early twentieth century to find the opinions of the English judges turning up as the guiding principles for American judges.

Rules of law passed by parliamentary, legislative or administrative bodies, known as statutes or regulations, are subject to statutory construction, or application of the facts of the case to the language of the statute. If the language of the statute is unclear, then the courts must try to ascertain the legislative intent behind the statute. Decisions of statutory construction are also subject to the same rule of *stare decisis*.

In order to facilitate the full application of the rule of *stare decisis*, it is fundamental that decisions of the courts be reported in a routine and systematic manner. In the early English courts, the judges read their opinions orally and these opinions were taken down verbatim by court reporters. They were published by the reporter and informally disseminated to the bench and bar. To date, England does not have an official reporter of the opinions of its courts.

However, in the United States, regular, routine, and current publication of court opinions has been established in every state court and in the federal courts for over 100 years. The reports of the opinions of the United States Supreme Court have been published since the first term of the Court. In the United States, the opinions of most state courts and the United States Supreme Court are officially published. In addition, a large number of unofficial commercial publishers publish opinions and administrative decisions of other courts and tribunals. This section will provide a brief overview of these various law reporting systems.

At the outset, it should be understood that the reports containing state court opinions are almost exclusively decisions of the appellate courts. In the federal system, the selected opinions of the United States District Courts (courts of original jurisdiction) are regularly published.

From the time the opinion of the court is announced until it ends up in a final bound volume, it goes through several stages. At first, the opinion may be read orally by its individual author during a session of court. The layman is probably most familiar with the announced decisions of the United States Supreme Court.

In many instances, when a single justice authors an opinion on behalf of the court, the justice will read the opinion from the bench in the courtroom. The author of a dissnet may also read his or her dissenting opinion in the courtroom. Copies of the opinion in its original form will be available in the clerk's office and will be sent to counsel for the parties. This first type of written opinion is called a slip opinion. Some state courts offer a subscription service which makes each decision of the state appellate courts available to interested members of the bar and the public.

The next form the opinion will take will be as part of an advance sheet. The advance sheet is the paperbound version of what will ultimately be the permanent bound volume of the reports. The advance sheet typically contains the same pagination that will be found in the bound reporter, but is not considered the final form of the opinion. Occasionally, an opinion published in the advance sheets is withdrawn by the court and a gap of pages will be found in the permanent bound edition.

The permanent bound edition of the reporter becomes part of the body of the law of the jurisdiction. In almost all jurisdictions, the number of bound volumes runs in the hundreds, and in some cases thousands.

In the federal judicial system, consisting primarily of the Supreme Court, courts of appeals, and district courts, only the Supreme Court has an official reporter system published by the Government Printing Office. This reporter is referred to as the United States Reports. It is published as an advance sheet and bound volume which is presently approaching its 500th volume. At the present, it takes as long as three years between the time an opinion by the Supreme Court is announced and the time it is set in the permanent bound edition of the reports.

In addition to the official United States Reports, there are also two unofficial reporters of decisions of the Supreme Court: The Supreme Court Reporter, published by West Publishing Company, and the United States Supreme Court Reports, Lawyers Edition (known as Lawyers Edition), published by the Lawyers Co-operative Publishing Company. These reporters are published in advance sheets and bound volume form. The advance sheets generally appear within a month or two of the announcement of the decision by the Supreme Court, while the official advance sheet may not come out for a year or more after the decision is announced.

The Supreme Court Reporter exceeds 100 volumes, while the Lawyers Edition is in its second series of volumes. They both contain every opinion, summary decision, and order contained in the official reporter.

In contrast, there are no official reporter systems for the federal courts of appeals or district courts. Rather, these opinions are found in two series of reporters published by West Publishing Company: the Federal Reporter and the Federal Supplement. The Federal Reporter, currently in its second series (800 plus volumes), reports the opinions of the federal courts of appeals. The first series of Federal Reporters, first published in 1880, also contains selected opinions from the United States District Court.

Since 1932, the Federal Supplement has published the selected opinions for the U.S. district courts. West also publishes the Bankruptcy Court Reporter, containing decisions of the U. S. bankruptcy courts, and the Federal Rules Decisions, containing district court opinions construing the Federal Rules of Civil and Criminal Procedure.

State court opinions are available in official and unofficial forms, the latter being published in the West National Reporter System, discussed below. To date, only about two-thirds of the states officially publish decisions of their appellate courts, and this number has been declining. For instance, in New York, the opinions of the state's highest court, the court of appeals, are published in the New York Reports, while decisions of the appellate division of the Supreme Court are found in the Appellate Division Reports. Reports from other lower courts in New York, such as the supreme court (trial court), criminal court or family court are found in the New York Miscellaneous Reports. In Michigan, the reports of the Michigan Supreme Court and Michigan Court of Appeals are published in the Michigan Reports and Michigan Appeals Reports, respectively.

The decisions of state appellate courts are also available in unofficial form, published exclusively by West Publishing Company, in its National Reporter System. The National Reporter System consists of seven regional reporters containing nearly all the appellate reports from each state in the nation. In some instances, the West Regional Reporter is the only source of a state's appellate reports. The state of Texas last officially published the opinions of the Texas Supreme Court in 1962. Since that time, the decisions of the Supreme Court, along with the Texas Court of Civil Appeals and Court of Criminal Appeals, have been published in West's Southwestern Reporter.

As is obvious to anyone who has seen a law library, the cost of maintaining it and keeping it up to date is prodigious in terms of actual cost and space requirements. Accordingly, even in the libraries of some prestigious law firms and law schools, reports are not kept in individual state series, except for indigenous states. For the most part, West's regional reports are most often cited. With the proliferation of computerized systems, the law library, as we now know it, may shortly become an anachronism.

The various regional reporters and the states they cover, are as follows:[1]

A. & A.2d, Atlantic Reporter: Connecticut, Delaware, District of Columbia, Maine, Maryland, New Hampshire, New Jersey, Pennsylvania, Rhode Island, and Vermont;

N.E. & N.E.2d, Northeastern Reporter: Illinois, Indiana, Massachusetts, New York, and Ohio;

N.W. & N.W.2d, Northwestern Reporter: Iowa, Michigan, Minnesota, Nebraska, North Dakota, South Dakota, and Wisconsin;

P. & P.2d, Pacific Reporter: Alaska, Arizona, California, Colorado, Hawaii, Idaho, Kansas, Montana, Nevada, New Mexico, Oklahoma, Oregon, Utah, Washington, and Wyoming;

S. or So. & So.2d, Southern Reporter: Alabama, Florida, Louisiana, and Mississippi;

S.E. & S.E.2d, Southeastern Reporter: Georgia, North Carolina, South Carolina, Virginia, and West Virginia;

S.W. & S.W.2d, Southwestern Reporter: Arkansas, Kentucky, Missouri, Tennessee, and Texas.

In addition to these regional reporters, West also publishes separate reporters for New York and California courts known as the New York Supplement (N.Y.S. & N.Y.S.2d) and the California Reporter (Cal. Rptr.). The New York Supplement reports the decisions of all of the New York courts and contains the same decisions as the Northeastern Reporter. However, the California Reporter is the only West publication containing the reports of the California courts and California decisions that have not appeared in the Pacific Reporter since 1959.

In addition to the official and unofficial reporter systems discussed above, which are the primary sources for the opinions of the nation's courts, there are dozens of specialized and looseleaf services available which report opinions of virtually every state and federal court and administrative agency. These services publish everything from the opinions of the United States Tax Court and Interstate Com-

---

[1] The reports of the California and New York courts are also contained in other reporters, discussed below.

§ 14.03[1] CASUALTY INSURANCE CLAIMS

merce Commission to decisions of state workers' compensation appeals boards and social security appeals boards. Particularly helpful is U.S. Law Week, published weekly by the Bureau of National Affairs (BNA). U.S. Law Week contains recent case summaries running the gamut of American law, and specialized articles discussing recent developments in separate areas of the law.

As has been evident throughout this text, cases are identified in citation form by regional reporters. Others are given as follows:

    United States Supreme Court—U.S., S. Ct. or L. Ed. 2d
        District Federal Court—F. Supp.
        Federal Circuit Court—F. & F.2d.
        Federal Rules Decisions—F.R.D.
        Bankruptcy Reports—Bankr.
    Commerce Clearing House Reports—CCH
        U.S. Law Week—U.S.L.W.

It is important to note that the federal court decisions are based upon the law of the state that would ordinarily have jurisdiction, as interpreted by the particular federal court.

[1] Available Computer Systems

Finally, the claim representative should be aware that as with many extensive compilations of writings, legal source materials have been reduced to computer database formats. Today there are several computer accessible databases available in the United States, the most widely available and well-known are Westlaw and Lexis.

Westlaw, as the name implies, is sold through West Publishing Company. These on-line computer databases have extensive holdings which are available through library and law office terminals.

Westlaw databases contain all of West's national and federal reporter systems and have access to federal court decisions not yet available in the advance sheets. The user is also able to access all state and federal statutes and regulations, attorney general opinions, and federal agency decisions from such a diverse alphabet soup as the FCC, FTC, NLRB, FERC, and SEC. In addition, Westlaw has databases from various state and federal reporter systems and commentaries published by CCH and BNA, such as CCH tax materials and BNA's U.S. Law Week and Blue Sky Reporter. Westlaw has access to Shepard's case citators and Black's Law Dictionary. Finally, Westlaw databases contain state topical libraries, including insurance case reports and statutes.

SUITS AND CASUALTY LITIGATION § 14.04

Lexis, Westlaw's largest competitor, is sold by the Mead Data Central Company of Dayton, Ohio. It has much the same state and federal databases as Westlaw and perhaps a broader section of treatises, bar journals, and law reviews. Lexis also accesses English, Commonwealth, and French legal source materials.

Lexis has a specific insurance law library containing insurance regulations, codes, attorney general opinions, and other miscellaneous materials. The user may also access the ABA Tort and Insurance Law Journal and the Proceedings of the National Association of Insurance Commissioners.

Others law related computer databases include Dialog, currently containing insurance abstracts from 1974 to 1984, and Wilson Line, containing an index to legal periodicals.

Finally, it goes without saying that if the claim representative is going to turn to legal source materials, he is going to have to have access to a law library. Most large metropolitan areas have one or more law schools, each of which have law libraries. As a matter of courtesy to the local bar, these law libraries are typically open to the public. In addition to law school libraries, public law libraries are typically found in most county seats and are also open to the public. An increasing number of university and community college libraries also contain legal holdings that may include the particular state reporter system, statutes, and the United States Supreme Court Reports. The claim representative will find that there are also many private law libraries maintained by various bar associations. Obviously, house counsel or outside counsel for the carrier will be a valuable source for legal source materials.

§ 14.04 Bibliography

A Uniform System of Citation. 14th ed. Cambridge, Mass.: Harvard Law Review Association, 1986.

Brenner, "A Comment as to Massive Pre-Trials and a Proposal for Pre-Suit Evaluation to Reduce Vehicle Accident Jury Cases,"Insurance Counsel Journal, January 1968.

Damsel, Jr., "Effective Delivery of Defense Counsel Services at a Price the Public Can Afford," F.I.C. Quarterly, Summer 1978.

Defense Research Committee's "Report and Recommendations for the Most Efficient Use of Legal Effort," Insurance Counsel Journal, October 1963.

Green, *Basic Civil Procedure* (2d ed. 1979).

"How an Active Law Firm Handles an Insurance Company Referral," F.I.C. Quarterly, Summer 1963.

Knapp, "Why Argue an Appeal? If So, How?", Insurance Law Journal, January 1960.

Long, "Problem Area Between Home Office and Trial Counsel," Insurance Counsel Journal, October 1965.

Moore, *Federal Practice*. New York: Matthew Bender & Company, 1986.

Sharratt, "What a Company Expects of Its Defense Trial Counsel," Insurance Law Journal, September 1962.

Shepherd, "How Long is the Long Arm of Due Process," Insurance Counsel Journal, April 1967.

Teply, *Program Materials on Legal Research* (1982).

Wright, Miller & Caine, *Federal Practice & Procedure*. Minn: West Publishing Co., 1986.

CHAPTER 15

Fraud

§ 15.01 Fraud by the Claimant Concerning the Facts of an Accident
§ 15.02 Fraud Regarding Allegations of Injury
§ 15.03 Fraud Practiced by Repairmen or Doctors Without Collusion by the Claimant
§ 15.04 Fraudulent Acts of an Insured
§ 15.05 Beware of Danger Signals
§ 15.06 Investigation of Claims Involving Fraud
    [1] Undercover Investigations
    [2] Index Bureau
§ 15.07 Medical Fraud and Psychosomatic Illness
§ 15.08 Medical Fraud—Overtreatment and Incompetence
    [1] Misused Medical Terminology
    [2] Iatrogeny
§ 15.09 Bibliography

Many articles, books, and discussions on the subject of fraud in casualty claims make some attempt to distinguish between falsification of the facts in an accident, as opposed to mere exaggeration of injury. Those attempting such a distinction have insisted that only the first category is fraud, and that the cases having to do with medical exaggeration are just malingering. This seems to make an unnecessary distinction between little evil and big evil. To be blunt—malingering is fraud.

The claim representative has no doubt heard these rationalizations: "There's a little larceny in all of us," and "It's only human nature to try to get something for nothing." These are half truths. The distinction between an honest man and a thief is that the honest man resists temptation. He does not deny that it exists.

There are many kinds of casualty claims susceptible to fraudulent allegations. Listing the more general types of fraudulent claims may aid the newcomer to the claims field in recognizing them and will certainly alert him to the various possibilities and exposures.

§ 15.01 Fraud by the Claimant Concerning the Facts of an Accident

1. **Complete fabricated accident involving collusion** between an insured, claimant, physician, and, possibly, attorney. This is what is commonly known as a fraud "ring" and is still a matter of concern to insurance companies. The type of fraud practiced today by some attorneys and physicians is of a much more subtle variety than the old "ring," which was as weak as its weakest link and involved too much risk for too little individual return. Although it is a matter of lesser importance today, it still does crop up and the claim representative should be alert to the possibility.

2. **Individual fraud of the claimant.** In this type of case, the claimant does not use accomplices to perform fraudulent acts. Examples of this type of fraud would be placing a mouse or other foreign body or matter in bottled beverages, or putting insects in canned foods, and then suing their packer.

3. **Fraudulent witnesses.** This type of case is usually encountered when an accident occurs in an area familiar to the claimant. An investigator will not often encounter witnesses who are completely phony; that is, witnesses who know nothing about the accident except what the claimant told them. Ordinarily, this type of fraud involves witnesses who either saw or may have heard about the accident, but who have changed their story at the claimant's behest, to indicate liability on the part of the insured.

4. **Change in the location of an accident.** An example of this type of fraud would be an allegation that the claimant fell on a defective part of the sidewalk whereas the fall actually happened in an area where there was no defect. Sometimes the scene of an accident may be changed from the property owned by one person to property a considerable distance away that was known to be insured.

5. **Change in condition.** In this type of case, the scene of an accident is changed to create the appearance of liability where none existed at the time of the accident. Prying up the metal nosing on a step after an accident had previously occurred would be an example of this type of fraud.

6. **Fraudulent allegation involving insured's automobile.** There have been many instances where injuries were sustained as a result of barroom brawls, falls, and other mishaps having absolutely no relationship to an automobile accident. The claimant in this type of case, having sustained an actual injury, usually picks as his victim a com-

FRAUD § 15.02

mercial vehicle, which he knows to be insured and which regularly travels in the area where he alleges the accident occurred. The alleged facts, as well as the circumstances, usually fall into a recognizable pattern. Since the hit-and-run driver is the exception in our society, the usual allegation is that the truck made a sharp turn around a corner, causing the rear end of a protruding part thereof, to strike the claimant and knock him down.

§ 15.02 Fraud Regarding Allegations of Injury

1. **Completely fabricated disability.** In this type of fraudulent claim, the claimant sustained no injury whatsoever, but is making up symptoms out of whole cloth. He may have false x-rays or "trick" medical conditions, such as joints that he can throw out of place at will.

2. **No causal relationship between the accident and the disability.** In this type of case, the claimant may be suffering from some disability either traumatic or organic in origin. This injury or disability, however, had nothing to do with the accident under investigation. Here the situation is a little more difficult because it becomes necessary to prove that the disability predated the accident or that the accident could not have caused that type of injury.

3. **Unduly prolonged treatment and alleged disability.** In this type of case, proof becomes even more difficult since it usually starts with some legitimate injury arising out of the accident under investigation, but where treatment and alleged disability are prolonged beyond the point where complete recovery should have been made.

4. **Completely subjective complaints.** Here the investigator may have a situation involving either a completely fabricated disability or one where there is some legitimate disability to which the claimant is attempting to add additional subjective complaints. These are often hard to detect, especially if the claimant has received good coaching or has done some medical research of his own.

5. **Alleged aggravation where none exists.** In this type of case, the claimant admittedly was suffering from some preexisting condition which he makes no attempt to hide. Here, however, he alleges that the preexisting condition was aggravated as a result of the accident. This is one of the most difficult medical allegations to disprove.

6. **Exaggerated aggravation.** Finally, we have the situation where a claimant was admittedly suffering from some preexisting condition

§ 15.03   CASUALTY INSURANCE CLAIMS

and where the accident under investigation did cause some slight aggravation. In this type of case, the claimant merely enlarges on the aggravation.

§ 15.03 Fraud Practiced by Repairmen or Doctors Without Collusion by the Claimant

Infrequently a claim representative will encounter instances where an unjustly high repair bill or bill for medical services is submitted without fault or collusion on the part of the claimant. Claims of this nature require very diplomatic handling because the repairman or doctor has usually gained the confidence of the claimant. The latter will suspect that the claim investigator has an ulterior motive when he questions the bills.

§ 15.04 Fraudulent Acts of an Insured

No race, creed, color, religion, profession, or economic group has any monopoly on fraud. It crosses all lines and all boundaries and is attempted by insureds as well as claimants. For instance:

1. **Post-dated policy.** This situation may arise with or without the collusion of a broker or agent. It involves an individual who has sustained an accident without insurance coverage. Usually where this type of fraud is practiced, the prospective insured will call a broker or agent and arrange for a binder or policy to be written, the inception to be indicated at some date or hour prior to the time of the accident which has already occurred. Sometimes the individual will attempt to get a broker or agent to pre-date the policy by some ruse or excuse. An agent is rarely party to this type of fraud, but occasionally he is. The reputation of the agent or broker is, of course, of primary importance in detecting this type of fraud. A careful check must always be made for this possibility if the inception date of a policy is close to the alleged date of accident.

2. **Uninsured auto.** Occasionally, an insured may own other vehicles in addition to the car which is insured. Prompt and proper identification of the vehicle involved in the accident can prevent any attempt to obtain coverage on an uninsured car. This today is a minor problem because of the automatic coverage feature for new cars in most automobile policies.

3. **Material damage losses.** These afford the greatest opportunity for an insured to present fraudulent claims:

   (a) Padded bills to cover the deductible feature on collision losses. It is amazing at the number of people who look upon this type of fraud as "legitimate." It is not an uncommon practice and, in some instances, garages and repair agencies are comparatively innocent victims who are told by their customers that if they don't pad the bill to cover the deductible, the business will be taken elsewhere.

   (b) A more blatant type of fraud is the attempt by an insured to get body paint, or motor damage caused by wear and tear, to be repaired as a result of an allegation of malicious mischief or other coverage under the comprehensive section of a physical damage policy. This will be discussed at greater length in § 22.05 covering physical damage claims.

   (c) Arson. Our concern in casualty matters is with arson in respect to automobiles. The claim investigator should beware of automobiles that apparently catch fire spontaneously in isolated areas.

§ 15.05 Beware of Danger Signals

Those who have been in insurance claim work for any length of time will sometimes tell a new claim representative that after a while he will acquire a knack somewhat on the order of an intuitive sense that indicates when there is something that needs special looking-into in a particular claim. What appears to be a sixth sense, however, is nothing more than an accumulation of past experience registering on a perceptive and intelligent mind.

There are innumerable signals that will automatically register caution to an experienced claim representative almost as a matter of reflex action. To list them all would be impossible, but as an illustration, here are some examples.

1. *Offers of favor from the claimant.* Bribery can be subtle as well as blatant. Offers of free or wholesale products or services preceding the disposition of a claim are usually suspect.

2. *Factual situations that seem too "pat".* It is very unusual for an insured's version to agree in all details with that of the claimant, let alone be also coincident with factual informa-

tion obtained from witnesses. Wherever there is too much agreement in a liability case, the case bears looking into.

3. *Claimant's desire for a quick settlement* in an amount that seems disproportionately small to the liability and the injury. Pressure to settle because the claimant "has to get out of town," or a slightly too frantic threat to turn the matter over to an outstanding negligence attorney, should be viewed with skepticism.

4. *Unwitnessed accidents.* These are what are commonly known in the industry as "blind accidents." Although it is obviously true that many accidents do occur at odd hours, and are not witnessed, seldom does someone not at least hear an outcry or see the injured person immediately or shortly after the accident. Blind accidents always warrant extra investigative effort.

5. *Complete denial of any knowledge of the accident by an insured.* Sometimes a driver, for fear of losing his job, or an insured who fears prosecution for "hit and run" driving, will deny knowledge of an accident that actually occurred. Usually, however, there are witnesses or other factors that will eventually reveal the truth. If the insured or driver, however, seems utterly sincere in their denial of the accident, there is a good chance that it never occurred.

6. *Claimants' or witnesses' stories that sound too well rehearsed.* To repeat, no two people will see an accident and report it in exactly the same manner. The honest witness will usually hesitate several times in an attempt to refresh his memory. The story that is rattled off as though it has been memorized is the story to suspect.

7. *Inability of claimant to produce proper identification,* prior addresses, employment history, etc.

8. *Unsavory reputation* of claimant, witnesses, doctor, or attorney.

9. *Claimant's unreasonable refusal to reveal medical details or detailed special damage information.* Vague allegations concerning injury or employment are certainly indicative of an attempt to hide something.

10. *Completely subjective complaints* of injuries which are peculiar or unusual. Because of a stringent attitude on the part of the insurance industry, strengthened by prosecutions fos-

tered by the Association of Casualty and Surety Companies (now the American Insurance Association), there are fewer claims arising from "trick injuries," such as knees and other joints that can be thrown out of alignment at will. Such claims are still a problem, however, especially in compensation cases.

11. *Undue delay by the claimant* in making a claim, coupled by an allegation of previous injuries from which he has allegedly recovered.
12. *Questionable accident* involving a claimant who is in financial difficulty.
13. *Unwarranted counterclaim* on an original action against a claimant for an unpaid bill, either by a doctor or a hospital.

§ 15.06 Investigation of Claims Involving Fraud

The investigation of a claim involving fraud should be as thorough as possible, whether the questionable feature be factual or involve the medical picture or special damages.

The investigator will encounter many claims which in the beginning will appear to be suspicious in one respect or another. In some instances, they will wash out clean. In others, his suspicions may remain but he will not be able to get the factual information to confirm them. He should avoid any acts, statements, or writings that may subject him or his company to an action for defamation.

The comments in this section will be confined to matters of a general nature. Where fraud is involved, emphasis in the investigation should be placed on the following points:

- ☐ Details of the claimant's background.
    - ○ General reputation and character.
    - ○ Financial condition.
    - ○ Employment.
    - ○ Hobbies and sports, such as gardening, golf, and so on.
    - ○ Social activities.
    - ○ Previous history.
        - — All previous addresses.
        - — All previous employers.
    - ○ Insurance, accident, and health policies.
    - ○ Police records.
    - ○ Index Bureau. Check on claimants, witnesses or any other parties under suspicion, such as doctors and attorneys.

- ☐ Complete medical investigation.
  - ○ Reputation of all attending physicians.
  - ○ Complete physical examination.
  - ○ X-rays.
  - ○ Physical activities that might be recorded by way of statements or motion pictures.
- ☐ Complete investigation of all special damages.
  - ○ Lost time and earnings and all details as previously outlined under the discussion of "special damages", in Chapter 3, *supra*.
  - ○ Complete check of all other special damages, including estimates, medical bills, and so on.

Important information may be obtained from almost any aspect of the investigation of a fraudulent case. Leads may also be obtained from depositions, interrogatories, and bills of particulars, if the claims have gone into suit.

Many medical tests can be made to detect malingering and fraud in medical allegations, but these are the province of the examining physician. The physician cannot, however, know what to look for unless he is given proper background information by the investigator. If malingering is suspected, the matter should always be discussed with the examining physician before the examination is made. Suspicions should be made clear to him.

If the physician wishes to discuss certain tests which he proposes to make, so much the better, but the claim representative should choose a competent physician in whom he has confidence.

[1] Undercover Investigations

Many private detective agencies specialize in doing undercover investigations for attorneys and insurance companies. It takes an expert who can testify in court, to take motion pictures that will be worthwhile. "Tailing" a suspect is another matter that is best left to the specialist in that field. If undercover investigation is advisable, engage the services of competent people and let them do the work. The claim representative should not, however, hire someone else to do an investigation that he could just as easily do himself with a little application and ingenuity. If the work definitely requires specialized training and experience, however, he should recognize his limitations.

In recent years, the courts have looked with an every-increasing jaundiced eye on information obtained under false pretenses. There are accordingly some definite boundaries within which the investigator should remain in order to be able to use in court the information that he obtains.

Obviously, if the claimant is represented by counsel the investigator has no business interviewing him at all, unless it is with the permission of his attorney.

If the claimant is not represented by counsel the investigator should be wary of using any disguise or false pretext in interviewing him.

In any event, no attempt should be made to induce a claimant to perform physical activities for the purpose of proving him to be malingering. The danger here is twofold. Even if the evidence could be used, there is always the possibility of aggravating a real disability, which could be disastrous.

In no event should the investigator commit an illegal act, or trespass on the claimant's property in order to obtain evidence.

A good investigator knows how to obtain valuable information without violating the law or the rights of the claimant. Movies of the claimant showing his normal activities can be obtained but must be used discretely. Judges and juries are prone to look upon evidence obtained by undercover means as an invasion of privacy. They do not always see the situation in the light of prevention of fraud.

In situations involving undercover investigations, it is always advisable to discuss all aspects of the proposed investigation with the insurer's counsel before, as well as after, it is made.

[2] Index Bureau

The Index Bureau of the American Insurance Association was set up for the purpose of making available the previous claim records of repeat claimants to member companies.

There are many occasions where reference to the Index Division will show that the claimant is a "repeater." In such cases, the leads furnished by the old cases are most important and should be diligently followed up. All too often this extremely important investigation is either neglected or completely ignored.

Once a lead has been obtained from the Index Bureau, the investigator should check through by personal contact with the insurance carrier on the previous accident to make certain that the claimant is the same one involved in his accident. He should obtain detailed information concerning the facts, injury, or any other pertinent data that may be available.

§ 15.07 Medical Fraud and Psychosomatic Illness

Psychosomatic illness is a physical disorder that is caused, or notably influenced, by the emotional state of the patient. Modern medicine is just beginning to scratch the surface of the interrelationship between the mind and bodily disability. A psychosomatic illness is just as real and can be just as painful as any other and it is the recognition of this fact that makes malingering so much more difficult to detect.

In the early days of liability insurance, doctors put little stock in ailments such as emotional distress. If the cause of the pain or disability was not readily apparent, short shrift was usually given to the complaints of such patients. As a result, doctors of standing were loath to get involved in situations where they felt that they could be held up to ridicule by opposing physicians, and courts and compensation boards were very skeptical of such allegations.

The fact that we are beginning to know how much effect the brain and the emotions may have on real physical disability and resultant pain, has created a field day for those claimants and their doctors and lawyers who are all too willing to covertly, and even actively, help the claimant or plaintiff to "prove" such allegations as post-traumatic stress syndromes, emotional distress, neuropsychological disabilities and depressive responses to injuries, or alleged injuries, among others.

In a very good article on this subject, Paul R. Lees-Haley, Ph.D.[1] states: "In the process of providing more humane treatment for real victims, we have opened the door for unethical claimants. Unfortunately, the individuals most likely to use deception . . . are also the best actors and the most adept liars." Such claimants learn from reading and from the reaction of their doctors and lawyers to the answers they give.

Let it be known that at present there are no completely fool-proof methods for detecting malingering, especially since today "most health care professionals are trained in helping orientation which emphasizes supportive, empathetic and healing forms of rapport building, rather than attempts to penetrate deception."[2]

The tried and true methods of detecting fraud such as neighborhood investigations, movies of the activities of allegedly disabled

---

[1] "Personal Injury Malingering," F.T.D., February 28, 1986.
[2] *Id.*

claimants, and witnesses' statements contradicting disability allegations are still available in most jurisdictions. The claims representative must, however, now be aware of the possible "back-lash" effect of such testimony on a jury intent on punishing an insurer who will be accused of taking unfair advantage of the claimant "while he or she wasn't looking," ludicrous though this may be.

Our best weapon is still the use of physician experts who can refute the allegations of the claimant and his or her doctors, but everyone is now well aware of the costs of such experts.

Dr. Lees-Haley gives a few clues that might help the adjuster to detect psychosomatic malingering. Persons truly suffering under these physical symptoms may exaggerate their problems in an effort to "cry for help," but they don't "ham it up" on cue and recover when the doctor or employer aren't looking. Genuinely mentally disturbed persons, says Dr. Lees-Haley, commonly exhibit behavior which is counterproductive, illogical and irrational, but this also is an area that I believe should be best left to psychiatrists. Trained physicians can give some tests to help detect malingering and such tests are often worth the expense involved, but the polygraph is not one of them. The polygraph has now become so discredited that it is only very rarely accepted in any court of law.

Unfortunately, these days, there are less and less areas where definite answers can be obtained in the ever ongoing fight against fraud, especially in the nature of malingering. Claim handling has become a much more complex occupation than it was in previous years.

Unnecessary use of a psychiatrist is sometimes likely to do more harm than good, but there is a real need to get psychiatric help where it is clearly called for.

§ 15.08 Medical Fraud—Overtreatment and Incompetence

As R. Kent L. Brown, in his article, "Overtreatment of Accident Patients,"[3] states:

> The problem is basically one of dual morality. Individuals who are apparently honest, suffer some types of an ethical and moral breakdown in certain legal cases. The physician who has had excellent training and is a superb surgeon, on the one hand, may be persuaded to color his legal reports and to "go along" in "building" [these] cases by making

---

[3] D.R.I. Monograph, October 1966.

fancy or questionable diagnosis and to require the use of braces, collars, traction or therapy with no real basis for such action.

Visible evidence of "injury" such as collars or braces are particularly effective in convincing a jury of the seriousness of an injury, and the only way of combating such allegations is intensive investigation and the use of the most effective medical specialists that can be obtained, where warranted, for the defense. A specialist of impeccable qualifications, however, can be quite ineffective on the witness stand, and can fall prey to a good fast-talking lawyer.

[1] **Misused Medical Terminology**

Dr. Wallace Duncan, in his article, "Excessive Treatment of the Automobile Accident Victim,"[4] states that many terms, some of which—like "whiplash"—were not even meant to be used as medical terminology, are now being used by plaintiff's doctors indiscriminately because of their effect on a jury. He states that: "Along with the misuse of the word 'whiplash,' other spurious 'medical' words have been promoted by some physicians to describe the claimed sequelae of soft tissue injuries. Such words as 'myositis, fascitis, fibrosis and myofascitis' . . . are inaccurate and misleading."

Dr. Duncan further states: "When (these) 'injured' victims of an automobile accident are placed under the care of the relatively few physicians who deliberately 'overtreat' them, such overtreatment sometimes results in permanent disability and psychologically prevents these individuals from regaining the same useful places in society they occupied before the injury." He gave some examples of overtreatment, such as:

1. Prolonged use of a cervical collar.
2. Prolonged use of traction or the use of a collar or traction when it is not called for.
3. Immobilization for too long periods of time.
4. Constant or repeated use of heat, short wave diathermy or ultrasound for prolonged periods.
5. Failure to reassure the patient and to place the patient in the proper mental attitude to help himself make a speedy recovery. (Here, I add that it must be remembered that in these days, fear of a possible malpractice suit may make a doctor

---

[4] D.R.I. Monograph, October 1966.

overcautious in his prognosis and can even stimulate overtreatment as a defensive tactic, all of which makes this problem even more complex.)

[2] Iatrogeny

Dr. Brown[5] states that:

Remarks or suggestions made by a physician directly, or even in an off-hand way can induce a pathological psychiatric condition in a patient. This process is known as iatrogeny. The patient takes a minimal suggestion and builds it to great proportions. He may develop a limp or adopt some other abnormal or mental response to adequately play the role he thinks he ought to assume. In fact, his whole personality may be warped to a degenerated state which does not always revert to complete normality even after the settlement of his case.

Just to make a complex problem even a little more difficult, the effect of an honest doctor's unintended suggestion may create an effect on a claimant, but such suggestions and innocent comments or questions can be and are an educational experience for anyone who wishes to use such information to fake his "symptoms."

§ 15.09 Bibliography

Brown, Dr. K.L., "Overtreatment and Incompetence," D.R.I. Monograph, October 1966.
Carney, "Investigations of Fraudulent Claims," F.I.C. Quarterly, Winter 1958.
Duncan, Dr. W., "Excessive Treatment of the Automobile Accident Victim," D.R.I. Monograph, October 1966.
Eaton, C.H., "Eleven Tips for Uncovering Claims Frauds," National Underwriter, March 13, 1970.
Lees-Haley, P.R. (Ph.D.), "Personal Injury Malingering," F.T.D., February, 28, 1986.
Perr, Dr. I.N., "Psychiatric Treatment and Litigation," D.R.I. Monograph, October 1966.
Shemoff, "The Demise of the Sub Rosa Investigation," F.T.D., April 1971.
Strabinger, B.E., "Unmasking of Fraudulent Claimants," Insurance Law Journal, September 1951.

---

[5] "Excessive Medical Treatment in Personal Injury Cases: The Causes and the Cures," D.R.I. Monograph, October 1966.

Warshawer, B., "Sub-Rosa Investigations," The Independent Adjuster, Summer 1964.

CHAPTER 16

Claims—Reserves, Reserving, and Statistics

§ 16.01 What Are Reserves?
§ 16.02 Various Types of Claims Reserves
    [1] Unearned Premium Reserves
    [2] Incurred But Not Reported Reserves (IBNR)
    [3] Actual Claim Reserves
    [4] Expense Reserves
    [5] One-Shot Cases
    [6] Delayed Reserving System
§ 16.03 Importance of Prompt Reserving
    [1] Automobile and General Liability Claim Reserving
    [2] Liability Suit Reserving
    [3] Fatal Cases Reserving
    [4] Property Damage Claims Reserving
    [5] Workers' Compensation Cases Reserving
§ 16.04 Reserve Revisions
§ 16.05 Claim Inventory or Reserve Reconciliation
§ 16.06 Reducing Outstanding Reserves
§ 16.07 Additional Factors to Consider in Reserving Policy
§ 16.08 Admissibility of Reserves in Evidence
§ 16.09 Claim Statistics
§ 16.10 Claim Department Responsibility
    [1] Claims
    [2] Suits
    [3] Average Reserves
    [4] Claim Expenses
    [5] Settlement Figures
    [6] Statistical Forms
§ 16.11 The Age of the Computer
§ 16.12 Bibliography

§ 16.01 What Are Reserves?

Reserves are those estimated sums of money that are set aside by an insurance company to cover known and unknown claim settlements and verdicts, as well as claim expenses.

There are few functions more important to an insurance company than maintaining proper balance between reserves and payments made on claims and suits. The solvency of an insurance company depends on its loss ratio, which is a comparison of premium amounts against claim payments. Reserves are the projection of claim payments plus suit verdicts yet to be experienced.

There are, of course, other factors that enter into the financial picture of an insurance company such as production commissions and costs, expenses of many kinds, including claim expenses and other factors, but if the pure loss ratio (premiums versus claims), is out of line, other factors may become incidental.

Other reasons for making every effort to keep reserves as close to claim payments involves:

1. The underwriting projections. Underreserving will give a distorted picture of the profitability of lines of business.
2. Even where the very existence of a company is not in question, the financial condition of a company can be affected by unnecessary higher taxes and less investment profit.
3. Retrospectively rated risks are distorted, which leads to bad customer relations.
4. Agency contingent fees become distorted and this too leads to a bad effect on production.

Accordingly, the old concept of a 15 percent redundancy or safety margin is no longer accepted as good claim practice by most insurance companies.

Evaluation of the ultimate cost of a claim or suit is an art based on experience, knowledge, and integrity. There is no crystal ball to look into for the answer. Obviously, the more training the claims personnel receive, the better the reserve picture will look.

A realistic reserve should, as far as possible, reflect an honest appraisal of the settlement value of a claim before it is in suit and a realistic appraisal of the verdict value in the particular jurisdiction in which the suit is being tried.

By and large, well-run insurance companies are willing to pay a fair value to settle a claim or suit. It would, however, be very naive to suggest that even among the established companies there is any uniformity in claim and suit settling policy.

There can be no denying that some companies still play their cards close to the vest and review each claim as though the claimant or his attorney was unscrupulous, greedy, and unreasonable. Their claim representatives are taught to search for any and every technicality that might give them the slightest advantage and fight to the

CLAIMS—RESERVES § 16.01

bitter end to save every penny that they can. Often the claim people in such companies fail to reserve realistically lest such reserving will color the thinking of the claim adjuster who is doing the negotiating.

Others take calculated risks and watch every dime that is spent on investigation as though it was wasted money. These companies gamble on winning enough cases to offset the risk of cursory investigations. As a result, their names are becoming prominent in "bad faith" suits that are proliferating.

Some companies require forms to be completed at the time a reserve is being set up or changed. These vary from forms that merely require the dollar amount, to detailed forms that require the answer to a few or many of the elements that go into reserving consideration. Such forms are only as good as the attitude of the claim representatives toward them. If completed properly and with thoughtfulness, they usually provide an excellent guide that focuses attention on important claim elements that should not be overlooked in making a proper reserve evaluation. If proper training and indoctrination has not been given however, the form will be looked upon as just another one that has to be completed as quickly as possible and gotten out of the way. Such an attitude only encourages sloppy claim work.

Detailed reserve forms serve an important purpose. There is the temptation by the claim representative handling a claim to make himself look good by overreserving a claim or suit so that he will be able to show an ultimate savings on the reserve. This is not only bad for the company, but will eventually catch up with the claim representative. Good reserve forms give supervisory staff a quick measure of a claim adjuster's integrity.

In an effort to arrive at a reasonably accurate appraisal, both extremes should be avoided. Unless justified by strong factual considerations, neither the extremely unusually high verdict nor the unjustified hopes of the claim representative should be guidelines.

The overall reserve figures are of prime concern to the accounting and statistical departments of an insurance company as well as to the claim, underwriting, and production departments. They include reserves not only on known cases, but also take into account those claims that have probably been incurred but which have not as yet been reported to the company.

Claim reserves also include claim expense factors as well as indemnity and first party payments. Some companies maintain separate reserve figures for each of these items but, since claim expenses run

§ 16.02   CASUALTY INSURANCE CLAIMS

pretty true to form, the claim representative's main concern will be with actual incurred case reserves.

§ 16.02   Various Types of Claims Reserves

There are three principal types of reserves that affect claims and claim handling, namely (1) unearned premium reserves, (2) incurred but not reported claim reserves, and (3) actual claim reserves.

Claim representatives are mainly concerned with the reserves on reported claims or losses, including reserves to cover the estimated cost on any claim report received of any event that *might* result in a loss.

[1]   Unearned Premium Reserves

These represent that part of the premium which has not been earned as of any given time. In other words, it is the amount of money that would have to be returned to the policyholders if the company stopped doing business at any particular time.

The entire annual premium is unearned when the policy is first written. As each month goes by, 1/12th of the premium is earned until the year is up.

While this is an important factor in the financial picture of a casualty or fire insurance company, it is not the particular concern of the claim department even though it does contemplate probable future claims.

[2]   Incurred But Not Reported Reserves (IBNR)

Incurred but not reported reserves, commonly referred to as IBNR reserves are those block or percentage reserves required by law to take care of accidents which have occurred, but which have not as yet been reported to the insurance company.

Every accident report is delayed to some extent since there is always a time lag between the time when the accident occurred and the time when the company received the report. This may range from an hour to a year or more. What is certain is that at any given time, a casualty insurance company has outstanding claims which have not been reported to it.

It is the duty of the statisticians to determine the average delay and the average value of such claims. This determination is usually made at the end of the year. Those claims which occurred before the last day of the year, but which were reported during the following year, are used as the basis for the IBNR report for the following year.

Here again, this is the primary concern of the accountants and statisticians, but it is a factor with which the claim representative should be familiar.

[3] Actual Claim Reserves

Claim reserves represent the best educated estimate of the amount of money that will be required to pay the outstanding claims at any given time. They are amounts put aside to pay claims that have been reported to the company, but which have not as yet been paid in full.

There are several ways of estimating actual claim reserves.

1. **Individual Case Reserves.** Here the claim representative who is reviewing the file must make the best possible appraisal of what the claim or suit will ultimately cost. As has already been said, this is a field in which the claim adjuster becomes proficient by experience. No two claims are exactly alike and every claim must be examined as a special case, with a reserve established and maintained in accordance with the facts at hand at the time of review.

2. **Formula Reserves.** The formula method involves the use of statistics to determine the average amount paid on a claim within a certain category. It is ordinarily used in those group of cases that involve a large volume of relatively small claims, such as compensation medical only, automobile property damage, minor accident and health claims, medical payments only, P.I.P., etc. This method is effective when there is a large enough volume of claims for the average payment to be meaningful and where the variants in amount are not such that any unusually large case will throw out of balance the average payment that might make the figures become meaningless.

Such reserves are usually placed on the basis of the three months' previous experience. In other words, the average payment is taken on the basis of a three-month period and that average is used in setting up each claim within the category that arises within the next three-month period.

Where the formula method is used, it is most important that a constant test be made as to its adequacy based on a specific period of time. All of this, however, is the province of the statisticians and the accountants. Our main concern is with the individual case reserves.

[4] Expense Reserves

Some companies set up separate reserves for the expenses incurred during the investigation and handling of claims and suits.

Ordinarily, items such as the cost of medical examinations, photographs and similar items are taken care of by formula reserves. In other words, a rough determination is made as to the percentage of these expense items as against the actual case reserves and this is then added on an overall basis to the reserve figures.

Where the company requires an actual expense figure in addition to a claim reserve figure, consideration should be given to the following items:

(a) Independent adjuster's fees (in some companies).
(b) Legal fees and expenses.
(c) Cost of physical examinations.
(d) Cost of photographs, plaques, etc.
(e) Cost of police, hospital and similar reports.
(f) Other out of pocket expenses.

[5] One-Shot Cases

Where the numerical claim volume is large and the amounts of each claim confined to a relatively small amount, some companies have instituted a system of recording the claim and the payment in one transaction.

Such a "one-shot" system avoids the necessity of certifying a claim mainly for the purpose of setting up a reserve and obviously saves much clerical time and effort by avoiding duplication. However, care must be used to confine such one-shot processing to those lines which usually involve first party claims, such as accident and health, motor vehicle, etc., where prompt reporting and quick disposition of the claim are the rule.

This again, is primarily an accounting and statistical problem, but is mentioned here merely to explain that when such a procedure exists, there is no need to be concerned about setting up a reserve in this category of cases.

[6] Delayed Reserving System

A delayed reserving system should not be confused with delayed reserves, which deals with incurred, but not reported claims.

A delayed system of reserving deals with reported claims on which there is insufficient information to warrant a good educated guess. This category may make up a substantial number of heavy cases.

Insurance companies handle this problem in various ways. Some companies set up a minimum figure for various classes and then adjust that figure as the information is developed. Some set up the best figure they can from the facts at hand and make a wild guess at the unknown quantities.

Others delay setting up the reserve for a period of 30, 60, or 90 days, during which time they make every effort to develop sufficient information to set up a realistic reserve. Obviously, in this method, it is essential to set up some bulk accounting reserve, based on recent past experience, to cover the gap which such delays create.

§ 16.03 Importance of Prompt Reserving

Reserves should be set up promptly. It is better to get the bad news behind you.

In setting up the reserve on each casualty claim, the individual reviewing the file must make the best possible appraisal of what the claim or suit may ultimately cost.

Very often, the first report of an accident will give a minimum of information. Wherever possible, a telephone call or an immediate personal investigation should be made so that sufficient facts are at hand for a proper evaluation of the claim.

Again, let it be clearly stated that when it comes to setting up the reserve, if there is any doubt concerning the liability or the injury, such doubt should be resolved in favor of the claimant, while taking care to avoid excessive reserving. Adjustments can always be made to cover subsequent developments.

[1] Automobile and General Liability Claim Reserving

There is no hard or fast rule or formula that is workable for setting up a reserve on an individual casualty claim. Many factors are involved and must be given consideration in proportion to their respective importance or application to the case at hand.

Some of the factors which should be given consideration in setting up a reserve on an automobile or general liability claim are:

1. **Coverage.** This is the paramount factor in every claim or suit. In this age of the computer, the majority of coverage determinations can be made by a push on the right keys. These are, however, the standard automobile, workers' compensation or other small claim variety where, if a policy exists, coverage is usually applicable. If, however, a policy doesn't exist, inquiry must be made as to why a report was made. The incident may have been reported to the wrong company. The company name may have been given in a deliberate attempt to mislead at least momentarily. A policy may be on binder. The policy may have been cancelled for lack of payment of the premium or for other reasons. The accident may have occurred shortly before or after the policy was in effect, or there may be no coverage for other reasons.

A policyholder may sincerely believe that he or she has proper coverage where none exists because of an exception, exclusion, or because of a breach of a policy condition. Great care must always be used before coverage is definitely denied, while at the same time delay in making a coverage decision can be just as dangerous, since such a delay may waive the right of the insurer to deny coverage later.

Much of this book will be devoted to coverage problems and their solution. Any doubt about coverage is not to be taken lightly since the consequences of a wrong decision can be costly to the company. All problems involving coverage should be discussed with the claim supervisor or manager.

2. **Liability.** Liability means legal fault or responsibility for the accident. Next to coverage, it is the most important factor to be considered in evaluating the reserve on a liability case. It must be realized, however, that whenever a question of fact requires the determination of a jury, the odds are usually against the defendant and this must be kept in mind when setting up a reserve.

Unless a company requires an initial formula figure, or works on a delayed reserving system, the initial reserve will depend on the facts given in the first report, or on what can be determined by a few telephone calls or immediate investigation. Some judgment can often be made concerning the severity of the accident from other information that may be available.

CLAIMS—RESERVES § 16.03[1]

If a serious accident report is required it is better to err a little on the serious side and make the report as called for.

3. **Comparative and Contributory Negligence.** These are factors to be considered at all times, but greater weight should be given against the insured in the initial reserving or early reserving, depending on the nature of the injuries. The more serious the injuries, the less weight should be given the defenses until the house counsel or the defense attorney have made their evaluation, especially if there is definite liability on the part of the insured.

4. **Other Legal Defenses.** Additional legal defenses such as assumption of risk, agency, fellow servant rule, and many others could have a definite bearing on the ultimate outcome of a suit. They are, however, usually of minor concern when it comes to setting up an early reserve. They may deserve some fair amount of weight when a case goes into suit, however, at which time the claim representative will have the opportunity to get legal advice.

5. **Injury and Disability.** It is, of course, important to learn the exact nature of the injury and probable disability as soon as possible. It may take time to get the doctor's and the hospital reports but unless an attorney is already representing the claimant, a few telephone calls can usually provide enough information to get a fairly good idea as to the severity of the injuries. It is then important to follow up in order to get as much solid medical information as possible, as soon as possible, and review the reserve at that time. (The timing of a physical examination has been discussed in Chapter 6, *supra.*) Disability is always an important factor in reserving a claim.

6. **Pain and Suffering.** Any pain must be taken into consideration in evaluating a case for the purpose of reserving it. Long and painful disability will increase the value of the claim considerably. It is an item which is closely tied in with the medical situation and the medical information will usually give some indication as to the extent and duration of the pain involved.

7. **Age of the Claimant.** It is obvious that an older person will suffer a greater disability from a certain injury than a younger person. It has been estimated, for instance, that every ten years over the age of forty increases disability by 10 percent. Age is also important in a death claim; the deceased's life expectancy is an important factor in establishing monetary loss to his dependents.

8. **Sex of the Claimant.** It has been reported that in most instances disability to a woman will be 20 percent to 25 percent greater than

to the average man. On the other hand, life expectancy of women is usually longer than that of men.

9. **Dependency.** This is an item to be particularly considered in death cases. The claimant may leave a dependent spouse, minor children, or other dependents.

10. **Loss of Salary.** This item speaks for itself. It is essential that the amount and the time lost be checked, preferably from payroll records. In cases of long disability or death it is important to consider the salary potential of the individual involved, as well as the salary at the time of the accident.

11. **Medical Expenses.** This is one of the items of special damage, along with loss of salary.

12. **Property Damage.** This item may include damage to a claimant's automobile, clothing, jewelry, or other personal effects.

13. **Economic Status.** This item is not one that can be pinned down to a definite amount, like some of those listed above. However, a claim involving a person in the higher income brackets is usually going to cost more than a similar claim sustained by someone whose income losses are not as large.

[2] **Liability Suit Reserving**

If a liability claim goes into suit, as it usually does in potentially serious cases these days, a complete review of the reserve previously placed on a case is warranted so that additional factors can be given proper consideration.

1. **The liability** should be reviewed with a more flexible attitude in the light of how a jury might react to the facts of the particular accident.

2. **Venue** is the jurisdiction where the case will be tried, and is a very important item to be considered in evaluating the reserve. While old guidelines are becoming blurred, it can still be expected that, generally speaking, juries in rural areas will be more conservative than those in the big cities. Experience also indicates that certain cities and states are more plaintiff-minded than others.

3. **The court** in which the case is to be tried is also important in determining the ultimate verdict value of a case. Juries in the federal courts are usually better educated and more likely to understand the complexities of involved cases, but this is obviously a generality and too much importance must not be given to this factor in and of itself.

It is also important to evaluate the tendencies of the courts of appeal in the jurisdiction involved and to become aware of the legal position which that jurisdiction has taken on any legal questions which might be involved.

The trial judge who is likely to be involved in the case should also be a factor to be considered in evaluating the suit. Some judges are very active in trying to arrange settlements and put a good deal of pressure on insurers to open wider the so-called "deep pockets" of insurance companies. Judges are human and all are conditioned to a greater or less degree by their backgrounds. It is always realistic to know whether a judge has been more prominent as a plaintiff or a defense lawyer and what his attitude has been on past cases, especially if the case is being tried without a jury.

4. **Realistic Appraisal of the Ability of Both Counsel.** This information may be at hand or the claim representative may have to dig for it, but, in any event, much of the verdict evaluation will depend on how good a trial lawyer represents each side of the case. This may depend on who is available in the area. It is usually advisable to engage a local lawyer in a rural community even though he may be a little less qualified. Otherwise the attorney who has built the best reputation in a particular specialty, should be appointed if available.

In the larger cities, the choice will probably be confined to larger law firms. In such instances, it is important to know the individual who is going to handle the case.

5. **Availability of Witnesses.** It is one thing to have discovered witnesses that are important in order to determine liability. It is another thing to make sure that these witnesses are willing and available to appear at the trial of the case when it comes up. The unavailability of an important witness, or a change in his attitude or a lack of desire to attend trial, can change the entire complexion of a case. Accordingly, when a case goes into suit, periodic check-ups on the witnesses is essential and should always be a consideration in evaluating or reevaluating the reserve.

6. **Coverage** should be reexamined if questionable. It should always be remembered that in any case of questionable coverage, the doubt will be resolved in favor of the policyholder.

In the past, attempts have been made to get a quick fix on a liability reserve by using various evaluation "formulas," such as:

1. *Three or four times the special damages.* This was never a good guide and is completely out of date today. There are many cases

where the special damages are comparatively low but where the jury verdict could be very high. If the special damages are legitimately high, the claim representative will soon realize that such a case will rarely settle out on any such percentage basis, and if a low demand is made, he should become immediately wary.

2. *A fixed amount per day* as an indication of payment for pain and suffering. Who is to judge what a jury will decide? Pain is too variable an item and its evaluation needs a lot of thought and experience.

3. *The point system.* Here, percentage points are given to each factor that goes into the evaluation of a case such as liability, injury or death, special damages, and other items previously mentioned, adding up to 100 percent and then dividing that figure by some percentage of comparative negligence. Such a formula simply formalizes the factors that enter into consideration for any evaluation, but as a formula it is too rigid for everyday use. The inexperienced claims person will be just as confused. No two cases are exactly alike, nor can they be evaluated with the same slide rule. As has been previously stated, individual liability reserving is an art, not an exact science.

[3] Fatal Cases Reserving

Although some of the factors involved in a consideration of the reserve figure for a fatal case have already been mentioned, there are others that apply only to this type of claim.

Some items to which special consideration should be given are:

1. Age and life expectancy of decedent.
2. Marital status (single, married, divorced, separated).
3. Number, age, and sex of dependents.
4. Economic status, to determine funeral and other expenses.
5. Health and habits.
6. Earnings.
7. Earning capacity and prospects of increases.

[4] Property Damage Claims Reserving

Reserves on property damage claims are not only easier to set up, but should come much closer to the ultimate amount paid on a claim. In dealing with property damage only, we avoid some of the nebulous items, such as pain and suffering, probable disability, and so forth.

CLAIMS—RESERVES § 16.03[5]

The three major factors in determining the reserve on property damage losses are:

1. Liability and coverage.
2. Determination of the exact extent of the property damage by survey, examinations, competitive estimates, and the like.
3. Possible claim for loss of use.

The last item is one with which the claim representative may have some trouble. Naturally if a claim is to be made for loss of use and proof is submitted corroborating this allegation, the reserve should consider the possibility that the company will have to pay for this item in third party claims. Otherwise, the same general principles apply to property damage as to other casualty claims.

[5] Workers' Compensation Cases Reserving

As in all other casualty claims, the reserve on workers' compensation cases should be based upon the best appraisal of what a claim will ultimately cost. Unlike other casualty claims, however, the workers' compensation acts of the various states do give some specific information that enables a slightly more exact figure or appraisal on the reserve.

Each state, for instance, lists the weekly benefits to which a particular employee may be entitled. Most states have a time limit for the running of such benefits and list lump sum benefits that may be payable. A thorough knowledge of the jurisdiction's particular workers' compensation act is essential for a proper appraisal of the reserve.

Compensation reserves are divided into two sections: (1) the amount of compensation or indemnity due; and (2) medical expenses.

Compensation or indemnity reserves should be based on the following factors:

1. Disability.
   a. Extent of injury. Whether the injury is an initial one or an aggravation of a preexisting condition, it is important to determine as quickly as possible the full extent of the injury so that some appraisal of the disability involved may be made. This simply means that the adjuster must make some determination of how long he believes such an injury would keep an employee away from work.

b. Age of the claimant. As in liability reserves in general, the age of the claimant is an important consideration in his recovery. As we have already said, an older person will be likely to have a greater disability than a younger person.
c. Sex of the claimant. Again, as in liability cases, it is important to remember that the disability of a woman is usually greater than that of a man.
2. Allowance under the compensation act.
a. Temporary total disability and number of weeks.
b. Temporary partial disability and number of weeks.
c. Permanency.
d. Dependency and death benefits.

It is important to know whether the compensation act of the particular state makes an award for permanent partial disability over and above the temporary disability allowed.

Medical reserves should be based on the following factors:

1. Doctor's and dentist's bills, including surgical expenses and cost of therapeutic or other treatments. Consult the fee schedule of the state for the extent of probable medical expense.
2. Hospital or sanatorium bills.
3. Nurse's bills.
4. X-rays.
5. Cost of practical nurse. In some instances, it is advantageous to pay for the cost of a practical nurse where hospitalization or registered nurse's care would otherwise be warranted.
6. Fee for surgical appliances.

§ 16.04 Reserve Revisions

It is not only important to evaluate a claim properly in the beginning so that a realistic reserve may be placed upon the case, but just as important to review reserves regularly in order to make proper adjustments as conditions change.

A claim must at all times be evaluated on the information at hand. Every effort must be made to enlarge upon this information and revise the reserve in accordance with the additional information obtained.

It is, therefore, important that the claim representative acquire the habit of thinking of the reserve every time he looks at a file. Additional medical information, new witnesses, high special damages, or any number of changing conditions may daily affect the value of a claim.

Finally, it is especially important to review old cases in the light of present day economic conditions. What may have been an adequate reserve last year, may be an insufficient one today.

§ 16.05 Claim Inventory or Reserve Reconciliation

In any clerical operation involving human manipulation, there will be a certain percentage of error. The process of transmitting claim statistics to the statistical or accounting departments involves many such operations. Ordinarily, the vast majority of the errors made in the clerical processing of claims are committed on cases of nominal value so that the overall effect is not too great, particularly since these errors usually involve "take-downs" in about the same proportions as they do "put-ups."

The more complex and higher reserved cases, particularly in the compensation field, involve many more clerical transactions since in compensation particularly, many drafts are issued on the same file. One major clerical error on any of these files can take down an outstanding reserve. Accordingly, just a handful of errors in this category of cases can mean a considerable imbalance of reserve figures.

As a result of these possibilities for error, it is common practice in most companies to make what is known as a claim inventory or reserve reconciliation as between claim files and statistical and accounting records at least once a year. Such an inventory is merely a comparison of the record maintained by the statistical and accounting departments against what the claim file actually shows to be the case. Imbalance can be caused by clerical errors whether in the claim department or in the computer or statistical unit. It is obvious that surveillance is necessary in order to correct such imbalances as soon as possible.

§ 16.06 Reducing Outstanding Reserves

Pressure from brokers or agents to reduce outstanding reserves may be brought for three possible reasons:

1. Business reasons payments where there is no other justification for making a payment on a claim.
2. Retrospectively rated risks where the premium depends on the past loss ratio.
3. Agency contingency contracts where claim and loss payments affect the agent's commission.

The claim representative handling a claim that is involved in any of the above categories should here have no decisionmaking authority, and should refer all such requests to higher authority.

§ 16.07 Additional Factors to Consider in Reserving Policy

Several elements that deserve consideration which have not previously been mentioned are:

1. Other Insurance. Where there is known co-insurance, this should of course, be given its full weight in setting up a reserve. There may, however, be factors that could nullify such co-insurance for many possible coverage or other reasons. The claim representative should not be overly optimistic unless he knows that the money is there.
2. Contribution from Joint Tortfeasors. Here again, one should be pretty sure of the liability of the joint tortfeasor or codefendant and of his insurance or financial position before giving this substantial consideration in setting up your reserve.
3. Subrogation. Here again, I not only urge caution, but warn the claim representative not to count his chickens before they are hatched. Each company has its own policy about considering possible subrogation in setting up reserves on a case. My own reaction is that I don't count the money until I have a definite commitment.

§ 16.08 Admissibility of Reserves in Evidence

One reason that a great deal of attention must be given to the setting up and revision of proper reserves on individual suits is the pragmatic consideration that in any bad faith suit for damages in excess of the policy limits, it is very likely that the claim file will get into the hands of the plaintiff's attorney. In such a case, an improper reserve can be a very damaging piece of evidence, whether the reserve be too high, too low, or improperly or not at all revised upon receipt of pertinent new information.

The admissibility of evidence concerning reserves varies from federal to state courts and from state to state, depending on the jurisdiction. There are very few decisions to guide the trial judge. Accordingly, he has a lot of leeway on this subject. My own experience has been that in the great majority of liability suits, permission to review the reserves on the claim file has been granted, although there is a difference of opinion where first party suits are involved.[1]

§ 16.09 Claim Statistics

Running a claim department without proper claim statistics is like trying to fly an airplane blind without an instrument panel.

While statistics are essential, figures can and do lie. There are many factors which can distort final figures if incidental elements are not given proper consideration. In speaking about average settlement costs for instance, it is most important that we know whether we are talking about individual claims or "cases" which means accidents that may involve many claims. It is also important to know if the statistics include claims closed without payment in the final figure. It is just as essential that the volume from which the statistics are taken is large enough to be meaningful. One catastrophic loss in any small volume can distort average figures to the point of absurdity. Finally, there must be some uniformity in the inclusion or exclusion of reinsurance and allowances for this must be made in reviewing the final figures.

Probably the most important factor in interpreting claim statistics is the promptness with which the figures are obtained. If the statistics are considerably delayed, the claim executive finds himself in the position of trying to lock the barn door after the horse has been stolen. In this age of the computer, there is no longer any valid excuse for any such delay.

---

[1] Groben v. Travelers Indem. Co., 266 N.Y.S.2d 616 (N.Y. Sup. Ct. 1967), *but see* first party decisions of Union Carbide Corp. v. Travelers Indem. Co., 61 F.R.D. 411 (Miss. 1973), and North Georgia Lumber & Hardware Co. v. Home Ins. Co., 82 F.R.D. 687 (Ga. 1979).

See also Howser & Zuck, "Insurance Claim Reserves: Are They Admissible?", Insurance Counsel Journal, January 1985. (While this article confines itself to first party cases, much of it is also applicable to third party liability suits.)

§ 16.10　　　　　　　　　CASUALTY INSURANCE CLAIMS

In order to be meaningful, and depending upon the size of the claim department, there is a need for a proper breakdown by area, region, city, line or other unit. There is, for instance, little point in learning that average claim costs are going up if the areas or lines causing the increase cannot be pinpointed. It is also important to recognize the fact that comparisons must be made on a similar basis in similar territories as well as lines. It is obviously pointless to compare average settlement costs in Lincoln, Nebraska or Lancaster, Pennsylvania with New York City, Los Angeles, or Chicago. It is just as unfair to measure average expense costs of a company with many branch claim offices, writing a large volume, as against one writing a small volume and handling its claims by independent adjusters.

§ 16.10　Claim Department Responsibility

While the claim department is vitally concerned with incurred but not reported claims, these figures are primarily the province of the statisticians. The areas which are the direct responsibility of the claim department are the following.

[1]　**Claims**

1. **Arising, Received or Newly Created Claims.** This category permits determination concerning the adjusters workload, the accident frequency and severity. New claims should be reported by line and should include:
   (a) Number of claims received in each line.
   (b) Initial aggregate reserves by line.
   (c) Cases referred to independent adjusters for handling.
   (d) Number of cases referred to other offices for handling.
   (e) Claims reported but not reserved either because there was no noticeable damage or because liability was unquestionably that of the claimant.
2. **Closed Cases.** This category should be broken down into those cases closed by payment and those cases closed without payment. This separation is necessary so that comparisons with the figures of other companies can be meaningful and also so that a determination can be made concerning the accumulation or turnover of claims which never should have been set-up in the first place. The closed cases should be subdivided as follows:

CLAIMS—RESERVES § 16.10[2]

  (a) Number of cases closed by line.
  (b) The aggregate amount paid by line.
  (c) The last meaningful reserve on the closed cases. This does not necessarily mean the last actual reserves since the final reserve can be set-up either the month preceding or even a day preceding the disposition of the claim.
  (d) Reserve savings on closed cases.

3. **Reopened Cases.** These should be listed as follows:
  (a) Numerically by line.
  (b) Aggregate amount of reserves on the reopened claims.

4. **Increases and Decreases in Reserves.**
  (a) Numerically by line.
  (b) Aggregate amount of increases or decreases.

5. **Pending or Outstanding Claims.**
  (a) Numerically by line.
  (b) Aggregate reserves.

6. **Subrogation.** The number of cases and the amount recovered will give some idea as to whether subrogation is being pursued diligently or not.

[2] Suits

Here again, it is important that the same yardstick be used in making any comparison concerning suits. Most companies use the definition of a suit promulgated by the New York Insurance Department in a special bulletin which they issued on this subject.

There is no way of knowing the allowable percentage in cases that should go into suit in the first place. There is, for instance, the matter of territory. It is obvious that the large cities will engender more suits than the rural areas. Again, the claim settling policy of a particular company will, of course, have a decided effect on the number of suits produced.

In making any comparison concerning the percentage of suits won and lost, it is essential that the percentage of suits tried be taken into consideration as an important element. The company that tries more cases is going to have an overall lower percentage of wins but this does not necessarily mean that the overall combined claim and suit payment will be greater.

Suit records can be divided into the following categories:

1. **Arising, Received or New Suits.**
   (a) Number of arising or new suits by line.
   (b) Percentage comparison of new suits to all arising claims.
   (c) Number of summons first notice cases received.
   (d) Percentage comparison of summons first notice cases to all of the new arising suits.
2. **Closed Suits.**
   (a) Number of suits tried.
   (b) Percentage of suits tried compared with outstanding suits.
   (c) Number of suits won.
   (d) Percentage of suits won compared to number of suits tried.
   (e) Aggregate amount of reserves taken down as a result of suits won.
   (f) Number of suits lost.
   (g) Percentage of suits lost compared with number of suits tried.
   (h) Number of suits dismissed.
   (i) Percentage of suits dismissed compared with number of suits tried.
   (j) Number of suits discontinued.
   (k) Percentage of suits discontinued as against the number of suits tried.
   (l) Number of suits settled.
   (m) Percentage of suits settled as against the outstanding suits.
3. **Pending or Outstanding Suits.**
   (a) Number of outstanding suits at the beginning and the end of each period reported on.
   (b) Percentage of outstanding suits as against overall outstanding claims and suits.
4. **Appeals.** A suit should not be considered finally won or lost as long as it is in appeal or as long as time for appeal has not run.
5. **Aggregate Legal Expenses.** This should be obtained by line and by territory. Averages should be obtained where meaningful.

CLAIMS—RESERVES § 16.10[4]

[3] **Average Reserves**

It is important to obtain regular figures concerning average rising reserves so that any violent pattern change can be detected that requires further investigation.

Where the volume warrants it, average reserves can be set up on minor cases based on a previous experience over a set period of time. However, unless the volume is large, such reserve averaging is warranted only in the following categories.

(a) Small property damage claims of all kinds.
(b) Compensation medical only claims, and P.I.P. cases.
(c) Small accident and health claims.
(d) Small inland marine claims.

[4] **Claim Expenses**

Claim expenses fall into two general categories, allocated and unallocated.

1. **Allocated expenses.** These are concerned with the handling of specific and particular claims. Generally speaking, they fall under the following categories:
    (a) Cost of physical examinations.
    (b) Cost of automobile surveys.
    (c) Cost of photographs, plaques, engineering and other special reports.
    (d) Police and motor vehicle reports.
    (e) Legal fees.
    (f) Other similar expenses.

Claim expenses should be maintained numerically and by aggregate amount in each category so that averages can be determined and compared where necessary. The number of physical examinations made or photographs ordered can tell management if these items are being ordered indiscriminately. The average amounts will suggest whether good judgment is being used and instructions are being followed.

2. **Unallocated Expenses.** These are generally concerned with the overall handling of the claim department and not confined to specific or individual claims. Unallocated expenses comprise chiefly such items as claim adjusters salaries, auto-

mobile costs and expenses, meals and hotel expenses, telephone and telegraph, postage, entertainment, building expenses, etc. A separate record should be kept concerning independent adjuster's fees.

[5] Settlement Figures

Properly used, average settlement figures can help to determine whether there has been any relaxation in claims settling policy, any increase in severity, and whether certain territories are becoming more claim conscious.

Separation should be made between suit settlements and claim settlements. These figures can be compared with average figures produced by certain companies that provide them as a regular service.

[6] Statistical Forms

Statistical figures should be kept as uncluttered as possible. Designing statistical forms is a specialized art and a great deal of thought and care should be given so that the forms will be most useful and intelligible to the person receiving them.

Recapitulation sheets should be devised as needed in whatever category required. Properly designed, such recapitulation sheets can impart a world of information almost at a glance.

§ 16.11 The Age of the Computer

It is probably difficult for a young person coming up the line in the claim department of an insurance company to realize that it wasn't all that long ago when claim statistics were gathered individually by hand, before the computer was envisioned and even before the IBM system came into universal acceptance.

In those days, statistics were still necessary in order to keep from "flying blind," but since the cost of gathering those figures was relatively high, they were kept at a minimum and were usually connected with workloads. Now that we are in the age of the computer there is no limit to the figures that can be obtained, assuming that proper programing has been arranged.

It is recognized that statistics, such as average settlement costs, numbers of cases that go into suit, and even expense costs must be broken down by area, city, state, and line of business. Volume also plays a large part in keeping statistics realistic.

Even small companies today have computerized programs available to them and are able to get many more meaningful figures within their own operations. They can now obtain claim statistical information on a regular and timely basis that can be charted to show the effects of inflation, personnel changes, company policy, and other factors that might affect reserves, settlement figures, verdicts, and expenses. In previous times, the most frustrating experience of insurance executives was the inability to get claim figures in time to take proper action. This is now a matter of history.

The problem now is not within the companies themselves. It lies in a failure of cooperation in the industry as a whole. Each company is reluctant to disclose figures that might open areas of possible question or investigation, whether it be from the upper echelons of the company itself or from state or federal sources.

Today there are organizations which, for a fee, will provide a great deal of information concerning verdict averages in individual localities. Such figures are obtained from court records and other open sources and are of course confined to figures which are a matter of public record.

The schedule figures presented to state insurance departments are a source of good information, but difficult to obtain and not always reliable for statistical purposes. They also do not cover the spectrum that should be essential to insurance executives. Such figures could, for instance, help to determine:

1. The percentage of increase in settlement values due to inflation.
2. Whether there has been an increase in claim severity in a given locality.
3. Whether there has been any change in claim settling attitudes.
4. Whether there has been a change in claims consciousness in any given locality.
5. Whether interim reserves are being set in accordance with present trends and values.
6. Whether old reserves need reviewing and increasing in view of recent trends and values.

Now that insurers have the means to obtain whatever figures are needed, some way should be found to cooperate in an exchange of information that could be helpful to all.

The computer is still in its infancy and while insurers have already seen some of its advantages in claim and policy processing, reserving and statistics, its ultimate value will be so great as to be unforeseeable.

There are already, several software companies that have training packages which, together with video tapes, make quality training courses available to any insurance company claim department, no matter how small, or to any independent adjuster. Such packages are now available in specialized fields such as property, liability, workers' compensation, and their subdivisions. In the workers' compensation field, for instance, there is at least one package[2] that can help to determine a claimant's eligibility, validate payments against state fee schedules, issue checks, and track a company's compensation reserves.

Large insurers, with proper programming systems, are able to determine personnel needs, show available experts in many fields, amass and process all kinds of claim statistics and accomplish much more, depending on the particular needs of that insurance company.

In the property field there are software packages that assist in the evaluation and settlement of losses and produce estimates that can be taken into the field to speed up the disposition of catastrophic losses. One company[3] advertises that on construction claims, estimates can be available on unit prices on a local basis. This company states that "each data base contains prices on multiple construction operations, created and maintained with local rates and material costs." Another software company[4] claims that "all room dimensions can be calculated automatically" in its package and includes depreciation and cash value information.

---

[2] Insurance Software Packages, Inc., Tampa, Fla. 33610.

[3] Comp-U-Claim, c/o Policy Management Systems Corp., Columbia, S.C. 29202

[4] Cost Engineering Technologies, Parsippany, N.J. 07054. The names and addresses of other software companies can be obtained in a "Special Report" on computers for the insurance claim industry, published by Insurance Adjuster Magazine, July 1986.

§ 16.12 Bibliography

Bownlee, "A Matter of Reserves," Insurance Adjuster Magazine, October 1984.

Brown, "Reserving—Who Cares?", Gustin Holdings, Milwaukee, Wis. 53202.

Forbes, "Automobile Bodily Injury Liability Loss Reserving Techniques and Simulation," Journal of Risk & Insurance, August 1968.

Hislop, "Reserves," F.I.C. Quarterly, Spring 1967.

Pennington, Jr., "Claims Departments Have an Alert System to Meet Challenges in 1980's," Independent Adjuster Magazine, Winter 1980.

CHAPTER 17

Settlements and Settlement Negotiations

§ 17.01 Introduction
§ 17.02 First-call Settlements
§ 17.03 General Rules Concerning Settlements
        [1]   Demands Made After Settlement
        [2]   Protecting Medical Bills
        [3]   Dealing With the Claimant's Attorney
§ 17.04 Evaluating Bodily Injury Claims
§ 17.05 Decisions Concerning Evaluation
§ 17.06 Control
        [1]   Maintaining Control of Death Cases
§ 17.07 The Proper Approach to Settlement Negotiations
§ 17.08 Offer Versus Demand
§ 17.09 Obtaining the Release
§ 17.10 Negotiating With Attorneys
§ 17.11 Disposition of Injury Claims Involving Minors
        [1]   Medical Information
        [2]   Indemnification Release
        [3]   Investigation
        [4]   Emancipated Child
        [5]   Settlement With Court Approval
        [6]   Closing Records
§ 17.12 Advance Payments
        [1]   Advantages
        [2]   Choosing the Cases
        [3]   Some Reasonable Limitations
        [4]   Method of Payment
        [5]   Admission of Liability
        [6]   Written Permission to Settle
        [7]   Statute of Limitations
        [8]   Follow-up
        [9]   Closing the Case
§ 17.13 Structured Settlements
        [1]   Introduction
        [2]   Tax Considerations
        [3]   Legal Aspects
        [4]   Model Structured Settlement Act
        [5]   Workers' Compensation Cases

§ 17.14 Bibliography

§ 17.01 Introduction

A conscientious claim representative must strive to close as many claims as possible in a manner that is fair to all concerned.

There are several ways in which a claim can be closed: the insured may have no coverage; the claimant may recognize the fact that the insured was not liable for the accident; a case may go to court and be disposed of through a decision; it may be amicably settled as a result of reasonable negotiations between the claim representative and the claimant, or his attorney.

One school of thought subscribes to the theory that if no action is taken on a claim, it will disappear into thin air. This is what is known as "the ostrich approach." Someone recently said that when you put your head in the sand, you not only miss what is going on around you, but you leave yourself very vulnerably exposed.

No matter what the insurance carrier has decided, a claimant is entitled to know where he stands with reference to his claim. If he is serious about pressing it, ignoring him will not put him in a better frame of mind.

If, therefore, a claim representative has completed his investigation and concluded that the claim is one to decline, he should do so promptly and courteously. If his investigation has progressed to the point where he has decided that it is a case to settle, then he should enter into settlement negotiations as soon as circumstances warrant it.

No hard and fast rules can be given with reference to settlement or settlement negotiations because, here again, as in other phases of claim work, a claim representative will be dealing with many diverse situations and people. He will have to pattern his actions upon the particular circumstances involved in any given situation. This discussion, therefore, must of necessity deal in generalities.

The experienced claim representative will learn little that will be new to him, but a restatement of proven principles should strike some responsive chords. The making of fair and ethical claim settlements is recognized as good business by the vast majority of the insurance industry. Grossly inadequate payments not only make for bad public relations, but, as we shall see, have led to an increasing tendency by the courts to limit the effectiveness of releases, especially if they are taken under circumstances which may be open to question.

§ 17.02 First-call Settlements

The advantage of first-call settlements has been previously discussed. It is a subject important enough to bear re-emphasizing.

Assuming that a claim representative is dealing with a case of liability, obvious injury, and a reasonable demand, the advantages of a first-call settlement are obvious. In those cases where the liability or the injury may be questionable, or where the demand is slightly high, first-call settlements may still be advantageous, even admitting that the amount paid may possibly be slightly in excess of the fair value of a claim. A troublesome claim usually becomes more troublesome the longer it continues to remain open. The necessity for continued investigation, the cost of examinations, photographs, travel expense, continued overhead, and expense involved in reporting and correspondence all add to the final cost of any claim, even if it does not go into suit.

This does not imply that a claim representative should rush into settlement of a claim if he has good reason to suspect fraud, merely because of the problem involved in ultimate disposition. Such cases should always be resisted to the limit; but if fraud is not involved, and the injury is not extensive, some consideration should always be given to the possibility of disposing of the case at the earliest possible time.

§ 17.03 General Rules Concerning Settlements

By and large, settlement of a claim by an insurance carrier is not an admission of liability on the party of the insured. As we will see, under some circumstances in a few jurisdictions, however, after a claim has gone to suit, settlement might act as an admission of liability. A claims representative should be sure, therefore, that he knows the law of his jurisdiction with reference to settlement of claims after they have gone into suit so that he does not prejudice the rights of the insured and inadvertently wipe out any right of action which the insured may have against the party with whom settlement is being negotiated.

[1] Demands Made After Settlement

Generally speaking, except for partial settlements or advance payments which will be discussed separately, once settlement has been agreed upon the claim against an insured should be closed in its entirety. There should be no loose ends that might imply an agreement to pay an additional sum. The release must contain a sum certain. It must be a full release for all claims—past, present, and future—arising out of the particular accident under investigation. It is, therefore, not only unwise but completely unrealistic to make any commitments for an unknown or indefinite amount of future expenses, unless it intended that the settlement is partial only and not final.

For this reason much stress has been laid on the proper manner of obtaining a release, the method of disposition of cases involving minors, and matters of a similar nature. Any request to pay a sum in addition to the amount agreed upon in settlement after a case is closed and a release obtained should be weighed extremely carefully. Payment made after the case is closed may be construed as waiver of the previous settlement and under certain circumstances may leave the company in as bad a position as it was before the release was obtained. This does not mean to imply that there are no circumstances under which a company might wish to reconsider a settlement previously agreed upon. However, this should be the rare exception, and if a fair and reasonable amount is paid in the first instance, there should ordinarily be no need for subsequent review.

[2] Protecting Medical Bills

Very often, because of a friendly relationship with the claimant's attending physician or hospital, a claim representative may wish to protect their bills when settlement is made. In this event, it would be unwise to issue a draft directly to the doctor or hospital alone.

The safest procedure is to issue a separate draft in the amount of the particular bill which is sought to be protected, to the doctor or hospital and the claimant, both being named on the draft. Where the claimant is represented by an attorney, a letter from the attorney authorizing payment of the bill directly, is just as effective.

[3] Dealing With the Claimant's Attorney

A claim representative should never advise a claimant against obtaining the services of an attorney. If he learns that the claimant is represented by counsel he should bow out as quickly and as gracefully as possible. Once he is aware of the fact that the claimant is represented by counsel, he no longer has any ethical right to take a written statement from the claimant or even to question him verbally about the accident. Until such time as the attorney in question indicates in writing that he is no longer interested in the case, his dealings and negotiations should be strictly confined to the attorney and not to the claimant.

This leads to the subject of commitments or admissions made to a claimant or his attorney. Particular care must be used in settlement negotiations to avoid misunderstanding in reference to any offer made or allegedly made. An interpretation may be placed upon comments which were never intended. Remarks such as, "If you can get your client interested in a figure of around $1,500, I'll see what I can do," are usually interpreted to mean a definite offer. A claim representative should be circumspect when he speaks, and doubly so when he puts words on paper. If he makes a settlement in an amount which exceeds his authority, he will bind the company to that settlement if the claimant or claimant's attorney has reasonable grounds for believing that he had proper authority to do so, assuming of course that fraud is not involved.[1]

There may be occasions when, because of a clash of personalities, a claim representative is obviously making no headway with the claimant or his attorney. An admission to this effect with the suggestion that another representative continue negotiations is a sign of strength rather than weakness and shows a recognition and awareness of a peculiar problem that can possibly be handled only by the intervention of another person.

§ 17.04 Evaluating Bodily Injury Claims

There is no set formula by which a bodily injury claim can be evaluated. In the course of future experience, a claim investigator will no doubt hear of some rule of thumb by which an evaluation is attempted by multiplying the special damages by some figure ranging

---

[1] Zager v. Gubernick, 208 A.2d 45 (Pa. 1965).

§ 17.04 CASUALTY INSURANCE CLAIMS

from 3 to 5 or more. Such so-called rules are not only worthless but misleading.

The blunt fact is that every case must be judged on its own merits. There are rarely two cases with an identical value, even though the injuries and liability appear similar.

The only thing that can be said with any certainty is that no proper evaluation can be made unless a claim investigator has obtained as much information as possible about the claim and has checked to verify the allegations.

What are the factors that enter into a proper evaluation of any bodily injury claim? These can generally be listed as follows.

1. **The facts.** First, it is essential that a determination be made whether the facts of the accident fall within the terms of the policy. In other words, is there proper coverage? If so, it must then be determined whether those facts spell out liability on the part of the insured. The degree of liability will of course affect the ultimate value of the claim, since the appraisal will be based on the probability of a jury verdict in the event of trial.

The claim investigator should determine the physical facts as accurately as possible and judge the statements of the witnesses in relation to those physical facts. In short, the better his investigation, the more able he will be to make a proper evaluation of a claim. When he tries to evaluate a claim without proper information, he is in effect buying a "pig in a poke."

2. **The evidence.** The claim investigator should judge the credibility and effectiveness of the witnesses. This includes not only the insured, claimant, and other witnesses to the accident, but physicians or other specialists who may be called upon to testify. He should determine all the known factors and realistically appraise those which are unknown, such as the possibility of a witness changing his story at trial, the possibility of surprise, unknown witnesses, or unexpected factual allegations.

He should further weigh the factual information against the actual evidence which he can produce to substantiate it. No matter what information he may have obtained, his position may still be vulnerable unless he has the evidence to substantiate the information.

3. **The law.** No proper evaluation of a claim can be made without knowledge of the law of the jurisdiction in which an accident occurred. Consideration must be given to primary negligence, contributory or comparative negligence, proximate cause, last clear chance,

family purpose doctrine, guest laws, assumption of risk, agency, traffic regulations, and other laws and doctrines of a similar nature. The various problems of adjective law concerning service and trial of a case, jurisdiction of the courts and appeal, must also be considered in making an evaluation.

4. **Injury or damage.** The extent of the injury and the possibility of permanent or partial disability and disfigurement must be considered. The age and sex of the injured will affect recovery and his occupation will have a direct bearing on the extent of his disability.

In death cases, dependency and age should play an important part in the evaluation. Since the same factors which enter into the reserve of a case also have a direct bearing on its settlement evaluation, a review of Chapter 16 regarding reserves is suggested.

5. **Special damages.** Special damages such as loss of salary, medical expenses, and other direct and tangible financial losses are a prime factor in the consideration of the value of a casualty claim.

6. **Conscious pain and suffering.** While important, this is one of the most difficult to evaluate in dollars and cents. Nevertheless, based on experience gained from previous verdicts in the area, a value must be placed on this item.

7. **Intangible elements.** These factors include the reasonableness of the claimant, his economic status and standing in the community, the attitude of all parties with reference to the trial, the caliber of attorneys on both sides, local feeling, sympathy engendered if the claimant is a widow or orphan, or the pitiful condition of the injured. The emotional factor should sometimes bear considerable weight in the evaluation of a particular claim.

8. **Expense factor.** Finally, consideration must be given to the economic factors involved. Would trial costs, for instance, exceed the amount demanded in settlement? In some instances, a decision to try a case may be made in spite of the fact that it may be poor economy on that particular case, because of the possibility of encouraging similar claims or because an important principle is involved. However, if after consideration of these factors, it is deemed advisable to settle a claim, then the economic factors of investigation, trial costs, and other expense items should be weighed against the demand.

§ 17.05 Decisions Concerning Evaluation

Occasionally, a decision has to be made quickly on information just obtained. This presents a situation in which pressing for a first-call settlement may be advisable.

Usually, however, settlement negotiations involve several calls and are often long drawn-out affairs. Before entering into any discussions of settlement, the claim representative must make some decision concerning the value of the claim, based upon the factors previously listed. The approximate figure which he decides upon must be based on sound reasoning, since only then will he be able logically to convince a claimant of its fairness.

The average claimant, a layman, usually has little idea of the true value of his claim. He is emotionally upset, has sustained some monetary loss which he may not be able to afford, and is convinced that there is merit to his claim, no matter what the facts. He has seen newspaper articles that publicized high verdicts and probably has talked with others who may have given him inflated ideas. Human nature being what it is, ego seems to lead some people to boasting, even on matters of claim settlement figures.

All of these factors present obstacles which the claim representative must surmount if he is to dispose of a claim at a fair figure. To do so, his thinking and his arguments must be logical, clear and concise.

If the value of a claim has been reasonably thought out, the amount will usually be an uneven figure. There is quite a controversy among claim representatives concerning the relative merits of odd versus round figure settlements. Frankly, I hold no brief for either side. If insistence on an uneven figure might antagonize a claimant to the point of jeopardizing settlement, or where the addition of a few dollars to reach the nearest round figure will make the claimant pleased with the ultimate settlement, I believe that the extra investment is worth the cost.

On the other hand, there are undoubtedly many instances where an offer of an uneven figure, backed by a logical explanation, will impress the claimant much more than an offer of a round figure. My suggestion is that the initial offer ordinarily be made on an uneven-figure basis, with a little leeway permitted in those instances where it is deemed advisable to increase the offer.

§ 17.06 Control

Control of a claim means that a claim representative has gained the confidence of the claimant. It implies first of all, that he has made prompt contact with the claimant so that he is aware of the claim adjuster's interest in the matter. It implies that he has acted in a manner that convinced the claimant of his sincere desire to do what is fair and proper. Finally, it implies that he has convinced the claimant that his word can be depended upon when it is given.

As has been said before, the claimant who has been involved in an accident is worried and somewhat emotionally upset, at least. He needs reassurance that he will be treated fairly. The claim representative should make no definite commitments until the case is ready for settlement, unless he has decided to make an advance payment. Reassurance can sometimes be given, however, to relieve the claimant's financial anxiety by assuring him that the claims representative intends to deal fairly with him when he is prepared to discuss settlement.

If the claimant is confined to a hospital and is in no condition to be interviewed, control may be maintained by paying a friendly visit to a wife, husband, parent, or other close relative residing in the claimant's household. It is unwise to press for an immediate interview with the claimant if he is obviously unable because of physical or emotional incapacity, to discuss his claim rationally. In order to arrive at a proper balance between "too early" and "too late," careful consideration should be given to determine the time for the initial interview with the injured claimant. There are also statutes which may have some bearing on when a claimant can first be seen.

Once initial contact has been made, the claim representative will find it just as important to make periodic and regular calls on the claimant or his family whether they be to a hospital or at home. The fact that the claimant may not be ready to discuss settlement for some time should not deter him from making calls on the claimant. A call made ostensibly to see how the claimant is getting along and to inquire about his health, without any discussion of the claim factor whatsoever, will go a long way toward convincing the claimant that a claim representative's interest in his welfare is sincere.

[1] Maintaining Control of Death Cases

Death cases always present difficult problems. There are, of course, some instances in which the death of an individual is not too emotionally disturbing a factor to the heirs, and others in which possible monetary gain is more important to them than the loss of the decedent. These, however, are obvious exceptions.

For the most part, the death of an individual as a result of a sudden accident creates an emotional shock that leaves the immediate family in no condition and with no desire to discuss the settlement of the claim, at least until enough time has elapsed for them somewhat to regain their perspective.

The courteous and decent thing to do in such an instance is to communicate with some member of the family. A claim representative can leave a note on a card at the house, make a telephone call, or write a very tactful and diplomatic letter. In this he can explain that he realizes that "this is not time to discuss the claim," but wishes to reassure them of his interest in the matter by expressing his sympathy and suggesting that someone get in touch with him at such time as they may wish to discuss the matter. This will inform the family of the interest of the insurance carrier and reassure them financially to some degree. At the same time, it will not be forcing them to discuss the claim before they are ready to do so.

To sum up, maintaining control is nothing more than acting in a courteous, sympathetic, and humane fashion, so that the claimant will be convinced that the claims representative has a sincere desire to be friendly and fair.

§ 17.07 The Proper Approach to Settlement Negotiations

Most people are inherently honest, but the claim representative must maintain an attitude of healthy skepticism because of some human tendencies that lie more or less dormant in all of us.

A proper attitude in approaching an individual with whom he is about to enter into settlement negotiations can be outlined as follows:

1. **Be friendly and above-board.** Maintain an even temper and do not give vent to anger or hostility. Show a sincere desire to do what is right and proper and avoid at all costs any signs of sarcasm or condescension.

SETTLEMENTS § 17.07

2. **Be courteous, tactful, and well-mannered.** General deportment will play an important part in the impression made on the claimant. Such details as removing a hat in a claimant's home and addressing the claimant properly are matters of common courtesy. If the claim representative is a cigar smoker, he should refrain from indulging while he is in a claimant's home.

3. **Be tolerant and avoid any show of bigotry or prejudice.** Never make slighting remarks, humorous or otherwise, about race, creed, religion, or politics. An apparently innocent remark made thoughtlessly can create a bad impression.

4. **Be sympathetic, understanding, and attentive.** A claimant will often be angry at the insured, whom he blames for his predicament or for the injury that a child or other relative has suffered. Let him blow off steam. However, be a good listener; avoid adding fuel to the fire. Silence and good temper can go a long way toward dispelling his anger, or at least avoiding its transference to the claim representative and the company he represents.

5. **Speak at the claimant's language level.** Avoid the use of legal phraseology or polysyllabic words that may be over the head of the particular individual. A claim representative should remember that he is not trying to impress the claimant with his education or vocabulary.

6. **Be confident, persuasive, and decisive,** but avoid an attitude of rigidity. Be firm, but don't close the door on further negotiations so tightly that the claimant or his attorney will have to start an action in order to save face. The claimant can very easily detect signs of weakness or indecision. One sign of weakness is an indication of over-anxiety.

7. **Be well-informed and have the facts at hand.** Otherwise the claim representative will be in no position to convince the claimant of his point of view.

8. **Be honest and keep your word.** Do not promise anything you cannot deliver. Never mislead, and be very careful in making commitments.

9. **Deal with the party who has control,** whether he be husband, wife, doctor, or friend, but try to do so in the presence of the claimant. A claim representative should not give the claimant the impression that he is unimportant or being by-passed.

In the ordinary case, try to see the claimant alone or in the presence of the spouse.

§ 17.08 Offer Versus Demand

Since settlement negotiations are a matter of judgment and common sense, any discussion of this subject will of necessity abound with generalities. For instance, in a discussion of settlement figures, a claim representative should usually obtain some demand from the claimant or his attorney before making any offer. Let us assume that the claim representative has already evaluated the claim from information he has been able to obtain. There are, however, many factors in every case of which the claimant alone is aware. The claimant's evaluation is possibly based on entirely different considerations from those to which the claim representative has given weight. Ordinarily, because of emotional involvement, inexperience, lack of familiarity with the law, or ill-advised counsel, the claimant's figure is usually greater than the insurers. Occasionally, however, because of factors which are unknown, the claim representative may have over-valued the claim and finds that the claimant's demand is lower than the insurer's appraisal.

It will occasionally be found that although the claimant is willing and ready to discuss settlement, he has not actually formulated any definite figure in his mind. If he has gained confidence in the claim representative he may rely on him to help evaluate his claim. In this exceptional instance, a claim representative may find it advisable to outline the basis for his evaluation and make an offer based on sound reasoning before the claimant has made a demand. Usually, in such an instance, a "cushion" should be allowed for normal bargaining. This again depends upon the appraisal of the individual with whom he is dealing.

Do not be gullible. Occasionally a claim representative may be lulled into a false sense of security by someone who is much more shrewd than he appears. Such a person will usually attempt to learn the figure that the insurer believes fair so that he can use it as a basis to start negotiations upward. Every claim representative has made errors in his appraisals of claimants. The best teacher will be the experience gained by numerous contacts.

The general demeanor of a claimant, what he says, and the manner in which he says it, will usually give reliable clues concerning

SETTLEMENTS § 17.09

his character. This, however, is not always true. Some of our best actors and actresses have never been on a stage or before a motion picture camera.

Initially, the new claim representative is ordinarily inclined to be a little too gullible and trusting. He must guard, on the other hand, against allowing a few unpleasant incidents to color his viewpoint and warp it too far in the opposite direction. An intelligent, tolerant individual will soon acquire a proper balance and perspective; a sense of humor is an invaluable aid that should help him to attain it.

The good claim representative is one who can settle a claim for a reasonable amount and leave the claimant content with the knowledge that he has been dealt with fairly and honestly.

§ 17.09 Obtaining the Release

While the subject of releases as legal instruments will be discussed separately, any discussion of settlement negotiations must of necessity concern itself with the obtaining of the claimant's signature to a release.

Here are a few rules which are applicable to obtaining a release from a claimant:

1. Settlement negotiations should be complete and a definite amount agreed upon before any release is produced or drawn.
2. The completion of a release, including signature, witnessing, or notarization should be treated as a matter of fact accompaniment to the settlement agreement.
3. Wherever possible a release should be completed and signature obtained at the time settlement is agreed upon. In claims involving husband and wife, it is advisable to arrive at a settlement agreement in the presence of both. If this is impractical, an individual release should be obtained from the injured party and a call-back made at a subsequent time to obtain the release for loss of services from the spouse.
4. A claim representative should make absolutely certain that the claimant understands that he is releasing all claims against the insured. He should read the release to the claimant and avoid making any statements that might in any way be construed as misleading. He must guard against misrepre-

senting the nature of the instrument the claimant is about to sign.
5. Occasionally, if future difficulty is suspected, he should have the claimant append a few lines at the bottom of the release in his own handwriting, or take a supplemental affidavit or signed statement from him, to the effect that he is aware that he is terminating any and all rights which he might have against the party being released.
6. If the claimant is illiterate, or does not read or write English, the same procedure should be followed as outlined in taking signed statements from such individuals.

§ 17.10 Negotiating With Attorneys

Very often, a claimant with whom a claim representative is dealing will be receiving advice from an attorney who is either a friend, relative or someone trying to obtain the case. If the connection is obviously a close one, it may be more advantageous to deal directly with the attorney rather than through the claimant, since the claimant in this instance is only acting as the mouthpiece for the attorney. An attorney will more readily understand a claim representative's language than will a claimant who is trying to talk like an attorney.

Attorneys do not like to be ignored any more than anyone else. Therefore, letters of representation should be acknowledged promptly. To refrain from doing this is not only impolite but poor claims handling because of the antagonism it invites.

Attorneys are cooperative too. In the ordinary case, it may safely be assumed that the attorney is just as anxious to settle the claim as is the insurer. Not only is he under personal economic pressure, but he is also being pressed by his client. He is therefore just as anxious to gain the insurer's cooperation as the claim representative is to gain his.

A claim representative should not be afraid to ask an attorney to substantiate his allegations. In order to justify his demand, he must convince the claim representative that his case is worth reasonably close to his asking figure. Obtain a complete list of special damage allegations. Ask for his theory of negligence. It is surprising how an attorney will be brought up short by this request. Find out what factual information he can give to back up his allegations.

The average attorney will not give his complete file, but he will ordinarily give enough information to attempt to justify his demand. Most attorneys, if approached in a proper and fair manner, will give medical information and permit the taking of a physical examination even in those states where this is not a legal requirement.

If the investigation indicates the case is one to deny, a claim representative should do so as soon as he has sufficient information to justify his decision. If suit is instituted, the file should be reviewed periodically for any change in conditions or factors which might affect a previous decision. The disappearance of a witness, a new allegation made by the attorney, or the very act of instituting suit may be important enough to warrant a review that might justify some payment on the claim.

Always be careful of the wording used in making offers or in mentioning figures. A tentative offer is usually interpreted as a definite offer.

Get to know your local attorneys. Continued negotiations with attorneys will soon make a claim representative familiar with their characteristics and peculiarities. Information obtained from other experienced claim people and his own personal experience will be the best teachers. There are as many types of attorneys as there are types of other people. For instance, there is:

1. The honest, conscientious attorney who is trying to make the best possible settlement for his client in a fair and ethical manner. He knows his law and is familiar with values. With this type of attorney, a claim representative will have the least amount of trouble. He should treat him courteously, fairly, honestly, and let him know that his word can be relied upon.
2. The substantially honest attorney who has been mislead or misinformed and is not too anxious to make any thorough investigation that might discredit his client. Here again, we are dealing with the pleasant type of person that can be reasoned with and whose reactions are those of the average human being.
3. The shrewd attorney whose sharp practices border on the dishonest. This person's reputation usually is well-known in the locality. With him, a claim representative will have to be on guard constantly. He should be careful not to reveal his

defenses and check all facts and special damages with extreme care.

4. The arbitrary, unreasonable, and antagonistic attorney. This person carries a grudge, usually against insurance companies and claim adjusters. Sometimes courtesy will break down his antagonism. With others, it may be so ingrained as to require a firm stand. Firmness, however, does not mean belligerence, which should be avoided at all costs.

5. The attorney who is inexperienced in the handling of negligence matters. This individual usually presents a tough problem because he has no realistic ideas of values. Usually he is handling a case because of other business connections with the claimant. No guiding rules can be set down in negotiations with this type of attorney. He is just as likely to go to one extreme as the other; dealings with him are simply catch as catch can.

6. The dilatory attorney is the one who can be the most aggravating. This attorney may want to settle a claim, but because of a congenital inability to do things at a proper time, will continue to procrastinate until everyone's patience is worn thin. There are some schools of thought that believe it is inadvisable to press an attorney for settlement, on the theory that it may give him the impression that the insurer is concerned about its position. I do not subscribe to this theory, and believe that there are many ways of approach that will open up settlement negotiations without giving the attorney the impression that the insurer's position is weak. All that is needed is to point out to the attorney that it is necessary to know in which direction the case is headed, so that if it is impossible to dispose of it by settlement, the investigation will have to be completed in good time in order to prepare a proper defense.

7. Finally, there is the plaintiff's negligence specialist to whom other lawyers refer cases and who is known for the high verdicts which he has obtained. This kind of attorney prefers to try a case before a jury rather than settle it out of court. He is the most difficult of all to deal with because he really doesn't care whether he settles the case or not. In fact, where the policy limits are high, he hopes that he will not be able to settle it and primes such a case for a bad faith action if he

has the slightest chance. Unless, therefore, he is fishing for such an opportunity, it is very difficult to get any settlement demand from him. On the other hand, where the policy limits are low and the insured is an individual who is not "well heeled," the insurer will ordinarily get a demand letter with a short time limitation, offering to settle for the policy limits within a short period of time. *A claim adjuster should always take such letters seriously.* If the liability is even questionable, and the injuries are evident, put the money on the line as fast as possible, even before a release is signed. See that the check and release or releases are hand delivered and a receipt obtained. Do not wait for written home office authority to be received, but do use the telephone to get it as quickly as possible, where warranted. Do not let such an attorney lull you into a false sense of security by accepting any remarks such as "Don't take this letter seriously, you understand that I have to protect myself," or "I know the time limitation is short, but I won't take any action that is unreasonable," or other such "assurances." This attorney is gambling that the insurer will delay reply until after the time limitation has passed, and if it does you can be sure that you will be "nailed." Even where the policy limit is fairly high, if you get such a demand letter, check the liability and injury as quickly as possible, and if the demand warrants settlement arrange to get confirmation of injury or damages after the settlement, and do not make it a condition of settlement, where warranted.

Sometimes, this kind of attorney is so busy that he may make a reasonable demand either because he doesn't believe his case is too good or because he hasn't had the time to give it proper consideration. With this kind of attorney, take every demand seriously and act upon it promptly. Where there has been no demand, courtesy and persistence will often get a demand where other things have failed. Don't fall into the trap of not trying.

§ 17.11 Disposition of Injury Claims Involving Minors

Though no hard and fast rules can be promulgated for handling bodily injury claims involving minors, certain guiding principles can be set forth that will help in the disposition of these cases.

Ordinarily one who has not attained his majority is as we have seen, legally incapable of making a binding contract. Accordingly, releases executed by a minor are not binding upon him. The age at which a person reaches majority varies in different states. Marital status, sex, and other factors may be determinative.

There is no way to definitely settle an infant's claim for bodily injury without court sanction. However, there are good reasons why it is sometimes advisable to dispose of claims involving infants without obtaining such court approval. The most obvious is the matter of expense often not warranted in claims where the injury is trivial.

Many such claims involve exceedingly minor injuries where the full extent of the medical bill is very small. In most of these cases the demand of the parents is confined to the actual amount of the medical bills, or a few dollars over this sum.

Complete recovery is usually normal if an infant has received trivial injuries. The parents certainly would not want to incur an expense that would be as great, or possibly greater than the amount of recovery. The insurance company, likewise, must consider expense factors in the disposition of this type of claim. A claim representative must, therefore, consider the following items in disposing of claims involving injuries to minors.

[1] Medical Information

The claim representative can and should obtain a detailed medical report from the attending doctor or hospital, and copies of all medical bills. Barring unforeseen circumstances and unexpected developments, he has then done everything possible to learn the full extent of the injury, short of obtaining a physical examination. Should he still have any doubt about the extent of the injury, he may then find it advisable to obtain a medical examination.

[2] Indemnification Release

Since a minor cannot give a binding release, claims involving slight injuries to children present a problem for the claim adjuster.

A parent can only release his or her personal claim for expenses, past, present, and future, and sometimes for the possible loss of a child's services, but he or she cannot release the basic claim of the infant. Accordingly, insurance companies instituted the practice of obtaining a release from the parents which included an indemnification agreement to the effect that the parents would reimburse the company for any monies that it might be required to pay the infant in addition to the amount specified in the release, in the event of a subsequent judgment. Almost immediately, however, the courts held such an agreement void as being against public policy, so the companies were right back where they started.

Nevertheless, many claims involving minors do not warrant the expense of obtaining a court approved settlement. In addition, such approval requires the services of an attorney and this in and of itself leads to further complications.

Most companies, therefore, take a calculated risk where the injuries are trivial, and hope that the moral effect of signing a release by the parents, even though ineffective as to the child, will be a deterrent to any further claim.

[3] Investigation

At the least, the obvious routine investigation should be made. Witnesses should be interviewed, the scene of the accident checked, diagrams made or photographs ordered, and so on, despite the fact that the claim representative intends to close out the claim. Remember that if an infant's claim has not been put through court it may always be subject to reopening until the statutory period has run after the infant has obtained his majority.

In completing the investigation the claim adjuster should, in all possible cases, obtain a signed statement concerning the facts of the accident directly from the infant. The primary concern here is not the legal or evidentiary value of the statement. Comments have often been heard to the effect that no attempt was made to question the infant because (a) children tell lies as a matter of course and are unreliable, (b) children are easily confused, (c) they cannot give coherent accounts of what they saw, (d) they are just too young, and so on. This is negative thinking. By and large, children are more honest and forthright than their parents. Frequently, they are much more observant than their elders and quite able to give a clear description of what they have witnessed.

If the child is too young to write, the claim representative should obtain the parents' account of what the child told them. This statement should include the fact that the child has fully recovered from the injury, since no attempt to close a case should be made unless complete recovery has been made.

[4] Emancipated Child

There are several means by which an infant can gain and prove emancipation. All of them involve economic independence. Living away from home may be partial proof. Being married usually denotes emancipation.

The only effect of a child's emancipation on a bodily injury claim is that a parent has no claim *of his own* for necessary expenses or loss of services. However, mere emancipation does not always make it possible for an infant to execute a valid and binding release for his own injuries.

If negotiations are being conducted with an emancipated minor, some proof of such emancipation should be obtained. This proof should include an affidavit from the minor himself, as well as one from his parents.

[5] Settlement With Court Approval

There are two effective ways of settling a claim involving injuries to a minor:

1. With approval of a court of proper jurisdiction. In this instance a guardian of the child is appointed by the court and an order for the distribution of the payment is usually made.
2. By satisfaction of a judgment duly entered in an action instituted by or on behalf of a minor, often called a "friendly suit," which is also a court approved settlement.

When an agreement is reached, the parents should understand that this is the final settlement figure and be apprised of a breakdown so that they will know approximately what proportion of the settlement figure will go as the attorney's fee. In some jurisdictions the fee is set by the court. In those instances the parents are to be fully informed of this fact. This procedure usually involves legal representation for the claimant.

[6] Closing Records

It is not unusual for an attorney to be unfamiliar with the procedures necessary to close an infant action. In those cases it is advisable to tell the attorney exactly what is needed in the way of court orders and releases to clear the records. Consultation with the insurer's attorney is advisable to make sure that all is in proper order.

§ 17.12 Advance Payments

The Advance Payment Program was instituted by the insurance industry in order to combat the allegations of hardship that arose as a result of the practice that required no payment to the claimant in negligence cases until a full and final release could be obtained from him. All too many claimants found it very difficult to weather the financial burden during their period of distress.

The turnabout came as a result of sudden social awareness plus a recognition that faith in human nature might be worth a gamble. I think, much to their surprise, the insurer's have found that the gamble paid off and that the trust which they have shown has been appreciated and reciprocated in varying degrees.

To be sure, when serious consideration is given to the matter, the gamble is not a great one and the odds are pretty small.

In any event, even where no written agreement of any kind has been obtained, and the matter goes to trial, the company is almost sure to get an offset for monies paid.[2]

Most states have enacted statutes that grant immunity from implied liability that might arise from making advance payments, and permit deductions of amounts paid to be made from any final judgment.

The decision in the case of *Ferris v. Anderson*,[3] summed it up very nicely when it stated that (1) the absence of a specific advance payment statute does not bar the trial court from incorporating the partial payment into the judgment, (2) the issue of offset must be properly pleaded, and (3) the offset issue must be separated from the liability issue to avoid prejudice.

---

[2] Edwards v. Passarelli Bros. Auto. Service, 221 N.E.2d 708 (Ohio 1966).
[3] 255 N.W.2d 135 (Iowa 1977).

While the court concluded that it need not decide whether advance payments constituted an admission of liability, it did make clear that it felt that such payments should be encouraged.[4]

[1] Advantages

An advance payment on deserving cases has the following advantages:

1. It immediately puts the claimant in a friendly and receptive frame of mind and creates the desire and sometimes the moral obligation to cooperate with the insurer. It makes it much more likely for the claim representative to maintain control of the case without forcing it into the hands of an attorney.
2. It creates immediate goodwill with the public at large and even with attorneys that represent claimants.
3. It relieves the claimant from financial anxiety which has a definite advantageous effect on his physical recovery.
4. It enables the claimant to get the best medical attention and accordingly helps to reduce the period of disability.
5. It enables the insurer to get complete and accurate medical information for a more realistic reserve and settlement evaluation.
6. It gives the insured a definite advantage in negotiating a final settlement.
7. It even has a social value in some instances in keeping the claimant from welfare relief dependency.

The usual objections that had the industry hidebound for years were of course voiced during the initial period when advance payments were first promulgated, and to my sincere regret, by myself as vociferously as anyone else. We argued that advance payments financed a suit, discouraged early settlement, encouraged overtreatment, etc, etc, etc. I am now convinced, and I believe as does the industry at large, that the advantages far outweigh the disadvantages.

Advance payments usually contemplate the following expenses:

---

[4] *See also* Byrd v. Stuart, 450 S.W.2d 11 (Tenn. 1969). D.R.I. Monograph, "Efficient Use of the Legal Effort for the Defense," October 1970.

1. Medical and hospital bills as they arise.
2. Salary, in the form of regular payments.
3. Property damage, but care must be used in those areas where payment of property damage may be construed as an admission of liability.
4. Other immediate financial needs such as day care for children, hospital services, and similar essential expenses as they arise.

[2] Choosing the Cases

I still retain enough of my hard-shell training to insist that care must be used in the selection of cases where a decision to make advance payments may be applicable:

1. Liability should be apparent in most instances.
2. Where the injury is severe, I still believe that the liability should be probable in contributory negligence states and at least 50-50 in comparative liability states. Again, of course, a matter of judgment.
3. The injury should be obvious or undisputed. I would never, of course, advise advance payments on a case in which there is a good chance of fraud or even malingering.
4. The claimant must be willing to cooperate by permitting full medical and special damage disclosure.

Here again each company has set its own guidelines with which the new claim representative must become familiar.

[3] Some Reasonable Limitations

The obligation of making advance payments should not be assumed lightly. Once having decided that the liability and injury warrant such action, it must always be uppermost in the mind of the claim representative that he must protect the interest of his company to the best of his ability. Accordingly, some stop-gap action or understanding should be had in the cases that warrant it, depending on the circumstances.

1. *Time limit.* It should be understood that the agreement to make advance payments cannot be on an indefinite basis. Some time limit must be set, after which reconsideration

should be given concerning extension. This of course depends on the amount of coverage as well as other factors.
   2. *Amount limit.* I believe it advisable to set reasonable figures as an amount limit, again to be reconsidered when the limit has been received, and again determined by the policy limits and other factors.
   3. *Reasonable expenses.* The claimant must be made to understand that he does not have carte blanche to go hog-wild on medical or other expenses and that any unusual expense item should be referred to the insurer for approval before authorization is given. In any event, all expenses should be measured by reasonable standards.
   4. *Credit for payments.* It should be understood that all payments made by the company will be credited and taken into consideration at the time final settlement is made.
   5. *Written agreement.* Company policy will have to guide the claim representative in the determination as to whether or not an effort should be made to obtain a written agreement from the claimant outlining the limitations set by the insurer. Anything requested of the claimant in writing during the time of stress will probably make him suspicious. If he is represented by an attorney the task becomes simplified since the attorney will be more knowledgeable and understanding concerning such an agreement.

If the claimant is not represented by legal counsel, then the claim representative must make the difficult decision whether or not to press for a written agreement. He can always confirm an oral agreement by way of a letter and this method appeals to me greatly. Once again, he will have to be guided by the individual policy set by the company for which he works.

It is absolutely essential that a complete investigation be conducted on all claims that warrant it regardless of whether or not advance payments are being made. In the latter case, the investigation should be easier in view of the claimant's cooperation on medical information and special damages.

[4] Method of Payment

Periodic payments can be made in several ways. The claimant can be paid directly with the reason for the payment stated on the draft.

It can also be made directly to the doctor or hospital or other individual rendering the service. My own recommendation is that the drafts or checks should be made out to the claimant and the individual or entity doing the billing for those items where the money is eventually to go to someone other than the claimant himself. This is just an extra precaution that requires very little effort. The drafts or checks should be sent with a covering letter so that a copy can be kept for the file records.

If it is the policy of the insurer to obtain signed receipts for the payments made, the claim representative must obviously comply with his company's requirements. Where such a receipt is required, the company usually has preprinted forms. The worst thing he could do would be to send a release type of draft to the claimant. The reaction would be justifiably negative.

[5] Admission of Liability

In some instances the fear has been voiced that making an advance payment, or even the offer of an advance payment on injury cases, might be interpreted legally as an admission of liability. The courts have, until recently, rejected such a view.[5] Judge Cardoza as long ago as 1914, held that such a payment is "a voluntary act of mere benevolence."[6]

A number of states have enacted legislation encouraging advance payments by holding that such payments are not an admission of liability.

Recently, however, an astonishing decision was made by the Oregon Court of Appeals in the case of *Bollam v. Fireman's Fund Ins. Co.*[7] In this case, the insurer proceeded to initiate and make advance payments to a seriously injured claimant for a period of about six months, at which time it became convinced that the claimant's expenses would probably exceed the insurer's policy limits. It so notified its insured, who hired his own attorney to protect his own interests. The insured then settled with the claimant for an amount which was $35,000 over his policy limits and had his attorney bring an ac-

---

[5] *See* Hughes v. Anchor Enterprises, Inc., 245 N.C. 131, 63 A.L.R.2d 685 (1956); Fields v. Rutledge, 284 S.W.2d 659 (Ky. App. 1955); Oldenburg v. Sears, Roebuck & Co., 152 Cal. App. 2d 773, 314 P.2d 33 (1957).

[6] Grogan v. Dooley, 211 N.Y. 30 (1914).

[7] 709 P.2d 1095 (App. 1985).

tion for reimbursement of this amount on the grounds of negligent handling of the claim.

The court of appeals held that while advance payments, of themselves, are not necessarily an indication of negligent delay in settling, there was evidence in the record that the insurer delayed tendering its full policy limit well after the damages were known to have exceeded such limit, and that there was evidence to support the jury's conclusion that more prompt behavior might have obtained a settlement within the policy limits.

This decision, in my opinion, is a gross miscarriage of justice and could well put a decided damper on the making of advance payments in cases where the injured has a real need for such payments. The court's argument that a settlement within the policy limit *might* have been possible and that such a settlement would have given the insured "peace of mind" would have been at the cost of depriving the injured claimant of the additional $35,000 which he obtained from the insured. All things considered, the balance of equities appear to me to favor the insurer. The arguments of the court were based on a mere possibility, which is, at best, gossamer law.

[6] Written Permission to Settle

Special precautions should be taken in those instances where the limits of liability may not be adequate in negotiating the final disposition of the claim. At this point, the individual interests of the insured must be given particular attention. Accordingly, it is most important in such cases to obtain written permission from the insured before any commitments are made that could possibly be construed as an admission of liability.

Such permission must always be obtained where the injury arose out of an allegation of malpractice arising out of a professional liability policy.

[7] Statute of Limitations

An insurer that is making advance payments is presumed to be acting with more than the average degree of good faith. Accordingly, any thought of taking advantage of the statute of limitations to avoid further payment on a claim on which advance payments have been made will be obviously unethical and ineffective.

SETTLEMENTS § 17.12[9]

Whether or not a written agreement to toll the statute should voluntarily be given to the claimant or his attorney is again a matter of company policy. In any event, even if it is not given, some verbal or written warning should be made concerning the statutory period. It seems pretty obvious that if no extension is given it can only drive the claimant to turn the matter over to an attorney or to institute suit to protect his interests.

California and perhaps some other states have enacted statutes which take care of this kind of situation by automatically tolling the statute of limitations where advance payments are being made unless written notice has been given.

[8] Follow-up

Once having made the decision to make advance payments, some diary or other follow-up system should be instituted to make absolutely sure that payments are made promptly and that the claim is reviewed regularly. All of the benefit that can be derived from such a system can be lost by dilatory practices.

[9] Closing the Case

When a claimant has reached a point in his recovery where he is willing to discuss settlement, he will make his attitude known to the claim representative. Should he reach the point of maximum recovery without broaching the subject of settlement, it then becomes a matter for decision as to whether the claim representative will take the initiative or whether to continue regular payments. This will depend upon the limits of liability coverage, the relationship that has been developed between the claim representative and the claimant, the question of possible malingering, and upon impartial medical advice. No set rules can be established. It is merely a matter of judgment.

In any event, I am not flexible enough to advocate open-end settlements except in unusual situations. Some companies permit a claim to be closed without obtaining a release from the claimant. I cannot reconcile myself to such a practice. It leaves open too many avenues for trouble, whether it be in the nature of fraud, or merely second thoughts by the claimant.

At some point, I think a decision should be made concerning final settlement, at which time a release of all further claims should be taken.

I cannot deny, however, that some companies have had success in terminating such claims with only a letter of understanding from the company in place of a release. Such a letter usually informs the claimant that he can contact the insurer for reconsideration of the claim in the event of unexpected further expenses or difficulties arising out of the injury and warns him of the statute of limitations.

§ 17.13 Structured Settlements

[1] Introduction

Generally speaking, an injured plaintiff who receives a large verdict or settlement is no more capable of handling a large sum of money than is the average person in our society. Most of us are not accustomed to the responsibility of a great deal of money and are, for the most part, possible victims of the human jackals and vultures that prey on anyone who has suddenly come into a "fortune."

Often, relatives and friends, even those who are well intentioned, may influence the injured to invest or lend some money in a project that is anything but financially sound.

In any event, to give such an individual a large sum of money without guidance, or without arranging for his or her financial security, is shameful. One answer to this problem has been, and is, the development of the so-called "structured settlement."

In effect, a structured settlement involves some method of payment to the injured and/or his family other than a lump-sum outlay of the entire settlement amount or verdict. It may be made in the form of a trust, or can involve the purchase of an annuity, or in several combinations. It can require a lump-sum payment to the plaintiff and his attorney, or to a dependent, in addition to regular payments from a trust fund or annuity.

Structured settlements are a fairly recent development. While insurance companies may not have been motivated solely by altruism for this development, the end result is commendable and certainly advantageous to the plaintiffs, as well as the insurer.

So far, I have been unable to corroborate alleged statistics that indicate that a large proportion of plaintiffs who receive high awards dissipate the money and are left indigent within a few years. Nevertheless, everyone has heard plenty of horror stories to this effect and whether the number of such caes is high or low, the fact that it does happen is reason enough to make some attempt to secure the financial position of the injured and his family.

[2] Tax Considerations

Under Section 104(a)(2) of the Internal Revenue Code,[8] a lump-sum payment of a claim for personal injuries (also a judgment) is not taxable to the plaintiff. However, income subsequently earned and received from that payment is subject to taxation. By comparison, periodic payments, even in the same amount as the aforementioned income, subsequently received from a structured settlement may not be taxable. It is not however a simple matter. Mr. R.A. Koseff[9] states that under a key ruling,[10] the annuity arrangement is held to be merely a matter of convenience to the obligor (insurer) and does not give the recipient (plaintiff) any right in the annuity itself.

In the event the original casualty insurer becomes insolvent, its receiver can redirect payments away from the plaintiff, who would then become a general creditor of the annuity insurance company. In such an event, in some states, guarantee funds have been set up to see that the injured does not "hold the bag."

Mr. Koseff goes on to state that if the plaintiff attempts to sever a direct interest in the annuity contract as part of the settlement to circumvent this possibility, he incurs the risk of losing the tax exclusion of the interest portion of the payments.

The original solvent casualty insurer does, however, carry the contingent liability of making any payments that the annuity company is unable to make.

In 1983, the above ruling was codified and, in addition, held that the original casualty insurer, with the consent of the plaintiff, could now assign its obligation to a third party who then would be obligated to make the payments to the plaintiff. As practiced, this is in effect a reinsurance agreement.

Despite what has been stated, the percentage of life insurance companies that have defaulted in their payments of annuities in

---

[8] *See* Croft, "The Decision to Appeal," F.T.D., February 1985.
[9] "Difficulties With Structured Settlements," F.T.D., September 1983.
[10] Rev. Rul. 79-220, 1979-2C.B. 74.

structured settlements has been very small, if at all, and as far as I can determine, no claimants have suffered any loss.

Enormous lump sum verdicts have always appeared to me to be unfair because in a great many instances the amount awarded, tax free, and even after legal fees have been deducted, permits the plaintiffs to live off the interest generated by the settlement or verdict without touching the principal, if invested wisely. This leaves a windfall fortune to the injured's heirs over and above any amount necessary to provide for the needs of dependents.

The beauty of structured settlements is that it can provide, as far as possible, security for the injured and his dependents without the inequitable excess windfall to those that might have no moral right to it.

There are, of course, no certainties in this world. It is possible that the insurance company that sells the annuity may fail, as was previously pointed out, and if it does the original defendent insurance company could and probably would be held responsible for any deficiency. That is one of the reasons why I would recommend that all structured settlements that are involved, should be made with the assistance of specialists who keep up with all of the latest developments in this complex field, and are particularly familiar with the financial status of the life insurance companies that write annuities in various forms.

Arrangements can be made to provide a regular periodic income or a lump-sum in addition, in order to pay outstanding medical or other bills, legal fees (although some attorneys prefer periodic payments of their bill for tax purposes), children's tuition fees, and even for payments of business enterprises which are sound investments. The amounts paid can be graduated up or down over a period of time, and can also provide for death benefits. The variations are unlimited, and with the active participation of the plaintiff's lawyer, if he really cares, together with the approval of the court, there is enough latitude to take care of almost any contingency that has at least been thought of up to now. For instance, structured settlements can be arranged to take care of:

1. All medical needs of the injured on a regular basis or on a graduated scale.
2. Adequate living expenses in lieu of salary on a graduated basis to take care of inflationary trends.
3. Household help.

4. Occupational therapy and rehabilitation training.
5. Educational needs of children on a graduated scale.
6. Lump-sum amounts for special needs.
7. Legal fees on a lump-sum or extended basis.
8. Trusts, endowments, or annuities to take care of all of the above contingencies.
9. Trusts, endowments, or annuities to take care of dependents.

Obviously, other needs may also be taken care of. As Mr. J.F. Cleary put it:[11]

> Just as no two cases are the same, no two structured settlements are the same. While certain principles remain unchanged, the defense must continually update its knowledge to be aware of the latest devices, legislation and products available to properly handle the needs of plaintiff's counsel and his client.

After a settlement agreement has been reached, some basic steps must be taken to start the ball rolling with the cooperation of the plaintiff's attorney:

1. Make a determination of the life expectancy by arranging a complete medical evaluation, which should include all medical records.
2. Make an appraisal of future medical expenses including rehabilitation, therapy, future operations, medical bills, nursing home confinement, nurses at home services, prosthetic devices, and similar expenses.
3. Make a determination of the reasonable living expenses so as to arrive at a monthly income figure. This should include such items as rent or mortgage payments and real estate taxes, home repairs and necessary improvements, household help, food, clothing, and other such items.
4. Needs of dependents.
5. Legal fees.
6. Lump sums for special contingencies.

Thereafter, I think that it is advisable to call on the expertise of a specialist, with the aid of a lawyer, if necessary. In an article on this subject entitled, "The Use of Annuities in Settlement of Personal In-

---

[11] "Structured Settlements: A Variation on a Theme," F.T.D., January 1984

jury Cases,"[12] the authors include exhibits of settlement agreements and particulars relating to annuities, which are well worth reviewing. All of which is obviously wasted breath if the plaintiff is represented by an attorney who is unconcerned about the welfare of his client. Most lawyers, however, like most other human beings, have a conscience that can be awakened if they are properly approached.

No article can teach a claim adjuster how to be intelligent and tactful in such a mission. I can only caution that it does require the best talents of which the adjuster is capable. The question that ultimately must be addressed concerns the fact that the cost of a structured settlement will cost the insurance company considerably less than the agreed settlement figure and plaintiff's lawyers and even judges are taking a skeptical view of this fact, as is the Internal Revenue Service. All parties must be convinced that structured settlements are best for the plaintiffs and their families and that is, after all, the bottom line, and, for this reason, judicial attitudes are changing rapidly.

[3] Legal Aspects

In an article by Professor M.L. Plant,[13] he states that the desirable features of periodic payment plans have also promoted interest in their incorporation into judgments in contested cases. Occasionally, the courts have done this by judicial decision.[14]

[4] Model Structured Settlement Act

The National Conference of Commissioners on Uniform State Laws drafted a statute on structured settlements entitled, "Model Periodic Payments of Judgments Act," which was approved in 1980.

Parties to an underlying suit may adopt the Act, or any part of it, in a settlement agreement filed in court, whether or not a suit has been instituted, provided that one or more sections of the Model Act shall apply. The court may then enter a consent judgment as desired by both parties.

Unfortunately, this Model Act has not been received with any great enthusiasm by either the insurance companies or the plaintiff's

---

[12] Sedgwick & Judge, Insurance Counsel Journal, October 1974.

[13] "Periodic Payment of Damages for Personal Injury," 44 La. L. Rev. 1327 (May 1984).

[14] **Idaho:** McGhee v. McGhee, 353 P.2d 760 (1960).
Okla. M.&P. Stores v. Taylor, 326 P.2d 804 (1955).

SETTLEMENTS § 17.13[5]

bar. Insurers have been reluctant to accept that part of the Act requiring the underlying insurer to issue the type of annuity (or other security) that would take account of the fluctuations in the purchasing power of the dollar in calculating the annual installment payments. The plaintiff's lawyers, according to Professor Plant,[15] do not believe that courts should be vested with the authority to impose periodic payments against the will of either of the parties or their attorneys.

Both arguments show more self-interest than consideration for the interests of the injured.

[5] Workers' Compensation Cases

In recent years, the benefits provided by the various workers' compensation acts have been increased at rates never before contemplated and lump-sum settlements are being advocated by self-seeking plaintiff's lawyers.

The same reasons for the need to protect the plaintiffs in suits resulting from liability claims apply to the victims of work-related injuries brought under workers' compensation acts.

Professor Arthur Larson, in his highly respected text[16] has this to say about this subject:

> In some jurisdictions, the excessive and indiscriminate use of the lump-summing device has reached a point at which it threatens to undermine the real purposes of the compensation system. Since compensation is a segment of a total income insurance system, it ordinarily does its share of the job only if it can be depended on to supply periodic income benefits replacing a portion of lost earnings. If a partially or totally disabled worker gives up these reliable periodic payments in exchange for a large sum of cash immediately in hand, experience has shown that in many cases the lump sum is soon dissipated and the workman is right back where he would have been if workers' compensation had never existed. One reason for the persistence of this problem is that practically everyone associated with the system has an incentive—at least a highly visible short-term incentive—to resort to lump-summing.

Professor Larson goes on to state that "The only solution lies in conscientious administration, with unrelenting insistence that

---

[15] "Periodic Payment of Damages for Personal Injury," 44 La. L. Rev. 1327 (May 1984).

[16] *The Law of Workers' Compensation.*

§ 17.14

lump-summing be restricted to those exceptional cases in which it can be demonstrated that the purpose of the Act will best be served by a lump-sum award."[17]

Another author, E.J. Kelly,[18] writes:

> The primary reason for the periodic payment settlement technique, in the opinion of a workers' compensation administrator, is to avoid a large lump-sum payment, which could be quickly dissipated, to provide some form of long term periodic payments as contemplated in wage replacement and to insure claimant of regular payments without delay or interruption and to allow insurance carriers to close their files.

The same variety of annuities, trusts, etc., that can provide security in regular payments for the liability plaintiff are also available to the injured worker under the compensation acts, and all such arrangements must be approved by the workers' compensation administrator.

§ 17.14 Bibliography

Advance Payments

Carpenter, "The Legal Aspects of Partial Payments Made on Liability Claims in Advance of Final Settlement," Defense Law Journal, 1967.

Corboy, "Advance Payments: A Superficial Analysis from the Vantage of a Plaintiff's Lawyer," Defense Law Journal, 1967.

Gallagher, "Advance Payments: A Defense Attorney's Viewpoint," Defense Law Journal, 1967.

Hinkle, "The Affluent Adjuster and the Bodily Injury Claim," Insurance Law Journal, October 1968.

Hislop, Avitabile, Welch, Majeski, O'Brien, "Advance Payments and Rehabilitation," F.I.C. Quarterly, Fall 1967.

McCartney, "Legal Aspects and Problems Involved in Advance Payment of Medical and Economic Loss Programs," F.I.C. Quarterly, Fall 1966.

Robinson & Due, "Advance Payments—Problems in Practice and Procedure," Insurance Counsel Journal, July 1968.

Snow, "Advance Payments Under Liability Policies," Defense Law Journal, 1967.

---

[17] *Id.*

[18] "Workers' Compensation and the Periodic Payment Settlement Technique," Insurance Counsel Journal, October 1981.

Settlements

Carter, "Handling Claims With the Senior Citizen," Insurance Law Journal, June 1963.
Clayton, "Creating Risk in Negotiation and Settlement Techniques," The Independent Adjuster, Spring 1967.
Foutty, "The Evaluation and Settlement of Personal Injury Claims," Insurance Law Journal, January 1964.
Gooch, "Personal Injury Litigation: Settlement or Trial, From the Defense Point of View," 14 Wash. & Lee L. Rev. 1 (1967).
Hermann, "The Partially Educated Guess and Claim Evaluation," Insurance Law Journal, February 1960.
Mayer, "When to Talk Settlement," Insurance Adjuster, December 1965.
Reeder, "Evaluation of Damages," Insurance Law Journal, April 1965.

Structured Settlements

Carestia, "Structured Settlements in Practice," 46 Mont. L. Rev. 25 (Winter 1985).
Cleary, "Structured Settlements: A Variation On A Theme," F.T.D., January 1984.
Comment, "Customized Compensation for Personal Injury Plaintiff's," 13 Stetson L. Rev. 309-42 (1983).
Hillard, "Alternative Recovery Methods: Structured Settlements and Periodic Payment of Judgments," F.I.C. Quarterly, Spring 1984.
Hindert, "Periodic Payment of Personal Injury Damage," F.I.C. Quarterly, Fall 1980.
Kelly, "Workers' Compensation and the Periodic Payment Settlement Technique," Insurance Counsel Journal, October 1981.
Lilly, "Alternatives to Lump-Sum Payments in Personal Injury Cases," Insurance Counsel Journal, April 1977.
Moore, "The Use of Annuities in the Settlement of Personal Injury Cases," Insurance Counsel Journal, January 1982.
Plant, "Periodic Payment of Damages for Personal Injury," 44 La. L. Rev. 1327 (May 1984).
Sedgwick & Judge, "The Use of Annuities in Settlement of Personal Injury Cases," Insurance Counsel Journal, October 1974.
Winslow, "Tax and Economic Consideration in Structured Settlements," F.I.C. Quarterly, Fall, 1984.

CHAPTER 18

Releases

§ 18.01 New Developments
§ 18.02 Contractual Aspects
§ 18.03 Release Forms
     [1] Execution of Release Forms
§ 18.04 Fraud
§ 18.05 Indecent Haste
§ 18.06 "Fairly and Knowingly Made"
§ 18.07 "In Full Satisfaction of All Claims Against Others"
§ 18.08 Mistake Concerning Injuries or Facts
§ 18.09 Respondeat Superior
§ 18.10 Joint Tortfeasors
     [1] Statutory Enactment—Uniform Contribution Acts
§ 18.11 Releases in Death Claims
§ 18.12 Alleged Subsequent Malpractice by Doctors
§ 18.13 Bad Faith Allegations to Induce Settlement
     [1] Assignment of Insured's Claim for Bad Faith
§ 18.14 Mary Carter Agreements
§ 18.15 Laches
§ 18.16 Bibliography

§ 18.01 New Developments

Aside from no fault legislation involving automobile insurance, no change in our industry has been as radical as that concerning settlements and releases of bodily injury claims. No more than three decades ago I could safely say that as a general principle, and with relatively few exceptions, a release absolves the insurer from all further liability. I have had to qualify this statement considerably.

Today, I would define a release as a unilateral (signed by one party only) legal document, which if properly executed, *ordinarily* absolves the party or parties being released from further liability arising out of an incident which caused the damage or injury.

The qualification is now necessary because the changes in the law have been twofold. First of all, there has been a gradual erosion in the effectiveness of releases by the courts as we shall note subsequently. Secondly, there has been a complete change in the attitude of insurance carriers. Advance payments and open-end agreements have turned our previous conceptions upside-down.

While some courts still hold to the original doctrines concerning the validity of releases, and have stated their special importance "in this age of voluminous litigation,"[1] many of the recent decisions have tended to erode what was once a fairly impregnable position.

A release is still, however, the only tangible property that an insurance company receives for the money paid on a claim. If it is not a proper release, or not properly drawn, the claim representative has in effect purchased a defective article that will not give the insured or the insurer protection from further liability.

§ 18.02 Contractual Aspects

A release is a contract to terminate a claim, but has not been so interpreted universally. By and large however, it must have all of the elements of a valid contract to be held effective.[2]

1. **Meeting of the minds.** There must, of course, be a "meeting of the minds," but here we get into difficulties immediately. In the past, a release was interpreted to mean what it said. When a court held that whether or not a release was effective depended upon the intent of the parties, it was making a very obvious statement.[3] The difficulty lies in determining the intent when we can no longer depend completely on the wording of the release.

Some courts still hold that in the absence of fraud, mutual mistake, or illegal contract, parol (oral) evidence will not be recognized in order to show that a release did not intend what it stated.[4]

As we will see, however, those courts that stress "intent of the parties" as a new doctrine, disregard the parol evidence rule almost completely.

2. **Consideration.** A release must show that some consideration has been given for the discharge of the claimant's legal right.

Consideration has been defined as being some detriment of the releasee or some benefit to the releasor received from the releasee or someone in his behalf. Aside from the situation where there may be an exchange of releases between the insured and the claimant,

---

[1] Thomas v. Hollowell, 20 Ill. App. 2d 288, 155 N.E.2d 827 (1959).
[2] 71 A.L.R.2d 88 (1960).
[3] Aronovitch v. Levy, 56 N.W.2d 570 (Minn. 1953).
[4] Cannon v. Pearson, 383 S.W.2d 565 (Tex. 1964).

the consideration shown in the release is represented by a payment of money in some specific sum.

At one time, the use of a legal seal (not to be confused with a corporate seal) avoided the necessity for the showing of consideration. This device today is merely a holdover from the old common law, and has been eliminated. For our purposes, we can safely assume that in all cases where a release is obtained, it must show some valid consideration given therefore.[5]

Consideration must be actual and not merely nominal. One dollar releases, accordingly, are worth no more than the paper they are written on.

It must have some equitable basis, and should include separate consideration for every right which is released. For instance, if a claim which involves injury is settled for the exact amount of the property damage, a court might hold that there was no intent to release the bodily injury claim. By the same token, a release giving consideration for the exact amount of the special damages could be attacked as lacking in consideration for pain and suffering. A husband and wife release must show separate consideration for each.

Although failure to show consideration may be grounds for rescinding a release, the mere fact that a check or draft was not tendered or received until several days after the signing of the release, is not an indication that consideration was not given and will not affect its validity. The release in the case of *Hoefland v. Gustafson*[6] was held effective, even though the releasor refused to endorse the check.

Such consideration, however, cannot be delayed indefinitely. It must be made within a reasonable time.[7]

3. **Release must be legal.** A release, like any contract, cannot be held valid if it is made for an illegal purpose or if it is against public policy.

The releasor must also be legally capable of giving a valid release. An incompetent, for instance, cannot do so, nor can an infant, except in a very few special circumstances. Even emancipation, which may free him from parental control, does not always confer upon him the legal responsibility to make binding contracts that cannot be rescinded.

---

[5] Ruggles v. Selby, 165 N.E.2d 533 (1960).
[6] 282 P.2d 1039 (Cal. App. 1955).
[7] Walsh v. Walsh, 42 Cal. App. 2d 287, 108 P.2d 765 (1940).

It is therefore absolutely necessary to get court approval, with the appointment of a guardian or committee where necessary, in order to make a binding settlement of a claim involving a minor or incompetent. This is often done by "friendly suit," which is a legal process whereby a preagreed judgment is entered by the court. In such instances the release should conform with the exact wording of the court order or judgment and a certified copy of the order or judgment should be attached.

§ 18.03 Release Forms

An individually worded release, tailored to suit the circumstances of a particular claim, must be drawn by an attorney.

Filling in the blank spaces on a preprinted release form, however, does not constitute the practice of law and is in accordance with the Statement of Principles on Respective Rights and Duties of Lawyers and Laymen.

All companies use printed release forms that are, for the most part, adequate in the ordinary claim. These forms vary somewhat in size and langauge. My own preference is for the shorter forms that use the least amount of legal verbiage and which are most easily understood by the laymen.

Some forms in general use follow.

1. **General release—individual.** A general release discharges the named individual, his "successors and assigns, heirs, executors, administrators, and all other persons, firms and corporations." This is the phraseology ordinarily found in most documents of this kind.

It is a combination bodily injury and property damage form that should be used if the claimant is unmarried, divorced, or legally separated. The marital status should always be clearly stated in the release. In the case of a married woman who is living apart from her husband and who is self-supporting, the release should be accompanied by an affidavit attesting to these facts.

It is most important that all insureds, including owners and drivers of vehicles who may be covered as additional insureds, be specifically named in the release, in some instances even though they may not have been personally involved in the accident. *The insurance company, however, should never be named in the release* except in the few jurisdictions that permit direct actions against the insurer, or where the insurer may otherwise be directly involved in the claim or suit.

2. **General release—husband and wife.** Wherever possible, in the event of a claim resulting from an injury to a married person, a husband and wife release should be obtained, signed by both parties to the existing marriage. The trend of recent decisions makes it almost as imperative to obtain the wife's signature on a claim arising out of injury to her husband as it is to get the husband's. This form also effectively releases any property damage claim by either the husband or wife where extra consideration can be shown.

If individual releases are obtained for an injury involving a married person, separate consideration should be shown on each of the releases with the major consideration being named in the release involving the person injured.

In lump-sum compensation settlements, where a separate right of action may exist in a spouse for loss of services or consortium, an individual release should be taken from the spouse where possible, even though the Act in a particular state does not permit a release to be taken on the original compensation claim from the injured party.

3. **Corporation release.** Corporate releases are subject to the same general rules as general releases except that, if feasible, the corporate seal should be affixed thereto. Care should be exercised to have the correct corporate name on the release and to have it signed by an authorized officer of the corporation. It should be properly attested or notarized where there is any doubt about its authenticity.

4. **Partnership release.** A partnership is a contractual relationship between two or more persons to do business on a joint basis. All that is needed to create a partnership is to make an agreement concerning what each individual will contribute to it and what each will in turn receive from it by way of profits. Assuming that it has been made in accordance with the legal requirements in any contract, and any licensing regulations, it requires no further legal sanction.

Since each partner may be the agent of the others as outlined in the agreement, for the purpose of conducting the joint enterprise, a release signed individually and as a partner for the firm, is binding on the partnership and on each individual member.

A claim representative must determine (1) that the individual signing the release is actually a working partner, and (2) that he is authorized to bind the partnership.

5. **Conditional release.** Separate conditional release forms are not available because of the obvious divergence of the possible "condi-

tions." This type of release is usually taken in order to reserve a right of action against or on behalf of some specific party, or to release only part of the claimant's rights. Any general or corporate release can be made into a conditional release by the addition of certain words describing the condition in the space allotted for this purpose.

A conditional release is important because of the general rule still prevalent in many jurisdictions that a release of one joint tortfeasor releases all, unless specifically excluded.

Whatever the reason for taking a conditional release, extreme care must be used in the wording so as to avoid any ambiguity or misunderstanding and to make certain that the release serves its purpose. A right of action reserved against a party who may have a good cross-action against the insured leaves him in little better position than he was before the release was taken. A conditional release should therefore seldom be taken without advice of counsel.

Recently, there have been several decisions which have held that, in certain circumstances, a release obtained on behalf of an insured may act as an admission of liability and bar his right of action against the claimant. If such an interpretation is possible in a jurisdiction it is obvious that some condition specifically reserving a right of action on behalf of the insured must be inserted in the release. Such a condition can read as follows:

> It is covenanted and agreed between the releasor and releasee that this release and settlement is not to be construed as an admission of liability on the part of the releasee. It is further agreed that this release and settlement shall not be used by the releasor or anyone on his behalf as a defense or estoppel in any action which is now pending or which may be brought hereafter by the releasee or anyone in his behalf against the releasor.

6. Covenant not to sue. A covenant not to sue is, as a practical matter, about the same as one form of conditional release; it amounts to a release of one party out of several who may be liable in an action at law.

It is an agreement by a party who has a right of action, with another party against whom such action may be brought; whereby the first party for a consideration covenants not to enforce such right.

Covenants not to sue are not acceptable in all jurisdictions. Some jurisdictions give them no legal import whatsoever. Others regard them as a conditional release; still others give them the same effect

RELEASES § 18.03

as a general release. Only in some jurisdictions are they given the recognition for which they were originally intended.

Obviously, before using this form the claim representative must determine its status in his particular jurisdiction in order to be absolutely sure of its effectiveness.

A covenant not to sue originated primarily in order to avoid any effect on the liability of the remaining parties, by a settlement with one of them. It presents only a partial settlement of all claims and at best has the effect of releasing only the one named in the covenant.[8] Joint tortfeasors not a party to the covenant are not released.[9] There may be difficulties, however, in those states which have statutes or which by decision permit contribution between joint tortfeasors. Some states, on the other hand, subscribe to the old Uniform Contribution Among Tortfeasors Act or the revised Act of 1955.

It must be remembered that covenants not to sue do not affect an insurer's duty to defend the insured in case suit is brought despite the covenant obtained. Such covenant can of course be set up as a defense.

7. **Release and indemnity agreement.** An injury to an unemancipated minor dependent involves two distinct and separate claims; one for loss of services and expenses by the parents, and the other for pain and suffering by the minor. This situation gave rise to an attempt to obtain a release of all claims involving a minor by obtaining, in addition to a release from the parents, an agreement from them (usually incorporated in the same form), to the effect that in consideration for the payment, the parents agree to indemnify the releasee for any additional amount it may be called upon to make as a result of the accident.

The courts have universally failed to give such an agreement its intended effect and have in fact held that such an agreement is wholly void as against public policy.[10] Nevertheless, some companies still authorize its use in the disposition of inconsequential injuries involving minors. Its only legal effect is to release the parents claim for loss of service and expenses. It does not release the claim of the minor himself who usually can bring suit up to the statutory limitations period after attaining the age of majority. We have already discussed, in

---

[8] Anderson v Kemp, 184 So. 2d 832 (Ala. 1966); Mills v. Inter Island Tel. Co., 416 P.2d 115 (1966).
[9] Bacon v. United States, 321 F.2d 880 (8th Cir. 1963).
[10] Valdimer v. Mt. Vernon Hebrew Camps, 210 N.Y.S.2d 520, 172 N.E.2d 283 (1961).

§ 18.03[1] CASUALTY INSURANCE CLAIMS

Chapter 17, the only legal method for closing an infant's claim; by court order or friendly suit.

8. **Policyholder's release.** A policyholder's release can be used when reimbursement is made to an insured if it is desired that no further liability extend to the company as a result of the incident involved. Ordinarily its use arises out of an unauthorized settlement of a third party claim made directly by the insured with the claimant. Although such settlement is a violation of the policy provisions, some companies will in certain instances make reimbursement.

This form of release can also be used on first party claims requiring a release from the insured.

9. **Open end agreements.** As we have already seen, in cases of liability with serious injury and protracted disability involving uncertain prognosis, many companies now believe that consideration should be given to making a conditional settlement with the proviso that future expenses or developments would not foreclose additional payment. Such an agreement ordinarily states specifically that the insurer will be responsible for future reasonable medical and/or other expenses and salary loss up to a time limitation or in some specified limit of amount.

An open end agreement is not a release, except in the sense that monies paid will be offset against any final verdict if suit is brought subsequently.

There is no uniform wording for such agreements. Some allow a specific amount for each day of disability, but I do not favor such agreements because of the temptation for malingering.

[1] Execution of Release Forms

While the release forms speak for themselves, some basic rules should be kept in mind in completing them so as to make the release as binding as possible.

1. **Name of claimant.** Include the full name, exact age, marital status, and address of the claimant. Most forms include a printed statement to the effect that the claimant is over the age of 18, 21 or "of lawful age." Often a woman or man may be reticent about giving their exact age. In those instances it is sufficient to let the matter stand by using phraseology in the printed release. However, in most instances the exact age of the claimant should be made a part of the release.

The marital status of the claimant must be stated in the release. In some forms this will have to be inserted by typing or writing it in. Under certain circumstances, particularly during a state of war when funds of aliens may be frozen, it may be advisable to include the fact that the claimant is a citizen of the United States of America.

2. **Sum paid.** The exact amount of the payment being made is to be written in the appropriate place on the release and the amount in numerical figures also placed therein. Be sure that the two correspond. Do not erase or correct these items. If an error has been made in the amount, destroy the form and prepare a new one.

3. **Name of insured.** Include the full name of the insured as written in the policy and the full name of any other party to be released properly from further liability.

Ordinarily (excluding cases of nonownership coverage or instances in which for proper legal reasons the driver is to be specifically excluded), be sure to include the name of the driver of the vehicle in a claim arising out of an automobile accident.

As we have seen, in some jurisdiction a general release of one party is a valid release of all, but even in those jurisdictions it does no harm to get into the habit of being specific and complete in making out releases.

In claims involving public or general liability policies it may in some instances be advisable to include parties to be released who may have claims over and against the insured as a result of secondary liability. In this type of case it is advisable to get legal advice before completing the release form.

Again, for emphasis, the name of the insurance company should never be placed on the release except in those states in which it may properly be made a party defendant in the first instance by statute or in which it may otherwise be an actual party defendant.

4. **Signature.** The release should be signed in full by the claimant. Ink should be used. Make sure that the signature corresponds exactly with the name of the claimant as designated in the body of the release.

If because of injury a claimant is unable to use the hand with which he ordinarily signs his name, use of the other hand is proper, provided the signature is witnessed or notarized.

In the event that the claimant is unable to read or write, he may make his mark, properly witnessed, or, more preferably, notarized. In such instance the release must be read to the claimant in the presence of the witnesses or notary. Be sure he understands the nature of the document to which he is affixing his mark.

It is not advisable to attempt to take a finger or thumb print unless the claim representative has the technical knowledge to do so properly.

A signature of someone unfamiliar with the English language may be taken in a foreign language, but in such instances a translator's affidavit should be appended to the release, attesting not only to the signature, but to the fact that the entire release was translated and read to the claimant in his native tongue and that he fully comprehended its meaning.

5. **Witnesses and notary.** Wherever possible, a release should be properly witnessed or notarized. The name of the company representative or independent adjuster handling the case should not appear as a witness on the release.

Although no hard and fast rule on this subject is advisable, it is always preferable to have a release notarized where the claim involves a substantial amount of damage or injury even when, because of the questionable nature of the liability, a substantial payment is not being made. Where it is difficult or impossible to have the release notarized, the names and addresses of two witnesses to the signature should be obtained.

6. **Date.** Extreme care should be exercised to see that all releases are properly dated.

7. **Completion.** Make sure that all releases are filled in completely before obtaining the signature and that they are properly witnessed or notarized after the signature has been affixed, where warranted.

8. **Corrections.** Minor corrections, if properly initialed by the claimant or made in his own handwriting, are not objectionable except where the correction involves the amount of the payment made.

9. **Attorneys.** Where an attorney is involved in a claim, it is advisable to have his signature appended to the release as witness or notary. Give him all the necessary information and instructions so that the release will be as complete and correct as one drawn by one of the company's own attorneys.

10. **Mailing.** As a general rule, a release for bodily injury should be signed in the presence of the representative handling the claim, unless an attorney is involved. If, because of distance, minor injury, or other good and sufficient reason, the release is mailed to the claim-

RELEASES § 18.05

ant, instructions for signing should be given, together with an explanation that draft or check will promptly follow receipt of completed release. A stamped, self-addressed envelope should be enclosed for its return.

11. **Extraneous marking.** Do not stamp, mark, or otherwise mutilate a completed release, since by doing so its value as court evidence may be lessened or destroyed. It should under no circumstances bear any markings indicating that an insurance company is involved in the transaction, except where the company is, of necessity, named in the release.

§ 18.04 Fraud

Fraud, or deliberate misrepresentation made to induce a claimant to sign a release will void such release. For instance, any attempt to withhold information in order to obtain a release has been held to be sufficient fraud to set aside the release.[11]

Some states have enacted statutes prescribing waiting periods, which vary but generally are around two weeks or more, before allowing any binding settlement to be made, or permitting an injured person to be interviewed in a hospital.

In any event, no settlement of a serious injury should be made before the claimant has had a chance to obtain a proper prognosis from his attending physician, as far as this is possible.

§ 18.05 Indecent Haste

Some comment has been made to the effect that a settlement made very shortly after the claimant received a serious injury, is made in "indecent haste." The clear implication is that a release so obtained is subject to attack and would be set aside on the basis that undue advantage was taken of the claimant.[12]

Some states have enacted statutes prescribing waiting periods, which vary but generally are around two weeks, before any binding settlement can be made, or a claimant can be interviewed in a hospital. No settlement of a serious injury should be made before the

---

[11] Casey v. Proctor, 59 Cal. 2d 97 (1963).
[12] Wise v. Prescott, 244 La. 157, 151 So. 2d 356 (1963).

§ 18.06   CASUALTY INSURANCE CLAIMS

claimant has a chance to obtain a proper prognosis from his attending physician.[13]

§ 18.06 "Fairly and Knowingly Made"

In recent years a doctrine has been propounded to the effect that a release must have been "fairly and knowingly made," without fraud or mistake.[14]

This is obviously a question of fact. The gist of the opinions seems to be that the claimant and the insurer are unequal bargainers and the insurer should be put in the position of having to show that it avoided using its superior position by having made full disclosure of all pertinent information.

In one case it was held that where insurance coverage over the amount paid was not revealed to the claimant, undue advantage was taken and the release was set aside.[15]

§ 18.07 "In Full Satisfaction of All Claims Against Others"

As has previously been stated, the general release form, which includes wording such as "in full satisfaction of all claims against the releasor and others," or similar wording, was in previous years interpreted to mean just what the words stated.

However, this same wording has specifically been criticized in more recent cases where it has been held that the release must fully compensate all parties and that all parties must be named in the release.[16]

A federal case in Maryland,[17] held that a general release of "all persons, firms and corporations" did not preclude a subsequent action by the releasor against attending physicians and the hospital for alleged negligent treatment of the plaintiff's injuries.

---

[13] Mitschelen v. State Farm Mut., 555 P.2d 707 (N.M. 1976).

[14] **Mich.:** Hall v. Strom Constr. Co., 118 N.W.2d 281 (1962); Ryan v. Alexey, 127 N.W.2d 845 (1964).

U.S.: Ricketts v. Pennsylvania Ry. Co., 153 F.2d 757 (2d Cir. 1946).

[15] La.: Cole v. Lumbermen's Mut. Cas. Co., 160 So. 2d 785 (1964).

[16] **N.H.:** Gagnon v. Lakes Region Gen. Hosp., 465 A.2d 1221 (1983); Pickering v. Frink, 461 A.2d 117 (1983).

N.Y.: Spector v. K-Mart Corp., 471 N.Y.S.2d 420 (1984).

[17] White v. General Motors Corp., 541 F. Supp. 190 (1982).

RELEASES § 18.08

Some courts still hold to the old doctrine that, in the absence of fraud or special knowledge withheld from the claimant, a general release disposing of "all claims," present and future, is ordinarily binding and final.[18]

§ 18.08 Mistake Concerning Injuries or Facts

Ordinarily, a mutual mistake that does not take into consideration an unknown injury at the time a release is taken, will void such release even if it is general in nature and states otherwise.[19]

The mistake, however, must relate to a past or present fact that is material to the release contract and not to an opinion respecting future conditions or disabilities resulting from present facts.[20]

Unforseen complications or disability arising out of known injuries are ordinarily not sufficient to void a general release that was given and taken in good faith.[21]

If the mistake concerns the facts of injury itself, at the time release was taken, and no consideration was made for bodily injury, the courts will usually hold the release ineffective against such a claim.[22]

---

[18] **Mo.:** Bozus v. Birenbaum, 375 S.W.2d 156 (1964).
N.J.: Raroha v. Earle Fin. Corp., 220 A.2d 107 (1966).
N.M.: Smith v. Loos, 431 P.2d 72 (1967).
Ore.: Wheeler v. White Rock Bottling Co., 366 P.2d 527 (1961).
Pa.: Emery v. Mackiewicz, 240 A.2d 68 (1968).
[19] **D.C.:** Wells v. Rau, 393 F.2d 362 (1968).
Idaho: Ranta v. Rake, 421 P.2d 747 (1966).
Mich.: Ware v. Geismar, 155 N.W.2d 257 (1968).
N.M.: Bennie v. Pastor, 393 F.2d 1 (10th Cir. 1968) (release taken for property damage only. Both parties unaware of injury).
N.Y.: Castenada v. Ruderman, 228 N.E.2d 822 (1967) (despite the fact that this was an infant settlement that was court approved).
S.D.: Bowman v. Johnson, 158 N.W.2d 528 (1968).
Utah: Reynolds v. Merrill, 460 P.2d 323 (1969).
[20] **Ariz.:** Melvin v. Stevens, 458 P.2d 977 (1969).
N.J.: Bauer v. Griffin, 250 A.2d 603 (Super. 1969).
[21] **Del.:** Reason v. Lewis, 250 A.2d 390 (1969).
Fla.: Swilley v. Long, 215 So. 2d 340 (Fla. App. 1968).
N.J.: Raroka v. Earle Fin. Corp., 220 A.2d 107 (1966).
Va.: Cotman v. Whitehead, 164 S.E.2d 681 (1968).
Contra: Martin v. Po-Jo, Inc., 104 Ill. App. 2d 462, 244 N.E.2d 851 (1969) (dicta indicated mutual mistake as to extent of injury will void release).
[22] DeWitt v. Miami Trans. Co., 95 So. 2d 898 (Fla. 1957); Barry v. Lewis, 20 N.Y.2d 88 (1940).

§ 18.09   CASUALTY INSURANCE CLAIMS

Some courts have voided a release where the nature and extent of the injury was due to faulty diagnosis.[23]

In some of the older cases, mistake as to the injury due to a doctor's diagnosis was considered a mistake of opinion only and not a fact sufficient to void release.[24]

However, a unilateral mistake concerning an injury will not void a general release where the mistake was made by the claimant,[25] especially if the insurance company relied on the information given by the claimant.[26]

§ 18.09   Respondeat Superior

In most jurisdictions, a general release includes unnamed agents or employees involved in the act for which the release has been obtained.[27] By the same token, a general release taken from an employee ordinarily includes an unnamed vicariously liable employer.[28]

However, a release of a general contractor did not release the subcontractor from a third party indemnity action by the general contractor which was based on a hold-harmless agreement.[29]

§ 18.10   Joint Tortfeasors

While most states have by common law decision or by statute modified the old holding that a general release in full satisfaction of all claims is good against all possible defendants, there are still jurisdictions that hold to the old ruling in cases involving joint tortfeasors.[30]

---

[23] Duch v. Giacquinto, 222 N.Y.S.2d 101 (1961); Rankin v. N.Y., NH & Hartford R.R. Co., 338 Mass. 178, 154 N.E.2d 613 (1958); Clancy v. Pacenti, 15 Ill. App. 2d 171, 145 N.E.2d 802 (1957); Mendenhall v. Vandeventer, 61 N.M. 277, 299 P.2d 457 (1956).

[24] LaRosa v. Union Pac. R.R. Co., 142 Neb. 290, 5 N.W.2d 891 (1942).

[25] Hutcheson v. Frito-Lay, Inc., 315 F.2d 818 (8th Cir. 1963).

[26] D.C.: Randolph v. Ottenstein, 238 F. Supp. 1011 (1965).
Ill.: Thomas v. Hollowell, 155 N.E.2d 827 (1959).
Mo.: Sosa v. Velvet Dairy Stores, 407 S.W.2d 615 (App. 1966).
Wash.: Pepper v. Evanson, 422 P.2d 817 (1967).

[27] Mich.: Willis v. Total Health Care of Detroit, 337 N.W.2d 20 (App. 1963).

[28] La.: Sampay v. Morton Salt Co., 388 So. 2d 62 (App. 1980).

[29] R.I.: Corrente v. Conforti & Eisele Corp., 468 A.2d 920 (1983).

[30] Ga.: Tomlin v. Yergin, 305 S.E.2d 665 (1983).
Ill.: Porter v. Ford Motor Co., 449 N.E.2d 827 (1983) (unless specifically stated otherwise); Lake Motor Freight v. Randy Trucking, Inc., 455 N.E.2d 222 (1983).
La.: Johnson v. Ford Motor Co., 707 F.2d 189 (5th Cir. 1983).

Several of these cases involved automobile accidents in which there was a question of possible defect in the automobile involved. The court ruled that any action against the automobile manufacturer arising out of the accident was released by the signing of a general release in full satisfaction of all claims by the releasor, even though the names of the automobile manufacturers were not included in the release.[31]

Other courts, however, have made a specific exception to the old general rule and have held that a release of one joint tortfeasor does not release other joint tortfeasors who are not named in the release.[32]

Thomas E. Brenner[33] states that

> the critical factor in molding a verdict to consider comparative negligence and joint tortfeasor concepts is the provisions of the joint tortfeasor release. This document should be carefully worded to maximize the payment made in exchange for the release and to underscore the possible contribution right from the nonsettling defendant.
>
> Language should be included which states "that the dollars tendered should be deemed to be the extent of the pro-rata share of liability or responsibility of the defendant or the proportionate share of the total amount awarded as damages under the Comparative Negligence Act, whichever is greater."

[1] Statutory Enactment—Uniform Contribution Acts

The Uniform Contribution Act was first promulgated in 1939 and subsequently adopted by some states. The Act states that:

> A release by the injured person by one joint tortfeasor, whether before or after judgment, does not discharge the other tortfeasors unless the release so provides; but reduces the claim against the other tortfeasors in the amount of the consideration paid for the release, or in any amount in proportion by which the release provides that the total claim shall be reduced if greater then the consideration paid.

Not all of the states that have adopted this uniform act have accepted the exact wording, but basically, the main provision and intent is the same.

---

[31] Ill.: Porter v. Ford Motor Co., 449 N.E.2d 127 (1983).
La.: Johnson v. Ford Motor Co., 707 F.2d 189 (5th Cir. 1983).
[32] Ky.: Lavada v. Eastland, 660 S.W.2d 7 (1983).
Tex.: Duncan v. Cessna Aircraft Co., 665 S.W.2d 414 (1984), *but see* General Motors Corp. v. Simmons, 558 S.W.2d 855 (1977).
[33] "Plaintiff's Windfall," F.T.D., October 1983.

This Act was revised in 1955 and the revision reads as follows:

Sec. 4. [Release or Covenant Not to Sue] When a release or a covenant not to sue to enforce judgment is given in good faith to one or two or more persons liable in tort for the same injury or the same wrongful death:

a. It does not discharge any of the other tortfeasors from liability for the injury or wrongful death unless its terms so provide; but it reduces the claim against the others to the extent of any amount stipulated by the release or the covenant or in the amount of the consideration paid for it, whichever is greater, and,

b. It discharges the tortfeasor for whom it is given from all liability for contribution to any other tortfeasor.

§ 18.11 Releases in Death Claims

The requirements necessary for the settlement of fatal cases vary greatly throughout the country. These differences apply not only to procedural matters but also with respect to those entitled to recover.

In some instances, a binding release can only be obtained from the appointed administrator of an estate. In others, the statutes authorize settlement to be made directly with the lawful heirs, in some cases.

The designation of those entitled to recover varies in some degree in almost every jurisdiction. Because of this, the adjuster must be thoroughly familiar not only with the wrongful death acts in his state, but also with the laws of descent and distribution. A release obtained from the wrong person or a settlement made without including all of the possible claimants, does not accomplish the purpose for which payment is made.

In all cases where settlement is made with an administrator or personal representative, evidence of his or her authority and legal capacity to make the settlement should be obtained. This usually involves a court order.

If releases may be obtained directly from the heirs, consult counsel to make sure that they are drawn properly and that all possible claims are released. If the plaintiff's attorney draws the papers, make sure that they are reviewed and approved by counsel for the insurer.

§ 18.12 Alleged Subsequent Malpractice by Doctors

Until recent years, it was usually held that a general release of a tortfeasor also released a doctor or surgeon from subsequent malpractice arising out of the underlying accident, which allegedly caused an aggravation of the original injury.[34]

Only a few courts held that such a general release did not include a doctor or surgeon who treated the injured, and that such a release did not release the doctor or surgeon unless there was specific wording to this effect by naming them in the release.[35] Recently, however, some courts have reversed their previous attitude and now hold that malpractice arising out of the treatment for the underlying injury for which a general release was given to the tortfeasor, is not contemplated or released.[36]

If the release is conditional, releasing specifically only the tortfeasor, then there seems to be no doubt that only he is released and such a release would not bar a subsequent action for malpractice in the treatment of the original injury.[37]

The New York Court of Appeals applied the "intent of the parties" test and held that whether or not a doctor or surgeon was released in the general release given by the tortfeasor, depended on the circumstances under which the release was obtained and whether or not the consideration given, did in fact constitute full satisfaction of all damages, and was intended as such.[38] The same general reasoning was applied in other cases.[39]

In attempting to arrive at the intent of the parties, the courts have listed as items for consideration "the presence of bargaining the ne-

---

[34] Some jurisdictions that held so are:
Ohio: Knight v. Strong, 140 N.E.2d 9 (1955).
Tex.: Cannon v. Pearson, 374 S.W.2d 453 (1964).
Wis.: Hartley v. St. Francis Hosp., 129 N.W.2d 235 (1964).
[35] **Cal.:** Ash v. Mortensen, 150 P.2d 876 (1944).
N.H.: Wheat v. Carter, 106 A. 602 (1910).
[36] **Ariz.:** Leech v. Bralliar, 275 F. Supp. 897 (1967).
Iowa: Smith v. Conn, 163 N.W.2d 407 (1968).
Md.: White v. General Motors Corp., 542 F. Supp. 190 (1982).
Ore.: Rudick v. Pioneer Mem. Hosp., 296 F.2d 316 (1961).
Wash.: De Nike v. Mowery, 418 P.2d 1010 (1966).
[37] **Wis.:** Greene v. Waters, 49 N.W.2d 919 (1951).
[38] Derby v. Prewitt, 236 N.Y.S.2d 953 (1962).
[39] **Miss.:** Pearson v. Weaver, 173 So. 2d 666 (1965).
N.Y.: Viskovitch v. Walsh-Fuller-Slattery, 225 N.Y.S.2d 100 (1962).
Wis.: Doyle v. Teasdale, 57 N.W.2d 381 (1953).

gotiation leading to settlement, the closeness of the issue of liability, whether the subject of personal injuries was discussed, and the reasonableness of the contention that the injuries were in fact unknown at the time the release was executed."[40]

§ 18.13 Bad Faith Allegations to Induce Settlement

As we have seen, where a release has been obtained by fraud, it is generally accepted that such a release is invalid. In addition, however, suits are now being brought by plaintiffs against insurers to whom they gave a release in the underlying action, on the grounds that such release was obtained by a breach of good faith in obtaining the release or on the basis that there was a breach of an Unfair Claim Practices Act.

The question as to whether a release that named the insurer, and even one where some specific sum was allocated for the release of the insurer in the underlying action, would be effective to release the insurer from this type of subsequent suit is moot and would depend on the jurisdiction involved. In Wisconsin, for instance, it was held that a general release of the tortfeasor only, did not release his or her insurer.[41]

Other states have also deemed such an action to be new and independent of the original underlying negligence suit and accordingly not effective to preclude a subsequent action for bad faith in the settlement negotiations leading to the release.[42]

[1] Assignment of Insured's Claim for Bad Faith

This matter is further complicated if an assignment of a bad faith cause of action is made by the insured defendant against the defendant's insurer.

With rare exceptions, it has been generally accepted that such an assignment, given with consideration (that the insured defendant will not be held personally responsible for any verdict in excess of his policy limits) is legal and will be enforced.

---

[40] Cal.: Casey v. Proctor, 28 Cal. Rptr. 307 (1963).
[41] Loy v. Bunderson, 320 N.W.2d 175 (1982).
[42] Alfuso v. U.S.F.&G. Co., 215 Cal. Rptr. 490 (App. 1985); Vega v. Western Employers Ins. Co., 216 Cal. Rptr. 592 (App. 1985).

As far as the insured defendant is concerned, such an assignment is not affected by the fact that the plaintiff in the underlying action has released the insured from further liability.[43]

A federal district court in New Jersey[44] held that an insured who made a conditional settlement with the injured plaintiff could assign his right of action for the liability in excess of the policy limits resulting from bad faith failure to settle within the limits.

This, however, is an entirely different matter from the right of the plaintiff in the underlying action, who has no contractual relationship with the defendant's insurer, to bring an action in his own name against the underlying insurer. Nevertheless, as has already been stated, such a right is being given by jurisdictions that have held that such a right can exist under the guise of the tort of bad faith in the settlement negotiations.

§ 18.14 Mary Carter Agreements

Mary Carter, or sliding scale agreements, are an extension of a conditional release or a covenant not to sue. All three instruments agree to release named party defendants, or not to release specific party defendants.

The Mary Carter type of agreement, however, goes a step further in that the released defendant agrees to remain in the proceedings after his personal liability is no longer in jeopardy. For this, he is released for a relatively minor sum, in exchange for which he is expected to assist in the suit against the other remaining defendants.

In the case of *Maule Industries v. Roundtree*,[45] the court stated that:

> The term arises from the agreement popularized by the case of *Booth v. Mary Carter Paint Co.* [citation omitted] and now appears to be used rather generally to apply to an agreement between the plaintiff and some (but less than all) defendants whereby the parties place limitations on the financial responsibility of the agreeing defendants, the amount of which is variable and usually in some inverse ratio to the amount of recovery which the plaintiff is able to make against the non-agreeing defendant or defendants.

---

[43] Steedly v. London & Lanc. Ins. Co., 416 F.2d 560 (3d Cir. 1976).
[44] Atlantic City v. American Cas. Co., 254 F. Supp. 396 (1966).
[45] 264 So. 2d 445, *reversed*, 284 So. 2d 389 (Fla. 1973).

§ 18.15

In the Insurance Counsel Journal,[46] it is stated that: "Many of the courts have concluded that the Mary Carter agreement is one of maintenance and champerty because agreeing defendants are primarily interested in obtaining a large verdict in order to relieve themselves of minimal liability, and are deemed sham parties, inimical to the adversary process."

There have been some statutory enactments on this subject and it is certainly enough to warrant advice from counsel if a claim representative gets involved in a case that even appears headed for a Mary Carter type of agreement.

§ 18.15 Laches

Unreasonable delay in bringing an action to set aside a release should be a good reason to deny the plaintiff's demand. The courts, in such instances, have sometimes applied the equitable doctrine of laches, since such delay opens many avenues to possible fraud.[47] In such a case, laches has the same effect as a statute of limitations.

§ 18.16 Bibliography

Mary Carter Agreements

Adler, "Allocation of Responsibility After American Motorcycle Association v. Superior Court, 6 Pepperdine L. Rev. 1 (1978).
Comment, "Mary Carter Agreements: A Viable Means of Settlement," 14 Tulsa L.J. 744-69 (1979).
Freeman, "The Expected Demise of 'Mary Carter': She Was Never Well," Insurance Law Journal, October 1975.
Guy, "Partial Settlements in Multiple Defendant Cases," F.T.D., February 1983.
Mullins & Morrison, "Who is Mary Carter?" F.T.D., December 1981.
Westierski, "Mary Carter Agreements and Good Faith Settlements: Are They Both Possible in California?" Insurance Counsel Journal, October 1981.

---

[46] July 1978, p. 344.
[47] **Minn.:** Aronovich v. Levy, 56 N.W.2d 570 (1953).
Mont.: Schantz v. Minow, 411 P.2d 362 (1966).
Pa.: Nocito v. Lanuitti, 167 A.2d 262 (1961).

Releases

Andrews, H., Jr., "The Personal Injury Release," Insurance Law Journal, April 1965.

Levit, "Validity of Claimant's Release with Respect to Unknown Injuries," Insurance Law Journal, March 1964.

Miller, "Does the Release of the Original Tortfeasor Release a Subsequent Negligent Attending Physician?" Insurance Counsel Journal, July 1969.

Weston, "The Indemnifying Release in the Settlement of Minors' Claims," Insurance Counsel Journal, April 1962.

CHAPTER 19

Coverage Problems

§ 19.01 Typical Coverage Problems
§ 19.02 Importance of Immediate Investigation
§ 19.03 Disclaimer of Coverage
§ 19.04 Reservation of Rights
    [1] Wording of the Letter of Reservation
§ 19.05 Nonwaiver Agreements
§ 19.06 Declaratory Judgment Actions
§ 19.07 Plain Language Policies
§ 19.08 The Doctrine of Reasonable Expectations
    [1] Ambiguity in the Policy Provisions
    [2] Existing Means for Balancing the Equities
    [3] Commercial Policies
§ 19.09 Bibliography

Since an insurance policy is a contract, the terms of the policy are the determining factors that outline the duties and obligations of the insured and the insurer, with a few exceptions.

Although the trend in recent years has been toward simplifying the language of the standard policies, there has also been a tendency to write more of the multiple line, comprehensive, and "tailor-made" policies. For this reason there will always be enough ambiguity to create coverage problems in doubtful or borderline cases. In addition, we will always have with us question-of-fact cases in which a determination of the facts presents a difficult problem. Finally, the law is a constantly changing factor that tends more and more to extend the actual provisions of the policy.

It has already been said that the duty of an insurance company is not only confined to the insured, but runs as well to the stockholders and the public at large, who ultimately pay the insurance premiums. Ours is a highly regulated industry. Insurance companies are subject to examination by the state insurance departments. Insurance companies must operate and discharge their obligations within the limits set by the policy contract, the courts, and the legislature.

Questions of coverage must be kept distinct; entirely apart from questions of the insured's liability, in determining the insurer's obligation to the insured under the policy.

§ 19.01 Typical Coverage Problems

Coverage questions may arise as a result of:

1. *A false declaration.* Example: Named insured is not the owner of the automobile.
2. *The facts not falling within the scope of the insuring agreements.* Example: Date of the accident does not fall within the policy period.
3. *The incident on which claim is based clearly falling within one of the exclusions.* Example: Property owned by, rented to, in charge of, the insured.
4. *A breach of the conditions.* Example: Delayed reporting.

The insurer may, by the acts or omissions of its agent, be stopped from denying coverage or may be declared to have waived a breach of the policy provisions. For instance, it has been held that the continued investigation of a claim together with settlement negotiations with the third party, without putting the insured on notice concerning his breach, amounts to a waiver of that breach.[1]

An insurer must, therefore, make a decision as soon as possible or take some affirmative action if an immediate decision cannot be made because of insufficient information. This may be done either by sending a letter reserving the company's rights pending investigation, or by entering into a nonwaiver agreement with the insured, by which both parties agree that the rights of neither party will be waived until a final decision is made by the insurance company.[2]

---

[1] **Cal.:** Miller v. Elite Ins. Co., 161 Cal. Rptr. 322 (App. 1980).
Ga.: Sargent v. Allstate Ins. Co., 303 S.E.2d 43 (App. 1983).
Ill.: Thornton v. Paul, 366 N.E.2d 1058 (1977).
N.Y.: Kansas City Fire & Marine Ins. Co. v. Hartford Ins. Group, 368 N.Y.S.2d 791 (1975).
See also Magarick, *Excess Liability* (New York: Clark Boardman Co. Ltd., 1982), Chapter 4.

[2] **Fla.:** Giffen Roofing Co. v. D.H.S. Developers, Inc., 442 So. 2d 306 (App. 1983).
Ga.: Continental Ins. Co. v. J.W. Weeks, 232 S.E.2d 80 (App. 1976).
Ill.: Western Cas. & Sur. Co. v. Brocher, 460 N.E.2d 832 (App. 1984).
Ohio: Motorists Mut. Ins. Co. v. Trainor, 294 N.E.2d 874 (1973).

Disclaimer of coverage or even the receipt of a reservation of rights letter may antagonize an insured or an agent. If such disclaimer or reservation of rights letter is sent unjustifiably, the damage to public and business relations can be considerable. For this reason, extreme caution should be exercised in making a determination of coverage questions.

It is therefore most important that the adjuster learn and know the policy provisions. Although it is virtually impossible to memorize the many policies dealing with casualty claims, the claim representative should familiarize himself with important provisions so that he can immediately recognize a coverage question when the facts indicate one.

§ 19.02 Importance of Immediate Investigation

As soon as a report is received indicating that a coverage question may be involved, immediate investigation must be made of the coverage question as well as preliminary investigation of the liability.

Separate signed statements should be taken with reference to the coverage question. For instance, where there is a question of considerable delayed notice, a separate signed statement concerning such delay should be obtained from the insured. The investigation should then be traced right back to the agent. If necessary, additional signed statements should be obtained from all intervening persons who allegedly received notice of the accident before the report came to the attention of the insurance carrier.

Prompt action on all coverage questions is necessary because:

1. Delay in asserting the company's rights under the policy may result in a waiver or estoppel of such rights.
2. Prompt disclaimer enables the defendant to prepare his own defense and get his own attorney much sooner. The insurer will also learn much more quickly whether the defendant intends to assume defense or whether he intends to press for coverage under the policy.
3. Prompt investigation lessens the possibility of collusion.

See also Magarick, *Excess Liability* (New York: Clark Boardman Co. Ltd., 1982), Chapter 6.

§ 19.03   CASUALTY INSURANCE CLAIMS

   4. Prompt action avoids the annoyances and irritations of uncertainty, thereby improving business and public relations.

In all claims involving coverage questions it is essential that the investigation be as comprehensive as possible. A decision with reference to coverage cannot be made on guess or surmise. All facts must be obtained. This, admittedly, requires initiative.

Possible action to be taken if coverage problems arise:
   1. Accept coverage fully. Handle the case in the regular manner if a decision on coverage has been made in favor of the insured.
   2. Disclaim coverage if the facts are clear-cut and unequivocal, and refuse to handle, negotiate, or defend the case.
   3. Issue reservation of rights letter or enter nonwaiver agreement if a determination is doubtful or if insufficient facts have been obtained to make a complete determination.
   4. Institute *declaratory judgment* action to determine the rights of the insured and the insurer under the policy in cases of doubtful coverage.
   5. Enter agreement to defend a suit without indemnity. This is an exceptional action taken in the rare case where the defendant agrees that there is no coverage, but where defense is offered because of extenuating circumstances. In such an instance, an agreement should be obtained in writing to the effect that while the carrier is defending the case, it will not be responsible for any judgment that may be rendered against the defendant.

§ 19.03 Disclaimer of Coverage

Disclaimer of coverage is the act by which an insurer takes the definite and unequivocal position that the claim or suit in question is not covered by the provisions of the policy of insurance. The company says in effect that there is no valid policy of insurance for the incident in question.

This decision may have been reached for one of three possible reasons:
   1. The claim or suit in question did not initially fall within the provisions of the policy.

2. The allegations or the facts fall within a definite exclusion or exception in the policy.
3. The conduct of the insured was such as to withdraw him from the protection of the coverage afforded, either because of an original material misrepresentation or a subsequent failure to comply with the provisions of the policy.

An example of the first classification is the commission of a deliberate act on the part of the insured that would not be construed as an accident under the terms of the policy.

An example of the second category is an accident arising out of the use of a vehicle or instrumentality definitely excluded and listed under the exclusions of the policy.

An example of the third occurs when the insured, because of his delay in giving notice of the accident to the company, or because of his lack of cooperation, has breached a condition of the policy except for which the original accident might otherwise have properly been covered.

A disclaimer letter should be carefully worded in order not to prevent the insurer from asserting all of its rights. When the situation calls for specifics, these should be named, but the letter should be broad enough to include any and all possible grounds for disclaimer.

When an agent is involved, he should be forewarned of the intended action of the company so that he can prepare for any repercussions from his client.

A disclaimer is the most drastic action a company can take. It should be used only where the company is sure of its position and cannot be harmed by a possible default judgment.

It could be not only embarrassing but extremely costly to allow a default judgment to be obtained and then find that the company's position on coverage is not too sound. The courts are not inclined to favor the insurer in an action on the policy unless the equities are clear-cut.

In addition, wrongful disclaimer could make an insurer responsible not only for a verdict against the insured, but also for the full amount of such a verdict, even in excess of the policy limits.

§ 19.04 Reservation of Rights

A *reservation of rights letter* is written notice to the insured that the company is conducting its investigation pending a determination of its possible right to disclaim (or accept) coverage under the policy. It is to be used if there is some reason to believe that the claim does not fall within the provisions of the policy and if time is needed in which to make an investigation to determine whether or not this is so. Its purpose is to prevent estoppel or waiver of a breach of policy conditions and to permit the company to make a thorough investigation before taking a definite stand on coverage.

Extreme care must be exercised in the use of the reservation of rights letter because:

1. The insured and the agent may be antagonized, resulting in consequent business repercussions.
2. Full cooperation of the insured may be lost.
3. Failure to send a proper letter may be held to waive the insurer's rights.

The law with reference to reservation of rights is as varied as many other legal problems confronting a claim representative. The question whether a reservation of rights letter should be sent immediately upon notice of an accident or after a preliminary investigation has been made is one that has been the subject of much discussion.

There has been some argument to the effect that investigation of an accident before sending a reservation of rights letter implicitly waives the insurer's right to deny coverage under the policy. It is my belief that the company is entitled to make an investigation before it reserves its rights in order to determine whether there is any possible justification for denial or acceptance of coverage. However, because of the many decisions holding that a lapse of time implies a waiver, promptness in the investigation is of utmost importance. If the insured is inclined to color the facts to fit the situation, the position of the insurer will not be enhanced by putting him on guard.

A claim representative cannot safely assume that because a policy condition was breached, the company can proceed with the normal handling of a case and then step out at any time it may desire. The courts have held that the insurer has a duty to take some affirmative action to let the insured know what his position is. This means that the insurer must either make an outright disclaimer or accept under some reservation of its rights.

If the latter course of action is taken it must be followed up by making a determination of position as soon as possible. In the event that a decision cannot be made until the trial of a case, then a non-

COVERAGE PROBLEMS § 19.05

waiver agreement should be executed between the insured and the company, if possible.

It is important to remember that a reservation of rights letter must be sent to all parties likely to claim coverage under the policy; for instance, those that might be covered under the Omnibus Clause of an automobile policy.

It is necessary that claim personnel become thoroughly familiar with the decisions of their courts with reference to this problem and be guided accordingly.

In handling a claim under a reservation of rights or nonwaiver agreement, great care must be used so that the company is not estopped or charged with a waiver of its rights because of some act on the part of its agent. In other words, estoppel and waiver may work against the company despite the fact that a reservation of rights letter has been sent or a nonwaiver agreement obtained. For example, if the claim representative of an insurance company entered into settlement negotiations and made an offer of settlement after reservation of rights letter was sent or nonwaiver agreement entered into, the courts would probably hold that the company had waived its rights to disclaim.

[1] Wording of the Letter of Reservation

Generally speaking, reservation of rights should be sufficiently broad so as to cover all points at issue. Extreme care should be used in the wording so that the company is not prevented from asserting any valid grounds for reserving its rights at a later time.

Care should be used in stating that a position is taken "pending completion of investigation" since such a statement makes it essential that the insurer assert its position as soon as investigation has been made, or in some instances, after a reasonable time has elapsed in which investigation could have been made.

No definite form can be used to fit all occasions. It can only be suggested that where warranted, such a letter should be drawn by an experienced and knowledgeable claim representative or counsel.

§ 19.05 Nonwaiver Agreements

A *nonwaiver agreement* is one in which the insured and the insurance company agree in writing that neither party will waive any of its rights under the policy as a result of the investigation or defense of an action brought against the insured.

Since several decisions have held that at least the implied consent of the insured is necessary to protect the company under a reservation of rights, particularly where suit has been instituted, it again becomes obvious that the claim representative must become familiar with the law on this subject in his particular jurisdiction.

When it is necessary to reserve the company's rights in the case of a claim which has gone into suit, every effort should be made to obtain a signed nonwaiver agreement before accepting the case for defense. Any delay on the part of the company in obtaining the nonwaiver agreement may act as a waiver or estoppel of its rights.

If the insured refuses to sign a nonwaiver agreement, then a decision must be made whether to disclaim or to send a reservation of rights letter. Here again, I would suggest that since the situations calling for a nonwaiver agreement may be so varied, and can become so complex, that drafting such an agreement be left to experienced claims personnel or counsel.

§ 19.06 Declaratory Judgment Actions

What if an insured refuses to sign a nonwaiver agreement and replies to a reservation of rights letter disagreeing with the position of the company and demanding full coverage?

Under authority granted by state and federal declaratory judgment acts, an insurer may bring an action against the insured for the sole purpose of determining their respective rights under the terms of a policy of insurance, whether or not a third party action has been instituted. In this way questions of coverage may be determined by a court of competent jurisdiction before the third party suit against the insured is brought to trial. By instituting a timely declaratory judgment action an insurer can avoid estoppel and can deny coverage if adjudication is favorable, despite having previously assumed defense of the case in behalf of the insured and assuming that no prejudice to the insured was involved.

Matters concerning primary or coinsurance can also be determined by declaratory judgment action. Such an action may usually be started at any time either before, during, or after a third party action against the insured has been instituted, regardless of any other statutory remedies that might be available.

COVERAGE PROBLEMS § 19.07

Delay in instituting a declaratory judgment action may, however, make a determination of the issues before the third party suit comes to trial technically impossible. This could be extremely prejudicial. It is therefore important that the claim representative be able to recognize situations in which a declaratory judgment action could be used advantageously. He or she should discuss the advisability of such an action with defense counsel and home office as soon as possible.

In the event that a reservation of rights letter elicits a reply from the insured rejecting an offer to handle or investigate a claim under a full reservation of rights, the declaratory judgment action may be the only means of avoiding a waiver or estoppel of the insurer's rights.[3]

§ 19.07 Plain Language Policies

It is not hard to understand the position of an illiterate person or that of an immigrant who has recently arrived from a country whose language is not English. He or she will need help, whether a policy is written in plain language or in legalese, and it is the duty of such people to get help from their agents or others who can give them an understanding of their insurance policies.

However, even lawyers, judges, claims people, and underwriters differ constantly over policy interpretation, and simplification of policy language may not perceptibly reduce the number of suits being brought to interpret policy provisions. Companies and insureds have financial stakes in such controversies and lawyers live on them.

Nevertheless, there is no arguing the fact that the present trend toward plain language policies, rather than the verbiage in which previous standard type policies were written, is in the right direction, especially where noncommercial policies are concerned. Enough pressure has been generated to affect even some legislators so that more states are enacting statutes that require some policies to be written in *plain* English.

The problem in translating legalese into plain understandable English, however, is quite complex. Academicians can be just as obfus-

---

[3] **Cal.:** Johanson v. California State Auto. Ass'n, 116 Cal Rptr. 546 (App. 1974).
Ga.: Richmond v. Georgia Farm Bur. Mut. Ins. Co., 231 S.E.2d 245 (App. 1976).
Ill.: Fidelity & Cas. Co. of N.Y. v. Envirodyne Eng'rs, Inc., 461 N.E.2d 471 (1983).
Utah: State Farm Mut. Auto. Ins. Co. v. Kay, 487 P.2d 852 (1971).
See also Magarick, *Excess Liability* (New York: Clark Boardman Co. Ltd., 1982), Chapter 7.

cating as lawyers, so while we need translators who can write good English, they must be able to write plain understandable common English and not the language they use for doctoral dissertations. Such writers must be problem solvers. An attempt must be made to have each provision stand on its own feet with as little reference to, or dependence on, other provisions as possible. Accordingly, such drafting requires the help of teams of underwriters, claims people, and lawyers, as well as advertisers and marketing people.

The price to accomplish a more understandable insurance policy may be high. Many old judicial decisions concerning policy intent will go by the board and much legislation will have to be modified.

However, the new policies do not appear to be creating more suits than previous forms. It may even be that controversy concerning intent may be reduced, as was intended. It is still too early to make any definitive judgment, but it appears obvious that there will be no turning back from the road that has been taken.

§ 19.08 The Doctrine of Reasonable Expectations

It is most important that claim people and defense counsel realize that when it comes to policy interpretation, what appears to be understandable and clear-cut, is often quite the opposite to our courts. Accordingly, as has already been stated several times, declination of coverage should never be made lightly. The possible consequences are too grave.

One reason for this confusion is the unreasonable doctrine of *reasonable expectations.* Although, for reasons that will become apparent subsequently in this discussion, most authorities agree that a satisfactory comprehensive definition of this doctrine has as yet not been given.

Professor Keeton[4] makes an attempt: "The objectively reasonable expectations of and intended beneficiaries regarding the terms of insurance contracts will be honored even though painstaking study of the policy provisions would have negated those expectations."

The rationale behind this doctrine is that the ordinary insurance policy is a contract of adhesion, which means that one party to the contract draws it up (policy is in a printed form) and presents it to the other party on a take-it-or-leave-it basis.

---

[4] *Insurance Law* (Basic Text, 1971), p. 351.

As Professor Williston put it,[5] "Contracts of adhesion are contracts (policies) drafted by a party of superior bargaining strength and offered to the weaker party on a take-it-or-leave-it basis." It has been held that an insurer that selects standardized contracts (policies) and offers them on this basis must assume responsibilities for the confusion created in the mind of a nonexpert insured,[6] and other courts agree with this attitude.[7]

[1] Ambiguity in the Policy Provisions

The doctrine of reasonable expectations has been applied for various specific reasons, but the decisions are mainly divided between those jurisdictions that hold that there must be an ambiguity in the policy provisions before this doctrine can be applied,[8] and those who hold that an ambiguity is not necessary in order to apply the doctrine.[9]

In a case involving a burglary policy, the burglary was allegedly committed without leaving any visible marks of forced entry, as required by the policy. There was no question concerning the fact that there were no visible signs of entry, but despite this fact the court held that there was coverage under the policy, stating that "no one purchasing something called burglary insurance would expect coverage to exclude skilled burglaries that leave no visible marks of entry or exit."[10]

Since it is the law in all jurisidctions that ambiguities in contracts of adhesion (printed policies) should be decided in favor of the policyholder, it appears to me that the requirement of ambiguity in the

---

[5] *A Treatise on the Law of Contracts,* 3d ed. (1963)
[6] **N.D.:** Mills v. Agricultural Aviation, Inc., 250 N.W.2d 663 (1977).
[7] **Ala.:** Lambert v. Liberty Mut. Ins. Co., 331 So. 2d 260 (1976).
Cal.: Miller v. Elite Ins. Co., 161 Cal. Rptr. 322 (1980).
Mass.: Davenport Peters Co. v. Royal Globe Ins. Co., 490 F. Supp. 286 (1980).
Mich.: Bradley v. Mid-Century Ins. Co., 294 N.W.2d 141 (1980).
N.H.: Trombley v. Blue Cross & Blue Shield, 423 A.2d 980 (1980).
Wis.: Patrick v. Head of the Lakes Coop. Elect. Assoc., 295 N.W.2d 205 (App. 1980).
[8] **Iowa:** Chipokas v. Travelers Indem. Co., 267 N.W.2d 393 (1978).
N.J.: Diorio v. New Jersey Mfrs. Ins. Co., 398 A.2d 1274 (1979).
See also Comment, Krider, "The Reconstruction of Insurance Contracts Under the Doctrine of Reasonable Expectations," 18 J. Marshall L. Rev. 155 (1984).
[9] **Alas.:** Stordahl v. Gov't Employees Ins. Co., 564 P.2d 63 (1977).
Cal.: Stewart v. Bohner's Estate, 162 Cal. Rptr. 126 (1980).
N.H.: Olszak v. Peerless Ins. Co., 406 A.2d 711 (1979).
[10] **Minn.:** Atwater Creamery v. Western Nat'l Mut. Ins. Co., 366 N.W.2d 271 (1985).

policy provisions to justify the application of the reasonable expectations doctrine is redundant.

Some courts, in rejecting the doctrine of reasonable expectations, persist in quoting the doctrine by holding that the insured's reasonable expectations are to be solely determined by the terms of the policy.[11]

[2] Existing Means for Balancing the Equities

In view of accepted doctrines that can and do for the most part balance the equities between the parties to an insurance contract, such as: (1) *unconscionability,* to correct situations where policy provisions are patently oppressive to the insured,[12] (2) *estoppel or waiver,*[13] (3) *reformation,*[14] (4) *ambiguity resolution,*[15] and (5) *public policy,*[16] I cannot see the need for a doctrine that shocks established rules of law without accomplishing much more than confusion. As the Idaho Supreme Court stated in its conclusion in the case of *Casey v. Highland Ins. Co.*[17]

> Reliance on (the) traditional approach avoids the danger that the court might create liability by construction of the contract terms of a new contract for the parties. In the event that there is an ambiguity in the terms of the policy, special rules of construction apply to insurance contracts to protect the insured.
>
> Since these rules protect the insured under more traditional approaches, it becomes unnecessary to adopt a new theory of recovery where, conceivably, the periphery of what losses would be covered could be

---

[11] **D.C.:** Mills v. Cosmopolitan Ins. Agency, 424 A.2d 43 (1980).
Ga.: Atlanta Int'l Prop's., Inc. v. Georgia Underwriting Ass'n, 256 S.E.2d 472 (1979).
Idaho: Casey v. Highlands Ins. Co., 600 P.2d 1387 (1979) (rule rejected because it is a rule of interpretation rather than a rule for avoiding inequitable policy provisions).
N.J.: Diorio v. New Jersey Mfrs. Ins. Co., 398 A.2d 1274 (1979), *but see* Jones v. Continental Cas. Co. 303 A.2d 291 (1973).

[12] **Iowa:** C. & J. Fertilizer, Inc. v. Allied Mut. Ins. Co., 227 N.W.2d 169 (1975).
N.Y.: Royal Indem. Co. v. Westinghouse Elec. Corp., 385 F. Supp. 520 (1974).

[13] **Ill.:** Armstrong v. United Ins. Co., 424 N.E.2d 1216 (1981).
N.J.: Bowler v. Fidelity & Cas. Co., 250 A.2d 580 (1969).

[14] Providence Wash. Ins. Co. v. Rabinowitz, 227 F.2d 300 (5th Cir. 1955).

[15] Keeton, *Insurance Law.*

[16] **Ill.:** Menke v. Country Mut. Ins. Co., 401 N.E.2d 539 (1980); First Nat'l Bank of Chicago v. Fidelity & Cas. Co., 428 F.2d 499 (7th Cir. 1970).

[17] 600 P.2d 1387 (1979).

extended by an insured's affidavit of what he "reasonably expected" to be covered.

When the majority opinion in *Collister v. Nationwide Life Ins. Co.*[18] states that the adhesionary nature of insurance documents is such that the insured is under no duty to read the policy sent by the company, I begin to fear for our entire judicial system.

The dissenting opinion by Justice Pomeroy makes much more sense: "Thus the problem in deciding an insurance claim seems no longer to be one of ascertaining what the contract as written means, but of somehow divining the 'reasonable expectations' of the insured as to what the contract should mean."

As Professor Keeton put it,[19] the doctrine of reasonable expectations goes beyond a mere rule of construction and is "a measure of judicial regulation of insurance contracts."

[3] Commercial Policies

Many large corporations are either self-insured or partners with their insurers on a deductible basis, or have insurance managers who deal with brokers that represent the insured in determining the insurance needs of the corporation. Insurance managers are technicians, usually with a high degree of knowledge about insurance and the company needs. If such a person is not competent in the job, the fault or negligence in keeping such a person is that of the insured corporation. Bad choice in procuring insurance may also be the fault of the broker who represents the insured, but it is not ordinarily the fault of the insurance company that must depend on the insured and its broker to provide necessary information.

In addition, many of the commercial policies are specialized, necessitating "tailor-made" policies in which all parties participate, including corporate attorneys. While the standard form of insurance policy may be viewed as a contract of adhesion, a custom drafted manuscript policy is a product of negotiation.[20]

Even preprinted forms like the new Commercial General Liability policy are so all-inclusive that decisions concerning specific cover-

---

[18] 388 A.2d 1346 (1978).

[19] Keeton, "Wayfaring Fool Doctrine," Insurance Advocate, July 24, 1971.

[20] *See* Ostrager & Ichel, "Should the Business Insurance Policy Be Construed Against the Insurer? Another Look at the Reasonable Expectations Doctrine," F.I.C. Quarterly, Spring 1983.

ages cannot be made without the active participation of the insured and his broker.

Where then, is the applicability of the doctrine of reasonable expectations in such situations? Neither party is taking advantage of the ignorance of the other. As Ostranger & Ichel state:[21] "Most fundamentally however, the independent brokerage firm's role in placing large volumes of insurance for its clientele provides the business insurance consumer with substantial bargaining power." They also outline the assessment of the relative bargaining powers of the parties to an insurance contract which involves consideration of the following factors:

1. A determination of the intent of the drafters of the policy contract.
2. The relative level of knowledge and sophistication of the contracting parties.
3. The extent to which the terms of the contract were the product of actual negotiation.

As an example, in the case of *School Dist. #1, Multnoham County v. Mission Ins. Co.*,[22] the court held that there was no evidence that the school district, in purchasing the policy, understood the "narrow meaning" of errors and omissions coverage. The court put the shoe on the wrong foot. It was up to the school district to prove that they were innocent "babes in the woods," and that is hardly likely. If the court had held the policy ambiguous or unclear the decision could have made sense, but there was no such issue.

Temporary Insurance. There is some merit to be recognized in the application of the doctrine of reasonable expectations cases involving prospective buyers of insurance who have paid a premium and are awaiting receipt of the policy, or to holders of insurance "binders" during the period between the date of the application or binder and a reasonable "reading time" after receipt of the actual policy.[23] While this is usually a matter of concern that has to do with life insurance, this situation could also apply to third party liability policies.[24]

---

[21] *Id.*
[22] 650 P.2d 929 (Ore. App. 1982).
[23] **Cal.:** Smith v. Westland Ins. Co., 123 Cal. Rptr. 649 (1975).
Idaho: Toevs v. Western Farm Bur. Life Ins. Co., 483 P.2d 682 (1970).
Md.: Simpson v. Prudential Ins. Co., 177 A.2d 417 (1962).
[24] For further discussion of this topic, *see* Magarick, *Excess Liability* (New York: Clark Boardman Co. Ltd., 1982).

§ 19.09   Bibliography

Plain-Language Policies

Harding, "The Standard Automobile Insurance Policy: A Study of its Readability," The Journal of Risk & Insurance.

Siegel, "Plain English Policies In Action," Best's Review, February 1980.

Reasonable Expectations

Abraham, "Judge-Made Law and Judge-Made Insurance: Honoring the Reasonable Expectations of the Insured," 67 Va. L. Rev. 1151 (1981).

Gardner, "Reasonable Expectations: Evolution Completed or Revolution Begun?", Insurance Law Journal, October 1978.

Goodhue, "The Doctrine of Reasonable Expectations in Massachusetts and New Hampshire: A Comparative Analysis," 17 New England L. Rev. 891 (1982).

Keeton, "Insurance Law Rights At Variance With Policy Provisions," 83 Harv. L. Rev. 961 (1970).

Krider, "The Reconstruction of Insurance Contracts Under the Doctrine of Reasonable Expectations," J. Marshall Law Rev., Vol. 18:155 (1984).

Lashner, "A Common Law Alternative to the Doctrine of Reasonable Expectations in the Construction of Insurance Contracts," 57 N.Y.U. L. Rev. 1175 (1982).

Magarick, *Excess Liability* (New York: Clark Boardman Co. Ltd. 1982).

Ostrager & Ichel, "Should the Business Insurance Policy Be Construed Against the Insurer? Another Look at the Reasonable Expectations Doctrine," F.I.C. Quarterly, Spring 1983.

CHAPTER 20

Some Important Casualty Policy Provisions

§ 20.01 Accident and Occurrence
    [1] Self-Defense
§ 20.02 Duties of the Insurer
    [1] Duty to Defend
    [2] Determination of Insurer's Duty
    [3] Duty to Appeal
    [4] Family Automobile Policy
§ 20.03 Notice of Accident or Occurrence
    [1] Prejudice
    [2] Notice by Others On Behalf of the Insured
    [3] "As Soon As Practicable"
    [4] Written Notice
    [5] Disclaimer Letter
    [6] Investigation of Delayed Notice Cases
§ 20.04 Assistance and Cooperation
    [1] Prejudice
    [2] Nonappearance at Trial
    [3] Statutory Protection for Injured Claimants
§ 20.05 "Other Insurance" Clause
§ 20.06 Policy Cancellation
    [1] Written Notice of Cancellation
    [2] Cancellation Because of Nonpayment of Premium
    [3] Renewal of Coverage

Casualty insurance policies are constantly undergoing change and consolidation. Some of these changes are drastic, resulting in a broadening or even, in some cases, a restriction of coverage. New policies are being issued regularly.

There are, however, a number of basic provisions that appear in most liability policies where the intent of these provisions remains basically the same, with only minor changes meant to conform to new decisions that interpret old clauses.

It is because of such changes that this book will discuss, and sometimes quote, several "variations on a theme": provisions which vary but basically intend to convey the same general principles.

Most provisions of a casualty liability policy must be interpreted in conjunction with other clauses that affect the intent of the provision under scrutiny.

For instance, in discussing the coverage provided by a liability policy, the word "accident" is of distinct importance. In the personal auto policy, the insurer promises to "pay damages for the bodily injury or property damage for which any covered person becomes legally responsible because of an auto accident." The previous edition of this policy used the word "occurrence" instead of "accident," as does the comprehensive general liability policy and others. However, since "occurrence" is defined as an "accident," we are back to defining an "accident," which some of the policies try to do by means of limitation such as "from the viewpoint of the insured."

There is also an exclusion in this policy that applies to "intentional bodily injury," previously known as the "Assault and Battery" exclusion. The intention that deliberate acts are not to be interpreted as "accidents" is present in almost all liability policies with the exception of professional liability. Accordingly, an "occurrence" provision must be read in conjunction with the definition of "occurrence."

As if that is not enough, the new commercial general liability policy has an exception to this exclusion for "bodily injury resulting from the use of reasonable force to protect persons or property," which also must be taken into consideration when judging whether the particular facts of an accident amount to coverage under the policy.

At first glance, a claim representative may become overwhelmed by the complexity of policy wording, even in the so-called plain language policies. Nevertheless, with some study and diligence, he will soon learn the fundamental coverage parameters within which most of his work will lie.

Where complex questions of coverage are involved, help must be sought from supervisors and counsel. If the adjuster uses such cases to learn from them, it won't be long before he or she will themself become a supervisor. What appears very complex initially will become less so by experience if one learns from such experience.

Following are some important policy provisions that can be discussed generally.

§ 20.01 Accident and Occurrence

Today, the great majority of casualty policies no longer use the expression "caused by accident" in describing the liability of an insured for which insurance coverage is provided. Most policies have either eliminated the word "accident" or have replaced it with "occurrence."

It is still present in the terminology of the standard basic automobile policy, the medical payments provisions, and certain others, including accident policies, but has recently become a matter of waning importance to the claim representative in the interpretation of casualty policies outside of the accident and health field. However, since the word "occurrence" is usually defined as an accident, I believe it important enough to warrant some discussion.

As usual, there is no uniformity in the decisions and no agreement concerning a definition of the word "accident." The courts have defined an accident as an event that takes place without one's foresight or expectations; an undesigned, sudden, and unexpected event. Some definitions have held that it must also be identifiable as to time and place.

It has been held that a long and continuous exposure to radiation, which caused an injury, did not fall within the definition of a "sudden" event.

Although the courts have not been definite or in agreement in their interpretation, and certainly cannot be relied upon to follow this theory in the future, damage which follows as a natural consequence of the performance of some deliberate act should not be considered as "accidental" within the meaning of the terms of the policy.

Some decisions have gone so far as to say that anything accidental *in respect to the injured party* must be considered as an accident within the terms of the policy. If this yardstick were universally followed, I can think of very few circumstances that would not fall within such a broad definition of the word. Under this definition, no matter how blatantly willful the act on the part of the insured, as long as the result was unexpected on the claimant's part, it would be considered an accident.

The definition of "occurrence" in the general liability policies tries to eliminate any ambiguity by stating that "occurrence means an accident, including exposure to conditions, which results, during the policy period, in bodily injury or property damage neither expected nor intended *from the standpoint of the insured."*

The questions concerning when an occurrence becomes effective, multiple events and other matters most often involved with products liability claims, will be discussed in more detail in the products liability section of this book.

There is no uniformity of opinion on whether or not the event must be sudden. For instance, corrosive fumes that damage neighborhood property after having been permitted to escape through the chimney of a chemical plant should not be considered an accident if the insured had knowledge of both the corrosive nature of the fumes and the fact that they were being permitted to escape through the chimney. The fact that the deterioration of the property was the result of continued exposure over a period of time would add to the weight of evidence against such an incident's being considered an accident. However, most public liability policies written today on an occurrence basis, would cover such an incident.

Deliberate acts, such as libel, slander, or false arrest are certainly not intended to be covered and cannot be considered as accidents or occurrences. Special coverage is provided for such liabilities under a personal injury policy or endorsement.

The question of assault must be treated separately because of the provision in the policy which deals with this specific subject.

Despite the fact that some courts have stated that words in an insurance policy should be given their usual, ordinary, popular meaning,[1] the courts, using legal reasoning (sometimes far-fetched in an effort to achieve a desired result), have interpreted this language in surprising ways such as whether "accident is to be perceived from the insured's viewpoint or from that of the claimant." These cases stress *cause* in some cases and *effect* (injury or damages) in others in making their determinations.[2]

[1] Self-Defense

Self-defense has been creating problems in the interpretation of what is or is not an accident for some time.

---

[1] **Ga.:** St. Paul-Mercury Indem. Co. v. Rutland, 225 F.2d 689 (1955).
N.J.: Wilkinson v. Providence Wash. Ins. Co., 307 A.2d 639 (1973).
[2] **Cal.:** Gogerty v. General Accid. Fire & Life Assur. Co., 48 Cal. 37 (1966).
N.Y.: McGroarty v. Great American Ins. Co., 351 N.Y.S.2d 428 (1974).

CASUALTY POLICY PROVISIONS § 20.02[1]

On the one hand, some courts have ruled that an injury or death resulting from the firing of a gun in self-defense is not an accidental act.[3] Other courts hold that where the insured causes an injury while acting in self-defense, the insured is not precluded from coverage by an "intentional injury" exclusion.[4]

Quite often the facts do not equate with the interpretation given them by the courts. An example of this kind of convoluted reasoning involves cases where manufacturing and processing plants dump waste materials into a river or on adjoining property belonging to someone else. Some of these cases hold that while the act was intentional, the resulting damage or injury was not.[5]

An interesting case that discusses "intended injury" is that of *Steinmetz v. National Amer. Ins. Co.*,[6] where the court states that "if the insured acts with the intent or expectation that bodily injury will result, even though the bodily injury that does result is different either in character or magnitude from the injury that was intended," the act that caused the injury is not to be considered as accidental.

§ 20.02 Duties of the Insurer

[1] Duty to Defend

Part IV A2 of the *1980 Basic* plain language Automobile policy reads:

> We have the duty to defend any suit asking for (these) damages. However, we have no duty to defend suits for bodily injury or property damage not covered by the policy. We may investigate and settle any claim or suit as we consider appropriate. Our payment of the Liability Insurance limit ends our duty to defend or settle.

This version of the defense clause does not specify that the insurer will pay for defense costs, although this is implied, nor does it put any cap on such costs. In addition, despite the fact that the insurers tried to terminate the duty to defend when "Our payment of the Liability Insurance limit" is made, most courts make an exception

---

[3] **Fla.:** Clemmons v. American States Ins. Co., 412 So. 2d 906 (App. 1982).
Ore.: Allstate Ins. Co. v. Simms, 597 F. Supp. 64 (1955).
[4] **Cal.:** Walters v. American Ins. Co., 8 Cal. Rptr. 665 (1960).
[5] Atlantic Cement Co. v. Fidelity & Cas. Co. of N.Y., 459 N.Y.S.2d 425 (1983).
[6] 589 P.2d 911 (Ore. App. 1978).

when the insured is left in a position of jeopardy in the middle of a trial, and in some other exceptions.

Part A - Liability Coverage Insuring Agreement of the *1980 Personal Auto* plain language policy reads:

> ... We will settle or defend, as we consider appropriate, any claim or suit asking for (these) damages. In addition to our limit of liability, we will pay all defense costs we incur. Our duty to settle or defend ends when our limit of liability for this coverage has been exhausted.

This version of the defense clause doesn't spell out what "exhausted" means.

The *Homeowners 76 Form HO-2* states in Section II-Liability Coverages:

> If a claim is made or a suit is brought against any insured for damages because of bodily injury or property damage to which this coverage applies, we will (b) provide a defense at our expense, by counsel of our choice. We may make any payment and settle any claim or suit that we decide is appropriate. Our obligation to defend any claim or suit ends when the amount we pay for damages resulting from the occurrence equals our limit of liability.

Here the argument concerning interpretation centers around the words "counsel of our choice," since most courts have held that if there is any conflict of interest between the insured and his insurer in the defense of the case, the insurer must supply the insured with his own counsel at the insurer's cost.[7]

In the Insuring Agreements of the *1966 and 1973 Comprehensive General Liability* forms, the policies read:

> ... the company shall have the right and duty to defend any suit against the insured seeking damages on account of such bodily injury or property damage even if any of the allegations of the suit are groundless, false or fraudulent, and may make such investigation and settlement of any claim or suit as it deems expedient, but the company shall not be obligated to pay any claim or judgment or to defend any suit after the applicable limit of the company's liability has been exhausted by payments of judgments or settlements.

---

[7] **Cal.:** Nike, Inc. v. Atlantic Mut. Ins. Co., 578 F. Supp. 948 (1983).
Ill.: Murphy v. Urso, 430 N.E.2d 1079 (1981).
N.Y.: Allstate Ins. Co. v. Long, 446 N.Y.S.2d 742 (App. 1981).

The new *1986 Commercial General Liability* policy presents some very notable changes from the former comprehensive forms which will be discussed in § 26.02, *infra*. The duty to defend provision of this new policy is embodied in the last portion of the Insuring Agreements which reads: "We shall have the right and duty to defend any suit seeking (those) damages. . . ."

The question as to whether defense costs should be a part of the overall limits of liability, or be in addition to the limits of liability as heretofore, is presently being debated. Such a change would be a radical departure from all previous forms and is being seriously considered because of the very high cost of defense in the last few years.

The wording of the defense clause has been the subject of so much litigation and involves enough points of controversy to warrant the number of such examples herein given.

As the F.C. & S. Bulletins put it:[8]

> The Insurer's duty to defend suits against the insured is generally regarded as being broader than the insurer's duty to pay damages. This is because the duty to defend is based not on the apparent facts of a claim but on the allegations of the complaint by a third party against the insured. As long as there is a *possibility* that one or more of the allegations is within the coverage of the policy, the insurer is obligated to defend. As a general rule, this is the case even if the complaint contains other allegations that are clearly not within the policy coverage. And, as stated in the insuring agreement, the insurer is obligated to defend even if the *allegations* of the complaint are "groundless, false or fraudulent."

[2] Determination of Insurer's Duty

If the facts alleged against the insured, no matter how false or fraudulent they may be, would have spelled out a claim that was covered under the policy had the facts been true, the insurer has an unequivocal duty to defend the insured. The question of disclaimer or reservation of rights does not enter into this picture.

For instance, the plaintiff may allege that as a result of an automobile accident, which occurred on a certain date, at a certain place, the plaintiff was seriously injured because of the insured's negligence. The fact that the insured could prove that he was not driving his automobile on that particular day, that his automobile was, as a matter of fact, in a different city, and that there was absolutely no

---

[8] Published by The National Underwriter Co., Cincinnati, Ohio.

possibility of the accident having occurred as alleged, would not affect the duty to defend the insured. This is the case because, had the facts alleged been true, the insurer would have properly covered the accident and assumed the insured's liability, if any, to the extent of the coverage. This is an example of a case which is entirely groundless because of either fraud or error, but which nevertheless calls for defense under the policy provisions.

On the other hand, if the complaint alleged that the insured deliberately and intentionally struck the plaintiff pedestrian with intent to injure him, such an incident would not be covered under the ordinary liability policy no matter what the insured's personal liability to the plaintiff might be. This is so because a specific clause in the policy says that an assault committed by or at the direction of the insured shall not be deemed an accident. In this latter instance, if the facts alleged in the complaint proved to be true, the carrier would owe no obligation whatsoever to the insured if the policy only afforded coverage for injuries or damage caused by accident, or by occurrence defined as accident.

Obligation determined by the complaint. The courts of most jurisdictions have held that the obligation of an insurance company to defend an insured is to be determined by the allegations of the complaint. Several decisions have in effect stated that this obligation (to defend) is not affected by facts ascertained before suit or developed in the process of litigation or by the ultimate outcome of the suit. If the allegations of the complaint state a cause of action within the coverage of the policy, the insurance company must defend. On the other hand, if the complaint alleges a liability not within the coverage of the policy, the insurance company is not required to defend.[9]

I cannot altogether agree with this line of reasoning. For instance, if the insured denied the allegations made by the plaintiff in his complaint and said that he did not deliberately injure or assault the plaintiff, but that it was merely an unintentional pedestrian knockdown accident, I believe that the burden would be on the insurance company to investigate the truth or falsehood of the insured's allegations before denying coverage. Should the ultimate outcome of the suit sustain the insured's contention that it was an accident rather than an assault, I believe that the insurer would be in a very precarious

---

[9] Hoffine v. Standard Accid. Ins. Co., 379 P.2d 246 (Kan. 1963); Kelly v. U.S.F.& G Co., 76 So. 2d 116 (La. App. 1954).

position in the event of a suit on the policy, had it denied coverage on the allegations in the complaint.

Certainly, if the insurer knew that the allegations of the complaint were false, and that the facts clearly fell within the policy coverage, the obligation to defend would be clear. The courts have so declared.[10]

Obligation after amount of policy has been paid. The obligation of an insurer to defend a third party action against the insured has been said to be separate and independent of its obligation to pay a claim or judgment and certainly is broader than the latter obligation.[11]

How far, then, must an insurer go to fulfill its obligations to an insured after the policy limits have been exhausted? Does the obligation to defend terminate when the policy limits have been paid?

The courts have held many times that the various provisions of an insurance policy must be read and interpreted in conjunction with each other. Thus it would seem that the theory of severability of the obligation to defend should be considered only in connection with the insurer's additional duty to defend, aside from its duty to pay a judgment.

In other words, it does not seem logical to believe that the insured's obligation to defend must go on indefinitely and with total disregard for the amount of coverage purchased, since the insured had the opportunity to purchase coverage at higher or lower limits depending upon the premium he wanted to pay. Several cases have held that upon making payment up to the full amount of the policy coverage, the company's duty to defend ceases to exist. This, however, is not the weight of authority although it seems to be the logical conclusion.

This does not necessarily mean that the insurer may elect to pay the full limit of its coverage and thereby rid itself of the duty to defend, nor that it could abandon the defense in mid-course under circumstances prejudicial to the insured. If the insurer has elected to defend it must do so completely and in good faith up to the point of final judgment. Having paid such judgment and incidental expenses to the limit of coverage, the insurer has then completely fulfilled its obligation and should owe no further duty to defend.

---

[10] Crum v. Anchor Cas. Co., 119 N.W.2d 703 (Minn. 1963).

[11] American Employers Ins. Co. v. Goble Air. Spec's, 131 N.Y.S.2d 394 (1954).

[3] Duty to Appeal

The question whether the insurer, upon request by the insured, owes the latter the duty to appeal from a decision is one upon which there is little authority to base any conclusion. The wording of the standard policy concerning the payment of accrued interest from the time judgment is entered until payment is made seems to imply that there is no absolute duty to appeal.

Again, however, we must qualify this statement by saying that the insurer must act in good faith and avoid placing its insured in unnecessary jeopardy by its refusal to appeal if requested.[12]

It has been held that since the right of an insurer to defend is absolute, so is *its right* to appeal a judgment that is within its policy limits,[13] but this attitude has been changing in recent years.

[4] Family Automobile Policy

The family automobile policy and some other policy forms have moved the defense clause so as to make it a part of the paragraph which refers to the bodily injury liability and the property damage liability coverages. There is no separate "Defense, Settlement, Supplementary Payments" clause. After stating the coverages (paragraph 1 of "Part 1—Liability"), the clause reads: "and the company shall defend any suit alleging such bodily injury or property damage and seeking damages which are payable under the terms of this policy, even if any of the allegations of the suit are groundless, false or fraudulent."

This is one more attempt to make it very clear that the insurer intends the defense obligation to be subordinated to the overall coverage provided. There is no intent to provide a defense where there is no coverage provided. There is no intent to provide a defense where there is no coverage under the policy and no duty to defend over and above the policy limits except in special circumstances already discussed.

More recently, the "groundless, false or fraudulent" wording has been dropped since the intent is already expressed throughout the policy and judicial interpretation of these words have succeeded only in beclouding this intent.

---

[12] Hawkeye-Security Ins. Co. v. Indemnity Ins. Co., 260 F.2d 361 (1958).
[13] Abrams v. Factory Mut. Liab. Ins. Co., 298 Mass. 141, 10 N.E.2d 82 (1937).

CASUALTY POLICY PROVISIONS § 20.03

§ 20.03 Notice of Accident or Occurrence

One of the most controversial conditions in casualty liability policies deals with the requirement for prompt notice of any accident or occurrence and suit.

In the commercial type of policies, while the wording sometimes varies somewhat, the following is a fair sample of such a Condition in which I have italicized some of the key wording which will subsequently be discussed:

> When an occurrence happens, *written notice* shall be given *by or on behalf of the insured* to the company *or any of its authorized agents as soon as practicable.* Such notice shall contain particulars sufficient to identify the insured and also reasonably obtainable information respecting the time, place and circumstances of the occurrence, the names and addresses of the injured and of available witnesses. If legal proceedings are begun in such a case, the insured shall forward to the company each paper therein, or copy thereof, received by the insured or the insured's representatives, together with copies of reports of investigations with respect to such claim proceedings.

In the personal automobile and other "plain language" policies, the wording is similar and the pertinent sections read as follows:

> Part E. *Duties After an Accident or Loss:* We must be notified promptly of how, when and where the occurrence (or accident) or loss happened. Notice should also include the names and addresses of any injured persons and of any witnesses.
>
> A person seeking any coverage must:
>
> 1. Cooperate with us in the investigation, settlement or defense of any claim or suit.
>
> 2. Promptly send us copies of any notice or legal papers received in connection with the occurrence or loss.

A delay in reporting an incident may make the investigation and defense of a claim much more difficult, if not impossible.

Although a constant program of education among insureds, brokers, and agents helps to lessen the problem of delayed reporting, it will always be a problem because of the physical impossibility of reaching or convincing everyone.

Originally, this clause of the policy was strictly construed by the courts. The only thing that had to be shown by the insurer was that notice was not given promptly or within a reasonable or specified time, depending upon the wording of the policy.

The tendency in an ever-increasing number of jurisdictions is to require that some prejudice to the insurer be shown as a result of the delayed notice before the delay will invalidate coverage.

The decisions concerning sufficiency of notice, or whether notice was given at all, are also becoming increasingly favorable to the insured.

Few cases have made much of a distinction between written and oral notice despite the wording of the condition calling for written notice. Today, it would not be wise for an insurance company to deny coverage on this basis alone.

Most courts have held that an insurance carrier by its actions or by its omissions may waive the provisions requiring prompt notice and certainly that requiring written notice. There are some instances where because of physical or mental incapacity, or because of no knowledge of the incident on the part of the insured, the delay in reporting is not considered to be a breach of the policy conditions. Lack of knowledge, however, must be reasonably explained.

In some instances it has been held that notice to an insured's broker is not notice to an insurance company if the broker is not an agent of the company or has not been declared so by law.

Some states have by statute set up a required time for the reporting of accidents. If definite time periods conflict with the policy provisions, the state statutes are, of course, paramount. However, if the policy is silent as to the exact time required for reporting, the courts will not necessarily construe the statutory time as being absolutely binding.

Because of this, and because the wording "reasonable time" or "as soon as practicable" have been variously interpreted by the different state courts, it becomes essential that the claim representative familiarize himself fully with the law concerning delayed notice in his particular jurisdiction.

The courts are in unanimous agreement that as a general proposition, policy Conditions that require notice of accident and forwarding of suit papers are valid and enforceable.

[1] Prejudice

A majority of the states, either by court decision or by statute, now hold that denial of coverage for reasons of delay in giving notice of an accident or occurrence is not valid unless it can be shown that the insurer's rights have been prejudiced thereby.[14] The burden of establishing such prejudice is on the insurer.[15]

Nevertheless, a minority of the states hold to the reasoning that where notice of accident is expressly made a condition precedent to an action against the insurance company, prejudice is immaterial.[16]

In certain situations that seem obvious, prejudice to the insurer may be presumed. For instance, notice given to an insurer for the first time after a default judgment where the insured has no logical explanation,[17] where the insured's investigation has been impaired because of a delay in reporting,[18] or unduly protracted delay in reporting, depending on the circumstances.[19] Such delays were held to be prejudice as a matter of law. However, if such a delay can be properly explained, even a lengthy delay in reporting may be excused.[20]

The sufficiency of the excuse and the diligence of the insured that determines prejudice are questions of fact for the jury to decide.[21]

---

[14] **Ill.:** Fremont Indemnity Co. v. Special Earth Equip. Corp., 474 N.E.2d 926 (App. 1985).
N.C.: Great American Ins. Co. v. Tate Constr. Co., 279 S.E.2d 769 (1981).
R.I.: Pa. Gen. Ins. Co. v. Becton, 474 A.2d 1032 (1984).
[15] **Alas.:** Weaver Bros., Inc. v. Chappel, 684 P.2d 123 (1984).
N.C.: Fortess Re, Inc. v. Central Nat'l Ins. Co., 595 F. Supp. 334 (1983) (reinsurer involved).
[16] **Ala.:** Big Three Motors, Inc. v. Employers Ins. Co. of Ala., 449 So. 2d 1232 (1984).
Ga.: Diggs v. Southern Ins. Co., 321 S.E.2d 792 (1984).
[17] **Mo.:** Anderson v. Slayton, 662 S.W.2d 575 (App. 1983).
[18] **Ind.:** Miller v. Dilts, 463 N.E.2d 257 (1984).
[19] **Ala.:** Big Three Motors, Inc. v. Employers Ins. Co. of Ala., 449 So. 2d 1232 (1984) (delay of three years and nine months).
Colo.: Emcasco Ins. Co. v. Dover, 678 P.2d 1051 (App. 1983) (delay of six weeks after counterclaim was filed).
Ga.: Bates v. Holyoke Mut. Ins. Co., 324 S.E.2d 474 (1985) (delay of forty-three months).
Ill.: Wausau Ins. Co. v. Valspar Corp., 594 F. Supp. 269 (1984) (delay of more than ten years).
N.Y.: Jenkins v. Burgos, 472 N.Y.S.2d 373 (App. 1984) (delay of one year and ten months).
[20] **N.Y.:** Van Buren v. Employers Ins. Co. of Wausau, 469 N.Y.S.2d 488 (App. 1983).
[21] **Ala.:** Weaver Bros., Inc. v. Chappel, 684 P.2d 123 (1984).
Ga.: North East Ins. Co. v. Townsend, 315 S.E.2d 463 (1984).
Ind.: Miller v. Dilts, 463 N.E.2d 257 (1984).

[2] Notice by Others On Behalf of the Insured

It appears to be the majority opinion that notice from any reliable source fulfills the requirement of notice "on behalf of the insured."[22]

Some jurisdictions hold that an injured claimant has an independent right to give notice of an accident to the tortfeasor's insurer.[23]

Even an injured claimant however, must use reasonable diligence in order to make a timely report.[24]

Other jurisdictions hold that notice from some source other than the insured or his representative does not relieve the insured of the duty to forward suit papers.[25]

A general agent of an insurance company has implied authority to accept notice of an accident and notice to the agency is tantamount to notice to the insurance company.[26]

[3] "As Soon As Practicable"

Requirement that the report of an accident or occurrence be made "as soon as practicable" means that it must be done within a reasonable time in view of the circumstances involved.[27]

In the case of *Jackson Housing Authority v. Auto-Owners Ins. Co.*,[28] the Tennessee Appellate Court ruled that a delay of three months did not invalidate coverage where there was a reasonable doubt that a claim would be made.

[4] Written Notice

For the most part, the requirement of "written" notice in a notice of accident or occurrence provision has not been given full faith and

---

[22] **Ill.:** Wausau Ins. Co. v. Valspar Corp., 594 F. Supp. 269 (1984).

Pa.: Philadelphia Elec. Co. v. Aetna Cas. & Sur. Co., 484 A.2d 768 (1984).

[23] **Me.:** American Home Assur. Co. v. Ingeneri, 479 A.2d 897 (1984) (report must be made in sufficient time to protect the insurer's interests and prejudice must be absent).

N.Y.: Hartford Accid. & Indem. Co. v. C.N.A. Ins. Co's., 472 N.Y.S.2d 342 (1984) (timeliness of notice is not judged by the same standard as that required from the insured).

[24] **N.Y.:** Jenkins v. Burgos, 472 N.Y.S.2d 373 (App. 1984).

[25] **Ga.:** Adwater v. Georgia Ins. Co., 316 S.E.2d 2 (App. 1984).

[26] **N.C.:** City of Greensboro v. Reserve Ins. Co., 321 S.E.2d 232 (1984).

[27] **D.C.:** Diamond Service Co., Inc. v. Utica Mut. Ins. Co., 476 A.2d 648 (1984).

[28] 686 S.W.2d 917 (App. 1984).

CASUALTY POLICY PROVISIONS § 20.03[6]

credence, despite the fact that decisions are not uniform, especially if a reasonable excuse is made for such failure.[29]

A New York case, on the other hand, held that a telephone notice, even assuming that it was made, was insufficient notice as a matter of law.[30]

[5] Disclaimer Letter

Disclaimer on the basis of delayed notice, must be written with a "high degree of specificity of the grounds on which the disclaimer is predicated."[31]

Here again, it is suggested that such a letter be drafted with the aid of counsel.

[6] Investigation of Delayed Notice Cases

Immediate investigation into the cause of the delayed reporting should be made. Separate signed statements should be obtained concerning the delay, and prompt decision made as soon as possible about what course of action the company intends to take.

Investigation of a delayed notice case, as in any other casualty investigation, must be made as the circumstances demand. It will naturally vary as the facts are developed. Its purpose is threefold: first, to obtain the allegations; second, to check their accuracy; and third, to obtain evidence which will stand up in court.

Although it isn't possible to set down any rigid pattern for such an investigation, an attempt has been made to outline some guiding material that will be helpful in a variety of situations that may be encountered where warranted.

1. Signed statement should be obtained from the insured, driver, or witness giving the details of the accident.
2. Separate signed statement should be obtained repeating the exact date, time, and location of the accident, for identification purposes. Include details of to whom, when, and how the accident was first reported. If it was reported by telephone, identify the person who took the call and get his recollection

---

[29] **Va.:** Hitt v. Cox, 737 F.2d 421 (4th Cir. 1984).
[30] **N.Y.:** Jenkins v. Burgos, 472 N.Y.S.2d 373 (App. 1984).
[31] **N.Y.:** Fabian v. Motor Vehicle Accid. Indem. Corp., 489 N.Y.S.2d 588 (1985).

§ 20.04   CASUALTY INSURANCE CLAIMS

of the conversation as exact as possible. Include the reason for the delay, if delay is admitted.

If the insured was not present at the scene of the accident, get complete information on how and when he first learned of it, including the name of the person who first gave him the details.

3. Signed statement should be obtained from the person who first reported the accident to the insured giving all of the surrounding circumstances and including the exact date and time of the report.
4. Examine the originals and obtain copies of all letters, telegrams, or memoranda that corroborate or deny the insured's allegations.
5. If a corporation or business firm is the insured, obtain a signed statement covering the details of the delayed notice along lines previously mentioned. The statement should be obtained from the person responsible for reporting accidents and should identify him as such.
6. Signed statements corroborating or denying allegations of reporting should be obtained from any alleged witnesses to the reporting.
7. If an agent or a broker is involved, a signed statement should be obtained from him or his secretary (if secretary is involved) concerning their knowledge of the matter. Original letters and records should be seen and copies obtained both of his receipt of the notice and his transmittal of it to the agent or company. A check should be made to determine that the broker is definitely not an agent of the company.
8. See that a signed statement or letter is received from the agent or his representatives concerning receipt of notice and its transmittal to the company. Letters and records should be examined where necessary and copies obtained both of the receipt and transmission of the information.

§ 20.04 Assistance and Cooperation

In the previous standard forms and in some other policies, a separate clause specifically entitled "Assistance and Cooperation" was included in the policy form. While wording differed in some policies, basically such a clause read as follows:

The insured shall cooperate with the company and, upon the company's request, shall attend hearings and trials and shall assist in effecting settlements, securing and giving evidence, obtaining the attendance of witnesses and in the conduct of suits. The insured shall not, except at his own cost, voluntarily make any payment, assume any obligation or incur any expense other than for such immediate medical and surgical relief to others as shall be imperative at the time of the accident.

In the newer "plain language" policies, the assistance and cooperation clause of the older standard forms has been incorporated into the "Duties After An Accident or Loss" provision with the "notice of accident" clause condensed into the one line requirement that: "A person seeking any coverage must: 1. Cooperate with us (the insurer) in the investigation, settlement or defense of any claim or suit."

Gone is all the specific verbiage that caused more harm than good and which was, in any event, a greater cause for controversy.

Cooperation has been defined by Justice Cardoza, in the case of *Coleman v. New Amsterdam Cas. Co.*,[32] as a "fair and frank disclosure of information reasonably demanded by the insurer to enable it to determine whether there is a genuine defense."

[1]   Prejudice

The majority of the courts now hold that in considering whether a breach of either the notice or cooperation clause would justify denial of coverage, the insurer must show prejudice to its interests and most of these decisions have ruled that the prejudice must be substantial.[33]

---

[32] 247 N.Y. 271 (1928).

[33] **Conn.:** O'Leary v. Lumbermen's Mut. Cas. Co., 420 A.2d 888 (1979) (no prejudice in this case).

Fla.: Travelers Ins. Co. v. Jones, 422 So. 2d 1000 (App. 1982).

Ill.: State Farm Mut. Auto. Ins. Co. v. McSpadden, 411 N.E.2d 121 (App. 1880) (prejudice not shown).

Ind.: Kosanovich v. Meade, 449 N.E.2d 1178 (App. 1983).

Md.: Fidelity & Cas. Co. v. McConnaughty, 179 A.2d 117 (1962).

Miss.: State Farm Mut. Auto. Ins. Co. v. Commercial Union Ins. Co., 394 So. 2d 890 (1981).

Mo.: Hendrix v. Jones, 580 S.W.2d 740 (1979) (substantial prejudice must be shown).

N.M.: Foundation Reserve Ins. Co. v. Esquibel, 607 P.2d 1150 (1980) (no prejudice shown).

§ 20.04[2]   CASUALTY INSURANCE CLAIMS

While the "notice" and "cooperation" clauses are now integrated into the "Duties After an Accident or Loss" provision, an Indiana court in the case of *Miller v. Hilts*,[34] ruled that the two clauses are not equivalent and do not serve the same objectives. Accordingly, prejudice must be shown on each allegation and the burden of proving prejudice is on the insurer.[35]

[2] Nonappearance at Trial

Probably the most contested reason for denial of coverage for lack of cooperation is the failure of the insured to appear at the trial of the suit against him or her.

The Virginia Supreme Court, in the case of *State Farm Mut. Auto. Ins. Co. v. Davies*,[36] stated that the insurer is not required to show that the appearance of the insured would have altered the outcome of the trial. Nor did the court approve the "per se" ruling that the insurer merely had to show that the insured did not appear. This court stated that "we favor neither [rule] . . . we believe that the proper rule lies midway between these two extremes." The court ruled that in an action on the policy, when the insurer shows that the insured's willful failure to appear would have deprived the insurer of some evidence that might have been material in the defense of the case, he has fulfilled his burden of proving prejudice. Other jurisdictions have reacted similarly.[37]

Other courts have felt that the unexplained absence of the insured from the trial would influence the attitude of the jury in favor of the plaintiff and have therefore felt that such absence was prejudicial in and of itself.[38]

[3] Statutory Protection for Injured Claimants

Because of the fact that injured parties that are plaintiffs may be innocent victims of the insured's failure to comply with policy provisions, some states have enacted statutes holding that any denial of

---

[34] 463 N.E.2d 257 (1984).
[35] **Kan.:** Watson v. Jones, 610 P.2d 619 (1980).
[36] 310 S.E.2d 167 (1983).
[37] **Ill.:** Johnson v. R.&D. Enterprises, 435 N.E.2d 1233 (1982).
Mo.: Hendrix v. Jones, 580 S.W.2d 740 (1979).
[38] **Ark.:** Firemen's Ins. Co. of Newark v. Cadillac Ins. Co., 679 S.W.2d 821 (1984).
Ga.: Young v. Allstate Ins. Co., 282 S.E.2d 115 (1981).
Mo.: Riffe v. Peeler, 684 S.W.2d 539 (1984).

coverage is not effective against such claimants.[39] Such decisions usually derive from compulsory automobile insurance laws.[40]

The argument of the courts that the insurer can still protect itself by suing its insured is a hollow advantage since in most instances where an individual insured is involved, he or she is not financially responsible.

In the case of *Huse v. Fulton*,[41] a Georgia court pointed out that since the purpose of the enactment was meant to be for the protection of the public, such purpose would be thwarted if the insurer was permitted to escape liability by raising his own failure to comply with the conditions of his policy as a defense.

The statutes obviously differ in important respects and knowledge of them is essential to the claims person.

Some courts hold that an insurer that attempts to show a breach of the cooperation condition must show that it made an effort to achieve compliance.[42] Other courts have held that where an insurer is forewarned that the insured might not cooperate in the trial, and still actively participates in the defense, it waives any right it might have had to disclaim coverage on that basis.[43]

§ 20.05 "Other Insurance" Clause

No insurer wants to bear the full burden of a claim or loss if there is other insurance that covers, in whole or in part, the same claim or loss. Accordingly, the Other Insurance or "escape" clause soon became commonplace in all casualty policies.

The wording of these clauses, while different in some specific details, is generally the same intent, which is to make the insurance primary, excess or coinsurance. This is not to say however that it always accomplishes its intent.

The General Comprehensive Liability form is similar to those used in other commercial casualty policies and reads as follows:

Other Insurance—The Insurance afforded by this policy is primary insurance, except when stated to apply in excess of or contingent upon

---

[39] Ill.: Johnson v. R.&D. Enterprises, 435 N.E.2d 1233 (1982).
Mich.: Coburn v. Fox, 350 N.W.2d 852 (App. 1984).
[40] Ga.: Young v. Allstate Ins. Co., 282 S.E.2d 115 (1981).
[41] 678 F.2d 132 (11th Cir. 1982).
[42] Ind.: Newport v. M.F.A. Ins. Co., 448 N.E.2d 1223 (1983).
[43] Mass.: Di Marzo v. American Mut. Ins. Co., 449 N.E.2d 1189 (1983).

the absence of other insurance. When this insurance is primary and the insured has other insurance which is stated to be applicable to the loss on an excess or contingent basis, the amount of the company's liability under this policy shall not be reduced by the existence of such other insurance.

When both this insurance and other insurance apply to the loss on the same basis, whether primary, excess, or contingent, the company shall not be liable under this policy for a greater proportion of the loss than that stated in the applicable contribution provision below.

(a) *Contribution by Equal Shares.* If all of such valid and collectible insurance provides for contribution by equal shares, the company shall not be liable for a greater proportion of such loss than would be payable if each insurer contributes an equal share until the share of each insurer equals the lowest applicable limit of liability under any one policy or the full amount of the loss is paid; and, with respect to any amount of loss not so paid, the remaining insurers then continue to contribute equal shares of the remaining amount of the loss until each such insurer has paid its limit in full or the full amount of the loss is paid.

(b) *Contribution by Limits.* If any such other insurance does not provide for contribution by equal shares, the company shall not be liable for a greater proportion of such loss than the applicable limit of liability under this policy for such loss bears to the total applicable limit of liability of all valid and collectible insurance against such loss.

Some of the wording of this provision has been changed from previous editions in order to make it conform to previous decisions.

The wording of the plain language Personal Auto policy reads as follows:

Other Insurance—If there is other applicable liability insurance we will pay only our share of the loss. Our share is the proportion that our limit of liability bears to the total of all applicable limits. However, any insurance we provide for a vehicle you do not own shall be excess over any other collectible insurance.

It is apparent at first glance that this clause is considerably less inclusive and easier to comprehend than the commercial form. However, in the Personal Auto policy there is a separate "Other Insurance" clause which is applicable to "Medical Payments" coverage, another for "Uninsured Motorists" coverage, and still another for "Coverage For Damage To Your Auto," with which the claim representative should at least be familiar.

CASUALTY POLICY PROVISIONS § 20.06

The different situations calling for an interpretation of the "Other Insurance" clause are myriad, but a few basic rules can be given.

Where both insurers have policies with similar "Other Insurance" clauses that do not conflict, the loss will usually be prorated in accordance with the limits of liability.[44]

Where the "Other Insurance" clauses are in conflict, several cases have recently held that the court must determine which policy is closest to the risk.[45] The problem is of course, to determine which is "closest to the risk."

There seems to be a tendency in recent decisions to hold that self-insurers are not to be considered as "other insurers."[46]

One final generalization holds that umbrella or excess policies, unless otherwise stated, are considered to be excess over primary insurance and not an "other insurer" as meant by this clause.[47]

§ 20.06 Policy Cancellation

The act of cancelling a policy is primarily the responsibility of the underwriting department of an insurance company. However, repercussions as a result of improper cancellation directly affect the claim department, since controversy arises only after an accident has occurred involving the effectiveness of the policy in question.

The law concerning cancellation has been variously interpreted by the courts so that only general principles can be discussed. In addition, most states have enacted statutes that require strict compliance in order to make cancellation by the insurer effective. Most jurisdictions, including those that have not legislated on this subject, are loathe to enforce cancellation against the insured and go to extremes to rule for the policyholder.

The pertinent wording of the clause commonly found in commercial liability policies is similar to the following:

---

[44] D.C.: Glacier Gen. Assur. Co. v. Continental Cas. Ins. Co., 605 F. Supp. 126 (1985).
Fla.: Gulf Ins. Corp. v. Continental Cas. Co., 464 So. 2d 207 (1985).
N.Y.: J.P. Realty Trust v. Public Service Mut. Ins. Co., 476 N.Y.S.2d 325 (1984).
Pa.: Liberty Mut. Ins. Co. v. Home Ins. Co., 583 F. Supp. 849 (1984).

[45] Minn.: Federated Mut. Ins. Co. v. American Family Mut. Ins. Co., 350 N.W.2d 425 (1984); Transamerica Ins. Co. v. Austin Farm Center, Inc., 354 N.W.2d 503 (1984).

[46] N.J.: American Nurses Ass'n v. Passaic General Hosp., 484 A.2d 670 (1984).

[47] Ga.: Atkinson v. Atkinson, 326 S.E.2d 206 (1985).

§ 20.06 CASUALTY INSURANCE CLAIMS

Cancellation:—This policy may be cancelled by the named insured by mailing to the company written notice stating when thereafter the cancellation shall be effective. This policy may be cancelled by the company by mailing to the named insured, at the address shown in this policy, written notice stating when not less than 30 days thereafter such cancellation shall be effective. The mailing of notice as aforesaid shall be sufficient proof of notice. The effective date of cancellation stated in the notice shall become the end of the policy period. Delivery of such written notice either by the named insured or by the company shall be equivalent to mailing.

The wording in the plain language Personal Auto policy reads as follows:

"Termination—This policy may be cancelled during the policy period as follows:

1. The named insured shown in the Declarations may cancel by:

a. returning this policy to us; or

b. giving us advance written notice of the date cancellation is to take effect.

2. We may cancel by mailing to the named insured shown in the Declarations at the address shown in the policy:

a. at least 10 days notice:

(1) if cancellation is for nonpayment of premium; or

(2) if notice is mailed during the first 60 days this policy is in effect and this is not a renewal or continuation policy; or

b. at least 20 days notice in all other cases.

3. After this policy is in effect for 60 days, or if this is a renewal or continuation policy, we will cancel only:

a. for nonpayment of premium; or

b. if your driver's license or that of:

(1) any driver who lives with you; or

(2) any driver who customarily uses your covered auto: has been suspended or revoked. This must have occurred:

(1) during the policy period; or

(2) since the last anniversary of the original effective date if the policy period is other than 1 year."

CASUALTY POLICY PROVISIONS   § 20.06[1]

The cancellation clause in this policy goes on to cover nonrenewal, automatic termination, and other termination provisions which are just as complex as the part already quoted.

The claim representative will, of course, read the particular policy involved in the coverage provided for the occurrence which is being investigated, but it can be seen that some provisions of the "plain language" policies do not do much to improve the ability of an insured to understand his policy.

[1] Written Notice of Cancellation

Although the clauses previously quoted call for "written" notice, in some policies this is not essential. Written notice is usually required because of the difficulty in establishing verbal notice.

Written notice may be given in three ways:

1. Personal Service.
2. Registered Mail.
3. Regular Mail.

The method of serving notice is also sometimes guided by statute and (as previously stated) if the statute is explicit, it is of course also paramount.

If a policy stipulates notice by mailing, the use of regular mail is usually sufficient compliance with the provision. Proof that such mailing was made may be obtained on a post office receipt form established for that purpose.

Ordinarily, if the policy does not designate the method of giving notice, proof of receipt of notice is usually necessary. When proof of receipt is necessary, registered mail (return receipt requested) is preferable.

In some instances, regular mail may even be preferable to registered mail, since it has been held that by sending the cancellation notice by registered mail, the company had undertaken the duty of seeing that the insured received the notification.

To whom notice is to be sent. Notice of cancellation must of course be sent to all proper parties. Is the insured's personal broker a proper person to receive notice in the absence of any direct notice to the insured? The answer is "no," since it has been held that the insured's broker is an agent of the insured only to the extent of obtaining the policy and that his agency terminates with the procurement of such policy.

§ 20.06[2]   CASUALTY INSURANCE CLAIMS

The ordinary cancellation clause requires the cancellation notice to be sent to the insured at the address shown on the policy. In some instances the last known address may be added or substituted.

As long as the insured does not deny receiving notice of cancellation, there is no problem. The difficulty arises when an accident has intervened and the insured denies receiving the cancellation notice. Strict compliance with the terms of the policy in this respect, is usually sufficient. However, if the last known address of the insured differs from that listed on the policy, it would certainly be preferable to send cancellation notice to both addresses in order to avoid any possible difficulties.

Effective date and time of cancellation. Once again the terms of the policy contract are controlling unless they conflict with statute, in which event the statutory time supersedes that given in the policy.

Occasionally, the wording in the policy will call for the effective date of termination to be some days after receipt of notice. Any such wording of course forces the carrier to prove that notice of cancellation was actually received.

The courts have ordinarily held that the expiration time is midnight of the day mentioned. It has also been held that an extra day is to be allowed if the last day falls on a Sunday or a legal holiday.

[2] Cancellation Because of Nonpayment of Premium

Probably the greatest number of suits concerning the cancellation provision have to do with the late payment of insurance premiums. Any notice of accident that is dated on the same date as a premium payment, especially where proper cancellation notice has been given together with the premium notice by the insurer, should be regarded with a proper degree of skepticism and investigated thoroughly.

In some instances the mere mailing of the premium is not enough, unless this was common practice in the company involved.[48]

In a Rhode Island case,[49] the court held that that cancellation was ineffective because receipt of cancellation notice had not been produced, despite the fact that the statute did not require it.

---

[48] Colo.: Thomason v. Schnorr, 587 P.2d 1205 (App. 1978).
[49] Liquori v. Aetna Cas. & Sur. Co., 384 A.2d 308 (1978).

In the case of *Norred v. Employers Fire Ins. Co.*,[50] the Louisiana court held that proof of mailing establishes a rebuttable assumption that the notice of cancellation was received.

Many jurisdictions hold that the notice of cancellation must actually be received by the insured to become effective, but some of them accept proof of mailing as being equivalent to receipt of the notice.[51]

In most jurisdictions, acceptance of the delayed premium waives any previous cancellation notice.[52]

Opinion is unanimous that cancellation may not be made retroactively.[53]

Courts have held that notice of cancellation must be given to all insureds, whether they be named, designated, or otherwise included as insureds.[54]

Cancellation notice must be definite and certain. Any ambiguities will be decided in favor of coverage and a mere request for payment of premium is not enough to enforce cancellation.[55]

[3] Renewal of Coverage

Renewal of policy coverage can be accomplished by incorporation in the policy provisions. The insured does not have to rely on a specific notice of renewal.[56]

---

[50] 460 So. 2d 1147 (App. 1984).
[51] **Kan.:** Richmeier v. Williams, 675 P.2d 372 (App. 1984).
[52] **Ga.:** Smith v. Allstate Ins. Co., 573 F.2d 707 (1983).
[53] **Ill.:** Green v. J.C. Penney Auto. Ins. Co., 722 F.2d 330 (7th Cir. 1983).
Mo.: Wright v. Newman, 599 F. Supp. 1178 (1984).
[54] **Mich.:** Lease Car of Amer. v. Rahn, 347 N.W.2d 444 (1984).
[55] **Conn.:** Travelers Ins. Co. v. Hendrickson, 472 A.2d 356 (1984).
Pa.: Federal Kemper Ins. Co. v. Commonwealth of Pa., 469 A.2d 344 (1984).
[56] **Ga.:** Wheeler v. Standard Guar. Ins. Co., 309 S.E.2d 805 (App. 1983); Prudential Property & Cas. Ins. Co. v. Pritchett, 313 S.E.2d 706 (1983).

CHAPTER 21

Liability for Bad Faith and Punitive Damages

§ 21.01 In General
    [1] Original Concept
    [2] Fraud or Bad Faith Doctrine
    [3] Negligence
        [a] Determining the Insurer's Negligence
        [b] Absolute Liability for Excess Verdict
        [c] Suggestions for Defensive Action
§ 21.02 Conditional Time Limitation Offers
§ 21.03 Guiding Principles for Primary and Excess Insurers
§ 21.04 Unfair Claim Settlement Practices Statutes
§ 21.05 Checklist for the Investigation of Excess Liability Claims
§ 21.06 Insurance Coverage for Punitive Damages
    [1] Public Policy
    [2] Insurance Coverage
    [3] Vicarious Liability—Employer-Employee Relationships
§ 21.07 Bibliography

§ 21.01 In General

Although the policy does not say this in so many words, the claim representative should not forget that besides the existence of the obligation to defend, the courts have held that the insurer, under certain circumstances, also has the duty to settle if the settlement is reasonable and commensurate with the liability, injuries and damages involved. The penalty for arbitrary refusal to do so may be the payment of a judgment not only up to the amount of the policy limit, but beyond it as well.

In recent years, the question of responsibility for a verdict in excess of the policy limits has been one of ever-increasing concern to insurance companies. Today, some attorneys for the plaintiff make it routine practice to inform the insured or his personal attorney that he has made a demand within the policy limits and that the case can therefore be settled by the insurance company without subjecting the insured to the risk of an excess verdict. The insured, understandably concerned, then brings pressure on the company to settle, even though the demand may be much more than the claim is worth.

[1] Original Concept

The insurance policy was originally interpreted strictly in accordance with the letter of the contract. This interpretation allowed for no deviation whatsoever. If an insurance company refused to settle a claim within the policy limits, for any reason or for no reason at all, the insured had absolutely no recourse against the company no matter how much in excess of the policy limits was the verdict rendered.

The courts soon recognized the inequity of such a rigid position. It was not long before they began to make exceptions to the strict contract interpretation.

[2] Fraud or Bad Faith Doctrine

The first deviations from this original concept were made on the grounds of fraud or bad faith.

In many of the early decisions, fraud and bad faith were used synonymously or with little differentiation. The definitions of both terms were vague and indefinite. Eventually, bad faith became defined almost synonymously with negligence.

In the early cases holding fraud or bad faith necessary to make an insurance company responsible for an excess verdict, the courts made it clear that the company could not be held for mere negligence, and that some act over and above negligence was necessary to constitute bad faith.[1]

It was considered bad faith on the part of a carrier if its representative refused to settle when he really felt that a verdict would be rendered within the policy limits, or even if it felt that there was a good chance of such verdict being rendered. The only requirement in these early cases was that the attitude of the insurance carrier must not have been arbitrary. The burden of proving fraud or bad faith was on the part of the plaintiff.

Gradually, however, the courts began to enlarge and expand their interpretation of the term "bad faith," until we find that in *Tyger*

---

[1] Abrams v. Factory Mut. Liab. Ins. Co., 298 Mass. 141, 10 N.E.2d 82 (1937).

River Pine Company v. *Maryland Casualty Company*,[2] the South Carolina Supreme Court held that if an insurer *negligently* failed to settle a case against the insured, such action could be interpreted as bad faith and the insurance company held responsible for an excess verdict. Other courts agreed.[3]

[3] Negligence

In recent years, the trend toward holding an insurer responsible for a verdict in excess of the policy limits on the grounds of negligence as such seems to be slowing down, but more cases seem to be using negligence in the investigation or settlement negotiations as evidence of bad faith.[4]

In December 1947, the New Hampshire Supreme Court in the case of *Dumas* v. *Hartford Accident & Indemnity Co.*,[5] handed down a decision reaffirming the position it had previously taken in 1919 and 1924, but stated it more clearly and comprehensively.

In this decision it was held that the carrier was responsible for an excess verdict because it was guilty of negligence in failing to settle the claim within the policy limits. No longer did the courts use the subterfuge of bad faith. It was flatly stated that negligence, and negligence only, was necessary to hold the insurance company responsible for the excess verdict. The sole question presented to the jury was whether the danger of adverse verdict was so great that a reasonable man in similar circumstances would have avoided going to trial and would have settled the claim. The court ruled that the standard of care is at least that which a reasonable man would exercise in the management of his own affairs. The *Dumas* decision was shortly followed by others which held similarly.

---

[2] 170 S.E. 346 (1933).
[3] Ala.: Nationwide Mut. Ins. Co. v. Smith, 194 So. 2d 505 (1967).
Ark.: Members Mut. Ins. Co. v. Blissett, 492 S.W.2d 429 (1973).
N.H.: Allstate Ins. Co. v. Reserve Ins. Co., 373 A.2d 339 (1977).
Ill.: Kavanaugh v. Interstate Fire & Cas. Co., 342 N.E.2d 118 (App. 1976).
S.C.: Chitty v. State Farm Mut. Auto. Ins. Co., 36 F.R.D. 37 (1965).
[4] Fla.: Thomas v. Lumbermen's Mut. Cas. Co., 424 So. 2d 36 (App. 1982).
Md.: Sobus v. Lumbermen's Mut. Cas. Co., 393 F. Supp. 661 (1975).
Tenn.: Perry v. U.S.F.&G Co., 359 S.W.2d 1 (1962).
[5] 56 A.2d 57 (1947).

[a] Determining the Insurer's Negligence

Since negligence is, of course, a question of fact for a jury to determine, one must be very realistic about the chances of an insurance company in such an action before the average jury. Decisions upon which a determination of negligence could be made have been based on the following factors:

1. Whether the case could have been justifiably settled within the policy limits.
2. Whether the investigation was adequate.
3. Whether there was a proper and thorough investigation.
4. Whether the insurance company was remiss in any way in settlement negotiations.
5. Whether there was adequate trial preparation.
6. Whether proper defense was made and whether there was proper defense counsel.
7. Whether the trend in verdicts in any particular locality is excessively high.
8. Whether the insured was kept advised of all negotiations.

[b] Absolute Liability for Excess Verdict

A great effort has been made to create responsibility for an excess verdict in *any* case where the insurer refused to settle within the policy limits. This is of course the ultimate situation that would surely destroy negligence as a measure for responsibility in automobile cases and would go far toward destroying our entire civil-tort system. It is ridiculous to the point of utter absurdity and yet some justices have given it serious consideration.

Another area of concern has been a recent rash of punitive damage awards with which the insurers have been saddled by so-called judicial reasoning which is indeed farfetched in this instance.

[c] Suggestions for Defensive Action

Aside from paying whatever may be demanded, there is no way of absolutely preventing the possibility of an excess suit except by having higher policy limits. This does not mean, however, that a claim adjuster should assume a defeatist attitude if faced with this situation. There are some steps that can be taken that should at least minimize the possibility of an excess verdict:

1. **Notify the insured.** This is the first step to be taken as soon as suit has been started and the insurer has notice that a judgment is demanded in excess of his policy limits. This notice should inform the insured that although the carrier will defend him and take every precaution to protect his interests, he nevertheless has the right to engage counsel in his own behalf and at his own expense to collaborate with the insurance company's defense counsel.

   Where there is any conflict of interests between the insured and the insurance company, most jurisdictions now hold that the insurer must pay the fee of separate counsel for the insured, even if the insured chooses his own counsel.[6]

2. **Prompt and adequate investigation** is an absolute must. When an insured accepts a policy of insurance, he agrees by the terms of the policy to leave the investigation, defense, and settlement negotiations in the hands of the insurance carrier. The courts, therefore, have held that it is the duty of the insurer to make prompt and adequate investigation, engage competent counsel, and make adequate trial preparation. It has further been held that the insurer must be fair and reasonable in its settlement negotiations and it is of utmost importance that no arbitrary or unreasonable position be taken with reference to these negotiations.

3. **Obtain comprehensive opinion of liability and settlement value** from counsel, and if this is done do not disregard it. Remember that the insurer's attorney's opinion may be read into the record on a suit for payment of an excess verdict.

4. **Keep the insured advised** of all developments so that there can be no question of bad faith or deception. It would obviously be bad faith on the part of an insurance company to attempt to avoid responsibility by trying to keep an insured from knowing about an offer of settlement made within the policy limits.

5. **In some instances it may be advisable to obtain an unbiased opinion** from some competent attorneys who have no connection with the action involved.

---

[6] **Cal.:** Nike, Inc. v. Atlantic Mut. Ins. Co., 578 F. Supp. 948 (1983).
Ill.: Murphy v. Urso, 430 N.E.2d 1079 (1981).
N.Y.: Allstate Ins. Co. v. Long, 446 N.Y.S.2d 742 (App. 1981).

6. **Make some reasonable offer** or counteroffer to a demand within the policy limits.[7]

Some courts have given consideration to the past practices and reputation of an insurance company, and have held that if an insurer can show an established policy of making fair settlements and a record that is absent from past unreasonable refusals to settle, it can be assumed that refusal to settle in the case under consideration was probably justified.[8]

Whether used as a defensive or offensive measure by an insurer, it can be effectively telling in any claim for excess liability, for that insurer to be able to show that it has done everything within reason to impress the need for fair dealing on its claim personnel.

Some important measures that it can take is for the insurer to send written notice, by way of bulletins, manuals, general memoranda, special notices, or all of these, instructing all claim personnel that the insurance company subscribes to a fair claim practices policy. This can be highlighted by reference to any unfair claim practices legislation or regulation that may be applicable, and to a general condemnation of those practices held to be unfair in these regulations, which are pretty uniform in nature.

§ 21.02 Conditional Time Limitation Offers

Just a few years ago, it was generally accepted that if an offer to settle within the policy limits was only conditional or indefinite, failure to accomplish settlement was not considered to be bad faith.[9] Attitudes of the courts have changed considerably and presently the trend is in the other direction. At the present it is generally accepted that a conditional offer to settle within a specified time is a valid offer to which an insurer must give proper consideration, and refusal to accept a reasonable offer in the alloted time may hold the insurer responsible for a verdict in excess of the policy limits unless there was no reasonable opportunity to settle within the time limitation. An offer made subsequent to the expiration of the time limitation may not even vitiate bad faith in some instances.

---

[7] *See* Magarick, *Excess Liability* (New York: Clark Boardman Co. Ltd., 1982).
[8] **N.H.:** Douglas v. U.S.F.&G. Co., 81 N.H. 371, 127 A. 708 (1924).
Vt.: Johnson v. Hardware Mut. Cas. Co., 109 Vt. 481, 1 A.2d 817 (1938).
Wis.: Berk v. Milwaukee Auto. Ins. Co., 245 Wis. 597, 12 N.W.2d 834 (1944).
[9] **Tex.:** Danner v. Iowa Mut. Ins. Co., 340 F.2d 427 (5th Cir. 1964).

In *De Laune v. Liberty Mut. Ins. Co.*,[10] the court held that the time limit of a conditional offer must be reasonable in order to hold the insurer responsible for nonacceptance of such an offer within the time limit set. This case further held that a ten-day limit which gave no reasonable opportunity for the insurer to make a proper investigation was unreasonable. To hold otherwise would provide an opportunity for the plaintiff's attorney to "set up" the insurer for just such an action without justification.

The time set for acceptance of a conditional offer must be reasonable in order to give the insurer a proper chance to investigate the claim or suit. All circumstances surrounding the conditional offer must be considered in order to determine if the time limitation was reasonable.[11]

A conditional offer with a twenty-eight-day deadline was held ineffective where an offer of the policy limit was made at a pretrial conference and refused. This delay of three months, and forty days after the expiration of the time limitation, was held to be unreasonable but the plaintiff failed to show why the offer made after the expiration date was not acceptable.[12]

On the other hand, a conditional offer of thirty days was held effective even though the insurers agreed to the figure two days after the expiration date.[13] The time limitation offer with a "short fuse" can be so obviously made with the object of setting-up the insurer for a subsequent suit for liability in excess of the policy limits that I believe the courts should take a good hard look at every such case to see if there was any reasonable cause for such a short time limitation, and to see if the insured was prejudiced in any way by a short delay in acceptance after the time limitation had run.

Where the policy limits are low compared to the nature of the injury and the liability, the conditional offer of settlement for the extent of the policy limits, with a "short-fuse" time limitation, is being received by insurance companies in ever increasing numbers.

In most instances such offers, usually in letter form, are set-ups for the instituing of a bad faith action with the hope that the offer will not be accepted within the time limit.

---

[10] 314 So. 2d 601 (Fla. App. 1975).

[11] Grumbling v. Medallion Ins. Co., 392 F. Supp. 717 (Ore. 1975) (nevertheless, the fifteen-day limitation in this case was held to be reasonable).

[12] Ill.: Adduci v. Vigilant Ins. Co., 424 N.E.2d 645 (App. 1980).

[13] U.S.: Kivi v. Nationwide Mut. Ins. Co., 695 F.2d 1285 (1983).

§ 21.03   CASUALTY INSURANCE CLAIMS

These types of letters deserve extra careful handling. The short time limitation puts the adjuster on the spot since he usually will not have the settlement authority to issue a check immediately. At this point it is a race to get the needed authority, and when supervisors and home office examiners begin to ask about confirmation of injury and liability in writing, the time has usually run out.

The claim adjuster should not be deceived by any off-hand, unwritten assurances that the lawyer's letter is merely pro-forma and will not be acted upon, or by any verbal extensions of the time limitation.

If the situation is such that the policy limits and the demand are not within the authority of the branch office, and there is no way that approval of the settlement figure can be obtained soon enough, then it is necessary to obtain an immediate reply to the plaintiff's attorney's letter.

It is suggested that such a letter be drafted by in-house counsel or some other counsel. The letter should point out that the time limitation is unreasonable and should explain why, giving a reasonable explanation. Assurance should be given the plaintiff's lawyer that the investigation will be completed as promptly as possible. If the plaintiff's lawyer is withholding vital information, this should be pointed out and request made for his cooperation. The letter should be drafted and sent as soon as possible.

In this kind of a situation, it is essential that a requirement that every "i" be dotted and every "t" be crossed should be waived, if warranted. A couple of phone calls may be able to confirm liability and injury, or they may be self-evident and if this is so, and it is suspected that this is an attempted set-up, a draft or check should be prepared with the release and hand delivered to the plaintiff's attorney and a receipt obtained. Then, if the plaintiff's counsel backs down on his offer, his bad faith hopes may well be finished, assuming nothing untoward happens thereafter. In any event the claim representative should make sure that acceptance of the offer made can be documented in court.

§ 21.03   Guiding Principles for Primary and Excess Insurers

A policy of fair dealing can also be highlighted by showing that the insurance company subscribes to the Guiding Principles for primary and excess insurers.

In 1974, the Claim Executive Council of the American Insurance Association, the American Mutual Insurance Alliance and some unaffiliated insurers proposed to their member companies the adoption of some guiding principles concerning the settlement and trial decisions of liability claims and suits in which both a primary and an excess insurer are involved. For those insureds that accepted the recommendations they would "provide standards of conduct which, if followed by insurers in the handling of claims, would reduce, if not eliminate the incidence of controversy between primary and excess insurers" and "provide a format for the resolution of problems involving the interaction of primary and excess insurance coverages and their applicable policy limits. It is implicit in these guiding principles that the primary insurer in its dealings with an excess insurer voluntarily adopt those standards of conduct which the law imposes upon the primary insurer in its dealings with the insured and that the excess insurer voluntarily refrain from any conduct which might create additional difficulty for the primary insurer in the handling of a case or increase the danger of the primary insurer's being liable in excess of its policy limits."

The recommendations continue with the statement that "nothing in these principles shall in any way abridge the rights or the duties owed to the insured, indeed it is believed that the insured's interest will be better served by adherence to these principles."

The recommendations are:

1. The primary insurer must discharge its duty of investigating promptly and diligently even those cases in which it is apparent that its policy limit may be consumed.

2. Liability must be assessed on the basis of all relevant facts which a diligent investigation can develop and in the light of applicable legal principles. The assessment of liability must be reviewed periodically throughout the life of a claim.

3. Evaluation must be realistic and without regard to the policy limit.

4. When from evaluation of all aspects of a claim, settlement is indicated, the primary insurer must proceed promptly to attempt a settlement, up to its policy limit if necessary, negotiating seriously and with an open mind.

5. If at any time, it should reasonably appear that the insured may be exposed beyond the primary limit, the primary insurer shall give prompt written notice to the excess insurer, when known, stating the results of investigation and negotiation, and giving any other informa-

tion deemed relevant to a determination of the exposure, and inviting the excess insurer to participate in a common effort to dispose of the claim.

6. Where the assessment of damages, considered alone, would reasonably support payment of a demand within the primary policy limit but the primary insurer is unwilling to pay the demand because of its opinion that liability either does not exist or is questionable and the primary insurer recognizes the possibility of a verdict in excess of its policy limit, it shall give notice of its position to the excess insurer when known. It shall make available its file to the excess insurer for examination, if requested.

7. The primary insurer shall never seek a contribution to a settlement within its policy limit from the excess insurer. It may, however, accept contribution to a settlement within its policy limit from the excess insurer when such contribution is voluntarily offered.

8. In the event of a judgment in excess of the primary policy limit the primary insurer shall consult the excess insurer as to further procedure. If the primary insurer undertakes an appeal with the concurrence of the excess insurer the expense shall be shared by the primary and the excess insurer in such manner as they may agree upon. In the absence of such an agreement, they shall share the expense in the same proportions that their respective shares of the outstanding judgment bear to the total amount of the judgment. If the primary insurer should elect not to appeal, taking appropriate steps to pay or to guarantee payment of its policy limit, it shall not be liable for the expense of the appeal or interest on the judgment from the time it gives notice to the excess insurer of its election not to appeal and tenders its policy limit. The excess insurer may then prosecute an appeal at its own expense being liable also for interest accruing on the entire judgment subsequent to the primary insurer's notice of its election not to appeal. If the excess insurer does not agree to an appeal it shall not be liable to share the cost of any appeal prosecuted by the primary insurer.

9. The excess insurer shall refrain from coercive or collusive conduct designed to force a settlement. It shall never make formal demand upon a primary insurer that the latter settle a claim within its policy limit. In any subsequent proceedings between excess insurer and primary insurer the failure of the excess insurer to make formal demand that the claim be settled shall not be considered as having any bearing on the excess insurer's claim against the primary insurer.

It is urgently further recommended by the Council that an attempt be made to reconcile any differences between a primary and an excess insurer by arbitration; and the Council outlines rules under which such arbitration should be arranged and carried out.

The Council's recommendations, in my opinion, encompass the heart of the present day law on the subject of excess liability and if adhered to by enough insurance companies would help the position of the insured because it would avoid much internecine squabbling that hurts all parties.

These principles are a fine basis for fair dealing and if similar principles were adopted in dealing with the insured, they would go a long way toward establishing an insurer's good faith and reputation in an action for excess liability.

Some excess claims executives agree that the principles are generally praiseworthy and should be adhered to, but explain their own reluctance to sign by stressing the fact that provision 9, forbidding the excess insurer from "coercive" conduct designed to force a settlement and making it improper for the excess insurer to make a formal demand upon a recalcitrant primary carrier to settle within the policy limits of the primary insurer, takes away an essential protection they feel they must retain as a last resort. I am inclined to agree with them.

§ 21.04 Unfair Claim Settlement Practices Statutes

On March 1, 1973, the Model Unfair Claim Settlement Practices promulgated by the National Association of Insurance Commissioners was adopted as law by the state of California, and, shortly thereafter, by many other states. The Model Act was revised somewhat in 1975, and generally speaking, this model has been the basis for all of the Unfair Claim Settlement Practices statutes that have been enacted.

In view of the fact that there are differences in the statutes, each must be scrutinized in accordance with the facts and with the jurisdiction of the suit involved.

Nevertheless, some general principles are evolving in the area of third party liability claims with which we are here chiefly concerned. The statutes usually specifically exempt certain types of coverage such as workers' compensation, marine, some accident and health and life policies, and a few others.

Usually, much legal verbiage is involved in the various statutes, but basically, the following acts and attitudes are proscribed as unfair practices:

1. Misrepresentation to claimants of pertinent facts or insurance policy provisions relating to any coverages at issue.

2. Failing to acknowledge and act reasonably promptly upon communications with respect to claims arising under insurance policies.

3. Failing to adopt and implement reasonable standards for the prompt investigation and processing of claims arising under insurance policies.

4. Failing to affirm or deny coverage of claims within a reasonable time after proof of loss requirements have been completed and submitted by the insured.

5. Not attempting in good faith to effectuate prompt, fair and equitable settlements of claims in which liability had become reasonably clear.

6. Compelling insureds to institute litigation to recover amounts due under insurance policies by offering substantially less than the amounts ultimately recovered in actions brought by such insureds, when such insureds have made claims for amounts reasonably similar to the amounts ultimately recovered.

7. Attempting to settle a claim by an insured for less than the amount to which a reasonable man would have believed he was entitled by reference to written or printed advertising material accompanying or made part of an application.

8. Attempting to settle claims on the basis of an application which was altered without notice to, or knowledge or consent of the insured, his representative, agent, or broker.

9. Failing, after payment of a claim, to inform insureds or beneficiaries, upon request by them, of the coverage under which payment has been made.

10. Making known to insureds or claimants a practice of the insurer of appealing from arbitration awards in favor of insureds or claimants for the purpose of compelling them to accept settlements or compromises less than the amount awarded in arbitration.

11. Delaying the investigation or payment of claims by requiring an insured, claimant, or the physician of either, to submit a preliminary claim report, and then requiring the subsequent submission of formal proof of loss forms, both of which submissions contain substantially the same information.

12. Failing to settle claims promptly, where liability has become apparent, under one portion of the insurance policy coverage in order to influence settlements under other portions of the insurance policy coverage.

13. Failing to provide promptly, a reasonable explanation of the basis relied on in the insurance policy, in relation to the facts or applicable

law, for the denial of a claim or for the offer of a compromise settlement.

As is obvious from a reading of the verbiage taken from the Model Act, it is a mixed bag of vague phrases, peppered with words like "reasonable" and "substantial." In many of the statutes subsequently enacted, such words and phrases have been replaced with specific wording giving time limitations where necessary.

It appears to be obvious that the underlying intent was to correct unfair practices in the handling and settlement of first party claims. In by far the most instances, the aggrieved party is referred to as the "insured," and even where the word "claimant" has been added or substituted, such a claimant could be a beneficiary under a first party claim.

At any rate, no reasonable person would deny that most of the transgressions listed warrant corrective action, if, as the statute usually states, the insurers are *"knowingly committing or performing (such acts) with such frequency as to indicate a general business practice."* (Italics added).

It did not take long for some states to add wording that permitted individual action for single transgressions, or for judges to disregard or circumvent the intent of the statutes. Most of the statutes by far, give evidence that the intent was to give some additional administrative power to the various state insurance commissioners to enforce, by way of warnings or fines, good settlement practices by insurers in first party claims.

In an excellent article on this subject, G. Robert Micherle and Donald Overton[14] wrote that "Since the N.A.I.C. drafters borrowed the form (Model Act) of the F.T.C. Act to create the same legislation at the state level, the interpretation of the F.T.C. Act by the federal judiciary is demonstrative of the intent of the drafters and legislators, federal and state." Such decisions overwhelmingly hold that no right of private individual action was ever intended under such Acts. The authors cite numerous cases confirming this position.[15]

Many of the recent decisions brought against insurers in third party liability claims, have held that the Unfair Claim Settlement

---

[14] "A New Extra Contractual Cloud Upon the Horizon: Do the Unfair Claim Settlement Practices Acts Create a Private Cause of Action?", Insurance Counsel Journal, April 1983.

[15] *Id.* pp. 263-64, fn. 4.

Practices statutes do not confer a private cause of action upon third party individuals resulting from alleged injury or damage caused by an alleged violation of such a statute.[16]

There are, however, a growing number of cases holding, to the contrary, that statutes with similar wording do permit individual suits to be brought against an insurer for breach of some section of the local Unfair Claim Settlement Practices Acts,[17] even in a state that has no direct action statute permitting suit by a third party directly against a liability insurer.[18]

The California case of *Royal Globe Ins. Co. v. Superior Court*[19] did restrict such an action by stating that it can only be brought after the original suit has been brought to a favorable conclusion. A Montana case, *Klaudt v. Flink,*[20] on the other hand, held that such an action could be brought simultaneously with the underlying original third party suit, as the Montana statute was interpreted by that court. A West Virginia case,[21] restricted recovery to those instances where the insurance company was held to have made repeated violations of the statute. The same result was implied when the Montana court decided that it was necessary to show that breaches of the statute were general business practices of a particular company before an action based on the statute could be successful.[22]

---

[16] **Colo.:** Farmers Group, Inc. v. Trimble, 691 P.2d 1138 (1984).
Ill.: Van Vleck v. Ohio Cas. Ins. Co., 471 N.E.2d 925 (App. 1985).
Kan.: Spencer v. Aetna Life & Cas. Co., 611 P.2d 149 (1980).
Mich.: Young v. Michigan Mut. Ins. Co., 362 N.W.2d 844 (1985).
Pa.: D'Ambrosio v. Pennsylvania Nat'l Mut. Cas. Ins. Co., 431 A.2d 966 (1981).
Vt.: Wilder v. Aetna Life & Cas. Co., 433 A.2d 309 (1981).
Wis.: Kranzush v. Badger State Mut. Cas. Co., 307 N.W.2d 256 (1981).
[17] **Ariz.:** Sparks v. Republic Nat'l Life Ins. Co., 647 F.2d 1127 (so stated in the statute).
Cal.: Royal Globe Ins. Co. v. Superior Court of Butts County, 153 Cal. Rptr. 842 (1979); Coleman v. Gulf Ins. Group, 200 Cal. Rptr. 619 (App. 1984).
La.: French Market Plaza Corp. v. Sequoia Ins. Co., 480 F. Supp. 821 (1979).
Mont.: Klaudt v. Flink, 658 P.2d 1065 (Mont. 1983).
Tex.: Allstate Ins. Co. v. Kelly, 680 S.W.2d 595 (App. 1985).
Va.: Morgan v. American Family Life Assur. Co., 559 F. Supp. 477 (1983).
W.Va.: Jenkins v. J.C. Penney Cas. Ins. Co., 393 N.E.2d 718 (1981).
[18] **Cal.:** Royal Globe Ins. Co. v. Superior Court, 153 Cal. Rptr. 842 (1979).
W. Va.: Jenkins v. J.C. Penney Cas. Co., 393 N.E.2d 718 (1981).
[19] 592 P.2d 329 (1979).
[20] 658 P.2d 1065 (Mont. 1983).
[21] Jenkins v. J.C. Penney Cas. Ins. Co., 393 N.E.2d 718 (1981).
[22] Klaudt v. Flink, 658 P.2d 1065 (Mont. 1983).

California, on the other hand, specifically stated that there need be only one violation to create an individual cause of action.[23] A New York decision,[24] while not directly involving the Unfair Claim Settlement Practices statute, did cite the New York Insurance Code as establishing a standard of conduct required by an insurance company in the pursuit of claim settlements.

In the case of *Farris v. U.S.F. & G. Co.*,[25] the Oregon court held that when the legislature prohibited certain claim settlement practices in their Unfair Claim Settlement Practices statute, there was nothing in the Act to indicate that the legislature intended to transform a breach of insurance contract into a tort. It further held that in the absence of any common law civil penalties having been recognized for the breach alleged in this case, the legislature provided for penalties which did not include punitive damages or damages for emotional distress.

§ 21.05 Checklist for the Investigation of Excess Liability Claims

The following checklist, suggesting steps to be taken in the event of a claim or suit for excess liability, should be helpful.

- ☐ Upon receipt of a complaint indicating an ad damnum in excess of the policy limits, if coverage is in order, an "excess ad damnum letter" should be sent to the insured containing the following essentials, and informing the insured that:
    - ○ Plaintiff has made demand in excess of the policy limits.
    - ○ Insurer will defend the action and take every precaution to protect the rights of the insured within the limits of the policy terms and conditions and within the limits of liability.
    - ○ Insurer cannot accept responsibility for any possible verdict in excess of the policy limits.
    - ○ If the insured so desires, he may engage his own counsel at his own expense (assuming there is no conflict of interests) and that the insurer will welcome collaboration with the insured's personal attorney, but that in any event, the insurer will obtain competent counsel to protect the interests of the insured.
    - ○ Call upon the insured for full cooperation and assistance.

---

[23] Royal Globe Ins. Co. v. Superior Court, 592 P.2d 329 (1979) (*but see* text accompanying note 19, *supra*).
[24] Frizzy Hairstylists, Inc. v. Eagle Star Ins. Co., 392 N.Y.S.2d 554 (1977).
[25] 587 P.2d 1015 (Ore. 1978).

§ 21.05 CASUALTY INSURANCE CLAIMS

- [ ] If the insured designates his own attorney to collaborate with the attorney appointed by the insurer, consider a request to the insured's attorney for his opinion in writing with reference to settlement value, and his attitude toward contribution to any settlement over the policy limits. Be aware of the danger of a possible over-evaluation, and never request contribution within the policy limits.
- [ ] Determine the financial responsibility of the insured.
- [ ] Make a prompt and adequate investigation of the facts of the accident, the medical information (including physical examination if advisable), and the special damages. Obtain signed statement from the insured giving his detailed version of the accident.
- [ ] Make a proper evaluation of the claim, and, where warranted, make a reasonable settlement offer. Act promptly on any reasonable demand. Do not take an arbitrary or unjustified position. Room should always be left for reasonable negotiations. If placed in an unreasonable situation by a demand which has a short time limitation, put the plaintiff's attorney and the insured on notice concerning insurer's reasonable grounds for being unable to act within the time mentioned.
- [ ] Keep the insured and his personal attorney advised of all settlement demands, offers and negotiations, and of any adverse developments of any kind.
- [ ] Appoint the best available outside defense counsel to protect the interests of the insured as well as the insurer.
- [ ] Determine if there is any conflict of interests, and if so, make sure that a separate attorney is appointed for each of the contesting parties that are covered.
- [ ] Be sure to keep defense counsel advised in writing of all developments concerning the investigation and negotiations conducted by company personnel.
- [ ] Be sure to give equal consideration to the interests of the insured as to those of the company.
- [ ] Obtain defense counsel's opinion concerning liability and settlement value, but in so doing, know that to disregard his advice may be perilous.
- [ ] In special cases, consider the advisability of obtaining legal consultation and evaluation from impartial and competent outside counsel. Use care since such opinion may put the insurer on the spot. Be prepared to follow the advice given.
- [ ] If decision has been made to try the case, make complete and adequate defense preparations.
- [ ] Establish and keep the reserve at a realistic level, commensurate with its settlement and verdict value. If the reserve greatly exceeds the last settlement offer, the position of the company may be imperilled. On the other hand a too low reserve implies improper evaluation.

- ☐ Make sure that defense counsel has sufficient settlement authority at trial or have someone with settlement authority in attendance at trial.
- ☐ Give particular consideration to any offers to settle within the policy limits after a verdict has been rendered in excess of those limits.
- ☐ Invite the insured and his personal attorney to collaborate on the advisability of making an appeal to an adverse decision.
- ☐ Upon receipt of a letter from the insured or his attorney demanding settlement within the policy limits, the letter in reply should point out:
  - ○ What actions have been taken by the insurer to protect the interests of the insured. This should include details concerning the investigation and defense of the claim or suit and any offers of settlement which were made by the insurer.
  - ○ That insured's opinion is requested concerning why he believes settlement should be made.
  - ○ That insured previously had indicated that he did not believe himself to be at fault in the accident, if this was so.
- ☐ In the event of a receipt of a demand letter which is conditioned on a reply within a limited time, make every effort to comply within the limitation set since such a letter is often a set-up where the injury is extensive and the limits low. If the settlement is advantageous, send a check or draft with the release and if necessary, hand deliver and get a receipt for the check.

§ 21.06 Insurance Coverage for Punitive Damages

[1] Public Policy

The principal argument against payment of punitive damages by an insurance company under a liability policy is that since punitive damages are awarded as punishment to the wrongdoer and as a deterrent and warning to others as well as the wrongdoer, it is therefore against public policy to permit the insured to avoid responsibility for his acts by passing the burden of punishment to his insurer. Many cases have so held. As one decision put it, insurance coverage for punitive damages is barred by the fundamental principle that one should not be permitted to take advantage of one's own wrongdoing.[26] Payment by an insurer of a judgment for punitive damages would enable people to insure themselves against punishment and gain freedom inconsistent with the establishment against their misconduct.[27]

---

[26] Jack Parker d/b/a Parman Co. v. Agricultural Ins. Co., 440 N.Y.S.2d 964 (1981).
[27] Crull v. Glebb, 382 S.W.2d 17 (Mo. App. 1964).

The cases that decide the issue on the grounds of public policy need give no further consideration to coverage or policy wording if they hold the incident is not covered by insurance. As usual, however, there is no uniformity of opinion on this subject and the present trend seems to be in the direction of simply holding that the payment of punitive damages by insurance companies is not against the public policy of that particular state, without delving too deeply into the rationale, unless there is a specific exclusion to that effect in the policy provisions.[28]

[2] Insurance Coverage

Some of the cases involving punitive damages have also based their decisions on the coverage provided by the insurance policy contract. The majority of the decisions that have stressed policy wording and coverage have ruled that the standard liability wording in which the insurance company agrees *"to pay all sums which the insured shall be obligated to pay by reason of liability imposed by law,"* includes sums awarded for punitive damages, in the absence of a specific exclusion. This line of reasoning holds that the insurance policy makes no distinction between actual and punitive damages, and in the absence of any public policy or statutory enactment to the contrary, such a controversy must be resolved in favor of the insured.[29]

Some of the early cases, decided under insurance policy wording that did not use today's standard phraseology ("legally obligated to pay"), held that punitive damage is "liability imposed by law" and therefore covered under the policy. Nevertheless, the decisions concerning the payment of punitive damages by an insurance company based on the policy wording have had strong minority support. These decisions hold that since punitive damages are not awarded as compensation (with very few exceptions) for injuries suffered because of the negligence of the insured resulting in injury to a third party, the insurance company incurs no responsibility for the payment of exemplary damages. Such decisions hold that the liability policies provide only for liability for bodily injuries.

In recent years, the insurance industry made a collective effort through its Insurance Service Office to introduce an exclusion to the

---

[28] Harrell v. Travelers Indem. Co., 567 P.2d 1013 (Ore. 1977).
[29] Abbie Uruguen Olds., Buick, Inc. v. U.S. Fire Ins. Co., 511 P.2d 783 (Idaho 1973); Grant v. North River Ins. Co., 453 F. Supp. 1361 (Ind. 1978).

liability policies that would have removed coverage for punitive damages. A few independent insurers introduced a similar exclusion. Various associations of insurance agents immediately raised vociferous objections on the basis of business disadvantage and because the proposed exclusion was too broad in that it eliminated even vicarious responsibility for punitive damages. In addition, a number of state insurance departments refused to permit any exclusion for punitive damages to be written into the policies in their states. As a result, the industry withdrew the exclusionary wording. The exclusion should have been reworded and resubmitted, but there is presently little indication that this will be done in the near future.

[3] Vicarious Liability—Employer-Employee Relationships

Suppose an insured employer, who is completely innocent of any wrongdoing, is held responsible under the doctrine of respondeat superior for the wrongful acts of an employee and an award is made for punitive damages which is payable by the employer. In a master-servant or principal-agent relationship, most often involving corporations, insurance policy coverage for damages resulting from the wrongful acts of the employee-agent would be provided to the innocent insured so long as the act was not committed at the employer's direction or ratified by him. The courts are almost unanimous in holding that any punitive damages for which the employer would be held responsible would also be properly covered by his insurance policy.

If a corporation is the insured, persuasive arguments can be made that since it can act only through its agents, it can act only vicariously and therefore should always be able to insure itself as an entity against awards for punitive damages as a result of acts of its employees or agents. In first-party cases, the courts have given this argument no real consideration. Ordinarily, in order to avoid payment of punitive damages, an insurer will have to show that the corporation, through its officers, directors or others authorized to act, either authorized or ratified the wrongful act of the employee that gave rise to the award. While some courts have held that an agent's malice may be imputed to his principal despite a lack of authorization, participation or ratification of the wrongful act, as long as such acts further the business of the principal, I cannot see any logic in imposing punitive damages on the principal while exonerating the actual wrongdoers.

Generally speaking, it has been held that if punitive damages are not recoverable against an agent, such damages may not be assessed against the principal on the basis of an agency relationship. Such rational principles of law, however, sometimes have little effect on some courts. The California Supreme Court for instance, in the case of *Egan v. Mutual of Omaha Ins. Co.*, [30] held that while the employee-agents of an insurance company who committed the wrongdoing were not liable for punitive damages, it was perfectly proper to clobber the insurance company for whom they were working with a huge punitive damage award. The question as to whether there should be any vicarious liability at all for punitive damages has, as far as I can determine, been ignored by both the courts and the legal writers.[31]

§ 21.07 Bibliography

Berg, "Losing Control of the Defense: The Insurer's Right to Select His Own Counsel," F.T.D., July 1984.

Day, "Insurer's Bad Faith Failure to Pay or Settle Insurance Claims," F.T.D., September 1983.

Fager, "Insured's Right to Independent Counsel in Conflicts of Interest Situations," Insurance Counsel Journal, January 1981.

Gallagher & German, "Resolution of Settlement Conflicts Among Insureds, Primary Insurers and Excess Insurers: Analysis of the Current State of the Law and Suggested Guidelines for the Future," 61 Neb. L. Rev. 284 (1982).

Griffin, "Excess Liability Insurance," 62 Marq. L. Rev. 375 (1979).

Harmon, "An Insurer's Liability for the Tort of Bad Faith," 42 Mont. L. Rev. 67 (1981).

Kornblum, "Plaintiff's Tactics in Extra-Contractual Damage Cases," F.T.D., August 1981.

Leair, "Insurer's Excess Liability: Evaluating Conduct and Decision in Refusal of Settlement Offers," F.I.C. Quarterly, Summer 1983.

Magarick, *Excess Liability*. New York: Clark Boardman Co. Ltd. (1982).

Mecherle & Overton, "A New Extra-Contractual Cloud Upon the Horizon: Do the Unfair Claim Settlement Acts Create a Private Cause of Action?", Insurance Counsel Journal, April 1983.

---

[30] 598 P.2d 452 (1979).

[31] For an in-depth study of Punitive Damages, *see* Magarick, *Excess Liability* (New York: Clark Boardman Co. Ltd., 1982).

Wall, "Bad Faith, Excess Liability Actions By or Against Excess Insurers," Insurance Counsel Journal, April 1981.

Williams & Jernberg, "Conflicts of Interest in Insurance Defense Litigation: Common Sense in Changing Times," F.I.C. Quarterly, Winter 1981.

CHAPTER 22

Automobile Policies and Coverages

§ 22.01　Introduction
§ 22.02　History of the Automobile Liability Policy
　　　　[1]　Indemnity versus Liability
　　　　[2]　The Omnibus Clause—Permissive User of the Automobile
　　　　[3]　Some More Recent Decisions Regarding the Omnibus Clause
　　　　[4]　Other Early Differences
　　　　[5]　Standardization
　　　　[6]　Legislation
§ 22.03　A Review and Comparison of the Family and Personal Auto Policies
　　　　[1]　Exclusions
　　　　[2]　Limits of Liability
　　　　[3]　Out of State Coverage and Financial Responsibility
　　　　[4]　Other Insurance
　　　　[5]　Reduction in Coverage in Personal Auto Form
§ 22.04　Medical Payments Coverage
　　　　[1]　Exclusions
　　　　[2]　Limit of Liability
　　　　[3]　Other Insurance
§ 22.05　Physical Damage—Motor Vehicle Claims
　　　　[1]　Coverage
　　　　[2]　Salvage
　　　　[3]　Insurable Interest
　　　　[4]　Subrogation
　　　　[5]　Decisions Concerning Policy Interpretation
　　　　[6]　Checklists
　　　　　　[a]　Total Loss Claims
　　　　　　[b]　Theft Losses Investigation
　　　　　　[c]　Fire Losses Investigation
§ 22.06　Uninsured Motorist Coverage
　　　　[1]　Exclusions
　　　　[2]　Differences in Coverage
§ 22.07　Underinsured Motorist Coverage
　　　　[1]　Multiple Claimants
§ 22.08　Conditions for All Parts of the Personal Auto Policy
　　　　[1]　Duties After an Accident
　　　　[2]　Other Conditions

§ 22.09 Business Auto Policy
§ 22.10 Garage Policy
    [1] Care, Custody or Control Exclusion

§ 22.01 Introduction

If volume of business is to be taken as a criterion, the most important policies with which the casualty insurance industry is concerned are those pertaining to the automobile. The changes that have taken place since the inception of insurance covering the automobile and its use have been many. Such changes include the addition of Medical Payments, Uninsured and Underinsured Motorists Coverage, Physical Damage, Automobile Death and Special Disability Benefits, and No-Fault (P.I.P.), among others.

Policy changes have been made in an attempt to clarify ambiguous provisions and provisions that the courts have held to be ambiguous, and because of other court decisions and statutes that have superceded the wording and even the intent of these policies.

§ 22.02 History of the Automobile Liability Policy

By 1898 the annual production of automobiles in the United States had reached the 200 mark. Speeds of 10 miles per hour were not uncommon and even 15 miles per hour was not unheard of. More and more, intrepid souls were braving the hazards of the horseless carriage and learning to drive. The hazards were many. Rearing horses, the weather, bumpy roads, and whims and temperaments of the new gasoline engine and steam boiler were some of them. Some forward-looking insurance underwriters began to believe that the automobile was here to stay and that it might provide a little sideline for the Teams policies then being sold.

The automobile liability policy, first written shortly before the turn of the century, was an outgrowth of the Teams Liability policy which preceded it by a few years and the early Automobile policies were written on Team forms.

[1] Indemnity versus Liability

Probably the greatest difference between the earliest automobile liability policies and the later forms was the fact that the early policies were indemnity contracts. This meant that the insured must have suffered a loss by payment of a judgment before he was entitled to make any recovery from his insurance carrier. Since coverage for defense costs came later, the indemnity form of contract worked a double hardship on the insured by making him go through the trouble of defending a suit and paying the defense costs as well. Accordingly, the state legislatures started to enact insurance laws requiring the "payment on behalf of" interpretation on all such policies. At the same time, insurers began to write liability policies as we now know them, rather than indemnity contracts.

Today, there are no indemnity policies in the ordinary liability coverages applicable in this country. They are all liability contracts and accordingly become effective as soon as an accident occurs.

[2] The Omnibus Clause—Permissive User of the Automobile

While it is apparent that the underlying underwriting theory in automobile liability insurance in this country right from its inception was that the hazard should follow the vehicle, up until 1918 the basic policy covered only the named insured. To be sure, additional coverage could be purchased for other drivers but these had to be added by endorsement.

The Omnibus Clause, in a form that we would recognize today and which we will discuss subsequently, first appeared in 1918 when the wording in the policy extended coverage on pleasure cars to include anyone operating the car with the knowledge or consent of the insured, or any adult member of his household, excluding domestic servants.

In the light of present day experience, it is interesting to speculate on the possible effect on loss ratios if the basic theory had centered on coverage for the individual, rather than the vehicle. Such a system would certainly have made it easier to keep more accurate statistics on the accident-prone driver and permit his isolation as an undesirable insured.

When it was determined that we would not follow the then English system of insuring the driver, it became obvious that in covering the automobile it would be necessary to stipulate coverage for others who might drive or otherwise use a vehicle with the permission of the named insured.

The clause that incorporates coverage for others besides the named insured was referred to as the "omnibus clause" because it included as covered in the named insured's policy, a number of other people who, in effect, were "going along for the ride." The limitation on "other insureds" was that he or she was driving with the *permission* of the named insured or his or her spouse. The key word was always "permission" and the courts were deluged with cases trying to determine whether permission was or was not given. The restrictions concerning purpose of the trip, time limitation, geographic limitation and others were hotly debated. Secondary permission and previous approval became factors to discuss.

In the Business Auto policy the clause referred to, under "Who is Insured," states under subheading 2: "Anyone else (in addition to the named insured) is an insured while using *with your permission* [italics added] a covered auto you own, hire or borrow," except for a list of three categories that are mentioned, which are not pertinent to this discussion. It is to be noted that the word "permission" is still a key word in the definition.

However, when we look at the Personal Auto policy, what should have been clarification, has come out as double talk and confusion.

In Part A—Liability Coverage, the following three paragraphs are listed under " 'covered persons," as follows:

"1. You or any family member for the ownership, maintenance or use of any auto or trailer." The only problem seems to be the determination of who is a family member, and under "Definitions" we learn that a family member means "a person related to you by blood, marriage or adoption who is a resident of your household. This includes a ward or foster child."

"2. Any person using your covered auto." First of all, this is a blunt statement without any qualifications whatsoever. What about a thief who has stolen your auto? To find a restriction that applies to such a situation, the reader must refer to paragraph 3 which follows.

"3. For your covered auto, any person or organization but only with respect to legal responsibility for acts or omissions of a person for whom coverage is afforded under this Part." This qualification of "legal responsibility" will also be found in the Insuring Agreement of this part of the policy where it states: "We will pay damages for bodily injury or property damage for which any covered person *becomes legally responsible....*" [Italics added.] Again we meet with the words "legally responsible" which rules out the car thief unless the courts place legal responsibility on the driver for negligence in leaving the keys in the car, or for some other reason. Whether the word "permission" is in or out, a determination of legal responsibility will still involve the owner's permission to drive the vehicle.

Now we come to Exclusion 8 which states that liability coverage is not provided for any person "using a vehicle without a reasonable belief that that person is entitled to do so," and that surely opens up a can of worms.

In any event, I do not think that the Personal Auto policy improved the understanding of this provision.

Providing coverage for an omnibus insured is an exception to many of the basic principles of insurance. This coverage is provided despite the fact that the omnibus insured was not a party to the policy contract, that he paid no consideration for the coverage, and that he was not even known to the insurer and could not have been involved in any underwriting decision. In addition, an insured is responsible for knowing the terms of the policy despite the fact that an omnibus insured may not even have been aware of the fact that the automobile was insured. Obviously, the omnibus insured is subject to the same limitations as the named insured and has no rights that are greater than his.

[3] Some More Recent Decisions Regarding the Omnibus Clause

A Georgia court held that an omnibus insured must comply with all of the policy conditions before an insurer has any duty toward him as an insured.[1]

Several courts have recently held that an omnibus insured must be provided with the same coverage as the named insured.[2]

By statute, the courts of some states usually invalidate clauses purporting to restrict omnibus coverage.[3]

It is generally agreed that where lawful possession has been shown, permission to drive is implied.[4] On the other hand, a person who has no access to the insured vehicle, such as not having possession of ignition keys, or control of the vehicle, cannot be considered as a "borrower."[5]

---

[1] Mattison v. Travelers Indem. Co., 307 S.E.2d 39 (1983).
[2] **Idaho:** Automobile Club Ins. Co. v. Tyrer, 560 F. Supp. 755 (1983).
Wis.: Miller by Grindell v. Amundson, 345 N.W.2d 494 (1984).
[3] **Pa.:** Nationwide Mut. Ins. Co. v. Walter, 434 A.2d 164 (1981).
[4] **N.C.:** Stanley v. Nationwide Mut. Ins. Co., 321 S.E.2d 920 (1984).
[5] **Cal.:** Home Indem. Co. v. King 182 Cal. Rptr. 490 (App. 1982).

§ 22.02[4]   CASUALTY INSURANCE CLAIMS

Finally, a Georgia court stated that if a driver was without reasonable grounds to believe that he was entitled to drive and knew that he was not entitled to drive, it could be presumed that this was not a "reasonable belief" as required by the policy.[6]

[4] Other Early Differences

Even when the wording of the early policies made an honest attempt at specific delineations of coverage provisions (and some did not), the number of differences in the coverages provided made it extremely difficult to make a fair evaluation of the different policies offered. For instance:

1. *Bonds:* Some of the policies provided for the payment of all premiums on bonds to release attachments. Others agreed to pay an amount not in excess of the policy limits and a few made no provisions to pay any amount whatsoever.
2. *Interest on judgments:* Some policies agreed to pay all of the interest while others provided only payment on the amount in excess of the policy limits.
3. *Notice of accident:* There was originally no uniformity in the provision requiring notice of accident to the insurer.
4. *Exclusions:* The exclusions in the early policies were varied and numerous. There was an exclusion for "fraud" in some policies and the definition of the word was very broad. Intoxication was excluded in some early policies. In others, even the violation of a traffic ordinance was an exclusion of coverage.

[5] Standardization

In the early 1920's, the more stable insurance companies began to realize that continuation of the existing conditions involving complete lack of uniformity in the automobile liability coverages could ultimately lead to chaos and a complete lack of respect for all automobile insurance. Accordingly some of the companies got together on an informal basis and started to collaborate on policy forms, ratings, and, shortly thereafter, loss statistics.

It was apparent that some degree of uniformity would present the following advantages: (1) uniformity of language, (2) uniformity in

---

[6] Nationwide Mut. Ins. Co. v. Southern Trust Ins. Co., 330 S.E.2d 443 (1985).

rate making, (3) economy for all companies, particularly in the collection of statistical information, (4) eliminate some unfair practices, and (5) a greater combined knowledge for each company.

[6] **Legislation**

State legislation gave impetus to the standardization development because of the enactment of laws requiring standard policy provisions for automobile liability coverage. The disadvantages to the public at large had become obvious. Unfortunately, as often happens, in their haste to correct an existing evil, they created some errors in the wording of policy provisions. Once the insurance industry recognized the need for change however, revisions shortly followed each other so that in many instances the new policy wording was even more liberal than the statutory requirements. In fact, much of the statutory insurance wording was taken from standard policy provisions.

The program for standardization of the automobile policy was the result of joint committee deliberations of the National Bureau of Casualty and Surety Underwriters, the American Mutual Alliance, and the Committee on Automobile Insurance Law of the American Bar Association. The main objectives were to be standardization of the liability or third party provisions of the automobile policy rather than of the entire policy itself.

The Basic Standard Automobile Liability policy has undergone many changes since it was first promulgated in 1936. In addition to these changes, a new major form was introduced under the name of the Family Automobile policy in 1956, which itself was subsequently revised several times. The Special and Package Automobile forms were introduced in 1959 and these policies have also been drastically revised over the years, followed by the Personal Auto policy.

The Garage Liability policy, which includes many elements of the public liability policies in addition to automobile coverage, was first promulgated in 1935 and this policy has also been drastically revised over the years.

In the early 1950's, Uninsured Motorists coverage was adopted by the insurance industry in answer to a great need for protection of some sort against injury arising out of an uninsured automobile.

Finally, the change which has not only rocked the insurance industry, but great segments of the legal profession and general public as well, is the trend toward "no-fault" legislation which is changing the entire concept of automobile liability insurance. All of these changes and developments will be discussed subsequently.

§ 22.03 A Review and Comparison of the Family and Personal Auto Policies

When a few of the independent insurance companies introduced automobile liability insurance policies in readable English rather than legalese, it became obvious that the rest of the industry would soon have to follow suit or suffer the economic consequences. Enter the Personal Auto policy, developed by the Insurance Services Office, which will replace both the Family Automobile and the Special Package liability policies.

The average insured who has no legal training, will inevitably encounter difficulties in understanding the meaning of policy provisions that have been variously interpreted, even by lawyers and judges.

While some of the coverages have been changed, we will discuss both the changes and the language of the provisions which have not been basically changed in intent. There is no better place to start than the introductory paragraph of both policies. The Family Automobile Liability policy reads as follows:

> (Insurer) agrees with the insured, named in the declarations made a part hereof, in consideration for the payment of the premium and in reliance upon the statements in the declarations and subject to all of the terms of this policy:

Forty words, full of legal jargon, which, translated into English in the Personal Auto policy, comes out as:

> In return for payment of the premium and subject to all the terms of this policy, we agree with you as follows:

Twenty-two perfectly good and understandable words that say exactly the same thing as the more complicated forty.

Under the heading "Definitions," the Personal Auto policy then goes on to explain what "you," "we," and similar terms mean. A spouse residing in the same household, is included as "you." A passenger auto, leased for at least six months, is deemed an owned auto, and covered autos are defined specifically. This section also defines "family member," "occupying" (which includes in, upon, getting in, on, out or off the vehicle), and "trailer."

The policy is divided into six parts, A to F. Part A includes "Liability Coverage," "Supplementary Payments," "Exclusions," "Limits of Liability," "Out of State Coverage," "Financial Responsibility Required," and "Other Insurance."

The introductory paragraph under "Liability Coverage" is clear and concise, but I am not at all sure that any wording, no matter how intelligible, will end the controversy concerning when an insurer's duty to defend the insured ends.

The duty to defend wording of the Family Automobile Liability form was the result of many changes, all intended to terminate the duty to defend when the policy limits were exhausted. The wording of the final Family form reads: "and the company shall defend any suit alleging such bodily injury or property damage and seeking damages which are payable under the terms of this policy." It was, in my opinion, a step backward in the attempt to define the limitations on the duty to defend, which the Personal Auto form tries to correct once again, as follows: "Our duty to settle or defend ends when our limit of liability for this coverage has been exhausted."

This is the kind of wording that I have been urging, and, to my mind, is the most explicit that the industry has come up with to date. There are, however, still some situations that will prevent an insurer from walking away from the defense of a suit if to do so will leave the insured in a precarious position.[7]

The latter part of the "Liability Coverage" section is, in my opinion, not well thought out and part of it is still written in turgid language.

"Covered person," for instance, is defined in part as "any person using your covered auto." I am sure that this wording was supposed to eliminate most of the legal ramifications involved in the omnibus clause concerning permissive use of the automobile and the question of second permittee, etc. Here is one example of oversimplification because, as previously stated, in order to be sure that a car thief is not a covered insured, one must refer to Exclusion 11 which states that "We do not provide liability coverage: For any person using a vehicle without a reasonable belief that the person is entitled to do

---

[7] For a full discussion of this subject, *see* Magarick, *Excess Liability* (New York: Clark Boardman Co. Ltd. 1982).

so." This exception could simply have been added to the definition of a "covered person."

[1] Exclusions

The Exclusions provisions of the Personal Auto policy are located in Part A of that policy. The exclusions are introduced very effectively by the statement that "We do not provide liability coverage" and are then followed by 12 exclusions, so numbered.

Exclusion number 1, involving intentional injury, has been changed from the Family form (b) which reads: "to bodily injury or property damage caused intentionally by or at the direction of the insured" to: "any person who intentionally causes bodily injury or property damage."

Other exclusions are self-explanatory and changes from the previous form are minor. It is obvious that any claim representative who handles automobile liability claims must have enough knowledge of the exclusions so as to recognize the need for further scrutiny when a pertinent coverage problem arises.

[2] Limits of Liability

The Family form has separate limits of liability for one person and for all persons in any one *occurrence,* and a separate limit for property damage. The liability limits include "damages for care and loss of services."

This provision has been radically changed to a single limit of liability which applies to one or any number of persons injured, and includes property damage as well, so long as all damages arise as a result of any one automobile "accident." It is to be noted that the word "occurrence" in the Family form has been changed to "accident," which replaced the former change from accident to occurrence.

This provision goes on to state that "this is the most we will pay regardless of the number of covered persons, claims made, vehicles or premiums shown in the Declarations, or vehicles involved in the auto *accident."* (Italics added).

If separate limits are required by state law, the policy states that "We will apply the limit of liability . . . . required by law for bodily and property damage liability. However, this provision does not change our total limit of liability."

The single limit, in use in England, is a good step forward in terms of understandability, but does enlarge the property coverage considerably.

[3] Out of State Coverage and Financial Responsibility

The clause entitled "Out of State Coverage" is new to the Personal Auto policy. Section 1 of this provision includes a part of the Family "Financial Responsibility Laws" provision and states:

> If an auto accident to which this policy applies occurs in any state or province other than the one in which your covered auto is principally garaged, we will interpret your policy for the accident as follows:
>
> 1. If the state or province has a financial responsibility or similar law specifying limits of liability for bodily injury or property damage higher than the limit shown in the Declarations, your policy will provide the higher specified limit.

It the goes on to add:

> 2. If the state or province has a compulsory insurance or similar law requiring a nonresident to maintain insurance whenever the nonresident uses a vehicle in that state or province, your policy will provide the required minimum amounts and types of coverage.
>
> No one will be entitled to duplicate payments for the same elements of loss as a result of the application of this provision.

Gone are the limitations of the Family form to the effect that the required limits be "in no event in excess of the limits of liability stated in this policy." In fact, as already quoted, the policy specifically states that the policy limits will, if necessary, be increased to the amount required in any out of state accident.

Omitted also is the agreement in the Family form "to reimburse the company for any payment made by the company which it would not have been obligated to make under the terms of this policy except for the agreement contained in this paragraph."

[4] Other Insurance

The intent of this provision has not been changed in the Personal form. The verbiage, however, has been reduced from a layman's nightmare of 84 confusing words to an understandable 51 words.

[5] **Reduction in Coverage in the Personal Auto Form**

Several minor reductions in coverage have been made in addition to those already mentioned. Payments for bail bonds required as a result of a traffic violation not related to an automobile accident will not be made under the Personal form.

The First Aid provision of the Family form has also been eliminated in view of the fact that Medical Payments coverage is still available and because first aid in effect, merely duplicated most of the liability areas already covering such an expenditure.

§ 22.04 Medical Payments Coverage

The wording of Part II of the Family Automobile Liability policy entitled "Expenses for Medical Services" has been simplified and condensed in the Personal form, Part B entitled "Medical Payments Coverage."

The Family form is divided into two parts, namely Divisions 1 and 2, with subdivisions (a) and (b) in Division 1 and further subdivisions (1) and (2) under (b) of Division 2.

All of this has been rearranged in the Personal form, which simply states that:

> We will pay reasonable expenses incurred for necessary medical and funeral services because of bodily injury caused by accident and sustained by a covered person. We will pay only those expenses incurred within three years from the date of the accident.

It will be noted that the Family form limiting payment for "all reasonable expenses incurred within *one* year from the date of the accident" has been increased to "those expenses incurred within *three* years from the date of the accident." (Italics added).

The same provision in the Personal form then goes on to define "Covered person" in this part, to include:

> 1. You or any family member while occupying, or as a pedestrian when struck by, a motor vehicle designed for use mainly on public roads or by a trailer of any type.
>
> 2. Any other person while occupying your covered auto.

Omitted from the introductory paragraph of the Personal form, are the qualifying words of the Family form limiting coverage "while occupying a non-owned automobile, but only if such person has, or reasonably believes he has, the permission of the owner to use the automobile and the use is within the scope of such permission," which is repeated at the end of Division 2, subdivision (b) (2) in the Family form.

These restrictions concerning permissive use have been transferred to Exclusion 7 in the Personal form, which covers the same ground in one simple sentence which will be quoted subsequently.

Another change from the Family form, which includes medical payments coverage under Division 1, subdivision (c) "through being struck by an automobile or by a trailer of any type" reads in the Personal form "when struck by, a motor vehicle designed for use mainly on public roads or by a trailer of any type." The apparent intent is to make clear that coverage is provided if the individual is *struck* by a motorcycle.

[1] Exclusions

There are ten exclusions in Part B of the Personal Auto policy that apply to Medical Payments coverage, and which are so numbered, in place of the rather involved lettered exclusions with subdivisions, contained in the Family form.

As with the liability exclusions, these use an introductory sentence to the effect that: We do not provide Medical Payments Coverage for any person:

"1. For bodily injury sustained while occupying a motorcycle." It has already been pointed out that Medical Payments coverage *is* provided for a person who is *struck* by a motorcycle, but this new exclusion makes it clear that injury or death sustained while *occupying* a motorcycle is *not* covered.

"2. For bodily injury sustained while occupying your covered auto when it is being used to carry persons or property for a fee. This exclusion does not apply to a share-the-expense car pool." Exclusion 2 replaces the old "public or livery" wording of the Family form in Exclusion (a)(1) and then specifically exempts share-the-expense car pools.

"3. For bodily injury sustained while occupying any vehicle located for use as a residence or premises." This exclusion replaces the second part of the Family form Exclusion (a) and is identical to it.

"4. For bodily injury occurring during the course of employment if workers' or workmen's compensation benefits are required or available for the bodily injury." The only mention of an exclusion for "workmen's compensation law" in the Family form is contained in (d) and refers to employment in the automobile business. The Personal form is specific in that it excludes double coverage where workers' compensation is *available* in any event, and in that respect, properly narrows the Family form coverage concerning medical payments.

"5. For bodily injury sustained while occupying or, when struck by, any vehicle (other than your covered auto) which is owned by you or furnished or available for your regular use." This exclusion is new to the Personal form. It narrows nonowned coverage when the auto is provided for the regular use of the named insured insofar as medical payments are concerned.

"6. For bodily injury sustained while occupying or, when struck by, any vehicle (other than your covered auto) which is owned by, or furnished or available for the regular use of any family member. However, this exclusion does not apply to you." This language is a little difficult to understand. It does not negate Exclusion 6 in its exception for the named insured and refers to vehicles available for the regular use of a *family member*. It too, is new to the Personal form and is an extention of Exclusion 5.

"7. For bodily injury sustained while occupying a vehicle without a reasonable belief that the person is entitled to do so." This exclusion, also new to the Personal form, incorporates the Family form provision concerning permissive use, as has already been discussed.

"8. For bodily injury sustained while occupying a vehicle when it is being used in the business or occupation of a covered person. This exclusion does not apply to bodily injury sustained while occupying a private passenger type of auto. It also does not apply to bodily injury sustained while occupying a pick-up, sedan delivery or panel truck that you own." This wording replaces Exclusion (c) (3) of the Family form and narrows it in that it is not confined to nonowned automobiles, but enlarges the types of vehicles which are excepted from this exclusion.

"9. For bodily injury caused by discharge of a nuclear weapon (even if accidental), war (declared or undeclared), civil war, insurrection, rebellion or any consequence of any of these." The only mention of any of these specific exclusions in the Family form is contained in Exclusion (e) which merely states that the policy does not apply "due to war." All else is new to the Personal form, but it is to be noted that the word "riot," usually associated with this kind of wording, is absent from this exclusion.

"10. For bodily injury from any nuclear reaction, radiation or radioactive contamination, all, whether controlled or uncontrolled or however caused, or any consequence of any of these." Here again, is a new exclusion not mentioned in the Family form.

The Family form Exclusion (b)(1) concerning "a farm type tractor or other equipment designed for use principally off public roads" and "(2) a vehicle operated on rails or crawler treads" has been eliminated in the Personal form.

However, we have already noted that "covered person 1" includes "a motor vehicle designed for use mainly on public roads or by a trailer of any type," so that the end result is about the same.

Omitted from the Personal form are also the two references to "automobile business" in the Family form Exclusions (c)(2) and (d).

[2] Limit of Liability

In addition to clarifying the intent of the policy that "This is the most we will pay regardless of the number of covered persons," etc., the Personal Auto policy adds a couple of new paragraphs not in the Family form.

For instance, a separate paragraph has been added to avoid possible duplication of expenses already payable under the Auto Liability or Uninsured Motorists coverages.

In addition, this new provision states that "No payment will be made under this coverage (medical payments) unless the injured person or his legal representative agrees in writing that any payment shall be applied toward any settlement or judgment that person receives under any Auto Liability or Uninsured Motorists Coverage provided by this policy." It thereby makes clear that the present intent of Medical Payments coverage is not meant to duplicate any payments made or to be made under any of the other bodily injury expenses, covered elsewhere.

[3] Other Insurance

While the intent of the Other Insurance provision in the Personal Auto form remains the same as in the Family form, the wording is considerably simplified and reduced by about one-third. It states that

"If there is other applicable auto medical payments insurance we will pay only our share" and explains what "our share" means.

This clause also provides that "any insurance we provide with respect to a vehicle you do not own shall be excess over any other collectible auto insurance providing payments for medical or funeral expenses," which wording is similar in intent to the more complicated wording of the Family form.

§ 22.05 Physical Damage—Motor Vehicle Claims

Claims under Automobile Physical Damage policies or coverage involve a direct contractual relationship between the insured and the insurance company. These are commonly called *first party* claims.

All claims should receive prompt and fair attention but because in this type of claim the claimant is also the insured, it presents problems of diplomacy which go a little beyond that of the ordinary liability claim, in dealing with the insured. In addition, most states have now enacted some form of Unfair Claim Practices Acts so that failure to make prompt and fair settlement, particularly of first party claims, can become extremely costly by inviting bad faith actions.

Most policies of this kind are written on an actual cash value (ACV) basis, with a deductible amount to be paid by the insured in the event of damage, in varying amounts. The coverage provides reimbursement for damage resulting from accidental loss to the automobile, its equipment and some other equipment that is permanently attached to the automobile. The policy does not cover damage intentionally or deliberately inflicted by the insured or at his direction.

[1] Coverage

Coverage for physical damage to the insured's automobile is similar enough to make some generalizations and because the mass volume of such coverage is provided under the Personal Automobile or a similar policy, it will be used as a example of this coverage.

Under the Personal Auto policy, it is provided under Part D and entitled "Coverage for Damage to Your Auto." The Insuring Agreement of Part D reads:

> We will pay for direct and accidental loss to your covered auto, including its equipment, minus any deductible shown in the Declarations.

However, we will pay for loss caused by collision only if the Declarations indicate that Collision Coverage is provided.

"Collision" is then defined as "the upset or collision with another object of your covered auto," and thereafter ten specific exceptions are made which are already otherwise stated in the insuring agreement.

In an effort to simplify previous wording which specifically defined "Comprehensive Property Damage" and "Collision," it seems to me that the result is more cumbersome than it was. "Collision" has now been excepted from all other coverages and the new definition of "Collision" excepts the formerly "Comprehensive" coverage. Nevertheless, the end result is the same and the policy provides comprehensive coverage plus collision coverage if purchased separately for an additional premium.

In former policies, there was a big to-do as to whether glass breakage fell under the comprehensive or the collision coverage. This has finally been put to rest by giving the insured the election to choose under which coverage he wants the loss to be paid.

Transportation charges are included as reimbursable charges, in the event of a total loss, in a specific amount per day for a specified number of days. What actually constitutes transportation charges is not defined.

The "Exclusions" section of this coverage lists ten exclusions which are pretty much self-explanatory. It is noteworthy to mention that while loss to equipment designed to reproduce sound is excluded, an exception is made for equipment which is "permanently installed in your covered auto."

The "mechanical breakdown" exclusion has caused quite a bit of controversy in the past since it has been argued that the exclusion referred only to the initial breakdown damage and not to any resulting or consequential damage. The weight of judicial opinion, however, favors the view that the exclusion includes the initial cause plus, in the absence of any intervening cause, any subsequent damage naturally resulting from the initial breakdown.[8]

The *Limit of Liability* clause is noteworthy since it agrees to pay "*actual cash value*" of the stolen or damaged property without defining what actual cash value means, despite all of the previous controversy revolving around these words. Then under Item 2 of this section, the insured is given the option of accepting the cost of necessary

---

[8] Fla.: Fireman's Fund Ins. Co. v. Cramer, 178 So. 2d 581 (1964).

repairs or replacement of the property. This clause no longer states that the insurer may replace the item, as previously, but that the limit of liability will be the lesser of the actual cash value or the replacement cost.

In fire claims, as well as automobile, actual cash value has been variously interpreted. Most courts hold it to mean "market value" and while definitions of market value have also often been complex, it boils down to the amount of money that it would cost to buy an automobile of the same make, model, year, and condition, together with the same covered equipment or permanent attachments and covered extras.

"Market value" already includes depreciation, which obviously depends on how many miles the car has been driven plus the care that was given to it. While guides such as the redbook have value in providing "ball park" figures as to market value, two cars of similar nature may vary greatly in the amount of depreciation that should be taken to arrive at its fair value. It's the story of the "little old lady who drives her car once a week to go to church" versus the traveling salesman.

It must be remembered that any "extras" not permanently attached to the automobile, are not covered.

[2] Salvage

If full payment has been made for the damaged automobile because the cost of repairs would exceed its market value, or because of damage that would affect its safety, the insured's car should be turned over to the insurance company along with properly executed title papers and keys and proof of loss or first party release.

In such an event it is preferable to transfer title directly from the insured to the salvage buyer if this can be arranged conveniently, since in this event storage costs are avoided and legal liability is not assumed for the wreck.

Large insurer's of physical damage policies usually have ongoing arrangements with firms that buy automobiles for parts or to reconstruct them, or they may make periodic sales of damaged automobiles on their own.

If the automobile has been stolen the insurance company has the right to return the automobile to the insured, within a reasonable or stated time when recovery has been made. In that event the insurance company must "pay for any damage resulting from the theft."

The *"Other Insurance"* clause states that "if other insurance also covers the loss, we will pay our share of the loss. Our share is the proportion that our limit of liability bears to the total of all applicable limits." In other words, a pro rata sharing.

Finally, the Physical Damage section has an "Appraisal" clause that outlines the method by which the value of the lost or damaged automobile is to be determined in the event of a disagreement that cannot be resolved between the insured and the insurance representatives.

[3] Insurable Interest

When a bank or other financial institution has loaned money to the insured to buy an automobile, it almost universally requires the insured to obtain a "Loss Payable" endorsement and to name the loss payee in the policy Declarations.

Such an endorsement must be honored by the insurance company and no first party physical damage settlement should be made without notice to the loss payee, preferably in writing. Failure to bring the loss payee into the settlement could result in double payment of the loss.

[4] Subrogation

The subject of "Subrogation, Salvage and Contribution" is discussed in a Chapter 43, *infra,* and the reader is referred thereto, for a general review of these subjects.

The first two editions of the Personal Auto policy made no special reference to subrogation, and a misunderstanding arose concerning the right of an insurer to make a subrogation claim against an insured other than the named insured. To correct this inadvertent misunderstanding, the third edition of the Personal Auto policy amended the General Provisions section so as to state specifically that the insurer does not have the right to take subrogation action against any person who is a permissive user of the covered automobile.[9]

---

[9] *See* the Personal Lines volume of the F.C. & S. Bulletins under Personal Auto, Apd-6, which states:

> The Personal Auto policy does not have a "No Benefits" clause. That of course strongly suggests that the policy drafters intended that the insurer retain its right of recovery against such entities in the event that they were at fault in damaging the covered auto. However, the Personal Auto policy does not except

[5] Decisions Concerning Policy Interpretation

Many Physical Damage insurance coverages still refer to "Comprehensive" as well as "Collision" damage and while the Personal Auto policy does not do so, this terminology will be used in this section for the sake of clarity and to make distinctions.

The usual definition of "Comprehensive Coverage" as loss "from any cause except the covered auto's collision with another object or its overturn" covers a lot of territory and leaves little room of denial of coverage.

While the glass breakage problem has been resolved, there will continue to be controversies as to whether a loss belongs under the comprehensive or the collision section of the policy, particularly because some deductibles on collision are quite high. An insured will obviously try to declare such a loss as comprehensive without any deductible if at all possible.

[6] Checklists

[a] Total Loss Claims

In settling a claim involving a total loss, the following items should be obtained:

- ☐ Original bill of sale or other evidence that title is held by the insured.
- ☐ Assignment of bill of sale from the insured to the company or salvage buyer.
- ☐ Motor Vehicle Registration Certificate properly endorsed if necessary.
- ☐ Keys to the car.
- ☐ Original insurance policy for cancellation.
- ☐ Completed Proof of Loss form and Subrogation Receipt.

In all cases involving a car declared to be a total loss due to fire, theft, or collision, report should be made to the National Automobile Theft Bureau by a representative of the member companies.

---

carriers and bailees for hire from its statement that it will not take legal action against persons using the car with a reasonable belief of being entitled to do so. The no-subrogation clause and the No Benefit to Bailee clause could very possibly be viewed by courts as being in conflict, to be resolved against the insurer.

AUTOMOBILE POLICIES AND COVERAGES § 22.05[6][c]

[b] Theft Losses Investigation

When a car insured by the company has been stolen and not recovered, the following investigation is necessary:

- ☐ The vehicle involved should be identified through the title papers and registration if available.
- ☐ If there is any reason to suspect uncertainty of ownership, change of title from the original dealer to the insured should be checked in order to be certain that the insured had lawful title to the vehicle.
- ☐ A description of the vehicle including its condition when last seen and a complete list of all accessories should be obtained. The claims person should also secure evaluation of a similar vehicle from several dealers in the locality where the loss occurred.
- ☐ A complete investigation of the facts must be made. Where there is any reason to suspect fraud, the financial status of the insured should be checked.
- ☐ The claims person should make sure that the theft has been reported to the police even though the car has been recovered.
- ☐ A report should be made to the National Automobile Theft Bureau where applicable.
- ☐ If recovery is made before the loss is paid, the policy provides that the stolen property may be returned to the insured with payment for any resultant damage thereto.

If the stolen vehicle is recovered the claims person should carefully check the damage alleged as a result of the theft against any possible old damage or wear and tear suffered while the vehicle was in the insured's possession.

[c] Fire Losses Investigation

A thorough investigation should be conducted in connection with a claim for total loss of an automobile by fire, especially if there is any suspicion of arson.

The following outline is suggested for an initial investigation of such loss:

- ☐ Details concerning the purchase of the car, including the date, cost, trade-in value, amount of mortgage due, and the amount of any payments that are past due, should be obtained.
- ☐ The mileage and general condition of the car at the time of the loss, including any defects in the motor, date last repairs were made and by whom, should also be obtained. The claims person should determine if any tools

§ 22.06   CASUALTY INSURANCE CLAIMS

or accessories were missing at the time of the inspection by the adjuster. He should check for evidence of previous collision damage.

☐ The claims person should obtain information concerning the insured's financial status in cases involving a suspicion of arson.

☐ Where warranted the claims person should obtain a signed statement from the insured of all the details of his itinerary on the date of the loss. He should check into the possible presence of any inflammatory materials that may have been in or around the car at the time of the fire. He should also get a full explanation for their presence. He should further determine if any valuable personal property was burned in the car.

☐ In the event of suspected arson, the National Automobile Theft Bureau suggests that a mechanical inspection of the vehicle be obtained to determine:

- ○ Whether the gas tank cap shows any sign of tampering or the drain plug at the bottom of the gas tank shows evidence of plier marks which would indicate that gasoline might have been drained off and used in setting a fire.
- ○ Whether there were any breaks in the gas line from the tank to the fuel pump or any tool marks that would indicate deliberate breaks or disconnections.
- ○ If there is any evidence of a short-circuit in the wiring.
- ○ Whether there is any evidence of fire on the front lower part of the motor. Accidental fire in this area can originate only in the fuel pump, carburetor, or wiring. Otherwise, the origin might be subject to suspicion.
- ○ Whether any attempt was made to extinguish the fire.

§ 22.06   Uninsured Motorist Coverage

The Family Automobile Liability policy includes "Protection Against Uninsured Motorists" in Part IV of that form. The Personal Auto policy includes it in Part C entitled "Uninsured Motorists Coverage," reversing the order and placing it before the Physical Damage coverage, rather than after.

The Personal form is much simpler, more understandable, and greatly condensed from the Family form.

The Uninsured Motorist provision in the Personal form reads:

> We will pay damages which a covered person is legally entitled to recover from the owner or operator of an uninsured motor vehicle because of bodily injury sustained by a covered person and caused by an accident. The owner's or operator's liability for those damages must arise out of the ownership, maintenance or use of the uninsured motor vehicle.

Any judgment for damages arising out of a suit brought without our consent is not binding on us.

The Personal form then goes on to define "Covered person" and "Uninsured Motor Vehicle." Surprisingly, the definition of "Uninsured Motor Vehicle" also includes what is *not* an uninsured vehicle by exception.

[1] Exclusions

There are only three specific exclusions, as such, in the Family form, with reference to this coverage, listed as (a), (b), and (c).

Exclusion 1 of the Personal form providing no coverage "While occupying, or when struck by, any motor vehicle or trailer of any type owned by you or any family member which is not insured for this coverage under this policy" replaces Exclusion (a) of the Family form which says basically the same thing in more involved language.

Exclusion 2 of the Personal form withholds coverage "If that person or the legal representative settles the bodily injury claim without our consent." This wording replaces Family form Exclusion(b).

Exclusion 3 of the Personal form provides no coverage "While occupying your covered auto when it is being used to carry persons or property for a fee." Except for share-the-expense car pools, it is a new exclusion, although not a new provision.

Exclusion 4 of the Personal form concerning "using a vehicle without a reasonable belief that the person is entitled to do so" is again a new exclusion but not a new provision since the same intent was covered elsewhere in the Family form as pointed out in the discussion of the liability provisions.

The Personal form also includes a section B in the exclusions to the effect that "This coverage shall not apply directly or indirectly to benefit any insurer or self-insurer under any workers' or workmen's compensation, disability benefits or similar law" and is similar to Exclusion (c) of the Family form.

Gone from the Personal form are the involved legal wording of the "Trust Agreement" in the Family form, which was considered redundant as a separate provision in the Personal form.

[2] Differences in Coverage

Both forms have an Arbitration clause but the Personal form no longer requires mandatory use of the American Arbitration Association in settling disputes.

Also, in accordance with the single limit form of the liability coverage in the Personal form, the Uninsured Motorists coverage in that policy follows suit.

In general, the differences in intent and scope of coverage are of a minor nature and need no further comment. The improvement in the Personal form is most obvious in the wording contained in the Uninsured Motorists provisions. Uninsured Motorist coverage will be discussed in more detail in Chapter 24, *infra*.

§ 22.07 Underinsured Motorist Coverage

For the most part, Underinsured Motorist coverage is an appendage to the Uninsured Motorist coverage, attached by endorsement. It is subject to statutory enactment, just as is the Uninsured Motorist coverage.

The endorsement defines an "Underinsured Motor Vehicle" as a "land motor vehicle of any type to which a bodily injury liability bond or policy applies at the time of the accident, but its limit for bodily injury liability is less than the limit of liability for this coverage."

This coverage is meant to cover an insured victim who is not sufficiently compensated:

1. Where the wrongdoer's liability limits conform with the financial responsibility law, but where those limits are inadequate to compensate the seriously injured victim.
2. Where the wrongdoer's limits are less than those required under the financial responsibility laws of the state within which the accident happened.
3. Where multiple claims against a wrongdoer's liability policy depletes the limits of liability so that the amount left is less than that required by the financial responsibility law or less than a fair recovery for the the victim's injury or damage.

Like Medical Payments and Uninsured Motorist coverage, Underinsured Motorist coverage is a type of first party coverage added on to an automobile liability policy, if purchased.

AUTOMOBILE POLICIES AND COVERAGES § 22.08[1]

In some states underinsured motorist coverage is mandatory, but in most, it is merely optional.

Confusion often exists as to whether a given situation falls under uninsured or underinsured coverage, but this depends on the statutes involved and the court decisions of that jurisdiction. It is advisable for the claim adjuster to realize that in some cases he may have to call for legal review in making a coverage decision.

There are two views of recovery under underinsured motorist coverage, and while both may be valid, the choice will sometimes greatly affect the victim insured. One view holds that the amount that has been paid under the underinsured liability policy should be offset by the amount paid by the wrongdoer's insurer. The other view holds that the victim's underinsured coverage is excess over the amount paid by the wrongdoer's insurer. The decision depends on the statute involved, where there is one.[10] Otherwise, it is again a matter of court interpretation of the coverage.

[1] Multiple Claimants

Where multiple claimants are involved, some decisions hold that the claimants share the policy limits on a pro rata basis, depending on the number of claimants.[11] This is unfair because a claimant with a minor injury would have a much greater chance of full recovery than one with a major injury. Other courts distribute the limits of liability on a first-come, first-served basis,[12] which, in my opinion, is even worse.

As usual, the amount recovered depends on the particular statute and the courts that are construing it, and the coverage. This could be the difference between the victim's limits and the amount received from the wrongdoer's insurer, or it could be the difference between the victim's damages and the amount received.

§ 22.08 Conditions for All Parts of the Personal Auto Policy

[1] Duties After an Accident

In the Family Automobile policy, as in other casualty policies promulgated before the Personal Auto policy, "Notice" (of accident) and

---

[10] **Minn.:** Schmidt v. Clothier, 338 N.W.2d 256 (1983).
[11] **Tenn.:** Rogers v. Farmers Mut. Ins. Co., 620 S.W.2d 476 (1981).
[12] **Ill.:** Hass v. Mid America Fire & Marine Ins. Co., 343 N.E.2d 36 (App. 1976).

"Assistance and Cooperation of the Insured" are two of the most important Conditions in these policies. These two provisions outline the duties and responsibilities of an insured to his or her insurer in the event of an accident.

In the Personal Auto policy, the Insurance Services Office has now made an intelligent change that should highlight the importance of these provisions by combining them into a separate section, Part E entitled, "Duties After an Accident or Loss." This section, in addition, has also incorporated the older provision entitled, "Insured's Duties in Event of Loss," which concerns only the Physical Damage aspects of the automobile.

These three long, involved provisions in the Family and similar forms have been condensed into a couple of simple introductory sentences followed by short, numbered duties. The intent has not been changed basically from that of the Family form.

[2] Other Conditions

Part F of the Personal Auto policy is the final section of it. It incorporates the Conditions of the Family and other casualty forms except for the ones previously mentioned.

1. *Policy Period and Territory* in the Personal form incorporates two provisions of the older forms which include a Premium clause. The wording has been changed a bit, but the intent remains the same.

2. *The Changes Clause* has been repositioned and reworded in a manner that is important in that the Personal form makes no reference to "Notice to any agent or knowledge possessed by any agent" not effecting a waiver or change in the policy.

The Personal form simply states that the terms of the policy "may not be changed or waived except by endorsement issued by us" and this means no matter by whom. In addition, the matter of company responsibility for the action of agents is such a complicated legal tangle, that the inclusion of the old wording has become almost meaningless.

The Personal form also includes comment concerning premium adjustment in the event of a change in the policy terms, which I think is very much in order in this clause.

3. *Legal Action Against Us* in the Personal form incorporates the intent of the "Action Against Company" provision of the Family and other forms, and while the wording has been greatly condensed, the

intent remains the same, except that the sentence concerning Bankruptcy in the older form has been removed from this provision and placed in a separate clause, numbered 8, of its own at the very end of the Personal Auto policy.

4. *Transfer of Your Interest in this Policy* is the new title for the former "Assignment" provision. It too has been repositioned and reworded in a condensed, simplified form, but the intent remains basically the same.

5. *Our Right to Recover Payment*, known in previously issued casualty policies as the "Subrogation" clause, has been reworded for better understanding by the lay public, without change in basic intent.

6. *Termination* in the Personal Auto policy includes the former Cancellation and Cancellation by Company provisions. It includes as subdivisions, A. Cancellation, B. Nonrenewal, C. Automatic Termination, and D. Other Termination Provisions.

This is the longest and most inclusive provision of the Personal form and warrants some detailed study. The wording has been completely rearranged for easier reference and understanding.

The wording concerning "short rate table" for determining the premium return if the insured cancels, has been properly omitted in the Personal form.

The section of the older forms concerning cancellation for nonpayment of premium has been greatly simplified. The Personal form also makes no mention concerning cancellation "(because) the insurance was obtained through fraudulent misrepresentation" or "(because) the insured violated any of the terms and conditions of the policy," presumably since such statements are redundant.

There is also no mention in this provision of the Personal form concerning epilepsy or heart attacks, nor does it mention conviction for a felony, criminal negligence, assault, intoxication, drugs and other specifics that were a part of the Cancellation by Company Limited of the Family and some other casualty forms previously promulgated.

7. *Two or More Autos Insured,* the seventh provision of Part F of the Personal Auto policy replaces the older provision entitled "Two or More Automobiles" and makes it much clearer that it is the intent of the policy that "the maximum limit of the company's liability under all the policies shall not exceed the highest applicable limit under any one policy."

8. *Bankruptcy* is the final clause of the Personal Auto policy, and as I have already pointed out, it is highlighted as a separate provision rather than being an appendage to the "Action Against Company" provision of the formerly promulgated forms.

Much redundancy in the older forms has been eliminated in the Personal Auto policy. The verbiage has been reduced by about 50 percent and the rewording is a vast improvement over the older forms. It is in larger type and altogether a great advancement on previously promulgated forms. The Insurance Services Office is to be congratulated.

§ 22.09 Business Auto Policy

In 1978, the Comprehensive Automobile Liability and the Basic Automobile policies were replaced by the Business Auto policy, which was written in the plain English style.

The Business Auto policy is written on a single limit basis but double limits are available by endorsement. It has many optional coverages for which additional premiums are required, including, among others, Personal Injury Protection, Medical Payments, and Uninsured Motorists coverages.

It is imperative for those handling claims under this policy to become familiar with the meaning of code numbers so as to know what types of coverages are included in the particular policy involved in the claim or loss.[13]

The policy is comprised of six parts.

"Part I—Words and Phrases With Special Meaning" is, in effect, the definitions section of this policy. The Business Auto policy has a Liability section, under which "accident" is defined as a "continuous or repeated exposure to the same conditions, resulting in bodily injury or property damage the insured neither expected nor intended."

The "continuous or repeated exposure" wording brings in the usual definition of "occurrence" within the definition of "accident" instead of the other way around, as is often found in other liability policies.

Subheading F, in defining "insured" refers the reader to the "Who Is Insured" section. It makes clear that "Except with respect to *our*

---

[13] *See* F.C. & S. Bulletins, Casualty Vol., section Auto B., National Underwriter Co., Cincinnati, Ohio.

AUTOMOBILE POLICIES AND COVERAGES § 22.09

limit of liability, the insurance afforded applies separately to each insured who is seeking coverage or against whom a claim is made or suit is brought." This was formerly a separate clause known as the "Severability" clause.

"Mobile equipment" is specifically defined in five subheadings, but the reader must refer to Part II under section C, subheading 2, to learn that "mobile equipment" is covered only "while being carried or towed by a covered auto." The catch-all phrase "other similar equipment" is meant to be broad enough to include items such as concrete mixers, sprayers and other nonspecifically named items of a similar nature.

"Part IV—Liability Insurance," contains a number of lettered subheadings such as:

A. We Will Pay:

1. We will pay all sums the insured legally must pay as damages because of bodily injury or property damage to which this insurance applies, caused by an accident and resulting from the ownership, maintenance or use of a covered auto.

2. We have the right and duty to defend any suit asking for these damages. However, we have no duty to defend suits for bodily injury or property damage not covered by this policy. We may investigate and settle any claim or suit as we consider appropriate. Our payment of the LIABILITY INSURANCE limit ends with our duty to defend or settle.

Part A 2 contains language that has produced much litigation and is discussed in more detail in Chapter 20 dealing with the duties of the insured and the insurer. The final sentence of this section is still another attempt to nail down the intent of the insured that "Our payment of the liability limit ends with our duty to defend or settle," but still leaves open exactly when "our duty to defend or settle" actually ceases.

Section B of this same Part IV entitled, "We Will Also Pay," lists the additional payments which the insurer contracts to pay, under seven subheadings. Subheading 5, second sentence, reads "Our duty to pay interest ends when we pay or tender our limit of liability," but "tender" will still engender litigation.

Subheading C under Part IV—"We Will Not Cover," lists the Exclusions in this policy and includes many that have been tested over the years with a few exceptions:

7. Bodily injury or property damage resulting from the handling of property:

a. Before it is moved from the place where it is accepted by the insured for movement into or onto the covered auto, or

b. After it is moved from the covered auto to the place where it is finally delivered by the insured.

This replaces the old wording of "loading or unloading" and is an attempt to end the controversy as to when loading begins and unloading ends and item 8 tries further to make a determination of this controversy.

The former exclusion concerning nuclear energy has been omitted in this policy. Other exclusions remain basically as they were in previous policies.

Subheading D under Part IV—"Who Is Insured," in section 2 still includes the phrase "while using with your permission, a covered auto you own, hire or borrow except . . . ." It then lists three exceptions to "Who Is Insured" which, it appears, could better have been placed under the Exclusions.

This section also attempts to define "omnibus" insureds as distinguished from the named insured. These are in fact, unnamed additional insureds.

Former policies agreed to pay "all expenses incurred by the company" in addition to the limits of liability. In Part IV, the Business Auto policy makes no such specific reference and the implications of sections A and B appear to indicate that defense costs are also subject to the limit of liability.

The F.C. & S. Bulletins[14] note however that:

> The insuring agreement has two parts; the first binds the insurance company to all sums the insured must pay as *damages* for (covered) bodily injury and property damage. The Limit of Liability clause stipulates that the specified limit is the "most we will pay for *all damages.*" [Emphasis added.]

It would appear as though the promulgators of this policy stuck their toe in the water to test the temperature, since the cost of defense has skyrocketed. There is enough ambiguity in the Business Auto policy about this point to make any such intent ineffective and

---

[14] Published by the National Underwriter Co., Cincinnati, Ohio.

if the industry wants to take this step it will have to do so in direct and unequivocal language.

Part V concerns coverage for "Physical Damage" to "a covered auto or its equipment" and specifies the various coverages available.

"Part VI—Conditions" under section "A 1—Your Duties After Accident or Loss," is the provision that was formerly called "Notice of Accident or Loss." As in the Personal Auto policy, the cooperation clause has been combined with the notice clause as items 2 a and b which refers to the Liability section. The other clauses of this Condition refer to first party claims.

Section B of the Conditions provisions, "Other Insurance," specifies when the coverage is primary and when it is excess. It also states that when two or more policies cover an insured on the same basis, whether they be primary or excess, the insurer (coinsurer), is only responsible for its pro rata share of the liability.

It is obvious that any reference to this section of the text must be in conjunction with the reading of a copy of the actual policy involved in the claim or suit.

§ 22.10 Garage Policy

The Garage policy has comprehensive coverage that includes elements of the Owners, Landlord and Tenants, Manufacturers and Contractors, Products and Completed Operations, Contractual, and most of all, Automobile Liability coverages.

In the Garage policy, whatever coverages are needed for the operation of automobile garages, repair shops, agencies or parking lots can be obtained by a payment of separate premiums. The choices are up to the named insured.

The Garage policy is one of the most complicated with which the claim representative will have to deal, principally because it covers both automobile and public liability areas and because it has special coverages and exclusions that apply specifically to this policy.

As in most standard type commercial policies, the Garage policy contains a jacket that includes the overall provisions that apply to all sections and enclosures that cover the specific coverages that were purchased. It has also been translated into plain English, and while it is perceptibly easier to understand than the previous forms, the complex nature of this policy still needs refining which it will probably get in future editions.

§ 22.10

Coverage applies to the ownership, maintenance or use of any automobile while being used in furthering the necessary or incidental operations of a garage, automobile repair shop, automobile sales agency, service station, or public parking place. In addition there is some coverage for other than business use and for automobiles furnished for the use of others. It can include medical payments, uninsured motorists, and no-fault coverages.

The definition of "automobile" in the Garage policy is different from other policy forms and includes "any land motor vehicle, trailer or semi-trailer."

The problem of defining what is or is not "incidental" to a garage business, however, is a tricky one. The F.C. & S. Bulletins cite several examples of problem situations.[15]

It must be noted, however, that automobiles as defined by the policy are covered, regardless of whether they are being used in connection with garage operations or not at the time of the accident. This differs from previous garage liability forms.

The Garage policy becomes effective only when injury or damage occurs within the policy period, which also differs from previous forms.

The requirement concerning *notice of accident* includes the word "promptly," which in my opinion leaves that requirement wide open to court and jury interpretation. The requirement that suit papers be forwarded to the insurer "immediately" at least gives the matter more urgency, as was intended.

The *Subrogation* provision of the Garage policy is important because it permits recovery of sums paid by the insurer from parties causing the loss. Exempted from subrogation in this clause are claims or suits involving employees of the named insured since they too are included insureds.

Damage to property in the *care, custody and control* of the insured is specifically excluded unless Garagekeepers Liability coverage has been purchased, and coverage for damage to a customer's car while on a hoist may also be purchased.

---

[15] Ill.: Great Central Ins. Co. v. Bennett, 351 N.E.2d 582 (1976) (involved a car-wash operation) (covered)).

Ind.: Automobile Under's, Inc. v. Hitch, 349 N.E.2d 271 (1976) (involved the sale of shotgun shells) (not covered)).

N.H.: Moore v. New Hampshire Ins. Co., 444 A.2d 546 (1982) (concerned car rental operations) (covered).

The *Contractual Liability* part of the Garage policy grants coverage to the insured for liability to third parties which is assumed by the insured because of hold-harmless agreements or other contracts.

To quote from the F.C. & S. Bulletins:

> The *Products and Completed Operations* coverage on the Garage policy is not detailed in (this) form. As in the CGL (Comprehensive General Liability) form, the promise to pay claims for bodily injury or property damage caused by the insured's products or work is implicit in the promise "to pay all sums legally owed as damages for bodily injury or property damage" when there is an accident "to which this insurance applies."

The insured is protected from claims for injury or damage to others, caused by a defective product or from faulty work, but the coverage is not intended to serve as a guarantee that the products are worthy or suitable for the intended purpose or that the insured's work is satisfactory. Accidents that arise from real or alleged defects in automobiles, gasoline, parts, etc., or out of defective work are covered. It is only claims that the product or work itself is defective that are not covered.

Otherwise, the general provisions of this policy are pretty much in line with others of a similar nature which we have or will discuss in other parts of this book.[16]

[1] Care, Custody or Control Exclusion

While the insuring agreements show what coverage the casualty policy gives, the exclusions inform the insured what is not covered. One of the most controversial exclusions which has been the cause of a great deal of controversy and litigation is the one concerning property in the "care, custody and control" of the insured.

This exclusion is especially pertinent in the Garage policy, particularly if garagekeepers legal liability coverage has not been purchased.

General rules are hard to apply to this exclusion because it is written in so many versions in the various casualty policies. In the plain language policies it is usually one sentence to the effect that "person-

---

[16] The policy is, as we have said, complex and warrants close reading. It is suggested that further insight can be obtained by a reading of the F.C. & S. Bulletins concerning the Garage policy found in the Casualty & Surety Volume section Auto, Garage Liability, Gla.

§ 22.10[1] CASUALTY INSURANCE CLAIMS

al property in your care, custody or control" is not covered. Some policies exclude "property owned or transported" by the insured. Other policies exclude "property rented to or in charge of the insured."

In any event, the burden of proof is on the insurance company to show that whatever the wording, the exclusion applies.[17]

Courts have held that the wording "care, custody or control" is clear and unambiguous,[18] and accordingly, the doctrine of "reasonable expectations" did not apply to this provision.[19]

The wording that has caused the most controversy is "property in charge of" the insured. It is generally agreed that this requires more than mere physical possession of the property.[20]

In my opinion, "control" does not imply any degree of permanency, but if the insured does not have the temporary authority to keep, handle, move or work on the property that is subsequently damaged, it could not logically be considered to be in his care, custody or control and the exclusion would not apply.

If the insured actually owns, rents, or leases the property in its entirety, the verbiage speaks for itself. It becomes much more complex however if the property is not rented in its entirety. For example, an insured may rent space in a garage building and damage a portion of the building adjoining the space that he leases. The exclusion has not been held applicable to this or other cases involving damage to property such as roofs, which have to be traversed in order to reach the property being worked on.

The property or objects actually being worked on, or expected to be worked on, have been declared as property in the care, custody or control of the insured.

Each case under consideration must be considered carefully, and, in my opinion, interpreted liberally since this is exactly what most of the courts are doing today.

---

[17] La.: State Farm Fire & Cas. Co. v. Zurich Amer. Ins. Co., 459 So. 2d 205 (App. 1984).

[18] Ill.: Insurance Co. of N. Amer. v. Adkisson, 459 N.E.2d 310 (App. 1984).

[19] Id.

[20] Fla.: Shankle v. VIP Lounge, Inc., 468 So. 2d 548 (App. 1985).
Ga.: Georgia Cas. & Sur. Co. v. Swearingen, 254 S.E.2d 735 (App. 1979).

CHAPTER 23

Some Laws Applicable to the Use of Automobiles

§ 23.01 Guest Statutes
    [1]   Purpose of the Guest Statutes
    [2]   Who Is a Guest?
    [3]   Joint Venture
    [4]   Share the Ride Arrangements
    [5]   What Does Payment or Compensation Comprise?
    [6]   Owner Occupant
    [7]   Contributory or Comparative Negligence of Guests
    [8]   Infants as Guests
    [9]   Entering, Leaving, or Outside the Vehicle
    [10]   Gross Negligence or Willful and Wanton Misconduct
    [11]   Examples of Gross Negligence or Willful and Wanton Misconduct
§ 23.02 Checklist for Investigation of Guest Statute Cases
§ 23.03 Liquor Law Liability
    [1]   Dram Shop and Liquor Control Statutes
    [2]   Exclusivity of Dram Shop Legislation
    [3]   Recent Trends
    [4]   Social Hosts and Company Parties
    [5]   Uninvited Guest
    [6]   Employer Hosts
    [7]   Minors or Incompetent Guests
    [8]   Common Law Defenses
    [9]   Noninnocent Participant
    [10]   Intoxication Defined
    [11]   Extraterritoriality in Dram Shop Jurisdiction
    [12]   Suit by the Intoxicated Person
    [13]   Insurance Coverage for Liquor Law Liability
§ 23.04 Seat Belt Defense
    [1]   Statutory Enactments
§ 23.05 Bibliography

§ 23.01 Guest Statutes

Before the era of guest statutes, the duty owed by a driver of an automobile to a guest passenger, was that of ordinary care with respect to the operation of the vehicle.

While more than half of the states that had previously enacted guest statutes have either repealed them or declared them unconstitutional or otherwise invalid, a number of states still have effective guest statutes, despite the fact that the trend is certainly in the other direction.

It took some courts an inordinate amount of time to discover that their statutes were unconstitutional or discretionary after years of holding them effective.

The statutes that still exist generally refer to the owner, operator or person responsible for the operation of a motor vehicle who shall not be liable for loss or damage arising from injuries to or death of a guest while being transported without payment while in or upon said vehicle, unless caused by:

(1) willful or wanton misconduct (most frequently used),
(2) intoxication,
(3) reckless disregard for the rights of others,
(4) intentional acts, and/or
(5) gross negligence.

The statutes specifically name any one or combination of the above. The Texas statute grants driver immunity only if guests are related. Another statute makes an exception for prospective purchasers of the vehicle. At least two states—Massachusetts and Virginia—specifically hold that nonpaying guests *may* recover for ordinary negligence and still another grants coverage for car pool operations.

Most statutes state, or at least imply, that the driver's partial immunity is lost only if the actions complained of, caused or contributed to the injury or death of a passenger.

As already noted, some states have declared their former guests statutes as being unconstitutional[1] and others have declared them in-

---

[1] Colo.: Clemens v. District Court, 390 P.2d 83 (1964).
Ky.: Ludwig v. Johnson, 49 S.W.2d 347 (1932).
Mich.: Mansitee Bank & Trust Co. v. McGowan, 232 N.W.2d 636 (1975).
N.M.: McGeehan v. Bunch, 540 P.2d 238 (1975).
See "Statutes Affecting Liability Insurance," American Insurance Association, January 1981.

effective for other reasons.[2]

[1] Purpose of the Guest Statutes

The purpose behind the enactment of guest statutes was principally twofold:

1. To prevent recovery for ordinary negligence by a guest who has accepted the hospitality of the owner.
2. To prevent collusion between friends or relatives.

It goes against the grain to allow a person who was being gratuitously helped or accommodated in a social way, to turn around and repay his benefactor by suing him for ordinary negligence.

[2] Who Is a Guest?

Any attempt to define the meaning of "guest" in absolute terms would be an impossibility. In any event, by a process of elimination and with the help of guidelines set by the decisions and the exercise of some degree of common sense, an attempt can be made to circumscribe the area within which a guest would fall after we have reviewed the limitations which fence it in.

It has been held that the word "guest" does not require more than the giving of hospitality without payment of any kind in order to place the person receiving hospitality and to be benefited by it, in that category.[3]

Social companionship, without any other consideration, even if primarily for the benefit of a host, is not payment for transportation and would not take the passenger out of the guest category.[4]

However, one who rides as a passenger in an automobile for the definite, tangible benefit of the owner operator, or for a definite mutual tangible benefit is ordinarily not held to be a guest. Another exception would be where the trip was primarily for business reasons resulting in some substantial or material benefit to the driver owner. Here again the passenger would not be held to be a guest.

---

[2] *E.g.,* Pimes v. Tyler, 335 N.E.2d 373 (Ohio 1975) (statute was held to be discriminatory).

[3] Lombard v. DeShance, 167 Ohio St. 431, 149 N.E.2d 914 (1958).

[4] Stiltner v. Bahner, 10 Ohio St. 2d 216, 227 N.E.2d 192 (1967).

[3] Joint Venture

A joint venture is an association of two or more persons to carry out a single business purpose for material gain or profit which may be the very transportation itself.

In actuality, however, the joint venture concept as it affects the status of the passenger is no longer applied in any strict sense. Generally speaking, joint ventures now fall into the same category as business ventures in general and are subject to the same interpretations.

In a 1968 decision it was held that if the trip was in the nature of a joint enterprise or was a venture of a business nature benefiting both parties, the passenger could not be held to be a guest.[5]

[4] Share the Ride Arrangements

A passenger who is riding in a car in a "Share the Ride Plan," serving a common economic need of the driver as well as the passengers without any social purpose, is not a guest within the meaning of the guest statutes. Such an arrangement need not necessarily be for the purpose of going to work. Where a passenger, for instance, had an agreement with the driver over some period of time to pay a definite sum each week to go back and forth to school, he was not considered to be a guest.

[5] What Does Payment or Compensation Comprise?

The vast majority of the statutes in attempting to define guest passengers require that the driver owner receive some payment in order to release the passenger from being considered a guest. A few statutes use the word "compensation" instead of "payment" and initially there was some controversy concerning the meaning of these two words. For a time it was felt that the word "compensation" was broader than "payment" but it was shortly generally agreed that the terms were synonymous.

An informal agreement to share expenses between friends or relatives in and of itself does not take a passenger out of the guest category.[6] The mere courtesy of a passenger in voluntarily paying for gasoline or in sharing expenses is not in and of itself sufficient to relieve the passenger from the status of a guest if the purpose of the

---

[5] Mukasey v. Aaron, 20 Utah 2d 383, 438 P.2d 702 (1968).
[6] Casas v. Moya, 193 So. 2d 60 (Fla. App. 1966).

LAWS APPLICABLE TO AUTOMOBILE USE § 23.01[7]

trip was primarily social or for pleasure. It is essential that the payment or the sharing of expenses must have been the motivating factor for receiving the transportation in order to take the passenger out of the guest classification.[7]

Ordinarily, the arrangement to share expenses on a trip of mutual benefit to the driver and the passenger must have been made before the trip started in order for the courts to hold that no guest relationship existed. It must be understood, however, that the payment or compensation need not be limited to money. Any real and tangible benefit to the driver owner could be sufficient to hold that the passenger was not a guest.[8]

The three factors usually necessary to determine the status of the passenger are:

1. Actual or potential benefit in a material or business sense resulting or to result to the owner or operator of the automobile;
2. That the transportation be motivated by the expectation of such benefit; and
3. That the presence of the occupant directly compensate the operator or owner in a substantial and material or business sense, though not necessarily with money, as distinguished from mere social benefit or nominal or incidental contributions to expenses,

[6] Owner Occupant

An owner occupant who is injured while riding in his automobile while it is being driven by another, is not a guest within the meaning of the guest statutes.[9] This seems to be by far the majority opinion. There have, however, been some indications to the contrary, holding that there could be some circumstances that might lead to a conclusion that he was a guest in his own car.

[7] Contributory or Comparative Negligence of Guests

The contributory negligence of a guest can be used against him in any action which he may bring for the negligence of the driver of the automobile in which he was riding. If a passenger had reason

---

[7] Joslyn v. Callison, 12 Cal. App. 3d 788 (1970).
[8] Martinez v. So. Pac. Co., 45 Cal. 2d 244, 288 P.2d 868 (1955).
[9] Summers v. Summers, 40 Ill. 2d 338, 239 N.E.2d 795 (1968).

to know of the driver's inability to drive safely, he would be guilty of contributory negligence if he accepted a ride despite such knowledge.[10]

By the same token where he accepted a ride without knowledge of any reckless propensities on the part of the driver and was then subjected to driving at a dangerous speed, he has the duty to object to the speed and request the driver to slow down. If the driver disregards his request he can be chargeable for gross negligence or willful and wanton misconduct.[11]

Obviously it is impossible to cover all of the circumstances which might involve a passenger or guest in contributory or comparative negligence. The action which he should take to protect himself from danger while riding as a passenger in someone else's car depends on the circumstances of each case.

[8] Infants as Guests

Generally speaking and in ordinary circumstances, it has been held that a minor can be a guest and subject to the guest statute of the particular state. However, a passenger who voluntarily accepts a ride in an automobile must have the mental capacity to understand what he is doing.[12] Ordinarily children under seven years of age are not considered mentally competent to accept or reject a ride and most courts have said that in this age bracket guest statutes are not applicable to them.

Some courts have held that a parent may confer guest status on a child by accepting a ride on the child's behalf.[13]

[9] Entering, Leaving, or Outside the Vehicle

There is no hard and fast rule for determining whether a guest relationship exists where the passenger is not fully seated in the vehicle at the time of injury.

It has been held that the guest relationship of a passenger is suspended when he leaves the car and is injured while he is on the outside. On the other hand, it has been held that the existence of a guest relationship does not depend solely on the physical position of the

---

[10] Zumwalt v. Lindland, 239 Ore. 26, 396 P.2d 205 (1964).
[11] Mann v. Good, 451 P.2d 233 (Kan. 1969).
[12] Rocha v. Hulen, 6 Cal. App. 2d 245, 44 P.2d 478 (1935).
[13] Welker v. Sorenson, 306 P.2d 737 (1957).

injured at the moment of the automobile accident, but the test is rather whether or not the driver's alleged negligence was performed in the course of carrying out the gratuitous undertaking that he had assumed.[14] The points at issue concern the questions as to exactly when a person becomes a "passenger" (entered upon) or ceases to be a "passenger" (leaving) and when he is being "transported" (during the ride). These are the key words in some of the decisions.

[10] Gross Negligence or Willful and Wanton Misconduct

There can be no precise definition of gross negligence or willful and wanton misconduct. The ordinary definition for gross negligence relates to a failure to use slight care. The courts have attempted to interpret it variously. Gross negligence has been defined as that degree of negligence which shows an utter disregard of prudence amounting to complete neglect for the safety of another.[15]

Willful or wanton misconduct must show that the defendant drove with a reckless indifference to consequences and consciously and intentionally did some wrongful act or omitted some duty which produced the injuries.[16]

In addition to willful acts, I think that wanton misconduct implies that a reasonably prudent man would realize that the conduct of the driver was such as would naturally and almost inevitably result in a serious accident, despite the fact that the driver may have had no deliberate intent to injure or kill.

[11] Examples of Gross Negligence or Willful and Wanton Misconduct

Once again we are in an area where we are trying to determine what twelve good and true jurors might decide in any given circumstance. The answer, of course, is that there is no way to look into the mind of the average juror, so the only thing we can do is to give some examples from past cases.

Surprisingly enough, under ordinary circumstances most juries have held that falling asleep at the wheel is not gross negligence. This of course is far from unanimous. Certainly, where it has been shown that the driver had insufficient sleep the night before and knew or

---

[14] Thomas v. Newsome, 211 So. 2d 46 (Fla. App. 1968).
[15] Sturman v. Johnson, 209 Va. 227, 163 S.E.2d 170 (1968).
[16] Lankford v. Mong, 214 So. 2d 301 (Ala. 1968).

should have known that he was likely to doze off, it was held willful and wanton misconduct and in my opinion rightfully so.[17]

Speed and road conditions are other factors which are often involved in the determination of gross negligence or wanton misconduct. Failure to stop at a stop sign has also been held to be wanton misconduct.

Conduct arising from momentary thoughtlessness, inadvertence, or from an error of judgment would not ordinarily indicate a reckless disregard for the rights of others and should not be considered as willful or wanton misconduct.[18]

§ 23.02 Checklist for Investigation of Guest Statute Cases

- ☐ Make the usual automobile investigation of the coverage, the complete facts, the injuries and damages and the liability. Interview all passengers where necessary.
- ☐ Interview the driver and the passenger separately and determine the following:
  - ○ Exact nature of the trip:
    - — Who suggested the trip?
    - — What was the purpose? Was it for business or pleasure?
    - — Was it a joint enterprise for the benefit of both?
    - — Did the driver receive any material benefit from the trip?
    - — Was the trip made for purely social reasons?
  - ○ Give the exact route, including starting point and exact destination. Check if necessary.
  - ○ Did the passenger make any contribution toward the expenses of the trip?
    - — Was any arrangement for contribution made before the trip was started?
    - — Who paid for the gasoline and oil?
    - — Did the passenger pay for road or bridge tolls, meals, or other items of expense?
    - — Was the trip part of a share-the-ride plan?
    - — Did the passenger make a cash payment or give other material consideration of any other kind?
  - ○ Get the names and addresses of all other occupants and possible witnesses to the financial or other arrangement of the trip and obtain corroboration of information given by the parties in interest.
  - ○ Was the passenger or driver intoxicated or under the influence of drugs? Get full details. Did the passenger know that the driver drank or took drugs regularly?

---

[17] Dunn v. Caylor, 218 Ga. 256, 127 S.E.2d 367 (1962).
[18] Ascher v. Friedman, 110 Conn. 1, 147 A. 263 (1929).

LAWS APPLICABLE TO AUTOMOBILE USE § 23.03

- ○ If the driver was going fast or driving recklessly, did the passenger object? In what manner? Obtain complete details.
- ○ Was the driver tired or sleepy? Did the passenger know this?
- ○ How well did the passenger know the driver?
  - — Were they related?
  - — Were they coemployees?
  - — Were they friends of long standing?
  - — Did the passenger know that the driver usually drove fast or recklessly?
  - — Did he know of any possible driving defects such as physical or mental incapacity, no driver's license, etc?
  - — Had passenger ridden with the driver previously? How often?
- ○ Determine the general condition of the automobile:
  - — Were the brakes, steering, or other vital mechanical parts defective? Did the passenger know or should he have known this?
  - — What was the general condition of the automobile?
- ○ Was the passenger an infant? If so:
  - — Give exact age.
  - — Determine if parent or parents were present in the car.
  - — Obtain full details of infant's presence in the car.

§ 23.03 Liquor Law Liability

The vast majority of the accidents arising out of the intoxication of an individual involve automobile driving, even though torts committed by drunkards are not altogether confined to driving. Accordingly, this subject is being treated in this general section.

It is most important for adjusters to determine the responsibility of those serving drinks to others since a Dram Shop Act or a common law decision may also place responsibility upon someone in addition to the principal tortfeasor. Liquor law liability can provide grounds for bringing into the action such a party as a co-defendant, or less likely, give rise to a possible subrogation action against him or her.

Historically, at common law, one who sold liquor to an intoxicated person or to one who became intoxicated as a result of such a sale, could not be held liable for the subsequent acts of the intoxicated person. The reasoning behind this opinion rested on the premise that it was the drinking of the liquor and not its sale that was the proximate cause of the injury or damage.[19]

---

[19] **Ark.:** Carr v. Turner, 385 S.W.2d 656 (1965).
Cal.: Brockett v. Kitchen Boyd Motor Co., 100 Cal. Rptr. 752 (1972).
Conn.: Nolan v. Morelli, 226 A.2d 383 (1967).
Ill.: Colligan v. Cousar, 187 N.E.2d 292 (1963).

Prohibition forced legislators to pass dram shop statutes aimed at those who sold liquor. At one time thirty-seven states had some form of dram shop statute. After prohibition was repealed, many states repealed their dram shop statutes and by the early 1970's the number of states still retaining dram shop statutes had been reduced to about half this number.

In recent years, as a result of the growing highway slaughter caused by drunken driving, the pressure of public opinion has forced courts and legislators to take a more strict attitude toward this evil. Today, all states have some form of liquor control statutes and most have some form of dram shop acts.

Decisions involving the liability of dispensers of alcoholic beverages are based on dram shop and liquor control statutes and on common law.

Despite all of the justified outcry against drunken driving, there is no uniformity in the decisions or the statutes and the resulting confusion is deplorable. The present trend has made all but very recent cases obsolete. Many jurisdictions now permit recovery based upon dram shop statutes, a violation of the liquor control statutes, or on common law negligence.

[1] Dram Shop and Liquor Control Statutes

As has already been said, the statutes vary greatly. A few require notice in writing from close relatives, guardians, or employers not to sell liquor to a specific individual before liability can be created on the part of the seller. A few restrict those who can be the beneficiary of such acts. Many of the acts include owners or lessees of the property, whether it be taproom, bar, restaurant, or liquor store. Most of the acts forbid the sale of liquor to minors and to those who are already intoxicated.

The majority of these acts are not meant to protect the intoxicated person himself, but a few specifically include "source of support" as a factor in establishing liability, and in those states a wife or child may bring an action based upon the sale to the husband or father.

Maine is one of the few states that permits recovery by the intoxi-

---

U.S.: Megge v. United States, 344 F.2d 31 (6th Cir. 1965); Campbell v. Village of Silver Bay, 315 F.2d 568 (8th Cir. 1963).

cated person or his representative. In a recent case,[20] an intoxicated patron of a tavern died as a result of alcohol poisoning after being served additional drinks when it was obvious that the patron was drunk. His representative recovered in an action against the tavern keeper.

California, as usual, is a special case. It has a statute placing responsibility for the injury or damage exclusively on the consumer of the alcoholic beverage, limiting the responsibility of the seller to liquor sold to an already intoxicated minor. A criminal statute in that state makes it a misdemeanor for a seller to provide liquor to a habitual or common drunkard and to one obviously intoxicated. Minnesota and Iowa have enacted similar but different legislation. Some states have legislated in the opposite direction.

Quite a few states that do not have dram shop statutes deal with this problem by way of statutes, ordinances or regulations under their alcohol control statutes, which are as varied as the dram shop acts. Most such statutes are criminal in nature and violation of them has been construed in some courts as negligence per se in common law actions.

As a prerequisite to obtaining a license to sell liquor, various statutes require an applicant to furnish a bond or an insurance policy guaranteeing compliance with the law in respect to payment for injuries or damage resulting from a violation of the liquor provisions of the statute. Today, however, the insurance policy has replaced the need for a bond in practically all jurisdictions.

It accordingly becomes obvious that the claims person must become familiar with the law in his jurisdiction in order to be able to understand all aspects of an accident which involved drunken driving.

[2] Exclusivity of Dram Shop Legislation

Generally speaking, dram shop statutes impose liability on individuals or establishments that sell alcoholic drinks illegally, and to patrons or customers that subsequently cause injury, death, or property damage as a result of drunken driving, or for other tortious acts.

Illegal sales are usually designated as sales to persons already obviously drunk, or to a minor or incompetent person or to a known habitual drunkard.

---

[20] Klingerman v. SOL Corp., 505 A.2d 474 (Me. 1986).

§ 23.03[3]   CASUALTY INSURANCE CLAIMS

A fair number of states have held that their dram shop acts are the exclusive remedy for those seeking recovery for injury or death against the provider of alcoholic beverages to persons already intoxicated.[21] Other courts have held that the dram shop statutes were not exclusive.[22]

[3] Recent Trends

Many of our courts have reversed their old rulings at common law and now hold commercial vendors of alcoholic beverages liable for the injury or damage caused by customers to whom alcoholic beverages were sold when they were already intoxicated.[23]

---

[21] **Ark.:** Carr v. Turner, 385 S.W.2d 656 (1965).
Ill.: Camille v. Berry Fertilizers, 334 N.E.2d 205 (App. 1975) (liquor served at company party).
Iowa: Connally v. Conlan, 371 N.W.2d 832 (1984) (common law suit barred).
Mich.: Behnke v. Pierson, 175 N.W.2d 303 (1970).
Minn.: Holmquist v. Miller, 367 N.W.2d 468 (1985), *but see* Trail v. Christian, 213 N.W.2d 618 (1973).
Mont.: Runge v. Watts, 589 P.2d 145 (1979).
Neb.: Holmes v. Circo, 244 N.W.2d 65 (1976).
Nev.: Yoscovitch v. Wasson, 645 P.2d 975 (1982).

[22] **Colo.:** Crespin v. Largo Corp., 698 P.2d 826 (1985) (court held that statutory dram shop act did not supersede the common law).
Ohio: Mason v. Roberts, 294 N.E.2d 884 (1973).
Wis.: Sorensen v. Jarvis, 350 N.W.2d 108 (1984).

[23] **Ala.:** Buchanan v. Merger Enterprises, 463 So. 2d 121 (1985) (common law).
Colo.: Kerby v. Flamingo Club, Inc., 532 P.2d 975 (1974).
Fla.: Armstrong v. Munford, Inc., 451 So. 2d 480 (1984).
Idaho: Algeria v. Payonk, 619 P.2d 135 (1980).
Ind.: Elder v. Fisher, 217 N.E.2d 847 (1966).
Iowa: Haafke v. Mitchell, 347 N.W.2d 381 (1984).
Ky.: Pike v. George, 434 S.W.2d 626 (1968).
Mass.: Michnik & Zilberman v. Gordon's Liquors, Inc., 453 N.E.2d 430 (1983).
Mich.: Thaut v. Finley, 213 N.W.2d 820 (1983).
Mo.: Carver v. Schafer, 647 S.W.2d 570 (App. 1983).
N.H.: Ramsey v. Anctil, 211 A.2d 900 (1965).
N.J.: Rappaport v. Nichols, 156 A.2d 1 (1959) (landmark case).
N.M.: Lopez v. Maez, 651 P.2d 1269 (1982).
N.C.: Hutchens v. Hankins, 303 S.E.2d 584 (1983).
Ohio: Mason v. Roberts, 294 N.E.2d 884 (1973) (despite statute).
Ore.: Chartrand v. Coos Bay Tavern, 696 P.2d 513 (1985) (liability only upon showing that customer was visibly intoxicated at the time he was served).
Pa.: Jardine v. Upper Darby Lodge, 198 A.2d 550 (1964).
Tenn.: Brookins v. The Round Table, 624 S.W.2d 547 (1981).
Wash.: Young v. Caravan Corp., 663 P.2d 834 (1983) (negligence per se).
Wis.: Sorensen v. Jarvis, 350 N.W.2d 108 (1981) (minor).
Wyo.: McClellan v. Tottenhoff, 666 P.2d 408 (1983).

[4] Social Hosts and Company Parties

In view of the fact that the various dram shop statutes are so diverse there must, of necessity, be some generalizations made, especially since many of the statutes are not specific as to the liability of the provider of the alcoholic drinks. Accordingly, the courts have great leeway in construing these statutes.

Where liquor is served by a host at a social gathering, the law is much more lenient to the host than it is to a seller of alcoholic drinks. It is generally accepted that a social host should not be held to the same degree of responsibility for acts of his guests as is required from those serving liquor for a profit, and most of the decisions have so held.[24]

After some decisions holding social hosts legally responsible for the negligence of intoxicated guests, California enacted legislation overruling the liability of social hosts in future cases except where alcoholic drinks are served to minors that are already intoxicated.[25]

The reasoning behind this leniency is based upon the fact that a social host does not have the profit motive for serving drinks, does not have as much control over the drinker, and is less experienced in exercising such control. It also seems to be the consensus of opinion that if such liability is to be imposed, it should be done by statute.

However, in a landmark decision, the Supreme Court of New Jersey held that

> Where a host provides liquor directly to a social guest and continues to do so even beyond the point at which the host knows the guest is intoxicated, and does this knowing that the guest will shortly thereafter be operating a motor vehicle, that host is liable for the foreseeable

---

[24] **Ala.:** De Loach v. Mayer Elec. Supply Co., 378 So. 2d 733 (1979).
Ariz.: Keckonen v. Robles, 705 P.2d 945 (1985).
Conn.: Slicer v. Quigley, 429 A.2d 855 (1981).
Fla.: Bankston v. Brennan, Jr., 480 So. 2d 246 (1986).
Ill.: Lowe v. Rubin, 424 N.E.2d 710 (1981) (court held that any extension to include liability for social hosts should be made by the legislature).
Mich.: Westcoat v. Mielke, 310 N.W.2d 293 (1981).
Minn.: Meany v. Newell, 367 N.W.2d 472 (1985) (company party).
Mo.: Harriman v. Smith, 697 S.W.2d 219 (1986).
Mont.: Runge v. Watts, 589 P.2d 145 (1979).
N.Y.: Kohler v. Wray, 452 N.Y.S.2d 831 (Supreme Ct. 1982).
Ohio: Settlemyer v. Wilmington Vet's Post, 464 N.E.2d 521 (1984).
Pa.: McCrery v. Scioli, 485 A.2d 1170 (1985) (no liability for landlord).
Wash: Halvorson v. Birchfield Boiler, Inc., 458 P.2d 897 (1969).
[25] Strange v. Cabrol, 209 Cal. Rptr. 347 (1984).

consequences to third parties that result from the guests's drunken driving.[26]

A previous case in Wisconsin,[27] had already held that "the necessity of drawing a line between a commercial vendor and a social host is a 'strawman' argument because social justice and common sense require that a social host not give an intoxicated guest more liquor." This was also reaffirmed in the case of *Sorensen v. Jarvis*.[28]

A few other states have construed their dram shop statutes to be broad enough to include liability of a social host as well as a commercial provider.[29]

[5] Uninvited Guest

It has been held that a social host who served alcoholic drinks to an uninvited guest was not liable for any resulting injury caused by the guest's drunken driving.[30]

[6] Employer Hosts

Most courts that have made a distinction between social hosts and employer hosts have usually done so on the basis of the employer-employee relationship which implies some intangible gain by the employer host even though he does not sell the drinks. The matter of vicarious liability is also involved.[31]

---

[26] N.J.: Kelly v. Gwinnell, 476 A.2d 1219 (1984); Davis v. Sam Goody, 480 A.2d 212 (1984) (agreeing).

[27] Garcia v. Hargrove, 176 N.W.2d 566 (1970).

[28] 350 N.W.2d 108 (1981) (involved a minor), *but see* Olsen v. Copeland, 280 N.W.2d 178 (1979).

[29] **Iowa:** Clark v. Mincks, 364 N.W.2d 226 (1985) (Iowa dram shop statute does not create liability for social hosts, but that did not deter the court from declaring that social hosts could be held liable at common law)

Minn.: Williams v. Klemesrud, 197 N.W.2d 614 (1982) (legislature thereafter amended the statute to limit liability to those that sell liquor. *See* Cole v. City of Spring Lake Park, 314 N.W.2d 836 (1982).

N.J.: Kelly v. Gwinnell, 476 A.2d 1219 (1984) (court held a social host liable in common law. It also rejected any distinction between licensees and social hosts).

N.M.: Walker v. Key, 686 P.2d 973 (App. 1984) (violation of statute construed as negligence per se).

Ore.: Wiener v. Gamma Phi Chapter of Alpha Tau Omega Frat., 485 P.2d 18 (1971).

[30] **Ill.:** Heldt v. Brie, 455 N.E.2d 842 (1983).

[31] Chastain v. Litton Systems, Inc., 694 F.2d 957 (4th Cir.), *cert. denied*, 462 U.S. 1106 (1983).

Drinks served at a social event sponsored by an employer for the benefit of his employees represents a situation that falls somewhere between a social host and a tavern operator.

While it is true that the employer gets no immediate short term profit from serving liquor which he makes available to his employees without charge, there can be said to be a benefit in establishing or keeping good employer-employee relationships. The same argument, however, could be used when a host entertains a customer or his boss in his home.

It must be kept in mind that we are not here discussing the liability of caterers or establishments that provide facilities for entertaining.

Where drinks were served at a Christmas party sponsored by an employer for the benefit of his employees and held on the premises of the employer's business property, the Minnesota Court of Appeals decided that a direct action for negligence could be brought against the employer as a result of injuries committed by his employee who was intoxicated.[32]

In several other cases involving suits brought under the Dram Shop Acts of their states, the courts held that the employers that held the parties for their employees were not subject to the dram shop or liquor control acts.[33]

[7] Minors or Incompetent Guests

Courts usually come down much harder on hosts that serve liquor to minors. In most states this is against the law, where such laws have been enacted. Some jurisdictions have limited recovery to situations where the guest is a minor or an incompetent person.[34]

---

[32] **Minn.:** Meany v. Cardinal I.G. Co., 352 N.W.2d 779 (Minn. App. 1984); Meany v. Newell, 352 N.W.2d 779 (App. 1984).

[33] **Ill.:** Miller v. Owens Illinois Glass Co., 199 N.E.2d 300 (1964).
N.Y.: Edgar v. Kajet, 375 N.Y.S.2d 548 (1975) (lower court decision).

[34] **Cal.:** Strange v. Cabrol, 209 Cal. Rptr. 347 (1984).
Ga.: Sutter v. Hutchings, 327 S.E.2d 766 (1985).
Iowa: Haafke v. Mitchell, 347 N.W.2d 381 (1984) (at common law).
Mich.: Thaut v. Finley, 213 N.W.2d 822 (1973); Lonstreth v. Fitzgibbon, 335 N.W.2d 677 (1983).
N.J.: Linn v. Rand, 356 A.2d 15 (1976) (no statute).
N.M.: Walker v. Key, 686 P.2d 973 (App. 1984) (new statute provides that violation can no longer be considered as negligence per se).
Ore.: Wiener v. Gamma Phi Chapter of Alpha Tau Omega Frat., 485 P.2d 18 (1971).

Some jurisdictions hold by statute that liability is confined to those that sell alcoholic beverages and courts have usually made no exception where this was clearly stated in the statute.[35]

[8] Common Law Defenses

Common law defenses such as contributory and comparative negligence and assumption of risk, formerly available in cases involving the liability of those serving alcoholic drinks, are, for the most part, no longer recognized by most of our courts.[36]

[9] Noninnocent Participant

The case of *Barrett v. Campbell*,[37] a Michigan Court of Appeals case, involved a plaintiff who had participated in purchasing "rounds" of drinks. He was subsequently a passenger in a car driven by one of the other participants who was intoxicated, resulting in injury to the passenger plaintiff.

The court held that the plaintiff was not an innocent party under the Michigan Dram Shop Act and therefore was not entitled to recover.

[10] Intoxication Defined

By far, most of the dram shop statutes refer to the serving of liquor to persons who are already intoxicated. The term has been variously defined.

In the case of *Sanders v. Officers Club of Conn.*,[38] a Connecticut court defined intoxication as

> an abnormal mental or physical condition due to the influence of imbibing intoxicating liquors; a visible excitation of the passions and impairment of judgment, or a derangement or impairment of physical

---

Pa.: Douglas v. Schwenk, 479 A.2d 608 (Superior 1984) (drinking companions joined as co-defendants with tavern operator).

[35] **Minn.:** Holmquist v. Miller, 352 N.W.2d 47 (App. 1984).

[36] **Conn.:** Sanders v. Officers Club of Conn., 493 A.2d 184 (1985).

Mich.: Barrett v. Campbell, 345 N.W.2d 614 (App. 1983).

Contra: **N.C.:** Brower v. Robert Chappell & Assoc., 328 S.E.2d 45 (App. 1985) (as a matter of law).

[37] 345 N.W.2d 614 (1983).

[38] 493 A.2d 184 (1985).

functions and energies. This may be reflected in the intoxicated person's walk or conversation, his common sense actions, or his lack of willpower.

[11] Extraterritoriality in Dram Shop Jurisdiction

In the case of *Baukford v. De Rock*[39] the federal court, moving away from lex loci delicta, decided that the Iowa Dram Shop Act should be applied in an accident that happened in Minnesota. The driver, already intoxicated, was sold liquor in Iowa in violation of the Iowa Dram Shop law. The court held that Iowa law should be given extraterritorial effect to cover an injury that occurred in Minnesota in the interest of deterring the selling of liquor to intoxicated persons.

[12] Suit by the Intoxicated Person

Although in the minority, at about the same time that some courts began to recognize a common law duty by a taproom operator to the general public, a few courts also came to the conclusion that there was also a duty owed to the person who was sold the intoxicating liquor.[40]

In the cases mentioned, the courts surprisingly brushed off the defense of contributory negligence, which a New Hampshire court refused to do.[41]

In some cases the duty to the patron was included in the overall responsibility of the tavern operator to both the customer and the general public.[42]

Frankly, I find it hard to understand why a person who voluntarily becomes intoxicated should not even be held responsible for his own

---

[39] 423 F. Supp. 602 (1976).
[40] **Ariz.:** Ontiveros v. Borak, 667 P.2d 200 (1983) (involved a minor).
Ky.: Nally v. Blandford, 291 S.W.2d 832 (death caused by overdrinking).
La.: Pence v. Ketchum, 326 So. 2d 831 (1976).
N.M.: Porter v. Ortiz, 665 P.2d 1149 (1982) (involved a minor).
Ohio: Mason v. Roberts, 294 N.E.2d 884 (1973) (case held that the selling establishment owed a duty to its customers.
Ore.: Sager v. McClendon, 650 P.2d 1002 (1982) (by statute).
Pa.: Schelin v. Goldberg, 146 A.2d 648 (1958).
[41] Ramsey v. Ancil, 211 A.2d 900 (1965) (statutory interpretation).
[42] **Colo.:** Crespin v. Largo Corp., 698 P.2d 826 (Colo. App. 1984).
Minn.: Cady v. Coleman, 315 N.W.2d 593 (1982).
N.J.: Rappaport v. Nichols, 156 A.2d 1 (1979); Soronen v. Olde Milford Inn, Inc., 218 A.2d 630 (1966) (no statute involved in either case).

condition, and further, should be able to recover from someone who certainly did not force the drinks down his throat. The better opinion, I think, holds that the dispenser of alcoholic beverages owes no duty to the one who becomes intoxicated at his own request. In any event, contributory or comparative negligence should be a most important factor.[43]

[13] Insurance Coverage for Liquor Law Liability

The Fidelity, Casualty and Surety (F.C. & S.) Bulletins published by the National Underwriter Company[44] states that:

> General Liability policies contain a liquor liability exclusion that eliminates coverage for persons or organizations involved in the alcoholic beverage industry if liability is imposed because of the violation of any statute or regulation pertaining to alcoholic beverages. Liability imposed because of the selling or serving of alcoholic beverages to minors or that causes or contributes to the intoxication of any person is also excluded. As the exclusion appears in the 1973 comprehensive general liability policy, owners and lessors of premises where alcoholic beverages are involved also fall subject to the liquor liability exclusion if liability arises out of the violation of any alcoholic beverages statute or regulation. This part of the exclusion was omitted from the 1986 commercial general liability policy, thereby providing coverage for owners or lessors who are not also operators of such premises. Because the exclusion is tied to statutes and regulations (and, in some instances the principles of common law) the scope of the exclusion varies in different jurisdictions.

The comprehensive personal liability coverages have no exclusions for the liquor liability of a social host. However, the definition of an accident, may cause coverage problems.

---

[43] **Mich.:** Klotz v. Persenaire, 360 N.W.2d 255 (App. 1985).
Minn.: Herrly v. Muzik, 374 N.W.2d 275 (1984), *but see* Cady v. Coleman, 315 N.W.2d 593 (1982).
N.Y.: Allen v. County of Westchester, 492 N.Y.S.2d 772 (App. Div. 1985) (suit by widow whose husband fell while intoxicated, following a visit to a bar on the campus of a community college); Matalavage v. Sadler, 432 N.Y.S.2d 103 (App. Div. 1980) and Delamater v. Kimmerle, 484 N.Y.S.2d 213 (App. Div. 1984) (the N.Y. dram shop act does not create a cause of action in favor of the person whose intoxication resulted from the unlawful sale of liquor.
N.C.: Brower v. Robert Chappell & Assoc., 328 S.E.2d 45 (App. 1985) (contributory negligence applied as a matter of law).
[44] Public Liability, section L.

LAWS APPLICABLE TO AUTOMOBILE USE   § 23.04

There are also special liquor law coverages and policies that give specific coverage for commercial establishments that provide alcoholic beverages.

Specific liquor liability coverage can be obtained by tavern, taproom, bar, or restaurant operators or owners from insurance companies that specialize in writing this type of coverage. Even restaurants whose license restricts the sale of liquor to 49 percent or less of total revenue are considered vendors of liquor who are subject to the liquor law exclusion in the policy.[45]

§ 23.04 Seat Belt Defense

Since seat belts have only been in existence since the early 1960's, the law involving their use is still in a state of development. The trend of legislative enactment concerning the use of seat belts appears to be on the increase, in view of the fact that continuing information is beginning to make it evident that in the overall their use does help to diminish the number and severity of injuries resulting from automobile accidents.

The major legal approaches to the failure to use available seat belts are whether such failure is negligence per se, whether such failure should be considered as contributory negligence, or whether it should be considered as comparative negligence.

There is also the problem involved in the failure by the owner of a vehicle to provide seat belts in proper working order, which can be an important element in bringing a suit as well as defending one.

Initially, the courts were very reluctant to even permit seat belt use as evidence since it was argued that seat belts merely mitigated damages but did not prevent accidents.[46]

There are those that believe that not only is the efficacy of seat belts in question, but that its use may, in some instances, actually be harmful, since the belt may delay or prevent escape to safety after an accident. Courts that hold to this view do not believe that evidence of failure to use seat belts as a defense is proper, even to indi-

---

[45] Heritage Ins. Co. v. Cilano, 433 So. 2d 1338 (1983).
[46] **D.C.:** McCord v. Green, 362 A.2d 720 (App. 1976).
Mich.: Romankewitz v. Black, 167 N.W.2d 606 (1969).
N.Y.: Spier v. Baker, 363 N.Y.S.2d 916 (1974).

§ 23.04[1]   CASUALTY INSURANCE CLAIMS

cate possible mitigation of damages.[47]

A minority of the decisions, however, hold that failure to use seat belts that are available can be admitted as evidence to mitigate damages.[48] These decisions were made on the basis that:

1. Plaintiff's conduct was a contributing cause in bringing about the injuries, or
2. Plaintiff failed to take any action to protect himself and should recover only for those injuries that would have occurred even if seat belts had been used, or
3. Plaintiff's injuries were aggravated by the fact that seat belts were not used.

In any event, the courts have generally agreed that failure to use seat belts is not negligence per se by any standard of an ordinarily prudent and reasonable driver or occupant, where there has been no legislation on that particular point.[49]

[1] **Statutory Enactments**

About one-third of our states have enacted some form of seat belt laws. Such states include those that follow the doctrine of contributory negligence (only a handful), and those that follow one or the other form of comparative negligence. Some have made seat belt use mandatory, others have legislated on the admissibility of the use of seat belts in evidence. Here again, no generalizations can be made since court decisions depend on the interpretation of their particular statutes. Most of the rulings are still made at common law.

---

[47] **Ariz.:** Nash v. Kamarath, 521 P.2d 161 (1974) (where there is no statutory or common law duty to use seat belts).
D.C.: McCord v. Green, 362 A.2d 720 (App. 1976).
Ind.: State v. Ingram, 427 N.E.2d 444 (1981).
Mo.: Miller v. Haynes, 454 S.W.2d 293 (App. 1970).
[48] **Conn.:** Remington v. Arndt, 259 A.2d 145 (1969) (but only in unusual circumstances).
Fla.: I.N.A. v. Pasakarnis, 451 So. 2d 447 (1984).
N.M.: Thomas v. Henson, 696 P.2d 1010 (1985).
N.Y.: Spier v. Parker, 323 N.Y.S.2d 164 (1974).
Okla.: Henderson v. United States, 429 F.2d 588 (10th Cir. (1970).
Pa.: Parise v. Fehnel, 406 A.2d 345 (1975).
Wis.: Bentzler v. Braun, 149 N.W.2d 626 (1967).
[49] **D.C.:** McCord v. Green, 362 A.2d 720 (1976).
Wash.: Derheim v. N. Fiorito Co., 492 P.2d 1030 (1972).

Some statutes have made express provision that failure to use seat belts when available does not constitute contributory negligence.[50]

In those states where the statute merely requires the installation of seat belts, the courts are reluctant to hold that failure to use seat belts is evidence of contributory negligence.[51]

An Iowa case held that where the defendant is under no statutory duty to provide seat belts in a taxi, failure to do so as evidence of negligence, is a matter of jury determination.[52]

Even in those states that have enacted some form of comparative negligence, there has been no concerted movement to apply the seat belt defense, except where causal relationship has been shown.[53]

In the case of *Twohig v. Briner*,[54] the plaintiff was a passenger in the car of the driver-owner who had removed the seat belts that were attached when the owner bought the car. The court ruled that the removal of the belts may have been a breach of the duty of care owed to a passenger and that this was a question of fact for jury determination.

§ 23.05 Bibliography

Guest Statutes

"Automobile Guest Laws Today," Report of the Automobile Insurance Commission, 1960, Insurance Counsel Journal, April 1960.

Foley, "Whatever Happened to the Guest Statute?", Insuransweek, May 9, 1980.

McAdams, "Automotive Guest Statutes—A Constitutional Analysis," Insurance Counsel Journal, July 1974.

Schlotthauer, "Assumption of Risk in Automobile Guest Cases," Insurance Law Journal, August 1962.

---

[50] **Kan.:** Hampton v. State Highway Commission, 498 P.2d 236 (1972).
Ky.: Statute of 1982.
Tenn.: Stallcup v. Taylor, 463 S.W.2d 416 (1970).
[51] **Mo.:** Miller v. Haynes, 454 S.W.2d 293 (App. 1970).
[52] Tiemeyer v. McIntosh, 176 N.W.2d 819 (1970) (no negligence found).
[53] **Pa.:** Parise v. Fehnel, 406 A.2d 345 (1979) (no causal relationship found in this case).
Wis.: Bentzler v. Braun, 149 N.W.2d 626 (1967) (there must be a causal relationship).
[54] 214 Cal. Rptr. 729 (App. 1985).

Liquor Law Liability

Comment, Lang & McGrath, "Third Party Liability for Drunken Driving: When 'One for the Road' Becomes One for the Courts," 29 Vill. L. Rev. 1119 (1983-84).

Comment, Levin, "The Liability of Social Hosts for Their Intoxicated Guests' Automobile Accidents—An Extension of the Law," 18 Akron L. Rev. 473 (Winter 1985).

F.C.& S. Bulletins, Casualty volume, Public Liability section, pp. L1 to L16. Contains excellent and comprehensive treatment on this subject, especially as to insurance coverage.

Gomulkiewicz, "Recognizing the Liability of Social Hosts Who Knowingly Allow Intoxicated Guests to Drive: Limits to Socially Acceptable Behavior," 60 Wash. L. Rev. 389 (1985).

Mishky, "The Liability of Providers of Alcohol: Dram Shop Acts?" 12 Pepperdine L. Rev. 177 (1984).

O'Meara, "Liquor Vendor Liability for Torts of Intoxicated Persons," Comment, 12 Baltimore L. Rev. 139 (Fall 1982).

Tish & Ream, "Social Host Liability," F.T.D., January 1985.

Zuger, "Liability for Liquor Suppliers," Insurance Information Service (Insurance Adjuster Magazine, October 1984).

Seat Belt Defense

Guldenschuh, "The Seat Belt Defense: A Comprehensive Guide for the Trial Lawyer and Suggested Approach for the Courts," Note, 56 The Notre Dame Lawyer (December 1980).

Marema, "A New Perspective on the Duty to Buckle Up," F.T.D., August 1985.

Miller, "The Seat Belt Defense Under Comparative Negligence," 12 Idaho L. Rev. 59-76 (1976).

"The Seat Belt Defense in Practice," D.R.I. Monograph (1970).

CHAPTER 24

Protection Against the Irresponsible Motorist

§ 24.01 Financial Responsibility Laws
    [1] Policy Wording
    [2] Motor Carrier Act of 1980
§ 24.02 Assigned Risk Plans
§ 24.03 Unsatisfied Judgment Laws
§ 24.04 Compulsory Insurance
§ 24.05 Uninsured and Underinsured Motorist Coverage
    [1] Stacking of Recoveries
    [2] Hit-and-Run Cases
    [3] Statute of Limitations
    [4] Investigation of Uninsured Motorist Claims
§ 24.06 No-Fault Automobile Plans and Legislation—Personal Injury Protection (P.I.P.) Coverage
    [1] Introduction
    [2] History
    [3] The Keeton–O'Connell Plan
    [4] Complete Personal Protection Automobile Insurance Plan
    [5] Present Trends—Personal Injury Protection (P.I.P.) Coverage
        [a] Policy Coverage
        [b] Multiple Coverages
        [c] Subrogation

The problem of the irresponsible motorist has been with us since the invention of the automobile. It took the insurance industry some time however to realize that the irresponsible uninsured driver was their concern as much as it was that of the responsible public that suffered the injuries and damages. The legislatures were just as nearsighted.

For many years, Financial Responsibility Laws (which did help to reduce the number of uninsured drivers) were accepted as the sole remedy, even though their inadequacies were obvious. In many instances, they did not take care of the situation arising from the first accident and they did not cope with hit-and-run drivers or stolen cars.

Assigned Risk Plans, Unsatisfied Judgment Funds, Compulsory Insurance Laws, and Uninsured Motorist Coverage were all subsequent palliatives which were tried with varying degrees of success. We will discuss them separately.

§ 24.01 Financial Responsibility Laws

The first Financial and Safety Responsibility Law was enacted by the Connecticut legislature in 1926. The statute required fault in order to become effective. It was not until 1937 that New Hampshire passed a law requiring proof of financial responsibility after an accident, regardless of who was responsible for the accident.

All states, including the District of Columbia, have now enacted some sort of financial responsibility laws. Their general intent is to protect the public at large from financial loss resulting from the operation of automobiles by reckless and financially irresponsible individuals. They provide that certain persons be required to furnish evidence of financial responsibility by way of an insurance policy, the posting of a bond, cash or securities. In the event of a failure to do so, the person so required may lose his driving privilege and the right to register an automobile.

Those required to post proof of financial responsibility fall within three general classifications:

1. Persons convicted of certain specified traffic violations or crimes involving the use or operation of an automobile.
2. Those who have judgments against them as a result of automobile accidents involving personal injury or property damage.
3. In some states, those involved in automobile accidents that resulted in some specified monetary damage to either car, or in bodily injury to anyone, regardless of liability.

The laws vary in the different states. Some require proof of financial responsibility relating to future accidents only. Others require proof for the initial accident regardless of liability, and some states run the gamut between the two. Obviously, therefore, the claims person must become familiar with the financial responsibility laws of his state and with the procedures required to prove such responsibility by means of insurance.

[1] Policy Wording

Previous casualty policies, such as the Family Automobile policy, contained a provision entitled, "Terms of Policy Conformed to Statute." In view of the fact that it is a well accepted principle of law that all insurance policies must conform to the statutes that refer to insurance coverage, such a clause was actually redundant and present policies tend to eliminate this clause entirely.

The Condition referring to "Financial Responsibility Laws" compounded the redundancy in this long involved clause that stated in effect that the policy would conform to any financial responsibility laws that were enacted.

The Personal Auto policy still contains a clause entitled, "Financial Responsibility Required," that reads "When this policy is certified as future proof of financial responsibility, this policy shall comply with the law to the extent required." The Business Auto policy has omitted any such reference altogether. Accordingly, the provisions of the financial responsibility laws of any particular jurisdiction in which the policy is issued are read into the policy contract.

These laws uniformly provide that the liability of the insurance carrier will be absolute in regard to third parties. By issuing the policy to enable an insured to meet the requirements of the financial responsibility laws, therefore, we are in effect saying that our denial of coverage will not affect any claim of third parties. Both the statutes and the provisions of the policy, however, limit this absolute liability to third parties only. Though coverage cannot be denied insofar as claims by third parties are concerned, the right to seek reimbursement from the insured for any amount paid as a result of a claim that ordinarily would not have been covered under the terms of the policy except for the requirements of the financial responsibility law, is specifically reserved.

Notice to the Motor Vehicle Bureau. Most financial responsibility laws also require notice to the motor vehicle bureau in some specified manner when a carrier wishes to cancel a policy. Again, since the laws are read into the policy, cancellation cannot be effective in respect to third party claims unless this provision of the law has been complied with.

Although the procedure for getting the information to the different motor vehicle state bureaus may vary, the forms generally require the same information and, for the most part, bear the same designations:

1. SR-21. This form is required only in the event the insured is involved in an accident. In effect, it states that the insured carries an existing automobile liability policy for the amounts stated with the designated insurance company. It is usually required where property damage over a certain amount, or bodily injury resulted from the accident.
2. SR-22. This form is one required from the insurance carrier to show that a policy has been issued *after* a noncovered accident has occurred.

Although some other forms may be necessary under certain conditions in order to meet the requirements of the financial responsibility laws, these are the two important ones with which the claim department is most directly concerned.

The consensus of opinion is that the filing of an SR-21 form does not affect the rights of the company under its policy and these rights are affected only by the filing of an SR-22 Form.

There are some decisions holding that if the insured was not *required* to qualify under the act at the time that the policy was issued, the policy defenses are preserved despite a change in the law at the time the accident occurred.

It is most important that any required filing of a form by the carrier be done promptly and carefully.

The person who receives a notice from the motor vehicle bureau informing him that his license will be revoked if he does not file proof of financial responsibility, is not going to be very tolerant of any excuse if he has reported the matter promptly to his carrier.

By the same token, a carrier may be estopped from later denying coverage if a form is completed carelessly and proof is filed for someone not intended to be covered by the policy. This is particularly important when there is any question of permissive use. If such permission, actual or implied, has not been extended to the driver of the automobile, this fact should be clearly indicated on the SR-21 form in the designated space, since the policy may provide no coverage for such a driver.

[2] Motor Carrier Act of 1980

The Motor Carrier Act of 1980 set new financial responsibility requirements on truckers that transport certain hazardous cargoes in interstate and intrastate destinations. The responsibility for the enforcement of these regulations was given to the Department of Transportation through the Bureau of Motor Carrier Safety.

The Interstate Commerce Commission (I.C.C.) accordingly modified its regulations so that there would be no overlapping and the Bureau of Motor Carrier Safety took jurisdiction in this area. Duties that were not affected by the Motor Carrier Act of 1980 were retained by the I.C.C.

Financial responsibility under the Act applies to three specified types of freight transport involving vehicles with a gross weight of 10,000 pounds or more. Compliance with these regulations may be met by: (1) insurance coverage by endorsement, as provided by the Bureau of Motor Carrier Safety, or (2) a bond guaranteeing payment of liability judgments up to the required amounts.

The insurance endorsement (MCS-90) is fairly comprehensive and includes Definitions of *accident, motor vehicle, bodily injury and property damage, environmental restoration,* and *public liability.*

Environmental Restoration is defined as:

> restitution for the loss, damage, or destruction of natural resources arising out of the accidental discharge, dispersal, release or escape into or upon the land, atmosphere, watercourse or body of water, of any commodity transported by a motor carrier. This shall include the cost of removal and the cost of necessary measures taken to minimize or mitigate damage or potential for damage to human health, the natural environment, fish, shellfish and wildlife.

As is now obvious, the old controversies concerning cleanup costs, particularly for oil spills, has finally been put to rest.

The MCS-90 endorsement, further, accepts coverage for any final judgment, under the requirements of Sections 29 and 30 of the Motor Carrier Act of 1980 "whether or not each vehicle is specifically described" or "whether or not such negligence occurs on any route or in any territory authorized to be served by the insured *or elsewhere."* (Emphasis added.)

Exclusions are incorporated for employees in the course of their employment and for property transported by the insured.

The paragraph in endorsement MCS-90 which incorporates the insuring agreement, states that: "no condition, provision, stipulation, or limitation in the policy, this endorsement, or any other endorsement thereon, or violation thereof, shall relieve the company from liability."

The only limitation is that of the Limits of Liability provision of the policy. In return, the insured, in this form, agrees to reimburse the insurer for any payment that the insurer would not have had to make under the terms of the policy itself.

§ 24.02 Assigned Risk Plans

When financial responsibility laws demanded insurance coverage for generally unacceptable risks, some means had to be devised to provide such insurance where needed. Accordingly, the legislatures and the insurance industry got together to grant coverage, in minimum limits as required by law, to those who could not get it elsewhere. Such risks might include either the too young or too old, those with bad driving or accident records, or merely individuals unfortunate enough to live in a high risk area. The Assigned Risk Plans thus came into being and are now operative in all states.

The various plans are operated by designated agencies who provide for the assignment of bodily injury and property damage liability insurance only, to companies in proportion to the amount of business which they write in a particular locality.

There is no provision under the Assigned Risk Plans for the writing of medical payments coverage, or physical damage coverages, or for bodily injury and property damage limits higher than the minimum requirements of the particular state where the named insured resides. There is some provision in some states permitting higher limits to be purchased under an "Excess Indemnity Policy." This is not uniform or universal.

In order to be eligible, an applicant must certify that he has attempted and failed to obtain the necessary insurance in the state where the application is being made. There are some situations where an insurer is not required to accept an assigned risk. This ordinarily involves an illegal enterprise or a driver who has been convicted of a felony or for other reasons specifically stated in the various acts.

§ 24.03 Unsatisfied Judgment Laws

Another method of attempting to combat the evils of the irresponsible motorist was the setting up of state funds to pay for unsatisfied judgments and hit-and-run claims, in some states.

The idea was originated in Manitoba, Canada, and first adopted in the United States by the state of North Dakota in 1947. Subsequently New Jersey, Maryland, and Michigan adopted some form of unsatisfied judgment statute.

There are two basic types of statutes, namely:

1. State operated and administered. North Dakota and Michigan follow this form.
2. Company administered under the direction of a board representing the state and the insurance companies. This type of statute is in effect in New Jersey, New York, and Maryland.

These funds are provided for by motor vehicle and individual driver taxation as requirements for registration of motor vehicles and driver's licenses, and in addition, in some cases, by taxation on insurance companies on a percentage of the premium written. The funds differ as to collection of monies, particulars of prosecution and defense of suits, requirements for collection and other details. With some exceptions, they cover hit-and-run accidents.

In the event that a claimant recovers all or a portion of his judgment from any other source, the amount to be recovered from the Unsatisfied Judgment Fund is reduced by the amount of such recovery from the other source. Default judgments require notice to the fund prior to the entry of judgment in order to be recognized for reimbursement.

The bad features of these laws are:

1. They are very cumbersome, involved, and costly.
2. The claimant is forced to take his claim to judgment.
3. The amount of recovery is limited and, in addition, there is usually a deductible feature.
4. There are many restrictions that prevent recovery in quite a few instances.

In my opinion such funds are not an adequate answer to the problem and apparently most state legislatures agree, since very few have instituted Unsatisfied Judgment Funds, and they have diminished in importance since the establishment of Uninsured Motorist Insurance.

§ 24.04 Compulsory Insurance

The first state to adopt a compulsory insurance law was Massachusetts in 1927. After many changes, including the drastic one to a "No-Fault" system, compulsory insurance is still in effect there and other states. The insurance is required at the time of registraton and runs from the duration of the registration. While there are some exceptions for surety bonds or deposit of cash in lieu of insurance, basically these are unimportant exceptions.

The one insurmountable hurdle involved in compulsory insurance is that it can apply only to the state in which registration is taken out and such laws cannot affect the hit-and-run driver. Out-of-state motorists are not affected, at least at the time of the registration of the motor vehicle. The acts are not uniform.

Some states have initiated legislation involving certain classes of commercial vehicles; for instance, automobiles held out for hire, requiring what amounts to compulsory insurance for them. These are special situations, however, with which the claim representative must familarize himself in his particular state.

§ 24.05 Uninsured and Underinsured Motorist Coverage

Insurance coverage for the protection of an injured against the acts of irresponsible motorists was the first really effective measure taken by the insurance industry to fill the voids still left despite the other measures that have already been discussed. It was designed in addition to take care of injuries resulting from out-of-state drivers, from hit-and-run drivers, and even from those who purchased insurance but whose insurers denied coverage for one reason or another.

The impetus that prompted the insurance industry to act was the continuing pressure for compulsory insurance, plus the fact that the first real rumblings concerning "No-Fault" legislation were being heard. New York was the first state to promulgate standard provisions for uninsured motorists coverage in 1956, at the recommendation of the insurance industry, although a proposed endorsement was already in being and had been for several years.

As with Medical Payments coverage, Protection Against Uninsured Motorists coverage is first party insurance bought directly by the insured for his own protection and for the protection of those riding in, or using his car with his permission as outlined in the policy. It is, however, superimposed upon third party liability since recovery can only be made from the insurer if the injured would have been entitled to recover against the uninsured motorist who caused the injury or damage. In other words, liability must have been in favor of the insured.

It must be made very clear that neither the uninsured's vehicle, its driver, owner, nor anyone responsible for its use is covered under the policy. Uninsured Motorists coverage is an addition to the regular policy which covers the insured vehicle and adds this extra protection for an additional premium. Some states make this coverage mandatory. Most states have enacted some statutes concerning Uninsured Motorists coverage and some make such coverage optional.

Uninsured Motorist coverage means exactly what it states. As long as the wrongdoer has some insurance, no matter how inadequate the limits, Uninsured Motorist coverage does not apply.[1] Subsequently, the insurance industry promulgated Underinsured Motorist coverage, which filled this gap.

[1] Stacking of Recoveries

Under the Uninsured Motorist coverage, in addition to the named insured, certain relatives, permissive users, and occupants of the insured vehicle are also covered. As a result, a covered insured may be entitled to recover under provisions in the same or other policies resulting from the same accident. To allow duplicate recoveries under the same or more than one applicable policy for the same accident is commonly referred to as "stacking" of recoveries.

It is generally agreed that most of the states that have enacted Uninsured Motorist statutes have done so in order to provide insurance protection for the insured who has had an accident with an uninsured vehicle or been involved with a hit-and-run driver. The purpose is to put the insured in the same position that he would have been in had the wrongdoing driver been covered by automobile liability insurance, and no more. Some courts have generally agreed

---

[1] **N.J.:** Gorton v. Reliance Ins. Co., 391 A.2d 1219 (1978).
Wash.: Strunk v. State Farm Mut. Auto. Ins. Co., 580 P.2d 622 (1978).

that under their statutes, stacking of recoveries is forbidden.[2] Other courts have interpreted their statutes to permit stacking, especially where a separate premium was paid for each additional coverage.[3]

[2] Hit-and-Run Cases

The Insuring Agreement of the Uninsured Motorist coverage in defining a "motor vehicle" states in part:

3. [A motor vehicle] which is a hit-and-run vehicle whose operator or owner cannot be identified and which *hits* [emphasis added]:

a. you or any family member;

b. a vehicle which you or any family member are occupying; or

c. your covered auto.

The key word in this clause is "hits," which replaces former wording that used "physical contact." The meaning was intended to be the same. Some courts have construed this clause strictly and have held that there must be actual contact between the vehicle causing

---

[2] **Ariz.:** Bakken v. State Farm Mut. Auto. Ins. Co., 678 P.2d 481 (1983).
Iowa: Tri-State Ins. Co. v.De Gooyer, 379 N.W.2d 16 (1986).
La.: Block v Reliance Ins. Co., 417 So. 2d 29 (App.), *cert. denied,* 420 So. 2d 978 (1982).
Minn.: Stenzel v. State Farm Mut. Auto. Ins. Co., 379 N.W.2d 674 (1986) (applying S.D. law).

[3] **Fla.:** General Accid. Fire & Life Assur. Corp. v. MacKenzie, 419 So. 2d 1197 (1982).
Ga.: State Farm Mut. Auto. Ins. Co. v. Hancock, 295 S.E.2d 359 (1982).
Miss.: State Farm Mut. Auto. Ins. Co. v. Nester, 459 So. 2d 787 (1984) (multiple premiums paid).
N.J.: Lundy v. Aetna Cas. & Sur. Co., 458 A.2d 106 (1983) (insurer cannot differentiate between separate or single policies involving different vehicles).
Ohio: Gomolka v. State Auto. Mut. Ins. Co., 472 N.E.2d 700 (1985) (multiple premiums paid).
Okla.: Lake v. Wright, 657 P.2d 643 (1983) (clause to prevent stacking is against public policy).
S.C.: Gambrell v. Travelers Ins. Co., 310 S.E.2d 814 (1983).
Wash.: Bradbury v. Aetna Cas. & Sur. Co., 91 Wash. 2d 504 (1979) (multiple premiums were paid).
For a more exhaustive study of this subject, I recommend N.N. Stott's, "Underinsured Motorist Coverage: Working Out the Bugs," F.I.C. Quarterly, Winter 1986, and in particular, Schermer, *Automobile Liability Insurance,* 2d ed. (New York: Clark Boardman Co. Ltd. 1981).

the damage or injury and the vehicle driven by an insured under the Uninsured Motorist coverage.[4]

There were, however, many situations where the wrongdoing driver's vehicle did not sustain direct contact with the Uninsured Motorist or the vehicle he was driving. For instance, where the vehicle responsible for the accident hit a car in the rear which was then pushed into the rear of the insured's car and then disappeared, an Arizona court held that there was no physical contact as required by the policy and accordingly no recovery was permitted.[5]

On the other hand, a California court decided that where a hit-and-run vehicle struck another car, causing it to cross over the median and hit the insured driver's vehicle, there was physical contact enough to warrant coverage.[6]

A similar case involved a rock that was thrown from under the wheels of an unidentified truck, striking the insured's windshield and killing a passenger in his car. An Indiana appellate court held that this constituted sufficient "contact" to satisfy the statutory and policy requirements.[7]

Other decisions follow the line of reasoning that holds that "where an intermediate vehicle transmits the impact from a hit-and-run car to the insured's car . . . the interference of an intermediate object does not negate physical contact."[8]

The hit-and-run case presents an extra problem in that it lends itself to the temptation of fraud. The same case that seemed to imply that physical contact was necessary,[9] very cogently stated that "Where force has been exerted from an unidentified vehicle through

---

[4] **Idaho:** Hammon v. Farmers Ins. Co. of Idaho, 707 P.2d 397 (1986).
Ill.: Cole v. Pekin Ins. Co., 453 N.E.2d 876 (App. 1983).
La.: Harrison v. Commercial Union Ins. Co., 471 So. 2d 922 (1985).
Mich.: Auto Club Ins. Assoc. v. Methner, 339 N.W.2d 234 (1983) (not against public policy to hold otherwise).
Ohio: Yurista v. Nationwide Mut. Ins. Co., 481 N.E.2d 584 (1985).
Wis.: Hayne v. Progressive Northern Ins. Co., 339 N.W.2d 588 (1983) (implied, since case involved required coverage under the statute).

[5] Anderson v. State Farm Mut. Auto. Ins. Co., 652 P.2d 537 (1982).

[6] Inter-Ins. Exch. v. Lopez, 47 Cal. Rptr. 834 (1985).

[7] Allied Fidelity Ins. Co. v. Lamb, 361 N.E.2d 174 (1977).

[8] Motor Vehicle Indemnification Corp. v. Eisenberg, 271 N.Y.S.2d 641 (1966). *See also* the following cases.
La.: Ray v. De Maggio, 313 So. 2d 251 (1975).
Mich.: Lord v. Auto-Owners Ins. Co., 177 N.W.2d 653 (App. 1970).
Tex.: Latham v. Mountain States Mut. Cas. Co., 482 S.W.2d 655 (App. 1972).
Wash.: Johnson v. State Farm Auto. Ins. Co., 424 P.2d 648 (1967).

[9] **Ariz.:** Anderson v. State Farm Mut. Auto. Ins. Co., 652 P.2d 537 (1982).

an intermediate object and *where this fact may be verified in such a way to provide safeguards against fraud* [emphasis added], we find that the physical contact requirement of the policy has been satisfied."

Accordingly, quite a few cases have affirmed the so-called "corroborative evidence" rule that physical contact is required only in cases where corroborative evidence is unobtainable.[10]

[3] Statute of Limitations

Once again, the policy provisions are always subject to the state laws. The applicable law is ordinarily where the policy was bought (where contract was made) rather than where the accident occurred. Accordingly it has been held that the proper statute of limitations would be the one applicable to contracts.

Some statutes provide for the time in which suit must be filed, agreement made between the parties, or arbitration instituted.

[4] Investigation of Uninsured Motorist Claims

The investigation of claims which fall, or could fall, under Uninsured Motorist Coverage presents some problems which are more complex than those ordinarily encountered by the claim representative.

Under this kind of coverage, first party and third party become mixed up and the ethics of such a situation can become very difficult. Such situations can lead to what may appear to the claim representative to be a conflict of interests. On the one hand he is pushed to try to prove liability on the part of the uninsured claimant—particularly in borderline cases involving serious injuries. On the other hand, he is pulled in the direction of proving liability on the part of his insured when the claim under the Uninsured Motorist coverage could be serious and the other claim not.

If ever, therefore, a claim representative must exercise the highest degree of ethical conduct in such a situation. In some instances, it

---

[10] Ala.: State Farm Fire & Cas. Co. v. Lambert, 285 So. 2d 917 (1973).
Colo.: Farmers Ins. Exch. v. McDermott, 527 P.2d 918 (App. 1974).
Del.: State Farm Mut. Auto. Ins. Co. v. Abramowicz, 386 A.2d 670 (1978).
Fla.: Brown v. Progressive Mut. Ins. Co., 249 So. 2d 429 (1971).
Hi.: De Mello v. First Ins. Co. of Hawaii, 523 P.2d 304 (1974).
N.J.: Commercial Union Assur. Co. v. Kaplan, 377 A.2d 957 (Super. 1977).
Pa.: Webb v. United Services Auto Assoc., 323 A.2d 737 (1974).

IRRESPONSIBLE MOTORIST § 24.05[4]

will even be up to him to inform the insured of his rights under this coverage when the insured himself is ignorant of the provisions of his policy.

The investigation is in some ways easier. If it becomes clearly a matter of the insured's claim under the Uninsured Motorist coverage, he then has advantages which he would not ordinarily have in dealing with a third party claimant. The policy gives him certain rights and imposes certain duties on the insured with reference to the time limit on reporting a claim, the requirement of cooperation and the obtaining of medical and other information that he would not otherwise have. It also gives him the advantage of dealing with a friendly insured (at least initially) rather than a suspicious claimant.

The ordinary third party investigation must be made—if anything, a little more promptly and perhaps a little more thoroughly. He must in addition be sure to determine:

- ☐ Whether there is absolutely no insurance coverage available to the driver or owner of the other car.
- ☐ If the other car is insured, whether there is any likelihood that the carrier will deny coverage for any reason.
- ☐ If coverage is denied, whether such denial is justified and likely to stick.
- ☐ Whether there is any other Uninsured Motorist coverage available to the insured, such as:
  - ○ Another policy issued to the owner of the car.
  - ○ Another or separate policy issued to the driver.
  - ○ Possible coverage for someone responsible for the use of the vehicle.
  - ○ Possible coverage for an injured passenger.
  - ○ Possible coverage for drive-other-cars, if applicable.
  - ○ Possible coverage for relatives or members of the same household, if applicable.
- ☐ Whether the injury falls within any workers' compensation, disability benefits or similar law.
- ☐ In hit-and-run cases:
  - ○ Whether it is possible to learn the identity of the driver or owner of the hit-and-run car.
  - ○ Whether the insured complied with the requirements concerning reporting and other duties required by the policy.

§ 24.06 No-Fault Automobile Plans and Legislation—Personal Injury Protection (P.I.P.) Coverage

[1] Introduction

The idea of payment regardless of negligence, is not a new one. Workers' compensation, which is paid to injured employees regardless of negligence, has been declared constitutional many times, and has been in existence since the turn of the century.

Two factors that have, in my opinion, had a great deal to do with the erosion of the negligence system are some of the excessive verdicts being rendered by judges as well as juries, and the continuing trend toward almost absolute liability in may of the decisions of our state and federal courts. The basic rule of "reasonableness" has been perverted to mean the highest degree of care. Contributory negligence, in those states which still nominally hold to this obsolete doctrine, has gone by the board in actual practice. Defense doctrines have been so watered-down as to be practically ineffectual. Some of the decisions concerning liability for verdicts in excess of policy limits haven't helped the situation. As a result, automobile liability insurance costs soared to the point where the legislatures had to listen to the protesting public.

[2] History

Massachusetts was the first state to adopt "No-Fault" automobile liability legislation in 1970. Although some thought had been given to the subject even earlier, the first serious no-fault proposal was the so-called *Colombia Plan* or, as it is sometimes called, the "Ballantine Report," named after the chairman of the committee that made the proposal. The plan followed lines set out by workers' compensation laws and an entire statute was outlined, patterned on them. This plan, proposed in 1932, was followed by a number of other plans, the major ones being:

Saskatchewan Plan, actually enacted in Saskatchewan, Canada, in 1946. This plan requires liability insurance in addition to the no-fault coverage. Insurance is compulsory and the no-fault section pays scheduled benefits.

Ehrenzweig "Full Aid" Plan proposed in 1954 by Professor A.A. Ehrenzweig in a book entitled, "Full Aid Insurance for the Traffic Victim—A Voluntary Compensation Plan." His plan provided for a system of voluntary insurance that would make stated benefit payments without regard to fault. It would do away with negligence as a basis for recovery and was to be written by private insurance companies.

Professor Leon Green in 1958, published a book entitled, "Traffic Victim—Tort Law and Insurance." It suggested an exclusive compulsory no-fault insurance law that included property damage and permitted no recovery for pain and suffering. It was an uncomplicated plan, but made no provision for compensating the victims of uninsured motorists.

Professors Morris and Paul, in 1962, proposed a system of supplementary insurance for automobile accidents where the victim had more than $800 in unreimbursed medical or lost earning expenses and would receive 85 percent of the amount above that sum. Here again, there was to be no reimbursement for pain and suffering.

Conrad Plan, proposed by Professor Alfred F. Conrad in 1964, made some recommendations as a result of a study conducted at the University of Michigan. His report indicated that no single plan for automobile accident compensation proposed so far was workable, and proposed that the problem be handled as an extension of social security with the retention of a modified tort system.

Keeton–O'Connnell Plan, otherwise known as the "Basic Protection Plan," was first promulgated in 1965 and was subsequently published in book form and created the waves that finally resulted in actual legislation. It was followed by the *California Plan* in 1967, the *Social Protection Plan of Puerto Rico* enacted in 1968, the *Complete Personal Protection Automobile Insurance Plan*, proposed by the American Insurance Association, and many others.

All of the proposed plans had some basic element of recovery that was not dependent upon negligence in order to be effective. Most of them suggested compulsory insurance, usually at the time of registration. A few were to be optionally under government control, but most recommended insurance from private carriers. Payments generally were to be made for medical and related expenses in a lump sum plus regular payments for loss of earnings. Most of them also contained the right of legal action for negligence above certain monetary limits. Some included property damage but most did not. Only a few were brave enough to opt for the complete elimination of payments for pain and suffering, but most permitted suit for pain and suffering over a certain amount. A few were what I call "either or" plans since they permitted either the acceptance of specified payments under "No-Fault" and/or permitted the institution of negligence actions at the choice of the insured.

[3] The Keeton–O'Connell Plan

This plan grants the injured what it refers to as Basic Protection in return for which the insured has a limited exemption for tort liability. The injured claimant makes his claim directly against his own insurance carrier, or if a guest against the carrier of the automobile in which he was riding.

Legal action based on negligence is permitted where the out-of-pocket expense exceeds $10,000 and where, in the opinion of the claimant, damages for pain and suffering exceed $5,000, but a specific limit was placed on the amount recoverable for this item. Recovery is reduced by the amounts payable under Basic Protection.

The plan was subsequently changed to allow some recovery for property damage by the purchase of separate insurance.

Reimbursement under this plan is limited to the net economic loss including reasonable medical expenses, loss of income, and some related items. The plan also contains some deductible features.

[4] Complete Personal Protection Automobile Insurance Plan

The problem with some of the proposed no-fault plans, in my opinion, is due in some measure to the fact that those who promulgated them did not have the practical experience necessary to see the problem in all of its facets.

It is perhaps for this reason that I, at least, believe that the American Insurance Association's "Complete Personal Protection Automobile Insurance Plan" is the most completely thought out, practical and workable of the plans heretofore proposed.

In this plan the injured would receive his payments, regardless of fault, from his own insurer. It would be a compulsory form and would operate in the manner of present day medical payment claims, including additional consideration for loss of salary and other economic loss. Payments would be made periodically as expenses are incurred.

The one serious criticism that I can make concerning this plan is in the area of duplicate payments. The very principle of no-fault, I believe, should preclude multiple recovery of medical, hospital bills, or other items of this nature. Where there is duplicate coverage, I believe it only fair that such items of expense should be prorated, except where accicent and health policies are purchased for additional income during disability or for extraordinary medical expenses.

The plan also includes recompense for expenses reasonably incurred for services in lieu of those the injured person would have performed without income. This could include, for instance, household services ordinarily performed by a spouse.

There is no monetary limit in this plan, except for a monthly limitation for loss of salary. Consideration is given for deduction of tax benefits. The plan includes payment for the usual expenses and losses in case of death.

An important part of the Complete Personal Protection Plan is that there is no provision for payment of pain and suffering in any amount and no provision for legal action for negligence after payment of any amount. The plan does recognize the need to compensate for dismemberment, permanent disfigurement, and total disability. It even has a provision to cover property damage.

The problem of out-of-state accidents or out-of-state drivers is handled by what is called "Residual Automobile Liability Coverage."

It is not a lengthy plan. It is terse, to the point, and in my opinion covers more contingencies than any other no-fault plan that has so far been promulgated. It is not an "either-or" plan but is a straight no-fault compensation type plan that proposes to do the job it was set out to do—to reasonably protect insureds at premium rates that they can afford.

In my opinion, this plan is the one that had the most influence on those that were subsequently enacted, and was the forerunner of the Personal Injury Protection (P.I.P) coverage which has become an integral part of many standard types of liability insurance policies.

[5] Present Trends—Personal Injury Protection (P.I.P.) Coverage

About one-half of our states have adopted some form of no-fault or personal injury protection acts. The one thing that is disturbing in reviewing these plans is their lack of uniformity in so many areas. What started out as a gallant attempt to correct our obviously defective system of making injured victims of accidents whole, has been perverted and diminished in importance to become another mere appendage to the automobile liability policy. Lawyers, insurance companies, and the greed of the public at large have all but destroyed the basic central premise of no-fault recovery. Many states have already amended their statutes to eliminate or emasculate the provisions that make the law mandatory and free of the problem of liability.

The areas of noneconomic recoveries in the last ten years, such as pain and suffering, bad faith actions, emotional distress, and punitive damages have blossomed into a veritable bonanza for lawyers and the lucky plaintiffs who have profited by the unwarranted verdicts in many cases.

The very lawyer-legislators who pointed the finger at what they called the failure of no-fault were the ones who sabotaged it and made it even less effective than it already was.

Some amendments have been made increasing the threshold amount for no-fault over which a legal action may be brought. Others have changed specific amounts to thresholds involving specific injuries, which I think is a move in the right direction.

Without the mandatory factor under which amount no legal action could be brought, fraud was encouraged in order to increase medical expenses. With a low threshold, claimants who were responsible for accidents and had little chance of recovery in the courts, took the no-fault payments and ran. Others simply saw to it that the medical expenses were increased so that they could bring legal actions. As a result the insurers got the worst end of the bargain. Accordingly, they were happy enough to attach the no-fault endorsements to the regular automobile liability policy for an extra premium, and that made everybody happy until it came time to pay the piper.

[a] Policy Coverage

At this time, no-fault coverage is provided as an endorsement to the automobile liability policy under the designation of Personal Injury Protection (P.I.P.).

As with other insurance policies and provisions, they are subordinate to any statutory provisions that differ substantially with those provisions. It is the statute that spells out the terms of the coverage and since the various statutes are quite different in many respects, so are the endorsements providing the coverage. For this reason, the endorsements will have to be discussed in the most general terms.

Since this coverage duplicates benefits obtained under the Medical Payments coverage, Section II of the P.I.P. endorsement states that:

> In consideration of the coverage afforded under Section I and the adjustment of applicable rates, any Medical Payments coverage afforded under this policy is deleted with respect to a motor vehicle on which coverage is provided under this endorsement.

Those who may recover benefits in the event of an accident, usually include, under "Covered Persons," the named insured, his or her spouse, other residents, relatives, and users or occupants who are there with the permission of someone who is authorized to give it, and any pedestrian who is struck by the covered automobile. There is some variance in those covered (if at all), when an accident occurs outside the jurisdiction of the state where the insurance was purchased.

Where no-fault statutes do not restrict the right to bring a liability suit, P.I.P. coverage is often called "add-on," since it is, in effect, additional coverage.

With the exception of one state—Michigan—property damage is not covered under the P.I.P. endorsement, probably because of the preponderence and availability of collision and comprehensive property damage coverages.

The usual bodily injury expenses that are covered include:

1. Medical expenses that are reasonable;
2. Rehabilitation expenses that are warranted and reasonable;
3. Funeral expenses usually up to a specified amount;
4. Loss of earnings, usually up to some specified time limit;
5. Replacement services, such as necessary housecleaning, home repairs and upkeep, and similar items within certain limitations; and
6. Survivor's loss, usually specified and for a limited time.

The amounts recoverable for medical and rehabilitation expenses run the gamut from unlimited to very little. Overall benefits run from a low of $2,000 to $50,000 at this time. Loss of earnings or "work loss" are usually on a percentage of regular earnings basis with a maximum time limitation.

Some states require insurers to offer increased no-fault benefits, on an optional basis for an additional premium, and other states permit optional deductibles in certain instances at a reduced rate.

Benefits that could be duplicated by other coverages may not be "stacked" in most cases and the rules and exceptions are outlined in the various statutes.

With some exceptions, benefits usually do not include noneconomic damages such as pain and suffering, emotional distress, etc.

[b] **Multiple Coverages**

It is possible, from the very nature of this coverage, that an occupant of an insured vehicle that is not his own, will be entitled to recover under the owner's policy and also under his own automobile policy. The same may hold for a pedestrian.

In situations such as these some statutes give priority to the insurer of the individual, while others require priority to be given to the insured vehicle. In either event, such coverage also applies to injuries sustained as a result of involvement with an uninsured vehicle.

[c] **Subrogation**

Under most no-fault statutes the insurer is subrogated to the rights, if any, of the insured. In some states, lien rights are available to an insurer.

These provisions are, as usual, not uniform and reference must be made to the specific statute which is involved. Controversies are usually required to be settled by arbitration.[11]

---

[11] For a state-by state review of the no-fault statutes and endorsements, *see* F.C.& S. Bulletins, Vol. entitled "Personal Lines," under section "Personal Auto," starting at pages Noa Co-1.

CHAPTER 25

Automobile Liability Investigation and Checklists

§ 25.01 Coverage Information
§ 25.02 Checklist on Policy Declarations
§ 25.03 Identification of the Insured's Vehicle
§ 25.04 Information to be Obtained from the Insured's Driver
§ 25.05 Information to be Obtained from the Claimant
§ 25.06 Witnesses
§ 25.07 Physical Facts or Objective Findings
§ 25.08 Further Details
§ 25.09 Evaluating Automobile Property Damage Claims
§ 25.10 Good Investigations Are Still Necessary
§ 25.11 Guide for Property Damage Settlement Decision
         [1]   Loss of Use

The basic principles of casualty claim investigation are the same whether they involve automobile, general liability, products liability or, in some measure, even workers' compensation claims. Therefore, the basic concepts covered heretofore, apply with equal force and merit to any of the separate categories included in this broad field. In order to avoid unnecessary repetition, it will be assumed that the reader has familiarized himself with the information contained in the previous chapters.

No two accidents are ever identical. It would therefore be impossible to make any investigation checklist that would be comprehensive enough to cover all of the contingencies that might be encountered. The checklists that follow cover most of the situations that the claim investigator will encounter. In reviewing them, he should apply whatever may be pertinent to the accident under investigation.

§ 25.01 Coverage Information

The initial report of an accident should be carefully reviewed for every bit of information that might be useful as a lead in the investigation of the incident. Comprehensive notes should be taken and an outline planned along the lines previously suggested.

Wherever possible, the policy application or daily should be carefully reviewed in an effort to determine whether the incident reported falls within the policy provisions. There may, of course, be many developments of which the claim investigator cannot be aware at the time he reviews the first report, which may call for additional investigation on coverage as leads develop. However, such items as making certain (1) that the incident occurred within the policy period, (2) that there was no delay in reporting the incident, (3) that the car listed in the report is properly covered, and similar items, are obvious points which can be checked immediately and noted for investigation, if they are not in order.

In reviewing the policy application, he should note the exact name of the insured and the limits of liability, check the basic coverage, and examine all endorsements very carefully to determine which, if any, apply to the accident under investigation.

Accidents close to inception or renewal date. An accident which allegedly occurred within a day or two of the inception date of the policy is one that should be checked carefully to determine whether the policy had actually been ordered before the accident occurred. If the alleged date of the accident is uncomfortably close to the inception date of the policy, the following investigation should be made:

- ☐ Signed statement from the insured, including:
  - ○ The exact date and time when the policy was ordered.
  - ○ The manner in which it was ordered, whether by telephone, mail, or otherwise.
  - ○ The exact name of the person from whom the policy was ordered.
  - ○ Conversations and surrounding circumstances of the order.
- ☐ Signed statement from the person with whom the original order was placed, covering the same information as 1.
- ☐ Check the date stamp of the binder in the agent's office.
- ☐ Check any other written notations or memoranda that the agent may be able to produce.
- ☐ Check the company's records, if necessary, to determine the exact date and time when notice was received by the company concerning the binder or policy.
- ☐ Check the date of the accident carefully through police records, witnesses, claimant's version, or other means that will definitely make the date conclusive.

AUTOMOBILE LIABILITY INVESTIGATION

§ 25.02 Checklist on Policy Declarations

- [ ] Determine who owns the vehicle involved in the accident.
  - Is it an individual, partnership, or corporation?
  - Is it an estate, trusteeship, municipality, or other entity?
  - Is the owner someone other than the named insured? If so, give details.
- [ ] Determine who regularly drives the vehicle named in the policy.
  - Is the vehicle driven by members of the insured's family or household?
  - Is it driven by employees of the insured?
  - Obtain the exact ages of all regular drivers of the vehicle.
- [ ] Determine the purposes for which the automobile is used.
  - Business or pleasure.
  - Other purposes.
  - Average number of miles per year the car is driven.
- [ ] Determine where the automobile is principally garaged.
- [ ] Determine whether there are any other automobiles in the same household.
  - How many?
  - Who owns them?
  - Does the insured own or regularly drive any other automobiles?
  - Are they insured?
  - In what company?
- [ ] If a commercial radius endorsement is involved:
  - Determine whether the truck is ever driven outside the allowed limits.
  - If so, how often?
  - Give locations and times as nearly exact as possible.

§ 25.03 Identification of the Insured's Vehicle

The purpose of making an identification of the insured's vehicle is to determine whether the vehicle involved in the accident is the one which is intended to be covered under the policy. This is today of much less importance than it was previously in view of the present automatic coverages under certain circumstances. However, if pertinent, the following checklist will help in most situations that the claim investigator may ordinarily encounter:

- [ ] Check the make, year, and model of the automobile.
- [ ] Check the registration certificate and compare it with the policy information.
- [ ] If necessary, check the motor and serial numbers, color of the car, and the license tag on the automobile.

§ 25.04   CASUALTY INSURANCE CLAIMS

- ☐ Examine the automobile for any marks or damage resulting from the accident in order to make sure that the automobile allegedly involved was the actual one.
- ☐ Check the speedometer mileage and compare it with the age of the automobile to determine the average number of miles driven per year.
- ☐ Check the condition of the vehicle, especially specific items that may have been involved in the accident like brakes, windshield wipers, lights, and so on. If an automobile is in poor general condition, the claim investigator may wish to make a Confidential Risk Report to the underwriting department.
- ☐ If the vehicle identified is not the one listed in the policy, determine:
  - ○ If it is a temporary substitute vehicle.
  - ○ Who owns it.
  - ○ Where the vehicle listed in the policy is located and why.
  - ○ If the vehicle involved in the accident is a replacement. If so, give details including exact dates of sale of the old vehicle and purchase of the new. In a separate signed statement, cover whether notice was given to the agent.
  - ○ If the vehicle involved in the accident is an additional automobile, give details including the exact date of purchase. Information concerning notice to the agent should also be covered in a separate signed statement.
  - ○ What primary insurance is carried on the vehicle and by whom, and determine if there is excess coverage.
- ☐ If the vehicle is not a temporary substitute vehicle and is not listed in the policy, determine:
  - ○ Who owns the vehicle.
  - ○ The purpose for which the car was used.
  - ○ Whether it is a hired vehicle. If so, who hired it, and how often it has been hired.
  - ○ What primary insurance is carried on the vehicle involved in the accident and by whom.

§ 25.04   Information to be Obtained from the Insured's Driver

A signed statement should be obtained from the insured's driver, incorporating as much of the following information and details as may be pertinent. There are obviously many points of information, such as general appearance, physical defects, and other such items, which do not belong in a signed statement and should not be incorporated in it, but should be commented on in the report.

A. Driver's background information and introductory information:

- ☐ Name and address.

AUTOMOBILE LIABILITY INVESTIGATION § 25.04

- ☐ If present address is temporary, obtain permanent address or the permanent address of a close relative through whom the driver may always be reached.
- ☐ Age, general appearance, and comments on mental or physical defects such as poor eyesight, poor hearing, crippling, amputation of fingers or other limbs, heart trouble, epilepsy, and so on.
- ☐ Marital status.
- ☐ Military status and how it may affect ability to appear as a witness.
- ☐ Nature of employment, and name and address of employer.
- ☐ If employed by the insured, obtain length of employment.
- ☐ Driving experience.
- ☐ Driver's or chauffeur's license or learner's permit.
  - How long obtained?
  - Is driver required to wear glasses? If so, was he wearing them?
  - Any recorded traffic violations? Any unrecorded? Obtain details.
  - Was license ever revoked or suspended? Obtain details.
  - If driver was a learner, was he accompanied by a properly licensed person? Did he have a proper learner's permit?
- ☐ Previous accident record, with dates, locations, and details.
- ☐ Possible driving distractions.
  - Was driver watching something or someone?
  - Was driver daydreaming?
  - Was radio in operation?
  - Was driver smoking?
  - Was driver worried or under emotional strain?
  - Was driver in a hurry?
- ☐ Possible fatigue.
  - How long had driver been driving before the accident?
  - What was his starting time?
  - What was the distance driven, including the point of departure, route and destination?
  - How much rest did the driver have immediately preceding the last driving?
- ☐ Alcoholic consumption.
  - How much?
  - When?
  - Where?
- ☐ If the accident involved injury to passengers in the insured's vehicle:
  - What was the exact nature of the trip? Obtain details.
  - What was the status of the passengers?
    - Did passengers make any contribution toward expenses?
    - Was this a joint venture?
    - Were the passengers guests, as interpreted by the law of your jurisdiction?
    - Who had control of the vehicle?

§ 25.04   CASUALTY INSURANCE CLAIMS

- [ ] Investigate permissive use of the vehicle. Corroborate all information obtained in the driver's statement by taking a signed statement from the named insured.
  - ○ Did driver receive direct permission from the named insured to drive the vehicle?
  - ○ Was any limitation placed on the use of the vehicle?
  - ○ Were there any material deviations from the permission granted?
    - — Exact places visited and the routes taken.
    - — Time consumed while the vehicle was in the driver's possession.
    - — Reasons for the deviation.
  - ○ If the driver was the second permittee, obtain a signed statement from the named insured and from both the first and second permittees.
    - — Did the named insured give express permission for the second permittee to drive?
    - — Did the named insured know the second permittee was going to drive?
    - — Was the named insured in the vehicle at the time?
    - — Had the named insured known the first permittee to allow the second permittee to drive on previous occasions?
    - — Did he ever forbid him to drive?
    - — Did the nature of the mission make it necessary for the second permittee to drive?
    - — Was he on business for the named insured?
- [ ] Was any report made to the motor vehicle bureau, police department or other official body? If so, what were the circumstances? Obtain copies.
- [ ] Report on your opinion concerning the insured's economic status and financial responsibility.
- [ ] Find out whether the insured intends to press any claim of his own.

B. Factual details:

- [ ] Obtain the exact date, time, and place of the accident.
- [ ] Obtain the direction of movement of all vehicles involved, including the name of the roads or streets and the locality:
  - ○ Was the driver familiar with the area?
- [ ] Find out the exact speed of the insured's vehicle and the approximate speed of any other vehicles involved:
  - ○ Was there a governor on the insured's vehicle?
  - ○ What gear was vehicle in?
  - ○ When did the driver last shift gears?
- [ ] Describe all traffic controls, including traffic police, signs, signals, or lights.
- [ ] Obtain the distance of the insured's car from the curb or its position with reference to traffic lanes and shoulders.
- [ ] The same should be found for any other vehicles involved.
- [ ] Obtain the position of all cars with reference to the nearest intersecting streets or highways.

AUTOMOBILE LIABILITY INVESTIGATION § 25.04

- ☐ Describe the physical facts in detail, including such items as weather conditions, road conditions, lighting, and other items specifically outlined in the following section entitled "Physical Facts."
    - ○ Did the accident occur during daylight, at dusk, or at night?
    - ○ Was it cloudy or foggy? Was there any moonlight?
    - ○ Describe proximity and lighting power of street or road lights.
    - ○ Was driver facing into the sun?
    - ○ Did approaching headlights blind driver?
    - ○ Were the insured's headlights in operation? What beam?
    - ○ Were windshield wipers in operation?
    - ○ Was the side window down?
    - ○ Were there any obstructions to the approach to the scene of the accident or to any of the vehicles?
- ☐ What first attracted the driver's attention to the claimant or the adverse vehicle or vehicles?
- ☐ How far away was the pedestrian or vehicle when first seen?
- ☐ If a pedestrian was involved, how was he or she dressed? Was he or she carrying any objects or packages?
- ☐ Obtain a complete description of the movements of the pedestrian or adverse vehicles during and after the impact, with distances and positions placed as exactly as possible.
- ☐ Did either driver sound horn?
- ☐ Was any attempt made to swerve or slow down? If not, explain why.
- ☐ Was other action taken by any of the parties when danger was first perceived?
- ☐ Were any arm or directional signals given before the accident?
- ☐ Were any skid marks made by any of the cars involved? If so, describe exact direction and length.
- ☐ Obtain the exact point of impact in relation both to the vehicles and the scene of the accident.
- ☐ Obtain the exact position of the pedestrian or vehicles, including the insured's vehicle, immediately after all motion had stopped.
- ☐ Quote any pertinent remarks made by anyone immediately after the accident, including any admissions of fault.
- ☐ In accidents involving bus passengers, obtain the following information:
    - ○ Was the passenger boarding or leaving the bus?
    - ○ If so, by what door? Was it opened or closed? Obtain details.
    - ○ Was the passenger seated, walking, or running toward or away from the bus?
    - ○ Was there any tripping or stumbling before entering or leaving the bus?
    - ○ Did any other passengers precede or follow the injured passenger?
    - ○ Did the bus make a sudden stop, or was it involved in any other unusual movement? Obtain details.
    - ○ Were there any warnings given or warning signs on the bus?
    - ○ How many other passengers were aboard?

§ 25.04   CASUALTY INSURANCE CLAIMS

     ○ Did any of the passengers witness the accident? If they did, obtain their names and addresses. Upon interview, if the witnesses deny having seen the accident, obtain signed statements.

C. Injuries:

- ☐ Obtain the names, addresses, and description of all persons injured.
- ☐ If possible, obtain the age, marital status, and occupation of all persons injured.
- ☐ If the injureds were occupants of the insured's car:
  - ○ Obtain their relationship to the driver or the named insured.
  - ○ List their previous disabilities, if known.
  - ○ Describe their exact position and seating arrangement in the vehicle immediately preceding the accident.
- ☐ Was there any visual evidence of injury?
  - ○ If there were any cuts or bleeding, give the exact location.
  - ○ Was first aid rendered at the scene? By whom?
- ☐ Did the police, hospital attendant, doctor, pharmacist, nurse, or anyone else who might have rendered first aid make any comment on the injuries?
- ☐ Did the injured make any outcries or show any other evidence of great pain?
- ☐ Where were the injured taken from the scene of the accident and how?
- ☐ Review Chapter 6, "Obtaining Medical Information."

D. Property damage:

- ☐ Describe the vehicles involved giving the make, model, year, color, license number, ownership, and so on.
- ☐ Obtain as detailed a description as possible of the damage to all cars involved.
- ☐ Were the cars able to move under their own power after the accident?
- ☐ If any car was towed away, where was it taken?
- ☐ If a pedestrian accident was involved, describe any scratches, marks or dents on the insured's vehicle resulting from the impact and give their exact location. Obtain immediate photographs when advisable.
- ☐ Describe damage to personal belongings, including luggage, contents of vehicles or trucks, clothes, jewelry, and so forth.

E. Witnesses:

- ☐ Obtain the names and addresses of all people in the insured's car and their locations in it.
- ☐ Explain their relationship to the driver or the named insured.
- ☐ The insured's driver may have received names and addresses of people in other vehicles involved, or of occupants of other vehicles in the area who may have witnessed the accident. These should be obtained.
- ☐ Obtain any outside witnesses' names that the driver may have gotten.

AUTOMOBILE LIABILITY INVESTIGATION § 25.05

- ☐ If there were witnesses whose names or addresses the driver did not obtain, get driver's best possible description of them and any leads that might be followed up to locate them.
- ☐ Obtain any pertinent comments or remarks made by the witnesses.
- ☐ Did any police officer witness the accident or get the names of any witnesses?
    - ○ Get the names and numbers of all police officers.
    - ○ Obtain the police organization and precinct number.
    - ○ Were there any traffic or other charges made against either party?
    - ○ Was there any police, motor vehicle, or coroner's hearing?
    - ○ Were any tests for alcoholism made?

§ 25.05 Information to be Obtained from the Claimant

A separate signed statement should be obtained from each claimant, including the drivers of all adverse vehicles, where warranted.

In order to avoid unnecessary repetition, it is suggested that the claim investigator review the previous section, "Information to be Obtained from the Insured's Driver," and apply whatever leads are pertinent, such as driving and accident records, complete facts, and so on, to obtain information from the claimant. In addition, the following checklist should be helpful.

NOTE: If the adjuster has learned that the claimant is represented by an attorney, no attempt should be made to interview him or her without that attorney's permission or presence. If the adjuster, upon first contact, learns from the claimant that he or she is represented by an attorney, the interview is over and any attempt to advise the claimant to dismiss the attorney could be disastrous.

- ☐ Claimant's name and all previous names or aliases under which the claimant was ever known, including maiden name of any married female claimants.
- ☐ Age, general appearance, and impression the claimant makes. Include any information on the claimant's moral character, industriousness, honesty, reputation, intelligence, education or other factors that might bear on his or her impression as a witness.
- ☐ Present address, and, if warranted, all previous addresses.
- ☐ Dependency.
    - ○ Name, age, and dependency status of spouse.
    - ○ Names, ages, and dependency status of all children.
    - ○ Marital status including details, and, if necessary, records of all previous marriages, separations, divorces, and children by former marriages.

§ 25.05 CASUALTY INSURANCE CLAIMS

- [ ] Employment history.
  - ○ Names and addresses of present and previous employers.
  - ○ Time employed by each.
  - ○ Nature of work.
  - ○ Salaries received.
  - ○ Time and earnings lost. (Review the "Special Damages" section in Chapter 3.)
- [ ] Obtain, but do not incorporate in the signed statement, information concerning workers' compensation status, automobile insurance, and names of the carriers.
- [ ] If the claimant was a pedestrian, determine:
  - ○ Whether claimant's attention was distracted at the time of the accident because of:
    - — The weather (rain, snow, sleet, or icy conditions).
    - — An umbrella, package or other object which he or she was carrying.
    - — Watching someone or something.
    - — Daydreaming or preoccupied for any reason.
    - — Worry or other emotional stress.
    - — Being in a hurry.
    - — Being unduly tired.
  - ○ What kind of clothes the claimant was wearing.
    - — Were they drab and did they blend in with the scenery?
    - — Did the claimant have a hat over his or her eyes?
    - — Did the claimant have his or her collar up over the ears?
- [ ] If the injury involves a passenger, interview all passengers separately and obtain signed statements from each. The information obtained should include:
  - ○ Relationship of the passengers to the driver or the named insured.
  - ○ Exact seating arrangement and positions immediately preceding the accident.
  - ○ Exact nature of the trip. For whose benefit was it being made? At whose request was it being made? Get all details.
  - ○ Exact nature of any contribution toward expenses.
  - ○ Who controlled the driving and destinations.
  - ○ Who invited the claimant to ride. Would he or she be considered a guest?
  - ○ Had the claimant ever ridden with the driver before. If so, how often and under what circumstances?
  - ○ If any objection was made concerning the driver or his driving. Any outcries or admonitions made by anyone.
  - ○ The claimant's previous knowledge of the driving ability of the driver.
  - ○ If the driver was driving carefully on this particular trip.
  - ○ Complete details of any alcoholic consumption, including amounts, places, and opinion about possible intoxication.
- [ ] Claimant's educational background, if pertinent, should be learned.

AUTOMOBILE LIABILITY INVESTIGATION § 25.07

- ○ Name and address of school attended, including previous schools, if necessary.
- ○ Year or grade in attendance and previous marks or grades.
- ○ Exact time lost from school as a result of the accident. Review appropriate parts of Chapter 5, "Securing the Physical Facts" concerning obtaining of school records.
- ☐ Obtain details of any welfare help that the claimant may be receiving or had received in the past. Be diplomatic.
  - ○ City, state, or federal relief or benefits, including social security.
  - ○ Private or public pensions of any kind.
  - ○ Disability benefits of any kind.
- ☐ Besides any previous accident record, obtain a record of any accidents in which the claimant may have been involved after the accident under investigation, with all details.
- ☐ Review all details of a possible criminal record.
- ☐ Get complete medical information, list of special damages, and other necessary information as previously outlined.

§ 25.06 Witnesses

The claim investigator can find detailed information on locating and interviewing witnesses in Chapter 3, "General Principles of Investigation," under the appropriate subheadings. This information, in conjunction with that contained in § 25.04, "Information to be Obtained from the Insured's Driver" and § 25.05, "Information to be Obtained from the Claimant" outline in detail a pattern to be followed for the proper investigation of a witness in an automobile claim.

In all cases involving serious injury, every attempt should be made to locate as many witnesses as possible and obtain individual signed statements even from those who allegedly did not see the accident.

The claim investigator should remember that every witness is a potential source of information for the location of other witnesses, since he is usually a resident of the neighborhood and may readily remember friends or acquaintances who were present at the time.

§ 25.07 Physical Facts or Objective Findings

It will be necessary for the claim investigator to review Chapter 5, "Securing the Physical Facts." The following checklist applies specifically to the investigation of automobile claims.

§ 25.07 CASUALTY INSURANCE CLAIMS

- [ ] Draw a complete diagram of the scene of the accident, giving measurements and locations of all pertinent objects, including the position of all vehicles before, during, and after the impact. Include the measurements of streets, traffic lanes, distances, distance from curb or shoulder, skid marks, distance from lights and intersections, positions of all marks or debris on the road or shoulders, and so on. Review § 5.01 on diagrams.
- [ ] Obtain snapshots or, if necessary, commercial photographs of both the scene of the accident and all vehicles involved where this is warranted. Review § 5.02.
- [ ] Report on the weather conditions and obtain a weather report if necessary.
  - Was there snow, rain, hail, fog, mist, sleet, wind, and so on?
  - Were the windshield wipers working?
  - Was side window down?
  - Was the windshield steamed up or frosted?
- [ ] Give a complete description of road conditions.
  - Dry, wet, slippery, icy, and so on.
  - Smooth, rough, bumpy, rutted, and so on.
- [ ] Description of streets, roads or highways.
  - Describe the main and secondary highways.
  - Describe all marks, gouges, or debris on the street, road, or shoulders.
  - Describe the area (city, urban, suburban, business or factory).
  - Was the road crowned or flat?
  - Was the road straight or curved? Give the directions, if curved.
  - Was the road level or inclined? Give directions.
  - Was the road paved with macadam, asphalt, concrete, cobblestone, brick, gravel, or dirt?
  - Give the widths of the roads or streets and the number of lanes? Were they marked? Describe markings.
  - Did the street contain trolley tracks?
  - Give the width, construction and type of shoulders or berms.
  - Describe the width, depth, and general nature of any ditches.
  - Describe the locality in respect to general visibility, and list obstructions such as parked vehicles, buildings, trees, and shrubbery.
  - Which street had the right of way?
- [ ] Traffic control.
  - Was a police officer directing traffic?
  - Were there any traffic lights or signals at the location of the scene? Were they in operation? Give exact location.
  - Describe any stop signs or other warning signs and give their exact location.
  - Was this within a hospital or school zone and were the proper signs posted?
- [ ] Description of skid marks.
  - Exact location.
  - Measurements.
  - Direction.

AUTOMOBILE LIABILITY INVESTIGATION § 25.08

- ☐ Description of any debris at the scene.
  - ○ Glass, oil stains, parts of the automobile, parts of any contents.
  - ○ Exact location.
- ☐ Complete description of the lighting in the area.
  - ○ Daylight, dusk, cloudy, night, moonlight. Include the position of the sun to indicate in which direction it was shining.
  - ○ Headlights (bright, medium, dim, parking, fog lights).
  - ○ Were approaching headlights blinding? Was traffic heavy?
  - ○ Road or street lights. Give exact power and distances as nearly as possible.
  - ○ Were flares needed? Were they available? Where were they placed? Were they properly placed?
- ☐ Condition of the vehicle.
  - ○ Age and general care given it.
  - ○ Detailed information on any specific items that might have contributed, such as brakes, headlights, directional signals, tires, tail lights, horn, steering, governor, and so on. If they were involved in the accident, find out when last checked, where, and by whom.
  - ○ Were chains or snow tires used or necessary?
- ☐ Determine whether there was any state inspection of any of the vehicles. If so, when and where?
- ☐ Complete description of the area, including the location of all buildings that might house possible witnesses.
- ☐ Police, sheriff, or state trooper reports:
  - ○ Interview all officers.
  - ○ Obtain photos, measurements and any special reports concerning alcoholism or reports by the homicide squad.
- ☐ Determine whether a criminal hearing will be held. If it will, determine the advisability of obtaining transcript of the hearing or attending as observer.
- ☐ Obtain motor vehicle report and determine whether there was a motor vehicle hearing. If so, determine advisability of obtaining transcript of the hearing or attending as observer.
- ☐ Obtain possible autopsy report.
- ☐ Obtain possible coroner's report or transcript of the coroner's hearing.
- ☐ Obtain complete newspaper accounts and photographs that may contain leads to witnesses. These may include films made for television, or photos of scene made by amateur neighborhood photographers.

§ 25.08 Further Details

Items like medical information, list of special damages, confidential risk report, and so on, have been covered in detail in previous chapters. All checks on specialized investigation should be reviewed under the appropriate subheadings.

As a final lead for obtaining essential information in the investigation of an automobile accident the claim investigator should be sure that he has a working knowledge of the municipal traffic laws, state statutes, or federal regulations involving lights on automobiles or trucks, parking regulations, flares, and so on. It may be advisable for him to obtain and quote the particular provisions applicable so that his investigation will be complete in all details should suit be instituted.

§ 25.09 Evaluating Automobile Property Damage Claims

The fact that the average automobile property damage claim may involve only a small sum of money does not mean that this type of claim is unimportant.

Handling of these claims can affect not only the financial status of a casualty company, but can reflect on its reputation as well. Even the reputation of the entire industry has suffered as a result of too-casual handling of such claims by some companies in the past.

Therefore, it is important that the industry claim people assume a fair, just, and courteous attitude under all circumstances. If a claim is to be declined, the adjuster should do so courteously and promptly after completing his investigation, but he should always keep in mind the possible ramifications of such declination, especially where injury claims may be in the offing.

§ 25.10 Good Investigations Are Still Necessary

The investigation of the average property damage claim does not justify the expenditure of a great deal of time or money. Nevertheless, the essential information necessary for the proper disposition of every claim must be obtained. Much time, money, and effort can be saved by a proper use of form letters. Such forms are not only very effective for obtaining the facts to determine liability, but will inform the claim representative of the possibility of any personal injury involvement as a result of the accident.

If a substantial amount of property damage is involved, or if fraud is suspected, a complete investigation, including signed statements, diagrams, police reports, and so on, should be made in the same manner as though a bodily injury claim were involved.

AUTOMOBILE LIABILITY INVESTIGATION § 25.11

Proper use of the telephone in adjusting small property damage losses where the accident does not warrant a personal call will lead to a considerable saving on this type of loss. When the claimant cannot be reached by telephone a postcard can be sent to him, suggesting that he call at an appropriate time.

§ 25.11 Guide for Property Damage Settlement Decision

Every disposition of a casualty claim involves the use of common sense and good judgment. No rule can be so rigid that it has no exception. A few general principles that can be followed to good advantage are here set out. *The following applies only to claims in which there is no bodily injury.*

Examples of cases in which the investigation discloses absolute liability on the part of the insured are:

> The claimant's car is legally parked or stopped.
> The insured's car strikes the rear of the claimant's car without any fault on the part of the claimant.
> The insured's car pulls out from the curb and strikes the claimant's car without any fault on the part of the claimant.
> The insured's car makes a left turn in front of the claimant, all other factors being equal, with no fault on the part of the claimant.
> The insured makes a right turn from the wrong lane cutting off the claimant, without fault on the claimant's part.

In an investigation of this type of claim the claim representative should:

- ☐ Ascertain the fair value of the damage done as a result of the accident.
  - ○ In claims involving a small amount, if there is no reason to suspect fraud, get two or more competitive estimates from reputable repair agencies. Scrutinize the listed items carefully and check these with the damage to the claimant's car as described in the insured's report. Multiple estimates are not necessarily competitive estimates. It is no trade secret that repair shops sometimes cooperate closely with each other. It is obvious that if a claimant has the inclination to submit one padded estimate, he will just as readily submit two or three. Therefore, the claim representative must know his repair shops and insist that at least one estimate be obtained from a firm whose integrity is known to him.

    Many reputable repair agencies will allow discounts on replaced parts. Determine whether discounts are available, then make an effort to take advantage of them.

§ 25.11   CASUALTY INSURANCE CLAIMS

- ○ If the estimate is questionable or the amount involved is more than nominal, get a property damage survey.
- ○ Settle promptly, basing your decision on a fair evaluation of the damage.

Examples of cases in which investigation discloses liability on the part of the insured, with some contributory or comparative negligence on the part of the claimant are:

The insured pulling away from the curb with some fault on the part of the claimant.
Right-angle collision after the insured passed a stop sign.
Right-angle collision when the claimant was on a main artery or had the right of way.
Right-angle collision when the insured struck the rear of the claimant's car after the claimant was almost across the intersection.
The insured making a left turn.
The insured "cut off" the claimant.

In investigating such cases, the claim representative may find it advisable to:

- ☐ Ascertain the correct amount of the damage as outlined in preceding checklist.
- ☐ Decline payment or make compromise settlement as the circumstances demand. (A compromise settlement is some amount more than the lowest estimate or survey of the actual damage done.)

Examples of cases in which the investigation discloses no liability on the part of the insured are:

The insured's car legally stopped or parked.
The insured's car struck in the rear.
Claimant's car pulling out from curb.
Claimant making left turn in front of insured.
Claimant making right turn from wrong lane or "cutting off" insured.
Right-angle collision when claimant did not heed stop sign or when insured is on a main artery.

In such cases the claim representative should:

- ☐ Determine the exact amount of the property damage by obtaining two or more estimates on small claims, obtaining appraisal on larger or question-

AUTOMOBILE LIABILITY INVESTIGATION § 25.11

able claims of any amount, and by other means generally outlined heretofore.

- [ ] After investigation is complete and the exact amount of property damage has been determined, decline payment promptly if no injury claims are or could be involved.
- [ ] In the event that the claim is pressed further, maintain his or her position unless he feels that suit will be brought. In that event the matter becomes one of using judgment on the course to follow. He should act in a manner that will be least expensive to his company in the long run, but he should remember that payment of an unjust claim sometimes leads to the appearance of two others that replace it, just for the nuisance value.

Suits should be avoided wherever possible. This does not mean, however, that the claim representative is to be intimidated into unjust settlement merely because of the threat of a suit. If there is sufficient justification, there is little point in trying a case that could have been settled for an amount less than it would cost to try it.

To repeat: if repairs have already been made be doubly careful on the check-up. If there is any doubt whatsoever, obtain an appraisal and have the appraiser check on the replaced parts. In this type of case it is often advantageous to see the repair agency or the person who made the repairs personally.

Check bills carefully. In checking the estimates or repair bills, it is important to watch for:

- [ ] Replacement of parts not damaged by the accident.
- [ ] Replacement of parts where the damage was caused by ordinary wear and tear.
- [ ] Charge made for new parts although used parts were actually installed.
- [ ] Overcharge on parts.
- [ ] Labor overcharge.
- [ ] Duplication of parts and labor items.
- [ ] Inclusion of previous damage.
- [ ] Incorrect addition.

The claim representative or his appraiser should where warranted insist upon seeing all parts which were allegedly replaced and examine the records of the repair shop, if necessary. Old damage can often be detected by rust. He should check the damage in relationship to the point of impact.

In the adjustment of total losses it is, of course, very important that the claim adjuster know what the general condition of the car was before the accident. It is also important to check on the accessories.

Such items as heater, radio, fog lights, and so on, will have a bearing on the amount of the loss.

Wherever possible, title to the salvaged automobile should not be taken over, but a proper deduction should be made from the settlement figure after bids have been received. Salvage should be disposed of in a manner calculated to obtain the most return for the company. It stands to reason that a prompt disposal of salvage will avoid incurring storage bills which will eat into the amount recovered.

It is understood that these suggestions may not apply to some claims involving personal injuries in which expediency and common sense might indicate the need for a more liberal interpretation. A claim representative should never lose the opportunity to conclude a reasonable settlement of a bodily injury claim because of an adamant or arbitrary stand taken on a property damage claim. However, the mere threat of an unjustified bodily injury claim should be met with firm resistance and intensified investigation to combat such allegation.

[1] Loss of Use

One of the elements of damages in a property damage claim may be the loss of use of the automobile or truck arising out of the damage to it. Even before the policy specifically covered this item, the courts had almost universally declared that a claim for loss of use was valid in cases of partial damage, whether the vehicle involved was a pleasure car or a commercial vehicle. The majority held that the period of time covered was the reasonable time required to make repairs.

A definition of "reasonable time" varies with the jurisdiction involved. Parts replacement may, for instance, hold up repairs to a car for months. While it does not seem equitable to charge a wrongdoer for conditions beyond his control, it has been argued that since the innocent party did what he could to mitigate damages and suffered an extraordinary loss, the wrongdoer who initiated the chain of events causing the loss should be charged with it. Certainly, the owner of the damaged property must do everything he can to minimize the period of disability.

The majority ruling concerning cases involving total loss of a vehicle holds that the measure of damages is the difference between the value of the vehicle before it was damaged, and after, disallowing any claim for loss of use.

Some courts have declared loss of use an item of damage in total losses and others have permitted "interest" in total loss cases. Generally, the courts have held that damages should not exceed the total value of the vehicle before it was involved in the accident.

In any event, although opinion seems to be divided on whether an actual out-of-pocket loss must have been sustained in order to uphold a claim for loss of use, I think the position of the insurance company is sound when it insists on proof of actual expenditures in the temporary replacement of the disabled vehicle.

Rental bills for the substitute vehicle should be requested when a claim is made for loss of use, and any charge for such a vehicle by a relative or friend should be looked at with extreme skepticism. The same attitude should be assumed for claims alleging taxi fares during the period when repairs are being made.

CHAPTER 26

Public or General Liability Policies and Coverages

§ 26.01   Introduction
§ 26.02   Commercial General Liability Policy
    [1]   The "Occurrence" Policy
    [2]   The "Claims-Made" Policy
    [3]   Extended Reporting Period
    [4]   Section I—Coverages
        [a]   Coverage A—Bodily Injury and Property Damage Liability
        [b]   Duty to Defend
        [c]   Exclusions in the Master Forms
    [5]   Section II—Who Is an Insured
    [6]   Section III—Limits of Insurance
    [7]   Section IV—Commercial General Liability Conditions
        [a]   Notice of Accident
    [8]   Section V—Extended Reporting Periods
§ 26.03   Personal and Advertising Injury Liability
    [1]   Definitions
    [2]   Privileged Communications
    [3]   Investigation of Personal Injury Cases
        [a]   Defamation
        [b]   False Arrest or Imprisonment
    [4]   Damages
§ 26.04   Advertising Injury
§ 26.05   Medical Payments
§ 26.06   Contractual Liability
§ 26.07   Products—Completed Operations
    [1]   Covered Territory
    [2]   Completed Operations
§ 26.08   Liquor Liability Coverage Form
§ 26.09   Pollution Liability Coverage
§ 26.10   Endorsements

§ 26.01   Introduction

Public Liability policies first appeared in this country in the late 1800's. They rapidly branched out to provide coverage for manufac-

§ 26.01

turers, retailers and wholesalers, contractors, landlords and owners of theatres, amusement parks, fairs, promoters of sports activities, and others.

As long as the law had created the liability, there was the obvious need for protection. The Public Liability policies as they exist today are extremely varied in scope and fall within five general categories:

1. Premises and Current Operations.
2. Products and Completed Operations.
3. Contractual.
4. Protective.
5. Personal.

Each of these categories may be represented in one or more of the Public Liability policy forms and the major ones will be discussed individually.

We have already discussed some of the major policy conditions that apply to practically all casualty policies, and we will also stress the differences and unusual features of the public liability provisions. In many respects, the various conditions are similar in wording to many of the clauses in the Automobile Liability forms, and here I refer principally to those provisions found in the jacket of the major forms.

The program of incorporating specific coverages within a uniform jacket, which applies to all of the policies, was inaugurated in 1966. The jacket includes such common provisions as Definitions, Supplementary Payments, and Conditions. It does not contain the Insuring Agreements or Exclusions under those headings.

The inserts, or specific policies, provide coverage under the following principal policy forms:

1. Owners', Landlords' and Tenants' Liability.
2. Manufacturers' and Contractors' Liability.
3. Contractual Liability.
4. Completed Operations and Products Liability.
5. Comprehensive General Liability.
6. Owner's and Contractor's Protective Liability.
7. Storekeeper's Insurance.
8. Comprehensive Personal Insurance.

In addition, coverage may be provided for specialty operations such as farmers, druggists, garages, hospitals, etc.

It will be more orderly, and lead to a better understanding of the policy forms if those provisions which are common to all are discussed first. A good place to start is with a discussion of the Commercial General Liability policies issued in 1986 by the Insurance Services Office.[1]

§ 26.02 Commercial General Liability Policy

The new Commercial General Liability policy is, of necessity, a very complex policy because of its comprehensive nature. There are many interrelated and interlocking provisions that require concentrated study. It is a lawyer's dream and a claim adjuster's nightmare.

Because it is a completely new and important form, it will be discussed in more detail, and in concurrence with some of the individual coverages that it encompasses.

In recent years, new developments in the courts and in the legislatures concerning products liability, malpractice, pollution, and other fields of law have been all but disastrous to insurance companies that write casualty coverages. The changes have come so fast and have been so far-reaching that the industry has been forced to review policy coverages and, in particular, the Comprehensive General Liability policy, which was, if not completely rewritten, changed in format as well as contents, although many of the original provisions are incorporated in the new forms. Even the name has been changed from Comprehensive to Commercial, apparently for the justified fear that the word "comprehensive" might lead to an even greater enlargement of the scope of coverage than was intended, despite denials by the drafters.

On January 1, 1986, the Insurance Services Office instituted a new standard Commercial General Liability policy. It must be noted, however, that this policy, despite the fact that it has already been promulgated and accepted (with proper state endorsements) in many jurisdictions, is still very much in a state of development. Amendments are being made as vociferous objections are being received from the various state insurance departments, agents, brokers, and insureds.

---

[1] Quotations from these policies are made with the permission of the Insurance Services Office in New York City, and while this policy, in two master forms and with many attachments, has not as yet been approved by all states at the time of this writing, it is well on its way.

Accordingly, what is here stated may, in some respects, be changed shortly hereafter, which makes it imperative for claim people to read carefully the policy version that was in effect at the time of the particular accident under investigation.

The Commercial General Liability policy comes in two major forms: the "occurrence" form, which comes into effect upon receipt of a notice of a covered accident or occurrence that happened during the effective policy period; the "claims-made" form, becomes effective at the time a claim is first made, or a suit initially instituted as first notice of a claim, regardless of when the accident or incident complained of happened. Both forms contain the following sections.

Section I contains the Insuring Agreements and related coverages as follows:

A. Bodily injury and property damage liability and supplementary payments provisions,
B. Personal and Advertising injury liability and supplemental payments provisions, and
C. Medical payments.

This section also includes the General Exclusions.

Section II defines who is an insured.

Section III describes the Limits of Insurance and how they apply.

Section IV contains the General Conditions.

Section V of the "occurrence" form contains the Definitions and that is the final Section in this form.

Section V of the "claims-made" form contains the Extended Reporting periods and in addition has a Section VI which contains the Definitions.

The Commercial General Liability policy, in both forms, covers bodily injury and property damage (third party) liability, personal and advertising injury liability, and medical payments. Not included in the master forms, but available for an additional premium are:

1. Owners and Contractors Protective Liability for Operations of Designated Contractor,
2. Liquor Liability (2 types),
3. Products/Completed Operations Liability (2 types),
4. Pollution Liability, in several forms, and
5. Railroad Protective Liability.

A few of the major coverages that may be included by endorsement include Nuclear Energy Exclusion, Deductible Liability, Hired Auto Liability, Non-Owned Auto Liability, Disaster Relief, many types of "additional insureds" including Vendors, Waiver of Charitable and Municipal Immunities (up to the limits of insurance coverage), Products/Completed Operations Exclusion, and many others of less frequent importance to the claim representative.

The new policy form incorporates some previous optional coverages, such as explosion, collapse and underground peril as an integral part.

Just as additional coverages may be obtained for additional premiums, so can some of the existing coverages such as Personal and Advertising Injury and Medical Payments be deleted for a reduced premium.

[1] The "Occurrence" Policy

This form, in which Coverage A states in part: "This insurance applies only to 'bodily injury' and 'property damage' which occurs during the policy period," expresses essentially the same intent as did the former 1977 CGL form.

The "occurrence" policy is by far the less complicated form. Its disadvantage stems from the fact that the insurer may have to pay a claim that happened as a result of an incident that occurred many years ago at claim values that are much higher when the claim is finally made, and at which time the insured may find that they are considerably underinsured.

[2] The "Claims-Made" Policy

The wording of the "claims-made" policy, in Coverage A (Bodily Injury and Property Damage) of the Insuring Agreements, paragraph b, reads as follows:

> This insurance applies to "bodily injury" and "property damage" only if a claim for damages because of the "bodily injury" or "property damage" is first made in writing against any insured during the policy period.
>
> (1) A claim by a person or organization seeking damages will be deemed to have been made when written notice of such claim is received by any insured or by us, whichever comes first.

It is to be noted that while the "occurrence" policy becomes effective when the incident happened, the "claims made" policy becomes effective only when a definite claim is made.

There is a definite limitation period however, even in the "claims made" form and that period is designated in the *Retroactive Date provision* of the policy, located in the Coverage A insuring agreement as follows: "This insurance does not apply to 'bodily injury' or 'property damage' which occurs before the Retroactive Date if any, shown in the Declarations."

In other words, the incident causing the injury or damage must have occurred after the retroactive date, if any, shown on the policy, but coverage is not available in any event if claim is made after the end of the policy period.

This retroactive date may either be the same as the inception date, sometime earlier, or there may be no retroactive date, depending on the premium chosen.[2]

[3] Extended Reporting Period

Since a "claims made" policy expires at the end of the policy period, and gives no coverage thereafter, the situation obviously poses a considerable problem for the insured if renewal is not requested or given for any one of a number of possible reasons.

The policy provides an "Extended Reporting Period" provision (Sec. V) for a period of sixty days after the expiration date of the policy if the accident or incident occurred before the end of the policy period and after the retroactive date stated in the policy. Since some time must, of necessity, elapse after an occurrence, this gives the insured sixty days in which to report such an occurrence. This is known as the "mini tail" on the policy.

The same provision gives the insured an option to extend the sixty-day "mini tail" for an indefinite period, for which an additional premium is charged, but again only if the occurrence happened before the expiration of the policy period and after the retroactive date.

The policy itself spells out the conditions under which the new "mini tail" becomes effective as follows:

> We will provide one or more Extended Reporting Periods, as described below, if:

---

[2] *See* F.C. & S. Bulletins, Cas. vol., Section Public Liability, pp. Aat 5 and Aat 9 to 12.

a. This Coverage Part is cancelled or not renewed, or

b. We renew or replace this Coverage Part with other insurance that:

(1) Has a Retroactive Date later than the date shown in the declarations of this Coverage Part; or

(2) Does not apply to "bodily injury" or "property damage" on a claims-made basis. . . .

This provision is further qualified by stating that: "The Basic Extended Reporting Period does not apply to claims that are covered under any subsequent insurance you purchase, or that would be covered but for exhaustion of the amount of insurance applicable to such claims."

In addition, a Supplemental Extended reporting Period may be obtained by endorsement for an extra premium. The policy in paragraphs 3 a. and 3 b. of Section IV gives the details of this extended coverage.

The F.C. & S. Bulletins explains that:

> A notable feature of the supplemental tail endorsement . . . is that it automatically provides separate aggregate limits equaling the policy's original aggregate limits. . . . However, neither the endorsement nor its separate limits take effect until the end of the basic 5 year tail (for claims resulting from occurrences reported to the insurer within 60 days after the end of the policy period), or the 60 day tail (for claims resulting from occurrences that were not previously reported to the insurer). Once it takes effect, the endorsement provides an extended period of unlimited duration.[3]

The introduction of the new Insurance Services Office (ISO) Commercial General Liability policies was accompanied by an "Introduction and Overview" pamphlet which further helps to explain some of the policy provisions.

In explaining the "occurrence" policy, the ISO notes state:

"Under the 'occurrence' form, the policy that is in effect when the bodily injury or property damage occurs, responds to the claim." This is not a change from ISO's previous Comprehensive General Liability policy. It is important to note that both the old and the new "occurrence" policies are triggered by *injury or damage* (italics added) that occurs during the policy period and not by the "occur-

---

[3] F.C. & S Bulletins, Cas. Vol., Section Public Liability, page Aat 8.

rence" that caused the injury or damage, or by the insured's negligent act or omission.

"Under the 'occurrence' forms—old and new:

"If the injury or damage occurs during the policy period, the coverage applies no matter when resulting claims are made.

"Cancellation or non-renewal after the injury or damage occurs does not affect coverage for the resulting claims.

"If the injury or damage is held to have occurred over several policy periods, all the policies in effect during these periods may be required to provide primary coverage for a single claim.

"Claims for injury that occurred long ago will be assigned back to previous policies that may have inadequate limits and/or coverages (if there were such policies).

"Policy records may need to be kept open indefinitely for possible future claims.

"Keeping limits current and adequate may be difficult.

"Disputes and litigation may arise in determining when the injury occurred."

Concerning the "claims-made" form, the ISO explanatory pamphlet states: "Under the 'claims-made' form, bodily injury or property damage is covered by the policy in effect when the *first claim for the injury or damage is made in writing* (italics added) against the insured."

In discussing the Retroactive Date of this form, the pamphlet explains that:

> The form excludes bodily injury and property damage that occurred before a Retroactive Date to be entered by the company on the Declarations page. Normally, the Retroactive Date will be the inception date of the insured's first "claims-made" policy. But the company may choose to eliminate this provision and provide retroactive coverage by writing "none" in the Retroactive Date blank, or choose to provide some retroactive coverage by using a retroactive date earlier than the first "claims-made" policy's inception date. In either case, coverage for a claim first made during the "claims-made" policy will be excess over the applicable prior insurance.

The pamphlet goes on to explain that:

"Under the 'claims-made' form:

"One and only one 'claims-made' policy will respond to a given claim. Coverage is pinpointed in the most recent applicable policy.

"Disputes over which policy applies will be reduced.

"Limits can be kept current to reflect expected claims patterns.

"Policy files need not be kept open indefinitely.

"There is complete continuity of coverage upon renewal or replacement.

"If the policy is cancelled or not renewed after injury or damage occurs, the built-in option to buy the extended reporting option 'tail' must be exercised to obtain coverage for resulting future claims, unless all those claims are first made within the automatic 60-day 'tail' period, or replacement 'claims-made' coverage can be found with the same retroactive date as the expiring policy, or no retroactive date."[4]

[4] Section I—Coverages

[a] Coverage A—Bodily Injury and Property Damage Liability

Insuring Agreement 1. a. (2) contains the usual provision giving the insurer the right to "investigate and settle any claim or 'suit' at our (the insurer's) discretion."

Insuring Agreement 1. a. (3) attempts, once again, to settle the question of when the insurer's duty to defend terminates by stating that: "Our right and duty to defend end when we have used up the applicable limit of insurance in the payment of judgments or settlements under Coverages A or B or medical payments under Coverage C."

The courts have held that the insurer nevertheless may not abandon an insured who is prejudiced thereby, before termination of that suit and there are still other legal problems involved in determining the extent of the insurer's duty to defend, which are discussed in Chapter 20, *supra*.

Insuring Agreement 1. b. defines "bodily injury" damages as including "damages claimed by any person or organization for care, loss of services or death resulting at any time from the 'bodily injury.'"

Insuring Agreement 1. c. states that "'Property damage' that is loss of use of tangible property that is not physically injured shall be deemed to occur at the time of the 'occurrence' that caused it," no matter when the damage becomes evident.

---

[4] Introduction and Overview of the Commercial General Liability policy, published and distributed by the Insurance Services Office, N.Y., N.Y.

[b] Duty to Defend

The duty to defend provision of the Commercial General Liability policy may be found in Section I—Coverage A—Bodily Injury and Property Damage Liability.

The last line of the first paragraph of the Insuring Agreement reads: "We will have the right and duty to defend any 'suit' seeking (those) damages," and goes on to state: "But: (1) The amount we will pay for damages is limited as described in Section III—Limits of Insurance."

The policy states that "suit" includes any arbitration proceedings.

The usual phrase in previous policies concerning the insurer's duty to defend a suit even if it is "groundless, false or fraudulent" is absent from this policy. The duty to defend such actions, however, is still present and the inclusion of these words would be redundant. In addition, this phrase has been so badly misinterpreted by some of our courts that its exclusion may actually more clearly delineate the boundaries of the insurer's duty to defend in this policy. The "duty to defend" clause of liability policies, in general, is discussed in Chapter 20, *supra*.

Coverage A, under Insuring Agreement 1a, states that "We will pay those sums that the insured becomes legally obligated to pay as damages because of 'bodily injury' or 'property damage' to which this insurance applies."

In addition, the policy provides for the payment of "Supplementary Payments—Coverages A and B" which are listed under that heading, positioned in the policy after Coverage C—Medical Payments. The "Supplementary Payments" section lists seven specific areas of expense incurred in the investigation of a claim and in the defense of a suit for which the company will be responsible, and certifies that "These payments will not reduce the limits of insurance."

The ISO[5] has been probing the acceptability of putting a cap on defense expense in view of the soaring increase in these costs. There has been some discussion of sharing the expense with the insured over a certain amount and some talk of including defense costs in the overall limits of liability.

The hue and cry from agents, brokers, insureds, and attorneys has been anguished and loud. It is my guess that the insurers will make

---

[5] Insurance Services Office, N.Y., N.Y.

the ISO back off, and at any rate, at the moment of this writing, the matter is in limbo.

Paragraphs 2 and 3 of the "Supplementary Payments" reiterate previous policy intent that while the *cost* (italics added) of bail bonds (up to $250) and bonds to release attachments (within the applicable limits of insurance) will be paid, the insurer is not required to furnish the bonds.

The Insuring Agreement of the "claims-made" form of the Commercial General Liability policy differs in some major respects from the "occurrence" form.

Section A in the "claims-made" form includes the wording that: "This insurance does not apply to 'bodily injury' or 'property damage' which occurred before the Retroactive Date, if any . . . or which occurs after the policy period."

Insuring Agreement 1 b. in the "claims-made" form is completely different from the "occurrence" form and states that the insurance applies "only if a claim . . . is first made against any insured during the policy period."

Subheadings (1), (2), and (3) of this section concern only the "claims-made" form and refer to the specific situation involved in determining when a claim is made.

In subheading 1. a. (2) of the "claims-made" form, the clause adds wording to the effect that the insurer may also investigate any "occurrence." The F.C. & S. Bulletins state that this additional wording

> is necessitated by the feature of the claims-made form that provides a five-year extended reporting period for claims resulting from occurrences during the policy period. Since the insurer may later need to defend resulting claims, it will of course want the right to investigate the occurrence as soon as possible.[6]

[c] **Exclusions in the Master Forms**

Part 2 of Coverage A—Bodily Injury and Property Damage Liability, under Section I—Coverages, contains the general Exclusions. Both the "occurrence" and the "claims-made" policies have fourteen identical general exclusions listed from "a" to "n."

The exclusions in the Commercial General Liability policies differ in some respects from the 1973 Comprehensive General Liability policy.

---

[6] F.C. & S. Bulletins, Casualty vol., Public Liability section, page A a - 4.

Exclusion "a," which refers to intentional injury, uses the wording "bodily injury or property damage expected or intended from the standpoint of the insured." It attempts to clarify the legal controversy as to whether the *act* or the *result of the act* was intended.

This exclusion was previously included in the definition of "occurrence" in the 1973 Comprehensive General Liability policy.

It is important to note that the second sentence of the exclusion creates an exception by stating that "This exclusion does not apply to 'bodily injury' resulting from the use of *reasonable* (italics added) force to protect persons or property."

Exclusion "b" applies to " 'bodily injury' or 'property damage' for which the insured is obligated to pay damages by reason of the assumption of liability in a contract or agreement." This exclusion makes an exception for (1) liability assumed under an "insured contract" as defined in the policy, and (2) for liability that the insured would have in the absence of the contract or agreement.

Exclusion "c" concerns liquor law liability and is self-explanatory, but it applies only "if you (the insured) are in the business of manufacturing, distributing, selling, serving or furnishing alcoholic beverages." This exclusion does not apply to a social host or an employer who serves free drinks at a party, or even to an owner-lessor of a liquor store who had no other business interest in the store other than as landlord.

Exclusions "d" and "e" refer to workers' compensation and employer's liability and are similar to those in the Comprehensive General Liability policy. They, too, are self-explanatory, but again, the exception that "This exclusion does not apply to liability assumed by the insured under an 'insured contract' " must be noted.

Exclusion "f " deals with pollution liability. It was first introduced in some areas as an optional endorsement to the 1973 edition of the Comprehensive General Liability policy. Its effect is intended to eliminate coverage for most incidents involving pollution, with some exceptions. This exclusion in the Commercial General Liability policies reads as follows:

> "Bodily injury" or "property damage" arising out of the actual or threatened discharge, dispersal, release or escape of pollutants:
>
> (a) At or from premises you own, rent or occupy;
>
> (b) At or from any site or location used by you or for you or others for the handling, storage, disposal, processing or treatment of waste;

(c) Which are at any time transported, handled, stored, treated, disposed of, or processed by you or for you or any person or organization for whom you may be legally responsible; or

(d) At or from any site on which you or any contractors working directly or indirectly on your behalf are performing operations:

(i) if the pollutants are brought on or to the site or location in connection with such operations; or

(ii) if the operations are to test for, monitor, clean up, remove, contain, treat, detoxify or neutralize pollutants.

The second part of this exclusion is intended to eliminate coverage for "any loss, cost or expense arising out of governmental direction or request that you test for, monitor, clean up, remove, contain, treat or neutralize pollutants".

This exclusion applies even if the cause was accidental, except for certain off-premises accidents and accidents that are included under the products/completed operations coverage. In any event, clean-up costs are specifically excluded.

Finally, this exclusion defines pollutants as: "any solid, liquid, gaseous or thermal irritant or contaminant, including smoke, vapor, soot, fumes, acids, alkalis, chemicals and waste. Waste includes materials to be recycled, reconditioned or reclaimed."

The pollution exclusion can be deleted by endorsement or the insured may purchase separate pollution liability coverage.

Exclusion "g" refers to: " 'Bodily injury' or 'property damage' arising out of the ownership, maintenance or entrustment to others of any aircraft, 'auto' or watercraft owned or operated by or rented or loaned to any insured."

The final sentence of the first paragraph "Use includes operation and 'loading or unloading' " puts the full burden of loading or unloading an auto under the auto policy where it belongs.

This exclusion then itemizes five specific exceptions which are self-explanatory. In addition to these specific exceptions, it may be necessary to refer to the Definitions section to learn whether the definitions fit the "aircraft," "watercraft" or "auto" under investigation.

Exclusion "h" refers to the "transportation of 'mobile equipment' by an auto owned or operated by or rented or loaned to any insured" or the use of such equipment "while in practice or preparation for, a prearranged racing, speed or demolition contest in any stunting activity."

Exclusion "i" is the usual exclusion of injury or damage due to war and then defines "war" as including "civil war, insurrection, rebellion or revolution." It then limits this exclusion as applying "only to liability assumed under a contract or agreement."

Exclusion "j" includes the old "care, custody or control" exclusion about which there has been much litigation, and includes six subdivisions that are themselves separate exclusions. They exclude damage to property as follows:

(1) Property you own, rent or occupy;

(2) Premises you sell, give away or abandon if the "property damage" arises out of any part of those premises;

(3) Property loaned to you;

(4) Personal property in your care, custody or control;

(5) That particular part of real property you or any contractors or sub-contractors working directly or indirectly on your behalf are performing operations if the "property damage" arises out of those operations; or

(6) That particular part of any property that must be restored, repaired or replaced because "your work" was incorrectly performed on it.

The language of this exclusion attempts to clarify the former wording of "premises alienated by the named insured."

In addition, this exclusion contains three separate paragraphs, at the end, which delineate the exceptions to some of these exclusions by number and which must be read in conjunction with the exclusion to which they refer.

Exclusion "k" refers to property damage to "your product arising out of it or any part of it." This exclusion does not include real property, and must be read in conjunction with the definition of "your product."

Exclusion "l" refers to damage "to 'your work' arising out of it or any part of it and *included in the 'products liability—completed operations hazard.'*" (Italics added.)

The exception to this exclusion applies "if the damaged work or the work out of which the damage arises was performed on your behalf by a sub-contractor."

The definition of "your work" includes "materials, parts or equipment furnished in connection with such work or operations."

Exclusion "m" reads:

PUBLIC OR GENERAL LIABILITY § 26.02[4][c]

"Property damage" to "impaired property" or property that has not been physically injured, arising out of:

(1) A defect, deficiency, inadequacy or dangerous condition in "your product" or "your work"; or

(2) A delay or failure by you or anyone acting on your behalf to perform a contract or agreement in accordance with its terms.

This exclusion does not apply to the loss of use of other property arising out of sudden and accidental physical injury to " 'your product' or 'your work' after it has been put to its intended use."

In order to interpret the difficult language of this exclusion, the reader must go back to the Definitions of "your work" and "your product."

To reiterate, if property is "impaired" because of reasons set forth in parts (1) or (2) of this exclusion, the exclusion applies.[7]

Exclusion "n," the last exclusion in the master forms, is sometimes called the "sistership liability" exclusion. It reads:

Damages claimed for any loss, cost or expense incurred by you *or others* (italics added) for the loss of use, withdrawal, recall, inspection, repair, replacement, adjustment removal or disposal of:

(1) "Your product";

(2) "Your work"; or

(3) "Impaired property,"

if such product, work or property is withdrawn or recalled from the market or from use by any person or organization because of a known or suspected defect, deficiency, inadequacy or dangerous condition in it.

The final paragraph under Exclusions reads as follows: "Exclusions c through n do not apply to damage by fire to premises rented to you. A separate limit of insurance applies to this coverage as described in Section III—Limits of Insurance."[8]

---

[7] For a more detailed explanation of this exclusion, *see* F.C. & S. Bulletin, Cas. vol., Public Liability, pages Aa14, 15, and CGL, 2d ed. published by The National Underwriter Co., Cincinnati, Ohio.

[8] Here again, I would refer the reader to the F.C. & S. Bulletins, Cas. vol., Public Liability, page Aa - 10, and the CGL pamphlet by Malecki and Flitner published by The National Underwriter Co., Cincinnati, Ohio.

[5] Section II—Who Is an Insured

This section specifies, in four major paragraphs, with subheadings in some cases, exactly who is to be considered as an insured under this policy. These include individuals, partnerships, organizations other than partnerships, employees, real estate managers, custodians, and legal representatives in some instances. Each category has its own exceptions and limitations which are self-explanatory.

[6] Section III—Limits of Insurance

Except for any damage covered under Products—Completed Operations insurance, this policy contains a general Limit of Insurance for all damages, including personal and advertising liability, and medical expenses incurred in any policy year. Both the Aggregate and Coverage A occurrence limits are combined single limits. The Products—Completed Operations Aggregate Limit has a special aggregate limit of its own. This differs from the 1973 Comprehensive General Liability policy which did not have any aggregate limits except for Products—Completed Operations and a few others.

It is to be noted that:

> The limits of this Coverage Part apply separately to each consecutive annual period and to any remaining period of less than 12 months, starting with the beginning of the policy period shown in the Declarations, unless the policy period is extended after issuance for an additional period of less than 12 months. In that case, the additional period will be deemed part of the last preceding period for purposes of determining the Limits of Insurance.

[7] Section IV—Commercial General Liability Conditions

[a] Notice of Accident

The notice of accident provision of other policy forms is to be found in the Commercial General Liability form in Section IV under the heading of "2. Duties in The Event Of Occurrence, Claim or Suit" and is self-explanatory.

It should be noted, however, that there is some difference between the "occurrence" and the "claims-made" forms. The "claims-made" form contains the statement that "notice of an occurrence is not notice of a claim." There must be specific notice of claims received by the insured or the insurer and, obviously, if only the insured receives such notice, he must transmit it to the insurer "as soon as practicable," assuming the occurrence was within the policy period.

The clause usually known as the "assistance and cooperation" clause is, in this policy, incorporated in subheading 2.c. of Section IV.

The provision prohibiting the insured from making settlement without the authority of the insurer is, in this policy, included in 2.d. of this section.

Paragraph 3 incorporates the "Legal Action Against Us" clause.

Paragraph 4—"Other Insurance" is divided into two main parts: "a. Primary Insurance" and "b. Excess Insurance," and states that "If other valid and collectible insurance is available to the insured for a loss we cover under Coverage A or B of the Coverage Part, our obligation is limited as follows:" The clause then gives the specifics of the contribution expected in the various situations where there is other insurance that covers the same incident.

Medical payments (Coverage C) is always primary insurance.

Condition "7. Separation Of Insureds," is a reinforcement of Section II—"Who Is An Insured" and seems to imply that if there is any conflict of interests between insureds, each insured is to be treated in a fashion that will best protect his or her individual interests. It specifically excepts "the Limits of Insurance and any rights or duties specifically assigned in this Coverage Part to the first named Insured."

Condition "8. Transfer of Rights of Recovery Against Others to Us," is a rewrite of the old "Subrogation" provision.

Conditions such as "1. Bankruptcy," "5. Premium Audit," and "6. Representations" are of lesser importance to the claim representative.

SECTION V of the "occurrence" form and *SECTION VI* of the "claims-made" form contain the Definitions which are an extremely important part of this (or any other) policy since practically all of the other provisions are dependent upon them for clarification of the intent of the policy.

Medical Payments and Personal Injury—Advertising Injury Coverages will be discussed hereafter since they are specific coverages and, in my opinion, should not have been sandwiched in between the general provisions, assuming there was a good reason for including them in the master forms.

[8] Section V—Extended Reporting Periods

This section of the "claims-made" policy form has already been commented upon in § 26.02[3], *supra*. It is a long, complex section that attempts to cover all the bases and, in the process, sometimes trips over its own feet. Paragraph 6 in particular needs special study, and I believe rewriting, although I wouldn't want to be the one to do it.

The attempt to cover so much and so many types of coverage, together with the attempt to avoid the legal pitfalls of the "occurrence" type of policy is so complex and difficult that it causes one to wonder whether such an attempt is productive. While it certainly narrows the number of individual policies that a commercial venture might need, there is a question as to whether this process accomplishes simplification and clarity, which are, or should be, the prime requisites of any insurance policy.

§ 26.03 Personal and Advertising Injury Liability

There must be some good business reason why Personal and Advertising Injury Liability coverage was placed under Coverage B of the Commercial General Liability policy and right in the middle of the "occurrence" and the "claims-made" master forms, although I am unaware of it. Instead of adding this coverage to the master form, it is automatically provided unless it is specifically excluded by endorsement and so indicated in the Application.

The courts and common usage have often confused the term "personal injury," as used in insurance terminology, with "bodily injury." Accordingly, the first prerequisite to an understanding of this coverage is to define "personal injury." Since Coverage B does not provide the Definition, we must turn to paragraph 10 of the Definitions section of the master forms, which defines "Personal injury" as:

> injury, other than "bodily injury," arising out of one or more of the following offenses:
>
> a. False arrest, detention or imprisonment;
>
> b. Malicious prosecution;
>
> c. Wrongful entry into, or eviction of a person from, a room, dwelling, or premises that the person occupies;

PUBLIC OR GENERAL LIABILITY § 26.03

d. Oral or written publication of material that slanders or libels a person or organization or disparages a person's or organization's goods, products or services, or

e. Oral or written publication of material that violates a person's right of privacy.

This policy excludes coverage for "bodily injury," so that if the injury to the person of someone being unlawfully or unjustly evicted or arrested is also physical, recovery for the "bodily injury" apparently is not intended to be covered, even though damages other than bodily injury arising from the same incident are covered under this policy. Whether Coverage A would pick up the "bodily injury" liability is a moot question. It would probably depend on the particular facts of the incident and the interpretation made by the courts, which usually favor the applicability of coverage where there is any doubt.

While I can understand the difficulties in defining legal terms such as "slander," "libel," "malicious prosecution," etc., no attempt has been made to do so in this policy.

Paragraph 1.b. of the Insuring Agreement of this coverage states that "This insurance applies to 'personal injury' only if caused by an offense: (2) Arising out of the conduct or your business, excluding advertising, publishing, broadcasting or telecasting done by or for you."

This exception to the application of coverage excludes coverage for businesses that are primarily in the categories mentioned under paragraph "1.b. (2)."

There are two separate sets of Exclusions: "a" for "Personal Injury or advertising injury," and "b" for "Advertising injury arising out of " four specific categories that are self-explanatory.

Under Exclusion "b. (4)," the policy reiterates the intent as expressed in the Insuring Agreement that coverage does not apply to "An offense committed by an insured whose business is advertising, broadcasting, publishing or telecasting."

As stated in the F.C. & S. Bulletins:[9]

> Under the new and old forms alike, there can be difficulty in determining when an alleged offense of malicious prosecution was committed. Some courts have held that "because a cause of action for malicious prosecution does not mature until a favorable determination in the underlying action, that date is used to determine whether there is cover-

---

[9] Casualty vol., Public Liability Section, page A b -5.

age under an insurance policy." Other courts have held that the offense of malicious prosecution is committed, for purposes of insurance coverage "when the alleged tortfeasor takes action resulting in the application of the State's criminal process to the claimant."[10]

The *Limit of Liability* on this coverage is not on an "each offense" basis, but applies to all damages because of all personal injury and advertising injuries sustained by *any one person or organization.* The aggregate limit applies to *all damages,* including those sustained under Coverage A (excluding Products and Completed Operations), plus Coverage C (Medical Payments).

[1] Definitions

As has already been noted, the policy provisions contain no specific definitions of the perils insured, since these acts are defined differently in various jurisdictions. In some states, the statutes specifically define some of the terms mentioned in the policy. In others, it is a matter of judicial interpretation, and since the decisions are based on text book definitions, we will use such definitions here.

False Arrest or Imprisonment is the intentional, unprivileged detaining of a person without his consent. It need not necessarily be a physical restraint. A show of apparent authority or the apparent threat of physical force is all that is usually necessary. It is most often involved in suspected shoplifting arrests.

Supermarkets of products other than food, and most department stores, now employ less sales people than in previous times. As a result, this serves as a temptation that has increased the incidence of shoplifting to the point where it has become a great problem in the retail business. This has increased the need for tighter security measures which, in turn, have increased allegations of false arrest since con artists have discovered that it is more profitable to fake shoplifting and sue for false arrest.

False arrest allegations usually include other allegations such as assault, battery, defamation, false imprisonment, and intentional or negligent infliction of emotional distress. These kinds of claims are usually repetitive. Accordingly, a careful check with the Index Bureau is essential and a careful investigation should be made where

---

[10] The different rules of interpretation are discussed in Southern Maryland Assoc. v. Bituminous Cas. Corp., 539 F. Supp. 1295 (1982), in which the U.S. District Court for the District of Maryland adopted the latter rule.

a repeater is suspected. Ordinarily, a quick payoff is what this kind of claimant is looking for, and the last thing he wants to invite is an intensive investigation.

Malicious Prosecution. Malicious prosecution has been held to involve (1) a criminal prosecution, (2) terminating in favor of the plaintiff, (3) actuated by malice, and (4) without probable cause.[11]

Juries are prone to be sympathetic to people who have been allegedly wronged, and because of the increase of actions that include emotional distress and punitive damages, it too has become a problem arising out of the increase in shoplifting.

Most states have recognized this problem and have enacted "reasonable cause" statutes. This has often been referred to as "reasonable grounds" (for the belief that wrongdoing has been committed) or probable cause, in the common law decisions on this subject. Again however, the facts that might lead to a conclusion of reasonable belief is a matter for jury determination.

Libel and Slander. In libel or slander suits, it is important to note that false statements of fact are not privileged (actionable),[12] while statements which are expressions of opinion are usually within the rights granted by the First Amendment and accordingly are privileged. Expressions such as "acted with greed to fleece customers" have been held to be a matter of opinion.[13]

For claims people it is of importance to note that reports of investigations by claim adjusters have been held to be conditionally privileged, which means privileged as long as such privilege is not abused, and the statements made with a proper motive, in a proper manner and based upon reasonable cause.[14] Statements made in the complaint of a suit are usually held to be absolutely privileged.[15]

Defamation is a word that almost defines itself. It includes either libel or slander and is any communication of any kind, made in any manner, which has the tendency of harming a person's reputation.

---

[11] Md.: Martz v. Alban, 349 A.2d 685 (1976).
S.C. Ruff v. Echkerds Drugs, Inc., 220 S.E.2d 644 (1975).
Va.: Tweedy v. J.C. Penney Co., Inc., 221 S.E.2d 152 (1975).
[12] U.S.: Gertz v. Robert Welch, Inc., 418 U.S. 323 (1974) (dictum).
[13] Mo.: Henry v. Halliburton, 690 S.W.2d 775 (1985).
[14] Pa.: Beckman v. Dunn, 419 A.2d 583 (1980).
[15] Cal.: Nichols v. Great American Ins. Cos., 215 Cal. Rptr. 416 (App. 1985) (disparaging statements in the investigator's report which were incorporated in the complaint do not state a cause of action for defamation).

Historically, defamation required the statements or published material to be false in order to be actionable, and damages had to be actual and proven. The more recent trend has breached both of these previous requirements in most jurisdictions.

[2] Privileged Communications

Privileged communications are those based on an intimate relationship between the parties and which the law recognizes as confidential. Information obtained as a result of such a relationship cannot be divulged in a court of law without the permission of the person for whom the privilege is granted.

Such privilege is most often granted in the following cases:

1. Husband and wife.
2. Clergyman and parishioner.
3. Physician or psychotherapist and patient.
4. Attorney and client.

The old common law rule, that one spouse may not testify against the other spouse, has been substantially modified by statute. Today, such testimony is admissible in most jurisdictions unless the information is of a very confidential nature.

On the contrary, at common law, communications between physician and patient were not held to be privileged. Here, a change has been made by statutes and by judicial decisions granting privilege to the patient under certain circumstances. In the field of tort law it is rare that any attempt is made to exercise such a privilege where the injured plaintiff is trying to establish verification of his or her injuries. The subject sometimes gets complicated, however, where a question of previous medical attention could have a detrimental effect on present allegations, but this is a matter for legal determination with which the claims person need not be too concerned.

In situations involving clergymen and parishioners there is almost unanimous agreement that statements made in confidence by such parishioner to a clergyman are privileged.

The lawyer-client privilege is much more involved in civil cases and requires a knowledge of local laws and judicial attitudes best left to the representing attorneys.

PUBLIC OR GENERAL LIABILITY § 26.03[3][b]

[3] **Investigation of Personal Injury Cases**

[a] **Defamation**

This category will include both libel and slander. In addition to the basic investigation indicated previously, the claim investigator should:

☐ Determine if the statement or publication was defamatory? Determine, if possible, the exact nature of the statements, pictures, printing, radio, television, etc.
☐ Attempt to discover whether the alleged statements or publication were true.
☐ Determine the exact nature, circumstances, and manner of publication. To whom and how and where?
☐ Determine if there was any malice involved? What exact reasons did the insured give for publication.

[b] **False Arrest or Imprisonment**

The false arrest or imprisonment coverage of personal injury insurance is ordinarily involved in cases of suspected theft or pilferage from a store.

In recent years a more devious and much more potentially lucrative con game has become prevalent. This involves the fraudulent actions of men or women who make it appear as though they have stolen some merchandise in order to invite a false accusation of theft and subsequent arrest or imprisonment. The danger to the perpetrator is almost nonexistent since the worst that can happen is the "embarrassment" of the incident itself. The rewards depend on the gullibility of a jury.

Of course there are cases of honest mistake, but it is the job of the claim representative not only to try to distinguish between the honest and the fraudulent claimant, but to determine whether the actions of an insured were justified, even when the mistake was honest. It is most important for the investigator to determine if there was probable cause and, if so, whether the action taken was reasonable under the circumstances.

I would suggest that the investigator:

☐ Examine the coverage carefully to determine exactly who is insured.
☐ Obtain the complete facts of the incident from all available parties to it.
☐ Obtain statements from all known witnesses and try to discover witnesses not reported by the insured.

§ 26.03[4] CASUALTY INSURANCE CLAIMS

☐ Determine, as closely as possible, the exact words used by the parties involved in the incident.
☐ Learn the exact nature of any physical acts or force used by all parties concerned.
☐ Make an exhaustive check of the claimants:
  ○ Background and reputation.
  ○ Police record of arrests and convictions.
  ○ Employment record.
  ○ Church affiliation.
  ○ Credit record.
  ○ Activities of any other kind that would help to determine whether the claim under investigation is an honest one and what approximate embarrassment such a claimant would have suffered.
☐ Try to determine damages, both actual and consequential.

[4] Damages

In some states, libel and slander are exceptions to the general rule that damages must be proven. Such instances are usually limited to vicious publications (verbal or in writing) which tend to hold the victim in scorn, or which affect his livelihood or business.

The measure of damages in cases of false arrest or imprisonment may include, in addition to actual financial loss, recovery for embarrassment, fright, mental pain and anguish, and similar items.

All categories within this coverage are subject to punitive damages, and here I depart from my usual opinion that punitive damages should not be assessed against the insurer. In Personal Injury coverage, malice is either the very element for which the insurance is provided or so closely interwoven with any possible action as to make it inseparable from the other elements. Accordingly, here I see no valid objection to payment of such damages by the insurance company.

§ 26.04 Advertising Injury

Advertising injury is defined in the master policy as:

[I]njury arising out of one or more of the following offenses:

a. Oral or written publication of material that slanders or libels a person or organization or disparages a person's or organization's goods, products or services;

b. Oral or written publication of material that violates a person's right of privacy;

c. Misappropriation of advertising ideas or style of doing business; or

d. Infringement of copyright, title or slogan.

While "defamation," "piracy," and "unfair competition" are not specifically mentioned in this policy, as they were in previous policies, the other categories that are mentioned take up the slack so as to cover incidents that fall within these groups.

Once again, coverage in the "B Advertising Injury" category, applies only if the insured's business is "other than advertising, publishing, broadcasting or telecasting." Coverage, in both forms, becomes effective when the alleged tort is committed, as long as it is within the policy period and within the covered territory.

§ 26.05 Medical Payments

Medical payments coverage, as has previously been stated, is, in fact, a bastard combination of accident coverage attached to a third party liability policy. Its accident insurance aspects involves a lack of any requirement of liability for this coverage to take effect. All that need happen is that an injury and resulting medical expense shall have occurred as a result of an accident arising out of the named insured's premises or operations that are covered by the policy. Coverage is provided only for third parties and not for any insured, named or otherwise.

Medical payments is included in both forms as an integral part of the master policies under Coverage C—Medical Payments, unless deleted by endorsement. It is a relatively short and uncomplicated coverage. The accident resulting in the medical expense must occur during the policy period in both the "occurrence" and the "claims-made" forms.

It differs from other coverages in that there is a specific requirement that "The expenses are incurred and reported within one year of the date of the accident."

The Limit of Liability for this coverage is the amount stated in the Declarations as to each person and to the general aggregate limits of the master policies.

The fact that Coverage C—Medical Payments is subject to the general applicable Exclusions of the master policies (besides having Exclusions of its own) is spelled out in Exclusion "g" of the Medical Payments Exclusions.

§ 26.06 CASUALTY INSURANCE CLAIMS

Exclusion "f" of the Medical Payments exclusions also notes that expenses arising out of any products-completed operations hazard are not covered under the Medical Payments Coverage C.

§ 26.06 Contractual Liability

Contractual liability coverage is required as a result of exposure to the liability of others, which was assumed by an insured because of actual or implied agreements between the insured and the other parties to the agreements.

Exclusion "b." of the master forms of the Commercial General Liability policies states that the insurance does not apply to: " 'Bodily injury' or 'property damage' for which the insured is obligated to pay damages by reason of the assumption of liability in a contract or agreement." This exclusion has 2 exceptions.

Accordingly, Contractual Liability coverage may be purchased as additional insurance under the Commercial General Liability policies.

The definition of "insured contract" makes no requirement that such contract be in writing and presumably if an otherwise valid oral contract could be proven, it would be covered under the Contractual Liability insurance.

This coverage specifically lists seven kinds of liabilities, from "a" to "g," most of which are self-explanatory.

Paragraph "g" covers "That part of any agreement pertaining to the insured's business under which the insured has assumed the tort liability of another, to pay damages because of bodily injury or property damage to a third person or organization." The tort liability assumed therefore, need not have originated from any agreement made by the other party. The original liability which is assumed may have been any tortious liability as long as it did not precede the date of the agreement upon which liability was assumed.[16]

§ 26.07 Products—Completed Operations

Since Products—Completed Operations insurance is ordinarily issued as an addition to other general liability policies, it is to be ex-

---

[16] For a more in-depth discussion of this coverage, the reader is referred to the F.C. & S. Bulletins, Casualty volume, Public Liability Section, pages C a - 1 to C a - 5.

pected that this coverage would be available as an additional coverage to the Commercial General Liability policies. It is available in separate forms for both the "occurrence" and the "claims-made" policies, and the two forms differ because of the "retroactive" requirements of the "claims-made" policy.

A discussion of the law of products liability is included in Chapter 29, "Products Liability."

The Products—Completed Operations Liability coverage is, in the Commercial General Liability policy, a complete policy, in and of itself and many of its provisions repeat the wording of much of the master form. It is even divided in the same way. There is no need to repeat sections of the policy already covered.

The Insuring Agreement of Section I—Coverages, for Bodily Injury and Property Damage, under paragraph "a." of the "occurrence" form states that: "We will pay those sums that the insured becomes legally obligated to pay as damages because of 'bodily injury' or 'property damage' included within the 'products—completed operations hazard to which this insurance applies.'"

The Insuring Agreement in the "claims-made" form includes the "Retroactive" coverage wording found in the master form. Otherwise, the wording is about the same as that of the master policies.

The Exclusions are self-explanatory and many are identical with the wording of the master forms. The Exclusion concerning faulty workmanship, however, deserves comment.

The intent of the general liability policies is to protect an insured from liability resulting from injuries to a third party resulting from the insured's faulty workmanship and material. It is not intended to protect an insured from liability for replacement or repair of the defective work itself.[17] Business risks assumed by the insured contractor in the ordinary normal course of business, are, in part, the consequences of not performing work well, which is part of every business venture; the replacement or repair of faulty goods and works is a business expense, to be borne by the insured-contractor in order to satisfy customers. Such risks are not intended to be covered by a liability insurance policy.[18]

---

[17] Ill.: Western Cas. & Sur. Co. v. Brochu, 460 N.E.2d 832 (1984).
Minn.: T.E. Ibberson Co. v. American & Foreign Ins. Co., 346 N.W.2d 659 (App. 1984).
N.J.: Weedo v. Stone-E-Brick, Inc., 405 A.2d 766 (1979).
[18] C.D. Walters Construction Co. v. Fireman's Ins. Co., 316 S.E.2d 709 (S.C. App. 1984).

§ 26.07 CASUALTY INSURANCE CLAIMS

In *C.D. Walters Construction Co. v. Fireman's Ins. Co.*,[19] it was held that "There exists another form of risk in the insured-contractor's line of work that is injury to people and damage to property *caused by* (italics added) faulty workmanship. Such losses are intended to be covered."

Products liability covers injury or property damage which occurs away from the insured's premises and it also covers liability for the use of the product when possession of it has been relinquished by the insured. Otherwise, injury or property damage which occurs from the insured's products *on the insured's premises* (italics added) is usually covered by the general provisions of the master policy to which the products liability coverage has been added.

The Definitions section of the master form defines the "Products—Completed Operations" hazard under paragraph "9. a." as including "all 'bodily injury' and 'property damage' occurring away from premises you (the insured) own or rent and arising out of 'your product' or 'your work' except: (1) Products that are still in your physical possession; or (2) Work that has not yet been completed or abandoned."

Thereafter, section "b." states when "your work" will be completed. There are also three exclusions under this definition for:

(1) The transportation of property [excepting the "loading and unloading"];

(2) The existence of tools, uninstalled equipment or abandoned or unused materials;

(3) Products or operations for which the classification in this Coverage Part or in our manual of rules includes products or completed operations.

The definition of "your product" as given in the master form is identically repeated in the Products—Completed Operations coverage as follows:

a. Any goods or products other than real property, manufactured, sold, handled, distributed or disposed of by:

(1) You;

(2) Others trading under your name; or

---

[19] *Id.*

PUBLIC OR GENERAL LIABILITY § 26.07[1]

(3) A person or organization whose business assets you have acquired; and

b. Containers (other than vehicles), materials, parts or equipment furnished in connection with such goods or products.

It is interesting to note that despite all of the litigation concerning what is or is not a "container," no attempt was made in this policy to define it.

" 'Your product' includes warranties or representations made at any time with respect to the fitness, quality, durability, or performance of any of the items included in "a" and "b" above." Vending machines or other property rented to or located for the use of others is not included as "your product."

"Exclusion h" states that there is no coverage for damage to "your product" or any part of it and "Exclusion i" states that there is no coverage for damages to "your work" arising out of and included in the Products—Completed Operations hazard, unless the damage resulted from work performed on behalf of the insured by a subcontractor.

[1] Covered Territory

The territory covered by this section of the Commercial General Liability policies which is usually found in a separate provision of the policy Conditions, is here found under paragraph 3, "Coverage territory" of the Definitions.

The wording of the same provision in the master policies differs somewhat from that of the Products—Completed Operations definition, but the intent is obviously the same. The intent of this provision can best be illustrated by an example given in the F.C. & S. Bulletins as follows:

> a product made by the insured in the U.S. but sold abroad would, under this new language, be covered (so long as the insured's liability was determined in a suit on the merits in the territory described in a. above. ("The United States of America including its territories and possessions, Puerto Rico and Canada.") If an insured did not make the product, but sold it in the U.S. and it later went abroad and caused injury, the resulting liability would likewise be covered. There would not be coverage if the named insured neither made nor sold the product in

26-29

the U.S., Canada or Puerto Rico.[20]

[2] Completed Operations

Definition 11 under the master policies defines "your work as having been completed at the earliest of the following times:

(1) When all the work called for in your contract has been completed;

(2) When all the work to be done at the site has been completed if your contract calls for work at more than one site.

(3) When that part of the work at a job site has been put to its intended use by any person or organization other than another contractor or subcontractor working on the same project.

Work that may need service, maintenance, correction, repair or replacement, but which is otherwise complete, will be treated as completed.

This wording makes it clear that the operations are completed, under the meaning of the policy, when the *work* (italics added) is completed and not when the work has been accepted, and even if there may be a further requirement for maintenance or correction of a defect.

It should be noted that the Products—Completed Operations coverage of the Commercial General Liability policies differ somewhat from other Products—Completed Operations policies and, while they are all basically similar, the facts of the incident under investigation must be measured by the particular policy that was issued and for which coverage is provided.

§ 26.08 Liquor Liability Coverage Form

The Liquor Liability Coverage Form, as with other attached coverages to the Commercial General Liability policies, comes in two types, one for the "occurrence" policy and the other for the "claims-made" policy, to take care of the retroactive features of this latter policy.

The master policies exclude coverage for those "in the business of manufacturing, distributing, selling, serving or furnishing alcoholic beverages." It is intended to exclude only those establishments

---

[20] Casualty volume, Public Liability Section, page A a-3, F.C. & S. Bulletins, The National Underwriter Co, Cincinnati, Ohio.

that serve liquor for a profit, and for such establishments or businesses, Exclusion C applies to "bodily injury" or "property damage" for which any insured may be held liable by reason of:

(1) Causing or contributing to the intoxication of any person;

(2) The furnishing of alcoholic beverages to a person under the legal drinking age or under the influence of alcohol; or

(3) Any statute, ordinance or regulation relating to the sale, gift, distribution or use of alcoholic beverages.

The Liquor Liability coverage does away with this exclusion and provides coverage for those businesses excluded in the master policies. Otherwise, the general provisions of this coverage are about the same as those in the master policies and are simply repeated in this attachment.

The law concerning the liability for those serving liquor is discussed in § 23.03, *supra*.

§ 26.09 Pollution Liability Coverage

Pollution liability coverage comes in two forms: (1) Pollution Liability Coverage, at designated sites, and (2) Pollution Liability Limited Coverage, at designated sites.

The Insuring Agreement of the Pollution Liability form "1. a. (3)" reads: "Our right and duty to defend end when we have used up the applicable limit of insurance in the payment of judgments, settlements or 'clean-up costs.'"

The Insuring Agreement of the limited form does not include "clean-up costs," nor does the limited form include Insuring Agreement 2 for Reimbursement of Mandated Off-Site "Clean-up Costs."

The pollution exclusion in the master policies is to be found in Exclusion "f" which reads:

(1) "Bodily injury" or "property damage" arising out of the actual, alleged or threatened discharge, dispersal, release or escape of pollutants;

(a) At or from premises you own, rent or occupy;

(b) At or from any site or location used by or for you or others for the handling, storage, disposal, processing or treatment of waste;

§ 26.09   CASUALTY INSURANCE CLAIMS

(c) Which are at any time transported, handled, stored, treated, disposed of, or processed as waste by or for you or any person or organization for whom you may be legally responsible; or

(d) At or from any site or location on which you or any contractors or subcontractors working directly or indirectly on your behalf are performing operations;

(i) if the pollutants are brought on or to the site or location in connection with such operations; or

(ii) if the operations are to test for, monitor, clean up, remove, contain, treat, detoxify or neutralize the pollutants.

(2) Any loss, cost, or expense arising out of any governmental directive or request that you test for, monitor, clean up, remove, contain, treat, detoxify or neutralize pollutants.

"Pollutants" are then defined in this exclusion and in the Pollution policy Definitions as being: "any solid, liquid, gaseous or thermal irritant or contaminant, including smoke, vapor, soot, fumes, acids, alkalis, chemicals and waste. Waste includes materials to be recycled, reconditioned or reclaimed."

"Pollution incident" is defined in the Pollution Definitions as being "emission, discharge, release or escape of pollutants into or upon land, the atmosphere, or any watercourse or body of water, provided that such emission, discharge, release or escape results in 'environmental damage.'"

Exclusion "f" of the Pollution policy excludes " 'Property damage' or 'environmental damage' to (1) A 'waste facility.' " Clean up costs at a waste facility are also excluded.

Another applicable Exclusion in the Pollution form excludes environmental damage arising out of a "pollution incident" from an insured site that was used

by you for the storage, disposal, processing or treatment of waste materials and was:

(1) Sealed off, closed, abandoned or alienated prior to the Retroactive date shown in the Declarations of this Coverage Part (if any) or;

(2) Sealed off or closed subject to statute ordinance or governmental regulation or directive requiring maintenance or monitoring during or after sealing off or closure.

Exclusion "m" refers to:

"Bodily injury," "property damage" or "environmental damage" arising out of a "pollution incident" which results from or is directly or indirectly attributable to failure to comply with any applicable statute, regulation, ordinance, directive or order relating to the protection of the environment and promulgated by any governmental body, provided that failure to comply is a willful or deliberate act or omission of: (1) The insured, or (2) You or any of your members, partners or executive officers.

Finally, Exclusion "n" excludes damage or injury "arising out of acid rain."

The repetition ad nauseam of synonyms is necessitated by legal decisions that make a mockery of policy intent and forces such otherwise redundant verbiage.

§ 26.10 Endorsements

As originally stated, the Commercial General Liability policies may be affected by many standard ISO endorsements such as Nuclear Energy Liability Exclusion, Cancellation by the Insured, Deductible Liability coverage, Hired and Non-Owned Auto Liability coverage, Disaster Relief coverage, Additional Insureds of many kinds, Waivers of Governmental and Charitable Immunities and many others.

All of these deserve careful review when the basic facts of an incident under investigation are reported so that the investigation can be directed toward a determination of coverage, not only under the policy itself, but under the endorsements that always supercede the policy to which they are attached.

CHAPTER 27

"Occurrence"

§ 27.01 Introduction
§ 27.02 "Occurrence" Is an "Accident"
§ 27.03 Manifestation Theory
§ 27.04 Exposure Theory
§ 27.05 Triple-Trigger Theory
§ 27.06 Injury In Fact
§ 27.07 "Cause of Injury" Determines Number of Occurrences
§ 27.08 Statute of Limitations
§ 27.09 Stacking and Proration
§ 27.10 Doctrine of Reasonable Expectations
§ 27.11 Neither Expected Nor Intended from the Standpoint of the Insured
§ 27.12 Self-Defense

§ 27.01 Introduction

The importance, in tort liability, of products liability and medical malpractice, and because of the litigation that the definition of "occurrence" has engendered, make it practical to devote a chapter of this book to this subject.

One of the principal factors in rephrasing the wording in the 1986 Commercial General Liability policy from the 1973 Comprehensive General Liability form resulted from judicial interpretations of the definition of "occurrence" in cases involving prolonged injuries or diseases.

The original 1966 CGL policy defined "occurrence" as follows:

> An accident, including injurious exposure to conditions, which results, during the policy period, in bodily injury or property damage neither expected nor intended from the standpoint of the insured.

"From the standpoint of the insured" was a phrase added many years ago after some courts interpreted "accident," before it was specifically defined, to mean an accident as far as the claimant was concerned and this was certainly not the intent of the policy drafters.

The former policies did make clear that "assault" and "battery" were not intended to be covered.

In the 1976 revision of the Comprehensive General Liability policy, "occurrence" was defined as follows:

> occurrence means an accident, including continuous or repeated exposure to conditions, which results in bodily injury or property damage neither expected nor intended from the standpoint of the insured.

The change from the 1966 form, while only slight, did eliminate the words "injurious" exposure, from the definition.

Despite the continued use of the word "accident," the 1973 wording made it clear that the definition of the word "accident" as a sudden incident that caused injury, no longer applied. This one stroke broadened the coverage considerably. Nevertheless, it also attempted to make clear that the insured's liability for injury by "continuous or repeated exposure," limited the "occurrence" to only one covered incident no matter how many exposures resulted in the particular injury to a particular claimant.

The intent was also to trigger coverage when injury or damage was done and not when the wrongdoing was committed.

The interpretation of the definition of "occurrence" in the 1973 CGL form in cases involving prolonged exposure to dangerous conditions resulting in injuries and damages that were not discovered until years after the exposure, was broadened beyond the foreseeability of the previous drafters of the policy. Liability was created by judicial decision where no such liability was intended, causing precedent with which the casualty insurance companies have had to live.

§ 27.02 "Occurrence" Is an "Accident"

A further attempt was made to clarify the intent of the policy drafters in the wording of the 1986 Commercial General Liability policy which reads in part, as follows:

An occurrence is "an accident, including continuous or repeated exposure to substantially the same general harmful conditions." The part of the previous definition referring to the result as being "neither expected nor intended" is contained in exclusion 2(a) which reads: "This insurance does not apply to bodily injury or property damage expected or intended from the standpoint of the insured."

§ 27.03

The three elements required by these definitions of "occurrence" were emphasized by the Washington Court of Appeals in the case of *Yakima Cement Products Co. v. Great American Ins. Co.*[1] as being (1) an "accident," (2) "damage," and (3) "neither expected nor intended by the insured."

The advent of the manifestation of the disease of asbestosis as a result of long exposure to the inhalation of asbestos fibers, followed by DES and the approaching agent orange cases are opening the floodgates to a new series of legal actions that has catapulted products liability suits into one of the most fertile grounds for plaintiff's lawyers and one of nightmarish proportions for the insurance industry.

Insecticides, pollutants, drug distribution and ingestion, new inventions in the computer, video and audio fields, and areas completely unknown today will provide injuries and diseases with which we will have to contend in the future, after the harm which they are doing will be discovered. Who knows, for instance, how many complicated suits will be instituted when the juniors of today learn that the earsplitting rock music has made them at least partially deaf.

At present, we must contend with the mostly standardized wording of the Comprehensive General Liability policies and the new Commercial General Liability policy, which basically in the definition of "occurrence" has not changed much since the 1966 forms.

In attempting to decide exactly when coverage comes into play in an "occurrence" type policy (when coverage was triggered), the courts have resorted to various theories which are often used to suit the needs of the plaintiff, and so openly admitted by some jurists.

§ 27.03 Manifestation Theory

The manifestation theory holds that coverage is not triggered until the injury or disease that arose out of an exposure to a deleterious substance, over a period of years, manifests itself and becomes known to the victim.[2]

---

[1] 590 P.2d 371 (1979).

[2] Eagle-Picher Indus. v. Liberty Mut. Ins. Co., 682 F.2d 12 (1982); Wolf Machin. Co. v. Insurance Co. of N. Amer., 183 Cal. Rptr. 695 (1982); Transamerica Ins. Co. v. Bellefonte Ins. Co., 490 F. Supp. 935 (Pa. 1980).

Four years after the decision in *Insurance Co. of N. Amer. v. Forty Eight Insulations*[3] held in favor of the manifestation theory, the same court of appeals in *Michigan Chemical Corp. v. American Home Assur. Co.*[4] declared that the law should not be oriented in the direction of who will be benefited, but that legal precedent should be applied without regard to the identity of the party who may benefit from the decision and should not be changed for that reason alone. Apparently the court had second thoughts about Justice Keith's comments in the *Forty Eight Insulations* case, but Justice Keith wrote a dissenting opinion showing that he still thought that justice depended upon who was benefited.

In the case of *Clutter v. Johns-Manville Corp.*,[5] the court specifically pointed out that in it's opinion "manifestation" is not the same as "discover." The opinion stated that "manifestation" occurs when some symptoms are present as a result of which the plaintiff *could have discovered* (italics added) the injury. "Discovery" is when the injury becomes evident. This case follows the *Eagle-Picher*[6] decision to the effect that "A disease 'results' under the occurrence policies when it becomes clinically evident, that is, when it becomes reasonably capable of medical diagnosis."[7]

While the decision in the case of *Ducre v. Mine Safety Appliances*[8] applied the "manifestation" theory, the court made a very important distinction holding coverage is also afforded for any "real but undiscovered injury in retrospect, to have existed at the relevant time ... irrespective of the time the injury became manifested," and cited *American Home Products v. Liberty Mut. Ins. Co.*,[9] as being in accord. It would appear as though these cases are going in both directions at the same time.

§ 27.04 Exposure Theory

Under the "exposure" theory, coverage under an occurrence policy is triggered when the claimant is first exposed to the deleterious substance.

---

[3] 633 F.2d 1212 (6th Cir. 1980).
[4] 728 F.2d 374 (6th Cir. 1984) *reversing* 530 F. Supp. 147 (1982).
[5] 646 F.2d 1152 (6th Cir. 1981).
[6] Eagle-Picher Indus. v. Liberty Mut. Ins. Co., 682 F.2d 12 (1982).
[7] *Id.*
[8] 573 F. Supp. 388 (La. 1983).
[9] 565 F. Supp. 1485 (1983).

The leading case on the exposure theory is the 1980 case of *Insurance Co. of N. Amer. v. Forty Eight Insulations,*[10] where the decision, interpreted as Illinois and New Jersey law, stated that it was obligated to construe the policies broadly in order to promote coverage, and that, therefore, the court held for the exposure theory, obviously because it felt that this theory was most beneficial to the plaintiffs in this case.

In his dissenting opinion, Justice Merritt stated that there were flaws in both the exposure and manifestation theories. He proposed a "discoverability" rule. If an injury can be discovered by x-ray or other means long before it actually manifests itself, coverage should be in order from the time of discovery. This, in effect, defines the "injury in fact" theory discussed hereafter.

The "exposure" theory is not limited to asbestos cases, but was also followed in cases involving the ingestion of drugs.[11]

§ 27.05 Triple-Trigger Theory

The first important case to favor the "triple-trigger" theory of coverage under the occurrence policies was *Keene Corp. v. Insurance Co. of N. Amer.*[12] which it called the "injurious process" theory.

This case held that coverage was triggered by (1) inhalation exposure (asbestos), (2) exposure in residence, and (3) manifestation. In effect, the triple-trigger theory holds that coverage is in order in an occurrence policy from the time of first exposure, through the period when the disease becomes manifested, and thereafter. Some other decisions have held likewise.[13]

The decision in the case of *Eli Lilly v. Home Ins. Co.,*[14] flatly held that any insurer that covered the risk between the initial exposure and the manifestation of the disease should be liable under an occurrence policy.

---

[10] 633 F.2d 1212 (6th Cir. 1980).

[11] Schwartz v. Heyden Newport Chem. Corp., 12 N.Y.2d 212 (1963); Thornton v. Roosevelt Hosp., 47 N.Y.2d 780 (1979).

[12] 667 F.2d 1034 (D.C. Cir. 1981).

[13] Vale Chem. Co. v. Hartford Accid. & Indem. Co., 490 A.2d 896 (Pa. Super. 1985); Schering Corp. v. Home Ins. Co., 554 F. Supp. 613 (N.Y. 1982) (court stated that the same standard did not apply to all cases; that DES differed from asbestos cases and that both exposure and manifestation theories might apply to permit coverage); AC&S, Inc. v. Aetna Cas. & Sur. Co., 576 F. Supp. 936 (Pa. 1983) (here too, the court very frankly stated that its interpretation was made in order to maximize coverage).

[14] 482 N.E.2d 467 (Ind. 1985).

§ 27.06 Injury In Fact

All too many justices promulgate legal "theories" under the impression that this is their way to immortality. The various theories concerning the meaning of "occurrence" is no exception.

In the case of *American Home Products Corp., v. Liberty Mut. Ins. Co.,*[15] the court interpreted an occurrence of "personal injury, sickness or disease" to mean "any point in time at which a finder of fact determines that the effects of exposure to a drug actually resulted in a diagnosable and compensable injury."

This case held that the trigger of coverage unambiguously provided coverage based upon the occurrence during the policy period of an "injury in fact." The court distinguished "manifestation" from "injury in fact" by stating that:

> The provision that the policies give coverage for occurrences that cause injury, read with the provision that the policies apply only to personal injury, sickness or disease ... which occurs during the policy period, clearly supports the court's conclusion that coverage is triggerd by "injury in fact." ... Some types of injury to the body occur prior to the appearance of any symptoms; thus, the manifestation of the injury may well occur after the injury itself. There is no language in the policies that purports to limit coverage only to injuries that become apparent during the policy period, regardless of when the injury actually occurred.[16]

In the case of *Hartford Accid. & Indem. Co. v. Aetna Life & Cas. Co.*[17] the court held that the trigger was when the claimant was actually injured. There was no evidence that the ingestion of the drug was immediate or immediately injurious. The court specifically rejected the "exposure theory."

§ 27.07 "Cause of Injury" Determines Number of Occurrences

The courts are practically unanimous in determining that the number of occurrences depends on the cause of the injury or disease

---

[15] 748 F.2d 760 (2d Cir. 1984).
[16] *Id.* at 764.
[17] 483 A.2d 402 (N.J. 1984).

rather than its effect.[18]

The *Appalachian* case[19] involved employment discrimination that occurred over a period of time and the one occurrence decision referred to the policy coverage only.

In the *Michigan Chemical Corp.*[20] decision, the case involved the interpretation of "per occurrence," which was the wording in all of the insurance company policies involved in this incident that lasted over a period of two policy years. Determination was required as to whether "occurrence" was triggered at the time damage resulted or whether the "occurrence" was triggered at the time of wrongdoing.

The Court of Appeals (Sixth Circuit) reversed the District Court and remanded the case, holding (1) that the majority of courts have concluded "that although injury must be suffered before an insured can be held liable, the number of occurrences for purposes of applying coverage limitations is determined by referring to the cause of the damage and not to the number of injuries or claims." In support of this statement, the court cited *Appalachian Ins. Co. v. Liberty Mut. Ins. Co.*;[21] (2) the policy definitions of "occurrence" reflect the majority approach in two ways, first that the language makes the accident constituting the occurrence, logically distinct from the injuries, and second, that because the policies afford coverage on an "oc-

---

[18] **Ala.:** U.S. Fire Ins. Co. v. Safeco Ins. Co., 444 So. 2d 844 (1983).

D.C.: Owens-Ill., Inc. v. Aetna Cas. & Sur. Co., 597 F. Supp. 1515 (1984).

Fla.: American Indem. Co. v. McQuaig, 435 So. 2d 414 (App. 1983).

Ill.: Aetna Cas. & Sur. Co. v. Medical Protective Co., 575 F. Supp. 901 (1983) (court held that a series of related injuries comprise a single occurrence where they all flow from a single cause. All injuries flowed from one diagnosis and one course of treatment).

Me.: Honeycomb Systems, Inc. v. Admiral Ins. Co., 567 F. Supp. 1400 (1983) (in this case there were two causes, hence two occurrences).

Mich.: Michigan Chem. Co. v. American Home Assur. Co., 728 F.2d 374 (1984).

Minn.: Cargill, Inc. v. Liberty Mut. Ins. Co., 621 F.2d 275 (8th Cir. 1980) (although the property damage happened over an extended period of time, it was one occurrence for the purpose of applying a deductible limit).

N.Y.: Champion Int'l Corp. v. Continental Cas. Co., 546 F.2d 502 (2d Cir. 1976).

Pa.: Appalachian Ins. Co. v. Liberty Mut. Ins. Co., 676 F.2d 56 (3d Cir. 1982).

Tex.: Transport Ins. Co. v. Lee Way Motor Freight, Inc., 487 F. Supp. 1325 (1980).

Wis.: Olsen v. Moore, 202 N.W.2d 236 (1972) (old policy wording); American Motorists Ins. Co. v. Trane Co., 544 F. Supp. 669 (1982).

[19] Appalachian Ins. Co. v. Liberty Mut. Ins. Co., 676 F.2d 374 (3d Cir. 1984).

[20] Michigan Chemical Corp. v. American Home Assur. Co., 728 F.2d 374 (6th Cir. 1984).

[21] 676 F.2d 56 (3d Cir. 1982).

currence" basis rather than a "claim made" basis, the policies were intended to gauge coverage by the underlying circumstances which resulted in the damage claims. For this holding, the court cited *Champion International Corp. v. Continental Cas. Co.*;[22] (3) because the courts have reached a uniform interpretation on the policy language, the term "occurrence" is held to be unambiguous; and (5) and (6) basically hold that "using the cause test in order to calculate the number of occurrences is consistent with looking to the time and place of injury in order to decide when and where an occurrence takes place for the purpose of applying either a products liability provision or assigning a claim to a particular policy period."

As James T. Ferrini says:[23]

> Identification of the occurrence for the purpose of determining the number of times the limits of liability will apply is made by reference to the cause or causes of the injury. Stated another way, an occurrence is inchoate until it culminates in injury or damage and it is the causal agency that determines the application of the limits of coverage; in contrast, the damage or injury aspect of the occurrence is determinative of the "when" of the occurrence, and that, in turn, determines the policy period to which the loss is assigned.

The case of *Maurice Pincoff's Co. v. St. Paul Fire & Marine Ins. Co.*[24] involved the sale of contaminated bird seed to eight dealers who sustained damage to birds, resulting from ingestion. The court held that the insured's liability resulted from the sale of the seed and that each sale was a different occurrence. Accordingly, the primary insurer had to exhaust its coverage on eight occurrences before the excess carrier's coverage came into play.

In another case, *Aetna Cas. & Sur. Co. v. Owens Ill. Co.*,[25] the decision was obviously made specifically to benefit the insured. The case involved hundreds of claims resulting from asbestos exposure, and since each occurrence was covered under a rather large deductible limit, the court ruled that the number of claimants was not relevant in determining the number of occurrences.

---

[22] 400 F. Supp. 978 (N.Y. 1975).
[23] "The Single-Multiple Occurrence Controversy—A Fair Resolution," Insurance Counsel Journal, April 1985.
[24] 315 F. Supp. 964 (Tex. 1971).
[25] 597 F. Supp. 1515 (1984).

§ 27.08 Statute of Limitations

The "occurrence" policies present another problem for determination concerning the date from which a statute of limitations begins to run. Here again, opinion is divided between those jurists holding to the "discovery" or "manifestation" theory and those following the "exposure theory."

The federal court in *Insurance Co. of N. Amer. v. Forty Eight Insulations* [26] was consistent in deciding what was best for the plaintiff while being inconsistent in its opinions. In deciding when the action accured for the purpose of coverage, it held for the "exposure theory." The court noted however, that the "manifestation theory" should govern the application of the statute of limitations "since a worker cannot know he has suffered injury until the disease manifests itself."

Other cases have also held that the statute begins to run when the plaintiff discovers, or, with reasonable diligence, should have discovered, not only the injury and its relation to the cause of exposure, but that the manufacturer engaged in wrongful conduct.[27]

Allegations of mere difficulty in identifying the defendants was not sufficient to toll the statute, nor was the fact that the injury was a continuing one.[28]

The case of *Locke v. Johns-Manville Corp.*,[29] held that the statute of limitations begins to run when the plaintiff has been injured, the date to be established by medical evidence that pinpoints the precise time, with a reasonable degree of medical certainty. This case further stated that if the evidence shows that the injury occurred before the onset of symptoms, the earlier date prevails. I cannot see how anyone can "pinpoint" an injury with a "reasonable degree of medical certainty."

---

[26] 633 F.2d 1212 (Mich. 1980).

[27] **Idaho:** Theriault v. A.H. Robins Co., 698 P.2d 365 (1985).

Ill.: Nolan v. Johns-Mansville Asbestos, 421 N.E.2d 864 (1981).

Ohio.: O'Stricker v. Jim Walters Corp., 4 Ohio St. 3d 84 (1981).

Pa.: Cathcart v. Keene Indus. Insul., 471 A.2d 493 (1984); Appalachian Ins. Co. v. Liberty Mut. Ins. Co., 676 F.2d 56 (1982) (manifestation determines "when"); Da Mato v. Turner & Newall, Ltd., 651 F.2d 908 (3d Cir. 1981).

R.I.: Anthony v. Abbott Labs., 106 F.R.D. 461 (1985); Romano v. Westinghouse Elec. Co., 336 A.2d 555 (1975).

Wis.: Hansen v. A.H. Robins, 335 N.W.2d 578 (1983) (reversing previous Wisconsin decisions).

[28] Cathcart v. Keene Indus. Insulation, 471 A.2d 493 (Pa. Super. 1984).

[29] 275 S.E.2d 900 (Va. 1981).

The *exposure theory* holds basically that the statute begins to run from the last date of exposure to the harmful substance.[30]

A federal court, interpreting Virginia law, held that exposures after the injury complained of, are irrelevant since the plaintiff suffered no new injuries or diseases that were not present on the date of the original harm.[31]

A federal district court, interpreting Illinois law, held that if the asbestos action had not accrued (been discovered) by the time of the decedent's death, there was no action to be kept alive. If it had survived, the court stated that the survivors had only two years from the date of the decedent's death to bring an action, in accordance with the Illinois Survival statute.[32]

§ 27.09 Stacking and Proration

Where more than one policy covers a claim or suit, the insured may designate the policy that will apply to the given claim and the limits of liability of that policy will be the total limits for which that insurer will be liable. There can be no "stacking" of policy limits.[33] In other words, no insurer is liable for any amount in excess of the highest one year limit in a policy in force during the period of exposure.[34]

In the case of *Hendrickson v. Cumpton*,[35] the Missouri Court of Appeals, in ruling that liability coverages could not be stacked, stated: "Courts in other jurisdictions . . . have uniformly denied stacking," and cited a number of cases as precedent.[36]

---

[30] Thornton v. Roosevelt Hosp., 47 N.Y.2d 780 (1979) (statute held to run from the time when an injection was made that caused the onset of cancer); Schwartz v. Heyden Newport Chem. Corp., 12 N.Y.2d 212 (1963); Steinhardt v. Johns-Manville Corp., 54 N.Y.2d 1008 (1981) (N.Y. made an exception for "agent orange" cases).

[31] Large v. Bucyrus Erie Co., 524 F. Supp. 285 (Va. 1981).

[32] McDaniel v. Johns-Manville Corp., 511 F. Supp. 1341 (Ill. 1981).

[33] Owens-Illinois, Inc. v. Aetna Cas. & Sur. Co., 597 F. Supp. 1515 (D.C. 1984); Keene Corp. v. Insurance Co. of N. America, 667 F.2d 1034 (D.C. Cir. 1981).

[34] Insurance Co. of N. Amer. v. Forty Eight Insulations, 633 F.2d 1212 (6th Cir. 1980).

[35] 654 S.W.2d 332 (Mo. App. 1983).

[36] **Ariz.:** Basso v. Allstate Ins. Co., 504 P.2d 1281 (App. 1973).
Fla.: Maine v. Hyde, 350 So. 2d 1161 (App. 1977).
Ky.: Butler v. Robinette, 614 S.W.2d 944 (1981).
Md.: Oarr v. Government Employees Ins. Co., 383 A.2d 1112 (1978).

OCCURRENCE § 27.09

While these cases did not involve products liability occurrences, the same general principles apply.

In the *Forty Eight Insulations case* [37] the court also pointed out that the twelve different policies that were involved in the suit all had the same definition of "occurrence" and the court accordingly adopted a prorata solution with reference to the apportionment of liability based on the time period that each insurer was on the risk, and applied the same rule with reference to the apportionment of defense costs.

In the case of *Eli Lilly v. Home Ins. Co.*,[38] the court held that where more than one policy provides coverage for the injury, the insured may select the policy under which payment is to be made. Where multiple insurers are involved, the payment is subject to the provisions governing the allocation of liability.

In a situation involving two policies issued by different insurers, both having the same policy limits and pertinent provisions, the court held that both insurers were jointly and severally liable.[39] On the other hand, the court in the *Forty Eight Insulations* case,[40] ruled that each insurer's liability is individual and proportionate and not joint and several where the policy provisions were not conflicting, and this, I think is by far the more equitable approach. This view was also accepted in the case of *Porter v. American Optical Corp.*[41]

In the *Keene* case,[42] the court stated that the allocation of the limits of liability involved in coverage by several insurers should be governed by the "other insurance" provisions of the policies. This does not give much help where all the "other insurance" provisions are alike, which is usually the case.

The case of *California Union Ins. Co. v. Landmark Ins. Co.*[43] involved damage caused by progressive saturation of adjoining compacted fill slopes as a result of leaking from a nearby swimming pool. The damage was discovered in July 1979, and repairs were improper-

---

[37] Insurance Co. of N. Amer. v. Forty Eight Insulations, 633 F.2d 1212 (6th Cir. 1980).
[38] 482 N.E.2d 467 (Ind. 1985).
[39] California Union Ins. Co. v. Landmark Ins. Co., 198 Cal. Rptr. 461 (1983).
[40] Insurance Co. of N. Amer. v. Forty Eight Insulations, 633 F.2d 1212 (6th Cir. 1980).
[41] 641 F.2d 1128 (La. 1981).
[42] Keene Corp. v. Insurance Co. of N. Amer., 667 F.2d 1034 (D.C. Cir. 1980).
[43] 193 Cal. Rptr. 461 (App. 1983).

ly made. The damage continued until November 1980, when the actual cause of the damage was discovered.

The court held that there was only one occurrence involving continuous and progressively deteriorating damage. Accordingly, the court held that the policy that covered the initial incident in July 1979, was also liable for the damage subsequently caused after the policy expired. The court also held the new insurer jointly responsible for the damage that occurred after the policy came into effect before November 1980.

§ 27.10 Doctrine of Reasonable Expectations

Under the most extenuating circumstances, "reasonable expectations" is a doctrine born out of contract violation. If there is any real ambiguity in an insurance policy contract, insurance and contract law justly hold that such ambiguity should be resolved against the maker, that is, the insurance company.

Even where the policy wording is stretched beyond the breaking point and favors an insurer against a naive and ignorant insured, there is at least some equitable basis for invoking this doctrine.

However, in dealing with insureds in these "occurrence" cases under general liability policies, such insureds are, for the most part, companies with knowledgeable and sophisticated personnel and often with special insurance managers or departments. If anyone can be presumed to have read and understood an insurance policy, such insureds or their brokers should be so charged.

Nevertheless, in the case of *Eli Lilly v. Home Ins. Co.*,[44] the court favored the triple-trigger theory on the basis that it was the reasonable expectations of an insured that purchased single triggered coverage.

In the previously mentioned case of *Keene Corp. v. Insurance Co. of N. Amer.*,[45] the court found that acceptance of manifestation as the sole trigger of coverage would violate an insured's reasonable expectations because it would permit insurers to terminate coverage prior to the manifestation of many future cases.

Other cases have also held that reasonable expectations include

---

[44] 482 N.E.2d 467 (Ind. 1985).
[45] 667 F.2d 1034 (D.C. Cir. 1981).

inception (exposure?), or discovery (manifestation?) as a trigger for coverage.[46]

In still another case, a federal court stated that "An examination of the [insured's] policies' large annual and per occurrence limit provisions also supports the conclusion that, when [the insured] purchased the policies, the parties [?] reasonably expected that [the insured] would be required to pay only one deductible for claims like these resulting from asbestos-related injury."[47]

§ 27.11 Neither Expected Nor Intended from the Standpoint of the Insured

Since the 1966 form, the definition of "occurrence" included the CGL phrase that the insured's act should be "neither expected nor intended from the standpoint of the insured." The 1986 CGL form incorporated this wording in Exclusion 2(a), using the same phrase. Apparently, no further attempt was made to resolve the differences of opinion in the legal decisions.

In the case of *Moss v. Champion Ins. Co.*,[48] damage was caused by rain that penetrated a roof which was left exposed while being repaired. The trial court's decision that there was no coverage because the damage could be expected under such circumstances, was unjustly, in my opinion, reversed. The upper court stated that since the roofer had instructed his employees to cover the exposed part of the roof, he could not have expected or forseen that they would not do so. That is a question that should have been decided by the jury. The statement that "occurrence" was defined as "repeated exposure to conditions" should have been irrelevant.

The case of *American States Ins. Co. v. Maryland Cas. Co.*,[49] involved deliberate and continuous dumping of toxic waste over an extended period of time. The court held that the dumping was deliberate and the resulting damage should have been expected. The acts were held to be intended to damage.

In a case where a builder of houses discovered after the first eight houses were built that the siding being used was defective, but continued to use the same siding thereafter, the court held that after

---

[46] Vale Chem. Co. v. Hartford Accid. & Indem. Co., 490 A.2d 896 (1985).
[47] Owens Illinois, Inc. v. Aetna Cas. & Sur. Co., 597 F. Supp. 1515 (D.C. 1984).
[48] 442 So. 2d 26 (Ala. 1983).
[49] 587 F. Supp. 1549 (Mich. 1984).

§ 27.11   CASUALTY INSURANCE CLAIMS

the first eight houses had been built and the damage discovered, because of the defective use of the siding it was thereafter not to be considered unexpected.[50]

Where the act or wrongdoing was deliberate, and even where the result could have been forseen, the intention for doing the act will continue to give trouble.

In the case of *State Farm v. Worthington*,[51] it may or may not have been the farmer's intent to kill some of the trespassers on his land, when he discharged a shotgun aimed at them. It could certainly be reasonably expected that a pellet might kill one or more of them but the intent would lay deeply buried in the mind of the insured, if he did so intend.

On the other hand, in the case of *Norman v. Insurance Co. of N. Amer.*,[52] an insured who, in a fight, apparently intending to scare his tenant and her brother, fired a revolver without even removing it from his pocket, and without even aiming it at anyone. He was found guilty of willfully and maliciously assaulting and wounding the brother of the tenant, despite the fact that the wound was caused by the ricocheting of the bullet. In this case the court held that an "intentional assault cannot be converted into an accident by a mere statement from the person making the assault that he did not intend the act or its consequences."

In a case involving an allegation of conspiracy to force a car off the road, the court held that "An intentional act is neither an "occurrence" nor an "accident" so as to provide coverage."[53]

Another case held that if any reasonable person would have realized that the injuries would have resulted from an assault (battery?) it was "expected or intended as excluded from policy coverage." In *Bohnsack v. Employers Ins. Co. of Wausau*,[54] the insured hit the claimant on the head with a two-by-four, causing his death. The court stated that "if the performance of an intentional act causes injury which may be said to be the natural and probable consequences of such an act, then the injury itself was intentional, even though it was not the injury intended." This statement, which should be obvious

---

[50] Economy Lumber Co. v. Insurance Co. of N. Amer., 204 Cal. Rptr. 135 (App. 1984).
[51] 405 F.2d 683 (1968).
[52] 239 S.E.2d 902 (Va. 1978).
[53] Utica Mut. Ins. Co. v. Travelers Indem. Co., 286 S.E.2d 225 (Va. 1982).
[54] 708 F.2d 1961 (8th Cir. 1983).

and which is so often ignored by our judiciary, was emphasized in the case of *Truck Ins. Exch. v. Pickering*,[55] where the court stated that "When an intentional act results in injuries which are natural and probable consequences of an act, the injuries, as well as the act are intentional." This clear and logical decision also stated that "an admission of specific intent is not the only way to show intent to cause harm; it can be inferred from facts and circumstances surrounding the act."

In agreement with this point of view was the case of *Horace Mann Ins. Co. v. Independence School Dist.*,[56] which involved sexual intercourse between a school counselor and a minor student who came to him for guidance. It was held that the trial court was entitled to infer that there was "an intent to injure or damage from the nature of the acts involved." The exclusion in the policy for intentional acts was upheld.

On the other hand, I think that the decision in the case of *Farmers Ins. Co. of Ariz. v. Vagnozzi*[57] to the effect that "the presumption that a person intends the ordinary consequences of his actions, has no application to the interpretation of insurance contracts," is without logic or justice. Summary judgment for the insurer was reversed, with which conclusion I agree, but not for the same reason. I think that the court could simply have decided that "intent" was a decision for the jury, which they did, and should have left it at that.

§ 27.12 Self-Defense

It should be noted that the 1986 Commercial General Liability policies, under Exclusion 2a states that " 'Bodily injury' or 'property damage' expected or intended from the standpoint of the insured" is excluded from coverage, but this exclusion has an exception that "does not apply to 'bodily injury' resulting from the use of reasonable force to protect person or property."

The cases involving self-defense belong in a special category. Even without the wording quoted above, it has been held that

> an exclusion of intentional injury in a liability policy does not apply to an insured who acts in self-defense . . . In such cases, the question

---

[55] 642 S.W.2d 113 (Mo. App. 1982).
[56] 355 N.W.2d 413 (Minn. 1984).
[57] 675 P.2d 703 (Ariz. 1983).

§ 27.12   CASUALTY INSURANCE CLAIMS

of intent must be resolved by a determination of the basic purpose or desire underlying the insured's conduct. . . . an act committed in self-defense should not be considered an intentional act.[58]

In another case involving alleged self-defense, the Georgia Court of Appeals held that

although a claim of self-defense may raise the criminal defense justification . . . it does not vitiate the actual intent to cause injury. "The defenses of self-defense and justification do not deny the intent to inflict injury. . . . Since an 'accident' defense involves the lack of intent to do the act at all, the two defenses are inconsistent."[59]

The court accordingly held that there was no coverage under the policy for this act of self-defense.

Nevertheless, the question as to what is "reasonable force" and what constitutes "protection of person or property" will continue to be debated by the lawyers and the courts.

---

[58] Fire Insurance Exch. v. Berray, 694 P.2d 191 (Ariz. 1984).
[59] Stein v. Massachusetts Bay Ins. Co., 324 S.E.2d 510 (Ga. App. 1984).

CHAPTER 28

Investigation of Public or General Liability Claims

§ 28.01 In General
§ 28.02 General Checklist for the Investigation of Public or General Liability Claims
§ 28.03 Checklists for Special Investigations
  [1] Claims Involving Tenancy
  [2] Sidewalk Claims
  [3] Waxed Floors
  [4] Stairways
  [5] Falling Objects
  [6] Elevators
  [7] Escalators
  [8] Construction Cases
  [9] Sports Events, Fairgrounds, and Amusement Parks
  [10] Golfing Accidents
  [11] Animals
  [12] Blasting Operations

§ 28.01 In General

The basic principles for the investigation of all casualty claims are the same. It is therefore essential that the claim investigator review those principles and checklists contained in the chapters on general claim handling and general investigation.

Such matters as planning and preparation, medical investigation, locating and interviewing witnesses, physical facts (photographs, diagrams and so on), have all been adequately covered. What we have previously said about signed statements applies equally to the investigation of public liability claims.

These claims fall into many classifications. They run the gamut from falling objects to falling people; they happen on floors, sidewalks, stairways, in factory buildings, stores, private homes, and in every other imaginable (and sometimes unimaginable) place. As a practical matter, therefore, it is impossible to outline investigation checklists that would cover all types of cases that might be encountered. We will, therefore, make a general checklist outline for the investigation of public liability claims. The list will be basic, and we will add to it pertinent additional investigation to be made in certain specific claims that are encountered rather frequently.

In public liability, more than in automobile, the claim investigator will encounter situations in which, because his company carries the contingent coverage, or because someone else is the primary wrongdoer, his insured may have a cause of action over against that other party. The routine information about the financial responsibility of the wrongdoer, and about his liability insurance must be obtained. In addition, the claim investigator must take particular care to put the wrongdoer and his carrier on notice concerning their responsibility, and request them to take over negotiations and, if necessary, defense of the suit or claim. This should be done in writing as soon as the information has been developed.

Since no investigation should properly be undertaken without an understanding of the basic principles of law involved in a particular claim, it is suggested that the claim investigator review those portions of the chapters on law applicable to the particular type of claim under consideration in the investigation checklists. He should direct his investigation toward obtaining all of the answers necessary to make a proper decision under the law governing the particular claim with which he is dealing.

§ 28.02 General Checklist for the Investigation of Public or General Liability Claims

A. Description and Identification of the Premises

- ☐ Exact location, giving street numbers and any other designation necessary to pinpoint the location.
- ☐ Type of building (one or two family house, apartment, store, factory, theatre, etc.).
- ☐ Age of the building. (If necessary, obtain the name of the original architect, contractor, or builder.)
- ☐ General condition of the building or area.
  - ○ Is the building or area in good general condition?
  - ○ Is the building or area well maintained?
  - ○ Is the building kept in good repair?
  - ○ If the building or area is not well maintained, or is in poor condition, make sure to advise the underwriting department.
- ☐ Determine use to which the building or area is put.

GENERAL LIABILITY INVESTIGATIONS § 28.02

- ○ Is the use proper in accordance with the facilities offered?
- ○ Is the use lawful and proper?
- ○ Is the use unusually hazardous in any way?
- ☐ Obtain the history of any previous accidents in the building or within the area.

B. Ownership and Control

- ☐ Obtain the complete and correct name of the insured (individual, partnership, corporation, trade name, estate, trust, etc.).
- ☐ What part of the building does the insured occupy?
- ☐ How long has the insured occupied that part of the building?
- ☐ Is the area or deficiency complained of completely within the part of the building or area controlled by the insured?
- ☐ If some other tenant may have been involved, obtain a complete list of the tenants occupying the building who may have been responsible or partially responsible.
- ☐ Obtain copies of any leases by or from the insured which may be pertinent to the investigation.
- ☐ Does the landlord (if he is other than the insured) control that portion of the building or area complained of?
- ☐ If the landlord is responsible for the area or portion of the building complained of, determine if he is insured and if so get the name of his carrier. See that the carrier is notified of the incident promptly and that the landlord is put on notice concerning responsibility.
- ☐ Is the rental, cleaning, and general maintenance and repair of the building under the control of a separate agency? If so, obtain the name, address and insurer.
- ☐ Was the maintenance agency if any, engaged by the insured, or by someone else? Obtain details.

C. Coverage (Review all endorsements carefully)

- ☐ Make sure that the location of the accident is within the territory covered by the policy.
  - ○ Determine whether the accident occurred inside or outside of the building, or in another area under the possible control of someone other than the insured.
  - ○ Determine whether the accident occurred on a public sidewalk. (The municipality may be involved.)
  - ○ If the accident occurred near a boundary line, make sure it occurred within the boundary line of the area controlled by the insured.
- ☐ Determine whether the incident falls within the contractual liability exclusion.
  - ○ Did the insured enter into any hold-harmless or other agreement assuming any liability of others?

- ○ Obtain photostat of the contract or agreement, if so, and review for possible disclaimer.
- ☐ If the insured's liability was contingent, determine the primary wrongdoer and put him and his insurance carrier on notice.
- ☐ Determine whether there was any employer-employee relationship or whether workers' compensation was involved that might bring the matter within the policy exclusion.
- ☐ Determine whether there was any new construction which might bring the incident within such exclusion.
- ☐ Check delayed notice and any other possible policy violation that might need consideration.
- ☐ If an edible product was involved, determine whether it was consumed on or off the premises.
- ☐ Check possible completed operations.
  - ○ Obtain the exact date when the last work was done.
  - ○ Was the job accepted as completed? If so, obtain any evidence of acceptance that may be available.
  - ○ Was payment made for the completed work? If so, how and when? Obtain any available evidence of such payment.
  - ○ Were any tools left at the job site? If so, were they involved in the incident? Obtain details.
  - ○ Did the insured leave any uninstalled equipment? If so, was it involved in the incident? Obtain details.
  - ○ Did the insured leave any unused materials and were they involved in the incident? Were they usable or merely debris? Did the insured intend to return for the materials, either to take them away or to clean up the area?
  - ○ Was there any complaint about the allegedly defective materials or workmanship? Did the insured have to return to correct or repair some condition? Obtain full details including exact dates.
  - ○ Was it necessary for the insured to return in order to make adjustments or subsequent inspections? Did he do so? Obtain exact dates and details.
  - ○ Did the operation involve a service or maintenance contract or agreement? If so, did the insured return pursuant thereto, and when? Obtain copy of any contract and all details with exact dates.

D. Information to be Obtained from the Insured

Detailed information concerning the incident and the surrounding circumstances that bear upon the insured's possible liability should be obtained from the insured, his rental or maintenance agent, superintendent or engineer of the building, janitor, porter, or anyone else who knows or should know anything about the matter. Signed statements should be obtained from each individual who can

GENERAL LIABILITY INVESTIGATIONS § 28.02

contribute material information necessary for the defense of the case. The information to be obtained should cover:

- ☐ Notice (actual or constructive)
  - o Who was responsible for the general maintenance and condition of the building? (Superintendent, engineer, agent, janitor, etc.).
  - o Was the individual aware of the condition complained of?
  - o How did it come to his attention?
  - o When did it come to his attention?
  - o How long had the condition been permitted to exist? Obtain dates as exactly as possible.
  - o Were any regular inspections made? If so, when and by whom? Obtain details.
  - o Was the condition open and obvious?
  - o If the insured did not know of the condition, could he have known of it if proper inspection had been made?
  - o Were any previous complaints ever made about the condition?
  - o Was there any record of previous accidents as a result of the same condition, or at the same site?
  - o How often was the area cleaned?
  - o How was it cleaned? Obtain complete details.
  - o Were proper safety precautions taken while cleaning?
- ☐ Physical facts
  - o Obtain complete description of the defect, obstruction, or other condition which allegedly caused the incident.
  - o Obtain the exact location of the condition complained of. Make sure to preserve any evidence by proper marking and control of the articles complained of, or by obtaining proper photographs of the alleged defect or condition.
  - o Describe the composition of the floor if it was involved. (Wood, cement, marble, terrazzo, linoleum, etc.).
  - o Describe the nature and condition of any floor coverings. (Carpets, rubber mats, paper, etc.).
  - o Describe the condition of the floor, if it was involved.
    - — Was the floor wet? If so, was the water tracked in? How far was the location of the accident from the outside entrance? Describe any other cause for the wet condition.
    - — Was there any debris on the floor? If so, give details and description.
    - — Did the accident involve excess wax on the floor? (Waxed floor will be discussed separately in more detail.)
    - — Was the floor broken, depressed, rough, or defective in any other way? Give details and exact description.
    - — Was the floor level or did it slope? Obtain measurements, as nearly as possible, including degree of slope.
    - — Was it customary to place a mat at the scene of the accident? If so, was it there at the time? If not, why?

- If cleaning was being done, were proper precautions taken during and after the cleaning period? Was the area blocked off? Was it perfectly dry before people were permitted to walk on it?
- Was there any obstruction in the floor area? (Signs, tables, counters, displays, etc.). Describe fully, and draw diagram.
○ What other conditions were complained of?
- Was the condition a nuisance or was it objectionable in any way?
- Was a defective object or product involved? Describe in detail if so.
- Was it defective owing to ordinary wear and tear or to the effect of the weather and natural elements?
○ Was faulty construction or construction defect involved? If so, follow through as outlined in the checklist for the investigation of construction claims.
○ Natural lighting
- Obtain the time of day when the incident occurred.
- Was it daylight, dusk, or dark?
- Was it sunny or cloudy?
- Determine the location of all windows.
- Describe the size of the windows.
- What type of glass was in the windows? (Transparent, opaque, colored, etc.).
- Was there any obstruction to natural light? (Furniture, counters, displays, shades, blinds, etc.).
- Did the color of the walls and the area blend in with the surroundings to create a light hazard? If so, describe in detail.
○ Artifical lighting
- Obtain the size and location of all fixtures in the area.
- Determine the size of the bulbs and give your opinion as to their adequacy.
- Were the lights in operation?
- Should they have been in operation?
- Who controlled the lighting?
- Was there any obstruction to the light reaching the area under investigation? Describe fully.
○ Weather conditions. (Review previous information on weather conditions and reports.)
○ Obtain complete description and photographs of any guards (human or mechanical), warning signs, roped-off areas, or warnings of any other nature, with photographs if advisable, and as soon as possible, before the condition changes.
○ Obtain any photographs that may have been made by anyone before arriving at the scene.
○ Obtain any blueprints, sketches, or plans that may become necessary for the proper defense of the case.
○ Was the scene of the accident used in common by anyone other than the insured? Obtain details.

GENERAL LIABILITY INVESTIGATIONS § 28.02

- ○ Building or area violations should be investigated as outlined in the checklist for the investigation of construction claims.
- ☐ Repairs
  - ○ Was it the insured's duty to repair?
  - ○ Were any repairs made?
  - ○ Who made the repairs?
  - ○ How were the repairs made?
  - ○ When were the repairs made? Why?
  - ○ At whose direction were the repairs made? Obtain details.
  - ○ Were the repairs made properly?
  - ○ Were any repairs made subsequent to the accident? Why? By whom and at whose direction? Obtain full details.
- ☐ Information obtained after the accident
  - ○ How was the accident called to the insured's attention? By whom?
  - ○ Who inspected the scene of the accident immediately after it occurred? Obtain signed statements from all parties.
  - ○ Obtain information concerning any conversations or admissions that occurred immediately after the accident.
  - ○ Get complete information concerning claimant's injuries; by whom he or she was helped immediately after the accident, and any medical information of a similar nature as previously outlined.
- ☐ Witnesses
  - ○ Obtain the names and addresses of all people who were with the claimant at the time.
  - ○ Obtain the names and addresses of any sales people or other employees who witnessed either the accident itself or the scene immediately before or after the accident.
  - ○ Obtain names and addresses of bystanders or other witnesses to the incident.
  - ○ Obtain names and addresses of any outside witnesses who can testify to the condition of the area at the time of the incident, or immediately thereafter.
  - ○ Obtain names and addresses of any police officers or other officials, doctors, nurses, or anyone else who may have been called to the scene after the accident.

E. Information to be Obtained from the Claimant

- ☐ Obtain the claimant's name and all previous names or aliases under which the claimant was ever known, including the maiden name of any married female claimant.
- ☐ Obtain the age, observe the general appearance and describe the impression made. Include any information concerning the claimant's moral character (although in this day and age, great care must be exercised to avoid possible action against the claim investigator and the company he represents for having overstepped the bounds of propriety), industriousness, honesty, reputation, intelligence, education, or other factors that might

§ 28.02   CASUALTY INSURANCE CLAIMS

bear on his or her impression as a witness. (Here again, I must caution the claim investigator to obtain information discretely and carefully so as to avoid any possible action for invasion of privacy or even defamation.)

- [ ] Obtain the present address, and, if warranted, any previous addresses of the claimant.
- [ ] Obtain the claimant's military status.
- [ ] Determine dependency.
  - Obtain the name, age, and dependency status of the wife or husband.
  - Determine the names, ages, and dependency status of all children.
  - Determine the marital status, including details and, if necessary, records of all previous marriages, "arrangements," separations, divorces, and children by former marriages.
  - Determine if there are any other dependents and whatever details can be determined.
- [ ] Employment history.
  - Get the names and addresses of present and previous employers.
  - Determine the time employed by each employer.
  - What was the nature of the work?
  - What salaries were received?
  - Determine the time and earnings lost. (Review the section on Special Damages.)
- [ ] If it is applicable, obtain information concerning the claimant's workers' compensation status and the name of the carrier.
- [ ] Possible distractions to the claimant.
  - The weather. (Rain, snow, sleet or icy conditions.)
  - Was the claimant carrying an umbrella, packages, or other objects?
  - If so, how large were they. Describe in detail.
  - Was the claimant watching someone or something?
  - Was the claimant talking to someone at the time?
  - Was the claimant daydreaming or preoccupied for any reason?
  - Was the claimant worried or under emotional stress?
  - Was the claimant in a hurry?
  - Was the claimant tired?
- [ ] Were the claimant's clothes material to the accident?
  - Did the claimant have a hat over his or her eyes?
  - Did the claimant have his or her collar up over the ears?
  - Was the claimant wearing a long dress or coat? Could it have been a tripping hazard? Was it involved in the accident in any way?
  - Did the claimant's shoes have anything to do with the accident? If so, describe the type and size of the shoes, giving the composition of the heels, soles, and the general condition. If the claimant lost a lift or a heel and it is available, preserve it as evidence.
- [ ] Claimant's educational background if pertinent.
  - Obtain name and address of school attended, including previous schools if pertinent.
  - Determine the year or grade in attendance and previous marks or grades. Interview former and present teachers if pertinent.

GENERAL LIABILITY INVESTIGATIONS § 28.02

- ○ Determine the exact time lost from school as a result of the accident. (Review § 5.08[7] concerning the obtaining of schools records.)
- ☐ Obtain details concerning any welfare help which the claimant may be receiving or has received in the past.
  - ○ City, state, or federal benefits, including social security, unemployment, or disability payments.
  - ○ Private or public pensions of any kind.
  - ○ Public relief or private charities of any kind.
- ☐ Obtain previous and subsequent accident records.
- ☐ Obtain criminal record, if any, and other background information that might be material.
- ☐ Obtain complete medical information, special damages, and other information outlined previously.
- ☐ If the accident under investigation is a so-called "blind" accident and the claimant cannot produce witnesses:
  - ○ Learn from the claimant the name of the person to whom he or she first spoke about the accident and the date, as exact as possible.
  - ○ If there was any delay in reporting the incident to the insured, obtain detailed explanation for the delay.
  - ○ Check the allegations of injury against the possibility that the claimant might have needed assistance at the scene of the incident. Obtain an explanation if no assistance was received.
  - ○ Check for any evidence of accident on the claimant's clothes, such as dirt, grit, grease, or oil stains, etc.
  - ○ Check the scene for any evidence of the alleged accident.
  - ○ Check the background of the claimant with special care in view of the questionable nature of the circumstances.
- ☐ Did the claimant's physical condition or possible deformities have any bearing on the accident? If so, describe as follows:
  - ○ History of epilepsy, heart disease, dizziness, fainting, etc.
  - ○ Alcoholic consumption.
  - ○ Use of drugs.
  - ○ Generally weakened condition due to illness or lack of sleep.
  - ○ Physical deformities:
    - — Crippled or needing prosthetic appliances which the claimant was wearing or should have been wearing.
    - — Amputation of a limb or other extremity.
    - — Overweight.
    - — Unsteady because of infirmity due to age or other cause.
    - — Defective eyesight. Did the claimant need glasses? Was he or she wearing them?
- ☐ Nature and purpose of the trip.
  - ○ What was the reason for making the trip?
  - ○ Determine the exact time, date, and place. Describe in detail.
  - ○ Was the claimant a guest, invitee, or trespasser? If the accident occurred in a building, why was the claimant there? Was he or she a customer, or merely someone trying to get in out of the rain?

- ☐ Obtain the name and address of anyone who was with the claimant immediately preceding, during, or after the incident.
- ☐ Determine how the claimant arrived at the scene:
  - ○ Was this the usual route? Was it the shortest?
  - ○ If not, why was the route taken?
  - ○ Were other routes available?
  - ○ Was the claimant familiar with the route taken? How often had claimant traveled route before?
- ☐ What was the cause of the fall?
  - ○ Was crowding or pushing involved?
  - ○ Did the claimant slip, trip, stumble, misstep, fail to step up or down, or turn his or her ankle? (Some people have congenitally weak ankles.)
  - ○ Was a trap or hidden defect of any kind involved?
  - ○ Was there debris, oil, water, vegetable matter, or obstruction of any kind? Describe in detail.
- ☐ Describe the exact position of the claimant immediately after the fall and all details concerning outcry, injury, and other matters of a similar nature as previously indicated.
- ☐ Previous knowledge of condition:
  - ○ Had the claimant ever been at the scene of the accident before?
  - ○ How often? Give dates, if possible, or approximations.
  - ○ Is it necessary for the claimant to pass the scene of the accident in order to get home, to work, school, shop, visit friends, etc?
  - ○ Did the claimant have any previous knowledge of the defect or allegedly dangerous condition? If so, why were no precautions taken?
  - ○ Was the claimant observant? Was any effort made to avoid the danger?

F. Witnesses

Interview and take signed statements from all witnesses, as previously outlined.

G. The Law

Consider the applicability of all defenses such as lack of notice, status of claimant (invitee, licensee, trespasser), negligence of a fellow servant, assumption of risk, contributory negligence, etc., and prepare the investigation in accordance with the defenses available.

As indicated in previous sections of this text, obtain all police reports, coroners' reports, reports of criminal hearings, autopsy reports, etc., that may be available and follow through with complete medical information and account of special damages.

GENERAL LIABILITY INVESTIGATIONS   § 28.03[1]

§ 28.03 Checklists for Special Investigations

We have covered the basic points of investigation generally required in most public liability claims of a serious nature. The checklists that follow are confined to suggesting avenues of investigation peculiar to the particular type of accident under which claim is being made. They are to be used in conjunction with the points that have already been developed.

Again, it is obviously impossible to cover all, or even most of the situations that may confront a claim representative. The checklists are therefore confined to those kinds of accidents most frequently encountered, and may be used as a guide to stimulate thinking along proper channels.

[1] Claims Involving Tenancy

- Determine the type of tenancy.
    - Yearly or more.
    - Month-to-month.
    - Written or oral.
    - Sub-lease.
- Obtain copy of the lease or terms of the oral agreement.
- How long has claimant lived there?
- Was the flat, apartment, or premises in good condition?
- When was it last repaired or redecorated? Exactly what work was done?
- Was it inspected before occupancy by either the tenant or the landlord?
- Was an inspection made after repairs had been completed? By whom?
- Were periodic inspections made? When and by whom? Did the landlord have the right to inspect?
- Report on the general condition in addition to the specific complaint.
- Could the defect or condition complained of have been caused by other tenants or by outsiders?
- Was the defect or condition open and obvious?
- Was the defect or condition known to the tenant? Could it have been caused by him or her either inadvertently or deliberately?
- Who controls the area complained of?
- Was the area in common usage by other tenants as for instance a hallway or stairway leading to several apartments? By whom was it used?
- Was notice of the defect or condition given to the landlord? By whom? When?
- Is any violation of local or state building codes involved?
- Does the building come within any multiple dwelling law?
- Was there any ill-feeling or trouble between the tenant, landlord or janitor?
- Did the tenant pay rent on time? Was any back rent due?

- [ ] Was the claimant a desirable tenant?
- [ ] Was any action started or contemplated to dispossess tenant?
- [ ] Did the tenant ever threaten to make trouble for the landlord or the janitor?

[2] Sidewalk Claims

The need for reinvestigation in the handling of sidewalk claims that go into suit is usually due to the fact that the claim investigator is unfamiliar with the law involved.

Most sidewalks are owned by the municipalities in which they are located. Sometimes, the owner of the abutting property does not have the primary duty to keep them in good repair. Nevertheless, there are many circumstances that create liability on the part of the abutting property owner. Generally, these are:

1. Cases in which the defective condition was created by the landowner. These might involve improper installation or maintenance of a coal hole, driveway, cellar doors, or other such objects or conditions.
2. Cases in which the condition was created as a result of an act which is for the benefit of the owner. A crack resulting from instruction to drive over the sidewalk in order to deliver fuel or topsoil, might be an example of this kind of situation.
3. Repairs made improperly by the landowner. Here he assumes an obligation which might not have existed before he tampered with the conditions.
4. In some jurisdictions, failure to repair after being instructed to do so by the municipality creates liability on the landowner. Here again, it is most important, where applicable, that the municipality be put on notice promptly and properly concerning any claim in which it may have some liability, especially since there may be a requirement of formal notice within a definite period of time.

With these points in mind, the following checklist for the investigation of sidewalk claims should be helpful:

- [ ] Obtain the exact location of the accident.
- [ ] Obtain complete description of the defect or obstruction complained of.
- [ ] Describe the composition of the sidewalk. (Cement, brick, stone, dirt, etc.).
- [ ] Describe the general condition of the sidewalk. (Cracked, broken, uneven, etc.).
- [ ] Determine the exact location of the building line, the private property boundary, and the boundaries of adjacent landowners.

GENERAL LIABILITY INVESTIGATIONS § 28.03[2]

- ☐ Make a complete diagram, with measurements.
- ☐ Determine whether the sidewalk is privately or publicly owned.
- ☐ If it is private, is an easement involved? Obtain details.
- ☐ If the municipality is involved, make sure that it is properly notified in time.
- ☐ Determine who or what caused the defect, condition, or obstruction complained of.
- ☐ Did the insured derive any benefit from the act which caused the defect? Get details.
- ☐ If the condition was dangerous, was any attempt made to guard or barricade it? Describe in detail.
- ☐ How long did the condition complained of exist before the accident?
- ☐ Who owned the abutting property when the defective condition was created?
- ☐ Was any attempt made to correct the condition?
- ☐ If so, were the corrections or repairs made properly? Obtain details of who made the repairs, when, and how made. By whom were they ordered?
- ☐ Who was in control of the abutting property at the time of the accident?
- ☐ Was a building or highway department violation placed against the abutting owner? If so, obtain a copy of the report.
- ☐ Were any repairs or corrections made in compliance with the violation?
- ☐ Were any warning signs or barricades placed around the defect or condition?
- ☐ Who originally constructed the sidewalk? How old was it?
- ☐ Did the defect involve trees or tree roots? If so, who planted and maintained them? Who owns them?
- ☐ If cellar doors, fuel outlets or holes, sidewalk hoists, gratings, or other items of a similar nature are involved in the accident:
  - ○ Give their exact location and make sure that they are within the property boundaries.
  - ○ Determine whether the object or objects are in good condition and were properly installed.
  - ○ Determine whether their presence and installation was in accordance with local regulations or ordinances.
- ☐ Snow and ice cases:
  - ○ Describe the slope of the sidewalk.
  - ○ Was the ice caused by leaking water?
  - ○ If so, was it due to a defective rain spout, plumbing, or other defect connected with the building?
  - ○ If snow is involved, when did the snowfall stop?
  - ○ Was the entire walk covered? To what depth?
  - ○ Was the snow fluffy or hard packed?
  - ○ Was it smooth or ridged?
  - ○ Did the snow cover any ice?
  - ○ Obtain complete weather report covering the temperatures and the amount of precipitation.

§ 28.03[3] CASUALTY INSURANCE CLAIMS

- ○ Determine if there was any defect under the snow or ice?
- ○ Was any attempt made to clean the snow or ice?
- ○ If so, by whom, when and how?
- ○ Was it properly cleaned? Was it piled so that melting snow would dribble onto the sidewalk and create an icy hazard if it froze?
- ○ Determine what the local regulation or ordinance is concerning the cleaning off of snow.
- ○ Is a claim being made against the city or municipality? If so, obtain whatever information is available from the proper authorities. If not, make sure that the city or municipality is put on notice promptly and properly where warranted.

[3] Waxed Floors

- ☐ Determine when the floor was last waxed.
- ☐ By whom? If not by the insured, obtain the name and the insurance carrier.
- ☐ Obtain the name of the wax product used and all available printed matter concerning its use.
- ☐ Who manufactured it? Who insures the manufacturer?
- ☐ How was the floor prepared for waxing? Obtain details.
- ☐ What was the exact method used in applying the wax?
- ☐ If necessary, obtain a chemical analysis of the wax.
- ☐ If warranted, have friction tests made by a properly qualified engineer before waxing, after waxing, and after buffing.
- ☐ Consider the advisability of placing the manufacturer and applier of the wax on notice.

[4] Stairways

- ☐ Obtain a complete description of the stairs:
  - ○ What is the composition and construction of the steps? (Wood, stone, marble, etc.).
  - ○ Obtain the measurements of the steps. (Height, width, and depth.)
  - ○ Are the steps of equal height?
  - ○ How many steps are there?
  - ○ What is the condition of the steps? (New, worn, slippery, firm, wobbly, abrasive, etc.).
  - ○ Did the stairs have any covering? (Rubber treads, carpeting, etc.). Describe the composition and its condition.
  - ○ Did the steps have any nosings? Describe in detail, giving their condition.
  - ○ Was the stairway straight, curved, winding, or unusual in any way?
  - ○ Give the location and description of any landings.
- ☐ Did the construction of the stairway and rails conform to local building code requirements?
- ☐ Was there any obstruction on the stairway? Describe in detail.

GENERAL LIABILITY INVESTIGATIONS § 28.03[5]

- [ ] Who was responsible for lighting the stairway?
- [ ] Was the stairway used in common? Who else used it?
- [ ] Obtain a description of the handrail:
  - Was there a handrail? Describe exactly.
  - How was it fastened?
  - What was its composition?
  - What condition was it in? Was it firm?
  - Exactly how high was it?
- [ ] Information to be obtained from the claimant:
  - What type of shoes was he or she wearing? Describe soles and heels and their condition.
  - What was he or she carrying?
  - What caused claimant to fall?
    - Tripping, slipping, or loss of balance?
    - Failure to use handrail? If so, why?
  - Determine how claimant fell.
    - Backwards or forwards?
    - Did claimant lurch?
    - Did claimant attempt to catch rail?
- [ ] Determine the exact location from which claimant fell. Between which floors and what step?
- [ ] Determine if there were any witnesses to the accident, as previously outlined.

[5] Falling Objects

- [ ] Determine from where the object fell, if possible.
- [ ] What was the exact spot where it landed?
- [ ] What was the name of the owner, tenant and their carriers?
- [ ] Describe in detail, the object which fell.
- [ ] Who owned it?
- [ ] What caused it to fall?
- [ ] If the object that fell was a piece of a building:
  - Determine who was in control of the building.
  - How old was the building?
  - When was the area last inspected? How often was it inspected?
  - Determine if pieces ever fell off before? Get details.
  - Determine when the area was last repaired.
  - Who made the repairs and what did they constitute? If possible, get copies of repair bills.
  - What was the general condition of the building?
  - Were weather factors involved?
- [ ] Was the area blocked off?
- [ ] Was a protective shed erected? Was it adequate and in good condition?
- [ ] Were warning signs or guard posted?

- [ ] In construction cases:
  - Were the floors above covered?
  - Determine who was working above. Obtain the names of all contractors, subcontractors, and employees.
  - Find out who was most likely to have used or needed the object which fell.
- [ ] If the object fell in a store:
  - How was it stacked?
  - Did some other person cause it to fall?
  - Was it stacked in line of traffic? Give exact description.

[6] Elevators

- [ ] Determine the exact location of the elevator.
- [ ] Determine the exact location of the accident.
- [ ] Obtain complete description of the elevator.
  - Kind and make.
  - Passenger or freight?
  - Determine the size, capacity, lifting weight, and age.
  - Obtain the details concerning its mechanical or automatic operation.
  - What automatic devices did it have?
  - Who was permitted to operate the elevator?
- [ ] Actions and qualifications of the operator:
  - Obtain the age and physical condition of the operator, if pertinent. When did operator have last physical examination? What was the result?
  - What was operator's length of employment and previous experience as an operator?
  - What was operator's previous employment record? Any previous complaints? Obtain details, if necessary.
  - What was the operator's previous accident record?
  - Did the operator do anything to cause the condition resulting in the accident?
  - Did the operator take any precautionary or preventive measures?
  - From what floor did the claimant enter or alight?
  - What was the height or depth at which the elevator stopped above or below the floor level?
- [ ] Control of the elevator:
  - Who hired the operator?
  - Does the owner have a maintenance contract for the operation and maintenance of the elevator? Get the name of the maintenance company, and its insurer.
  - Did the owner lease the entire building? If so, does the tenant have an elevator maintenance contract?
  - Put on notice anyone who might be directly or indirectly responsible. (Elevator service or maintenance company, manufacturer or installer of the elevator, building maintenance agency, owner or tenant of the building, or whomever.)

GENERAL LIABILITY INVESTIGATIONS § 28.03[6]

- ☐ Cause of the deficiency:
  - ○ Were the elevator doors involved?
    - — Describe their type and the mechanics of their operation.
    - — Can they be stopped, accelerated, or slowed by hand? Should they be?
    - — What closing pressures do they exert?
    - — Were they properly closed?
    - — Was a mirror attached to the elevator if manually operated? Was it used?
    - — Can the elevator be in motion while the doors are open? Were they so open?
    - — Can the shaft door be opened when the elevator is not at floor level? If so, what precautions were taken to avoid opening it at the wrong time?
  - ○ Was the defect due to natural wear and tear? What was the condition of the elevator and its component parts?
  - ○ Was an unexpected breakdown involved? (Machinery, cable, etc.). Obtain complete details.
  - ○ Was it a known or unknown defect? Should it have been found by proper inspection?
  - ○ Was improper operation involved?
  - ○ Were any safety devices missing or inoperative?
  - ○ Was the elevator overloaded or overcrowded?
    - — Did the elevator stop unexpectedly?
    - — On what floor did it last start or stop properly?
    - — How many floors did it fall? Did it stop between floors?
    - — Was there any unusual noise before it fell?
  - ○ Was another passenger responsible or involved in any way? Obtain details.
  - ○ Was there any debris on the elevator floor? Describe.
  - ○ Was there any defect in the elevator floor, if pertinent? Describe in detail.
  - ○ Was there a mat on the elevator floor? Describe, if pertinent.
- ☐ Inspection:
  - ○ When was the last Building Department inspection made before the accident? Was it inspected after the accident? When?
  - ○ Obtain copies of all inspection reports.
  - ○ Interview the inspectors.
  - ○ Were any violations filed? If so, were the conditions corrected? When and by whom? Obtain details.
  - ○ Obtain previous accident record.
  - ○ Obtain the name of the elevator service company and its carrier.
  - ○ When was the last service inspection made before the accident? Was any inspection made after the accident? When? Obtain report.
  - ○ Obtain a copy of the service contract.
  - ○ Interview the serviceman and obtain full details.
  - ○ Find out what inspections were made by the building superintendent or engineer.

§ 28.03[7]   CASUALTY INSURANCE CLAIMS

    — Were any made before the accident? How often and when?
    — Was an inspection made after the accident? When? Obtain all details and findings.
- Consider the advisability of an examination by an outside expert.

☐ Witnesses:
- Obtain the names and addresses of everyone in the elevator.
- If the names are not known, obtain the number of people as closely as possible, and their description. Canvass the building in an effort to locate and interview them. (It is not too unusual to get 15 claims arising out of an accident where the elevator can hold only 10 people.)

[7] **Escalators**

☐ Review the checklist on elevator accidents covering service, maintenance, control, and inspection.
☐ Give complete description of the escalator:
- Was it going up or down?
- Was the handrail properly synchronized with the movement of the steps?
- Was the movement smooth or jerky?
- What was the exact speed?
- Obtain measurements, including height, width and depth of the steps and the height of the handrail.
- Describe the landing and takeoff platforms.

☐ Determine how the accident happened:
- Was the claimant getting on or off?
- Was a child involved? If so, was child attended? Was an adult in front of or behind the child to help child on or off?
- Was the claimant holding onto the handrail?
- How was the claimant standing?
- Was the claimant running on, off, or up and down the escalator?
- Was horse-play involved?
- Was the escalator crowded? Was the claimant jostled or pushed?
- Was there any sudden cessation of power or movement?

☐ How did the claimant fall? Describe in detail.
☐ If a foreign substance was involved, make the usual investigation as previously outlined.
☐ Was an attendant in charge? If so, interview him or her.
☐ Find and interview anyone who was with the claimant at the time.

[8] **Construction Cases**

These are among the most difficult and complicated cases that the casualty claim investigator will encounter. Not that there is any particular mystery involved, but the mere physical difficulty in locating and interviewing witnesses and interested parties makes the han-

GENERAL LIABILITY INVESTIGATIONS   § 28.03[8]

dling of this type of claim somewhat unusual. If you have ever tried to take a signed statement on the top floor of an unfinished building on a cold windy day, you have an idea of what I mean. Furthermore, no one is particularly anxious to admit responsibility for an accident, and the bricklayer who has just dropped a brick is no exception. Labor turnover is high. Subcontractors leave a job and workers are hard to trace once they are gone. Conditions change overnight and unless the photograph is taken today, it may be too late.

Then there is the matter of determining liabilities of the owner, contractor, and subcontractors. The contracts themselves are usually involved and sometimes ambiguous. Very frequently a contract will require liability insurance that has not been purchased. If all parties have insurance there is often controversy among them concerning primary and secondary liabilities. Disposition of a claim is often held up because of a squabble over percentages of contribution.

These cases present a definite challenge to the new claim representative. If he has gotten this far in the book, he will probably accept the challenge with enthusiasm, because an assignment that is unusual can also be more exciting and certainly a lot more satisfying if done well.

Here again, it will be necessary to review the general checklists for the investigation of public liability claims. Particular attention should be payed to the possibilities of completed operations and contractual obligations which may not be covered. The policy and every endorsement must be read carefully before outlining the plan for investigation.

- [ ] Is the insured the owner or principal, architect, general contractor, or subcontractor? Obtain the names and insurance carriers of all parties.
  - Who controlled the operation?
  - Who supervised the work? Who gave instructions and directions? How were they given?
- [ ] Obtain copies of all contracts, and report on any oral agreements. Obtain copies of specifications, if necessary.
- [ ] Was the work unusually hazardous?
- [ ] Were the workers experienced?
  - Were they licensed, if so required? If not, why?
  - Were they properly supervised? Obtain details.
  - Were they engaged in any unusual practices? If so, explain in detail.
- [ ] What was the nature of the tools or equipment?
  - Who furnished them?
  - Were they proper for the work to be done?

- ○ Were they in good working order?
- ○ Were they regularly inspected before being given to the workers? When, how, and by whom? When were they last inspected?
- ○ Were any defects noted? Should they have been?
- ○ Were any repairs made? When, by whom, and how? If not, why?
- ○ Who furnished the work clothes, uniforms, or other personal equipment?
- ☐ What safety measures were taken? By whom? (Lanterns, signs, barricades, walkways, overhangs, etc.).
- ☐ Were all safety regulations observed? If not, why?
- ☐ Was special safety equipment available? Was it used? If not, why?
- ☐ Obtain progress sheets giving the exact dates and locations where specific work was to be done.
- ☐ Obtain any progress photographs which may be available.
- ☐ Obtain report from first aid station.
- ☐ Obtain full details and medical reports from the compensation carrier.
- ☐ Arrange for immediate photographs before condition has changed.
- ☐ Were plans properly filed with Building Department? Were they approved?
- ☐ Was permit granted to build or construct? Obtain copy.
- ☐ Was the job done in accordance with plans, specifications, and building permit? Does it conform with the Building Code? If necessary, have this checked by an architect.
- ☐ Were periodic inspections made by the Building Department? Were any violations ever filed? Obtain details and reports.
- ☐ Was Certificate of Completion issued by the Building Department? If so, obtain copy. If not, why?
- ☐ Was the federal government involved in any way? If so, obtain copy of the Government Inspector's report. (FHA, loan, housing project, etc.).
- ☐ Put on notice everyone who might possibly be involved.
- ☐ If a preexisting condition in a finished building is alleged to be structurally defective:
  - ○ Determine whether the structure or portion of it which is being complained of conforms with local and state building codes.
  - ○ If not, determine if the building was erected before such laws went into effect.
  - ○ Are any part of the laws retroactive? (In respect to fire prevention, for instance.)
  - ○ Did the complaint involve new construction on an old building? (Watch for possible violations.)

[9] Sports Events, Fairgrounds, and Amusement Parks

These events may be subdivided into two categories: (1) those in which the claimant is a participant, and (2) those in which the claimant is a spectator.

GENERAL LIABILITY INVESTIGATIONS § 28.03[9]

Where the claimant is a participant, the investigation should be directed toward determining:

- ☐ Whether the premises was constructed and maintained in a manner which is accepted as reasonably safe by others engaged in a similar business.
- ☐ Whether the usual and ordinary safety precautions were taken to protect participants in a manner considered reasonably proper by those engaged in a similar business.
- ☐ Whether the accident was precipitated by an act of another participant or spectator.

Assumption of risk plays an important part in determining liability in all accidents of this kind. The degree of importance is a matter with which the claim representative should become familiar in his own jurisdiction. Investigation should proceed along the following lines:

- ☐ Does the insured own the premises? If not, who does?
- ☐ Does the insured operate or promote the event?
- ☐ Who maintains the premises?
- ☐ Who controls the premises? Obtain copies of all leases, contracts, or agreements.
- ☐ Was the claimant a paying spectator?
  - ○ What kind of a ticket did claimant purchase?
  - ○ Where did claimant sit?
  - ○ Did claimant have a choice of seats?
- ☐ Describe the object, contrivance, or area complained of.
  - ○ Was it in proper working order?
  - ○ Was it properly constructed?
  - ○ Did it have proper safety contrivances, screens, or rails? Were they operating properly and in good condition? Describe in detail.
  - ○ Was it properly maintained?
  - ○ Were there any warning signs? Did claimant heed them?
- ☐ Was a guard or attendant present? Should there have been? If not, explain.
- ☐ Was the failure or defect due to the intervention of someone else? If so, obtain details.
- ☐ Had claimant been there before? If so, try to determine when and how often.
- ☐ Was claimant aware of the danger?
- ☐ Was the danger unusual or extraordinary, considering the circumstances.
- ☐ How was the claimant injured? Obtain full details.
- ☐ Did the claimant do anything to place himself in a position of jeopardy? Explain fully.

§ 28.03[10]

[10] Golfing Accidents

- ☐ Was claimant a participant, caddy, or spectator?
- ☐ Was claimant on the course for any other reason?
- ☐ Was claimant outside the course either as a pedestrian, or in a vehicle? Explain fully.
- ☐ Has claimant ever played golf before? How often?
- ☐ What was the exact position of the claimant? Why was claimant there?
- ☐ What was the exact position of the insured?
- ☐ Did the insured look to see if anyone was in his or her line of play?
- ☐ Did the insured cry "fore" or give any other warning before or after hitting the ball?
- ☐ Was the claimant aware of the danger? Should he have been?
- ☐ Did the claimant see the ball as it was hit or after it was in flight?
- ☐ Did the claimant move after the ball was struck?
- ☐ What club did the insured use?
- ☐ Was the ball hooked or sliced? Did it rebound or go straight?
- ☐ Obtain signed statements from those who were playing golf with the insured, including caddies and any other witnesses.

[11] Animals

Some jurisdictions have enacted laws that go so far as to impose absolute liability on an owner for the acts of his dog. If this is the situation, the problem is a comparatively simple one. The claim investigator's energies should best be expended in determining the extent of the injury and damage, and attempting to reach a reasonable settlement.

Although most localities do not go quite so far, many do have some ordinance or statute governing the responsibility of owners of domestic and wild animals. In order to make a proper investigation of this type of claim, the claim investigator must learn the law not only as it reads, but also as the courts have interpreted it. For instance, practically no two courts agree on whether some animals, other than household pets commonly accepted as such, are wild or domestic. Since the law governing the two categories is quite different, the distinction is very important.

With this in mind, here is a checklist which will start the investigation in the right direction. It should include:

- ☐ Exact location of the incident.
- ☐ Description of the animal:
  - ○ Species

GENERAL LIABILITY INVESTIGATIONS § 28.03[12]

- ○ Domestic or wild?
- ○ Size
- ○ General condition and health
- ○ Nature and reputation. (Vicious, gentle, snappy, playful, etc.) Check with neighbors.
- ☐ Does the insured own the animal? If not, who does?
- ☐ Does the insured have control of the animal? How and why?
- ☐ Is the claimant a mailman, door-to-door salesman, meter reader, customer, invitee, trespasser, etc?
- ☐ Why was the claimant there?
- ☐ Was the animal provoked? If so, who or what provoked it? Did the animal react to striking, threatening, or sudden movement?
- ☐ What control, if any, was being exercised over the animal at the time? By whom?
- ☐ Was the animal on a leash? Should it have been?
- ☐ Was another animal or animals involved? Were they controlled or running loose?
- ☐ Did the claimant intervene with the animals or try to stop them from romping or fighting? How?
- ☐ Had the claimant been on the premises before? Was he aware of the presence of the animal?
- ☐ Was the claimant warned about the presence of the animal?
- ☐ Did the claimant try to avoid the animal?
- ☐ Were there any warning signs?
- ☐ Was the claimant aware of the nature of the animal?
- ☐ Was the animal enclosed, caged, chained, or tied? If so, was it a proper enclosure or restraint?
- ☐ Was the animal muzzled? Should it have been?
- ☐ Was there a violation of any ordinance or statute?
- ☐ Was the animal involved in any other previous incident or incidents? Were any previous complaints made against the animal?
- ☐ Was the insured aware of any previous incidents or complaints indicating possible vicious propensities? If so, did he take any precautions to protect the public? Details.
- ☐ Describe the injury in detail.
- ☐ Was the animal checked for rabies? Was the Health Department notified?
- ☐ If so, did they take any action? Were laboratory tests made? What was the result? Obtain any available reports.

[12] Blasting Operations

- ☐ Was a permit or license issued for the blasting? If so, obtain copy.
- ☐ What was the past experience of the person handling the explosives?
- ☐ Describe the explosive and give the exact amount of the charge. Was the amount unusual?

- [ ] Describe the exact manner in which the charge was placed. Did it conform to ordinary safety standards?
- [ ] What method of detonation was used?
- [ ] Exactly what safety precautions were taken?
  - What was the manner of counting the explosives and the caps?
  - Who was in charge of the operation?
  - What warning signs were erected, if any? Where were they placed?
  - What other warnings were given, if any?
- [ ] Were vibration tests made? If so, obtain reports.
- [ ] Learn the local laws concerning blasting.

CHAPTER 29

Products Liability

§ 29.01　Coverage
§ 29.02　Products Hazard
§ 29.03　Containers
§ 29.04　Exclusions
§ 29.05　Limits of Liability
§ 29.06　Territorial Extension
§ 29.07　Persons Insured
§ 29.08　Vendor's Endorsement
§ 29.09　Legal Aspects of Products Liability
　　　　[1]　Intervening Acts
§ 29.10　Sales—Breach of Warranty
　　　　[1]　Express Warranty (U.C.C. § 2-313)
　　　　[2]　Merchantability and Fitness for Use
　　　　[3]　Implied Warranty—Merchantability Code (U.C.C. § 3-316)
　　　　[4]　Implied Warranty—Fitness for Particular Purpose
　　　　[5]　Multiple Grounds for the Same Action
　　　　[6]　Statute of Limitations in Warranty Actions
§ 29.11　Strict Liability
　　　　[1]　Vendor's Liability
　　　　[2]　Statutory Enactments
　　　　[3]　Insurance Protection
§ 29.12　Design Defects
　　　　[1]　Unreasonably Dangerous
　　　　[2]　Crashworthiness and Second Injury Liability
　　　　[3]　Seat Belts
　　　　[4]　Strict Liability in Design Defect Cases
　　　　[5]　Open and Obvious Danger
　　　　[6]　State-of-the-Art Defense

　　The Products-Completed Operations attachment to the Commercial General Liability policies has already been discussed in § 26.07. As previously stated, products liability coverage, together with completed operations of which it is a part, may be included as a part of other general liability policies and this chapter will be devoted to this very important coverage. The basic coverage will again be reviewed as a necessary introduction to a detailed study of this insurance.

§ 29.01 Coverage

Products Liability insurance covers the insured's liability for occurrences resulting from real or alleged defects arising out of the handling, use or existence of any condition in goods or products manufactured, sold, or distributed by the named insured providing that the incident occurs after the insured has relinquished possession of the product to others, and also providing the incident occurs away from the insured's premises. It also covers accidents due to misdelivery of the products.

§ 29.02 Products Hazard

The policy defines "products hazard" to include "bodily injury and property damage arising out of the named insured's products or reliance upon a representation or warranty made at any time with respect thereto."

§ 29.03 Containers

The policy defines "named insured's products" as including "any container of the product other than a vehicle and it does not include a vending machine or any property other than such container, rented to or located for use of others but not sold." It should be noted that coverage for liability arising out of defective containers is included. Such containers might be bottles, cans, cartons, drums, cylinders, etc.

Usually, such containers are manufactured by someone other than the named insured. Sometimes, containers such as drums or cylinders for bottled gas may be owned by others. *In these instances it becomes most important, where a defect in such a container is alleged or indicted, to determine who is the owner and its insurance carrier and to put them on notice in writing that they will be held responsible for any ultimate damages.* This also holds true where the allegedly defective product itself is sold or distributed by the named insured, but manufactured wholly or in part by someone else.[1]

---

[1] *See* Gardner v. Coca Cola Bottling Co., 127 N.W.2d 557 (Minn. 1964).

§ 29.04 Exclusions

In addition to the applicable exclusions in the policy jacket to which the products coverage may be attached, there are specific exclusions applying only to the Products coverage, as follows:

a. While coverage does not apply to liability assumed by the insured under any contract or agreement, "this exclusion does not apply to a warranty of fitness or quality of the named insured's products or a warranty that work performed by or on behalf of the named insured will be done in a workmanlike manner." The positive part of this exclusion however, must be interpreted in conjunction with the definition of "occurrence" and together with exclusion (e) referring to design, error, etc., and exclusion (f) which refers to damage to the named insured's own products.

b. This exclusion refers to the manufacture, distribution or sale of alcoholic beverages in violation of a law, or to a minor or intoxicated person, or which contributes to such intoxication.

c. and d. are the ordinary exclusions applying to employees and workers' compensation benefits.

e. The 1972 revision of this "Business Risk" exclusion, completely rewritten, now reads:

> To loss of use of tangible property which has not been physically injured or destroyed resulting from (1) a delay in or lack of performance by or on behalf of the named insured of any contract or agreement, or (2) the failure of the named insured's products or work performed by or on behalf of the named insured to meet the level of performance, quality, fitness or durability warranted or represented by the named insured; but this exclusion does not apply to loss of use of other tangible property resulting from the sudden and accidental physical injury to or destruction of the named insured's products or work performed by or on behalf of the named insured after such products or work have been put to use by any person or organization other than an insured.

The previous wording of this exclusion stressed the difference between property damage caused by management mistake (design error) as opposed to active malfunctioning of the product. The new wording eliminates this distinction but creates ambiguities of its own, especially since it must be interpreted in conjunction with the definition of "occurrence" and the new definition of "property damage" which now reads:

> (1) physical injury to or destruction of tangible property which occurs during the policy period, including the loss of use thereof at any time

resulting therefrom, or (2) loss of use of tangible property which has not been physically injured or destroyed provided such loss of use is caused by an occurrence during the policy period.

If this doesn't lead to some further arguments, I'll be very surprised.

f. Under no circumstances is there any coverage for injury or damage to the named insured's product itself. There must be some specific damage to property *arising out of the use of the named insured's product*. The wording of this exclusion reads: "This insurance does not apply to property damage to the named insured's products arising out of such products or any part of such products."

This wording substantially changes the former wording which left room for a great deal of doubt as to whether the exclusion applied only to the *defective parts* of the named insured's product. It now appears to be the clear intent of the policy to exclude the entire product of the named insured, and not only its defective part.

g. The exclusion "to property damage to work performed by or on behalf of the named insured arising out of the work or any portion thereof, or out of materials, parts or equipment furnished in connection therewith" applies to completed operations of the named insured.

The example given in the F.C. & S. Bulletins is that of a plumber who installed a faulty joint as part of the entire plumbing job. It now seems to be the intent of the policy that no part of the plumbing repair work necessitated by the leakage, or to the joint itself, is covered.

h. The exclusion "to damage claimed for the withdrawal, inspection, repair, replacement or loss of use of the named insured's products or work completed by or for the named insured or of *any property* of which such products or work form a part, if such products, work or property are withdrawn from the market or from use because of any known *or suspected* defect or deficiency therein" is commonly known as the "Sistership" exclusion. (Italics mine.)

This exclusion makes it clear that "Recapture and Recall" coverage was never intended to be given under the ordinary Products Liability policy.

The exclusion applies to the costs in recalling a defective product from the market from which it was distributed.

The importance of this exclusion is certainly obvious in this day and age of massive recall of products such as automobiles, drugs, etc.

PRODUCTS LIABILITY § 29.06

It is noted that this exclusion applies not only to the named insured's products or work but to any property of which such products or work form a part. It is also important to note that any consequential damages, such as loss of business *from the withdrawal of a product,* are not covered under the policy.

While consequential damages arising out of a covered peril are also covered, it is important to note that there is no coverage for consequential damages arising out of an incident that is not covered. For instance, any consequential damages arising out of damage to the product itself would not be covered, since damage to the product is not covered. The section of the policy dealing with this subject must be read in conjunction with the exclusion and other parts of the policy to determine the obvious intent.

The General Liability policies require the named insured to take prompt action, at his own expense, to use all reasonable steps to prevent other bodily injury or property damage from arising out of the same or similar conditions.

§ 29.05 Limits of Liability

Products liability coverage provides a bodily injury liability limit per person, a limit per occurrence, and an aggregate limit of liability for the annual policy period. The aggregate limit applies regardless of the number of claims made against the insured. Once the aggregate has been reached within the year there is no further coverage. There is no carryover beyond the annual period.

The limit of liability is restricted to all injuries or accidents arising out of any one batch or lot of the prepared or acquired product. The amount each person may recover under the policy is also restricted. However, note Chapter 26, *supra,* on the 1986 Commercial Liability policies, that have important differences.

§ 29.06 Territorial Extension

The Products Liability coverage in the United States extends coverage to bodily injury or property damage occurring outside the territorial limits of the United States with two important limitations:

1. The product must have been sold for ordinary use or consumption within the United States or Canada.

2. The original suit must be brought within the United States or Canada.

The intent here is to cover products which are purchased in the United States, but which are taken abroad for ordinary consumption when the purchaser travels. Such items might include toothpaste, mouthwash, razors, drugs and cosmetics, or similar products or equipment. This territorial extension has no relationship to products sold and/or distributed for consumption outside the United States or Canada.

§ 29.07 Persons Insured

Those insured under the policy are:

a. if the named insured is designated in the declarations as an individual, the person so designated but only with respect to the conduct of a business of which he is the sole proprietor;

b. if the named insured is designated in the declarations as a partnership or joint venture, the partnership or joint venture so designated and any partner or member thereof but only with respect to his liability as such;

c. if the named insured is designated in the declarations as other than an individual, partnership or joint venture, the organization so designated and any executive officer, director or stockholder thereof while acting within the scope of his duties as such;

d. any person (other than an employee of the named insured) or organization while acting as a real estate manager for the named insured.

The policy emphasizes the fact that it does not apply to damages arising out of the conduct of any partnership or joint venture of which the insured is a partner if it is not designated in the policy as a named insured.

§ 29.08 Vendor's Endorsement

Large retail merchandising organizations often insist that the insured from whom they purchase goods, carry a vendor's endorsement to protect them in the event of a claim or suit resulting from an actual or alleged defect in the product. Ordinarily such endorsement does not cover liability arising out of the negligence of, or the express warranty given by the vendor which is not authorized by the named insured.

There are two basic types of vendor's endorsements, namely the limited and the broad forms. In both forms the vendor is added as an additional insured "only with respect to the distribution or sale in the regular course of the vendor's business of the named insured's products," and both exclude coverage for the supplier of the product or container or any part of it, if other than the named insured.

The Limited Form Vendor's Endorsement Specifically Excludes:

a. any express warranty, or any distribution or sale for a purpose, unauthorized by the named insured.

b. bodily injury or property damage arising out of

1. any act of the vendor which changes the condition of the products,

2. any failure to maintain the product in merchantable condition,

3. any failure to make such inspections, adjustments, tests or servicing as the vendor has agreed to make or normally undertakes to make in the usual course of business, in connection with the distribution or sale of the products, or

4. products which after distribution or sale by the named insured have been labeled or relabeled or used as a container, part or ingredient of any other thing or substance by or for the vendor,

5. bodily injury or property damage occurring within the vendor's premises.

The Broad Form Vendor's Endorsement Excludes:

a. any express warranty unauthorized by the named insured;

b. bodily injury or property damage arising out of

1. any physical or chemical change in the form of the products made intentionally by the vendor,

2. repacking unless solely for the purpose of inspection, demonstration, testing or the substitution of parts under instruction from the manufacturer and then repacked in the original container,

3. demonstration, installation, servicing or repair operations, except such operations performed at the vendor's premises in connection with the sale of the product, or

4. products which after distribution or sale by the named insured have been labeled or relabeled or used as a container, part or ingredient of any other thing or substance by or for the vendor.

The broad form does not have the exclusion for bodily injury or property damage occurring within the vendor's premises.

In trying to determine ultimate responsibility so as to put the wrongdoer on notice, if the wrongdoer is other than the named insured, it can, of course, be most important in some instances to determine whether the policy contained a vendor's endorsement. It could become most embarrassing to put the vendor on notice, only to learn that he is an additional insured.

§ 29.09 Legal Aspects of Products Liability

Even more than in other fields of non-static law, products liability has been one of constant and frequent change, evolving from a contract theory into a negligence doctrine and more and more into the field of strict liability.[2]

Since we are discussing "products," it stands to reason that this word should at least be subject to some specific definition. My conclusion is that a product is anything that a particular court chooses to name as such. In addition to such obvious objects as automobiles, machinery, foods and cosmetics, and other products of like familiarity, some courts have held that: (1) a heating, ventilating and air conditioning unit permanently attached to real property was a product;[3] (2) a defective component part of a prefabricated assembly-line building was a product;[4] (3) a silo that did not provide proper ventilation was declared a product;[5] and (4) a defect in the design of a residential home was also held to be a products liability case.[6]

Legal responsibility for defects in a product may rest with the assembler, distributor, wholesaler or retailer as well as with the manufacturer of the product itself. Ultimate responsibility, however, in an action for negligence, remains with the wrongdoer. This must constantly be borne in mind *in the event that the named insured is not the wrongdoer.* As soon as the determination has been made that the

---

[2] *See* Funston, "The 'Failure to Warn' Defect in Strict Products Liability: A Paradigmatic Approach to 'State of the Art' Evidence and 'Scientific Knowability,' " Insurance Law Journal, January, 1984.
[3] Trent v. Brasch Mfg. Co., 477 N.E.2d 1312 (Ill. 1985).
[4] Kaneko v. Hilo Coast Processing Co., 654 P.2d 343 (Hawaii 1982).
[5] Cox v. Shaffer, 302 A.2d 456 (Pa. Super. 1973).
[6] Hyman v. Gordon, 111 Cal. Rptr. 262 (App. 1973).

wrongdoer is someone other than the named insured, notice must be given to him that he will be held responsible for the resultant damages.

An action can be brought against the responsible party resulting from an accident arising out of a defect in a product on the basis of strict liability, negligence, or breach of warranty. Negligence, of course, is based on the principle of reasonable care in the manufacture, distribution, or sale of the particular product involved.

An action for breach of warranty is based on an express or implied promise concerning the fitness of a product, arising out of the sale of that product. Whereas such an action was previously limited to the purchaser only, this doctrine has been broadened beyond recognition to apply to almost anyone who rightfully uses the product. In addition, we have seen the advent of the *strict liability* rule applied in just about all of our jurisdictions. This rule imposes almost absolute liability on the manufacturer, processor, or assembler of a product that is used for human consumption or is considered inherently dangerous.

In the area of inherently dangerous items such as insecticides or similar products which are poisonous upon contact or when taken internally, there is an additional duty on the manufacturer and seller to give prominent warning of the dangers which the use of a product may create. Here again, the courts have gone far beyond what I consider to be reasonable care in the labeling of such products, as a measure of legal responsibility. Courts are today interpreting the doctrine of reasonableness to its ultimate limit, almost to the point of strict accountability, particularly where the product involved is one that might get into the hands of children. This will be discussed in greater detail in Chapter 30.

[1] Intervening Acts

The investigator must always be alert to determine whether someone other than the named insured or an additional insured did something to the product that may have made it defective or contributed toward any defect. The legal yardstick used in determining ultimate responsibility is whether the intervening act of another broke the chain of causation in such a manner as to create an independent injury. In other words, was the change made to the product the principal and direct cause of the injury or damage? This is often involved in compounding of insecticides or drugs, in the assembling of machines which use component parts supplied from various sources, or modifying equipment which affect its design safety.

§ 29.10 Sales—Breach of Warranty

A *warranty* is more commonly known as a guarantee concerning the fitness, quality, or durability of a product.

Strictly speaking, an action based on breach of warranty is not an action in tort, but one based on contract. However, some courts recognize a cause of action in tort for breach of an implied warranty of fitness.

Warranties may be *express* or *implied*. An express warranty may be created either orally or in writing by the seller if he asserts that the product is fit for a certain definite purpose or that it will or will not do certain things.

An implied warranty is one which the law imposes on the seller under certain circumstances, with reference to certain products. For instance, in some states the owner of a restaurant is held to warrant implicitly that the food served is wholesome, fit for human consumption, and free from foreign substances. In accordance with recent trends, an absolute warranty may also be created by statute as evidenced by some of the pure food and drug acts.

In order to recover in an action for breach of warranty, whether express or implied, the plaintiff must prove (1) that he was injured or damaged as a result of the alleged breach, and (2) that the product complained of was used properly.

Most jurisdictions no longer hold that privity of contract is an essential element to an action for breach of warranty. Thus an action against the seller or manufacturer may be available to someone other than the purchaser of a product. Accordingly, warranties may be made to the purchaser by the retailer, distributor or manufacturer.

Must the injured be the consuming purchaser? Must the seller be the retailer, distributor, or manufacturer? That depends upon the jurisdiction in which the action is being brought.

The courts that have overruled the doctrine of privity have extended the warranty to the foreseeable user, even though he did not actually purchase the article. Other courts make little distinction between warranty and negligence.

Most of our states have adopted the "Uniform Commercial Code." This act has codified many of the common law concepts concerning warranty. Some important provisions of the act are worth repeating.

[1] Express Warranty (U.C.C. § 2-313)

1. Express warranties by the seller are created as follows:

a. Any affirmation of fact or promise made by the seller to the buyer which relates to the goods and becomes the basis of the bargain creates an express warranty that the goods shall conform to the affirmation or promise.

b. Any description of the goods which is made a part of the basis of the bargain creates an express warranty that the goods shall conform to the description.

c. Any sample or model which is made part of the basis of the bargain creates an express warranty that the whole of the goods shall conform to the sample or model.

2. It is not necessary to the creation of an express warranty that the seller use formal words such as "warranty" or "guarantee" or that he have a specific intention to make a warranty, but an affirmation merely of value of the goods or a statement purporting to be merely the seller's opinion or commendation of the goods does not create a warranty.

[2] Merchantability and Fitness for Use

These two terms have become common legal phraseology in warranty actions, and have caused much controversy resulting in no uniformity or interpretation. The Uniform Commercial Code further states that acceptance of the product does not bar an action for damages in the absence of any agreements to the contrary. However, it requires the buyer to notify the seller of any breach of warranty within a reasonable time. The form of notice and what constitutes a reasonable time is subject to judicial interpretation.

The fact that a purchaser may have a right of action as a result of a breach of warranty does not destroy any right of action which he may have on grounds of negligence. Since negligence, however, is often so hard to prove in most food products cases, the doctrine of *res ipsa loquitur* has come to play a very prominent part in this type of action. These three words mean "the thing speaks for itself."

[3] Implied Warranty—Merchantability Code (U.C.C. § 3-316)

1. Unless excluded or modified, a warranty that the goods shall be merchantable is implied in a contract for their sale if the seller is a merchant with respect to goods of that kind. Under this section the serving for value of food or drink to be consumed either on the premises or elsewhere is a sale.

2. Goods to be merchantable must at least:

a. Pass without objection in the trade under the contract description; and

b. in the case of fungible goods, are of fair average quality within the description; and

c. are fit for the ordinary purpose for which such goods are used; and

d. run, within the variations permitted by the agreement, of even kind, quality and quantity within each unit and among all units involved; and

e. are adequately contained, packaged and labeled as the agreement may require; and

f. conform to the promises or affirmations of fact made on the container or label if any.

3. Unless excluded or modified, other implied warranties may arise from course of dealing or usage of trade.

4. U.C.C. Sec. 2-318 extends express and implied warranties to certain third parties that allows a cause of action for economic loss.

[4] Implied Warranty—Fitness for Particular Purpose

The appropriate subsection of Section 2-315 of the Uniform Commercial Code concerning implied warranty—fitness for particular purpose, reads as follows:

> Where the seller at the time of contracting has reason to know any particular purpose for which the goods are required and that the buyer is relying of the seller's skill or judgment to select or furnish suitable goods, there is, unless excluded or modified under the next section an implied warranty that the goods shall be fit for such purpose.

This section of the U.C.C. deals with the situation where a buyer purchases an item and relies on the special knowledge of the seller. This may involve choosing one item over another, or where the buyer relies exclusively on the knowledge and recommendations of the seller when the item is for a particular, as opposed to an unspecified, use.

[5] Multiple Grounds for the Same Action

Actions on products liability cases based on warranty have in recent years become blurred with actions sounding in negligence and strict liability. As a matter of fact, some courts have recently held that as far as adequacy of warning of product hazard is concerned, actions brought in negligence and implied warranty involve identical evidence and proof of exactly the same elements.[7] In an action brought in warranty and strict liability, it was held that the warranty part of the action presents unnecessary burdens to a plaintiff's case. The court accordingly eliminated the warranty action that was based on an alleged breach of an implied warranty.[8]

Warranty theories are becoming excess baggage and this is spilling over onto the multiple theories of liability in products liability cases even where warranty is not involved. For instance, in an action based on negligence and strict liability involving alleged faulty product design and manufacture, the trial court refused to submit the negligence count to the jury on the ground that instructions on theories of negligence, as well as strict liability, would be unnecessarily confusing to the jury. This decision was ultimately affirmed by the supreme court.[9]

As Professor John W. Wade[10] wrote:

> Torts scholars would agree, I think, that the *Greenman-Restatement* approach provides the better rationale. Tort is the right milieu for redress for physical injury to person or property; contract is the appropriate milieu for redress for the failure of a product to accomplish the purpose for which it was sold. The incidents of the contract or sales remedy are different from those in tort. Sales law has been codified in uniform acts first under the Uniform Sales Act and now the Uniform Commercial Code. These acts are attuned to the law of sales and the remedies of injured consumers ought not be made to depend on the intricacies of the law of sales.[11]

---

[7] **Mich.:** Smith v. E.R. Squibb & Sons, Inc., 245 N.W.2d 52 (1976).
[8] **Wis.:** Austin v. Ford Motor Co., 273 N.W.2d 233 (1979).
[9] **N.J.:** Masi v. R.A. Jines Co., 394 A.2d 888 (1978).
[10] "Strict Tort Liability for Products: Past, Present and Future," 13 Cap. U.L. Rev. 335 (Spring 1984).
[11] *See also* Ketterer v. Armour & Co., 200 F. 322 (N.Y. 1912).

§ 29.10[6]   CASUALTY INSURANCE CLAIMS

Under the Code, liability for personal injuries is included as a mere afterthought, in the form of consequential damages. Appellate judges throughout the country have recognized the tort-contract distinction and, with a single exception—Delaware—declined to accept the argument that the Uniform Commercial Code has preempted the field so as to constitutionally disable courts from adopting strict tort liability for products.[12]

[6] **Statute of Limitations in Warranty Actions**

About the only advantage in bringing a products liability suit in warranty is that the warranty statute of limitations under the U.C.C. is four years rather than the shorter tort limitation which is usually two years.[13] Even these decisions have been questioned by other courts that hold, to the contrary, that in products liability cases warranty claims are basically tortious in nature, and fall within the tort statutes of limitation.[14]

A third group of decisions have held that the U.C.C. statutory period is applicable only if there is privity of contract between the plaintiff and the defendant.[15]

§ 29.11 **Strict Liability**

Strict liability, as a cause of action in products liability suits permeates all aspects of such actions. It has already been discussed in a gen-

---

[12] There are numerous cases and much writing on the subject. They are cited and discussed in Wade, "Tort Liability for Products Causing Physical Injury and Article 2 of the U.C.C.," 48 Mo. L. Rev. 1 (1983).

[13] **Ala.:** Simmons v. Clemco Indus., 368 So. 2d 509 (1979).
Alas.: Sinka v. Northern Commercial Co., 491 P.2d 116 (1971).
Del.: Johnson v. Hockessan Tractor Co., 420 A.2d 154 (1980).
Ore.: Redfield v. Mead, Johnson & Co., 512 P.2d 776 (1973).
Pa.: Williams v. West Penn Power Co., 467 A.2d 811 (1983) (Pennsylvania had been a mixed bag until the court held in this case that the four year statute of limitations of the U.C.C. applied to all breach of warranty actions, regardless of whether or not there was privity of contract).

[14] **Mich.:** Waldron v. Armstrong Rubber Co., 235 N.W.2d 722 (1975).
Ohio: Lee v. Wright Tool & Forge Co., 356 N.E.2d 303 (1975).
Okla.: Kirkland v. General Motors Corp., 521 P.2d 1353 (1974).
W. Va.: Maynard v. General Elec. Co., 486 F.2d 538 (4th Cir. 1973).

[15] **N.J.:** Heavner v. Uniroyal, Inc., 305 A.2d 412 (1973).
R.I.: Kelly v. Ford Motor Co., 290 A.2d 607 (1972).

PRODUCTS LIABILITY § 29.11

eral way and will again be discussed more specifically as the various aspects of products liability are examined.

Strict liability is a very broad brush. It was imposed where a jury found that "the product left the supplier's control lacking any element necessary to make it safe for its intended use."[16] This accordingly is a general statement that defines and delineates nothing.

It has been observed that strict liability does not mean absolute liability and that a manufacturer accordingly is not an insurer of his product.[17] That is what strict liability is not, but searching for a specific definition of strict liability is an impossible task. This author has never found a satisfactory definition, nor, from a reading of many cases, can I come up with such a definition. All I can say is that strict liability has been applied in certain instances, and is being increasingly applied by courts, especially in products liability cases. A clear definition is left in limbo.

In a typical products liability case based on strict liability, the plaintiff must show that (1) the product was defective at the time it left the possession of the seller, (2) it was in an unreasonably dangerous condition, (3) the defect was the cause of the injuries, and (4) the product reached the consumer without substantial change in its condition.[18] The basic difference between suits brought in negligence and those brought in strict liability is that in the latter situation, negligence does not have to be proven.

The differences between strict liability and liability based on negligence are more theoretical than real, "and (that) judicial adoption of one or the other rationale results more from a perception of what is fair in the allocation of the burden of proof than from a conscious judicial choice between competing jurisprudential theories."[19]

Another writer[20] states that strict liability for certain products liability cases has been based essentially on three grounds:

---

[16] Azzarello v. Black Bros. Co., 391 A.2d 1020 (Pa. 1978) (the court failed to define what constitutes a "safe product," nor did it attempt to define what strict liability encompasses).

[17] Courtois v. General Motors Corp., 182 A.2d 545 (N.J. 1962); Lartique v. R.J. Reynolds Tobacco Co., 317 F.2d 19 (5th Cir. 1963).

[18] Kelley v. R.G. Industries, Inc., 497 A.2d 1143 (Md. 1985).

[19] Davis, "Strict Liability or Liability Based Upon Fault? Another Look," 10 U. Dayton L. Rev. 5 (Fall 1984).

[20] Henderson, "Strict Products Liability and Design Defects in Arizona," 26 Ariz. L. Rev. 261 (1984).

1. The cost to the victims of accidents attributable to defective and dangerous products should be distributed through the marketplace by first charging those costs to manufacturers and distributors who, in turn, pass those costs on to purchasers,[21]
2. The imposition of strict liability will serve the cause of accident prevention by inducing improvements in products and information provided about those products,[22] and
3. The burden of proving fault or negligence which is often present in defective product situations, is too difficult and expensive where the manufacturing process is not open to public view and, in many cases, not readily understandable without expert testimony.[23]

Reasoning such as this led to the adoption of the rule as set out in Restatement (Second) of Torts § 402A which will be discussed in dealing with design defect cases.

[1] **Vendor's Liability**

It appears obviously inequitable to hold a vendor to the same degree of liability for harm to a purchaser of a product that was not manufactured by the seller, as the manufacturer himself. Even though the vendor has a right of common law indemnity, in most cases, against the manufacturer, he is forced to face the expense of defense and the unforeseeable consequences of litigation.

The courts have generally held that the seller of a product nevertheless, was equally responsible in strict liability, with the manufacturer for injury caused by a defective and dangerous product that was properly used or consumed.[24] This has been so held, especially if the product has been reconstructed or altered by the seller without the compliance or consent of the manufacturer,[25] and in some cases,

---

[21] Turner v. Bituminous Cas. Co., 244 N.W.2d 873 (Mich. 1976); Greenman v. Yuba Products, Inc., 27 Cal. Rptr. 697 (1962).
[22] Phillips v. Kimwood Machine Co., 525 P.2d 1033 (Ore. 1974).
[23] Phipps v. General Motors Corp., 363 A.2d 955 (Md. 1976).
[24] Cal.: Green v. City of Los Angeles, 115 Cal. Rptr. 685 (1974); Vandermark v. Ford Motor Co., 37 Cal. Rptr. 896 (1964).
Ill.: Dunham v. Vaughan & Bushnell Mfg. Co., 247 N.E.2d 401 (1969).
See Restatement (Second) of Torts § 402A.
[25] Jordan v. Sunnyslope Appliance Propane & Plumb. Supplies, 660 P.2d 1236 (Ariz. App. 1983).

PRODUCTS LIABILITY § 29.11[2]

even if the vendor is an independent contractor.[26]

Vendor liability may be predicated on warranty, negligence, or strict liability. It is obviously more convenient to bring an action against the vendor than it is to bring such action against the manufacturer.[27] To be able to reach the manufacturer, "Tracing is required to show that the particular product or component part has not been altered by the manufacturer's agents, at his instructions, with his aquiescence, or with parts supplied by him."[28]

While the sellers' position in the marketplace enables them to exert pressure on the manufacturer to enhance the safety of the product, "where the seller does not create the risk or assume it by representations, he is entitled to indemnity from the manufacturer so that the loss will ultimately be borne by the party that caused the risk."[29]

In the Mississippi case of *Shainberg v. Barlow*,[30] the court held that the vendor was not strictly liable for latent defects that could not readily be discovered by the vendor.

[2] Statutory Enactments

Much of the product liability legislation enacted at state level refers to the issue of nonmanufacturer liability, and many of these statutes come within three basic limitations:

1. A specific limitation on liability.
2. A time limitation in which an action may be brought.
3. A requirement that the manufacturer assume the cost of defense and the cost of any liability on a nonmanufacturer defendant down "the stream of commerce."

Specific provisions have ranged from excluding nonmanufacturers from suit (Nevada 1979), providing indemnity schemes (Arizona 1982), shifting to a negligence requirement for funding nonmanufac-

---

[26] Michalko v. Cooke Color & Chem. Corp., 451 A.2d 179 (N.J. 1982).

[27] Cal.: Green v. City of Los Angeles, 115 Cal. Rptr. 685 (1974).

[28] *See* Danielski, "Manufacturer's Liability for Defects in Used Products," F.T.D., December 1980.

[29] Cal.: Hessler v. Hillwood Mfg. Co., 302 F.2d 61 (6th Cir. 1962).

Ill.: Suvada v. White Motor Co., 210 N.E.2d 182 (1965); Peterson v. Lou Backrodt Chem. Co., 329 N.E.2d 785 (1975).

But see Turner v. International Harvester Co., 336 A.2d 62 (N.J. Super. 1975). *See also* Danielski, *supra* note 28.

[30] 258 So. 2d 242 (1972).

turers liability (Tennessee 1980), and distinguishing between manufacturer's and nonmanufacturer's amenability to suit (Kentucky 1982).[31]

Colorado, Illinois, Idaho, Nebraska, North Carolina, Ohio, and Washington have also enacted statutes dealing with vendor's liability and it is likely that other states will soon follow suit.

A model Uniform Products Liability Act (1979) contains a provision which limits the liability of a seller who is not a manufacturer of a defective product, but there has been resistance to the adoption of this model act by the states. The tendency at this time is toward protection for the vendor and limiting its liability for defects in the products manufactured by others.[32]

[3] Insurance Protection

The article, "Limiting Sellers' Exposure to Product Liability: Vendors' Endorsement,"[33] deals at length with the insurance coverage available to a vendor either in the body of a liability policy purchased by the manufacturer who may name the vendor as an additional insured, or by way of several types of endorsements giving protection to the vendor against liability imposed as a result of the manufacturer's defective product.

§ 29.12 Design Defects

A production or manufacturing defect is almost self-explanatory. Faulty fabrication, assembly, or quality control are manufacturing defects and are usually obvious, or should be. A manufacturing defect is caused by a production breakdown on what otherwise could have been a safe product.

A design defect, on the other hand, may be present despite the fact that the product was perfectly manufactured, with the best materials and with no breakdown in either the product's manufacture or use.

---

[31] *See* George, "In the Stream of Commerce: The Liability of Non-Manufacturers in Products Liability Actions," 13 Cap. U.L. Rev. 335-477 (1984); Utt, Note, "S136: Ohio's New Law Limiting the Liability of Nonmanufacturing Sellers in Certain Products Liability Actions," 10 U. Dayton L. Rev. 181 (Fall 1984).

[32] *See* Dillmann, "Limiting Sellers' Exposure to Product Liability: Vendors' Endorsement," F.T.D., September 1984.

[33] *Id.*

The case law evolving in design defect litigation indicates that this is a very troublesome and controversial area; even more so than other aspects of products liability law. Unlike a manufacturing defect, a design defect is rarely self-evident, nor is it a result of an aberration in the production line where every unit coming off the line is defective in the same manner.[34]

A design defect arises when a product has been placed in the marketplace by a manufacturer in the condition intended by the manufacturer, but nevertheless causes injury to the reasonably prudent user who used it for the purpose for which it was intended. The Restatement (Second) of Torts § 402A states that a product is defectively designed if it is unreasonably dangerous for its intended use. Accordingly, under this definition we are left to define, as specifically as the courts permit, what is "unreasonably dangerous" and what is "intended use."

An "unreasonably dangerous" condition has been defined in the Restatement (Second) of Torts § 402A comments g and i to the effect that it depends on the "reasonable expectations" of the average consumer or user of a product, and not by the particular consumer of the product involved in the specific accident involved in the suit.[35]

[1] **Unreasonably Dangerous**

Generally speaking, there are three major types of defects that can make a product unreasonably dangerous:

1. *Manufacturing defects.* These involve an abnormality or condition that was unintended. Here, the manufacturer can be subject to liability without regard to negligence.[36]
2. *Defective or inadequate instructions, warnings or other similar communications about a product.* Here, the generally accepted view is that proof of inadequacy or error requires a showing of fault.

---

[34] Phillips v. Kimwood Mach. Co., 525 P.2d 1003 (1974) ("The courts continue to flounder" while attempting to determine whether a product is in a defective condition); Caterpillar Tractor Co. v. Beck, 593 P.2d 871 (Alas. 1979). *See also* Babcock, "Products Liability: A Problem in Jurisprudence," F.T.D., February 1981, wherein the author quotes Professor Fuller and outlines the judicial traps in design defect cases.

[35] Gray v. Manitowac Co., 771 F.2d 665 (5th Cir. 1985).

[36] International Harvester Co. v. Chiarello, 555 P.2d 670 (1976).

3. *Design defect.* Will be discussed here in some detail. It is more involved since it is usually not open and obvious and because of the difficulty of proof. An action for design defect may be brought on the theory of negligence or strict liability.[37]

Three factors to be considered in determining whether a product was unreasonably dangerous were discussed in the New Hampshire case of *Thibault v. Sears, Roebuck & Co.*,[38] and listed as follows:

1. Social utility and desirability.
2. Presence or absence of adequate warnings sufficiently covering dangers of normal or foreseeable use.
3. Obvious or latent nature of the defect.

This court made it clear, however, that the most obvious dangers, the most explicit warnings, and the highest degree of usefulness cannot absolve a manufacturer from liability where the risk of danger could have been reduced without significant impact on the product's effectiveness and manufacturing cost.

In an effort to determine whether a design is unreasonably unsafe, some decisions have relied on evidence as to alternative designs which could have been safer.[39]

The test propounded by the Restatement (Second) of Torts has come to be known as the *"Consumer Expectation"* test, and has been followed in a number of jurisdictions.[40] Other jurisdictions have re-

---

[37] *See* Henderson, "Strict Products Liability and Design Defects in Arizona," 26 Ariz. L. Rev. 261 (1984).

[38] 395 A.2d 843 (1978).

[39] Carpinin v. Pittsburgh & Western Bus Co., 316 F.2d 404 (9th Cir. 1954); Boeing Airplane Co. v. Brown, 291 F.2d 310 (9th Cir. 1961); McCormick v. Hankscraft Co., 154 N.W.2d 488 (Minn. 1957).

[40] **Ariz.:** Byrns v. Riddell, Inc., 550 P.2d 1065 (1976).
Conn.: Slepski v. Williams Ford, Inc., 364 A.2d 175 (1975).
Idaho: Rindlisbaker v. Wilson, 519 P.2d 421 (1974).
Ill: Huebner v. Hunter Packing Co., 375 N.E.2d 763 (1978).
Iowa: Eickelberg v. Seere & Co., 276 N.W.2d 442 (1979).
Kan.: Lester v. Magic Chef, Inc., 641 P.2d 353 (1982).
N.M.: Skyhook Corp. v. Jasper, 560 P.2d 934, *reversing* 547 P.2d 1140 (1977).
Nev.: Ginnis v. Mapes Hotel Corp., 470 P.2d 135 (1970).
Okla.: Kirkland v. General Motors Corp., 521 P.2d 1352 (1974); Hagan v. FZ Mfg. Co., 674 F.2d 1047 (5th Cir. 1982).
Vt.: Menard v. Newhall, 373 A.2d 505 (1977).
U.S.: Rigby v. Beech Aircraft Co., 548 F.2d 288 (10th Cir. 1977); Latimer v. General Motors Corp., 535 F.2d 1020 (7th Cir. 1976).

jected the "unreasonably dangerous" yardstick and have accepted the *"Risk-benefit"* test, which basically holds that a product may be found defectively designed if either of two alternative tests are satisfied: (1) if the product failed to perform as safely as an ordinary consumer would expect when used as intended or in a reasonably foreseeable manner, or (2) the product causes injury and the defendant fails to establish, after relevant factors are balanced, that the benefits of the design outweigh the risk inherent in it.[41]

However, the two tests are not necessarily exclusive. The difficulty arises when a jury is forced to determine whether a product could or should have been designed more safely *at the time it was made* and whether its utility is more important than the risk involved in its use, and the jurists must decide whether strict liability applies. Accordingly, some decisions embody elements of both tests and both grounds for liability in their decisions.[42]

In the case of *Barker v. Lull Engineering Co.*,[43] for instance, the California Supreme Court defined design defect as being present "(1) if the product has failed to perform as safely as an ordinary consumer would expect when used in an intended or reasonably foreseeable manner, or (2) if the benefits of the challenged design are outweighed by the risk of danger inherent in such design." In *Phillips*

---

[41] **Colo.:** Union Supply v. Pust, 583 P.2d 276 (1978).
Del.: Martin v. Ryder Truck Rental, Inc., 353 A.2d 581 (1976).
Mo.: Keenor v. Dayton Elec. Mfg. Co., 445 S.W.2d 362 (1969).
Neb.: Kohler v. Ford Motor Co., 191 N.W.2d 601 (1971).
N.Y.: Codling v. Paglia, 345 N.Y.S.2d 461 (1973).
N.D.: Olson v. A.W. Chesterton Co., 256 N.W.2d 530 (1977).
Pa.: Azzarello v. Black Bros. Co., 391 A.2d 1020 (1978) (court stated that it was error to use the term "unreasonably dangerous" to instruct the jury in design defect case).

[42] **Ala.:** Atkins v. American Motors Corp., 335 So. 2d 134 (1976).
Alas.: Caterpillar Tractor Co. v. Berk, 593 P.2d 871 (1979).
Cal.: Barker v. Lull Eng'g Co., 143 Cal. Rptr. 225 (1978).
N.J.: Cepeda v. Cumberland Eng'g Co., 386 A.2d 816 (1978).
Ore.: Phillips v. Kimwood Mach. Co., 525 P.2d 1033 (1974).
Tex.: Turner v. General Motors Corp., 584 S.W.2d 844 (1979).
Wis.: Heldt v. Nicholson Mfg. Co., 240 N.W.2d 154 (1976).
U.S.: Welch v. Outboard Marine Corp., 481 F.2d 252 (5th Cir. 1973).
See also Fowler, Comment, "Products Liability: Kansas Adopts the Consumer Expectation Test to Define 'Unreasonably Dangerous' in Design Defects Cases," 22 Washburn L. J. 397 (1983) from which some of the above cases were cited.

[43] 143 Cal. Rptr. 225 (Cal. 1978).

v. Kimwood Machine Co.,[44] the Oregon Supreme Court stated that the test for whether strict liability will apply "is whether a reasonably prudent manufacturer would have so designed and sold the article in question had he known of the risk which injured the plaintiff." This is an example of a case allegedly decided not in strict liability, but in terms of negligence.

In *Hagans v. Oliver Mach. Mfg. Co.*,[45] the court pointed out that many products have both utility and dangerous characteristics and that such a product becomes unreasonably dangerous only if the danger outweighs its utility.

[2] Crashworthiness and Second Injury Liability

"Crashworthiness" is a term used in design defect cases involving a product that is a vehicle. It is a nebulous measure that relates to the ability of a vehicle to protect its occupants from injuries or aggravation of injuries due to "second impact" after an accident has occurred.[46]

"Second injury," "second impact," and "enhanced injuries" are terms used to describe injuries that have been caused or aggravated by some failure in the design of a vehicle, after an initial accident has occurred. They typically occur when the occupants of a vehicle are thrown out of, or about the inside of the vehicle subsequent to a collision. These are injuries that would not have happened in their final form but for some danger created by the design defect. Such defects render the vehicle uncrashworthy and may spell out liability for its manufacturer, distributor, and seller.[47]

The problem invites the question of whether the manufacturer has created an unreasonable risk of causing or increasing injury to occupants of a vehicle in the event of a statistically probable collision. This was discussed in detail in the case of *Dreisonstok v.*

---

[44] 525 P.2d 1033 (1974).

[45] 576 F.2d 866 (5th Cir. 1985).

[46] Dreisonstok v. Volkswagenwerk, 489 F.2d 1066 (4th Cir. 1974).

[47] Dreisonstok v. Volkswagenwerk, 489 F.2d 1066 (4th Cir. 1974); Larsen v. General Motors Corp., 391 F.2d 495 (8th Cir. 1968); Higginbotham v. Ford Motor Co., 540 F.2d 762 (5th Cir. 1976). *See also* David & Richard, "Defective Design and the Uncrashworthy Vehicle," Insurance Counsel Journal, April 1983, Appendix A, for a list of cases that follow the *Larsen* decision.

Contra: Evans v. General Motors Corp., 359 F.2d 822 (7th Cir. 1966); Edgar v. Nachman, 323 N.Y.S.2d 53 (1971).

Volkswagenwerk,[48] in which case the following factors were listed as a measure of liability in crashworthy cases:

1. The obviousness of the danger.
2. The style, type, purposes and intended use of the vehicle, noting that it is commonplace that utility of design and attractiveness of style are elements after which manufacturers seek and by which buyers are influenced in their selections.
3. Price, "for if a change in design would appreciably add to cost, add little to safety, and take an article out of the price range of the market . . . it may be 'unreasonable' as well as 'impractical' for the courts to require the manufacturer to adopt such a change."
4. The circumstances of the accident itself, noting that "it could not reasonably be argued that a car manufacturer should be liable because its vehicle collapsed when involved in a head-on collision with a large truck at high speed."

While I can basically agree with the court's opinion the overall impression that I get from this decision is that the court places a little too much emphasis on property values and a bit too little on the value of life. I think the automobile industry, for one, should make safety its first priority, rather than what it perceives is the taste of the buying public for the appearance of its vehicles.

In recent years, because of the difficulty of proving uncrashworthiness, more courts have begun to permit a strict liability theory rather than negligence while, in actuality, using negligence as a yardstick to determine strict liability without the necessary proof otherwise required.[49]

Except for California, most states that have adopted strict liability in defective design cases follow Restatement (Second) of Torts § 402A which requires a showing of both "defective product" and "unreasonably dangerous" condition.[50] It has been held that an automobile manufacturer has a duty to design a vehicle that will not aggravate the user's injury in case of an accident.[51]

---

[48] 489 F.2d 1066 (4th Cir., 1974).
[49] Barker v. Lull Engineering Co., 143 Cal. Rptr. 225 (1978).
[50] *See* Davis and Richard, "Defective Design and the Uncrashworthy Vehicle," *supra* note 47.
[51] N.M.: Duran v. General Motors Corp., 688 P.2d 779 (1983).

[3] Seat Belts

While the law concerning seat belts has been discussed elsewhere in this text, I believe it is worthy of mention here since its very invention was based on the premise that it would reduce the risk of "second injury." In those jurisdictions that recognize the seat belt defense, it can pose some problems. On the one hand, it can provide a basis for recovery from the manufacturer of the seat belt and the vehicle for injuries sustained by a plaintiff in an accident which was caused by the negligence of a third party. On the other hand, it can prevent an injured plaintiff from recovering from the negligent defendant for those injuries which would not have occurred if the plaintiff had been using his seat belt.[52]

In an early seat belt case,[53] the Wisconsin Supreme Court stated that:

> While we agree it is not negligence *per se* to fail to use seat-belts where the only statutory standard is one that requires the installation of seat-belts in a vehicle, we nevertheless conclude that there is a duty, based on the common law standard of ordinary care, to use available seat belts *independent of any statutory mandate*. [Emphasis added.]

Attitudes have changed drastically since this early decision. Legislators have changed the laws and justices have changed their attitudes in interpreting these new statutes to make the seat belt defense more viable.

[4] Strict Liability in Design Defect Cases

We have already seen that even when some courts are applying the principles of negligence to determine liability in design defect cases, they have labelled the cause of action as being in strict liability simply because of the difficulty of proving negligence in most alleged defective designs,[54] while some jurisdictions hold to negligence and

---

[52] *See* Hagarty, "Design Defects, Seat Belts & Second Injury," F.I.C. Quarterly, Fall 1973.

[53] Bentzler v. Braun, 149 N.W.2d 626 (1967).

[54] **Ariz.:** Embry v. General Motors Corp., 565 P.2d 1294 (1977). *But see* Brady v. Melody Homes Mfg., 589 P.2d 896 (1978). *See also* Rocky Mt. Fire & Cas. Co. v. Biddulph Olds., 640 P.2d 851 (1982).

Cal.: Rowlings v. D.M. Oliver, Inc., 159 Cal. Rptr. 119 (App. 1979).

Ill.: Harms v. Caterpillar Tractor Co., 399 N.E.2d 722 (1980).

refuse to permit such actions to be brought in strict liability.[55]

In at least one case, the court was honest enough to state that strict liability may be applied in all products liability suits whether the defect was one of design or manufacture *and even though a negligence analysis is used in arriving at a design defect.*[56]

There is just about unanimous opinion that a manufacturer is not under a duty in strict liability to design a product that is totally incapable of injuring those who foreseeably come in contact with it, even though some of the decisions do not reflect this statement of obvious fact. A fundamental tenet of products liability law is that a manufacturer is not an insurer of his product.[57]

[5] **Open and Obvious Danger**

An early New York decision,[58] setting forth the defense of open and obvious design error, held that if a manufacturer does everything necessary to make his product function properly for the purpose for which it was designed, if the product is without latent defects, and if it functions without danger other than what is inherent in its purpose and which is known to the user, the manufacturer has satisfied the demands of the law. Other cases have also held that the open and obvious danger defense is valid.[59]

In 1976, another New York court, in *Micallef v. Miehle*,[60] overruled the *Campo* decision[61] and held that the "open and obvious danger" defense amounted to an assumption of risk defense as a matter of law, putting the burden of proof on the plaintiff and accordingly

---

[55] **Ariz.:** Brady v. Melody Homes Mfg., 589 P.2d 896 (1978). *But see* Embry v. General Motors Corp., 565 P.2d 1294 (1977).
  N.J.: Cepeda v. Cumberland Eng'g Co., 386 A.2d 816 (1978).
  U.S.: Bruce v. Martin-Marietta Corp., 544 F.2d 442 (10th Cir. 1976).

[56] Ford Motor Co. v. Hill, 404 So. 2d 1049 (Fla. 1980) (court refused to distinguish between products that cause a primary collision and those that merely enhance further injury because it would be unreasonable to have strict liability depend on the cause of the accident rather than the cause of the injury).

[57] Hunt v. Blasius, 384 N.E.2d 368 (1978).

[58] Campo v. Scofield, 95 N.E.2d 802 (1950).

[59] **Ga.:** Pressley v. Sears, Roebuck & Co., 738 F.2d 1222 (11th Cir. 1984).
  Ill.: Genaust v. Illinois Power Co., 343 N.E.2d 465 (1976); Holecek v. E-Z Just, 464 N.E.2d 696 (1984).
  Ind.: Estrada v. Schmutz Mfg. Co., 734 F.2d 1218 (7th Cir. 1984).

[60] 348 N.E.2d 571 (1976).

[61] Campo v. Scofield, 95 N.E.2d 802 (1950).

decided that it did not apply to cases brought in strict liability. Other courts have followed this reasoning.[62]

[6] State-of-the-Art Defense

"State of the art" has been defined, in the case of *Sturm, Ruger & Co.*,[63] "to mean nothing more than the customery practice of the defendant's industry. Others consider state of the art as the utmost in scientific advances for a particular product. Still others use governmental agency approval as the state of the art."

In the case of *Murphy v. Owens-Illinois, Inc.*,[64] state of the art was defined as the "available scientific and technological knowledge, customary practice and industry standards."

In most cases, state of the art boils down to evidence of standard industry practices and customs which were available at the time the product was manufactured or concocted.[65]

It has been held that there is a difference between "state of the art" and "custom in the industry." "'Custom' refers to what was being done in the industry and 'state of the art' refers to what feasibly *could have been done.*" (Emphasis added.)[66]

In a landmark Texas case,[67] the court stated that "The 'state of the art' with respect to a particular product refers to the technological environment at the time of manufacture. This technological environment includes the scientific knowledge, economic feasibility, and the practicalities of implementation when the product was manufactured."

A federal district court case[68] held that the state of the art defense is a good and full defense.[69]

---

[62] **Mont.:** Kuiper v. Goodyear Tire & Rubber Co., 673 P.2d 1208 (1983).
Tenn.: Ellithorpe v. Ford Motor Co., 503 S.W.2d 516 (1973).
Wash.: Palmer v. Massey-Ferguson, Inc., 476 P.2d 713 (1970).
Wis.: Gracyalny v. Westinghouse Elec. Corp., 723 F.2d 1311 (7th Cir. 1983).
Wyo.: Caterpillar Tractor Co. v. Donahue, 674 P.2d 1276 (1983).
[63] 594 P.2d 38 (Alas. 1979).
[64] 779 F.2d 340 (6th Cir. 1985).
[65] Bruce v. Martin-Marietta Corp., 544 F.2d 442 (10th Cir. 1976). *See* Weinberger, "The State of the Art and Products Liability," 28 Duke L.J. 303 (1979).
[66] Chown v. USM Corp., 297 N.W.2d 218 (Iowa 1980).
[67] Bailey v. Boatland of Honston, Inc., 609 S.W.2d 743 (1980).
[68] Carter v. Johns-Manville Sales Corp., 557 F. Supp. 1317 (1983).
[69] *But See* Flatt v. Johns-Manville Sales Corp., 488 F.2d 836 (1980).

State of the art evidence does not apply to manufacturing defects. It does apply in design cases and may apply in failure to properly warn cases.[70]

According to the theory set forth in comment J of the Restatement (Second) of Torts § 402A, followed by most jurisdictions, there is a duty on the manufacturer to warn of inherent dangers in the use of his product if he had, or should have had, knowledge of such dangers.[71]

It has been generally held that there is no duty to warn of a risk in using a product in a foreseeable manner unless this risk is scientifically known either in the industry or the scientific community.[72] This is commonly referred to as "the state of the art" defense.

Some jurisdictions, however, argue that "state of the art" is irrelevant in a failure to properly warn case that has been brought in strict liability and hold that it is a proper defense only in actions brought in negligence.[73] Other courts have considered such evidence admissable, but not controlling.[74]

In the context of strict liability, there appears to be a shift in focus away from the defendant's conduct toward the defectiveness of the

---

[70] S.C.: Reed v. Tiffin Motor Homes, Inc., 697 F.2d 1192 (4th Cir. 1983).

U.S.: Raney v. Honeywell, Inc., 540 F.2d 932 (1976); Hoppe v. Midwest Conveyor Co., 485 F.2d 1196 (1973); Welch v. Outboard Marine Corp., 481 F.2d 252 (1973).

See Funston, "The 'Failure to Warn' Defect in Strict Products Liability: A Paradigmatic Approach to 'State of the Art' Evidence and 'Scientific Knowledge,' " Insurance Counsel Journal, January 1984.

[71] Alas.: Caterpillar Tractor Co., v. Berk, 593 P.2d 871 (1979).

Cal.: Burke v. Almaden Vineyards, Inc., 150 Cal. Rptr. 419 (App. 1978).

Ill.: Woodill v. Parke Davis & Co., 412 N.E.2d 194 (1980).

[72] U.S.: Ferebee v. Chevron Chem. Co., 736 F.2d 1529 (D.C. Cir. 1984); Hendrix v. Raybestor-Manhattan, Inc., 776 F.2d 1492 (11th Cir. 1985); Koloda v. General Motors Parts Div., 716 F.2d 373 (6th Cir. 1983); McMahon v. Eli Lilly & Co., 774 F.2d 830 (7th Cir. 1985); Woodill v. Parke Davis & Co., 374 N.E.2d 683 (1978).

[73] La.: Halphen v. Johns-Manville Sales Corp., 788 F.2d 247 (1986).

Mass.: Hayes v. Oriens Co., 462 N.E.2d 273 (1984).

Mo.: Elmore v. Owens-Illinois, 673 S.W.2d 434 (1984) (asbestos case).

N.J.: Beshada v. Johns-Manville Prods. Corp., 447 A.2d 539 (1980). *But see* Johnson v. Salem Corp., 477 A.2d 1246 (1984).

[74] Ill.: Murphy v. Chestnut Mt. Lodge, 464 N.E.2d 818 (App. 1984).

Neb.: Erickson v. Monarch Indus., Inc., 347 N.W.2d 99 (1984) (state of the art may be considered as a factor in risk-utility analysis).

N.J.: Johnson v. Salem Corp., 477 A.2d 1246 (1983). *But see* Beshada v. Johns-Manville Prods. Corp., 447 A.2d 539 (1980).

Tex.: Flatt v. Johns-Manville Sales Corp., 488 F.2d 836 (1980). *But see* Carter v. Johns-Manville Sales Corp., 557 F. Supp. 1317 (1983).

§ 29.12[6]　　　　　　　　　　　　CASUALTY INSURANCE CLAIMS

product itself.[75] In a drug related case, it was held that drug manufacturers should not be held strictly liable for failing to warn of side effects that were unknown by the industry when the drug was sold.[76]

---

[75] **Cal.:** Folgio v. W. Auto Supply, 128 Cal. Rptr. 545 (1976).
N.D.: Olsen v. A.W. Chesterton Co., 256 N.W.2d 520 (1977).
Tex.: Gonzales v. Caterpillar Tractor Co., 571 S.W.2d 867 (1978) (Texas seems to be shifting in all directions); Carter v. Johns-Manville Sales Corp., 557 F. Supp. 1317 (1983).

[76] Feldman v. Lederle Labs., 479 A.2d 374 (N.J. 1984).

CHAPTER 30

Products Liability—Duty to Warn and Recall

§ 30.01 Duty to Warn
    [1] Negligence and Strict Liability in Duty to Warn
    [2] Foreseeability
    [3] Open and Obvious Condition
    [4] Design Defects
    [5] Dangers That Are Common Knowledge
    [6] Adequacy of Warning
    [7] Proximate Cause
    [8] To Whom the Duty is Owed
    [9] Alterations
    [10] Component Part
    [11] Continuing Duty to Warn
    [12] Continuing Duty to Warn in Drug Cases
    [13] Method of Warning in Drug Cases
    [14] Post-Accident Warnings
    [15] Pre-Accident Governmental Standards Compliance
    [16] Model Act—Duty to Warn
§ 30.02 Recall
    [1] Coverage from Loss Resulting from Recall
    [2] "Sistership" Exclusion
    [3] Recall Letter
    [4] Recall as a Defense
    [5] Assumption of Risk in Recall Cases
    [6] Admissibility in Evidence of Recall Letter

§ 30.01 Duty to Warn

It has been held that proper marketing of a product contemplates, generally, three basic duties:[1]

  1. To give appropriate instructions or directions for the products safe and proper use or assembly. While instructions may contain warnings, and often do, the instructions properly

---

[1] Sales, "The Marketing Defect (Warning and Instructions) in Strict Tort Liability," D.R.I. pamphlet on Products Liability (1980).

§ 30.01 CASUALTY INSURANCE CLAIMS

focus on the appropriate use to avoid injury. Warnings focus on the avoidance of unsafe handling or use.[2]

2. To give proper warning of any inherent dangers when a product is used properly and for its intended purpose. This "basic duty" really opens up a can of worms and will be discussed in more detail subsequently.

3. To give proper warning of dangers and hazards inherent in a reasonably foreseeable, though unintended, use of a product.[3]

We will discuss foreseeability separately.

While the duty to properly warn is, in most instances, a question of fact,[4] it can, in some flagrant and obvious circumstances, be considered a matter of law for the judge to decide.[5]

---

[2] **Cal.:** Midgley v. S.S. Kresge Co., 127 Cal. Rptr. 217 (App. 1976).
Colo.: Anderson v Heron Eng'g Co., 604 P.2d 674 (1979).
Ill.: Kerns v. Engelke, 369 N.E.2d 1284 (App. 1977), *aff'd as modified*, 390 N.E.2d 859 (1979).
N.D.: Schmidt v. Plains Elec., Inc., 281 N.W.2d 794 (1979).
Ore.: Harris v. Northwest Natural Gas Co., 588 P.2d 18 (1978) (mere directions do not satisfy the duty to warn).
U.S.: Hagens v. Oliver Mach. Co., 576 F.2d 97 (8th Cir. 1978); Reyes v. Wyeth Labs., Inc., 498 F.2d 1264 (5th Cir. 1974), *cert. denied*, 419 U.S. 1046 (1974).

[3] **Cal.:** Canifax v. Hercules Powder Co., 46 Cal. Rptr. 552 (1965).
N.D.: Seibel v. Systems Corp., 221 N.W.2d 50 (1974).
Tex.: Technical Chem. Co. v. Jacobs, 480 S.W.2d 602 (1972).
U.S.: Borel v. Fiberboard Paper Prods. Co., 493 F.2d 1076 (5th Cir. 1973), *cert. denied*, 419 U.S. 869 (1974).

[4] **Mass.:** Wolfe v. Ford Motor Co., 376 N.E.2d 143 (App. 1978).
N.Y.: Baker v. St. Agnes Hosp., 421 N.Y.S.2d 81 (1979).
Tex.: Lopez v. Aro Corp., 584 S.W.2d 333 (App. 1979).
Wash.: Berry v. Coleman Systems Co., 596 P.2d 1365 (App. 1979) (trial court may rule as a matter of law that warnings are inadequate only when the danger is clearly latent).
Wis.: Gracyalny v. Westinghouse Elec. Corp., 723 F.2d 1311 (7th Cir. 1983).
U.S.: Stapleton v. Kawasaki Heavy Indus., Ltd., 608 F.2d 571 (5th Cir. 1979); Westerman v. Sears, Roebuck & Co., 577 F.2d 873 (5th Cir. 1978); Dougherty v. Hooker Chem. Corp., 540 F.2d 174 (3d Cir. 1976).

[5] **Cal.:** Barrett v. Atlas Powder Co., 150 Cal. Rptr. 339 (App. 1978).
Ill.: Genaust v. Illinois Power Co., 343 N.E.2d 465 (1976).
Wash.: Berry v. Coleman Systems, Inc., 596 P.2d 1365 (App. 1979) (if danger is clearly latent).

See also Sales, "The Marketing Defect (Warning and Instructions) in Strict Liability," D.R.I pamphlet on Products Liability, 1980.

[1] Negligence and Strict Liability in Duty to Warn

In addition to using reasonable care (which may be great care in many instances) in the design and manufacture of a product that is or can be dangerous in its consumption or use, the manufacturer may have an additional duty to warn prospective buyers or users of any latent foreseeable dangers in its use (or sometimes even in the misuse) of a product.

Such products might include drugs—both prescription and "over-the-counter"—vehicles of all kinds, housewares, appliances, motorized tools and gardening equipment, sports equipment, agricultural and construction equipment, and other such products too numerous to list. There is no more uniformity in the decisions concerning the duty to properly warn than in other products liability decisions, even where it involves statutory interpretation.

An action based on duty to properly warn may be brought in negligence or in strict liability, but the difference appears to be only that in an action brought in strict liability there is no requirement of *proof* of fault, which, of course, is an integral part of any negligence suit. Otherwise, while there is little logic in this situation, the negligence yardstick is almost always used to impose the duty to properly warn in strict liability cases.[6]

In negligence, we are talking about the reasonableness of the manufacturer's action in selling the article without a warning. In a strict liability case, we are talking about the (dangerous) condition of an article which is sold without a warning,[7] at least so say some of these cases that try to justify the distinction. It has been held, for instance, that under the negligence theory, a manufacturer must test adequately, in order to discover any possible latent design defects, and if any are found he has the additional duty to properly warn the consumer or ultimate user of any dangers that were discovered.[8] In ef-

---

[6] **Minn.:** Karjala v. Johns-Manville Prods. Corp., 525 F.2d 155 (8th Cir. 1975).
Ore.: Anderson v. Klix Chem. Co., 472 P.2d 806 (1970).
Tex.: Bristol Myers Co. v. Gonzales, 561 S.W.2d 801 (1978).
[7] **Colo.:** Hamilton v. Hardy, 549 P.2d 1107 (App. 1976) (court rejected foreseeability).
Ore.: Phillips v. Kimwood Mach. Co., 525 P.2d 1033 (1974).
U.S.: Borel v. Fiberboard Paper Prods. Co., 493 F.2d 1076 (5th Cir. 1973) (foreseeability required as indicated by Restatement (Second) of Torts § 402A).
[8] Ford Motor Co. v. Russel & Smith Ford Co., 474 S.W.2d 549 (App. 1970).

fect, however, if not in so many words, so say many other decisions that are also brought in strict liability.[9]

In the case of *Temple v. Wean United, Inc.*,[10] the court held that "The rule imposing obligation on the manufacturer or seller to give suitable warning of a dangerous propensity in a product is a rule fixing a standard of care, and is accordingly an action based on negligence and not strict liability."

[2] Foreseeability

In *Karjalla v. Johns-Manville Prods. Corp.*,[11] quoting from *Rose v. Phillip Morris & Co.*,[12] the court stated that under the negligence theory a manufacturer must warn only of foreseeable dangers and that "Liability will not attend those injurious consequences resulting from the use of a product, the harmful effects of which no developed human skill or foresight can afford knowledge."

It has also been held that foreseeable use of a product implies use in the manner intended by the manufacturer,[13] but even in *Suchomajcz v. Hummel Chem. Co.*[14] the court qualified its holding by stating that misuse of a product is not always an absolute bar to recovery if the misuse is foreseeable.

In another case, the court made a further qualification by holding that the duty to warn, even though foreseeable, must be balanced against the cost of preventing the magnitude of the risk.[15]

Accordingly, strict liability has been held to be inapplicable in the duty to warn, where the manufacturer could not have reasonably an-

---

[9] **Cal.:** Barker v. Lull Eng'g Co., 143 Cal. Rptr. 225 (1978).
N.J.: Beshada v. Johns-Manville Prods. Corp., 447 A.2d 539 (1982).
Ore.: Phillips v. Kimwood Mach. Co., 525 P.2d 1033 (1974).
Wash.: Little v. PPG Indus., Inc., 579 P.2d 940 (1978), *modified,* 594 P.2d 911 (1979).
See Jackson, "The Duty to Warn and Strict Liability," Insurance Counsel Journal, July 1981.

[10] 364 N.E.2d 267 (Ohio 1977).

[11] 523 F.2d 155 (8th Cir. 1975).

[12] 388 F.2d 3 (8th Cir. 1964).

[13] Suchomajcz v. Hummel Chem. Co., 524 F.2d 19 (3d Cir. 1975); Moran v. Faberge, Inc., 332 A.2d 11 (Md. 1975); Spruill v. Boyle-Midway, Inc., 318 F.2d 79 (2d Cir. 1962); McLaughlin v. Sears, Roebuck & Co., 281 A.2d 587 (1971).

[14] *Id.*

[15] Hohlenkamp v. Rheem Mfg. Co., 601 P.2d 298 (1979).

PRODUCTS LIABILITY—DUTY TO WARN   § 30.01[3]

ticipated the dangers inherent in the product, or anticipated the use to which the product was put by the use of reasonable skill and foresight.[16]

[3] **Open and Obvious Condition**

While a manufacturer has a duty to warn of dangerous properties in his product, there is usually no duty to warn of conditions in the product that are open and obvious and apparent even to ignorant or careless users.[17]

The court in *Collins v. Ridge Tool Co.*,[18] stated that "Whether a danger is open and obvious to a user of a particular instrumentality is not a matter which should be determined in a vacuum. Rather, the unique facts of each case should bear on the question . . . (includ-

---

[16] **Ga.:** Vance v. Miller-Taylor Shoe Co., 251 S.E.2d 52 (App. 1978).
Ill.: Peterson v. B/W Controls, Inc., 366 N.E.2d 144 (App. 1977).
Ind.: Ortho Pharmaceutical Corp. v. Chapman, 388 N.E.2d 541 (App. 1979).
Kan.: Prentice v. Acme Mach. & Supply Co., 601 P.2d 1093 (1979).
Ky.: Ford Motor Co. v. McCamish, 559 S.W.2d 507 (App. 1977).
N.H.: Thibault v. Sears, Roebuck & Co., 395 A.2d 843 (1978).
N.J.: Mohr v. B.F. Goodrich Co., 371 A.2d 288 (Super. 1977).
Tex.: Bristol-Myers Co. v. Gonzales, 561 S.W.2d 801 (1978).
Wash.: Little v. PPG Indus., Inc., 579 P.2d 940 (App. 1978), *aff'd as modified*, 594 P.2d 911 (1979) (foreseeability abrogated in strict liability).
U.S.: Wisconsin Elec. Power Co. v. Zallea Bros., Inc., 606 F.2d 697 (7th Cir. 1979); Ezagui v. Dow Chem. Corp., 598 F.2d 727 (2d Cir. 1979); Harrison v. Flota Mercante Columbiana, 577 F.2d 968 (5th Cir. 1978).
See also Restatement (Second) of Torts § 402A comment j which holds that in order to prevent the product from being unreasonably dangerous, the seller may be required to give directions or warning, on the container, as to its use. The seller is required to give warning against a danger not generally known if he has knowledge, or by the application of reasonable, developed human skill and foresight, should have had knowledge of the danger.

[17] **Cal.:** Barrett v. Atlas Powder Co., 150 Cal. Rptr. 339 (1978); Price v. Niagara Mach. & Tool Works, 136 Cal. Rptr. 535 (App. 1977).
Colo.: Bookout v. Victor Comptometer Corp., 576 P.2d 197 (App. 1978).
Idaho: Rindlisbaker v. Wilson, 519 P.2d 421 (1974).
Ill.: Zideck v. General Motors Corp., 384 N.E.2d 509 (App. 1978); Genaust v. Illinois Power Co., 343 N.E.2d 465 (1976).
N.H.: Thibault v. Sears, Roebuck & Co., 395 A.2d 843 (1978).
Vt.: Menard v. Newhall, 373 A.2d 505 (1977).
Wash.: Haysom v. Coleman Lantern Co., 573 P.2d 785 (1978).
U.S.: Hagans v. Oliver Mach. Co., 576 F.2d 97 (5th Cir. 1978).
See also German, "Product Design Negligence and Duty to Warn," 13 F.T.D. 67, June 1971.

[18] 520 F.2d 591 (7th Cir. 1975).

§ 30.01[4]   CASUALTY INSURANCE CLAIMS

ing) the status, intelligence and more importantly, the training of the particular user involved."

Where a dangerous condition is equally within the technical knowledge of the supplier and the employer of the injured, there is no duty on the part of the supplier to warn the employer of an obvious danger inherent in the use of the product.[19]

[4] Design Defects

"The drafters of Restatement (Second) of Torts § 402A, the various state and federal courts and commentators on the concept, have been extremely successful in making the word defect into a jurisprudential quagmire."[20]

Dictionary definitions of "defect" are "a fault or imperfection," "an irregularity . . . that spoils the appearance or causes weakness or failure." While such definitions tend to describe a manufacturing defect, they leave something to be desired when applied to design defects.[21]

Design defect was defined in *Barker v. Lull Eng'g Co.*,[22] as the products failure to perform "as safely as an ordinary consumer would expect when used as intended in a reasonably foreseeable manner."

[5] Dangers That Are Common Knowledge

When a product is not defectively designed or manufactured and when the possibility of injury arises only from a dangerous property of the product which is open and obvious, there is no duty to warn about the danger in the use of such a product.[23] Such knowledge may

---

[19] Lockett v. General Elec. Co., 376 F. Supp. 1201 (Pa. 1974).

[20] Baldwin, Hare & McGovern, "The Preparation of a Product Liability Case," as quoted by Funston, "The 'Failure to Warn' Defect in Strict Products Liability: A Paradigmatic Approach to 'State of the Art' Evidence and 'Scientific Knowledge,' " Insurance Counsel Journal, January 1984.

[21] *See* Wade, "On the Nature of Strict Tort Liability for Products," Insurance Law Journal, March 1974.

[22] 143 Cal. Rptr. 225 (1978). *See also* Suter v. San Angelo Foundry, 406 A.2d 140 (1979).

[23] **Cal.:** Bojorquez v. House of Toys, 133 Cal. Rptr. 483 (1976).

Ill.: Morgan v. Bethlehem Steel Corp., 481 N.E.2d 836 (1986); Holecek v. E Z Just, 464 N.E.2d 696 (1984).

Okla.: Berry v. Eckhardt Porche, Audi, Inc., 578 P.2d 1195 (1978).

Tenn.: Temberton v. American Distilled Spirits Co., 664 S.W.2d 690 (1984) (duty to warn is not required where the risk of use, if abused, is widely known).

be common to all users of an ordinary product or to a specific common industry, profession or other such group of which the injured is a member.[24]

[6] Adequacy of Warning

The duty to warn of latent, inherent, production, or design dangers are now accepted as a fact of life in the business community. The overwhelming majority of cases do not focus on the need for *any* warning, but rather on whether or not a particular warning was adequate to apprise the consumer or user of a dangerous product under the particular circumstances.

An adequate warning has been described as:

1. Being in such a form as to be reasonably expected to catch the attention of a reasonably prudent person in the circumstances of the product's ordinary and expected use.
2. Having a content of such a nature as to be comprehensible to the average user and to convey a fair indication of the nature and extent of any danger to the mind of a reasonably prudent person.[25]

More specifically, the wording of the warning must be unambiguous and the lettering clear and easily readable.[26]

The warning should inform anyone who is able to read and understand what he has read. Some courts also consider the nature of the product, the manner in which it was used, the "intensity" of the

---

Vt.: Menard v. Newhall, 373 A.2d 505 (1977).
U.S.: McIntyre v. Everest & Jennings, Inc., 575 F.2d 155 (8th Cir. 1978); Martinez v. Dixie Carriers, Inc., 529 F.2d 457 (5th Cir. 1976) (common knowledge within the industry trade group).

[24] Martinez v. Dixie Carriers, Inc., 529 F.2d 457 (5th Cir. 1976).

[25] *See* Hirsch & Zimmerman, "Duty to Warn and Adequacy of Warning in Products Liability Cases," 20 F.T.D. 135, June 1979, quoting from Bristol-Myers Co. v. Gonzales, 548 S.W.2d 416 (Tenn. App. 1977) and Muncy v. Magnolia Chem Co., 437 S.W.2d 15 (Tex. App. 1968).

[26] **N.J.:** d'Arienzo v. Clairol, Inc., 310 A.2d 106 (Super. 1973).
N.M.: Michael v. Warner, Chilcott Co., 579 P.2d 183 (App. 1978).
U.S.: Harrison v. Flota Mercante Grancolumbiana, 577 F.2d 968 (5th Cir. 1978).

warnings and the liklihood that a warning will be communicated adequately to any foreseeable user.[27]

This may be all well and good, but what about the 25 percent or more of our population that cannot read, or cannot read well enough to understand beyond the primitive level, or cannot read English? In such a case, symbols such as those internationally recognized in the form of a skull and crossbones in a prominent black or red setting, or other such symbols should be used.[28]

In any event, the warning must be conspicuous.[29] The warning must also communicate the risk of harm other than the normal expectations of a consumer or user as to hazardous performance.[30] Advertising promotions that give "warnings" and which emphasize the effectiveness of a drug while underestimating its dangers or side effects are inadequate and misleading.[31]

Where the occasion demands it, warnings of danger must be comprehensive.[32] Nevertheless, in spite of all that has been said, there are still a few courts that have not recognized a cause of action in strict liability for injuries incurred as a result of inadequate warnings.[33]

---

[27] **Ariz.:** Tucson Indus. v. Schwartz, 487 P.2d 12 (Ariz. 1971).
Tex.: Bituminous Cas. Corp., v. Black & Decker Mfg. Co., 518 S.W.2d 868 (App. 1974).
U.S.: Dougherty v. Hooker Chem. Corp., 540 F.2d 174 (3d Cir. 1975).
[28] Hubbard-Hall Chem. Co. v. Silverman, 340 F.2d 402 (1st Cir. 1965).
[29] **Ariz.:** Shell Oil Co. v. Gutierrez, 581 P.2d 271 (App. 1978).
Idaho: Rindlisbaker v. Wilson, 519 P.2d 421 (1976).
Iowa: Miller v. Bock Laundry Mach. Co., 568 S.W.2d 648 (1977).
Tex.: West v. Broderick & Bascom Rope Co., 197 N.W.2d 202 (1972).
U.S.: Dougherty v. Hooker Chem. Corp., 540 F.2d 174 (3d Cir. 1976); Stapleton v. Kawasaki Heavy Indus., Inc., 608 F.2d 571 (5th Cir. 1979) (warning in manual of instructions is not enough); Griggs v. Firestone Tire & Rubber Co., 513 F.2d 851 (8th Cir. 1975), *cert. denied,* 423 U.S. 865 (1975).
[30] **Cal.:** Cavers v. Cushman Motor Sales, 157 Cal. Rptr. 142 (1979).
N.M.: Skyhook Corp. v. Jasper, 560 P.2d 934 (1977).
Tex.: Bituminous Cas. Corp. v. Black & Decker Mfg. Co., 518 S.W.2d 868 (App. 1974).
[31] Incollingo v. Ewing, 282 A.2d 206 (1971).
[32] **La.:** Chappas v. Sears, Roebuck & Co., 358 So.2d 926 (1978).
Tex.: Schering v. Geisecke, 589 S.W.2d 516 (App. 1979).
U.S.: Johnson v. Husky Indus., Inc., 536 F.2d 645 (6th Cir. 1976).
[33] **Ohio:** Hardiman v. Zep Mfg. Co., 470 N.E.2d 941 (1985); Temple v. Wean United, Inc., 364 N.E.2d 267 (1977).

[7] Proximate Cause

In suits brought for failure to warn or give adequate warning of dangers in products, most courts require that the plaintiff show that the *proximate* cause of the injury was a direct result of such failures.[34] In some jurisdictions, however, the courts have held that it is sufficient if the cause is *contributing* to or "producing" the injury, rather than being the proximate cause of it. The duty to warn may run to a user of a product who need not be one of the persons to whom the manufacturer had an initial duty to warn, as long as the breach was the proximate cause of the injury.[35]

[8] To Whom the Duty is Owed

The duty to warn of any dangerous propensities in a product runs to all whom the manufacturer or supplier should reasonably expect might use or consume the product or be endangered by its use, including customers, users, consumers, and handlers of the product.[36]

Most decisions hold that the duty to warn runs to the ultimate user or consumer,[37] except for prescription drugs where most jurisdictions hold that the duty to warn is reasonably owed to the doctor, rather than the patient.[38]

---

[34] **Ariz.:** Dyer v. Best Pharmacal, 577 P.2d 1084 (1978).
Ill.: Wenzell v. MTD Products, 355 N.E.2d 99 (App. 1977).
Ind.: Nissen Trampoline Co. v. Terre Haute First Nat'l Bank, 332 N.E.2d 820 (App. 1975).
Pa.: Greiner v. Volkswagenwerk, 429 F. Supp. 495 (1977).
Wash.: Little v. PPE Indus., Inc., 579 P.2d 940 (App. 1978), *aff'd as modified,* 594 P.2d 911 (1979).

[35] Burton v. L.O. Smith Foundry Products Co., 529 F.2d 108 (7th Cir. 1976).
Tex.: C.A. Hoover & Son v. Franklin Serum Co., 444 S.W.2d 596 (1969).
U.S.: d'Hedouville v. Pioneer Hotel Co., 552 F.2d 886 (9th Cir. 1977).

[36] *See* Restatement (Second) of Torts § 388 comment a.

[37] **N.D.:** Seibel v. Symons Corp., 221 N.W.2d 50 (1974).
Ore.: Schneiser v. Truss Joint Corp., 540 P.2d 998 (1975).
Wash.: Reed v. Pennwalt Corp., 591 P.2d 478 (App. 1979).
Wis.: Koslowski v. Johns E. Smith's Sons Co., 275 N.W.2d 915 (1979).
U.S.: Reyes v. Wyeth Labs., 498 F.2d 1264 (5th Cir. 1974), *cert. denied,* 419 U.S. 1046 (1974); Jackson v. Coast Paint & Lacquer Co., 499 F.2d 809 (9th Cir. 1974).

[38] **Md.:** Chambers v. G.D. Searle & Co., 441 F. Supp. 377 (1975).
Mich.: Smith v. E.R. Squibb & Sons, 245 N.W.2d 52 (App. 1976), *aff'd,* 273 N.W.2d 476 (1979).
Neb.: McDaniel v. McNeil Labs., 241 N.W.2d 822 (1976).
N.Y.: Lindsay v. Ortho Pharm. Corp., 481 F. Supp. 314 (1979).

[9] Alterations

If a product is safe as manufactured and distributed, it has usually been held that the manufacturer has no duty to warn about subsequent alterations that he did not make or sanction,[39] although even here, there is opinion to the contrary.[40]

[10] Component Part

Ordinarily, "the supplier of a component part which contains no latent danger" is not required to "warn the subsequent assembler and his employees of any danger which might arise after the components are assembled."[41]

[11] Continuing Duty to Warn

The duty to warn may be a continuing one, even after a product has been sold,[42] and in some cases, even where the dangerous conditions were not the fault of the original manufacturer.[43]

Ordinarily, and aside from drug products, some jurisdictions have held that to require a manufacturer to be responsible for a continuing duty to warn of dangers subsequently discovered, is tantamount to insuring the product that the manufacturer markets and no such requirement is valid.[44]

Ore.: McEwen v. Ortho Pharm. Corp., 528 P.2d 522 (1974).
Tex.: Bristol-Myers Co. v. Gonzales, 561 S.W.2d 801 (1978).
Wash.: Terhune v. A.H. Robbins Co., 577 P.2d 975 (1978).
[39] Ariz.: Rodriguez v. Besser Co., 565 P.2d 1315 (1977).
Minn.: Westerberg v. School Dist. 702, 148 N.W.2d 312 (1967).
Ohio: Temple v. Wean United, Inc., 364 N.E.2d 267 (1977).
Wis.: Shawver v. Roberts Corp., 280 N.W.2d 226 (1979).
[40] Colo.: Bradford v. Bendix-Westinghouse Auto. Air Service Co., 350 P.2d 1044 (1960).
[41] Burton v. L.O. Smith Foundry Prods. Co., 529 F.2d 108 (7th Cir. 1976).
[42] Canto v. Ameteck, Inc., 328 N.E.2d 873 (1975); Braniff Airways, Inc. v. Curtis-Wright Corp., 411 F.2d 451 (2d Cir. 1969), *cert. denied,* 400 U.S. 829 (1970) (no notice was given to a purchaser of an airplane motor about a defect that was discovered after the purchase, but eight months before the accident); Noel v. United Aircraft Corp., 342 F.2d 232 (3d Cir. 1964).
[43] Basco v. Sterling Drug, Inc., 416 F.2d 417 (2d Cir., 1969); Bly v. Otis Elevator Co., 713 F.2d 1040 (4th Cir. 1983) (in an action brought in *negligence,* the duty to warn is continuous); Sterling Drug Co. v. Yarrow, 408 F.2d 978 (8th Cir. 1969).
[44] N.J.: Jackson v. N.J. Manufacturers Ins. Co., 400 A.2d 81 (Super. 1979).
Tex.: Bell Helicopter Co. v. Bradshaw, 594 S.W.2d 519 (App. 1979).

PRODUCTS LIABILITY—DUTY TO WARN § 30.01[13]

[12] Continuing Duty to Warn in Drug Cases

If dangerous side effects from the use of a drug are subsequently discovered, the manufacturer must take steps to warn doctors or users of the drug concerning the hazards of the newly discovered side effects.[45] In addition, the manufacturer of drugs, which, by the very nature of its position is considered to be an expert in its field, must keep abreast of the latest developments concerning its products, including continued research. It has the further duty to inform the medical profession of any adverse findings or developments.[46]

[13] Method of Warning in Drug Cases

Drug manufacturers communicate information and warnings to the medical profession about their products in different ways:

1. By employing a "detail" man who is a sales representative and who distributes literature concerning the product.
2. The Physician's Desk Reference, which contains a listing and description of prescription drugs and describes their side effects, if any.
3. Product cards and advertisements mailed to doctors and distributed at medical conventions, seminars, etc.
4. Special mailings when pertinent new information is obtained.
5. Package inserts.

Each of these methods has been commented on as being individually or collectively adequate or not, to constitute sufficient warning to determine the liability of the manufacturer.[47]

---

[45] Basco v. Sterling Drug Co., 416 F.2d 417 (2d Cir. 1969); Davis v. Wyeth Labs, Inc., 399 F.2d 121 (9th Cir. 1968); Sterling Drug, Inc. v. Cornish, 370 F.2d 82 (8th Cir. 1966). *See also* Frumer & Friedman, Products Liability, § 8.01 (1983).

[46] **N.J.:** Ferrigno v. Eli Lilly & Co., 420 A.2d 1305 (1980).
Ore.: McEwen v. Ortho Pharm. Corp., 528 P.2d 522 (1974).
Va.: Stanback v. Parke Davis & Co., 502 F. Supp. 767 (1980).
U.S.: Dalke v. Upjohn Co., 555 F.2d 245 (9th Cir. 1977); Werner v. Upjohn Co., 628 F.2d 848 (4th Cir. 1980).
See also Royal, "Post Sale Warnings: A Review and Analysis Seeking Fair Compensation Under Uniform Law," 33 Drake L. Rev. 817 (1983-84).

[47] **Md.:** Chambers v. G.D. Searle & Co., 441 F. Supp. 377 (1975).
N.Y.: Baker v. St. Agnes Hosp., 421 N.Y.S.2d 81 (1979).
U.S.: Lindsay v. Ortho Pharm. Corp., 637 F.2d 87 (2d Cir. 1980).

[14] Post-Accident Warnings

A manufacturer or seller of a product has a duty to warn previous purchasers of any defects or hazards that have been discovered by them after the sale of the product.[48] This duty requires the manufacturer to keep current on its own research and on technical and scientific publications so as to warn the consumer or user of dangers about which it has discovered or should reasonably have discovered.[49]

Evidence of a manufacturer's post-accident warning to consumers to take safety precautions was held admissible in an action brought in strict liability.[50] However, changes in warnings made subsequent to the accident are usually not admissible to establish warning inadequacy in the individual case.[51]

Evidence of subsequent remedial warnings by the manufacturer, however, has been deemed admissible in some states in actions brought in strict liability.[52]

Generally speaking, subsequent governmental regulations are not admissible as evidence if the case is brought either in negligence or strict liability.[53]

---

[48] Basco v. Sterling Drug, Inc., 416 F.2d 417 (2d Cir. 1969); La Belle v. McCauley Indus. Corp., 649 F.2d 46 (1st Cir. 1981); Feldman v. Lederle Labs., 479 A.2d 374 (N.J. 1984). *See* pertinent federal and state legislation.
See also Royal, "Post Sale Warnings: A Review and Analysis Seeking Fair Compensation Under Uniform Law," 33 Drake L. Rev. 817 (1983-84).
[49] McKee v. Moore, 648 P.2d 21 (Okla. 1982); Borel v. Fiberboard Paper Prods. Co., 493 F.2d 1076 (5th Cir.), *cert. denied*, 419 U.S. 869 (1973).
[50] Schelbauer v. Butler Mfg. Co., 52 U.S.L.W. 2414 (1984) (despite statute that applies to negligence or culpable conduct).
[51] **Fla.:** Ellis v. Golconda Corp., 352 So. 2d 1221 (App. 1977).
Mich.: Smith v. E.R. Squibb & Sons, 273 N.W.2d 476 (App. 1979).
N.J.: Price v. Buckingham Mfg. Co., 266 A.2d 140 (Super. 1970).
Wash.: Hayson v. Coleman Lantern Co., 573 P.2d 785 (1978).
U.S.: Smyth v. Upjohn, 529 F.2d 803 (2d Cir., 1975).
[52] **Cal.:** Burke v. Almaden Vineyards, Inc., 150 Cal. Rptr. 419 (App. 1978); Ault v. International Harvester Co., 528 P.2d 748 (1974).
U.S.: d'Hedouville v. Pioneer Hotel Co., 552 F.2d 886 (9th Cir. 1977); Robbins v. Farmers Union Grain Term. Ass'n, 552 F.2d 788 (5th Cir. 1977).
[53] **Ariz.:** Gaston v. Hunter, 588 P.2d 336 (1978) (negligence action).
Cal.: Ault v. International Harvester Co., 528 P.2d 1148 (1974) (strict liability case).
Tex.: Simons v. Southwest Texas Methodist Hosp., 535 S.W.2d 192 (App. 1976).
Wis.: Chart v. General Motors Corp., 258 N.W.2d 680 (1977) (strict liability case).
U.S.: d'Hedouville v. Pioneer Hotel Co., 552 F.2d 886 (9th Cir. 1977) (strict liability case).

The case of *Fish v. Georgia-Pacific*[54] held that admission of evidence concerning measures taken subsequent to an event (accident or occurrence) is barred by Federal Rule of Evidence 407.

[15] Pre-Accident Governmental Standards Compliance

Compliance with governmental agency requirements concerning labeling quality standards of products is admissible on the issue of adequate warning, but is ordinarily not accepted as conclusive evidence.[55]

In general, with reference to compliance with governmental standards that were subsequently established, a study reported on by Stephen Van Voorhis[56] states:

> Contrary to popular assumptions, the body of LSI (Litigation Sciences, Inc., N.Y. City) research seems to show that the jurors are not impressed by claims of standards compliance. Jurors, in fact, appear to lend no special approval to defendants who plead compliance, a finding that should arouse concern in defense counsel.

> In contrast, research also indicates that plaintiff's charges of non-compliance on the part of defendants dispose jurors quite negatively toward those defendants.

> Indeed, the whole subject of compliance with standards appears to be a problematic one, for it presents defendants with a no-win situation in which demonstration of compliance may yield no positive results at trial, while plaintiff's charges of non-compliance can pose a grave threat to the defense.

Mr. Voorhis also reports that "failure to meet standards in pharmaceuticals was judged more negatively than the same failure in the auto industry."

---

[54] 779 F.2d 836 (2d Cir. 1985).

[55] **Ariz.:** Shell Oil Co. v. Gutierrez, 581 P.2d 271 (1978) (governmental regulations must be applicable).
Cal.: Stevens v. Parke Davis & Co., 507 P.2d 653 (1973).
Tex.: Bristol-Myers Co. v. Gonzales, 551 S.W.2d 801 (1978).
U.S.: Raymond v. Riegel Textile Corp., 484 F.2d 1025 (1st Cir. 1973); Simien v. S.S. Kresge Co., 566 F.2d 551 (5th Cir. 1978).

[56] "Compliance as a Defense in Products Cases: Risks and Pitfalls," F.T.D., 8 July 1985.

[16] Model Act—Duty to Warn

The recent explosion of products liability claims and suits and the concomitant increase in the amounts of the verdicts have had a drastic result on insurance company loss ratios. As insurance premiums increased greatly, there has been an increasing clamor for legislative relief.

Congress has enacted a model products liability act which has been adopted by some states. Section 104(c)(6) regarding post sale warnings reads as follows:

> In addition to the claim provided in subsection (c)(1), a claim may arise under the subsection where a reasonably prudent manufacturer should have learned about a danger connected with a product after it was manufactured. In such a case, the manufacturer is under an obligation to act with regard to the danger as a reasonably prudent manufacturer in the same or similar circumstances. This obligation is satisfied if the manufacturer makes reasonable efforts to inform product users or a person who may be reasonably expected to assure that action is taken to avoid harm, or that the risk of harm is explained to the actual product user.[57]

§ 30.02 Recall

"Recall" with which most people are familiar, are notices sent by automobile manufacturers to customers that certain defects in the automobiles sold to them have been discovered and that these defects require correction because continued driving of the vehicle, without the correction could be hazardous to life and limb. There are different types of "recall." Recall may refer to a governmental directive, or because the manufacturer himself voluntarily issued a recall order. It is to be noted that recall is somewhat different from "withdrawal" where the product is simply withdrawn from the market with no attempt intended to make any correction on the recalled product, as was the case with Tylenol and some other drug products that were tampered with.

---

[57] Mr. R.A. Royal, in his article "Post Sale Warnings: A Review and Analysis Seeking Fair Compensation Under Uniform Law," 33 Drake L. Rev. 817 (1983-84) says about this Model Act that it "leaves as many unanswered questions as the case law and is little help in specifically defining the duty to issue post sale warnings, to whom they should be communicated, and the method of communication." For details concerning the various state enactments, I would refer the reader to pages 853 to 856 of this article.

PRODUCTS LIABILITY—DUTY TO WARN § 30.02[2]

There have also been recalls or withdrawals because of fire hazards of dolls and other toys, because of unsafe packaging, and for many other reasons and including many types of products. For the most part, however, when we see the word "recall," we usually are concerned with automobiles.

[1] Coverage from Loss Resulting from Recall

The intent of the product's liability policies is, and always has been, to provide third party liability coverage for injury or damage resulting from the insured's wrongdoing. There is, and never was any intent to pay for the cost of repairs or replacement of the defective product itself, or the economic loss resulting therefrom. Such a loss is covered only by a product guarantee policy, which is usually provided by companies specializing in this type of coverage.

In an attempt to make this intent clear, the 1986 Commercial General Liability policy, which provides for a product's liability attachment, contains the specific exclusion "n" which states that there is no coverage for: "Damages claimed for any loss, cost or expense incurred by you (insured) or others for the loss of use, withdrawal, recall, inspection, replacement, adjustment, removal or disposal of (1) your product." Together with the exclusion of damage to the insured's product, the intent not to cover "recall" loss should now be beyond doubt.

Nevertheless, government instigated recall does put the manufacturer, vendor, and purchaser on notice that the recall itself places some responsibilities and further duties on all these concerned parties.

Recall puts the purchaser of the product on notice that the product is or may be defective. The recall notice does not ordinarily go into details concerning the alleged defect, especially in mechanical products, nor does it usually specify the extent of the danger. Finally, most of the items recalled are not generally found to be defective.

[2] "Sistership" Exclusion

Products liability policies are not standard or uniform. Some of them still contain the "sistership" exclusion. It usually states that

> this insurance does not apply: (a) to liability assumed by the insured under any contract or agreement, but this exclusion does not apply to a warranty of fitness or quality of the named insured's products or a

warranty that work performed by or on behalf of the named insured will be done in a workmanlike manner.

Because of this exception within the exclusion and in spite of another specific exclusion in the policy which states that property owned by the insured is not covered, some courts have decided that the exclusion gives rise to an ambiguity in the policy that should be construed against the insurer.[58]

With the advent of new policy wording, the question of coverage for product damage and economic loss as a result of recall or withdrawal will become a matter of history. Nevertheless, the issuance of, or failure to issue recall notices as evidence of defects that are discovered by the manufacturer or distributor of a product will remain a problem in the handling of products liability cases.

In 1959, the Michigan Supreme Court, in *Comstock v. General Motors Corp.*,[59] held that the duty of a manufacturer exists at common law to notify a purchaser of known danger in the use of its product and that this duty extends to it to give prompt warning when a latent defect that is hazardous becomes known to it shortly after the product has been put on the market.

The problem then arises as to the content of such a recall notice and how it can be used to further the plaintiff's suit, or help the manufacturer or distributor in its defense.

[3] **Recall Letter**

In determining the individual liability (not coverage) of the manufacturer, wholesaler, or retailer of the product, there are certain requirements in the letter of recall which must be met. First, it must be determined whether mailing must be proved, or whether receipt is required. It has been held by some courts that proof of mailing is

---

[58] *See* International Hormones, Inc. v. Safeco Ins. Co., 294 N.Y.S.2d 260 (1977); Paper Mchy. Corp. v. Nelson Foundry Co., 323 N.W.2d 160 (La. App. 1982); Yakima Cement Prods. Co. v. Great Amer. Ins. Co., 590 P.2d 771 (Wash. App. 1979); Thos. J. Lipton, Inc. v. Liberty Mut. Ins. Co., 314 N.E.2d 37 (1975). *See also* Soden, "Judicial Recall of the Product Withdrawal Exclusion," F.I.C. Quarterly, Summer 1984 and "Products Impairment, Recall, Replacement & Rehabilitation," Excess & Surplus Lines Bulletin 11-B 1.8, published by The Merritt Co.

[59] 99 N.W.2d 627 (1959).

PRODUCTS LIABILITY—DUTY TO WARN   § 30.02[5]

not enough to insure that proper warning has been given.[60]

It has also been held that that the recall letter should be as specific as possible in order to inform the recipient of the true nature of the danger.[61]

[4] Recall as a Defense

Ordinarily, recall has not been very effective as a defense to a products liability claim. Such a defense, however, is not impossible. As Mr. Ramp points out in his article:[62]

> Each recall campaign is unique. A variety of factors will determine the scope of the manufacturer's duty to his consumers and determine the ease with which recall campaigns can be used as a defense. These factors include the degree of negligence of the manufacturer, the number of products recalled, the age of the product at the time of recall, whether the product was a necessity and whether the defect was common to all recalled items or merely found in a few.[63]

It would also be appropriate to determine how many previous recall campaigns of the product were conducted by the manufacturer. In some instances, continued use of a product without heed to a recall letter may be considered as misuse by the consumer.[64]

[5] Assumption of Risk in Recall Cases

Although the defense of assumption of risk has been highly restricted in recent years, it may still be effective in some situations

---

[60] Nevels v. Ford Motor Co., 439 F.2d 251 (5th Cir. 1971). Section 1402 of the National Traffic & Motor Vehicle Safety Act of 1970 requires notification to be made by certified mail to the first purchaser of the product. *See* Ford Motor Co. v. R. J. Poeschal, 98 Cal. Rptr. 702 (1971).

[61] Spruill v. Boyle-Midway, Inc., 308 F.2d 79 (4th Cir. 1962); Tampa Drug Co. v. Wait, 103 So. 2d 603 (Fla. 1968); Post v. American Cleanup Equip. Corp., 437 S.W.2d 576 (Ky. 1968); Incollingo v. Ewing, 382 A.2d 222 (Pa. 1971) (warning held inadequate as a matter of law). *See also* Smith, "Recall Campaigns: A Possible Defense to Product's Liability," Insurance Counsel Journal, January 1975.

[62] "The Impact of Recall Campaigns on Products Liability," Insurance Counsel Journal, January 1977.

[63] *See* Caskey v. Olympia Radio & Tel., 343 F. Supp. 969 (S.C. 1972).

[64] Larson v. General Motors Corp., 391 F.2d 495 (8th Cir. 1968); Mazzi v. Greenline Tool Co., 320 F.2d 821 (2d Cir. 1963).

involving recall campaigns.[65]

[6] Admissibility in Evidence of Recall Letter

As a general rule, state courts have permitted recall letters to be introduced as evidence of post-accident repairs.[66]

There is also a distinct difference in the attitude of courts between recall letters issued as a result of governmental requirement,[67] and those issued voluntarily.[68] Mere compliance with safety standards, however, does not ordinarily provide a defense to a products liability suit, nor is it conclusive proof that a product is safe.[69]

The courts have been almost unanimous in forbidding the admissibility of recall letters for the purpose of proving that the automobile involved in a specific accident or occurrence contained the specific defect involved in the recall letter.[70] The recall letter is ordinarily admissible only to indicate that the defect may have existed at the time the automobile or other product was sold by the manufacturer.[71]

---

[65] Messick v. General Motors Corp., 460 F.2d 485 (5th Cir. 1972); Mooney v. Massey Ferguson, Inc., 429 F.2d 1184 (9th Cir. 1970); Rhoads v. Service Co., 329 F. Supp. 367 (Ark. 1971).

[66] Ill.: Millette v. Radosta, 404 N.E.2d 823 (App. 1980).
Mass.: Carey v. General Motors Corp., 387 N.E.2d 583 (1979).
Mo.: Rinker v. Ford Motor Co., 567 S.W.2d 655 (App. 1978).
N.Y.: Barry v. Manglass, 389 N.Y.S.2d 870 (App. 1976).

[67] Ill.: Millette v. Radosta, 404 N.E.2d 823 (App. 1980).
Mass.: Carey v. General Motors Corp., 387 N.E.2d 583 (1979).
N.Y.: Barry v. Manglass, 389 N.Y.S.2d 870 (App. 1976).

[68] La.: Landry v. Adam, 282 So. 2d 590 (App. 1973).
Okla.: Fields v. Volkswagen, 555 P.2d 48 (1976).

[69] H.P. Hood & Sons, Inc. v. Ford Motor Co., 345 N.E.2d 683 (Mass. 1976); Larson v. General Motors Corp., 391 F.2d 495 (8th Cir. 1968).

[70] Fla.: Harley-Davidson Motor Co. v. Carpenter, 350 So. 2d 360 (App. 1977).
La.: Landry v. Adam, 282 So. 2d 590 (1973).
Mich.: Comstock v. General Motors Corp., 99 N.W.2d 627 (App. 1954).
N.Y.: Barry v. Manglass, 389 N.Y.S.2d 870 (App. 1976).

[71] Mass.: Carey v. General Motors Corp., 387 N.E.2d 583 (1979).
N.J. Munieri v. Volkswagenwerk, 376 A.2d 1317 (Super. 1977).
N.Y.: Iadicicco v. Duffy, 401 N.Y.S.2d 557 (App. 1978).
Okla.: Fields v. Volkswagen, 555 P.2d 48 (1976).

CHAPTER 31

Products Liability—Some Defenses and Related Problems

§ 31.01 Some Products Liability Defenses
    [1] Assumption of Risk in Products Liability Cases
    [2] Contributory Negligence
    [3] Comparative Negligence as a Defense to Strict Liability
    [4] Comparative Causation
§ 31.02 Used, Rebuilt, Reconditioned, or Altered Products
    [1] Liability of Manufacturer for Reconditioned Products
    [2] Dealer Preparation
    [3] Drugs and Related Products
    [4] Duty to Warn in Prescription Drug Cases
    [5] Hypersensitivity to Certain Drugs
    [6] Pre-Marketing Testing
    [7] Drug Addiction
    [8] Statutes of Limitation in Drug Related Cases
    [9] Handguns
    [10] Subsequent Modification or Repair
§ 31.03 Federal Rules of Evidence
§ 31.04 Post-Settlement Problems
§ 31.05 Changes in Standards
§ 31.06 "Market Share" Liability and Similar Theories
§ 31.07 Successor Corporations
    [1] Punitive Damages Against Successor Corporations
§ 31.08 Statutes of Limitations or Repose
    [1] Statutes of Repose
    [2] Implantations or Insertions
§ 31.09 Service versus Product

§ 31.01 Some Products Liability Defenses

[1] Assumption of Risk in Products Liability Cases

The defense of assumption of risk is still regarded as valid in a few jurisdictions under some circumstances. It must first of all be shown that the plaintiff proceeded unreasonably in the face of a known danger. Secondly, he must have understood and appreciated the risk involved and must have accepted the risk as well as the inherent possibility of danger because of the risk.[1]

According to *Prosser & Keeton on Torts*, the principal requirements of the assumption of risk defense are (1) the plaintiff knew of, and understood the danger, and (2) voluntarily undertook the risk, which (3) resulted in injury to him.[2] The great majority of the courts, however, have rejected assumption of risk as a defense in actions brought in strict liability as being out of step with present thinking.[3] Indeed, the adoption of comparative negligence usually infers the abolition of the doctrine of assumption of risk.[4]

In *McConville v. State Farm. Mut. Auto. Ins. Co.*,[5] the Wisconsin court merged assumption of risk into contributory negligence and held that such conduct would be treated as comparative negligence.[6]

Restatement (Second) of Torts § 402A comment "n" provides that the user of a product must discover a defect and must be aware of its danger in order to invoke the defense of assumption of risk.[7]

In the Illinois Appellate case of *Pell v. Victor J. Andre High School*[8] the court appears to retain both "assumption of risk" and "misuse of product" as valid defenses, but implies that neither of these doctrines applies to actions brought in strict liability.

Some courts made a distinction between knowledge of a defect and awareness of a dangerous condition.[9] Others have interpreted

---

[1] Colo.: Jackson v. Harco Corp., 673 P.2d 363 (1983).
La.: Doffelmijer v. Gilley, 384 So. 2d 435 (1980) and cases cited therein.
Okla.: Bingham v. Hollingsworth, 695 F.2d 445 (10th Cir. 1982).
U.S.: Lambert v. Will Bros. Co., 596 F.2d 799 (8th Cir. 1979).

[2] *Prosser & Keeton on Torts* (5th ed. 1984).

[3] *See* Greenlee & Rochelle, "Comparative Negligence and Strict Liability: A Marriage of Convenience," Land & Water Law Rev., vol. XVIII (1983).

[4] Tex.: Farley v. MM Cattle Co., 529 S.W.2d 751 (1975).
U.S.: Bell v. Jet Wheel Blast., 717 F.2d 181 (5th Cir. 1983).

[5] 113 N.W.2d 14 (1962).

[6] *See also* Comment, "Coney v. J.L.G. Industries: Applying Comparative Negligence to Strict Products Liability: Should Ohio Follow?", 13 Cap. U.L. Rev. 335-477 (Spring 1984).

[7] Ms. Cloud, in her article, "Setting the Standards for the Sufficiency of an Assumption of Risk in Oklahoma Manufacturer's Products Liability Actions," Okla. City U.L. Rev., vol. 8, Spring, 1983, argues convincingly in footnotes 26, 27, and 28 that there is an inconsistency in the Restatement. *See also* Smith, "Recall Campaigns: A Possible Defense to Products Liability," Insurance Counsel Journal, January 1975.

[8] 462 N.E.2d 858 (1984).

[9] Ellis v. Moore, 401 S.W.2d 789 (Tex. 1966).

"dangerous condition" to be synonymous with "defect."[10]

In the defense of assumption of risk, direct evidence would be almost impossible for the defendant to present. Accordingly, most courts that give credence to this defense have permitted circumstantial evidence to prove the plaintiff's case, making this defense a question of fact.[11]

In discussing the various defenses of assumption of risk, contributory and comparative negligence, it is difficult, if not impossible, to keep them in separate categories since they are conceptually interrelated.

[2] **Contributory Negligence**

Generally speaking, contributory negligence is conduct on the part of the plaintiff that falls below the standard to which he should conform for his own protection, and that is a legally contributing cause cooperating with the negligence of the defendant in bringing about the plaintiff's harm. A comment to Restatement (Second) of Torts § 402A states that contributory negligence is not a defense to an action in strict liability except when it takes the form of a voluntary and unreasonable assumption of risk. R.E. Nielsen[12] states that "It may be argued (therefore) that the Restatement recognizes as a defense to strict liability, only the overlap area which includes elements of assumption of risk and contributory negligence, while rejecting the pure forms of both."[13] Most courts, however, have rejected contributory negligence as a defense to strict liability, while some apparently permit the assumption of risk defense in actions brought on other grounds.[14]

---

[10] Henderson v. Ford Motor Co., 519 S.W.2d 87 (1974).

[11] **Okla.:** Jordan v. General Motors Corp., 590 P.2d 193 (1979); Bingham v. Hollingsworth, 695 F.2d 445 (10th Cir. 1982).

U.S.: Campbell v. Norco Products, 629 F.2d 1258 (7th Cir. 1980).

[12] "Strict Liability Actions—Defenses Based on Plaintiff's Conduct," F.I.C. Quarterly, Winter 1982.

[13] **Fla.:** Blackburn v. Dorta, 348 So. 2d 287 (1977).

U.S.: Borel v. Fiberboard Paper Products Corp., 493 F.2d 1076 (5th Cir. 1973).

[14] **Ill.:** Williams v. Brown Mfg. Co., 261 N.E.2d 305 (1970).

Ind.: Gregory v. White Truck & Equip. Co., 323 N.E.2d 280 (1975).

Iowa: Hughes v. Magic Chef, Inc., 288 N.W.2d 542 (1980).

Tenn.: Holt v. Stihl, Inc., 449 F. Supp. 693 (1978).

[3] Comparative Negligence as a Defense to Strict Liability

Since the Wisconsin Supreme Court expressed its opinion in *Dipple v Sciano,* [15] most states have adopted both the principles of strict liability in products liability cases and some form of comparative negligence. Since comparative negligence is a negligence doctrine and strict liability is supposedly not, these jurisdictions were and are faced with an apparent contradiction.

After the adoption of the Uniform Comparative Fault Act, some states applied comparative negligence in strict liability actions and this has simply added to the confusion.[16] Nevertheless, as we have already noted, the courts involved have either directly or implicitly held that strict liability and comparative negligence are not incompatible.[17]

---

[15] 155 N.W.2d 55 (1967).

[16] *See* Wade, "Product Liability and Plaintiff's Fault—The Uniform Comparative Fault Act," 29 Mercer L. Rev. 373 (1978). *See also* Daly v. General Motors Corp., 144 Cal. App. 380 (1978).

[17] *See* "Applying Comparative Fault to Strict Liability Actions," D.R.A. article in the Insurance Adjuster Magazine, June 1985, listing most of the following cases:

Alas.: Butard v. Surburban Marine & Sporting Goods, Inc., 555 P.2d 42 (1976).

Ark.: Brewer v. Jeep Corp., 546 F. Supp. 1147 (1982), *aff'd,* 724 F.2d 650 (8th Cir. 1983).

Cal.: Daly v. General Motors Corp., 144 Cal. Rptr. 380 (1978); Li v. Yellow Cab Co., 119 Cal. Rptr. 858 (1975) (involving "pure" form of comparative negligence).

Fla.: West v. Caterpillar Tractor Co., 336 So. 2d 80 (1976).

Hi.: Kaneko v. Hilo Coast Processing Co., 654 P.2d 343 (1982).

Idaho: Sun Valley Airlines v. Avco Lycoming Corp., 411 F. Supp. 598 (1976).

Ill.: Coney v. I.L.G. Industries, 454 N.E.2d 197 (1983).

Kan.: Albertson v. Volkswagenwerk, 634 P.2d 1127 (1981).

La.: Wesley v. City of Durham Springs, 455 So. 2d 1183 (1984).

Minn.: Hudson v. Snyder Body, Inc., 326 N.W.2d 149 (1982).

Miss.: Edwards v. Sears, Roebuck & Co., 512 F.2d 276 (5th Cir. 1975).

Mont.: Zahrte v. Sturm, Ruger & Co., 661 P.2d 17 (1983).

N.H.: Thibault v. Sears, Roebuck & Co., 395 A.2d 843 (1978) (applies only to products liability actions), *but see* Algyer v. Lincoln, 484 A.2d 1079 (1984).

Nev.: Aetna Cas. & Sur. Co. v. Jeppesen & Co., 642 F.2d 339 (9th Cir. 1981).

N.Y.: Dole v. Dow Chem. Co., 282 N.E.2d 288 (1972).

Ore.: Sandford v. Chevrolet Div. of General Motors Corp., 642 P.2d 624 (1982).

R.I.: Fiske v. MacGregor, 464 A.2d 719 (1983).

Utah: Mulherin v. Ingersoll-Rand Co., 628 P.2d 1201 (1981).

Wash.: Davis v. Globe Mach. Mfg. Co., 684 P.2d 692 (1984).

W. Va.: Star Furn. Co. v. Pulaski Furn. Co., 297 S.E.2d 854 (1982) (applies to products liability only).

Wis.: Dippel v. Sciano, 155 N.W.2d 55 (1967) (first state to hold that strict liability was applicable to comparative negligence).

PRODUCTS LIABILITY—DEFENSES § 31.01[3]

Some jurisdictions, however, still refuse to recognize comparative negligence as a defense in strict liability cases.[18]

The two types of comparative negligence, "pure" and "modified," have been discussed in §§ 9.06[a], [b], *supra,* dealing with strict liability. Merely as a reminder, under the "pure" form, the plaintiff may recover his total damages reduced by the percentage of fault attributable to him. In the "modified" form, his recovery ceases altogether if his fault is 50 percent or more of the total, depending on the particular Act.[19]

Restatement (Second) of Torts § 402A has also been discussed in § 29.12, *supra,* dealing with strict liability as applied to products liability cases. In those jurisdictions that follow Section 402A, most of the courts have accepted comparative negligence as a full or partial defense.[20]

In at least one state, comparative negligence may be held as a valid defense in strict products liability cases at the discretion of the trial judge.[21] Comparative fault recognizes that injuries are often due to a variety of causes-in-fact and allows juries to apportion cause among the parties involved in an accident.[22]

See also Kulig, "Comparative Negligence and Strict Products Liability: Where Do We Stand?" 29 Vill. L. Rev. 695 (1983-84).

[18] **Colo.:** Kinard v. Coats Co., 553 P.2d 835 (App. 1976), *but see* Welch v. F.R. Stokes, 555 F. Supp. 1054 (1983).

Ga.: Deere v. Brooks, 299 S.E.2d 704 (1983).

Iowa: Speck v. Unit Handling Div., Litton Systems, 366 N.W.2d 543 (1985).

Ky.: Anderson v. Black & Decker, 597 F. Supp. 1298 (1984).

Mass.: Melia v. Ford Motor Co., 534 F.2d 795 (8th Cir. 1976).

Ohio: Robinson v. Parker-Hannifin Corp., 447 N.E.2d 781 (1982).

Okla.: Kirkland v. General Motors Corp., 521 P.2d 1353 (1974).

S.D.: Smith v. Smith, 278 N.W.2d 155 (1979).

[19] *See* Elder v. Orluck, 483 A.2d 474 (Pa. Super. 1984) wherein this subject is discussed in some detail.

[20] **N.H.:** Hagenbuch v. Snap-On-Tool Corp., 339 F. Supp. 676 (1972).

Wis.: Dipple v. Sciano, 155 N.W.2d 55 (1967).

See also Feinberg, "The Applicability of a Comparative Negligence Defense in a Strict Products Liability Suit Based on Section 402A," Insurance Law Journal, January 1975.

[21] Bell v. Jet Wheel Blast., 717 F.2d 181 (5th Cir. 1983). *See* Robertson, "Ruminations on Comparative Fault," 44 La. L. Rev. 1352-56 (1984).

[22] *See* Twerski, "The Many Faces of Misuse: An Inquiry Into the Emerging Doctrine of Comparative Causation," 29 Mercer L. Rev. 403 (1978).

[4] Comparative Causation

Some jurisdictions have distinguished between comparative negligence and comparative causation, which reflects the degree to which each party is a *cause of the injuries,* rather than in proportion to the fault of each party in strict products liability cases.[23]

§ 31.02 Used, Rebuilt, Reconditioned, or Altered Products

Commercial sellers of used products which are rebuilt or reconditioned may be strictly liable for injuries to the user,[24] as may the maker of a component part of a finished product who is held to the same duty as an assembler of the finished product.[25]

"Any product," as stated in Restatement (Second) of Torts § 402A includes used, modified, rebuilt, or altered products.[26]

Where there was no warranty or guaranty of the product, however, some courts have been reluctant to hold the reconditioner strictly liable.[27]

[1] Liability of Manufacturer for Reconditioned Products

Manufacturers of the original product are not ordinarily held strictly liable for injuries or damages resulting from accidents that occurred after substantial modifications were made, without the con-

---

[23] **Idaho:** Sun Valley Airlines v. Avco-Lycoming Corp., 411 F. Supp. 598 (1976).
Ill.: Coney v. J.L.G. Indus., 454 N.E.2d 197 (1983).
Kan.: Kennedy v. City of Sawyer, 618 P.2d 788 (1980).
N.H.: Thibault v. Sears, Roebuck & Co., 395 A.2d 843 (1978).
Ore.: Sandford v. Chevrolet Div. of General Motors Corp., 642 P.2d 624 (1982) (when the court states that causation can be scientifically apportioned while fault cannot, I question its logic).
Tex.: Duncan v. Cessna Aircraft Co., 665 S.W.2d 414 (1984).
Utah: Mulherin v. Ingersoll-Rand Co., 628 P.2d 1301 (1981) (statute was held inapplicable).

[24] Jordan v. Sunnyslope Appliance Propane & Plumbing Supply Co., 660 P.2d 1236 (Ariz. App. 1983); Crandell v. Larkin & Jones Appliance Co., 334 N.W.2d 31 (S.D. 1983) (product was guaranteed).

[25] Smith v. Peerless Glass Co., 181 N.E.2d 576 (N.Y. 1932) and many subsequent cases.

[26] Danielski, "Manufacturer's Liability for Defects in Used Products," F.T.D., December 1980, quoting from Metzgor, "Products Liability and the Seller of Used Goods," 15 American Bus. Law Journal 159 (1977).

[27] **Ariz.:** Rix v. Reeves, 532 P.2d 185 (App. 1975) (despite decision that favored defendant).
Ore.: Tillman v. Vance Equip. Co., 596 P.2d 1299 (crane was bought "as is").

sent of the manufacturer, that resulted in an unusually dangerous product.[28] One case hedges the strict liability question with several qualifications. Where repairs were made on a television set that was four years old, by technicians authorized and trained by the manufacturer, and where only parts made by the manufacturer were used, the manufacturer was held liable for the resulting damage.[29]

In at least one case, even where the original product was substantially damaged by fire and rebuilt by the salvager with original parts, the manufacturer was held liable despite a warning that was sent to all dealers that a part was defective.[30]

Ordinarily proof of wear and tear and improper maintenance will relieve the original manufacturer of liability.[31]

[2] Dealer Preparation

An automobile manufacturer may not escape liability by delegating responsibility for final adjustments and corrections to its authorized agents,[32] and in some cases, even after substantial repairs were made after the owner had been using the automobile, because the dealer is an agent of the manufacturer.[33]

There are, of course, requirements that must be met in order to relieve a manufacturer of a product that has been altered, from being held for strict liability, after the product was put in the marketplace:

1. The alteration must have been done by someone other than the manufacturer, in some instances and with some exceptions.[34]
2. They must not have been done at his direction or supervision.[35]

---

[28] King v. K.R. Wilson Co., 455 N.E.2d 1282 (1983).

[29] Bombardi v. Pochel's Appliance & Tel. Co., 515 P.2d 540, *aff'd*, 518 P.2d 202 (Wash. App. 1973) (in addition, the defendant was unable to show any substantial change in the product).

[30] Ford Motor Co. v. Matthews, 291 So. 2d 169 (Miss. 1974).

[31] Gibbs v. General Motors Corp., 445 S.W.2d 589, *aff'd*, 450 S.W.2d 827 (Tex. 1970).

[32] Vandermark v. Ford Motor Co., 37 Cal. Rptr. 896 (1964).

[33] Goodrich v. Ford Motor Co., 525 P.2d 130 (Ore. 1974).

[34] **Cal.:** Vandermark v. Ford Motor Co., 37 Cal. Rptr. 896 (1964).
Mo.: Swindler v. Butler Mfg. Co., 436 S.W.2d 78 (1968).

[35] **Mo.:** Winters v. Sears, Roebuck & Co., 554 S.W.2d 565 (App. 1977).
Wash.: Bombardi v. Pochel's Appliance & Tel. Co., 515 P.2d 540 (App. 1973).

3. Repairs must have been made with parts that were not made or originally assembled by the manufacturer.[36]
4. The alterations must result in a dangerous condition which was not reasonably foreseeable when the product was manufactured.[37] (Some cases have held that the manufacturer is not required to foresee that the user will alter his product so as to make it dangerous.)[38]
5. The dangerous condition must have caused, or have been a contributing factor, of the injury or damage.[39]
6. The alteration must have been substantial.[40]

These requirements usually overlap and overlap in varying degrees.[41]

[3] **Drugs and Related Products**

As stated by Munsey,[42] "Regrettably, drugs and vaccines powerful enough to combat disease also have the capacity to produce adverse side effects. The danger is sharply increased if the product is misused or if the patient happens to be a particularly sensitive individual. Proper warnings conveyed to the physician are essential."

Actions involving drugs or vaccines and related products may be brought in warranty, negligence, or strict liability. Even in strict liability, however, most courts use a negligence yardstick to measure liability.

It has been held, for instance, that liability will only be imposed for failure to properly warn, if side effects or other injurious consequences to the user of the drug were known to the manufacturer or could have been known by reasonably obtainable information at

---

[36] Wash.: Bombardi v. Pochel's Appliance & Tel. Co., 515 P.2d 540 (App. 1973).
[37] Colo.: Bradford v. Bendix-Westinghouse Auto. Brake Co., 517 P.2d 406 (1973).
U.S.: Griggs v. Firestone Tire & Rubber Co., 513 F.2d 851 (8th Cir. 1975).
[38] Ariz.: Rodriguez v. Besser Co., 565 P.2d 1315 (1977).
Ill.: Wells v. Webb Mach. Co., 315 N.E.2d 301 (1974).
Ohio: Temple v. Wean United, Inc., 364 N.E.2d 267 (1977).
[39] Tex.: General Motors Corp. v. Hopkins, 535 S.W.2d 880 (1976).
U.S.: Kessler v. Bowie Mach. Works, Inc., 510 F.2d 617 (8th Cir. 1974).
[40] Ind.: Cornette v. Searjeant Metal Prods., Inc., 258 N.E.2d 652 (1970).
Pa.: D'Antona Hampton Grinding Wheel Co., 310 A.2d 307 (1973).
[41] *See* Lauwers, "The Defense of Product Alteration," F.I.C. Quarterly, Spring 1981.
[42] "Products Liability: Drugs, Vaccines, Blood," 21 Defense Law Journal 1 (1972).

PRODUCTS LIABILITY—DEFENSES § 31.02[3]

the time of manufacture.[43]

Munsey further states[44] that "Strict liability has limited application in prescription drugs, as shown by comment (k) in the rule set forth by the Restatement (Second) of Torts," as follows:

> There are some products which, in the present state of human knowledge, are quite incapable of being made safe for their intended and ordinary use. These are especially common in the field of drugs. An outstanding example is the vaccine for the Pasteur treatment of rabies, which not uncommonly leads to very serious and damaging consequences when it is injected. Since the disease itself inevitably leads to a dreadful death, both the marketing and the use of the vaccine are fully justified, notwithstanding the unavoidable high degree of risk which they involve. Such a product, properly prepared, and accompanied by proper directions and warning, is not defective, nor is it unreasonably dangerous. The same is true of many other drugs, vaccines and the like, many of which, for this very reason, cannot legally be sold except to physicians, or under the prescription of a physician. It is also true in particular of many new or experimental drugs as to which, because of lack of time and opportunity for sufficient medical experience, there can be no assurance of safety, or perhaps even of purity of ingredients, but such experience as there is justifies the marketing and the use of the drug notwithstanding a medically recognizable risk. The seller of such products, again with the qualification that they are properly prepared and marketed, and proper warning is given, where the situation calls for it, is not to be held to strict liability for unfortunate consequences attending their use, merely because he has undertaken to supply the public with an apparently useful and desirable product, attended with a known but apparently reasonable risk.

Munsey[45] then goes on to state:

> The language in comment (k) has thus carved out an exception for drugs and vaccines to the strict liability theory, assuming proper testing, labeling, and manufacture. This means that inadequate-warning cases brought in strict liability actually are no different from warning cases on negligence. Inadequate warning must be proved in order for a manufacturer to lose the exemption rank.

---

[43] Feldman v. Lederle Labs., 479 A.2d 374 (N.J. 1984) (knowledge of an "unknowable danger" may not be imputed to the manufacturer, but the burden of proof is on him. Determination of "unreasonably unsafe" should be made on a case-by-case basis).

[44] *Supra,* note 42.

[45] *Supra,* note 42.

Generally speaking, a vendor of a prescription drug may not be held strictly liable for side effects or other defects if he has used due care in compounding or processing the prescription.[46]

[4] Duty to Warn in Prescription Drug Cases

Most prescription cases based on products liability deal with the duty to properly warn the doctor concerning the correct dosage or possible side effects. In most instances this duty is fulfilled when the physician is given proper warning.[47]

Under strict liability it has been held that where there is a proper warning of possible side effects or other dangers, the manufacturer of a prescription drug cannot be held liable, as has already been indicated.[48]

Once again there is a difference of opinion, this time as to whether detailed warning must be given as to drugs whose dangerous propensities are well-known to the medical profession. In the case of *Davis v. Wyeth Labs.*,[49] the court held that detailed, proper warning must be given to the physician. However, in the case of *Mulder v. Parke Davis*,[50] the court stated that "We agree that where the only issue is failure to communicate a warning, the manufacturer is not liable if the doctor was fully aware of the facts which were the subject of the warning.[51]

[5] Hypersensitivity to Certain Drugs

Courts generally have made a distinction between side effects to drugs that affect many users and allergic effects to some skin preparations that affect a very few people because of a physical peculiarity or because they are hypersensitive to such products, and those people who have only the average reactions to such products. The warranty with respect to drugs does not run in favor of a person who

---

[46] Murphy v. E.R. Squibb & Sons, Inc., 221 Cal. Rptr. 447 (1986); Sindello v. Abbott Labs., 607 P.2d 924 (1986).

[47] Love v. Wolf, 38 Cal. Rptr. 183, *aff'd*, 58 Cal. Rptr. 42 (1967).

[48] Leibowitz v. Ortho Pharm. Corp., 307 A.2d 449 (Super. 1973) (I would be much more at ease with such a statement if the words "should not" had been used instead of "cannot").

[49] 399 F.2d 121 (Cal. 1968).

[50] 181 N.W.2d 882 (Minn. 1970).

[51] *See also* § 30.01, *supra*, dealing in general with the duty to warn.

PRODUCTS LIABILITY—DEFENSES § 31.02[7]

suffers from allergic reaction to it unless such reaction is common to a substantial portion of possible users.[52]

It has also been held under a strict liability theory, that a manufacturer is not liable for failure to warn for uncommon reactions to a drug by a hypersensitive user. The same rule applies if such a case is brought in negligence.[53]

Some courts have made no such distinction.[54]

[6] Pre-Marketing Testing

Suppose a drug is discovered which proves to be effective against a life-threatening disease for which no other cure is known, but which has not received extensive testing. Is it the manufacturer's duty to withhold this vitally important drug until long-range studies on its safety can be completed? According to Munsey,[55] the answer seems to be that a manufacturer has a duty to make a reasonable effort to learn the nature and effect of his product before it is placed in the marketplace. However, this approach does not take into account FDA regulation of drug marketing and those jurisdictions that hold drug manufacturers strictly liable for injury. (In my opinion, there should be a weighing of considerations in each such case; the merits of the product against the possibility and the degree of harm that may result.) Negligence in testing, however, is a factor that should always be a consideration for recovery.[56]

Since the *Tinnerholm*[57] decision, state legislatures have enacted various statutes with reference to blood transfusions and transplantations as being a service rather than a sale of a product and have similarly treated potent drugs and vaccines.

[7] Drug Addiction

Just to touch upon this vital subject, the court in *Crocker v. Winthrop Labs.*[58] stated that:

---

[52] Magee v. Wyeth Labs., Inc., 29 Cal. Rptr. 322 (1963). Similar holding in Cudmore v. Richardson-Merrell, Inc., 398 S.W.2d 640 (Tex. 1965).
[53] Griggs v. Combe, 456 So. 2d 790 (1984).
[54] Esborg v. Bailey Drug. Co., 378 P.2d 298 (Wash. 1963).
[55] "Products Liability: Drugs, Vaccines, Blood," 21 Defense Law Journal 1 (1972).
[56] Tinnerholm v. Parke Davis & Co., 285 F. Supp. 432, *aff'd*, 411 F.2d 48 (2d Cir. 1969).
[57] *Id.*
[58] 514 S.W.2d 429 (Tex. 1974).

Whatsoever the danger and state of medical knowledge, and however rare the susceptibility of the user, when the drug company positively and specifically represents its product to be free and safe from all dangers of addiction, and when the treating physician relies upon that representation, the drug company is liable when the representation proves to be false and harm results.

[8] Statutes of Limitation in Drug Related Cases

Again the usual controversy. Some jurisdictions have adopted the discovery rule holding that the statute of limitations in a drug related case runs from the date on which the injury was first recognizable, rather than the date on which the drug was taken.[59] Other jurisdictions have held that the statute begins to run on the last day on which the drug was used, despite the time at which the injury or disease was discovered.[60]

[9] Handguns

If there was ever an area where my own inclinations and prejudices would suggest the application of strict liability, it is against the vendors of handguns. Some of these merchants of death, while giving lip-service to local and state regulations, wink at what they consider minor irregularities, in order to sell handguns which instinct must tell them, will be put to criminal use.

Vendors are not always brought into the action because in many instances, they are unknown, or uninsured or uncollectable.

Heretofore, it has just about universally been held that strict products liability applies to a manufacturer only when the handgun is defective. If it was in normal use at the time of the injury and functioned precisely as designed, and because its dangers are open and obvious, the courts have not held the manufacturers in strict liability.[61]

For example, in an action brought under a strict liability theory, alleging defective marketing, distribution and design, a Maryland

---

[59] Ark.: Schenebeck v. Sterling Drug, Inc., 423 F.2d 919 (8th Cir. 1966).
La.: Breaux v. Aetna Cas. & Sur. Co., 272 F. Supp. 668 (1967).
[60] Schwartz v. Heyden, Newport Chem. Corp., 188 N.E.2d 142 (1963).
[61] Perkins v. F.I.E. Corp., 762 F.2d 1250 (5th Cir. 1985); Riordon v. International Armament Corp., 477 N.E.2d 1293 (Ill. App. 1985).

PRODUCTS LIABILITY—DEFENSES § 31.02[9]

court of appeals, in the case of *Kelley v. R.G. Indus.*,[62] ruled that the plaintiff must establish that the product (handgun) itself was defective at the time it left the possession of the seller. Since the handgun did not malfunction, strict liability was held inapplicable, and its misuse was irrelevant. This court did, however, make an exception for "Saturday night specials."

In the *Riordan* case,[63] the plaintiffs brought wrongful death actions against the manufacturer and the distributor of handguns, arising out of deaths caused by third-party criminals. The court ruled that the defendants owed no duty to control the distribution of handguns that it manufactured, that the sale of the guns did not constitute ultrahazardous activity, and that the guns were not defectively made.

A comprehensive and important decision, previously mentioned,[64] discusses many aspects of handgun liability. Ordinarily, if there is no defect of any kind in a handgun, the manufacturer is not liable for injury caused by its improper use by a purchaser, especially since Maryland statutes permit persons to possess and carry handguns in certain instances. This follows Restatement (Second) of Torts, § 402A, adopted by the Maryland courts.

As has already been noted, this court did state, however, that Saturday night specials were clearly not sanctioned as a matter of public policy. Such handguns were, in this decision, described as having short barrels, being of light weight, easily concealable, made of cheap quality materials, of proof manufacture, unreliable, and low in cost. These characteristics, the court went on to state, render them particularly attractive for criminal use and make them virtually useless for legitimate purposes. This court also noted that the federal Gun Control Act of 1968 prohibits the importation of Saturday night specials. It further admitted that apparently no other jurisdiction has either distinguished between Saturday night specials and handguns in general, or has expressly refused to make such a distinction. It further stated that a handgun should never be designated as a Saturday night special as a matter of law, since distinctions (such as its own?) are relative.

Finally, the court ruled that once a trier of fact determines that a handgun is a Saturday night special, liability may be imposed

---

[62] 497 A.2d 1143 (1985).
[63] Riordan v. International Armament Corp., 477 N.E.2d 1291 (Ill. App. 1985).
[64] Kelley v. R.G. Indus., 497 A.2d 1143 (Md. App. 1985).

against a manufacturer or anyone else in the marketing chain. The shooting must be a criminal act and neither contributory negligence nor assumption of risk will be recognized as defenses and the plaintiff must not have been a participant in the criminal activity.[65]

The Supreme Court of Oregon, on the other hand, ruled that the design, manufacture, sale and marketing of a small, easily concealable handgun does not constitute abnormally dangerous activity rendering the manufacturer strictly liable for injuries suffered by an individual who was shot during a jail escape.[66]

[10] Subsequent Modification or Repair

In many instances, a manufacturer may want to make a design change in a product, or in its assembling, either by way of correction, to make it safer, or as a matter of improved performance, after an accident. In such a situation, the manufacturer may be reluctant to do so for fear that evidence of such a change might be construed by a jury in a subsequent case as a defect in the former design or assembly of the product.

Since it has also been held that failure to make a change when a defect has been called to the attention of the manufacturer may be interpreted as evidence of a disregard for the health or welfare of prospective customers, the manufacturer is caught between the frying pan and the fire.

§ 31.03 Federal Rules of Evidence

Rule 407 of the Federal Rules of Evidence holds that:

> When, after an event, measures are taken which, if taken previously, would have made the event less likely to occur, evidence of subsequent measures is not admissable to prove negligence or culpable conduct in connection with the event.

---

[65] *See also* Turley & Harrison, "Strict Tort Liability of Handgun Suppliers," 6 Hamline L. Rev. 285 (1983).

[66] Burkett v. Freedom Arms, Inc., 704 P.2d 118 (Ore. 1985). This case cited the following cases in support:
Cal.: Martin v. Harrington & Richardson, 743 F.2d 1200 (1984).
Ill.: Riordon v. International Armamment Corp., 447 N.E.2d 1293 (Ill. App. 1985).
See also Note, "Handgun and Products Liability," 97 Harv. L. Rev. 1219 (1984).

PRODUCTS LIABILITY—DEFENSES § 31.05

The notes of the Advisory Committee to Rule 407 state that the grounds for exclusion rests "on social policy of encouraging people to take, or at least not discourage them from taking, steps in furtherance of added safety."[67] However, Rule 407 applies to actions based on negligence, and some courts have ruled that it does not apply to actions brought in strict liability.[68]

Just as many cases, if not more, however, do not so interpret Rule 407 and hold that Rule 407 is effective to bar such evidence in cases brought in strict liability.[69]

Ordinarily, when there is a conflict between a state ruling and Rule 407 in a products liability action, the state rule will control.

§ 31.04 Post-Settlement Problems

Settlement of a products liability case involving an alleged design defect can leave a manufacturer in a position of jeopardy in the future. The fact that a suit was previously filed against the manufacturer will be subject to discovery, and this is a serious consideration. Failure to disclose facts in a discovery proceeding, involving a previous claim or suit, may constitute grounds for reversal and the granting of a new trial.[70]

§ 31.05 Changes in Standards

There is a difference of opinion concerning the admission of evi-

---

[67] *See* Tish & Reams, "Does Rule 407 Apply to Strict Liability Actions?", F.T.D., October 1984.

[68] Robbins v. Farmers Union Grain Term. Ass'n, 552 F.2d 788 (8th Cir. 1980); Unterberger v. Snow Co., 630 F.2d 599 (8th Cir. 1980); Herndon v. Seven Bar Flying Service, Inc., 716 F.2d 1322 (10th Cir. 1983).

[69] Grenada Steel Indus., Inc., v. Alabama Oxygen Co., 695 F.2d 883 (5th Cir. 1983); Werner v. Upjohn Co., 628 F.2d 848 (4th Cir. 1980); Roy v. Star Chopper Co., 584 F.2d 1124 (1st Cir. 1978); Josephs v. Harris Corp., 677 F.2d 915 (3d Cir. 1982); Hill v. American Steamship Co., 688 F.2d 1062 (6th Cir. 1982).

[70] **Kan.:** Powers v. Kansas Power & Light Co., 671 P.2d 491 (1983).
Ky.: Rhodes v. Michelin Tire Corp., 542 F. Supp. 60 (1982).
Mo.: In re Multi-Piece Rims Product Liability Litigation, 545 F. Supp. 149 (1982).
Wash.: Gammon v. Clark Equip. Co., 686 P.2d 1102 (1984).
U.S.: Robinson v. Audi, 739 F.2d 1481 (10th Cir. 1984); Weeks v. Remington Arms Co., 733 F.2d 1485 (11th Cir. 1984); Rexrode v. American Laundry Press Co., 674 F.2d 826 (10th Cir. 1982).

dence that standardized codes for the manufacture or assembling of a product have been changed after an accident.[71]

§ 31.06 "Market Share" Liability and Similar Theories

"Market share" liability came into prominence in the case of *Sindell v. Abbott Labs.*,[72] when a suit was brought in strict liability against eleven drug companies on behalf of a group of women who had allegedly suffered injurious consequences as a result of in utero exposure to DES, used to prevent miscarriage. The plaintiff was unable to identify which company had manufactured the particular drug that her mother had used and sued all of the identifiable manufacturers of the drug.

In a detailed opinion, the California Supreme Court listed and evaluated three exceptions to the general rule that the plaintiffs were required to prove that their injuries were caused by an act of a specific defendant, as follows:

1. *Alternative liability,* addressed in Section 433 B, subsection 3 of the Restatement (Second) of Torts to the effect that:

   Where the conduct of two or more actors is tortious, and it is proved that harm has been caused to the plaintiff by only one of them, but there is uncertainty as to which one had caused it, the burden is upon each actor to prove that he has not caused the harm.

The fact in this case was that *all* the parties that could have been responsible for the harm were not joined as party defendants.

Alternative liability addresses the causation problem. Although it involves conduct by more than one defendant, the conduct of one must have caused the injury. The burden of proof (the attribution requirement) shifts to each defendant to prove it has not caused the injury. In this particular case, *all* of the parties that could have been responsible for the harm were not joined as party defendants.

---

[71] *See* "Post-Accident Revisions to Standards," F.T.D. August 8, 1982, in which is listed Hassan v. Stafford, 472 F.2d 88 (3d Cir. 1973) and Lambertson v. Cincinnati Corp., 257 S.W.2d 679 (Minn. 1979). In both cases, the court refused to permit introduction of evidence concerning a change in standards promulgated after the accident. In another case, Scott v. Dreis & Krump Mfg. Co., 326 N.E.2d 74 (Ill. App. 1975), such evidence was deemed admissible.

[72] 607 P.2d 924, *cert. denied,* 449 U.S. 912 (1980).

PRODUCTS LIABILITY—DEFENSES § 31.06

2. *Concert of action* theory as stated in Section 876 of the Restatement (Second) of Torts, which holds:

For harm resulting to a third person from the tortious conduct of another, one is subjected to liability if he:

(a) does a tortious act in concert with the other or pursuant to a common design with him, or

(b) knows the other's conduct constitutes a breach of duty and gives substantial assistance or encouragement to the other so to conduct himself, or

(c) gives substantial assistance to the other in accomplishing a tortious result, and his own conduct, separately considered, constitutes a breach of duty to the third person.

3. *Enterprise liability* or, as this court puts it, *industry-wide* liability. In this situation, the industry-wide practices become the cause of the plaintiff's injury.

The court rejected this approach because of the large number of possible defendants in DES cases against the small number involved in the *Sindell* case.

This decision also held that a plaintiff need only join a sufficient number of manufacturers to represent a "substantial share" of the market, after which the burden of proof shifts to each manufacturer to exculpate itself by showing that it could not have supplied the drug (DES). Those unable to do so were liable for only the proportion of damages represented by its share of the market.

In *Cousineau v. Ford Motor Co.*,[73] the court found the "concert of action" theory applicable if the plaintiff can prove that the defendants acted tortiously in furtherance of a common design and that such action was the proximate cause of the injury.

In the *Sindell* case,[74] the court, having ruled out all three approaches to imposing liability, then fashioned still another doctrine, called it "market share" liability and rationalized it by stating that "in the light of an increasingly complex industrial society, it is virtually impossible to trace fungible goods harmful to consumers, to a specific producer," and decided that "some adaptation of the rules of causation and liability" are accordingly called for.

---

[73] 363 N.W.2d 721 (Mich. App. 1985).
[74] Sindell v. Abbott Labs., 607 P.2d 924, *cert. denied,* 449 U.S. 912 (1980).

§ 31.06

The court was, in my opinion, obviously looking for a "deep pocket" and this is typical of the rationalizations of so many courts today that come to a conclusion which they then try to justify, even when they practically prove, in the process, that their conclusion was not legally logical, as Justice Richardson so ably demonstrated in his dissent.[75]

Most cases decided since *Sindell*[76] have relied on traditional tort concepts in denying relief to the plaintiffs on the basis of market share liability.[77]

Some jurisdictions, however, did adopt some form of market share liability.[78]

The Supreme Court of Florida, in a thorough and well thought-out decision,[79] ruled that the market share theory of proximate liability was inappropriate where an asbestos worker was able to identify several of the manufacturers that supplied asbestos to which he was exposed. The court stated that:

---

[75] *See* Hirsch, "Market Share Liability for Manufacturers," F.T.D., October 1980.
[76] *Supra,* note 74.
[77] **Cal.:** In re Related Asbestos Cases, 543 F. Supp. 1152 (1982).
 D.C.: Tidler v. Eli Lilly & Co., 95 F.R.D. 332 (1982).
 Fla.: Conley v. Boyle Drug Co., 477 So. 2d 600 (1985); Morton v. Abbott Labs., 538 F. Supp. 594 (1982); Celotex Corp. v. Copeland, 471 So. 2d 533 (1985) (market share theory inappropriate if asbestos manufacturers are identifiable).
 Ga.: Starling v. Seaboard Coast Line R. Co., 533 F. Supp. 183 (1982).
 Iowa: Mulcahy v. Eli Lilly & Co., 386 N.W.2d 67 (1986).
 La.: Hannon v. Waterman Steamship Corp., 567 F. Supp. 90 (1983).
 Mass.: Payton v. Abbott Labs., 512 F. Supp. 1031 (1980).
 Minn.: Mason v. Spiegel, Inc., 610 F. Supp. 401 (1985).
 Mo.: Zafft v. Eli Lilly & Co., 676 S.W.2d 241 (1984).
 N.J.: Namm v. Chas. E. Frost & Co., 427 A.2d 1121 (1980), *but see* Ferrigno v. Eli Lilly & Co., 420 A.2d 1305 (1980).
 Pa.: Prelick v. Johns-Manville Corp., 531 F. Supp. 96 (1982); Klein v. Council of Chem. Assoc's., 587 F. Supp. 213 (1984).
 S.C.: Ryan v. Eli Lilly & Co., 514 F. Supp. 1004 (1980).
[78] **Mich.:** Abel v. Eli Lilly & Co., 343 N.W.2d 164 (1984) (allegations sufficient to support "concert of action" and "alternate liability").
 N.J.: Ferrigno v. Eli Lilly & Co., 430 A.2d 1305 (1980), *but see* Namm v. Chas. E. Frost & Co., 427 A.2d 1121 (1981).
 N.Y.: Bichler v. Eli Lilly & Co., 436 N.Y.S.2d 625 (App. 1980) (court basically accepted "concert of action" theory).
 S.D.: McElhaney v. Eli Lilly & Co., 564 F. Supp. 265 (1983) (alternate liability adopted).
 Wis.: Collins v. Eli Lilly & Co., 342 N.W.2d 37, *cert. denied,* 469 U.S. 826 (1984).
 See also Hirsch, "Identifying the Generic Product: Market Share and Related Theories of Liability," F.T.D., May 20, 1983.
[79] Celotex v. Copeland, 471 So. 2d 533 (1985).

PRODUCTS LIABILITY—DEFENSES § 31.07

It is important to note that there are inherent differences between asbestos products and the drug DES, for which the market share theory was developed, which further make the market share theory extremely difficult in asbestos-injury cases. DES was produced by hundreds of companies pursuant to one formula. As a result, all DES had identical physical properties and chemical compositions and, consequently, all DES prescribed to pregnant women created the same risk of harm to the women's female offspring.

The court went on to point out that the asbestos cases were entirely different since asbestos products are made up of different physical characteristics and content of asbestos fibers, and since the asbestos cases are confined to only a relatively few companies.

§ 31.07 Successor Corporations

A manufacturer that acquires the business of another, and continues to produce the same product as its predecessor, generally speaking, assumes liability for defects in that product.[80]

The Washington Supreme Court adopted what it called the *Ray* rule,[81] under which a court must determine:

(1) whether the successor has acquired substantially all the predecessor's assets, leaving no more than a mere corporate shell,[82]

(2) whether the successor is holding itself out to the general public as a continuation of the predecessor by producing the same product line under a similar name, and

(3) whether the successor is benefitting from the good will of the predecessor.

To which *I* might add:

(4) any legally enforceable terms in any agreement between the predecessor and the successor corporations,

(5) continuity of officers, directors, shareholders or management personnel, in the successor corporation, and

---

[80] Martin v. Abbott Labs., 689 P.2d 368 (Wash. 1984).
[81] Ray v. Alad Vorp., 560 P.2d 3 (Cal. 1977).
[82] *See* Kline v. Johns-Manville, 745 F.2d 1217 (1984).

(6) if fraud was involved to escape such liability.[83]

Under the "product line" theory, developed by the court in *Ray v. Alad,* [84] "the broad and sweeping principles of social policy which underlie this theory look primarily to the availability of a remedy . . . and implicitly to the location of a 'deep pocket' to furnish the remedy."[85]

In a case involving a table saw, the court held that since the new corporation never manufactured or sold such a product, there was no continuity of liability.[86]

The court, in *Hickman v. Thomas C. Thompson Co.,* [87] stated that:

> The traditional general rule of successor liability, as adopted in Colorado, provides for non-liability on the part of a successor corporation. The risk of loss falls upon the injured party in the breach of contract or tortious injury case. The rule is solely based on corporation and contract law. This rule provides as follows:
>
> "where one company sells or otherwise transfers all assets to another company the latter is not liable for the debts and liabilities of the transferor, except where: (1) the purchaser expressly or impliedly agrees to assume such debts; (2) the transaction amounts to a consolidation or merger of the seller and purchaser; (3) the purchasing corporation is merely a continuation of the selling corporation; or (4) the transaction is entered into fraudulently in order to escape liability for such debts."[88]

This court went on to state that:

> A number of jurisdictions are moving away from the strict corporations and contract view of successor liability. These states have adopted the so called product line exception to the general rule. See *Ray v. Alad Corp.,* 19 Cal. 3d 22, 560 P.2d 3, 136 Cal. Rptr. 574 (1977); *Ramirez v. Amsted Industries, Inc.,* 86 N.J. 332, 431 A.2d 811 (1981); *Dawejko*

---

[83] Ala.: Rivers v. Stihl, Inc., 434 So. 2d 766 (1983).
Fla.: Kelly v. American Precision Indus., 438 So. 2d 29 (App. 1983).
Ill.: Gonzales v. Rock Wool Eng'g & Equip. Co., 453 N.E.2d 792 (1983).
Iowa: Weaver v. Nash Int'l, Inc., 562 F. Supp. 860 (1983).
Mich.: Fenton Area Public Schools v. Sorensen-Gross Constr. Co., 335 N.W.2d 221 (1983).

[84] 560 P.2d 3 (Cal. 1977).

[85] *See also* Dawejko v. Jorgensen Steel Co., 434 A.2d 106 (1981) which rejected both theories on behalf of a case-by-case approach.

[86] Bullington v. Union Tool Corp., 328 S.E.2d 726 (Ga. 1985).

[87] 592 F. Supp. 1282 (1984).

[88] *Id.* at 1283-84.

v. Jorgensen Steel Co., 290 Pa. Super. 15, 434 A.2d 106 (1981). The product line exception provides:

> "That where one corporation acquires all or substantially all the manufacturing assets of another corporation, even if exclusively for cash, and undertakes the same manufacturer's operation as the selling corporation, the purchasing corporation is strictly liable for injuries caused by defects in units of the same product line, even if previously manufactured and distributed by the selling corporation or its predecessor."[89]

[1] Punitive Damages Against Successor Corporations

Once again, there is a difference of opinion. It has been held that a successor corporation is not liable for punitive damages to persons injured by asbestos materials manufactured by its predecessor because (1) punitive damages are a windfall to a plaintiff, not a part of a remedy for his injury, (2) punitive damages could seriously deplete successor's assets, (3) possible lack of insurance, and (4) liability for defective products is sufficient assumption of the burden that runs with the predecessor's good will.[90]

The Supreme Court of Florida, in *Celotex Corp. v. Pickett*,[91] ruled that a successor corporation, pursuant to Florida's merger statute, succeeds to "all of the duties and liabilities" of the predecessor corporation and may be held liable for punitive damages in a product liability action involving a product manufactured by the predecessor corporation.

§ 31.08 Statutes of Limitations or Repose

The rationale for the tolling of statutes of limitation or repose in products liability suits are as varied as the products themselves. The reasoning in asbestos or DES cases is of necessity, different from that concerning products that are implanted or inserted permanently, or at least for a long time period, for the purpose of preserving or enhancing life. Both are different from a situation involving an external danger resulting from an unknown design defect which is again dif-

---

[89] *Id.* at 1284.
[90] In re Related Asbestos Cases, 566 F. Supp. 818 (Cal. 1983). *See also* "Ten Rules for Acquiring Corporate Assets Without Successor Liability," F.T.D., July 1982; Ware, "Recent Development in the Law of Successor Products Liability," 19 F.T.D. 95, June 1978; Liebo, "Products: Successor Liability," F.T.D., February 6, 1984.
[91] 490 So. 2d 35 (Fla. 1986).

ferent from a manufacturing defect that resulted from carelessness in its manufacture.

Accordingly, the subject of statutes of limitations in products liability cases has, in some instances, been dealt with in discussing the subjects of "occurrence versus claims-made" policies, as well as within this discussion of products liability. In addition, there is much difference as to actions brought in warranty as against those brought in negligence or strict liability.

Recently statutes of limitations or repose have also been enacted in many states specifically directed at products liability and their constitutionality is constantly being tested in the courts with mixed results.[92]

[1] Statutes of Repose

According to Thomas J. Dennis:[93]

> Courts are inconsistent and imprecise in their use of the term "statute of repose." The term has no standard definition, and several definitions are currently in use. Generally though, it can be said that these statutes (of repose) set a designated event for the statutory period to start running and they provide that at the expiration of the period, any cause of action is barred regardless of the usual reasons for tolling.[94]

"Statutes of repose are analytically similar to traditional tort statutes of limitation," and we will so treat them for the purposes of this discussion.[95]

[2] Implantations or Insertions

With respect to products that are implanted or inserted into the body, but not assimilated by it, and where such products have a continuing function (such as pacemakers or penile implants), some cases have held that the statute of limitations runs from the time of implantation or insertion of the device.[96] Other courts hold that the statute

---

[92] *See* Dennis, "Products Liability Statutes of Repose as Conflicting with State Constitutions: The Plaintiffs Are Winning," 26 Ariz. L. Rev. 363-76 (1984).
[93] *Id.*
[94] *See* Restatement (Second) of Torts § 889 comment g (1979).
[95] *See* Dennis, *supra* note 92.
[96] *See* Martin v. Edwards Labs., 60 N.Y.2d 417, 457 N.E.2d 1150, 469 N.Y.S.2d 923 (1983).

PRODUCTS LIABILITY—DEFENSES § 31.08[2]

runs from the time injury or harm is discovered from the breakdown of the product.[97]

In the case of *Martin v. Edwards Labs,*[98] the court made what I believe is a fair analysis of the concept involved in implant cases by stating:

> In the instant cases, we deal with products intended to be implanted or inserted in, but not to be assimilated by, the human body, and there to remain, until removed for repair or other reason, in order to perform a continuing function. There is no need on the recipient's side of the equation for a discovery rule as in foreign objects cases, for the implantation or insertion is with the recipient's knowledge and consent; knowledge which he or she can pass on to a physician seeking to diagnose the cause of later developing bodily problems and which, under normal circumstances, will include instructions concerning when repairs may be required or replacement parts have to be inserted. But, on the other hand, to protect the manufacturer by a date of insertion or implantation rule is both unrealistic and unnecessary. In the inhaled, ingested or injected substances cases in which such a rule does apply, the forces of harm are inexorably set in motion when the substance enters and is assimilated into the body. An implanted or inserted device intended to perform a continuing function, to the contrary, causes no injury until the product malfunctions. Until that time, the recipient, like the remote user . . . has no cause to complain. If through malfunction the product is thought to have caused harm, it can in most cases be removed and examined to ascertain whether in fact it malfunctioned and, if so, whether that was the cause of the harm. Thus, again like the remote user situation . . ., the age of the claim is no greater disadvantage to the manufacturer than it is to the recipient. Credibility thus plays a lesser part in the determination of the claim than it does with assimilated substances, and though complicated medical questions may be involved and professional diagnostic judgment implicated, that normally will concern only recent events rather than the remote implantation. Moreover, because of the availability of the product, the danger of feigned or frivolous claims will no much less.
>
> We conclude therefore, that the proper rule to be applied with respect to products implanted or inserted . . . is neither the time of implantation . . . nor the time of discovery (but is the) "date of injury rule," which will most often be the date when the product malfunctions.

---

[97] **N.Y.:** Victorson v. Bock Laundry Mach. Co., 37 N.Y.2d 395, 335 N.E.2d 275, 373 N.Y.S.2d 39 (1975); Martin v. Edwards Labs, *supra* note 96, which concluded after discussing the reasoning on both sides, that the statute begins to run with the injury-causing malfunction of the product.

[98] *Supra,* note 96.

§ 31.09 Service versus Product

Some courts have applied strict liability where a plaintiff is injured by a defective product even though it was supplied in the course of the performance of a commercial or professional service.[99]

Other courts have been reticent in applying the theory of strict liability to situations where the sale of a tangible product was not involved, nor was the service performed by a professional.[100]

If the defective service did not involve a defective product, most courts have not permitted recovery under strict liability.[101]

A hospital and a radiation technician were not held liable for radiation burns resulting from cobalt therapy under the doctrine of strict liability since the therapy was a service rather than a product.[102]

---

[99] **N.J.:** Newmark v. Gimbels, Inc., 258 A.2d 697 (1969) (case involved a defective permanent wave solution applied by a hairdresser).
Wash.: Carpenter v. Best's Apparel, Inc., 481 P.2d 924 (1971).
[100] *See* Goodman, "Strict Liability and the Professional Service Transaction," Insurance Counsel Journal, April 1983.
[101] **Alas.:** Pepsi Cola Bottling Co. v. Superior Burner Service, 427 P.2d 833 (1967).
Ill.: Jeffreys v. Hickman, 269 N.E.2d 110 (1971).
Tex.: Barbee v. Rogers, 425 S.W.2d 342 (1968).
Wis.: Hoven v. Kebble, 256 N.W.2d 379 (1977).
[102] Nevauex v. Park Place Hosp., 656 S.W.2d 923 (Tex. App. 1983).

CHAPTER 32

Products Liability—Punitive Damages

§ 32.01 Punitive Damages
    [1] Multiple Exposure
    [2] First Come, First Served
    [3] Justification for Punitive Damages
    [4] Phraseology Used in Justifying Punitive Damage Awards
    [5] Settlement of Underlying Suit
    [6] Collateral Estoppel
    [7] Wrongful Death Statutes
    [8] Strict Liability
    [9] Negligence as a Basis for Awarding Punitive Damages
    [10] Breach of Warranty
    [11] Insurance for Punitive Damages
    [12] Amounts Awarded—Model Uniform Products Liability Act

§ 32.01 Punitive Damages

[1] Multiple Exposure

In the case of *Maxey v. Freightliner Corp.*,[1] the court pointed out the effect of multiple exposure to punitive damage awards of the manufacturer, stating that even if each jury in a products case will faithfully follow the applicable legal principles "it is the aggregate effect of the following juries that poses the risk of ultimate destruction," to the manufacturer.

While there is no doubt that the wrongdoing involved in many of the products liability suits that resulted in the awarding of punitive damages has been of such a nature as to warrant criminal prosecution, the cumulative effect of such verdicts in civil suits in multiple products liability claims may do injury and harm to many innocent people, including employees and stockholders.

Even under our present system, it has been said that

---

[1] 450 F. Supp. 955, *aff'd*, 623 F.2d 395 (5th Cir. 1980).

Justice requires that limits be placed on punishment; that one jury's mulct should be enough; that the windfall of punitive damages designed originally to punish once, be limited to its original purpose. Justice requires that when society has punished once by criminal sanctions, society should be content. It should not demand or permit successive punishment by the device of punitive damages.[2]

In the case of *Roginsky v. Richardson Merrell, Inc.*,[3] the court said that the possibility of multiple suits and even class actions for substantial compensatory damages would be deterrent enough without having the defendant face multiple punitive damage actions in addition to the compensatory verdicts.

On the other hand, where the manufacturer did not correct the defect in subsequent sales of the product, it appears obvious that the previous verdicts and awards did not act as a deterrent to future misconduct.[4] The court further reasoned that even if a manufacturer has discontinued production of a defective product, there is no guarantee that his greed will change his practice of putting the profit motive ahead of any public considerations.[5]

Well and good, but such statements apply to punitive damages in general. Punishment should benefit the general public and criminal prosecution should result in meaningful fines that would go into the general coffers that could benefit society as a whole. They should not be in the form of an individual windfall to the claimant who has presumably already been compensated adequately by compensatory and consequential damages.

In addition, the legal cost of defending multiple suits can be devastating to the defendant, and while consolidation has been attempted in some jurisdictions, it has not been very successful for obviously self-interested reasons. Where such consolidation has been attempted in state courts, the plaintiffs have usually moved to have the case placed under federal jurisdiction, resulting in even more suits.[6]

In the federal circuit court case of *Cathey v. Johns-Manville Sales*

---

[2] Tozer, "Punitive Damages and Products Liability," 39 Insurance Counsel Journal 300 (1972).

[3] 378 F.2d 832 (2d Cir. 1967).

[4] **Minn.:** Gryce v. Dayton-Hudson Corp., 297 N.W.2d 727 (1979).

[5] *See also* **Alas.:** Sturm, Ruger & Co. v. Day, 594 P.2d 38 (1979).
Minn.: Gryce v. Dayton-Hudson Corp., 297 N.W.2d 38 (1979).

[6] Ghiardi & Kircher, "Punitive Damage Recovery in Products Liability Cases," 65 Marq. L. Rev. 34 (Fall 1981).

Corp.,[7] decided under Tennessee law, the court stated that the danger that repeated awards of large sums for punitive damages would exhaust the resources of defendants and insurers, depriving future litigants of a source of compensatory recoveries was noted, but the court did not believe that such "public policy" concerns present a proper basis to limit punitive damages. This court also held that the imposition of multiple awards for punitive damages in asbestos cases did not violate due process.

[2] First Come, First Served

There is no law regulating punitive damage claims or suits by successive plaintiffs, even though all claimants have been injured in the same way by the same product.[8]

In discussing this subject, in the case of *Roginsky v. Richardson-Merrell*,[9] the court stated that it does not seem either fair or practical to limit punitive damage recoveries to "an indeterminate number of first-comers, leaving it to some unascertained court to cry 'hold-enough,' in the hope that others would follow." In the same opinion, the court also stated that there is "grave difficulty in perceiving how claims for punitive damages in such multiplicity of actions throughout the nation can be so administered as to avoid overkill."

Nevertheless, that is exactly where the situation seems to stand at the present time, with no practical solution in sight.

[3] Justification for Punitive Damages

Prosser & Keeton on Torts, quoting from the Restatement (Second) of Torts, state that punitive damages are awarded when the defendant's behavior amounts to intentional or malicious wrongdoing or where there was a conscious or reckless disregard for the safety of others. Similar wording has been expressed by many courts to justify the awarding of punitive damages, but in noting the actual facts that have been held to be "malicious conduct" or "conscious disregard

---

[7] 776 F.2d 1565 (6th Cir. 1985).

[8] Greenberg, "Punitive Damages in Mass-Marketed Products Litigation," 14 Loy. L.A.L. Rev. 405 (1981).

[9] 378 F.2d 832 (2d Cir. 1967).

of the safety of others," it would be naive indeed to think that the dictionary limitations on these words have any real effect on many of our courts and juries.[10]

After discussing the subject and the cases involved at great length, Professor Owens sums it up by stating:

> Indeed, misbehavior akin to negligence and misbehavior deserving of punitive damages are similar in products liability cases in that both expose consumers to unreasonable risk of harm. Two additional elements are necessary however, before a manufacturer's exposure of consumers to such risks may appropriately be punished by a punitive damage award. First, the manufacturer must be either aware of, or culpably indifferent to an unnecessary risk of injury, Second, knowing that its product is or might be excessively dangerous, the manufacturer must intransigently refuse either to determine the seriousness of the danger or to reduce it to an acceptable level.[11]

It has been held, for instance, that pre-marketing knowledge of the dangerous propensities of a product, coupled with a failure to warn consumers or reduce the hazard, justified the awarding of punitive damages.[12]

Post-marketing knowledge of product-related injuries together with a failure to warn consumers, recall the product, develop more accurate safety tests, or correct the defect have also been held sufficient to warrant the awarding of punitive damage verdicts.[13]

An Ohio court ruled that a jury may determine whether a manufacturer's indifference to consumer risks was flagrant enough to justi-

---

[10] G.D. Searle & Co. v. Superior Court, 122 Cal. Rptr. 218 (1975) (malice was implied from a "conscious disregard for the safety of others").

[11] Owen, "Punitive Damages in Products Liability Litigation," 74 Mich. L. Rev. 1257 (June 1976).

[12] **Cal.:** Grimshaw v. Ford Motor Co., 174 Cal. Rptr. 348 (1981), *but see* Magallanes v. Superior Court (E.R. Squibb), 213 Cal. Rptr. 574 (App. 1985).
Ill.: Moore v. Jewel Tea Co., 253 N.E.2d 636 (1969), *aff'd,* 263 N.E.2d 103 (1970).
Minn.: Gryce v. Dayton-Hudson Corp., 297 N.W.2d 727 (1969).

[13] **Alas.:** Sturm, Ruger & Co. v. Day, 594 P.2d 38 (1979) (defectively designed handgun).
Ill.: Moore v. Jewel Tea Co., 253 N.E.2d 636 (1969), *aff'd,* 263 N.E.2d 103 (1970) (defendant was aware of numerous injuries caused by the defective product).
Minn.: Gryce v. Dayton-Hudson Corp., 297 N.W.2d 727 (1969) (manufacturer was aware of injuries caused by flammable material in clothing).
Mo.: Rinker v. Ford Motor Co., 567 S.W.2d 655 (App. 1978) (manufacturer knew of numerous accidents caused by the defective product).

fy an award of punitive damages.[14] Thereafter, a federal circuit court followed suit and stated that juries should be at liberty to weigh the gravity of harm against the onerousness of the manufacturer's failures. This court also made the rather peculiar statement that while actual malice is not essential in order to justify the awarding of punitive damages, evidence of malice must be shown.[15]

[4] Phraseology Used in Justifying Punitive Damage Awards

Phraseology used by the judiciary to justify the awarding of punitive damages in products liability cases include: "conscious or reckless disregard for the safety, welfare or rights of customers";[16] "willful and wanton conduct";[17] "malice, oppression or ill-will";[18] "outrageous conduct";[19] and clearly defined standard;[20] but, I wonder if this is even possible.

When there is a situation that is so flagrant that the facts speak for themselves, as in the case of *Toole v. Richardson-Merrell, Inc.*,[21] the actual wrongdoing will fit into any and all of the categories used by the courts. In that case, the defendant drug manufacturer distributed a drug called ME/29 to about 400,000 users, through the usual channels. Complaints started to come in almost immediately concerning dangerous side effects, including the development of cataracts. The evidence indicated that the defendant knew of the poten-

---

[14] Leichtamer v. American Motors Corp., 424 N.E.2d 568 (1981).
[15] Moran v. Johns-Manville Sales Corp., 691 F.2d 811 (6th Cir. Ohio 1982).
[16] **Alas.:** Sturm, Ruger & Co. v. Day, 594 P.2d 38 (1979).
  Ill.: Moore v. Jewel Tea Co., 253 N.E.2d 636 (1969) (Drano can exploded. Defendant had knowledge of such a possibility and could have corrected the defect by installing an excess pressure release).
  Minn.: Gryce v. Dayton-Hudson Corp., 297 N.W.2d 727 (1979) (testing procedure inadequate).
  Mo.: Rinker v. Ford Motor Co., 567 S.W.2d 655 (1978).
  Wis.: Wangen v. Ford Motor Co., 294 N.W.2d 437 (1980).
  U.S.: Gillham v. Admiral Corp., 523 F.2d 102 (6th Cir. 1975); d'Hedouville v. Pioneer Hotel, 552 F.2d 886 (1977).
[17] **Ill.:** Moore v. Jewel Tea Co., 253 N.E.2d 636 (1969).
  Ohio.: Gillham v. Admiral Corp., 523 F.2d 102 (6th Cir. 1975).
[18] **Cal.:** Toole v. Richardson-Merrell, Inc., 60 Cal. Rptr. 398 (1967); G.S. Searle v. Superior Court, 122 Cal. Rptr. 218 (1975).
  Hi.: Volert v. Summar Corp., 398 F. Supp. 134 (1975).
[19] **Alas.:** Sturm, Ruger & Co. v. Day, 594 P.2d 38 (1979).
  Wis.: Wangen v. Ford Motor Co., 294 N.W.2d 437 (1980).
[20] Owen, *supra* note 11, at 1365.
[21] 60 Cal. Rptr. 398 (1967).

tial danger even before marketing the product. Previous tests had all shown dangerous side effects. The defendant altered the test conclusions and lied in its report to the F.D.A. It also advertised to doctors that the drug was "virtually nontoxic" and remarkably free of side effects. Continued complaints had no effect on the manufacturer and the product was only withdrawn after the F.D.A. made a surprise investigation and confiscated the actual test records.

No amount of punishment is too great for such outrageous (and I use the word advisedly) behavior and it fits into any condemnatory wording that can be used.

Generally speaking, however, such wording as "wilfull and wanton" and similar verbiage give little assistance to honest, humane manufacturers who strive to produce a good, safe product. In additions, such loose language permits uncaring manufacturers to find avenues of doubt sufficient to let them squeeze by in some courts.

The recent Manville cases are a good example of the gray area where the same kind of judicial language resulted in defendant's verdicts or no cause of action in about 40 percent of the cases tried, according to the defendant's own figures. In other cases, the verdicts ranged all over the lot, from very insufficient to highly exorbitant.

Nevertheless, taking some of Professor Owen's guidelines as a starting point, the following failures and violations have been used to justify the awarding of punitive damages:

1. Deliberate violation of safety standards set by federal and/or state regulatory bodies and federal acts or state statutes.[22]
2. Failure to correct a known defect.[23]
3. Failure to warn about known danger or to recall the defective product.[24]
4. Deliberate concealment of known defects or dangers.[25]
5. Inadequate testing or quality control.[26]

---

[22] Owen, "Punitive Damages in Products Liability Litigation," 74 Mich. L. Rev. 1335 (June 1976).

[23] Braniff Airways, Inc. v. Curtiss-Wright Corp., 411 F.2d 451 (1969); Hoffman v. Sterling Drug, Inc., 485 F.2d 132 (1973).

[24] Cal.: Toole v. Richardson-Merrell, Inc., 60 Cal. Rptr. 398 (1967).
Pa.: Hoffman v. Sterling Drug, Inc., 485 F.2d 132 (1973).

[25] Cal.: Toole v. Richardson-Merrell, Inc., 60 Cal. Rptr. 398 (1967).
N.Y.: Roginsky v. Richardson-Merrell, Inc., 378 F.2d 832 (2d Cir. 1967).

[26] *Id.* cases cited in notes 23-25 *supra.*

PRODUCTS LIABILITY—PUNITIVE DAMAGES § 32.01[6]

6. Improper design, where proper design was reasonably possible and feasible.[27]
7. Improper or deficient labeling on dangerous products.[28]
8. Misleading advertising that fails to warn of known danger.
9. Failure to give correct instructions or warn of possible dangers where deficient manuals or instructions are given on products that require detailed instructions.[29]

[5] Settlement of Underlying Suit

It has been held that punitive damages constitute only one of a variety of remedies that a plaintiff can recover, each in its own right. Accordingly, if settlement is made in satisfaction of a claim for compensatory damages, the remaining, or additional action for punitive damages may be continued separately, so long as the underlying cause of action continues to exist.[30] If, however, no compensatory, or only nominal compensatory damages have been awarded, there should be no recovery for punitive damages.[31] To find otherwise, again, seems to me to be completely illogical and contradictory, despite the fact that several jurisdictions have permitted awards for punitive damages in similar circumstances.[32]

[6] Collateral Estoppel

In jurisdictions where standards similar to those discussed above apply for the awarding of punitive damages, it has been held that a conclusive previous judgment may be asserted in a subsequent suit

---

[27] **Cal.:** Sabich v. Outboard Marine Corp., 131 Cal. Rptr. 703 (1976) (verdict for $600,000 compensatory and $1,254,000 punitive damages reversed on erroneous instruction by trial court).
Ill.: Moore v. Jewel Tea Co., 253 N.E.2d 636 (1969).
[28] **Ill.:** Moore v. Jewel Tea Co., 253 N.E.2d 636 (1969).
[29] Kritser v. Beech Aircraft Corp., 479 F.2d 1089 (5th Cir. 1973) (punitive damage award denied by judge); Hoffman v. Sterling Drug, Inc., 485 F.2d 132 (3d Cir. 1973).
[30] **Fla.:** Stephenson v. Collins, 216 So. 2d 433 (1968).
Wis.: Wussow v. Commercial Mechanisms, Inc., 293 N.W.2d 897 (1980).
[31] **Wis.:** Barnard v. Cohen, 162 N.W.2d 840 (1971).
[32] **D.C.:** Wardman-Justice Motors v. Petrie, 39 F.2d 512 (1930).
Iowa: Pringle Tax Serv. v. Knoblauch, 282 N.W.2d 151 (1971).

to bar relitigation of identical issues, even though the theories of recovery may differ.[33]

While in the past, the doctrine of collateral estoppel had to be applied mutually so that the judgment in the original suit was binding on both litigants before one party could subsequently assert it, such mutuality was abolished in California, where one party to a judgment not involved in the previous suit, can use the doctrine against the other party who was bound by the previous judgment.[34]

An Illinois case[35] held that the plaintiff in the later suit against the original manufacturer must establish that the same issue that was essential in making the prior determination is essential in the present suit, and that the defendant had full opportunity to contest the issue in the prior action.

While collateral estoppel may only be applicable if the situation is identical,[36] in some instances, the rule was held applicable even where all users of the product were not adversly affected by it.[37]

[7] **Wrongful Death Statutes**

The majority of the decisions on the subject appear to be interpreting their death statutes as precluding recovery of punitive damages by the heirs of the deceased.[38]

Some jurisdictions have indicated that they would permit recovery, but only if the culpability was very obvious.[39]

---

[33] **Tex.:** Flatt v. Johns-Manville Sales Corp., 488 F. Supp. 836 (1980) (doctrine barred manufacturer of asbestos from contesting the issue of whether products containing asbestos were unreasonably dangerous).

See Siliman, "Punitive Damages Related to Multiple Litigation Against a Corporation," Fed. of Ins. Counsel Quarterly, Spring 1966.

Contra: Roginsky v. Richardson-Merrell, Inc., 378 F.2d 832 (2d Cir. 1967).

[34] Bruszewski v. United States, 181 F.2d 413 (3d Cir), *cert. denied,* 340 U.S. 865 (1950); Bernhard v. Bank of America, 122 P.2d 892 (1942).

[35] Moore v. Jewel Tea Co., 253 N.E.2d 636 (App. 1969).

[36] **Ore.:** Williams v. Lawrence-David, Inc., 534 P.2d 173 (1975) (during compensatory damage phase of case).

[37] **Cal.:** Toole v. Richardson-Merrell, Inc., 60 Cal. Rptr. 398 (1967).

[38] **Cal.:** Ford Motor Co. v. Superior Court, 175 Cal. Rptr. 39 (1981); Georgie Boy Mfg., Inc. v. Superior Court, 171 Cal. Rptr. 382 (1981); Grimshaw v. Ford Motor Co., 174 Cal. Rptr. 348 (1981); Stencil Aero-Engineering Corp. v. Superior Court, 128 Cal. Rptr. 691 (1976); Pease v. Beech Aircraft Corp., 113 Cal. Rptr. 416 (1974).

Ill.: Moore v. Jewel Tea Co., 253 N.E.2d 649 (1969).

Mo.: Rinker v. Ford Motor Co., 567 S.W.2d 655 (App. 1978).

[39] **Ala.:** Casrell v. Altec Indus., Inc., 335 So. 2d 128 (1976).

Tex.: Maxey v. Freightliner Corp., 623 F.2d 395, *rev'd,* 634 F.2d 1008 (5th Cir. 1980) (punitive damage award reversed); Heil v. Grant, 534 S.W.2d 916 (App. 1976)

[8] Strict Liability

It would seem, on the face of it, that the awarding of punitive damages, which ordinarily requires a showing of a high degree of fault, is completely incompatible with the doctrine of strict liability, standing alone, but there are practically no decisions that have so held.[40]

In most other jurisdictions that permit the awarding of punitive damages the courts have held that it is proper to submit the question of punitive damage awards to the jury where the underlying suit has been brought on the basis of strict liability,[41] and in some cases, even where the action was brought on the basis of strict liability alone.[42]

Some jurisdictions that permit punitive damage awards brought on the basis of strict liability make an effort to temper the apparent contradiction by making strict requirements for the awarding of punitive damages in such cases.[43]

(submission of punitive damages denied); Kritser v. Beech Aircraft Corp., 479 F.2d 1089 (5th Cir. 1973).

[40] **La.:** Commercial Union Ins. Co. v. Upjohn Co., 409 F. Supp. 453 (1976) (even this case was decided in one of the few states that prohibits the awarding of punitive damages in all civil cases).

[41] **Alas.:** Sturm, Ruger & Co. v. Day, 549 P.2d 38 (1979).

Cal.: Toole v. Richardson-Merrell, Inc., 60 Cal. Rptr. 398 (1967); Greenman v. Yuba Power Products, Inc., 27 Cal. Rptr. 697 (1962); Grimshaw v. Ford Motor Co., 174 Cal. Rptr. 348 (1981) (other grounds included).

Fla.: American Motors Corp. v. Ellis, 403 So. 2d 459 (1981) (action included allegation of negligence).

Hi.: Vollert v. Summa Corp., 389 F. Supp. 1348 (1975) (action included allegation of negligence).

Ill.: Moore v. Jewel Tea Co., 253 N.E.2d 636 (1969), *aff'd,* 263 N.E.2d 103 (1970) (other grounds included).

Md.: American Laundry Mach. Industries v. Horan, 412 A.2d 407 (1980).

Minn.: Gryce v. Dayton-Hudson Corp., 297 N.W.2d 727 (1979).

Mo.: Rinker v. Ford Motor Co., 567 S.W.2d 655 (1978).

Ohio: Leichtamer v. American Motors Corp., 424 N.E.2d 568 (1981).

Pa.: Hoffman v. Sterling Drug Co., Inc., 374 F. Supp. 850 (1974).

Tenn.: Cathey v. Johns-Manville Sales Corp., 776 F.2d 1565 (6th Cir. 1985).

Wis.: Wangen v. Ford Motor Co., 294 N.W.2d 437 (1980).

[42] **Alas.:** Sturm, Ruger & Co. v. Day, 594 P.2d 38 (1979).

Cal.: Grimshaw v. Ford Motor Co., 174 Cal. Rptr. 348 (1981).

Minn.: Gryce v. Dayton-Hudson Corp., 297 N.W.2d 727 (1979).

Ohio: Leichtamer v. American Motors Corp., 434 N.E.2d 568 (1981).

[43] **Ariz.:** d'Hedouville v. Pioneer Hotel, 552 F.2d 886 (9th Cir. 1977) (jury failed to award punitive damages).

Cal.: Pease v. Beech Aircraft Corp., 113 Cal. Rptr. 416 (1974) (oppression, fraud or malice required. New trial ordered because of error in instruction to jury).

Ohio: Moran v. Johns-Manville Sales Corp., 691 F.2d 811 (6th Cir. 1982) (evidence of malice must be shown).

§ 32.01[8]   CASUALTY INSURANCE CLAIMS

Punitive damages relates to the conduct of the defendant and not to the theory of liability, as some courts have confirmed.[44] In other words, if the facts show malice, willful, wanton or outrageous conduct, or fit into the definition of any of the other verbiage used by the courts to warrant a punitive damage award, then such an award may be made even if the suit is brought on strict liability.

Even where punitive damage awards have been permitted in actions based on strict liability, there is no uniformity in the decisions, and it is obvious that the same facts and circumstances could, and probably would, result in different conclusions, depending on the jurisdiction in which the suit was brought.[45]

While there is a similarity in much of the wording used by the courts to justify an award for punitive damages, there is a wide divergence in the exact language used. It is as though each judge wanted to make his own imprint on his decision. The wording used in cases based on strict liability has, for example included the following.

"Complete indifference to, or conscious disregard for the safety of others";[46] "reckless, wanton, willful and gross acts";[47] "fraud, malice or insult";[48] "oppression, fraud or malice";[49] "willfulness, reckless-

---

Pa.: Thomas v. American Cystoscope Makers, Inc., 414 F. Supp. 255 (1976) (recklessness required, even gross negligence is not enough to warrant a punitive damage award); Hoffman v. Sterling Drug, Inc., 485 F.2d 132 (3d Cir. 1973) (suit based on strict liability, negligence and fraud. Appeals court decided that the issue of punitive damages should have been submitted to the jury).

Tenn.: Johnson v. Husky Indus., Inc., 536 F.2d 645 (6th Cir. 1976) (court upheld submission of punitive damages to jury but set aside the verdict. Punitive damages permitted where the manufacturing was done "so recklessly as to imply disregard for social obligations, or where there is such willful misconduct or entire want of care as to raise a presumption of conscious indifference to consequences." The evidence in this case was held to be inadequate to support punitive damages as a matter of law).

Tex.: Newding v. Kroger Co., 554 S.W.2d 15 (App. 1977) (alleged wrongdoing did not meet standards justifying the awarding of punitive damages).

[44] **Tex.:** Heil v. Grant, 534 S.W.2d 916 (1976).
Wis.: Drake v. Wham-O Mfg. Co., 373 F. Supp. 608 (1974); Draeger v. John Lubotsky Motor Sales, 202 N.W.2d 20 (1972).

[45] Roddy, "Punitive Damages in Strict Liability Litigation," 23 Wm. & Mary L. Rev. 333 (1981); Greenberg, "Punitive Damages in Mass-Marketed Products Litigation," 14 Loy. L.A.L. Rev. 405 (1981).

[46] **Mo.:** Rinker v. Ford Motor Co., 567 S.W.2d 655 (App. 1978).

[47] **Ill.:** Moore v. Jewel Tea Co., 253 N.E.2d 636 (1969), aff'd, 263 N.E.2d 103 (1970) ("willful and wanton").
Ohio: Gillham v. Admiral Corp., 523 F.2d 102 (6th Cir. 1975).

[48] **Ohio:** Leichtamer v. American Motors Corp., 424 N.E.2d 568 (1981).

[49] **Cal.:** Grimshaw v. Ford Motor Co., 174 Cal. Rptr. 348 (1981).

ness, maliciousness, outrageous conduct, or oppression or fraud."[50]

In the case of *G.D. Searle & Co. v. Superior Court*,[51] an action brought on strict liability and negligence, the court held that the California statutory requirement of "malice in fact" in order to warrant punitive damages, is met by the defendant's "conscious disregard for the safety of others" or could be the equivalent of "intent to injure."

[9] **Negligence as a Basis for Awarding Punitive Damages**

Having reviewed the wording used by the courts to justify the awarding of punitive damages in products liability cases, it would appear that, generally speaking, an action based on mere negligence alone will not justify such an award.[52]

In some cases, even gross negligence alone has been held insufficient to warrant the awarding of punitive damages.[53]

[10] **Breach of Warranty**

Breach of warranty is a hard road to take in any attempt to recover punitive damages in products liability suits. Most jurisdictions hold breach of warranty actions to be in contract, which ordinarily does not support an action for punitive damages.[54]

Even in those jurisdictions that do not make the ordinary contract distinction, the courts have failed to permit punitive damages on the sole basis of breach of warranty.[55] In addition, the Uniform Commercial Code,[56] adopted by all states except Louisiana, states that "neither consequential nor penal damages may be had except as specifically provided in this Act or by other rule of law."

---

[50] **Fla.:** American Motors Corp. v. Ellis, 403 So. 2d 459 (1981).

[51] 122 Cal. Rptr. 218 (1975).

[52] **D.C.:** Knippen v. Ford Motor Co., 546 F.2d 993 (1976).
Fla.: Ellis v. Calconda Corp., 352 So. 2d 122 (App. 1971).
Ind.: Hibschman Pontiac, Inc. v. Batchelor, 340 N.E.2d 377 (1976).
Tex: Newding v. Kroger Co., 554 S.W.2d 15 (App. 1977).

[53] Kirschnik v. Pepsi-Cola Metro. Bottling Co., 478 F. Supp. 849 (1979); Walbrun v. Berkel, Inc., 433 F. Supp. 384 (1976).

[54] **Ind.:** Hibschman Pontiac, Inc. v. Batchelor, 34 N.E.2d 377 (1976).

[55] Ghiardi & Kirchner, "Punitive Damage Recovery in Products Liability Cases," 65 Marq. L. Rev. 34 (Fall 1981).

[56] Sec. 1 - 106 (1).

I therefore find it hard to understand why many cases add to other grounds, breach of warranty, in an effort to obtain a punitive damage award.

[11] Insurance for Punitive Damages

Along with others, I have argued that if the purpose of punitive damages is to punish and deter, allowing the defendant to insure against such awards defeats these purposes since the defendant effectively escapes the consequences of his wrongdoing.[57]

It has, however, been suggested that this argument is falacious because many industrial policies are written with extremely high deductibles and because they are written on a loss-rated basis, depending on the insurance experience of the manufacturer who is then punished by having to pay higher rates for insurance.[58]

While both statements are true, they do not negate the conclusion that, to a greater or lesser degree, any part of the punitive damage award that is paid by the insurer still relieves the wrongdoing defendant of some of his responsibility and passes it on to the nonwrongdoing insurer.

[12] Amounts Awarded—Model Uniform Products Liability Act

While punitive damage awards are subject to judicial review, there are no adequate guidelines that limit or even delineate boundaries for the assessment of the amounts awarded.

The proposed Model Uniform Products Liability Act[59] provides as follows:

> (B) If the trier of fact determines that punitives should be awarded, the court shall determine the amount of those damages, in making this determination, the court shall consider:
>
> 1. The likelihood that at the relevant time, serious harm would arise from the product seller's misconduct;

---

[57] Knippen v. Ford Motor Co., 546 F.2d 993 (D.C. Cir. 1976).

[58] *See* Magarick, *Excess Liability*, §16.06; Sprentail, "Insurance Coverage for Punitive Damages," 84 Dick. L. Rev. 221 (1980); Chilcoat, "Punitive Damages in Products Liability: A Layman's Guide for the Manufacturer's Protection," 13 Cap. U.L. Rev. 435 (1984); Owen, "Punitive Damages in Products Liability Litigation," 74 Mich. L. Rev. 1257 (June 1976).

[59] 44 Fed. Reg. 62714 & 62748 (1979).

2. The degree of the product seller's awareness of that likelihood;

3. The profitability of the misconduct to the seller;

4. The duration of the misconduct and any concealment of it by the product seller;

5. The attitude and conduct of the product seller upon discovery of the misconduct and whether the conduct has been terminated;

6. The financial condition of the product seller;

7. The total effect of other punishment imposed or likely to be imposed on the product seller as a result of the misconduct including punitive damage awards to persons similarly situated to claimant and the severity of criminal penalties to which the product seller has been or may be subjected;

8. Whether the harm suffered by the claimant was also the result of the claimant's own disregard for personal safety.

So far, there has been no great rush by any state to adopt this proposed model act.

David L. Chilcoat, in his excellent article, "Punitive Damages in Products Liability: A Layman's Guide for the Manufacturer's Protection,"[60] gives a checklist of actions to be taken by a manufacturer in order to avoid culpability that might lead to the awarding of punitive damages, as follows:

1. He should place a high priority on the safety of his product.
2. He must not allow lack of functional coordination to result in behavior which can be deemed constructive malice.
3. He should never overestimate the understanding of any possible users of the product. (To which I might add misusers, including children, illiterates, and foreigners who cannot understand instructions and warnings written in English.)
4. He should avoid relying too heavily on governmental or industrial standards which are usually minimum standards.
5. He should keep proper records of sales and deliveries. Manufacturers should develop a system to track any products that have a long-lasting capacity.
6. He should keep a line of communication open with customers.

---

[60] 12 Cap. Univ. L. Rev. 435 (1984).

7. He should designate a high-level officer to give priority to the safety of his products and make sure that all personnel are aware of their proper function in the safety chain.
8. He should keep informed of all new safety developments in his industry.
9. He should keep informed of all new governmental requirements.
10. If necessary, he should develop a comprehensive disaster plan similar to that effectuated by Johnson & Johnson in the Tylenol situation.

CHAPTER 33

Investigation of Products Liability Claims

§ 33.01 In General
§ 33.02 Strict Liability—Areas for Investigation
§ 33.03 Products Liability Investigation—General Checklist
§ 33.04 Products Liability—Some Specific Investigations Checklists
      [1]   Automobiles
      [2]   Bottling Claims
      [3]   Crop Dusting
      [4]   Drugs and Cosmetics
      [5]   Food Consumption on Premises of Vendor
      [6]   Design Defect Cases
      [7]   Warning Defects Cases
      [8]   Altered Products—Liability of Original Manufacturer
      [9]   Product Recall
      [10] Market Share Liability for Fungible Products
§ 33.05 Bibliography

§ 33.01 In General

The investigation of products liability claims can tax the imagination, ingenuity, and mental versatility of the claim representative. For one thing, aside from those accidents which occur in restaurants, the claims arise, for the most part, out of what are known as "blind" accidents, or those to which there are no witnesses other than the claimant, his relatives or close friends. For another, a products liability claim may involve any one of a vast variety of unrelated products; the claim representative may have to learn much in a short time about fields which are entirely new to him. Products claims, for instance, involve not only drugs, cosmetics, food products, and beverages, but also vehicles and other mechanical devices, ladders and tools, electric appliances, insecticides (with or without pressure containers), dyes in clothing, home permanents, pressure cookers, gas and oil stoves, matches, inflammable gases like butane, and other products too numerous to mention.

The insured may be the manufacturer, wholesaler, jobber, distributor, retailer, or maintenance, repair, and service agency. It is important to remember that the defect complained of may have occurred anywhere along the line from the manufacturer down to and including the consumer.

The quickest way to learn about a product manufactured by the insured is to call on the insured and make a thorough inspection of the plant under the guidance of someone who can properly explain the various processes, after reading all of the available advertising and instructional material and manuals available. Such calls serve not only to familiarize the claim representative with the information he must have, but permits him, when a claim is presented, to make arrangements for obtaining specific information in the shortest possible time and with the least friction. They can also afford the opportunity to make arrangements for handling claims, a matter of public relations.

Often, products liability claims do not involve serious injury. In many instances it is more a matter of outrage than actual damages. A courteous, considerate, and understanding person, who calls on the claimant in the capacity of representative of the firm which his company insures, can very often nip a claim in the bud by offering to replace the allegedly defective product.

Very often the alleged defect complained of is nothing more than something which is quite natural to the product, such as salmon crystals which may be mistaken for glass, burnt cracker dust which may be mistaken for mouse excrement, or things of a similar nature. A courteous explanation, sincere regret for the misunderstanding, and the offer of several cans or packages in replacement for the one that was allegedly defective, will very often turn a prospective claim into good publicity, with the resultant feeling on the part of the claimant that the company is interested in maintaining his good will.

There are, however, occasions when a claim or claims can involve many individuals who may have sustained serious injuries or death, or where the property damage may be very extensive with considerable consequential loss of business. Such claims or suits can become very complex, and in these cases every lead must be explored, every contract reviewed, and all advertising and technical instructional material carefully examined to determine where the ultimate responsibility, if any, lies.

If someone other than the insured may have been involved in the claim, whether it be the manufacturer of the product or container, or a distributor, the claim representative should make sure to put that other firm on notice through the insured's demanding that they take over and hold the insured harmless. They should also be requested to notify their insurance carrier immediately.

The relatively recent flood of publicity which asbestos, DES, and Agent Orange cases have spawned has focused attention on a comparatively small area of products liability, despite the fact that such claims have greatly affected coverage interpretation and have produced some of the highest verdicts on record. Nevertheless, their numbers compared to all products liability claims must be kept in proper perspective.

The companies that insure the former asbestos, DES, and Agent Orange manufacturers have had to deal with multiple plaintiffs long after the injuries or diseases were initially triggered. Many of these manufacturers are no longer in business and most, if not all of the rest, no longer manufacture these products in any form. Investigation of these cases has been formalized and has been directed by highly specialized counsel. Literature on this subject is voluminous and comprehensive.

§ 33.02 Strict Liability—Areas for Investigation

Professor Wade, in his article, "On the Nature of Strict Liability for Products,"[1] lists seven factors which he thinks are significant in applying the doctrine of strict liability in products liability cases:

1. The usefulness and desirability of the product—its utility to the user and to the public as a whole.
2. The safety aspects of the product—the liklihood that it will cause injury, and the probable seriousness of the injury.
3. The availability of a substitute product which would meet the same need and not be as unsafe.
4. The manufacturer's ability to eliminate the unsafe character of the product without imparing its usefulness or making it too expensive to maintain its utility.
5. The user's ability to avoid danger by the exercise of care in the use of the product.

---

[1] Insurance Law Journal, March 1974.

§ 33.03   CASUALTY INSURANCE CLAIMS

    6.   The user's anticipated awareness of the dangers inherent in the product and their avoidability, because of general public knowledge of the obvious condition of the product, or of the existence of suitable warnings or instructions.
    7.   The feasibility, on the part of the manufacturer, of spreading the loss by setting the price of the product or carrying liability insurance.

The items listed above should be a good guide to compare investigations made under negligence actions against suits brought in strict liability. Although the burden of proof has shifted from the plaintiff to the defendant in a strict liability suit, it is obvious that the investigation of a products liability suit requires intensive digging in either case.

§ 33.03 Products Liability Investigation—General Checklist

As has been said, we are here dealing with a field that is exceedingly varied. Obviously it is impossible to outline the investigation for every product which might be made the subject of a claim. The following checklist must, therefore, deal in generalities which it is hoped will give leads that may stimulate the claim representative to use his own imagination and initiative and permit him to branch out in whatever direction the investigation calls for. He should determine:

- [ ] Name of the product.
- [ ] Name and address of the manufacturer.
- [ ] Name of all jobbers, retailers, wholesalers, and distributors that may be involved.
- [ ] Names of the insurance carriers for the manufacturer, wholesaler, retailer, and so on.
- [ ] Complete description of the product. Obtain copies of all advertising and descriptive printed matter including manuals and charts.
- [ ] Name and address of the person who purchased the article.
- [ ] Where was the purchase made? From whom? (Retailer, wholesaler, manufacturer, and so on.)
- [ ] Name and address of the sales person who sold the article.
- [ ] Name and address of the person for whom the purchase was made. Obtain details if the claimant was not the purchaser.
- [ ] Exact date and time of purchase.
- [ ] Date and time of the delivery of the article.

PRODUCTS LIABILITY INVESTIGATION § 33.03

- ☐ How was it delivered? Give details including the name of the delivery service.
- ☐ If the article was not purchased, determine how it was obtained by the claimant.
  - ○ From whom was it obtained?
  - ○ When was it obtained?
- ☐ Give the exact price of the product.
- ☐ Who paid for it?
- ☐ How was payment made? (Check, cash, money order.)
- ☐ Was the product asked for by trade name?
- ☐ Did the salesperson recommend the product? Details of any conversation between the salesperson and the purchaser.
- ☐ When was the defect first discovered? How?
- ☐ Describe defect in detail. Was it natural to the product, like a fishbone?
- ☐ What tests were made to determine the safety of the product? Describe in detail.
- ☐ Was the article inherently dangerous in any way? If so, how?
- ☐ What became of the article?
  - ○ Was the evidence preserved?
  - ○ Was it properly identified?
  - ○ How much of the article was used?
- ☐ Try to obtain its possession for the purpose of taking laboratory tests, chemical analysis, bacteriological counts, and so on.
- ☐ Obtain other packages of the product from the same batch, carton, or case, for the purpose of examination and analysis.
- ☐ Did the product conform with all Pure Food and Drug or other applicable laws?
- ☐ How was the product used?
- ☐ Was it examined before being used?
- ☐ Did it appear in good condition?
- ☐ Was the product used properly, or was it abused?
- ☐ The claim representative should use his imagination to think of the ways in which, through improper use, the product could have become in the condition complained of.
- ☐ Obtain local Health Department report and examination.
- ☐ What was the injury or reaction complained of?
- ☐ When did it first manifest itself? Describe symptoms in detail.
- ☐ How many people suffered these symptoms?
- ☐ Give the names of all the people who consumed the product or had anything to do with it.
- ☐ If food is involved, what else was eaten at that particular meal? What was eaten at prior and subsequent meals? How many people ate the same things? What was the common factor? (Food eaten by all persons who became ill.)

§ 33.04[1] CASUALTY INSURANCE CLAIMS

- ☐ When was the first complaint made? To whom?
- ☐ If glass or other sharp object was alleged to have been taken into mouth:
  - ○ Obtain the objectionable object for examination or get detailed description of it.
  - ○ Was there any evidence of blood?
  - ○ If the sharp object was allegedly swallowed, obtain complete description of any complaints or symptoms.
- ☐ Details regarding packaging or canning:
  - ○ Describe packing in detail.
  - ○ Was package properly sealed?
  - ○ Could package have been refilled or tampered with?
  - ○ Was it received in the original wrapper?
  - ○ Describe label and markings. The package is usually coded for identification by the manufacturer or packer.
  - ○ Check the coding to determine the packer and put him on notice if necessary.
  - ○ Was there any warning on the label? Get the exact wording and a copy of the label.
  - ○ Was it purchased in the original container or wrapping? If not, obtain details.
- ☐ Describe the methods of storage and handling, from the factory to the purchaser.
- ☐ Get complete details regarding manufacturing, canning, or packing including bottling, inspection and method, testing, wrapping, or capping and so on.
- ☐ Get complete details of transportation, including a description of all places where tampering with the product might have occurred.

§ 33.04 Products Liability—Some Specific Investigations Checklists

[1] Automobiles

Negligence has been accepted as creating a liability on the manufacturer or assembler of automobiles since the decision in the case of *MacPherson v. Buick Motor Co.*[2] This has subsequently led many jurisdictions to the acceptance of the doctrine of strict liability for design as well as for manufacturing or assembling errors.

In recent years, a new tendency has also developed, in an attempt to separate a second injury inside the vehicle, after the effects of the initial impact. It has been argued that in addition to the duty of a designer or manufacturer to produce a roadworthy and safe vehicle,

---

[2] 217 N.Y. 382, 111 N.E. 1050 (1916).

there is the further duty to produce a vehicle that is crashworthy and free of defects or weaknesses that may make it unreasonably unsafe for passengers after an impact occurs.[3]

The effect of recall letters on the liability of a manufacturer for admitted defects can also be a complicated matter that could either aid in the defense of a case, or be used with possible deadly effect in the prosecution of the claim.[4] In making the investigation of such cases, special attention must, of course, be given to the sending and receipt of recall letters, and whether such a letter was called for, if not sent.

The investigation of Products Liability claims involving automobiles can focus on the designer, manufacturer, assembler, sales agency, and repair shop. Obviously, it is impossible to cover the whole field. The following checklist is meant to help stimulate the imagination of the investigator.

- [ ] Get the name of the manufacturer of the allegedly defective part. Determine the conditions of the contract between the automobile manufacturer and the manufacturer of the subcontracted part.
- [ ] Find out if any tests were made by the parts manufacturer. Determine what tests were made by the automobile assembler, either before or after installation of the part, and whether or not any tests were made at the factory if the part was manufactured by the automobile manufacturer.
- [ ] Determine where, when, and by whom the part was installed.
- [ ] Determine if car had seat belts and if they were being used.
- [ ] Determine if car was equipped with air bags and whether they were available.
- [ ] Determine if bumpers met governmental requirements.
- [ ] Find out if there were any previous complaints concerning the part or its operation. Automobiles have such wide distribution that a defective part is soon noticed by many people. Find out whether the automobile company made any attempt to call in the defective part or issued any notice of warning concerning it.
- [ ] Find out if there was any mention of the defective part in any of the instructions given out with the automobile or in any of its advertising.
- [ ] Determine whether or not the allegedly defective part was vital to the safe operation of the vehicle.
- [ ] Determine whether the alleged defect was obvious or hidden.
- [ ] Find out if bad driving played any part in the accident.

---

[3] Larson v. General Motors Corp., 391 F.2d 495 (8th Cir. 1968).
[4] Comstock v. General Motors Corp., 358 Mich. 163, 99 N.W.2d 627 (1959).

§ 33.04[2] CASUALTY INSURANCE CLAIMS

In checking a brake failure it is important to determine the following:

- [ ] When did the plaintiff purchase the car?
- [ ] How many miles was it driven safely?
- [ ] Was the car purchased when it was new or used?
- [ ] Was it ever involved in a collision before the accident?
- [ ] When were the brakes last adjusted and inspected?
- [ ] Could the adjustment have been improper?
- [ ] What system of brakes was used?
- [ ] Was there a defect in the brake mechanism?
- [ ] Were there double brakes?

[2] **Bottling Claims**

One of the most common types of products liability claims involves the manufacture, sale, and distribution of carbonated bottled beverages. Flying glass fragments can do a lot of harm. It is seldom indeed that an explosion of a bottled beverage occurs without some sharp change in temperature and external bruising or contact with hard objects.

While cases concerning foreign substances in bottled beverages do not usually involve serious injury, the number of these claims has reached such major proportions that the careful and prudent attorney for plaintiff and defendant will take unusual care in order to determine that there is substance behind the allegations made by the plaintiff. In cases alleging foreign substances, it is particularly important to check the manner in which the bottles are cleaned before they are filled and capped. Quite often there is an allegation of swallowing of glass particles dislodged as a result of defective capping. Such cases should be viewed with particular skepticism, since it is very difficult to dislodge small particles of glass from a bottle containing liquid until all of the liquid has been drained from it.

If a broken bottle or foreign substance is involved, the following checklist should be helpful:

- [ ] Obtain the bottle fragments for examination. You can assure the claimant or the claimant's attorney that these fragments will not be disturbed and will be returned to him in the same condition in which they were given. Proper laboratory examination can determine:
  - O Whether some outside force was applied to the bottle that may have nicked or cracked it causing weakening sufficient for it to explode.

33-8

- ○ Whether there was a defect in the bottle that made it weaker than normal.
- ○ Whether there was a defect in the cap or in the capping process.
- ☐ Determine the manner in which the bottle was handled and stored by all previous parties, from the manufacturer to the consumer.
- ☐ Obtain report on previous similar accidents from parties anywhere along the line between the consumer and the manufacturer.
- ☐ Determine where the claimant stored the bottle and whether it was kept near artificial heat or in the sunlight.
- ☐ Obtain a description of the sound of the explosion and the manner in which the flying fragments separated.
- ☐ In cases where a mouse allegedly was in the bottle, determine the advisability of:
  - ○ Autopsy to determine whether there was any liquid in the lungs of the mouse.
  - ○ X-ray to see if any bones of the mouse were fractured. These are two means that are almost fool-proof in helping to determine whether the mouse was pushed into the bottle after it was dead or whether it actually drowned in the liquid.
- ☐ Complete description of the bottling process, including:
  - ○ Temperature and pressure control.
  - ○ Use of returned bottles and their inspection.
  - ○ Washing of previously used bottles.
  - ○ Inspection of the bottle before and after filling.
  - ○ Capping process.
- ☐ Determine the name of the manufacturer of the bottle from the markings on it and put him on notice to take over the claim or suit if necessary.

[3] Crop Dusting

The laws governing the responsibility of an owner or independent contractor for damage or injury resulting from crop dusting vary from statutes imposing strict liability to the ordinary rules of negligence. The following checklist will serve as a guide to the adjuster investigating such a cause of action:

- ☐ Obtain a copy of the contract between the owner and the person or firm that performed the crop dusting. If the contract was oral, obtain as many details as possible. Find out what specific directions were given and by whom they were given. Determine how payment was made, who owned the equipment, and other details that might establish whether or not the person or firm performing the work was an independent contractor.
- ☐ Determine the applicable local laws and whether there was compliance with them.

§ 33.04[4]   CASUALTY INSURANCE CLAIMS

- ☐ Find out if any preliminary testing was made to insure safety to other plants and animals.
- ☐ Determine if any warnings were issued, if necessary.
- ☐ Find out the exact weather conditions with particular emphasis on wind velocity and drift. Determine if weather conditions were properly checked in advance, and whether or not a sudden, unexpected and unpredicted wind helped to cause the damage.
- ☐ Determine the exact nature and inherent danger of the insecticides used. Determine whether or not any other product of a less dangerous nature could have been used. Find out if the product was properly labeled and packaged, and arrange for a chemical analysis of the compound to determine its nature, ingredients, and concentration. Preserve a sample of the compound so that it may be used in evidence.
- ☐ Find out from whom the compound was purchased.
- ☐ Determine the method of application, and whether or not it was in accordance with ordinary standards. Determine whether or not the application or the applicator was defective in any way and find out whether or not the operator or pilot confined himself within the proper area. Determine whether or not the operators or pilot were experienced and competent.
- ☐ Investigate the condition of similar plants outside range of contamination. Determine if harm might have been due to causes other than dusting, such as drought, poor farming methods, insufficient or improper fertilizer, plant disease, insect infestation, age, or delicate nature.
- ☐ Have an inspection made by an expert of the injured plants, trees, or crops.

[4] Drugs and Cosmetics

- ☐ Determine when the drug was first put on the market.
- ☐ Find out if any professional papers or articles have been written on the particular drug and get copies.
- ☐ Determine what tests were made by the manufacturer. Obtain full details.
- ☐ Determine if the product received the approval of the Federal Food and Drug Administration and whether this administration made any tests of its own.
- ☐ Find out if the product received the approval of any local state authorities and whether it complied with the laws of the state in which it was sold.
- ☐ Determine if the product was subject to the regulations of the Federal Trade Commission and, if so, whether it complied with any such regulations.
- ☐ Find out if any restraining order of any kind was ever issued against the product by any governmental authority.
- ☐ Determine the manufacturer's experience with the product since it has been on the market. Were any previous complaints made? If so, determine

PRODUCTS LIABILITY INVESTIGATION § 33.04[5]

their number and exact nature. Were there side effects or were allergies involved?

- [ ] If previous complaints were made, what action did the manufacturer take concerning them?
- [ ] Determine if there was any error in the manufacture or compounding of the drug. Had it ever been recalled?
- [ ] Determine if the instructions for use were clear and adequate. Find out if warning labels were adequate or misleading in any way. Was any change made in the literature or labeling. Obtain a copy of any advertising material, labels, etc.
- [ ] Find out who prescribed the drug and whether prescribed instructions were strictly followed. Exactly when was it first prescribed? How often was the drug taken and in exactly what quantities? If a cosmetic, how did it first come to the claimant's attention?
- [ ] Determine if allergy or other sensitivity tests were ordered or made.
- [ ] Find out if the doctor gave any warning concerning possible side effects.
- [ ] Determine when the first manifestation of side effects or allergy were first noticed. Obtain full details.
- [ ] Determine if the claimant's reaction was unusual. Could it be considered an abnormal reaction?
- [ ] Find out if the claimant reported the reaction to his doctor and if so what countermeasures were taken if any. What drugs were taken or prescribed as treatment? Obtain complete medical history.
- [ ] Find out what previous experience the doctor has had with the drug. How did it come to his attention?
- [ ] Determine if the drug was taken in combination with, or at the same time other drugs were imbibed. Get full details.
- [ ] Interview the manufacture's representative (detail man).

[5] **Food Consumption on Premises of Vendor**

The particular information referred to in the following checklist should be elicited in the investigation of injuries due to food consumption on the premises of a vendor thereof:

- [ ] Obtain the date, time, and place of food consumption.
- [ ] Determine the exact nature of the food. Determine the exact foods and beverages consumed immediately preceding and after the period complained of.
- [ ] Obtain the date and time of the onset of symptoms. Describe the nature of the symptoms. If there was vomiting, determine duration and contents. Find out if there was diarrhea. Check the prior medical history carefully to determine whether or not a chronic ailment may have been involved.

§ 33.04[6]   CASUALTY INSURANCE CLAIMS

- ☐ Obtain the number of others who ate the food complained of and get the names and addresses of as many as possible.
- ☐ Obtain Health Department report if notification was made.
- ☐ Make laboratory testing of the stools if pertinent.
- ☐ Complete investigation of the processing, storing, and serving of the food.
  - ○ Check the conditions of cleanliness.
  - ○ Learn how and for how long the food was cooked.
  - ○ Determine the exact ingredients that went into the food and where they were obtained.
  - ○ Find out if the food was left for any unusually long duration without proper refrigeration.
  - ○ If frozen food was involved, determine from whom it was purchased, and whether or not it was refrozen after defrosting.
  - ○ If a steam table was involved, determine how long the food was on the steam table and at what temperature the food was kept.

[6] Design Defect Cases

- ☐ Determine if the product is dangerous to use by ordinary reasonably prudent purchasers.
- ☐ Find out if the danger was open and obvious and describe.
- ☐ Determine if the product could become dangerous if used improperly. Obtain details.
- ☐ Learn if it could have been foreseen that a child or someone deficient of adult reasoning would have used the product.
- ☐ Describe the user in detail and the nature of the failure in the product. Is he or she a knowledgeable user?
- ☐ Learn the "state-of-the-art" concerning the product under investigation and if there are other products of a like nature being marketed that are safer. Describe in detail.
- ☐ Find out if guards or other safety devices are necessary or might interfere with the utility of the product.
- ☐ Determine, if possible, whether a safer product could have been designed without pricing the product out of the market.
- ☐ Find out if the product was tamper-proof, or easily opened, if pertinent.
- ☐ Determine if the product met all governmental and industry standards.
- ☐ Determine if any post-accident changes were made in the product and get reasons for the change. Determine if the post-accident changes were pertinent in any subsequent claim.

[7] Warning Defects Cases

- ☐ Find out if the product is dangerous if used properly.
- ☐ Determine if it could be dangerous if not used properly, and how.
- ☐ Learn if the product contained a warning concerning its danger:

PRODUCTS LIABILITY INVESTIGATION § 33.04[9]

- ○ Determine if the warning was on the product or on a container.
- ○ Determine if warning was prominent.
- ○ Find out and describe exact position of warning and whether it was easily visible and understandable. Describe its contents, size, and other features.
- ☐ Determine if adequate instructions were given for safe use or assembly.
- ☐ Find out if any warnings were given concerning ingestion, if this is pertinent. Learn if any antidotes were given with reference to any poisonous substances.
- ☐ Determine if all governmental rules and regulations were complied with.
- ☐ Where drugs are concerned, determine if proper instructions concerning side effects or allergies, with proper warnings, were issued to doctors and pharmacists. Determine how this was done.
- ☐ Where poisonous products are involved, determine if the warnings would have been understood by people who were illiterate, retarded, or who simply could not read the English language. Were practical visual warnings available?
- ☐ Learn if any post-accident changes in the warnings were made and describe in detail. Find out if such changes were pertinent to any other suits.

[8] Altered Products—Liability of Original Manufacturer

- ☐ Determine if the insured made the changes, or whether they were made under insured's supervision, instructions, or with parts supplied by insured.
- ☐ Determine if the insured was ever consulted about such changes.
- ☐ Determine the previous use and age of the product and all facts concerning its history.
- ☐ Determine exactly what broke down and if there was a defect in a part manufactured by someone other than the original manufacturer. Follow up with notice to him if appropriate. Was the breakdown foreseeable?

[9] Product Recall

- ☐ If recall of a product is involved, determine the method of recall and if the plaintiff received proper notice.
- ☐ Determine if plaintiff took action upon receipt of the recall notice and, if not, why?
- ☐ Obtain full details concerning the defect and whether it was the proximate cause of the accident.
- ☐ Determine if the defect could have been discovered sooner by the manufacturer.

[10] Market Share Liability for Fungible Products

☐ Make every effort to determine the actual manufacturer of the product involved.
☐ If this is not possible, determine as many manufacturers as possible who manufactured the same product at the time the plaintiff used or consumed, or was subjected to the product.
☐ Review the corporate structures of successor companies and determine whether they accepted liability by agreement or because they continued to manufacture the same product. Try to find out if any transfer of the corporation was made for the purpose of escaping liability.
☐ Determine if any of the manufacturers of the product either sold or might have sold the product to the plaintiff, either directly or indirectly. Get complete details.
☐ Determine if any wholesaler or distributor was involved and determine the chain of distribution.[5]

§ 33.05 Bibliography

Altered or Used Products

Danielski, "Manufacturer's Liability for Defects in Used Products," F.T.D., December 1980.
Lauwers, "The Defense of Product Alteration," FIC Quarterly, Spring 1981.

Asbestos

Boydstun, "Asbestos Property Damage Cases: Has the Statute Run?", F.T.D., June 1986.
Locks, "Asbestos-Related Disease Litigation: Can the Beast Be Tamed?", 28 Vill. L. Rev. 1184 (1982-83).
Peeples, III, "Asbestos Litigation and Theories of Insurance Coverage," FIC Quarterly, Summer 1982.
Phillips, "Asbestos Litigation: The Test of the Tort System," 36 Ark. L. Rev. 343 (1982).
Special Report, "An Analysis of the Legal, Social and Political Issues Raised By Asbestos Litigation," 36 Vand. L. Rev. 573 (1983).
Wojcik, "Tracing the Fibers of Asbestos Litigation: When Do An Insurer's Duties of Defense and Indemnity Arise?", FIC Quarterly, Spring 1986.

---

[5] For some additional checklists, *see* Spacone, "A Practical Guide to Controlling Products Liability Costs," DRI Monogram # 6, vol. 1984.

Zeman, "The Asbestos Crisis: Thoughts on Proposed Solutions," FIC Quarterly, Summer 1984.

Assumption of Risk

Clowd, "Setting the Standards for the Sufficiency of an Assumption of Risk in Oklahoma Manufacturer's Products Liability Actions," 8 Okla. City U.L. Rev. (Spring 1983).
Nielsen, "Strict Liability Actions—Defenses Based on Plaintiff's Conduct," FIC Quarterly, Winter 1982.

Comparative Fault

"Applying Comparative Fault to Strict Liability Actions," DRI article in Insurance Adjuster Magazine, June 1985.
Feinberg, "The Application of a Comparative Negligence Defense in a Strict Product Liability Suit Based on Section 402A of the Restatement (Second) of Torts," Insurance Comm. Journal, January 1975.
Greenlee & Rochelle, "Comparative Negligence and Strict Liability: A Marriage of Necessity," Land & Water L. Rev. vol. XVIII (1983).
Kroll, "Comparative Fault: A New Generation in Products Liability," Insurance Law Journal, August 1977.
Kulig, "Comparative Negligence and Strict Products Liability: Where Do We Stand? Where Do We Go?", 29 Vill. L. Rev. 695 (1983-84).
Pinto, "Comparative Responsibility—An Idea Whose Time Has Come," Insurance Counsel Journal, January 1978.
Robertson, "Ruminations on Comparative Fault," 44 La. L. Rev. 1352 (1984).
Twerski, "The Many Faces of Misuse: An Inquiry into the Emerging Doctrine of Comparative Causation," 29 Mercer L. Rev., 1978.
Wade, "Products Liability and Plaintiff's Fault—The Uniform Comparative Fault Act," 29 Mercer L. Rev. 373 (1978).

Corporate Successor Liability

Fegan, "Ten Rules for Acquiring Corporate Assets Without Successor Liability," 24 F.T.D. 10, July 1982.
Liebo, "Products Successor Liability," F.T.D., February 6, 1984.
Nielsen, "Liability of Successor Corporations," FIC Quarterly, Fall 1981.
Ware, "Recent Developments in the Law of Successor Products Liability," 19 F.T.D. 95, June 1978.

Coverage Problems

Cayten, "CGL Product Liability Clauses," F.T.D., October 1985.

Kroll, " 'Claims Made'—Industry's Alternative: 'Pay As You Go' Products Liability Insurance," Insurance Law Journal, February 1976.

Oshinsky, "Comprehensive General Liability Insurance: Trigger and Scope of Coverage in Long-Term Exposure Cases," 17 Forum 1025 (1982).

Peeples III, "Asbestos Litigation and Theories of Insurance Coverage," FIC Quarterly, Summer 1982.

Wojcik, "Tracing the Fibers of Asbestos Litigation: When Do An Insurer's Duties of Defense and Indemnity Arise?", FIC Quarterly, Spring 1986.

Design Defects

Birnbaum, "A Re-evaluation of the Concept of Design Defects in Products," FIC Quarterly, Winter 1979.

David & Richard, "Defective Design and the Uncrashworthy Vehicle," Insurance Counsel Journal, April 1983.

Fowler, Comment, "Products Liability: Kansas Adopts the Consumer Expectation Test to Define 'Unreasonably Dangerous' in Design Defect Cases," Washburn L.J., vol. 22 (1983).

Hagarty, "Design Defects, Seat Belt and Second Injury," FIC Quarterly, Fall 1973.

Henderson, "Strict Products Liability and Design Defects in Arizona," Ariz. L. Rev., vol. 26 (1984).

Hoenig, "Product Designs and Strict Tort Liability: Is There a Better Approach?," Insurance Law Journal, May 1976.

Keeton, "Products Liability—Design Hazards and the Meaning of Defect," 10 Cumb. L. Rev. 293 (1979).

Patterson, "Design Defect Cases: The True Cost of Settling," F.T.D., May 20, 1985.

Vandall, " 'Design Defect' in Products Liability: Rethinking Negligence and Strict Liability," 43 Ohio State L.J., 61 (1982).

Drugs and Other Toxic Products

Comment, "Overcoming the Identification Burden in DES Litigation: The Market Share Liability Theory," 65 Marq. L. Rev. 609 (1982).

Elser, "Medical Products—An Area of Growing Concern," Insurance Law Journal, October 1974.

PRODUCTS LIABILITY INVESTIGATION § 33.05

Note, "Beyond Enterprise Liability in DES Cases," 14 Ind. L. Rev. 695 (1981).
Note, "Sindell v. Abbott Laboratories—A Market Share Approach to DES Causation," 69 Cal. L. Rev. 1179 (1981).
Obrenski," 'Toxic Torts' Litigation and the Insurance Coverage Controversy," FIC Quarterly, Fall 1983.

Duty to Warn

Funston, "The Failure to Warn Defect in Strict Products Liability: A Paradigmatic Approach to 'State-of-the-Art' Evidence and 'Scientific Knowability,'" Insurance Counsel Journal, January 1984.
Hirsch & Zimmerman, "Duty to Warn and Adequacy of Warning in Product Liability Cases," 20 F.T.D. 135, June 1979.
Jackson, "The Duty to Warn and Strict Liability," Insurance Counsel Journal, July 1981.
Keeton, "Products Liability—Inadequacy of Information," 48 Tex. L. Rev. 398 (1970).
Manta, "Proximate Causation in Failure to Warn Cases: The Plaintiff's Achilles Heel," F.T.D., October 1984.
Royal, "Post Sale Warnings: A Review and Analysis Seeking Fair Compensation Under Uniform Law," Drake Univ. L. Rev., vol. 33 (1983-84).
Sales, "The Marketing Defect (Warning and Instructions) in Strict Liability," DRI Monograph on Products Liability (1980).

General

Babcock, "Products Liability: A Problem in Jurisprudence," F.T.D., December 1980 & February 1981.
Bowman, "Multiple Defendant Problems in Products Liability Cases," F.T.D., January 1983 & February 1983 (2 part article).
Dickerson, "The ABC's of Products Liability—With a Close Look at Section 402A and the Code," 36 Tenn. L. Rev. 439 (1969).
Goodman, "Strict Liability and the Professional Service Transaction," Insurance Counsel Journal, April 1983.
Kircher, "Products Liability—The Defense Position," Insurance Counsel Journal, April 1977.
Sachs, "A Survey of Product Manufacturers, Insurers and Attorneys," F.T.D., October 1985.
Scheid & Papalia, "Resisting the Irresistible: Defending a Products Liability Case," Insurance Counsel Journal, April 1978.
G. Schwartz, "Understanding Products Liability," Cal. L. Rev., May 1979.

Y.E. Schwartz & Bares, "Federal Reform of Product Liability Law: A Solution That Will Work," 13 Cap. Univ. L. Rev. 251 (1984).

Treece & Mead, " 'Open and Obvious Dangers' in Consumer Products Actions," F.T.D., October 1985.

Walker, "Police Dogs, Pickup Trucks and Other Plaintiff Inspired Products: Today's Expanding Areas of Liability," F.T.D., October 1985.

Handguns

Note, "Handguns and Products Liability," 97 Harv. L. Rev. 1219 (1984).

Turley & Harrison, "Strict Tort Liability of Handgun Suppliers," 6 Hamline L. Rev. 285 (1983).

Investigation of Products Liability Claims

Sorenen, "Initial Investigation of Products Liability Claims," Insurance Law Journal, May 1974.

Spacone, "A Practical Guide to Controlling Products Liability Costs," DRI Monograph, # 6, vol. 1984.

Market Share Liability

Comment, "Market Share Theory and the Asbestos Suits: Should the Industry Bite the Dust?", 14 Stetson L. Rev. 239 (1984).

Comment, "Market Share Liability for Defective Products: An Ill-Advised Remedy for the Problem of Identification," 76 Nw. U.L.R. 300 (1981).

Comment, "Overcoming the Identification Burden in DES Litigation: The Market Share Liability Theory," 65 Marq. L. Rev. 609 (1980).

Hirsch, "Identifying the Generic Product: Market Share and Related Theories of Liability," F.T.D., May 20, 1983.

_____, "Market Share Liability for Manufacturers," F.T.D., October 1980.

Post Accident Evidence

Davis, "Evidence of Post Accident Failures, Modifications and Design Changes in Products Liability Litigation," 6 St. Mary's L.J. 792 (1975).

Note, "Evidence of Subsequent Remedial Measures in Products Liability Actions: Recent Conflict in the Circuit Courts," 35 Mercer L. Rev. 1389 (1984).

"Post-Accident Revisions to Standards," F.T.D., August 1982.
Tish & Reams, "Does Rule 407 Apply to Strict Liability Actions?", F.T.D., October 1984.

Punitive Damages

Comment, Chilcoat, "Punitive Damages in Products Liability: A Layman's Guide for the Manufacturer's Protection," 13 Cap. Univ. L. Rev. 435 (1984).
Comment, Greenberg, "Punitive Damages in Mass-Marketed Product Litigation," 14 Loy. L.A.L. Rev. 405 (1981).
Comment, Roddy, "Punitive Damages in Strict Products Liability," 23 Wm. & Mary L. Rev. 333 (1981).
Ghiardi & Kircher, "Punitive Damage Recovery in Products Liability Cases," 65 Marq. L. Rev. 1 (1981).
Owen, "Punitive Damages in Products Liability Litigation," 74 Mich. L. Rev. 1257 (June 1976).

Recall

Ramp, "The Impact of Recall Campaigns on Products Liability," Insurance Counsel Journal, January 1977.
Smith, "Recall Campaigns: A Possible Defense to Products Liability," Insurance Counsel Journal, January, 1975.
Soden, "Judicial Recall of the Product Withdrawal Exclusion," FIC Quarterly, Summer 1984.
Witker & Phipps, "The Automobile Recall or 'Campaign Letter,'" Insurance Counsel Journal, October 1971.

State-of-the-Art

Comment, "The State of the Art Defense in Products Liability: 'Unreasonably Dangerous' to the Injured Consumer," 18 Duq. L. Rev. 915 (1980).
Lindgren & Ream, " 'State-of-the-Art' Defense," F.T.D., July 1985.
Voorhis, "Compliance as a Defense in Product Cases: Assessing Risks and Pitfalls," F.T.D., July 1985.
Weinberger, "The State of the Art and Products Liability," 28 Def. L.J. 303 (1979).

Strict Liability in Products Liability Cases

Davis, "Strict Liability or Liability Based Upon Fault? Another Look," 10 Univ. of Dayton L. Rev. 1 (1984).
German, "Seller Beware—Strict Liability But Not Absolute Liability," Insurance Counsel Journal, January 1970.

Goodman, "Strict Liability and the Professional Service Transaction," Insurance Counsel Journal, April 1983.
Nielsen, "Strict Liability Actions—Defenses Based on Plaintiff's Conduct," FIC Quarterly, Winter 1982.
Sales, "An Overview of Strict Liability and Its Effects On Property Damage," Insurance Counsel Journal, July 1974.
Tish & Ream, "Does Rule 407 Apply to Strict Liability Actions?", F.T.D., October 1984.
―――――, "The Open and Obvious Danger Defense in Strict Liability Actions," F.T.D., November 1984.
Wade, "On the Nature of Strict Tort Liability for Products," Insurance Law Journal, March 1974.
―――――, "Strict Tort Liability for Products: Past, Present and Future," 13 Cap. Univ. L. Rev. 335 (1984).

Vendor's Liability

Comment, George, "In the Stream of Commerce: The Liability of Non-Manufacturers in Product Liability Actions," 13 Cap. Univ. L. Rev. 405 (1984).
Dillmann, "Limiting Seller Exposure to Product Liability: Vendor's Endorsement," F.T.D., September 1984.
Jursik, " 'World-Wide' Without 'Minimum Contracts': An Analysis of Product Seller's Amenability to Suit," FIC Quarterly, Spring 1981.

CHAPTER 34

Environmental Pollution

§ 34.01 Introduction
§ 34.02 Class Actions
§ 34.03 Mass Tort Litigation
§ 34.04 State Rules
§ 34.05 Federal Acts and Statutes Concerning Pollution
§ 34.06 Grounds for Bringing Environmental Pollution Actions
§ 34.07 Insurance Coverage
    [1] Occurrence and Accident Defined
    [2] Sudden and Accidental Discharges
    [3] Completed Operations Hazard Exclusion
    [4] Policies Intended to Cover Pollution Damage
    [5] First-Party Cases
    [6] Emotional Distress
    [7] Clean-up Costs
§ 34.08 Statutes of Limitation
§ 34.09 Investigation of Environmental Pollution Claims Checklist
§ 34.10 Bibliography

§ 34.01 Introduction

In recent years, cases involving land, water, and air pollution have suddenly attained national prominence. Before the days of nuclear energy, proliferation in the manufacture of hazardous chemicals, and more complete knowledge of the long-term dangers involved in the disposal of hazardous wastes and other pollutants such as industrial smoke, noxious odors and other objectionable byproducts of some industries were accepted as a way of life and the price that must be paid for economic progress.

The attitude today, while concerned with employment opportunities, has changed abruptly and dramatically about the long-term effects involved in the use of carcinogens, dangerous chemicals, and the disposal of hazardous wastes. Such dangers are being found in homes, places of employment, schools, and other buildings that were constructed during the time when asbestos and polyurithane were not known to be dangerous or harmful. We have only recently discovered the extreme dangers of previous careless or deliberate disposal of hazardous wastes. Nor did we realize that many of the chemicals used in farming would later be found to be more harmful then helpful.

Actions have been brought for the removal of lead paint, polyurithane, and asbestos from schools, other public buildings, and homes as a result of injury and damage from the hazards of these and other pollutants in individual and class actions.

§ 34.02 Class Actions

Class actions evolved where there were common questions of law or fact that could be tried in one suit so that the burden of multiple litigation could be reduced. It originally involved claims that could be made where the amount of damages in each was so small as not to warrant individual suits.

Such an action is also useful where a unitary adjudication prevents prejudice to the position of any individual claimant, had he been acting on his own.[1]

Where a court must decide separate substantial questions before it can determine if a person is a member of a class, a class action is inappropriate.[2] Where, however, proof of membership is simple and obvious, the fact that a member's identity is not known should not prevent a class action from being certified.[3]

§ 34.03 Mass Tort Litigation

Asbestos, DES, birth control pills and devices, various drugs, menstrual products, carcinogens, pollutants, environmental waste products and their disposers, highly toxic and flammatory chemicals and other such products and their manufacturers, have been the cause of thousands of new suits.

Such products and the injuries and diseases they have spawned, some of which involved numerous people who were subjected to the same conditions, drugs, pollutants and products that allegedly and

---

[1] Newman v. Tulatin Dev. Co., 597 P.2d 800 (1979) (class action certified for negligence but not for warranty).
[2] Weaver v. Pasadena Tournament of Roses Ass'n, 198 P.2d 514 (Cal. 1948).
[3] Daar v. Yellow Cab Co., 63 Cal. Rptr. 724 (1967).

ENVIRONMENTAL POLLUTION § 34.03

actually caused injury and damages, created a fertile ground for the development of mass tort litigation.

Most of the class actions were instituted in the federal courts, under Rule 23, which governs the certification of federal class actions.

The Rivkin & Silberfeld[4] article lists four requirements for certification as follows:

1. "Numerosity"—the class must be so numerous that joinder of all members is impractical;
2. "Commonality"—there must be questions of law or fact common to the class;
3. "Typicality"—the claims or defenses of the representative parties must be typical of all the class members; and
4. "Adequacy of representation"—the named parties must fairly and adequately protect the interests of unnamed class members.

Under Rule 23, subsection (b)(3), an action may be certified if questions of law or fact, common to the class members predominate over individual questions and if a class action is superior to other available methods for adjudicating the controversy. Four factors are listed in this subdivision for consideration when certification is sought thereunder:

1. The extent that each individual class member would have an interest in controlling the prosecution of his claim in a separate action;
2. The extent and nature of any litigation concerning the controversy already commenced;
3. The desirability of concentrating the litigation in one form; and
4. The difficulties to be encountered in the management of a class proceeding.

Initially, the attitude of the courts was that torts actions had too many variables for them to be included in class actions, but this attitude seems to have changed in recent products and pollution actions,

---

[4] "To Certify or Not to Certify: The Use of the Class Action Device in Mass Tort Litigation," FIC Quarterly, Winter 1983.

§ 34.03   CASUALTY INSURANCE CLAIMS

as well as other mass tort actions.[5] Other cases also failed to get certification.[6] Certification has also been denied in some early pollution and environmental suits.[7]

Mr. O.J. Weber, in his article, "Mass Tort Litigation—The Pot Boils Over,"[8] states: "The tremendous expansion in types and numbers of mass tort litigation has fostered many new procedural developments and tactics. Courts, overwhelmed by mountains of paper and multitudes of suits are impelled to innovate. . . . Therefore we see many, and sometimes all the following tactics employed on a broad scale": [*The following condensed drastically by the writer from the original fifteen observations to eight.*]

1. Expanded use of discovery, interrogatories, and depositions.
2. Increasing attempts to use offensive collateral estoppel.
3. A literature explosion in virtually all of the fields of major mass tort litigation.
4. Institution of uniform procedures by judges for the handling of particular types of litigation and issuance of omnibus orders.
5. More effective use of counsel with specific areas assigned to each.
6. Mass settlements.
7. Assertion of novel and revolutionary (and bizarre) theories of recovery, some of which will no doubt be adopted.
8. The use of multiple juries at the same time in the same courtroom, with each jury deliberating separately and returning answers to interrogatories structured by the court for each jury.

---

[5] In re "Agent Orange" Products Liability Litigation, 506 F. Supp. 762 (N.Y. 1980) (certified for a limited purpose only); In re Northern Dist. of Cal. Dalkon Shield IUD Products Liability Litigation, 526 F. Supp. 877 (Cal. 1981); In re Skywall Cases, 93 F.R.D. 415 (Mo. 1982), *rev'd*, 680 F.2d 1175 (8th Cir. 1982).

[6] Yandle v. PPG Indus., 65 F.R.D. 566 (Tex. 1974); Payton v. Abbott Labs., 83 F.R.D. 382 (Mass. 1979); Hernandez v. Motor Vessel Skyward, 61 F.R.D. 558 (Fla. 1973), *aff'd*, 507 F.2d 1278 (5th Cir. 1975); In re Three Mile Island Litigation, 87 F.R.D. 433 (Pa. 1980); Quellette v. International Paper Co., 86 F.R.D. 476 (Vt. 1980); Penthowski v. Marfuerza Compania Maritime, S.A., 70 F.R.D. 401 (Pa. 1976).

[7] Boring v. Medusa Portland Cement Co., 63 F.R.D. 78 (Pa. 1974); Wojciechowski v. Republic Steel Corp., 413 N.Y.S.2d 70 (1979); Markiewicz v. Salt River Valley Water User's Ass'n, 576 P.2d 517 (Ariz. 1978); Dimond v. General Motors Corp., 97 Cal. Rptr. 639 (1971); McDonnell Douglas Corp. v. United States Dist. Ct., 523 F.2d 1083 (9th Cir. 1975), *cert. denied*, 425 U.S. 911 (1976).

[8] FIC Quarterly, Winter 1983.

§ 34.04 State Rules

State class action rules vary greatly and reflect the historical development of the federal rules. More than two-thirds of the states have adopted some form similar to Federal Rule 23, previously mentioned.[9]

§ 34.05 Federal Acts and Statutes Concerning Pollution

The federal Solid Waste Disposal Act of 1965 provided assistance to local governments in regulating dumpsites used for the disposal of hazardous waste materials. The Act was amended in 1970 to authorize studies that resulted in the enactment of the Resource Conservation and Recovery Act (RCRA) of 1976.[10]

In 1980, the Comprehensive Environmental Response, Compensation and Liability Act (CERCLA) was enacted to fill the gaps that were noted in previous environmental protection laws. CERCLA has been characterized as a "cradle-to-grave" system of controlling toxic chemicals through regulation of generators, transporters, treaters, storers, and disposers of toxic chemicals.[11]

The congressionally avowed purpose of enacting CERCLA was "to provide the beginning of an equitable solution to the environmental and health problems created by reckless and irresponsible disposal of chemical wastes." It was also intended to clarify and codify longstanding common law theories as they relate to liability for damages caused by hazardous waste disposal activity.

A "superfund" was created for the purpose of covering the expense of hazardous waste site response costs. Action can be brought under this Act for liability to refund costs paid by the superfund or by a state or any other entity within certain limitations, and for damages for injury resulting from release of hazardous substances. This Act has been criticized for vagueness, especially as to the circumstances under which a successor owner may be liable for cleanup costs incurred by previous owners and for damages resulting from a failure to clean up hazardous wastes on newly acquired property.

---

[9] *See* Haskell, "Class Actions and the Defense," DRI Seminar Course Book, 85-5, May 17, 1985.

[10] *See* Cyphert & Key, "Hazardous Waste Facility Successor Liability: The Ultimate in Guilt by Association," F.T.D., November 18, 1985.

[11] *See* id.

At a recent congressional hearing on the reauthorization of CERCLA, the American Insurance Association stated that insurers have three major concerns about the Act:

1. Insurance policies drafted long before the enactment of CERCLA would be called upon to pay "superfund" losses and defense costs which the policies intended to exclude, and for which coverage no premium was collected.
2. The Act uses retroactive, strict, joint and several liability which the Association said "cannot be insured" as a matter of underwriting practicality.
3. It was stated that the present system allows no reduction of liability for good conduct.

What effect criticisms like these will have on the Act in the future remains to be seen.

§ 34.06 Grounds for Bringing Environmental Pollution Actions

Generally speaking, actions for injury or damage resulting from environmental pollution, are based upon several theories of recovery.

1. *Negligence.* As in any negligence action, the plaintiff must prove that the defendant owed him a duty to use care in an effort to avoid injury or damage to him, that the defendant acted in a manner not consistent with that of the ordinary prudent person under similar circumstances, and, as in all suits, that there is causal connection between the wrongdoing and the injury or damage.

Where the action is brought on negligence, the usual negligence defenses are available in actions brought for environmental pollution.

2. *Statutory Enactments.* The acts or omissions complained of must fall clearly within the purpose of the environmental act or statute.

3. *Nuisance.* Quite some time ago, our courts recognized the rights of habitation to be superior to the rights of trade, and that when they conflict, the rights of trade must yield to the primary right of habitation.[12] However, while these rights were occasionally recog-

---

[12] American Smelting & Refining Co. v. Godfrey, 158 F. 225 (8th Cir. 1907).

nized judicially, in actuality they were given mere lip-service until recent years.

Doctrines such as the "right to pollute" (where tolerence levels had been set by municipal or other governmental agency), *"prescriptive right to pollute"* (where pollution had continued over many years), and *"reasonable use doctrine"* (where upstream pollution was permitted if it was not "unreasonable"), have become outmoded and, for the most part, outdated.

There are still, however, some defenses that are considered as legitimate in some jurisdictions:

(a). *Coming to a Nuisance.* There is some justice in the defendant's position when he can prove that the operation complained of, was in the neighborhood long before the plaintiff came to it.[13]

(b). *Zoning Ordinances.* Where local zoning ordinances permit businesses and manufacturing plants of a certain type, and in some cases invite such plants into the area, knowing by their very nature that there will be the possibility of pollution, the defense may be a valid one.[14]

(c). *Balance of Convenience.* Here, we are involved chiefly with the economy of a particular area. As long as actual health is not involved, the main question is whether the inconvenience created by the defendant is greater than the benefits which the people in the area will derive from the presence of business or manufacturing plant. Such a balance may include positive items such as the benefit which the industrial operation has upon the public by way of producing jobs, the necessity of the product—particularly at a time of civil commotion or war—plus consideration to be given to the cost of correcting the situation.

While these defenses are still given some weight, and certainly deserve proper consideration as long as health hazards are not involved, it is obvious that recent trends will continue to liberalize judicial decisions, particularly in areas of pollution where we have learned that pollutants are a lot more toxic than had originally been suspected. In addition, we as a nation are much more conscious of protecting the ecology.

---

[13] Ky.: West Va. Gas Co. v. Lafferty, 174 F.2d 848 (6th Cir. 1949).
[14] Weltsche v. Graf, 82 N.E.2d 795 (Mass. 1948).

Obviously, where the plaintiff has contributed to the injury or the damage done by a failure to take available remedial action, or where he has acted in a manner likely to invite or provoke the injury or damage, such actions would either mitigate damages or destroy his right of action.

A major advantage in bringing a pollution action in nuisance, is that the plaintiff does not need to prove that the defendant failed to exercise ordinary care. The nuisance theory also has the effect of focusing more on the injury or damage aspect of the action, rather than on the conduct of the defendant.

4. *Trespass.* Black's Dictionary defines trespass as the commission of a wrongful act, or the doing of a lawful act in a wrongful manner so as to injure the person or property of another. It has also been defined as an invasion of one's interest in the possession of land.[15]

Pollution may occur in the air,[16] on water, or directly onto the land itself.

As in cases based upon nuisance, suits based in trespass are also based upon intentional acts. The fact that harm was not intended is immaterial.[17]

The advantage of bringing the action in trespass, as with nuisance, is that it is not necessary to prove that the injury or damage was caused by negligence. It is the wrongful conduct of the defendant that is paramount.[18]

In an action based upon trespass, a defendant has frequently been held liable even for the indirect or reasonably unforeseeable consequences of his acts while trespassing.[19]

Those who use another's land without permission, may have "risk of losses" imposed on them far beyond those normally imposed in actions based upon negligence.[20]

---

[15] Beck, "The Defense of an Environmental Lawsuit Between Private Litigants," Insurance Counsel Journal, October 1976. *See also* Reynolds Metals Co. v. Martin, 337 F.2d 780 (9th Cir. 1964).

[16] **N.C.:** Hall v. Neweld Mica Corp., 93 S.E.2d 56 (1956).
Ore.: Martin v. Reynolds Metal Corp., 342 P.2d 790, *cert.* denied, 362 U.S. 918 (1960).
Tex.: Gregg v. Delhi-Taylor Oil Corp., 344 S.W.2d 411 (1960).

[17] *Prosser & Keeton on Torts* (5th ed. 1984).
Cal.: Wardrup v. City of Manhattan Beach, 326 P.2d 15 (1958).
Ga.: Montego Corp. v. Hazelrigs, 189 S.E.2d 421 (1982).

[18] **Tex.:** Mountain State Tel. Co. v. Vowels Constr. Co., 341 S.W.2d 148 (1960).

[19] Kopka v. Bell Tel. Co., 91 A.2d 232 (Pa. 1952).

[20] *Prosser & Keeton on Torts* (5th ed. 1984).

ENVIRONMENTAL POLLUTION § 34.07

Continuing tresspass may result from a failure to remove a hazardous condition created by the defendant or by continuing invasions, as, for instance, in the seepage of gasoline or contaminated water onto the property of the plaintiff.[21]

5. *Strict Liability.* The doctrine of strict liability as applied to situations of unusual danger is not a recent development.[22] It is accordingly not surprising that this doctrine has been adopted by more and more jurisdictions, particularly in situations involving pollution.[23]

The defendant's conduct does not have to be intentional in order to justify the awarding of punitive damages for wanton conduct in environmental pollution cases.[24]

Strict liability has been imposed on a defendant as a result of damage resulting from pollution of a water supply because of spillage of waste material,[25] and in many other cases involving pollution.

§ 34.07 Insurance Coverage

Insurance coverage for cases involving pollution was initially granted under the comprehensive general liability policies if the incident complained of could be defined as an "accident."

When the policy language was changed and broadened in 1966, substituting "occurrence" for "accident," the judicial attitude considered it a minor matter since "occurrence" was still defined as an "accident, including continuous or repeated exposure to conditions, which results, during the policy period, in bodily injury or property damage neither expected nor intended from the standpoint of the insured."[26]

The various rating bureaus formulated some exclusions which were usually attached as endorsements. The comprehensive general liability and the special multi-peril policy wording was as follows:

> It is agreed that the insurance does not apply to bodily injury or property damage arising out of the discharge, dispersal, release or escape

---

[21] Sixth Ave. Corp. v. New York City Transit Author., 255 N.Y.S.2d 89 (1964); Restatement (Second) of Torts § 161.

[22] **Cal.:** Luthringer v. Moore, 190 P.2d 1 (1948); *Prosser & Keeton on Torts* (5th ed. 1984).

[23] **Tex.:** Atlas Chem. Indus's., Inc. v. Anderson, 514 S.W.2d 309 (1974).

[24] **Ore.:** McGregor v. Barton Sand & Gravel, Inc., 660 P.2d 175 (1983).

[25] **Ill.:** Indiana Harbor Belt R.R. v. American Cyanamid Co., 517 F. Supp. 314 (1981).

[26] Cardwell, "Insurance and Its Role in the Struggle Between Protecting Pollution Victims and the Producers of Pollution," 31 Drake L. Rev. 913 (1981-82).

of smoke, vapors, soot, fumes, acids, alkalis, toxic chemicals, liquids or gases, waste materials or other irritants, contaminations or pollutants into or upon land, the atmosphere or any water course or body of water; but this exclusion does not apply if such discharge, dispersal, release or escape is sudden and accidental.

This wording was not uniform. Some policies included the words "neither expected nor intended by the insured," but there is little doubt today that the courts found reasons enough, despite the new language, for holding most pollution incidents covered under the liability policies. The 1986 Commercial General Liability policy permits specific coverage against pollution for an extra premium.

[1] Occurrence and Accident Defined

As already noted, the use of the word "occurrence" instead of "accident" did not, for the most part change the attitude of the courts. Many decisions held that long-term series of acts were covered under the liability policy.[27]

One type of exclusion, also usually applied by endorsement, excludes coverage under any circumstances and regardless of whether the discharge was accidental. This type of endorsement usually reads as follows: "any bodily injury or property damage arising out of the discharge, dispersal, release or escape of oil or other petroleum substances or derivatives into or upon any water course or body of water."

This endorsement was specifically aimed to prevent coverage for the rash of oil spills that were creating havoc over a large area of shoreline.

---

[27] **Ala.:** Employers Ins. Co. of Ala. v. Rives, 87 So. 2d 653 (1955) (gasoline seepage over long period of time, causing contamination).

Cal.: Moore v. Fidelity & Cas. Co. of N.Y., 259 P.2d 154 (1956) (unexpected and unforeseen consequences held to be "accident from plaintiff's point of view." Damage over long period of time did not affect court's decision).

Mo.: White v. Smith, 440 S.W.2d 497 (App. 1969) (nuisance involving obnoxious odors, noise, and well contamination over six-year period held covered since resulting damage was unintentional).

Ore.: Aetna Cas. & Sur. Co. v. Martin Bros. Container & Timber Prod's Corp., 256 F. Supp. 145 (1966) (change of endorsement from "accident" to "occurrence" did not exclude coverage since "occurrence" was defined in terms of "accident").

Pa.: Moffat v. Metropolitan Cas. Ins. Co., 238 F. Supp. 165 (1964) (nuisance arising out of gases and waste products).

See also Wilmarth, "Outline of Insurance Developments," 21 Federal Insurance Counsel Quarterly, #4, Summer 1971, from which the above cases were culled.

[2] Sudden and Accidental Discharges

The pollution exclusion holds that discharge of waste materials on land, water, or in the air is not covered unless "such discharge, dispersal, release or escape is sudden and accidental." The majority of the decisions interpreting these words hold that this exclusion is ambiguous and should be interpreted in consistence with the definition of "occurrence" which states that the injury or damage should be "neither expected nor intended" as to *results* (italics mine). In other words, coverage will not be provided for intentional results from unintentional acts but should be provided for unintended results of intentional acts.[28]

Some cases have held that where hazardous waste material is illegally dumped over a protracted period of time and contamination therefrom is likely to continue for some indefinite time, the dumping cannot be considered as sudden or accidental. Accordingly such dumping is not covered under the liability policy containing any such exclusionary wording.[29] The new Commercial General Liability policy defines "occurrence" more specifically.

[3] Completed Operations Hazard Exclusion

It has been held that coverage for hazardous waste disposal that was not intended for consumption, sale, or use by others, are not "products" so as to preclude coverage under the completed operations provision.[30]

---

[28] **Mass.:** Shapiro v. Public Service Mut. Ins. Co., 477 N.E.2d 146 (1985).
  N.J.: C.P.S. Chem. Co., Inc. v. Continental Ins. Co., 489 A.2d 1265 (Super. 1985); Jackson Township Munic. Utilities Author. v. Hartford A. & I. Co., 451 A.2d 990 (1982).
  N.C.: Waste Management of Carolinas, Inc. v. Peerless Ins. Co., 323 S.E.2d 726 (App. 1985).
  Ohio: Buckeye Union Ins. Co. v. Liberty Solvents & Chem. Co., Case # 11598 (C.A. Ohio, July 11, 1984).
  Utah: Branch v. Western Petroleum, Inc., 657 P.2d 267 (1983) (liability can be predicated on the basis of strict liability or nuisance).
  Wash.: United Pacific Ins. Co. v. Van's Westlake Union, Inc., 664 P.2d 1262 (App. 1983).
[29] **Ind.:** Barmet of Indiana, Inc. v. Security Ins. Group, 425 N.E.2d 201 (App. 1980) (discharge of gases was not sudden and accidental and hence, not covered).
  Mich.: American States Ins. Co. v. Maryland Cas. Ins. Co., 587 F. Supp. 1549 (1984).
  Contra: **N.Y.:** Evans v. Aetna Cas. & Sur. Co., 435 N.Y.S.2d 953 (1981).
[30] **Md.:** Steyer v. Westvaco Corp., 450 F. Supp. 384 (1978).

[4] Policies Intended to Cover Pollution Damage

In 1981, the Insurance Services Office (ISO) promulgated its first pollution liability policy, which was an optional, claims-made policy covering injury and/or damage resulting from pollution, and for clean-up costs imposed by law or voluntarily assumed with the consent of the insurer.

Similar forms were promulgated by independent insurers that did not subscribe to ISO. Originally this coverage was mainly provided by companies that specialized in this type of policy.

The new 1986 Commercial General Liability policy, also promulgated by ISO, has substantially revised the provisions dealing with pollution coverage. There has been much criticism concerning the new forms and I would guess that further substantial changes will be made in this form in the near future, as courts interpret the new language in a manner not as yet suspected by the underwriters.

The judicial trend concerning injury and damage resulting from pollution has clearly been toward finding some reasoning that would justify insurance coverage when the incident involved was unquestionably intended and the resulting damage known or predictable by any reasoning being.

Since many of the new claims and suits involve older policy forms, it is vitally necessary that each case be carefully scrutinized as to the exact wording of any references to pollution coverage. Such cases should be referred for legal opinion so that the claims person will have some direction and guidelines for investigation.

[5] First-Party Cases

First-party claims or suits involving pollution losses may arise under "All-risk," Homeowners or Multi-peril formats, as well as named peril coverages.

Some pertinent questions of coverage may involve:

1. Definition of property damage.
2. Determination of what is a "direct physical loss."
3. Definition of "occurrence."
4. Determining the boundaries of "all-risk" versus all losses.
5. Determining the time of occurrence and whether or not the loss was within the time limitation of the policy coverage.

6. Applicability of certain exclusions such as "inherent vice" or "inherent defect," "ordinary wear and tear," or "intentional misconduct."

[6] Emotional Distress

The Restatement (Second) of Torts § 920 states:

(1) If one is entitled to a judgment for harm to land resulting from a past invasion and not amounting to a total destruction of value, the damages include compensation for (c) discomfort and annoyance to him as an occupant.

This section of the Restatement cites in support, some cases involving pollution.[31]

The Supreme Court of Montana, in an action based in nuisance, trespass and negligence, arising out of a leakage of gasoline from negligently installed tanks at a neighborhood gasoline station, ruled that the plaintiffs could recover for mental anguish.[32] In this case, the court stated that: "Where there has been a trespass to land, damages for the discomfort and annoyance to the occupant, in addition to damage to the land or for the use of the land itself, have long been recognized."

In recent years, the theory of strict liability has invaded the area of products liability with a vengeance, with the result that there has been a distinct change in attitude concerning recovery for emotional distress in pollution-related cases that also involve products liability. In the case of *Wetherill v. University of Chicago*,[33] for instance, the court held that damages for emotional distress due to the fear of cancer on an action brought in strict liability, was recoverable.

On the other hand, the Federal District Court in Rhode Island[34] held that women who had DES injected during their pregnancies could not recover for emotional distress because it was not accompanied by a physical manifestation.

---

[31] **Cal.:** Kornoff v. Kingsburg Cotton Oil Co., 288 P.2d 507 (1955) (case involved dust pollution from a ginning mill that caused damage and discomfort, amounting to mental anguish).

Mont.: Nelson v. C.& C. Plywood, 465 P.2d 314 (1970) (this case involved dumping of glue wastes resulting in noxious odors and damage to the water supply).

Ore.: Edwards v. Talent Irrigation District, 570 P.2d 1169 (1977).

[32] French v. Ralph Moore, Inc., 661 P.2d 844 (1983).

[33] 565 F. Supp. 1553 (Ill. 1983).

[34] Plummer v. Abbott Lab's, 568 F. Supp. 920 (1983).

In a New Jersey case, the superior court held that persons who alleged cancer-phobia due to toxic wastes leaking into their wells from a municipal landfill must show that it was foreseeable that escaping contaminants would cause a fear of cancer and that the emotional distress resulted in substantial bodily injury or sickness.[35]

In the case of *Wisniewski v. Johns-Manville Corp.*,[36] the U.S. Court of Appeals, predicting what the Pennsylvania Supreme Court would hold, ruled that a claim for negligent infliction of emotional distress caused by the illness and subsequent death of workers from asbestos exposure did not state a valid cause of action in the absence of allegations of any injuries that stemmed from exposure to the asbestos itself.

[7] Clean-up Costs

In the North Carolina Appellate case of *Waste Management of Carolinas, Inc. v. Peerless Ins. Co.*,[37] the court asks whether the policy language that "the company shall have the right and duty to defend any suit against the insured seeking *damages* (italics mine) on account of . . . bodily injury or property damage" means that the insurer is obligated only to defend the insured when legal, monetary damages are demanded, or whether the insurer must also defend when a suit seeks only the costs of complying with an injunction.

The court held that "Although such action is called equitable relief, (such) cleanup costs are essentially compensatory damages for injury to community property. . . . They are covered by the general liability policies."

As a matter of practical economics and good business and public relations, insurers have, in many instances, accepted coverage and paid for clean-up costs. Such payments have no doubt avoided further damage which probably would have instigated additional claims that could have become much more costly.

§ 34.08 Statutes of Limitation

A cause of action in nuisance, for pollution damage, arises when the harm is done,[38] while one brought in trespass usually begins from

---

[35] Ayers v. Jackson Township, 461 F.2d 184 (1983).
[36] 759 F.2d 271 (3d Cir. 1985).
[37] 323 S.E.2d 726 (App. 1985).
[38] **Tex.:** Barakis v. American Cyanamid Co., 161 F. Supp. 25 (1958).

ENVIRONMENTAL POLLUTION § 34.09

the first time of the wrongful act.[39]

In *Reynolds Metals v. Yturbide*,[40] brought in nuisance, the court held that under the *continuing nuisance* theory, each incident of pollution comprises a new tort and the statute of limitations may apply separately to each incident.

In recent years, the belated discovery concerning carcinogenic and other hazardous toxic chemicals and substances, has resulted in masses of new products liability suits. It is accordingly suggested that a review of the Products Liability section of this book be made for more information concerning pollution and insurance coverage therefore, as well as more information concerning the applicability of the statutes of limitation in pollution cases.

§ 34.09 Investigation of Environmental Pollution Claims Checklist

Even more than in other cases, an investigation of claims involving pollution must include a complete investigation of the physical facts in the situation. In these cases it is essential that a determination of the exact nature of the alleged pollution, its duration, the extent of the contamination or alleged contamination, and all other aspects of the physical facts be obtained in detail. The following investigation is a suggested starting point:

- ☐ Determine if there was actual damage to tangible property belonging to the plaintiff and/or others.
- ☐ Determine if any alleged injury is actually of a physical nature and the extent of the injury.
- ☐ Find out if the insured's plant or operation has any public or economic value to the area in which it is located. Determine if the insured is the owner, lessor or what his connection is to the wrongdoing.
- ☐ Learn how many people are employed at the plant or operation, what group or groups were subjected to the same contamination and for how long.
- ☐ Determine if there was any reasonable way to abate the pollution and whether the insured has attempted to stop or abate it. If so, determine how and at what cost and effectiveness.
- ☐ Find out who came to the area first and whether the plaintiff moved into it fully aware of the condition.

---

[39] *Id.*
[40] 258 F.2d 321 (9th Cir. 1958).

§ 34.10 CASUALTY INSURANCE CLAIMS

☐ Determine if the plant or operation complies with all federal and state requirements and those of all regulatory agencies.
☐ Find out if the insured or his plant or operation has ever been in violation of any such acts, statutes, or regulations and, if so, obtain full details.
☐ Determine if the insured ever obtained specific permission to act in the manner complained of and, if so, obtain proof.
☐ Determine whether the insured was invited to build a plant or to operate in the area by local, state, or federal agencies, or anyone else.
☐ Learn if the insured's operation is vital to the defense or welfare of the people or any governmental agency.
☐ In toxic waste cases, learn how often and when such wastes were dumped at the location in question. Find out if permission was given by the landholder or anyone else.
☐ Determine whether there is coverage under your policy and if any other policies could possibly have provided coverage. Get underwriting and legal help in making such a determination.
☐ Check the medical aspects very carefully in any allegation of injury.
☐ Find out if others who were subjected to the same condition suffered similar injuries or disease.
☐ Submit your ongoing investigation on a regular basis for legal and medical review and follow through as directed.

§ 34.10 Bibliography

Beck, "The Defense of an Environmental Lawsuit Between Private Litigants," Insurance Counsel Journal, October 1976.
Brookmeier, "Pollution—The Risk and Insurance Problem," 12 F.T.D. #7, September 1971.
Conley & Paynter, "Basic Aspects of Defending Pollution Suits," 12 F.T.D. # 5, May 1971.
Currie, "State Pollution Statutes," 48 U. Chi. L. Rev. 27 (1981).
Cyphert & Key, "Hazardous Waste Facility Successor Liability: The Ultimate in Guilt By Association," F.T.D., November 18, 1985.
"Environmental Pollution: Liability and Insurance," Monogram, Insurance Information Institute.
Goulka, "The Pollution Exclusion," Insurance Adjuster Magazine, June 1984.
Morrissey, "Private Nuisance: A Remedy Against Air Pollution," Insurance Counsel Journal, July 1971.
"Symposium on Ecology and Environmental Control," 21 Fed. of Insurance Counsel Journal, #4, Summer 1971.

Whitehead, "Hazardous Wastes and Toxic Torts: Handling Litigation and Insurance Coverage Issues," Insurance Counsel Journal, April 1984.

CHAPTER 35

Professional Liability—Physicians

§ 35.01 Introduction
§ 35.02 Physicians, Surgeons and Dentists Professional Liability Policies
    [1] Insuring Agreements
    [2] Persons Insured
    [3] Limits of Liability
    [4] Medical Incident
    [5] Exclusions
    [6] Consent of Insured to Settle
    [7] Each Claim
    [8] Protracted Treatment
    [9] Coverage for Insured's Employees
    [10] Notice of Accident
    [11] Claims-Made Policies
    [12] Sexual Wrongdoing
§ 35.03 Some General Principles of Medical Malpractice Liability Law
    [1] Standard of Care
    [2] *Res Ipsa Loquitur*
    [3] Honest Error in Judgment
    [4] Informed Consent
        [a] Exceptions to the "Informed Consent" Doctrine
        [b] Forms and Videotapes
    [5] Defenses to Actions for Medical Malpractice
    [6] Referral to Specialist
    [7] Abandonment
    [8] Psychiatrist and Psychotherapist Responsibility for Wrongful Release of Mentally Ill Patients
    [9] Second Injury
    [10] Respondeat Superior or Captain-of-the-Ship Doctrine
    [11] Contracts to Cure
    [12] Multiple Defendants
    [13] Good Samaritan Doctrine
    [14] Malpractice Actions for Wrongful Birth and Wrongful Life
        [a] Wrongful Birth
        [b] Wrongful Life
        [c] Wrongful Pregnancy or Wrongful Conception
        [d] "Benefits of Parenthood" Doctrine
        [e] Damages Recoverable for Wrongful Birth Cases

[15] Actions Based on Contract
[16] Statutes of Limitations
    [a] Discovery Rule—Foreign Substance Left in Body
    [b] Continuing Negligence Rule
    [c] Fraudulent Concealment
§ 35.04 Arbitration of Medical Malpractice Cases
§ 35.05 Recent Medical Malpractice Legislation
§ 35.06 Action for Wrongful Suit by Physicians
    [1] Malicious Prosecution

§ 35.01 Introduction

Professional Liability insurance, commonly known as Malpractice insurance, is also sometimes called Errors and Omissions coverage. This kind of insurance provides liability protection not only for physicians and hospitals, but for a variety of other professions and even some trades. For instance, in addition to dentists, nurses, druggists, lawyers, and accountants, professional liability coverage may be obtained in some companies designed to protect architects, teachers, insurance agents and adjusters, corporate officers and directors, social workers, psychotherapists, real estate and security brokers, and even beauticians and undertakers among others.

According to one commentator,[1] "A professional is one who continually must exercise intellectual judgment predicated upon high educational achievement in the performance of his duties, and whose clients rely on that judgment."

Some cases have made a distinction between commercial services of a beautician, undertaker, or other commercial ventures, and those of professionals such as doctors, lawyers and similar professions. A few of these cases that make such a distinction hold that strict liability should be imposed on commercial ventures only.

The common denominator is that each holds himself out as a specialist who has some knowledge peculiar to his or her field of endeavor. The general principles of law governing the professional liability of an attorney arising out of his practice, for instance, is similar, with some notable exceptions, to that of a doctor and other specialists.

As with other areas of insurance costs, the complaints from those who have to pay high premiums, and from the general public who helps to pay those premiums indirectly, has been heard by legislators.

---

[1] "Professional Negligence," 121 Univ. Pa. L. Rev. 627 (1973).

As a result, most states have enacted statutes that were intended to give some relief to insurers in the hope that it would help to reduce insurance premiums.

In handling claims and suits that fall within the professional liability policies, particularly those dealing with the medical sciences, consideration must always be given to the possibility of overlapping coverage in those borderline cases that lie somewhere between the Professional Liability policy and the General Liability policy.

If, for instance, a patient is injured while getting off of an examining table, the demarcation line is so thin that the case could possibly fall within either or both policies. The claim representative must always therefore be alert to the possibility of at least contribution from the carrier of another policy and, in some cases, even the likelihood that the other carrier might take over the case entirely.

Professional liability policies are designed to protect the practitioner from liability for acts or omissions performed as a result of his or her practice. With the exception of the medical arts and Lawyers Liability policies, many of the other policies do not follow a standard format, even though most of them have more similarities than differences.

The professional liability policies differ from the general liability policies in that the latter are designed to cover an insured for liability arising out of premises incidents or out of the insured's actions or omissions that do not result from his or her professional practice.

While there are usually no specific exclusions in either policy with reference to the other, the medical professional liability policies usually do specify that the insured is covered for "All sums for which the insured (specified in the policy) shall become legally obligated to pay as damages because of injury to which this (insurance) applies, *caused by a medical incident* (italics added) . . . in the practice of the insured's profession as a physician," etc. Other professional policies usually have similar wording.

Where both the general liability and the professional liability policies are written in the same company, the problem is resolved internally. It does, however, become of major importance to scrutinize both policies where they are written in different companies, especially since many, if not most, of the professional liability policies are nonstandard.

The big question as to which policy covers a given situation then involves a determination as to whether or not the incident arose out of the professional act or omission.[2] This major distinction between professional and liability policies will be discussed in greater depth as the specific fields of professional liability coverage are examined.

§ 35.02 Physicians, Surgeons and Dentists Professional Liability Policies[3]

In a discussion of the Physicians, Surgeons and Dentists Professional Liability policy, as with similar professional policies, it is the professional services or the failure to render them that is covered. These policies do not cover liability resulting from premises and other incidents not connected with professional activities.

Physicians, Surgeons and Dentists Professional Liability policies are written on a "claims-made" as well as on the usual "occurrence" form. These two types of policies have already been discussed in § 26.02 *supra*, concerning professional liability coverage in general.

The Physicians, Surgeons and Dentists Professional Liability policy also comes in two other forms: Coverage M for individual physicians and Coverage N for partnerships, associations or corporations.

Since Coverage M insures the individual liability of each person named in the Declarations, such insureds may be practicing alone or he or she may be a member of a partnership, association or corporation.

---

[2] The following illustrative list of cases was taken from the F.C. & S. Bulletins, Casualty vol., Public Liability section, pp. Dma - 3 to 12:

Cal.: Northern Ins. Co. v. Superior Court of San Francisco, 154 Cal. Rptr. 198 (1979).
Fla.: The Foremost Ins. Co. v. Hartford Ins. Group., 385 So. 2d 110 (1980).
La.: Grant v. Touro Infirmary, 223 So. 2d 148 (1969).
Neb.: Marx v. Hartford A. & I. Co., 157 N.W.2d 870 (1968).
N.Y.: Hartford A. & I. Co. v. The Regent Nursing Home, 413 N.Y.S.2d 195 (1979); Brockband v. Travelers Ins. Co., 207 N.Y.S.2d 723 (1960).
Okla.: Gulf Ins. Co. v. Gold Cross Ambulance Service, 327 F. Supp. 149 (1971).
Ohio: American Policyholders Ins. Co. v. Michota, 103 N.E.2d 817 (1952).
Pa,; Knoor v. Commercial Cas. Ins. Co., 90 A.2d 387 (1952).
Wash.: Harris v. Firemen's Fund Indem. Co., 257 P.2d 221 (1953).

[3] The policies used in this discussion are those promulgated by the Insurance Services Office (ISO), New York, NY, and parts are reprinted with their permission. Due credit must also be given to the Fidelity, Casualty & Surety (F.C.&S.) Bulletins, National Underwriting Co., Cincinnati, Ohio, from which we have liberally quoted and paraphrased.

[1] Insuring Agreements

The Insuring Agreement under Coverage M includes "all sums which the insured shall be legally obligated to pay as damages because of injury to which this insurance applies, caused by a medical incident . . . arising out of the insured's profession as a physician, surgeon or dentist."

The deficiency of individual coverage for members of any group is that individual coverage will not protect the insured from his or her responsibility *as a member of the group.* Therein lies the need for Coverage N and the Insuring Agreement for Coverage N reads the same, except that Coverage N provides for the insured's liability for damages arising out of injury caused "by any person for whose acts or omissions the professional partnership, association or corporate insured is legally responsible."

[2] Persons Insured

Persons insured under Coverage N are

the partnership, association or corporation described in the Declarations and any member, partner, officer, director or stockholder thereof, with respect to acts or omissions of others, provided that no such member, partner, officer, director or stockholder . . . shall be an insured . . . with respect to acts or omissions in the furnishing of professional services by the insured or any person acting under the insured's personal direction, control or supervision."

In other words, a practicing physician who is a member of a partnership, association or corporation needs both Coverage M and N, unless he alone comprises the corporation.

[3] Limits of Liability

Initially, Physicians Professional Liability coverage was written on a per claim limit of liability and an aggregate limit. It was not material how many claims arose out of a single act or omission. The aggregate limit was and still is on a yearly basis. Subsequently, in 1977, a modified form was introduced in many territories (not all) on a per "medical incident" limit. This was intended to restrict the number of claims that might arise from one act or omission.

Coverage M provides protection arising out of "The furnishing of professional medical or dental services by the insured, an employee of the insured, or any person acting under the personal direction, control or supervision of the insured."

[4] Medical Incident

"Medical incident" is defined as any act or omission "in the furnishing of professional medical or dental services by the insured, an employee of the insured, or any person acting under the personal direction, control or supervision of the insured."

The term "medical incident" also provides coverage to the insured when an insured's liability arises out of acts of employees such as nurses and technicians acting under the direction or control of the insured.

This coverage does not include an employee or other person *for his or her own personal liability*. An endorsement can be provided for this purpose.

Coverage N defines "medical incident" as any act or omission "in the furnishing of professional medical or dental services by (1) any member, partner, officer, director, stockholder or employee of the insured, or (2) any person acting under the personal direction control or supervision of the insured."

[5] Exclusions

The current Physicians, Surgeons and Dentists Professional Liability policy contains five exclusions.:

(a) to injury arising out of the performance by the insured of a criminal act;

(b) to injury for which the insured may be held liable as a proprietor, hospital administrator, officer, stockholder, or member of the board of directors, trustees or governors of any hospital, sanitarium, clinic with bed and board facilities, laboratory, nursing home or other business enterprise;

(c) under Coverage M—individual Professional Liability—to injury arising out of the rendering or failure to render professional services of any other person for whose acts or omissions the insured may be held liable as a member, partner, officer, director or stockholder of any professional partnership, association or corporation;

(d) to bodily injury of any employee of the insured arising out of or in the course of that person's employment by the insured;

(e) to any obligation for which the insured or any carrier acting as insurer may be held liable under any workers' compensation law or under any similar law.

The 1973 edition of this policy included only a modified version of exclusion (b). Coverage for criminal acts were never intended to be covered but were not specifically excluded, nor were exclusions (c), (d), and (e) in the 1973 edition.

Another exclusion which is either contained in the jacket of comprehensive liability policies or added as an essential endorsement, deals with Nuclear Energy.

[6] Consent of Insured to Settle

As has already been stated in general, the Physicians, Surgeons and Dentists Professional Liability policy has, until recent years, required the written consent of the insured before any settlement with the claimant could be consummated.

This provision of the policy was dropped from this and other professional liability policies in 1977 and 1981 and has not been replaced. The old provision caused many complications where the insurer felt it expedient to settle and the insured professional interpreted the claim as a personal affront.

The Insurance Services Office form of Physicians, Surgeons and Dentists Professional Liability policy is, in many respects, similar to other forms of medical malpractice coverage. We will here discuss some of the principle aspects of this coverage.

[7] Each Claim

In the case of *St. Paul Fire & Marine Ins. Co. v. Hawaiian Ins. & Guar. Co.*,[4] the court held that: (1) Separate acts of negligence constitute separate claims, even though they may result in one death; and (2) Claims made against several individuals under the same policy constitute separate claims.

Another case,[5] held that the factor that determines the limits of liability under a malpractice policy is the number of patients injured by the alleged malpractice and not the number of persons that were adversely affected as a result of the injury. In other words, derivative

---

[4] 637 P.2d 1146 (1981).
[5] Chicago Ins. Co. v. Pacific Indem. Co., 566 P.2d 954 (Pa. 1982).

§ 35.02[8]   CASUALTY INSURANCE CLAIMS

claims of husbands for loss of consortium and others of a like nature do not constitute additional claims.

This case also held that "The fact that the physician's alleged failure to make a proper diagnosis which may have extended over several years does not mean that the failure gave rise to more than one claim."

[8] **Protracted Treatment**

When treatment is given over a protracted period of time so that the exact date of the malpractice cannot be determined, it has usually been held that as long as any part of the treatment occurred within the limits of coverage, the resulting injury is covered.[6]

[9] **Coverage for Insured's Employees**

In the case of *National Union Fire Ins. Co. v. Medical Liability Mut. Ins. Co.*,[7] a doctor's nurse, employed by the doctor, rendered certain medical services to a patient, after which the patient delivered a premature baby. A malpractice action was brought as a result, against the doctor and the nurse. The doctor's insurer refused to cover the nurse's individual exposure.

Despite the fact that the case made no mention of a specific exclusion for employees of the insured, the policy did define "insured" as "the licensed physician or surgeon named in the declarations."

The court held that the phrase "persons for whose acts or omissions the insured is legally responsible" does not include an employee nurse.

Under the ISO form,[8] the doctor's vicarious liability as a result of the nurse's malpractice, if any, would have been covered in an action against him, but the personal liability of the nurse would not have been covered.

[10] **Notice of Accident**

In the Illinois Appellate case of *Sisters of Divine Providence v. In-*

---
[6] Glacier General Assur. Co. v. Continental Cas. Co., 605 F. Supp. 126 (1985).
[7] 448 N.Y.S.2d 480 (N.Y. App. 1981).
[8] Insurance Services Office, New York, NY.

terstate Fire & Cas. Co.,[9] the Notice of Accident provision of the policy required that: "Whenever the insured has information from which the insured may reasonably conclude that an occurrence covered hereunder involves injuries or damages which . . . (are) likely to involve this policy, notice shall be given by, or on behalf of the insured to the company as soon as practicable."

The court held that:

1. The insured's duty to report an incident or occurrence is a condition precedent to coverage.
2. The duty to report arose once the insured had "actual knowledge" from which it could reasonably conclude that a claim would be made.
3. Since there was no acceptable reason for the delay in reporting, it was not made "as soon as practicable."
4. Prejudice need not be established.

[11] Claims-Made Policies

The Louisiana Appellate court case of *Hunter v. Office of Health Services*,[10] held that a "claims-made" policy covers the insured from the time a claim is made, or from the time the injury or the damage was discovered.

This case also held that unless there was specific wording to the contrary, an excess policy is derivative of the primary policy. In this case, both policies were accordingly restricted to claims made during the policy period. The fact that "occurrence" wording was used does not make the policy ambiguous.

Finally, the case also held that the doctrine of estoppel in Louisiana "has not been allowed . . . to extend or enlarge coverage beyond that set forth in the policy."

[12] Sexual Wrongdoing

Sexual wrongdoing comes in several fashions. Sometimes, it is a direct assault that has nothing to do with medical treatment. Even where there is no explicit exclusion for intentional or criminal acts,

---
[9] 453 N.E.2d 36 (N.Y. 1983).
[10] 385 So. 2d 928 (1980).

the courts have generally agreed that where the act was clearly not a part of any alleged diagnosis or treatment, such acts were not covered by a professional liability policy.[11]

In the case of *Aetna Life & Cas. Ins. Co. v. McCabe*,[12] the court held that since the malpractice policy did not contain an explicit exclusion for intentional injury, public policy usually prevents an insurer from profiting at the expense of an innocent beneficiary. Accordingly, sexual assaults were held to be covered. The court apparently felt that there was no public policy objection to the criminal insured's profiting from his own wrongdoing.

Other courts have used public policy more logically, as a reason for not granting coverage because the wrongdoer should not be permitted to profit from his wrongdoing.[13]

Psychiatrists are in a class by themselves. It has been held by the majority of the opinions that since the malpractice policies cover "injury arising out of a rendering of, or failure to render professional services," the professional liability policy does not make an exception for this kind of malpractice where sex is induced as an alleged part of the treatment. This has been construed as failure to give proper treatment and, accordingly, covered.[14]

A recent case[15] held that sexual conduct, if related to therapy by a psychiatrist, is covered as "professional services." The court further held that even if the psychiatrist is aware of the potential harm of his acts, it is not the same as intended harm and cannot therefore be considered as "intentional injury." The intent of the decision was to declare that sex performed as part of the psychiatric treatment is covered by the malpractice policy.

---

[11] **Idaho:** Hirst v. St. Paul Fire & Marine Ins. Co., 683 P.2d 440 (1984).
Minn.: Smith v. St. Paul Fire & Marine Ins. Co., 353 N.W.2d 130 (1984).
[12] 556 F. Supp. 1342 (Pa. 1983).
[13] *See supra* note 10.
[14] **Ga.:** St. Paul Fire & Marine Ins. Co. v. Mitchell, 296 S.E.2d 126 (1982).
Mich.: Vigilant Ins. Co. v. Kambly, 319 N.W.2d 382 (1982).
Mo.: Zipkin v. Freeman, 436 S.W.2d 763 (1968).
Pa.: Aetna Life & Cas. Co. v. McCabe, 556 F. Supp. 1342 (1983).
Wis.: L.L. v. Medical Protective Co., 362 N.W.2d 174 (1985).
[15] Vigilant Ins. Co. v. Employers Ins. of Wausau, 626 F. Supp. 262 (N.Y. 1986).

§ 35.03 Some General Principles of Medical Malpractice Liability Law

[1] Standard of Care

Initially, the standard for evaluating the conduct of a physician in a malpractice suit was that degree of skill and care of a "reasonably skilled practitioner" in the same or similar locality.[16] The "locality rule" was initially promulgated in order to protect those doctors who were practicing in rural communities who did not have the education or skill of urban doctors. However, since the advent of state medical licensing, many courts have recognized the fact that, at least in family medicine, the skill and education of the rural practitioner is at least the equivalent of the urban doctor, if not greater.

While some jurisdictions still follow the "locality" rule,[17] many of the more recent cases have accepted instead, the national standard.[18]

---

[16] Ariz.: Fiske v. Soland, 448 P.2d 429 (1968).
Del.: Di Filippo v. Preston, 173 A.2d 333 (1961).
Md.: Dunham v. Elder, 306 A.2d 568 (1973).
Mass.: Brune v. Belinkoff, 235 N.E.2d 793 (1968).
Mich.: Naccarato v. Grob, 180 N.W.2d 788 (1970).
Mo.: Aiken v. Clary, 396 So. 2d 668 (1965).
Neb.: Mecham v. McLeay, 227 N.W.2d 829 (1975).
Tex.: Karp v. Cooley, 493 F.2d 408 (3d Cir. 1974).
Va.: Bly v. Rhods, 222 S.E.2d 783 (1976).
Wis.: Shier v. Freedman, 206 N.W.2d 166 (1973).
[17] Ark.: Gambill v. Stroud, 531 S.W.2d 945 (1976).
D.C.: Haven v. Randolph, 342 F. Supp. 538 (1972).
Ill.: Hirn v. Edgewater Hosp., 408 N.E.2d 970 (1980).
Ind.: Stanley v. Fisher, 417 N.E.2d 932 (1981).
N.C.: McPherson v. Ellis, 287 S.E.2d 892 (1982).
Pa.: Cooper v. Rogers, 286 A.2d 647 (Super. 1971).
R.I.: Young v. Park, 417 A.2d 889 (1980), cert. denied, 449 U.S. 1119 (1981).
U.S.: Rees v. Shaughnessy, 570 F.2d 309 (10th Cir. 1978).
[18] Ga.: Sullivan v. Henry, 287 S.E.2d 652 (1982).
Ky.: Blair v. Eblen, 461 S.W.2d 370 (1970).
Md.: Shilkret v. Annapolis Emerg. Hosp., 349 A.2d 245 (1975).
Miss.: Hall v. Hillbun, 466 So. 2d 856 (1985).
Wash.: Pederson v. Dumouchel, 431 P.2d 973 (1967).
W. Va.: Plaintiff v. City of Parkersburg, 345 S.E.2d 564 (1986).
See also 99 A.L.R.3d 1133 (1980); Decyk & Hirsch, "The Medical Standard of Care," DRI Monograph #4, 1977; King & Coe, "The Wisdom of the Strict Locality Rule," 3 Univ. Balt. L. Rev. 221 (1974); Note, "An Evolution of Changes in the Medical Standard of Care," 23 Vand. L. Rev. 729 (1970); Walty, "The Rise and Gradual Fall of the 'Locality' Rule in Medical Malpractice Litigation," 18 De Paul L. Rev. 408 (1969).

§ 35.03[1]　　　　　　CASUALTY INSURANCE CLAIMS

Most jurisdictions accept the premise that locality should have no bearing in judging the competency of medical specialists.[19]

Since there are limits as to how much information a doctor should disclose to a particular patient, the bottom line is what is reasonable under all of the circumstances, to disclose, and that is a question for jury determination.[20]

In the case of *Stepakoff v. Kantar*,[21] the court held that the negligence of a physician who practices a specialty, consists of a failure to exercise the degree of care and skill of the average qualified physician practicing that specialty, taking into account the advances in the profession and the resources available to the physician.

This case also held that a psychiatrist, after diagnosing a patient as suicidal, does not have the additional duty to take preventive measures, under the "reasonableness" standard.[22]

There has been some legal discussion as to whether the standard of reasonable care "as practiced by other doctors" is a standard of custom by the profession rather than a reasonable standard in the minds of the jurors or trial judges. This is a matter of evidence and I find these discussions of little value to an understanding of the basic premise of malpractice. There are, I think, rather few situations of blatant negligence that would be "customary practice" unless it was confined to an extremely small backwards community.[23] More logical is the decision in the case of *Darling v. Charleston Community Mem. Hosp.*,[24] where the court held that medical custom is only one factor to be used in resolving the negligence issue.[25]

---

[19] **Mont.:** Aasheim v. Humberger, 695 P.2d 824 (1985).
Okla.: Spellman v. Mount, 696 P.2d 510 (1984).
[20] **Cal.:** Cobbs v. Grant, 502 F.2d 1 (1972).
D.C.: Canterbury v. Spence, 464 F.2d 772 (D.C. Cir. 1972).
Kan.: Collins v. Meeker, 424 P.2d 488 (1967).
Ore.: Holland v. Sisters of St. Joseph's, 522 P.2d 208 (1974), *vacated on other grounds*, 536 P.2d 577 (1974).
Pa.: Copper v. Roberts, 286 A.2d 647 (Super. 1971).
Vt.: Small v. Gifford Mem. Hosp., 349 A.2d 703 (1975).
Wash.: Hunter v. Brown, 502 P.2d 1194 (1972).
[21] 473 N.E.2d 1131 (Mass. 1985).
[22] *See also* Helling v. Carey, 519 P.2d 981 (1974) where an ophthalmologist was held guilty of malpractice as a matter of law for not testing for glaucoma.
[23] *See* Favalora v. Aetna Cas. & Sur. Co., 144 So. 2d 544 (La. App. 1962).
[24] 211 N.E.2d 253 (1965).
[25] *See* Pearson, "The Role of Custom in Medical Malpractice Cases," 51 Ind. L.J. 528 (1976).

It has been held that the duty of a general practitioner to refer a patient to a specialist arises when a reasonably careful physician, under similar circumstances, would have done so.[26]

[2] Res Ipsa Loquitur

Requirements commonly associated with the application of the doctrine of *res ipsa loquitur* in negligence cases include:

1. An injury or resulting condition which does not ordinarily occur in the absence of negligence.
2. The injury or condition must be the result of an agency or instrumentality within the exclusive control of the doctor.
3. The injury or condition must have occurred without the voluntary action or the contributory negligence of the plaintiff.[27]

The standard of care for evaluating the conduct of a doctor in a medical malpractice case is the skill and care of the "reasonably skilled practitioner" and not that of the "reasonable person," as is usual in a situation not calling for specialized skills.

Expert testimony is commonly an essential requirement for proving both breach of the duty to use due care and proximate causation.[28]

Even though *res ipsa loquitur* raises only the inference of negligence, the courts had generally been reluctant to tamper with the basic requirement of showing negligence by accepting this doctrine in medical malpractice cases, until recent years.[29] However, because of the generally known difficulty in obtaining expert testimony by plaintiffs and because in many instances expert testimony is not essential to recognize negligence by doctors, the courts are increasing-

---

[26] **Cal.:** Simone v. Sabo, 231 P.2d 19 (1951).
Minn.: Larsen v. Yelle, 246 N.W.2d 841 (1976).
Mont.: Collins v. Itoh, 503 P.2d 38 (Mont. 1972).
[27] *See Prosser & Keeton on Torts* (5th ed. 1984).
[28] *See* Podell, "Application of Res Ipsa Loquitur in Medical Malpractice Litigation," Insurance Counsel Journal, October 1977.
[29] *See* Salgo v. Leland Stanford Univ. Bd. of Trustees, 317 P.2d 170 (Cal. 1957).

ly recognizing the validity of the doctrine of *res ipsa loquitur* in medical malpractice cases.[30]

Ordinarily, bad result of a treatment or operation is not, of itself, enough to warrant the acceptance of *res ipsa loquitur*.[31]

The situations involving the acceptance or rejection of the doctrine of *res ipsa loquitur* are numerous and divergent and, as always, depend on the views of the particular courts involved. It is difficult to set any definite rules with regard to this doctrine.[32]

[3] Honest Error in Judgment

It has been held that in order to fully state the standard of care applicable to a physician, the jury must be instructed that a doctor is not responsible for an honest error in choosing accepted methods of diagnosing and treatment.[33] Some jurisdictions, however, have discarded the "honest error in judgment" wording in the instructions to a jury under the belief that such wording is potentially misleading and exculpatory.[34]

[4] Informed Consent

The doctrine of informed consent is often said to be based upon the philosophy that "Every human being of adult years and sound mind has a right to determine what shall be done with his own body, and a surgeon who performs an operation without the patient's con-

---

[30] **Cal.:** Ybarra v. Spangard, 154 P.2d 687 (1944).
 La.: Grant v. Touro Infirmary, 223 So. 2d 148 (1969).
 Md.: Jefferson v. United States, 77 F. Supp. 706 (1948), *aff'd*, 178 F.2d 518 (4th Cir. 1949) and 340 U.S. 135 (1950).
 N.Y.: Berdoff v. Kessler, 135 N.Y.S.2d 696, *reversed on other grounds*, 135 N.Y.S.2d 717 (1954); Fogal v. Genesee Hosp., 344 N.Y.S.2d 552 (1973).
 Tex.: Harle v. Krchnak, 422 S.W.2d 310 (App. 1967).
[31] George v. City of New York, 268 N.Y.S.2d 325 (1966).
[32] *See* Podell, "Application of Res Ipsa Loquitur in Medical Malpractice Litigation," Insurance Counsel Journal, October 1977. *See also* Pearson, "The Role of Custom in Medical Malpractice Cases," 51 Ind. L.J., 550 1974) and the following cases:
 Ariz.: Riedisser v. Nelson, 534 P.2d 1052 (1975).
 Del.: Coleman v. Garrison, 327 A.2d 757 (Super. 1974).
 Iowa: Perin v. Hayne, 210 N.W.2d 609 (1973).
 Kan.: Funke v. Fieldman, 512 P.2d 539 (1973).
[33] **Minn.:** Ouellette by Ouellette v. Subak, 379 N.W.2d 125 (1986).
[34] **Conn.:** Logan v. Greenwich Hosp. Ass'n, 465 A.2d 294 (1983) (court held that "bona fide error in judgment" wording serves only to confuse the jury).
 N.C.: Wall v. Stout, 311 S.E.2d 571 (1984).
 Va.: Teh Len Chu v. Fairfax Emerg. Med. Ass'n, 290 S.E.2d 820 (1982) (court held that such wording conflicts with "departures from ordinary care" requirement).

sent commits an assault (battery?) for which he is liable in damages."[35]

While liability arising out of a lack of informed consent can rest on either battery or negligence, the ground of battery in modern cases is so seldom used that for the purposes of this text it does not warrant undue discussion and is merely a matter of historical interest.[36]

The case of *Natanson v. Kline*[37] is credited with being the first important modern case that was principally concerned with the doctrine of "informed consent."[38]

In this case, the patient suffered from side effects from treatment as a result of cobalt therapy. He had not been informed of the hazards involved in this treatment. The court stated that physicians must disclose that which a reasonable medical practitioner would disclose under the same or similar circumstances. This is also the prevailing view of other courts.[39]

Some cases have been decided on the basis that it was or was not the custom for physicians to disclose the risks in the particular situation involved.[40]

Some cases show a decided trend toward a standard of disclosure measured by what patients need to know in order to make intelligent decisions of their own.[41] In these cases, the measure of liability is the

---

[35] H.E. Still-Caris, "Informed Consent: What Doctors Should Understand About Their Duty to Disclose," F.I.C. Quarterly, Fall 1985, in which is cited Schloendorf v. Society of N.Y. Hosp., 105 N.E.92 (N.Y. 1914).

[36] **Hi.:** Nishi v. Hartwell, 473 P.2d 116 (1970).
Me.: Woolley v. Henderson, 418 A.2d 1123 (1980).
Mich.: Zoterell v. Repp. 153 N.W. 692 (1915).
Nev.: Corn v. French, 289 P.2d 173 (1955).

[37] 350 P.2d 1093, *rehearing denied*, 354 P.2d 670 (Kan. 1960).

[38] Comment, "Informed Consent and the Material Risk Standard: A Modest Proposal," 12 Pacific L.J. 915 (1981).

[39] **Ark.:** Fuller v. Starnes, 597 S.W.2d 88 (1980).
Colo.: Bloskas v. Murray, 618 P.2d 719 (App. 1980), *aff'd in part*, 646 P.2d 907 (1982).
Ill.: Ziegart v. S. Chicago Commun. Hosp., 425 N.E.2d 450 (App. 1981).
Tenn.: Watkins v. United States, 482 F. Supp. 1076 (1980).
Va.: Dessi v. United States, 489 F. Supp. 722 (1980).

[40] **Ariz.:** Reidisser v. Nelson, 534 P.2d 1052 (1975).
N.C.: Butler v. Berkeley, 213 S.E.2d 571 (1975).
Ohio: Congrove v. Hilmes, 308 N.E.2d 765 (App. 1973).

[41] **Cal.:** Cobbs v. Grant, 104 Cal. Rptr. 505 (1972).
Conn.: Logan v. Greenwich Hosp., 465 A.2d 294 (1983).
D.C.: Canterbury v. Spence, 464 F.2d 772 (D.C. Cir. 1972) (respect for the patient's

§ 35.03[4] CASUALTY INSURANCE CLAIMS

ordinary one of negligence, namely, what is reasonable under the same or like circumstances.[42]

The common law elements usually required in a case involving duty to disclose are:

1. The nature of the procedure;
2. The risks and possible aftereffects of the procedure;
3. Any alternative procedures; and
4. The anticipated benefits of the procedure.[43]

In addition, it would seem pretty obvious that the doctor would already have informed his patient of his diagnosis and prognosis and the purpose of his treatment.

A landmark case concerning informed consent, *Salgo v. Laland Stanford Univ. Board of Trustees*,[44] stated that a plaintiff could not validly consent to an operation unless all of the information concerning the risks were explained. His right to determine the disposition of his body triggers the necessity for informed consent. However, where the plaintiff is required to establish that the medical community would inform a patient of a risk inherent in a procedure, this right is diminished, since it must be established by evidence.[45]

A recent Georgia decision held that ordinarily, the informed consent doctrine is not a viable principle of law in that state and a doctor who has informed a patient in general terms about a specific treatment has no further duty to disclose the risks of such treatment.[46]

---

right of self determination demands a standard (of disclosure) set by law for physicians rather than one which physicians may or may not impose upon themselves).

Md.: Sard v. Hardy, 379 A.2d 1014 (1977).
La.: Goodwin v. Aetna Cas. & Sur. Co., 294 So. 2d 618 (App. 1974).
Ore.: Holland v. Sisters of St. Joseph, 522 P.2d 208 (1974).
R.I.: Wilkinson v. Vesey, 295 A.2d 676 (1972).
Wash.: Miller v. Kennedy, 522 P.2d 852, *aff'd*, 530 P.2d 334 (1975).
Wis.: Scaria v. St. Paul Fire & Marine Ins. Co., 227 N.W.2d 647 (1975).

[42] Canterbury v. Spence, 464 F.2d 772 (D.C. Cir. 1972), *cert. denied*, 409 U.S. 1064 (1972); McPherson v. Ellis, 287 S.E.2d 892 (N.C. 1982).

[43] *See* Waltz & Scheuneman, "Informed Consent for Therapy," 64 Nw. U. L. Rev. 628 (1970).

[44] 317 P.2d 170 (Cal. 1957).

[45] Alsobrook, "Informed Consent: A Right to Know," Insurance Counsel Journal, October 1973.

[46] Padgett v. Ferrier, 323 S.E.2d 166 (1985), *citing* Hyles v. Cockrill, 312 S.E.2d 124 (1983); Young v. Yarn, 222 S.E.2d 113 (1975); and Simpson v. Dickson, 306 S.E.2d 404 (1983).

It appears to me that this decidedly minority view restricts rather than repudiates the informed consent doctrine. As was said by one commentator:[47] "A definitive statement on informed consent is difficult to make since there is much diversion of opinion. . . . the legal profession should be charged with the responsibility of defining informed consent."

Actually, there is no dearth of definitions. It is merely that there is a lack of uniformity in these definitions. In addition, a majority of states have by now enacted some form of informed consent statutes, while very few of them are completely uniform, many are adaptations of the AMA's Model Informed Consent Law.[48]

[a] Exceptions to the "Informed Consent" Doctrine

Over the years, it has become obvious that the doctrine of informed consent, no matter how defined, required some very essential exceptions, as follows:

1. *Emergency situations,* where the patient is not capable of giving consent and where no one else is available to give it.[49]
2. *Mental or physical incapacity* of the patient, with no one else available to give consent.[50]
3. *Remote and not reasonably foreseeable consequences,* which has been recognized in many jurisdictions.[51]
4. *Psychological reasons.* Exceptions to the doctrine of in-

---

[47] Roth, "The Medical Malpractice Insurance Crises: Its Causes, the Effects, and Proposed Solutions," Insurance Counsel Journal, July 1977, p. 481.

[48] *See* Still-Caris, "Informed Consent: What Doctors Should Understand About the Duty to Disclose," F.I.C. Quarterly, Fall 1985, pp. 60-63.

[49] Canterbury v. Spence, 464 F.2d 772, *cert. denied,* 409 U.S. 1064 (1972); Crouch v. Most, 432 P.2d 250 (N.M. 1967).

[50] Crouch v. Most, 432 P.2d 250 (N.M. 1967).

[51] **D.C.:** Flannery v. President & Directors of Georgetown Coll., 679 F.2d 960 (1982).
Fla.: Bowers v. Talmadge, 159 So. 2d 888 (1963).
Kan.: Yates v. Harms, 393 P.2d 982, *modified,* 401 P.2d 659 (1965).
Mont.: Doerr v. Movius, 463 P.2d 477 (1970).
N.C.: Starnes v. Taylor, 158 S.E.2d 339 (1968).
Pa.: Salis v. United States, 522 F. Supp. 989 (1981).
S.D.: Block v. McVay, 126 N.W.2d 808 (1964).
Tenn.: Longmire v. Hoey, 512 S.W.2d 307 (App. 1974).
Tex.: Scott v. Wilson, 396 S.W.2d 532 (App. 1965).
Wash.: Mason v. Ellsworth, 474 P.2d 909 (1970).

formed consent have been made where the emotional stability of a patient warranted it.[52]

5. *Patient's desire not to be informed*, where he or she makes known such a desire to the physician.[53]

6. *Commonly known danger* is another exception recognized in some jurisdictions.[54]

Obviously, consent obtained by fraud is not valid consent if it consists of a misrepresentation of a material fact.[55]

[b] Forms and Videotapes

The doctrine of informed consent has led to the creation of many different types of forms for consent to particular treatment and operations by physicians and hospitals—long, short, specific, tailor-made, or copies from law books are all being used. Obviously, any such forms should be referred to counsel for approval before being used.

In some cases, even videotape recordings by professional actors have been used to describe in detail the risks involved in some medical procedures. This can pose a problem where specific questions are left unanswered. In addition, some patients may have psychological problems that makes it inadvisable to show such videotapes to them without causing more problems than the showing attempts to evade.[56]

[5] Defenses to Actions for Medical Malpractice

The obvious and best defense to an action for malpractice is that no wrongdoing was committed. As long as there was no guarantee of a cure, either explicit or implied, and so long as the treatment or operation is accepted as good and reasonable medical practice in that locality, and the patient was properly informed, there was no mal-

---

[52] Ala.: Roberts v. Wood, 206 F. Supp. 579 (1970).
Cal.: Salgo v. Leland Stanford Univ. Bd. of Trustees, 317 P.2d 170 (App. 1957).
N.C.: Watson v. Clutts, 136 S.E.2d 617 (1964).
U.S.: Canterbury v. Spence, 464 F.2d 772, *cert. denied,* 409 U.S. 1064 (1972).
[53] Putensen v. Clay Adams, Inc., 91 Cal. Rptr. 319 (App. 1970).
[54] Canterbury v. Spence, 464 F.2d 772, *cert. denied,* 409 U.S. 1064 (1972).
[55] Spikes v. Heath, 332 S.W.2d 889 (1985) (medical risk of inserting an intrauterine device was not properly explained).
[56] *See* Havener, "Observations Regarding Investigation and Preparation of Medical Malpractice Litigation," DRI Monograph #4, 1977.

practice. The fact that the result was disappointing, bad or otherwise unexpected, is in itself immaterial.

There are, in addition, other valid defenses:

1. *Assumption of risk.* Assuming that the patient was fully informed of the dangers of the treatment or operation, he is aware of the possible unexpected results and assumes the risk of such results.
2. *Failure of the patient to give full information to the doctor.* A doctor cannot make a complete diagnosis unless he has all of the information available to the patient, including complete medical history, present complaints, previous treatment, and any other pertinent information. Failure of a patient to fully disclose such information upon request, could relieve a doctor from ultimate responsibility for unfortunate results.
3. *Failure to comply with the doctor's or nurse's instructions.* A patient's failure to take prescribed medicine, or follow other specific orders or directions of a doctor, or a nurse who has in turn received instructions from the doctor, may be a good defense to an action based on alleged malpractice.
4. *Failure to return for treatment.* Essential follow-up treatment can often mean the difference between proper recovery and bad results. If proper instructions were given, failure to heed them could be a good defense.
5. *Tampering with treatment.* Any unauthorized changing of a doctor's instructions could be unfortunate and could possibly provide a valid defense for the doctor.
6. *Statute of limitations.* Without discussing the time when such a statute might begin to toll, it is of the utmost importance for the claim representative to give this factor full consideration.
7. *Contributory and comparative negligence* of a patient is rarely an issue in an action for malpractice. Nevertheless, both may be factors in a malpractice action.
8. *Written consent* by patient absolving doctor from liability.

[6] Referral to Specialist

A general practitioner has the duty to refer his patient to a specialist if in his judgment the situation is beyond his knowledge, experience or capacity to treat, or if he believes that his opinion and diagnosis need corroboration. Failure to do so under certain circumstances can result in a verdict against him for malpractice.[57]

If, however, he honestly believes that referral to a specialist would not benefit his patient, he is under no duty to make such referral.[58]

This situation opens even more areas of danger for the general practitioner. He must choose competent specialists, and if he does not there could be the possibility of vicarious liability for not doing so.

[7] Abandonment

Once a doctor undertakes treatment—even emergency treatment (assuming no Good Samaritan statutes), he must exercise the same degree of skill and care as is rendered by others of similar qualifications, and may not thereafter abandon his patient.

Failure to make a return visit to a bedridden patient, declining to attend a pregnant woman, and unreasonable delay in hospital attendance have all been held to be abandonment, since in all of these cases the doctor had already entered into a doctor-patient relationship with the patient.

[8] Psychiatrist and Psychotherapist Responsibility for Wrongful Release of Mentally Ill Patients

Ever since the battle for the rights of inmates of mental institutions has led to hastefully drawn-up legislation, those who fought so hard to alleviate injustices have lived to regret rash actions by state-run and other "charitable" institutions under the guise of complying with the law. These institutions used the opportunity to evade political pressure for budget reductions and reform by dumping thousands of mentally ill patients onto the streets of our cities.

Prisons are overcrowded, so mentally ill inmates who are very dangerous to society have also been released to prey upon innocent victims. The net result has been a wave of crimes committed by irresponsible people who never received proper medical treatment and who are now adding to the social problems of this age.

From a legal point of view, the result has been a rash of civil malpractice suits against hospitals, mental institutions, psychiatrists, and

---

[57] Manion v. Tweedy, 100 N.W.2d 124 (Minn. 1959).
[58] Tucker v. Stetson, 123 N.E. 239 (Mass. 1919).

psychotherapists who have approved the release of mentally ill patients who have then injured or killed "enemies" conjured up out of their sick minds.

Some recent cases have approved a cause of action based on a psychiatrist's or psychotherapist's failure to warn of the violent propensities of patients that were released.[59]

Some cases were disallowed on the basis that the patient had not made specific threats against readily identifiable victims.[60]

I suppose that even justices read newspapers, or at least listen to the television news about deranged people who for no reason kill innocent victims in shooting or bludgeoning sprees. Must the victim be "readily identifiable" before a doctor is held responsible for releasing a homocidal maniac?

In an action by a mother whose son was killed by a patient on a two day pass from a state mental hospital, the Supreme Court of Missouri ruled that she had no cause of action against treating physicians for the patient's release. The court stated that:

> This court assumes . . . that the jury could find that the patient was a dangerous person with severe mental illness and could also find that danger to members of the public . . . could be reasonably anticipated if he were released. Nevertheless, the treating physicians should not be held liable for even foreseeable civil damages simply because they might be found to have exercised negligent professional judgment.[61]

After all, his negligence resulted in the mere death of an innocent victim!

A California court, in *Tarasoff v. Regents of the Univ. of*

---

[59] **Cal.:** Hedlund v. Superior Court, 669 P.2d 41 (1983) (foreseeable victim).
Mich.: Davis v. Lhim, 335 N.W.2d 481 (App. 1983); Jablonski v. United States, 712 F.2d 391 (9th Cir. 1983); Christie v. United States, 564 F. Supp. 341 (1983).
S.C.: Sharpe v. South Carolina Dep't of Mental Health, 315 S.E.2d 112 (1984) (liability for failure to warn despite statute).
[60] **Cal.:** Doyle v. United States, 530 U.S. 1278 (1982).
Colo.: Brady v. Hopper, 570 F. Supp. 1333 (1983).
Iowa: Estate of Votteler, 327 N.W.2d 759 (1982) (since the victim had independent knowledge of the plaintiff's violent propensities, the case was considered one of no liability).
Minn.: Cairl v. State, 323 N.W.2d 20 (1982).
N.C.: Currie v. United States, 644 F. Supp. 1074 (M.D.N.C. 1986).
[61] Sherrill v. Wilson, 653 S.W.2d 661 (Mo. 1983).

California,[62] in my opinion, approached the problem more rationally. In this case, a psychotherapist was found liable for failure to warn an unnamed, but readily identifiable, victim that the patient had threatened. The court stated that (1) a psychotherapist and his or her patient have a special relationship that can impose on the therapist an affirmative duty to exercise reasonable care; (2) public policy considerations justify imposing a duty to warn as a component of reasonable care when a psychotherapist knows, or should have known that a patient is dangerous; (3) therapists owe this duty (at least) to readily identifiable third persons that the patient had threatened.

[9] Second Injury

If, as a result of an accident, the medical treatment subsequently received aggravated the initial injury, it has been held that a separate action may be brought against the doctor who was guilty of medical malpractice despite the fact that a previous verdict was rendered or a settlement made of the underlying case.[63]

[10] Respondeat Superior or Captain-of-the-Ship Doctrine

The *captain of the ship doctrine*, propounded by some courts to hold a surgeon responsible for the acts of his assistants[64] has, in my opinion, always been fallacious because no surgeon has ever had the authority of a captain, and because under the stress of performing an operation, no surgeon is capable of supervising the actions of all of those who are assisting him. In addition, the surgeon neither hired them (generally speaking), nor have any exact knowledge of their capabilities until after having worked with them.

Nevertheless, many decisions still hold that in the operating room, assisting hospital doctors, nurses, and other technicians all become the temporary agents of the surgeon within the limits of their duties as assistants.[65]

However, the tide is turning, and the complexities of modern operating procedures are being recognized as beyond the possible con-

---

[62] 551 P.2d 334 (1976).

[63] N.Y.: Derby v. Prewitt, 236 N.Y.S.2d 953 (1962). *See also* Comment, "Release of Original Tortfeasor for Injury Caused—Effect on Subsequent Action Against Physician for Malpractice," 3 Washburn L.J. 75 (1984).

[64] McConnell v. Williams, 65 A.2d 243 (Pa. 1949).

[65] Ybarra v. Spangard, 154 P.2d 687 (Cal. 1960).

trol of any surgeon. This is particularly so in the case of anesthesiologists and other specialists not under the immediate direction of the surgeon.

While assisting physicians and nurses may be employed by the hospital where treatment is given or an operation performed, they normally are legally held to be temporary servants or agents of the operating surgeon who is in charge while the operation is in progress. Accordingly, liability may be imposed on the surgeon for the negligent acts of the assistants under the doctrine of *respondeat superior*.[66] This doctrine was founded on the surgeon's power and resulting duty to direct nurses and assisting doctors under his supervision. Consequently, a surgeon's reliance on assistants or nurses, no matter how reasonable, does not extinguish his own personal vicarious liability.[67]

However, if the nurses or an assisting physician were under the supervision of an anesthesiologist, the negligence or malpractice of that team would no longer be the responsibility of the surgeon.[68]

The captain-of-the-ship doctrine has become of less importance since practically all hospitals and registered nurses carry individual professional liability insurance of their own. Accordingly, they are usually made codefendants under their own coverage for their own personal liability instead of falling under the vicarious liability of the surgeon.

[11] Contracts to Cure

It is very rare that any doctor would, in today's malpractice climate, make a written contract with a patient specifically guaranteeing cure. A valid contract, however, need not be in writing if a verbal contract can be proved or is admitted. If such verbal assurance is given the doctor can be held for breach of contract in a malpractice case.[69]

Obviously, if this becomes a matter of fact for jury determination,

---

[66] Schultz v. Mutch, 211 Cal. Rptr. 445 (1985).
[67] Tonsic v. Wagner, 289 A.2d 138 (Pa. Super. 1972).
[68] **Cal.:** Marvulli v. Elshire, 103 Cal. Rptr. 461 (1972); Kennedy v. Gaskell, 78 Cal. Rptr. 753 (1969).
[69] **Cal.:** McKinney v. Nash, 174 Cal. Rptr. 642 (1981) (no liability).
D.C.: Scarzella v. Saxon, 436 A.2d 358 (1981).
Pa.: Mason v. Western Pa. Hosp., 428 A.2d 1366 (Super. 1981).
See also 43 A.L.R. 1221, 1980 annotations.

the case may resolve itself into a question of who the jury believes. It has been suggested that the plaintiff's testimony alone should be insufficient to spell out a case for jury determination.[70]

As a general rule, in the absence of a specific contract to cure, a physician is neither a warrantor of cure nor a guarantor of the result of treatment.[71] He is not an insurer,[72] and the law does not require him to obtain perfect or near perfect results.[73]

It has been said that the great majority of contracts to cure are implied from the very nature of the doctor-patient relationship and, as previously stated, need not be in writing.[74]

Assurances by a surgeon that a patient will be recovered and back to work in a short time, or that the operation is a simple one when in fact it may not be, have been held to be verbal "quasi contracts to cure," sufficient to hold him liable for damages.[75]

A surgeon who assured a patient that an operation would result in hairline scars of a minor nature, was held to have contracted such a result when the actual result of the operation produced disfiguring scars.[76]

[12] Multiple Defendants

In an excellent article,[77] Darrell L. Havener has stated the advantages of cooperation by multiple defendants very succinctly, as follows:

> Study of the pleadings will reveal any possibility of cross-claims or third party actions, and subsequent discovery will confirm or negate their

---

[70] Note, "Express Contracts to Cure: The Nature of Contractual Malpractice," 50 Ind. L.J. 377 (1975).

[71] **Ill.:** Greenberg v. Michael Reese Hosp., 415 N.E.2d 390 (1980).
Ind.: Stanley v. Fisher, 417 N.E.2d 932 (1981).
Mich.: Berwald v. Kasal, 301 N.W.2d 499 (1980).
Pa.: Salis v. United States, 522 F. Supp. 989 (1981).
R.I.: Young v. Park, 417 A.2d 889, *cert. denied,* 449 U.S. 1119 (1980).

[72] Hayes v. Brown, 108 Ga. App. 360 (1963).

[73] Hopper v. McCord, 115 Ga. App. 10 (1967). *See also* Roth, "The Medical Malpractice Insurance Crises: Its Causes, the Effects and Proposed Solutions," Insurance Counsel Journal, July 1977, p. 479.

[74] *See* Tierney, "Contractual Aspects of Malpractice," 19 Wayne L. Rev. 1457 (1973).

[75] Guilmet v. Campbell, 385 Mich. 57, 188 N.W.2d 601 (1971).

[76] Campsano v. Claiborn, 196 A.2d 129 (Conn. 1964).

[77] "Observations Regarding Investigation and Preparation of Medical Malpractice Litigation," DRI Monograph # 4, 1977, p. 13.

existence. Should there be a colorable and potential cross-claim against non-parties, it may be more beneficial to the defendant *not* to join them but to establish early contact with the potential third party defendants, apprise them of the circumstances and count on their cooperation to defend the suit rather than to muddy the waters by bringing them in on only a colorable claim at best. Thorough consideration at least, should be given to the tactical advantage of non-joinder.

Even where there are multiple defendants, and cross-claims among them, it may be more advantageous for all defendants to unite in a cooperative defense effort to prevent a plaintiff's recovering more than fair or reasonable compensation, rather than to become embroiled in a "dog fight" among themselves. In such a fight, as the defendants prove each other's negligence, they also make the plaintiff a third party beneficiary before the jury. Many plaintiffs' attorneys will candidly admit that one of the primary reasons they name multiple defendants is their hope that the defendants will point the finger of blame at each other and forget to defend themselves against the plaintiff.

Where such cooperative efforts are impossible, it may be beneficial to the interests of all defendants—and still afford fair compensation to a deserving plaintiff—if the defendants can agree to defer, until disposition of the plaintiff's case, their intraparty dispute as to the amount or percentage of liability each defendant owes. Lawyers who have participated in a "no holds barred" dispute between multiple defendants will agree that such a dispute often increases the amount of the verdict substantially, solves nothing as to the dispute between the codefendants, and should never be allowed to occur, if possible.

Another problem raised by multiple defendants is that of possible conflict of interest where a single insurer represents several of the named defendants. There may be instances where, absent any conflict of interest between the defendants, and with full knowledge and consent of the insurer and its insureds, a single attorney might represent more than one defendant. This problem will likely arise with frequency in direct proportion to the diminution of the number of carriers writing such liability coverage. The problems created by this circumstance will likely proliferate, and will require greater attention.

Mr. Havener's remarks speak for themselves and need no further comments.

[13] Good Samaritan Doctrine

Before the good samaritan laws were enacted, a doctor was under no duty to help an injured person in the event that he was fortuitously present when an emergency situation arose. On the contrary, if he did volunteer to help, he could be held accountable for his negligence in rendering medical assistance.

In most cases, consideration was given to the circumstances under which the doctor was working, but no doctor wants to depend on a jury to determine his negligence, if any, under emergency circumstances. The wonder is not that some doctors refused to give medical assistance, but that so many did.

At present, all states, including the District of Columbia, have adopted some form of good samaritan statutes.[78]

The typical good samaritan statute grants immunity from civil liability to physicians and nurses (and sometimes paramedics) who, in good faith, render medical care or treatment at the scene of an emergency where someone was injured.

In the light of the limited judicial interpretation of these statutes, their lack of uniformity, and their imprecise wording, serious questions remain regarding the limits of protection which they give to conscientious doctors.

Only time will tell how effective such statutes are.

[14] Malpractice Actions for Wrongful Birth and Wrongful Life

Kevin L. Mayo, in an article on the subject of wrongful birth and wrongful life,[79] states that "Wrongful life, dissatisfied life [which term I found hardly ever used], wrongful death and wrongful birth suits should each be distinguishable from the other. Each rests its claim for damages upon distinguishable factual premises."

[a] Wrongful Birth

Wrongful birth actions are brought by the parents of usually (but not always) healthy, "normal" children who were unwanted and usually resulted from the failure of contraceptive devices, or as a result

---

[78] *See* Note, Lieb, "The Good Samaritan Statute, Wisconsin (1977)," 62 Marq. L. Rev. 469 (1979).

[79] "The Legal Recognition of Medical Malpractice Tort Claims Based Upon Theories of Wrongful Birth and Wrongful Life," 15 No. Carolina Central L.J. 274, 286 n.80 (Winter 1985).

of unsuccessful sterilization operations.[80]

Wrongful birth suits have also been brought against a physician who has performed an ineffective abortion, as a result of which a child may have been born unhealthy or impaired.[81] Such an action may also be brought against a doctor who negligently gives incorrect advice regarding the possibility or probability of the birth of a defective child, born as a result of failed or improperly made tests, or failure to make proper tests initially.[82]

There is also a large category of claims that can and have been brought against drug manufacturers and retailers in products liability claims for failed contraceptive drugs or devices or for contraceptive drugs that caused the birth of an impaired child, but such claims are not the subject of this discussion regarding malpractice.

An action for wrongful birth by parents has been recognized as proper in many jurisdictions.[83]

Until recently, however, courts had been reluctant to recognize wrongful birth claims and even less willing to accept claims of wrongful life.

Legalized abortion, increased use of birth control methods, and medical advances that improve the chances of detecting birth defects early in pregnancy have increased the ability to terminate un-

---

[80] **Cal.:** Custodio v. Bauer, 59 Cal. Rptr. 463 (1967).
Me.: Macomber v. Dillman, 505 LA.2d 810 (1986).
Md.: Sard v. Hardy, 379 A.2d 1014 (1977).
Minn.: Martineau v. Nelson, 247 N.W.2d 409 (1976).
Ohio: Bowman v. Davis, 356 N.E.2d 496 (1976).
[81] **Cal.:** Stills v. Gratton, 127 Cal. Rptr. 652 (1976).
[82] **N.Y.:** Becker v. Schwartz, 413 N.Y.S.2d 895 (1978).
Tex.: Jacobs v. Theimer, 519 S.W.2d 846 (1975).
Wis.: Deimer v. St. Michael's Hosp., 233 N.W.2d 372 (1975), *but see* Gleitman v. Cosgrove, 227 A.2d 689 (N.J., 1967) (both cases involved German measles).
[83] **Conn.:** Ochs v. Borelli, 448 A.2d 883 (1982).
Ill.: Wilczynski v. Goodman, 391 N.E.2d 479 (1979).
Me.: Macomber v. Dillman, 505 A.2d 810 (1986).
Mich.: Troppi v. Scarf, 187 N.W.2d 511 (1971).
Minn.: Sherlock v. Stillwater Clinic, 260 N.W.2d 169 (1977).
N.Y.: Sala v. Tomlinson, 448 N.Y.S.2d 830 (1982).
Tex.: Terrell v. Garcia, 496 S.W.2d 124 (App. 1973), *cert. denied*, 415 U.S. 927 (1976).
Va.: Naccash v. Burger, 290 S.E.2d 825 (1982) (recovery allowed for expenses and care and treatment as well as for emotional distress).
W. Va.: Bishop v. Byrne, 265 F. Supp. 460 (1967); James G. v. Caserta, 332 S.E.2d 872 (1985) (W. Va. recognizes action for wrongful pregnancy).
Wyo.: Beardsley v. Wierdsman, 650 P.2d 288 (1982).

§ 35.03[14][b] CASUALTY INSURANCE CLAIMS

desired pregnancies. These social changes and medical advances should lead courts that previously rejected the theories of wrongful birth and wrongful life to reevaluate the validity of such claims.[84]

[b] Wrongful Life

Wrongful life claims usually involve the birth of a defective or disabled child and are ordinarily brought by the parents or guardian on behalf of the child. They often accompany an action for wrongful birth as well.[85]

Wrongful life claims have also been brought (usually without success) by illegitimate children for emotional distress and other effects of bastardy.[86]

As usual, however, confusion reigns supreme in this, as in many other legal doctrines. In many cases, jurists have either made no distinction in their decisions concerning wrongful birth and wrongful life or have confused them. Most jurisdictions, in fact, do not even recognize an action for wrongful life.[87]

---

[84] Mayo, "The Legal Recognition of Medical Malpractice Tort Claims Based Upon Theories of Wrongful Birth and Wrongful Life," 15 No. Carolina Central L.J. 274 (Winter 1985).

[85] **Cal.:** Turpin v. Sortine, 182 Cal. Rptr. 337 (1982).
N.H.: Smith v. Cote, 513 A.2d 341 (1986).
N.C.: Azzolino v. Dingfelder, 337 S.E.2d 528 (1985).
Wash.: Harbeson v. Parke-Davis, Inc., 656 P.2d 483 (1983).

[86] Comment, "Illegitimate Child Denied Recovery Against Father for 'Wrongful Life': Zepeda v. Zepeda," 49 Iowa L. Rev. 1005 (1964); Comment, "Illegitimate Child Allowed Action for Wrongful Life: William v. State," 50 Minn. L. Rev. 593 (1966).

[87] **Ala.:** Elliott v. Brown, 361 So. 2d 546 (1978).
Fla.: Moores v. Lucas, 405 So. 2d 1022 (App. 1981).
Idaho: Blake v. Cruz, 698 P.2d 315 (1984) (quite an illogical decision).
Ill.: Goldberg v. Ruskin, 471 N.E.2d 530 (App. 1985).
Mich.: Strohmaier v. Associates in Obstetrics & Gynecology, 122 Mich. App. 116 (1983) (this court reasoned that "it is impossible to weigh the difference between life with suffered defects against the alternative of non-existence"); Eisbrenner v. Stanley, 308 N.W.2d 209 (1981).
Mo.: Miller v. Fuhart, 637 S.W.2d 183 (App. 1982).
N.J.: Gleitman v. Cosgrove, 227 A.2d 689 (1967).
N.Y.: Weintraub v. Brown, 470 N.Y.S.2d 634 (1983); Becker v. Schwartz, 413 N.Y.S.2d 895 (1978).
Pa.: Ellis v. Sherman, 478 A.2d 1339 (Pa. Super. 1984) (court stated that "faced with the almost impossible question of whether non-existence is preferable to existence in an impaired state, and the inability either to answer the question or to ascertain the appropriate calculation of damages, we must hold that (the child's) cause of action for 'wrongful life' is not cognizable in law").
Tex.: Nelson v. Krusen, 678 S.W.2d 918 (1984) (Texas does not recognize a *child's*

Nevertheless, a few courts braved the wrath of the fundamentalists and judicially recognized an action for wrongful life by a child in some cases.[88] A decision worth noting, *Azzolino v. Dingfelder*,[89] involved a child born with Down's Syndrome. Suit was brought in the name of the child, parents, and siblings alleging malpractice for failing to advise the mother of the availability of aminocentesis and genetic counseling. Of the various actions, one was for wrongful birth by the parents and wrongful life in the name of the defective child.

The Supreme Court of North Carolina held that neither the claims for wrongful life nor wrongful birth were cognizable. The decision stated that life, even with serious defects is not an injury in the legal sense, absent legislation on the matter. There was unanimous agreement that the siblings had no valid claim.

[c] **Wrongful Pregnancy or Wrongful Conception**

Yet another category of wrongful birth cases has been created by some courts which is called "wrongful pregnancy" or "wrongful conception."[90]

Some of the decisions differentiate wrongful pregnancy resulting in the birth of a healthy child from wrongful birth of a child born with defects; others do not. Some note should be made of the decisions that made such a distinction.[91]

(emphasis added) cause of action for having been born mentally or physically deformed. This court loftily stated that "(it) refuses to hold that life with defects is undesirable and that non-existence would have been preferred. . . . It seeks to protect and preserve all human life without inquiring into a person's physical abilities, disabilities or deformities." Who speaks for the child?

W. Va.: James G. v. Caserta, 332 S.E.2d 872 (1985) (in the absense of a statute).
Wis.: Diener v. St. Michael's Hosp., 233 N.W.2d 372 (1975).
Wyo.: Beardsley v. Wierdsma, 650 P.2d 288 (1982).

See also Kohnen & Zoellner, "Wrongful Life: Existence or Nonexistence—Is Life Always Preferable?", FIC Quarterly, Spring 1986, for an excellent and exhaustive treatment.

[88] Cal.: Turpin v. Sortini, 182 Cal. Rptr. 337 (1982).
N.J.: Procanik v. Cillo, 478 A.2d 755 (1984).
Wash.: Harbeson v. Parke-Davis, Inc., 656 P.2d 954 (1983).

[89] 337 S.E.2d 528 (N.C. 1985).

[90] *See* Rose & Ream, "Wrongful Pregnancy," F.T.D., September 2, 1986; Chestic, "Wrongful Conception," FIC Quarterly, Spring 1985.

[91] Nelson v. Parrot, 333 S.E.2d 101 (Ga. 1985) (decision favored the physician); Garrison v. Foy, 586 N.E.2d 5 (Ind. App. 1985); Byrd v. Wesley Medical Center, 699 P.2d 459 (Kan. 1985) (child rearing costs disallowed); Macomber v. Dillman, 505 A.2d 810 (Me. 1986); Szekeres v. Robinson, 715 P.2d 1076 (Nev. 1986) (no action allowed);

[d] "Benefits of Parenthood" Doctrine

It has been argued that since the benefits of having a healthy, "normal" child defy precise measurement, its value always outweighs any economic expense as a matter of law. The Appellate Division of New York for instance, stated that:

> As a matter of public policy, we are unable to hold that the birth of an unwanted, but otherwise healthy and normal child constitutes an injury to the child's parents and is, therefore, compensable in a medical malpractice action. Such a holding would be incompatible with contemporary views concerning one of life's most precious gifts—the birth of a normal and healthy child.[92]

This kind of fallacious reasoning is apparent to anyone who has had any contact with large families of poor people. The "benefit" is questionable in and of itself so long as the parents who already found it difficult, if not impossible, to properly feed, clothe, and educate the children they already had. There is no law that forces or even requires parents to have children and in some very civilized countries quite the opposite is true. What about the child itself who may rue the day that it was born, or society that has to pay the price ultimately for its care? It has in fact been stated[93] that "no court can say, as a matter of law, that every mother seeking wrongful birth damages, wed or unwed, is required to abort or place the child up for adoption."

The "benefits" rule in the Restatement (Second) of Torts (1977), is one involving a mitigation of damages, while the "overriding benefits of parenthood" theory used by other jurists is one of "public policy" (as they see it) that could result in a complete bar to recovery.[94]

Nevertheless, not a few courts continue, from "cloud 8" to mouth

---

O'Toole v. Greenberg, 488 N.Y.S.2d 143 (N.Y. 1985) (no recovery for birth of healthy child); Miller v. Johnson, 343 S.E.2d 301 (Va. 1986); James G. v. Vaserta, 332 S.E.2d 872 (W. Va. 1985) (no recovery for child rearing).

[92] Weintraub v. Brown, 470 N.Y.S.2d 634 (1983).

[93] Troppi v. Scarf, 187 N.W.2d 511 (Mich. 1971).

[94] Terrell v. Garcia, 496 S.W.2d 124 (Tex. App. 1973). *See also* Mayo, "The Legal Recognition of Medical Malpractice Tort Claims Based Upon Theories of Wrongful Birth and Wrongful Life", 15 No. Carolina Central L.J. 274 (Winter 1985); Comment, " 'Wrongful Life,' The Right Not to be Born," 54 Tul. L. Rev. 480 (1980).

such platitudes as reason for denying any recovery.[95]

[e] **Damages Recoverable for Wrongful Birth Cases**

While there are many subdivisions and all kinds of damages which are and are not allowable in wrongful birth cases brought successfully by parents against a doctor for malpractice, some of these cases do fall into recognizable categories.

1. Cases involving an unsuccessful sterilization procedure or operation and where the baby is born healthy and without serious defects. In such cases, where the action was successful some courts have permitted recovery for the cost of the unsuccessful sterilization, and in some instances even for a resterilization operation, the mother's lost wages, and the economic costs of rearing the child to maturity.[96]

2. Cases where only limited recovery has been allowed that was directly related to the pregnancy and the birth, but where child support has been disallowed for the birth of a healthy baby.[97]

---

[95] **Fla.:** Public Health Trust v. Brown, 388 So. 2d 1084 (App. 1980), *review denied*, 399 So. 2d 1140 (1981).
Iowa: Nanke v. Napier, 346 N.W.2d 520 (1984).
N.J.: Berman v. Allan, 404 A.2d 8 (1979) (parents recovered damages for emotional anguish of seriously defective child but not for medical expenses and support costs. Whether for technical reasons or not, the logic of this decision eludes me).
Wis.: Rieck v. Medical Protective Co., 219 N.W.2d 242 (1974) (court listed six reasons for denying recovery).

[96] **Cal.:** Custodio v. Bauer, 59 Cal. Rptr. 463 (1967).
Ill.: Cockrum v. Baumgartner, 425 N.E.2d 968, *rev'd*, 447 N.E.2d 385 (1983).
Wyo.: Beardsley v. Wierdsma, 650 P.2d 288 (1982) (recovery allowed for hospital and medical abortion expenses, pregnancy and childbirth expenses and pain and suffering connected therewith, loss of mother's wages, but no recovery for birth of healthy child or its rearing nor for emotional stress of childbirth). *See* Sala v. Tomlinson, 448 N.Y.S.2d 830 (1982), in accord.

[97] **Ala.:** Boone v. Mullendore, 415 So. 2d 718 (1982).
Ark.: Wilbur v. Kerr, 628 S.W.2d 568 (1982).
Cal.: Robak v. United States, 658 F.2d 471 (1981).
Del.: Coleman v. Garreson, 349 A.2d 8 (1975).
D.C.: Flowers v. District of Columbia, 478 A.2d 1073 (1984).
Fla.: Public Health Trust v. Brown, 388 So. 2d 1084 (1980); Fassoulas v. Ramey, 450 So. 2d 822 (1984).
Ga.: Fulton-DeKalb Hosp. Author. v. Graves, 314 S.E.2d 653 (1984) (child born with defect).
Idaho: Blake v. Cruz, 698 P.2d 315 (1984).
Ill.: Cockrum v. Baumgartner, 447 N.E.2d 385 (1983).
Kan.: Byrd v. Wesley Med. Center, 699 P.2d 459 (1985).
Ky.: Schock v. Huber, 648 S.W.2d 681 (1983).
Me.: Macomber v. Dillman, 505 A.2d 810 (1986).

§ 35.03[14][e]   CASUALTY INSURANCE CLAIMS

3. Recovery allowed for usual damages flowing from a physician's negligence but offset by the benefits of having a healthy baby.[98] Such an offset requires placing a definite monetary value for damages on the birth of a child and destroys the argument that damages for the birth of a child are incalculable and therefore not compensable.

4. Damages recoverable for the support of a child born with serious disabilities against a doctor for malpractice include child support until he or she is able to be self-supporting, or forever.[99]

Minn.: Sherlock v. Stillwater Clinic, 260 N.W.2d 169 (1977).
Mo.: Miller v. Duhart, 637 S.W.2d 183 (App. 1982).
N.H.: Kingsbury v. Smith, 442 A.2d 1003 (1982).
N.J.: P. v. Portadin, 432 A.2d 556 (Super. 1981).
Pa.: Mason v. Western Pa. Hosp., 453 A.2d 974 (1982).
Tex.: Terrell v. Garcia, 496 S.W.2d 124 (App. 1973), *cert. denied,* 415 U.S. 927 (1976).
Va.: McNeal v. United States, 689 F.2d 1200 (4th Cir. 1982); Naccash v. Burger, 290 S.E.2d 825 (1982).
Wash.: McKernan v. Aasheim, 687 P.2d 850 (1985).
W. Va.: James G. v. Caserta, 332 S.E.2d 872 (1985) (court held that wrongful birth cases may allow damages for (1) cost of initial unsuccessful sterilization operation, (2) resterilization operation, (3) prenatal and post natal care, including childbirth, (4) loss of consortium, and (5) loss of wages. Court further stated that ordinary care for raising a healthy child is not damages, but if child is born defective, recovery may include extraordinary expenses such as the cost of rearing the child, even beyond minority and until child is self-supporting, if ever).
Wis.: Rieck v. Medical Protective Co., 219 N.W.2d 242 (1974).
Wyo.: Beardsley v. Wierdsma, 650 P.2d 288 (1982).
[98] **Ariz.:** University of Ariz. Health Services Center v. Arizona Super. Court, 667 P.2d 1294 (1983).
Cal.: Stills v. Gratton, 123 Cal. Rptr. 652 (1976).
Conn.: Ochs v. Borelli, 445 A.2d 883 (1982) (child born with minor, but mostly correctable orthopedic defects. While on general principles, the "benefit" theory was rejected, court did allow "benefits of child" as an offset to other damages).
Idaho: Blake v. Cruz, 698 P.2d 315 (1985) (court held that in the birth of a defective child, parents may recover damages for child support, emotional injury, medical and hospital expenses, but all benefits to be offset by "benefits of child." Very odd decision. What benefits can ordinarily accrue upon birth of a seriously defective or disabled child to most parents?).
Md.: Jones v. Malinowski, 473 A.2d 429 (1984).
Mich.: Troppi v. Scarf, 187 N.W.2d 511 (1971).
Minn.: Sherlock v. Stillwater Clinic, 360 N.W.2d 169 (1977).
[99] **Idaho:** Blake v. Cruz, 698 P.2d 315 (1985).
N.H.: Smith v. Cote, 513 A.2d 341 (1986).
W. Va.: James G. v. Caserta, 332 S.E.2d 872 (1985).

5. Emotional distress not allowed to parent of a child born with serious disabilities.[100]

There is absolutely no uniformity as to the damages which a parent may recover in a successful action for malpractice against a physician for the wrongful birth of a child, despite the categories listed above. In the recent case of *Smith v. Cote*,[101] the Supreme Court of New Hampshire stated that a new special rule of damages has developed in wrongful birth cases to the effect that parents may recover only the extraordinary medical and educational costs attributed to birth defects. They may not recover ordinary child bearing costs, but only extraordinary costs including those incurred after a child reaches maturity, as in category 4 above, and not for emotional distress as listed in category 5.

An interesting case[102] intelligently defines wrongful birth cases and its various subdivisions and concludes that where a healthy child results from a wrongful pregnancy, the mother may recover medical expenses, pain and suffering, lost wages for a reasonable period of time and emotional distress. This decision agrees with most courts that child rearing costs are not recoverable because of the speculative nature of the damages. In fact, isn't every damages action for prospective medical expenses, rehabilitation, and lost wages speculative? What about life expectancy?

[15] Actions Based on Contract

While there are a few advantages in bringing an action for malpractice against a doctor on contract, the contract theory has a number of distinct disadvantages which appear to make the tort theory of recovery the plaintiff's more favorable option in most cases.[103] Nevertheless, some such actions have been instituted.[104]

[16] Statutes of Limitations

The limitation period for bringing a suit in medical malpractice is governed by statute. These statutes, some pertaining expressly to

---

[100] **N.H.:** Smith v. Cote, 513 A.2d 341 (1986).
N.Y.: Howard v. Lecher, 397 N.Y.S.2d 363 (1977).
[101] 513 A.2d 341 (1986).
[102] Miller v. Johnson, 343 S.E.2d 301 (Va. 1986).
[103] Robertson, "Civil Liability Arising From 'Wrongful Birth,' Following an Unsuccessful Sterilization Operation," 4 American Journal Law & Medicine 131 (1978).
[104] **Cal.:** Custodio v. Bauer, 59 Cal. Rptr. 463 (1967).
W. Va.: Bishop v. Byrne, 265 F. Supp. 460 (1967).

malpractice actions and others to tort actions in general, set the time limit after the accrual of a cause of action, in which the suit must be brought, and after which date it will be barred, except in those situations where the statute is tolled.[105]

Traditionally, the statute begins to operate at the time of the negligent act or omission by the physician.[106]

In more recent years, this rather harsh rule has been either abrogated or drastically modified.[107]

[a] Discovery Rule—Foreign Substance Left in Body

The traditional rule for the running of the statute of limitations was subsequently discarded where foreign substances were left in the body of a patient after an operation.[108]

The more equitable rule holds that the statute of limitations in this kind of case does not begin to run until the patient either discovers, or in the exercise of reasonable care and diligence, should have discovered the malpractice (foreign body).[109]

In 1953, a California Appellate Court, in the case of *Costa v. Regents of Univ. of Cal.*,[110] broadened the discovery rule to include its application to *any* medical malpractice situation involving medical wrongdoing and held that the statutes of limitations did not apply until the patient discovered, or, by means of reasonable diligence,

---

[105] *See* Maynard & Kinney, "The Statute of Limitations in Medical Malpractice Law," DRI Monograph 34, 1977.
[106] Ark.: Owen v. Wilson, 537 S.W.2d 543 (1976).
Ga.: Wolfe v. Virusky, 306 F. Supp. 519 (1969).
Ill.: Mosby v. Michael Reese Hosp., 199 N.E.2d 633 (App. 1964).
Ind.: Blank v. Comm. Hosp., 240 N.E.2d 562 (App. 1968).
Md.: Jackson v. United States, 182 F. Supp. 907 (1960).
Mich.: Eschenbacher v. Hier, 110 N.W.2d 731 (1961).
Mo.: Laughlin v. Forgrave, 432 S.W.2d 308 (1968).
N.M.: Roybal v. White, 383 P.2d 250 (1963).
Tenn.: Clinard v. Pennington, 438 S.W.2d 748 (1969).
W. Va.: Bolen v. Bolen, 409 F. Supp. 1374 (1976).
[107] Ill.: Lipsey v. Michael Reese Hosp., 262 N.E.2d 450 (1970).
[108] Huysman v. Kirsch, 57 P.2d 908 (Cal. 1936).
[109] Del.: Layton v. Allen, 246 A.2d 794 (1968).
Ga.: Parker v. Vaughn, 183 S.E.2d 605 (App. 1971).
Hi.: Yoshizaki v. Hilo Hosp., 433 P.2d 220 (1967).
Idaho: Billings v. Sisters of Mercy of Idaho, 389 P.2d 224 (1964).
N.J.: Fernandi v. Strully, 173 A.2d 277 (1961).
N.Y.: Flanagan v. Mt. Eden General Hosp., 248 N.E.2d 871 (1969).
Ohio: Melnyk v. The Cleveland Clinic, 290 N.E.2d 916 (1972).
[110] 254 P.2d 85 (1953).

could have discovered the malpractice. This was shortly followed by other cases that held likewise.[111]

Many cases stressed the fact that recovery should not be permitted if the plaintiff could have discovered the malpractice by reasonable investigation or discovery.[112]

Where the alleged malpractice resulted from continuing treatment, some courts hold that the statute does not begin to run until treatment has been completed.[113]

The decisions run the gamut, from the date of the act or omission to the time of injury, the date of discovery, or the date when discovery could reasonably have been made. They run from the date of last treatment to the last day of successive contributing injury. As usual, the problem for the claim representative is to learn the position taken by the courts in his jurisdiction.

The statute of limitations for malpractice is often different from that involving other negligence. In addition, the time may be the period applying to contracts, where a doctor or surgeon may be interpreted to have contracted to produce certain results.[114]

---

[111] **Cal.:** Neel v. Magana et al, 98 Cal. Rptr. 837 (1971).
La.: Dauzat v. St. Paul Fire & Marine Ins. Co., 336 So. 2d 540 (App. 1976).
Md.: Jones v. Sugar, 305 A.2d 219 (App. 1973) (nurse's claim barred because her medical training should have made her conscious of the malpractice sooner).
Mich.: Johnson v. Caldwell, 123 N.W.2d 785 (1963).
N.J.: Rankin v. Sowinski, 291 A.2d 849 (Super. 1972); Mant v. Gillespie, 460 A.2d 172 (Super. 1983).
Ore.: Frahs v. Greene, 452 P.2d 564 (1969).

[112] **Ariz.:** Ashley v. United States, 413 F.2d 490 (1969) (the fact that the plaintiff did not know that the condition was permanent did not extend the statutory period).
Ark.: Johnson v. United States, 271 F. Supp. 205 (1967).
Cal.: Wozneak v. Pennsylvania Hosp., 82 Cal. Rptr. 84 (1969).
D.C.: Burke v. Washington Hosp. Center, 293 F. Supp. 1328 (1968).
Ill.: Mathis v. Hejna, 248 N.E.2d 767 (1969).
La.: Berrios v. Sara Mayo Hosp., 224 So. 2d 846 (1969) (injury so apparent, it was "beyond belief" that plaintiff did not discover it sooner).
Neb.: Acker v. Sorensen, 165 N.W.2d 74 (1969).
N.Y.: Flanagan v. Mt. Eden Gen. Hosp., 301 N.Y.S.2d 23 (1969).
Okla.: Lewis v. Owen, 395 P.2d 537 (1968).
Ore.: Frohs v. Greene, 452 P.2d 564 (1969).
R.I.: Wilkinson v. Harrington, 243 A.2d 745 (1968).
Tex.: Coyne v. United States, 411 F.2d 987 (1969).
Utah: Christiansen v. Rees, 436 P.2d 435 (1968).
Wash.: Ruth v. Dight, 453 P.2d 631 (1969).

[113] Schwenn v. Cacho, 319 N.Y.S.2d 674 (1971).

[114] Camposano v. Claiborn, 196 A.2d 129 (Conn. 1964).

[b] Continuing Negligence Rule

The "continuing negligence rule" enunciates the principle that the statute of limitations does not begin to run until the termination of the treatment by the physician or the doctor-patient medical relationship has ceased.[115]

In the case of *Koenig v. Group Health Corp. of Puget Sound*,[116] the court was faced with the problem as to whether the statute of limitations was tolled by a continuous course of non-negligent treatment after the plaintiff had actual knowledge of a negligent operation.

Holding the action time-barred, the court stated that the statute of limitations is tolled by a continuous course of non-negligent treatment years after a completed disclosure of facts by the operating surgeon, which would have put a reasonable person on notice that the acts of the surgeon were negligent. The court so held despite the fact that in this case the non-negligent treatment was given by a different surgeon and not by the original negligent surgeon.

It must be again noted that in the new type of "claims-made" policies, the physician is required to have a valid malpractice liability policy at the time a claim is made against him.

[c] Fraudulent Concealment

It has been stated that:

In malpractice actions against doctors, the law is . . . that a higher standard is applied in determining whether a doctor fraudulently concealed a cause of action from a patient than is applied where fraudulent concealment is alleged in cases between two corporations or two businessmen dealing at arms length. The law does critically examine the relationship between patient and doctor, the disparity between

---

[115] **Md.:** Waldman v. Rohrbaugh, 215 A.2d 825 (1966) (statute begins to run at termination of treatment for specific injury).

Ohio: Wyler v. Trippi, 267 N.E.2d 419 (1971); Amer v. Akron City Hosp., 351 N.E.2d 479 (1976).

Tenn.: Frazor v. Osborne, 414 S.W.2d 118 (App. 1966) (despite fact that date of malpractice was clearly determinable).

See also Kroll, "The Etiology, Pulse and Prognosis of Medical Malpractice," 8 Suffolk U.L. Rev. 598 (1973-74).

[116] 491 P.2d 702 (Wash. App. 1971).

them in knowledge and experience, and the reliance placed upon the doctor by the patient.[117]

Accordingly, the statute of limitations will not begin to run until the concealment is no longer practiced or until the patient becomes aware of the malpractice.

§ 35.04 Arbitration of Medical Malpractice Cases

Arbitration is a process, subject to law, whereby both parties to a dispute agree to submit controversies to a neutral party or panel for final determination. A statement of the nature of the dispute, and a possible reply replaces formal pleadings and, generally, pre-trial procedures are abolished. The arbitrator or panel judges, the relevancy of evidence, and formal rules of evidence are usually suspended. The award granted is final and enforceable in the same manner as a court judgment.[118]

There are several kinds of arbitration programs. Some have been set up by local and state bar associations, some by the insurance industry, and a few operate independently.

In the case of *Madden v. Kaiser Foundation Hospitals*,[119] the California Supreme Court held that (1) an agent or fiduciary has implied power to agree to binding arbitration; (2) such a contract is not a contract of adhesion if the weaker party has a strong agent to represent him; (3) surrendering the opportunity for a jury trial is balanced by the advantages of arbitration such as speed, lower costs, relaxed rules of evidence, potential for a reduced health premium, and feasibility of making a determination in small claims.

On the other hand, an appellate court, in *Wheeler v. St. Joseph Hosp.*[120] held that a patient's alleged agreement at the time of hospital admission, was a contract of adhesion and accordingly unenforceable.

Each arbitration agreement must be carefully scrutinized in the light of local statutory and case law.

---

[117] Eschenbacher v. Hier, 110 N.W.2d 731 (Mich. 1961) at 732. *See also* Emmett v. Eastern Dispensary & Cas. Hosp., 396 F.2d 931 (D.C. Cir. 1967); Kauchik v. Williams, 435 S.W.2d 342 (Mo. 1968); Lopez v. Sawyer, 279 A.2d 116 (N.J. Super. 1971).

[118] Ladimer & Solomon, "Medical Malpractice Arbitration: Laws, Programs, Cases," Insurance Law Journal, June 1977.

[119] 17 Cal. 3d 699 (1976).

[120] 133 Cal. Rptr. 775 (1977).

The question of whether or not punitive damages may be awarded in arbitration is moot. In the case of *Garrity v. Lyle Stuart, Inc.*[121] the court held that an arbitrator was not permitted to award punitive damages since this was a social sanction reserved to the state in order to punish wrongdoers in civil actions.

§ 35.05 Recent Medical Malpractice Legislation

The recent outcry concerning medical costs and malpractice insurance has reached the ears of our legislators and spawned a rash of new statutes, some of which were long overdue, and others that were hastily drawn up and ill considered.

Some of these statutes have rightly or wrongly already been declared unconstitutional and others are in litigation. All fifty states have enacted some form of medical malpractice legislation which runs the gamut from too little to too much. The basic areas at issue in these statutes generally cover in total:

1. Good samaritan laws.
2. Immunity for participants in mass immunization programs.
3. Establishing standards for informed consent.
4. Mandatory and voluntary arbitration programs for the institution and appeals from malpractice suits.
5. Placing limits on contingency fees.
6. Placing limits on recovery amounts.
7. Concerning collateral source doctrine.
8. Denying subrogation rights against malpractice benefits.
9. Disallowing punitive damages.
10. Revising statutes of limitation.
11. Setting up funds for partial payment of some judgments.
12. Confining the doctrine of res ipsa loquitur.
13. Limiting liability in medical emergency situations.
14. Limiting recovery to economic losses only.
15. Permitting the establishment of professional liability funds.
16. Elimination of ad damnum clauses in legal pleadings.
17. Requiring prior notification before suit is instituted.
18. Requiring contracts insuring results to be in writing.
19. Providing immunity for testing or examinations made at the request of the patient.

---

[121] 353 N.E.2d 793 (N.Y. 1976).

20. Immunity for doctors for medical services rendered at free clinics.
21. Providing for periodic payments of verdicts or settlements.

In addition, some forms of "no-fault" laws are being proposed for medical malpractice liability insurance.

A Texas appellate court invalidated a statute that placed a cap on the amount of damages that a malpractice victim could recover from a hospital, holding that such a statute violated the equal protection clause of the state and federal constitutions by singling out a specific class of tort victims.[122] Just the opposite was decided on an even more restrictive statute, by a Louisiana court of appeals.[123] Other courts have also upheld damage limitations in their statutes.[124]

On the other hand, some courts have followed the Texas example and held such statutes unconstitutional.[125]

Other statutes have also been tested and such suits are proliferating daily.

§ 35.06 Action for Wrongful Suit by Physicians

It is small wonder that doctors who feel betrayed by patients who bring suits for malpractice against them, after what they consider an unfortunate turn of events despite all of the doctor's efforts to cure, should feel vengeful. Is it not only human for them to use the same means that were used against them, to put both the patient and his lawyer in a defendant's posture and in addition help reduce other such actions?

In recent years, this has been tried by way of suits and countersuits, but not with any great degree of success.

In a detailed and excellent article on this subject, Sheila

---

[122] Baptist Hosp. of Southeast Texas v. Baker, 672 S.W.2d 296 (1984).
[123] Williams v. Lalli Kemp Charity Hosp., 428 So. 2d 1000 (1983).
[124] **Ind.:** Johnson v. St. Vincent Hosp., 404 N.E.2d 585 (1980).
Neb.: Pendergast v. Nelson, 256 N.W.2d 657 (1971).
[125] **Ill.:** Wright v. Central Dee Page Hosp. Assoc., 347 N.E.2d 736 (1976).
N.H.: Carson v. Maurer, 424 A.2d 825 (1980).
N.D.: Arneson v. Olson, 270 N.W.2d 125 (1978).
Ohio: Simon v. St. Elizabeth Medical Center, 355 N.E.2d 903 (1976).
See also Richards, "Statutes Limiting Medical Malpractice Damages," FIC Quarterly, Spring 1982.

Birnbaum[126] lists the grounds upon which a lawyer may be subjected to an action by a doctor, who felt that the underlying suit against him was unjustified, as follows:

1. If such underlying action was brought solely because of a patient's malice or ill will.
2. Where the plaintiff's lawyer has not used reasonable skill and diligence to learn pertinent facts or applicable law prior to instituting the malpractice suit.
3. Where the lawyer has continued the suit after learning that such an action was frivolous or unjustified.
4. Where the lawyer brings an action solely to extort a "nuisance settlement."
5. Where the lawyer learns that such an action was brought in an attempt to avoid payment of the doctor's fee or to have it reduced.
6. Where the doctor has been made a codefendant for the sole purpose of securing his testimony or for purposes of "fishing."

Obviously, not all of these "causes" are actionable and some of them are just about impossible to prove. However, this article discusses in detail the traditional tort remedies that have been utilized to counterattack in cases of frivolous malpractice suits that were brought against a physician.

[1] Malicious Prosecution

Many jurisdictions now recognize actions for malicious prosecution where the suit was maliciously instituted and without probable cause.[127] Such an action may also be maintained against the patient.[128]

---

[126] Birnbaum, "Physicians Counterattack: Liability of Lawyers for Instituting Unjustified Medical Malpractice Actions," FIC Quarterly, Winter 1978.

[127] **Ariz.:** Carroll v. Kalar, 545 P.2d 411 (1976).
Cal.: Babb v. Superior Court, 92 Cal. Rptr. 179 (1971).
La.: Spencer v. Burglass, 337 So. 2d 596 (App. 1976) (failed to prove malice).

[128] **Idaho:** Allen v. Moyle, 367 P.2d 579 (1961).
Ore.: Patupoff v. Vollstedt's, Inc., 369 P.2d 691 (1962); O'Toole v. Franklin, 569 P.2d 561 (1977) (failed to show "special injury").
Tex.: Wolfe v. Arroyo, 543 S.W.2d 11 (App. 1976).
Wyo.: Consumers Filling Station v. Durante, 333 P.2d 691 (1958).
Tex.: Wolfe v. Arroyo, 643 S.W.2d 11 (App. 1976).

In such an action or counterclaim, it is usually necessary for the underlying malpractice suit to have terminated in favor of the underlying defendant.[129]

In the case of *Tappen v. Ager*,[130] Ager brought a malpractice and wrongful death action against Dr. Tappen for the latter's alleged negligence at the birth of Ager's daughter. Without waiting for the disposition of the case, Dr. Tappen brought an action against Ager for abuse of process. The federal court, applying Kansas law, held that there is no recognizable tort of negligence arising from the prosecution of a lawsuit, since there is no duty running from the plaintiff to the defendant to use reasonable care in filing such a suit. The court found that abuse of process was inapplicable since there was no ulterior purpose in filing the malpractice action and because there was no malice and, finally, because the complaint failed to state a cause of action for outrageous, gross or wanton conduct.

As a practical matter, it is very difficult to establish malice. In the case of *Field v. Goldstein*,[131] the court listed six criteria which must be met to establish a case for malicious prosecution, namely:

1. Commencement or continuation of an original civil or criminal judicial proceeding;
2. Its legal causation by the present defendant against the plaintiff;
3. Its bona fide termination in favor of the present plaintiff;
4. The absence of probable cause for such underlying prosecution;
5. The presence of malice; and
6. Damages conforming to legal standards resulting to the plaintiff.

However, as was pointed out in "Physician's Countersuits: A Reply,"[132] in the few cases mentioned, because of the "special injury" rule, this requirement makes malicious prosecution virtually unavailable in some, but not most, jurisdictions.

This article also points out that a number of countersuits by doctors have been settled at trial level and that there are appellate deci-

---

[129] **Cal.:** Babb v. Superior Court, 92 Cal. Rptr. 179 (1971).
Ill.: Schwartz v. Schwartz, 8 N.E.2d 668 (1937).
[130] 599 F.2d 376 (10th Cir. Kan. 1979).
[131] 379 So. 2d 410 (Fla. App. 1980).
[132] F.T.D., March 1981.

sions affirming the right of a physician to countersue,[133] and where countersuits and awards have been affirmed by the Supreme Court.[134]

---

[133] Weaver v. Superior Court, 156 Cal. Rptr. 745 (App. 1979).

[134] Bull v. McCloskey, 615 P.2d 957 (Nev. 1980). *See also* Freeman, "Endless Litigation: Justice or Revenge?", Insurance Counsel Journal, April 1978; Comment, Janzer, "Countersuits to Legal and Medical Malpractice Actions: Any Chance of Success?", 65 Marq. L. Rev. 93 (1980); Birnbaum, "Physicians Counterattack: Liability of Lawyers for Instituting Unjustified Medical Malpractice Actions," FIC Quarterly, Winter 1978; Comment, "Attorney Liability for Malicious Prosecution and Legal Malpractice: Do They Overlap?", 8 Pacific L.J. 897 (1977); Notr, "Malicious Prosecution: An Effective Attack on Spurious Medical Malpractice Claims?", 26 Case W. Res. L. Rev. 653 (1976).

CHAPTER 36

Professional Liability—Dentists, Nurses, Hospitals, and Druggists—and the Investigation of Medical Malpractice Claims

§ 36.01 Dentists
    [1] Duty of Care
    [2] Expert Testimony
    [3] Contributory and Comparative Negligence
    [4] Releases
    [5] Statutes of Limitations
§ 36.02 Nurses
    [1] Duty of Care
    [2] Locality Rule
    [3] Some Areas of Responsibilities
    [4] Charitable Immunity
§ 36.03 Hospitals
    [1] Coverage
    [2] Who is Covered
    [3] Hospital Liability
    [4] Corporate Liability
    [5] Standard of Care—Locality Rule
    [6] Vicarious Liability of a Hospital
    [7] Ostensible Agency Doctrine
    [8] Product/Service Distinction
    [9] Negligent Release of Mental Patient
    [10] Blood Transfusions
    [11] Charitable Immunity
    [12] Pleadings
§ 36.04 Druggists
§ 36.05 Investigation of Medical Malpractice Claims
    [1] In General
    [2] Checklists
        [a] Qualifications of the Insured
        [b] Factual Details
        [c] Information to be Obtained from or Concerning the Injured
        [d] Hospital Records
        [e] Druggist's Malpractice Claims

§ 36.06 Bibliography

§ 36.01 Dentists

Dentists Professional Liability insurance is provided on the Physicians and Surgeons form, and the rules involving dental malpractice are the same rules of medical malpractice applied in a dental context.

While the general principles in medical malpractice claims are very similar to those of the dental profession, as the profession of dentistry made vast strides in both treatment and diagnosis, the amount of new knowledge and technology that has been developed has warranted the growth in dental specialists. The entire area of specialization in this field is very recent and some aspects of it, such as root canal work, extractions, gum and other mouth diseases, teeth straightening and major jaw operations, among other developments, require such detailed skills that specialization became inevitable.

As with other medical practitioners, dentists are not insurers or guarantors (unless they so contract) of a specific result.[1]

[1] **Duty of Care**

The general duty of care owed by a dentist is that usually applied in professional liability cases which is that degree of care and knowledge exercised by others in the same profession or area of specialized practice.[2]

The standard of care and skill used *in a comparable community* is a standard more often used in dental cases than in that of medical cases,[3] probably because the quality and amount of dental care varies more widely by community than does medical care.

State dental licensing boards set up standards of care in the form of statutes in most states that are a good guide of what is required in the defense of dental malpractice cases.[4]

---

[1] Kent v. Henson, 330 S.E.2d 126 (Ga. App. 1985). *See also* Yee & Ream, "Dental Malpractice," F.T.D., February 2, 1986, from which article most of the citations in this section were taken.

[2] Gurdin v. Dongieux, 468 So. 2d 1241 (La. App. 1984).

[3] *Id.;* Storm v. Costa, 682 S.W.2d 599 (Tex. App. 1984).

[4] *See* In re Proposed Disciplinary Action Against the Dentist License of Schultz, 375 N.W.2d 509 (Minn. App. 1985); James v. Board of Dental Examiners, 218 Cal. Rptr. 710 (1985); Engel v. Dep't of Professional Regulation, 477 So. 2d 11 (Fla. App. 1985).

PROFESSIONAL LIABILITY—MEDICAL AREAS § 36.01[5]

[2] Expert Testimony

The only situation in which an absence of expert testimony is excused, generally speaking, is when the lack of skill or care of the dentist is so apparent that the average layman could understand and recognize it,[5] and where express warranties of results were made.[6]

[3] Contributory and Comparative Negligence

Defenses of contributory and, more often, comparative negligence are usually available in cases involving dental malpractice.[7]

[4] Releases

In dentistry, as well as in other forms of medical malpractice, the courts are usually strict in interpreting "release" forms which are tendered to a patient before a procedure or treatment without full explanation and without giving the patient time for consideration.[8]

[5] Statutes of Limitations

It has been stated that there are at least four theories concerning the time when the statutory period of limitations begins, as follows:

1. *The traditional rule,* which holds that the statute of limitations begins to run on the date of the occurrence of the malpractice, regardless of the discovery date.[9]

2. *The last act doctrine,* which holds that the date of the last act of the treatment, which can be after the treatment and post-treatment check-up have been completed.[10]

3. *The discovery doctrine* is the same as in a doctor's or surgeon's malpractice and holds that the statute does not begin to run until the patient discovers, or reasonably could have discovered, the malpractice.[11]

4. *The fraudulent concealment rule* tolls the running of the statute

---

[5] Steinmetz v. F.J. Lowry & Assoc's., 477 N.E.2d 671 (1984).
[6] Cirafici v. Goffen, 407 N.E.2d 633 (Ill. App. 1980).
[7] *See* Gumper v. Bach, 474 So. 2d 420 (Fla. App. 1985).
[8] Abromowitz v. University Dental Center, 494 N.Y.S.2d 721 (1985).
[9] Masi v. Seale, 682 P.2d 102 (Idaho 1984).
[10] Schneider v. Brunk, 324 S.E.2d 922 (N.C. App. 1985).
[11] Pittman v. Hodge, 462 So. 2d 332 (Miss. 1980).

if the dentist knowingly conceals his negligence in order to avoid the consequences of his wrongdoing.[12]

§ 36.02 Nurses

A nurse, in the discharge of duties, must obey and diligently execute the orders of the doctor or surgeon in charge of a patient, unless such order is so obviously incorrect or negligent as to lead others of like training and experience to conclude that harm would result from the execution of such an order.[13]

Under proper orders, a nurse may administer drugs, give hypodermic injections, take temperature and pulse, place dressings and bandages, apply medication and perform many other duties peculiarly within the ministrations of healing and for which the nurse has been specifically trained.

A nurse, although obviously trained for skills, is not in the same category as a doctor who is required to exercise independent judgment on medical matters. A nurse is not authorized to practice medicine. A nurse's primary function is to follow the doctor's orders and to record and keep the doctor advised of observations.

In determining what statute of limitations was applicable to the negligence of a nurse in the care of a patient, the court held that it was ordinary negligence and not malpractice.[14] The line to be drawn concerning what statute of limitations applies is, as we have said, often a very fine one.

Nurses who are employed, or being trained by a hospital, are employees of the hospital, and their negligence is accordingly also attributable vicariously to the hospital for which they work. This is not true of nurses specially hired by a patient or someone on the patient's behalf, who has been called into the hospital for special duty involving that patient only and who has no other association with the hospital.

The fact that a nurse's negligence occurs while acting under orders from the personal doctor of the patient does not insulate the hospital from liability, assuming the nurse is an employee of the hospital. There are, however, some circumstances in which the nurse may be considered as the temporary employee of the doctor or sur-

---

[12] Weaver v. Witt, 561 S.W.2d 792 (Tex. 1977).
[13] Byrd v. Marion General Hosp., 202 N.C. 337 (1932).
[14] Richardson v. Doe, 199 N.E.2d 878 (Ohio 1964).

geon. This is usually when the nurse is acting in the capacity of an assistant at an operation, or at the birth of a child. In such instances, the hospital has, until recently, ordinarily been absolved of responsibility for the nurse's negligence if there was no question of general incompetence.[15]

There appears to be a trend away from the "borrowed servant" rule, however, and a holding of liability on the part of a hospital, even where the employee nurse was temporarily under the direct control of a doctor or surgeon.[16]

[1] Duty of Care

Formerly, the liability of nurses was predicated on that of the ordinary reasonably prudent person. In recent years, however, registered nurses, for the purpose of malpractice liability at least, have been given professional recognition. Today, for the most part, the duty of care imposed on a nurse is the duty to use reasonable professional skill and care commensurate with that used by other nurses, and, sometimes, in the same or similar locality.

The duty of nurses differs from that of physicians in that nurses are subject to the orders and instructions of physicians and their duty to follow such orders is limited only to the use of independent judgment commonly attributed to others in the same profession. Accordingly, it is possible for a nurse to make an error in judgment or to be unsuccessful in treatment (at least theoretically), without being negligent.[17]

The duty of a nurse has also been held to be the rendering of professional services and to exercise that degree of skill and caring commonly applied under all circumstances (in the community or nationally) by the average prudent reputable member of the profession.[18]

In the Louisiana Supreme Court case of *Tankersley v. Ins. Co. of*

---

[15] Beadles v. Metayka, 135 Colo. 366, 311 P.2d 711 (1957).

[16] Kemalyan v. Henderson and the Deaconess Hosp., 45 Wash. 2d 693, 277 P.2d 372 (1954).

[17] Fraijo v. Hartland Hosp., 160 Cal. Rptr. 246 (App. 1979). *See also* "A Revolution in White—New Approaches in Treating Nurses as Professionals," 30 Vand. L. Rev. 839 (1977).

[18] Matthews v. Walker, 296 N.E.2d 569 (Ohio App. 1973); Shilkret v. Annapolis Emerg. Hosp., 349 A.2d 245 (Md. 1975).

North America,[19] the court stated that "nurses are classified as professional persons employed to exercise their calling on their own responsibility, and that nurses are grouped with physicians and surgeons and not with chambermaids and cooks,"[20]

This is certainly as it should be for registered and licensed nurses who have received college level professional training and education. Today, however, as any patient knows, the great majority of those called nurses, and who attend to them in hospitals, are not qualified or registered nurses. They are called "practical nurses," and their training is minimal, haphazard, and in many cases rudimentary, depending on the hospital in which they work. They and "orderlies," to whom they are related, cannot be held to the same degree of responsibility as a registered nurse. Such people are direct employees of the hospital and are not, nor should they be, given professional status. The hospital should be held accountable not only for choosing them, but for their training and supervision. They are supposedly working under the direct supervision of a registered nurse and the question arises as to whether the registered nurse or the hospital, or both, should be accountable for their acts of malpractice.

[2] **Locality Rule**

Most jurisdictions have now abandoned the "locality rule" as a standard in judging the negligence of a nurse.[21] It has been recognized in medical malpractice generally, that the locality rule has become obsolete, but, in my opinion, hospitals, as will be pointed out, should not be judged on the same basis as others connected with the medical sciences.

[3] **Some Areas of Responsibilities**

Nurses have been held liable for malpractice in many areas of responsibility, some of which have been:

1. Failure to follow the doctor's instructions.[22]
2. Leaving a patient unattended when attention was called for.[23]

---

[19] 216 So. 2d 333 (App. 1968).
[20] Louie v. Chinese Hosp. Ass'n, 57 Cal. Rptr. 906 (1967).
[21] Shilkret v. Annapolis Emerg. Hosp., 349 A.2d 245 (Md. 1975).
[22] City of Somerset v. Hart, 549 S.W.2d 814 (Ky. 1977).
[23] Cavenaugh v. South Broward Hosp. Dist., 247 So. 2d 769 (Fla. App. 1971).

3. Using unsterile instruments.[24]
4. Improper removal of catheters.[25]
5. Errors in blood transfusion.[26]
6. Failure to record vital information on charts.[27]
7. Failure to call vital changes in the patient's condition to the immediate attention of a doctor.[28]

[4] **Charitable Immunity**

An employee-nurse of a hospital that has been granted charitable immunity in the few jurisdictions that still hold to this antiquated doctrine, does not have the immunity granted to the hospital for which he or she works.[29]

§ 36.03 Hospitals

[1] **Coverage**

We have already discussed the "claims-made" policy forms and their differentiation from the usual "occurrence" forms in Chapter 26. In hospital professional liability policies, the insured has the option of purchasing either form, although not all states have as yet approved the latest Insurance Services Office (ISO) forms.

The older forms still require the insured's consent to settle a claim before the insurer may do so and this provision has been dropped from the newer forms.

All of these policies, for reasons previously outlined in differentiating general liability coverage from malpractice, contain protection from both types of claims. The general and products liability coverage comes into play when injury arises out of such general activities as housekeeping, the making and serving of meals, and other hospital responsibilities not connected directly with medical care and treatment of patients. As previously pointed out, there are many areas of uncertainty as to which part of the policy would provide protection in specific incidents.

---

[24] Kalmus v. Cedars of Lebanon Hosp., 281 P.2d 872 (Cal. 1955).
[25] Zach v. Centro Espanol Hosp., 319 So. 2d 34 (Fla. App. 1975).
[26] Kyte v. McMillion, 259 A.2d 532 (1969).
[27] Lhotka v. Larson, 238 N.W.2d 870 (Minn. 1976).
[28] Karrigan v. Nazareth Convent and Academy, 510 P.2d 190 (1973).
[29] Watson v. St. Anne's Hosp., 386 N.E.2d 885 (Ill. 1979).

Coverage for liability arising out of the furnishing of food, beverages, medications, or appliances in connection with professional services gives, in effect, products liability, as well as general and malpractice coverage if connected with professional services. Accordingly, as stated in the F.C. & S. Bulletins,[30] liability arising out of food served to patients is covered, but food served to relatives or other visitors, is not.

[2] Who is Covered

Coverage applies to the personal liability of any partner, executive officer, hospital administrator, stockholder or member of the board of trustees, directors or governors of the named insured hospital, while acting within the scope of their duties as such. This policy does not cover the liability of individual doctors who may be owners or directors, etc., for their own acts of malpractice.

The Hospital Professional Liability policy contains the usual general liability exclusions found in other policies.

[3] Hospital Liability

The liability of a hospital may rest on its corporate responsibility (administrative acts), or on the doctrine of agency or master and servant (respondeat superior).

Responsibility for its administrative or corporate acts usually falls within three categories: (1) defective equipment; (2) selection or retention of incompetent personnel; and (3) unsatisfactory maintenance of buildings, grounds, furnishings, medical, and other equipment, and defective food and drink.

Hospitals may be government owned, privately run for profit, or privately run on a nonprofit or charitable basis. I would suggest a review of Chapter 12 dealing with charitable and governmental immunities in connection with our discussion of the liability of hospitals, since all three categories present different legal problems.

Hospitals run for profit are responsible for the wrongdoing of their employees, generally to the same degree that ordinary corporations, partnerships, or other business entities would be held accountable.

---

[30] Published by The National Underwriter Co., Cincinnati, Ohio.

[4] Corporate Liability

As already indicated, one theory used to impose liability on a hospital is that of corporate liability, which is predicated on the notion that a hospital owes a direct duty to its patients to render good and adequate medical care.[31]

Most hospitals are corporations and their duties encompass responsibility for their administrative staffs and their medical staffs. Generally speaking, such duties include:

1. The exercise of reasonable care in providing proper medical equipment, supplies, medication; and food, beds and other sheltering equipment (proper medical equipment these days can depend on next week's new inventions, but in view of the enormous costs of items such as scanners and others of a like complexity, I should think that reasonableness would be a guide);
2. The providing of safe physical premises for patients and invitees;
3. The use of reasonable care in the procuring of a proper staff, both administrative and medical; and, most of all,
4. Making sure that proper care is being given to patients.

While, in some instances, it is still important to distinguish administrative from professional duties and acts, the prevalence of hospital insurance which provides both general liability and professional liability coverage makes this distinction of less importance than it was previously.

In addition, relatively fewer cases are being brought on the basis of corporate liability than in previous years.

[5] Standard of Care—Locality Rule

The standard of care required of a hospital is the usual lack of negligence required, measured against the standards of other

---

[31] Cal.: Elam v. College Park Hosp., 183 Cal. Rptr. 156 (1982).
Minn.: Sandhofer v. Abbott-Northwestern Hosp., 283 N.W.2d 362 (1979).
Tenn.: Crumley v. Memorial Hosp., 509 F. Supp. 531 (1979).
Wis.: Johnson v. Miserecordia Community Hosp., 301 N.W.2d 156 (1981).

See also Moore, "Medical Staff—Corporate Account Liability," Insurance Counsel Journal, January 1976; Note, "Theories for Imposing Liability Upon Hospitals for Medical Malpractice: Ostensible Agency and Corporate Liability," 11 Wm. Mitchell L. Rev. 561 (1985).

well-run hospitals and, in some jurisdictions, in the same or like community.

Although locality is a measure less frequently used, there is logic for having it play a larger part in the measuring of hospital malpractice than in other branches of medicine for the obvious reason that hospital costs are so extremely high that their facilities must be judged by the funds available to buy the latest equipment in a particular locality.

[6] **Vicarious Liability of a Hospital**

Access to hospital facilities is essential to the practice of a doctor. Licensing and review procedures provide some measure of quality control of the physicians who are connected with a hospital, but the burden is on the hospital to make its own investigation (with the help of medical boards) concerning the competency of any doctor who is accepted on its staff.

The well-documented expansion of a hospital's liability for the acts of it's servants (respondeat superior), or independent contractors (physicians or other medical practitioners who practice in the hospital), received added impetus as a result of the 1978 Michigan court decision in *Greive v. Mt. Clemens General Hosp.*[32]

"The person who avails himself (or herself) of hospital facilities expects that the hospital will attempt to cure him, not that its nurses or other employees will act on their own responsibility," says the court in *Bing v. Thunig.*[33] Not any more, I am sorry to say. Patients of today are, to some extent, grateful that they don't come out of some hospitals more ill or diseased than they were when they were admitted. The advent and proliferation of the "practical nurse" was a good and practical idea in theory, but the failure to properly train and supervise such employees and the free reign which seems to be so prevalent for nurses, and particularly for doctors and surgeons, would indicate a possible return to the legal position of the court in

---

[32] 273 N.W.2d 429 (1978) (case involved the liability of a hospital for the acts of an independent contractor-physician who was not named in the complaint and a defendant employee-intern, who was exonerated).

See also Stanczyk & Moffett, "Hospitals, Physicians and their Liability Carriers: Ostensible Authority, Enterprise Liability, and Beyond," FIC Quarterly, Spring 1981 (this article quotes numerous other articles on this subject in footnote 1).

[33] 163 N.Y.S.2d 3 (1957).

PROFESSIONAL LIABILITY—MEDICAL AREAS § 36.03[6]

Schloendorff v. Society of N.Y. Hosp.[34] Nevertheless, our courts seem more and more inclined to hold a hospital responsible for the free-wheeling acts of doctors and surgeons who roam the hospital corridors as "kings of the walk."[35]

On the other hand, as one writer pointed out:[36]

> Today's hospitals are larger and more complex than ever before and operate as highly integrated systems utilizing a team approach to medical care. . . . As the larger hospitals treat more patients, the potential for negligence by the hospital increases. A patient commencing a malpractice action will probably sue the hospital in addition to the treating doctor. . . .
>
> The changing nature of hospitals has not gone unnoticed by the courts. These changes have precipitated a reevaluation of the traditional legal analysis regarding hospital's liability for the negligence of their physicians.

As this situation has developed, some hospitals are beginning to realize that they must now begin to exercise some real degree of control over the physicians who use their facilities.[37]

Besides the usual maintenance and service staffs, some hospitals also include resident physicians such as internists, anesthesiologists, radiologists, and pathologists, under various arrangements.

I surely agree with the opinion of the court in *Beck v. Tuscon Gen. Hosp.*[38] when it stated that "The care and service dispensed . . . however technical, complex and esoteric its character may be, must meet standards of responsibility commensurate with the undertaking to preserve and protect the health and indeed, the very lives of those placed in the hospital's keeping."

True enough, but is that not extending the liability of hospitals when it is now being measured by what a hospital should be, rather than what the average hospital really is?

The hospital does, it has been held, assume certain non-delegable

---

[34] 105 N.E.2d 92 (1914).

[35] *See* Schagrin v. Wilmington Medical Center, 304 A.2d 61 (Del. Super. 1973); Breck v. Tucson Gen. Hosp., 500 P.2d 1153 (App. 1972) (radiologist was held to be an employee of the hospital).

[36] Note, "Theories for Imposing Liability Upon Hospitals for Medical Malpractice: Ostensible Agency and Corporate Liability," 11 Wm Mitchell L. Rev. 561 (1985).

[37] *See id.*

[38] 500 P.2d 1183 (Ariz. App. 1972).

duties for the care of a patient which are owed directly to him.[39]

In the area of maintenance responsibilities a hospital has a duty to all invitees to use reasonable care in the maintenance of buildings, grounds, and furnishings, which are usually referred to as administrative duties, as distinguished from medical duties.[40]

[7] Ostensible Agency Doctrine

If a patient's lawyer fails to prove an actual master-servant or agency relationship between a doctor and the hospital involved, liability may still be held to be that of the hospital under the doctrine of "ostensible agency."

This doctrine requires that the hospital has given the impression that the medical treatment was given by a doctor who was employed by the hospital.[41]

In order for the court to recognize the doctrine of "ostensible agency" as applied to a particular case, the defendant must prove that the person dealing with the agent must *reasonably* have believed in the agency relationship and that such an alleged agent had the authority to act on behalf of the hospital.[42]

This doctrine is sometimes referred to as the "holding-out" or "agency estopped" ruling as set forth in the Restatement (Second) of Agency § 267 as follows:

> One who represents that another is his servant or other agent, and thereby causes a third person justifiably to rely upon the skill or care of such apparent agent is subject to liability to the third person for harm caused by the lack of care or skill of one appearing to be a servant or other agent as if he were such.[43]

---

[39] Darling v. Charlestown Community Hosp., 211 N.E.2d 253 (Ill. 1965), *cert. denied*, 383 U.S. 946 (1966).

[40] Bellaire Hosp. v. Campbell, 510 S.W.2d 94 (Tex. App. 1974); Hill v. James Walker Mem. Hosp., 407 F.2d 1036 (4th Cir. 1968).

[41] *See* Payne, "Recent Developments Affecting a Hospitals' Liability for Negligence of Physicians," 18 S. Tex. L. J. 389 (1977) and Howard v. Park, 195 N.W.2d 39 (Mich. 1972).

[42] Seneris v. Haas, 291 P.2d 915 (Cal. 1955).

[43] **Cal.:** Quintal v. Laurel Grove Hosp., 41 Cal. Rptr. 577 (1964).
Del.: Vanamaut v. Milford Mem. Hosp., 272 A.2d 718 (Super. 1972).
Mich.: Howard v. Parke, 195 N.W.2d 39 (1972).
Mont.: Kober v. Stewart, 417 P.2d 476 (1966).
Ohio: Lundberg v. Bay View Hosp., 191 N.E.2d 821 (1963).

[8] Product/Service Distinction

In making a determination of the malpractice liability of a hospital, it is sometimes necessary to make a distinction as to whether the alleged negligence involved the sale of a product or providing a medical service. This differentiation is very important since strict liability is often imposed in products liability cases and rarely in medical malpractice.[44]

In *Newmark v. Gimbels, Inc.*,[45] the court stated that the applicability of an old common law distinction between the sale of goods and the rendering of services, was regarded by this court as "highly artificial." Nevertheless, most subsequent decisions disagreed.

The Supreme Court of Texas,[46] in a case involving a plaintiff who sustained an injury to his eye following the fitting and sale of contact lenses, also had lenses prescribed for him by one of their many optometrists. The same price was charged despite the possible involvement of eye problems and the number of subsequent eye examinations. In this case there was little doubt that the charges were made for the product, as advertised, and not for the services of the optometrist. Nevertheless, the court held this to be a professional service rather than a sale of a product and the defendant was not held strictly liable.

In the case of *Dubin v. Michael Reese Hosp. & Medical Center*,[47] the facts involved a plaintiff who brought an action to recover for a thyroid cancer allegedly caused by x-ray treatments administered thirty years before the onset of cancer. The Illinois Appellate Court ruled that the x-ray treatment given by the hospital constituted the sale of a product. Accordingly, the hospital was held to a strict degree of liability.

It has also been held that the product must be supplied, rather than merely used.[48]

---

[44] Immergluck v. Ridgeview House, 368 N.E.2d 803 (Ill. 1977) (nursing home offered services); Shepard v. Alexian Bros. Hosp., 109 Cal. Rptr. 132 (1973); Greenman v. Yuba Power Prods., 27 Cal. Rptr. 697 (1963).

See also Weyna, "Dublin v. Michael Reese Hosp. and Med. Center: Seeing Through the Products/ Service Distinction," Insurance Counsel Journal, July 1981.

[45] 258 A.2d 687 (N.J. 1979).

[46] Texas State Optical, Inc. v. Barbee, 417 S.W.2d 750, *aff'd sub nom.* Barbee v. Rogers, 425 S.W.2d 342 (1968).

[47] 393 N.E.2d 588 (Ill. 1979).

[48] Magrine v. Krasnica, 227 A.2d 539, *aff'd sub nom.* Magrine v. Spector, 241 A.2d 637 (N.J. 1968).

§ 36.03[9] CASUALTY INSURANCE CLAIMS

The decisions on this subject appear to have no uniformity at all, and what is or is not a product sold or a service rendered seems to be at the whim of the particular court involved.[49]

[9] Negligent Release of Mental Patient

We have seen that some jurisdictions may hold a psychiatrist liable, under some circumstances, for the release of a mental patient who has exhibited violent propensities. It has also been held that a cause of action for medical malpractice can be maintained against staff doctors of a state mental institution who negligently released a mental patient who had shown violent propensities.[50] Private mental hospitals and their psychiatrists have similarly been held liable.[51]

[10] Blood Transfusions

It has been aptly stated that:

> It is impossible to give a definite answer as to what acts or omissions would constitute actionable negligence in the blood transfusion process. What is financially and administratively feasible, what customs and procedures are in a particular area, what situation, emergency or otherwise is facing the actors, all bear on the question of actionable negligence (in blood transfusion cases). The test is hindsight evaluation of the conduct of the actor, weighed against standards of reasonableness. The cases in the courts and suggestions in the medical literature can only be illustrative of the myriad possible ways in which liability might arise.[52]

This is another area in which there is a great deal of controversy as to whether the hospital is providing a product or a service and the

---

[49] Ill.: Dubin v. Michael Reese Hosp. & Med. Center, 393 N.E.2d 588 (1979).

Wash.: Helling v. Carey, 519 P.2d 981 (1974) (lack of test for glaucoma during the performance of an eye examination subjected the doctor to a higher standard, somewhere between reasonable care and strict liability).

Wis.: Hoven v. Keble, 256 N.W.2d 379 (1977) (services of "a relatively routine or simple nature" can be subject to strict liability); Johnson v. Sears, Roebuck & Co., 355 F. Supp. 1065 (1973) (distinction made between administrative and professional services).

[50] Durflinger v. Artiles, 727 F.2d 888 (10th Cir. 1984) (inmate subsequently killed several members of his family).

[51] Tarasoff v. Regents of the Univ. of Cal., 17 Cal. 3d 425 (1976) (the court held that in such cases, the general rules of negligence and medical malpractice apply).

[52] Zipser, "Liability for Negligence in Blood Transfusions," based on a study prepared for the Ridge Borough Medical Society. (No date available or further source.)

question of strict liability may come into play. As a product, the hospital is responsible for the proper preservation, freedom from infection, infusion procedure, typing, and labeling of the blood.

The Uniform Commercial Code may become an important factor, as adopted by various states. Recent statutory enactments may be controlling. The situation becomes all the more complicated where hepatitis is alleged to have been contracted as a result of a blood transfusion.

This subject has been the focus of much legislation to relieve hospitals from malpractice liability which otherwise might be imposed.

[11] Charitable Immunity

As previously noted, early in this century, hospitals in general were exempted from vicarious liability since they were considered to be charitable institutions. They were protected from suit by the doctrine of charitable immunity.

Almost all of our states have repudiated completely, or in part, this doctrine. In any event, the number of private hospitals operated for profit has proliferated. An early landmark case, *President of Georgetown College v. Hughs*,[53] set the stage, after numerous exceptions and qualifications, by rejecting outright the charitable immunity doctrine for hospitals.

[12] Pleadings

Proper drafting of pleadings may be critical to a plaintiff's suit against a hospital for medical malpractice. Where, for instance, the plaintiff's complaint failed to plead a theory of respondeat superior, a verdict in favor of the physicians allowed accelerated judgment for the defendant in view of the fact that the plaintiff pleaded no theory of liability against the hospital that had not been predicated against the individual doctors.[54]

---

[53] 130 F.2d 810 (D.C. Cir. 1942).

[54] Ellison v. Wayne County Gen. Hosp., 300 N.W.2d 392 (Mich. 1980). *See also* Johnson v. Children's Hosp., 307 N.W.2d 371 (Mich. 1981). *See also* Note, "Theories for Imposing Liability Upon Hospitals for Medical Malpractice: Ostensible Agency and Corporate Law," 11 Wm. Mitchell L. Rev. 561 (1985).

§ 36.04 Druggists

Druggists liability insurance, as written today, for the most part is not written as a professional liability policy. It can be written as a liability policy, either separately or as an attachment to some of the general and products liability policies.

As with hospital liability insurance, it is important that the general liability and products liability coverages be written in the same company so that coverage problems in borderline cases will be kept at a minimum.

It must be remembered that druggists liability policies do not cover a druggist's errors in, or failures of, services that might fall outside the scope of products liability, except as covered under premises and operations liability stemming from incidental operations arising out of the ownership, maintenance, or use of the insured premises, if there is no pertinent professional liability exclusion in the policy or if such exclusion has not been endorsed out.

The Businessowners policy also incorporates liability coverage. In an exception to an exclusion in this policy, liability coverage applies to bodily injury and property damage claims against an insured retail drug store "due to rendering or failure to render any professional service."

In my opinion, there must be a better way to provide full coverage to the owner of a pharmacy, including malpractice coverage specifically so named. The methods of coverage indicated above,[55] appear to be shot full of ambiguities, as a result of which full professional liability coverage would probably attach in any event, but don't bet on it.

§ 36.05 Investigation of Medical Malpractice Claims

[1] In General

The investigation of claims arising out of Professional Liability policies, commonly known as malpractice claims, obviously requires some specialized knowledge of the professional field which is involved. The handling of medical malpractice claims, for instance, requires a greater knowledge of basic medical terminology than does the handling of other ordinary types of negligence claims.

---

[55] As outlined in the F.C. & S. Bulletins (National Underwriter Co., Cincinnati, Ohio), Public Liability Section, pp. Rd 1 to 4.

The attorney or investigator who specializes in this field, or who has a complicated medical malpractice case, better do his homework carefully by referring to, and studying some of the many medical texts written especially for the legal profession. By the same token, the attorney or investigator handling a professional liability claim involving engineering, accounting, architecture, or any other profession better familiarize himself with the professional aspects of the claim from whatever source material is available. Aside from a certain degree of technical knowledge that may be required of an attorney or investigator in this field, there is nothing particularly complicated or mysterious about it.

Certain fundamentals of the law concerning professional liability must be constantly borne in mind. The investigation will be geared to the precept that a professional person, such as a doctor or surgeon, is held to the same degree of care and skill as is usually exerted by other reputable people in the same profession. The attorney or investigator must also make sure to determine that the professional involved did not in any way enlarge his or her scope of responsibility by making a guarantee of cure or by any other irresponsible words or actions.

Since the vast majority of malpractice claims fall within the province of the physician, surgeon, druggist, nurse, or other medical practitioner, the outline of investigation will stress these professions. In many instances, an investigator who is concerned with a professional liability claim involving some other profession can substitute basic principles of investigation without too much orientation.

It must always be remembered that in some professional liability policies, one of the conditions of the policy may require the permission of the insured before any settlement may be negotiated. It is therefore essential that the attorney representing an insurance company, establish a close liaison with the insured and keep him advised of all discussions and negotiations with the attorney for the plaintiff, which is good practice in any event.

As with other areas of casualty claim investigation that deal with subjects that require a knowledge of the particular law, it is essential to claims involving professional liability. It is the law that determines what facts are needed and in what form these facts must be obtained in order to be admissible in evidence.

This is one area where the necessity for a thorough and complete investigation is commonplace. The claim representative is dealing not only with all of the ordinary aspects of a casualty investigation, but, in addition, with the very reputation of the insured himself. While he will get the complete cooperation of the insured, the investigator must be wary of the information he gets from him because he is so personally involved. It is essential that he corroborate information in a manner that can be presented in court if necessary.

An area of particular concern for the claim representative is the situation where a spite claim is made to offset an allegedly excessive bill for services, or where a claimant will sometimes bring an unfounded claim merely for the purpose of avoiding payment for services rendered. An area that must be watched involves the Medicare-Medicaid programs.

It is most important for the investigator never to lose sight of the fact that bad results do not necessarily spell out malpractice. Doctors are not little gods, despite the opinion to the contrary of some of them. The measure of negligence for a medical professional must never be lost sight of; was the treatment in conformity with good medical practice?

Once a claim representative has determined that the case is one for settlement consideration, he should never forget to obtain the insured's written consent if such settlement is effected, if this is called for by the policy. It is good practice to probe this question with the insured if necessary, even before negotiations are in order, so as to know his attitude. If a doctor is unreasonably stubborn, it may call for a letter to be sent to him or her stressing possible personal exposure over the policy limits (which should be done in any event where suit has been instituted) and, if the policy is so written, advise him or her that the company's liability will be limited to the amount of possible settlement.

Most malpractice actions require the review, if not the active supervision, of a staff or consulting physician and an attorney, for guidance in the investigation and preparation for defense. It is rare that these cases do not require highly specialized knowledge, and to refer such a claim to a consultant is evidence of good judgment rather than an admission of incompetence. In addition, the rules of discovery have been so liberalized as to require the protection of defense counsel even in advance of actual suit in some cases.

An excellent tool for obtaining information on the background, education, and standing of doctors and specialists is the American Medical Association Directory, which lists every physician and in-

PROFESSIONAL LIABILITY—MEDICAL AREAS § 36.05[2][a]

cludes their address, year of birth, medical school, year of admission to practice, specialty certifications, medical societies and boards, and much other useful information.

The best sources for defense material in medical malpractice cases are the local or state medical associations, societies, and committees. It therefore behooves the investigator to become familiar with any such group in his locality and to call upon them for the help which he may need.

[2] Checklists

[a] Qualifications of the Insured

The competence and educational background of the individual involved will have a great bearing on the investigation of professional liability claims. Accordingly, a good deal of the investigation will be concerned with a determination of the qualifications of the professional practitioner. The following are some suggested lines of investigation:

- ☐ Obtain the complete name, address, and age of the individual, association, hospital, clinic, or other entity that may be involved. If it is a corporation, determine the state of incorporation. If a trade name, trust or other local entity, obtain full details.
- ☐ If an individual, check his or her qualifications and background:
  - ○ Obtain the name of the professional schools attended and their rating. Determine the year of graduation and whether graduated with honors.
  - ○ Find out when and where internship or other apprenticeship was served.
  - ○ Find out if he or she has license to practice, and, if so, in what states. Determine when and where these licenses were obtained.
  - ○ Determine what medical or honorary societies he or she belongs to and what hospital connections he or she has. If the profession is other than medical, make appropriate similar determinations.
  - ○ If the professional is a doctor, find out what field of medicine is specialized in, qualifications, and how he or she is rated. Determine how long he or she has practiced as a physician and in the specialty. Learn where practiced. Determine the extent of practice and the type of clientele.
  - ○ By general inquiry among laymen and fellow professionals, determine the reputation of the professional being investigated, both as a person and as a technician. Find out if he or she has written any papers, articles, or books in his field which have been accepted as authoritative.

§ 36.05[2][b] CASUALTY INSURANCE CLAIMS

- ○ Find out whether any previous claims or suits have ever been made against him or her, and, if so, what disposition was made of them. Obtain complete details and check them thoroughly.
- ○ If advisable, obtain written consent to settle.

[b] Factual Details

- ☐ Obtain the exact date, time, and place of the incident.
- ☐ Obtain complete factual details from all available sources.
- ☐ Obtain complete medical or other records that may be available, such as supervisory reports, police reports, medical records, etc. If medical or hospital malpractice is involved this investigation should cover the history of the incident, previous medical history, diagnosis, treatment rendered, x-rays taken, operations performed, consultations made and an exact list of all visits. *See* § 36.05[2][d], Hospital Records.
- ☐ Obtain an itemization of the professional bill. Determine whether there was ill feeling or controversy concerning it. If so, obtain complete details.
- ☐ Obtain statements from any associates, assistants, nurses, attendants, or anyone else involved in the incident. If applicable, determine their qualifications. If an independent contractor is involved, determine whether separate insurance is carried and, if so, obtain the name of the carriers and see that proper notification is given.
- ☐ Determine whether any medical practitioner made any promise of definite cure or made any statement or took any action which might have broadened the scope of his or her liability.
- ☐ Determine whether the professional was under the influence of intoxicants or narcotics at the time of the alleged malpractice.
- ☐ Find out if any equipment failure was involved. If so, refer to the checklist for suggested investigation of Products Liability claims in Chapter 33. If warranted, put the retailer, wholesaler, or manufacturer on notice.
- ☐ Obtain the opinion of legal practitioners in the same profession in order to determine whether the services performed or the treatment rendered was in accordance with ordinary good practice. If medical malpractice is involved, enlist the aid of local medical societies. This is ordinarily more easily obtained by the defense than by the plaintiff.
- ☐ Determine if the insured held out any promise of definite results and, if so, get full details.

[c] Information to be Obtained from or Concerning the Injured

- ☐ Find out who referred the doctor, surgeon, hospital, etc. to the injured.
- ☐ If surgery was performed determine whether consent was obtained and, if so, how, when, and from whom. If consent was obtained in writing, obtain a copy. If no consent was obtained, find out why.

PROFESSIONAL LIABILITY—MEDICAL AREAS § 36.05[2][d]

- ☐ Find out whether the injured followed the doctor's, surgeon's, or nurse's instructions. Obtain complete details.
- ☐ Determine when the injured made the first complaint after the alleged malpractice and why such complaint was directed at the specific doctor, surgeon, or nurse involved.
- ☐ Determine what subsequent treatment was received and obtain complete medical reports from all available sources as previously outlined in making a medical investigation.
- ☐ Find out whether the injured received a settlement or was awarded compensation or a judgment as a result of an injury which necessitated the medical treatment presently being investigated. Obtain full details, including copies of all releases, checks or drafts issued, court orders, or other records.
- ☐ Determine whether the injured ever made a previous medical malpractice claim, and, if so, obtain complete details.
- ☐ Determine the advisability of obtaining a physical examination by a specialist. Make a complete background investigation of the injured, including complete medical history as previously outlined.

[d] Hospital Records

Whether or not the hospital is a party defendant to an action for malpractice or other liability, hospital records are of vital importance to any investigation where the plaintiff received care that could be involved in the liability, medical treatment, or the factual situation of a case.

Unless the case calls for only a summary report from the hospital, the hospital records should, where warranted, include copies of the complete hospital records, which will usually require the cooperation of the hospital legal advisor, who is usually not the attorney chosen by the insurer to defend the action.

Complete hospital records should include:

A. General records:

- ☐ Patient's complete medical chart and doctor's notes
- ☐ Admission sheet
- ☐ Admitting history
- ☐ Admitting physical examination
- ☐ Doctor's order sheets
- ☐ Nurse's notes
- ☐ Laboratory sheets
- ☐ X-ray reports and films

B. Accessory records:

- ☐ Emergency room records, if any
- ☐ Out-patient records, if any
- ☐ Psychotherapy or other therapy records, if any
- ☐ Clinic records, if any
- ☐ Pathology and autopsy records if pertinent

In some cases, where warranted, the investigator may want a medical review of the following:

C. Notes from which the records were made.:

- ☐ Laboratory notes:
  - ○ Work notebooks
  - ○ Log entries
  - ○ Rewriting slips
- ☐ Pathology notes:
  - ○ Work notebooks
  - ○ Slides
  - ○ Parafin blocks
  - ○ Amputated parts, where essential
- ☐ Operating room:
  - ○ Log schedules
  - ○ Material schedules
  - ○ Financial charges, if called for
- ☐ Equipment and supply records:
  - ○ Purchase orders
  - ○ Maintenance and service records, if called for
- ☐ X-ray notes:
  - ○ Films
  - ○ Therapy dosage, if applicable
  - ○ Charts

D. Applicable hospital regulations:

- ☐ Check with the Joint Commission on Accreditation, if necessary:
  - ○ Determine if the hospital and/or the doctors and nurses were accredited
  - ○ Find out when the hospital was last inspected and get a copy of the report and recommendations
  - ○ Check to see if all recommendations were complied with
  - ○ Check to determine if hospitals own regulations were followed

E. Manuals and handbooks:

- ☐ Regarding nursing procedures and regulations
- ☐ Regarding operating procedures
- ☐ Any others

PROFESSIONAL LIABILITY—MEDICAL AREAS § 36.05[2][e]

☐ Check any standing orders of attending doctors

F. Personnel records:

☐ Obtain personnel records where necessary

G. Identify all personnel involved in the incident:

☐ Doctors and specialists
☐ Registered and practical nurses, orderlies, and other attendants, whether employed by the hospital or not
☐ Therapists—physical and mental
☐ Any observers at the operation including interns, students, and others
☐ Any maintenance or other service personnel that may be able to give information concerning the incident
☐ Hospital roommates of the patient
☐ Possible visitors, including religious persons, social workers, etc.

H. Equipment:

☐ Check equipment age and condition, and purchase and maintenance records if pertinent

I. Photographs or diagrams:

☐ Take photographs (professional, where warranted), make diagrams, etc. of the operating room or other pertinent area

J. Hospital ownership:

☐ Determine the ownership of the hospital, including any corporate officers, directors and/or stockholders

K. Hospital's previous records:

☐ Determine the hospital's previous experience with similar incidents and equipment

In the event that important records are not legible, get help to make them so.[56]

[e] Druggist's Malpractice Claims

☐ If a patented product is involved, proceed with the investigation as outlined under the Products Liability section in Chapter 33.

---

[56] *See* Morris, "Appendix" and "Strategy of Discovery," DRI Monograph # 4, 1977, which contains excellent investigation suggestions, some of which are incorporated above.

§ 36.06

- [ ] If a prescription is involved, obtain a photostat of the prescription. Determine if it was intelligible, properly filled and labeled, and if filled by a qualified and properly licensed pharmacist as required by the law of the state.
- [ ] Obtain the remainder of the filled prescription for analysis to determine if it conforms with the written prescription. Determine whether it was inherently dangerous. If it did conform to the prescription and was incorrectly prescribed, determine whether the pharmacist should have caught the error. If the prescription was not intelligible or if was questionable for any other reason, determine if the druggist checked with the doctor concerning contents, quantities, or directions.
- [ ] Find out if local and federal laws were involved in dispensing the prescription and, if so, whether proper records were kept.
- [ ] Determine whether this was a new prescription or a refill. If it was a refill, obtain the date and number of the original prescription or the previous refill.
- [ ] Determine whether the pharmacist prescribed the medication or treatment and, if so, obtain complete details.
- [ ] How and when was the error discovered?
- [ ] If a narcotic or poison was involved, determine if it was properly labeled and registered.
- [ ] Determine whether the pharmacist actually treated the injured in any way, and, if so, obtain complete details.

§ 36.06 Bibliography

Actions for Wrongful Malpractice Suits

Birnbaum, "Physicians Counterattack: Liability of Lawyers for Instituting Unjustified Medical Malpractice Actions," FIC Quarterly, Winter 1978.

Comment, Janzer, "Countersuits to Legal and Medical Malpractice Actions: Any Chance for Success?", 65 Marq. L. Rev. 93 (1981).

Freeman, "Endless Litigation: Justice or Revenge?", Insurance Counsel Journal, April 1971.

Note, "Physicians' Countersuits: A Reply," F.T.D., March 1981.

Arbitration

Bassis, "Arbitration of Medical Malpractice Disputes—Some Problems," Insurance Law Journal, May 1979.

Gilmore, "Medical Malpractice Arbitration: Insurance Developments," Insurance Law Journal, June 1977.

Heintz, "Medical Malpractice Arbitration: A Successful Hospital-Based Application," Insurance Law Journal, September 1979.

PROFESSIONAL LIABILITY—MEDICAL AREAS § 36.06

Ladimer & Solomon, "Medical Malpractice Arbitration: Laws, Programs, Cases," Insurance Law Journal, June 1977.

Contracts to Cure

Note, "Express Contracts to Cure: The Nature of Contractual Malpractice," 50 Ind. L. J. 377 (1975).

Tierney, "Contractual Aspects of Malpractice," 19 Wayne L. Rev. 1457 (1973).

Counterattack by Doctors

Birnbaum, "Physicians Counterattack: Liability of Lawyers for Instituting Unjustified Medical Malpractice Actions," FIC Quarterly, Winter 1978.

Comment, "Attorney Liability for Malicious Prosecution and Legal Malpractice: Do They Overlap?", 8 Pac. L.J. 897 (1977).

Comment, Janzer, "Countersuits to Legal and Medical Malpractice Actions: Any Chance for Success?", 65 Marq. L. Rev. 93 (1980).

Freeman, "Endless Litigation: Justice or Revenge, Insurance Counsel Journal, April 1978.

Note, "Malicious Prosecution: An Effective Attack on Spurious Medical Malpractice Claims?", 26 Case W. Res. 653 (1976).

General

Comment, "Agreements to Arbitrate in Hospital Admission Forms: Are They Contracts of Adhesion?," 2 Western State L. Rev. 104 (1974).

Havenor, "Observations Regarding Investigation and Preparation of Medical Malpractice Litigation," DRI Monograph #4, 1977.

Havenor & Lieb, "Discovery and Evidentiary Use of Hospital Staff Committee Materials in Medical Malpractice Actions," DRI Monograph # 4, 1977.

Lieb, "The 'Good Samaritan' Statute, Wisconsin (1977)," 62 Marq. L. Rev. 469 (1979).

Moore & O'Connell, "Foreclosing Medical Malpractice Claims by Prompt Tender of Economic Loss," 44 La. L. Rev. 1267 (1984).

Pearson, "The Role of Custom in Medical Malpractice Cases," 51 Ind. L.J. 528 (1976).

Hospitals and Nurses' Liability

Moore, "Medical Staff—Corporate Account Liability," Insurance Counsel Journal, January 1976.

Morris, "The Negligent Nurse—The Physician and the Hospital," 33 Baylor L. Rev. 109 (1981).
Note, "Theories for Imposing Liability Upon Hospitals for Medical Malpractice: Ostensible Agency and Corporate Liability," 11 Wm. Mitchell L. Rev. 561 (1985).
Payne, "Recent Developments Affecting a Hospitals' Liability for Negligence of Physicians," 18 S. Tex. L.J. 389 (1977).
Stanczyk & Moffitt, "Hospitals, Physicians, and Their Liability Carriers: Ostensible Authority, Enterprise Liability and Beyond," FIC Quarterly, Spring 1981.
Weyna, "Dubin v. Michael Reese Hospital and Medical Center: Seeing through the Products/Service Distinction," Insurance Counsel Journal, July 1981.

Informed Consent

Alsobrook, "Informed Consent: A Right to Know," Insurance Counsel Journal, October 1973.
Comment, "Informed Consent and the Material Risk Standard: A Modest Proposal," 12 Pacific L.J. 915 (1981).
Comment, "Informed Consent as a Theory of Medical Liability," 1970 Wis. L. Rev. 879.
Havenor, "Observations Regarding Investigation and Preparation of Medical Malpractice Litigation," DRI Monograph # 4, 1977.
Marks, "Informed Consent in Medical Malpractice Cases," DRI Monograph # 4, 1977.
Meisel, "Informed Consent to Medical Treatment: An Analysis of Recent Litigation," 41 Pittsburgh L. Rev. 407 (1980).
Note, "Failure to Inform as Medical Malpractice," 23 Vand. L. Rev. 754 (1970).
Note, "Informed Consent—A Proposed Standard for Medical Disclosure," 48 N.Y.U. L. Rev. 548 (1973).
Plante, "An Analysis of 'Informed Consent,'" 36 Fordham L. Rev. 639 (1968).
Roth, "The Medical Malpractice Insurance Crises: Its Causes, the Effects, and Proposed Solutions," Insurance Counsel Journal, July 1977.
Still-Caris, "Informed Consent: What Doctors Should Understand About Their Duty to Disclose," FIC Quarterly, Fall 1985.

Locality Rule v. National Standard

Decyk & Hirsch, "The Medical Standard of Care," DRI Monograph # 4, 1977.

King & Coe, "The Wisdom of the Strict Liability Rule," 3 U. of Balt. L. Rev. 221 (1974).
Note, "An Evolution of Changes in the Medical Standard of Care," 23 Vand. L. Rev. 729 (1970).
Waltz, "The Rise and Gradual Fall of the 'Locality' Rule in Medical Malpractice Litigation," 18 De Paul L. Rev. 408 (1969).

Res Ipsa Loquitur

Podell, "Application of Res Ipsa Loquitur in Medical Malpractice Litigation," Insurance Counsel Journal, October 1977.

Second Injury

Comment, "Release of Original Tortfeasor for Injury Caused—Effect on Subsequent Action Against Physician for Malpractice," 3 Washburn L.J. 75 (1964).

Statutes of Limitations

Kroll, "The Etiology, Pulse and Prognosis of Medical Malpractice," 8 Suffolk U.L. Rev. 598 (1973-74).
Maynard & Kinney, "The Statute of Limitations in Medical Malpractice Law," DRI Monograph # 4, 1977.
Richards, "Statutes Limiting Medical Malpractice Damages," FIC Quarterly, Spring 1982.

Wrongful Birth and Wrongful Life

Cheslik, " 'Wrongful Conceptions' " FIC Quarterly, Spring 1985.
Comment, Cochran, "Wrongful Life: The Tort That Nobody Wants," 23 Santa Clara L. Rev. 847 Summer (1983).
Comment, "Damages for the Wrongful Birth of Healthy Babies," 21 Duq. L. Rev. 605 (1983).
Comment, De Walt, "Wrongful Life and Wrongful Birth: The Current Status of Negligent Genetic Counselling," 3 Cooley L. Rev. 175 (1985).
Comment, "Illegitimate Children Allowed Action for 'Wrongful Life': William v. State," 50 Minn. L. Rev. 593 (1966).
Comment, "Illegitimate Children Denied Recovery Against Fathers for Wrongful Life: Zepeda v. Zepeda," 49 Iowa L. Rev. 1005 (1964).
Comment, "Liability for Failure of Birth Control Methods," 76 Colum. L. Rev. 1187 (1976).
Comment, "Recovery of Childbearing Expenses in Wrongful Birth Cases: A Motivational Analysis," 32 Emory L.J. 1167 (1984).

Comment, "The Right Not to be Born," 54 Tulane L. Rev. 480 (1980).

Comment, "The Trend Toward Judicial Recognition of Wrongful Life: A Dissenting View," 31 U.C.L.A. L. Rev. 473 (1983).

Gross, "Strict Liability: A 'Lady in Waiting' for Wrongful Birth Case," 11 Cal. W. L. Rev. 136 (1974).

Kohnen & Zoellner, "Wrongful Life: Existence v. Nonexistence—Is Life Always Preferable?", FIC Quarterly, Spring 1986.

Mayo, "The Legal Recognition of Medical Malpractice Tort Claims Based Upon Theories of Wrongful Birth and Wrongful Life," Comment in 15 No. Carolina Central L.J. 274 (Winter 1985).

Note, "Wrongful Birth: A Child of Tort Comes of Age," 50 U. Cin. L. Rev. 65 (1981).

Robertson, "Civil Liability Arising From 'Wrongful Birth' Following an Unsuccessful Sterilization Operation," 4 American J.L. and Med. 131, 145 (1978).

Rose & Ream, "Wrongful Pregnancy," F.T.D., September 2, 1986.

Scheid, "Benefits v. Burdens: The Limitation of Damages in Wrongful Birth," Journal of Family Law, vol. 23 (1984-85).

CHAPTER 37

Professional Liability—Lawyers

§ 37.01 In General
§ 37.02 Policy Coverages
    [1] Occurrence Policies
    [2] Claims-Made Policies
    [3] Exclusions
    [4] Other ISO Policy Provisions
    [5] Nonstandard Policy Forms
    [6] Professional Services
§ 37.03 Grounds Upon Which Actions May Be Brought
    [1] Privity of Contract
    [2] Actions in Negligence—Standard of Care
    [3] "Errors-in-Judgment" Rule
    [4] Duty to Research the Law
    [5] The Age of the Computer
    [6] The Doctrine of "Informed Consent"
    [7] The "But For" Rule
    [8] Conflict of Interests
    [9] Statute of Limitations
§ 37.04 Some Suggestions for the Investigation of Lawyer's Malpractice Cases
§ 37.05 Checklist for Avoiding Legal Malpractice
§ 37.06 Bibliography

§ 37.01 In General

Historically, the courts have granted lawyers a more favored position than other professionals with respect to claims for malpractice liability. The more cynical observer might attribute this phenomenon to the notion that judges, having themselves been lawyers, consciously or unconsciously are taking care of their own. There is also a reluctance to encourage an atmosphere in which losing clients might habitually respond to their loss by suing their attorneys,[1] despite the fact that the proliferation of suits where lawyers were not defendants, doesn't seem to have bothered most judges at all.

---

[1] From "Lawyers' Professional Liability: The Experience in New York and Elsewhere," by Albert L. Bases and Charles Engros, FIC Quarterly, Fall 1977.

The major difficulty in lawyers legal liability, even more so than in other professions, is the difficulty in determining what is a reasonable degree of professional competence.

The climate is changing very rapidly and the pressure is becoming so great that lawyers can no longer hide behind the judicial robes, and the robes themselves are shrinking considerably.

As with other professionals, an attorney is not an insurer of results. The fact that he or she may lose a case will not ordinarily involve the lawyer in an action for malpractice. The lawyer can be held liable only for wrongdoing in the course of his or her practice as a lawyer.

§ 37.02 Policy Coverages

The Insurance Services Office (ISO), New York, N.Y., Lawyers Professional Liability insurance policies are presently issued in two forms: the regular "occurrence" form and the more recent "claims-made" form. These policies follow the general format of the Physicians, Surgeons and Dentists malpractice policy except that lawyers professional liability is not concerned directly with liability for bodily injury.

The Lawyers Professional Liability policy has separate insuring clauses for individual coverage and for partnerships, associations, or corporations and the "Persons Insured" provision gives automatic coverage for both. Older policy forms may differ in this respect.

All lawyers professional liability policies give coverage to the insured in his or her capacity as a lawyer, whether the suit is brought in contract or negligence.

The new policies do not define "the profession of law." The second paragraph of "Coverage—Lawyers Professional Liability," does however state that:

> When the insured acts as an administrator, conservator, executor, guardian, trustee, or in any other similar fiduciary capacity, the insured's acts or omissions in such capacity shall be deemed to be the performance of professional services for others in the insured's profession as a lawyer, but only to the extent that such acts or omissions are those for which in the usual attorney-client relationship the insured would be legally responsible as attorney for a fiduciary.

[1] Occurrence Policies

Incidents which are alleged to have occurred within the policy period of an "occurrence" policy are covered regardless of when claim is made or suit is filed so long as it is within the "Notice of Accident" meaning. There is otherwise, no time limitation. This policy also provides protection from incidents that allegedly occurred before the inception date of the policy if:

(a) they were discovered during the policy period;
(b) claim is made or suit is brought during the policy period;
(c) the insured did not know or could not reasonably have foreseen that such acts or omissions might be expected to be the basis for a claim or suit at the time of the inception of the policy; or where
(d) no other insurance is involved.

[2] Claims-Made Policies

The "claims-made" policies require the reporting of a claim within the time that the policy is in effect and state that:

A claim shall be considered as being first made at the earlier of the following times:

(a) when the insured first gives written notice to the company that a claim has been made, or,

(b) when the insured first gives written notice to the company of specific circumstances involving a particular person or entity which may result in a claim.

Not all lawyers professional liability policies follow the same wording. Some policies require reporting of an incident that "might be expected to be the basis of a claim or suit," instead of "which may result in a claim." In any event, this type of wording has been considered as "unambiguous and presents no question of law."[2]

While the word "claim" is not usually defined in the policy, it has been held that a claim is simply a demand for something due, and a lawsuit is not necessarily a condition of it.[3]

---

[2] Cal.: Phoenix Ins. Co. v. Sukut Constr. Co., 186 Cal. Rptr. 513 (1982).
[3] Katz Drug Co. v. Commercial Standard Ins. Co., 647 S.W.2d 831 (Mo. App. 1983).

At this time, it seems to be the consensus of opinion that to give acceptance to claims-made policies is not against public policy.[4] A few courts have in some cases, however, held that the restriction inherent in these policies was ineffective on the basis of "reasonable expectations."[5]

The doctrine of "reasonable expectations" is peculiar enough under most circumstances, but to hold that a lawyer who is supposed to be a specialist in policy interpretation can hide behind such a judicial shield with reference to his own insurance policy is, to me, beyond reason.[6]

In a case where an attorney did not report a suit until after the claims-made policy period expired, the court held that prejudice to the insurance company was immaterial as long as a known claim or suit was involved.[7] To the contrary, a federal district court in Michigan held that an insurer was not entitled to disclaim under a claims-made policy where the insurer failed to show that it was unfairly prejudiced by the insured's failure to report within the policy period.[8]

[3] Exclusions

The Lawyers Professional Liability policy has eight exclusions, of which the first applies to "any dishonest, fraudulent, criminal or malicious act or omission of any insured or employee of any insured."

The second exclusion applies to any claim "made by an employer or, if the employer is a corporation, its parent or subsidiary, or by a director, officer or stockholder thereof against an insured who is a salaried employee of such employer." The F.C. & S. Bulletins,[9] give an example, that this exclusion "would apply to a case where an employed attorney (not a partner), who is covered as an additional insured, commits some act that the employing attorney believes has caused him financial loss."

---

[4] **Ala.:** James Hackworth v. Continental Cas. Co., 522 F. Supp. 785 (1980).
Fla.: Gulf Ins. Co. v. Dolan, Fertig & Curtis, 433 So. 2d 512 (1983).
[5] **Cal.:** Gyler v. Mission Ins. Co., 110 Cal. Rptr. 139 (1973).
N.J.: Jones v. Continental Cas. Co., 303 A.2d 91 (Super. 1973).
[6] *See* Cline, "Professional Liability Insurance: Retiring Lawyers," FIC Quarterly, Spring 1985, for a good discussion of policy coverage.
[7] Zuckerman v. National Union Fire Ins. Co., 495 A.2d 395 (1985).
[8] Sherlock v. Perry, 605 F. Supp. 1001 (1985) (in accordance with the court's interpretation of a Michigan statute).
[9] Published by The National Underwriter Co., Cincinnati, Ohio.

Damage to tangible property, however remote this may be, is also not covered nor would be "any loss sustained by the insured as the beneficiary or distributee of any trust or estate" involving several specifically named acts or omissions.

Activities arising out of business enterprises, other than the practice of law, and any activities in the capacity of officer, director, partner, etc. of any corporation, association, partnership and other specifically named enterprise, are also not covered.

The policy also does not apply to any claim "arising out of or in connection with the insured's activities as a fiduciary under the Employees Retirement Income Securities Act of 1974" and amendments or regulations of that Act.

Finally, the "claims-made" form contains an additional exclusion concerning acts or omissions occurring prior to the effective date of the policy, if the insured knew of or could have reasonably foreseen that a claim or suit might be made as a result thereof.

[4] Other ISO Policy Provisions

Suits include arbitration proceedings entered into with the insurer's consent.

The *duty to defend* terminates when the applicable limit of the company's liability has been exhausted by payment of judgments, settlements, or *claim expenses,* which are defined in the policy.

Supplemental payments, in addition to the applicable limits of liability include premiums on appeal bonds and all reasonable expenses other than loss of earnings, incurred by the insured at the insurer's request in assisting in the investigation or defense of a claim or suit.

The newer Lawyers Professional Liability forms do not have a "consent to settle" provision. They contain two *"Limits of Liability"* (1) applicable to all claims arising out of the same or related professional services, and (2) an aggregate limit which is the total liability for all damages and claim expenses. Expenses must be deducted first, after which the remainder is left for the payment of damages. If the limits of liability are exhausted before settlement or judgment, the insurer may withdraw from further investigation and/or defense by tendering to the insured, control of the case. It is my opinion, however, that should the insured refuse to take over, the insurer better make absolutely sure that it is not abandoning the insured in mid-suit despite this and another clause that requires the insured to return any sums paid in excess of the applicable limits.

[5] Nonstandard Policy Forms

Many Lawyers Professional Liability policies are not written on an ISO or other "standard" form. Some provide that the insurer pay all sums which the insured becomes legally obligated to pay as damages. Others provide that the insurer indemnify the insured in the event of losses incurred by the insured. Whatever the wording, courts just about unanimously hold such policies to be liability policies even where the wording specifically calls for indemnification.[10]

An attorney-insured must also be aware of the fact that some professional liability policies may not include coverage for defense costs, rare though this may be.

Coverage for "groundless, false or fraudulent" claims is not unique in the older liability policies, and is contained in some professional forms. Such wording was dropped from "standard" forms when it became obvious that this wording was being misunderstood and was accordingly dropped as being redundant.

[6] Professional Services

Of great concern to some attorneys whose policy protects them from claims or suits "arising out of the performance of professional services," is whether or not they were indeed acting in a professional capacity when the alleged malpractice occurred.[11]

The situations in which an attorney could get involved in possible malpractice are myriad. A few examples are:

1. Failure to properly identify and sue the actual tortfeasor.[12]
2. Failure to give proper attention and adequate preparation.[13]
3. Failure to follow express instructions of the client.[14]

---

[10] *See* Gribaldo, Jacobs, Jones & Assoc's. v. Agrippina Versicherunges A.G., 476 P.2d 406 (Cal. 1970).

[11] **Mo.:** Sager v. St. Paul Fire & Marine Ins. Co., 461 S.W.2d 704 (1971).
Neb.: Marx v. Hartford Marine & Indem. Co., 157 N.W.2d 870 (1968).
See also Comment, "Insurance for Lawyers: Professional Liability," 8 S.U.L. Rev. 301 (Spring 1982).

[12] **N.Y.:** Siegel v. Kranis, 288 N.Y.S.2d 831 (1968).

[13] **La.:** Lewis v. Collins, 260 So. 2d 357 (App. 1972).
Utah: Milliner v. Elmer Fox & Co., 529 P.2d 806 (1974).
Wash.: Hansen v. Wightman, 528 P.2d 1238 (1975).

[14] **Ore.:** Schaefer v. Fraser, 290 P.2d 190 (1955).

4. Failure to properly defend an action.[15]
5. Actions brought for bad faith refusal to settle within the policy limits.[16]
6. Actions which result in default judgments.[17]
7. Dismissals resulting from failure to prosecute.[18]
8. Failure to appeal, or to properly appeal.[19]
9. Actions brought by physician defendant in underlying case, for malicious prosecution.[20]
10. Failure to observe the statute of limitations.[21]

§ 37.03 Grounds Upon Which Actions May Be Brought

Actions for malpractice brought against a lawyer, may be brought in contract, express or implied.[22]

[1] Privity of Contract

Privity of contract is usually brought into play when a malpractice suit is brought against an attorney by a third party. In days of yore, lack of privity to the contract of hire was sufficient grounds for dismissing an action for malpractice against an attorney.[23] Surprisingly, some fairly recent decisions still hold to this position.[24]

In 1958, a California court, in the case of *Biakanja v. Irving*,[25] was already radically hedging its bets. It stated that:

---

[15] Outboard Marine Corp. v. Liberty Mut. Ins. Co., 536 F.2d 730 (7th Cir. 1976) (case remanded for trial on the issues).

[16] **Cal.:** Lysick v. Walcom, 65 Cal. Rptr. 406 (1968).
Ill.: Smiley v. Manchester Ins. & Indem. Co., 364 N.E.2d 683 (1977).

[17] Masters v. Dunstan, 124 S.E.2d 574 (N.C. 1962).

[18] **Del.:** Spring v. Sullivan, 361 F. Supp. 282 (1973).

[19] **Ore.:** Bryant v. Seagrace, 526 P.2d 1027 (1974).

[20] *See* Note, "Malicious Prosecution: An Effective Attack on Spurious Medical Malpractice Claims?", 26 Case W. Res. 653 (1976).

[21] Christy v. Saliterman, 179 N.W.2d 288 (Minn. 1970); Boechler v. Borth, 377 N.Y.S.2d 781 (1976).

[22] **Cal.:** Lucas v. Hamm, 15 Cal. Rptr. 281 (1961), *cert. denied*, 368 U.S. 987 (1962) (breach of express contract).
Md.: Woldarek v. Thrift, 13 A.2d 774 (1940) (breach of implied contract).
Ohio: Taylor v. Sheldon, 173 N.E.2d 892 (1961).

[23] *See* 45 A.L.R.3d 1187 (1972).

[24] **N.Y.:** Victor v. Goldman, 344 N.Y.S.2d 672, *aff'd*, 351 N.Y.S.2d 956 (1974).
Pa.: Sachs v. Levy, 216 F. Supp. 44 (1963).
Tex.: Bryan & Amidei v. Law, 435 S.W.2d 587 (App. 1968).

[25] 320 P.2d 16 (1958).

§ 37.03[2]   CASUALTY INSURANCE CLAIMS

The determination whether in a specific case, the defendant will be held liable to a third person not in privity, is (a) matter of policy and involves the balancing of various factors, among which are the extent to which (the) transaction was intended to affect the plaintiff, the foreseeability of harm to him, the degree of certainty that the plaintiff suffered injury, the closeness of the connection between the defendant's conduct and the injury suffered, the moral blame attached to the defendant's conduct and the policy of preventing future harm.

Many courts have since completely abandoned this outmoded concept.[26]

[2] Actions in Negligence—Standard of Care

While an action can be brought against a lawyer for malpractice by a client on the grounds of contract, most such actions, by far, are brought in negligence. The basis for such an action depends on the degree of skill and care shown by the attorney.

The degree of care, skill, and knowledge required of an attorney is that of the reasonably careful and competent attorney and commonly possessed by other lawyers, usually within the same jurisdiction or area of practice.[27] To which I would add, in an effort to be more comprehensive: (a) *diligence,* which includes such matters as timely filing of actions, motions, appeals, answers, etc.; (b) *proper and sufficient investigation;* and (c) *integrity and ethics* in all transactions, particularly where there may be a conflict of interests.

Prosser & Keeton on Torts[28] defines standard of care as that degree used to determine whether an attorney has properly performed his duty to his clients, which is derived from the reasonable standard of tort law. As defined in the case of *Lucas v. Hamm,*[29]

> an attorney must use such skill, prudence and diligence as lawyers of ordinary skill and capacity commonly possess and exercise in the per-

---

[26] **Cal.:** Lucas v. Hamm, 15 Cal. Rptr. 821 (1961), cert. denied, 368 U.S. 987 (1962).
Conn.: Ticata v. Spector, 225 A.2d 28 (1966).
La.: Woodfork v. Sanders, 252 So. 2d 455 (App. 1971).
[27] **Ariz.:** Martin v. Burns, 429 P.2d 660 (1967).
Cal.: Smith v. Lewis, 520 P.2d 589 (1975).
Fla.: Warwick, Paul & Warwick v. Potter, 190 So. 2d 596 (1966).
La.: Ramp v. St. Paul Fire & Marine Ins. Co., 254 So. 2d 79 (1976).
Wash.: Flanagan & Berst v. Clausing, 438 P.2d 865 (1968).
See also Mallen & Levit's *Legal Malpractice* (2d ed. 1981).
[28] 5th ed. 1984.
[29] 15 Cal. Rptr. 821 (1961).

formance of the tasks they undertake. The jury must judge the attorney's conduct by its determination of what a reasonable and competent lawyer would have done in similar circumstances.[30]

Lawyers who claim to be specialists are held to a higher degree of knowledge in their field of specialty.[31]

In measuring the degree of competence required, most courts hold to some locality rule, usually that of the state where the lawyer practices,[32] although some courts use the yardstick of rural versus metropolitan area.[33]

While some courts hold that the question of whether or not an attorney has breached his professional duty to his client is a matter of fact for jury determination,[34] this opinion is by no means unanimous.[35]

Some courts require expert testimony in order to maintain the burden of proof,[36] while others have completely abandoned this requirement.[37]

In the case of *Sanders v. Smith*,[38] the decision stated that "A lay witness does not have the experience, knowledge and wisdom to opinionate on the complexities of trial practice."

As in all tort cases, the breach of the lawyer's duty must have been the proximate cause of the damage to him.[39]

[3] "Errors-in-Judgment" Rule

Lawyers are always required to use judgment concerning the law, which is hardly ever specific, and legal tactics, which also may vary greatly, so as to achieve client satisfaction. This is the very lifeblood of our adversary legal system. Accordingly, courts have historically

---

[30] *See also* Collins v. Greenstein, 595 P.2d 275 (Hawaii 1979).
[31] **Cal.:** Wright v. Williams, 121 Cal. Rptr. 194 (1975); Horne v. Peckman, 158 Cal. Rptr. 714 (1979).
Wash.: Walker v. Bangs, 601 P.2d 1279 (1979).
[32] **N.D.:** Rolfstad v. Winkjer, Suess, McKennett & Kaiser v. Hansen, 221 N.W.2d 734 (1974).
Wash.: Hansen v. Weightman, 538 P.2d 1238 (1975).
[33] **Tex.:** Cook v. Irion, 409 S.W.2d 475 (App. 1966).
[34] Ishmael v. Millington, 50 Cal. Rptr. 592 (Cal. App. 1966).
[35] Martin v. Hall, 97 Cal. Rptr. 730 (App. 1971).
[36] Walters v. Hastings, 500 P.2d 186 (N.M. 1972).
[37] Survitz v. Kelner, 155 So. 2d 831 (Fla. 1963); Central Cab Co. v. Clarke, 270 A.2d 662 (Md. 1970).
[38] 496 P.2d 1102 (N.M. App. 1972).
[39] Lewis v. Collins, 260 So. 2d 357 (App. 1972).

and almost unanimously held that an attorney is not liable for honest errors in judgment, so long as they were in the "reasonably competent lawyer" category,[40] although even here, in some instances, there are differences of opinion.[41]

It has often been stated that the law is not an exact science and, consequently, no lack of skill exists for which all differences of opinion or doubts will be removed from the minds of lawyers and judges.[42] In fact, our adversary system depends on those differences.

Courts have recognized that a trial lawyer should have substantial discretion in the trial of a case.[43]

Competent lawyers who have an honest belief that their actions and advice were well founded and in the best interests of their clients, should not be held liable for mere mistakes in judgment.[44]

Evaluation of a client's bodily injury case for purposes of settlement was held to be protected by the "error-in-judgment" rule.[45]

A qualification that must be made is that an attorney is required to use ordinary skill in determining the law, where it is well defined,[46] or when the facts and/or the law can readily be determined.[47]

---

[40] **Cal.:** Lucas v. Hamm, 364 P.2d 685 (1961), *cert. denied,* 368 U.S. 987 (1962).

Tex.: Cook v. Irion, 409 S.W.2d 475 (App. 1966) (as a matter of law); Medrano v. Miller, 608 S.W.2d 781 (App. 1980).

U.S.: Frank v. Bloom, 634 F.2d 1245 (10th Cir. 1980).

See also Beck, "Legal Malpractice: Trial Lawyers and the Errors-in-Judgment Rule," Insurance Counsel Journal, January 1985; Mallen & Evans, "Attorneys' Liability for Errors of Judgment—At the Crossroads," 48 Tenn. L. Rev. 283 (1981).

[41] **Cal.:** Smith v. Lewis, 118 Cal. Rptr. 621 (1975).

Minn.: Togstad v. Vesely, Otto, Miller & O'Keefe, 291 N.W.2d 686 (1980).

[42] George v. Caton, 600 P.2d 822 (N.M. App.). *cert. quashed,* 598 P.2d 215 (1979); Smith v. Lewis, 118 Cal. Rptr. 621 (1975); Woodruff v. Tomlin, 616 F.2d 924 (6th Cir.), *cert. denied,* 449 U.S. 888 (1980).

[43] Shores Co. v. Iowa Chem. Co., 268 N.W.2d 581 (Iowa 1936); Federal Fuel Co. v. Macy, 223 N.Y.S.2d 710 (Supreme Ct. 1927).

[44] **Ariz.:** Martin v. Burns, 429 P.2d 660 (1967).

N.C.: Hodges v. Carter, 80 S.E.2d 144 (1954) (as a matter of law).

Okla.: Wabaunsee v. Harris, 610 P.2d 782 (1980).

[45] Glenna v. Sullivan, 245 N.W.2d 869 (Minn. 1976).

[46] Smith v. Lewis, 118 Cal. Rptr. 621 (1975); Boss-Harrison Hotel Co. v. Barnard, 266 N.E.2d 810 (Ind. App. 1971).

[47] **Cal.:** Metzger v. Silverman, 133 Cal. Rptr. 355 (1976); Horne v. Peckham, 158 Cal. Rptr. 714 (1979).

Fla.: Dillard Smith Constr. Co. v. Greene, 337 So. 2d 841 (App. 1976).

Minn.: Togstad v. Vesely, Otto, Miller & O'Keefe, 291 N.W.2d 686 (1980).

[4] Duty to Research the Law

One of the most controversial problems involving legal malpractice concerns the amount and quality of research which a lawyer must reasonably do on behalf of his client.[48]

Attorneys are expected to know well-established and clearly defined principles of law.[49] As a corollary, liability should not be imposed on a lawyer where there is no established law on the point at issue.[50]

The decision in the case of *Horne v. Peckham*[51] made a broader interpretation of the duty to research which stated that the duty extends to helping the client avoid "murky areas of the law" by identifying alternative causes of action. However, as one court put it, reasonable minds do differ concerning the quantity and quality of the research required,[52] and therein lies the rub. Time and more decisions may help.[53]

[5] The Age of the Computer

The cases cited heretofore, zero in on the failure to research. The question of adequate research has remained mostly moot until very recently. Prior to the introduction of the computer, legal research was conducted solely through books and periodicals as well as the case reporters. The case of *Smith v. Lewis*[54] opened the possibility that printed matter might not be sufficient to satisfy the research re-

---

[48] **Cal.:** Aloy v. Mash, 192 Cal. Rptr. 818 (1983) (where the court held that the issues should have been referred to the jury);Smith v. Lewis, 118 Cal. Rptr. 621 (1975); Davis v. Damrell, 174 Cal. Rptr. 257 (1981).
Fla.: Dillard-Smith Constr. Co. v. Greene, 337 So. 2d 241 (App. 1976).
La.: Muse v. St. Paul Fire & Marine Ins. Co., 328 So. 2d 698 (App. 1976).
Minn.: Togstad v. Vesely, Otto, Miller & O'Keefe, 291 N.W.2d 686 (1980).
[49] **Cal.:** Starr v. Mooslin, 92 Cal. Rptr. 583 (1971).
La.: Ramp v. St. Paul Fire & Marine Ins. Co., 254 So. 2d 79 (App. 1971).
Neb.: State v. Holscher, 230 N.W.2d 75 (1975).
U.S.: Woodruff v. Tomlin, 616 F.2d 924 (6th Cir. 1980).
[50] Brown v. Gitlin, 313 N.E.2d 180 (Ill. 1974); Martin v. Burns, 429 P.2d 660 (Ariz. 1967).
[51] 158 Cal. Rptr. 714 (1979).
[52] Wright v. Williams, 121 Cal. Rptr. 194 (1975).
[53] *See* Miller, "The Myth of Objectivity in Legal Research and Writing," 18 Catholic U.L. Rev. 290 (1964).
[54] 118 Cal. Rptr. 621 (1975).

quirement for a lawyer to avoid legal malpractice. If not now, computer legal research will shortly become a measure of reasonable research in some instances.[55]

Computerized research also offers unpublished opinions, which some courts permit, and one commentator noted that the weight of precedent on a point of law hardens it, making it more difficult to overturn. Professor O'Connell observes[56] "in some cases an unpublished opinion may be the only favorable or decisive authority concerning the legal problem being researched."

[6] The Doctrine of "Informed Consent"

The doctrine of "informed consent," while quite established in the field of medical malpractice, is in its infancy as applied to legal malpractice. It is obviously of less importance in legal malpractice since the latter is a matter of property rights rather than life itself. Nevertheless, the courts are beginning to recognize that a client, as well as a patient, should have the right to make vital decisions concerning his own economic welfare.

The Model Rules of Professional Conduct (1983), give greater emphasis to a lawyer's responsibility as an advisor than did earlier promulgated disciplinary rules.[57]

Rule 1.4(b) provides that a "lawyer shall explain a matter to the extent reasonably necessary to permit the client to make informed decisions regarding the representation." Comment on this rule holds that the "client should have sufficient information to participate intelligently in decisions concerning the objectives of the representation and the means by which they are to be pursued, to the extent the client is willing and able to do so."

Another Comment (to rule 2.1) states that "In rendering advice, a lawyer may refer not only to law, but to other considerations such as moral, economic, social and political factors that may be relevant to the client's situation. Purely technical legal advice therefore, can sometimes be inadequate."

---

[55] *See* Ruchiti v. Goldfein, 170 Cal. Rptr. 375 (1980). *See also* O'Connell, "Legal Malpractice: Does the Lawyer Have a Duty to Use Computerized Research?", FIC Quarterly, Fall 1984.

[56] "Legal Malpractice: Does the Lawyer Have a Duty to Use Computerized Research?", FIC Quarterly, Fall 1984.

[57] *See* Peck, "A New Tort for Lack of Informed Consent in Legal Matters," 44 La. L. Rev. 1289 (May 1984).

While the rules themselves include a disclaimer to the effect that "Violation of a Rule should not give rise to a cause of action nor should it create any presumption that a legal duty has been breached," it is unlikely that the courts will give heed to this restriction which is imposed on the rights of others.

Liability can also exist because an attorney has failed to provide advice. While the obligation does not extend to every possible alternative, discussion is required in those situations likely to result in adverse consequences.[58]

Failure to advise a client that the law in California was unsettled, was held not to be excepted from the error-in-judgment rule and accordingly the court decided that the lawyer was not guilty of malpractice.[59]

[7] The "But For" Rule

In order to recover for his attorney's malpractice, the client must obviously prove that in addition to the attorney's negligence, the action initiated would have succeeded *but for* the malpractice of the defendant attorney and that the judgment would have been collectable.[60]

[8] Conflict of Interests

The problem of conflict of interests between an attorney chosen by an insurance company to represent the insured, and the insured, has been discussed in Chapter 21 dealing with the subject of bad faith.

Where there is any conflict of interests that prevents an attorney from fully and competently protecting the interests of his client in-

---

[58] *Id. See also* Martyn, "Informed Consent in the Practice of Law," 48 Geo. Wash. L. Rev. 307 (1980).

[59] Davis v. Damrell, 174 Cal. Rptr. 257 (1981).

[60] Cal.: Lysick v. Walcom, 65 Cal. Rptr. 406 (App. 1968).

Colo.: Coon v. Ginsburg, 509 P.2d 1293 (1973).

N.C.: Masters v. Dunstan, 124 S.E.2d 574 (1962).

Ore.: State v. Yates, 302 P.2d 719 (1956).

Tenn.: Sutton v. Clements, 257 F. Supp. 63 (1966), *aff'd*, 385 F.2d 869 (6th Cir. 1967).

Tex.: Rice v. Forester, 415 S.W.2d 711 (App. 1967); Jackson v. Urban, Coolidge, Pennington & Scott, 516 S.W.2d 948 (App. 1974).

sured, the attorney should promptly recommend that the insured obtain independent counsel of his own, despite the fact that full disclosure was made to all parties concerning any possible conflict.[61]

An attorney should not represent multiple insureds whose interests conflict.[62]

Whenever there is a situation where the underlying litigation will determine a conflict between the insured and the insurer regarding coverage, there is an obvious conflict of interests.[63]

In increasing jurisdictions, a right to independent counsel means that the insured has a right to choose his own counsel,[64] although the insured, in some instances, may delegate that duty to his insurer.[65] In either event, the insurance company is obligated to pay the counsel's fee for the defense of the insured where there is a conflict of interests,[66] unless a declaratory judgment action is initiated by the policyholder.

Most actions involving conflicts between an insurance company and its insured are actions brought by an insured against the insurer on the basis of bad faith. In some instances the defense attorney is brought in as codefendant. On occassion, the action is for malpractice directly against the attorney who represented the insured in the underlying action.[67]

Rarely will a suit for malpractice be brought by an insurer against the counsel it chose to defend the insured, but it has been done.[68]

---

[61] **Cal.:** Executive Aviation, Inc. v. National Ins. Under's., 94 Cal. Rptr. 347 (1971).
N.J.: Yeomans v. Allstate Ins. Co., 296 A.2d 96 (1972).
N.Y.: Hartford Fire Ins. Co. v. Masternak, 390 N.Y.S.2d 949 (1977).
Tex.: W. Hill & Sons, Inc. v. Wilson, 399 S.W.2d 152 (App. 1966) (conflict involved several insureds).

[62] **Pa.:** Aluminum, Inc. v. Aetna Cas. & Sur. Co., 402 N.Y.S.2d 877 (1978).

[63] Executive Aviation, Inc. v. National Ins. Under's., 94 Cal. Rptr. 347 (1971).

[64] Burd v. Sussex Mut. Ins. Co., 267 A.2d 7 (N.J. 1970); Utica Mut. Ins. Co. v. Cherry, 358 N.Y.S.2d 519 (1974), aff'd, 143 N.E.2d 758 (1975).

[65] Brohawn v. Transamerica Co., 347 A.2d 842 (Md. 1975).

[66] Maryland Cas. Co. v. Peppers, 355 N.E.2d 24 (Ill. 1976); Employers Fire Ins. Co. v. Beals, 240 A.2d 397 (R.I. 1968).

[67] **Ariz.:** Fulton v. Woodford, 545 P.2d 979 (1976).
Cal.: Kirtland & Packard v. Superior Court, 131 Cal. Rptr. 418 (1976).
Ill.: Public Taxi Service v. Barrett, 357 N.E.2d 1232 (1976).
Md.: Central Cab Co. v. Clarke, 270 A.2d 662 (1970).
Wash.: Hamilton v. State Farm Mut. Auto. Ins. Co., 511 P.2d 193 (1974).

[68] **Ill.:** Smiley v. Manchester Ins. & Indem. Co., 364 N.E.2d 683 (1977).
Okla.: Royal Crown Cola Bottling Co. v. Aetna Cas. & Sur. Co., 438 F. Supp. 39 (1977).
Tex.: Fireman's Fund Ins. Co. v. Patterson & Lambert, 528 S.W.2d 67 (App. 1975).

[9] Statute of Limitations

The differences in the decisions concerning the time at which the statute of limitations begins to run in legal malpractice actions is so varied that it is most important for the novice to make sure that he or she has his eye on the right ball.

Some states make it easy by setting a time limitation for all malpractice actions at a specific and separate date. Otherwise, a determination must be made as to whether the date for contract or tort actions applies.

If an action for legal malpractice is brought in tort, and there is no specific statute for malpractice cases, the variations proliferate as follows:

1. Some courts hold that the statute of limitations begins to run from the date when the malpractice was committed.[69]
2. More cases have favored the discovery date of the wrongdoing.[70]
3. Other decisions have been made on the basis of the date on which the malpractice was discovered or should reasonably have been discovered.[71]
4. Still other decisions have set the time for the running of the statute when the claimant first suffered injury or damage.[72]
5. Several decisions have held that the continued representation by the attorney tolls the statute until such representation has ceased.[73]
6. At least one court held that the statute begins to run from the date of the lower court's decision if the malpractice was committed at or before the trial level.[74]

In the case of *Neel v. Magana*,[75] the court stated that

---

[69] Goldberg v. Bosworth, 215 N.Y.S.2d 849 (1961) (in the absence of fraud).

[70] Corley v. Logan, 192 N.W.2d 319 (Mich. 1971); Boechler v. Borth, 377 N.Y.S.2d 788 (1976); Busk v. Flanders, 468 P.2d 695 (Wash. 1970).

[71] Neel v. Magana, Olney, Levy, Cathcart & Gelfand, 98 Cal. Rptr. 837 (1972); Mumford v. Staton, Whaley & Price, 255 A.2d 359 (Md. 1969); Kohler v. Woollen, Brown & Hawkins, 304 N.E.2d 677 (Ill. 1973); Hendrickson v. Sears, 310 N.E.2d 131 (Mass. 1974).

[72] Budd v. Nixen, 491 P.2d 433 (1971); Marchand v. Miazza, 151 So. 2d 372 (1963).

[73] Siegal v. Kranis, 288 N.Y.S.2d 831 (App. 1968).

[74] Watson v. Dorsey, 290 A.2d 530 (Md. App. 1972).

[75] 98 Cal. Rptr. 837 (1972).

the rule as to legal malpractice (being the date of the running of the statute of limitations) contrasts with the rule as to the accrual of causes of action against practitioners in all other professions; it ignores the right of the client to rely upon the superior skill and knowledge of the attorney; it denigrates the duty of the attorney to make full and fair disclosure to the client; it negates the fiduciary character of the attorney-client relationship. We conclude that the statute of limitations for legal malpractice should be tolled until the client discovers, or should discover his cause of action.

§ 37.04 Some Suggestions for the Investigation of Lawyer's Malpractice Cases

In addition to the suggested investigation concerning the handling of cases involving professional liability, the following can specifically apply to attorneys:

- ☐ Determine the experience and educational background of the attorney, including the state and federal courts in which he or she is licensed to practice, the legal associations belonged to, etc.
- ☐ Obtain a copy of the retainer, including the names of all parties. If there was no written retainer obtain the details concerning the hiring of the attorney's services.
- ☐ Obtain all the details concerning the case that brought about the allegations of negligence including details concerning such allegations. Check these carefully.
- ☐ If the claim involves the tolling of the statute of limitations obtain all the facts concerning the original action so that a decision can be made as to whether there was any real merit to the original action.
- ☐ If abandonment was involved, find out exactly why the attorney abandoned the case and what, if any, justification there was for so doing.
- ☐ If default, erroneous pleading, or other similar omission or commission was involved, obtain complete details.
- ☐ Determine whether the attorney was involved in any previous claim or suits and, if so, what determination was made of them.

§ 37.05 Checklist for Avoiding Legal Malpractice

Mr. Victor B. Levit[76] made a list for attorneys for the purpose of avoiding actions for legal malpractice which I believe is an excellent guide (which I have changed somewhat) as follows:

---

[76] "The Legal Malpractice Crisis," Insurance Law Journal, October 1977.

PROFESSIONAL LIABILITY—LAWYERS § 37.05

- ☐ Make no guarantees about results—either in writing or verbally—or over-optimistic predictions.
- ☐ Have a complete understanding of legal costs and fees.
- ☐ See that a complete investigation is made and adequately research the law.
- ☐ Make sure that your client understands his responsibilities and confirm in writing where advisable, trial dates and requirements to which he must conform or as to assistance needed.
- ☐ Keep the client informed of all material matters, and especially any offers or demands made, as the case progresses.
- ☐ Obtain the client's written consent before employing specialists or experts and make sure that the client understands their cost and the need for their testimony. With that in mind, call on such experts and specialists as needed.
- ☐ Make no settlement offers or agreements without the client's authorization
- ☐ Keep adequate records of time spent, telephone calls, conferences, interviews, etc.
- ☐ Answer all inquiries from your client promptly, whether by phone, or, if called for, in writing.
- ☐ File all legal papers on time.
- ☐ Keep current on active cases. Always diary case and review as called for
- ☐ Mark all changes in any records carefully so as to avoid any misunderstandings concerning corrections or additions.
- ☐ Do not withhold any discouraging information from your client.
- ☐ Keep up to date on the latest cases and other information relating to your active case.
- ☐ Remember that in any situation where you represent an insured, the insured is *your* client, no matter who assigned the case or is paying the bill.
- ☐ In any conflict of interests situation, make sure that the client is fully advised of all of the facts and of any possible conflicts of interest. If all facts are known and the client agrees to your continued representation, confirm this in writing so that there will be no future misunderstanding.
- ☐ Where separate counsel is obtained for the insured, keep him or her fully informed of the progress of the case.
- ☐ Respect the duty of confidentiality.
- ☐ If there are long periods of delay because of congested trial calendar, explain the reason for the delay to your client.
- ☐ Where there are alternative strategies or options that involve risks, inform your client and let him or her make their own choice after a full explanation.
- ☐ Do not release or dismiss a party without your client's consent, in writing if necessary.
- ☐ Do not undertake representation in matters beyond your experience and advise the client of the necessity for enlisting the aid of a specialist when called for.

§ 37.06 Bibliography

Averill, "Attorney's Liability to Third Persons for Negligent Malpractice," 2 Land & Water L. Rev. 379 (1967).

Bases & Engros, "Lawyers' Professional Liability: The Experience in New York and Elsewhere," FIC Quarterly, Fall 1977.

Beck, "Legal Malpractice: Trial Lawyers and the Error-in-Judgment Rule," Insurance Counsel Journal, January 1985.

Cline, "Professional Liability Insurance: Retiring Lawyers," FIC Quarterly, Spring 1985. (Contains a good discussion of policy coverage.)

Comment, Irving, "Insurance for Lawyers: Professional Liability," S.U.L. Rev. 494 (1982).

Cullen, "Attorneys' Professional Liability Insurance Coverage Problems," FIC Quarterly, Summer 1978.

Levit, "The Legal Malpracitce Crises," Insurance Law Journal, October 1977.

Mallen, "Insurance Counsel: The Fine Line Between Professional Responsibility and Malpractice," Insurance Counsel Journal, April 1978.

Mallen & Evans, "Attorneys' Liability for Errors of Judgment—At the Crossroads," 48 Tenn. L. Rev. 283 (1981).

Martyn, "Informed Consent in the Practice of Law," 48 Geo. Wash. L. Rev. 307 (1980).

Miller, "The Myth of Objectivity in Legal Research and Writing," 18 Cath. U.L. Rev. 290 (1969).

Note, "Liability of an Attorney for the Conduct of Litigation," 12 Syracuse L. Rev. 494 (1960).

O'Connell, "Legal Malpractice: Does the Lawyer Have a Duty to Use Computerized Research?", FIC Quarterly, Fall 1984.

Peck, "A New Tort Liability for Lack of Informed Consent in Legal Matters," 44 La. L. Rev. 301 (May 1984).

Richards, "Lawyer Malpractice—The Duty to Perform Legal Research," 32 FIC Quarterly 199 (Winter 1982).

Schwartz, "The Professionalism and Accountability of Lawyers," 66 Calif. L. Rev. 669 (1978).

Wade, "The Attorney's Liability for Negligence," 12 Vand. L. Rev. 755 (1959).

Wallach & Kelly, "Attorney Malpractice in California: A Shaky Citadel," 10 Santa Clara Lawyer 257 (1970).

Weithers, "A Defense Lawyer Looks at the Professional Liability of Trial Attorneys," FIC Quarterly, Summer 1978.

Wilkins, "Malpractice and the Under-Informed Lawyers, or, What You Don't Know May Really Hurt You After All," Insurance Counsel Journal, April 1977.

CHAPTER 38

Other Areas of Professional Liability

§ 38.01 Accountants
   [1]   Definition of the Practice of Accounting
   [2]   Liability to Client—Standard of Reasonable Care
   [3]   Restatement (Second) of Torts
   [4]   Liability to Third Parties—Privity of Contract
   [5]   Statutory Liability—Federal Security Act
   [6]   Accountants' Professional Liability Policy
§ 38.02 Claim Adjusters
   [1]   Agency Obligations
§ 38.03 Architects and Engineers
   [1]   General Areas of Possible Liability
   [2]   Hold Harmless Agreements
   [3]   Statute of Limitations
   [4]   Legislation Concerning Statutes of Limitations
   [5]   Checklist for Investigation of Cases Involving Architects and Engineers
§ 38.04 Directors and Officers
   [1]   Indemnification
   [2]   Insurance
   [3]   The Insurance Policy
§ 38.05 Educators
   [1]   In General
   [2]   Students Participation in Sports or Other Athletics
§ 38.06 Insurance Agents
   [1]   Standard of Care
   [2]   Insurance Agent's Authority
   [3]   Ratification
   [4]   Professional Liability Coverage for Insurance Agents
   [5]   Binders
   [6]   Actions By Company Against Agent
   [7]   Actions By Insured Against Agent
   [8]   Actions By Third Parties Against Agent
   [9]   Some Defenses for Malpractice Actions
   [10] Checklist for Agents to Prevent Some Actions for Malpractice
§ 38.07 Bibliography

§ 38.01 Accountants

[1] Definition of the Practice of Accounting

Most professions, including those of doctor, lawyer, teacher, and others require no specific definitions since their activities are generally well-known. Accountants are different in that their activities range over a wide area, including bookkeeping, auditing and certifying for a large group of business enterprises. To define the profession of accountant succinctly is almost impossible. The typical statutory definitions are so involved in legal language, that to make some sense of them is in itself a formidable task. Shorn of its legal garbage, one such statute can be boiled down to mean that one who offers accounting services for a fee, and issues financial, accounting or auditing reports and holds himself out to be an expert in this field, is an accountant. That isn't much help. Legal dictionaries add very little. Accordingly, case discussion has involved the professional duties and responsibilities of an accountant, who may or may not be certified or be an auditor.

Ordinarily, Professional Liability insurance involves the relationship between the insured and his patient or client. The accountant, however, is subject to claims and suits by third parties who may have been damaged as a result of his malpractice, in addition to his client. An accountant's statements are relied upon by many individuals and other legal entities with whom his client is doing business or intends to do business. The accountant's errors or omissions could affect many third parties.

Some of the principal areas of responsibility might concern:

1. Misappropriation of funds by employees.
2. Improperly prepared tax returns.
3. Failure to file proper tax returns on time.
4. Incorrect financial status reports.

What we can cull from case law, is that there are three major areas of responsibility of an accountant that can be grouped as follows:

1. Liability to his or her client or someone who "stands in the shoes" of the client;
2. Liability to third parties who have not retained the services of the accountant and who have no privity of contract relationship with him; and
3. Statutory liability, particularly under federal securities acts.

[2] Liability to Client—Standard of Reasonable Care

As in other professions, the standard of care expected of an accountant "requires (that he) exercise that degree of skill and competence reasonably expected of persons in his profession," and sometimes, within the community, state or nation where he practices.[1]

The accounting profession itself has established standards by which a member can be measured according to guidelines published by the American Institute of Certified Accountants.[2]

In addition, some states have also enacted guidelines for accountants, and while the violation of such acts may not constitute negligence per se, they would in any event be an indication thereof.

Ordinarily, the establishment of an act of malpractice could be achieved by presenting expert evidence, unless such malpractice is so obvious as to be recognized without it, by the layman.[3]

There is so little agreement concerning correct accounting and auditing procedures so that establishing specific boundaries as to which is right, is very difficult.[4]

Once again, as in other professions, an accountant or auditor is not legally responsible for honest errors in judgment made on a non-negligent reasonable basis.[5]

At the other extreme are cases involving fraud by the accountant which, whether perpetrated directly on clients or indirectly on third parties, has from an early date been held to be actionable malpractice.[6]

For the most part, malpractice actions against accountants are based on negligent misrepresentation.

[3] Restatement (Second) of Torts

Section 552 of the Restatement (Second) of Torts adopts a limited approach to liability. It rejects the requirement of privity of contract and requires instead "knowing reliance" as a yardstick. Liability is

---

[1] Bancroft v. Indemnity Ins. Co. of N. Amer., 203 F. Supp. 49 (La. 1962).

[2] *See* Eizenstat & Speer, "Accountants' Professional Liability: Expanding Exposure," DRI Monograph, #6 (1972).

[3] *See* Kurland, "Accountant's Legal Liability: Ultramares to *Bar Chris*," 25 Business Lawyer 155 (1969).

[4] Eizenstat & Speer, "Accountants' Professional Liability: Expanding Exposure," DRI Monograph #6, 1972.

[5] Levy, *Accountants' Legal Responsibility*.

[6] Security-First Nat'l Bank of L.A. v. Lutz, 322 F.2d 348 (9th Cir. 1963).

§ 38.01[4] CASUALTY INSURANCE CLAIMS

not extended to all parties whom the accountant might reasonably foresee as using the information he disseminates. It merely extends causes of action to a limited number of third parties who are expected to gain access to the financial statement information in an expected transaction.[7]

[4] Liability to Third Parties—Privity of Contract

A growing number of states have rejected the privity of contract requirement established in the *Ultramares* case,[8] and have ruled that accountants may be held liable for professional negligence affecting third parties whose reliance on the accountant's representations was reasonably foreseeable.[9]

Nevertheless, some jurisdictions still follow the *Ultramares* decision,[10] to the effect that privity of contract is a necessary requirement to establish malpractice liability by an accountant.[11]

In New York, an appellate court established three prerequisites to be met before an accountant can be held liable to third parties who relied on inaccurate financial statements to their detriment: (1) the accountants must have been aware of the particular purpose for the report, (2) there must have been a relying party who was known, and (3) there must have been some conduct by the accountants linking them to the third party or parties.[12]

Where foreseeability is present, the tendency is to abrogate the privity of contract rule.[13]

---

[7] Spherex, Inc. v. Alexander Grant & Co., 451 A.2d 1308 (1982); Ryan v. Kanne, 170 N.W.2d 395 (Iowa 1969); Haddon View Investment Co. v. Coopers & Lybrand, 436 N.E.2d 212 (Ohio 1982); Shatterproof Glass Corp. v. James, 466 S.W.2d 879 (Tex. App. 1976); Bonhiver v. Graff, 248 N.W.2d 291 (Minn. 1976).

[8] Ultramares v. Touche, 174 N.E.2d 441 (N.Y. 1931).

[9] **Cal.:** International Mtg. Co. v. John P. Butler Accounting Corp., 177 Cal. App. 3d 806, 223 Cal. Rptr. 218 (1986).
Iowa: Ryan v. Kanne, 120 N.W.2d 395 (1969).
Ohio: Haddon View Invest. Co. v. Coopers & Lybrand, 436 N.E.2d 212 (1982).
Tex.: Shatterproof Glass Corp. v. James, 466 S.W.2d 873 (1971).
Wis.: Citizens State Bank v. Timm, Schmidt & Co., 335 N.W.2d 361 (1983).

[10] Ultramares v. Touche, 174 N.E.2d 441 (N.Y. 1931).

[11] **Colo.:** Stephens Indus., Inc. v. Haskins & Sells, 438 F.2d 357 (10th Cir. 1971).
Fla.: Investment Corp. of Florida v. Buchman, 208 So. 2d 291 (App. 1968).
Ga.: G.P. MacNederland v. J.A. Barnes, 199 S.E.2d 564 (App. 1973).

[12] Credit Alliance Corp. v. Anderson & Co., 65 N.Y.2d 536 (1985).

[13] **Minn.:** Bonhiver v. Graff, 248 N.W.2d 291 (1976).
Neb.: Seedham, Inc. v. Safranek, 466 F. Supp. 340 (1979).

[5] Statutory Liability—Federal Security Act

A corporation offering, or firms or individuals selling, stock through a secondary offering are subject to the provisions of the Federal Securities Act of 1933.

Section XI of this Act imposes liability on the parties to the registration for material misstatements made in the registration documents and for omissions of material facts.

Parties who may be liable under this section of the Act include:

1. The issuer of the securities,
2. Others who sign the registration statement,
3. Directors of the corporation that issues the stock,
4. Underwriters of the stock issue, and
5. Auditors whose reports give erroneous and misleading information provided in the registration documents.[14]

As quoted in an excellent article by Eizenstat and Speer:[15]

> The role of the accountant is central to the administration of the Federal Securities Act. In enacting the Securities Act of 1933, Congress rejected the notion that financial statements of filing companies should be reviewed by government auditors, in favor of certification by independent public accountants . . . the "responsibility of a public accountant is not only to the client who pays his fee, but also to investors, creditors and others who may rely on the financial statements which he certifies."

[6] Accountants' Professional Liability Policy

There is not standard form for accountants' professional liability insurance. Generally speaking, such policies follow other professional liability forms, but differences abound. Therefore, more than ever, the claim representative or attorney assigned to such a case must re-

---

Pa.: Coleco Industries, Inc. v. Berman, 423 F. Supp. 275 (1976), *aff'd*, 567 F.2d 569 (3d Cir. 1977).

[14] *See* Escott v. Bar Chris Constr. Corp., 284 F. Supp. 643 (N.Y. 1968); Blakely v. Lisac, 357 F. Supp. 255 (Ore. 1972); Herzfeld v. Laventhol, Krekstein, Horwath & Horwath, 378 F. Supp. 112 (N.Y. 1974). *See also* "Day Lee's," "S.E.C. Liability Insurance," Insurance Adjuster Magazine, February 4, 1983.

[15] "Accountants' Professional Liability: Expanding Exposure," DRI Monograph #6, 1972).

§ 38.02　　　　　　　　　　　CASUALTY INSURANCE CLAIMS

view the specific policy involved very carefully.[16]

Ordinarily, coverage is provided for the named insured, partners, officers, directors, stockholders, and employees while acting in the scope of their duties.

While the exclusions vary, fraudulent, criminal or dishonest acts committed by or at the direction of a named insured are not covered and no coverage is provided for any insured *who commits a dishonest act.* Most policies do cover a partner who has no knowledge of the dishonest or criminal act of the wrongdoer. In addition, bodily injury and damage to tangible property are also usually excluded.

§ 38.02　Claim Adjusters

In the case of *Gruenberg v. Aetna Ins. Co.,*[17] a California court, following the doctrine of privity of contract, held harmless the company claim representatives who were primarily responsible for the wrongdoing that led to a verdict against the insurance company for bad faith refusal to settle and for punitive damages. There seems to be little doubt that this verdict was due to the "deep pocket" belonging to the insurance company for which the claim representatives worked as employees.

Since plaintiff's lawyers see some strategic advantage to the inclusion of claim representatives who actually handle settlement negotiations for the insurer, they will continue to make them party defendants in such actions. As a result, the exposure of claim representatives is increasing. In addition, the enactment of Unfair Claim Settlement Practices Acts that in some states permit personal actions against insurers and claim representatives, increased that exposure.

California was in the forefront in holding that an independent insurance adjuster was within the meaning of "persons engaged in the business of insurance" and subject to liability for violations of the Unfair Claim Settlement Practices Act.[18] Claim representatives who are

---

[16] *See* Seyold, "Accountants' Professional Liability Policies," DRI Monograph #6, 1972.

[17] 108 Cal. Rptr. 480 (1973).

[18] Bodenhamer v. Superior Court, 178 Cal. App. 3d 180 (1986); Davis v. Continental Ins. Co., 178 Cal. App. 3d 839 (1986); Nelson v. G.A.B. Business Services, Inc., 179 Cal. App. 3d 610 (1986). *See also* Glad, "Liability for Individuals in the Claim Handling Process," Insurance Adjuster Magazine, September, 1986.

insurance company employees, however, have for the time being remained exempt from liability under this statute in California.[19]

[1] Agency Obligations

As agents for a disclosed principal, it has been held that the claim adjuster is acting for and on behalf of the insurance company and is not held personally responsible for any malfeasance.[20]

In *Huddock v. Donegal Mut. Ins. Co.*,[21] it was held that as long as the principal was disclosed, the claim adjuster remained immune from professional liability even when he exceeds his authority.

The article "Thinking Without a License,"[22] named three hazards that cause errors and omissions problems for claim adjusters: (1) unclear communications, (2) procrastination, and (3) improper documentation. From personal experience, I would give the first three places to "procrastination" and go on from there to:

2. Lack of courtesy and diplomacy to all with whom the adjuster comes in contact, which includes failure to reply promptly to all inquiries.
3. Improper or incomplete investigation.
4. Improper evaluation and failure of continued reevaluation of settlement values. Too many adjusters assume a rigid attitude.
5. Incorrect coverage interpretation leading to improper disclaimers of coverage.
6. Failure to properly reserve insurer's rights where there is a conflict of interests with the insured.
7. Failure to make honest recommendations to supervisors and home office.
8. Failure to use defense attorney's services properly and within proper economic bounds.
9. Failure to keep insured and company supervisors properly and promptly advised and failure to respond properly to home office inquiries.

---

[19] Grief v. Superior Court, 178 Cal. App. 3d 984 (1986).
[20] Falcon Flying Service v. McKamey, 193 So. 2d 402 (S.C. 1966).
[21] 264 A.2d 668 (Pa. 1970). *See also* Iconoclast, "Thinking Without a License," Insurance Adjuster Magazine, June 1983.
[22] *See id.* note 21, *supra*.

§ 38.03 Architects and Engineers

It is generally agreed that any distinction between an architect and an engineer is irrelevant to the question of tort liability. Both are required to be certified by the state before being permitted to practice their professions. The standard of care for both professions is similar to that of other professions except for the greater duties assumed by contract.

Many of the duties assumed by architects and engineers are based upon the oral or written contract between them, their clients, contractors, and subcontractors. Accordingly, the first and prime duty of the attorney representing the architect or engineer in the event of suit for professional malpractice is to obtain and carefully review all contracts and agreements.[23]

In recent years, the law concerning the liability of architects and engineers for their professional liability has, to quite a degree, paralleled the development in the law of products liability. Privity of contract has ceased to be an important factor in both fields of law.

In 1957, in the landmark case of *Inman v. Binghamton Housing Authority*,[24] the court confirmed the demise of privity of contract as a defense for an architect or builder as to a structure erected on real property. It also decided, as a matter of law, that neither the architect nor the builder were liable to third parties for defects in buildings or other structures on real property, once they were accepted by the owner, where the defect or danger was known, obvious, and could have been discovered by reasonable inspection.[25]

By the early 1970's, nearly every jurisdiction had discarded the privity of contract defense for architects and engineers.[26]

[1] General Areas of Possible Liability

More than in any other profession, architects and engineers may be held liable for their professional liability to third parties as well as to their first party clients. Accordingly, the following areas of possi-

---

[23] *See* Goodwin, "Architects and Malpractice," Insurance Council Journal, April 1967.

[24] 164 N.Y.S.2d 699 (1957).

[25] *See* Gouldin, "Liability of Architects and Contractors to Third Persons: Inman v. Binghamton Housing Authority Revisited," Insurance Counsel Journal, July 1966.

[26] Conklin v. Cohen, 287 So. 2d 56 (1973). *See also* Neeson, "The Current Status of Professional Architects' and Engineers' Malpractice Liability Insurance," Insurance Counsel Journal, January 1978.

ble liability for architects and engineers includes aspects of both first and third party liability.

1. Liability for defects attributed to plans and specifications. This usually involves dangerous conditions that could cause injury or death resulting from:

- (a) Foundation of a building being inadequate.
- (b) Roof, floors, or walls that may crack, buckle, or collapse.
- (c) Fixtures that may be inadequate or badly installed.
- (d) Waterproofing, heating, or air conditioning inadequacies.
- (e) Liability arising out of improper certification of partial or total completion. The architect must certify to the owner and/or the lending bank or financial institution, the progress made in the construction of the building. If he negligently or fraudulently certifies more progress than has actually been made he may be liable for any resulting loss.
- (f) Improper specification of materials.
- (g) Improper supervision of construction, if called for in the contract.
- (h) Deviations from plans or specifications without previous agreement.

[2] Hold Harmless Agreements

The chance of an architect or engineer being asked to indemnify one or several contractors, subcontractors, or suppliers for damages resulting from a liability claim or suit are considerable. The case of *New York Central R.R. v. General Motors Corp.*,[27] defined "hold harmless" as the assumption of "all expenses incident to the defense of any claim and to fully compensate an indemnitee for all loss or expense, undiminished by the costs of defending a claim or litigation."

A good definition may be found in the California Civil Code, Section 2772 (West 1973) which states that "Indemnity is a contract by which one engages to save another from a legal consequence of the conduct of one of the parties, or of some other person." Basically, as one commentator put it "Generally speaking, the indemnitor as-

---

[27] 182 F. Supp. 273 (Ohio 1960).

sumes responsibility for protecting the indemnitee against liability."[28]

The wording of hold harmless clauses is limited only "by the imagination of creative lawyers." Ordinarily, hold harmless clauses can be categorized into five basic types:[29]

1. Indemnitor agrees to hold the indemnitee harmless from liability arising out of the indemnitee's own negligence.
2. Indemnitor agrees to hold indemnitee harmless from all liability arising out of the negligence of both parties except for the sole negligence of the indemnitee.
3. Indemnitor agrees to hold indemnitee harmless from all liability arising out of either party, without regard to fault.
4. Indemnitor agrees to hold the indemnitee harmless from all liability arising out of the negligence of anyone in the performance of the work.
5. Indemnitor agrees to hold indemnitee harmless from all injury, loss or damage, regardless of fault or cause.

The question of hold harmless agreements can be, and usually is, a very involved subject requiring expert legal guidance and I would suggest that it be obtained when it appears advisable.[30]

[3] **Statute of Limitations**

Until recent years, it had generally been held that the statute of limitations in professional liability cases involving architects and engineers ran from the date of the malpractice.[31] More recently, however, the "discovery rule" has become much more prevalent.[32]

Discounting any statutory enactment on the subject, the statutory period would also be affected by whether the action was brought in contract or tort.

Some cases hold that the statute begins to run from the time of completion of the construction.[33]

---

[28] *See* Maurer, Jr., "Architects, Engineers and Hold Harmless Clauses," Insurance Law Journal, December 1974.

[29] *See* Maurer, *id.* and Rossmor Sanitation, Inc. v. Pylon, Inc., 119 Cal. Rptr. 449 (1975).

[30] *See* Maurer, *id.*

[31] Wellston Co. v. Sam N. Hodges, Jr. & Co., 151 S.E.2d 481 (Ga. App. 1966).

[32] **Cal.:** Budd v. Nixen, 98 Cal. Rptr. 849 (1971).
Fla.: Downing v. Vaine, 228 So. 2d 622 (App. 1969).
Iowa: Chrischilles v. Griswold, 150 N.W.2d 94 (1967).

[33] Wills v. Black & West, Architects, 344 P.2d 581 (Okla. 1959).

[4] Legislation Concerning Statutes of Limitations

As a result of pressure brought by architects and engineers through their professional organizations, many states have adopted special periods of time limitation within which an action may be brought against architects and engineers for malpractice.

While most of them have been declared constitutional, the time period (usually four to seven years) was felt to be inadequate by the organizations representing the architects and engineers, since many malpractice actions are brought many years after the completion of the buildings involved.

[5] Checklist for Investigation of Cases Involving Architects and Engineers

Architects and engineers do not warrant that their plans and specifications are foolproof, nor do they warrant the durability of the structures involved, under ordinary circumstances.

Some suggested avenues for the investigation of accidents allegedly caused by the professional negligence of architects and engineers follows:

- ☐ Read the contracts and other papers attached carefully.[34]
- ☐ Find out who drew up the plans and specifications. Get his or her complete academic and experience background and length of service with the insured's firm.
- ☐ Obtain complete details concerning the names and correct legal entities of all parties to the suit, including the names of their attorneys.
- ☐ Determine the correct legal names of all contractors, both general and subcontractors, and their insurance carriers. See that they are put on notice if necessary.
- ☐ Find out exactly what supervision was called for and what was exercised by the insured and get complete details. Determine whether there was any failure to properly supervise the operation.
- ☐ Check any alleged negligence thoroughly and make a determination as to whether any alleged defect was hidden or open and obvious. Find out if the allegations or facts involved defective materials, improper materials, or improper or defective plans or construction.
- ☐ Determine whether the construction involved any deviation from the plans, blueprints or specifications and, if so, obtain complete explanation and details. Obtain signed statements from the workmen involved.

---

[34] *See* Kaskell, Jr., "Possible Avenues of Liability of the Architect and Engineer to Contractors and Subcontractors," Insurance Counsel Journal, July 1980.

§ 38.04   CASUALTY INSURANCE CLAIMS

☐ Obtain copies of all progress reports and certifications of work completed and check these against the contract requirements.

☐ Determine whether all proper and required permits were obtained and whether the work was done in compliance with all local, state, and federal laws.

☐ Find out if there were any "hold harmless agreements" between any of the parties and, if so, obtain copies and refer for legal advice. Determine whether there was any contractual insurance and obtain names of the insurance carriers. Put them on notice if advisable.

☐ Determine if the structure was formally accepted by the owner and obtain proof of such acceptance, including the exact date.

§ 38.04   Directors and Officers

The great difficulty in handling errors and omissions claims involving corporate directors is the common misconception that a board of directors actually manages a corporation. While such an impression is created in most corporation acts, including Section 35 of the Model Business Corporation Act, nothing is further from the reality of the situation.

In actuality, most directors know very little about the day by day operation of the corporation with which they are involved as directors, and yet some courts have held directors to a high standard of knowledge and responsibility for such daily operations. The courts have generally held directors to be obligated to act in good faith, and with diligence and loyalty. The degree of skill and care is the usual one required of the prudent person under similar circumstances in the conduct of their personal business affairs. They are regarded as fiduciaries of their corporations and stockholders.

Some directors perform special duties requiring specific skill or knowledge, and such directors are held to a much higher degree of responsibility.[35]

Some of the grounds upon which actions have been brought against corporate directors and officers involved the following:

(a)   Conflicts of interest.
(b)   Misuse of funds.
(c)   Inefficient administration.
(d)   Payment of unwarranted dividends.

---

[35] Escott v. Bar Chris Const. Corp., 283 F. Supp. 643 (D.C.N.Y. 1968).

PROFESSIONAL LIABILITY—OTHER AREAS § 38.04[2]

(e) Failure to comply with state and federal laws and regulations.
(f) Failure to attend meetings regularly.
(g) Misstatement of financial reports.

[1] Indemnification

In view of the ever increasing degree of accountability to which directors were being held, the situation was fast becoming untenable for any individual who assumed such a responsibility. Accordingly, the by-laws of most corporations now state that an officer or director will, in certain circumstances, be indemnified for expenses and even some damages for which a director has been held personally responsible. Many states have also enacted statutes agreeing with this position where fraud or illegal gain was not involved.

The statutes are far from uniform. Some authorize corporations to make indemnification, some require indemnification, and others require court approval on an individual basis. A few even permit indemnification for expenses involved in criminal defense, where the defendant has been successful.

Where the civil defense is successful, it is obviously just a matter of reimbursing a director or officer for legal expenses involved in defending himself. However, where a director is held responsible, his acts may run the gamut where indemnification may be mandatory to the other extreme, where indemnification could be outrageously unjust.

[2] Insurance

Once the problem of the legality of indemnification has been hurdled, it becomes obvious that the hazards of personal liability by directors and officers is insurable.

It has been argued that since the law imposes certain duties and obligations on directors, it should not permit them to evade those obligations by the purchase of insurance. This is a very untenable position to take. All liability insurance could be subject to the same argument, whether the policy be one of automobile liability, public liability, products or any other coverage of this nature. Why should insurance for directors and officers be different? The obvious answer is that it should not.

Some states have specifically enacted statutes permitting corporations to purchase insurance for the protection of officers and directors from financial disaster resulting from actions brought against them in their capacities as such. Other states permit such insurance without specific legislation on the subject.

[3] The Insurance Policy

There is no standard form for this insurance, but there is a great deal of uniformity in the policy provisions. The two general forms in common use in this country are the so-called "Mini" policy for financial institutions of modest size, and the blanket or "Maxi" policy for large corporations and conglomerates. Both policies are ordinarily written on a deductible basis requiring some participation by the insured. In addition, some companies issue a reimbursement or indemnification policy form which is tied in with the liability form.

These policies provide protection for any "wrongful act" of a director or officer and wrongful act is ordinarily defined as an actual or alleged error, misstatement, act of omission or breach of duty by the insured while acting in an individual or collective capacity, solely by reason of being a director or officer. The wording is not uniform but the intent is quite similar.

The wrongful act, in some policies, must occur during the policy period, and claim or suit concerning that act must also be made or brought within the policy period.

Notice of the wrongful act committed during the policy period is required to be given when committed, or if the insured is unaware that his act was wrongful, then notice must be given as soon as claim is made or suit is brought.

Some policies provide coverage for wrongful acts committed before the effective date of the policy period if claim is first made or suit first instituted during the policy period, assuming the insured had no previous knowledge of the impending claim or suit and could not reasonably have foreseen it, and also assuming that there was no other applicable insurance. This is in the nature of a discovery clause.

The exclusions in most Officer's and Director's malpractice policies cover similar areas. They all exclude claims or suits that were insured by another policy or policies. This is sometimes put in the form of an "Other Insurance" condition which is found in most liability policies.

Claims based upon, or attributable to bodily injury, disease or death, or to damage to or destruction of tangible property is also usually excluded, as is dishonesty of an insured, or of his acts which result in personal profit to which he was not legally entitled. Here it must be noted that alleged acts of dishonesty, denied by an insured, might have to be defended, preferably under some reservation of rights, unless the company knows and can prove that the allegations are correct, which is at best a difficult matter.

Some policies exclude claims or suits brought on the grounds of libel or slander, and a few exclude claims or suits based on a failure to obtain or maintain insurance.

Some of the original forms excluded violations of the Securities Exchange Act, but this has been eliminated from recent policy forms that I have seen, no doubt due to the increasing importance of such protection to directors and officers. Special forms have also been promulgated to fit this specific requirement by some insurers.

The limits of the policy usually include expenses and damages in a lump sum. If the limits are exceeded the problem becomes sticky, but the intent is probably to apportion such expenses.[36]

While the ordinary liability policy conditions are not usually spelled out in this policy, most of them do contain a subrogation clause.

In the last few years, the trend of the courts and the elimination of the Securities Exchange exclusion have necessitated considerable increases in the premiums for this coverage. In order to keep costs in line, it may be necessary to refine the policies far beyond their present terms. As the market for this type of insurance continues to grow, there will also be the need for more uniformity of provisions and standardization of policy forms.

§ 38.05 Educators

[1] In General

More than other professions, teaching is an art even more than it is a science. Volumes have been written on "how to teach" and more volumes have informed prospective teachers not to pay too much attention to the former.[37]

---

[36] The claims person or lawyer facing this and other problems dealing with this policy should read William Knepper's excellent book, *Liability of Corporate Officers and Directors* published by The Allen Smith Company of Indianapolis, Indiana.

[37] Peter W. v. San Francisco School Dist., 131 Cal. Rptr. 854 (1976) (recovery denied).

In past years, by and large, the teaching colleges and institutions for the training of grammar and high school teachers have been rigidly narrow and unimaginative. It is indeed odd that certification is required to teach at the primary and high school levels, but not in colleges or universities, where some of our best teachers have never taken "teaching" courses.

It is essential for the good teacher to have wide latitude in his or her profession. Every few decades, however, we witness the resurgence of fundamentalism that pits religion against science and in this battle, the losers include the teachers.

It is rightfully expected that teachers and educational institutions be expected to educate. This is theoretically just, and in days long gone, the teacher was a respected professional who did not have to worry unduly about discipline or the cooperation of parents.

While there has been no general acceptance of educational malpractice as a cause of action, it doesn't take a soothsayer to see that this attitude will soon change.[38]

Negligence and misrepresentation are the two most likely areas for a possible cause of action. In the area of negligence, sports and athletic activities present the greatest dangers. As to misrepresentation, the most likely candidates for becoming defendants are the "for profit" commercial institutions that imply in their advertising much more than they do or can produce.

[2] Students Participation in Sports and Other Athletics

The area that has produced the most claims and suits in dealing with educational malpractice has involved gymnastics or sports. Complaints have generally encompassed the following deficiencies:

1. Failure to provide safe facilities and equipment.
2. Failure to institute prompt and proper medical attention.
3. Failure to provide proper supervision and training.
4. Failure to segregate pupils by size and age.

---

[38] **Md.:** Doe v. Board of Educ., 453 A.2d 814 (1984).
N.Y.: Hoffman v. Board of Educ., 424 N.Y.S.2d 376 (1979); Donahue v. Copiague Union Free School Dist., 418 N.Y.S.2d 375 (App. 1979).
See also Di Liberto, Jr., "An Apple for the Teacher: Educational Malpractice Fails Judicial Test But Core Problem Remains," Insurance Counsel Journal, April 1986.

5. Pupils forced to take tumbling or other types of physical exercise that could cause injury if the pupil is not sufficiently coordinated.
6. Pupils coerced to play football, or other potentially dangerous contact sports.

In the case of *Carava v. Anacortes School Dist.*,[39] the school district was held liable for negligence in the supervision of a wrestling match.

§ 38.06 Insurance Agents

The duties and responsibilities of an insurance agent are different from other professionals because the insurance agent has duties to the insurance companies that write the policy, as well as to clients who buy the insurance. Often these duties conflict over matters of coverage, when claims are presented. In addition, independent agents represent more than one company and such agents may have to make a choice in placing good or mediocre risks.

Furthermore, since the agent receives a fee for placing a risk and is not immediately affected by loss ratio on that risk, it becomes more difficult for him to abide strictly to company authorization and the code of ethics to which he should be bound. The National Association of Insurance Agents (NAIA) Code of Ethics II, obligates the insurance agent to use care in the selection of risks, merit the confidence of the insurers by obtaining full information, and refrain from withholding any information that is detrimental to the interests of the insurer. These responsibilities have legal as well as moral effect.[40]

In order to practice as an insurance agent, most states require an applicant to pass an examination in order to obtain a necessary license. Such an agent has been given professional status by our courts.[41]

In addition, as the nature of insurance developed from relatively simple to highly complex contracts, the position of the insurance agent rapidly changed from that of a salesman to professional advisor

---

[39] 435 P.2d 936 (Wash. 1967).
[40] Oppenheim, "Professional Malpractice: Welcome Insurance Agents and Brokers," Insurance Law Journal, December 1979.
[41] **N.M.:** Butler v. Scott, 417 F.2d 471 (10th Cir. 1969).
Pa.: Fiorentino v. Travelers Ins. Co., 448 F. Supp. 1364 (1970).
Wash.: Roberts v. Sunen, 229 P.2d 542 (1951).

on matters of insurance needs. This change made the insurance agent a target for malpractice suits. Such a suit may be based on neglect, inattention, indifference, or other forms of negligence,[42] as well as on contract, written or implied.[43]

The old nominal distinction between an agent (of the insurance company) and a broker (for the insured) has fallen by the wayside. An agent or broker, whatever his or her designation, may incur malpractice liability. Accordingly, no differentiation will be made between the two in this discussion.[44]

[1] Standard of Care

The standard of care required of insurance agents is the usual one applied to professional liability; to exercise the degree of skill and knowledge of the reasonably prudent insurance agent under similar circumstances. Locality plays a very minor part in determining the professional liability of an insurance agent.

Again, as with other professional liabilities, an agent does not undertake to render perfect service, and mere errors of judgment, where negligence or fraud are not involved, should not warrant recovery against him for malpractice.

[2] Insurance Agent's Authority

The authority of an insurance agent to act on behalf of the insurance company that he represents is determined by the agency contract, the underwriting rules of the company, and past relationship with it.[45] An agent is usually granted specific written authority and, in addition, has implied authority to act in a proper manner to accomplish the usual purposes of an insurance agent where it does not contradict his or her written authority, with some exceptions to be noted hereafter.

Apparent agency arises out of an agent's acting in a reasonable manner which indicates that he or she has the necessary authority,

---

[42] *See* Restatement (Second) of Torts § 299A.
[43] Kamikawa v. Kerkinen, 172 N.W.2d 24 (Wis. 1969). *See also* O'Connor, "Liability of Insurance Agents and Brokers," DRI Monograph, 1970.
[44] *See* Maurer, "A Primer for Preventing Errors and Omissions of Insurance Agents and Brokers," Bests Review, September 1978.
[45] Austin v. Fulton Ins. Co., 498 P.2d 702 (1972) (implied authority).

and where the client has no reasonable grounds for doubting that the agent has such authority.[46]

An agent has the authority that a reasonably prudent person, using ordinary diligence would assume he has because of the insurer's conduct or tacit approval.[47]

[3] Ratification

Ratification of the acts of an insurance agent supercedes any lack of authority that may be claimed. Despite an insurer's directions for an agent to cancel a policy, subsequent contradictory instructions to continue negotiations will waive the company's right to stand on its previous order to cancel.[48]

Ratification may also arise out of knowledge of previous acts of the agent to which the company never objected.[49]

Acceptance of the premium and even the issuance of a policy may not, in and of itself, always act as a ratification.[50]

In the absence of ratification or other reason for waiver, an agent may be held liable to his insurance company principal for any loss resulting from unauthorized conduct.[51]

[4] Professional Liability Coverage for Insurance Agents

As with many other professional liability policies, there is no standard policy form, although the policies of those companies that write this coverage have many common provisions.

Exclusions usually include libel and slander, fraud, criminal or malicious acts.

Most such policies are liability forms, but in some of the older forms these were written as indemnity contracts, though often not interpreted as such by our courts.

---

[46] Lumbermans Mut. Ins. Co. v. Slide Rule & Scale Engineering Co., 177 F.2d 305 (1949) (secret limitations on the agent's authority not known to the insured are not effective).

[47] Hooker v. American Indem. Co., 54 P.2d 1128 (Cal. App. 1936); Bankers Protective Life Ins. Co. v. Addison, 237 S.W.2d 694 (Tex. App. 1951).

[48] Wujcik v. Globe & Wreckers Fire Ins. Co., 250 N.W.2d 820 (Wis. 1975).

[49] Minn.: Hockemeyer v. Pooler, 130 N.W.2d 367 (1964).
N.H.: Kolbilick v. Hartford Accident & Indem. Co., 63 A.2d 228 (1940).

[50] Mission Ins. Co. v. Enger Ins. Co., 513 P.2d 765 (Ore. 1973).

[51] Manufacturer's Cas. Ins. Co. v. Martin-Labartin Ins. Agency, 242 F.2d 851 (5th Cir. 1957).

[5] Binders

By agreeing to bind a risk, the agent impliedly warrants that he has the authority to do so. The issuance of binders creates a serious legal responsibility. Oral binders are subject to the ordinary legal requirements of valid contracts.

Insurance laws usually limit the time within which a binder is effective and agency authorizations often limit an agent's authority to issue binders. Any such limitations must be reported to the client, if applicable. It is important that there is agreement on all of the essential terms of the policy to be issued and that confirmation be sent to the client and the insurer, with all essential information including the exact time of the day on which the binder was issued.[52]

[6] Actions By Company Against Agent

Actions brought by an insurance company against an agent are, for the most part, indemnity suits brought to recover payments made by the insurer because of the malpractice of the agent, since knowledge of the agent is usually imputed to the insurer.[53]

While, for business reasons, indemnity actions are not of the greatest concern to the average agent, such suits are not at all unusual for the following reasons:

1. Fraud involving intentional concealment of material facts concerning a risk;[54]
2. Binding unauthorized risks;[55]
3. Failure to follow instructions;[56]

---

[52] *See* Tye, "Legal Problems of Insurance Agents—Binders," Insurance Law Journal, March 1957.

[53] Ill.: Frangos v. U.S.F. & G. Co., 312 N.E.2d 688 (App. 1974).
Md.: Bogley v. Middleton Tavern, Inc., 421 A.2d 571 (App. 1980).
Wis.: Estate of Ensz, 223 N.W.2d 903 (1974).

[54] Campbell v. St. Paul Fire & Marine Ins. Co., 480 S.W.2d 233 (Tex. App. 1972); Mittor v. Granite State Fire Ins. Co., 196 F.2d 988 (10th Cir. 1952).

[55] Millers Cas. Ins. Co. v. Cypress Ins. Agency, 273 So. 2d 602 (La. App. 1973); State Auto. Under's v. Salisbury, 494 P.2d 529 (Utah 1972).

[56] United States Liability Ins. Co. v. Haidinger-Hayes, Inc., 463 P.2d 770 (Alas. 1970) (failure to make adequate investigation of client); Hanover Ins. Co. v. St. Paul Fire & Marine Ins. Co., 359 F. Supp. 591 (La. 1973) (failure to cancel); Transamerica Ins. Co. v. Parrott, 531 S.W.2d 306 (Tenn. App. 1975) (failure to obey underwriting instructions).

4. Failure to disclose adverse information to company.[57]

[7] Actions By Insured Against Agent

The area of greatest danger and exposure to malpractice actions for insurance agents involves suits brought by clients or prospective clients against them for a number of reasons:

1. Failure to procure or renew insurance that the agent had contracted to obtain;[58]
2. Failure to advise client promptly concerning inability to obtain renewal, rejection, or cancellation;[59]
3. Failure to apply for coverage promptly with a solvent and authorized carrier;[60]

---

[57] Chicago Ins. Co. v. Connors, 296 F. Supp. 1335 (Ga. 1969) (acceptance of premium after cancellation); Insurance Co. of N. America v. J.L. Hubbard Co., 318 N.E.2d 289 (Ill. 1975) (negligent failure to place limitations on renewal policy); Hanover Ins. Co. v. St. Paul Fire & Marine Ins. Co., 359 F. Supp. 591 (La. 1973); Reserve Ins. Co. v. Netzer, 621 F.2d 314 (8th Cir. 1980) (failure to disclose full information re prospective insured. No recovery by insurer).

[58] Waldon v. Commercial Bank, 281 So. 2d 279 (App. 1973); Martin v. Langley, 477 S.W.2d 473 (1972); Northwestern Ins. Agency v. Courson, 274 S.E.2d 714 (Ga. App. 1980) (no duty established in this case); Wolfswinkel v. Gesink, 180 N.W.2d 452 (Iowa 1970); Keith v. Schiefen-Stockman Ins. Agency, 498 P.2d 265 (Kan. 1972); Ballon v. Smith, 299 So. 2d 501 (La. App. 1974) (failure to secure coverage after accepting partial premium and assuring client that she was covered by renewal policy); Security Ins. Agency v. Cox, 299 So. 2d 192 (Miss. 1974); Hanz Coiffures Int'l v. Hejna, 469 S.W.2d 38 (Mo. App. 1971) (failure to obtain one section of package coverage); Johnson v. George Tenuta & Co., 185 S.E.2d 732 (N.C. 1972); Arley v. Chaney, 496 P.2d 202 (Ore. 1972); Taylor v. Republic Grocery, 483 S.W.2d 293 (Tex. App. 1972) (failure to obtain renewal); Bates v. Bowles White Co., 353 P.2d 663 (Wash. 1974); Robertson v. Krupp, 260 N.E.2d 849 (Ill. 1970) (failure to obtain coverage requested); Rider v. Lynch, 201 A.2d 561 (N.J. 1964) (failure to obtain coverage requested).

[59] Burns v. Ramsey, 520 P.2d 137 (Colo. 1974) (no duty to notify re expiration date in absence of established precedent with insured); Board of Trustees of Phillip Mem. Methodist Church v. F & M Ins. Co., 306 So. 2d 777 (La. App. 1974) (failure to give personal notice of cancellation); Pittman v. Great Amer. Life Ins. Co., 512 S.W.2d 857 (Mo. App. 1974); Weathers v. Hartford Accid. & Indem. Group, 380 A.2d 742 (N.J. App. 1977); Taylor v. Republic Grocery, 483 S.W.2d 293 (Tex. App. 1972); Hardcastle v. Greenwood Savings & Loan Assoc., 516 P.2d 228 (App. 1973); Ingalls v. Commercial Ins. Co., 118 N.W.2d 178 (Wis. 1962) (agent instructed to disregard cancellation notice that he had no authority to issue); National Bank of Commerce v. Royal Exch. Assur. Co., 455 F.2d 892 (8th Cir. 1972).

[60] Bordelon v. Herculean Risks, Inc., 241 So. 2d 766 (La. App. 1970) (insolvent carrier not authorized to do business in La.); Ritchie v. Smith, 311 So. 2d 642 (Miss. 1975) (unauthorized insurer); Bates v. Gambino, 336 A.2d 1 (N.J. 1975) (agent applied to state plan for insurance but was not aware he could issue binder which would have covered subsequent fire); Master Plumbers Mut. Liab. Co. v. Cormany & Bird, 255 N.W.2d

4. Failure to explain the boundaries and exclusions of coverage—misrepresentations of coverage;[61]
5. Failure to advise insured about differences in coverage because of renewal changes, or mistakes of which the agent was, or should have been, aware;[62]
6. Failure to obtain adequate coverage;[63]
7. Failure to process application in time.[64]

[8] Actions By Third Parties Against Agent

While it is still uncommon, a few cases have held that an agent may be liable for malpractice against innocent third parties. In one such case,[65] the plaintiff was a passenger in a vehicle which struck the rear of a tractor-trailer. She brought suit against the owner and operator of the car in which she was riding and against the owner and operator of the tractor-trailer. The plaintiff subsequently amended her complaint and asserted a direct action against the insurer and the agent of the tractor-trailer for improper termination of its liability policy. The New Jersey Superior Court denied the defendant's motion to dismiss, holding in effect that the plaintiff was a potential third party beneficiary of the liability policy and was therefore a third party beneficiary of the agreement between the agent and his client.

---

533 (Wis. 1977) (agent not liable when at time he placed the insurance, he knew or should have known of financial difficulties of the insurance company).

[61] U.S.F. & G. Co. v. McKinnon, 356 So. 2d 600 (Ala. 1978); Nowell v. Dawn-Leavitt Agency, 617 P.2d 1164 (Ariz. App. 1980) (in absence of specific payment for advice and in absence of longstanding relationship, agent was held not liable); Bramson v. Chester Jordan & Co., 379 A.2d 730 (Me. 1977); Morgan v. Wartenbee, 569 S.W.2d 391 (Mo. 1978); Portella v. Sonnenberg, 181 A.2d 385 (N.J. 1962); Rempel v. Nationwide Life Ins. Co., 323 A.2d 193 (Pa. Super. 1974); Moore v. Kluthe & Lane Ins. Agency, 234 N.W.2d 260 (S.D. 1975); Hardt v. Brinck, 192 F. Supp. 879 (Wash. 1961) (landmark case); Estate of Jerry Ensz v. Brown Ins. Agency, 224 N.W.2d 963 (Wis. 1974).

[62] Greenfield v. Insurers, Inc., 97 Cal. Rptr. 164 (App. 1971).

[63] Wright Body Works v. Columbus Interstate Ins. Agency, 210 S.E.2d 801 (Ga. 1974); Karan v. St. Paul Fire & Marine Ins. Co., 281 So. 2d 728 (La. 1973); American Home Assur. Co. v. Osbourn, 422 So. 2d 8 (Md. App. 1980).

[64] Talbot v. Country Life Ins. Co., 291 N.E.2d 830 (Ill. App. 1973); Riley v. Carver General Ins. Agency, 279 So. 2d 698 (La. App. 1973).

[65] Eschle v. Eastern Freight Ways, Inc. 319 A.2d 786 (N.J. Super. 1974).

In another case,[66] a permissive user of an automobile recovered from the owner's liability insurance agent who negligently failed to renew the owner's policy on time.

Still another case[67] involved an action by a widow against an agent who persuaded an insured to cancel a life policy as a result of his false statements.

In a recent case,[68] the court was called upon to decide the malpractice liability of an insurance agent in a situation where he failed to procure insurance in an amount requested and in line with the limits of similar policies that he had previously obtained on other vehicles owned by the insured.

The court held that there was an implied promise to procure higher limits derived from past experience and that a third party duty arose because the third party was a beneficiary of the liability policy that had insufficient limits. It was further held that the agent's negligence sparked a cause of action for malpractice arising out of a direct duty owed to the third party.

[9] Some Defenses for Malpractice Actions

There are obviously many defenses that an agent can make to an action for malpractice that are as extensive as the allegation of malfeasance. A few of the major ones are as follows.

In actions brought by the client against the agent: for nonpayment of premium;[69] failure to receive sufficient information to procure policy.[70]

In actions brought by the insurance company against its agent: failure of insurer to prove negligence; ratification by insurer of allegedly unauthorized acts:[71]

Where an agent failed to submit an application for life insurance in proper time, the court nevertheless held in his favor since the

---

[66] Midcentury Ins. Co. v. Hutsel, 89 Cal. Rptr. 421 (App. 1970).

[67] Lewis v. Citizens Agency of Medalia, 235 N.W.2d 831 (Minn. 1975).

[68] Flattery v. Gregory, 489 N.E.2d 1257 (Mass. 1986).

[69] Boyle v. Colonial Life Ins. Co., 525 S.W.2d 811 (Mo. App. 1975).

[70] Bohn v. Abbott, 339 N.E.2d 253 (Ohio 1975); Williams Fruit Co. v. Hanover Ins. Co., 474 P.2d 577 (Wash. App. 1970).

[71] Farmers & Bankers Life Ins. Co. v. Allingham, 457 F.2d 21 (Colo. 1972); Prudential Ins. Co. v. Clark, 456 F.2d 932 (Fla. 1972) (apparent ratification); General Fidelity Life Ins. Co. v. Bank of Callao, 145 S.E.2d 212 (Va. 1965).

plaintiff did not prove that the insurance company would have issued the policy even if the application had been properly submitted.[72]

In a case in Colorado,[73] a corporation bought a house from a private individual. When the insurance agent was notified of the new ownership, he told the seller that he would request that his client's homeowners policy be assigned to the new owner but neglected to do so. After a subsequent fire, the corporation found itself uninsured. However, no recovery was made against the agent since the insurance company would, in any event, not have accepted assignment of the policy to a corporation and the corporation did not prove that it could have obtained coverage otherwise.

[10] Checklist for Agents to Prevent Some Actions for Malpractice

- ☐ Make sure of client's needs, including adequate limits.
- ☐ Make sure that proper policies are issued on time and as requested. Same for renewals.
- ☐ Make no gratuitous promises of coverage where there is any doubt whatsoever.
- ☐ Make sure that proper limits are procured on policies and renewals.
- ☐ Obtain appraisals to confirm values where necessary.
- ☐ Make sure the insured understands the policy coverage when it is issued.
- ☐ Let the client make the final decision after all options have been discussed. Confirm in writing and keep written record of all phone calls or other discussions that are pertinent.
- ☐ Promptly carry out all obligations as called for in applications, renewals, binders, notices of cancellation, requirements for further information, etc.
- ☐ Understand the limits of your authorization and do not exceed them, without written permission where advisable.
- ☐ Adhere to NAIA Code of Ethics.
- ☐ Be extremely careful about acceptance of premiums after cancellation and make absolutely sure there have been no accidents in the intervening period.
- ☐ Check the information given on the application for any indication of misrepresentation.
- ☐ Make sure that all active policies are renewed on time, and that inactive ones are properly terminated with the insured's permission. Return any excess premiums promptly.

---

[72] Brunt v. Standard Life Ins. Co., 259 So. 2d 575 (La. 1972).
[73] Heller Mark & Co. v. Kassler & Co., 544 P.2d 995 (1976).

PROFESSIONAL LIABILITY—OTHER AREAS § 38.07

☐ Use special care in issuing binders and follow up to see that a proper policy is properly issued. Keep records and stay within the authorization granted.
☐ Carefully explain any policy changes made at the time of renewal, or the need for additional limits.
☐ Document significant events with letter, memos, or notations.
☐ Prepare authorized endorsements carefully and promptly and send copies to the insured and the company immediately.

§ 38.07 Bibliography

Accountants

Bergadano, "Recent Developments and Perspectives in Accountant's Professional Liability," Paper prepared for the annual ABA Meeting, August 1972.

Besser, "Privity?—An Obsolete Approach to the Liability of Accountants to Third Parties," 7 Seton Hall L. Rev. 507 (1976).

Carroll, "Accountant's Third Party Liability," Insurance Counsel Journal, April 1966.

Comment, Pace, "Negligent Misrepresentation and the Certified Public Accountant: An Overview of Common Law Liability to Third Parties," 18 Suffolk U. L. Rev. 43 (1984).

Fifles, "Current Problems of Accountants' Responsibilities to Third Parties," 28 Vand. L. Rev. 31 (1975).

Kurland, "Accountant's Legal Liability: Ultramares to Bar Chris," 25 Business Lawyer 155 (1969).

Mess, "Accountants and the Common Law: Liability to Third Parties," 52 Notre Dame L. Rev. 838 (1977).

Seybold, "Accountant's Professional Liability Policies," DRI Monograph #6 (1972).

Wiener, "Common Law Liability of the Certified Public Accountant for Negligent Misrepresentation," 20 San Diego L. Rev. 233 (1983).

Architects and Engineers

Allen, "Liability of an Architect or Engineer to Third Parties," DRI Monograph on Professional Liability of Architects and Engineers, 1969.

Carey, "Assessing Liability of Architects and Engineers for Construction Supervision," Insurance Law Journal, March 1979.

Goodwin, "Architects and Malpractice," Insurance Law Journal, April 1967.

Gouldin, "Liability of Architects and Contractors to Third Persons: Inman v. Binghamton Housing Authority Revisited," Insurance Counsel Journal, July 1966.

Hoeveler, "Architects' and Insurance Agents' Professional Liability," Insurance Law Journal, December 1966.

Kaskell, Jr., "Possible Avenues of Liability of the Architect and Engineer to Contractors and Subcontractors or How Claimants Will Try to Anticipate and Overcome the A/E's Favorite Defenses," Insurance Counsel Journal, July 1980.

Legal Handbook for Architects, Engineers, and Contractors, A. Dib. and H. Block eds. Vol. 2. New York: Clark Boardman Co. Ltd., 1986.

Maurer, Jr., "Architects, Engineers and Hold Harmless Clauses," Insurance Law Journal, December 1976.

Neeson, "The Current Status of Professional Architects' and Engineers' Malpractice Liability Insurance," Insurance Counsel Journal, January 1978.

Seybold, "Liability of Architects or Engineers to their Clients," DRI Monograph on Professional Liability of Architects and Engineers, 1969.

Truinfol, "Professional Liability of Architects and Engineers," Insurance Law Journal, August 1964.

Witherspoon, "When is an Architect Liable?", Miss. L. J., December 1960.

Wolf, "Architects, Engineers and the Statute of Limitations," DRI Monograph on Professional Liability of Architects and Engineers, 1969.

Claim Adjusters

Glad, "Liability for Individuals in the Claims Handling Process," Insurance Adjuster Magazine, September 1986.

Iconoclast, "Thinking Without a License," Insurance Adjuster Magazine, June 1983.

Sargeant, "Package Liability Insurance Protection for Adjusters Often False Security," Insurance Adjuster Magazine, December 1985.

Directors and Officers

Brown, "The Not-For-Profit Corporation Director: Legal Liabilities and Protection," FIC Quarterly, Fall 1977.

Comiskey, "Directors' and Officers' Liability Insurance—A Hypothetical Case," Insurance Counsel Journal, January 1976.

German & Gallagher, "Liability of Corporate Officers and Directors: A Brief Survey of an Expanding Field," FIC Quarterly, Spring 1980.

Kenney, Jr., "Bank Directors' and Officers' Liability," Insurance Counsel Journal, October 1971.

Knepper, "An Overview of D. & O. Liability for Insurance Company Directors and Officers," Insurance Counsel Journal, January 1978.

Wever, Jr., "Liabilities of Officers and Directors of Insurance Companies," Insurance Law Journal, July 1973.

Educators

Di Liberti, Jr., "An Apple for the Teacher: Educational Malpractice Fails Judicial Test, But Core Problem Remains," Insurance Counsel Journal, April 1986.

Kelly and McCarthy, "Educational (sic) Malpractice Worying (sic) You? You Can Breath (sic) Easier if Your Students Can Spell Better Than This," 4 Update 16, Winter 1980.

Patterson, "Professional Malpractice: Small Cloud But Growing Bigger," 62 Phi Beta Kappa 193, November 1980.

Rapp, *Education Law* (1984) §12.03.

Reddick & Peach, "What Secondary School Teachers Should Know About Tort Liability," 55 Clearing House 392, May 1982.

Insurance Agents

Hume, "Errors and Omissions Liability as Affecting Insurance Agents and Brokers," 40 Insurance Counsel Journal 379 (1973).

Maurer, "A Primer for Preventing Errors and Omissions of Insurance Agents and Brokers, " Bests Review, September 1978. Provides an excellent review for adjusters and lawyers, despite lack of citations.

O'Connor, "Liability of Insurance Agents," DRI Monograph 1970.

O'Neill, "Liability of Insurance Agents and Brokers—A Supplement," 18 F.T.D., January 1977.

Oppenheim, "Professional Malpractice: Welcome Insurance Agents and Brokers," Insurance Law Journal, December 1979.

Redenbough, "Liability Considerations Concerning Insurance Agents and Brokers," 22 Drake L. Rev. 738 (1973).

CHAPTER 39

Handling Workers' Compensation Cases

§ 39.01 General Principles
    [1] Types of Compensation Acts
    [2] State Provisions for Obtaining Coverage
§ 39.02 Administration
§ 39.03 Benefits
    [1] In General
    [2] Medical Benefits
    [3] Indemnity Benefits
    [4] Benefits to Dependents in Fatal Cases
    [5] Waiting Period
    [6] Second Injury or Special Disability Funds
§ 39.04 Those Entitled to Coverage
    [1] Exempted Groups
    [2] Injured Must Be an Employee
    [3] Determining Who is an Employee and Who is an Employer
        [a] General Contractors
        [b] Subcontractor
        [c] Independent Contractor
        [d] Checklist for Determining Claimant's Status
        [e] Partners and Corporate Officers
        [f] Dual Employment
        [g] Loaned Employees
        [h] Volunteers
        [i] Casual Employees
        [j] Statutory Employers
        [k] Checklist for Determining Type of Employee
§ 39.05 Personal Injury By Accident Arising Out of and In the Course of the Employment
    [1] Personal Injury
    [2] Accident
    [3] "Arising Out of the Employment"
    [4] "In the Course Of"
§ 39.06 Exclusive Remedy in Workers' Compensation
    [1] Remedy Exclusive Even Where No Compensation Award is Made
    [2] Derivative Suits
    [3] Action for Loss of Consortium

CASUALTY INSURANCE CLAIMS

        [4] Recent Trends in California
        [5] Dual Capacity Doctrine
        [6] Insurance Coverage Dilemma
        [7] Intentional Injury
        [8] Sexual Harassment
        [9] Exclusivity in Occupational Disease Cases
        [10] Election to Sue Employer
§ 39.07 Third Party Action
§ 39.08 Punitive Damages Arising Out of Compensation Cases
§ 39.09 Jurisdiction and Extraterritoriality
        [1] Jurisdiction
§ 39.10 Notice of Accident or Disease
§ 39.11 Liability of Successive Insurers
§ 39.12 Illegal Employment of Minors
§ 39.13 Malpractice as Related to Workers' Compensation
§ 39.14 Final Determination
§ 39.15 Rehabilitation
§ 39.16 Structured Settlements in Workers' Compensation Cases

Before workmen's (now referred to as workers') compensation laws were enacted in the various states in this country, an employee's action against his employer for damages arising out of injury sustained during the course of his employment had to be brought at common law. The basis for such an action had to be an allegation of negligence on the part of the employer.

In answer to such an action, the employer had three possible defenses: (1) contributory negligence of the employee; (2) assumption of risk; or (3) fellow servant doctrine.

Contributory negligence and assumption of risk have already been discussed in Chapter 9. The fellow servant defense, which was subsequently added by the courts, stated that if the accident occurred by reason of the act of a fellow employee, and not through any act or omission of the employer, no recovery could be made by the injured employee against the employer.

The first modification of the old common law action and defenses was made by the enactment of Employer's Liability Acts (in some states). These acts tended to minimize some of the three basic common law defenses, in certain circumstances. The employee, however, still had to prove negligence on the part of the employer before any recovery could be made.

The basic theory of compensating an injured employee regardless of his own negligence or the negligence of the employer, as long as the injury arose out of and in the course of his employment, was first promulgated in Germany, and subsequently adopted in England.

The first workmen's compensation laws in the United States were passed in 1911. In that year eleven states adopted some form of workmen's compensation act.

Despite the fact that the spread of workmen's compensation laws was temporarily halted by the courts of three states, which declared them unconstitutional, subsequent decisions by the Supreme Court upholding the constitutionality of various types of workmen's compensation laws soon spurred their enactment throughout the country. The last state to fall in line was Mississippi, which enacted a workmen's compensation law in 1948.

§ 39.01 General Principles

Unfortunately, although most of the Acts follow the same general pattern and agree in basic principles, the uniformity ends there. Details as to what is compensable, amounts covered, time limits, procedural set up, and so on, differ in almost all of the fifty states.

It is, therefore, obviously impractical to attempt to give even an outline of the specific workers' compensation laws in the various states. Each state furnishes a pamphlet on its own specific workers' compensation law. The claims person handling these cases must become familiar with the workers' compensation act of his or her particular state and the judicial interpretations relating to it.

There are, however, certain general principles that apply to all of the Workers' Compensation Acts. The information contained here will deal with those general principles and their application to claim handling.

Workers' compensation laws, since their inception, have been consistently liberalized in both benefits and coverage afforded. The only employments generally excepted from the acts are agricultural, some domestic employees, and casual laborers. Compensation acts today require practically unlimited medical expenses in almost all states.

[1] Types of Compensation Acts

Workers' Compensation Acts can be divided into three types.

1. *Elective Acts.* For the most part, the states that have adopted elective acts have done so in name only. There are few so-called elec-

§ 39.01[2]   CASUALTY INSURANCE CLAIMS

tive acts that do not provide for a penalty of some sort should an employer "elect" to remain outside the provisions of the Act. Should he do so, the employer would still be subject to suit at common law. In most of the elective acts, a further penalty is provided for the employer by removing his three common-law defenses to such an action.

2. *Compulsory Acts.* In those states operating under compulsory Workers' Compensation Acts, neither the employee nor the employer has any choice in the matter. As long as none of the exceptions (such as the number of employees or the type of their work) are applicable, both must comply with the provisions of the Act of the particular state.

3. *Compulsory or Elective Acts.* Some Workers' Compensation Acts combine features of both the elective and compulsory acts. In these cases, certain specifically described employments fall within the compulsory provisions, though others not so described are elective.

[2] **State Provisions for Obtaining Coverage**

Provision for obtaining workers' compensation coverage under the various acts falls into four general categories:

1. *Monopolistic state-managed insurance.* In the states operating under this system, an employer has no option and, with rare exceptions, cannot either be a self-insurer or obtain insurance from a private insurance company.

2. *Competitive state funds.* In some states an employer can make a choice between state-managed insurance and that of a private carrier. In some instances he may become a self-insurer.

3. *Private insurance only.* An employer must obtain insurance from a private carrier; under certain circumstances, he may become a self-insurer.

4. *Partial-monopolistic state-managed insurance.* Under some statutes, employers, upon certain expressed conditions, may be permitted to carry their own risks or insure in private companies.

§ 39.02 **Administration**

The Workers' Compensation Acts of the various states are not uniformly administered. In some states the courts are the initial administrative body. In others a commission or board is the body of initial administration. States that have no administrative set-up other than the regular courts of law are by far in the minority.

The administrative bodies usually have considerable authority, since they not only have a right of determination on the facts but may also apply these facts to the law. Although it is true that their decisions on the law are subject to review by the courts, their findings of fact are ordinarily final. There are exceptions. A few states have made their administrative bodies so weak that they are almost completely ineffectual.

Procedure before the various Workers' Compensation Boards or Industrial Commissions is very informal and not bound by technical rules of evidence.

Most states require an injured employee to notify his employer concerning an accident within a certain specified time. Some states require notice to the Industrial Commission or Workers' Compensation Board by the insurance carrier.

Most boards or commissions require that actual claims for compensation be filed with them. All states have some time limitation for the filing of such claims.

Despite the fact that most states definitely require the employee to notify his employer of an accident within a specified time, many of the acts allow an additional period known as an "excusable time" within which notice may be made. In many instances, the courts, in interpreting the various statutes, have excused late claims as well as late notice. This is especially true in those jurisdictions in which time limitations are not altogether clear and specific. Errors of fact may in some instances justify late notices or claims. The employer's knowledge of an accident has been held to excuse late notice or even no notice at all. The courts have (in some instances) excused late notice if it was not prejudicial to the employer or the insurer.

Every state has its own requirements on the type and number of forms to be completed, as well as the time limit for filing. There is certainly no dearth of forms. It is the responsibility of the claims person to learn the requirements of the Act in his particular state and to make every effort to comply to the fullest possible extent with those requirements.

§ 39.03 Benefits

[1] In General

The basic benefits provided by the workers' compensation laws include (1) medical and hospital expenses; (2) payment for lost wages; (3) payment for loss of bodily members or loss of sight; (4) continued payments, sometimes including a lump sum, or sometimes in lieu of regular payments, for total disability; (5) cost of prosthetic devices; (6) rehabilitation costs; (6) death benefits for dependents; lump sum payments in the event of certain partial disabilities and in applicable cases; and (7) custodial care where necessary.

While the law was never intended to compensate an injured employee for complete loss of wages (to minimize malingering and to encourage recuperation), it is fast approaching that level in some states and in certain instances.

The workers' compensation laws provide no payment for such nebulous damages as pain and suffering or emotional distress. Disfigurement, however, does usually call for a monetary award in some cases, in some instances, and in certain jurisdictions.

[2] Medical Benefits

Most Acts do not specify the exact amount payable for doctor's or hospital bills. Many states, however, do have what is known as a "fee schedule" for some types of medical services. These statutes usually have a list of approved physicians who are required to keep their charges within the fee schedule.

The various states run the gamut for amounts allowable under medical benefits, from certain small amounts limited to a comparatively minor period of time up to unlimited amounts for an unlimited time.

For the most part, the Acts specify the particular expenses that fall within this category. Such items as doctors' fees, surgeons' fees, hospital expenses, and nurses' fees are universally considered proper medical expenses. In some states, however, the courts have enlarged the meaning of this term to include such items as practical nurses' care in the home, convalescent home expenses, and even room and lodging where greater expense would have been incurred, possibly necessitating confinement to a hospital, had these items not been provided for.

In cases of prolonged disability, insurance companies have gone far afield and have even considered such items as expenses incurred for morale-boosting visits to the injured, and have paid for such items under the medical expense provision.

The question whether fees of a chiropractor or osteopath are justifiable medical expenses depends upon the wording of the Act or the interpretation placed upon it by the courts of a particular jurisdiction. For the most part, expenses for treatment by faith healers, naturopaths, and the like, are not considered medical expenses.

[3] Indemnity Benefits

The benefits paid to the injured employee as a direct result of his loss of weekly earnings are known as indemnity or compensation benefits. These benefits are a portion of the employee's wages; they are paid to him while he is unable to perform the regular duties of his employment.

Usually, the Act specifies what percent of the regular salary will be paid to the injured, subject to a specified maximum. Most states also specify the duration in number of weeks for which benefits are to be paid. In some states, under certain circumstances, benefits may be continued for life.

Payments may be made on the basis of temporary total, permanent total, or permanent partial disability.

Most states have what are known as "scheduled" injuries that provide for the payment of a stipulated amount for certain permanent partial disabilities. Some provision is usually made in the Act to permit a small saving on lump sum settlements by discharging the entire liability in one payment.

In some jurisdictions, settlements are permitted if the percentage of disability has been agreed upon between the injured and the carrier. In other jurisdictions, this figure must meet with Board approval, and, in some instances, must be set by the Board. Such settlements are final in many jurisdictions, but there are some states in which no final settlement can ever be made.

The claims person must, of course, be careful to learn whether a temporary disability is allowed in addition to permanent partial, or whether the temporary disability is to be deducted from the permanent partial allowance. Many states have variations in limitation with which he must become familiar.

§ 39.03[4]　　　　CASUALTY INSURANCE CLAIMS

In some states the Act leaves room for doubt; the courts have held that the allowance for permanent partial is in addition to the amount already paid or allowed for temporary disability.

[4] Benefits to Dependents in Fatal Cases

All states make some provision for benefits to be paid a dependent spouse and minor children in fatal cases, but, as usual, the range of benefits is wide.

It is not always, however, an easy matter to determine who is a dependent spouse and who are dependent minors that come within the various Acts. Some states recognize common law marriages, others do not. Legitimacy of offspring sometimes has a bearing on whether they can recover under the Act. Divorce often affects dependency.

Dependents may not necessarily mean spouse or children only. In some states, close relatives and even relatives by marriage, and people totally unrelated to the deceased may, under certain circumstances, be considered dependents. In some jurisdictions, a distinction is made between a total and partial dependent. In some Acts, benefits to the dependent spouse cease if he or she remarries.

All the Acts make some provision for paying at least a part of the funeral expenses.

[5] Waiting Period

Aside from some loss of a member, or other scheduled disability, the various workers' compensation laws require some time lost from work before permitting indemnity recovery, usually ranging from one to seven days.

There are two types of waiting periods. In one type, indemnity is never paid for the waiting period. In the other type, the waiting period is paid for if the disability lasts beyond a required specified time.

[6] Second Injury or Special Disability Funds

Very often, a claimant who has received a previous partial disability becomes totally disabled as a result of an additional injury, which to a normal person would only have been partially disabling. For instance, an injury to an eye might totally and permanently incapacitate someone who had already lost the sight of his other eye as a result of some previous injury or disease. Most courts have held that the employer at the time the second injury was incurred is responsible for permanent and total disability.

It is only natural, therefore, that some employers are reluctant to hire persons who suffer some previous disability. The legislatures of many states have recognized this problem; it directly affects the disabled person and places a handicap on him in addition to his disability. These states have set up what are known as "Second Injury Funds." To varying degrees they relieve the employer and his carrier from carrying the full burden of a permanent and total disability in the event of injury to an already partially incapacitated individual. The Funds are usually set up from special taxes or assessments levied against all companies doing business in the state.

It is therefore quite evident that the claims person should familiarize himself with the provisions of the Act governing the Second Injury Fund, if it contains such provisions.

§ 39.04 Those Entitled to Coverage

[1] Exempted Groups

All the Acts contain some provision that may exclude certain employees from coverage. These provisions are generally as follows.

1. *Exceptions for numerical reasons.* Some Acts may exempt an employer and his employees from coming within the provision if the employer has fewer than two people in his employ. The number may range as high as ten or more. In any event, unless an employer has more employees than the number numerically excepted in the Act, neither the employer nor his employees come within the provision of the Act.

It should be noted that the required number of employees must exceed the minimum amount for those workers who would ordinarily fall within the Act. In other words, if agricultural or domestic workers were exempt from the Act, it would not matter how many such employees the employer had. They would not add to the numerical count.

2. *Farm and agricultural workers.* Many of the Acts make some provision for exempting certain types of farm or agricultural workers.

3. *Domestic servants.* Many acts exempt domestic servants from the provisions of the Act.

4. *Certain nonhazardous occupations.* Some Acts make exception in the case of some usually specified occupations which are ordinarily considered as nonhazardous.

5. *Various other exceptions.* These run the gamut from athletes to employees of charitable organizations, depending on the particular Act involved. The claims person must learn the excluded occupations in his own Workers' Compensation Act.

[2] **Injured Must Be an Employee**

Once we have gotten by the exempted groups, we find that the principal prerequisite for recovery under Workers' Compensation Acts is, of course, that the injured be an employee.

Ordinarily, employment is so obvious that it presents no unusual difficulties. There are, however, many instances in which the relationship is questionable. It is to these unusual circumstances that we now devote our attention.

Usually, the original report of accident and the preliminary investigation will indicate that there is no question concerning employment. The problem of obtaining confirmation from the employer is then a relatively simple one.

The questionable case, however, contains many pitfalls for the unwary claim representative. In the serious cases at least, an extensive investigation should be completed if there is any reason to suspect anything other than a direct employer-employee relationship.

There is no simple definition of "employee" that will fit all of the circumstances. The principal consideration is control. To determine control, the claim representative must look into the character and conditions of the employment in all its aspects.

[3] **Determining Who is an Employee and Who is an Employer**

Workers' compensation policies may be written that designate the following as employers: individuals, partnerships, corporations, individuals operating under trade names, municipalities, school districts, corporations engaged in joint ventures, estates, receiverships, or other legal entities.

There are many people who perform services for another but do not qualify for benefits under the Workers' Compensation Acts of many states because they are independent contractors, volunteers, subcontractors, or others who are not considered employees within the meaning of the Workers' Compensation Act.

We will therefore discuss those categories in which the line is not clear-cut and in which detailed investigation must be undertaken in order to make a definite determination.

[a] General Contractors

A general contractor is one who has been entrusted with the completion of an over-all operation. He may have direct employees on his payroll doing all of the work, a part of the work, or he may operate entirely through subcontractors.

Under the Workers' Compensation Acts, general contractors are usually held responsible for injuries to employees of uninsured subcontractors as well as to their own direct employees.

If the state Act so holds, you may be required to make payment to the injured worker of an uninsured subcontractor. In such case, however, you would have the right to proceed against the subcontractor for reimbursement, or, on audit of the premium, receive remuneration as a basis for the premium rate.

It is important in this respect to distinguish between owners and general contractors, since an owner may have no responsibility to the employees of contractors if he, the owner, could not be said to have met the legal definition and requirements of a general contractor.

[b] Subcontractor

A subcontractor is one who agrees to complete one part of an over-all job. This part may be assigned to him either by the owner or the general contractor. He is, of course, primarily responsible for injuries that occur to his workers within the scope of the Workers' Compensation Act. However, as has previously been stated, if he does not obtain compensation insurance to cover his employees, the Act may hold the general contractor responsible for payments.

[c] Independent Contractor

It is often very difficult to distinguish between employer-employee and independent contractor relationships. Generally speaking, the right of direction and control and the right to hire and fire will go a long way toward making this determination.

§ 39.04[3][d]   CASUALTY INSURANCE CLAIMS

In some instances, employers will enter into a written contract that attempts to establish an independent contractor relationship without meeting the usual tests for this relationship. The courts and administrating agencies will not usually recognize any such attempted subterfuge. They will, in any event, hold that the injured person is an employee rather than an independent contractor if the facts do not meet the requirements they have set up.

[d] Checklist for Determining Claimant's Status

The following checklist should help to determine the status of the injured individual:

- ☐ Was the claimant engaged in work that required specialized skill?
- ☐ Who hired the claimant?
- ☐ Who paid claimant?
- ☐ On whose payroll records is claimant listed?
- ☐ Who controlled claimant's activities?
- ☐ Who had the right to fire claimant?
- ☐ Was claimant paid by the hour, day, week, or month?
- ☐ Did claimant receive a regular salary or was claimant on piecework or commission? Was claimant paid through a combination of these?
- ☐ Was claimant on an expense account? How did claimant have to account for expenses?
- ☐ Was there any other consideration in lieu of salary, such as board, lodging, use of a car, or other expenses?
- ☐ Was there any contract in existence between the parties, either oral or written? If written, obtain a copy.
- ☐ Was the contract made in advance for a definite consideration?
- ☐ Was there any regulation concerning the hours worked? What were the hours?
- ☐ Who directed the method of operation?
- ☐ Who had the right of inspection?
- ☐ Was a lump sum agreed upon in advance for the entire job?
- ☐ Who furnished the materials, supplies, and work clothes? Who paid for them?
- ☐ Whose tools were being used?
- ☐ Who furnished transportation?
- ☐ Was the claimant permitted to hire extra help? If so, who did the hiring and who paid the help?
- ☐ Does the claimant maintain a separate business establishment, either at an office or at home?
- ☐ Does the claimant pay the maintenance costs, such as rent, electricity, water, telephone, and so on?

- [ ] Does the claimant have a business card or a sign at his place of business that advertises his services to the general public?
- [ ] Does the claimant hold himself out to hire by the public?
- [ ] Does the claimant perform similar work for others on a contract basis?
- [ ] Was it necessary to obtain an official license or special permit to perform the work that the claimant was doing? Obtain copy.
- [ ] Does the claimant have a social security number?
- [ ] Was social security deducted from pay or any other withholdings made for tax purposes such as unemployment insurance, and so on?
- [ ] Is the claimant on any pension plan?

[e] Partners and Corporate Officers

Injuries involving partners and officers of corporations require careful investigation and close scrutiny. Many states permit them to be considered employees, with certain limitations.

There is always the moral risk to be considered, since the officer or the partner is the person to whom we usually go for confirmation of a fact. There is always the possibility of fraud and certainly a greater temptation toward it.

Some jurisdictions require that a partner, in order to be considered an employee coming within the Act, must receive wages independent of profits.

Both partners and corporate officers must, of course, be performing work that meets all the other requirements of the Act.

[f] Dual Employment

Quite often the claims person will run into a situation of dual employment; for instance, the case of a commissioned salesperson who works for more than one employer.

It is, of course, imperative in these instances that the claims person determine whose interests were being served at the time the injury occurred. In some jurisdictions the law holds that all employers must share in the cost of the claim if the salesperson intended selling any of their products during the trip, even though he may not have been doing so at the time of the injury. This, however, is the minority view.

[g] Loaned Employees

Under certain conditions, one employer may loan an employee to another. The first thing to determine is whether the Act makes specific provision for liability in cases of loaned employees. In some instances it has been held that either employer may be held liable. Usually, the general employer will be held liable for an injury to a loaned employee if the employee is loaned with machinery or equipment and the injury arises directly out of the use of such machinery or equipment.

[h] Volunteers

Compensation benefits are usually denied to most persons who are mere volunteers and who render some service to an employer without pay or hiring agreement of any kind. The tendering or acceptance of a gratuity, in most cases, will not affect the status of the volunteer. Some states have held that under certain emergency conditions a volunteer may be considered as an employee. This may also be true if an employee has been given the authority to hire additional help.

It is important in cases of this kind, that the claim adjuster determine not only the conditions under which the injured person rendered the assistance, but also whether the person to whom the assistance was rendered has the authority to hire additional help. This situation arises quite frequently when truck drivers require assistance in loading or unloading a vehicle, or when trucks become temporarily disabled and require assistance so that the assigned job may be completed.

[i] Casual Employees

Casual employees may be defined as those who are sporadically employed in connection with the employer's business, or employed merely by chance. The provision presumes that the employment is not regular, periodic, or recurrent. The essential test under most statutes is whether the work performed is outside the usual business of the employer.

Although some states exclude this class of employee, many states have now revised their Act so as to bring them within its jurisdiction.

[j] Statutory Employers

Under certain circumstances, the compensation acts of many states hold that independent contractors and their employees are employees of the general contractor or owner of the business or premises upon which they are working. An owner or general contractor is, under the scope of these acts, made an employer by statute.

Some states accomplish a similar purpose by making the owner or general contractor responsible for compensation insurance coverage for a subcontractor's employees if the former has not required the subcontractor to carry his own compensation insurance.

[k] Checklist for Determining Type of Employee

The following checklist should help to make a determination concerning what type of employee the injured is:

- ☐ Was claimant a loaned employee?
- ☐ What were the circumstances involved in the lending?
- ☐ Was there a transfer of payroll and tax deductions?
- ☐ What was the understanding of the injured?
- ☐ Who directed the claimant's work?
- ☐ Was there a transfer of the right to hire and fire?
- ☐ Was any specific time limit or job limit specified?
- ☐ What type of work was claimant doing?
- ☐ Was there a general or special employer?
- ☐ Was claimant working for more than one employer?
- ☐ Was claimant either a subcontractor or the employee of a subcontractor? Get a copy of the original contract.
- ☐ Was claimant a volunteer?
- ☐ Was claimant a casual employee not engaged in the regular course of the employer's trade?
- ☐ Was work performed at home? If so, was a certificate of permission necessary and has one been issued?

§ 39.05 Personal Injury By Accident Arising Out of and In the Course of the Employment

Most Workers' Compensation Acts in this country require that disability must result from *personal injury by accident arising out of and in the course of the employment.*

This sentence has probably been the cause of more litigation than anything else in the field of worker's compensation. It has, as a matter of fact, caused so much controversy that we will have to discuss the sentence in four separate parts.

[1] Personal Injury

There is of course no problem if a direct and accidental force is applied to the body of the claimant resulting in obvious injury. There is, however, a definite question whether shock or neurosis resulting from fright is considered personal injury within the meaning of the statutes. At the present time, although some states refuse to recognize shock without impact as injury, most states do recognize it.

Some jurisdictions have held that a disease is not an injury. Most have modified this, and permit awards if there was unusual exposure to the disease itself or to a condition which might lead to contraction of the disease.

Most states now hold to the theory that any damage to the body may be considered as personal injury. They have, in fact, gone so far as to include damage to false eyes, teeth, arms, and other prosthetic appliances, so long as some accompanying injury has been sustained to the body in the area of the damaged property.

[2] Accident

A few of those states that adopted the wording of the original English Act have eliminated the words "by accident" entirely, or have somewhat modified it. Most of the Acts, however, include "accident" in the wording.

In the discussion of coverage under the Automobile and Public Liability policies, we have already considered the meaning of the word "accident." The courts, in interpreting Workers' Compensation Acts, have gone far afield from the liability requirement of a sudden, unexpected, or unforeseen event.

Those states that still use the word "accident" have, by and large, made other provisions for the inclusion of occupational diseases under their Acts.

Assaults have been pretty uniformly interpreted as accidents under the broad theory that anything which occurs unexpectedly to the claimant is accidental, at least as far as he is concerned.

[3] "Arising Out of the Employment"

Although some of the Workers' Compensation Acts have somewhat modified this wording, most of them still contain the original phraseology of the English Act.

WORKERS' COMPENSATION CASES   § 39.05[3]

There is no definite yardstick that can be used to determine whether an injury arose out of the employment. The great majority of cases that occur in factories or as a result of motor vehicle accidents are unquestionably covered; these present no particular problem. There is also a small, ever decreasing group of disabilities that are clearly personal to the claimant and have no relationship whatsoever to the employment, such as death because of old age, or disease contracted away from work and not aggravated by it.

The claim adjuster's chief difficulty will lie with those claims that fall between these two extremes. There is an ever-increasing tendency to hold them compensable. Examples of this class are injuries resulting from an epileptic fit during which some object was struck before the claimant reached the floor, or tornado or windstorm incidents during which injury was inflicted when some object was blown onto the claimant.

Originally, our administrative bodies and courts held that an injury, in order to be compensable, had to be caused by an accident or exposure which was peculiar to the employment, or which resulted from a risk which was increased by reason of employment, as distinct from a hazard which the general public might encounter under ordinary circumstances. It was not necessary that employment increase the *kind* of exposure; if employment increased the *degree* of exposure, any resulting injury was compensable.

For instance, an employee doing hard manual labor in the hot sun is subject to the same kind of exposure that a member of the general public might encounter. It is presumed, however, that the general public will not ordinarily remain in the heat for any length of time; the laborer's exposure is inherent in the nature of his work, and injury arising from such exposure is compensable since it arises out of the employment.

This concept is being modified by an ever-increasing body of decisions which hold that an accident or incident is compensable as long as it can be shown to have arisen as a result of the employment, despite the fact that the kind or even the degree of risk was common to the general public. The trend is best exemplified by the large body of decisions concerning sidewalk accidents. An overwhelming majority of these are held to be compensable as long as the employee was in the course of his employment at the time of injury.

The courts in a few jurisdictions have applied the "positional risk" rule which in effect holds that recovery can be made if the accident could not have happened had not the nature of the employment placed the employee in a situation in which he could be injured.

The tendency today is to follow the broadest concept, or *actual risk* rule. This in effect holds that if the injury was an actual risk arising out of the claimant's employment it is covered, regardless of other factors.

If the cause either of death or injury is unknown, the problem is quite complex. Decision must be arrived at on an individual basis, depending upon the interpretations previously given and the trend of the local courts and administrative bodies.

Ordinarily, if horseplay is involved, the innocent victim is permitted recovery if he has not taken part in the horseplay. Courts have generally denied recovery to the instigator unless the employer previously condoned such practice.

Some statutes prevent recovery if intoxication can be shown to be the cause of the injury. In those states in which the statute is silent on this subject, it is ordinarily necessary to prove that intoxication was the sole or at least the primary cause of injury.

The cases falling within the scope of injuries sustained as the result of an *Act of God* have also been quite controversial in nature. Originally, a majority of the decisions indicated that the claimant had to be placed in a position of danger greater than that of the ordinary person in order to come within the Act.

The overwhelming trend today, however, is toward liberalizing this interpretation. Some courts still require that an additional intervening cause contribute to the injury, such as the collapse of a wall after a hurricane strikes the building, or the fall of a tree after lightning strikes it. Most are now leaning toward the interpretation that if the claimant would not have been there but for the fact that his work required him to be there, recovery can be made.

Some of the Acts deny recovery if the employee has been guilty of serious or willful misconduct. Failure to obey an instruction, or ordinary neglect, is hardly ever sufficient grounds for denying coverage.

[4] "In the Course Of"

The words "arising out of" are ordinarily construed to refer to the causal connection between the act and the employment. The latter part of the phrase, "in the course of," is ordinarily interpreted to refer to the time, place, or general circumstances surrounding the incident.

It has been held that an accident occurs "in the course of" employment if it occurs while the employee is doing what a person so employed may reasonably do within a time during which he is employed, and at a place where he may reasonably be, during that time.

There is usually little question about "in the course of" when the injury occurs during regular working hours. There is also little question about incidents which occur while the employee is working overtime, so long as he is actually furthering his employer's business with the employer's tacit or actual consent.

There has been a good deal of controversy concerning injuries which occur during the lunch hour. Most courts have held these to be covered if the injury occurred on the insured's premises, and have usually so held if it occurred on the way in or out of the premises.

A majority of our courts have held that in order for an employee to come within the Act while on his way to or from work, he must have reached the employer's premises or at least that area adjacent to it. Some exceptions to this general rule are as follows:

1. If traveling is part of the employment itself, as in the case of salespeople, deliver people, and other outside workers.
2. If the employee is subject to call for duty at any hour during the day or night.
3. If transportation to and from work is supplied by the employer.
4. If there is a contract of hire that runs from portal to portal.
5. In some instances, if the employee is either permitted to take work home with him or has been instructed to do so.

§ 39.06 Exclusive Remedy in Workers' Compensation

In promulgating the Workers' Compensation Acts, the legislatures and Congress tried to balance the equities between the employer and the employee by removing some rights from the employee in return for the creation of a new limited obligation upon the employer. Accordingly, most Workers' Compensation Acts provide that if the employee falls within the provisions of the Act, the original intent of the Acts was that recovery under them was to be an exclusive remedy against the employer. In other words, by becoming a beneficiary under the Workers' Compensation Act, the employee of necessity

§ 39.06　　　　　　　CASUALTY INSURANCE CLAIMS

was supposed to give up any common law right of action against his employer.

While we will see that the general principle is as full of holes as a sieve, many courts still give lip-service to the general precept that if a workers' compensation act is applicable, it provides the exclusive remedy for the injury sustained by an employee against his or her employer and insurer.[1]

Several federal courts applying the law of direct action states, followed the same general interpretation of the exclusive remedy section of the Act.[2]

The constitutionality of this section of the compensation acts has been tested to the point where there is little doubt that this provision, as it has appeared in the compensation laws, is constitutional.[3]

---

[1] **Ariz.:** Vineyard v. Southwest Eng'g & Contracting Co., 570 P.2d 823 (App. 1977).
Ark.: Campbell v. Waggoner, 360 S.W.2d 124 (1962).
Cal.: Benjamin v. Ricks, 132 Cal. Rptr. 758 (1976); Balido v. Improved Mach., Inc., 105 Cal. Rptr. 890 (1973).
Conn.: Horney v. Johnson, 356 A.2d 879 (1975).
Ga.: Mitchell v. Hercules, Inc., 410 F. Supp. 560 (1976).
Idaho: Provo v. Bunker Hill Co., 393 F. Supp. 778 (1975).
Ill.: Vansickle v. Summers, 304 N.E.2d 132 (App. 1973).
Iowa: Kerrigan v. Firestone Tire & Rubber Co., 207 N.W.2d 578 (1973).
Kan.: Griffin v. United States, 644 F.2d 846 (10th Cir. 1981).
Me.: Davis v. Bath Iron Works Corp., 338 A.2d 146 (1975).
Mo.: Leicht v. Venture Stores, Inc., 562 S.W.2d 401 (App. 1978).
Nev.: Snow v. United States, 479 F. Supp. 936 (1979).
N.Y.: Canty v. Graer Children's Community, 387 N.Y.S.2d 292 (1976), 394 N.Y.S.2d 883 (1977); Brinkman v. Buffalo Bills Football Club, 433 F. Supp. 699 (1977).
Pa.: Turner v. Southeastern Pa. Trans. Authority, 389 A.2d 591 (1978); Shaner v. Caterpillar Tractor Co., 483 F. Supp. 705 (1980).
P.R.: Rodriguez v. Litton Industries Leasing Corp., 574 F.2d 44 (1st Cir. 1978).
Tenn: McBride v. Tennessee Valley Authority, 395 F. Supp. 1181 (1974), *aff'd*, 513 F.2d 632 (1975).
Wyo.: Jordan v. Delta Drilling Co., 541 P.2d 39 (1975) (exception applies to fellow employees and manufacturer of any product involved).

[2] **La.:** Hughes v. Chitty, 283 F. Supp. 734, *aff'd*, 415 F.2d 1150 (1969).
P.R.: Rodriguez v. Litton Industries Leasing Corp., 574 F.2d 44 (1978).
See also "The Law of Workmen's Compensation" by Arthur Larson, chapter XII, which covers this subject excellently and in much greater detail.

[3] **Ga.:** Williams v. Byrd, 247 S.E.2d 874 (1978).
La.: Flynn v. Devore, 373 So. 2d 580 (App. 1980).
Utah: Star v. Industrial Commission, 615 P.2d 436 (1980).

[1] Remedy Exclusive Even Where No Compensation Award is Made

There are, of course, many instances where no recovery is made under compensation despite the fact that the accident itself fell within the provisions of the Act.

In some states, even though recovery for intentional infliction of emotional distress is not compensable, such an action may not be brought at common law where it may be recoverable, if the incident out of which the alleged distress was caused, fell within the Act.[4]

A leading case on this subject[5] involved a claimant who had suffered an injury to his pubic nerve in an accident arising out of and in the course of his employment. As a result of his injury, the claimant was rendered impotent.

While he was not entitled to compensation because his injury did not render him disabled, he was denied the right to bring a common law suit because the Act was held to be exclusive in remedy.

Under the Georgia Act, no recovery can be made for disfigurement, but the Georgia courts have held that, again, since the accident out of which the disfigurement arose fell within the Act, the exclusive feature of the Act prevented the injured from bringing an action at common law.[6]

In Pennsylvania, injuries caused by a violation of the law are excepted from the Compensation Act, but the federal court has held that the exclusionary provision of the Act was nevertheless, effective.[7]

Occupational disease acts often have many exceptions and restrictions on recovery or the amount to be recovered. In Montana, an injured workman did not receive a compensation award because he was exposed to silicon dust less than the required 1,000 work shifts required under the Montana Act. He was denied the right to sue under common law.[8]

A few decisions have held that even occupational diseases that were not listed in the Act nevertheless fell within the exclusive provi-

---

[4] Mich.: Cowan v. Federal Mogul Corp., 273 N.W.2d 487 (1979).
[5] Minn.: Hyett v. Northwestern Hosp., 180 N.E. 552 (1920).
[6] Nowell v. Stone Mountain Scenic Ry., 257 S.E.2d 344 (1979).
[7] Carey v. Electric Mut. Liab. Ins. Co., 500 F. Supp. 1227 (1980).
[8] Anaconda Co. v. District Court of S.J.D., 506 P.2d 81 (1973).

sions of the Occupational Disease Act under consideration.[9] These were undoubtedly exceptional situations.

Compensation awards are frequently denied because of a failure to prove the accident, or that it did not happen as alleged, or because of a failure to prove compensable injury, etc., and in most such instances, the courts have disallowed recovery at common law where the alleged incident fell within the general provisions of the Act.[10]

[2] Derivative Suits

Many compensation acts, or the court's interpretation of them, consider derivative suits by relatives or other dependents to be based upon the injury covered under the Act and hold that the exclusive provisions of such Acts apply to derivative suits at common law as well as to suits by the injured personally.[11]

In Massachusetts, the court held that a previous recovery by an injured worker under compensation did not bar a liability suit by his wife and children.[12]

In Kentucky, a wife was permitted to bring a common law action by statutory enactment.[13]

---

[9] **Ind.:** Brewington v. Radio Corp. of America, 210 F. Supp. 204 (1962).
N.C.: Murphy v. American Enka Corp., 195 S.E.2d 536 (1928).
[10] **D.C.:** Tredway v. District of Columbia, 403 A.2d 732 (App. 1979).
Md.: Decius v. Marriott Corp., 402 A.2d 841 (1979).
N.Y.: Fetterhoff v. Western Block Co., 373 N.Y.S.2d 920 (1975).
[11] **Ala.:** Phillips v. Unijax, Inc., 462 F. Supp. 942 (1978), *reversed on other grounds*, 625 F.2d 54 (1980) (action by widow); Slagle v. Reynolds, Metals Co., 344 So. 2d 1216 (1977) (suit by father).
Alas.: Wright v. Action Vending Co., Inc., 544 P.2d 82 (1975) (suit by wife).
Ariz.: Mariscal v. American Smelting & Refining Co., 548 P.2d 412 (1976).
Cal.: Casaccia v. Green Valley Disposal Co., Inc., 133 Cal. Rptr. 295 (1976) (suit by wife); Soil Eng'g Constr., Inc. v. Superior Court, 136 Cal. 3d 329 (1982) (suit by parents of deceased).
Ill.: Collier v. Wagner Casting Co., 388 N.E.2d 265 (1979) (suit by wife).
Kan.: Stonecipher v. Winn-Rau Corp., 545 P.2d 317 (1976) (suit by parents).
La.: Branch v. Aetna Cas. & Sur. Co., 370 So. 2d 1270 (App. 1979) (suit by parents); Shepard v. Louisiana Power & Light Co., Inc., 369 So. 2d 1196 (App. 1979) (suit by parents).
Me.: Abshire v. City of Rockland, 388 A.2d 512 (1978) (suit by wife.)
Mo.: Leicht v. Venture Stores, Inc., 562 S.W.2d 401 (App. 1978) (action by husband).
Utah: Star v. Industrial Commission, 615 P.2d 436 (1980) (suit by mother).
Wash.: West v. Zeibell, 550 P.2d 522 (1976) (suit by parents).
[12] Ferriter v. O'Connell's Sons, Inc., 413 N.E.2d 690 (1980).
[13] Johnson v. Lohre, 508 S.W.2d 785 (1974).

[3] Action for Loss of Consortium

Another important instance of a breach of the exclusive remedy provisions of the compensation acts, and one that stirred quite a bit of controversy in legal circles, was the case of *Hitaffer v. Argonne Company.*[14]

In this case, the wife of an employee brought an action in her behalf for loss of consortium arising out of an accident for which compensation had already been paid under the Longshoremen and Harbor Worker's Compensation Act. The federal court declared that a wife not only had the right to recover for loss of consortium, but that the exclusive remedy provision of the Act did not bar her recovery because this was a separate and independent cause of action that was not directly related to the rights of the employee, under the Act.

Hitaffer v. Argonne Co.[15] was the first case to hold (1) that a wife has a common law right of action for loss of her husband's consortium despite a long string of previous decisions to the contrary, and (2) that such an action was not barred by even a severely exclusionary provision in the Act.

This case was followed by many courts in the following years.[16]

---

[14] 183 F.2d 811, *cert. denied,* 340 U.S. 852 (1950).

[15] *Id.*

[16] **Ala.:** Williams v. Alabama Neon Sign Co., 304 So. 2d 895 (1974).

Alas.: Schreiner v. Fruit, 519 P.2d 462 (1974), *but see* Wright v. Action Vending Co., 544 P.2d 82 (1975).

Ariz.: Glendale v. Bradshaw, 503 P.2d 803 (1972).

Ark.: Missouri Pacific Transp. Co. v. Miller, 299 S.W.2d 41 (1957).

Cal.: Pesce v. Summa Corp., 126 Cal. Rptr. 451 (1975); *but see* also Casaccia v. Green Valley Disposal Co., Inc., 133 Cal. Rptr. 295 (1976).

Colo.: Crouch v. West, 477 P.2d 805 (App. 1970).

Del.: Yonner v. Adams, 167 A.2d 717 (1961).

D.C.: Rollins v. District of Columbia, 265 F.2d 347 (1959).

Fla.: Gates v. Foley, 247 So. 2d 40 (1971).

Ga.: Brown v. Georgia-Tenn. Coaches, Inc., 77 S.E.2d 24 (1953).

Idaho: Rindlisbaker v. Wilson, 519 P.2d 421 (1974), *but see also* Coddington v. City of Lewiston, 525 P.2d 330 (1974).

Ill.: Dini v. Maiditch, 170 N.E.2d 881 (1960).

Ind.: Troue v. Marker, 252 N.E.2d 800 (1969).

Iowa: Acuff v. Schmit, 78 N.E.2d 480 (1956).

Ky.: Johnson v. Lohres, 508 S.W.2d 785 (1979) (by statute).

Md.: Deems v. Western Maryland Ry. Co., 231 A.2d 514 (1967).

Mass.: Diaz v. Eli Lilly & Co., 302 N.E.2d 555 (1973).

Mich.: Montgomery v. Stephan, 101 N.W.2d 227 (1960).

Minn.: Thill v. Modern Erecting Co., 170 N.W.2d 865 (1969).

Miss.: Tribble v. Gregory, 288 So. 2d 13 (1974).

In 1957, the federal court overruled the *Hitaffer* decision[17] and some other courts have also refused to follow in the footsteps of *Hitaffer,* continuing to hold that the exclusive provision of the Compensation Act is clear and applicable in this kind of a situation.[18]

[4] Recent Trends in California

In the last few years some additional major inroads have been made to the exclusive remedy provisions of the California Workers' Compensation Act by the California courts, never hesitant to erode legislative intent by judicial subversion.

Heretofore, and generally speaking, employees who are subject to the California Workers' Compensation Act could recover only under the Act where (1) both the employer and the employee are subject to California jurisdiction, (2) if the employee was within and during the course of his employment and was performing some duty or service arising out of such employment, and (3) if the injury was caused proximately by such employment.

Mo.: Novak v. Kansas City Transit, Inc., 365 S.W.2d 539 (1969).
Mont.: Duffy v. Lipsman-Fulkerson & Co., 200 F. Supp. 71 (1961).
Neb.: Luther v. Maple, 250 F.2d 916 (8th Cir. 1958) (statute).
Nev.: General Electric Co. v. Bush, 498 P.2d 366 (1972).
N.J.: Ekalo v. Constructive Service Corp., 215 A.2d 1 (1965).
N.Y.: Millington v. Southeastern Elevator Co., 293 N.Y.S.2d 305 (1969).
N.C.: Nicholson v. Hugh Chatham Memorial Hosp., 266 S.E.2d 818 (1980).
N.D.: Hastings v. James River Aerie, 246 N.W.2d 747 (1976).
Ohio: Clouston v. Remlinger Olds. Cadillac, Inc., 258 N.E.2d 230 (1970).
Okla.: Duncan v. General Motors Corp., 499 F.2d 835 (10th Cir. 1974) (by statute).
Ore.: Ross v. Cuthbert, 397 P.2d 529 (1965).
Pa.: Hopkins v. Blanco, 320 A.2d 139 (1974).
S.D.: Hoekstra v. Helgeland, 98 N.W.2d 669 (1959).
Tenn.: Burroughs v. Jordan, 456 S.W.2d 652 (1970).
Tex.: Copelin v. Reed Tool Co., 596 S.W.2d 302 (App. 1980).
Wash.: Lundgren v. Whitney's, Inc., 614 P.2d 1272 (1980).
W. Va.: King v. Bittinger, 231 S.E.2d 239 (1977).
Wis.: Moran v. Quality Alum. Casting Co., 150 N.W.2d 137 (1967).
See Larson "The Law of Workmen's Compensation", Supp. 2A.
[17] Smither & Co. v. Coles, 242 F.2d 220 (1957).
[18] **Kan.:** Fritzson v. City of Manhattan, 528 P.2d 1193 (1974).
Me.: Abshire v. City of Rockland, 388 A.2d 512 (1978).
N.H.: O'Keefe v. Associated Grocers of New England, Inc., 370 A.2d 261 (1977) (1971 amendment to Act makes it exclusive), *but see also* Ahern v. Laconia Country Club Inc., 392 A.2d 587 (1978), holding contra.

Sections 3600 and 3601 were intended to make it quite clear that the compensation remedy was exclusive and in lieu of any other liability of the employer.

Nevertheless, California now recognizes three exceptions to the exclusive remedy provisions in addition to those mentioned heretofore, as follows:

1. Where the employer is charged with an intentional act that caused an injury to his employee for which compensation benefits are not the sole remedy, such as the intentional infliction of emotional distress.
2. Where the employer is guilty of aggravation of the original work connected injury by intentional misconduct through concealment or misrepresentation.
3. Where the injury was caused by the conduct of the employer acting in the capacity other than that of employer, usually involving the manufacture or distribution of a product which the employee was coincidentally using and which caused the injury.

[5] Dual Capacity Doctrine

The dual capacity doctrine holds that an employer may lose his exclusivity immunity after an award is made in favor of his employee if he exercises a secondary association with his employee, as a result of which he assumed duties and obligations in addition to those imposed on him as an employer.[19]

Most jurisdictions have rejected the dual capacity rule which Professor Arthur Larson has sharply criticized.[20]

In an article on this subject,[21] the authors stated that:

> Rather than viewing dual capacity as an exception to the exclusive remedy provisions of Workers' Compensation Acts, it appears to (them) more apt to categorize a situation where the doctrine applies as a situation that is not covered by the Workers' Compensation Act.

---

[19] Kosowan v. MDC Industries, Inc. 465 A.2d 1069 (Pa. Super. 1983).

[20] *The Law of Workmen's Compensation* § 72.81 (1983).

See also Quinn v. National Gypsum Co., 469 A.2d 136 (N.H. 1983); Linzee v. New York, 470 N.Y.S.2d 97 (N.Y. 1983); Horne v. General Elec. Co., 716 F.2d 253 (4th Cir. 1983); Weber v. Armco, Inc., 663 P.2d 1221 (Okla. 1983); Kosowan v. MDC Industries, Inc., 465 A.2d 1069 (Pa. Super. 1983).

[21] Tish & Ream, "Dual Capacity Revisited," F.T.D., September 1984.

By definition, if the dual capacity doctrine applies, the normal employer-employee relationship does not exist. Therefore, the Workers' Compensation Act won't bar the common law liability of the employer because the injury suffered by the employee was not work related.

California, as is not unusual, takes a contrary position.[22] In the case of *D'Angona v. County of Los Angeles*,[23] the claimant contacted a disease in the course of her employment at the hospital where she was employed. During the course of treatment for this condition at the hospital, she developed gangrene resulting in the amputation of almost all of her fingers and toes.

After applying for workers' compensation benefits, the board awarded her compensation for her disability resulting from the disease plus additional compensation for her disability resulting from the alleged aggravation and negligent treatment.

The injured employee then brought a liability suit against the county for negligence of the hospital. The trial court dismissed the suit on the basis that the employee was confined to recovery under the workers' compensation act exclusively.

The Supreme Court of California reversed the lower court and affirmed that the underlying rationale for the application of the dual capacity doctrine is a determination of whether the injury arises from a relationship which is distinct from that of employer and employee so as to invoke a different set of obligations than those involved in the employer-employee relationship of the parties.

In this case the court held that there was such a difference and that in treating its employee, it did not act in the capacity of employer.

The court also found that the defendant was entitled to a setoff for payments made under the compensation claim.[24]

In the case of *Bell v. Industrial Van Gas Co.*,[25] the injured brought a liability suit against Industrial Van Gas, his employer, and others on the basis of strict liability in a products liability suit. The employee alleged that his employer, among others, was engaged in the business of designing, manufacturing, purchasing, producing, etc., the prod-

---

[22] Bell v. Industrial Vargas, Inc., 179 Cal. Rptr. 30 (1981).

[23] 27 Cal. 3d 661 (1980).

[24] *Id.* citing Douglas v. E. & J. Gallo Winery, 69 Cal. 3d 103 (1977); Reed v. The Yaka, 373 U.S. 410 (1963).

[25] Bell v. Industrial Van Gas Co., reported in January 1, 1981 issue of Insuranceweek by Low, Bell & Lynch.

uct complained of. The majority opinion granted him the right to his action on the basis of dual capacity of his employer.

In his excellently written and very logical dissenting opinion, Justice Frank Richardson states:

> [I]n my view, the workers' compensation laws afford the sole and exclusive remedy to the employee against his employer in such a situation. . . . The legislature has been very clear . . . this suggestion of a lack of causal relationship between Bell's injury and his employment is, frankly, absurd.
>
> Indeed it is uncontradicted that Bell has already successfully pursued to a finality his workers' compensation remedy against Vargas, which requires as a prerequisite that the injury occur during the course of employment.
>
> Yet the majority wholly fails to explain how we properly may ignore the plain, specific and unambiguous language appearing in both sections 3600 and 3601, statutorily mandating the exclusive remedy rule. It is not our function to tinker with these laws for the purpose of "improving them." . . . If sections 3600 and 3601 are to be abolished, and the employee's remedy is no longer to be "exclusive," it is the authors of the sections, the legislature, and not the courts which should do the erasing.
>
> Unlike the ordinary consumer or user of manufactured goods the employee-user under the workers' compensation laws is given an assured protection from impairment of earning capacity and payment of medical expenses, without regard to any principles of comparative fault.[26]

In the *Johns Manville* case,[27] the plaintiff, who was an employee of Johns Manville for twenty-nine years, sued his employer in negligence for illness allegedly resulting from exposure to asbestos. He further alleged that the employer knew of the danger and concealed it from its workers, and failed to provide protective devices.

The court held that if an employer goes beyond mere failure to provide a safe place to work and if additional injury or aggravation of the original injury is involved, it creates the climate for an exception to the exclusive remedy situation. The court held that the incident causing the injury or aggravation must involve intentional mis-

---

[26] In support, Justice Richardson cites: Johns Manville Products Corp. v. Superior Court, 27 Cal. 3d 465 (1980); Daly v. General Motors Corp., 20 Cal. 3d 725 (1978); Barker v. Lull, 20 Cal. 3d 413 (1978); Wright v. F.M.C. Corp., 81 Cal. App. 3d 777 (1978).

[27] Johns Manville Products Corp. v. Superior Court, 27 Cal. 3d 465 (1980).

conduct and aggravation or additional injury, which were found in this case.

[6] Insurance Coverage Dilemma

The coverage dilemma in dual capacity and intentional misconduct cases, which includes the three exceptions to the exclusive remedy provisions of the Workers' Compensation Act in California, is that intentional acts and injuries covered by the Act are excluded from coverage under the liability policies, including the employers liability section of the workers' compensation policy.

If the court interprets an employer's act, or failure to act, as having been intentionally wrongful, would that be considered res adjudicata in a subsequent action by the employer who is trying to obtain coverage under his liability policy?

Again, if the court declares the act that allegedly caused the injury to have been a separate and independent act other than that as employer, would that act circumvent the workers' compensation exclusion in the liability policies?

Frankly, I do not know, nor would I attempt to guess the circumlocutions that the California courts might indulge in.

[7] Intentional Injury

Another rule often invoked as an exception to the exclusivity rule is that where an "intentional" injury has been committed. The questions this exception raises are (1) what actions imply "intention," and (2) whose act is it?

In the case of *Jones v. VIP Development Co.*,[28] the court held that merely because the employer might have known of high voltage wires that could injure the employee, it does not make his failure to warn the employee of this condition an intentional act.

Where the injury was caused by a coemployee, a Louisiana decision ruled that the injured employee must prove that the coemployee tortfeasor either consciously intended the injury or knew that such a result was substantially likely to follow the acts of the coemployee.[29]

---

[28] 472 N.E.2d 1046 (Ohio 1984).
[29] Fallo v. Tuboscope Inspection, 444 So. 2d 621 (La. 1984).

Boudeloche v. Grow Chem. Coating Corp.,[30] involved a case of flagrant disregard of a health hazard which was brought to the attention of the employer's supervisor several times, and disregarded with instructions to the employee to continue the work without essential protection. The court held this to be an intentional act within the exception to the exclusivity provision.

An attempt was made by Supreme Court of Connecticut, in the case of *Mingachos v. C.B.S., Inc.*,[31] to put some specific boundaries around the word "intentional" by holding that the exclusivity provision of the workers' compensation law provides an employer with immunity from employee suits for accidental injuries caused by the "gross, wanton, willful, deliberate, reckless, culpable or malicious negligence, breach of statute, or other misconduct of the employer *short of genuine intentional* injury." [Italics added.]

This court also held that neither state nor federal law provide a private cause of action for work-related injuries which result from alleged violations of safety standards.

[8] Sexual Harassment

In my opinion, a Florida appellate court rendered a very unfair decision by holding that sexual harassment that caused a female employee emotional distress was a type of accidental injury that was subject to the Workers' Compensation Act and hence she was precluded from bringing an action against her employer, whether or not she could recover under the compensation act.[32]

[9] Exclusivity in Occupational Disease Cases

A U.S. District Court, applying Pennsylvania law,[33] ruled that an asbestos insulation manufacturer's failure to warn its former employees that they might have acquired asbestos-related diseases during their period of employment constituted an intentional tort. Accordingly such former employees were permitted to bring a tort action against their employer despite the tort immunity provision of the compensation law.

---

[30] 728 F.2d 759 (5th Cir. 1984).
[31] 491 A.2d 368 (1985).
[32] Brown v. Winn-Dixie Montgomery, Inc., 469 So. 2d 155 (1985).
[33] Neal v. Carey Canadian Mines, Ltd., 548 F. Supp. 357 (E.D. Pa. 1982).

On the other hand, an Alabama supreme court ruled that the mere fact that a workers' compensation *insurer* (italics added) may have some knowledge of the potential health hazards (cotton dust in this case) did not of itself impose a legal duty upon the insurer to inform the insured's employees of the potential danger.[34] This case obviously must be distinguished from *Neal*[35] since that case was brought against the employer and *Barnes* was brought against the employer's workers' compensation insurer.

[10] Election to Sue Employer

Under certain circumstances, some Acts permit an employee either to accept the jurisdiction of the Act or permit him to sue at common law with or without some restrictions.[36]

The circumstances may involve a default against the employer or because the employee falls into a classification that requires some overt act by him, the employer, or both, to indicate an election. Such a choice is usually activated against the employer for some wrongdoing on his part, as a result of which some of the common law defenses may be removed from the employer.

Elective situations are many and varied, depending on the jurisdiction involved.

§ 39.07 Third Party Action

An employee's right to elect either to come within the Workers' Compensation Act or to bring an action against his employer at common law, should not be confused with the employee's right of election in third party actions. If an injury to an employee (that arose out of his employment) was caused by the negligence of someone other than his employer, he may have a right of action against the third party wrongdoer as well as a right to accept benefits under the Workers' Compensation Act.

In most states, if the employee chooses to accept compensation, his employer becomes subrogated to whatever rights he had against the third party, at least to the extent of the employer's liability under the Act. This simply means that the employee ordinarily cannot re-

---

[34] Barnes v. Liberty Mutual Ins. Co., 468 So. 2d 124 (1985).
[35] *See* note 33, *supra*.
[36] Freeman v. SCM Corp., 316 S.E.2d 81 (N.C. 1984).

cover under the Act and then make an additional recovery in a damage suit against the third party, unless he pays back to his employer whatever he has received by virtue of the Compensation Act.

Some of the Acts require the employee to bring a third party action in his own name. Others permit the employer or his carrier to bring the action. In some instances, the right of recovery is restricted to the amount of compensation paid or received. In others, a recovery is permitted over this amount, with the excess to be paid to the injured employee.

In the event that no compensation has been paid, some Acts hold that an election to sue the third party becomes binding once the employee makes his choice known. In these states, if he starts suit against the third party he loses all further right to make any claim under the Compensation Act, even though he may subsequently lose the third party action.

If the employee has the right to take compensation and also to sue the third party the Act usually requires him to notify his employer or his employer's carrier before the third party case is settled. Failure to do so may nullify his right to additional compensation. By the same token, the carrier is also required to put the third party on notice concerning the fact that a lien for compensation paid is outstanding.

§ 39.08 Punitive Damages Arising Out of Compensation Cases

When an injury to an employee is caused by an accident arising out of, and in the course of his employment, most of the courts that have ruled on the subject have made it clear that recovery for punitive damages are not allowed since they do not fall within the scope of the Compensation Acts. The exclusionary provisions of the Act do not permit a separate suit for such damages.[37]

§ 39.09 Jurisdiction and Extraterritoriality

With our ever-expanding industrial growth beyond city and state limits, and with the increasing growth of industrial branch offices throughout the country, the problem of what particular state act con-

---

[37] **Cal.:** Nelson v. Metalclad Insulation Corp., 118 Cal. Rptr. 725 (1975).
Ind.: North v. United States Steel Corp., 495 F.2d 810 (7th Cir. 1974).
Ohio: Roof v. Velsicol Chem. Corp., 380 F. Supp. 1373 (1974).
Pa.: Woodell v. Washington Steel Corp., 269 F. Supp. 958 (1967).

trols a given situation is becoming of major proportions. This problem is particularly pertinent not only because of the great divergence of benefits permitted under the various Acts, but also because of the many other variations in covered employees, hazards, and circumstances. This problem is commonly known as extraterritoriality, although the actual question is one of jurisdiction.

Some states make an attempt to regulate jurisdiction within the terms of the Act itself. Others are silent on the question and decision must be made on the basis of previous court rulings.

[1] Jurisdiction

There are ordinarily six basic grounds upon which a particular state may take jurisdiction. These are:

1. Residence of the employee.
2. Place of the accident.
3. Place where the employee was originally hired.
4. Local business office of the employer.
5. Place of principal employment at the time of the injury.
6. Agreed state of jurisdiction by contract between employer and employee.

No hard and fast rule can be set. Jurisdiction may be accepted in some states because of any one or a combination of the above factors.

What then is the situation when one state accepts jurisdiction and makes an award? Must the employee accept such an award as final, or can he make an additional claim in another state that might accept jurisdiction because of the presence of some factor that would ordinarily bring the claim within its scope?

For example, an award may be made in one state because the employee resided in that state and the local place of business of his employer was in that state. The accident, however, may have occurred in a different state in the course of a temporary job that he was doing in that state. Can the employee then make an additional claim in the state where the accident occurred?

Before the Supreme Court attempted to rule on the subject, it was generally held that a claimant could make a second recovery for the same accident in another state which previously accepted jurisdiction, but that his second recovery would be limited to the additional amount granted over and above the award of the first state. In other words, the only restriction was that he could not recover the same amount twice.

Two decisions by the Supreme Court have confused the situation somewhat. In the case of *Magnolia Petroleum Company v. Hunt*,[38] the Supreme Court refused to permit the second state to take jurisdiction, but in a subsequent decision, *Industrial Commission of Wisconsin v. McCartin*,[39] the court seems to have reverted to the original position, which permits an additional recovery in another jurisdiction over and above the amount of the first award.

Apparently, the only definite exception to this interpretation is an award obtained in those few states in which the Workers' Compensation Act expressly forbids recovery under any other Workers' Compensation Act.

§ 39.10 Notice of Accident or Disease

The Workers' Compensation Acts of most of our states provide certain time limitations within which notice of claim, accident, or both, are to be made. Ordinarily, such notices are required to be filed upon the employer, although the Act may also require notification to the Compensation Board as well.

The time limitations within which notice must be filed vary from a set number of days, to a period of two years. The wording of the Act may require notice "within a reasonable time" or "as soon as practicable."

Exceptions. Some of the Acts now permit exceptions by express provision. In other states, the courts have declared certain exceptions.

1. Prejudice plays an important part in the waiving of delayed notice on compensation claims, as well as in liability claims, as we have previously seen. The question of what is considered prejudice depends of course on the interpretation of the courts of the particular locality in which the claim is being brought.
2. Knowledge of the incident or injury by the employer or insurer is often an excuse for delayed notice under certain cir-

---

[38] 320 U.S. 430 (1943).
[39] 330 U.S. 622 (1947).

cumstances. Knowledge by the employer may even excuse total lack of notice.
3. Mistake of fact may be an excuse in certain jurisdictions.
4. Reasonable cause, which is a rather broad term, has been propounded to excuse delayed notice. This has been held to apply where an employee had no immediate knowledge that his condition was a result of an injury received at work.

The doctrines of waiver and estoppel have also been applied to compensation cases in which the employer has not raised the question of delayed notice within a reasonable time. Similarly, payment of compensation is usually held to estop the employer or his carrier from presenting the defense of delayed notice, as well as certain other defenses.

§ 39.11 Liability of Successive Insurers

Some states have attempted to fix by statute the responsibility of successive insurance carriers in those instances where a second injury aggravated or reactivated a former injury or disease.

Determination of an insurer's responsibility is of course made a lot easier if there is a definite statute on the subject. Ordinarily, such statutes require a certain minimal period of coverage exposure in those cases which fall within the occupational disease category before the insurance carrier can be held.

Even though there is some statute law on the subject, the claims person will probably have to refer to the court decisions in many of the situations that may confront him.

In most jurisdictions, if a second injury reactivates a previous injury or disease, the second carrier (the insurer at the time of the second injury) is usually held responsible for the full consequences of the aggravated or reactivated condition, as long as there is causal relationship between the second accident and the disability.

Some jurisdictions make an attempt to apportion responsibility. This is always a difficult matter.

The situation is especially confusing if the claimant has returned to work but is still complaining of recurrent symptoms of the original accident, such as continued backaches, and subsequently sustains another accident as a result of a heavy strain of lifting operation which again disables him. Most jurisdictions will consider this as a continuing disability even though the claimant did return to work, as long as he continued to have recurrent symptoms. The original carrier will usually be held responsible for all the disability. Each case, however, must rest on its own merits. There is absolutely no way to predict how the particular administrating or judicial body in any jurisdiction will hold on one of the borderline cases.

If the second injury is a result of the original disability (such as in the case of a claimant who loses his balance while on crutches and falls, causing additional injury) there is no question about the original carrier's responsibility, since the second injury did not arise out of any employment hazard and was simply a direct result of the initial injury or disability.

Ordinarily, in cases involving occupational disease the responsibility rests on the insurance carrier who was on the risk at the time disability payment was first necessitated.

§ 39.12 Illegal Employment of Minors

An employer who knowingly (and sometimes even innocently) hires underage employees, places himself in a particularly vulnerable position. Most states permit the minor to accept the benefits of the workers' compensation law if he is injured while at work, but impose some penalty on the employer which he ordinarily cannot transfer to his carrier.

In some instances in which coverage is not granted, the employer may be deprived of one or more of his defenses in a common law action brought against him.

Under the wording of the former policy, the employer also ran the risk of disclaimer by his carrier in a common law action brought by an employee under section 1(b), unless coverage for "employees as are legally employed" was changed.

The recent situation involving an influx of millions of illegal immigrants into this country has created a condition that could undermine our entire workers' compensation system to some extent.

Employment of such illegal immigrants is a financial boon to some employers who do not have to pay for workers' compensation insurance and who know that the illegal employee is too fearful to report even serious injuries.

The courts and legislatures will soon have to deal with this problem in a realistic manner, which at present is in a state of flux.

§ 39.13 Malpractice as Related to Workers' Compensation

Most of our courts hold that an employee who is receiving benefits under a Workers' Compensation Act is entitled to continued benefits made necessary by additional injury or aggravation, due to malpractice that resulted from the original treatment.

The employee may, of course, have an independent common law right of action against the physician or hospital, but in most states he cannot make double recovery.

The employee may also, under certain circumstances, have a common law right of action against the employer if the employer provided the medical care and was negligent in so doing, or derived a profit from such medical care. Such remedy against the employer is admittedly rare.

Finally, the employer or his insurer may have a right of subrogation against the doctor or hospital for the additional injury or aggravation caused by their malpractice.

§ 39.14 Final Determination

Unlike the situation in liability claims, in which the signing of a proper release ordinarily terminates a claim, there are many instances in compensation where there is no absolute way of definitely closing a claim.

In some states, even a lump-sum settlement agreed upon by both parties with the approval of the Board does not prevent a claimant from reopening a case if he can present new evidence of further or additional disability.

Some states do not permit reopening after a definitely limited time has elapsed from the date of the last payment. There is absolutely no uniformity on this subject and the claims person must familiarize himself with the provisions of the Act in his particular jurisdiction.

§ 39.15 Rehabilitation

The philosophy in this country, and that to which the insurance industry subscribes, is that every partially disabled person who wants to work should be given the maximum help and opportunity to do so.

It is good business and just plain common sense for the insurance industry to do everything reasonably possible to help rehabilitate those who have become incapacitated by employment injury. Scientific progress in this field has been tremendous in recent years and almost no one today is considered hopeless. It is often cheaper in the long run to make a greater initial expenditure for proper medical service.

The extent to which any particular company may go depends of course on the type and volume of compensation business it writes. The claim representative should, however, become familiar with all of the available rehabilitation facilities in his locality so that he can make recommendations on an intelligent basis and the home office can pool the knowledge received from all its branches.

§ 39.16 Structured Settlements in Workers' Compensation Cases

In some states, structured settlements have been accepted by the Workers' Compensation Boards and the courts in lieu of lump-sum payments. However, this matter requires expert advice and guidance since there could be many tax, as well as other, ramifications. There are some specific federal laws under the IRS Code that must be considered.

This device, in workers' compensation settlements, is so complex that before entering into negotiations, I would suggest that the claim representative or attorney take a good look at all alternatives to see if a structured settlement is really warranted.[40]

---

[40] John F. Clearly, "Structured Settlements: A Variation on a Theme," 26 F.T.D. 25 (1984). Despite Mr. Clearly's statement to the effect that "the method is simple—once you get used to it," I find the explanatory quotation in his article, as quoted by Kelly, "Structured Settlement in Workers' Compensation Revisited," Insurance Counsel Journal, October 1984, anything but simple. I recommend a careful reading of both articles for more information on this subject.

CHAPTER 40

Workers' Compensation-Employers' Liability Policy and Investigation

§ 40.01 In General
    [1] Coverage A—Workers' Compensation
    [2] Coverage B—Employers' Liability
    [3] Occupational Disease
    [4] Voluntary Compensation Endorsement
    [5] Extra-Legal Medical Benefits Endorsement
§ 40.02 Workers' Compensation Investigation
    [1] Unfair Claim Practices Acts
    [2] Index Bureau Reports
    [3] Checklists
        [a] Coverage
        [b] Factual Information
        [c] Information to be Obtained from Insured
        [d] Information to be Obtained from Claimant
        [e] Medical Investigation
    [4] Physical Facts
    [5] Subrogation
§ 40.03 Occupational Disease Investigation
    [1] Checklist
§ 40.04 Non-Occupational Disability Laws
§ 40.05 Bibliography

§ 40.01 In General

Before 1954, when a uniform standard Workmen's Compensation-Employers' Liability policy was promulgated, the policies previously issued applied to the workmen's compensation acts of the states in which the insurance was purchased, assuming that is where the insured was located. Where there was any indication that the insured might be subject to the workmen's compensation acts of other states, endorsements were added to the policy in order to provide the necessary additional coverage. There were some situations that could not have been easily foreseen and because of this and because the policies differed from state to state, there was much confusion.

The present Workers' Compensation policy gives automatic coverage for all operations and locations of the insured within the scope of any state compensation law named in the Declarations. The specific workers' compensation law becomes a part of the policy.

Although all casualty policies must conform with the laws of the jurisdictions where they apply, none is so tied in, hand and foot, with any particular statute as the workers' compensation policy. The provisions of this policy are the provisions of the Workers' Compensation Act of the state in which it is applicable. It differs again from liability policies in that it is actually a combination of two separate and distinct policies.

Coverage A concerns the obligation of the insurance company under the workers' compensation provisions of the Act. It requires the carrier to pay promptly all compensation and other benefits required of the insured by the Workers' Compensation Law.

Coverage B provides employers liability protection for the insured in addition to the workers' compensation coverage provided under Coverage A. This feature of the policy will be discussed subsequently.

[1] Coverage A—Workers' Compensation

Employees covered are those whose salaries are included in the payroll upon which the policy premium is based, and all employees entitled to receive benefits under the particular Workers' Compensation Act or Acts.

Under this section of the policy, the obligation of the insurance company is a *direct* one, running from the carrier to the employee, instead of the employer.

The policy states that

> the obligations of the company may be enforced by such person, or for his benefit by any agency authorized by law, whether against the company alone or jointly with the insured. Bankruptcy or insolvency of the insured or of the insured's estate, or any default of the insured, shall not relieve the company of any of its obligations under Coverage A.

The policy goes on to state that notice or knowledge of the injury on the part of the insured shall be notice or knowledge on the part of the company, and that the company will be bound by the findings, awards and judgments rendered against the insured, within the provisions of the Workers' Compensation Law.

However, if payment is made in excess of the regular benefits because of the serious and willful misconduct of the insured, or because of employment in violation of the law (underage employment, etc.) with the knowledge of the insured or any executive officer, then the company is entitled to reimbursement for such excess from the insured.

The limits of liability are the limits contained in the various benefit provisions of the particular Workers' Compensation Act. There is no specified monetary limitation other than that provided by the Act.

The policy contains a Definitions section (III) in which Workers' Compensation Law is defined as including any Occupational Disease Law of the state designated in the Declarations, but does not include any provisions for nonoccupational disability benefits.

Under the same section, the policy distinguishes between bodily injury by accident and bodily injury by disease, and gives the standard definition for assault and battery.

Section IV of the policy states that it applies to any accident occurring during the policy period and to any disease caused or aggravated by exposure provided that the last day of the last exposure in the employment of the insured to the conditions causing the disease occurs during the policy period.

The only exclusions which apply to Workers' Compensation coverage are:

(a) To operations conducted at or from any workplace not described in the declarations if the insured has, under the Workers' Compensation Law, other insurance for such operations or is a qualified self-insurer. Accordingly, the policy provides automatic coverage for all locations and operations subject to this qualification.

(b) To domestic employment or to farm or agricultural employment unless required by law or described in the declarations.

The policy conditions require the insured to give notice of injury "as soon as practicable" and notice of suit immediately, but as with all of the provisions of this policy, if there is any contradiction between the statute and the policy, the statute always prevails.

The interpretation of "as soon as practicable" by our courts has made a shambles of any effective defense for failure to properly report a workers' compensation claim.

In any event, with rare exceptions, the injured employee is hardly ever held to any strict reporting responsibility to his employer.

The policy follows the format of the casualty policies and some of its conditions are similar to other policies.

[2] Coverage B—Employers' Liability

The Employers Liability section of the combined policy properly falls within the Public Liability group. It covers the employer for his legal liability.

Before the Workmen's Compensation Acts became widespread in this country, the casualty insurance industry was already issuing Employers Liability policies for the protection of employers against claims and suits by their employees. With the continued growth of the Workmen's Compensation Acts, and the development of Workmen's Compensation insurance, Employers' Liability policies became less important until today they play a relatively minor part in the casualty insurance field. However, as long as Workers' Compensation Acts continue to restrict some types of employment and certain numbers of employees from coverage, there will be a continuing need for Employers' Liability insurance.

It must be remembered that the Employers' Liability policy was primarily designed for the protection of the insured, and not for the benefit of his employee, as with Workers' Compensation insurance. Coverage is restricted to the liability imposed by law upon the insured employer. The insurance carrier can avail itself of all the common law defenses open to the employer, unless those defenses were modified by statute.

The Insuring Agreements in the Employers Liability section of the policy state that the insurer will pay damages which the employer is legally obligated to pay because of "bodily injury by accident or disease . . . by any employee of the insured arising out of and in the course of his employment by the insured either in operations in a state designated in . . . the declarations or in operations necessary or incidental thereof.

As in the Workers' Compensations section, the policy provides that it will cover the liability for disease to which the last exposure which caused or aggravated the disease in the employment of the insured occurred during the policy period.

The Employers Liability provisions specifically state that "the limit of liability stated in the declarations for coverage B is the total limit of the company's liability for all damages."

It must be specifically emphasized that Coverage B (Employers Liability) *does not apply to liability under any workers' compensation law.* Its sole purpose is to protect the insured from his possible liability to employees outside of, and distinct from, any Workers' Compensation Act.

In addition to the two exclusions mentioned in Coverage A, and which also apply to Coverage B, the Employers Liability section of the policy excludes:

(c) "liability assumed by the insured under any contract or agreement, but this exclusion does not apply to a warranty that work performed by or on behalf of the insured will be done in a workmanlike manner."

(d) "punitive or exemplary damages on account of bodily injury to or death of any employee employed in violation of law" or so employed with the knowledge or acquiescence of the insured.

(e) "bodily injury by disease, unless prior to thirty-six months after the end of the policy period, written claim is made or suit is brought against the insured for damages because of such injury or death resulting therefrom."

(f) "any obligation for which the insured or any carrier as his insurer may be held liable under the workman's compensation or occupational disease law of a state designated in . . . the declarations" or similar law.

These exclusions pretty well speak for themselves.

[3] **Occupational Disease**

The Workers' Compensation policy gives complete coverage for occupational disease. There is, however, great variance on this subject in different jurisdictions. In some states, practically all occupational diseases are covered in either the Workers' Compensation Act or in a separate Occupational Disease Act. In others, certain specified diseases only are covered.

§ 40.01[3]

The policy, as we have said before, follows the laws of the state or states in which it is applicable.

As already indicated, the Employers Liability section of the policy covers liability for bodily injury by *accident or disease,* so it is quite clear that coverage is provided for occupational disease. There is, however, a limitation. Claims must be brought against the employer within thirty-six months after the policy period and the last day of the last exposure to a disease during the employment of the insured and must have occurred during the policy period.

Although it is sometimes technically difficult to distinguish injury from disease, ordinary usage makes us think of injury as being related to accident and applying more specifically to a disability resulting from some specific outward force. On the other hand, we ordinarily think of disease as a bodily disability that is the result of gradual exposure or deterioration.

Under the various statutes, diseases contracted by reason of employment are generally considered as injuries. They are not, however, ordinarily construed as being contracted by accident. Accordingly, those states which still use the word "accident," provide no coverage for occupational disease unless separate occupational disease statutes have been enacted.

By and large, however, some provision has been made in all jurisdictions for disability resulting from occupational disease.

An occupational disease is one definitely associated with some employment hazard which, in the ordinary course of events, is not likely to be incurred by a member of the general public. It may range from industrial skin conditions that are not usually too serious, to diseases which affect the vital organs and are deadly in nature. Some of the more common occupational diseases are silicosis, radium poisoning, lead poisoning, mercury poisoning, benzene poisoning, and arsenic poisoning, and more recently, asbestosis and others.

Benefits provided for occupational diseases do not necessarily correspond with those provided for injuries that fall within the regular provisions of the workers' compensation laws.

The statutes dealing with occupational diseases generally require a time limitation within which notice of the incidents or claim must be given. This usually commences when the disease or injury first manifested itself. Some courts have interpreted the time limitation to run from the last day of exposure to the disease.

Some statutes involving occupational disease provide for the obtaining of complete and detailed information from a prospective employee concerning previous exposure. This is important to remember when setting up claim-servicing procedures on large new risks.

[4] **Voluntary Compensation Endorsement**

Most of the Workers' Compensation Acts exempt certain classes of employees such as domestics, and others specifically listed, from coverage. The employer may nevertheless obtain Workers' Compensation coverage for such employees by endorsement, for an additional premium.

By issuing such an endorsement, the carrier agrees to pay the benefits stipulated in the Workers' Compensation Act, as though the employee was actually covered under it. The employer and his insurer retain such defenses as would be available under the Act and, in most instances, the employee retains his right to pursue an action under common law if he does not choose to accept the Compensation benefits. Since the endorsement covers both sections of the policy (A and B), the company would of course defend the employer should the employee choose to bring an action at common law. The liability limits of coverage are specifically stated in the policy.

[5] **Extra-Legal Medical Benefits Endorsement**

More and more states are today placing no limitation on the amount of medical benefits available under Workers' Compensation. There are, however, some that still do limit not only the amount, but also the time which these benefits cover. An employer may choose to provide additional medical coverage in those states, and if he so desires, such coverage can be purchased by endorsement for an additional premium.

§ 40.02 **Workers' Compensation Investigation**

As we have seen, the basic principles of casualty investigation are the same whether the subject matter be Automobile, Public Liability, or Workers' Compensation. There is, therefore, no need to repeat the information contained in the sections of this book covering the general principles of investigation. It is suggested however, that these chapters be thoroughly reviewed.

The information and checklists contained in the Chapter 6, "Obtaining Medical Information," and Chapter 5, "Securing the Physical Facts," for instance, could be entirely duplicated since they would be applicable in practically all respects. However, there are certain specific avenues of investigation particularly pertinent to workers' compensation. These will be developed later on in this chapter.

Ordinarily, the run-of-the-mill Compensation claim will not require detailed investigation, nor does the expense involved warrant it. The average claim involving little or no lost time can and should be handled by mail or telephone. If, however, there is any question of compensability on an injury case, or if fraud is suspected, the investigation should be complete, detailed, and thorough. This is particularly true if there is any possibility of subrogation.

There is one major difference between the handling of Compensation and Liability claims. There are some states in which a Compensation claim cannot be finally terminated, even though a compromise lump-sum settlement amount has been approved by a Board or Commission.

In workers' compensation work, the claim representative will be thrown in contact with more semi-literate and economically poor claimants than he would be in other types of casualty claims handling. That should be no reason or license to forget good manners. A poor or illiterate person is often just as sensitive as his more fortunate compatriots. So, be courteous and considerate.

If promptness is a virtue in handling Liability claims, it is an even greater one in handling Compensation claims. Prompt decisions on compensability must be made, and prompt payment started in those cases that should properly be paid. An ever-increasing number of Industrial Commissions are maintaining records of late payments. Not only is it embarrassing to the claim representative and to his company if he persistently fails to get payments out on time, but it is also unfair to, and can work a great hardship upon, a claimant and his family whose very existence may depend upon the receipt of the check or draft.

It is true that delay is very often the fault of the insured employer rather than the insurance company. The claim representative must then do a little educating. It is just as much his duty to instruct an employer on the necessity for (and the advantages of) prompt reporting and full cooperation in all future cases, as it is to handle the immediate claim under investigation. This means that the claim representative should do all he can to see to it that all forms that are the employer's responsibility are completed fully, properly, and promptly.

If he is unable to get reasonable cooperation from an insured, or if for any other reason the risk appears undesirable, he should file a Confidential Risk Report promptly, just as he should in a Liability case.

[1] Unfair Claim Practices Acts

The subject of Unfair Claim Practices Acts has been discussed in Chapter 21.

Originally, the delayed payment of workers' compensation claims, and some blatantly unfair refusals to pay some claims, was one of the prime motivations for the enactment of Unfair Claim Practices Acts that have been adopted in practically all of the states. As previously stated, however, the courts have greatly enlarged the scope of these acts.

Since the previous discussion of this topic is fairly detailed, it serves little purpose to repeat the information here and the reader is accordingly referred to Chapter 21.

[2] Index Bureau Reports

Many companies believe that there is no need to report Workers' Compensation claims to the Index Bureau. I cannot subscribe to this belief. Obviously, there is no point in reporting claims involving little or no lost time, but experience has shown that there are enough fraudulent Compensation claims to warrant diligence in those cases in which protracted disability is alleged.

Although prompt payment of Compensation claims is essential, a claim representative should not make premature payment if there is good reason to controvert a claim. By making payment he may jeopardize his position. Even here, however, he should make every effort to resolve the problem as quickly as possible.

It is very essential that the claim representative make proper arrangements to be notified by the insured immediately upon the claimant's return to work. Overpayments are not only a clerical and accounting nuisance, but they may also be difficult or impossible to recover. For the same reason, regular check-ups should be made to

§ 40.02[3][a]   CASUALTY INSURANCE CLAIMS

determine whether a surviving spouse who is receiving Compensation payments has remarried.

The field of workers' compensation, more than others in the casualty claim category, requires attention to detail, especially on the computations of amounts due. The claim representative or his clerical assistant should be sure that the figures are correct before issuing a check or draft.

The following checklists must of necessity be broad and general. The claim representative should take from them what he needs for the investigation of his particular case and permit them to stimulate his thinking along proper channels.

[3] Checklists

[a] Coverage

It is difficult to determine exact categories for investigation checklists. The present heading of "coverage" could, for instance, include almost every phase of compensation investigation. For this reason, the list under this caption has been confined to those items which might affect coverage in respect to the endorsements to the policy.

A. **Jurisdiction or Extraterritoriality**

☐ Where is the insured's principal place of business, or home office?
☐ Where is the claimant principally engaged in doing most of his or her work?
☐ Where was the claimant hired? By whom?
☐ How was the claimant hired? Was there an oral agreement or written contract of hire? If written, obtain copy.
☐ In what state did the accident occur?
☐ In what state does the claimant maintain principal residence?
☐ What is the nature of the claimant's regular duties?
☐ What was the exact nature of the work at the time of the accident?
☐ Is coverage provided for all of the states that might be involved?

B. **Occupational Disease.** This topic will be covered in more detail subsequently. Our concern here is merely with coverage under the policy.

☐ Has an Occupational Disease Law been enacted?
☐ If so, is it part of the Workers' Compensation Law?
☐ Is the employer subject to the law?
☐ Is the employee subject to the law?
☐ Is the particular disease involved subject to the law?

WORKERS' COMP.-EMPLOYERS' LIABILITY § 40.02[3][a]

☐ Was an Occupational Disease endorsement attached to the policy, if necessary?
☐ File confidential risk report, if necessary.

C. Dual or Multiple Employment

☐ Names and addresses of all employers.
☐ Occupation or business engaged in by all employers.
☐ Was claimant working for more than one employer at the time? If so, list all employers for whom he was working. Check all necessary records.
☐ Was such employment known to all employers?
☐ What were the salary arrangements?
☐ Was there a definite separation of duties?
☐ Check with customer/employer to determine on whose business claimant was engaged at the time.

D. Voluntary Compensation

☐ What is the nature of the claimant's duties?
☐ Does the claimant's occupation fall within the coverage of the Act?
☐ If not, did the insured and claimant comply with the elective requirements of the Act? Was such election required?
☐ Did the claimant indicate a desire to come within the scope of the Act?
☐ Does the policy contain a proper endorsement?

E. General

☐ Determine the nature and location of all operations engaged in by the insured. Are they properly covered under the policy?
☐ If insurance was terminated, was proper notice of it given to the Commission, where such notice is necessary?
☐ Was proper notice of termination of insurance given by previous insurance carrier, if notice was necessary?
☐ Check auditing department to determine whether premium was paid on claimant's salary.

Some states require a termination notice by the insurance carrier before such carrier may be relieved of responsibility on the policy despite the fact that the policy period may have ended. It is therefore obviously essential that you determine whether such termination was given either by your own company or by the previous carrier in those instances where concurrent coverage is possible.

[b] Factual Information

Details of the manner in which the incident took place and of the surrounding circumstances must of course be obtained from all available sources, including the insured, the claimant, and witnesses. Corroboration or refutation must be made by comparison, not only with various versions, but also with the physical facts. If warranted, therefore, the same ground must be repeatedly covered with each separate interview. For this reason, the following checklist is given under this caption rather than repeated under information to be obtained from the insured, claimant, or other witness.

The facts may of course be as varied as the circumstances of any particular accident can be. As the need arises, you should accordingly review the specific checklists previously given, depending on the type of accident under investigation. The following list will be confined to avenues of investigation that concentrate on the Compensation feature in addition to the ground already covered.

A. Exact date and time of occurrence

- ☐ Was it a regular working day?
- ☐ Did it occur before opening time?
- ☐ Did it occur after closing time?
- ☐ Did it occur during overtime period?
- ☐ Did it happen during the lunch period?
- ☐ Determine the claimant's exact working days and hours.

B. Place of the incident

- ☐ Did it occur on the premises?
- ☐ Did it occur in the area adjacent thereto?
- ☐ Was the insured conducting an operation there?
- ☐ Was the claimant where he was supposed to be at the time?

C. Complete details as to how the incident occurred. (Review liability checklists that fit the specific circumstances.)

- ☐ Was claimant engaged in his regular duties?
- ☐ Was there any deviation from those regular duties?
- ☐ If so, were they authorized? By whom? When?
- ☐ Did claimant violate any rules or regulations?
  - ○ Were the rules oral or written?
  - ○ Were they posted? Where? How long had they been?
  - ○ Was the claimant aware of them?
  - ○ Were the rules enforced by the employer?

D. Likelihood of self-inflicted injury

☐ Was there any willful misconduct?
☐ Was there any possible motive such as suicide, or fear of losing job?

E. Cases of assault

☐ Was the act obviously intentional?
☐ What precipitated or provoked the original assault?
☐ Did it have anything to do with the business of the employer?
☐ Who was the aggressor?
☐ Was there any previous ill-feeling between the claimant and the one who allegedly committed the assault?

F. Cases involving horseplay

☐ Who started the horseplay?
☐ Was the claimant an instigator or was he the victim?
☐ Did the employer know of the horseplay? Did he object?
☐ Had the employer condoned such practices in the past?
☐ Had the employer expressly forbidden such practice?
☐ Had the employer previously discharged or penalized an employee for similar acts?

G. Cases involving the influence of alcohol

☐ Did the insured permit drinking on the job?
☐ Exactly how much did the claimant have to drink?
☐ Did the claimant know of any prohibition against drinking?
☐ Was anyone with claimant at the time? Who?
☐ Did the claimant appear to be intoxicated?
☐ Were any tests made to determine intoxication?

H. Illegal operations on the part of the insured

☐ Were minors employed without proper certificate?
☐ Were other Department of Labor, Health, or Building regulations disregarded or violated?
☐ Were required safety devices wanting? If present, were they disregarded?
☐ Was the insured engaged in gambling or other illegal activities?
☐ Submit Confidential Risk Report, if necessary.

I. Incidents resulting from Acts of God

☐ Was incident a result of lightning, tornado, hailstorm, hurricane, and so on?
☐ Was the injury a direct result of a force of nature?
☐ Was there an intervening cause of injury?

§ 40.02[3][c]   CASUALTY INSURANCE CLAIMS

[c] **Information to be Obtained from Insured**

A. **Background information**

- [ ] Is the insured an individual, corporation, partnership, trustee, or other legal entity?
- [ ] Is the insured an owner, general contractor, or subcontractor?
- [ ] If the insured is an owner or general contractor, does his subcontractor carry his own compensation insurance?
- [ ] What is the exact nature of the insured's business or operations?
- [ ] Does the claimant work at the plant, outside, or at home? If home, has a license been obtained?
- [ ] Check days and hours of employment. Obtain records.
- [ ] Determine whether incident occurred within regular employment time.
- [ ] Have other accidents of a similar nature occurred previously? Obtain details and make out Confidential Risk Report if necessary.
- [ ] Is claimant related to insured or any member of the firm?
- [ ] If necessary, check background information and previous employment of claimant.
- [ ] How long has claimant been employed by insured?
- [ ] How long has claimant been employed in the present position?
- [ ] Does insured intend to pay claimant's salary or any part of it during disability? If so, does he expect reimbursement from claimant or insurer? Check payroll records.

B. **Check details of incident.** Obtain signed statements where necessary.

- [ ] Did insured or member of firm personally witness the incident?
- [ ] Did insured come on scene shortly thereafter?
- [ ] When did insured first learn of the incident or disability? How?
- [ ] Did insured make any investigation? If so, obtain results.

C. **Type of employment.** (Complete checklists for the determination of "independent contractor" and other categories listed in this section are to be found in Chapter 39, "Handling Workers' Compensation Cases.")

D. **Employment status determination**

- [ ] Was claimant on part-time work?
  - ○ Did he have definite hours of employment?
  - ○ Did he have a definite place of employment?
- [ ] Was claimant a casual employee?
  - ○ Was he regularly employed at definite place of employment?
  - ○ Was he periodically employed at indefinite periods?

WORKERS' COMP.-EMPLOYERS' LIABILITY § 40.02[3][c]

- ○ Obtain account from records of his employment during the past year.
- ☐ Was claimant a special employee?
  - ○ Was he hired for this particular job only?
  - ○ Did the job require special skills?
  - ○ Review requirements concerning salary, tax deductions, control, and so on.
- ☐ Was claimant a volunteer?
  - ○ Did he offer his services without request?
  - ○ Did he ask for or receive any compensation?
  - ○ Was there any understanding concerning salary?
  - ○ Were his services needed?
- ☐ Was claimant a loaned employee?
  - ○ What was the understanding between regular and temporary employer?
  - ○ Who maintained control? (Right to direct work, to hire or fire.)
  - ○ Who paid salary?
  - ○ Was there any transfer on the books?
  - ○ What was the duration of employment? How long was it supposed to have lasted?
- ☐ Was claimant a partner or corporate officer?
  - ○ Did he receive a separate salary in addition to a share in the profits?
  - ○ Did he have any duties as an employee? Check all records carefully.
- ☐ Was claimant an employee of a subcontractor?
  - ○ Obtain name and address of subcontractor.
  - ○ Was he insured? What company? If so, see that company is properly notified.
  - ○ If there is no insurance, place subcontractor on notice that will hold him responsible for any amount paid. Request that he take over.
- ☐ Was claimant an independent contractor? (Review checklist.)

E. Complete salary details directly from the insured's records

- ☐ Was claimant paid by the hour, day, week, month, year, or any fraction thereof?
- ☐ Was claimant on straight salary or on piecework?
- ☐ If piecework, obtain rate.
- ☐ Did claimant work on commission basis?
  - ○ Commission only?
  - ○ Commission against drawing account?
  - ○ Commission plus regular salary?
  - ○ Determine the rate of commission.
- ☐ Did claimant receive any tips or other gratuities?
  - ○ Were they considered part of claimant's salary?
  - ○ Was an accounting kept? Obtain copy of records.
- ☐ Did claimant receive other benefits? Obtain copy of records.
  - ○ Bonuses.
  - ○ Board (meals).

§ 40.02[3][d]   CASUALTY INSURANCE CLAIMS

- ○ Lodging.
- ○ Transportation. If so, obtain details concerning the exact arrangements.
- ☐ Did claimant receive an allowance for expenses?
  - ○ Automobile. Company or personally owned?
  - ○ Hotel, meals, other transportation and incidentals.
  - ○ Did he receive a definite sum allowance for expenses?
- ☐ Will claimant return to work at same salary? If not, obtain details including salary expected to be paid and reasons therefore.

F. **Forms.** Explain need for prompt filing.

- ☐ Were proper forms completed?
- ☐ Were they filed on time?
- ☐ Were they completed properly?

[d] **Information to be Obtained from Claimant**

A. **Background information.** (Review previous checklists for detailed information which will not be repeated here.)

- ☐ Name, address, social security number, and so on.
- ☐ Previous addresses, if necessary.
- ☐ Age. If claimant is a minor determine whether or not certificate of employment was obtained.
- ☐ Union affiliations.
- ☐ History of previous accidents.
- ☐ Complete employment history, if necessary.

B. **Dependency.** Who may properly claim dependency under the Act is not always obvious. Occasionally, all the dependents will not be revealed unless careful investigation is made. A former marriage may not have been properly dissolved, or children by former marriage may be in existence but unknown to the investigator. It is therefore essential that all avenues of investigation be checked thoroughly before payments are made on a fatal claim.

In some instances, dependency for certain classes of persons is presumed under the Act. In other jurisdictions, dependency must be proven. In the latter cases, it will be necessary to determine the exact extent of the dependency. If records of marriage, birth, death, separation, divorce, and annulment are available, copies should be obtained. Do not rely on the word of an interested party. The following checklist should stimulate thinking along these lines.

- ☐ Present marital status of the claimant.

WORKERS' COMP.-EMPLOYERS' LIABILITY § 40.02[3][d]

- [ ] Name, address and age of last spouse.
- [ ] Names, addresses and details concerning previous spouses and those alleged to have been married to the claimant.
- [ ] Names, addresses, and ages of all children by all marriages.
- [ ] Names and addresses of any children born out of wedlock.
- [ ] Names and addresses of any incompetent or disabled dependents. Obtain details.
- [ ] Determine whether the claimant had any common-law marriage relationships.
  - Are common-law marriages recognized in the jurisdiction?
  - Did the claimant and the alleged spouse live together?
  - Did they hold themselves out as husband and wife?
  - Were they recognized in the locality as husband and wife?
  - Did they undergo any previous ceremony or, by personal vows, otherwise evidence intent to be husband and wife?
  - Did they intend to undergo a ceremony in the future?
  - Determine why no marriage ceremony was ever performed.
- [ ] Obtain complete details concerning any divorce, separation, or annulment.
- [ ] Determine whether there are other dependents, (father, mother, other close relatives, ward, adopted children, and so on).
  - Names, addresses, and ages of all such alleged dependents.
  - What was their relationship to the claimant?
  - Determine the exact degree of dependency.
    - Was the claimant their sole source of support?
    - If not, exactly how much did claimant contribute, including board and lodging?
    - Who else contributed? How much?

C. General information

- [ ] Corroborate salary and employment information obtained from the insured.
- [ ] When did claimant first make claim? To whom? How?
- [ ] Obtain the names of any witnesses the claimant may have.
- [ ] Determine whether the claimant is related to the insured.
- [ ] Determine whether the claimant is a partner or officer of the insured's corporation. If so, corroborate information concerning his status as an employee, in addition to his financial interest.
- [ ] Determine whether the claimant expects to return to the same employer and the same occupation.
- [ ] Corroborate all factual information as previously outlined.
- [ ] Corroborate all medical information along lines previously and subsequently outlined.

[e] Medical Investigation

It would be well for the claim representative to review the material previously covered in Chapter 6, "Obtaining Medical Information." That chapter is comprehensive enough so that there is no need to repeat the information here.

In the investigation of Compensation claims, the claim representative will be particularly interested in the treatment received by the claimant and in his rehabilitation. More than ever, therefore, it will be necessary for him to check the background and capabilities of the attending physician and to determine whether the claimant is fully carrying out all of the physician's orders and instructions.

In some areas, the Act permits the employer or the insurance carrier to select the attending physician. Other jurisdictions permit the employee to pick his own doctor from a panel approved by the local commission. In the matter of physical examinations, some states employ their own doctors on a full- or part-time basis. Others rely only on the claimant's attending physician and the examining doctor to furnish the insurance carrier with conclusions concerning the medical disability.

It is important that the claim representative make periodic check-ups on the claimant's progress, and determine, with the advice of the examining physician, whether he is receiving proper and adequate medical attention.

The Acts of some jurisdictions may set a limit on the employer's liability for medical care. The claim representative is often confronted with the problem of paying for additional medical care over and above that called for by the Act; the alternative is the possibility of protracted disability because medical attention might be discontinued. Very often an insurance company will accept the responsibility for additional medical bills if they are confronted with such a problem, but this is ordinarily a matter which must be faced individually and usually one which requires home office approval.

It is important that all bills be scrutinized carefully and checked against any fee schedules available. Although it is naturally of primary importance to see that the claimant obtains the best medical care, it is also important to see that this is done at the most reasonable cost. As recovery progresses, the extent of necessary treatment should diminish and the medical bills should become progressively smaller. This should be particularly evident if treatment involves x-rays, diathermy, or physiotherapy.

WORKERS' COMP.-EMPLOYERS' LIABILITY § 40.02[4]

In addition to the checklists previously outlined, the following points of investigation in compensation claims are suggested.

- ☐ Determine whether any pre-employment physical examinations were made. If so, obtain copies.
- ☐ Determine who engaged the doctors and who authorized medical treatment and hospitalization.
- ☐ Make a thorough check on the qualifications of the examining physicians.
- ☐ Obtain detailed information about the immediate symptoms.
- ☐ Make periodic check-ups on recovery.
- ☐ Determine at regular intervals what further medical attention is needed.
- ☐ Make an effort to determine whether there will be any degree of permanent disability.
- ☐ Determine when the claimant is expected to return to work.
- ☐ Try to determine whether the claimant will be able to carry out his regular duties or whether he will have to be assigned to lighter work for some period of time.
- ☐ In fatal cases, determine the advisability of an autopsy and obtain permission for one, if possible. If an autopsy has been made, obtain copy of the report.

[4] Physical Facts

Physical facts will of course be as diverse as the type of claim under investigation. Review not only Chapter 5, "Securing the Physical Facts," but the checklists previously outlined for the investigation of various types of liability claims. Particular emphasis should be placed on local ordinances and state laws on safety measures. Determine whether or not those measures were properly enforced. The claim representative should, for instance, find out whether there were any definite rules or regulations governing the manner of work or affecting safety measures, and if so, whether they were posted. He should determine whether the employees were aware of the rules and regulations, and whether disobedience of them was tolerated by the employer.

Such details as complete description of the scene of the accident, including a comprehensive description of the machine or device involved, are of course elementary. In general, investigation of the physical facts on a compensation case should parallel that on a liability claim. There is little point in repeating checklists already contained in this volume.

[5] Subrogation

Any accident involving vehicles, products, machinery, or subcontractors may have subrogation possibilities. The field of subrogation is a rather broad one and will be covered in more detail in Chapter 43. For our purposes here, it should be pointed out that every compensation investigation must be conducted with an eye to subrogation possibilities.

If a claimant is determined to accept compensation, no coercion should ever be used to persuade him to seek his remedy against a third party. It is, however, the duty of a claim representative to explain to the claimant the full extent of his rights and remedies so that he may make an intelligent decision.

The claim representative should be sure to place the third party on notice wherever he intends to press subrogation rights and, as far as possible, try to see to it that the insurance carrier is informed. He must search his own records initially to see if his company carries the liability coverage for the third party.

If there is a possible third party involvement, he should make sure, before he begins to make compensation payments, that no settlement has already been consummated.

§ 40.03 Occupational Disease Investigation

Investigation of Occupational Disease claims may fall within either the Workers' Compensation or the Employers' Liability sections of the policy. If the investigation is being conducted under the Employers' Liability provisions, the claim representative will have to determine whether or not there was any negligence on the part of the employer. If there was, the investigation must be just as comprehensive as that of any other public liability claim.

It is always difficult to determine the degree of exposure necessary to contract a disease. Often, disability must begin within a specified time from the date of last exposure in order to bring such a claim within the Workers' Compensation Law. It is essential that the length of exposure be determined and verified and the names of any previous carriers that may have possible overlapping or concurrent coverage for the claimant's disability ascertained.

WORKERS' COMP.-EMPLOYERS' LIABILITY   § 40.03[1]

[1] **Checklist**

In addition to the ordinary investigation as previously outlined, it is suggested that the following details be checked when investigating Occupational Disease claims.

- ☐ Determine the exact nature of the materials with which the claimant worked.
- ☐ Determine the amount of material used and the duration of use.
- ☐ If claimant did not work directly with or on the questionable material, what contact did he have with it?
- ☐ What was the size and location of the room or area in which the claimant worked?
- ☐ How many people worked in the same room or area?
- ☐ What was the duration of the exposure? Obtain the hours per day, days per week, and so on.
- ☐ What was the date of last exposure?
- ☐ Describe all safety devices.
    - ○ Were mask or gloves required? If they were not used, why not?
    - ○ Describe all ventilation facilities such as fans, blowers, windows, exhaust, air conditioning, and so on.
    - ○ Describe all other safety measures.
- ☐ Were any safety measures required by the Building, Health, or other local or state departments or authorities?
- ☐ Is a chemical or dust analysis necessary? If such analyses were previously made, obtain copies of reports.
- ☐ Obtain complete record of the claimant's previous employments.
- ☐ Obtain detailed information concerning claimant's previous medical condition.
- ☐ Obtain record of previous illnesses of any employee in same place of employment.
- ☐ Obtain complete report from your company's safety engineering department.
- ☐ Check local or state Building and Factory Inspection Department.
- ☐ Determine whether employer's physical examinations were given, and obtain copies of results, if available.
- ☐ When did claimant first show any manifestations of illness or disease? When and to whom did he report it?
- ☐ Obtain physical examination after your doctor has made a complete review of the medical and x-ray reports.

§ 40.04 Non-Occupational Disability Laws

Some states have enacted Non-Occupational Disability Benefits statutes which in effect supplement the workers' compensation laws in that they provide benefits to employees who are injured or who become ill as a result of non-occupational pursuits.

The laws vary. They are patterned either as unemployment benefits and similarly administered, or on workers' compensation laws and made a part of the workers' compensation administration.

The disability laws, like workers' compensation, are either monopolistic (entirely state-controlled) or elective. Benefits are computed in a manner similar to compensation; that is, a percentage of the weekly wage, after a waiting period, for a certain number of weeks not to exceed a definite limitation in any one year.

The problem on borderline cases involving the question of "arising out of or in the course of employment" would, of course, become much less acute if an insurance carrier were to cover an employer for both Workers' Compensation and Disability Benefits.

§ 40.05 Bibliography

While accepted texts often do not get the acknowledgment that they deserve, the comprehensive and learned work of Professor Arthur Larson on Workmen's Compensation, which is the undisputed authority in this field, must be mentioned.

Following are articles of note on the subjects of Workers' and Workmen's Compensation and Employers Liability:

Arthur, "Workmen's Compensation," 13 Ind. L. Rev. 439 (1980).

Burnett, "Workmen's Compensation Claims 'Arising Out Of' and 'In the Course Of,'" The Forum, October 1966.

Calzaretta & Hoffman, "Intentional Act Exceptions to Workers' Compensation," F.T.D., August 1985.

Clearly, "Structured Settlements: A Variation on a Theme," 26 F.T.D. 25 (1984).

Comment, Stump, "Michigan Workers' Disability Compensation, Intentional Torts and the Exclusive Remedy Provision," 3 Cooley L. Rev. 159 (1985).

Comment, Sweeney, "The International Act Exception to the Exclusivity of Workers' Compensation," 44 La. L. Rev. 1507 (May 1984).

Couch, "The Loaned Employee Doctrine as Applied to Workers' Compensation Cases," Insurance Counsel Journal, January 1959.
De Leon, "Workmen's Compensation: A Legal System in Jeopardy," FIC Quarterly, Summer 1979.
Galiher, "Conflicts and Problems of the Workers' Compensation Attorney in Representing the Employer and Insurer Before Federal and State Boards," Insurance Counsel Journal, January 1981.
Ghiardi, "Dual Capacity—An Exception to the Exclusivity of Workers' Compensation," FIC Quarterly, Spring 1983.
Kelly, "Structured Settlement in Workers' Compensation-Revisited," Insurance Counsel Journal, October 1984.
Liebo, "Dual Capacity Doctrine and Employers' Products," F.T.D., January 1983.
Micherle & Overton, "A New Extracontractual Cloud Upon the Horizon: Do the Unfair Claim Settlement Acts Create a Private Cause of Action?", Insurance Counsel Journal, April 1983.
Note, Antenucci, "Permanent Partial Disability Under Workers' Compensation: Schedule Exclusivity v. Impaired Earning Capacity," 33 Drake L. Rev. 885 (1983-84).
Soule, "Toward an Equitable and Rational Allocation of Employee Injury Losses in Cases with Third Party Liability," Insurance Counsel Journal, April 1979.
Tish & Ream, "Dual Capacity Revisited," F.T.D., September 1984.
_____, "Employer Immunity Under Workers' Compensation," F.T.D. August 1984.
"Workmen's Compensation: Occupational Diseases," DRI Memo #6, June 1968.

Employer Liability

Brooks, "Tort Liability of Owners and General Contractors for On-the-Job Injuries to Workmen," 13 U.C.L.A. L. Rev. 99 (1965).
Casey, "The Relationship Between Products Liability and Workers' Compensation—Third Party Rights Against Negligent Employers," FIC Quarterly, Fall 1981.
Diehm, "Liability for Loaned Employees," Insurance Counsel Journal, April 1958.
Employment of Under-Age Persons," F.C. & S. Bulletins, Casualty volume, Workers' Comp. Section Page Ua-1.
Forney, "Employers Liability Extending Beyond the Compensation Act," Insurance Adjuster Magazine, August 1963.

CHAPTER 41

Federal Employer-Employee and Other Federal Legislation

§ 41.01 Federal Employees' Compensation Act (FECA)
§ 41.02 Federal Employers' Liability Act
§ 41.03 Longshore and Harbor Workers' Compensation Act
§ 41.04 Defense Base Act
§ 41.05 War Hazards Compensation Act
§ 41.06 Economic Opportunity Act
§ 41.07 The Jones Act (Merchant Marine Act, Revised 7th ed. 1976)
§ 41.08 Seaworthiness
§ 41.09 Federal Tort Claims Act
§ 41.10 Occupational Safety and Health Act (OSHA)
§ 41.11 Death On The High Seas Act (1976) (DOHSA)
§ 41.12 Racketeer Influenced and Corrupt Organizations Act (RICO)
§ 41.13 Bibliography

There are some federal acts which regulate the rights of an employee who has been injured, disabled, or killed while acting in the course of employment, with which a claim representative should be at least somewhat familiar.

Some of these acts are in the nature of Workers' Compensation legislation and others are strictly Employers' Liability laws.

While Non-Occupational Disability Benefits laws are presently state enactments, and do not fall within the federal category, a brief discussion of this subject has been included in this chapter because of its allied nature.

Once again, we find a good deal of controversy in the law. There is sometimes no sharp line that enables the claim representative to determine if a borderline case falls within the province of a state Workers' Compensation Act or the Non-Occupational Benefits Act, or occasionally, even the Longshoremen's and Harbor Workers' Act. I can only repeat, where necessary, help from counsel should be obtained.

§ 41.01 Federal Employees' Compensation Act (FECA)

Since federal employees do not come under the jurisdiction of the state workers' compensation laws, the Federal Employees' Compensation Act was passed to provide the necessary coverage for federal employees who are injured in the course of and arising out of their employment.

The first federal act dealing with workers' compensation was enacted in 1908 and granted coverage to a limited group of federal employees. The scope was broadend in 1916 to include all civil employees of the federal government. It was revised again in 1966, and is administered under the supervision of the Secretary of Labor.

The government runs its own program which is not privately insured and the claim representatives only contact with this Act will probably be confined to subrogation. The Act provides the government with the right of subrogation in the event that injury was caused through the wrongful act of a responsible individual or entity.

If an insured has an accident with a government employee who was injured as a result of such an accident, while in the course of his employment, the claim representative must be aware of the rights of the government under this Act. In the event of a payment disregarding such rights, his company may be in double jeopardy.

§ 41.02 Federal Employers' Liability Act

The Federal Employers' Liability Act, enforced in 1908 and subsequently amended in 1939, applies to railroad employees who are engaged in furthering interstate commerce. It provides that a railroad, as a common carrier, while engaging in interstate or foreign commerce, is liable in damages to any person who, while employed by the carrier in such commerce, suffers an injury disability or death: (1) resulting in whole or in part from the negligence of any of the officers, agents, or employees of the carrier; or (2) resulting from any defect or insufficiency due to the negligence of the carrier in regard to its cars, engines, machinery, track, roadbed, or other equipment.

The 1939 amendment brought within the Act: employees, any part of whose duties are in furtherance of interstate commerce, or which directly or closely and substantially affect it.

The Federal Employers' Liability Act is strictly Employers' Liability legislation, and is not patterned upon any workers' compensation laws. There is no limitation on death benefits, or for pain and suffering, but loss of consortium is not covered. The basis for a claim or suit depends on the negligence of the employer, his officers, agents, or employees. The family of the injured or deceased employee have an action only if they have been deprived of a reasonable expectation of financial benefits, assistance, or support.

The common law defenses of an employer of "assumption of risk" and "negligence of a fellow servant" have been eliminated. The Act further provides that contributory negligence shall not be a bar to complete recovery, but may be set up in diminution of damages proportionate to the degree of fault shown. In effect, this is comparable to the doctrine of comparative negligence as followed in some of our states.

§ 41.03 Longshore and Harbor Workers' Compensation Act

Despite the fact that all states have enacted Workers' Compensation Acts, there are areas of federal jurisdiction which are not affected by state laws. Such areas include the navigable rivers and harbors within the United States and other waters extending from the United States to an internationally agreed limit.

Congress therefore enacted a law, in 1927, known as the Longshoremen's and Harbor Workers' Compensation Act which provides compensation benefits to designated employees who work upon such federal territories. Employers operating in these areas are required to comply with the law and usually purchase insurance coverage for this purpose.

The Longshore and Harbor Workers' Compensation Act is administered by the Bureau of Employees' Compensation, which is a subdivision of the Department of Labor. It is modeled in many respects on the various Workers' Compensation Acts.

In order to fall within the provisions of the Act, disability or death must result from injury which occurred on any navigable waters of the U.S., including any dry dock, provided the employee does not have the right to proceed under any state compensation act.

The Act specifically excludes the master and crew of a ship, officers, and employees of the U.S. government or an agency thereof, and employees of a state, foreign government, or political subdivision thereof.

§ 41.03

Although it was originally intended that employees must be engaged in maritime work at least partly, the courts have, by decision, practically eroded this requirement.

The many fine distinctions in the decisions concerning the difference between an employee and a member of a crew, and definitions of "maritime," "navigable waters," "dry docks," and other wording of the Act, had better be left to counsel.

The amendments of 1972 to the Longshoremen's (became Longshore in 1984) and Harbor Workers' Compensation Act were drastic and far reaching. They extended coverage beyond the water's edge to certain specific adjoining shore areas, to include longshoremen who are engaged in loading or unloading a ship, but are not necessarily upon it at the time of injury. The Act now also includes those who may be repairing or building a vessel on a dry dock.

Benefits were increased greatly and the increases were even made retroactive to cover employees with disabilities at the time the amendments went into effect.

As drastic as any change was that which tolled the death of two decisions that made a mockery of the original intent that the Act was to be an exclusive remedy.

In the case of *Seas Shipping Co. v. Sierocki*,[1] the court held that longshoremen were entitled to bring an action against a shipowner on the basis of "unseaworthiness" rather than to be confined to negligence. "Unseaworthiness" was then stretched to the breaking point until it was almost synonymous with absolute liability.

Shipowners then started to take "hold harmless" agreements from stevedoring companies with whom they were doing business.

In 1956, in the case of *Ryan Stevedoring Co. v. Pan Atlantic S.S. Corp.*,[2] the court held that a vessel may implead the stevedoring company for whom the injured longshoreman worked, on the theory that the stevedoring company breached an express or implied warranty of workmanlike performance to the vessel owner, or because it was held to have been the negligent cause of the injury. Thus the exclusive remedy intent of the Act was circumvented.

The present wording of the new amendments now makes it clear that *exclusive remedy* was meant to be just that, and that *seaworthiness* was no longer grounds for action against even the ship-

---

[1] 328 U.S. 25 (1946).
[2] 350 U.S. 124 (1956).

owner. Both decisions were accordingly made obsolete and ineffective.

The 1972 amendments provided:

1. Negligence as the sole basis for an action against the shipowner.
2. Seaworthiness was no longer grounds for actions against the shipowner by a longshoreman.
3. The shipowner could no longer implead or bring an action against the stevedore company on express or implied warranty or on any other grounds.
4. Hold-harmless, indemnity, or contribution agreements between the shipowner and the stevedore company became invalid and unenforceable.
5. A longshoreman who was employed directly by the shipowner had no cause of action if the injury was caused by the negligence of persons engaged in performing longshoring services.
6. Federal laws apply in any action brought by a longshoreman.

The Act was extended to cover injuries that accurred on adjoining piers, wharves, dry docks, terminals, building ways, maritime railways, and other areas adjoining navigable waters customarily used in loading, unloading, repairing, or building a vessel. While coverage for longshoremen at the water's edge was enlarged, there is no intent to cover employees who are not engaged in loading, unloading, repairing, or building a vessel merely because they happened to have been in the areas adjoining navigable waters.

The expansion of the shoreward area covered by the Act increased the insured's exposure beyond expected limits. In addition, coverage for occupational illnesses and for workers that developed disabilities during retirement created unforeseen gaps in coverage. Administrative problems also developed in the issuing of benefits. These concerns and some others were addressed in the 1984 amendments to the Longshore and Harbor Workers' Compensation Act, which in deference to today's touchy attitude concerning gender, was renamed "Longshore" in place of the previous "Longshoremen's."[3]

---

[3] For an excellent and detailed discussion of the effects of the 1984 amendments *see* the article by David G. Davies, "A Survey of Maritime Tort Exposure for Personal Injuries After the 1984 Longshore and Harbor Workers' Compensation Act Amendments," Insurance Counsel Journal, July 1985.

§ 41.04 Defense Base Act

The Second World War created the necessity to provide compensation for civilians employed at U.S. military bases overseas and in occupied or allied foreign territories.

The Defense Base Act, enacted by Congress at that time, extended the provisions of the Longshoremen's and Harbor Workers' Compensation Act to apply to such employees. United States Government contractors working abroad are now required to provide insurance in accordance with the provisions of the Act and this is ordinarily done by a Defense Base Act endorsement to a Standard Workers' Compensation policy.

Upon application, the Government Contracting office can recommend, and through the Labor Department, grant a waiver with respect to employees who are nationals of the country in which the work is being performed, or other noncitizens of the U.S. Such employees would be covered under the local workers' compensation laws of the country of their nationality, or where the work is being performed.

The Defense Base Act is an exclusive remedy and supersedes all other liability of the employer.

§ 41.05 War Hazards Compensation Act

The War Hazards Compensation Act differs from the usual compensation type of law in that it provides for payment by the Bureau of Employees' Compensation directly to the employees or their families, those benefits which the Act stipulates as a result of injury, disability, death, or enemy detention caused by a hostile force.

War risk is defined in the Act as "any hazard arising during a war in which the U.S. is engaged; during an armed conflict in which the U.S. is engaged, whether or not war has been declared; or during a war or armed conflict between military forces of any origin, occurring within any country in which a person covered by this Act is serving."

Employees who are exempted from the Defense Base Act because of waiver are also exempted from the War Hazards Compensation Act.

The benefits of the War Hazards Act are the same as those provided in the Defense Base Act. The claim representative must remember that any payments made under a policy providing Defense Base

FEDERAL EMPLOYER-EMPLOYEE LEGISLATION § 41.07

Act coverage, might be recovered from the Federal Bureau if the injury, disability or death resulted directly from a war hazard.

However, if premium is taken for a War Hazard endorsement on the policy, the insurer thereby waives any right of recovery from the government.

§ 41.06 Economic Opportunity Act

In 1964, Congress passed the Economic Opportunity Act as part of the Federal Anti-Poverty Program, which provides for the creation of a number of programs that offer opportunities for education, training, and work.

Our interest in this program deals with the requirement of a special endorsement for Workers' Compensation in many states, which is administered by the Department of Labor.

The endorsement, applicable to enrollees under these programs, makes unlimited total disability and medical expense benefits mandatory. Accordingly, any limitation placed on these benefits by the local Workers' Compensation Act would be superseded by the program, where effective. There is no requirement for change in the weekly benefits.

§ 41.07 The Jones Act (Merchant Marine Act, Revised 7th ed. 1976)

Here again, we are concerned with federal legislation in the nature of Employers' Liability rather than Workers' Compensation.

The Jones Act of 1915 placed seamen on the same basis as railway employees under the Federal Employers' Liability Act.

Before the Act became effective, members of a crew had no cause of action against their employer for injuries received during a voyage unless the employer could be held responsible for sending the ship to sea in poor condition. The negligence of the captain or mates were not imputable to the employer shipowner. The employee's sole right of action was for cure (which in effect meant care) and wages to the end of the voyage. This right of action was not based on negligence.

The Jones Act provides that a seaman injured in the course of his employment may, at his election, sue his employer for negligence. As we said, it extends the rights given to railway employees, as well to seamen.

The Act does not remove the seaman's former right to sue his employer for the unseaworthiness of a vessel, but permits him an election. Here again, his right under the Act is based on negligence; the employer cannot bring up the defenses of "assumption of risk" or "negligence of a fellow servant," and there is no right to recover for loss of consortium. The admiralty rule of comparative negligence, and not the common law doctrine of contributory negligence, is applicable.

The term "seaman" is broad enough to cover not only one who is a member of a crew, but any one on board a vessel who has some permanent connection with it, and whose labor contributes to the accomplishment of the main objective of a voyage, as long as the ship is being navigated.

The Jones Act also permits a seaman's personal representative to maintain a cause of action for the seaman's death due to negligence. The place of the tort is irrelevant so long as the injury or death resulted within the scope of the seaman's employment.[4]

The Jones Act must be construed in conjunction with the Federal Employers' Liability Act (FELA). Accordingly, a seaman's personal representative may only sue on behalf of certain specified beneficiaries.[5]

This Act permits jurisdiction in either the appropriate federal or state courts. The statutory period for bringing such action is three years. Since there are no restrictions on damages, non-pecuniary damages may also be recovered, but the award may be reduced under the application of comparative negligence.

§ 41.08 Seaworthiness

Seaworthiness, in tort terminology, means that a ship, including its hull, gear, appliances, and all other parts of the ship and its equipment and crew members are reasonably fit for their intended purposes and jobs. The standard of liability for seaworthiness is, theoretically at least, not perfection, but merely reasonable fitness.[6]

---

[4] Ivy v. Security Barge Lines, 606 F.2d 524 (5th Cir. 1979 (involving place of accident); Williams v. McAllister Bros., Inc., 534 F.2d 21 (2d Cir. 1976) (involved employment).

[5] Comment, Lewis, "Seaman's Death Actions Under the Jones Act, DOHSA, and the General Maritime Law: A Comparison," 37 Wash. & Lee L. Rev. (1980).

[6] Mitchell v. Trawler Racer, 362 U.S. 539 (1960).

A warranty of seaworthiness means that the vessel is competent to resist the ordinary attacks of wind and weather, and is competently equipped and manned for the voyage, with sufficient crew and with sufficient means to sustain them, and with a captain of general good character and natural skill.[7]

A warranty of seaworthiness extends not only to the condition of the structure of the ship itself, but requires that it be properly laden and provided with competent master, a sufficient number of officers and seamen, and the requisite appurtenances and equipments such as ballast, cables and anchors, cordage and sails, food, water, fuel and lights, and other necessary or proper stores and implements for the voyage.[8]

Under general maritime law, if a vessel is in fact unseaworthy, and the injury is proximately caused by such condition, the owner is liable regardless of fault. Due diligence on the part of the owner will not relieve him of liability for injury or death.

§ 41.09 Federal Tort Claims Act

In view of the fact that the federal government was immune from suit resulting from injuries or damages arising out of its governmental functions unless it specifically consented to such suit, Congress enacted the Federal Tort Claims Act in 1946 which permits suit in certain instances. The Act avoids responsibility for interest prior to judgment and for punitive damages, unless punitive damages are the only remedy.

There are ten exceptions to the Act:

1. Any claim or suit based upon an act or omission of an employee of the government, exercising due care, in the execution of a statute or regulation, whether or not valid, or based upon the performance or failure to perform a discretionary function or duty on the part of a federal agency or an employee of the government, whether or not the discretion involved be abused.
2. Any claim arising out of the loss, miscarriage or negligent transmission of letters or other postal matter.

---

[7] 3 Kent Comm. 287.
[8] *Black's Law Dictionary.*

3. Any claim concerning the assessment or collection of any tax or customs duty, or the detention of any goods or merchandise by any officer of customs or other law enforcement officer.
4. Any claim for damages caused by the imposition of a quarantine by the U.S.
5. Any claim arising out of assault, battery, false imprisonment, false arrest, malicious prosecution, abuse of process, libel, slander, misrepresentation, deceit, or interference with contract rights.
6. Any claim for damages caused by the fiscal operations of the Treasury or by the regulation of the monetary system.
7. Any claim arising out of the combatant activities of the military or naval forces, or the Coast Guard, during time of war.
8. Any claim arising in a foreign country.
9. Any claim arising from the activities of the Tennessee Valley Authority, Panama Railroad Company, or the Panama Canal Company.
10. Any claim arising from the activities of a federal land bank, a federal intermediate credit bank, or a bank for cooperatives.

The amendments of 1962 provided for governmental protection of federal employees who were involved in motor vehicle accidents while acting within the scope of their employment. Accordingly, the claim representative is faced with a problem if the same accident falls within the coverage provided by a policy issued by his company. This had best be left to a determination by counsel.

The Act sets up its own time limitations in which an action may be brought, namely two years after a claim accrues or unless action is begun within six months after the date of mailing or notice of a final denial of the claim by the agency to which it was presented.

§ 41.10 Occupational Safety and Health Act (OSHA)

An Act that may have far-reaching effects on compensation claims is the Occupational Safety and Health Act of 1970. This Act gives the federal government the right to examine the operations of private industry and indicate corrections for any failures or alleged failures involving the safety of the operations and the health of employees in such operations.

It also provided for the appointment of a National Commission on State Workers' Compensation Laws to evaluate these laws. The report is now in, and while it approves of the general idea of Workers' Compensation as such, it makes many recommendations, particularly for the enlargement of both the scope and the benefits, that will vitally affect insurers.

The object of the Act is to provide a job environment that is safe and to minimize recognized hazards that cause injury, disability, or death. Employers are required to comply with the safety and health standards set forth in the Act and also those promulgated by the Department of Labor.

It is generally agreed that in the years that the Occupational Safety and Health Act has been law, it has become increasingly clear that in its current form, OSHA isn't working. One *New York Times* article notes that:

> The mood of Congress and of the public in the late 1960's and through 1970 resulted in legislation that is extremely difficult to interpret.
>
> For example, the stated purpose of Congress in setting up OSHA was "to assure so far as possible every working man and woman in the nation safe and healthful working conditions and to preserve our human resources. Each employer shall furnish each of his employees employment and a place of employment which are free from recognized hazards that are causing or are likely to cause death or residuous physical harm to his employees."
>
> Note should be taken of the phrase "free from recognized hazards." Does this mean totally free, nearly, or substantially free, "recognized" and "hazards" are not defined. . . .
>
> Clearly, it is time for Congress to consider a major review of the language of the bill.

§ 41.11 Death On The High Seas Act (1976) (DOHSA)

DOHSA grants a cause of action in admiralty for the death of a person or a seaman due to a shipowner's negligence or for either unseaworthiness or negligence in the case of a seaman, occurring outside of U.S. waters.

Under DOHSA the decedent's personal representative can only sue on behalf of the decedent's spouse, parents, children, or dependent relatives. The decedent's representative must prove that the

§ 41.12   CASUALTY INSURANCE CLAIMS

defendant's "wrongful act, neglect or default" caused the seaman's death.

While recovery can be made based on unseaworthiness or negligence in the case of a seaman, any other person may recover only on the basis of negligence.

Jurisdiction may be accepted by a federal admiralty court or by a state court. The statutory period for bringing an action under DOHSA is two years from the death causing act and recovery is limited to pecuniary losses suffered by the beneficiaries in a death case. Comparative negligence may reduce the amount of an award.

§ 41.12   Racketeer Influenced and Corrupt Organizations Act (RICO)

RICO is encompassed within Title IX of the Organized Crime Control Act of 1970. This Act creates a relatively new cause of action for many old wrongs, ranging from business fraud to bribery, and allows treble damages and attorney's fees to prevailing plaintiffs.[9]

Section 1962 of this Act lists four activities that are proscribed:

1. It prohibits a person from using or investing income derived from a pattern of racketeering activity in an interstate enterprise.
2. It prohibits a person from acquiring or maintaining an interest in, or control of an interstate enterprise through a pattern of racketeering activity.
3. It prohibits a person from conducting or participating in the affairs of an interstate enterprise through a pattern of racketeering activity.
4. It prohibits a person from conspiring to violate any of the provisions listed above.

Racketeering activity is defined as any act or threat involving certain itemized state or federal crimes. *Pattern of racketeering* is interpreted to mean two or more racketeering acts within a period of ten years. *Enterprise* includes "any individual, partnership, corporation, association or other legal entity" or "group of individuals associated in fact."

---

[9] Cooper & Rice, "The Statutory Liability of Attorneys Under Rico," Insurance Counsel Journal, October 1986, from which article much of the material in this section was taken.

In addition to criminal penalties, this Act also authorizes civil penalties. It is the civil area with which we are here concerned and where activity has proliferated in just the last few years.

As is not unusual, some lawyers and courts have used this Act in a way that appears to me to subvert its original intent. Respected corporations and other legal entities have been sued under civil RICO despite some limitations set by some courts.

These limitations were an important factor in court decisions until the Supreme Court left many previous decisions in shambles, in the case of *Sedima, S.P.R.L. v. Imrex Co.*[10] In this case, the court stated that "Congress wanted to reach both 'legitimate' and 'illegitimate' enterprises. . . . (RICO) makes it unlawful for 'any person—not just mobsters' to engage in the prohibited activities." The court seemed to forget that there are remedies galore which have consistently and successfully been used against legitimate enterprises that can be reached easily by the arms of the law.

In his dissenting opinion, Justice Marshall stated that "The court's interpretation of the civil RICO statute quite simply revolutionizes private litigation. . . . (it) federalizes important areas of civil litigation that until now, were solely within the domain of the states."

As Cooper and Rice so aptly state:[11]

> By inviting plaintiffs to bring commercial cases in the form of RICO actions, *Sedima* also puts increased pressure upon defendants to settle. The complexity and expense of defending RICO actions, the potential of having to pay treble damages and the stigma of being labelled a "racketeer" . . . will lead many defendants to think twice before following their cases through to trial.

Justice Marshall made the same point in his dissent, "It is thus not surprising that civil RICO has been used for extortive purposes, giving rise to the very evil that it (RICO) was designed to combat."

On the other hand, Stephen P. Eisenberg[12] states that "looking beyond the language (of Rico) and more into the purpose of the statute, the insurance industry has an effective tool to use not only as a deterrent to fraud, but as a recovery vehicle. The industry suffers from billions of dollars in fraudulent claims annually." The thrust of his

---

[10] 741 F.2d 482 (2d Cir. 1984), *reversed*, 473 U.S. 479 (1985).

[11] "The Statutory Liability of Attorneys Under Rico," Insurance Counsel Journal, October 1986.

[12] Partner of Leahy & Eisenberg, Ltd., Chicago, Ill., as reported in the Insurance Adjuster Magazine, September 1986.

argument, however, is aimed at property losses and I certainly agree with him that the industry does not use all of the tools at its disposal even in property claims, although in this field much progress has been made in the last several years. However, while such cases are important and should not be neglected, in the bodily injury liability field, especially since the decision in the *Sedima* case,[13] there is little doubt in my mind that Justice Marshall's dissenting opinion was much more on target than the majority decision.

Concurrent Jurisdiction in RICO Cases. The question of concurrent jurisdiction of state and federal courts in RICO cases was recently considered in the case of *Greenview Trading Co. v. Hershman & Leicher.*[14] In this case the court stated that

> Congress consciously patterned the RICO section after the antitrust prototype. Legislators must have known that courts have construed virtually identical language as giving federal courts exclusive jurisdiction over antitrust claims. It would be anomalous for this court to hold that the jurisdictional grant in the RICO statute did anything other than create exclusive federal jurisdiction over civil claims by persons injured by violation of (RICO).

The court concluded by stating that "Congress did not intend to involve state courts so deeply in the interpretation of a host of federal statutes and we are persuaded that the better conceptual analysis of the problem points against concurrent jurisdiction for the state courts." This view, however, is not unanimous.[15]

§ 41.13 Bibliography

Bernstein, "The Federal Role in Meeting Consumer Insurance Needs," Address of the Federal Insurance Administrator, U.S. Dept. of Housing & Urban Development, before the N.Y. City Bar, March 29, 1971.

Bue, Jr., "Admiralty Law in the Fifth Circuit—A Compendium for Practitioners," Houston L. Rev., Winter 1968.

---

[13] Sedima, S.P.R.L. v. Imrex Co., Inc., 741 F.2d 482 (2d Cir., 1984), *reversed,* 473 U.S. 479 (1985).

[14] 108 A.D.2d 468, 489 N.Y.S.2d 502 (1st Dept. 1985).

[15] *See* Luebke v. Marine Nat'l Bank of Neenah, 567 F. Supp. 1460 (Wis. 1983); Cianci v. Superior Court of Contra Costa Cty., 40 Cal. 3d 903, 710 P.2d 375, 222 Cal. Rptr. 575 (1986).

Comment, Lewis, "Seaman's Death Actions Under the Jones Act, DOHSA, and the General Maritime Law: A Comparison," Wash. & Lee L. Rev., vol. XXXVII (1980).

Davies, "A Survey of Maritime Tort Exposure for Personal Injuries After the 1984 Longshore & Harbor Workers' Compensation Act Amendments," Insurance Counsel Journal, July 1985.

"Farewell to Sieracki, Ryan and Other Water Sports," Insurance Adjuster Magazine, December 1972.

Leonard, "Remedies Available to Injured Parties: Offshore Oil Operations and Litigations," Voorhies & Labbe, Lafayette, La.

Long, "The Federal Tort Claims Act," FIC Quarterly, Summer 1962.

Ray, "The Warranty of Seaworthiness Extended to Maritime Workers—Is Its Application Unlimited?", Insurance Counsel Journal, January 1973.

Troy, "Loss of Consortium in Federal Employers' Liability and Other Federal Act Cases," 11 F.T.D. 9, November 1970.

Wrightson, "Procedures Required Under the Federal Tort Claims Act," Insurance Adjuster Magazine, October 1963.

RICO

Cooper & Rice, "The Statutory Liability of Attorneys Under RICO," Insurance Counsel Journal, October 1986.

Gors, "RICO—Does It Need Major Surgery?", Insurance Adjuster Magazine, March 1986.

Lorentzen & Huppert, "Blame It On RICO: The Impact of the Racketeer Influenced and Corrupt Organization's Act on the Insurance Industry Following Sedima," FIC Quarterly, Fall 1985.

Mrozek & Sullivan, "Defending RICO Claims: A 'Pattern' of Activity," F.T.D., 18 November 1986.

CHAPTER 42

Wrongful Termination of Employment

§ 42.01 Introduction
§ 42.02 Actions Brought in Contract
§ 42.03 Implied Contracts—Personnel Manuals
§ 42.04 Public Policy Exceptions to the "At-Will" Doctrine
§ 42.05 Implied Covenant of Good Faith and Fair Dealing
§ 42.06 Tort of Wrongful Discharge
    [1] Fraud
    [2] Intentional Infliction of Emotional Distress
    [3] Employment Discrimination
    [4] Other Grounds for Tort Actions
§ 42.07 Some Insurance Problems in Termination of Employment Cases
    [1] Umbrella Policies
    [2] Errors and Omissions and Directors and Officers Liability Policies
    [3] Comprehensive and Commercial General Liability Policies
    [4] Occurrence—Pattern and Practice
    [5] "Civil Suit"
    [6] Public Policy in Insurance Coverage
    [7] Workers' Compensation Policy
§ 42.08 Checklist for Handling Termination Cases
§ 42.09 Bibliography

§ 42.01 Introduction

For more than a century, the doctrine of "employment at will" has been about as unquestioned a rule of law as there was on the books. Exceptions to the doctrine arose out of state and federal civil service laws, express employment contracts, or the terms of collective bargaining agreements.

Employment at will meant that absent an express and definite agreement to the contrary, an employer had the right to terminate the employment of an employee for any reason, no reason, or even a malicious reason. In recent years, a large majority of the state courts have carved out common law exceptions to the employment at will doctrine.

Most states have by now made serious inroads into the employment at will doctrine, either by judicial or legislative decision. The decisions and statutes run the gamut from protecting an employee for refusing to follow an employer's directive to break the law, to the requirement that the employer must show good faith and fair dealing before firing a long-time employee.

Actions for wrongful termination of employment today rest not only on a steady erosion of the employment at will doctrine, but also on the complex web of state and federal fair employment and civil rights legislation enacted in recent years.

This trend is, I believe, a step in the right direction. Recent decisions should help to prevent the arbitrary and ill will termination of employees who have a reasonable expectation of continued employment based on some contractual or statutory right, absent good cause for termination. It should encourage better systems of evaluation, greater care in the definition of employment terms and conditions, and generally provide fair treatment of employees who are not otherwise protected by the civil service rules or the terms of collective bargaining agreements.

Actions for wrongful termination of employment may be brought alleging breach of contract, written or implied, or in tort. An action brought in contract is usually more difficult to establish and will not permit an award of punitive damages.

§ 42.02 Actions Brought in Contract

Generally speaking, an express employment contract has not been strictly construed to guarantee permanent employment. A written contract including this type of promise or a promise of "employment for life" is typically not enforced because the promise has been found to be indefinite or lacking in mutuality. Courts have reasoned that since the employee is not bound to remain in the job permanently, that the contract lacked mutuality of obligation.[1]

In the absence of legislation to the contrary, a contract for wages at some specific amount per year or month, does not create a con-

---

[1] **Fla.:** Hamlen v. Fairchilds Indus's., Inc., 413 So. 2d 800 (App. 1982).
Mass.: Maddaloni v. Western Mass. Bus. Lines, Inc., 438 N.W.2d 351 (App. 1981).
N.M.: Gonzales v. United Southwest Nat'l Bank, 602 P.2d 619 (1979).

tract for the term specified, but is merely indicative of the term of employment.[2]

The same refusal to strictly construe the contract terms has been demonstrated by courts refusing to enforce a promise to discharge for good cause only, because the employee is free to leave at will,[3] unless additional consideration has been given, such as giving up one employment in return for a new job.[4]

Other interpretations of contract language have been construed in favor of employment at will, but this attitude is changing.

§ 42.03 Implied Contracts—Personnel Manuals

There is a growing tendency to consider employer's statements found in personnel manuals, advertising material, and other company publications concerning employee benefits and security as an implied contract, varying the otherwise at-will status of an employee. For instance, the Colorado Court of Appeals recently held that the specific procedures set forth in a company personnel manual become binding when relied on by employees to whom they are distributed.[5] In this respect, Colorado falls in line with some other jurisdictions.[6]

The New Jersey courts have recently held that employees have the right to rely on the language in a company personnel manual

---

[2] **Colo.:** Justice v. Stanley Aviation Corp., 530 P.2d 984 (1974).
D.C.: Sullivan v. Heritage Foundation, 399 A.2d 856 (1979).
[3] **Fla.:** Russell & Axon v. Handshoe, 176 So. 2d 909 (1965).
N.D.: Wadeson v. American Family Mut. Ins. Co., 343 N.W.2d 367 (1984) (verdict for defendant).
[4] **Mo.:** Lopp v. Peerless Serum Co., 382 S.W.2d 620 (1964).
N.J.: Rognozinski v. Airstream by Angell, 377 A.2d 807 (1977).
Contra: **Alas.:** Eales v. Tanana Valley Med.-Surg. Group, 663 P.2d 958 (1983); **Iowa:** Moody v. Gogue, 310 N.W.2d 655 (1981).
[5] Salimi v. Farmers Ins. Group, 684 P.2d 264 (Colo. Ct. App. 1984).
[6] **Mich.:** Toussaint v. Blue Cross & Blue Shield of Mich., 292 N.W.2d 880 (1980) (landmark case).
Mo.: Arie v. Intertherm, Inc., 648 S.W.2d 142 (App. 1983).
Neb.: Morris v. Lutheran Med. Center, 340 N.W.2d 388 (1983) (despite verdict for defendant in this case).
Nev.: Southwest Gas Corp. v. Ahmad, 688 P.2d 661 (1983).
N.J.: Wooley v. Hoffman-La Roche, Inc., Case No. A-98-82 (May 9, 1985).
N.Y.: Weiner v. McGraw-Hill, Inc., 57 N.Y.S.2d 458 (1982).
N.D.: Hammond v. N. Dakota State Personnel Bd., 345 N.W.2d 359 (1984).
Ore.: Yartzoff v. Democrat-Herald Pub. Co., 576 P.2d 356 (1978).

even if they never saw the manual.[7] The court further stated that if there was no clear and prominent disclaimer, an employment manual's promise that an employee will be fired for just cause only, is enforceable. Conversely, a North Carolina appellate court[8] held that an employer is not obligated to follow its personnel policies if they are not expressly incorporated in a written employment contract. Other courts have adhered to the traditional rule that company manuals and personnel statements do not create an exception to the at-will doctrine.[9]

In any event, the question of whether a personnel manual affords any protection to at-will employees has been held to be a question of fact.[10] Even where the manual contained disclaimer language expressly intended to establish employment-at-will, such a disclaimer is not "written in stone," and can be changed by subsequent company action.

In the case of *Longley v. Blue Cross & Blue Shield of Mich.*,[11] the court stated that:

> We recognize that the absence of an initial expectation of termination only for just cause, would not bar an employee's claim that his or her employer subsequently modified the employment contract, i.e., at some point during the course of employment, the employer instituted policies or practices which give rise to a legitimate expectation of contractual rights.

§ 42.04 Public Policy Exceptions to the "At-Will" Doctrine

In many jurisdictions, the courts have held that an employer may not discharge an at-will employee if, to do so, would frustrate and subvert the clear public policy of the state. Such an action is usually brought in tort,[12] but some jurisdictions also permit such a cause of

---

[7] Wooley v. Hoffman-LaRoche, Inc., Case No. A-98-82 (May 9, 1985).

[8] Griffin v. Housing Authority of Durham, 303 S.E.2d 200 (1984).

[9] **Del.:** Heideck v. Kent General Hosp., 446 A.2d 1095 (1982).
Kan.: Johnson v. National Beek Packing Co., 551 P.2d 779 (1976).
Pa.: Richardson v. Chas. Cole Mem. Hosp., 466 A.2d 1084 (1983).

[10] Leikvold v. Valley View Comm. Hosp., 688 P.2d 170 (Ariz. 1984).

[11] 356 N.W.2d 20 (Mich. App. 1984).

[12] **Md.:** Moniodis v. Cook, 494 A.2d 212 (1984) (employee discharged for refusing to take polygraph test).
N.H.: Clouter v. Great A. & P. Tea Co., 436 A.2d 1140 (1981) (malice must also be shown).

action to be brought in contract.[13] The New Jersey Supreme Court has recognized that such a cause of action may be brought in either tort or contract.[14] Some cases involve bad faith conduct resulting in the breach of an implied contract.[15]

While some courts require a showing of malice in addition to a violation of public policy, other courts hold that the mere showing of malice is, of itself, a violation of public policy.[16]

The application of the public policy exception to at-will employment varies from state to state. In addition, problems of definition are present. For instance, the New Hampshire court, in the case of *Howard v. Door Woolen Co.,*[17] stated that the public policy exception applies only when an employee is discharged for doing an act which public policy would encourage, or for refusing to do what public policy would condemn. The courts have consistently failed to spell out the policy sought to be fostered or condemned.[18]

Public policy exceptions have been upheld for such obvious reasons as sexual harassment and incitement to a crime,[19] to discharge for reasons of age or sickness,[20] or for joining a union.[21] Some courts, however, have rejected public policy as a basis for recovery altogether.[22]

Pa.: Geary v. United States Steel Corp., 319 A.2d 174 (1974) (action may also be brought on malice).

Wis.: Brookmeyer v. Dun & Bradstreet, 335 N.W.2d 834 (case nevertheless decided in favor of the defendant).

[13] **Cal.:** Peterman v. International Brotherhood of Teamsters, 344 P.2d 255 (1959).
N.H.: Monge v. Beebe Rubber Co., 316 A.2d 549 (1974).

[14] Pierce v. Ortho Pharmaceutical Corp., 417 A.2d 505 (1980).

[15] Lucas v. Brown & Root, Inc., 736 F.2d 1202 (1984) (applying Arkansas law. Case involved sexual harassment).

[16] Boreson v. Rohm & Haas, Inc., 526 F. Supp. 1230 (1981) (applying Pennsylvania law).

[17] 414 A.2d 1140 (1981).

[18] *See* the New Jersey Supreme Court's discussion of sources of public policy in Pierce v. Ortho Pharmaceutical Corp., 417 A.2d 505 (1980). *See also* Tameny v. Atlantic-Richfield Co., 610 P.2d 1330 (1980) (this case held that federal antitrust law may be a source of public policy).

[19] Lucas v. Brown & Root, Inc., 736 F.2d 1202 (8th Cir. 1984).

[20] Howard v. Door Woolen Co., 414 A.2d 1273 (N.H. 1980).

[21] **Cal.:** Glenn v. Clearman's Golden Cock Inn, 13 Cal. Rptr. 769 (1961).
S.C.: Gregory Elec. Co. v. Custodis, 312 F. Supp. 300 (1970).

[22] **Colo.:** Lampe v. Presbyterian Med. Center, 590 P.2d 513 (1978).
Del.: Heideck v. Kent Gen. Hosp., 446 A.2d 1095 (1982).
N.Y.: Murphy v. American Home Prod's., 461 N.Y.S.2d 232 (1983).
Vt.: Jones v. Keogh, 409 A.2d 581 (1979) (public policy recognized only when there is a clear and compelling case).

A prime example of a court's refusal to recognize a public policy exception to at-will employment is found in the U.S. District Court case of *Perdue v. J.C. Penney Co.*[23] In that case, members of the company's internal audit committee were discharged for their attempts to investigate a bribery and kickback scheme within the company. The court held that there was no cause of action since under Texas law an improper motive does not make an otherwise lawful act unlawful.

One of the most helpful summaries of the scope of the public policy exception may be found in the Michigan Supreme Court's opinion in *Suchodolski v. Michigan Consolidated Gas Co.*[24]

> In general, in the absence of a contractual basis for holding otherwise, either party to an employment contract for an indefinite term may terminate it at any time for any, or no, reason. However, an exception has been recognized to that rule, based on the principle that some grounds for discharging an employee are so contrary to public policy as to be actionable. Most often these proscriptions are found in explicit legislative statements prohibiting the discharge, discipline, or otherwise adverse treatment of employees who act in accordance with a statutory right or duty.
>
> The courts have also occasionally found sufficient legislative expression of policy to imply a cause of action for wrongful termination even in the absence of an explicit prohibition on retaliatory discharges. Such a cause of action has been found to be implied where the alleged reason for the discharge of the employee was the failure or refusal to violate a law in the course of employment. . . .
>
> In addition, the courts have found implied, a prohibition on retaliatory discharges when the reason for a discharge was the employee's exercise of a right conferred by a well-established legislative enactment.

§ 42.05 Implied Covenant of Good Faith and Fair Dealing

In California and a few other jurisdictions, the courts have recognized that an implied covenant of good faith and fair dealing is an essential factor in any employment relationship, regardless of wheth-

---

[23] 470 F. Supp. 1234 (1979) (applying Texas law).
[24] 316 N.W.2d 710 (1982).

er any specific promises were made.[25] Here again, there is a question as to what constitutes good faith and fair dealing. In the case of *Crosier v. U.P.S., Inc.*,[26] the California court held that an employer could be legitimately concerned with appearances of favoritism and possible allegations of sexual harassment, that could negate any allegation of bad faith in dismissing an employee.

§ 42.06 Tort of Wrongful Discharge

More and more courts are beginning to recognize the tort of wrongful discharge if termination of employment is based on malice or bad faith on the part of the employer.[27]

[1] Fraud

In an action for wrongful termination based on an employer's fraudulent inducement, the road is far from smooth for an employee pressing such a claim. Ordinarily, the employee must not only show that representations were made by the employer leading him to believe that termination of employment would be for just cause only, but also that such assurances were made by the employer, knowing them to be false and fraudulent.

In the case of *Harrison v. Fred S. James*,[28] the court listed the essential elements of fraud as: (1) misrepresentation, (2) communicated with fraudulent intent, (3) with the intent that another person will thereby be induced to act or refrain from acting, (4) with justifiable reliance upon such communication, and (5) with resulting damage to that person. The elements of a cause of action for fraud vary from state to state in more, or less, extrapolated forms.

Several jurisdictions have recognized a cause of action for wrongful discharge on the basis of fraud on the part of the employer.[29]

However, old thinking dies hard, and some courts have refused to permit an employee to bring an action for fraudulent inducement

---

[25] **Cal.:** Cleary v. American Airlines, 168 Cal. Rptr. 722 (1980); Pugh v. See's Candies, 171 Cal. Rptr. 917, *modified,* 117 Cal. App. 3d 520 (1981).
Idaho: Rosencrans v. Intermountain Soap & Chemical Co., 605 P.2d 963 (1980).
[26] 198 Cal. Rptr. 361 (App. 1983).
[27] *See* McNulty v. Borden, Inc., 474 F. Supp. 1111 (1979) (applying Pennsylvania law).
[28] 558 F. Supp. 438 (1983) (applying Pennsylvania law).
[29] **Fla.:** Hamlen v. Fairchilds Indus., Inc., 413 So. 2d 800 (1982).
Va.: Sea-Land Service, Inc. v. O'Neal, 297 S.E.2d 647 (1982).

§ 42.06[2]   CASUALTY INSURANCE CLAIMS

of an employment relationship, refusing to recognize an exception to at-will employment in such a case. One reason for this is the perceived difficulty in establishing damages.[30]

[2] Intentional Infliction of Emotional Distress

Intentional infliction of emotional distress is another basis for bringing an action for wrongful termination of employment.[31]

[3] Employment Discrimination

In this day and age, any allegation of termination of employment on the basis of race, religion, sex, age, marital status, or any other discriminatory classification must be regarded as serious, and investigated thoroughly. An action for discrimination of employment may be brought under any number of state and federal legislative enactments such as:

1. The Age Discrimination Employment Act of 1967.
2. The Equal Pay Act of 1963.
3. The Pregnancy Discrimination Act of 1978.
4. The Civil Rights Act of 1871.
5. Title VII of the Civil Rights Act of 1964.
6. The Equal Opportunity Act of 1972.
7. State and Local Fair Employment Statutes or Ordinances.

It has been stated that the multiplicity of potential forums for claims of employment discrimination makes it very tempting for complainants and their attorneys to take more than "one bite of the judicial apple."[32]

---

[30] **N.Y.:** Waldman v. Englishtown Sportswear, Ltd., 460 N.Y.S.2d 552 (1983).
N.C.: Briggs v. Mid-State Oil Co., 280 S.E.2d 501 (1981).
[31] **Ala.:** American Products Serv. Co. v. Inmon, 394 So. 2d 361 (1980).
Mass.: Agis v. Howard Johnson Company, 355 N.E.2d 315 (1976).
Ore.: Hall v. May Dept. Stores Co., 637 P.2d 126 (1980) (evidence of abusive conduct in trying to obtain confession of theft).
Pa.: Shaffer v. National Can Corp., 565 F. Supp. 909 (1983) (sexual harassment).
S.C.: Hudson v. Zenith Engraving Co., 259 S.E.2d 812 (1979).
See also Larson, "Employment Discrimination" published by Matthew Bender & Co., and "Probing the Wrongful Termination Claim," by G.E. Fleming, CAIIA Newsletter, December 1985.
[32] Jauvtis & Callender, "Applicability of Res Judicata to Employment Law Cases," F.T.D., April 1983.

Actions for employment discrimination have been brought on the basis of age,[33] inter-company employee dating,[34] sex,[35] and joining a union,[36] among others.

[4] Other Grounds for Tort Actions

While some termination of employment claims have been based on negligence and other theories, their success rate has been minimal.[37]

§ 42.07 Some Insurance Problems in Termination of Employment Cases

Aside from the policies or endorsements written to grant specific coverage for wrongful termination of employment, the problem of insurance coverage is very complex. The present trend seems to indicate that the wording of many policies that were written with no intent to cover such incidents are being interpreted in ways not previously contemplated by the insurers.

[1] Umbrella Policies

Umbrella policies are not standard and vary considerably. A few offer discrimination coverage without limitation. Some neither mention discrimination as a covered offense under the term "personal injury," nor specifically preclude discrimination as a covered offense or subject to certain limitations.

Donald S. Malecki, in his series of articles on "Employment Bias"[38] lists some limitations that appear in umbrella policies:

"Discrimination, except that committed by or at the direction or consent of the insured.

---

[33] **Colo.:** Rawson v. Sears, Roebuck & Co., 585 F. Supp. 1393 (1984).
[34] **Mich.:** Sears v. Ryder Trust Rental, Inc., 596 F. Supp. 1001 (1984) (held not to be discriminatory).
[35] **Ore.:** Holien v. Sears, Roebuck & Co., 677 P.2d 704, *aff'd and remanded*, 689 P.2d 1292 (1984).
[36] **Cal.:** Glenn v. Clearman's Golden Cock Inn, Inc., 13 Cal. Rptr. 769 (1961).
[37] For a detailed discussion, *see* Larson, "Employment Discrimination," published by Matthew Bender & Co.
[38] National Underwriter, April and May 1983.

"Racial or religious discrimination not committed by or at the direction of the named insured, executive officers, directors, stockholders, or partners.

"Liability arising out of the violation of any statute, law, ordinance or regulation prohibiting discrimination or humiliation because of race, religion, national origin, sex, color, or age.

"Liability for personal injury arising out of discrimination, including fines or penalties imposed by law, if insurance coverage thereof is prohibited by statute or committed at the insured's direction.

"Racial, religious, sex or age discrimination committed by or at the direction of the insured, or when insurance is prohibited by law.

"Liability for violation of civil rights acts or violation of constitutional rights."

Personal injury in these policies is usually defined as including "mental injury," "mental anguish," "humiliation," and terms of a similar nature. Some policies require that such conditions arise out of physical injuries, and some do not.

Claims of sexual harassment, libel, or slander before or after discharge causing damage to reputation or making reemployment difficult, and invasion of privacy are not uncommon, and these kinds of actions would warrant at least defense, and in many cases, even settlement, depending on the policy wording.

Accordingly, defense and duty to pay would depend on the particular policy involved and the interpretation that the courts would give to its wording. This is a wide-open area.

The broad form of the 1973 CGL policy also includes wording that could be questioned, but it does have a specific exclusion that is related to the employment of a person by the named insured.

[2] Errors and Omissions and Directors and Officers Liability Policies

Errors and Omissions policies are professional liability coverage, designed to provide coverage for the legal obligations of a professional or trade nature. They agree to pay for "breach of duty" because of any negligent act or omission of the insured.

In the case of *Multnomah County v. Mission Ins. Co.*,[39] the court stated that claims of a disparate impact which do not require discriminatory intent could encompass actions, judgments, or decisions that

---

[39] 650 P.2d 929 (Ore. 1982).

might be considered as negligent acts which would then be covered under an errors and omissions policy.

Officers and Directors policies cover only the liability of the individual directors and do not provide coverage for the corporation itself. In my opinion, many courts would grant coverage for a suit based on wrongful termination of employment that is brought against an officer or director.

[3] Comprehensive and Commercial General Liability Policies

Claims for wrongful termination of employment have alleged that "wages, salary and other benefits" are covered as "property" under the CGL policies.

The definition of "property" in these policies means "(1) physical injury to or destruction of tangible property . . . or (2) loss of use of tangible property which has not been physically injured or destroyed. . . ."

Several cases have, in fact, held that wrongful discharge and claims made for "loss of wages, salary and other benefits" could not ordinarily be interpreted as a loss of tangible property.[40]

Another coverage problem under the CGL policies has involved the definition of "bodily injury," which in the policies is defined as "bodily injury, sickness or disease sustained by any person which occurs during the policy period, including death at any time, resulting therefrom."

Emotional distress has been held in some jurisdictions to be bodily injury only if there are also physical manifestations of disability.[41]

On the other hand, there have been some cases that have held to the contrary that mental or emotional distress alone constitutes "bodily injury."[42]

---

[40] **Ga.:** Southeastern Color Lith's., Inc., v. Graphic Arts Mut. Ins. Co., 296 S.E.2d 378 (App. 1982).
Wyo.: Oyler v. State of Wyoming, 618 P.2d 1042 (1980).
[41] **Cal.:** Employers Cas. Ins. Co. v. Foust, 29 Cal. App. 3d 382 (1972) (this case however, has left a legacy of doubt).
Fla.: Skroh v. Travelers Ins. Co., 227 So. 2d 328 (1969).
N.D.: Rolette County v. Western Cas. & Sur. Co., 452 F. Supp. 125 (1978) (court specifically stated that embarrassment, humiliation, mental anguish, and emotional disturbance, in and of themselves, are not bodily injury as defined in the policy).
[42] **La.:** Levy v. Duclaux, 324 So. 2d 1 (1975).
U.S.: Commercial Union Ins. Co. v. Gonzales Rivera, 358 F.2d 480 (1st Cir. 1966).

In my opinion, where there is an element of doubt concerning physical injury resulting from, or accompanying emotional distress, there would certainly be a duty to defend, and in certain jurisdictions, this would be so even without any physical manifestation of injury.

[4] Occurrence—Pattern and Practice

The definition of "occurrence" in the CGL policies states that it means "an accident, including continuous or repeated exposure to conditions which results in bodily injury or property damage, neither expected nor intended from the standpoint of the insured." Wording in the umbrella policies is usually quite similar. Several decisions have held that termination of employment is not an "accident."[43] I doubt, however, whether these decisions will have much effect on other courts.

The question of whether wrongdoing such as "discrimination" or "sexual harrassment" was the cause of the wrongful termination of employment, does not ordinarily involve a determination as to whether there was one or more occurrences, which could have a bearing on coverage other than for termination of employment.

In a termination case, there is one act upon which the suit is brought, so the question as to whether there was one or more occurrences becomes academic. If, however, there is a question involving a statute of limitations, the question of when the termination occurred does become of vital importance.

The question of one or more occurrences may have a bearing in making a determination of discrimination, since some cases have held that to prove discrimination there must be a showing of a "pattern and practice" rather than a proof of a single act.[44]

In the case of *Appalachian Ins. Co. v. Liberty Mut. Ins. Co.*[45] the court held that an "occurrence" takes place when the plaintiff is damaged, and not necessarily when the wrongful act was committed.

---

[43] Cal.: St. Paul Fire & Marine Ins. Co. v. Superior Court, 161 Cal. App. 3d 1199 (1984).

N.Y.: Mary & Alice Ford Nursing Home Co., Inc. v. Firemen's Ins. Co. of Newark, 439 N.E.2d 883 (1982).

[44] Transport Ins. Co. v. Lee Way Motor Freight, Inc., 487 F. Supp. 1325 (1980) (this case also involved coverage questions in different policies).

[45] 676 F.2d 56 (1982).

Damages, in this case which was subsequently settled, were based on periods of employment during the policy periods.

[5] "Civil Suit"

An action for discrimination may be brought under a federal act or state statute, or before a commission or board set up for the purpose of hearing and deciding such cases.

Insurers have questioned actions brought for termination of employment before such administrative bodies on the grounds that a "civil suit," as used in the insurance policy, is confined to a suit that is filed in a common law court only, and not in any administrative tribunal.

The court, in the case of *Community Unit School Dist. v. Country Mut. Ins. Co.*,[46] held that "civil suit," in the strict sense of a suit filed in a common law court is a "term of art" in the legal profession and that a narrow specialized meaning is not the common understanding of the term. This case stated that the common understanding is that a civil suit is any attempt to gain legal redress or to enforce a right that may be brought before adminstrative or quasi-judicial bodies such as workers' compensation boards, police and fire commissions or human rights commissions. The word "civil" merely denotes the noncriminal nature of the action.

[6] Public Policy in Insurance Coverage

Insurance against suits alleging wrongful termination of employment, or employment discrimination, have usually been held not to violate public policy,[47] despite allegations to the contrary made by insurers. The argument has also been made that while public policy may, in some jurisdictions, prohibit insurance coverage resulting in intentional injury, it should not prohibit coverage involving intentional acts resulting in unintended injury.

---

[46] 419 N.E.2d 1257 (1981).

[47] U.S.: Solo Cup Co. v. Federal Ins. Co., 619 F.2d 1178 (7th Cir. 1980); Union Camp Corp. v. Continental Cas. Corp., 452 F. Supp. 565 (Ga. 1978).

[7] Workers' Compensation Policy

Suits have been brought under both Part 1 (Coverage A) and Part 2 (Coverage B) under the Workers' Compensation policy of which Coverage B is for Employers Liability.

Under Coverage A, some actions have been brought on the allegation that the wrongful discharge was retribution for the filing of a workers' compensation claim.

In the case of *Wojciak v. Northern Package Co. & Nat'l. Sur. Co.*,[48] for instance, a former employee alleged that his employment was terminated by his employer in retaliation for his having made just such a workers' compensation claim. The employee's action sought compensatory and punitive damages and the employer turned his claim over to both his compensation and general liability insurers, both of whom refused to defend this suit. This action was then brought against both insurers under a Minnesota statute. The insurers contended that retaliatory termination of employment, forbidden by the statute, could not be covered by insurance as a matter of public policy.

Both insurers appealed the decision by the trial court holding that both policies covered the incident. The supreme court affirmed the decision against the compensation carrier (holding for coverage) and reversed in favor of the general liability carrier (holding no coverage). In this decision, the court stated that wage loss, medical treatment, vocational rehabilitation, and penalties are all benefits encompassed by the word "compensation." All other rights granted an employee by law, including the right to recover damages because of retaliatory acts were held to be "other benefits" also covered by the compensation policy.

By some convoluted reasoning, the court also permitted the award of punitive damages under the compensation policy and held that the exclusion of the CGL policy should be held valid.

Much of the "reasoning" in this case is frankly beyond me, but this decision is nevertheless, now on the books.

The ruling on "other benefits" mentioned in the policy: "To pay all compensation *and other benefits* (italics added) required of the insured by the workers' compensation law" has also been litigated

---

[48] 310 N.W.2d 675 (1981).

in other suits.[49]

Under Coverage B (Employers Liability), terms such as "bodily injury" and "accident or disease" are loosely defined when questions of coverage arise. The question of "accident" as to whether the act or the result was intended, is up for discussion.[50]

In interpreting "arising out of" and "in the course of" employment, it has been stated that:

> In our view, the wrongful discharge, or related conduct, may be found to "arise out of" and "in the course of" the employment, because (any) emotional distress may begin before "employment" ends or may otherwise be sufficiently related to it.[51]

§ 42.08 Checklist for Handling Termination Cases

- ☐ Check coverage thoroughly:
  - ○ Determine the grounds upon which suit is being brought; whether for breach of written or implied contract, tort, discrimination, or any combination.
  - ○ Check allegations against coverage available.
- ☐ Interview personnel director:
  - ○ Determine reason for termination and who requested action.
  - ○ Identify immediate supervisor and interview.
- ☐ Check personnel file carefully:
  - ○ Determine if file is complete.
  - ○ Review original job application for possible false statements. Find out if any check was made of the allegations on the application.
  - ○ Find out how long the employee had been employed with the company and previous employment record if available. If advisable, make investigation of previous employment record.
  - ○ Carefully review any performance reports. Obtain copies.
  - ○ Determine whether the employee was ever promoted, received any salary increases or bonuses for good work, or other commendations.
  - ○ Find out if any complaints were recorded against the employee and get full details.
  - ○ Determine if any previous warnings were given for inadequate performance and what action was taken.

---

[49] **Ill.:** Rubenstein Lumber Co. v. Aetna Life & Cas. Co., 462 N.E.2d 66 (App. 1984).
Minn.: Wojciak v. Northern Package Co. & Nat'l Surety Co., 310 N.W.2d 675 (1981).
Tex.: Artco-Bell Corp. v. Liberty Mut. Ins. Co., 649 S.W.2d 722 (App. 1983).
[50] *See* Mary & Alice Ford Nursing Home Co., Inc. v. Fireman's Ins. Co. of Newark, 57 N.Y.2d 656 (1982).
[51] Wrongful Discharge Seminar Outline compiled by Sedgwick, Deter, Moran & Arnold, Los Angeles, Ca.

§ 42.09   CASUALTY INSURANCE CLAIMS

- ○ Find out if any time limitation was given for correction and what subsequent action was taken, if any.
- ☐ Review any written contract of employment. Determine if any oral assurances were given and get details. Check personnel manuals, advertising material, and bulletins for pertinent material.
- ☐ Carefully investigate any allegations of wrongdoing on the part of the employer, such as:
  - ○ Discrimination for reasons of sex, race, religion, foreign background, politics, union activities, etc.
  - ○ Employer's abusive conduct, malice, or retribution.
  - ○ Employer's request to perform unlawful acts.
  - ○ Employer's fraud or misrepresentations.
- ☐ Find out if employee was given severance pay or time to get a new job. Get details and learn if employee did indeed get another job. Where and at what salary? Was a release signed in exchange for severance pay?
- ☐ Interview department head:
  - ○ Determine if he or she was the one who graded employee's performance. If not, interview supervisor who did. Determine if there was any animosity between them and get details.
- ☐ If warranted, interview coworkers to check any details.
- ☐ Determine if there was an adequate training program, if pertinent, and get details. Was proper supervision and training given?
- ☐ Determine if employee was an activist or union organizer. Did employee exhaust union grievance process?
- ☐ Place all records for safekeeping with corporation counsel or other reliable officer.
- ☐ Learn whether employee was recruited, how and what promises were made to him or her.
- ☐ If employment agency was involved, get details.

§ 42.09 Bibliography

Comment, Elder, "Erosion of the Employment-At-Will Doctrine: Choosing a Legal Theory for Wrongful Discharge," 14 Capital Univ. L. Rev. 461 (1985).

Jauvtis & Callender, "Applicability of Res Judicata to Employment Law Cases," F.T.D., April 1983.

Larson, "Employment Discrimination," published by Matthew Bender & Co.

Malecki, "Employment Bias," series of articles for The National Underwriter, Cincinnati, Ohio, April and May 1983.

CHAPTER 43

Subrogation—Salvage—Contribution

§ 43.01 Subrogation
    [1] Policy Wording
    [2] Applicable Insurance Lines
    [3] Third Party Recovery
    [4] Third Party Settlement by Insured
    [5] Sample Form Lien Letters
    [6] Other Subrogation Rights
    [7] Right of Action
    [8] Defenses to Subrogation Actions
    [9] Voluntary Payment
    [10] Waiver of Subrogation Rights
    [11] Loan Receipts
    [12] Practical Application of Subrogation Rights
    [13] Some Factors to Consider
    [14] Subrogation Receipt
    [15] Knock-For-Knock Agreements
    [16] Subrogation Agreement
    [17] Arbitration
    [18] Deductible Feature of Collision Policy
    [19] Subrogation Apportionment—Excess Carrier
    [20] Recovery Expenses
    [21] A Few Recent Cases Involving Subrogation
    [22] Subrogation Under the Workers' Compensation Acts
§ 43.02 Salvage
    [1] In General
    [2] Checklist for Claims Involving Salvage
§ 43.03 Contribution
§ 43.04 Bibliography

§ 43.01 Subrogation

Subrogation, in the insurance industry, is the term used to describe the right of an insurance carrier who has paid a claim as a result of an accident or loss covered under a policy, to recover from a wrongdoer for the damage caused, up to the amount paid by the insurer. In other words, the insurer is substituted for the insured for the purpose of making a claim against the third party wrongdoer to recover the money paid under the policy.

Subrogation plays a very important part in claim work. Proper handling of this phase of insurance can make the difference between a profitable and an unprofitable operation. Every dollar recovered after expenses, is pure profit. Unlike the premium dollar, there are no commissions or other fees that must be deducted.

While the right of subrogation does not arise until after payment has been made to or for the insured by his insurance carrier, the claim representative must be alert to the possibilities of subrogation from the very inception of the claim and must prepare his investigation accordingly.

The right of subrogation may arise in law as a matter of equity or by contractual agreement. We are of course particularly concerned with the rights arising out of insurance policies.

[1] Policy Wording

Most casualty policies, where subrogation is a factor, contain a subrogation condition which reads, in effect, as follows:

> In the event of any payment under this policy, the Company shall be subrogated to all the insured's rights of recovery therefore against any person or organization and the insured shall execute and deliver instruments and papers and do whatever else is necessary to secure such rights. The insured shall do nothing after loss to prejudice such rights.

A similar provision appears in the workers' compensation policies. Many of the state insurance statutes incorporate this or similar wording in their workers' compensation laws.

The basic wording in the newer "plain language" policies reads:

> A. If we make a payment under this policy and the person to or for whom payment was made has a right to recover damages from another we shall be subrogated to that right. That person shall do:
>
> 1. Whatever is necessary to enable us to exercise our rights, and
>
> 2. Nothing after loss to prejudice them.
>
> B. If we make a payment under the policy and the person to or for whom payment is made recovers damages from another, that person shall:
>
> 1. Hold in trust for us the proceeds of the recovery, and
>
> 2. Reimburse us to the extent of our payment.

Where subrogation rights are asserted under the conditions of the policy, such conditions become the sole measure of the insurer's rights. The insurer is limited to the rights of the insured and only to the extent of the amount paid by the insurer.[1]

[2] Applicable Insurance Lines

Subrogation may apply to the following kinds of insurance policies or bonds:

1. Motor Vehicle
2. Workers' Compensation
3. Marine and Inland Marine
4. Fire
5. Fidelity-Surety

The basic principle of subrogation is the same in each instance. The insurer is substituted for the insured in any right of recovery against a wrongdoer.

In workers' compensation claims, subrogation rights are subject to the laws of the various states. While these may and do differ in their requirements for bringing actions against the wrongdoer, their purpose is uniform in attempting to deny double recovery to the injured and in protecting whatever subrogation rights an insurer may have.

The right of subrogation does not apply to life insurance or usually to accident and health policies unless the latter contain a specific subrogation clause, which is rare.

[3] Third Party Recovery

In all first party claims involving a third party wrongdoer, the insured has a choice of recovery, either under his first party policy, or against the third party wrongdoer, or his carrier. Recovery, however, can only be made once. Therefore if the insured chooses to press his claim against the third party, and makes recovery without the consent of the insurer, he relinquishes his right to make a claim under his first party policy.

---

[1] Merchants Fire Assur. Corp. v. Hamilton Co., 69 A.2d 551 (R.I. 1949).

[4] Third Party Settlement by Insured

In the event that the insured recovers under his first party policy, he loses the right to recover against the wrongdoer to the extent of the amount paid him by his first party insurer. Accordingly, if settlement is made under a first party policy, the claim representative should be certain that his insured is advised that he must not try to recover for his own benefit against the third party for the same damage. If he does make a recovery from the third party (or the third party carrier) after the claim has been paid under his first party policy, the first party carrier is entitled to repayment from the insured, assuming that such recovery is made without the knowledge or consent of the insurer.[2]

On the other hand, the tortfeasor or wrongdoing third party could remain liable to the first party insurer if he knew of the first party insurer's rights of subrogation at the time the latter settled the claim. It is therefore obvious that the company must notify the third party and his carrier of its interest in the matter as soon as possible after receiving a report of an accident. A release given by an insured ordinarily voids the right of subrogation unless a lien or some notice has been filed with the wrongdoer.

It has been held that a mere sending of a lien letter in advance of payment of a claim is not sufficient to hold the third party wrongdoer or his insurance carrier in double jeopardy unless the carrier that has the subrogation rights notifies the wrongdoer or his carrier that payment has actually been made on the claim.

The court held in *National Surety Corp. v. Bimonte*[3] that the plaintiff's right to subrogation did not actually arise until the claim had been paid and since the lien letter preceded any payment made, and did not give the amount of any expected payment, it was ineffective.

Accordingly, the letter notifying the wrongdoer or his carrier of subrogation rights should be followed by a notification that payment has been made including the amount of such payment.

It is just as essential that the claim representative keep possible subrogation involvement in mind when making a property damage settlement. As we have indicated, payment of such a claim to a third party claimant where notice of subrogation rights has been received could put the company in a position of double jeopardy.

---

[2] Western Fire Ins. Co. v. Phelan, 179 Kan. 327, 295 P.2d 675 (1956).
[3] 143 So. 2d 709 (Fla. 1962).

[5] Sample Form Lien Letters

No single form can be devised to fit all situations. The following two letters therefore are given as examples only, and should be used as and where they fit the situation. They can be edited as needed.

1. Claims Involving First Party Property Damage

John J. Jones, insured under [Insurance Co.] Policy No. _____ has made claim for damage to his [automobile] caused by the negligent operation of your car resulting from the accident which occurred on [date of accident] at [place of accident]. The [Insurance Co.] because of its subrogation rights, hereby makes claim against you for the amount [state amount if known] which it has been or will be required to pay and requests prompt settlement of this claim.

If, at the time of this accident, you were insured against loss arising out of claims of this kind, we suggest that you forward this letter to your insurance company without delay.

Please let us know when this has been done and send us the name and address of your insurance company. We shall appreciate it if you will let us hear from you by return mail.

2. Workers' Compensation Form

A claim for workers' compensation benefits has been filed by [employee] in which he alleges that the injuries which he sustained were caused by your negligence.

As the compensation insurer for this employer, we hereby inform you and put you on notice to the effect that it is our intention to assert all rights which we now have, or which we may acquire against you for reimbursement of any sum we have, or may be required to expend in the payment of compensation, medical expenses or other items of expense.

If you have insurance covering this accident, please notify your insurance carrier at once.

Our rights in this matter are incorporated in the workers' compensation law and your attention is directed thereto.

[6] Other Subrogation Rights

Subrogation rights are not necessarily limited to first party (collision, fire, theft, etc.) or workers' compensation policies only. They may arise because of vicarious liability imposed upon a third party insured under a financial responsibility statute or in some instances because of agency.

For example, if payment is made under a nonownership policy because of the negligence of the driver-owner of the automobile, the carrier may bring an action to recover the amount paid against the driver-owner.

[7] Right of Action

In subrogation actions, suits may be brought in the name of the insured or may be required to be brought in the name of the carrier, depending upon the law of the jurisdiction involved, and the nature of the action being brought. In either event, investigation should be completed as soon as possible and action to recover should be taken without too much delay after payment has been made.

In workers' compensation cases, some state acts provide a lien in favor of the compensation carrier against the third party or his carrier if they are put on notice. Such a letter of notification must be drawn to fit the requirements of the particular Act. It is, of course, important that the claim representative take advantage of any lien rights that may have been granted. Failure to give notice in such a case may waive the subrogation rights.

[8] Defenses to Subrogation Actions

Any defense which a tortfeasor could ordinarily maintain, can also be asserted against the insurer in a subrogation action. The insurer does not lose its right of subrogation by waiving any of its policy defenses for breach of policy conditions such as late notice or failure to cooperate.[4]

However, the tortfeasor can defend a subrogation action against the insurer on the grounds that there was no coverage in the first place or that coverage was specifically excluded.[5]

[9] Voluntary Payment

Subrogation rights do not extend to voluntary payments made by the insurer. Payment of a claim properly covered by an insurance policy, however, is not construed as a voluntary payment. It is merely the fulfillment of a legal or contractual obligation.

---

[4] Potomac Ins. Co. v. Nickson, 231 P. 445 (Utah 1924).
[5] Inland Empire Ins. Co. v. State Farm Mut. Auto. Ins. Co., 86 So. 2d 247 (La. App. 1956).

If the insurer chooses to pay a claim that is not covered, with full knowledge of this fact, he thereby becomes a mere volunteer and is not entitled to subrogation rights.[6]

[10] Waiver of Subrogation Rights

An insurer may waive his right of subrogation either by express agreement or by failure to act.

If an insurer pays a claim with full knowledge of a settlement that has already been made between the insured and the wrongdoer, he waives his right of subrogation.[7]

Even more so, if he induces the insured to make settlement with the third party, he loses his right of subrogation.[8]

Furthermore, if an insurer unreasonably delays a settlement, knowing that the insured has financial need, he may waive his right to subrogation in the event that settlement does not take care of the complete obligation under the policy.[9]

[11] Loan Receipts

As already stated, an action against the wrongdoer, ordinarily brought under a subrogation clause, is usually brought in the name of the insured, although, in some other instances, it may be brought in the name of the insurance company.

A loan receipt is sometimes obtained for the purposes of:

1. Permitting the insurer to bring an action against the wrongdoer in the name of the insured where this might otherwise be contested.
2. In order to enable the insurer to pay the claim promptly before third party liability has been established.
3. To further protect the insurer's rights of subrogation.

After a first party claim has been paid by an insurance carrier, recovery against the wrongdoer becomes a primary concern of the insurer. Since the insured cannot make double recovery, it is obvious that his interest in any further action is greatly diminished, if not altogether extinguished.

---

[6] Employers Mut. Fire Ins. Co. v. Piper, 334 S.W.2d 925 (Ky. 1960).
[7] Weaver v. New Jersey Fid. & Plate Glass Ins. Co., 56 Colo. 12, 136 P. 1180 (1913).
[8] Mims v. Reid, 98 So. 2d 498 (Fla. 1957).
[9] American Auto Ins. Co. v. Clark, 122 Kan. 445, 252 P. 215 (1927).

§ 43.01[11] CASUALTY INSURANCE CLAIMS

In view of the fact that the insurance company becomes at this point, the real party in interest, under the laws of most states, its action must be prosecuted against the wrongdoer in its own name. The danger in doing so is obvious. Consciously, or not, most juries will side with an individual against a corporation, especially if the corporation is an insurance company.

The loan receipt is an instrument designed to permit the insurance company to bring such action against the wrongdoer in the name of the insured despite the fact that the insured no longer has a financial interest in the outcome. It provides in effect that the amount of the loss is advanced to the insured as a loan which is repayable only to the extent of any recovery made from the wrongdoer. The insured further agrees to enter and prosecute a suit against the wrongdoer in his own name. Such a receipt substitutes a "loan" for a "payment."

The wording of a loan receipt has become fairly standard and an example of such wording is as follows:

> Received from [Insurance Co.], the sum of _____ Dollars as a loan, without interest, under Policy No. _____ repayable only in the event and to the extent that any net recovery is made by [insured] from any person or persons, corporation or corporations, or other parties because of loss by fire, windstorm or other casualty for which this company may be liable occurring to [insured's] property on or about the [date].
>
> As security for such repayment [insured] hereby pleges to [insurer] whatever recovery may be made and deliver to it herewith all documents necessary to show the undersigned hereby agree to promptly present claim and, if necessary, to commence, enter into and prosecute suit against such persons, corporations or others through whose negligence the aforesaid loss was caused, or who may otherwise be responsible therefore, with all due diligence, in the undersigned's name, but at the expense of, and under the exclusive direction and control of the said [insurer].
>
> It is further agreed that the making of this loan by the [insurer] shall not be construed as a waiver of any of its rights and defenses under Policy No. _____ issued to [insured].

While there have been conflicting decisions as to the validity and effectiveness of such a loan receipt, for the most part it has been held to serve its purpose, despite the fact that it has been attacked as a sham in an effort to hide the real party in interest.

[12] Practical Application of Subrogation Rights

Judgment must be used in determining whether or not to press any subrogation rights that the company may have.

If the amount involved is small and the liability doubtful, it would be patently unwise to press subrogation rights when by so doing an otherwise quiescent claim for bodily injury or extensive property damage may be activated. Even if the amount involved is substantial, it is sometimes inadvisable to press subrogation rights if this might result in a retaliatory claim for serious bodily injury on a case of doubtful liability. Any question about the advisability of asserting subrogation rights should ordinarily be discussed with the claims manager or home office before taking any definite action.

The problems involved in subrogation, and the economic effects of good subrogation handling has caused many of the larger insurance companies to set up separate subrogation departments within their claim or legal departments. This is usually warranted where the subrogation volume is considerable. In these situations, a settled claim is referred to the subrogation department where standard procedures have usually been set up to handle such claims.

[13] Some Factors to Consider

Some factors which should be given consideration before making a final decision concerning subrogation are:

1. **Amount recoverable.** A substantial amount will of course warrant the expenditure of more time and effort than will a nominal amount.

2. **Expense.** The effort and expense involved in an attempt to recover should be warranted by the amount recoverable. It is not common sense to spend $20.00 worth of time in an effort to recover $10.00 in money. This does not mean, however, that no effort should be made to collect claims involving small amounts if this can be done through your own efforts and without undue expense. Some effort should always be extended to make recovery by mail, telephone, or personal contact where warranted.

Expense factors to be considered are: (a) cost of investigation in both time and money; (b) legal fees; and (c) suit expenses such as reimbursement for witnesses' fees, expert's testimony, and so forth.

3. **Insurance.** An attempt should always be made to find out whether the wrongdoing third party carries insurance and if so with

what company and to what extent. Always be sure to check your own underwriting files to make sure that such coverage is not being carried in your own company.

4. **Identity of third party.** It is of course essential to establish the exact identity of the wrongdoer and determine whether he is an agent or an individual, copartnership, corporation, or whatever.

5. **Financial responsibility.** If the individual or his principal does not have insurance an investigation should be made, in cases that warrant it, to determine the extent of financial responsibility of both the individual and his principal. This can be done fairly reasonably through one of the companies that specialize in this sort of work. There is little point in spending time and money to obtain a worthless judgment.

6. **Potential antagonisms.** The claim representative should check with the insured to determine whether there will be any business repercussions if an action is brought against the wrongdoer. In some instances, the insured's right may arise out of a manufacturer-wholesaler, manufacturer-retailer, or similar relationship in which the goodwill of the wrongdoer may be important to the insured in a business way. Although this should not be the determining factor in the final analysis, as far as the Claim Department is concerned, it is always good business practice to discuss such matters with the Underwriting Department so that they can have the opportunity of deciding whether any possible recovery would be worth the antagonism that might be created.

7. **Retaliation.** Give primary consideration to the possibility that prosecution of subrogation rights might stir up a retaliatory large property damage or bodily injury claim. If this is at all possible, it is well to give serious consideration before awakening sleeping dogs.

8. **Liability.** Even though other factors prove favorable to pressing a subrogation action, lack of liability on the part of the third party can of course defeat all other considerations. It is usually inadvisable to spend the time, effort, and money to press a subrogation claim unless it is felt that the chances of success are at least 50–50 or better.

[14] **Subrogation Receipt**

The right of subrogation arises normally through common law, but, as we have previously stated, is reaffirmed in the policy provisions.

Actually a subrogation receipt adds nothing to the subrogation clause already provided for in the policy. In the event that the claim representative may encounter the unusual circumstances in which there is no subrogation provision in the policy, he would be wise to obtain a subrogation receipt. Such receipt may be worded as follows:

> Received from [insured] through [insurer] _____ Dollars in full satisfaction, compromise and discharge all claims for loss and expense sustained to property insured under Policy No. _____ by reason of [describe the accident] which occurred [date] and in consideration of which the undersigned hereby assigns and transfers to the said company each and all claims and demands against any person, persons, corporation, or property arising from or connected with such loss or damage and the said company is subrogated in the place of and to the claims and demands of the undersigned against the said person, persons, corporation, or property in the premises to the extent of the amount above named.

[15] Knock-For-Knock Agreements

Agreements whereby the insurer does not press subrogation rights against another insurer as a matter of reciprocity are prevalent in the British Commonwealth of Nations and are known as Knock-For-Knock Agreements. Such agreements assume that in the long run the subrogation rights which an insurer may have are equalized by the claims which might be made against it as a result of which both parties avoid the time and expense necessary to press subrogation rights against each other.

There are several kinds of Knock-For-Knock Agreements that operate in various parts of the world and the idea has also caught on in some parts of the United States where it has sometimes been sponsored by local claim associations of various kinds.

[16] Subrogation Agreement

In 1958, a claim executive's association in Wisconsin designed a subrogation agreement that would apply to insurers who had claims against each other. This agreement outlines some thirteen specific instances which illustrate applicability of subrogation rights and the percentages of recovery in each instance. The same agreement or others patterned after it were adopted by other claim organizations.

The advantage of these agreements is obvious in that it not only avoids unnecessary time and expense of individual collections, but also avoids cluttering the courts with numerous property damage claims that are disposed of without the necessity of litigation.

[17] Arbitration

One of the programs previously sponsored by the American Insurance Association is the Inter-Company Arbitration Agreement. The purposes of this agreement are to improve claims service, to afford relief to the courts, and to prevent litigation of disputes between member companies as much as possible, thereby enhancing the confidence of the public in the insurance industry.

The vast majority of inter-company cases can and are quickly resolved by arbitration. These comprise, for the most part, property damage claims, usually in relatively small amounts, that would otherwise tend to clog the court calendars unnecessarily.

There are also arbitration programs set up by the American Bar Association and the Defense Research Association.

Proper use of arbitration machinery avoids legal expense and tends to lessen misunderstandings and friction among companies in the insurance industry, in addition to other advantages previously mentioned.

[18] Deductible Feature of Collision Policy

Practically all motor vehicle policies today covering collision losses are written on a deductible basis.

Ordinarily, an insurer has no right to represent an insured in pressing the insured's claim against the third party. As a practical matter, the deductible feature of the policy is usually the smallest part of the claim and is tied in with the subrogation claim of the insurer. The general practice therefore is for both carriers to treat the claim as a unit and dispose of the insured's as well as the insurer's claims in any settlement negotiations.

Where recovery for the deductible amount has been made, the amount due to the insured is to be determined by the general practice followed in any particular locality. In some areas legal fees involved in the recovery are apportioned. In others, the insured will receive a proportionate share in the settlement and now, in most jurisdictions, the insured's deductible is paid first and the remainder kept by the insurance company.

The amount involved is so small that there are few legal precedents to follow. It becomes a matter of business and public relationships in each particular area.

[19] Subrogation Apportionment—Excess Carrier

Ordinarily any recoveries made by a carrier under a subrogation action would make the excess carrier whole first.

Under a 1963 district court decision in the District of New York, however, the court permitted first recovery by the primary insurer because the primary insurer had taken a loan receipt. The court stated that the position of the excess insurer is no better than of the insured. The decision furthermore gave no weight to the "custom" in the insurance industry for the proceeds of a subrogation recovery to be applied first to the payment made by the excess underwriter.[10]

[20] Recovery Expenses

It is only logical that if the insured's personal attorney brings an action in which he makes a recovery for the insurer as part of that action, he should be reimbursed for a proportionate amount of his fees and expenses as a representative of the insurer.[11]

[21] A Few Recent Cases Involving Subrogation

A Wyoming Supreme Court held that unless one makes a payment that he is legally obligated to make, or for which he is liable, he becomes a volunteer, and a volunteer is not entitled to subrogation.[12]

In a case decided by the Kansas Supreme Court, subrogation was held to be within the restrictions of a two year statute of limitations for torts, since the two year limitation was applicable to the insured's cause of action against the tortfeasor and since the insurer stands in the shoes of its insured.[13]

In a case decided by a court in Nevada, an action for damages was instituted which included a subrogation action by a fire insurer. The

---

[10] City Gen. Ins. Co. Ltd. v. St. Paul F. & M. Ins. Co., 11 Fire & Cas. Cases 923 (1963).
[11] Tennessee Farmers Mut. Ins. Co. v. Pritchett, 32 Auto Cases 2d 288 (Tenn. App. 1964).
[12] Commercial Union Ins. Co. v. Postin, 610 P.2d 1095 (1980).
[13] Farmers Ins. Co. v. Farm Bur. Mut. Ins. Co., 608 P.2d 923 (1980).

court ruled that the policy included all losses "due to the negligence of any insured." Based on this interpretation, subrogation was not available against its own insured.[14]

A widow's recovery for the death of her husband was found to be out of the reach of an insurer's claim for death benefits and medical expenses.[15]

An Arizona court held that a reimbursement agreement was in fact an assignment of a personal injury claim and precluded recovery by the insurer after settlement by the insured with the third party wrongdoer.[16]

[22] Subrogation Under the Workers' Compensation Acts

Since the matter of subrogation under the Workers' Compensation Acts has already been discussed in § 39.07, *supra*, "Third-Party Action," we will not here go into the subject in great detail.

The right of subrogation in Workers' Compensation insurance is derived from the Workers' Compensation Acts of the various states. In addition, the Workers' Compensation Policy specifically provides for subrogation within its provisions.

Practically every Workers' Compensation Act makes some provision for the employer or the insurer to be subrogated to the rights of the injured claimant against the wrongdoer for medical payments or compensation paid to him or on his behalf.

In most states, the action to recover the amount paid may be brought in the name of the employee. In a few states the action under certain circumstances must be brought in the name of the real party in interest.

If the employer or carrier sues in its own name and recovers more than it has paid it must, in the overwhelming majority of states, return the excess after expenses have been deducted, to the injured claimant.

If an employee lives in a state in which he is permitted to take compensation and thereafter sue the third party, he must always reimburse his employer or the insurance carrier in full out of the sum

---

[14] Harvey's Wagon Wheel, Inc. v. MacSween, 606 P.2d 1095 (1980). *See also* Transamerica Ins. Co. v. Gage Plumbing & Heating Co., 433 F.2d 1051 (10th Cir. 1970); Baugh-Berlarde Constr. Co. v. College Utilities, 561 P.2d 1211 (Alas. 1977); Truck Ins. Exch. v. Transport Indem. Co., 591 P.2d 188 (Mont. 1979).

[15] In re Schmidt, 398 N.E.2d 589 (Ill. App. 1980).

[16] Brockman v. Metropolitan Life Ins. Co., 609 P.2d 61 (1980).

he received from the third party. If he does not make full recovery, some apportionment is made depending upon the provisions of the particular Act.

In some states, the claimant has a right of election, but even in a few of these, if he sues the third party initially and does not recover as much as he would under the Compensation Act, he can make a claim for the difference under the Act.

The duty to notify the wrongdoer of the amount paid (usually in the form of a lien) has previously been discussed. To repeat (merely for the sake of emphasis): it is essential to follow the prescribed rules set up by your particular Act and to given prompt notice that you will hold the third party responsible for any moneys paid out on the claim.

There is so little uniformity in the procedures and in the rights granted under the various subrogation provisions that it is futile, for our purposes, to go into the matter in any greater detail. It can only be suggested once again that the claim representative become familiar with the provisions of the Act with which he is working.

§ 43.02 Salvage

[1] In General

Property upon which the total value has been paid as a result of a claim under an insurance policy, rightfully belongs to the insurance company. Such property is commonly known as salvage. Properly handled, it can be an important source of revenue for an insurance company.

Despite the fact that an article may be considered a total loss for settlement purposes, more often than not the damaged article has some monetary value. It sometimes takes a little ingenuity to find a market for some articles, but it can ordinarily be done with the use of a little imagination and effort.

Salvage is a matter to be considered not only in the disposition of first party claims but in the settlement of third party claims as well. The claim representative will often find that a claimant may be willing to settle a claim for a lesser amount if he is permitted to keep the article that the company is paying for. In such an event it is usually more practical and economical to permit the claimant to retain the salvage if adequate deduction is being made for the value of the property in its damaged condition. Automobile salvage is a highly specialized field in which there is usually some buyer available whether the market be high or low at the time. It must become part of a claim representative's routine to become acquainted with dealers in wrecked cars so that he can always obtain a number of competitive bids on automobile salvage.

If the salvage involves a large object, like an automobile, make sure that it is protected from weather damage as well as from theft. It is of course important that the claim representative arrange for economic storage until such time as he can dispose of the article so that the eventual amount recovered will at least be more than the storage charges. For this reason, it is also advisable to dispose of salvage as soon as possible after having carefully explored the available market. Many insurers dispose of their salvaged items through salvage companies set up for this purpose.

[2] Checklist for Claims Involving Salvage

The following summarization is an outline of steps to be considered in the handling of a claim involving salvage.

- ☐ Whenever you have paid for the total loss of an article, either obtain credit for it from the claimant or take it in salvage, assuming that it is available and has some value.
- ☐ Protect the salvage from theft, further deterioration, and the elements.
- ☐ Arrange for storage at the lowest possible cost.
- ☐ Explore the market for all possible buyers.
- ☐ Dispose of the salvage as soon as possible. Retention increases depreciation as well as storage charges.
- ☐ Ordinarily, avoid selling salvage to coemployees or buying it yourself. You may both become dissatisfied customers and may, in addition, leave yourself open to unwarranted suspicion of favoritism.

§ 43.03 Contribution

Although the subject of contribution does not properly belong in the category of subrogation or salvage, proper attention to it can be an important item of possible financial gain to a company. This is reason enough to make some mention of it here.

The good claim representative should always be conscious of the possibility that someone else's responsibility for the payment of a loss may be equal to his company's or even greater than it. In many instances, the automobile and public liability policies may overlap: the claim representative must be awake to the possibility of such a situation. For example, an insured's automobile may have been involved in an accident while on the premises of the insured. In such instance, the public liability carrier would very likely be in as coinsurer, depending on the terms of the policies.

Ordinarily (excluding the operation of guest statutes), a passenger involved in a two-vehicle accident has a right of action against the owner and driver of the car in which he was a passenger as well as the owner and driver of the opposing car. Sometimes two cars will collide and injure a pedestrian or damage property belonging to someone else.

Occasionally, there will be two similar policies covering the same insured. There may be other instances, as well as these mentioned, in which it is advisable to check the possibility of contribution. This should be prominent in the thinking of the claim representative during the investigation of any casualty claim.

It is well to remember that a jury does not ordinarily try to determine the degrees of negligence if the plaintiff has an action against two tortfeasors.

If there is a question of contribution between insurance companies, every effort should be made to determine the matter amicably and, if possible, without resort to the courts. In the event of an honest difference of opinion, both may be willing to arbitrate the matter.

§ 43.04 Bibliography

Bybee, "Profits in Subrogation: An Insurer's Claim to Be More Than Indemnified," FIC Quarterly, Spring 1980.

Denenberg, "Subrogation: Recovery: Who Is Made Whole?", FIC Quarterly, Winter 1979.

Ferrini, "Commercial Law—An Effective Alternative to Tort Principles in Pursuing Subrogation," Insurance Adjuster, January 1980.

Horton, "Subrogation Suits: After Berlinski," Insurance Law Journal, September 1973.

"Insurer's Subrogation Rights—Recent Insurance Cases," F.T.D., September 1980.

Kimball & Davis, "The Extension of Insurance Subrogation," 60 Mich. L. Rev. 841 (1962).

Procaccia, "The Effect and Validity of Subrogation Claims in Insurance Policies," Insurance Law Journal, October 1973.

§ 43.04

Snyder, "Towards A New Theory of Subrogation," Insurance Counsel Journal, July 1976.

"Subrogation: Is It Worth The Effort?", Insurance Adjuster, May 1984.

CHAPTER 44

Reporting and Reports

§ 44.01 Introduction
§ 44.02 Reporting
    [1] Necessity for Reporting
    [2] Necessity for Prompt Reporting
    [3] Manner and Form of Reporting
    [4] The Art of Dictating a Report
    [5] Objectionable Material
§ 44.03 Reports
    [1] Casualty Claim Investigation Report Outline (Other than Compensation)
        [a] Suits
    [2] Compensation Claim Investigation Report Outline
    [3] Special Report Outlines
    [4] Interim Reports
    [5] Final Reports

§ 44.01 Introduction

As with every other facet of claim handling, reporting on a claim or suit should be done with a common sense approach.

The handling of minor claims where the amounts involved are small and of a routine nature, with little possibility of serious developments, are today mostly done by telephone, or form letters. Obviously, such claims do not require detailed reporting. To do so on a minor claim would be a waste of time and effort. Personal Injury Protection (P.I.P.) and medical payment claims of a minor nature would fall into this classification.

Sometimes, however, a claim that on the surface appears to be routine, may contain aspects that could result in a sizeable claim because of possible medical developments or because of suspected fraud. In such event, the file should contain enough information to put a supervisor or subsequent handler on notice.

The magnitude of the liability combined with the seriousness of the injury plus other possible complications will suggest the amount of detail which a report should contain and this is a matter of common sense judgment.

The following instructions, outlines, and checklists are based on the needs involved in handling a major claim. It is easier to eliminate unnecessary captions than it is to remember to include all important details. So—take from this section what you need but do not overburden a file with useless details.

Some companies have form reports for small claims which can be completed by hand. In doing so care should be taken to make the handwriting legible. Other companies use a preprinted form for all reports. Obviously, the claim representative should follow the procedures established by his company. Within most forms, however, there is opportunity for enlargement if necessary.

After a first full report, subsequent follow-up reports need only highlight any new or additional information obtained. If the new information contradicts previous reported material or adds to the seriousness of the claim, such information should be highlighted.

For reasons of economy and storage, most companies today do not transcribe reports or make copies of statements immediately, even in the serious category. Tapes and discs are kept in storage until needed. If this is the case, it is important for a claim representative to make a complete enough summary of his full report as is necessary for him, or someone following him, to give proper attention to the case.

§ 44.02 Reporting

[1] Necessity for Reporting

The following points further emphasize the absolute need for a file to show the work which has been done on a case. The file is invaluable:

1. In the event that something happens to the investigator, such as his resignation or transfer from a particular job, sudden illness, or other incapacity.
2. If the investigation has been requested by another branch office and the information must be relayed to that branch.
3. So that the investigation may be reviewed while the claim representative is away from the office and proper instruction and guidance given by the local supervisor or manager.

4. So that the home office may properly direct any additional investigation, submit instructions, and give educational guidance.
5. For trial counsel's review in the event that trial preparation becomes necessary.
6. So that a complete chronological record will be available if needed for the defense of a claim in court.
7. For the purpose of maintaining a long-term record if there is the possibility of a claim being pressed in the future.

Hence, it is obvious that reporting is a very important part of a claim representative's duties. It is also one of the most important means by which his work and efficiency are judged. If the reports do not reflect all the work being done on a case they are of little value to anyone, because a claim representative can be rated only by the work he can show as having been done. The report is not only a reflection of his capabilities as an investigator and adjuster, but is also a good indication of his ability to make himself convincing and understandable.

[2] **Necessity for Prompt Reporting**

The reporting requirements of no two companies are identical. Some prefer prompt reporting at the expense of completeness. Others will permit a longer lapse of time between reports as long as more material is eventually contained in them. It is a good rule not to delay reporting too long when there is information that is important enough to place on the file. If the information is incomplete, the claim representative can always make some comment under an appropriate caption concerning the work he intends to do in the near future.

A prompt initial report, giving as much information as is available at the time, is essential in order that a proper reserve may be placed against a claim. Very often a telephone call to a doctor or hospital will give just that additional bit of information that will enable the insurer to place a more realistic figure on a case, which would not have been possible without it. It is therefore essential that the claim representative gather as much information as he can in the shortest possible time for his initial report, and that it be forwarded promptly so that a proper reserve may be set up immediately.

Prompt reporting is also essential so that prompt determination may be made of any coverage problems. Protracted delay in taking any action may subsequently be interpreted as a waiver of the company's rights. This has been previously discussed and is emphasized here only to point out the absolute necessity for making a prompt report of the investigation on any coverage problem.

Finally, prompt reporting enables a supervisor, branch manager, or home office examiner to review the information carefully and issue instructions and immediate guidance concerning any additional investigation necessary, settlement negotiations, or instructions before conditions change. Supervisors and examiners will often be able to guide a claim representative around certain pitfalls. They may direct his attention toward avenues of investigation that might not have otherwise occurred to him because he lacked experience or because he was too close to the trees to see the forest.

[3] Manner and Form of Reporting

Most companies have an outline form of reporting that they favor. Some uniformity in the outline makes for much more efficient reading and permits the supervisor or examiner to spot details quickly upon review.

The captions that may be required for reporting run the gamut from the barest outline sketch to a complete 50-point formula that covers reams of paper just in listing all the headings. It is my belief that rigidity at either extreme is unreasonable. A report should be complete, but it should not be cumbersome. The main purpose of a claim representative is to dispose of claims. An effort should always be made to keep paper work at a minimum, necessary though it may be.

For this reason, a certain minimum nucleus of general headings should be used with latitude for the additions of as many subheadings as necessary to fit particular or special circumstances. The use of certain minimum general headings in chronological form makes for orderly reporting and results in easy reading and selection for the examiner.

Reports should at all times be logical. Where discrepancies appear, the claim representative should either explain them or point out why they cannot be explained. He should never leave contradictory statements hanging in the air, so that the reader is not certain that the claim representative is even aware of the discrepancies.

Use simple language. This does not mean to imply that the claim representative is to confine himself to two or three-syllable words. However, a forced attempt to create a literary masterpiece out of an ordinary report on a casualty claim usually results in bad reporting and worse writing. Never forget that the main purpose of the report is to convey factual information. Short concise sentences, proper paragraphing, and fairly simple language are much more effective in a report than involved and colorful phraseology. Good writing does not mean involved or tortured writing.

Avoid unnecessary verbiage and long-windedness. Be brief and concise, but not at the expense of completeness. Include every bit of information that is essential to a proper understanding of the circumstances, but do not add unnecessary detail that adds nothing of importance to the necessary information.

Although an occasional bit of humor is certainly not misplaced, no conscious attempt should ever be made to be funny. Such forced humor not only detracts from the information which the claim representative is attempting to convey, but may very often be in bad taste.

If signed statements speak for themselves they do not ordinarily need to be repeated in entirety in the body of the report. A brief outline, highlighting the essentials and commenting on contradictions, should suffice as long as reference is made to the original or copy attached to the report.

Finally, be sure to cross-reference the dictation if more than one file is involved in the investigation, such as files on compensation and liability, or public liability and automobile.

[4] The Art of Dictating a Report

Most companies provide some sort of recording equipment for their field claim representatives. Whether they are dictating to a stenographer or into a machine, there are certain fundamentals of good practice which should be observed. For instance:

1. *Plan the dictation in advance.* A considerable amount of time is wasted if the dictator must gather and arrange material and try to plan his dictation while in the process of doing it. Such haphazard dictation reflects itself in the finished product. A brief outline and a proper arrangement of papers in advance will not only save time in the long run, but is much more likely to produce a good report.

2. *Speak clearly and concisely.* If someone mumbles, slurs words, or talks too fast, his report will contain errors and will necessitate much closer proofreading than otherwise. He should remember that the stenographer to whom he is talking or the one who will transcribe the material, may not have much technical knowledge. Very often, what appears perfectly obvious to a claim representative may not be intelligible to the transcriber.
3. *Be brief and say only what is essential.* Garrulousness is not only a waste of the claim representative's time, but a waste of the stenographer's and the ultimate reader's time as well.
4. *Spell out all involved words.* Again what appears to be elementary may certainly not be so to the stenographer. Names and proper nouns should always be spelled out.
5. *Be sure to mark all corrections carefully when dictating into a machine.* Make proper notations in accordance with instructions. A little extra effort in this respect will be very helpful to the transcriber and will result in a much better finished product.

[5] **Objectionable Material**

As we have pointed out in many parts of this text, the conduct of a claim representative must at all times be exemplary. His company requires from him a high standard of ethics, and he must follow that standard in his every day dealings with insureds, claimants, and the general public.

It is obvious, therefore, that nothing should be placed on file which might possibly be misconstrued as improper by anyone reading it. As we have previously pointed out, files are examined periodically by representatives of the state insurance departments. They are also subject to subpoena. Derogatory remarks concerning race, religion, or national origin have no more place in a file than they do anywhere else. Unwarranted malicious comments that have no bearing on the claim should not be placed in the file.

§ 44.03 Reports

[1] Casualty Claim Investigation Report Outline (Other than Compensation)

The suggested report forms which follow are not intended as investigation outlines. Suggestions for the investigation of various types of casualty claims have previously been given in detail. The suggested captions on the report form are intended to serve merely as a guide for reporting, and any information concerning details of the investigation of the subject matter of the caption or subcaption, should be referred back to the chapters on investigation.

1. **Introductory Matter.** Introductory material such as the file number, names of the insured and claimants, date of assignment and date of the report, should be included in the introductory material.

2. **Reserve.** This caption should be included in all reports of investigation. The initial report should contain a suggested reserve with a brief explanation giving reasons therefor. All subsequent reports should contain at least a short comment under the same caption on the adequacy of the reserve at that particular time, or the need for increasing or decreasing it.

3. **Coverage.** This caption should be included in all reports involving any coverage problems. If necessary, it should in effect cover the following information:

(a) Policy information, such as the effective dates of the policy, the limits of liability, and the kind of policy involved.
(b) Legal entity of the insured. (Individual, corporation, copartnership, trust, trade name, estate, and so on.)
(c) Pertinent endorsements.
(d) Medical payments limits, P.I.P., etc., if any.
(e) Primary excess or concurrent insurance. Indicate any possible deductible. Check any other possible coverage which the insured might have with your company.
(f) Delayed reporting, lack of cooperation, or any other breach of policy conditions, declarations or other policy provisions. If delayed reporting is involved, this subheading should contain detailed information along with the claim representative's opinion as to whether the company's position has been prejudiced, and his recommendation concerning waiving the delay. It should also indicate whether or not a reservation of rights letter has been forwarded or a nonwaiver agreement

obtained, and, if not, whether he recommended that either of these measures be taken.

4. Identification (Automobile), or Ownership and Control (General Liability). Some identification of the insured's vehicle may be necessary on an automobile claim to make sure that the vehicle covered was the one involved in the accident.

In Public or General Liability claims it is just as essential to make an identification of the area or building where the accident occurred and to make certain that the location is covered under the policy. Adequate description of the building or locality should be given in addition to its location and information on whether the building is owned, leased, or subleased. Number and kind of tenants should also be included under this caption. If manufacturing or contracting is involved, a complete description of the operations should be included here.

5. Facts. As has previously been stated, it is not necessary to repeat verbatum the information obtained in signed statements. This caption should, however, include a general review of the insured's, claimant's, and witness' versions, highlighting any discrepancies which may be found in them. If no written statement has been obtained, it is of course essential to give the detailed information that would ordinarily have been contained in the statement.

This caption should also include an evaluation of the insured (or any other witness) as a witness. Each should be listed separately; it should include a complete description and comment concerning appearance, intelligence, credibility, veracity, and other pertinent personal traits.

Subheadings under this caption may read as follows:

(a) Insured's version.
(b) Insured's driver's or foreman's version.
(c) Claimant's or claimant's driver's version.
(d) Witnesses' versions:
  (i) Occupants of all vehicles.
  (ii) Witnesses obtained by the insured.
  (iii) Witnesses obtained by the claimant.
  (iv) Witnesses obtained by the police.
  (v) Witnesses obtained from motor vehicle or other reports.
  (vi) Witnesses obtained by neighborhood investigation or canvass.

6. **Physical Facts.** The information to be contained under this caption should include such items as a complete description of the scene of the accident, whether it be a street intersection, building, open lot, or whatever.

In the investigation of an automobile accident, the information should include street measurements, composition of the paving, general condition of the street, lighting conditions, weather, and other details mentioned in the investigation sections of this text. Similar information on Public Liability claims should include measurement and condition of stairways, areas, lighting conditions, and similar details.

Subheadings under this caption may be listed as follows:

(a) Complete description:
  (i) Scene of the accident.
  (ii) All vehicles, including description of the damage to them.
  (iii) Description of any other pertinent objects.
  (iv) Lighting.
  (v) Weather conditions and weather reports.
(b) Diagram attached. Comment on it.
(c) Photographs, snapshots, plaques, and so on. Comment.
(d) Index bureau reports.
(e) Police, detective, sheriff, state highway, or any other reports of a similar nature and comments concerning them.
(f) Motor vehicle reports.
(g) History of the accident as obtained from the hospital records.
(h) Traffic or criminal hearing information.
(i) Inquest report and comments.
(j) Autopsy report and comments.
(k) Pertinent records, such as birth, marriage, death, divorce, or separation certificates.
(l) Inspection reports by local, state, federal, or private agencies or concerns.

7. **Medical Information.** This caption should include any material that bears on the injury, such as the claimant's or attorney's allegations and any medical reports from any source whatsoever, including attending physician's examination reports, x-rays, hospital records, or a physical examination made at the company's request.

The names of all physicians and specialists should be given, along with an opinion as to their qualifications, reputation, and integrity, if known.

Subheadings under this caption may include:

(a) Visual evidence, from any source, of injury.
(b) Claimant's subjective allegations of injury.
(c) Reports or information from the claimant's doctors, dentists, surgeons, or specialists. List each individually and give an opinion on their qualifications, reputation, integrity, and so on, if known.
(d) Information on any other practitioners, such as chiropractors, naturopaths, faith healers, and so on.
(e) Hospital records, including x-rays.
(f) Medical examination by company-chosen physician.

8. **Damages.** Comment on the insured's or claimant's property damage as it is described by others or as it is visually observed by the adjuster or appraiser may be included under this heading. It should also include comment on any survey, appraisal, or expert examination made by any other specialists (engineers, chemists, contractors, and so on).

In addition, this caption can include subheadings concerning other special damages allegedly suffered by the claimant, such as lost time and earnings, hospital or doctor's bills, personal property damage loss, and similar expenses.

Suggested subheadings are as follows:

(a) Medical bills (doctors, dentists, nurses, surgeons, and so on).
(b) Insured's property damage, where pertinent, including estimates, bills, and appraisals.
(c) Claimant's property damage.
(d) Other property damage such as personal effects, including clothes, jewelry, etc.
(e) Lost time and earnings.
   (i) Employer's report and records.
   (ii) Income tax returns.
   (iii) Personal records and business accounts.
   (iv) Other sources.

9. **Liability.** This caption should include a brief review of the law, including comment on any applicable traffic regulations, building

codes, pure food laws, or other pertinent statutes or ordinances. It is always well to remember that the claim representative is not the trial counsel and is not required to give a detailed legal opinion. He should, however, have a general understanding of the legal situation and make some comment on it in his report.

10. **Subrogation and Salvage.** Some comment should be made on both of these items, if pertinent. The following information can be included under appropriate subheadings:

(a) Name of the adverse party's insurance carrier.
(b) Report on the financial responsibility of the adverse party.
(c) Settlement possibilities.
(d) Recommendations for further action.
(e) Complete description of any salvage and an indication of intended disposition including storage and care.

11. **Remarks.** This paragraph can be used as a "catch-all" to include any information not previously commented upon. It should include details of settlement negotiations with the claimant or his attorney, and an opinion on settlement evaluation.

Information of interest to the underwriting department with reference to the advisability of continuing on a risk can be reported here, as well as Index Bureau details.

Subheadings may be broken down into the following categories:

(a) Confidential Risk report.
(b) Index Bureau report.
(c) Liens (hospital, doctor, compensation carrier, and so on).
(d) Status (report on control of claimants and progress of settlement negotiations including last demand and offer).
(e) Recommendations (concerning final settlement figure, and trial or future strategy).
(f) Other information not previously reported on.

12. **Work to be Completed.** If further investigation is needed, it should be itemized here in the form of a specific paragraph for each step of the proposed investigation, such as:

(a) Police report to be obtained.
(b) Medical report from Dr. [claimant's attending physician].
(c) Check with [claimant's employer] for claimant's lost time and earnings.

§ 44.03[1][a]   CASUALTY INSURANCE CLAIMS

(d) Call on claimant before [date], to obtain additional medical information, and to maintain control, and so forth.

13. **Enclosures.** List all attachments in chronological order. Include statements, police or other reports, photographs, or any other material which should become a permanent part of the file.

[a] **Suits**

Some companies require some special form of report in the event that a case goes into suit. This may be requested as soon as suit has been instituted, after trial date has been ascertained, shortly before trial, or any combination of the three. In addition to the ordinary report form captions, information is usually required as previously discussed, under the following subheadings:

1. Title of the suit.
2. Docket and court numbers.
3. Service of summons.
4. Trial court.
5. Plaintiff's counsel.
6. Defense counsel.
7. Local court and jury conditions.
8. Availability of witnesses.
9. Attorney's opinion and recommendations.
10. Estimated cost of trial.
11. *Excess ad damnum* letter.
12. Possibility of excess verdict.
13. Counterclaim.

[2] **Compensation Claim Investigation Report Outline**

Here again it must be pointed out that the suggested form for reporting is not intended as a comprehensive guide for the investigation of Compensation claims.

The captioned material, including the file number, name of insured and claimant, date of the assignment, and date of report are to be included for Compensation as they are for liability.

Once again, we find that the suggested form has elasticity. Subheadings can be added or left out as the particular investigation demands.

1. **Reserve.** This caption should be included in all reports. The initial report should contain suggested reserves for both Indemnity and Medical benefits, with a brief explanation giving reasons therefor.

It should include the employee's wages and the compensation rate applicable in your state. Comment should be made on the exact time and wages lost, and whether or not the employee has received his salary or any portion of it during his disability.

If the claimant has returned to work, indicate whether there has been any reduction in wages or any change in occupation, and whether such reduction or change was due to the injury.

In arriving at a suggested reserve figure, the explanation should include a breakdown in the following categories:

(a) Temporary total.
(b) Temporary partial.
(c) Permanent partial.
(d) Permanent total.
(e) Specific items, such as loss of a member or disfigurement.
(f) Death benefits, including funeral expenses.
(g) Dependency, if applicable.

Subsequent interim reports should contain some comment under this caption concerning the adequacy of the reserve at that particular time, or the need for increasing or decreasing it.

2. **Compensability.** If the case involves any of the listed subheadings, comments should include all information concerning the Act of each state in which jurisdiction may be applicable.

If occupational disease is involved, report on whether the policy is endorsed to cover in those states where coverage is not automatically included in the Act. Comment can be made if necessary under the following subdivisions:

(a) Particular and peculiar endorsements, such as additional medical, occupational disease, and so on.
(b) Classification.
(c) Jurisdiction or extraterritoriality.
(d) Violations or illegal employment, including the employment of minors.
(e) Casual or temporary employment.
(f) Independent contractor relationship.

3. **Facts.** This caption should include all of the various versions of the incident itself and can be broken down into the following subdivisions:

   (a) Insured's version.
   - (i) Personal data such as name and location.
   - (ii) Business data such as the nature of the insured's business, his legal status (individual, partnership, corporation, estate, trustee, and so on).
   - (iii) Notice of the accident. The report should include the date when the insured first received notice of the injury, by whom and to whom such notice was given, in what manner, and when the injury was first reported to the company and to the Workers' Compensation Bureau.
   - (iv) Delayed reporting. This should include information on any delay on the part of the insured, either in reporting to the company or to the Board. Comment on any reasons for delay, and give an indication of corrective measures to be taken in the future.
   - (v) Factual information. This includes the insured's detailed version of how the incident occurred.

   (b) Claimant's version.
   - (i) Personal data such as name, address, age, nationality, and social security number.
   - (ii) Employment record, including the nature of the claimant's position, employment history, salary information, and so on.
   - (iii) Marital status and dependency.
   - (iv) Factual information, including complete history of the accident and information concerning any previous accidents or injuries that might have a bearing on the present case.

   (c) Witness's version.
   - (i) Personal data, including an explanation of how the incident was witnessed and why the incident was witnessed and why the witness was present.
   - (ii) Factual information about the incident itself.

4. **Physical Facts.** Complete description of the area, machinery, and so on should be included, if warranted. Lack of proper guard masks or other protective devices or failure to use them should be

commented on in detail. Subheadings can be designated as previously outlined in the Liability report form.

5. **Medical Information.** This section should include all details of the history of the accident, the nature of the injuries or disability, diagnosis and prognosis, including x-ray reports. Comment should be made on treatments rendered by all doctors, specialists, hospitals, clinics, and other practitioners.

If legible reports are attached, it should not be necessary to repeat the information contained in them, but explanatory comments should be made as needed. Any discrepancies found in the history of the accident as given on the various reports should be commented on.

Some comment should also be made on the qualifications, reputation, and integrity of all doctors, as well as the examining doctor's opinion on the effectiveness of the treatments rendered.

If there is any question of aggravation of a preexisting condition, the report should contain some information on the past medical history of the claimant and possible connection with the present condition. If there is any question of a congenital condition, comment should be made not only on the past medical history of the claimant, but also on that of claimant's immediate family. The report should also indicate who authorized or engaged the services of the physician or hospital, and include an opinion as to the advisability of obtaining an independent medical examination by an impartial doctor.

This caption may be broken down into the following subheadings:

(a) Visual evidence of injury.
(b) Claimant's subjective allegations of injury or pain.
(c) Claimant's doctors, dentists, etc., reports and some indication of their qualifications, reputation, etc.
(d) Previous medical history.
(e) Other practitioners.
(f) Hospital records, including x-ray reports.
(g) Medical examination by company-chosen physician.

6. **Fatal Cases.** In fatal cases, it is especially important to comment on the marital status and any history of previous marriages. Include the name, address, and age of the surviving spouse, the possibility of remarriage, age of all dependents, their relationship, and their degree of dependency. The report should also indicate whether these persons are conclusively presumed to be dependents under your Act,

or whether their dependency is a question of fact. The names and addresses of all possible dependents should be included. Whenever possible, all information should be corroborated by the procurement of death certificates, birth certificates, marriage certificates, and other applicable documents.

Autopsy report and coroner's findings, if any, should be attached and mentioned in the body of the report. This caption may include the following subheadings:

(a) Marital status and dependency of spouse.
(b) Other dependents, including details of dependency.
(c) Applicable provisions of your Act regarding dependency.
(d) Certified copies of all necessary certificates (marriage, divorce, separation, birth, death, adoption, and so on).
(e) Funeral expenses.

7. **Subrogation.** If there are any subrogation possibilities the claim should be investigated as though it were a regular liability case. If an insurance carrier is involved, give full details, including the name of the carrier, coverage available, and what attitude they are taking with reference to the subrogation claim. If no third-party insurance is involved, comments should completely identify the third party and indicate his financial responsibility.

The report should show whether a lien has been filed and, if so, a copy of the lien or letter notifying the third party should be attached to the report.

If a particular Act is elective, the report should indicate whether or not the employee intends to press a third-party claim. Comment on the action he may take in a particular state; state how and by whom such action can be brought. This caption may contain the following subheadings:

(a) Liability carrier for the third party, and the details of the coverage involved.
(b) Financial responsibility of the third party.
(c) Settlement possibilities.
(d) Law, which might include comment on the peculiarities of your particular Act.

8. **Other Reports.** Comment may be made here under the following subheadings:

(a) Index Bureau report.

(b) Police report.
(c) Motor vehicle hearing.
(d) Traffic and criminal hearings or trials.
(e) Confidential Risk report.

9. **Remarks and Recommendations.** This paragraph should include recommendations concerning voluntary payment, compromise, or denial. It should also include whether or not an attorney is involved, as well as any additional information not contained in any of the foregoing captions.

The final subheading under this caption should include the status of the case at the time of dictation.

10. **Work to be Completed.** This caption should include a numbered outline of the investigation to be completed and a report of intentions concerning the future handling of the claim.

11. **Attached Papers.** This caption should list individually all signed statements, reports, and other papers which are being attached to the dictation.

[3] Special Report Outlines

In outlining the general report forms for Liability and Compensation claims, it was pointed out that elasticity is essential because particular types of claims will always require slight revisions or additions to the captions suggested.

A report on an automobile property damage claim, for instance, will be a more abbreviated form of the regular liability report, whereas a report on a malpractice claim will include some subheadings not listed in either of the report forms given.

Proper reporting must of necessity allow some leeway. Once an orderly pattern of reporting has been established, however, choosing the particular subheadings that may be necessary to round out a specific report becomes second nature.

[4] Interim Reports

It is my opinion that all interim reports should contain some comment on the reserves. Unless this habit pattern is formed, it has been observed that this very important function of claim work is easily neglected.

Interim reports may contain whatever appropriate captions or subheadings are necessary to cover the information reported.

All interim reports should include the caption "Work to be Completed," and should list the investigation yet to be made.

Finally, some indication should be made of when the next report on the claim is to be expected. In other words, a general idea should be given to anyone who reviews the file of the approximate diary date that should be placed on it.

[5] Final Reports

Again, final reports vary with the requirements of the particular company. Some have rather rigid formulas which must be followed to the letter. Others may hold that the closing papers speak for themselves and require nothing further.

It is may opinion that a closing report on a bodily injury claim should at least give a brief account of the settlement negotiations and should contain enough information to justify the action taken, whether it involved a settlement or a closing without payment.

Index

References are to sections

A

Accountant's, liability of, 38.01 et seq.
  Bibliography as to, 38.07
  Client, liability to, 38.01[2]
    Standard of reasonable care owed, 38.01[2]
  Definition of practice of accounting and, 38.01[1]
  Federal Security Act and, 38.01[5]
  Privity of contract, liability to third parties and, 38.01[4]
  Professional liability policy, 38.01[6]
  Restatement (Second) of Torts and, 38.01[3]
  Statutory liability and, 38.01[5]
    Federal Security Act, 38.01[5]
  Third parties, liability to, 38.01[4]
    Privity of contract and, 38.01[4]
Acts of God
  Applicability, 9.10
  Causation due to, 9.10
Advertising injury, 26.04
Agency
  Authority of agent, 2.05
  Deviation from scope of authority granted, 10.05[1][c]
  Distinguished from brokers, 2.05
  Family purpose doctrine and, 10.05[4]

Agency—*Cont.*
  Implied
    Creation by statute, 10.05[3]
  Imputed, 10.05[1]
  Independent contractors and, 10.05[5]
  Joint venture and, liability, 10.05[1][d]
  Sub-agency, 10.05[1][a]
  Temporary or special employee, 10.05[1][b]
Ankylosis
  Causation, 8.01[1]
  Described, 8.01[1]
Architects and engineers, liability of, 38.03 et seq
  Bibliography as to, 38.07
  Checklist for investigation of cases involving, 38.03[5]
  General areas of possible liability, 38.03[1]
  Hold harmless agreements, 38.03[2]
  Investigation of cases involving, checklist, 38.03[5]
  Legislation concerning statutes of limitations, 38.03[4]
  Statutes of limitations and, 38.03[3]
    Legislation concerning, 38.03[4]
Arthritis
  Causation, 8.01[2]
  Described, 8.01[2]
Assigned risk plans, 24.02
Assumption of risk doctrine, 9.14
  Applicability, 9.14

References are to sections

Assumption of risk doctrine—*Cont.*
Elements of, 9.14
Sports activities, applicability to, 9.14
Attorneys, liability of, 37.01 *et seq.*
Bibliography as to, 37.06
Generally, 37.01 *et seq.*
Grounds for actions, 37.03 *et seq.*
"But for" rule, 37.03[7]
Computers, effects, 37.03[5]
Conflicts of interest and, 37.03[8]
Duty to research the law and, 37.03[4]
"Errors-in-Judgment" rule, 37.03[3]
"Informed consent", effect, 37.03[6]
Negligence, actions in; standard of care and, 37.03[2]
Privity of contract and, 37.03[1]
Standard of care in negligence cases, 37.03[2]
Statute of limitations and, 37.03[9]
Investigation of, suggestion, 37.04
Legal malpractice, checklist for avoiding, 37.05
Policy coverages, 37.02 *et seq.*
Claims-made policy, 37.02[2]
Exclusions, 37.02[3]
ISO policy provisions, 37.02[4]
Nonstandard policy form, 37.02[5]
Professional services, as to, 37.02[6]
Automobile guest statutes
Bibliography, 23.06
Checklist for investigation of cases, 23.02
Comparative negligence of guest, 23.01[7]

Automobile guest statutes—*Cont.*
Compensation, what constitutes, 23.01[5]
Entering, leaving or outside of vehicle, 23.01[9]
Investigation of cases, checklist, 23.02
Joint ventures, effect, 23.01[3]
Owner-occupant, effect, 23.01[6]
Payment or compensation, what comprises, 23.01[5]
Purpose of, 23.01[1]
Share the ride arrangements and, 23.01[4]
What does payment compensation comprise, 23.01[5]
Who is a guest, 23.01[2]
Willful or wanton misconduct and, 23.01[10]
Example, 23.01[11]
Automobile policies, generally
See also specific subject headings; Automobile guest statutes
Auto property damage claims
Evaluating, 25.09
Guidelines for settlement, 25.11
Loss of use, 25.11, [1]
Business automobile policies, 22.09
Comprehensive Automobile Liability and Basic Automobile policies, as replacement for, 22.09
Coverage, 22.09
Exclusions, 22.09
Parts, 22.09
Changes in, 22.01
Differences in, historically, 22.02[4]
Family Automobile Liability policy, 22.02; 22.03
Duties of insurer, 20.02 *et seq.*

INDEX

References are to sections

Automobile policies, generally
—*Cont.*
Family Automobile Liability policy—*Cont.*
Limitations of liability, 22.03[2], [3]
Medical payments coverage, 22.04 *et seq.*
Open insurance, 22.03[4]
Out-of-state coverage, 22.03[3]
Uninsured motorist coverage, 22.06[1] *et seq.*
Garage policy, coverage, 22.10
Exclusions, 22.10[1]
Notice of accident, 22.10
Subrogration, 22.10
Guest statutes. *See* Automobile guest statutes
History of, 22.02
Importance in casualty insurance industry, 22.01
Indemnity v. liability coverage, 22.02[1]
Irresponsible motorists, protection against, 24.01 *et seq.*
See also Irresponsible motorists
Laws applicable to, 23.01 *et seq.*
See also specific subject headings
Legislation as to standardization, 22.02[6]
Liability investigation coverage information, 25.01
Claimant, information to be obtained from, 25.05
Details of incident, investigation, 25.08
Insured's driver, information to be obtained from, 25.04
Insured's vehicle, identification of, 25.03
Investigation, value of, 25.10
Objective findings, 25.07
Physical facts, eliciting, 25.07

Automobile policies, generally
—*Cont.*
Liability investigation coverage information—*Cont.*
Policy declaration, checklist, 25.02
Property damage claims, evaluating, 25.09
Witnesses; locating; statements to be obtained, 25.06
Liquor law liability. *See* Liquor law liability
Medical payments coverage, 22.04 *et seq.*
Exclusions, 22.04[1]
Limits of liability, 22.04[2]
Other insurance, 22.04[3]
Omnibus clause, 22.02[2]
Coverage, extension, 22.02[2]
Historically, 22.02[2]
Limitations, 22.02[2]
Permissive user of auto and, 22.02[2]
Recent decisions regarding, 22.02[3]
Personal auto policies, 22.02[3] *et seq.*
Conditions for all parts, 22.02 *et seq.*
Duties after accident, 22.08[1]
Exclusions, 22.03[1]
Incorporation of provisions in other policies, 22.08[2]
Limits of liability, 22.03
Medical payments coverage, 22.04 *et seq.*
Reduction in coverage, 22.03[5]
Uninsured motorist coverage, 22.06[1] *et seq.*
Physical damages, policies or coverage, claims under, 22.05 *et seq.*
Actual cash value (ACV), 22.05
Checklist, 22.05[6]

Automobile policies, generally
—*Cont.*
Physical damages, policies or coverage, claims under—*Cont.*
Limits of liability, 22.05[1]
Salvage, provisions as to, 22.05[2]
Total loss claims, checklist, 22.05[6]
Review and comparison of family and personal policies, 22.03 *et seq.*
Seat belt defense, 23.04
Statutory enactments, 23.04[1]
Standardization, 22.02[5]
Legislation as to, 22.02[6]
Underinsured motorist coverage, 22.07
Uninsured motorist coverage, 22.06
Differences in coverage, 22.06[2]
Exclusions, 22.06[1]
Family form, 22.06[1] *et seq.*
Personal form, 22.06[1] *et seq.*
Autopsy reports
Information contained in, use, 5.08[6]

B

Back and spinal injuries
Backaches, causation, 8.01[3]
Diagnosing, 8.01[3]
Herniated discs, causation, 8.01[3]
Investigating, 8.01[3]
Treatment, 8.01[3]
Bad faith, liability for, 21.01[2]
Conditional time limitation offers and, 21.02
Form, 21.02
Fraud and, 21.01[2]

Bad faith, liability for—*Cont.*
Insured's claim for, assignment of, 18.13[1]
Settlement, use to induce, 18.13
Bailment
Acts of employees, 10.06[2]
Classes of, 10.06[1]
Comparative negligence as defense, 10.06[3]
Contributory negligence as defense, 10.06[3]
Custody
Release of, 10.06
Versus bailment, 10.06[1][a]
Kinds of, 10.06[1]
Particular, 10.06[4]
Release of custody, 10.06
Rental versus, 10.06[1][b]
Theft versus, 10.06[1][c]
Bibliographies. *See* specific subject headings
Binders
Issuance of, 2.10
Nature of, 2.10
Birth certificates, use of information contained in, 5.08[4]
Brokers distinguished from agents, 2.05
Burns, categories of, 8.01[4]
Bursitis
Described, 8.01[5]
Trauma causing, 8.01[5]
Business Auto Policy. *See* Automobile policies, generally

C

Carriers
See also specific subject headings
Types, 20.04
Casualty insurance, generally, 2.01 *et seq.*

INDEX

References are to sections

Casualty insurance, generally
—*Cont.*
See also specific subject headings
Carriers, 2.04
Coverage, 2.01[1]
Kinds of insurance, 2.01[1]
State regulation and control, 2.01[2]
Charitable immunity
Abolishment of, trend towards, 12.04[1]
Bibliography as to, 12.05
Importance of, 12.04
Insurance coverage, effect, 12.04[2]
Retention of doctrine, arguments for, 12.04
Status of doctrine, 12.04
Trust fund, rationale as to, 12.04
Checklists. *See* specific subject headings
Children, actions involving. *See* specific subject headings; Intrafamily immunity
Civil Aeronautics Board reports, use
Information contained in, 5.08[10]
Claim adjusters, liability of, 38.02
Agency obligations, 38.02[1]
Bibliography as to, 38.07
Claimants, generally
Claimant's attorney, interviews during investigation, 3.04[2], [4]
Claim handling
See also specific subject headings; Claim representatives
Adequate reporting, 1.02[4]
Confidentiality of files, 1.02[2]
Decision and action, 1.02[3]
Files, confidentiality of, 1.02[4]
Procedures, 1.02

Claim handling—*Cont.*
Procedures—*Cont.*
Investigation, prompt and thorough, 1.02[2]
Proper preparation, 1.02[1]
Representation by attorney and, 1.02
Claim representatives
See also Claim handling
Education and training, 1.01[2]
Good representatives, 1.01[1], [3]
Factors affecting, 1.01[1]
Qualifications, 1.01[1]
Training and education, 1.01[2]
Principles of law, need to know, 9.01 *et seq.*; 10.01 *et seq.*
Qualifications, 1.01[1]
Role in re suits, 13.10
Self-discipline, need for, 1.02[5]
Training and education, 1.01[2]
Comparative negligence,
bibliography as to, 9.18
Complete Personal Protection Automobile Insurance Plan, 24.06[4]
Compulsory insurance, effect on irresponsible motorists, 24.04
Conflict of laws, 10.01
Best interests rule, 10.01[2]
Conformity to jurisdiction where suit being tried, 10.01, [1]
Lex loci delicti rule, 10.01[1]
Contracts, generally
See also specific subject headings
Arbitration agreements as, 10.02[1]
Contractual liability coverage, 26.06
Endorsements, legal effects, 2.09
Exculpatory, 10.02[4]
Generally, 10.02[1]
Hold harmless agreements, 10.02[3]

Ind.-5

References are to sections

Contracts, generally—*Cont.*
  Indemnity and, 2.08
  Insurance polies, status as, 10.02[1]
  Land purchasing agreements and leases as, 10.02[1]
    Structured settlements and, 10.02[1]
  Legal retainers and contingent fee agreements as, 10.02[1]
  Policies as to, 2.06
  Parts, 2.07
  Principles of contract law, 10.02[2]
  Release as, 10.02[1]

Contribution in actions, 43.03

Coroners reports, information contained in, use, 5.08[5]

Corporate officers and directors, liability of, 38.04
  Bibliography as to, 38.07
  Indemnification and, 38.04[1]
  Insurance and, 38.04[2]
    Insurance policy, 38.04[3]

Court reporters, statements taken by, 4.12
  Limitations of, effects, 4.12[3]
  Objections to use, 4.12[1]
  Reasons for, 4.12[2]

Covenant not to sue, 9.15[7]
  See also Releases

Coverage, generally
  Bibliography, 19.09
  Denial of
    Nonappearance at trial, effect, 20.04[2]
  Disclaimers, 19.03
    Other insurance clause, 20.05
    Plain language requirement and, 20.05
  Injured claimants, statutory protection for, 20.04[3]
  Problems of, 19.01 *et seq.*

Coverage, generally—*Cont.*
  Problems of—*Cont.*
    Declaratory judgment actions and, 19.06
    Disclaimers and, 19.03
    Immediate investigation, need for, 19.02
    Nonwaiver agreements and, 19.05
    Plain language policies, 19.07
    Reasonable expectations doctrine and, 19.08
    Rights, effect of reservation of, 19.04, [1]
    Typical problems, 19.01
  Rights, effect of reservation, 19.04

D

Damages, generally
  See also specific subject headings
  Ad damnum defined, 10.03[1]
  Apportionment among joint tortfeasors, 9.15[2]; 10.03[11], [12]
  Bodily injury, 10.03[4]
  Collateral source rule and, 10.03[8]
    Medical payments and, 10.03[8]
    P.I.P. (no fault) payments and, 10.03[8]
  Compensatory damages, 10.03[2], [5]
  Consequential damages, 10.03[2], [6]
  Consortium, loss of, 10.03[9]
  Determining amount of, 10.03[1]
    Jury's role, 10.03[1]
  Emotional distress or fright as grounds for award, 10.03[13]
  Exemplary damages, 10.03[7]

INDEX

References are to sections

Damages, generally—*Cont.*
  Fright or emotional distress as grounds for award, 10.03[13]
  Generally, 10.03[1]
  Joint tortfeasors, liability for damages, 9.15[2]; 10.03[11], [12]
  Jury's role in determining amount, 10.03[1]
  Property damage, 10.03[3]
  Punitive damages, 10.03[7]; 32.01 *et seq.*
    See also Punitive damages, availability
  Survival rights, actions for, 10.03[10]
  Wrongful death actions and, 10.03[10]

Dangerous activities
  Care required, 9.16[2][b]
  Determining extent of danger, 9.16[2][b]

Dangerous instrumentalities
  Degree of care required, 9.16[2][a]

Death certificate, information contained in, 5.08[4]

Death claims and cases
  Maintaining control in, 17.06[1]
  Releases in, 18.11
    Who may make, 18.11

Defense counsel
  Claims representatives, dealings with, 14.02
  Relationships, checklist in, 14.02[1]
  Review of case by, 14.02[2][a]

Defenses
  See also specific subject headings
  Comparative negligence doctrine and, 9.06[2]
    Adoption, 9.06[2]
    Damages available, 9.06[2][a]
    Modified form, 9.06[2][b]

Defenses—*Cont.*
  Comparative negligence doctrine and—*Cont.*
    Pure comparative negligence, 9.06[2][a]
    "Slight," 9.06[2][c]
  Contributory negligence doctrine and, 9.06[1]
    Abolishment of doctrine, 9.06[1]
    Described, 9.06[1]
    Infants and incompetents, rule as to, 9.06[1]
  Willful and wanton misconduct and, 9.12

Dentists, liability of, 36.01 *et seq.*
  Comparative negligence rule and, 36.01[3]
  Contributory negligence and, 36.01[3]
  Duty of care required, 36.01[1]
  Expert testimony as to, 36.01[2]
  Investigation of claims against, 36.05[1]
  Release, 36.01[4]
  Statutes of limitations and, 36.01[5]

Depositions, use of, 14.01

Diabetes
  Described, 8.01[6]
  Psychological effects, 8.01[6]
  Treatment, 8.01[6]

Directors and officers of corporations. *See* Corporate officers and directors, liability of

Disclaimers, notice of
  Delayed notice cases, investigation of, 20.03[6]
  Disclaimer letters, 20.03[5]

Diseases and injuries. *See* Injuries and diseases

Doctors. *See* Physicians, liability of

Dram Shop legislation. *See* Liquor law liability

Drug and alcohol abuse, 8.02
Druggists, liability of, 36.04
  Investigating claims against, checklist, 36.05[2][e]

E

Economic Opportunity Act provisions, effect on employer-employee relations, 41.06
Educators, liability of
  Bibliography as to, 38.07
  Generally, 38.05[1]
  Student participation in sports or other athletics, effect, 38.05[2]
Employer-employee relations
  Federal legislation affecting, 41.06
Employment, wrongful termination of, 42.01 *et seq.*
  Actions brought in contract, 42.02[2], [3]
  "At-will" doctrine, public policy exception, 42.04
  Bibliography, 42.09
  Checklist for handling, 42.08
  Contract, action brought in, 42.02[2], [3]
    Implied contract, 42.03
    Personnel manuals, 42.04
  Implied covenant of good faith and fair dealing, 42.05
  Insurance problems in, 42.07 *et seq.*
    Civil suit, 42.07[5]
    Comprehensive and commercial general liability policies, 42.07[3]
    Errors and omission and directors and officers liability policies, 42.07[2]

Employment, wrongful termination of—*Cont.*
  Insurance problems in—*Cont.*
    Occurrence, pattern and practice, 42.07[4]
    Public policy in coverage, 42.07[6]
    Umbrella policies, 42.07[1]
    Writer's comprehensive policy, 42.07[7]
  Public policy exception to the "at-will" doctrine, 42.04
  Wrongful discharge, tort of, 42.06 *et seq.*
    Emotional distress, intentional infliction, 42.06[2]
    Employment discrimination and, 42.06[3]
    Fraud, 42.06[1]
    Other grounds for tort actions, 42.06[4]
Environmental pollution
  Bibliography as to, 34.10
  Class actions in re, 34.02
  Federal acts and statutes as to, 34.05
  Generally, 34.01 *et seq.*
  Grounds for actions, 34.06
    Statute of limitations as to, 34.08
  Insurance coverage, 34.07 *et seq.*
    Accident and occurrence, definition, 34.07[1]
    Clean-up costs and, 34.07[7]
    Completed operations hazard exclusion, 34.07[3]
    Emotional distress and, 34.07[6]
    First party cases, 34.07[5]
    Occurrence and accident, defined, 34.07[1]
    Policies intended to cover damage, 34.07[4]

INDEX

References are to sections

Environmental pollution—*Cont.*
  Insurance coverage—*Cont.*
    Pollution damage, policies intended to cover, 34.07[4]
    Sudden and accidental discharges, 34.07[2]
  Investigation of claims, checklist, 34.09
  Mass tort litigation in re, 34.03
  State rules as to, 34.04
  Statute of limitations as to actions, 34.08
Evidence
  See also Witnesses
  Best Evidence Rule, 10.04[3]
  Burden of proof, 10.04[2]
  Classifications of, 10.04[1]
  Defined, 10.04
  Hearsay, 10.04[1][b]
    Admissibility, 10.04[1][a]
    Defined, 10.04[1][a]
    Res gestae and, 10.04[1][b]
  Judicial notice, matters for, 10.04[1][c]
  Opinion versus fact, 10.04[4]
    Exception, 10.04[4]
  Res gestae and, 10.04[1][b]
    Defined, 10.04[1][b]
    Hearsay rule and, 10.04[1][b]
  Res ipsa loquitur doctrine, 10.04[5]
    Invoking, 10.04[5]
Expert witnesses
  Choosing, 5.10
    Bibliography as to, 5.11
    Factors affecting, 5.10
  Defined, 10.04[8]
  Qualification of, 10.04[8]
Eye injuries and diseases
  Malingering as to, possibilities, 8.01[7]
  Medical history of patient, importance of obtaining, 8.01[7]

Eye injuries and diseases—*Cont.*
  Seriousness, 8.01[7]
  Trauma causing, 8.01[7]

F

Facial injuries, 8.01[8]
Family auto policy, 20.02; 20.03
  See also Automobile policies, generally
Fatalities, claims as to, investigating, 3.07
Federal Employees' Compensation Act (FECA) provisions, 41.01
Federal Employers' Liability Act provisions, 41.02
  Bibliography as to, 41.13
Federal legislation affecting employer-employee interaction, 41.01 *et seq.*
  Bibliography, 41.13
Federal Tort Claims Act provisions, effect on employment, 41.09
  Bibliography, 41.13
Files, confidentiality of, 1.02[4]
Financial responsibility laws, 24.01
  Motor Carrier Act of 1980, 24.01[2]
  Policy wording, 24.01[1]
Fraud
  See also specific subject headings
  Accident, claimant's fraud as to facts of, 15.01
  Allegations of injury, as to, 15.02
  Bibliography as to, 15.09
  Claims involving, investigation of, 15.06
    Index Bureau and, 15.06[2]
    Undercover investigation, 15.06[1]
  Danger signals of, beware of, 15.05

Ind.-9

References are to sections

Fraud—*Cont.*
  Doctor's fraud without collusion of defendant, 15.03
  Iatrogenic injuries, 15.08[2]
  Insured, fraudulent act of, 15.04
  Liability for, 21.01[2]
    Bad faith and, 21.01[2]
  Medical, 15.03; 15.07; 15.08
  Overtreatment and incompetence and, 15.08
  Psychosomatic illnesses and, 15.07[1]
  Repairman's, without collusion by defendant, 15.03

G

General or public liability policies and coverage, 26.01 *et seq.*
  See also Public or general liability policies and coverage
Governmental immunity
  Acts of quasi-communities, 12.01[4]
  Adoption in the United States, 12.01[1]
  Bibliography, 12.05
  Civil disturbance, 12.01[5]
  Discretionary acts, defense of, 12.01[7]
  Eleventh Amendment, effects, 12.01[2]
  Exceptions, 12.01 [1] *et seq.*
  Federal immunities, 12.01[2]
    Discretionary acts, exception for, 12.01[2]
    Federal Tort Claims Act, effect, 12.01[2]
    Governmental or proprietary duties of employees, effects, 12.01[2]
    Judicial immunity, 12.01[2][a]

Governmental immunity—*Cont.*
  Federal immunities—*Cont.*
    Legislative immunity, 12.01[2][a]
  Historically, 12.01[1]
  Insurance coverage, effect, 12.02
  Introduction of, 12.01[1]
  Municipal immunity, 12.01[3]
  Proprietary or ministerial acts versus governmental acts, 12.01[6]
    Exception, 12.01[6]
  Punitive damages, availability, 12.03
  Riots, injuries or damages resulting from, 12.01[5]
Guest statutes. *See* Automobile guest statutes

H

Head injuries
  Dangerous potential, 8.01[8]
  Fractures, symptoms, 8.01[8]
  Prompt medical attention, need for, 8.01[8]
Heart disease and attacks
  Blood pressure and, 8.01[9]
  Terms associated with, 8.01[9]
  Trauma causing, 8.01[9]
Hernias
  Causes, 8.01[10]
  Employment, during course of, 8.01[10]
  Kinds, 8.01[10]
  Symptoms, 8.01[10]
Hospitals, liability of, 36.03 *et seq.*
  Bibliography as to, 36.06
  Blood transfusions, 36.03[10]
  Charitable immunity, effect, 36.03[11]
  Corporate liability, 36.03[4]
  Coverage, 36.03[1]
    Who is covered, 36.03[2]

INDEX

References are to sections

Hospitals, liability of—*Cont.*
  Investigating claims against, 36.05
  Locality rule, 36.03[4]
  Bibliography as to, 36.06
  Mental patient, negligent release of, 36.03[9]
  Ostensible agency doctrine, effect, 36.03[7]
  Pleadings in actions, 36.03[12]
  Product/service distinction, 36.03[8]
  Records, use in investigations; checklist, 36.05[2][d]
  Standard of care and, 36.03
Husband/wife immunity. *See* Intrafamily immunity

I

Immunity, generally. *See* specific types of immunity
Income tax reports, use of information contained in, 5.08[8]
Incompetents
  Liability for acts of, 11.01
  Liquor liability law and, 23.03[7]
Injuries and diseases
  See also specific subject headings
  Bibliography as to, 8.05
  Common injuries and diseases, examples, 8.01 *et seq.*
  Diagnostic tools and procedures as to, 8.03
    Angiography, 8.03[1]
    Balloon angioplasty of the arteries, 8.03[3]
    Computerized tomography (CAT Scan), 8.03[5]
    Digital subtraction angiography (DSA), 18.03[2]

Injuries and diseases—*Cont.*
  Diagnostic tools and procedures as to—*Cont.*
    Doppler equipment, use, 8.03[7]
    Magnetic resonance imagery (MRI), 8.03[6]
    Tomography, 8.03[4]
    Ultrasound, 8.03[7]
  Rehabilitation of seriously injured and crippled, 8.04
    Advances in, 8.04
    Workers' compensation cases, 8.04
Insurance agents
  Liability of, 38.06 *et seq.*
  Authority of, 38.06[2]
  Bibliography as to, 38.07
  Binders and, 38.07[5]
  Checklist for agents to prevent some actions for malpractice, 38.07[10]
  Company, actions against agent by, 38.06[6]
  Defenses for malpractice actions, 38.06[9]
  Insured, actions against agent by, 38.06[7]
  Professional liability coverage for, 38.06[4]
  Ratification, 38.06[3]
  Standard of care required, 38.06[1]
  Third parties, action by against agent, 38.06[8]
Insurance, generally
  See also specific subject headings
  Carriers, 20.04
  Governance, 2.01[2]
  Kinds of, 2.01[2]
  Major subdivisions of insurance companies, 2.03
  State regulation and control, 2.01[2]
  Types of, 2.01[2]

References are to sections

Insureds. *See* specific subject headings
Insurers. *See* specific subject headings
Intervening cause defined, 9.09
Interviews by investigators, 3.04
  Claimant, 3.04[2]
  Claimant's attorney, 3.04[2]
  Insured, 3.04[1]
Intrafamily immunities
  Bibliography, 11.07
  Husband/wife privilege
    Abrogation of, 11.04[3]
    Bibliography, 11.07
    Historically, 11.04[1]
    Jurisdictions that hold fast to doctrine, 11.04[4]
    Married Women's Emancipation statutes, 11.04[2]
    Torts committed before marriage, 11.04[5]
    Torts committed by husband or wife against each other, 11.04[2]
    Torts committed by wife, husband's liability for, 11.04[1]
  Minor children, liability for torts committed by, 11.01; 11.02
    Age as factor, 11.01; *See also* subhead: Parent's liability for torts of children
  Parent's liability for torts of children, 11.01; 11.02
    Age as factor, 11.01
    Automobile consent statutes, 11.02
    Dangerous instrumentalities and, 11.02
    Parental responsibility statutes, 11.02
  Parental and spousal immunities, doctrines of, 11.03

Intrafamily immunities—*Cont.*
  Parental and spousal immunities, doctrines of—*Cont.*
    Abolition of, 11.03[2][a], [3], [8]
    Collusion and, 11.03[2][a]
    Curtailment of, 11.03[3]
    Death of party in action between child and parent, effect on doctrine, 11.03[5]
    Drunken driving and, 11.03[7]
    Effectiveness, 11.03[2]
    Emancipation of child, effects, 11.03[4]
    Fraud as factor, 11.03[2][a]
    Gross negligence and, 11.03[7]
    Historically, 11.03[1]
    Intentional, willful and wanton torts, effects, 11.03[6]
    Legislative changes, need for, 11.03[8]
    Widespread insurance coverage, effects, 11.03[2][a], [b]
  Prenatal injuries, right of child to recover for, 11.05[1] *et seq.*
    Bibliography, 11.07
    Born alive and injured while viable, requirement for recovery, 11.05[4]
    Cause of action, recognition of, 11.05[2]
    Conception defined; viability at, 11.05[2][c]
    Early decision as to right of child to recover, 11.05[2]
    Fetus is "quick"; definition and requirement as to, 11.05[2][b]
    Injuries to child born alive resulting in death, right of action, 11.05[3][b], [4]

INDEX

References are to sections

Intrafamily immunities—*Cont.*
  Prenatal injuries, right of child to recover for—*Cont.*
    Pecuniary loss, limit for death of unborn child, 11.05[3]
    Stillborn child, right to recover for death of, 11.05[3] *et seq.*
    Viable condition of fetus, requirement as to, 11.05[2] [a], [b], [4]
  Women's right of privacy as to own body, recognition of, 11.06
  Decision to abort and, 11.06
  Wrongful life, child's right of action for, 11.06

Investigation of claims
  Confidential report to underwriters, 3.08
    Elements of, 3.08
  Contacts of investigator, effectiveness, 3.02
  Discovery witnesses, 3.05 *et seq.*
  Fatal claims, 3.07
  Immediacy of, need for, 19.02
  Interviews, use of, 3.04
    Claimant, 3.04[2]
    Claimant's attorney, 3.04[3]
    Insured, 3.04[1]
  Locating witnesses, 3.05 *et seq.*
  Planning for, 3.01
  Precision and objective of, 3.01
  Prompt and thorough investigation, 1.02[2]
  Public and general liability claims, 28.01 *et seq.*
  Special damages, investigating, 3.06
    Elements of, 3.06
    General principles, 3.06
  Thoroughness and precision required, 3.01
  Timing the investigation, 3.03
  Witnesses, discovery of, 3.05

Irresponsible motorists, 24.01 *et seq.*
  Compulsory insurance and, effect, 24.04
  No-fault auto plans and legislation: Personal Injury Protection (P.I.P.) coverage, 24.06 *et seq.*
  See also No-fault auto plans
  Uninsured/underinsured coverage, 24.05 *et seq.*
    Claims, investigation of, 25.05[4]
    Hit and run cases, 24.05[2]
    Stacking of recoveries, 24.05[1]
    Statute of limitations and, 24.05[3]

J

Joint tortfeasors
  See also Multiple defendants
  Contribution among, 9.15[2]
    Apportionment, 9.15[2]
    Inequities of, 9.15[2]
  Joint and several liability, 9.15[1]
    Confusion created by, 9.15[1]
  Uniform Contribution Among Tortfeasors Act, 9.15[5]
Joint ventures, liability, 10.05[1][d]
Jones Act, effect on employer-employee interaction, 41.07
  Bibliography, 41.13
Jurisdiction. *See* specific subject headings

L

Laches
  Application where unreasonable delay in action to set aside release, 18.15
Last Clear Chance Doctrine, 9.13

References are to sections

Last Clear Chance Doctrine
—*Cont.*
  Abolishment, 9.13
  Humanitarian doctrine, as, 9.13
  Invoking, conditions for, 9.13
  Use, 9.13
Legal reporting systems, use
  Insurance law library, availability on Lexis, 14.03[1]
  Lexis, 14.03[1]
  Westlaw, 14.03[1]
Legislative sanctions, ensuring effectiveness, 9.11
Liability, generally, 21.01 *et seq.*
  See also specific subject headings
  Creation of, 9.05[1]
  Excess claims, checklist for investigation of, 21.05
  Guiding principles for primary and excess insurers, 21.03
  Joint and several, 9.15[11]
  Model Unfair Claim Settlement Practices Statutes, 21.04
    Effects of, 21.04
    Promulgation, 21.04
    Revision of, 21.04
  Negligence, determining, 21.02[3][a]
    Defensive actions, suggestions for, 21.01[3][c]
    Excess verdict, absolute liability for, 21.01[3]
  Original concept of, 21.01[1]
  Public and general liability claims, investigation, 28.01
    Checklists, 28.02
    Generally, 28.01
Liquor law liability
  Automobile cases, 23.03 *et seq.*
  Bibliography, 23.05
  Common law defenses, 23.03[8]
  Company parties, 23.03[4]
  Dram Shop legislation, 23.03[1]
    Exclusivity of, 23.03[2]
    Extraterritoriality, 23.03[11]

Liquor law liability—*Cont.*
  Dram Shop legislation—*Cont.*
    Recent trends, 23.03[3]
  Employer hosts, 23.04[6]
  Extraterritoriality in Dram Shop jurisdiction, 23.03[11]
  Form, 26.08
  Hosts
    Company parties, 23.03[4]
    Employer, 23.03[6]
    Social, 23.03[4]
  Intoxicated person, suit by, 23.03[12]
  Intoxication defined, 23.03[10]
  Suit by intoxicated person, 23.03[13]
  Liquor control statutes, 23.03[1]
    Recent trends, 23.03[3]
  Minor or incompetent guests, 23.03[7]
  Noninnocent participant, 23.03[9]
  Recent trends, 23.03[3]
  Social hosts and company parties, 23.03[4]
Longshore and Harbor Workers' Compensation Act, provisions; effect on employer-employee interaction, 41.03
  Bibliography, 41.13
Loss defined, 2.01

M

Mail
  Statements from parties or witnesses obtained by, 4.09
Manufacturer's liability. *See* Products liability
Marriage certificate, information contained in, use, 5.08[4]

INDEX

References are to sections

Married Women's Emancipation
    statutes, 11.04[2]
Mary Carter Agreements, 9.15[6]
Master and servant
    See also Employer-employee
        relations; Employment,
        wrongful termination of
    Deviations from scope of
        authority granted,
        10.05[1][c]
    Imputed agency, 10.05[1]
    Respondeat superior, 10.05[1]
    Sub-agency and, 10.05[1][a]
    Temporary or special employee,
        10.05[1][b]
Medical information
    See also specific subject
        headings; types of medical
        personnel
    Attending physician, information
        to be obtained from, 6.03
    Autopsy and coroner's reports,
        use, 6.08
    Bones and bone structure, 7.06
    Branches of medicine, 7.04
    Dental reports
        Information required, 6.04
        Use, 6.04
    Fractures, 7.07
        Combination, 7.07[1]
        Effects, 7.07[3]
        Kinds, 7.07[1]
        Locations and shape,
            designation of, 7.07[2]
    Fundamentals, 7.01 *et seq.*
    Hospital record, information
        contained in, 6.06
    Personal interviews with
        hospital personnel,
        usefulness, 6.06
    Human body, structure of, 7.05
    Medical examinations, 6.07
        Advisability of, 6.07

Medical information—*Cont.*
    Medical examinations—*Cont.*
        Background of allegations and
            complaints, doctor's
            knowledge of, 6.07
        Diagnostic procedures,
            expense as factor, 6.07[2]
        Examining doctor, choosing,
            6.07[1]
        Knowledge of, 6.07
        Medical specialties, 6.07[1]
        Specialist, by, 6.07[1]
        Use, 6.07
    Medical liens, use, 6.02
        Procedure, 6.02
    Medical report form, 6.04
        Categories of information
            desired, 6.04
    Medical terminology, use and
        understanding, 7.02
    Military records, usefulness, 6.09
    Nurses, interviewing, 6.06
    Obtaining, 6.02 *et seq.*
        Attorney representing
            claimant, 6.01
        Claimant, from, 6.01
        Signed statement from
            claimant, 6.01
        Types of information
            necessary, 6.01
    Trauma, as to, 7.01
        Infectious disease resulting
            from, 7.01
    Veteran's records, usefulness,
        6.09
Medical malpractice
    See also specific medical
        specialties
    Actions for, bibliography, 36.06
    Arbitration of, 35.04
    Bibliography, 36.06
    Arbitration of case, 35.04
    Bibliography, 36.06
    "Benefits of Parenthood"
        doctrine and, 37.03[14][d]

Medical malpractice—*Cont.*
  Captain of the Ship doctrine
    and, 35.05[10]
  Checklists, 36.05[2] *et seq.*
  Continuous negligence rule,
    statute of limitations and,
    35.05[16][b]
  Contracts as basis for action,
    35.03[15]
  Contracts to cure and, 35.03[11]
  Counterattacks; Bibliography,
    36.06
  Damages recoverable for
    wrongful birth cases,
    37.03[14][e]
  Discovery rule: foreign substance
    left in body; statute of
    limitations, 35.05[16][a]
  Foreign substance left in body,
    discovery rule and,
    35.05[16]
  Forms for informed consent,
    35.03[4][b]
  Fraudulent concealment, statute
    of limitations and,
    35.05[16][c]
  Generally, 36.05[1]
    Bibliography, 36.06
  General principles, 35.03 *et seq.*
  Good Samaritan doctrine and,
    35.03[13]
  Honest error in judgment,
    35.03[3]
  Informed consent doctrine, 36.06
    Exceptions to, 35.03[4][a]
    Forms for, 35.03[4][b]
    Videotapes, use, 35.03[4][b]
  Investigation of claims
    Druggists claims, 36.05[2][e]
    Hospital records, 36.05[2][d]
    Information to be obtained
      from or concerning the
      injured, 36.05[2][c]
    Qualifications of the injured;
      checklist, 36.05[2][a]

Medical malpractice—*Cont.*
  Multiple defendants, 35.05[12]
  Recent legislation as to, 35.05
  Res ipsa loquitur, 35.03[2]
    Bibliography, 36.06
  Second injury and, 35.03[9]
    Bibliography, 36.06
  Standard of care requirements,
    35.03[1]
  Statute of limitations and,
    35.05[16]
    Bibliography, 36.06
  Videotapes, use in informed
    consent doctrine,
    35.03[4][b]
  Wrongful birth, actions for,
    35.03[14][a]
    Bibliography, 36.06
  Wrongful conception,
    35.03[14][c]
  Wrongful life, actions for,
    35.03[14][b]
    Bibliography, 36.06
  Wrongful pregnancy, actions for,
    35.03[14][c]
  Wrongful suit by physician,
    action for, 35.06
    Malicious prosecution and,
      35.06[1]
Medical payments coverage, 26.05
Merchant Marine Act provisions,
  effect on
  employer-employee
  relations, 41.07
  Bibliography, 41.13
Military record, using information
  contained in, 5.08[9]
Model Unfair Claim Settlement
    Practices Statutes, 21.04
  Effects of, 21.04
  Promulgation, 21.04
  Revision, 21.04
Motor Carrier Act of 1980,
  24.01[2]

INDEX

References are to sections

Motor vehicle records
  Information contained in, use, 5.08[3]
    Driving records, as to, 5.08[3][a]
Multiple defendants
  See also specific subject headings
  Classifications, 9.15
  Counterclaims and, 9.15[3]
  Declaratory judgment actions, 9.15[4]
  Degree of fault, division into categories, 9.15
  Mary Carter Agreements, 9.15[6]
  Problems in re, 9.15
  Set-offs, 9.15[3]
  Settlements under doctrine of comparative negligence, 9.15[5]
Multiple sclerosis, 8.01[12]
  Investigating cases where involved, 8.01[12]
  Trauma, effects, 8.01[12]

N

Negligence, generally
  Applicability to casualty claims, 9.05 *et seq.*
    See also specific subject headings
  Defined, 9.05[1], [2]
  Degrees of, 9.05[1][a]
  Establishing, 9.05[1][a]
  Presumption of, effect, 9.06
Nerves, injuries to, 8.01[11]
  Traumatic neurosis, 8.01[11]
Newspaper reports, use of information contained in, 5.08[11]
No-fault auto plans
  Complete Personal Protection Automobile Insurance Plan, 24.06[4]

No-fault auto plans—*Cont.*
  Generally, 24.06[1]
  Historically, 24.06[2]
  Keeton-O'Connell Plan, 24.06[3]
  Personal Injury Protection (P.I.P.) coverage
    Multiple coverages, 24.06[5][b]
    Policy coverage, 24.06[5] *et seq.*
    Present trends, 24.06[5] *et seq.*
    Subrogation and, 24.06[5][c]
Nuisance, doctrine of, 9.16
  Attractive nuisance, 9.16[1]
  Defined, 9.16
Nurses, liability of, 36.02 *et seq.*
  Areas of responsibility and, 36.02[3]
  Bibliography as to, 36.06
  Charitable immunity as affecting, 36.02[4]
  Duty of care requirements, 36.02[1]
  Investigating claims against, 36.05
  Locality rule and, 36.02[2]
  Bibliography as to, 36.06

O

Occupational diseases, 8.01[13]
  Anthrax, 8.01[13]
  Arsenic poisoning, 8.01[13]
  Asbestosis, 8.01[13]
  Benzene poisoning, 8.01[13]
  Carbon monoxide poisoning, 8.01[13]
  Lead poisoning, 8.01[13]
  Mercury poisoning, 8.01[13]
  Radium poisoning, 8.01[13]
  Silicosis, 8.01[13]
Occupational Safety and Health Act (OSHA) provisions, effects; Bibliography, 41.10

References are to sections

Occurrence policy coverage
  Accident, status as, 27.02
  "Cause of injury determines number of occurrences," 27.07
  Definition, 27.01
  Exclusions and, 27.12
  Exposure theory, 27.04
  Manifestation theory and, 27.03
  Neither expected nor intended from point of view of the insured, 27.11
  1986 Commercial Liability policy, 27.01
  Reasonable expectations, doctrine of, 27.10
  Self-defense, injuries resulting from, 27.12
  Stacking where more than one policy covers, 27.09
    Proration and, 27.09
  Statute of limitations and, 27.08
  Triple trigger theory, 27.05
Officers and directors of corporations, liability of. *See* Corporate officers and directors, liability of
Osteomyelitis
  Described, 8.01[14]
  Trauma causing, 8.01[14]
Osteoporosis
  Defined, 8.01[15]

P

Parent/child immunity. *See* Intrafamily immunity
Parties. *See* specific subject headings
Personal auto policies. *See* Automobile policies, generally
Personal injury
  Liability for, 26.03

Personal injury—*Cont.*
  Liability for—*Cont.*
    See also Public and general liability policies and coverage
  Personal Injury Protection (P.I.P.). *See* No-fault auto plans
Physical facts in the case, securing, 5.01 *et seq.*
  Bibliography as to, 5.11
  Instrumentalities of, 5.01 *et seq.*
Physicians, liability of, 35.01 *et seq.*
  See also specific subject headings; Medical malpractice
  Professional liability policies, 35.02 *et seq.*
    Claims-made policies, 35.02[11]
    Consent of insured to settle, 35.02[6]
    Coverage for insured's employee, 35.02[9]
    Each claim coverage, 35.02[7]
    Exclusions, 35.02[5]
    Insuring agreements, 35.02[1]
    Limits of liability, 35.02[3]
    Medical incidents and, 35.02[4]
    Notice of accident, 35.02[10]
    Persons insured, 35.02[2]
    Protracted treatment and, 35.02[8]
    Settlement, consent of insured as to, 35.02[6]
    Sexual wrongdoing and, 35.02[12]
    Treatment, protracted, 35.02[8]
Pleadings. *See* Service of process
Pleadings in actions
  Basic documents, 13.04
  Demurrer on, 13.04
  Judgment on, 13.04
  Motion on, 13.04

INDEX

References are to sections

Pleadings in actions—*Cont.*
  Bill of particulars, 13.04
  Defense counsel and, 13.10
  Discovery pleadings, 13.04
    Devices, 13.04
  Dispositive motions, 13.04
  Excess *ad damnum* letters, 13.11
  Summary judgment, motion for, 13.04

Police reports
  Information contained in, use, 5.08[2]

Policies, generally
  See also specific subject headings
  Accident or occurrence, 20.01 *et seq.*
    Notice of, 20.03 *et seq.*
  Assistance and cooperation clause, 20.04
    Plain language clause, effect, 20.04
    Prejudice, showing; substantiality of, 20.04[1]
  Binders, issuance of, 2.10
  Cancellation, 20.06
    Improper, effects, 20.06
  Contract, as, 2.06; 2.07
  Indemnity aspects, 2.08
  Injured claimants, statutory protection of, 20.04[3]
  Insurer, duties of, 20.02
  Legal effects of endorsement, 2.09
  Nonpayment of premiums as cause of cancellation, 20.06
  "Other insurance" clause and, 20.05
  Plain language wording, 20.06
  Public or general policies and coverage, 26.01 *et seq.*
    See also Public or general liability policies
  Renewal of coverage, 20.06[3]

Policies, generally—*Cont.*
  Written notice of cancellation, 20.06[3]

Pollution liability, coverage, 26.09
  See also Environmental pollution

Practice and procedure
  See also specific subject headings
  Attorney's fees as costs, 13.09
    Rule 11, Federal Rules of Civil Procedure and, 13.09
  Award of costs, determination of, 13.09
    Rule 11, Federal Rules of Civil Procedure and, 13.09
  Costs, determination of awards, 13.09
    Attorney's fees, 13.09
  Courts and their jurisdictions, 13.01
    Classifications, 13.01
    Limitations on jurisdiction, 13.01
    Original jurisdiction, courts of, 13.01
  Defense counsel action, 13.10
    Basis for, 13.10
    Claim representative, role of, 13.10
  Exclusion of mention of insurance policies, 13.05
  Forum, choice of, 13.03
    Forum non conveniens, motions for, 13.03
  Forum non conveniens, motions for, 13.03
  Insurance policy as evidence, 13.05
  Liens, use in re casualty claims, 13.08
  Procedure for appeal, 13.07
    Federal Rules of Civil Procedure and, 13.07
  Service of process, 13.02
  Trial, preparation for, 13.06

Prenatal injuries, child's right to recover. *See* Intrafamily immunity
Principles of law, generally, 9.01 *et seq.*; 10.01 *et seq.*
  See also specific subject headings
  Common and statutory law as basis for United States law, 9.04
Privileged communications, 10.04[7]
  Categories of privilege, 10.04[7]
Products-completed operations insurance, 26.07
Products liability, generally
  Altered or used products
    Bibliography as to, 33.05
  Assumption of risk
    Bibliography as to, 33.05
  Bibliography as to, 9.18; 33.05
  Claims, investigation of. *See* subhead: Investigation of claims
  Comparative fault, as to
    Bibliography, 33.05
  Containers, as to, 29.02
  Corporate successor, liability of, 33.05
  Coverage problems, 29.01
    Bibliography as to, 33.05
    Extension, 29.04
    Persons insured, 29.07
    Recapture and recall, as to, 29.04
  Dealer preparation of product, liability for, 31.02[2]
  Design defects and, 29.12
    Bibliography, 33.05
    "Consumer Expectation" test, use, 29.12[1]
    "Crashworthiness," 29.12[2]
    Custom in the industry, 29.12[6]
    Open and obvious danger, 29.12[5]

Products liability, generally—*Cont.*
  Design defects and—*Cont.*
    "Risk-benefit" test, use, 29.12[1]
    Seat belt defense, 29.12[3]
    Second injury liability, 29.12[2]
    Strict liability and, 29.12[4]
    Unreasonably dangerous product, 29.12[1]
    When arises, 29.12
  Drugs and related products
    Addiction, 31.02[7]
    Alteration of, 31.02[5] *et seq.*
    Bibliography, 33.05
    Checklist for investigation, 33.04[4]
    Hypersensitivity to certain drugs, 31.02[5]
    Pre-market testimony and, 31.02[6]
    Prescription drugs, duty to warn, 31.02[4]
    Statute of limitations in drug related cases, 31.02[8]
  Exclusions, 29.04
  Federal Rules of Evidence, effect on actions, 31.03
  Food and drugs, responses for, 9.16[2][g]
  Generally
    Bibliography, 33.05
  Handguns: used, rebuilt, reconditioned or altered, liability for, 31.02[9]
  Investigation of claims
    Altered product, original manufacturer's liability, checklist, 33.04[8]
    Areas of investigation, strict liability, 33.02
    Automobiles; checklist as to, 33.04[1]
    Bottling claims; checklist, 33.04[2]

INDEX

References are to sections

Products liability, generally—*Cont.*
  Investigation of claims—*Cont.*
    Crop dusting; checklist, 33.04[3]
    Drug defect cases; checklist, 33.04[6]
    Drugs and cosmetics; checklist, 33.04[4]
    Food consumption on vendor's premises; checklist, 33.04[5]
    Generally, 33.01
    Recall, investigations as to; checklist, 33.04[9]
    Specific areas; checklist, 33.04 *et seq.*
    Strict liability and, 33.02
    Warning defects cases; checklists, 33.04[7]
  Legal aspects, 29.09 *et seq.*
    Intervening acts, effects, 29.09[1]
  Limitations of liability, 29.05
  Market share liability
    Bibliography, 33.05
    Fungible products; checklist, 33.04[10]
    Similar theories and, 31.06
  Persons insured, 29.07
  Post-accident evidence, 33.05
  Post-settlement problems, 31.04
  Product hazard defined, 29.02
  Product versus service, 31.09
  Products-completed attachment to commercial general liability policies, 25.07
  Punitive damages. *See* Punitive damages
  Recall. *See* Recall of products in products liability cases
  Reconditioned products, liability of manufacturer for, 31.02[1]
  Service versus product, 31.09

Products liability, generally—*Cont.*
  Standards, effects of changes in, 31.05
  State of the art
    Bibliography, 33.05
  Statutes of limitations or repose, 31.08, [1]
    Implantation or insertions and, 31.08[2]
  Strict liability. *See* Strict liability in tort
  Subsequent modification or repair of product, liability for, 31.02[10]
  Successor corporations, liability of, 31.07
    Punitve damages against, 31.07[1]
  Territorial extension, 29.06
  Toxic products
    Bibliography, 33.05
  Trichinosis and, 8.01[16]
  Vendor's endorsement, 29.08
    Bibliography, 33.05
    Broad form exclusion, 29.08
    Limited form exclusions, 29.08
  Warning of danger. *See* Warning of danger, duty in products liability cases
  Warranties on sales, breach of, 29.10 *et seq.*
    Express warranty, 29.10[1]
    Fitness for particular purpose, implied warranty and, 29.10[4]
    Fitness for use and, 29.10[2]
    Implied warranty, 29.10[3]
    Merchantability and, 29.10[2], [3]
    Multiple grounds for same action, 29.10[5]
    Statute of limitations and, 25.10[6]
Professional liability, 38.01 *et seq.*
  See also specific subject headings

Ind.-21

CASUALTY INSURANCE CLAIMS

References are to sections

Proximate cause, yardsticks for measuring, 9.08
Psychological and psychiatric malpractice, 35.03[8]
Public or general liability policies and coverages, 26.01 et seq.
  Commercial general liability policies, 26.01; 26.02
    Bodily injury and property damage liability, 26.02[4][a]
    "Claims-made" policy, 26.02[2]
    Conditions, 26.02[7]
    Contractual liability coverage, 26.06
    Coverage A, 26.02[4][a]
    Coverage B, 26.03 et seq.
    Duty to defend, provisions as to, 26.02[4][b]
    Endorsements, 26.10
    Exclusions, 27.12
      In master forms, 26.02[4][c]
    Extended reporting period, 26.02[3], [8]
    Forms, 26.02
    Limits of insurances, 26.02[6]
    Liquor Liability Coverage Form, 26.08
    Medical payments coverage, 26.05
    Notice of accident, 26.02[7][a]
    "Occurrence policy," 26.02[1]; 27.01. *See also* Occurrence policy coverage
    Pollution liability coverage, 26.09
    Products-completed operations insurance, 26.07. *See also* Products liability, generally
    Section I coverage, 26.02[4]
    Section II coverage, 26.02[5]
    Section III coverage, 26.02[6]
    Section IV coverage, 26.02[7]

Public or general liability policies and coverages—*Cont.*
  Commercial general liability policies—*Cont.*
    Section V coverage, 26.02[8]
    Who is an insured, 26.02[5]
  Personal injury liability, 26.03 et seq.
    Damages, 26.03[4]
    Definitions, 26.03[1]
    Investigation of personal injury case, 26.03[3]
    Privileged communications and, 26.03[2]
Punitive damages, availability, 10.03[7]; 32.01 et seq.
  Amounts awarded
    Model Uniform Products Liability Act, 32.01[12]
  Bibliography, 33.05
  Breach of warranty and, 32.01[10]
  Collateral estoppel and, 32.01[6]
  First come, first served theory, 32.01[2]
  Governmental immunity, in action involving, 12.03
  Insurance for, 32.01[11]
  Justification for, 32.01[3], [4]
  Model Uniform Products Liability Act, 32.01[12]
  Multiple exposure, effect, 32.01[1]
  Negligence as basis for awarding, 32.01[9]
  Phraseology used in justifying awards, 32.01[4]
  Settlement of underlying suit, 32.01[5]
  Strict liability and, 32.01[8]
  Successor corporations, against, 31.07[1]
  Underlying suit, settlement, 32.01[5]
  Warranty, breach of, 32.01[10]

INDEX

References are to sections

Punitive damages, availability
—*Cont.*
  Wrongful death statutes, 32.01[7]

R

Recall of products in products liability cases, 30.02 *et seq.*
  Admissibility in evidence of recall letter, 30.03[6]
  Assumption of risk in recall cases, 30.02[5]
  Bibliography, 33.05
  Coverage from loss resulting from, 30.02[1]
  Defense, as, 30.02[4]
  Investigation checklists, 33.04[9]
  Letters, admissibility in evidence, 30.02[6]
  "Sistership" exclusion, 30.02[2]
Recording devices, use, 4.13 *et seq.*
  Statements taken by, use, 4.13
Release
  Alleged subsequent malpractice by doctors, effects on, 18.12
  Bad faith allegations to induce settlement, 18.13
    Assignment of insured's claim for bad faith, 18.13[1]
  Bibliography as to, 18.16
  Contractual aspects, 18.02
  Death claims, in, 18.11
  Deliberate misrepresentation as to, effect, 18.04
  Faulty diagnosis, where nature or extent of injuries not known due to, effect, 18.08
  Forms, 18.03
    Elements of, 18.03[1]
    Execution of, 18.03[1]
    Wording, effects, 18.03; 18.07
  Fraud in re, 18.03[4]

Release—*Cont.*
  General release from employment, effect, 18.09
  "Indecent haste," made in, effect, 18.05
  Indemnification release, use when dealing with injuries to minors, 17.11[2]
  "In full satisfaction of all claims against others," 18.07
  Joint tortfeasors, cases involving, 18.10
    Uniform Contribution Acts, 18.10[1]
  Laches, application of doctrine of where unreasonable delay in bringing action to set release aside, 18.15
  Mary Carter Agreements, 18.14
  Mistake concerning injuries or facts and, 18.08
    Mutual mistakes, 18.08
    Past or present fact, in re, 18.08
  Multiple defendants, actions in re, 9.15[7]
  Mutual mistakes concerning injuries or facts, 18.08
  New developments as to, 18.01
  Pierringer release, 9.15[7]
  Unforeseen complications or disability arising from known injuries, 18.08
  Uniform Contribution Acts, cases involving joint tortfeasors, 18.10[1]
  Waiting periods, reasons behind enactment, 18.05
Repairment, fraud committed by without client's collusion, 15.03
Reports and reporting
  Art of dictating, 44.02[4]
  Casualty claim investigation, report outline, 44.03

Ind.-23

References are to sections

Reports and reporting—*Cont.*
  Casualty claim investigation, report outline—*Cont.*
    Other than compensation, 44.03[1]
    Suits on casualty claims, 44.03[1][a]
  Compensation claim investigation, report outline, 44.03[2]
  Dictating a report, the art of, 44.02[4]
  Final reports, 44.03[5]
  Form of reports, 44.02[4]
  Generally, 44.01 *et seq.*
  Interim reports, 44.03[4]
  Manner of reporting, 44.02[3]
  Necessity for, 44.02[2]
  Objectionable material, as to, 44.02[5]
  Prompt reporting, necessity for, 44.02[2]
  Special report outline, 44.03[3]

Reserves
  Actual claim reserves, 16.02[3]
  Admissibility of into evidence, 16.08
    Factors affecting, 16.08
    Responsibility of claims departments, 16.10[1]
  Auto claims, 16.03[1]
  Average reserves, 16.10[3]
  Bibliography as to, 16.12
  Claim department, responsibility of, 16.10 *et seq.*
    Claims, as to, 16.10[1]
    Closed claims, 16.10[1]
    Newly created claims, 16.10[1]
    Pending claims, 16.10[1]
    Received, 16.10[1]
    Suits as to, 16.10[2]
  Claim expenses and, 16.10[4]
    Allocated expenses, 16.10[4]
    Unallocated expenses, 16.10[4]
  Claim inventorying, 16.04

Reserves—*Cont.*
  Claim statistics
    Breakdowns, 16.09
    Effects of, 16.09
    Forms, 16.10[6]
    Interpretation, 16.10
    Necessity for, 16.09
  Computers, effect, 16.11
  Defined, 16.01
  Delayed reserving system, 16.02[6]
  Expense reserves and, 16.02[4]
  Fatal cases, 16.03[8]
  Forms for, 16.01
  General liability claims and, 16.03[1], [2]
    Factors affecting, 16.03[1], [2]
  Incurred but not reported reserves, 16.02[2]
  Keeping close to claims payments, need for, 16.01
  One-shot cases, 16.02[5]
  Outstanding reserves, reducing, 16.06
  Policy as to, factors for consideration, 16.01 *et seq.*
  Prompt reserving, importance, 16.03
  Property damage claims, 16.03[4]
  Realistic, factors affecting, 16.01
  Reconciliation of reserve, 16.05
  Reserve revisions, 16.04
  Types, 16.02 *et seq.*
  Unearned, premium reserves, 16.02[1]
  Workers' compensation cases, 16.03[5]

Res ipsa loquitur doctrine, 10.04[5]
  Invoking, 10.04[5]

S

Salvage, generally, 43.02[1]

INDEX

References are to sections

Salvage, generally—*Cont.*
  Checklist for claims involving, 43.02[2]
School records and information
  Use, 5.08[7]
Seat belt defenses, 23.05
  Statutory enactment, 23.05[1]
Service of process, 13.02
  Long arm statutes, 13.02[2]
  Personal service, 13.02
  Proper service, waiver of, 13.02[1]
  Publication, service by, 13.02
  Substituted service, 13.02
Settlements and settlement negotiations
  See also Release
  Advance payments, 17.12
    Advance payment program, 17.12
    Advantages, 17.12[1]
    Bibliography, 17.14
    Choosing the cases, 17.12[2]
    Closing the case, 17.12[9]
    Follow-up system, need for, 17.12[8]
    Liability, as admission of, 17.12[5]
    Methods of payment, 17.12[4]
    Payment methods, 17.12[4]
    Reasonable limitation, 17.12[3]
    Written permission, importance of, 17.12[6]
  Attorneys, negotiations of, 17.10
    Demand letters, dealing with, 17.10
  Bad faith allegations to induce, 18.13
    Assessment of insured's claim for bad faith, 18.13[1]
  Bibliography as to, 17.14
  Demand, offer versus, 17.08
  Demands made following settlement, 17.14
  First call settlements, 17.02

Settlements and settlement negotiations—*Cont.*
  General rules as to, 17.03 *et seq.*
  Medical bills, protecting; procedure, 17.03[2]
  Minors, claims involving injuries to, disposition of, 17.11
    Closing records, 17.11[6]
    Court approval, 17.11[5]
    Emancipated children, 17.11[4]
    Indemnification releases, 17.11[2]
    Investigating, 17.11[3]
  Negotiations, proper approach to, 17.07
    Attorneys, with, 17.10
    Elements of, 17.07
  Release, obtaining, 17.09
    Rules for, 17.09
  Structured settlements, 17.13
    Generally, 17.13[1]
    Legal aspects, 17.13[3]
    Model Periodic Payments of Judgments Act, 17.13[4]
    Model Structured Settlement Act, 17.13[4]
    Tax considerations, 17.13[2]
    Workers' compensation cases, in, 17.13[5]
    Bibliography, 17.14
Special damages
  Investigating claim, 3.06
  Elements of, 3.06
Spinal injuries. *See* Back and spinal injuries
Spousal immunity. *See* Intrafamily immunity
Statements from parties or witnesses
  Signed and recorded, 4.01 *et seq.*
  Approach to witness interview, 4.02
  Better statements, rules for, 4.03

References are to sections

Statements from parties or witnesses—*Cont.*
  Signed and recorded—*Cont.*
    Children, from, 4.10
    Construction of statement, 4.04
    Court reporter, taken by, 4.12
    Elements, 4.03; 4.04
    Format, 4.03
    Illiterate witnesses, treatment, 4.07
    Mail, statements obtained by, 4.09
    Narrative statement; sample, 4.03; 4.04
    Negative statements, use, 4.08
    Obtaining, 4.01[1] *et seq.*
    Preparation and planning, 4.01[1]
    Question and answer statement, 4.11
    Recording devices, use of, 4.13
    Rules for better statements, 4.03
    Translation required, translator's affidavit, 4.06
State regulation and control, 2.02
Statutes of limitations. *See* specific subject headings
Strict liability in tort, actions involving
  Actions, grounds for, 29.11
  Aircraft, as to, 9.16[2][f]
  Animals, dealing with, 9.16[2][e]
  Bibliography, 33.05
  Blasting operations, care required, 9.16[2][d]
  Dangerous activities
    Care required, 9.16[2][b]
    Determining extent of danger, 9.16[2][b]
  Dangerous instrumentalities
    Degree of care required, 9.16[2][a]
  Definitions, 9.16[2]; 29.11

Strict liability in tort, actions involving—*Cont.*
  Investigation, areas for, 33.02
  Meaning, 29.11
  Notice requirements and, 9.16[2][c]
  Products liability cases and, 9.16[2][g]
    See also Products liability
  Punitive damages, availability, 32.01[8]
  Qualifications of, 9.16[2]
  Spread of, 9.16[2][g]
  Statutory enactments, 29.11[2]
  Ultrahazardous activities, 9.16[2][g]
  Vendor's liability, 29.11[1]
Subrogation
  Agreement, 43.01[16]
  Applicable insurance lines, 43.01[2]
  Application of rights, 43.01[12]
  Apportionment, excess carrier, 43.01[19]
  Arbitration and, 43.01[17]
  Collision policy, deductible feature, 43.01[18]
  Deductible feature of collision policy, 43.01[18]
  Defenses to action, 43.01[8]
  Excess carrier and apportionment, 43.01[19]
  Factors to consider, 43.01[13]
  Generally, 43.01[4] *et seq.*
  Knock-for-knock agreements, 43.01[15]
  Lien letters, sample form, 43.01[5]
  Loan receipts, 43.01[11]
  Receipt, 43.01[14]
  Recent cases involving, 43.01[21]
  Recovery expenses, 43.01[20]
  Rights of action, 43.01[7]
  Third parties
    Recovery, 43.01[3]

INDEX

References are to sections

Subrogation—*Cont.*
  Third parties—*Cont.*
    Settlement by insured,
      43.01[4]
    Voluntary payment, 43.01[9]
    Waiver of rights, 43.01[10]
    Workers' Compensation Acts,
      under, 43.01[22]
Suits
  Bibliography as to, 14.04
  Practical considerations of, 14.01
    et seq.
  Appeal, 14.02[7]
  Checklist for preparation for
    suit, 14.02[8]
  Claim manager's review of
    case, 14.02[2][b]
  Claim representative, role of,
    14.02
  Costs, 14.01
  Defense counsel, dealing with,
    14.02
  Law reporting systems, use,
    14.03 *et seq.*
  Legal expenses, as to, 14.01
  Nonwaiver agreements,
    14.02[3]
  Review of case, 14.02 *et seq.*
  Supervisors, review of case by,
    14.02[2][b]
  Trial preparation, 14.02[7]
  Witnesses, availability, 14.02[4]

T

Torts, 9.05[1]
  See also specific subject headings
  Definitions, 9.05[1]
Trauma
  Injuries and diseases, effects on,
    8.01 *et seq.*
  See also specific subject
    headings
Traumatic neurosis, 8.01[11]

Trial, preparation for, 13.06
  Appeal, procedure, 13.07
  Federal Rules of Civil Procedure
    and, 13.07
  Liens, use in re casualty claims,
    13.08
Trichinosis
  Cause of, 8.01[16]
  Described, 8.01[16]
  Products liability claims and,
    8.01[16]
Tuberculosis
  Overwork causing, 8.01[17]
  Trauma causing, claims of,
    8.01[17]
Tumors
  Benign, 8.01[18]
  Malignant, 8.01[18]
  Trauma causing, 8.01[18]

U

Underinsured motorist. *See*
  Automobile policies,
  generally
Underwriters
  Confidential report to by claim
    investigator, 3.08
  Elements of, 3.08
Unforeseeability
  Liability for
    Acts not those of ordinary
      prudent person, 9.07
    Reasonable foresight
      distinguished, 9.07
Uninsured motorist. *See*
  Automobile policies,
  generally
Unsatisfied judgment laws, 24.03

CASUALTY INSURANCE CLAIMS

References are to sections

W

**War Hazards Compensation Act
provisions, effect on
employer-employee
relations, 41.05**
**Warning of danger, duty in
products liability cases**
  Adequacy, 30.01[6]
  Alterations as to, 30.01[9]
  Bibliography, 33.05
  Checklist for investigation of
cases, 33.04[7]
  Component parts, as to,
30.01[10]
  Continuing duty as to, 30.01[11],
[12]
  Dangers that are common
knowledge and, 30.01[5]
  Design defects, as to, 30.01[4]
  Drug cases, continuing duty to
warn, 30.01[12], [13]
  Foreseeability and, 30.01[2]
  Method of warning in drug
cases, 30.01[13]
  Model Act, 30.01[16]
  Negligence and strict liability in,
30.01[1]
  Open and obvious condition,
effect, 30.01[3]
  Post-accident, 30.01[14]
  Pre-accident governmental
standards compliance,
30.01[15]
  Prescription drug cases, 31.02[4]
  Proximate cause and, 30.01[7]
  Strict liability and negligence in,
30.01[1]
  To whom duty is owed, 30.01[8]
**Weather reports, use of
information contained in,
5.08[1]**
**Willful and wanton misconduct
doctrine, 9.12**

Witnesses
  Age as factor, 10.04[6]
  Antagonistic, 10.04[6]
  Approach to interview, 4.02
  Availability, 14.02[4]
  Bibliography, 9.18
  Children, 4.10
  Competency, 10.04[6]
  Discovery witnesses, 3.05 *et seq.*
  Illiterate witnesses, treatment of,
4.07
  Locating, 3.05 *et seq.*; 25.06
  Past criminal record, effect,
10.04[6]
  Perjury and, 10.04[6]
  Statements to be obtained, 4.07
et seq.; 25.06
Workers' compensation cases
  Accident, notice of, 39.10
  Administration of claims, 39.02
  Benefits available, 39.03 *et seq.*
  Generally, 39.03[1]
  Bibliography as to, 40.05
  Coverage, who is entitled to,
39.04
    Casual employees, 39.04[3][i]
    Checklist for determining
claimant's status,
39.04[3][d]
    Claimant's status, checklist for
determining, 39.04[3][d]
    Corporate officers and
partners, 39.04[3][e]
    Dual employment, effect,
39.04[3][f]
    Employee status of injured
party, requirement for,
39.04[2]
    Employer/employee,
distinguishing between,
39.04[3] *et seq.*
    Exempted groups, 39.04[1]
    General contractors,
39.04[3][a]

Ind.-28

INDEX

References are to sections

Workers' compensation cases
—Cont.
  Coverage, who is entitled to
      —Cont.
    Independent contractors,
        39.04[3][c]
    Loaned employees, 39.04[3][g]
    Partners and corporate
        officers, 39.04[3][e]
    Statutory employers,
        39.04[3][j]
    Subcontractors, 39.04[3][b]
    Volunteers, 39.04[3][h]
  Dependents in fatal cases,
      benefits to, 39.03[4]
  Disease, notice of, 39.10
  Employer's liability, 40.01[1], [2]
    Bibliography, 40.05
    Coverage, 40.01[1], [2]
    Extra-legal medical benefits
        endorsement, 40.01[5]
    Generally, 40.01 *et seq.*
    Occupational disease and,
        40.01[4]
    Voluntary compensation
        endorsement and, 40.01[4]
  Exclusive remedy, 39.06 *et seq.*
    California, recent trends in,
        39.06[4]
    Consortium, actions for loss of,
        39.06[3]
    Derivative suits, 39.06[2]
    Dual capacity doctrine,
        39.06[5]
    Employer, election to sue,
        39.06[10]
    Exclusivity in occupational
        disease cases, 39.06[9]
    Insurance coverage dilemma,
        39.06[6]
    Intentional injury, 39.06[7]
    Sexual harassment and,
        39.06[8]
    Where no compensation award
        is made, 39.06[1]

Workers' compensation cases
—Cont.
  Extraterritoriality and
      jurisdiction, 39.09[1]
  Final determination, 39.14
  General principles in, 39.01
    Compensation Acts, types of,
        39.01[1]
    State provisions for obtaining
        coverage, 39.01[2]
  Illegal employment of minors,
      39.12
  Indemnity benefits, 39.03[3]
  Investigation of claims, 40.02 *et
      seq.*
    Checklists, 40.02[3] *et seq.*
    Coverage; checklist, 40.02[3][a]
    Factual information; checklist,
        40.02[3][b]
    Index Bureau reports, 40.02[2]
    Information to be obtained
        from claimant; checklist,
        40.02[3][d]
    Information to be obtained
        from insured; checklist,
        40.02[3][c]
    Medical investigation,
        40.02[3][e]
    Occupational disease, 40.03,
        [1]
    Physical facts, as to, 40.02[4]
    Subrogation and, 40.02[5]
    Unfair Claims Practices Act,
        40.02[1]
  Jurisdiction and
      extraterritoriality, 39.09,
      [1]
  Liability of successive insurers,
      39.11
  Malpractice as related to, 39.13
  Medical benefits, 39.03[2]
  Minors, illegal employment of,
      39.12
  Non-occupational disability laws,
      40.04

Workers' compensation cases
—*Cont.*
  Notice of accident or disease, 39.10
  Occupational disease, investigation of, 40.03
    Checklist, 40.03[1]
  Personal injury by accident arising out of and in the course of employment, 39.05 *et seq.*
    Accident and, 39.05[2]
    "Arising out of the employment," 39.05[3]
    "In the course of," 39.05[4]
  Punitive damages arising out of, 39.08
  Rehabilitation of injured and crippled, 8.04; 39.15
  Second injury or special disability funds, availability, 39.03[6]
  Structured settlements, 17.13 *et seq;* 39.16
    Bibliography, 17.14
    Generally, 17.13[1]
    Legal aspects, 17.13[3]

Worker's compensation cases
—*Cont.*
  Model Periodic Payments of Judgments Act, 17.13[4]
  Model Structured Settlement Act, 17.13[4]
  Tax considerations, 17.13[2]
  Successive insurers, liability of, 39.11
  Third party actions, 39.07
  Type of employee, checklist for determining, 39.04[3][k]
  Waiting period for benefits, 39.03[5]
Wrongful death, action for recovery, 10.03[10]
Wrongful discharge. *See* Employment, wrongful termination of
Wrongful life; child's right to action for, 11.06
Wrongful termination of employment. *See* Employment, wrongful termination of